The **Rough Guide** to

The Pyrenees

written and researched by

Marc Dubin

NEW YORK • LONDON • DELHI

www.roughguides.com

Contents

◁◁ Coma de Vaca mountain refuge ◁ Cloisters, Saint-Bertrand-de-Comminges

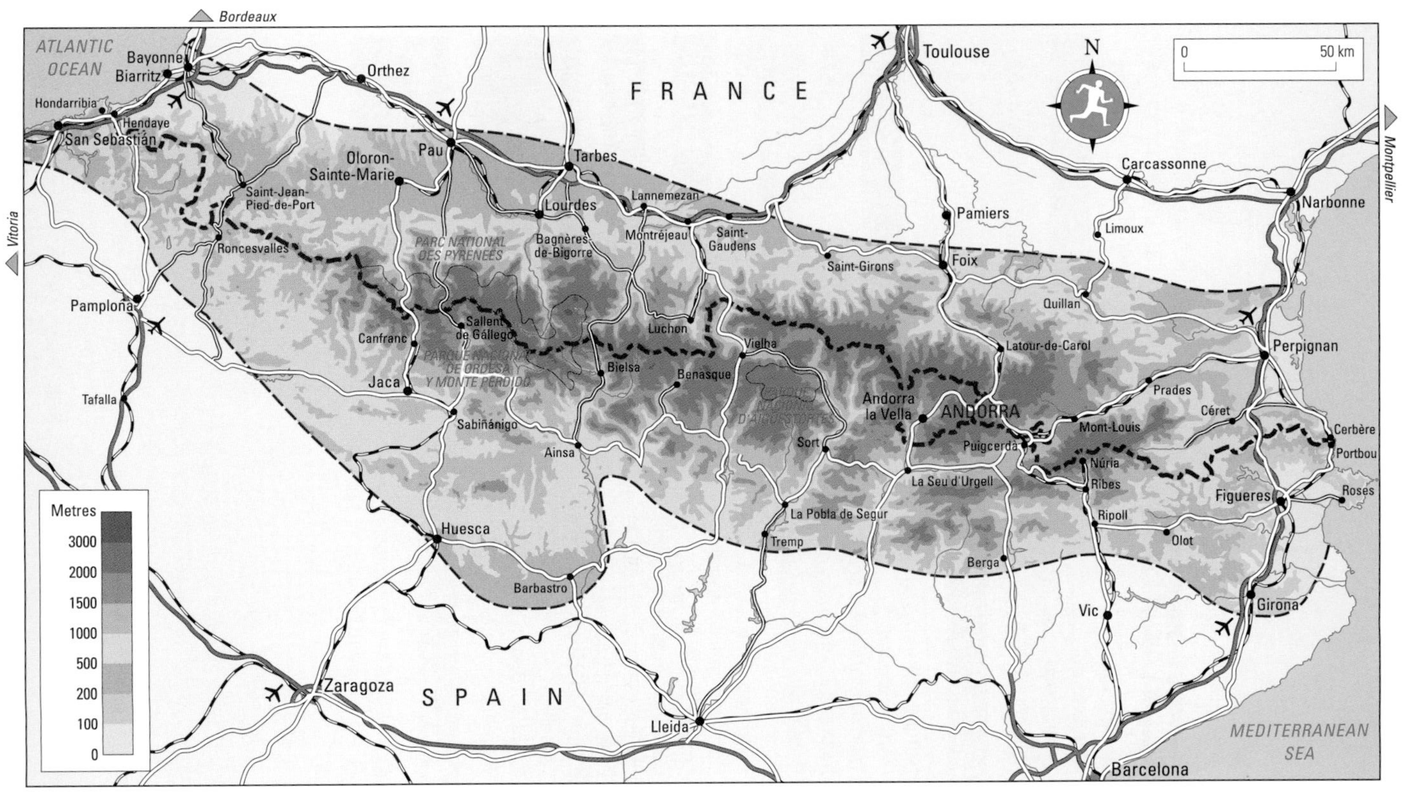

Bordeaux
Montpellier
Vitoria
ATLANTIC OCEAN
MEDITERRANEAN SEA
FRANCE
SPAIN
N
0
50 km
Metres
3000
2000
1500
1000
500
200
100
0
Bayonne
Biarritz
Hondarribia
Hendaye
San Sebastián
Orthez
Pau
Oloron-Sainte-Marie
Saint-Jean-Pied-de-Port
Roncesvalles
Pamplona
Tafalla
Tarbes
Lourdes
Bagnères-de-Bigorre
PARC NATIONAL DES PYRENEES
Lannemezan
Montréjeau
Saint-Gaudens
Luchon
Sallent de Gállego
Canfranc
Jaca
Sabiñánigo
PARQUE NACIONAL DE ORDESA Y MONTE PERDIDO
Bielsa
Benasque
Vielha
Ainsa
Huesca
Barbastro
Zaragoza
Lleida
Toulouse
Pamiers
Foix
Saint-Girons
Sort
La Pobla de Segur
Tremp
Andorra la Vella
ANDORRA
La Seu d'Urgell
Puigcerdà
Berga
Latour-de-Carol
Quillan
Limoux
Carcassonne
Narbonne
Perpignan
Prades
Céret
Mont-Louis
Núria
Ribes
Ripoll
Olot
Vic
Barcelona
Figueres
Girona
Roses
Cerbère
Portbou

Introduction to

Pyrenees

Anyone could find their perfect retreat in the Pyrenees, a mountain range comprising a diversity of landscapes rarely equalled in Europe. Between herb-scented Mediterranean slopes and the damper, stormier Atlantic coast lie iridescent green meadows, snow-clad peaks, canyons of sinuously sculpted rock, dense broadleaf forest, weirdly eroded limestone pinnacles and sheer, overgrown valleys that get two hours of sun daily.

These mountains challenge and invite rather than intimidate. Generally rounded and crumbling, their peaks – including 3404-metre **Aneto**, the highest Pyrenean summit, plus runners-up **Posets** and **Vignemale** – are attainable by any determined, properly equipped walker. Other natural wonders beckon to the averagely fit: the **Valle de Ordesa**, the most spectacular of many canyons, can be traversed on gentle footpaths, as can the great glaciated amphitheatre of the **Cirque de Gavarnie** just north. The water-moulded **canyons** of the **Sierra de Guara** in the Aragonese foothills invite both expert and novice equipped with little more than neoprene suits. You can raft down various foaming rivers on both sides of the range, including the **Noguera Pallaresa** in Catalunya and the **Gállego** in Aragón, as well as several tamer ones on the French side.

Walking the Pyrenees from end to end has become a classic endeavour. Thousands annually follow the **Haute Randonnée Pyrénéenne** (HRP) to either side of the watershed; the more circuitous but less demanding **Grande Randonnée 10** (GR10) entirely within France; or the equally spectacular Spanish **Gran Recorrido 11** (GR11). Detailed maps for the entire range show numerous other, briefer itineraries, suitable for hikers at all levels.

Fact file

- The Pyrenees, approximately 435km **long** as the crow flies and 50km **broad** at the widest points exceeding 1000m elevation, spans two national states – **France** and **Spain** – while entirely incorporating a third, **Andorra**. On the Spanish flank, Pyrenean territory makes up significant parts of the **autonomías** (autonomous regions) of Catalunya, Aragón, Navarra and País Vasco (Euskadi), which are further subdivided into the provinces of (from east to west) Girona, Lleida, Huesca, Pamplona and Gipuzkoa. In France, the **départements** of (from west to east) Pyrénées-Atlantiques, Hautes-Pyrénées, Ariège, Aude and Pyrénées-Orientales incorporate substantial tracts of high mountain.
- **Population** density averages less than ten individuals per square kilometre, and the total number of year-round inhabitants on both sides of the Pyrenees does not exceed 1.5 million – the vast majority living in the largest towns or conurbations of Pau, Perpignan, Bayonne-Anglet-Biarritz, Girona, San Sebastián, Tarbes, Huesca, Jaca, Figueres and Olot.
- The main Pyrenean employers are tourism, pastoralism and local government. Otherwise, hydroelectric power generation, coastal fishing, light industry in the towns and timber are the only other significant **economic activities**. Mining and farming are no longer practised on any significant scale.

Pyrenean **wildlife** is exceptionally rich, despite the devastating impact of human activity on many species. **Deer** and **wild boar** hide in the forests; the ubiquitous **isard** (Pyrenean chamois) abounds, as do shy **wildcats**; **marmots** are plentiful (and audible); majestic **birds of prey** patrol the skies. The **capercaillie**, a bird now extinct in the French Alps, still (just) survives in the Pyrenees, while the tiny **desman**, an aquatic mole, is unknown elsewhere in western Europe, except the Picos de Europa.

Traces of **human habitation** in the Pyrenees pre-date recorded history by millennia, with artefacts found (and displayed) at various caves in the Ariège, the Couserans and the Comminges regions. Among the prehistoric **caves** around **Tarascon-sur-Ariège**, the **paintings** in the **Grotte de Niaux** rank as the best open to public view worldwide.

△ Corncobs drying, Aínsa

△ Romanesque church, Axiat

Marmots

Throughout the high Pyrenees you will hear, though probably not see, the **marmot** (*marmotte* in French; *marmota* in Castilian), a now-common dweller above the tree line that once disappeared from these mountains after being hunted for centuries for its fur. This robust rodent – reaching a length of 75cm – was reintroduced to the French Central Pyrenees from 1948 onwards, and has now spread to both sides of the range. The rather indiscriminate manner of this restocking, and its few natural enemies, has led to an explosion in marmot populations, with control measures – especially after gnawing damage was discovered to hydroelectric pipes – now being considered.

The shrill alarm shriek emitted by "sentry" individuals sends colony members scurrying down their extensive tunnel system, generally dug on warm, south-facing scree slopes at 2000m – a habitat where the creature's fawn-grey fur makes it almost invisible. Since their rapid increase in numbers, however, colonies are now found down to the 1600-metre contour, the tunnels the venue for five months of annual hibernation. Despite their cuddly appearance and anthropomorphic habit of standing on two legs, marmots can be fierce, fighting to the death in territorial disputes.

△ Congost de Mont-Rebei gorge

Hundreds of extraordinary **Romanesque churches and monasteries** constitute the Pyrenees' architectural highlights, including such renowned examples as Saint-Michel-de-Cuixà, Serrabona, Santa Maria de Ripoll, Sant Climent de Taüll and a host of others in the Vall de Boí, Saint-Bertrand-de-Comminges, San Juan de la Peña and Saint-Engrâce in the Haute-Soule. So-called "Roman" **bridges** still linking isolated villages are even older, though not always pre-Christian. In the west of the range, numerous monuments attest to the thousands who followed the **pilgrimage trail** during the Middle Ages to Santiago de Compostela in Galicia via the fabled Puerto de Ibañeta near Roncesvalles, or the nearby Col du Somport. From the Mediterranean to the Ariège, the strength of the **Cathar** heresy is reflected in several immensely evocative ruined **castles**, notably the crag-top citadel of Montségur, site of this faith's effective extinction.

The **people** of the Pyrenees are as disparate as the landscape. The eastern and western Pyrenees are the respective homelands of Catalans and Basques, each with a tenaciously preserved cultural vitality embodied in the sombre *sardana*, the Catalan communal dance, or the lightning-quick Basque game of *pelota/pelote*. As you traverse the Pyrenees you'll hear Catalan, Aranese, Aragonese and Euskera (the Basque tongue), plus others – notably the Gascon dialect of Occitan – not officially accorded the status of a distinct language. For centuries before the final unifications of France and Spain, every valley effectively constituted a mini-republic, jealously guarding customary privileges against encroachment from distant central governments, further defying them with a thriving trade in **smuggling**. Remoteness and neglect always made the mountains a refuge for political as well as religious dissidents, most recently during the Spanish Civil War and

As you traverse the Pyrenees you'll hear Catalan, Aranese, Aragonese and Euskera (the Basque tongue), plus others...

△ Castillo de Loarre, Spanish Pyrenees

World War II when thousands of **refugees** took advantage of shepherds' and smugglers' knowledge to evade capture. After 1968, many disillusioned French protesters and "alternative" types again took up residence in the back country, swelling the traditional local vote for the political Left – and adopting the enduring local habit of **self-sufficiency**. Indeed the Pyreneans' historical disregard for the oft-altered boundaries between France and Spain has been vindicated and accentuated by the post-1993 European Union, as old border posts lie abandoned and a strong regional identity bridging the watershed has reasserted itself.

After decades of being eclipsed by the Alps, the Pyrenees have come into their own as a **travellers' destination**. Infrastructure and amenities improve each year, exemplified by increasing numbers of quality lodgings, ever-multiplying adventure-sport outfitters and a plethora of no-frills airlines offering service into previously sleepy regional airports.

Regional languages

Since the 1980s, Pyrenean regional languages have made a dramatic comeback. The process is more advanced in Spain, whose 1978 constitution devolves considerable discretion to the country's autonomous regions. In Catalunya, Catalan has officially displaced Castilian on everything from road signs to transport schedules to museum labelling – not to mention in map-publishing undertaken by the *Generalitat* (regional government). In Aragón, the process is confined largely to the odd village outskirts sign, though mountaineering maps often show all features in Aragonese, and local nationalists suitably "edit" Castilian road signs with spray paint. In Navarra, Euskera (Basque language) nomenclature is more prominent in the north, but in neighbouring Gipuzkoa Euskera signage reigns supreme. In traditionally centralized France, minority languages have limited official status, formerly restricted to "folkloric" manifestations, but now Gascon street-naming is prevalent, and all toponyms are indicated bilingually in French/Euskera; Pays Basque events are publicized strictly in the Basque language, and even local *mairies* are identified as *herriko etxea*. Bilingual road signage is common in Catalan-speaking Roussillon, and Catalan place names are even beginning to appear on those paragons of Gallic rectitude, the Cartes des Randonnées.

Where to go

If you've only got two weeks in hand, the Pyrenees are too vast to tour in their entirety, but **public transport** is good enough to explore a region roughly corresponding to one of this book's chapters. Rail lines will get you at least into the foothills, and buses will take you deeper into the mountains. A circuit of the eastern Pyrenees could begin at Perpignan, continue south by train along the Mediterranean coast, move west by road through the verdant Garrotxa to the Ripollès, then north by rail to the sunny plain of the Cerdanya/Cerdagne, and finally return to Perpignan by another train through the dramatic Têt valley. Circular itineraries can be constructed in other parts of the range – around Andorra or in the Basque country, for example – and even isolated, underpopulated zones such as the Maladeta and Posets massifs lend themselves to loops on foot from trailhead villages served by buses. With a **car** or **bicycle**, you could see the best of two consecutive chapters in two to three weeks.

For walks and climbs on the highest summits further east, make the all-purpose resorts of **Benasque** or **Luchon** your bases, while the westernmost high peaks can also be easily explored from villages such as **Lescun** or **Sallent de Gállego**.

The **Ariège** region suits most tastes with fabulous scenery, cave art, ruined castles and almost every form of outdoor activity. Over the border in Catalunya, the **Parc Nacional de Aigüestortes i Sant Maurici**, easily accessible from the Val d'Aran, Vall de Boí or the Noguera Pallaresa, makes a fine introduction to the glacially sculpted high peaks. **Gavarnie**, **Barèges** or **Cauterets** in France, and **Torla** or **Bielsa** in Spain, are comfortable, respective gateways for the French **Parc National des Pyrénées** and the Spanish **Parque Nacional de Ordesa y Monte Perdido**, contiguous national parks in the heart of the range. For walks and climbs on the highest summits further east, make the all-purpose resorts of **Benasque** or **Luchon** your bases, while the westernmost high peaks can also be easily explored from villages such as **Lescun** or **Sallent de Gállego**. During winter, these settlements are conveniently close to many of the best **ski resorts**, including **Astún**, **Candanchú**, **Gourette**, **Barèges-La Mongie**, **Espiaube**, **Cerler**, **Peyragudes**, **Baqueira-Beret** and **Boí-Taüll**, rivalling the better-known winter-sports centres in more commercialized **Andorra**.

Towards the west, **Pau** is the largest, most cosmopolitan Pyrenean city, straddling a main route to **Jaca**, historic county town of the Aragonese mountains. They're the most logical and congenial gateways to the surreal karst country extending between the French **Vallée d'Aspe** and the Spanish valleys of **Echo** and **Ansó**. Southeast of Jaca, the **Sierra de Guara** is available for visits most of the year owing to lower altitude. Inland from the surf-pounded Atlantic coast, with its elegant resorts of **San Sebastián** and **Biarritz**, the seductively green horizons and sumptuous domestic architecture of the **Basque country** await, with graceful **Bayonne** and atmospheric **Saint-Jean-Pied-de-Port** as focuses. Mediterranean beaches are more intimate – for example at the picturesque port-resorts of **Collioure** or **Cadaqués** – and the climate reliably sunny. From here you can make forays inland to Catalunya's volcanic **Garrotxa basin** or the gorge-slashed foothills of Rousillon's **Canigou Massif**. Whichever part of the range you visit, sample both sides of the border if possible – the north-to-south change of landscape, climate and culture is one of the delights of the Pyrenees.

When to go

The best time to visit depends on what you want to do. Snowfall permitting – and some recent years have been better than the Alps – the **downhill/cross-country ski season** gets under way by Christmas, lasting until mid-April. With the spring thaw, **rafting** and **canoeing** become practicable, and wildflowers are at their height from late May to early June, start of the summer **walking** season – and also a good time for riding, cycling and the more extreme pursuits of **canyoning** and **paragliding**. In autumn the crowds depart and the mountain trails are left to solitary walkers not afraid of the odd snow flurry.

△ Barn with hay bales, Spanish Tella

△ Belle Époque building, Eaux-Bonnes

Try to **avoid the French and Spanish national summer holidays** from mid-July to the end of August. It's better to come after this stampede rather than before: spring and autumn offer equal solitude, but May is muddy and many businesses are shut, while high passes may still be blocked until July. **Thunderstorms** also cause problems in summer: the Pyrenees are beset by them, with several storms a week guaranteed during July and August. In

Average temperatures (°C)

	Jan	Mar	May	Jul	Sep	Nov
Perpignan (Mediterranean coast)						
	12.4	12.5	20.1	28.4	26.1	15.8
Ransol (Andorra)						
	-2.1	1.4	7.3	13.6	10.9	2
Panticosa (Alto Aragón)						
	0.1	2.6	8.2	15.5	12.3	4.1
Bayonne (Atlantic coast)						
	10	12.2	18	27.2	24.2	15.4

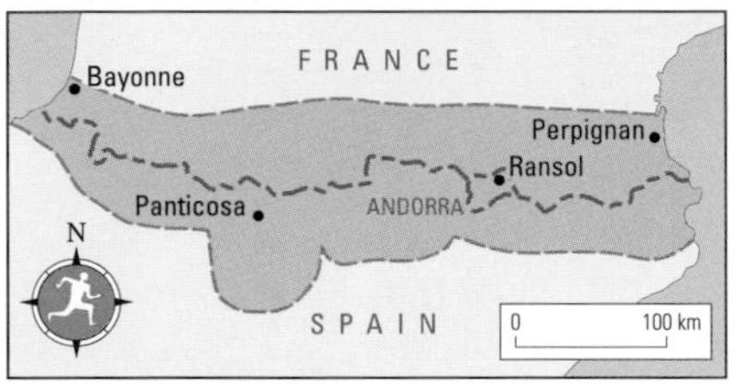

September you'll have complete freedom of the mountains, with most refuges still open. During **winter**, the **February half-term break** is pretty frantic in or near any ski resort, while March at the same spots can be comatose, as many proprietors close down for all or part of the week until the **Easter rush**. The French tend to **stagger** their late February and Easter breaks, so the north slopes are not quite so busy then as the Spanish side.

Pyrenean **weather** resists generalization, as microclimates abound. The Barèges valley, for example, has particularly idiosyncratic conditions, where a warm May can be followed by heavy June snowfall. In summer, marine cooling gives each coastal strip a temperature several degrees lower than a few miles inland, while for every 100–200m of ascent, temperature falls by as much as one degree Celsius. The French slopes are especially prone to the converse phenomenon of temperature inversion, when valleys become colder than the peaks, which protrude like islands from a sea of cloud.

things not to miss

It's not possible to see everything that the Pyrenees have to offer in one trip – and we don't suggest you try. What follows is a selective taste of the region's highlights, listed in no particular order: spectacular hikes, outstanding natural features, exquisite Romanesque churches and alluring resorts. They're arranged in five colour-coded categories, which you can browse through to find the very best things to see and experience. All highlights have a page reference to take you straight into the guide, where you can find out more.

ACTIVITIES | CONSUME | EVENTS | NATURE | SIGHTS

01 Valle de Ordesa Page **414** • Torla village is a popular gateway to the dramatic Ordesa valley with its banded-limestone walls.

02 Notre-Dame des Tramezaygues, Audressein Page **309** • Fourteenth-century frescoes at this riverside Couserans church are some of the most charming – and easily visible – on the French side.

03 Camino de Santiago/ Chemin de Saint-Jacques Page **479** • This millennial pilgrimage route, crossing the Pyrenees at several points, is enjoying a resurgence in popularity.

04 Château de Puilaurens Page **96** • Among the many magnificent "Cathar" castles in the eastern Pyrenees, though the Cathar sect didn't originally build every one of them.

05 Summer festivals Page **36** • You'd be exceptionally unlucky not to coincide with at least one saint's-day bash or musical programme during your stay.

06 Canyoning in Sierra de Guara Page **443** • Don a wetsuit and plumb the water-polished depths of Europe's mecca for this family-friendly sport.

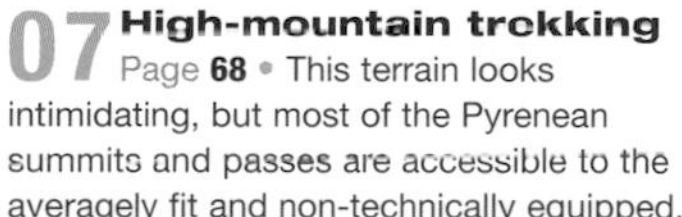

07 High-mountain trekking Page **68** • This terrain looks intimidating, but most of the Pyrenean summits and passes are accessible to the averagely fit and non-technically equipped.

08 Tour de France Page **350** • Almost every year, the world's most famous bicycle race visits the central Pyrenees in several days of gruelling stages.

09 Gliding and parapenting Pages **75 & 363** • Thermal conditions over much of the range are perfect for realizing your dreams of non-motorized flight.

10 Gorges of Haute-Soule Page **466** • The karstic country here is slashed by four breathtaking gorges; the Gorges d'Olhadybia is spanned by a famously bouncy suspension bridge.

11 Nive quais, Bayonne Page **495** • Quirky shopfronts and restaurants huddle below residential facades in a hybrid Basque/Gascon style.

12 High-altitude spas Page **222** • The Pyrenees are well sown with elegant thermal pools, both indoor and out, such as these at Dorres, ideal for soaking away post-trek or *après*-ski aches.

13 Plaza Mayor, Aínsa Page **401** • The most perfect extant example of an arcaded central plaza on the Spanish side.

14 Cremallera de Núria Page **177** • This narrow-gauge railway line is one of three in the Catalan Pyrenees providing an unforgettable ride up a steep river valley.

15 San Juan de la Peña Page **432** • The column-capitals of this twelfth-century cloister, carved by an anonymous master, constitute a *tour de force* of Pyrenean Romanesque art.

16 "Roman" bridges Page **167** • This graceful span at Llierca is one of many "Roman" bridges in the range: some indeed pre-Christian, some much later.

17 Spanish turismo rural Page **50** • Restored rural properties usually offer the most characterful and best-value accommodation across the Spanish Pyrenees.

18 Grotte de Niaux, Ariège valley Page **231** • Prehistoric cave paintings here are the most vivid of several in the region.

19 Cirque de Lescun Page **396** • The old stone village of Lescun perfectly offsets the eponymous karstic cirque topped by jagged summits.

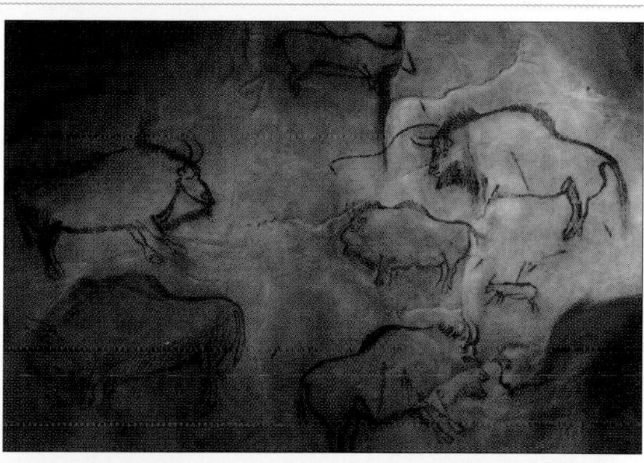

20 Basque country beaches Pages **500 & 515** • The blonde-tan sands of the Pyrenean Basque coast, from the Adour to San Sebastián, are both sheltered and wave-buffeted.

21 Cadaqués Page **135** • One of the most attractive and congenial Mediterranean resorts, and a welcome goal at the end of a GR11 traverse.

22 Wildflowers Page **557** • Few European ranges can match the Pyrenees in their variety of summer flora at all altitudes.

23 High-altitude lakes Page **270** • The Pyrenees have several hundred of these beauties, left behind by the last Ice Age, on both sides of the frontier.

24 White-water sports Pages **74 & 256** • Some of Europe's best kayaking and rafting attract enthusiasts during spring and early summer to both sides of the range.

25 Skiing Page **366** • Barèges-La Mongie is the largest and (usually) most reliable snow ski domain in the underrated Pyrenees, where facilities are beginning to rival the Alps.

26 Cirque de Gavarnie Page **369** • Overhyped it may be, but this, one of the largest glacial formations in Europe, still impresses mightily.

Basics

Basics

Getting there

From the UK and Ireland the most convenient way of reaching the Pyrenees is by flying – flights from London take just under two hours to Girona, Zaragoza or Lleida, less to Biarritz, Pau, Toulouse, Carcassonne and Perpignan. Reaching the Pyrenees overland is easy by combined use of Eurostar/Eurotunnel services with onward TGV trains from Paris or Lille, though plane fares usually cost less than rail tickets. There are also two ferry routes direct to northern Spain, bypassing France. From North America, choice of quasi-Pyrenean airports will be limited to Barcelona, Bilbao and Toulouse, usually via busier European hubs. From Australia or New Zealand, indirect routings via Asia arrive in the same cities, plus Paris or Madrid. Fly-drive deals are well worth considering, too, as a combined air ticket and car rental arrangement can be excellent value.

Airfares to the Pyrenees depend on the **season**, with the highest fares applicable from June to early September (plus Easter week); fares drop during the "shoulder" seasons – April/May and late September/October. You'll get the best prices during the low season, November to March (excluding Christmas and New Year weeks, plus – from Europe – February half-term when prices are hiked up for eager skiers and seats are scarce). Australian and New Zealand fares have their low season from mid-January to the end of February and October/November; high season is mid-May to August, plus December to mid-January; and shoulder season the rest of the year. You can often cut costs by using a **specialist/discount flight agent** who also offers a range of other travel-related services such as travel insurance, rail passes and car rental.

Don't overlook the possibility of reaching the Pyrenees on **frequent-flyer** miles. There are numerous ways to accumulate the required amount, and such tickets have powerful advantages over purchased tickets: they are usually valid for up to a year, and most (though not all) schemes allow you to change the return date for a reasonable fee, typically £40/$75. Even short-haul routings may be indirect (eg London–Frankfurt–Toulouse), and you remain liable for all taxes.

Flights from the UK and Ireland

Air travel to Pyrenean foothill airports has been revolutionized through year-round direct flights both by no-frills airlines and the major national carriers. You can pretty much pinpoint the valley you're visiting, or even purchase advantageous one-way tickets with all the no-frills (and some national) carriers and get the train back (or vice versa). No-frills airlines fly from remote, minor airports, charge for rudimentary food and drink on board and have severe baggage restrictions; phone bookings, as opposed to online bookings, are heavily penalized price-wise. The earlier you book, the better; you can easily pay as much as with a major airline (or more) if you leave it too late. Most no-frills airlines let you change the date of each travel leg for a modest fee (*c.* £17/€25) – plus any difference in the prevailing fare since the time of original booking.

With five airlines piling in from Britain, **Toulouse** is the major gateway airport on the French side. Fares from London vary from £60 return in low season to over £170 at peak times. Air France has the most varied daily schedule, but all flights from UK airports route via Paris CDG/Paris Orly and missed connections are common. British Airways provides three daily direct flights year-round from **London Gatwick**, while from **Manchester**, bmi is a better bet with its daily peak-season direct service. flyBE goes from **Birmingham** four to five times weekly at fairly civilized times. Among true no-frills carriers, easyJet has two daily services from London Gatwick and one from Bristol.

Biarritz (to/from Stansted, Dublin, Shannon) **Pau** (Stansted), **Carcassonne** (Dublin,

Stansted, East Midlands, Shannon, Liverpool) and **Perpignan** (Stansted) are all served at least daily year-round by Ryanair (with feeder flights to Stansted from Glasgow and Edinburgh, though Ryanair takes no responsibility for missed connections). Low-season fares begin at £15 one way – but £40–50 is typical, rising to over £100 each way during peak times. This airline also charges a per-bag luggage fee, and for checked weight in excess of 15 kilos (though carry-on allowances are normal), potentially wiping out any savings, especially if you're taking skis. bmibaby flies daily into **Perpignan** from **Manchester**, while flyBe goes from **Southampton**.

Girona vies with Toulouse on the south flank of the range as a gateway, at least as far as Ryanair goes – it's one of their major hubs, with daily (or more frequent) flights to/from London Stansted/Luton, Shannon, Dublin and just about every other regional UK airport except Manchester or Birmingham. **Ryanair** also serves **Zaragoza** (from Stansted), often the cheapest but the least convenient destination; **Vitoria-Gasteiz** (from Dublin and London), handy for the west of the range; and (from 2008, unless easyJet grabs the slot) **Lleida**. Return fares from the UK are rarely much under £100, and can rise to well over £200 in peak skiing or summer season. From Ireland, budget a minimum of €200, double that at prime times.

Bilbao is a good two-hours-plus by train from San Sebastián and the edge of the Pyrenees, but is reasonably served by nearly year-round scheduled flights: one daily from **London Heathrow** on British Airways/Iberia (same aircraft) at £100 minimum round-trip, plus one daily on easyJet from Stansted.

Airlines

Aer Lingus UK ⓣ0870 876 5000, Republic of Ireland ⓣ0818 365 000, ⓦwww.aerlingus.com.
Air France UK ⓣ0870 142 4343, ⓦwww.airfrance.com.
bmi UK ⓣ0870 607 0555, Ireland ⓣ01 407 3036, ⓦwww.flybmi.com.
bmibaby UK ⓣ0871 224 0224, Republic of Ireland ⓣ1890 340 122, ⓦwww.bmibaby.com.
British Airways UK ⓣ0870 850 9850, Republic of Ireland ⓣ1890 626 747, ⓦwww.ba.com.
easyJet UK ⓣ0905 821 0905, ⓦwww.easyjet.com.
flyBE UK ⓣ0871 700 0535, Republic of Ireland ⓣ1890 925 532, ⓦwww.flybe.com.
Iberia UK ⓣ0870 609 0500, Republic of Ireland ⓣ0818 462 000, ⓦwww.iberia.com.
Ryanair UK ⓣ0871 246 0000, Republic of Ireland ⓣ0818 303 030, ⓦwww.ryanair.com.

General flight agents

ebookers UK ⓣ0800 082 3000, Republic of Ireland ⓣ01 488 3507, ⓦwww.ebookers.com. Low fares on an extensive selection of scheduled flights.
North South Travel ⓣ01245 608291, ⓦwww.northsouthtravel.co.uk. Friendly, competitive flight agency, offering discounted fares – profits are used to support projects in the developing world, especially the promotion of sustainable tourism.
Rosetta Travel Belfast ⓣ028 9064 4996, ⓦwww.rosettatravel.com. Agent specializing in deals direct from Belfast.
STA Travel ⓣ0870 160 0599, ⓦwww.statravel.co.uk. Worldwide specialists in low-cost flights for students and under-26s.
Trailfinders UK ⓣ020 7938 3939, ⓦwww.trailfinders.com, Republic of Ireland ⓣ01 677 7888, ⓦwww.trailfinders.ie. One of the best-informed and most efficient agents for independent travellers; branches in all the UK's largest cities, plus Dublin.

Packages and specialist operators

There are various high-quality, specialist hiking, skiing or rural-accommodation-based packages available on both sides of the range.

Alto Aragón ⓣ01869 337339, ⓦwww.altoaragon.co.uk. The best and most varied offerings for the Spanish Pyrenees: spring/autumn horse-riding in the Sierra de Guara, cross-country skiing and snowshoeing near Benasque and well-planned one-week hiking tours, including the Posets/Maladeta area or the Ordesa region. Also self-guiding holidays from selected quality hotels. Prices from £640, land only.
La Balaguère ⓣ0033 5.62.97.46.46, ⓦwww.balaguere.com. Well-respected adventure travel outfit based at a *gîte* in Arrens-Marsous, France; they offer a wide variety of treks and expeditions in the Pyrenees, though English-language guiding cannot be guaranteed.
Borderline Holidays ⓣ0033 5.62.92.68.95, ⓦwww.borderlinehols.com. Friendly and small

British-run, Luz-Saint-Sauveur-based company offering guided walking and wildlife holidays in summer, and affordable, quality skiing packages in winter from £350 half-board per person for one week, based in hotels or apartments in Barèges or Luz. You arrange your own flights on Ryanair; pick-up service from Pau airport or Lourdes SNCF.

Exodus Expeditions ⓣ0970 950 0039; ⓦwww.exodus.co.uk. Broad array of year-round, eight-day holidays, most beginning at their own lodge near Luchon but taking in the Spanish side too. Winter offerings in small groups include snowshoeing trips (from £525) and cross-country skiing out of Ax-les-Thermes (from £459). Summer outings include a variety of walks on both sides of the border from day strolls to tough HRP traverses (£499–639) or a multi-activity holiday based near Luchon. All prices land only.

Iglu ⓣ020 8542 6658, ⓦwww.igluski.com. General marketers of skiing holidays at most of the Andorran resorts; from £350 per person per week including flights.

Inntravel ⓣ01653 617949, ⓦwww.inntravel.co.uk. Upmarket summer programme includes supported seven- to ten-day hikes in the French Basque foothills, the Garrotxa and the Catalan Pyrenees (including the French Cerdagne). Also horse-riding at *Can Jou* (see p.167) and cross-country skiing holidays based at *Auberge les Ecureuils* in Valcebollère (see p.222).

Jonathan's Tours ⓣ0033 561046447, ⓦwww.jonathanstours.com. Fully supported five- to seven-day snowshoeing tours (Jan–March) and summer walks in the Couserans, the Aude and the Ariège, based at a magnificent Napoleonic mansion-B&B in the Couserans or in mountain

Fly less – stay longer! Travel and climate change

Climate change is the single biggest issue facing our planet. It is caused by a build-up in the atmosphere of carbon dioxide and other greenhouse gases, which are emitted by many sources – including planes. Already, flights account for around three to four percent of human-induced global warming; that figure may sound small, but it is rising year on year and threatens to counteract the progress made by reducing greenhouse emissions in other areas.

Rough Guides regard travel, overall, as a global benefit, and feel strongly that the advantages to developing economies are important, as are the opportunities for greater contact and awareness among peoples. But we all have a responsibility to limit our personal "carbon footprint". That means giving thought to how often we fly and what we can do to redress the harm that our trips create.

Flying and climate change

Pretty much every form of motorized travel generates CO_2, but planes are particularly bad offenders, releasing large volumes of greenhouse gases at altitudes where their impact is far more harmful. Flying also allows us to travel much further than we would contemplate doing by road or rail, so the emissions attributable to each passenger are greater. For example, one person taking a return flight between Europe and California produces the equivalent impact of 2.5 tonnes of CO_2 – similar to the yearly output of the average UK car.

Less harmful planes may evolve but it will be decades before they replace the current fleet – which could be too late for avoiding climate chaos. In the meantime, there are limited options for concerned travellers: to reduce the amount we travel by air (take fewer trips, stay longer!), to avoid night flights (when plane contrails trap heat from Earth but can't reflect sunlight back to space) and to make the trips we do take "climate-neutral" via a carbon offset scheme.

Carbon offset schemes

Offset schemes run by **climatecare.org**, **carbonneutral.com** and others allow you to "neutralize" the greenhouse gases that you are responsible for releasing. Their websites have simple calculators that let you work out the impact of any flight. Once that's done, you can pay to fund projects that will reduce future carbon emissions by an equivalent amount (such the distribution of low-energy lightbulbs and cooking stoves in developing countries). Please take the time to visit our website and make your trip climate-neutral.

www.roughguides.com/climatechange

refuges. Typical per person price (nearly full board) €800 per person, land only.

Naturetrek Ⓦwww.naturetrek.co.uk (no phone). One-week butterfly, botanical and birding trips on both sides of the border, based either in Gèdre (France) or Berdún/Espot (Spain); fairly pricey at £985 land only.

Pyrenean Mountain Tours Ⓣ01635 297209, Ⓦwww.pyrenees.co.uk. Extensive summer hiking programme, using Luz-Saint-Sauveur as a focus: includes eight- or fifteen-day outings around Mont Perdu/Monte Perdido, the HRP between Pic du Midi and Vignemale, the GR10 and GR11, Sierra de Guara and the "Valleys of Lavedan", mostly priced at £525 per person land only. Also winter/spring eight-day ski-tours along the HRP in the French Parc National, and around Posets/Maladeta.

Ski Miquel Holidays Ⓣ01457 821200, Ⓦwww.miquelhols.co.uk. One- or two-week packages, with English-speaking instructor, at Baqueira-Beret in the Val d'Aran.

Flights from the US and Canada

The only Pyrenean gateway airports that feature advantageously on North American travel websites are Toulouse, Bilbao and Barcelona. Whether you fly into one of these, or to Paris or Madrid and travel onward overland, will depend on your budget and your schedule.

If you don't mind spending a few days in a big city first, or if you were planning to visit other parts of Europe anyway, it's usually not worth flying all the way to the Pyrenees. Discounted flights to London, Paris and Madrid are easy to find, and from London you can explore the various no-frills or overland options outlined on pp.27 & 32–34.

Of the gateway airports cited above, **Barcelona** is much the biggest, and usually the most economical choice; Continental has a direct service from Newark and Delta goes straight from JFK, while a dozen other airlines fly there via major European hubs. But through fares to **Toulouse** and **Bilbao** can be surprisingly attractive and shouldn't be overlooked – though Bilbao is well over two hours' land journey from the mountains.

Fares to **Barcelona from the US** are slightly more than those for Madrid, which is served non-stop at competitive rates by Iberia from Chicago, Miami and New York; Continental or Delta straight to Barcelona is a bit pricier than the typical indirect figures from New York of $500 in low season, $1000 in high season, perhaps via Frankfurt on Lufthansa or via Rome on Alitalia. To **Bilbao**, routes will unavoidably be one-stop at the very least (eg via Milan or Frankfurt), but fares are little different from those for Barcelona. **Canadian fares** are competitive; count on CDN$800/CDN$1400 from Toronto or Montréal to Barcelona via New York or a European hub, CDN$1030/CDN$1480 to Bilbao hubbing through Paris or London.

On the French side of the Pyrenees, there's a good selection of direct flights **into Paris** from most points in the US, and the strong links between France and Canada's Francophone community keep Canadian fares reasonable too. American Airlines and Air France offer direct service from New York JFK, Continental from Newark and Houston, with AA also flying non-stop from Chicago and Air France offering direct links from Miami and San Francisco, though as ever direct flights attract a premium, exceeding $1700 in high season from the west coast (versus *c.* $500 low season from the east coast). From Montréal or Toronto, expect to pay CDN$800/CDN$1300 direct to Paris on Air France, Air Transat or Air Canada, while one-stop flights from Vancouver clock in at CDN$1000/CDN$1700.

Closer to the mountains, **Toulouse** may prove a worthwhile target for a through fare: $560/1150 low/high season from New York, $650/1500 from San Francisco, $680/$1330 from Chicago, all via hubs such as Amsterdam, Munich or Milan. Flights from Canada to Toulouse should cost CDN$870/CDN$1400 from Montréal.

Airlines

Air Canada Ⓣ1-888 247–2262, Ⓦwww.aircanada.com.

Air France Ⓣ1-800 237-2747, Canada Ⓣ1-800 667-2747, Ⓦwww.airfrance.com.

Air Transat Canada Ⓣ1-877-872-6728, Ⓦwww.airtransat.com.

Alitalia US Ⓣ1-800-223-5730, Canada Ⓣ1-800-361-8336, Ⓦwww.alitalia.com.

American Airlines Ⓣ1-800 433-7300, Ⓦwww.aa.com.

British Airways Ⓣ1-800 AIRWAYS, Ⓦwww.ba.com.

Continental Airlines domestic ⓣ1-800/523-3273, international ⓣ1-800/231-0856, ⓦwww.continental.com.
Delta Air Lines ⓣ1-800 221-1212, ⓦwww.delta.com.
Iberia ⓣ1-800 772-4642, ⓦwww.iberia.com.
KLM/Northwest US domestic ⓣ1-800 225-2525, ⓦwww.klm.com, ⓦwww.nwa.com.
Lufthansa US ⓣ1-800 645-3880, Canada ⓣ1-800/563-5954, ⓦwww.lufthansa.com.
Swiss ⓣ1-877 FLY-SWIS, ⓦwww.swiss.com.
United Airlines ⓣ1-800 UNITED1, ⓦwww.united.com.
Virgin Atlantic Airways ⓣ1-800 821-4538, ⓦwww.virgin-atlantic.com.

Travel agents

Airtech ⓣ212/219-7000, ⓦwww.airtech.com. Standby and courier flights.
Educational Travel Center ⓣ1-800 747-5551 or 608/256-5551, ⓦwww.edtrav.com. Youth fares, rail passes.
STA Travel US ⓣ1-800 329-9537, Canada ⓣ1-888/427-5639, ⓦwww.statravel.com. Youth fares to everywhere; also student IDs, travel insurance, car rental, rail passes, etc.
Student Flights ⓦwww.isecard.com/studentflights. Youth fares, plus student IDs and European rail passes.
TFI Tours ⓣ1-800 745-8000 or 212/736-1140, ⓦtfitours.com/mars.asp. Established flight consolidator.
Travel Cuts Canada ⓣ1-886 246-9762, ⓦwww.travelcuts.com. Long-established student-travel organization.
Travelosophy ⓣ248/557-7775, ⓦwww.itravelosophy.com. Good range of student/teacher fares worldwide.

Specialist operators

If time is limited and you want to get straight up into the Pyrenees, it might be worth having a company make all arrangements. That said, not many North American companies feature the Pyrenees. Most that do specialize in vehicle-supported **hiking trips**, which – given the dollar's current woes – cost a hefty $3400–4300 per week.

Agama Taller de Viatges ⓣ00 34 932 157 320, ⓦwww.agama.net. Enthusiastic Catalan agency running Aragonese, Catalan and trans-border Pyrenean treks. Consult their website for current US/Canadian agents.
Backroads ⓣ1-800/GO-ACTIVE, ⓦwww.backroads.com. Offers an eight -day jaunt through the Basque foothills, with light walking.
Mountain Travel/Sobek ⓣ1-888/MTSOBEK, ⓦwww.mtsobek.com. eight-day whistle-stop tour of the central Pyrenees.
Saranjan Tours ⓣ1-800/858-9594, ⓦwww.saranjan.com. Spain specialists offering a ten-day, "Cathars in Catalunya" cycling tour from Sant Feliu de Guixols to Carcassonne.

Flights from Australia and New Zealand

There are no direct flights to anywhere in France or Spain from Australia or New Zealand, so you'll aim for **Paris**, **Barcelona**, **Toulouse** or **Madrid** on a two- or three-stop itinerary. Reckon on 24 hours' flying time via Asia, or 30 hours via North America – not counting time spent on stopovers – with flights via Asia cheaper and the more popular option. Travel agents or Australia-based websites offer better deals than the airlines direct and have the latest information on limited specials and stopovers.

Return fares to Barcelona, Madrid, Paris or Toulouse start at about AUS$2000 from Melbourne, Brisbane or Sydney; from Perth or Darwin expect to pay AUS$150–200 less. Most flights are routed via Singapore, and fares tend to be valid one year. Fares from Auckland to the same points, a few routing more expensively via North America, begin at NZ$2200 and are again good for one year. For a few hundred dollars more, Australasian travellers may want to consider a **round-the-world ticket** with a French or Spanish airport included amongst several stops.

Airlines

Air France Australia ⓣ1300/390 190, ⓦwww.airfrance.com.
Air New Zealand Australia ⓣ13 2476, ⓦwww.airnz.com.au; New Zealand ⓣ0800/737 000, ⓦwww.airnz.co.nz.
British Airways Australia ⓣ1300/767 177, New Zealand ⓣ09/966 9777, ⓦwww.ba.com.
Cathay Pacific Australia ⓣ13 17 47, New Zealand ⓣ09/379 0861; ⓦwww.cathaypacific.com.
Emirates Australia ⓣ1300 303 777 or 02/9290 9700, New Zealand ⓣ09/968 2200, ⓦwww.emirates.com.
Gulf Air Australia ⓣ1300/366 337, ⓦwww.gulfairco.com.

JAL (Japan Air Lines) Australia ⓣ02/9272 1111, New Zealand ⓣ09/379 9906, ⓦwww.jal.com.
KLM Australia ⓣ1300/303 747, New Zealand ⓣ09/921 6040, ⓦwww.klm.com.
Lufthansa Australia ⓣ1300/655 727, ⓦwww.lufthansa.com.
Malaysia Airlines Australia ⓣ13 26 27, New Zealand ⓣ0800/777 747, ⓦwww.malaysia-airlines.com.
Qantas Australia ⓣ13 13 13, New Zealand ⓣ0800/808 767, ⓦwww.qantas.com.
Singapore Airlines Australia ⓣ13 10 11, New Zealand ⓣ0800/808 909, ⓦwww.singaporeair.com.
Thai Airways Australia ⓣ1300/651 960, New Zealand ⓣ09/377 3886, ⓦwww.thaiair.com.

Travel agents

Flight Centre Australia ⓣ13 31 33, ⓦwww.flightcentre.com.au; New Zealand ⓣ0800 243 544, ⓦwww.flightcentre.co.nz.
STA Travel Australia ⓣ1300/733 035, New Zealand ⓣ0508/782 872, ⓦwww.statravel.com.
Trailfinders Australia ⓣ02/9247 7666, ⓦwww.trailfinders.com.au.

Specialist operators

Peregrine Adventures Australia ⓣ03/8601 4444, ⓦwww.peregrine.net.au. Offers at least one annual itinerary in the Pyrenees, typically a week's worth of day hikes. AUS$1895 land only.
Walkabout Gourmet Adventures Australia ⓣ02/9980 2928, France ⓣ04.92.75.15.60, ⓦwww.walkaboutgourmet.com. Nicely routed fourteen-day, off-season walking trip through the Pyrenees from the Mediterranean to Biarritz; day walks on both sides of the range, bracketed by vehicle transfers and gourmet meals. AUS$4745 land only.

Online Booking

Even if you don't actually buy your ticket online, a web search will clue you up on what the prevailing published economy fares are. However, the airlines' own websites tend to show only nonchangeable/nonrefundable and full economy fares; for the numerous options in between, you'll have to ring them or consult a general discount travel site. The cheapest fares require a minimum stay of three days away, and over a Saturday night, with a typical maximum period of thirty or sixty days. They're subject to penalties (including total loss of ticket value) if you miss your outbound departure or change your return date. Sometimes student/youth tickets are available to those under 26, as are "Senior" or "Golden" fares for those over 60.

Some general travel sites like Expedia or Travelocity offer "special bargain" fares – the catch with these being that you don't see the scheduling, or the airlines used, until after you've bought the ticket.

Online travel booking sites

ⓦ**www.cheapflights.co.uk** (UK & Ireland), ⓦ**www.cheapflights.com** (US) or ⓦ**www.cheapflights.ca** (Canada) Fare-comparison site providing links to the airline or agent offering the deals.
ⓦ**www.etn.nl/discount.htm** A hub of consolidator and discount agent web links, maintained by the nonprofit European Travel Network.
ⓦ**www.expedia.co.uk** (UK & Ireland), ⓦ**www.expedia.com** (US) or ⓦ**www.expedia.ca** (Canada) Discount airfares, all-airline search engine and daily deals.
ⓦ**www.kelkoo.co.uk** (UK) Useful price-comparison site, checking numerous sources of flights for a given day.
ⓦ**www.lastminute.com** (UK & Ireland), ⓦ**www.lastminute.com.au** (Australia) or ⓦ**www.lastminute.co.nz** (New Zealand) Good package and flight-only deals available at short notice.
ⓦ**www.opodo.co.uk** Popular source of cheap UK airfares, run by a group of airlines.
ⓦ**www.orbiz.com** (US). Good generalist fare site.
ⓦ**www.skyauction.com** (US). Flight-only and travel packages up for auction.
ⓦ**www.travel.com.au** and ⓦ**www.goholidays.co.nz.** Flights-only and holidays from Australasia.
ⓦ**www.travelocity.co.uk** (UK & Ireland), ⓦ**www.travelocity.com** (US) or ⓦ**www.travelocity.ca** (Canada) Long established for deals on car rental and lodging as well as fares.
ⓦ**www.travelselect.com** An easy-to-use subsidiary of lastminute.com (see above).
ⓦ**www.zuji.com.au**, ⓦ**www.zuji.co.nz** Antipodean sites with all the usual range of offers.

By rail

Getting to the French side of the Pyrenees from London takes nine to eleven hours using Eurostar from London to Paris or Lille, and then an onward TGV (*train à grande vitesse*); you'll change platforms in Lille (to

Lille-Europe), and stations in Paris, from Nord to Montparnasse, Lyon or Austerlitz, but it's an otherwise congenial itinerary, typically leaving London between 9am and 1pm, arriving in the foothills early or late the same evening. The useful **Rail Europe** website only allows booking through to the major TGV termini of Biarritz, Lourdes, Tarbes, Toulouse and Perpignan; for anywhere else, like Girona in Spain, you'll need to ring them. **Tickets** can be bought anywhere from seven to sixty days in advance; off-season return fares to southern French destinations vary from about £110–135 for a non-changeable, non-refundable Leisure ticket, to £180 for a partly changeable Leisure Semi Flexi fare. In summer or peak skiing season you'll need to add at least £30 to each of these figures, but provided you buy well in advance, prices compare well to peak no-frills airfares when you remember that you're not paying £30 return to reach a remote airport.

Booking by phone, you can get a couple of **add-ons** to bring you that little bit closer to the hills. Alighting from the Lourdes-bound TGV at Pau, you could change to the service up the Aspe valley via Oloron-Sainte-Marie, with rail-bus service beyond Oloron to Canfranc in the Aragonese Pyrenees. Rail Europe can also get you an add-on ticket continuing past Toulouse (where the TGV service stops) up to Latour-de-Carol in the French Cerdagne; here you must change trains and buy another ticket for the Spanish network, entering Spain at Puigcerdà. This route gives handy access to the Ariège and the Carlit massif, as well as Andorra (by connecting bus from L'Hospitalet près L'Andorre).

Rail contacts

In the UK

Eurostar ⓣ08705 186 186, ⓦwww.eurostar.com. Just the first leg of the journey, to Paris or Lille.
International Rail UK ⓣ08700 841 410, ⓦwww.international-rail.com. Best for rail passes rather than tickets.
The Man in Seat 61 ⓦwww.seat61.com. Named after British rail buff Mark Smith's favourite seat on the Eurostar, this invaluable non-commercial site helps you plan a train journey from the UK to anywhere in Eurasia. You can't buy tickets here, but all necessary links are provided.
Rail Europe ⓣ08708 371 371, ⓦwww.raileurope.co.uk. Good web-booking facility for major, TGV-served Pyrenean stations.

In North America

Europrail International Inc Canada ⓣ1-888 667-9734, ⓦwww.europrail.net. Rail passes only.
Rail Europe US ⓣ1-877 257-2887, Canada ⓣ1-800/361-RAIL, ⓦwww.raileurope.com. Tickets and passes.

In Australia and New Zealand

Rail Plus Australia ⓣ03 9642 8644, New Zealand ⓣ649 377 5414, ⓦwww.railplus.com.au. Rail passes and tickets.

By car: Channel Tunnel or ferry

The fastest way for **drivers** to reach **the continent** is the **Eurotunnel** service via the Channel Tunnel; the alternative is one of the time-honoured **ferry** crossings (see below). Eurotunnel operates shuttle trains 24 hours a day, for vehicles and their passengers. The service runs continuously between Folkestone and Coquelles, near Calais, with one to four departures per hour and takes 35min (45min for some night departure times), though you must arrive at least 30min before departure. It's possible to just turn up and buy your ticket at the toll booths (after exiting the M20 at junction 11a), though during busy seasons booking is advisable. **Rates** depend on the time of year, time of day and length of stay; it's cheaper to travel between 10pm and 6am (from £49 one way), while the highest fares apply for weekend departures and returns in July and August. For current information, contact the **Eurotunnel Customer Services Centre** at ⓣ0870/535 3535, ⓦwww.eurotunnel.com.

Traditional cross-Channel options are the **ferry** links between Dover and Calais or Dunquerque (quickest and cheapest) and Newhaven and Dieppe. If you're headed for the Western Pyrenees, consider crossing to Cherbourg, Caen, St Malo (from Portsmouth or Poole) or even Roscoff (from Plymouth). These latter routes cut out the long detour around Paris, and point you towards some interesting drives through Brittany and along the French Atlantic coast. Irish drivers may prefer the lines bypassing Britain, direct to Cherbourg or Roscoff.

Ferry **prices** vary according to the time of year and, for motorists, the size of your car; prices have tumbled lately owing to competition among conventional and high-speed craft and the Eurotunnel. Dover–Calais runs, for example, start at about £49 one way for a car and two adults; from Ireland to France (eg Cork–Roscoff), allow €250 minimum for a car and two passengers with just pullman seats. Return fares are always better value, even more so if you're able to book well in advance. It's worth tinkering with dates and times to find the best deals; midweek, midday sailings are usually cheapest. Two good cut-price fare outlets are Ferry Savers (ⓣ0870 066 9612, ⓦwww.ferrysavers.com) and EuroDrive (ⓕ020 8324 4030, ⓦwww.eurodrive.co.uk).

Ferries to Santander and Bilbao

Direct car and passenger ferry services from England to Spain are convenient but expensive, and seem designed primarily for individuals hauling chattels to Spanish second homes. Ticket prices vary enormously according to the season, the number of passengers in the car and the length of your stay. Both foot passengers and drivers have to book some form of accommodation, even if just a pullman seat (or a cabin).

The ferry **from Plymouth to Santander** (four hours' drive from the west end of the Pyrenees) is operated by Brittany Ferries, takes 20hr 30min and runs on Wednesdays and Sundays all year except for maintenance periods. Prices for two passengers in an inside double cabin plus a car start at £523 return.

P&O provides a nearly year-round ferry service every three days from **Portsmouth to Bilbao** (35hr journey time), ninety minutes closer to the mountains than Santander. Return fares for a car and two people start at £560, including the cheapest double cabin (mandatory), though watch for transient offers of about £240 each way. Quicker Acciona Transmediterranea sails the same route every three days during summer, twice weekly late September to late June (29hr), and sometimes has offers of about £300 return or £200 one way for two adults in a car.

Ferry companies

Acciona Transmediterranea UK ⓣ 0871 720 6445, ⓦwww.atferries.com.

Brittany Ferries UK ⓣ0870 366 5333, Republic of Ireland ⓣ021 4277 801, ⓦwww.brittanyferries.com. Portsmouth to Caen; Portsmouth to St Malo; Plymouth to Roscoff; Poole to Cherbourg; Cork to Roscoff; Plymouth to Santander.

Condor Ferries UK ⓣ0870 243 5140, ⓦwww.condorferries.co.uk. Poole to St Malo via Guernsey or Jersey; Weymouth to St Malo via Guernsey & Jersey; Poole to Cherbourg; Portsmouth to Cherbourg.

Norfolkline UK ⓣ0870 164 2114, ⓦwww.norfolkline.com. Dover to Dunquerque.

Irish Ferries UK ⓣ0870 517 1717, Ireland ⓣ0818/300 400, ⓦwww.irishferries.com. Rosslare to Cherbourg and Roscoff (early Feb to late Dec).

P&O Ferries UK ⓣ0870 598 0333, Ireland ⓣ1800/409 049, ⓦwww.poferries.com. Dublin to Liverpool; Dover to Calais; Portsmouth to Bilbao.

SeaFrance ⓣ0870 443 1653, ⓦwww.seafrance.com. Dover to Calais.

Transmanche UK ⓣ0800 917 1201, ⓦwww.transmancheferries.com. Newhaven to Dieppe.

Getting around

If you're not driving, cycling or walking, getting around the Pyrenees requires organization and attention to detail. There are adequate bus services (and sometimes trains) along the main valley floors and between major centres, but few otherwise – especially between valleys. Approximate journey times and frequencies can be found in the "Travel Details" at the end of each chapter.

If you intend to hitch in the Pyrenees, it's always safest to try and arrange a lift in advance at your hotel, *gîte* or refuge. However, this guide **does not recommend hitching** as a reliable means of transport; in peak season you can wait for hours for a ride, as scores of crammed-full vehicles pass you by. The same safety risks apply as for hitching anywhere else.

France

France has the most **extensive rail network** in western Europe, although rural services have been severely cut back since the 1980s. Trains are excellent for travelling parallel to the line of the mountains and along the coasts, but lines tend to give out as the gradients increase and the populations dwindle. However, where the train stops, an **SNCF** (the French rail company) **bus** often continues the route. Private bus services can be uncoordinated and poorly publicized – where possible, it is simpler to use SNCF. If you have the time and the vehicle, **driving** or **cycling** are both excellent ways of seeing the Pyrenean foothills.

Trains

SNCF trains are clean, fast and frequent, and their staff usually courteous and helpful; all but the smallest stations have an information desk/ticket window. Slower trains, stopping at most stations, are often marked on timetables with a bicycle symbol – meaning you can travel with a bike as free accompanied luggage. "Car" at the top of a timetable column means it's an SNCF bus service, for which train tickets and passes are valid.

Regional **rail maps** and complete **timetables** are on sale at tobacconist shops, though you will find them for free at the biggest tourist offices. Leaflet timetables for a particular line are available free at stations, and again many tourist offices. Complete timetables and fare quotes are also available at Ⓦwww.sncf.fr (English version available).

All **tickets** – though not passes – must be **date-stamped** in the orange machines at station platform entrances or foyers. It is an offence if you don't "*compostez votre billet*", and people caught riding without tickets are liable to heavy spot fines. Train journeys may be broken any time, anywhere, but after a break of 24 hours you must date-stamp your ticket again upon resuming your journey.

While **InterRail** and **Eurail** passes are valid on all trains, and worth investigating before you leave home, the SNCF itself offers a range of **discount fares** on *Période Bleue* (Blue Period) days – effectively most of the year. **Couples or groups** of up to nine are entitled to a 25 percent discount on return fares if they travel together and outbound on a blue-period day. **SNCF discount passes** are available only in France from major stations, or online. If you're **over 60**, a one-year *Carte Senior* (€50) will give you up to half off most journeys starting in a blue period, including TGVs, and a 25 percent reduction on white-period fares. Identical reductions are available for under-26s with the one-year **Carte 12–25** (€49).

Buses

With the exception of SNCF services, **buses** play a generally minor role in the Pyrenees. Their most frustrating characteristic is that they rarely serve regions outside the SNCF network – which is precisely where you need them. Where they do exist, timetables are designed to suit working, school and market schedules – it will be a real stroke of luck if one is going where and when you want. Buses are, generally speaking, cheaper and slower than trains.

Larger towns usually have a **halte routière** (bus station), often next to the train station. However, private bus companies may leave from an array of different kerbside points around town. Their locations and schedules are usually available from tourist offices, or there will be a timetable posted at the stop.

Driving and car rental

Using a car gives you enormous advantages of access to remote areas. If you're camping or trekking, the ability to carry extra equipment can make driving an attractive proposition, but you will only save money – especially with a rented vehicle – if there are several people sharing the cost. Breakdown liability and the complication of point-to-point treks are other minuses.

Car rental arranged on the spot costs upwards of €250 per week; you need to be at least 21. It's normal to leave an indemnity against any damage to the car not covered by the CDW premium; this is usually done on a credit-card slip which should be destroyed upon safe return of the vehicle. We strongly suggest that you either pay a top-up premium (sometimes called a Franchise Waiver or Super Collision Damage Waver) to eliminate this liability, or – if you rent frequently – arrange **annual excess insurance** through Insurance 4 Car Hire (Ⓣ020/7012 6300, Ⓦwww.insurance4carhire.com), which will cover all UK- and North-America-based drivers. Cars are delivered with a full fuel tank and must be returned full; there's usually a surcharge to pick the car up on arrival at one airport and leave it at another. Among the UK rental agencies listed opposite, Skycars usually has the best rates for the French Pyrenees. You'll need at least Group B standard for mountain gradients – don't accept offers of underpowered compacts.

Any EU drivers' licence is valid in France, but North Americans and antipodeans require an International Driving Permit (available from the AAA or CAA for a small fee) as a supplement to their home licence. Vehicle registration, road tax and insurance documents must be carried in your own or a rented car. If you bring your own car with **right-hand drive**, have your headlight dip adjusted to the right before you go – it's a legal requirement – and, as a courtesy, paint them yellow or stick on black glare deflectors. If you need to be towed, look under *Dépannages* (Breakdowns) in the *Pages Jaunes* (Yellow Pages). If you have an accident or break-in, make a report to the local police (and keep a copy) in order to make an insurance claim.

The main **rule of the road** to remember in France is the law of *priorité à droite*, which means that you must give way to traffic coming from your right, even from a minor road. As a major cause of accidents, it is being phased out, and now only applies in built-up areas. Watch the roadside for signs with a yellow diamond on a white background, which means that you have the right of way; the same diamond with an oblique black line through it means you must yield to right-hand traffic. Signs saying STOP or CEDEZ LE PASSAGE also mean you must give way. Roundabouts (*rond-points*), of which there are many in Pyrenean towns, work just like those in Britain, except in the opposite direction: signs always warn you VOUS N'AVEZ PAS LA PRIORITÉ. Other common warning signs are BOUE (mud), CHAUSSÉE DÉFORMÉE (uneven surface), DÉVIATION (diversion), ÉBOULEMENT (landslide debris), GRAVILLONS (loose chippings), NIDS DE POULES (potholes), SAUF RIVERAINS (residents only), and VERGLAS FRÉQUENT (frequent ice slicks).

Major highways swarm with gendarmes (see p.66) manning drunk-driver checkpoints (especially at night after restaurants close) and speed traps; failure to wear a seatbelt nets you a spot fine of €50. The minimum fine for speeding is €90; go 40kph over the limit and you'll have a court appearance scheduled as well. **Speed limits** are as follows: 130kph/80mph on toll *autoroutes*; 110kph/68mph on dual carriageways; 90kph/56mph on other roads; and 50kph/37mph in towns. For all drivers in bad weather, and those with less than two years' experience, the out-of-town limits are 110kph, 100kph and 80kph respectively. All this said, driving in France may prove a stressful experience.

The country has the dubious honour of being tied with Spain for third place amongst pre-2004 EU states for levels of **unsafe driving** and accident fatalities (Portugal and Greece are first and second, respectively). If you're not doing at least 20kph over the applicable speed limit, you'll definitely have someone crawling up your rear bumper, except on the remotest and narrowest roads.

Motorway – **autoroute** – driving, though fast, is very boring when it's not hair-raising, and the **tolls** are expensive: Paris to Perpignan, for example, costs around €60. Unless you've a plane to catch, don't waste your money on the toll routes, of which there are few in the Pyrenees anyway; a French N (*nationale*) or RN (*route nationale*) **road** is the equal of a good UK "A" road, or a well-maintained state highway in the US. In the Pyrenees, you will become acquainted of necessity with the D (*départmentale*) roads: many quite good, with two lanes (but no verge), others one-lane and barely paved. Some have been constructed over high passes or along corniches with spectacular views; minor roads over the passes are typically **snowed up** between November and May, though giant signboards may advise you of opened, snowploughed corridors and chain requirements, especially near ski resorts.

Fuel (*essence*) prices are currently in a state of flux – ie inching steadily upwards from 2006 levels of about €1.20 per litre, whether for lead-replacement "super", 95–98 octane "normal", or diesel (*gas-oil*); it's notably cheaper to fill up at out-of-town supermarket chains like Leclerc, Carrefour or Champion.

Car-rental agencies

Britain

Avis ⓣ0870 606 0100, ⓦwww.avis.co.uk.
Budget ⓣ0844 581 9998,ⓦwww.budget.co.uk.
Hertz ⓣ0870 844 8844, ⓦwww.hertz.co.uk.
National ⓣ0870 536 5365, ⓦwww.nationalcar.co.uk.
Sixt ⓦwww.e-sixt.com.
Skycars ⓣ0870 789 7789, ⓦwww.skycars.com.
Thrifty ⓣ01494/751 540, ⓦwww.thrifty.co.uk.

Ireland

Avis Northern Ireland ⓣ028/9024 0404, Republic of Ireland ⓣ01/605 7500, ⓦwww.avis.ie.
Budget Republic of Ireland ⓣ0903/277 11, ⓦwww.budget.ie.
Cosmo Thrifty Northern Ireland ⓣ028/9445 2565, ⓦwww.thrifty.com.
Hertz Republic of Ireland ⓣ01/676 7476, ⓦwww.hertz.ie.
Sixt Republic of Ireland ⓣ1850 206 088, ⓦwww.irishcarrentals.ie.
Thrifty Republic of Ireland ⓣ1800 515 800, ⓦwww.thrifty.ie.

North America

Alamo ⓣ1-800/462-5266, ⓦwww.alamo.com.
Auto Europe ⓣ1-800/223-555, ⓦwww.autoeurope.com.
Avis US ⓣ1-800/230-4898, Canada ⓣ1-800/272-5871, ⓦwww.avis.com.
Budget ⓣ1-800/527-0700, ⓦwww.budgetrentacar.com.
Dollar US ⓣ1-800/800-3665, ⓦwww.dollar.com.
Europe by Car ⓣ1-800/223-1516, ⓦwww.europebycar.com.
Hertz US ⓣ1-800/654-3131, Canada ⓣ1-800/263-0600, ⓦwww.hertz.com.
National ⓣ1-800/962-7070, ⓦwww.nationalcar.com.
Thrifty ⓣ1-800/847-4389, ⓦwww.thrifty.com.

Australia

Avis ⓣ13 63 33 or 02/9353 9000, ⓦwww.avis.com.au.
Budget ⓣ1300 362 848, ⓦwww.budget.com.au.
Hertz ⓣ13 30 39 or 03/9698 2555, ⓦwww.hertz.com.au.
National ⓣ13 10 45, ⓦwww.nationalcar.com.au.
Thrifty ⓣ1300 367 227, ⓦwww.thrifty.com.au.

New Zealand

Apex ⓣ0800 93 95 97 or 03/379 6897, ⓦwww.apexrentals.co.nz.
Avis ⓣ09/526 2847 or 0800 655 111, ⓦwww.avis.co.nz.
Budget ⓣ080/652 227, ⓦwww.budget.co.nz.
Hertz ⓣ0800 654 321, ⓦwww.hertz.co.nz.
National ⓣ0800 800 115, ⓦwww.nationalcar.co.nz.
Thrifty ⓣ09/309 0111, ⓦwww.thrifty.co.nz.

Cycling

Bicycles (*vélos*) have high status in France. All the car ferries from Britain carry them for free (with advance warning); SNCF makes minimal charges; and individual French people respect cyclists, both as traffic and potential customers. Restaurants and hotels are nearly always obliging about looking after your bike, while local motorists normally give you plenty of room – it's the lumbering foreign camper van you have to watch out for.

You can normally load your bike straight onto the train at your **ferry port of disembarkation**, though you must first go to the ticket office of the station. Eurostar allows you to take your bicycle within your normal baggage allowance, provided it's dismantled and stored in a special bike bag (ring ⓣ08702 649 899 for current rules). It's probably easier to send it unaccompanied, with guaranteed arrival within 24 hours (register it up to 10 days in advance – book through Esprit Europe on ⓣ0870 850 850); the fee is £20 each way. All airlines, however, are getting progressively stingier about transporting bikes, which will probably incur a set charge (cheaper if paid in advance, not at check-in). You may also have to box them, and you should deflate the tyres.

The SNCF runs various schemes for cyclists, all detailed in the free leaflet *Train et Vélo*, available from most train stations. Trains marked with a bicycle in the timetable are usually the only ones on which you can travel with an intact bike as free accompanied luggage in dedicated bike racks or in the luggage van if space is available. Otherwise, you have to send your bike bundled as registered luggage for a fee of €39: two-day delivery is promised, though this service doesn't operate at weekends.

For about €15/day, you can **rent bikes** from campsites and *gîtes d'étape*, as well as from specialist bike shops (which are more likely to have mountain bikes). Most rental bikes are **not insured**, however, and you will be billed for replacement or repair if it's stolen or damaged; check whether your travel insurance policy covers this.

More and more cyclists are using **mountain bikes** (*VTT* or *Vélos Touts Terrains* in French) for touring holidays. However, it's actually less strenuous, and much quicker, to cycle long distances on asphalt and carry luggage on a traditional touring or racing model.

Most sizeable foothill towns have well-stocked **retail and repair shops**, where parts are normally cheaper than in Britain or the US. However, it's wise to carry spare tyres for foreign-made bikes, as French sizes differ. It's also not always easy to find mountain-bike parts, as opposed those for to road-racers. Inner tubes are not a problem, as they adapt to either tyre size, though make sure you have the right valves.

Spain

On the Spanish side, there are few trains into the central Pyrenees; rail services mainly connect the towns of the Atlantic and Mediterranean coasts. On shorter or secondary routes buses tend to be quicker, and will also take you closer to your destination; some train stations are well outside the town or village they serve, with no connecting bus. Car rental may also be worth considering, with costs (if prearranged) among the lowest in Europe.

Trains

RENFE, the Spanish rail company, operates a horrendously complicated variety of train services. The main surviving Pyrenean foothill services are *regionales* or *trenes regional diesel* (R and TRD respectively on schedules), equivalent to buses in speed and cost. Slightly faster and better – and usually double the price – are **largo recorrido** (long-distance) services, sub-rated as IC (inter-city), such as the Barcelona–Lleida–Huesca line. On a few lines, buses susbstitute for trains, as on the French side. To sort out conflicting or missing schedules, ring RENFE's infor-

EuroDomino

One of the more useful rail passes for Pyrenean travel is the **EuroDomino pass**, available only to European residents of six months' standing. It offers unlimited rail travel on any three to eight days of a given calendar month, within a particular country, ie either Spain or France. You probably won't, however, get full value out of one unless you're planning to reach the Pyrenees by train from the UK, as well as travelling a few days along the foothills, rather than just travelling between a Spanish or French arrival airport and your mountain base.

mation/reservations line on ⓣ902 240 202 – you'll need to speak Spanish – or consult ⓦwww.renfe.es (English version available).

RENFE **fares** are discounted by 25–40 percent for those over 60, the disabled, children aged 4 to 11 years and groups of more than ten. Return fares are also discounted by ten percent on *regionales* (valid fifteen days) and twenty percent on *largo recorridos* (valid sixty days).

Tickets can be bought at stations between sixty days and fifteen minutes before the train leaves, from the *venta anticipada* window, or in the final two hours from the *venta inmediata* window. If you board the train without a ticket the conductor may charge you up to double the normal fare. Many of the stations on the three surviving mountain lines (Barcelona–Puigcerdà, Lleida–La Pobla de Segur and Huesca–Canfranc) are no longer staffed or keep very limited hours; if you do get on these trains without a ticket, find the conductor first and explain, rather than wait to have the conductor find you. Avoid such situations entirely by buying tickets beforehand at **travel agents** displaying the RENFE logo – they have a sophisticated computer system which can also make seat reservations, obligatory on *largo recorrido* trains; the cost is the same as at a station. You can **change** the departure date of an electronically issued, reserved-seat, *largo recorrido* ticket up to one hour before your originally scheduled departure, for a token charge. A full **cancellation** of the same type of ticket entails losing fifteen percent of the purchase price, provided it's done at least half an hour before scheduled departure.

InterRail and **Eurail** passes are valid on all RENFE trains (though not on the Núria *cremallera*), but there's a supplement for the fastest trains. The apparently random nature of these **surcharges** can be a source of considerable irritation. Learn what you're letting yourself in for by reserving a seat in advance, obligatory anyway on the best trains. For a few euros you'll get a computer-printed ticket which will satisfy any guard.

Buses

Buses will probably meet most of your public transport needs; most small Pyrenean villages are accessible by services originating in the provincial or *comarcal* (county) capital. Service, especially in Catalunya, is generally reliable, with prices pretty standard at around €6.50 per 100 kilometres. All Pyrenean towns have a single main bus station; newer terminals are often on the fringes of town. Services are drastically reduced **on Sundays and holidays**, when you shouldn't plan on travelling to remote places. The applicable Castilian words on timetables are *diario* (daily), *laborables* (workdays, including Saturday) and *domingos y festivos* (Sundays and holidays). On Catalan timetables, the equivalent expressions are *diari* (daily), *feiners* (workdays), *festius* (holidays), *dissabtes* (Saturdays) and *diumenges* (Sundays).

Driving

The advantages and disadvantages of having a car on the Spanish side are as for France, though slightly cheaper fuel prices are offset by significant vehicle crime – never leave anything of value visible in the car. Major river-valley roads are generally good, the mountain corniches more than serviceable, and traffic, while a little hectic in the cities, is moderately well behaved – though see the comment on p.37 about Spanish and French accident rates.

Driving licence requirements are as for France (see p.36). Away from main roads you yield to vehicles approaching from the right, but at roundabouts (*rondadores*) you yield to those approaching from the left. **Speed limits** are posted – the maximum on urban roads is 50kph, other roads 90kph, motorways (*autopistas*) 120kph – and (on the main highways at least) speed traps are common, especially in the morning. If you're stopped for any violation, the Spanish police can and usually will levy a stiff **on-the-spot fine** (cash only) before letting you go on your way, especially since as a foreigner you're unlikely to make a court appearance. Motorcycle-borne *policía* or Guardia Civil *Tráfica* are also on the lookout for non-belt-wearers, though unlike in France you may get off with just a warning. **Parking laws** are rigorously enforced in large towns, and any illegally parked vehicle (especially ones left in taxi zones) will be impounded promptly – with a sticker left on the road telling you where to pay the hefty fine (€100 and up, in cash only) to retrieve it.

Fuel currently costs about fifteen percent less than in France for Súper *Sín Plomo* (lead-free) 98, lead-replacement Súper 97, *Sin Plomo* (95 or diesel (*gasoleo*), though in villages off the main routes, you may not get this range of choice. In **Andorra**, you'll save roughly another fifteen percent, or nearly a third off compared to France. **Credit cards** are accepted at almost all stations on main highways. They are also taken at the motorway toll gates either side of Girona, though the amount is often trivial; stick the card in the reader and the bar opens. Otherwise you must have exact change for the coin slots, or go to the few attended gates. The **tolls** themselves add up quickly so these motorways are best avoided unless you're in a hurry.

Car rental

You'll find a limited choice of car rental companies in large towns, with the biggest ones like Hertz and Avis represented at Girona, Lleida and Zaragoza airports, or Huesca RENFE station. You'll need to be 21, with a licence held for a year minimum, and you're looking at from €30 per day for a small car (much less by the week). As in France, Skycars (see p.37) is among the best prebooking agencies, substantially undercutting the large companies – rates from Girona, for example, are about £100–130 a week. Again as in France, avoid compacts with engines of under 1.1L – simply not feasible with two adults and luggage going up a mountain gradient.

Cycling

Touring the Spanish Pyrenees by **bicycle** can be rewarding, though paradoxically the often superior state of the roads compared to the French side means nerve-wracking, higher-speed traffic. Cars tend to toot horns before they pass, which can be alarming at first but useful once you're accustomed to it. Always ride single file in any case – roads, while well surfaced, rarely have verges or multiple lanes. Remember also that even the foothills are horrifically steep – and torrid in summer, with none of the moderating mist of the French slopes.

That said, in the wake of Miguel Indurain's multiple Tour de France triumphs, the Spanish are keen cycling fans – which means that you'll be well received and find reasonable facilities. There are bike shops in the larger towns and parts can often be found at auto repair shops or garages. Cycle-touring guides to most of the Pyrenees can be found in good bookshops – written in Spanish, Catalan or Euskera, of course. The Castilian for "mountain bike" is BTT (*Bici Todo Terreno*).

Getting your bike there should present few problems. For arrival by air, see p.38. Spanish **trains** are also reasonably accessible, though bikes can only go on a train with a guard's van (*furgón*) and must be registered – go to the *Equipajes* or *Paquexpres* desk at the station. Most *hostales* will offer secure overnight storage.

Tourist information and maps

The national tourist organizations of both France and Spain have numerous overseas outlets, well stocked with literature, and are also conspicuously represented in towns at home. Both sides of the Pyrenean range are meticulously mapped, though French products have a slight edge over Spanish in terms of quality.

French information offices

Overseas branches of the **French Government Tourist Office** (ⓦwww.franceguide.com) give away numerous maps and glossy brochures for every region of France, including useful lists of accommodation and festival programmes.

In the French Pyrenees you'll find a tourist information centre – **Office du Tourisme**, as it's usually called – in practically every town and larger village. From these you can get specific local information – including, most importantly, the **météo** or daily weather report, posted in the window – and as a rule a useful free town plan. Many bureaux also publish hotel and restaurant listings, bus and train timetables and local car and walking itineraries, and they are often a few steps from local trekking and adventure-activity organizers. Most regions or major towns have useful websites, given in the text as appropriate.

French Government Tourist Offices abroad

Australia Level 20, 25 Bligh St, Sydney ⓣ02/9231 5244, ⓔinfo.au@franceguide.com.
Britain 178 Piccadilly, London ⓣ09068/244 123 (60p/min), ⓔinfo.uk@franceguide.com.
Canada 1981 Avenue McGill College, Suite 490, Montréal ⓣ514/876 9881, ⓔcanada@franceguide.com.
Ireland ⓣ1560/235 235, ⓔinfo.ie@franceguide.com. No walk-in info.
New Zealand contact the office in Australia.
US 9454 Wilshire Blvd, Suite 715, Beverly Hills ⓣ310/271 6665, ⓔinfo.losangeles@franceguide.com; 1 Biscayne Tower, Suite 1750, 2 South Biscayne Building, Miami ⓣ305/373 8177, ⓔinfo.miami@franceguide.com; 205 North Michigan Ave, Suite 3770, Chicago ⓣ312/751 7800, ⓔinfo.chicago@franceguide.com; 444 Madison Ave, 16th Floor, New York ⓣ212/838 7800, ⓔinfo.us@franceguide.com.

Spanish information offices

The **Spanish National Tourist Office** (SNTO; ⓦwww.tourspain.info) has a less broad array of maps, pamphlets and special-interest leaflets; walk-in offices are history in many countries, with petitioners expected to use the website or email for queries. **In the Spanish Pyrenees** itself you'll find instead separately administered provincial or municipal **Turismos** (*Turismes* in Catalan). These vary enormously in quality – those of the Basque country and Catalunya are usually excellent – but while useful for regional information, they seldom know anything about what goes on outside their patch. Like their French counterparts, they post **weather reports**, often for three days at a time, on their windows.

SNTO offices abroad

Britain ⓣ020/7486 8077, ⓦwww.tourspain.co.uk. No walk-in premises.
Canada 2 Bloor St West, 34th Floor, Toronto, Ontario M4W 3E2 ⓣ416/961-3131, ⓦwww.tourspain.toronto.on.ca.
Netherlands Laan Van Meerdervoor 8A, The Hague, ⓣ 703465900, ⓦwww.spaanverkeersbureau.nl.
USA New York, ⓣ212/265-8822, ⓔnuevayork@tourspain.es; Los Angeles, ⓣ323/658-7192, ⓔlosangeles@tourspain.es; Chicago, ⓣ312/642-1992, ⓔchicago@tourspain.es; Miami, ⓣ305/358-1992, ⓔmiami@tourspain.es. No walk-in premises.

Pyrenean trekking maps

Maps specifically for the Pyrenees are a problem if you want to trek through the entire range. A scale of at least 1:50,000 is essential, and the **1:25,000 TOP 25** series published by the French **Institut Géographique National** (IGN) would be ideal for the northern slopes. But apart from the significant expense of thirty-odd sheets at that scale, they're heavy. In principle, it's best to buy maps (typically €8–9) as you need them, because of the stiff mark-up overseas; in practice, however, try to buy indispensable maps before arrival, as they're often sold out in their area of use.

A compromise for the GR10/HRP traverse on the **French side** would be the **1:50,000 Cartes de Randonnées** published jointly by the IGN and Randonnées Pyrénéennes (Rando Éditions), numbered from 1 to 11 going from west to east. They cover the entire range from coast to coast, with *gîtes d'étape*, refuges and recommended GR, HRP and Tour routes highlighted. Note that no. 9, "Montségur", is out of print, though you can often find backstock in Spanish bookshops and outdoor equipment retailers. These maps are generally excellent, though not perfect – a few paths are shown incorrectly, partly owing to last revision dates for a few of 1990–93, though most were revised in the period 1998–2001. At about €9 apiece (£8.95 in the UK) though, the complete set of 1:50,000 sheets still represents a substantial investment in money and pack weight. For both IGN and Cartes de Randonnées maps, relevant titles are quoted throughout the text.

The most widely available Spanish productions for the **Spanish** side of the range are the maps of Catalunya-based **Editorial Alpina**, at scales of 1:25,000 to 1:40,000, covering the most popular walking areas between the Catalan coast and Navarra (relevant titles are quoted throughout the text; ⓦwww.editorialalpina.com). The accompanying booklets (Castilian or Catalan, rarely in English) supply useful information about accommodation, walking routes, winter mountaineering and caves, but the series omits most of the Basque country, and trail tracings are often woefully inaccurate, scarcely changed since the maps first appeared in the late 1940s. It's better to buy Editorial Alpina titles in Spain: not only are they much cheaper there (€8–9 versus £8–9), but you'll want the most current versions – overseas stocks are often obsolete. New editions have predominantly green booklet jackets, waterproof maps (with ten-metre contour intervals) and some detail on the French side of the border (where applicable).

The only serious alternative to Editorial Alpina, now preferred by many, are the 1:50,000 **Mapas Excursionistas**, produced jointly by the Institut Cartogràfic de Catalunya and Rando Éditions, and mimicking the French 1:50,000 *Cartes des Randonées*. They're numbered 20 to 24 from east to west – from the Garrotxa region to Ansó/Echo – and retail for €8–9 in Spain (£8.95 in the UK). What you lose in terms of scale compared to the Alpinas, you more than gain in accuracy and clarity. The ICC (ⓦwww.icc.es, Catalan only) also produces two of its own series of maps: the **Mapa comarcal de Catalunya**, large 1:50,000 folding sheets for each county (*comarca*), and the **Mapa topogràfic de Catalunya** at 1:25,000. Where necessary, the above can be supplemented by the range of **topographical maps** issued by the Spanish government's **Instituto Geográfico Nacional** (IGN), the Mapa Topográfico Nacional de España. These are available at scales of 1:100,000, 1:50,000 and occasionally 1:25,000. Though not quite up to the standard of French products, the maps have improved notably since the late 1990s, replacing Castilian with local place names, indicating magnetic declination from true north and including useful regional language vocabularies in the margins. Moreover, a plain-blue-jacketed folding series, analogous to the French Série Bleue and produced together by IGN and MOPU (the ministry of public works), covers many areas at scales of 1:50,000 and occasionally 1:25,000. Many bookshops in Spain, and a few specialist overseas stores, stock these maps, though as with Editorial Alpina products, you'll find them much cheaper on arrival – typically €4 – and again less accurate than their French equivalents.

Pyrenean road maps

In terms of **road maps covering the entire range**, only two products rate consideration. Firestone's "Pireneos" 1:200,000 map shows both sides of the border at the same level of detail, even indicating parts of the French GR10 and Spanish GR11. Although two-sided, it's easy to unfold and use, but available only in Spain (€5) – look for the blue-fringed red cover. Despite not having been updated since the mid-1990s, it remains reasonably accurate – but coverage in the most recent printing is incomplete (the "eastern" and "western" halves of coverage don't meet up, while parts of the French side are missing). If you want to try and special-order it from a specialist retailer, the product number is T-33, and the ISBN is 9788486907167. Rough Guides' very own "The Pyrenees & Andorra" (1:250,000; £5.99/$9.99), also two-sided (but again not "meshing" correctly), is harder-wearing and waterproof, including the Sierra de Guara, all French towns and current road numberings (as well as obscure churches), but excluding San Sebastián and Los Mallos. For the **French side** only, two one-sided IGN "TOP 250" *Série Rouge* 1:250,000 maps document the entire range: no. 113, "Pyrénées Languedoc Roussillon", and no. 114, "Pyrénées Occidentales". A better French production, and perhaps a good compromise – especially for **cyclists** – between a small-scale road map and a bulky stack of *randonnée* maps is the IGN 1:100,000 Série Verte. This shows contours and the GR10, covering the whole French side (and some of Spain) in four one-sided sheets: no. 69 "Pau Bayonne", no. 70 "Tarbes Bagnères-de-Luchon", no. 71 "Saint-Gaudens Andorre" and no. 72 "Perpignan Béziers". Road maps for the **Spanish side** of the range are best bought in bookshops (*librerías*), street kiosks or service stations in Spain itself. Among the best are those published by Almax (ⓦwww.almax-editores.com), which also produces reliable indexed street plans for the main cities.

> When using a **compass** in the Pyrenees, the magnetic declination from true north is a maximum of 3° west.

Map outlets

In the UK and Ireland

Blackwell's Map Centre Oxford ⓣ01865 793 550, ⓦwww.maps.blackwell.co.uk. Branches in Bristol, Cambridge, Cardiff, Leeds, Liverpool, Newcastle, Reading and Sheffield.
The Map Shop Leicester ⓣ0116 247 1400, ⓦwww.mapshopleicester.co.uk.
National Map Centre London ⓣ020 7222 2466, ⓦwww.mapsnmc.co.uk.
National Map Centre Ireland Dublin ⓣ01 476 0471, ⓦwww.mapcentre.ie.
Stanfords London ⓣ020 7836 1321, ⓦwww.stanfords.co.uk. Also in Manchester ⓣ0161 831 0250, and Bristol ⓣ0117 929 9966.
The Travel Bookshop London ⓣ020 7229 5260, ⓦwww.thetravelbookshop.co.uk.
Traveller Newcastle-upon-Tyne ⓣ0191 261 5622, ⓦwww.newtraveller.com.

In the US and Canada

110 North Latitude US ⓣ336 369-4171, ⓦwww.110nlatitude.com.
Book Passage Corte Madera, CA ⓣ1-800 999-7909, ⓦwww.bookpassage.com.
Distant Lands Pasadena, CA ⓣ1-800 310-3220, ⓦwww.distantlands.com.
Globe Corner Bookstore Cambridge, MA ⓣ1-800 358-6013, ⓦwww.globecorner.com.
Longitude Books New York, NY ⓣ1-800 342-2164, ⓦwww.longitudebooks.com.
Map Town Calgary, AB ⓣ1-877 921-6277, ⓦwww.maptown.com.
Travel Bug Bookstore Vancouver, BC ⓣ604 737-1122, ⓦwww.travelbugbooks.ca.
World of Maps Ottawa, ON ⓣ1-800 214-8524, ⓦwww.worldofmaps.com.

In Australia and New Zealand

Map Centre ⓦwww.mapcentre.co.nz.
Map Shop Adelaide ⓣ08 8231 2033, ⓦwww.mapshop.net.au.
Map World Sydney ⓣ02 9261 3601, ⓦwww.mapworld.net.au. Also in Perth ⓣ08/9322 5733.
Map World Christchurch ⓣ0800 627 967, ⓦwww.mapworld.co.nz.
Mapland Melbourne ⓣ03 9670 4383, ⓦwww.mapland.com.au.

Insurance

Even though EU reciprocal healthcare privileges apply across the Pyrenees (except Andorra), you'd do well to take out a travel insurance policy against theft, loss and illness or injury. Before paying for a new policy, however, check whether you are already protected: some all-risks home insurance policies may cover your possessions when overseas, and many private medical schemes offer supplemental cover for abroad.

In Canada, provincial health plans usually provide partial cover for medical mishaps overseas, while holders of official student/teacher/youth cards in Canada and the US are entitled to meagre accident coverage and hospital in-patient benefits.

After exhausting the possibilities above, you might want to contact a **specialist travel insurance** company, or consider the travel insurance deal we offer (see box below). A typical travel insurance policy provides cover for the loss of baggage, tickets and – up to a certain limit – cash or cheques, as well as **cancellation** or curtailment of your journey. If you take medical coverage, ascertain whether benefits will be paid as treatment proceeds or only after return home, whether there is a 24-hour medical emergency number and how much the deductible excess is. When securing baggage cover, make sure that the per-article limit – typically under £400 – will cover your most valuable possession. Receipts for medicines and medical treatment are needed to make a claim, and in the event you have anything stolen or lost, you must obtain an official statement from the police or the airline that lost your bags.

Extra cover

Ordinary travel insurance policies are rarely valid for sporting activities such as skiing, trekking, whitewater rafting, climbing or horse-riding, and certainly not for paragliding, canyoning or caving. For these you'll have to take out extra cover such as the French Carte Neige, which can be obtained in sports centres, equipment shops and clubs. It's inexpensive (about €35 for a year) and valid countrywide, but meets just the cost of recovery, offering only limited medical reimbursal (whatever your state or private insurance refuses to cover, up to about €4000) and no property protection – consult the web for current cautionary articles on the scheme's limitations. Spanish ski resorts offer similar recovery insurance as a top-up to lift-pass prices. In Britain, Snowcard Insurance Services (Ⓣ01327/262805, Ⓦwww.snowcard.co.uk) specializes in more comprehensive mountaineering and activity holiday travel insurance.

Health

Nationals of all EU countries are entitled to take advantage of each other's health services under the same terms as residents of the country. Traditional form E111 has been replaced by the EHIC (European Health Insurance Card), which you apply for at post offices or on-line at ⓦwww.dh.gov.uk/travellers – allow two to three weeks for delivery.

Only citizens (and with some restrictions permanent residents) of EU and EEA member states are covered under this scheme; anyone else is strongly advised to take out travel insurance (see opposite) with adequate medical and repatriation cover. If you're travelling in your own vehicle, you may want to get breakdown cover which includes return of the vehicle if you're incapacitated.

France

General healthcare in France, despite funding woes, remains among the best in the world. Under the French health system every hospital visit, doctor's consultation, ambulance callout and prescribed medicine incurs a **charge**. EU/EEA citizens are entitled to a refund (usually between 70 and 100 percent) of expenses incurred, providing the doctor is government-registered (a *médecin conventionné*). This can still leave a hefty shortfall, especially after a stay in hospital.

For minor complaints, a **pharmacie**, indicated by an illuminated green cross, should suffice. There's at least one in every small town and even some villages. They keep normal shop hours except for those doing a 24-hour shift (the *pharmacie de garde*); rota details are displayed in windows. To find a **doctor**, consult a pharmacy, tourist office or hotel where they should provide you with an address. Consultation fees are €23–27 and you'll be given a **Feuille de Soins** (Statement of Treatment) for subsequent insurance claims. Any prescriptions fulfilled by the pharmacy must be paid for; little price stickers (*vignettes*) for each medication will be stuck on your *Feuille de Soins*. In serious emergencies you will always be admitted to the nearest **hospital** (*hôpital*) – an ambulance can be summoned nationwide by dialling ⓣ15.

Spain

Public health standards and care in Spain are similarly high; the worst that's likely to happen to you is that you might fall victim to an upset stomach. Wash fruit and avoid *tapas* that look like they were prepared last week.

For minor complaints, go to a **farmacia** – you'll find one in all but the smallest villages. Pharmacists are willing to give advice (often in English) and able to dispense many drugs that would be available only on prescription in most other countries. They keep usual shop hours but some open late and at weekends, while a rota system keeps at least one in every area open 24 hours. The rota is displayed in the window of every pharmacy, or check in local newspapers under *Farmacias de guardia*.

In more serious cases, get the address of an English-speaking **doctor** from a *farmacia*, the local police or tourist office. In emergencies dial ⓣ091 for the *Servicios de Urgencia*, or look up the *Cruz Roja Española* (Red Cross) which runs a national ambulance service. Treatment at (often excellent) public hospitals for EU/EEA citizens is free; otherwise you'll be charged at private hospital rates, which can be expensive.

Spas

On both sides of the Pyrenees, but especially in France, you'll come across thermal spas. These were the original, eighteenth- or nineteenth-century impetus for tourism in these parts, and while many have been remodelled in Brutalist style, others retain their Belle Époque decor. They used to be the exclusive preserve of the elderly and/or the unwell – the *curistes*, in French – who would stay for weeks on end, with the French social security system footing the bill. Since the millennium, however, the authorities have made it clear that they will no longer subsidize indefinite taking of the waters, and in order to survive economically the spas have had to reinvent themselves. *Remis en Forme* (Get in Shape) programmes, with gyms, yoga classes and similar trappings, are now the rule, designed to attract a younger, more active clientele. Spas are typically open only during summer, with morning hours reserved for the dwindling numbers of *curistes*, and late afternoons for casual trade. But increasing numbers of thermal stations near ski resorts – Barèges, Luchon, St-Lary-Soulan, Eaux-Bonnes, Cauterets, for example – have a late-afternoon session in winter, aimed at chilled and muscle-sore skiers. Take advantage, when available.

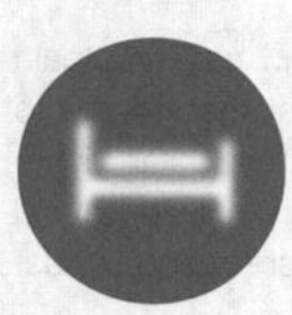

Accommodation

Finding a place to stay in the Pyrenees presents few problems, as long as you avoid the peak seasons. On both sides of the range, these are: Christmas and New Year, the February half-term week, Easter week, and mid-July to mid-August. Campsites are less of a problem in peak season, though drivers of caravans and camper vans should book ahead.

France

Almost every French Pyrenean town (excepting the notoriously pricey Basque coast) has at least one budget hotel, and a handful of more comfortable ones. Even during low season, reserving a room in advance saves trudging around on arrival. Full **accommodation lists** for each province are available from any French Government Tourist Office (see p.41) or from local tourist offices. It's worth getting hold of these, together with **Logis de France**'s (ⓦ www.logis-de-france.fr) handbook, which lists hotels, renowned for their consistently salubrious – if not always innovative – food and good-value rooms (each one is surveyed annually); they're recognizable on the spot by a logo of one to three green-and-yellow hearths. A growing number of hotels are **non-smoking** (*non fumeur*), especially once smoke alarms have been fitted.

Hotels and chambres d'hôtes

All French Pyrenean **hotels** are graded from zero to four stars. Prices more or less correspond to the number of stars, though the system is a bit haphazard, having more to do with ratios of bathrooms per guest, and the presence or absence of lobbies, than with genuine quality; renovated single-star hotels are often very good. However, unless you patronize fairly expensive, modernized hotels, you may have to contend with traditional French **pillows**, best described as sausages or long sacks of cement, often elaborately worked into the bedding; consider bringing your own small inflatable or orthopedic pillow. At the budget level, for rooms with a shower an extra charge of about €2–3 may be made each time you use the shower down the hall. A **taxe de séjour** of €0.50–€1 per person per day, according to the star rating, may be added to the final bill.

Breakfast, too, can add €4.50–10 per person to costs – though there is no obligation to take it and you will usually do better at a café. In busy resorts you may not find a room unless you agree to **demi-pension** (half-board). This can work in your favour, however, as *demi-pension* rates will often save you twenty percent of the cost of room and board taken separately. **Single rooms** – or more properly, less favoured rooms considered most suitable for a lone person

– are only marginally less expensive than more generously proportioned quarters, so sharing always slashes costs. Most hotels willingly provide rooms with extra beds, for three or more people, at good discounts.

Many Pyrenean hotels take a **month or so off** per year – usually sometime between November and May, unless they're in a major skiing area. You may also find that their restaurant and reception close one night, plus one day, a week. We've given days and months of closure as last known, but check as they change often.

In country areas, in addition to standard hotels, you will come across **chambres d'hôtes**, bed-and-breakfast accommodation in someone's house or farm. These vary in standard but are certainly affordable, falling mostly into the ❸ category; in some instances they are good sources of traditional home-cooking. Leaflets available in tourist offices list most of them.

Hostels, gîtes d'étape and refuges

Bona fide *Auberges de Jeunesse* (**youth hostels**) are confined to Biarritz, Bayonne and Pau, and for groups of two or more won't be cheaper than a basic hotel. For single travellers, however, they are invaluable (at €10–17 per night for a dormitory bunk), and allow you to cut costs by self-catering, or eating in inexpensive canteens. Stays are usually limited to three consecutive nights, though off-peak this may be negotiable. To use them, you are supposed to be a member of the International Youth Hostel Federation, but you can often join on the spot.

Far more useful for budget travellers in the countryside is the **gîte d'étape**, especially popular in walking areas. In the Pyrenees, *gîtes* are administered under the aegis of the publishing and outdoors activities organization Randonnées Pyrénéennes, established to create a chain of medium-category hostelries for trekkers, cyclists and horse-riders. All *gîtes* have self-catering kitchen facilities, some form of heating, bunks in dormitories or private rooms (bedding provided only for the latter), laundry, shower and toilet facilities; opening seasons vary. A bunk will be €9–16, a hot evening meal will rarely cost more than €13, and doubles, where available, generally fall in category ❶ or the lower half of ❷. Description of a *gîte* as a **Rando'Plume** means either that rooms are of extraordinarily high standard – typically with some en-suite facilities, and a low number of bunks per dorm, with proper linen – and/or that the *gîte* is affiliated to some upmarket activity centre in the area (a trekking or winter-sports outfitter, horse-riding, etc), whose devotees make up the main clientele.

Although *gîtes* must give priority to long-distance travellers on a traverse, it is sometimes possible to use one as a base for several nights; the manager will almost certainly be able to share an intimate knowledge of the region. Rando Éditions walkers' maps show *gîte* locations (sometimes obsolete), and they are noted in the individual GR *topo-guides*.

Most **mountain refuge huts** are open only in summer (June–Sept), though otherwise there is nearly always at least a simple annexe with sleeping platforms and perhaps a fireplace or stove. A few refuges are still extremely basic and antiquated, while most others are passably comfortable and modern – with hot showers in some cases. Almost all of them have cooking facilities and offer meals, though these are often not the best value (€11–16 with the emphasis on wine and carbohydrates), reflecting the fact that foodstuffs usually have to be brought in by mule or helicopter. Especially in or around the Parc National des Pyrénées, refuges are packed to the seams in summer, with the overflow having to sleep on and under tables – at full price. Costs range from €11 to €15 per night, half-price if you're a member of a climbing organization affiliated to the Club Alpin Français; either a membership card or your passport will be held as security against payment. A few refuges are affiliated not with the CAF (Ⓦwww.caf.fr) but with CIMES (Centre d'information Montagne et Sentiers).

Rando Éditions publishes a complete guide, *Gîtes d'étape et Refuges*, available in French bookshops or online at Ⓦwww.gites-refuges.com (English version available).

Camping

Practically every village and town in the Pyrenees has at least one **campsite** cater-

Accommodation price codes

All the accommodation establishments listed in this book, on both sides of the Pyrenees, have been **price-graded** according to the following scale. Spanish prices include seven percent IVA (VAT) where applied. Youth hostels, mountain refuges, *albergues* and *gîtes d'étape*, all in the range of €9–17 per person, fall outside this scheme. Categories indicate the **cheapest available double room** in each hotel during high season. Many of the budget places will also have more expensive rooms including en-suite facilities; in France the cheaper rooms are often the first to fill. Where dinner is included in the price of the room, the price code will be suffixed 'HB' (half-board). In the case of **apartments** intended for 4–6 persons, actual current prices are given in the text.

In Spain, rooms in the ❶ band correspond to the **most basic** *pensiones* without private bath, as well as the older non-en-suite *turismos rurales*; there will, however, often be a washbasin in the room, along with the minimum of furniture besides a decently firm bed. In France, ❶ means the most basic hotel rooms, often unmodernized: exposed wiring, saggy beds, interwar wallpaper, musty carpets, and – enthroned in one corner – a so-called *cabinette de toilette*, a sink side by side with a bidet. In Spain, ❷ rooms, whether in a *hostal* or a better class of *turismo rural*, will be bigger and probably have a **private bathroom**, with a so-called *medio baño* or very short bathtub meant to be used as a shower; there will also be a modicum of extra furniture, possibly a balcony, maybe a telephone. In France, ❷ will almost certainly have a partitioned area – possibly even a proper separate room – with a sink, shower and bidet, but the toilet may still be down the hall. Some Spanish ❸ and all ❹ rooms will be **impeccably furnished**, with telephones, full bathtubs, TV, built-in closets and heating plus double glazing; at ❹, **on-site restaurants** (as opposed to just breakfast provision) are pretty certain, while **sizeable common areas** and swimming pools make their appearance. Spanish ❺ will get you all these goodies, plus **swish accoutrements** like spot lighting, parquet floors, hardwood furniture, original artwork, designer fixtures and probably key-cards to work the electric switch. At French ❸, **full en-suite facilities** with a toilet are just about guaranteed, as are sizeable gardens and common areas, but you won't see bathtubs – or proper pillows, as opposed to the dreaded "cement sacks" (see p.46) – until ❹, which should also give such benefits as swimming pools and off-street parking, and sometimes a building of outstanding **architectural interest**. In category ❺, French facilities will be completely modernized – maybe a bit bland and sterile – while ❻ in both countries, away from the coast at least, guarantees most creature comforts and distractions. You don't get much extra for your money once beyond ❼'s lower limits, and except for a few unusual spots in the Central Pyrenees, or famously pricey San Sebastián, this book does not include many such.

❶ Under €30
❷ €30–45
❸ €45–60
❹ €60–80
❺ €80–100
❻ €100–125
❼ over €125

ing for the thousands of French who spend their holiday under canvas – or in a caravan. The cheapest – at €4–6 per person per night – is usually the **camping municipal**, run by the local municipality. When officially open, they are always clean and situated in prime locations, though hot water can be unreliable. Out of season, many managers don't even bother to collect the overnight charge.

On the coast especially, there are **superior categories** of campsite, where you'll pay prices similar to those of a *gîte d'étape* or hostel for the facilities: bars, restaurants, sometimes swimming pools. These have rather more status than the *campings municipals*, with people often spending a whole holiday in one place. If you plan to do the same, and particularly if you have a caravan or camper, or a substantial tent, it's wise to reserve in advance. Count on €8 a head all-in with a tent, €10 with a camper van.

Inland, **camping à la ferme** – on somebody's farm – is another possibility, though facilities often leave much to be desired. **Never camp rough** (*camping sauvage*, as the French call it) on anyone's land without first asking permission. In many parts of the Pyrenees *camping sauvage* on public land – including the beaches – is not tolerated, or is subject (as in the Parc National des Pyrénées) to severe restrictions.

Spain

Do you remember an Inn,
Miranda?
Do you remember an Inn?
And the tedding and the spreading
Of the straw for a bedding,
And the fleas that tease in the High
Pyrenees,
And the wine that tasted of tar?

The quality of Spanish Pyrenean lodging (and wine, see p.57) has improved immeasurably since Hilaire Belloc penned this doggerel in the early 1900s. Salubrious, reasonably priced rooms are the norm in the Spanish Pyrenees, and in almost any inland town you'll be able to find a double in the ❷ category. Only in major coastal resorts, particularly in San Sebastián or the Costa Brava ports, will you have to pay more. Festivals mean accommodation filling quickly rather than outrageous rate hikes.

In Spain you don't tend to pay a premium for a central location, though you do get a comparatively bad deal travelling on your own. There are relatively few bona fide **single rooms**, and you will often get charged sixty to seventy percent of the double rate. In Catalunya particularly, **half-board** is often encouraged or obligatory, and usually very good value.

There's little scope for **bargaining** in high season, when peak prices are adhered to; during the rest of the year, official rates (always posted in the entry hall) may be half to two-thirds as much. Most places have triples or quads at not much more than the double-room price – good value when travelling with children. Remember always to establish whether quoted rates include the seven percent **IVA** (Value Added Tax) or not; usually they don't, but proprietors may waive it as a small concession.

Fondas, pensiones, hostales and hoteles

The least expensive category of accommodation, all but extinct in the Pyrenees, is a **fonda** (identifiable by a square blue sign with a white "F" on it), often above a bar or restaurant), closely followed up the price scale by **pensiones** (*pensió* in Catalan singular; "P"). Most surviving *fondas*, even if they keep the name, have been officially reclassified as one- or two-star *pensiones*; the original meaning of *fonda* (from the Arabic *funduq*), now reverted to, is a roadside taverna in an isolated area (not offering beds). *Pensiones* usually serve food, and an increasing number may offer rooms only on a half-board basis. Even two-star *pension(e)s* and one-star *hostal(e)s* may have bathrooms larger – and more sumptuous – than the often sparsely furnished sleeping area.

Slightly more expensive are **hostales** (*hostals* in Catalan; marked "Hs") and **hostal-residencias** ("HsR"). These are categorized from one to three stars, but prices vary according to location and facilities – a place in a slightly down-at-heel medieval quarter with no car-parking facilities will cost less than new premises on a suburban street or the town's access road. Most *hostales* offer good if functional rooms, often with private shower, and, for doubles at least, can be excellent value. The *residencia* designation means that no meals other than perhaps breakfast are served. Faced, however, with competition from *turismos rurales* (see p.50), many town-centre *hostales* in the budget range have folded.

Moving up the scale you finally reach fully fledged **hoteles** ("H"), again star-graded (from one to five). One-star hotels cost no more than three-star *hostales* – sometimes they're actually less expensive, and remain officially rated as *hostales* – but at three stars you pay a lot more, and by four or five you're in luxury facilities with prices to match.

Outside all these categories you will sometimes find **habitaciones** (rooms; *habitacions* in Catalan) advertised in private houses or above bars. If you're on a very tight budget these can be worth seeking out – particularly if you're offered one at a bus station and the owner is prepared to bargain. In Catalunya, look for signs reading *dormir i esmorzar* (bed and breakfast) or *dormir i menjar* (bed and meal).

The approximate equivalent of the Logis de France scheme in Spain is the Catalunya-based **Casa Fonda** (www.casafonda.com), a fifty-strong chain of *fondas*, *hostals* and hotels. At these you're guaranteed certain standards, specifically hands-on management, up-to-date lodging and an often excellent *menjador*.

Turismo rural

Each of the autonomous communities featured in this book – Catalunya, Aragón, Navarra and Gipuzkoa – give official support to **"agroturismo"** programmes, akin to French *chambres d'hôtes*, but by no means equivalent. *Turismos rurales*, as they're better known, are either a private residence where extra rooms are rented out; self-contained, self-catering flats or cottages; or, at their best, a bed-and-breakfast or half-board-basis inn occupying a medieval farmhouse. They have gone from strength to strength in Spain since the early 1990s, booked months in advance for peak times. The fad for them – especially among big-city yuppies – shows little sign of abating, and understandably so: top-drawer *turismos rurales* comprise some of the best accommodation the Spanish Pyrenees have to offer. A few are still working cattle or pig-farms, with all the barnyard smell and noise that entails.

In Catalunya they are termed *cases de pagès*, or belong to the Girona province *turisme rural* scheme. In Aragón and Navarra they're variously called *casas de payés*, *casas rurales*, *viviendas de turismo rural*, or *landa etxeak*, while in Gipuzkoa they are identified by a rectangular green sign with white lettering, or a sun-and-sea-scape in a circular plaque with the word *nekazalturismoa*. Each autonomous region publishes comprehensive guide-booklets or lists to all their *agroturismo* outfits, available from the better-stocked tourist offices. To have been included in our guide, they satisfy certain criteria: they are attended most of the year (too many proprietors just erect an unstaffed modern villa, call it an *agroturismo*, and post the keys to advert-answerers); possess some architectural merit; are near points of interest or along a major trail; welcome walk-in, short-term trade; and offer breakfast if not half-board, providing regional and/or vegetarian specialities.

Albergues, refuges and pilgrim accommodation

Most Spanish **albergues juveniles** (youth hostels) have curfews, are often block-reserved by school groups for weeks on end, and demand production of a YHF membership card. At €9–13 per bunk, you can pay nearly as much as for sharing an inexpensive double room in a *casa rural* or one-star *pensión*.

There are, however, a number of privately run, similarly priced but less institutional **albergues** conforming to the notion of a French *gîte d'étape*, strategically sited in select mountain villages. These are often aimed more specifically at trekkers or those pursuing a particular local activity (skiing, canyoning, etc).

Additionally, in the high Pyrenees the Federación Aragonesa de Montañismo, the Federación Navarra de Montaña, the three Catalunyan clubs – the FEEC, the CEC and the UEC – plus a handful of private individuals all run a number of **refugios** (refuges; *refugis* in Catalan). Like their French counterparts, these are simple, inexpensive dormitory huts for climbers and trekkers, generally equipped with bunk-beds, a common room and cooking space (except in the CEC huts where self-catering is forbidden). Toilets are sometimes outside, and (hot) showers occasionally available. As in France, some sort of emergency adjacent shelter is occasionally open all year, and the most popular refuges are generally staffed from mid-June to late September, plus selected weekends and holiday weeks (Christmas, Easter) during the snowy months.

As on the French side, quite a number of elderly Spanish *refugios* have been renovated and/or enlarged, often with little regard for the immediate environment. Critics note that many such new facilities resemble roadhouses rather than alpine huts, and just encourage what's disparagingly called **dominguismo** in Castilian – "Sunday-tripping" by those with little knowledge of, or affection for, the mountains. At the same time, smaller, unstaffed huts in strategic high-altitude locales become progressively more derelict.

The cost of **accommodation** in the staffed refuges is €9–14, unless you're a member of a reciprocally recognized alpine club, in which case you'll get half off at club-affiliated refuges. At a typical cost of €13–16, **meals** should consist of at least three courses – soup and/or salad, a meat dish, dessert or fruit, and wine.

Pilgrims following the **Camino de Santiago** can take advantage of basic, dorm-style accommodation specifically reserved for pilgrims along the route; the best places, often attached to medieval churches, are detailed in the text. Lice infestations, however, have become a chronic problem and many are sporadically closed for fumigation.

Albergues aside, if you have any **problems** with Spanish rooms – overcharging, most obviously – you can usually encourage an immediate resolution by asking for an *hoja de reclamaciones* (complaints sheet). By law all establishments must stock these in a prominent place and provide them on demand to an unhappy customer. Once filled out (neatly, in English, is acceptable), you send it off to the government of the province or autonomous region – the results are occasionally gratifying.

Camping

There are scores of authorized **campsites** in the Spanish Pyrenees, including coastal areas. In peak season, sites charge €5–6.50 per person on the coast, €3–4.50 up in the hills, plus as much again for a tent and a similar amount for car or caravan. However, visitors will find the majority of Pyrenean sites biased towards use by (permanently anchored) **caravans**, and equipped with amenities (electric power hook-up, sewage purge tanks, etc) that they don't really need or want. Many sites, even some newer ones, are squalid, shadeless and packed out at peak times. Tent-friendly and attractive deviations from this norm are noted in the text. Of potential interest for trekkers are the various **áreas de acampada libre** or "free camping zones" dotted about the Catalan and Aragonese Pyrenees. Some are not "free", levying a token charge, but all are fairly basic, at or below the level of the most modest *camping à la ferme* or *camping municipal* in France. But you always get toilets and cold running water, possibly picnic furniture and a tiny drinks bar. Throughout the guide we've given exact opening months for campsites (often May to September); where not indicated, the campsite is (theoretically) open all year round.

Camping outside campsites (*acampar por libre*) is legal – with certain restrictions. Your group must number fewer than ten, and you're not allowed to camp in urban areas, areas "prohibited for military or touristic reasons" or within 1km of an official campsite. In practice this means that you can't camp on developed beaches, but with a little sensitivity you can set up a tent for a short period almost anywhere in the mountains above 2000m elevation. (Notable exceptions are the Ordesa/Monte Perdido, Posets-Maladeta and Aigüestortes national/natural parks and the Valle de Echo's river flood-plain, where camping is prohibited outside designated areas.)

Food and drink

For French and Spanish menu readers see p.578 and p.590 respectively.

Restaurants within easy reach of major centres are often popular and consequently expensive, but elsewhere Pyrenean eateries are low-key, informal and reasonably priced. Go wherever large numbers of locals go – the favourites will be particularly easy to spot at Sunday lunch time. See also the *Pyrenean Food and Drink* colour section.

France

In the mountains, ordinary restaurants often rely on a small fixed menu, with little in the way of *à la carte* dishes. Except in the foothill towns, which often have at least one Chinese/Vietnamese, Indian and Moroccan eatery apiece, you'll find little in the way of non-European food.

Breakfast, snacks and picnics

A croissant, *pain au chocolat* or a hard-boiled egg in a bar or café, with a hot chocolate or coffee, is generally the best way to eat **breakfast** – at a fraction of the price charged by most hotels, where for €4.50–7 you'll usually just get a pile of stale if toasted bread and foil-sealed jam, plus a pot of tea or coffee. For €8–10 you should have a better-value buffet breakfast comprising cereals, fruit and yoghurt.

At **midday** you may find cafés offering a *plat du jour* (chef's daily special) for €8–12, or set-price *formules*, typically a main dish and either starter or dessert. *Croque-Monsieurs* or *croque-Madames* (variations on the grilled-cheese sandwich) are on sale at cafés, brasseries and street stalls, along with *frites*, *crêpes*, *gaufres* (waffles), *glaces* (ice creams) and assorted sandwiches.

Crêpes or filled pancakes are popular as light meals, but at €3–7 each aren't the best value as you need two (or three) to fill up. The pricier, savoury-buckwheat variety (*galettes*) are main courses, the sweet light-flour ones desserts. Pizzerias, often *au feu du bois* (in a wood-fired oven), are also common and somewhat better value at €8.50–12.50, though quality varies.

For **picnics**, the local *halles* (covered produce market) or supermarket will provide cheese, *pâté* and salad ingredients. For more elaborate **takeaway food**, try the *charcuteries* (delicatessens), which you'll find even in small villages. Such shops sell meat dishes (mostly pork-based), salads and fully prepared main courses. You buy by weight, or ask for *une tranche* (a slice), *une barquette* (a carton) or *une part* (a portion). *Boulangeries* or **bakeries** often sell not just bread but baked snacks with meat or cheese in them, such as quiche, eminently suitable for a lunch on the hoof.

Full meals and restaurants

In the Pyrenees, the main eateries are restaurants, also known as *auberges* or *relais*, with *brasseries* comparatively rare. The few **brasseries** there are will serve quicker meals at most hours of the day, while **restaurants** tend to stick to the traditional meal times of noon–2pm (or 2.30pm in the larger towns) and 7–9pm (10pm in towns). After 9pm or so, restaurants may serve only the à la carte. **Serving hours** can be extremely inflexible, to the sorrow of unsuspecting novice visitors; you won't be seated or served even in a place still packed at its 10pm closing time. If you're staying in a hotel with a restaurant, you'll be asked at the outset whether you're planning to dine there. While the 35-hour work week lasts, staff are sent home early at slow times to avoid their going over the statutory limit, and in such cases you again won't be served, even well within the stated hours. Out of season, establishments may close altogether even on days they're nominally open – ring ahead if you're intent on eating there, to avoid driving around for miles looking for any place open. In summary, assume that you're guaranteed to be fed only between 12.15–1.30pm and 7.45–8.30pm; we've highlighted establishments whose kitchen functions later than usual. In small villages it will be impossible to find much other than a bar sandwich after 9.30pm; in major cities or busy resorts like Biarritz, town-centre **brasseries** will serve until 11pm or even midnight.

For more upmarket places it's wise to book – easily done the same day. Hotel restaurants are open to nonresidents, and are often very good value; in many small Pyrenean villages, the sole hotel may also have the only restaurant. As noted under "Accommodation" (p.46), *Logis de France* establishments are a safe bet, if unadventurous in the menu. Avoid places that are half-full at peak time and be suspicious of overlong menus (whose ingredients will rarely be fresh); asking locals will usually elicit strong views and sound advice.

Prices and menus are almost always posted outside. Normally there's a choice between one to four **menus** – with a set number of courses and limited choices within those. At the bottom of the price range, menus revolve around standard dishes such as steak and chicken served with fried potatoes, or various concoctions involving innards. Look for the *plat du jour*, which may be a more appealing regional dish. Increasingly, however, restaurants are offering a range of menus, the more expensive of which allow wider choice, and run to four or five courses. For €23 and up, you should expect an array of regional dishes, or *haute cuisine* dining. Weekend or evening menus are always pricier than mid-week lunch ones.

Going **à la carte** is always more expensive but offers greater flexibility and unlimited access to the chef's specialities. A perfectly legitimate tactic is to have just two courses instead of the expected three or four. You can share dishes or just have several starters – a useful strategy for vegetarians; there's rarely a minimum charge.

In the French **sequence of courses**, any salad – sometimes vegetables, too – arrives separately from the main dish, and cheese precedes – or is the alternative to – dessert. You will be offered coffee, which almost always costs extra, to finish off the meal. The waiter/waitress will approach with the words *Ça-y-était?* to take finished plates away, which inevitably throws some people as the expression isn't in most phrasebooks. Incidentally, you address staff as *monsieur* or *madame* (*mademoiselle* if a young woman), not *garçon*.

On menus or bills, *TTC* means that all local taxes and sales tax (IVA) are included; *service compris* or *s.c.* means the service charge is included (less common). *Service non compris*, *s.n.c.* or *servis en sus* means that it isn't and you need to allow for an additional fifteen percent. Wine (*vin* – see below for more) or a drink (*boisson*) may be included, though rarely on menus under €23.

The French are well disposed towards **children** in restaurants, not just in the ubiquitous offering of cut-price *menu enfants*, but by fostering an atmosphere – even in otherwise fairly snooty establishments – that welcomes kids. More difficult to accept may be the idea of **dogs** in the dining room, considered quite normal (though more and more places have signs up forbidding the practice, as well as **smoking**). The French are absolutely besotted with their pooches, and you may soon realize that a significant number of your fellow diners are concealing pets under the table.

Alcoholic drinks

Drinking is done at a leisurely pace whether as a prelude to food (*apéritif*), a sequel (*digestif*) or accompanying a meal, and **café-bars** are the standard places to do it. Every café-bar has to display its full price list (usually without a fifteen percent service charge added), with the cheapest drinks at the bar (*au comptoir*), increasing progressively for sitting at a table inside (*la salle*), or on the terrace (*la terrasse*). You pay when you leave, and it's quite acceptable to sit for an hour over one cup of a coffee, though in that case leave a tip.

Wine (*vin*) is drunk at just about every meal or social occasion. Red is *rouge*, white *blanc*, or there's *rosé*. *Vin de pays* or *vin ordinaire* – house wine – or *vin vrac* (in bulk) is generally drinkable and always cheap; it may be disguised, bottled and marked up as the house *cuvée*. In wine-producing areas the local *vin de pays* can be very good. In bars you normally buy wine by the glass – just ask for *un verre de rouge* or *de blanc* – though in restaurants you generally order *un quart* or *un pichet* (250ml), *un demi-litre* (half a litre) or *une carafe* (a litre jug). The basic terms are *brut*, very dry; *sec*, dry; *demi-sec*, sweet; *doux*, very sweet; *mousseux* or *pétillant*, sparkling; *méthode champenoise*, mature and sparkling.

AOC *(Appellation d'Origine Contrôlée)* wines are another matter. They can be excellent value at the lower end of the quality scale, at €4–6 a bottle, but move up and you're soon paying serious prices; restaurant mark-ups of any AOC label can be well over 100 percent. Popular Pyrenean AOC wines include red, white and rosé Côtes-de-Saint-Mont from north of Tarbes; the ubiquitous but palatable Buzet (red and rosé); and Bi Dou Rey, an excellent sparkling rosé from Béarn. From the central Pyrenees is the more specialist Madiran, a high-tannin, full-bodied red used also in cooking; from the environs of Pau comes Jurançon, a dry, almost vinegary white, also used at the stove. Irouléguy, from the *domaine* of the namesake village in the Pays Basque, is excellent, and available as rosé, a rather tannin-y red and white. At the opposite end of the range, Banyuls is found in both Spain and France near the namesake town, as either a dry or sweet dessert wine.

Alsatian brands such as Kanterbrau, Karlsbrau, Kronenbourg and Gold (small bottles, up to 6.1 percent) account for most of the **beer** served in the Pyrenees, though there's also Eki in the Basque country, and the refreshing, tequila-flavoured Desperados (5.9 percent). Draught (*à la pression*) is the cheapest drink you can have next to coffee and wine – although the smallest glass, *un demi* (330ml) rarely costs less than €2.50. **Cider** (*cidre*) is fairly common in the Pyrenees, as *brut* or *doux* – six percent is the usual strength, €8 the usual bottle price.

Stronger alcohol is consumed right through the day according to inclination, though less so since a clampdown on drink-driving. *Pastis*, the generic term for aniseed-flavoured drink such as Pernod or Ricard, is served diluted with water and ice (*glaçons*) – refreshing and not expensive. **Cognac** or **Armagnac** brandies and dozens of *eaux de vie* (brandies distilled from fruit) are **digestifs**. **Liqueurs**, flavoured with *ginepi*, assorted wild berries or *chataigne*, are popular **aperitifs**, as are *pineau* (cognac and grape juice) and *kir* (sweet white wine with a dash of blackcurrant syrup), or with champagne for a *kir royal*. In the central/western Pyrenees, **sweet dessert** wines such as Murançon are popular. A Pays Basque speciality distilled in Bayonne is **Izarra** liqueur, available in green (48-herb, peppermint) and yellow (32-herb, almond-flavour) varieties.

Water, soft drinks and hot drinks

In cafés bottled (sweetened) nectars such as apricot (*jus d'abricot*) and blackcurrant (*cassis*) still prevail, but you can buy unsweetened **fruit juice** in supermarkets; the best brand, with 30–40 percent fruit pulp in assorted flavours, is Pago. You can also get fresh orange and lemon juice (*orange/citron pressé*) at a price; otherwise it's just the standard fizzy canned stuff, such as Rio (based on blood-orange juice), or Fun Tea, essentially Lipton's peach- or lemon-flavoured iced tea. Rather better are **siropes** – concentrated pure-fruit essences dissolved in soda water, served at many mountain refuges and cafés. Bottles of mineral **water** (*eau minérale*) and spring water (*eau de source*) – either sparkling (*gazeuze*) or still (*plate*) – abound, but there's usually nothing wrong with tap water (*l'eau du robinet*).

Coffee is usually very strong espresso in small cups. *Un café* or *un express* is black; *un crème* is with milk; *un grand café* or *un grand crème* is a large cup; *une noisette* is a small one. In the morning you can ask for *un café au lait* – espresso in a large cup or bowl filled up with hot milk. *Un déca* is decaf, now widely available. Ordinary tea (*thé*) is usually Lipton's, though choice is improving with the arrival of speciality tea-shops and *salons de té*; to have it served with milk, ask for *un peu de lait frais* (a bit of fresh milk).

The most common varieties of **herbal teas** (infusions or tisanes) are *verveine* (verbena), *tilleul* (linden blossom), *menthe* (mint) and camomille (chamomile). Unlike tea, *chocolat chaud* – **hot chocolate** – lives up to the high standards of French food and drink and can be had in any café.

Spain

There are two ways to eat out in Spain: go to a *restaurante* or *comedor* (dining room; *menjador* in Catalunya) and have a full meal, or have a succession of *tapas* (small snacks) or *raciones* (larger ones) at one or more bars. Bars work out pricier but are sometimes more interesting, as you do the rounds and sample different local or house specialities. **Smoking**, incidentally, is banned in the majority of Spanish Pyrenean bars and restaurants unless an area is specifically set aside for puffers – this trend is most pronounced in Catalunya.

Breakfast, snacks and sandwiches

For **breakfast** you're best off in a bar or café, though *hostales* and *pensiones* serve the "Continental" basics. Especially at hotels in Catalunya, you may be offered a heartier **savoury breakfast** (*esmorzar de forquilla* in Catalan, *desayuno salado* in Castilian): instead of coffee and pastry, you'll be given a spread of ham, salami, cheese and wine, sometimes with omelettes and sausages too, at roughly the same price. Another typical Catalan snack or breakfast dish is **pa amb tomaquet**, "bread with tomato" – see "*Pyrenean food and drink*" colour section.

Other places will just serve *tostadas* (toast) with oil (*con aceite*), butter and jam (*con mantequilla y mermelada*), or more substantial dishes such as fried eggs (*huevos fritos*). *Tortilla* (potato omelette) also makes an excellent breakfast, perhaps along with *magdalenas* (little cupcakes).

Coffee and pastries (*pasteles*) are available at most cafés, too, though for a wider selection you should head for one of the many excellent *pastelerías*. In larger towns, especially in Catalunya, there will often be a *panadería* or *croissantería* serving an array of appetizing (and healthier, whole-grain) baked goods besides the obvious bread, croissants and pizza.

Most bars offer **sandwiches** (*bocadillos*), usually outsize affairs in French bread. If you want them wrapped to take away, ask for them *para llevar*. Incidentally, don't ask for a *sandwich* – in Spain this means a toasted cheese and ham sandwich on limp processed bread slathered with mayonnaise.

Tapas

One advantage of eating in **bars** is that you can experiment. Many places have food laid out on the counter, so you can see what's available and order by pointing without necessarily knowing the names; others have blackboards (see the lists in the box on pp.590–91). **Tapas** (**pintxos** in the Basque Country) are small platters – two to four small chunks of fish or meat, or a dollop of salad – which traditionally used to be served free with a drink. These days you have to pay for anything more than a few olives, but a single helping rarely costs more than €2.50 unless you're somewhere very flash. In much of the Pyrenees, alas, *tapas* more often than not consist of just a cube of cheese or some tinned shellfish – there just isn't as much range of choice as further south, or on the coast.

Raciones, literally "portions" (€6–9), are simply bigger plates of the same, intended for sharing among a few people, and can be enough in themselves for a light meal. Half a dozen *tapas* or *pintxos* and three *raciones* can make a varied and quite filling meal for three or four diners.

Bodegas, tascas and **cervecerías** are types of bar where you'll find *tapas* and *raciones*. Different prices apply depending on whether you stand at the bar to eat (the basic charge) or sit at tables (up to fifty per cent more expensive – and even more if you sit out on a terrace).

Wherever you have *tapas*, it is important to find out what the local "**special**" is. Spaniards commonly move from bar to bar, having just the one dish that they consider each bar does best. A bar's "non-standard" dishes can all too often be microwaved – not a good way to reheat fried squid.

Full meals and restaurants

For a full meal, **comedores** (called **menjadors** in Catalunya) are the places to go if your main criteria are price and quantity. In the Pyrenees you'll find them attached to a bar (often in a room behind), or more likely as the dining room of a *pensión* or *hostal*. You'll pay €10–18 for a **menú del día**, a complete meal of several courses, usually with house wine; many *pensiones* and *hostales* offer only this, and no **a la carta**. At the upper end of this price range, you should expect four courses – a salad, then usually a soup, a main course and a dessert, and unlimited access to a soup tureen and wine bottle. You'll be gently pushed to take coffee after the *postre* (dessert), and it will almost always be charged extra. Incidentally, the *comedores* of the **fancier hostales** share only the name with their humbler cousins; they can be upmarket indeed, with table linen, uniformed waiting staff and fare – plus bills – to match. Off the beaten tourist track, menus in Catalunya are often **in Catalan only** – thus the translations on p.594.

Only in the largest towns such as San Sebastián, Huesca or Olot will you find **cafeterías** or snack bars. These can be good value, especially the self-service places, but their emphasis is more on rather dull northern European fare. Food here often comes as a **plato combinado** – literally "combined plate", *plats combinats* in Catalan – which will be something like egg and chips or calamares and salad, often with bread and a small drink included. This will cost in the region of €6–9 per *plato*; *cafeterías* often serve some kind of *menú del día* as well. You may prefer to get your *plato combinado* at a bar, which in small towns with no *comedores* may be the only way to eat inexpensively.

Moving up the scale, the humbler *restaurantes* are often not much different in price and ethos to *comedores*, and may also have a *menú del día* or *menú de la casa* available. Patronize a flash restaurant, or one with an extensive seafood menu, and prices escalate rapidly.

To avoid confusion, ask for **la carta** when you want a menu; *menú* is short for the fixed-priced *menú del día*. In all but the most rock-bottom establishments it is customary to leave a small **tip** if service merits it; ten percent of the bill is quite sufficient, though service is normally included in a *menú del día*. The other thing to take account of is the addition of IVA, a seven percent sales tax on your bill. It should say on the menu (thus, *IVA no incluido*; in Catalan, *IVA no inclòs*) if you have to pay this. *Menús* sometimes include this; *a la carta* meals never do.

Spaniards **eat very late** by Anglo-Saxon or French standards, so many places serve food from around 1pm until 4 and from 8pm to 11.00. However, as in France, stricter labour laws and the phasing out of exclusively family-staffed businesses mean that 1.30–3.15pm and 8.30–10.30pm are now more realistic schedules, with 3pm and 10pm last orders not uncommon. **Andorra** is more French in its dining habits than Spanish; you'll have trouble finding lunch after 2.30pm or supper after 9.30pm, and hotel breakfast is served at 8am, not 9am as in Spain. Many restaurants close on Sunday evening and Monday all day.

What to eat

If you like **fish and seafood**, you'll be in heaven in Spain, since this forms the basis of a vast variety of *tapas* and proves fresh and excellent even hundreds of kilometres from the sea – though a 2006 health scare introduced a new, and hopefully not permanent, requirement to freeze all seafood before cooking it. It's not cheap, though, so rarely figures in low-price *menús* (though you may get the most common fish: cod, hake or squid). Fish stews (*zarzuelas*) and rice-based *paellas* (which also contain meat, usually rabbit or chicken) are often memorable. Paella comes originally from Valencia, but you'll find versions of it all over the Pyrenees – regrettably much of it prepackaged and microwaved.

Meat is typically grilled and served with a few fried potatoes and a couple of salad leaves, or cured/dried, served as a starter or in sandwiches. *Jamón serrano*, the Spanish version of Parma ham, is superb, though the best varieties from Extremadura and Andalucía are extremely expensive. **Game** is quite common in the hills – typically venison, rabbit or boar – and almost always freshly hunted.

Vegetables seldom amount to more than a token garnish to the main dish, though at the better restaurants a few more elaborate vegetable-based recipes will be offered. It's more usual to start your meal with a **salad**, or hearty vegetable soups. **Dessert** in the less expensive places is nearly always fresh fruit or *flan*, the Spanish *crème caramel*. There are also assorted kinds of *pudín* – rice pudding or various blancmange mixtures. Even in fancy restaurants you'll seldom find much else – if necessary make a separate foray to a *pastelería* (cake shop). Worth a mention, if only for their grotesqueness, are certain **dessert oddities**: frozen citrus fruit (*limon* and *naranja*) stuffed with sorbet of the corresponding flavour; *músic* (nuts in muscatel); *trufes* (frozen "truffles"); and other decadent ice-cream concoctions made by nationwide factories. Indeed, if offered ice cream it's best to go up to the glass-front chiller and point to your choice; descriptions are complicated, and trade names none too informative. If you encounter a genuine *heladería* (ice-cream parlour) that whips up its own, count your blessings. *Gelats casolans* is Catalan for ice cream (or sorbets) made in-house; Jinonenca is a Pyrenees-wide brand of decent *gelato*.

Alcoholic drinks

Vino (wine), either *tinto* (red) – *ví negre* in Catalunya – *blanco* (white, *ví blanc* in Catalan) or *rosado/clarete* or *rosat* (rosé), invariably accompanies every meal. *Jóven* means new or unaged, while *con crianza* means a minimum of two years' ageing before sale. Curiously, there's a very **limited choice of white wine** in Spain, where it's just not popular – perhaps three labels on a list versus twenty reds. Among notable vintners, from Navarra try Viña Orvalaiz (also as white and rosé), while from the Rioja region, around Logroño near the Basque country, Marqués de Caceres is a good mid-range label. There are also dozens of Pyrenean (foothill) wines, from Catalunya (Bach, Sangre de Toro or the excellent Penedès Castell Gornall white) and the Somontano domaine of Aragón (Viñas del Vero, Fabregas or Bodega Pirineos/Montesierra red/rosé), which you will often find as the house wine.

Bulk/barrelled wine is rare nowadays – most establishments serve a full, sealed container of the house-bottled or special-ordered vintage (*caserío* or *de la casa*). This can be great – especially the very light rosé or red wines from around Tremp – or mediocre, but at least it will be distinctive. In a bar, a small glass of wine will generally cost around €1.20–1.80; in a restaurant, if wine is not included in the *menú*, prices start at around €5 a large bottle. If it is included, you'll usually get a whole bottle for two people, a *media botella* (a third to a half of a litre) of red or rosé – never white – for one. Wine may appear in a *porrón* (*porró* in Catalan), a glass vessel which looks like a melted salad-dressing cruet. Uncork the larger opening on top, brandish it aloft, and potentially make a mess by aiming a stream of wine from the narrow jet into your waiting mouth. Or take the easy way out by filling glasses through the top hole. **Cava** is the generic term for sparkling wine and champagnes (*champaña*) that dare not speak their name lest they attract the wrath of the French. Freixenet will be familiar to Britons; Reimat Brut, Codorniu, Torelló, Juve y Camps and Castillo de Perelada less so, but the latter five are equally worthy. *Marc de cava* is the distilled spirit made from the spent pressings of the *cava* process.

Probably the most famous Spanish wine is **sherry** or *vino de jerez*, made exclusively in Andalucía in a triangular region west of Jerez de la Frontera. Served chilled or at room temperature, it's perfect for washing down tapas; the main distinctions are *fino* or *seco* (dry sherry), *amontillado* (medium dry) and *oloroso* or *dulce* (sweet).

Cerveza, lager-type beer, is generally good, though more expensive than wine. It comes in 300- to 330-ml bottles (*botellines*) or, for about the same price, on tap – a *caña* of draught beer is a small, 125-ml glass, a *caña doble* 250 ml. Many bartenders will assume you want a *doble*, so if you don't, say so. You get a *tubo* (tall narrow glass) or a *jarra media* (squat stein); 500-ml measures – a full *jarra* – are also available. Locally brewed brands, such as Ambar in Aragón, or Estrella Damm and Vell Damm (strongest at 7.2 percent) in Catalunya, tend to be more exciting than nationally available ones. **Cider** (*sidra*) is common in the western Pyrenees; the best commercial brand is Zapiain.

At mid-afternoon many Spaniards take a *copa* of **liqueur** with their coffee. The best are *orujo*, distilled from grape pressings like

Italian *grappa*, and 45 percent alcohol; or *coñac*, excellent local brandy with a distinct vanilla flavour ry Magno, Soberano, or Carlos III '*Tercero*' to get an idea of the variety). Most brandies are produced in Jerez, but an equally good Catalan one is Mascaró, resembling armagnac. In the Western Pyrenees, the Navarran specialty *pacharan* (or *patxaran*) is blackthorn sloes marinated in anisette with vanilla and coffee beans, not to be confused with the French wine Pacherenc. In the Garrotxa, try *ratafia*, a nut- and spice-based apéritif.

Most **spirits** are ordered by brand name, specifically the less expensive Spanish equivalents for standard imports; otherwise specify *nacional* to avoid getting an expensive foreign brand. Mixed drinks, universally known as *copas*, can be very expensive at the trendier bars, though measures tend to be generous.

Water, soft drinks and hot drinks

In the Pyrenees you can drink the **water** almost everywhere, and a *jarrón* or carafe of tap water (*agua de grifa*) will be provided in restaurants and cafés – unless there's something wrong with the local supply, in which case bottled water will be offered instead, often on the house. Such *agua mineral* comes either as sparkling (*con gas*) or still (*sin gas*). Among soft drinks, try *granizado* (fruit-syrup-flavoured slush), the ubiquitous Bitter Kas (like non-alcoholic Campari, very refreshing) or *horchata* (a milky drink made from *chufa-* or tiger nuts). You can get such drinks from *horchaterías* and *heladerías* (ice-cream parlours), or in Catalunya from the wonderful milk bars known as *granjas*. Fruit juices, typically orange, are called *zumos*.

Café (coffee) – served in cafés, *heladerías* and bars – is invariably espresso, slightly bitter and, unless you specify otherwise, served black (*café solo*). If you want it white ask for *café cortado* (*café tallat* in Catalan), a small cup with a drop of milk, or *café con leche* (made with lots of hot milk). For a large cup ask for a *doble* or *grande*; decaf is *descafeinado*. Coffee is also frequently mixed with brandy or cognac as a *carajillo*. Spanish **hot chocolate** (*chocolate caliente*) can be very good indeed as long as you avoid the Cola Cao brand – an insipid formula aimed at small children.

Té (tea) is also available at most bars, although Spaniards usually drink it black. If you want milk it's safest to ask afterwards, since ordering *té con leche* might well get you a glass of warm milk with a teabag floating on top. Most bars keep herbal teas such as *manzanilla* (chamomile), *hierba luisa* (lemon verbena) and *menta poleo* (spearmint).

Communications and the media

Both the French and Spanish postal and telecommunications systems work reasonably well, and with a smattering of secondary-school or university language study, you can derive enjoyment – or at least information – from French and Spanish newspapers and magazines.

France

French **post offices** are signed as *La Poste* in bright yellow and blue. Pyrenean post offices are generally open 9am to noon and 2pm to 5pm, Monday to Friday and Saturday 9am to noon, though in the smaller villages lunch hours and closing times can vary. You can receive letters at main post offices; they should be addressed (preferably with the surname underlined and in capitals) **Poste Restante**, Poste Centrale, followed by the name of the town and its postcode. To collect mail you need a passport and there'll be a charge of €0.50 per item. Ask for all your names to be checked, as filing systems tend to be idiosyncratic; letters may only be held for fifteen days.

Stamps (*timbres*) can be bought from tobacconists (*tabacs*), as well as from post offices, while large letters or small packets are best sent at a main *poste*, where they'll probably be more conversant with overseas rates. Standard postcards and letters (under 20gm) within the EU cost €0.50, or €0.90 to North America and the Antipodes.

Telephones and Internet

You can make **domestic and international phone calls** from any phone box (*cabine*) and can receive calls – the number is at the top right-hand corner of the information panel. **Phone cards** (*télécartes*), obtainable from PTT branches, train stations and some *tabacs*, are issued as 50 units and 120 units. **Coin-op phones** are now found only in cafés and bars. You can also use **credit cards** in many call boxes, subject to a minimum charge.

For all calls within France, dial all ten digits of **the number**. Numbers beginning with ⓣ08.00–05 are toll-free; those beginning ⓣ08.10 and 08.11 are charged as local calls; while those beginning with ⓣ08.36 are premium rate (typically €0.34/minute), while those beginning with ⓣ06 are mobiles.

Cheap rates apply from 7pm to 8am Monday to Friday, and all day Saturday and Sunday. Charging structures are complicated and change frequently – fortunately, in the downward direction as a whole. A good way to beat stiff overseas call charges is to buy a **pre-paid phone card** (*carte à codes*), sold at tabacs, post offices and newsagents, which you can use with any public or private fixed phone – they permit a couple of hours of chat overseas for well under €10.

Coverage for roaming dual-band **mobile phones** (*portables* in French) is adequate in the Pyrenees – at least one of several local networks will be accessible even in the depopulated Ariège. Whichever one your handset automatically selects, all cost around the same: a whopping £0.55 per minute, wherever you're calling to. Many UK providers, however, offer discount plans which lower the price of receiving calls to about £0.30/min. You might also consider having the phone unblocked and inserting either a universal, pay-as-you-go SIM (consult ⓦwww.oneroam.com) or (even cheaper) a French SIM. North Americans need a triband apparatus to enjoy any service in Europe.

The low population density of the Pyrenees means that there are very few **Internet** cafés, though a few post offices, cafés and tourist offices are beginning to offer access. If you can't live without your email, one possible strategy is to carry a laptop with you; however French phone sockets are wired differently from the RJ-11 standard plug (Spain, US) or the UK's flat plug. Adaptors are not easily available, so you'll have to find **wi-fi** zones (easiest in Pau and the Vallée d'Aspe).

Useful telephone numbers

Speaking clock ⓣ36.99
Directory enquires ⓣ12 (free for up to two requests)
International operator ⓣ31.23
Mountain weather Météo France – the national meteorological service – operates a 24-hour weather forecast hotline, with special extensions for snow conditions, avalanche risk, etc. For the basic forecast, dial ⓣ08.92.68.02.xx (€0,46/min) – the last two variable digits are uniquely assigned to each *départment*. For example ⓣ08.92.68.02.65 for Midi-Pyrénées (basically the central Pyrenees), ⓣ08.92.68.02.64 for Pyrénées-Atlantiques (the west of the range, including the Pays-Basques), ⓣ08.92.68.02.66 for Pyrénées-Orientales (the east around Perpignan) and ⓣ08.92.68.02.09 for the Ariège.

Phoning abroad from France

NB After dialling the country code, omit any initial zeroes before the local code and subscriber number.
Australia dial ⓣ00 + 61 + area code + number.
Britain dial ⓣ00 + 44 + area code + number.

Phoning France from abroad

To call a French phone number from abroad, dial the international access code for your country followed by the French country code (33), then the ten-digit local number minus the initial '0'; numbers beginning 08 cannot be reached from overseas.

Ireland dial ⓣ00 + 353 + area code + number.
New Zealand dial ⓣ00 + 64 + area code + number.
North America dial ⓣ00 + 1 + area code + number.

The media

A reasonable selection of **foreign newspapers** is on sale in selected resorts and larger towns such as Pau or Perpignan. Among **French national dailies**, *Le Monde* (ⓦwww.lemonde.fr) is the most intellectual and somewhat austere, though it now has colour photos. *Libération* (*Libé* for short, ⓦwww.liberation.com) is moderately left-wing, pro-European, independent and more colloquial, with good, selective, feature coverage and a colour format; it tends to sell out quickly. *L'Humanité* (ⓦwww.humanite-presse.fr) is the far-left, Communist-affiliated paper, struggling to survive. Among various right-of-centre papers, *Le Figaro* (ⓦwww.lefigaro.fr) is the most respected and readable.

Weeklies include the left-leaning *Le Nouvel Observateur* (ⓦwww.nouvelobs.com), its conservative counterweight *L'Express* (ⓦwww.lexpress.fr) and the centrist *Marianne* (ⓦwww.marianne-en-ligne.fr). The best investigative journalism can be found in the satirical weekly *Canard Enchaîné*, while *Charlie-Hebdo* fits the mould of the UK's *Private Eye* or *Spy* in the US.

Nationwide **monthlies** include the young and trendy *Nova* (ⓦwww.novaplanet.com), with excellent listings for cultural events. The bimonthly **Pyrénées** (widely available, €5.90) is worth a browse for destination features, news snippets and suggestions for obscure trekking or touring routes; periodically there are *hors série* special issue devoted to distinct topics (eg the Basque country, Cathar castles, family day walks).

French **TV** has six terrestrial channels, three public – F2, F5/Arte and F3 – one subscription – Canal Plus, with some unencrypted programmes – and two commercial open broadcasts – TF1 and M6. F5/Arte is devoted to high-brow fare including opera, films and critics' panels. Canal Plus is the main movie channel (and funder of the French film industry), though F3 screens a fair selection of serious films, especially (undubbed) late Sunday after midnight. The main news broadcasts are at 8pm on F2 and TF1, the most watched channels. The usual **cable/satellite** networks are available in better hotels.

Spain

Post offices in Spain – marked *Correos* in Castilian, *Correus* in Catalan – are generally open Monday to Friday 8.30am–2.30pm and Saturday 9.30am–1pm, though you may encounter idiosyncratic schedules in the Pyrenees, and main branches in the largest towns may have longer hours.

You can have letters sent **poste restante** (*Lista de Correos*) to any Spanish post office: they should be addressed (preferably with the surname underlined and in capitals) to *Lista de Correos* followed by the name of the town and province. To collect, take along your passport and, if you're expecting mail, ask the clerk to check under all of your names – letters are often misfiled.

Telephones and Internet

Spanish public **phone boxes** work well, though you can't phone them back. If you can't find one, many bars also have pay phones you can use. Phone boxes take euro coins, but it's less hassle to buy a **phone card** from a *kiosko* or *tabac*, or use the most common **credit cards** (subject to a minimum charge). With credit cards, the swipe readers are rather temperamental; you've succeeded when the LCD display says "processing" in the local language. Spanish provincial (and overseas) dialling codes are displayed in most cabins, as well as dialling – and credit card – instructions in English. Spain no longer has area codes *per se*, but nine-digit unitary numbers. The first three digits are particular to each province or type of service (eg ⓣ901 is akin to the UK's 0845 local-rate prefix, ⓣ906 is equivalent to UK 0870). The local **ringing tone** is long, **engaged** is shorter and rapid; the standard Castilian response is *dígame* (speak to me).

For **international calls**, you can use any phone box, or (in larger foothill towns) go to a shopfront *locutorio*, where you pay afterwards. International and domestic rates are slightly cheaper on Saturday and Sunday, and after 6pm (within Spain) or midnight (international) on weekdays.

Dual-band **mobile phones** (*moviles* in Castilian) from the UK roam easily in Spain; the Spanish are obsessed with them and coverage, especially in Catalunya, is respectable. There are three local networks, but as in France it matters not which one you use – call charges are the same £0.55/min – with the same remedies as suggested for France (unblock phone, insert universal or Spanish SIM). North Americans will require triband handsets.

As for the **Internet**, *cibercafés* are as lacking in the Spanish Pyrenees as on the French side. If you're addicted to your email, see the advice under France; RJ11 phone sockets are standard in Spain, and the better hotels tend to offer wi-fi access cheaply or for free.

Useful telephone numbers

Directory enquiries ⓣ1003
International operator (Europe) ⓣ1008
International operator (rest of world) ⓣ1005
Time ⓣ093
Mountain weather: Catalan Pyrenees (general) ⓣ933 256 391; Girona province ⓣ906 365 317; Lleida province ⓣ906 365 325; Huesca province (Aragón) ⓣ906 365 322; Navarra province (western Pyrenees) ⓣ906 365 331. You can also check snow and weather conditions online at ⓦwww.inm.es.

Phoning abroad from Spain

NB After dialing the country code, omit any initial zeroes before the local code and subscriber number.
Australia dial ⓣ00 + 61 + area code + number.
Britain dial ⓣ00 + 44 + area code + number.
Eire dial ⓣ00 +353 + area code + number.
New Zealand dial ⓣ00 + 64 + area code + number.
North America dial ⓣ00 + 1 + area code + number.

Phoning Spain from abroad

To call a Spanish phone number from abroad, dial the international access code for your country followed by the Spanish country code (34), then the nine-digit local number.

The media

British newspapers and the *International Herald Tribune* are on sale during the summer season in most large foothill towns, particularly Girona and San Sebastián.

Among **Spanish newspapers** the best are currently Madrid's *El Mundo* and Barcelona's *La Vanguardia*, both fairly liberal in outlook and having good arts and foreign news coverage, including comprehensive regional "what's on" listings and supplements each weekend. Madrid's *El País*, long the top-ranked quality daily, has become a somewhat boring read, though it still employs exceptional (and independent) columnists. Regional nationalist, mostly centre-right dailies include *Avui* in Catalunya, printed largely in Catalan, and the Basque papers *El Diario Vasco* and *Deia*.

If you can read Spanish, glossy bimonthly **El Mundo de los Pireneos** (ⓦwww.elmundodelospirineos.com; €5.15) offers excellent news analyses, hiking or skiing tips and features on Pyrenean personalities, cuisine, festivals and impending ecological/development crises on both sides of the border. It is issued by outdoor publishers SUA Edizoak in Bilbao, which offers certain back issues at six copies for €15 plus shipping costs (on website, ⓣ902 181 171, ⓔcliente@elmundodelospirineos.com), as well as annual special issues on walking and climbing.

Even up in the mountains, you'll catch more **TV** than you expect (or want to) sitting in bars and restaurants; older Spaniards are reckoned to be the continent's champion tube-heads in terms of annual hours per person spent in front of the box. Soaps – known as *culebrones* in Castilian – are a particular speciality, interspersed with truly awful game shows, cheesy retro galas and talking-heads programming. Sports fans are better catered for, with regular live coverage of **football/soccer** and basketball matches. In Catalunya, channels 3 and 4 broadcast exclusively in Catalan.

The FM **radio** dial is often rewarding, particularly *Catalunya Música* (88.6 or 103FM), a mix of classical and world-music programming, which can even be picked up in the high-altitude wilds of the Cerdanya or Aigüestortes.

Opening hours and public holidays

Almost everything on either side of the Pyrenees – shops, museums, churches, tourist offices, most banks – closes for a siesta of at least two hours in the hottest part of the day. There's considerable variation, but basic summer working hours are 9.30am to 1.30pm and 4.30 to 8pm in Spain, and 9am to noon or 1pm, and 2 or 3pm to 6.30 or 7.30pm in France. In both countries certain shops do now stay open all day, and the French 35-hour week (if it lasts) has meant a move towards shorter, "normal" working hours.

France

Food shops in France often don't reopen until halfway through the afternoon, closing between 7.30 and 8pm or just before the evening meal. Sunday and Monday are the standard French **closing days**, though you'll always find at least one *boulangerie* (baker's) open. Street markets only operate until about 1.30pm.

Museums open between 9 and 10am, close for lunch at noon until 2pm or 3pm, with an afternoon shift until 5pm or 6pm. Summer times differing from winter times are indicated where relevant in the guide. **Summer hours** usually extend from early June to mid-September, occasionally even from Palm Sunday to All Saints' Day, but sometimes they apply only during July and August. **Closing days** are usually Monday or Tuesday, sometimes both.

Cathedrals are almost always open all day, with charges only for the crypt, treasuries or cloister, and little fuss about how you're dressed. Small village **churches**, however, can often be closed except during Mass on Sunday morning or at other times which you'll see posted up on the door. In small towns and villages, however, getting the key is not difficult – ask anyone nearby or hunt out the priest, whose house is known as the *presbytère*.

Spain

Most **museums** observe the siesta with a break between 1 and 4 in the afternoon, and close on Sunday afternoons and all day on Monday. Summer hours usually run from May until September. Anywhere managed by the Patrimonio Nacional, the national organization that preserves monuments, is free to EU citizens on Wednesday.

Getting into **churches** can be problematic. Important ones, including most cathedrals, operate in much the same way as museums and almost always have some entry charge to see their treasury or their cloisters. Other churches, though, are usually kept locked, opening only for worship in the early morning and/or the evening (between around 6 to 9pm). For all

French national holidays

There are thirteen **French national holidays** (*jours fériés*), when most shops and businesses, some museums, though not (usually) restaurants, are closed. They are:

January 1 New Year's Day
Easter Sunday
Easter Monday
Ascension Day (forty days after Easter)
Pentecost/Whitsun (seventh Sunday after Easter, plus the Monday)
May 1 May Day/Labour Day
May 8 Victory in Europe Day
July 14 Bastille Day
August 15 Assumption of the Virgin Mary
November 1 All Saints' Day
November 11 1918 Armistice Day
December 25 Christmas Day

Spanish national holidays

January 1 *Año Nuevo* (New Year's Day)
January 6 *Tres Reyes* (Three Kings; Epiphany)
Maundy Thursday *Jueves Santo* (not in Catalunya)
Good Friday *Viernes Santo*
Easter Sunday *Pascua*, *Domingo de la Resurección*
Easter Monday *Lunes de Pascua*
May 1 *Fiesta de Trabajo* (May Day/ Labour Day)
Corpus Christi (early or mid-June)
June 24 *Día de San Juan* (St John's Day, the king's name-saint)
July 25 *Día de Santiago* (St James; patron saint of Spain)
August 15 *Assunción de la Virgen* (Assumption of the Virgin)
October 12 *Virgen del Pilar* (National Day)
November 1 *Todos Santos* (All Saints' Day)
December 6 *Día de la Constitución* (Constitution Day)
December 8 *Día de la Concepción Inmaculada* (Immaculate Conception)
December 25 *Navidad* (Christmas Day)
December 26 *Sant Esteve* (St Stephen; in Catalunya)

churches "decorous" dress is required, ie no shorts, bare shoulders, etc.

Public holidays can (and will) disrupt your plans at some stage. Besides the Spanish national holidays listed above, there are scores of **local festivals** (different in every town and village, usually marking the local saint's day); any of them will mean that everything except bars (and *hostales*, etc) locks its doors.

In addition, **August** is Spain's own holiday month, when the big cities are semi-deserted, and many shops and restaurants close. In contrast, it can prove nearly impossible to find a room in the more popular coastal and mountain resorts at these times; similarly, seats on planes, trains and buses at this time should be booked well in advance. **Easter**, incidentally, is worse; whereas people's summer breaks are slightly staggered – and indeed July is becoming nearly as busy as August – over Easter weekend the entire population is on vacation for five days, and every desirable (and most undesirable) accommodation is booked literally months ahead.

Festivals

Especially in July and August, it's practically impossible not to stumble on some sort of festival during your stay: either a tourist-board-organized concert series in a wonderful medieval venue, or a brass band and drinks in a decked-out village square. On both sides of the Pyrenees religion and folk history are the main launching platforms for a party, but apart from the occasional Mass to ensure everybody is spiritually insured, the festivities rarely dwell on solemn matters. Even pilgrimages are often celebrated with great gusto and, like many of the town and village celebrations, involve a colourful and photogenic procession. Festivals in major resorts tend to be more visitor-oriented, featuring music, art and theatre programmes.

Although you'll find the major festivals noted in the appropriate town accounts, there are hundreds of other minor ones. **Saints'-day** festivals can vary, often being observed over the weekend closest to the actual date. In many cases the fun occurs on the evening before the date given, with only a Mass taking place on the morning concerned. Local tourist offices should have more information about what's going on in their area at any given time. Outsiders are always welcome at festivals, the main problem being that during popular ones it might be difficult to find a bed. If you're planning to coincide with a major festival, reserve accommodation well in advance.

France

Catholicism is still deeply ingrained in the culture of the French Pyrenees; thus saints' days bring people out in all their finery, ready to indulge before or after Mass. Such occasions, along with the celebrations focused on wine and food production, are usually very genuine affairs intended for a local audience. Other festivals, based on historical events, harvest of a local commodity, folklore or literature, are more obviously money-spinners and forums for municipal prestige. Finally, there are the cultural seasons of the larger towns and resorts, centred on film, music or drama.

Easter Week is normally marked by special church services and processions. One of the most striking is the *Procession de la Sanch* at **Perpignan**, where masked penitents parade in red robes and tall pointed hats reminiscent of Ku Klux Klan garb; by contrast there are nocturnal processions of black-robed penitents at Arles-sur-Tech, Collioure and Céret. **Saint John's Eve** (*Día de Sant Joan*, June 23–24) sees fervent observance in the Catalan regions, with *Fêtes des Feux* celebrated on various summits throughout Roussillon, most notably a torchlit procession from Castillet to Canigou peak, and a giant bonfire at Banyuls-sur-Mer. Throughout the French Pyrenees, **Bastille Day** (July 14) is commemorated by marvellous firework displays. Many late-summer processions venerate an image from the parish church – a popular example is the *Procession de la Vierge* at **Font-Romeu** on September 8.

Sports events are great crowd-pullers, none more so than the **Tour de France** bike race, which visits the Pyrenees in July – even the police relax and enjoy themselves, loosening collars and accepting cool drinks. In Basque areas, bullfights, *force Basque* (rural games) and *pelote* tournaments punctuate the summer season.

Spain

It's hard to beat the experience of arriving in some Spanish Pyrenean village, expecting no more than a meal and bed for the night, only to discover the streets festooned with pennants and streamers, a band playing in the plaza and the entire population out celebrating the local fiesta. Every place, from the tiniest hamlet to the great cities, will devote at least one day off a year to partying. Usually it's a local saint's day, but there are also celebrations of harvests, of deliverance from the Moors, of safe return from the sea. It's often the more obscure and unpublicized events which prove most fun, with music, dancing, traditional costume and an immense spirit of enjoyment. The heart of most fiestas is a parade, either a solemn one behind a revered holy image or a more light-hearted affair with fancy costumes and *gigantones* (*gegants* in Catalan), grotesque giant figures which trundle down the streets terrorizing children.

Easter, perhaps the major national religious feast, is observed in a particularly poignant manner in Catalunya, where several municipalities have elaborate and vivid Good Friday eve processions, including hooded penitents in Girona and Camprodon. Several towns enact Passion plays, involving a *Via Crucis* (Stations of the Cross), culminating in a mock Crucifixion with local volunteers as Christ and the Two Thieves.

Many Spanish Pyrenean festivals are more conspicuously **religious** than on the French side, with emphasis given to the procession of the revered holy image before the partying begins. Better-known Catalan events include *Carnival* at various villages along the Noguera Pallaresa, the festival of *Sant Marc* at the shrine of Queralt on April 25 and – all over Catalunya – bonfires as the centrepiece of *Día de Sant Joan* (June 23–24) observances. The Corpus Christi **Festa de Patum** at **Berga** is the biggest late-spring bash in Catalunya, renowned for its high spirits and outrageous *gigantones*. The late-summer Marian festivals of August 14–15 and September 7–9 are also notable in the uplands of Catalunya, especially villages along the approaches to the Aigües Tortes area.

Folkloric and **rural** festivals often feature demonstrations of vanished traditional trades in addition to the normal shenanigans: examples include Rialp's sheep-shearing contest in June, log-rafting at La Pobla de Segur on the first Sunday in July and trials of sheepdogs (*gossos de altura*) across Catalunya in autumn. An unusual **historical** event is an all-female mock-battle, fought on the first Friday in May at Jaca, celebrating the role played by townswomen in a defeat of a Muslim army in 795.

Spain also has a succession of **musical events** in July and August, particularly at **San Sebastián**, and near **Sallent de Gállego** in Aragón, where the *Pirineos Sur* world music festival is now an established fixture on the tours of top performers.

Bullfights

Bullfights (*corridas*) are part of many Pyrenean festivals on both sides of the frontier, ironically nowadays more so in France than Spain. Spanish patronage of *Los Toros*, which has declined steadily since an early 1970s peak, is particularly slack in Catalunya, where animal-rights bodies oppose it as a barbarism from the south, and most bullrings have closed down.

In France, the resurgence of *Les Taureaux*, as it's called there, has sparked fierce debate over whether *corridas* are really a traditional folkloric manifestation of the regions concerned: Languedoc-Roussillon and the Basque country – precisely those areas with a large population descended from Spanish immigrants settled there since the beginning of the twentieth century. Thus advocates have assiduously demonstrated evidence of bullfighting in France from before 1900; it appears that the first *corrida* north of the border was staged at Bayonne in 1853, and spectacles still take place south of a line approximately joining Bayonne, Toulouse and Nîmes.

If you attend a bullfight, choose the biggest and most prestigious event available (tickets €20 and up), where star performers are likely to dispatch the bulls with "art" and a successful, "clean" kill. There are few sights worse than a matador making a prolonged and messy kill, while the audience whistles and hurls cushions into the ring – unfortunately more likely in France, where there's not as yet significant homegrown talent in man or beast, and often second-rate bullfighters (and bulls) have to be imported. In Spain, a government proposal for Portuguese-style bullfighting – which bans killing of the bull in the ring – is currently under discussion.

Crime, police and personal safety

In general, both sides of the Pyrenees are remarkably safe, with weather and terrain posing the greatest threats. In foothill towns and busy ski resorts, take normal precautions: keep your wallet in your front pocket and your handbag under your elbow, and you won't have much to worry about. In both Spain and France you are required to have ID (passport or equivalent) on you at all times, and police can stop you and request it.

France

All the comments about leaving cars unattended under "Spain", see p.66, apply to France as well, with extra vigilance needed in Perpignan, Pau and Bayonne. Foreign cars with their distinctive numberplates are easy to spot, rental vehicles much less so. Good insurance is the best answer, but do not tempt fate by leaving vehicles unlocked or valuables in plain sight, either lapse probably invalidating the best of policies.

Police and possible offences

There are two main types of police: the **Police Nationale**, covering large and mid-sized towns, and the **Gendarmerie Nationale**, covering everywhere else. If you need to report a theft, or other incident, you can go to either to fill out a *constat du vol* (required by most insurance companies). Although the police are not always as cooperative as they might be, it is their duty to assist you if you've lost your passport or all your money. The police have powers to search you and your car without a warrant; specifically in the Pyrenees, **game wardens** patrol on the look-out for people fishing/hunting out of season or without a licence, and you can be asked to open backpacks or large camera cases to prove you've no contraband on you.

In the Pyrenees you may come across specialized **mountaineering sections** of the **CRS** (*Compagnies Républicaines de Sécurité*); unlike their riot-gear-clad urban brethren, whose brutality in the events of 1968 is legendary, these are unfailingly helpful, friendly and approachable, providing rescue services and guidance.

If you have an **accident while driving**, you are required to fill in and sign a *constat à l'aimable* (jointly agreed statement); UK-based car insurers are supposed to give you this with a policy, as are French car rental agencies (along with the usual sheaf of registration papers). For non-criminal **driving violations** such as speeding or not wearing seat belts, the police used to levy on-the-spot fines, but are now equally likely to issue citations which must be paid at the applicable municipality within a certain number of days. Should you be arrested on any charge, you have the right to contact your consulate or embassy.

Personal safety and racial issues

Lone women travellers may be warned about "*les Arabes*" – routine French **racism**. If you are Arab, Asian or black your chances of completely avoiding unpleasantness are slim. Empty hotels claiming to be full, suspicion from shopkeepers or police arbitrarily demanding your papers are distinctly possible. In the Pyrenees specifically, locals are slowly getting used seeing to school outings including members of minorities, or people of colour out on the trail or the ski slopes, but French nationals of Arab or black African descent are still a rarity in the region.

Spain

While you're unlikely to encounter any trouble during the course of a normal visit to the Spanish Pyrenees, there are a few chronic problem points.

If you have a **car**, and especially if you're doing loop treks with the vehicle left at a trailhead, leave as little as possible in view, or indeed in the car at all. At the very least take the tape deck with you, or hide it well. In the lonelier valleys organized gangs rifle parked cars, and they're not picky about what they steal: tools, clothing and registration papers in particular. Glass shards all over the ground where you intend to park are a good indication there's a problem; the vehicles themselves are rarely stolen, if that's any consolation. Rental vehicles, fortunately, are not conspicuously labelled as such. **Cars with French numberplates** are at slight risk of being vandalized in the Spanish Basque country – apparently retaliation by ETA sympathizers for the French crackdown on them.

When **looking for accommodation**, don't leave any bags unattended anywhere. This applies especially to buildings where the *pensió(n)* or *hostal* is on a higher floor, and you're tempted to leave baggage in the hallway or ground-floor lobby.

If your car or room is burgled, **go to the police** to report it, not least because your insurance company will require a police report. Don't expect a great deal of concern if your loss is relatively small – and expect the process of completing forms and formalities to take ages. In the unlikely event that you're **mugged**, police will probably be more sympathetic.

Police and possible offences

There are three basic types of Spanish **police** – the *Guardia Civil*, the *Policía Municipal* and the *Policía Nacional*. Polite enough in the usual course of events, they can be extremely unpleasant if you get on the wrong side of them.

The **Guardia Civil**, in green uniforms, are the most officious and the ones to avoid. Though their role has been drastically cut back since they operated as Franco's right hand – you'll see many of their barracks abandoned in the Pyrenees – they remain a reactionary and distrusted force.

If you do need the police – especially if reporting a serious crime – go to the more sympathetic **Policía Municipal**, who wear blue-and-white uniforms. In the countryside there may be only the *Guardia Civil*, who can resent the suggestion that any crime exists on their turf. The blue-uniformed **Policía Nacional** are mainly seen in cities, armed with submachine guns and guarding key installations such as transport stations, post offices and their own barracks. They also control crowds and demonstrations. In Euskadi there's an additional autonomous **Basque police force**, the *Ertzaintaz*, distinguished by their red berets and blue-and-red uniform; in Catalunya, the *Mossos d'Esquadra* wear blue uniforms with red-and-white trim – both forces are important in traffic control.

Nude bathing on beaches not set aside for it or **unauthorized camping** are likely to bring you into contact with officialdom, though a warning to cover up or move on is more likely than any real confrontation. See p.51 for a summary of the rules governing rough camping. **Topless** (and often bottomless) tanning is commonplace at trendier coastal resorts, but by Pyrenean streams and lakes, where attitudes are rather more traditional, you should take care not to upset local sensibilities.

If you have an **accident while driving**, don't make a statement to anyone who doesn't speak English. Car rental agencies should provide you, along with the registration/insurance papers, with a bilingual statement to be filled in by both drivers if another car is involved.

Spanish **drug laws** are somewhat ambiguous at present. In 1983, cannabis use (possession of up to 8g of hashish, *chocolate* in Castilian) was decriminalized. Subsequent pressures, and an influx of harder drugs, changed that policy and – in theory at least – any drug use is now forbidden. However, the police are in practice little worried about personal use; larger quantities (and other drugs) are a different matter.

Should you be **arrested** you have the right to contact your **consulate**, and although they're notoriously unhelpful they are required to assist you if you have your passport stolen or lose all your money. If you've been detained for a drugs offence, don't expect any sympathy.

Personal safety and racial issues

Spain's macho image has faded dramatically since Franco's passing and there are now few parts of the country where foreign women travelling alone are likely to feel threatened or attract unwanted attention. In the **larger towns**, a culture of outdoor *terrazas* (terrace bars) and the tendency of Spaniards to move around in large, mixed crowds, filling central bars and streets late into the night, help to make you feel less exposed.

More isolated regions, separated by less than a generation from desperate poverty (or still starkly poor), can be dodgier. In some areas you can walk for hours without reaching an inhabited farm or house, or meeting anyone. It's rare that this poses a threat – help and hospitality are much more the norm – but you are more vulnerable. That said, many women happily trek the Pyrenees from end to end without incident.

Despite – or because of – having been at the receiving end of prejudice during their several decades of emigration to northern Europe, Spaniards are beginning to display some of the **racist attitudes** long espoused by their French neighbours. This has been aggravated by continual, large-scale illegal immigration of African "boat people" across the Straits of Gibraltar and to the Canaries, though not necessarily by the March 2004 Madrid Al-Qaeda bombings, to which most Spaniards reacted admirably and with dignity, without scapegoating. But anyone darker than expected for "tourists" should perhaps anticipate some raised eyebrows in the Pyrenees, where most people of colour tend to be Arab or black African immigrants in menial jobs in the foothill towns of Catalunya and Aragón.

The great outdoors

Although high-rise chalet-apartments and wide pistes make skiing the most conspicuous outdoor pursuit of the Pyrenees, walking is a more widely practised Pyrenean recreation, and much of the range is crossed with well-maintained footpaths. In addition, the mountains and their coastal fringes offer a range of variously energetic diversions, whether gentle cross-country rides on horseback, scuba plunges in the Mediterranean or the thrills of paragliding.

Walking

The Pyrenees rank among the top half-dozen walking areas in Europe. Unlike the Alps, where the high peaks are inaccessible to the average person, any fit, determined walker can reach most of the major summits. Throughout the Pyrenees, paths and trails of varying length are marked and (variably) maintained, some by activity clubs and mountaineering federations, others by local government. Most tourist offices will have map-leaflets or booklets describing shorter itineraries.

Long-distance routes

The principal **long-distance routes** are listed below; summaries are given where applicable throughout the Guide, and recommended specific trail guides are listed in Books.

• **Haute Randonnée Pyrénéenne** (HRP) is the shortest and toughest traverse from Atlantic to Mediterranean, sticking close to the frontier on either side of it. It's planned as a 45-day hike covering nearly 500km, staying in mountain refuges and unstaffed shelters. Not all of it is difficult but some (especially unmarked) sections call for map-reading skills, a head for heights and the use of crampons and ice-axe for much of the season.

• **Grande Randonnée 10** (GR10) is a lower-level traverse, entirely in France, about 300km longer than the HRP. Most nights can be spent in *gîtes d'étape*, huts or village accommodation, but there are sections where a tent or bivouac are necessary. The GR10 is marked in its entirety with red-and-white paint bars.

• **Gran Recorrido 11** (GR11), or *La Senda Pirenaica* as it's called locally, is the Spanish equivalent of the GR10, a well-marked itinerary – again with red-and-white bars – which mostly uses well-established footpaths. Much of this route – some of the wildest, most spectacular scenery in the Pyrenees, and a good compromise between the HRP and GR10 – is served by a mix of attended refuges and unstaffed huts, though again a tent or the willingness to bivouac is occasionally required. The Basque-country section of the trail west of Isaba is, alas, less than brilliantly marked and maintained.

• **GR15**, the *Sendero Prepirenaico*, runs parallel to the GR11 at a much lower altitude, and can thus be followed when the higher elevations are inaccessible due to snow; in this guide it is described only at the southern fringes of the Ordesa region, and in the Valle de Gistau.

• **GR19** is a short trail confined to Alto Aragón, which crosses the GR15 and is most useful as a pleasant way between Biadós, the Valle de Gistau and Ordesa.

• **GR36/GR4** is one of several major north–south traverses of the Pyrenees, in this case from Albi in France to Montserrat in Spain, via Canigou and the Cerdagne/Cerdanya. GR36 is the French designation, GR4 the Spanish.

• **GR7** is the second major north–south traverse, reaching the Pyrenees in the Pays de Sault, curving through Andorra and into Spain. It is described in both a French *topo-guide* and a Catalan-produced *topoguía*.

• **GR107**, from Montségur (France) to Berga (Spain), claims to follow the route of fleeing Cathars (see p.240). Some of its variants share the GR7.

• **GR65**, the modern version of the medieval Camino de Santiago/Chemin de Saint Jacques pilgrimage route, crosses the Pyrenees from Saint-Jean-Pied-de-Port in the French Basque Country, via the Ibañeta pass and Roncesvalles, to Pamplona and then across northern Spain to Santiago de Compostela. The traditional Aragonese spur of the main route is now marked as the GR65.3, which enters Spain from the Vallée d'Aspe at the Somport pass, then descends to Jaca where it turns ninety degrees west, joining the GR65 southwest of Pamplona at Puenta la Reina.

• **Le Sentier Cathare** is a traverse, well marked and well served by *gîtes d'étape*, linking all sites from the Mediterranean to Foix that were significant to the Cathar religion. You pass through some fantastic scenery in Corbières and the Pays de Sault and visit great ruined fortresses such as Quéribus, Peyrepertuse, Puilaurens and Montségur. Because of the modest altitude, it's another good trek for spring or autumn rather than summer.

Mention must be made of **variants** (*variantes* in both French and Castilian), which are exactly what they sound like: alternative routings diverging briefly from the main GR, often of greater difficulty or providing necessary side links to villages just off the principal trail. Both the GR11 and GR10 have been substantially rerouted in spots during recent years, in response to requests from both walkers and farmers, the latter no longer wanting people traipsing through or past their land. Old sectors, if not altogether abandoned, tend to be demoted to *variante* status.

On both sides of the frontier there exist PR trails (**pequeño recorrido** in Castilian, **petit randonnée** in French), usually marked in yellow and white (in Spain), in yellow and red (France), or sometimes blue and yellow or even green and blue; these are itineraries designed to be completed within a day by persons with limited experience of high-mountain walking. Nonetheless, they are also of use to long-haul trekkers, often sparing you some fairly miserable road-tramping, and frequently sharing, or running parallel to, the course of a GR route. They are found in greatest numbers around Benasque and Ansó/Hecho in Spain, and Ax-les-Thermes, Luchon or Cauterets in France, though any tourist board worth its salt seems to be devising these for their resort or valley. Locally produced guidelets describe most of them.

In the French Pyrenees, there are also over twenty **local circuits** called Tours, lasting from three to seven days. These are all indicated with varying precision on the 1:50,000 maps published by Rando Éditions (Randonnées Pyrénéennes) and some of the IGN ones, and most are also described in Rando Éditions guidebooks. The best of these loops are summarized in the relevant chapters of this guide. On the Spanish side, you'll have to devise your own itineraries, using the recommended maps (see p.42) and titles recommended in "Books".

Walking skills and equipment

Gauging the **distance** that can be covered in a day depends on one's level of fitness, type of terrain and load carried. Most people can walk about 4.5km per hour over flat country with a fairly light load, and climb 500m/1550ft per hour off-road; with a full (15- to 20-kilo) pack, they rarely exceed 350m/1150ft per hour climbing off-road. You should knock off 50m per hour from these figures for bad trail surface or heavy loads, and always assume that going downhill is no quicker than ascending – if you love your knees, it won't be. You should reckon on **10km horizontally and 1000m of ascent as a sustainable daily average** at first. If you are reasonably fit you could doubtless manage 20km and/or 2000m of climb, but you probably won't feel much like walking the next day. **Trailhead signs** on the Spanish side of the range often predict wildly optimistic times for the hikes ahead – take them with a grain of salt; by contrast, French estimates are often rather slower than reality.

As a rule of thumb you can carry a quarter of your own body weight comfortably in a **backpack**. Increasingly rare frame packs take loads more easily but one of the hi-tech soft packs with internal struts is more versatile, closer fitting and with nothing to get caught on rocks when scrambling.

You shouldn't skimp on **boots**. Although serious mountain footwear weighs 800–1100 grammes each foot, you don't notice it on the trail. High-tech, synthetic boots not only tend to be hotter than leather ones, but fail to provide vital ankle support – as do trainers, which should never be worn on anything other than a level stroll. As a compromise between flimsy trainers and rigid, expensive monsters designed to accommodate crampons, there are all- or part-leather designs with knobbly tread, moisture-wicking liner and some degree of stiffening around the ankle. **Socks** should be mixed-composition: cotton plus synthetic fibres for warmer conditions, wool plus polypro for colder ones.

If you love your knees, you'll also need a **walking stick** or a pair of **telescopic poles.** If you're following the GR10 or GR11 from west to east, simple sticks or the more elaborate pilgrim's *makila* are easy to buy in the Basque country. In the central part of the range, hi-tech, light-weight telescoping poles are widely sold in the busier trailhead resorts. Make sure they can telescope down to fit *inside* your luggage; airlines are adept at bending or losing them if checked loose, and they're banned as carry-ons. If you've a choice, cork handles are less sweaty than synthetic ones. Alternatively, find some deadfall or abandoned cuttings in a **beech grove**, and fashion your own stick with the saw attachment of a pocket knife. It will take fifteen minutes to strip the bark and sharp nubbins down to the pale yellow wood, but the result is superbly strong.

Unless you're going above 2500m or are camping in winter, there's no need for a specialist **tent**, though always pick one that's self-supporting. Contemporary two-person tents can weigh less than four kilos, if optimistically rated for capacity: two people will fit snugly, with no room for gear inside. Six or seven kilos is a more realistic allowance. You can manage most traverses with a good poncho or waterproof shell and the use of caves, huts, refuges and *gîtes d'étape*. Besides its use on the trail, a big poncho can be rolled around your sleeping bag, or rigged as a canopy. It's not too comfortable, but many consider the saving on weight and bulk worthwhile.

As for **clothing**, follow the **layer** principle. Ascending on a hot day, you'll want only shorts and a T-shirt (plus a dry spare for after lunch). Silk ski tops are also excellent in middling temperature conditions, as they wick sweat out and dry quickly, but in colder conditions you'll also need a long-sleeved shirt. All kinds of part-synthetic **pile/fleece** garments exist, warm and easy to wash. A fleece vest over a wool shirt, with long underwear as the lowest layer, should be as much warmth as you'll need; for freak storms add a **water/wind-proof** shell on the outside. For the HRP or **winter** walking you'll need gaiters, crampons (which fit only stiff mountaineering boots) and an ice-axe.

A good **sleeping bag** is essential. Down gives the best insulation relative to weight and bulk, but its efficiency falls drastically when it gets damp, which it's bound to do unless you have a proper tent, and a poncho over your pack. Artificial filling withstands moisture better, though much heavier and less compressible. Underneath either sort of bag you'll need a foam **mat**; also get a sleeping-bag **liner** – cotton or thermal – which you can wash and dry easily en route.

Complete your personal gear with a brimmed **sun hat**, a warmer ski-type **cap** for higher altitudes, **gloves**, **sunglasses, sunscreen**, including **lip-balm** with a sun-protection factor, and some sort of **insect repellent** – Pyrenean biting flies can be fierce. For navigation, a **compass** and **pocket altimeter** are both vital, together with the appropriate **maps**; a **GPS device** is optional.

Water and food

Per hiking day you need up to four litres of water as liquid or from food; in the mountains you can usually get fresh water along the way. Check your map for habitation upstream, as some villages have cesspits leaking into rivers; if there's nothing upstream a vigorous flow will be safe. If in doubt – ie if there are signs of livestock – add water purification tablets.

On an easy walk you'll need forty **calories** minimum per day per kilo of body weight – fifty for a tough hike and as much as sixty for ski touring. Fats provide the most energy, at around 7500 calories per kilo; dehydrated main-meal foods can give you 5000 calories per kilo; nuts and chocolate work out at around 4500 calories per kilo. **Re-supplying** on the GR10, GR7 or GR65 is easy, as they're designed to pass through plenty of villages; on the HRP or the GR11 you'll have to make diversions. It's possible to pick wild food along the way – in season you'll find edible mushrooms, wild spinach, wild strawberries, wild raspberries and hazelnuts – but these have low caloric value and should be regarded only as supplements to the trekking diet.

The best **stove** is an MSR type: light, powerful – and expensive. Next best are French-made Bleuet 206 or English-made Coleman 3001 HPX butane-cartridge stoves, as their fuel is light and almost universally available – the Coleman cartridges somewhat less so, though they are self-sealing and can thus be safely removed if necessary. However, butane stoves don't burn well at low temperatures or when the cartridge is running out. For supper, packet soups, dried potatoes, couscous or thin pasta, supplemented with dry cheese or cured meat, are high-calorie, lightweight and fuel-efficient. Although there's often little else to buy in high villages, avoid canned goods, as they're not only heavy but aggravate Pyrenean litter problems no matter where you dispose of them. For short excursions, a vacuum flask of hot water rehydrates dried foods.

Climbing

Although the principal summits of the Pyrenees can be reached with only rudimentary climbing skills, the range has plenty of demanding technical routes. Particularly good areas include Aigüestortes, Maladeta and the entire Ordesa country in Spain, and the Haute-Garonne, Vallée d'Aure, Cirque de Gavarnie and the tops of the Aspe and Ossau valleys in France. There are plenty of climbing courses on offer to summer visitors throughout the Pyrenees, most of them charging in the region of €70 for four to six hours' tuition.

Caving

The northern and southern foothills of the Pyrenees are largely Cretaceous or Jurassic **limestone**, and some of the high peaks are too, for example Monte Perdido, Europe's highest limestone mountain. Although limestone is soluble, it's also nonporous, which means it dissolves only at tiny cracks where water can penetrate. Over millennia, this action produces vertical potholes and vast caverns. Below the bizarrely eroded limestone around Pic d'Anie yawns the deepest cave system yet discovered in the Pyrenees, and one of the deepest in the world: the **Gouffre Pierre-Saint-Martin**. The Pyrenees also shelters the world's highest **ice-caves** (caves hung with frozen waterfalls), at the top of the Cirque de Gavarnie. If you've never done any caving, but would still like to experience it, a good introduction is **L'Aguzou** in the Aude, where small pre-booked, fully equipped parties are guided around (see p.99).

If you're intent on caving as a sport, you need to contact your closest caving club or sign up with a commercial school. It's possible to head off with your own gear if you know what you're doing, but many of the best caverns are locked, and only approved people can get the key. Rewarding areas, besides the above-cited Pic d'Anie and Monte Perdido regions, include, the **Comminges** and northern **Couserans**, the **Pays de Sault**, the **Ariège**, the **Aude**, the **Serra del Cadí**, the **Alta Garrotxa** region and the **Têt valley** around Villefranche-de-Conflent.

Snowshoeing and skiing

The comparatively gentle slopes of the Pyrenees are perfectly suited for **ski mountaineering** and **cross-country** skiing, and you're pretty well guaranteed solitude whilst ski-traversing. Compared with the Alps, the risk of avalanche is less, and the chance of falling into a crevasse or having a similar accident is minimal. To learn, sign on with a guide in a resort like Barèges or Gavarnie, both spots giving access to marvellous itineraries ranging from one day to several. If you're already a mountain walker and a competent downhill skier, you're well on the way. **Snowshoeing** is even less demanding, and is also booming of late, especially in areas like the Couserans which have few downhill ski resorts.

In terms of **downhill skiing**, snow quality on prepared runs seldom approaches the powder standard more often found in the Alps or North America – late in the season things get downright mushy and/or thin near the bottom. As a general rule, resorts in the eastern half of the range have these problems compounded by low precipitation and strong sun (also a problem on much of the Spanish side of the border), and by wind, which either packs the snow hard or scours it away. In the west there is a tendency to mist and rain, brought in by the Atlantic weather systems. Don't set out specially for a week's holiday without checking conditions at your chosen resort first. Always worth a look is the Ski Club of Great Britain's website, Ⓦwww.skiclub.co.uk; they feature about ten of the top Pyrenean resorts (including all those in Andorra), with current snow reports, frank resort profiles, customer comments and links to package operators, though you have to log on as a member for full functionality. For the Catalan Spanish slopes, an excellent website is Ⓦwww.catski.net/comunicat/partdeneu, with up-to-the-minute snow condition reports for seventeen downhill and cross-country resorts (Castilian or Catalan only, but interpretation of the lists isn't rocket science).

Snowboarding – *surfismo* in *Castilian*, *surfisme* in French/Catalan – is now a big thing in the Pyrenees, and boarders – *surfistas/surfistes* respectively – are well catered for in virtually every resort. **Snow-blading** is somewhat less widespread.

Eastern resorts

Proximity to the Mediterranean means that snow can be unreliable at the eastern resorts of **Vallter 2000, Núria and Massella/La Molina** in Spain, and **Cambre d'Aze** or **Puigmal 2600** in France. For ski mountaineering and cross-country skiing, on the other hand, the higher reaches of this region are a delight.

Pas de la Casa offers the most reliable snow immediately around **Andorra**, but the development – slowly expanding into France – itself is unaesthetic. Best all-rounders within Andorra are **Ordino-Arcalis**, set amongst magnificent high-mountain wilderness, or **Soldeu El Tarter**, with one of the best (British-dominated) beginners' schools in Europe. Andorra in general is busy reinventing itself as a family/upscale skiing destination, shedding its enduring reputation as a downmarket, wintertime Club 18–30.

Back in France, **Ax-Bonascre** has particularly appealing scenery. Just south, in the contiguous Capcir and Cerdagne regions, the most famous resort is **Font-Romeu**, though **Porté-Puymorens**, **Les Angles**, **Formiguères** and **Puyvalador** are all superior. For **cross-country skiing** (*ski de fondo* in Castilian, *ski de fond* in French and Catalan), much of the Cerdagne/Cerdanya and the Serra del Cadí are criss-crossed by trails, with famously sunny spring days.

Central and western resorts

Spain has several serious resorts near the Val d'Aran; the best of these are **Port-Ainé**, in the Noguera Pallaresa valley, **Boï-Taüll**, beside the Aigüestortes park, and **Baqueira-Beret**, at the head of the valley and the only one with an international reputation. Ski resorts in **Aragón**'s stretch of the Pyrenees – following massive investment and thus-far unsuccessful bids to host various Winter Olympics – are well equipped, particularly **Cerler**, **Formigal**, and **Candanchú-Astún**. Usually, however, the **north slope** of the **central French Pyrenees** provides the most reliable conditions; **Barèges-La Mongie** comes first for its size and recent infrastructure improvements. Other normally dependable destinations in this area include **Piau-Engaly**, **Saint-Lary Soulan**, **Peyreagudes** and **Gavarnie-Gèdre**. In the far west, both **Gourette** and **Arette-la-Pierre-Saint-Martin** have a reasonable snow record owing to their Atlantic exposure.

Every significant resort in the Pyrenees is described in the Guide, with details of top-point elevation and the number and type of pistes. The system for **grading pistes** is based on a universal **colour code**: green for beginners, blue for easy, red for intermediate and black for advanced skiers. It's not a completely dependable system – a red run in one resort might rate only as blue in another – but it should give a fair idea of what to expect. **Beginners** are usually well looked after – Gavarnie-Gèdre, Soldeu and Port-Ainé, for example, all have long green runs from their top lifts.

Mountain rescue phone numbers

The true utility of **mobile phones** as a mountain safety device is debatable. They do have reception in surprisingly remote places, particularly on top of ridges. But you cannot count on them to be working exactly when and where you need them – especially if they've been damaged in an accident – and they should never encourage you to take chances which you otherwise wouldn't. Take them along by all means, but they are only an aid to safety, not a guarantee of it.

Spain and Andorra

Navarra ⓣ112
Aragón ⓣ062
Catalunya ⓣ085 (also for forest fires)
Roncal ⓣ948 893 248
Jaca ⓣ974 311 350
Snowpack and avalanche risk (Dec–April; Navarra) ⓣ906 365 331
Snowpack and avalanche risk (Dec–April; Huesca) ⓣ906 365 322
Snowpack and avalanche risk (Dec–April; west Catalunya) ⓣ935 671 577
Snowpack and avalanche risk (Dec–April; east Catalunya) ⓣ935 671 576
Andorra ⓣ112

France

Oloron-Sainte-Marie ⓣ05.59.39.86.22
Central Pyrenees, general ⓣ05.62.92.41.41
Pierrefitte-Nestalas ⓣ05.62.92.75.07
Gavarnie valley ⓣ05.62.92.48.24
Luchon ⓣ05.61.79.83.79
Perpignan ⓣ04.68.61.79.20
Ariège ⓣ05.61.64.22.58
General alpine conditions (Dec–April) ⓣ08.36.68.04.04
Snowpack and avalanche risk (Dec–April) ⓣ08.36.68.10.20

Costs and packages

Pyrenean skiing, especially on the French side, **costs marginally less** than in the Alps because the range lacks international cachet and the **clientele** is almost totally local and family-oriented. There's little of the snootiness or nocturnal excess occasionally met with in the Alps, and as a foreigner (particularly in Spain) you'll be the object of benign curiosity or outright friendliness – though again in Spain you may have trouble finding English-speaking **instruction**. In France, the local *École du Ski Français* will have at least one multilingual instructor per resort; rates hover around €30 for one or two persons per lesson at a less popular spot. On the Spanish side, rates charged by the *Escuela Española de Esquí* are comparable; in Andorra, English instruction is guaranteed, though at a price premium. **Infrastructure** is adequate to quite good, best wherever sums have been spent on snow cannons, new lifts or piste extension. But especially in eastern Spain and Andorra, *pistes/pistas* can be **poorly marked**; the margin "lollipops" (*espiolettes/espiolets*) may not be colour-keyed, so it's fairly easy to stray onto the wrong run.

Package holidays are often the cheapest way of skiing – you may well find a UK-based deal offering tuition, equipment rental, accommodation and insurance at under £350 per person for a week, though more realistically allow £450–500. Be sure to check the resort's piste diagram carefully – if a run ends below 1800m it's unlikely that you'll get snow, whether natural or artificial, all the way down. The main destination promoted in Britain is Andorra, though some agents offer Baqueira-Beret and Barèges-La Mongie. Whether you arrive on a package or under your own steam (see p.28), you should take advantage of the slower mid-week periods and avoid the weekends and major holiday breaks when all accommodation is booked months in advance.

Arranging matters **on the spot**, expect to pay (in Spain or Andorra) €24–39 for a peak-season day **lift pass**, and in France €21–33 depending on the complexity and quality of the lift and piste scheme – some of the Mickey-Mouse French resorts can be very cheap indeed (under €20). Skis, boots and poles typically **rent** at €15 daily for anything medium-perfomance and above, including **"carving"** – adapted skis some 10cm shorter than conventional ones, which are much more manoeuvrable, confidence-building and forgiving of minor mistakes. Slope evacuation **insurance** tends to be pushed in Spain; at €1–2 per day it's probably a good idea. Obviously multi-day passes or long-term rental are more advantageous (eg €160 for a week); you'll usually need to present a passport-sized photo for three days or over. Many resorts offer the possibility of arranging on-the-spot **"mini-packages"**: local tourist offices list valley hotels which offer all-in deals of half-board and lift pass which save a good 25 percent compared to doing it piecemeal, even more if you restrict yourself to weekdays.

Cross-country skiing is altogether less costly – reckon on €7–10 per day for access; gear rental is also about a third cheaper than downhill.

Cycling

Cyclists shouldn't be daunted by the Pyrenees. You can find plenty of rolling hills and even almost flat terrain – the Cerdanya/Cerdagne, for example. There are numerous recognized circuits on the French side and recommended mountain-biking routes are marked in red on the Randonnées Éditions maps. On the Spanish side there aren't as many planned routes – though more and more Spanish guides to bike-touring are being published – and the hotter weather discourages all but the hardiest from cycling inland, though you should find company as you approach the sea, particularly on the Santiago de Compostela route. For more information on cycling, see pp.37–38 & 40.

Horse-riding

Horse-riding is available across the Pyrenees, mostly in the foothills. The classic mount of the high mountains is the native Mérenguais breed – the Ariège is the place to ride these stocky horses, especially at **Aulus-les-Bains** in the Couserans. There's also a prominent stable at **L'Estanguet** in the Vallée d'Aspe. On the Spanish side, there are renowned stables at **La Miana** in the Garrotxa, as well as two near **Puigcerdà** in the Cerdanya, and two at **Sarvisé** in Aragón, plus one in the northern **Sierra de Guara**. A full day in the saddle should cost around €80, while part-day rates of €15 per hour are standard.

River sports

The Pyrenees have plenty of rivers suitable for **canyoning**, **kayaking** and **rafting**, especially in the east of the range and in Aragón around the Ordesa park and the Sierra de Guara.

Canyoning involves jumping into a suitably smooth watercourse and letting it take you along, sometimes whooshing down waterfalls, occasionally abseiling down vertical drops, usually merely wading through near-freezing water. For the easier rivers you don't need any special abilities or equipment other than a wet suit and knowing how to swim, but tougher sections require helmets, inflatables, ropes and abseiling skills. Obviously it can be dangerous, so unless you're experienced, it's best to go in an escorted group, with gear and guidance included (see the box on p.443 for more on this). The undisputed canyoning centre for the Pyrenees, if not all of Europe, is the **Sierra de Guara** though it's also practised in the **Garganta de Escuaín** (both in Spain).

The Spanish **Noguera Pallaresa** is the most celebrated **rafting and kayaking** river of the whole range, but there are plenty of others, just as good and less crowded, where tuition and equipment are also available for about €40 a go. These include the **Têt**, **Aude**, **Ariège**, **Salat**, **Adour**, **Aure**, **Louron**, **Gave d'Oloron**, **Gave de Pau**, **Ossau**, **Aspe** and **Nive** in France, and the **Veral**, **Aragón**, **Ara**, **Gállego**, **Ésera**, **Noguera Ribagorçana** and **Segre** in Spain.

Scuba diving

While there are two centres in Biarritz on the French Atlantic, most Pyrenean **scuba facilities** line the Catalan coast, between Collioure and Roses. These take advantage of the clearer Mediterranean, and in particular the marine reserve off Cap de Creus. The thermocline here is about 12m deep, where the temperature dips to 12°C all year (versus 22°C at the surface in summer), so you'll want a 7mm wetsuit.

There are several centres on the Spanish side between Roses and Llança, most of them both CMAS and PADI certified and many (in theory) operating year-round on demand. Although many centres only quote rates as part of an all-inclusive package with an affiliated hotel, per-dive prices (where available) for qualified divers cost €21–25 (equipment not included) while a full PADI or CMAS Open Water Diver course will typically set you back just over €300. Under-16s are subject to legal restrictions for scuba diving in many parts of Spain; Catalunya now allows over-14s to dive, but double-check before booking a family holiday.

Airborne sports

Hot-air ballooning is practised in the Cerdanya and the Garrotxa, with standard rates of about €145 for 60–90 minutes, champagne breakfast in mid-air included. Airfields at Cerdanya and Luchon are the main venues for **light aviation** and **glider flights**; typical charges are €58 for 20 minutes, €110 for 40 minutes.

Paragliding (*parapente*) is a blend of hang-gliding and parachuting, the arc-shaped contraption steering something like a hang-glider but having no rigid parts. You take off by running or skiing down a slope until you get enough lift; in 1000m of descent you might cover a distance of 4–6km. Improvements in design and teaching since the sport's early, chequered days now make it relatively safe, if a bit expensive. A single introductory flight costs €45–80, but a full two-week course, taking you to a stage where you should be able to go off on your own, amounts to well over €700.

Major venues in the central Pyrenees include **Accous**, **Barèges, Saint-Lary-Soulan**, **Val Louron**, **Luchon** and **Guzet-Neige** in France, and **Ager** and **Castejón de Sos** in Spain. Areas closer to the coast tend to be unsuitable because of unpredictable winds, though **Baigura**, near Saint-Jean-Pied-du-Port in the French Pays-Basque, is an exception.

Travel essentials

Addresses

French ones are written as: 18 bis rue Henri-Foucault 1er, which means an annexe or sub-premises of no.18 Henri-Foucault Street, on the first floor. Common abbreviations – used in this book – are rte for *route*, av for *avenue* and bd for *boulevard*. Spanish addresses (except in San Sebastián and Hondarribia) are written as: c/Picasso 2, 4° izda. – which means Carrer or Calle Picasso no. 2, 4th floor, left- (*izquierda*) hand flat or office (dcha. – *derecha* – is right; cto. *centro* or centre). Other confusions in Spanish addresses result from the different spellings, and sometimes words, used in Catalan, Aragonese and Euskera – all of which are steadily replacing their Castilian counterparts – and from the removal of Franco and other Falangist heroes from the main *avenidas* and plazas. A dwindling number of maps – including some official ones – haven't yet caught up with either local-language or post-Falangist renaming. In some towns dual numbering systems are also in effect, and looking at the house plates it's difficult to tell which is the old and which the new scheme.

Travelling with children

Children/babies don't pose great travel problems in either country. Local tourist offices do a good job of detailing attractions or activities for kids. Both rail systems charge nothing for under-4s, and offer heavily discounted fares for under-11s/under-12s. All Pyrenean accommodation welcomes them: French hotels charge by the room, with small supplements for extra beds, while Spanish lodgings offer triples and quads. The more old-fashioned family-run places in both countries may offer baby-sitting services, or least keep an ear cocked while you go out briefly. Disposable nappies (*couches à jeter* in French) and feeding materials are widely available, though baby foods and milk powders tend to be heavily sweetened or very rich. In both countries, kids are allowed in all bars and restaurants, and on the French side there's usually a *menu enfants* (basically steak, chips and ice cream). Spanish *hostales* and *pensiones* may prepare food specially on request – or provide self-catering facilities to do so.

Cinema

There are just a few cinemas in the French Pyrenees – notably in Luchon – with others in the foothill or gateway towns. Students get discounts, and foreign films are sometimes shown subtitled in their original language (look for *version originale* or *v.o.* in the listings). On the Spanish side, there are again cinemas in larger foothill and coastal towns, like San Sebastián and Girona, as well as Huesca, Puigcerdà and Andorra. The majority of what's screened is Hollywood mainstream poorly dubbed into Spanish; you'll sometimes find films in their original language with subtitles. Look for *voz original* or *versión original (subtitulada)*, abbreviated "*v.o.*", in the listings; "*v.e.*" means *versión español.*

Consulates

Closest UK consulates to the Pyrenees are in Bilbao, Toulouse and Barcelona; the US is represented in Barcelona and Toulouse.

Costs

Prices in the Pyrenees don't differ greatly from those in towns away from the mountains. If you do spend less than you anticipate on a mountain holiday, it will be because there's less scope to go financially wild once you're off the beaten track. If you're travelling alone you'll end up spending much more than you would as a couple or group – sharing rooms (and wine) saves considerably.

French costs

Because of the reasonable cost of accommodation and eating out, at least by northern European standards, the French Pyrenees are not outrageously expensive to visit. **On average**, staying exclusively at *gîtes* or refuges, or camping, and being disciplined about denying yourself cups of coffee and culture, you could just about survive on £27/US$52 per person per day, including one inexpensive restaurant meal. For a more comfortable existence, including a basic double room, two meals out and café stops, you need to budget about £40/$78 per person per day. If you're planning to stay in fancier lodgings, and eat and drink to your heart's content, £58/$113 per day per head wouldn't be an unreasonable estimate.

Spanish costs

The Spanish Pyrenees, like northern Spain generally, are no longer a budget destination; especially in the more popular parts of the Catalan Pyrenees and the developed lowlands of Euzkadi, you can easily spend more than on the French side.

On average, if you're prepared to picnic at lunch, stay in inexpensive *pensiones* or *casas rurales* and partake the most frugal suppers, you could get by on £24/US$46 per person per day. If you intend to upgrade your accommodation, experience town nightlife and eat fancier meals then you'll need more like £48/$94 a day. At £66/$130 a day and upwards you'll only be limited by your energy reserves – though of course if you're planning to stay in the best hotels, this figure won't even cover your room.

One thing to look out for is the addition of value added tax – **IVA** – which may come as an unexpected extra when you pay the bill for food or accommodation; most establishments tend to quote prices without IVA. The magic words, often in small print at the bottom of the menu, are *IVA (no) incluido* in Castilian or *IVA (no) inclós* in Catalan.

Credit/debit cards

Credit/debit cards are widely accepted in France and Spain by major retailers, car rental firms, petrol stations and expensive hotels or restaurants; always check first, however, in smaller establishments. CHIP-and-PIN is all but mandatory nowadays in France (not yet so in Spain). Visa – known locally as Carte Bleue – is universally recognized in France; Mastercard and American Express rank considerably lower. In Spain, American Express and Visa have most status, while Mastercard is less widely accepted. Any Visa or Mastercard credit card, as well as any **debit card** that is part of the Cirrus/Maestro, Visa Electron or Link systems can be used to obtain cash while travelling from one of the numerous autotellers (**ATM**s) dotted across the Pyrenean foothills. The French words for "ATM" are *guichet automatique* or *distributeur de billets*, the Catilian is *cajero automatico*. Debit cards are cheaper to use in this manner than credit cards, but your home bank will probably levy a minimum charge of about £1.50/$2.50, so you don't want to be constantly withdrawing small sums. Lost or stolen cards should be reported either to your home country emergency number, or one of the following hotlines: in France, Carte Bleue (Visa) ⓣ08.00.90.11.79; American Express ⓣ01.47.77.72.00; Mastercard ⓣ01.45.67.84.84; in Spain, American Express, ⓣ915 720 303; Visa, ⓣ900 974 445; Mastercard, ⓣ900 971 231.

Electricity

In both France and Spain, electricity is 220V out of double, round-pin wall sockets. Travellers from Britain and Australasia will need the appropriate three-to-two adaptors for appliances, and North Americans will additionally require a step-down transformer.

Equipment

Equipment for skiing, climbing and other mountain activities is slightly more expensive in France or Spain than in the US, but usually much less than in the UK – and you'll find some bargains in Andorran megastores. The range of products is also striking; addresses of some shops are given in the Guide.

Laundries

Laundries are not that common outside the bigger towns of the French Pyrenees – look in the Yellow Pages under "*Laveries Automatiques*" or "*Laveries en libre-service*". If you want to wash your own, carry handwash powder or cold-water laundry liquid, and keep quantities small and inconspicuously dried in hotels, as it's often expressly forbidden to wash clothes in rooms. On the Spanish side, you'll find a few self-service *lavanderías automáticas* in towns like Jaca, Benasque or Olot, but otherwise they're absent – you normally have to leave your clothes for the full (and somewhat expensive) works. You're not allowed by law to leave laundry hanging out of windows over a street, though this is widely ignored. A dry cleaner is a *tintorería*.

Money

French banking hours are Monday to Friday 9am–4.30pm, mostly closing at midday (noon–2pm or 12.30–2.30pm). A few open Saturday 9am–noon, many rural branches shut on Mondays, but all close on Sundays and holidays. The Crédit Mutuel usually offers the best rates and takes the least commission.

There are **money-exchange counters** (*bureaux de change*) at airports and big-city train stations. You'll also find **automatic bill-changer machines** in such places, accepting notes in major non-euro currencies. However, rates for both such facilities tend to be poor and commissions high.

Spanish banks (*bancos*) and **savings banks** (*cajas de ahorro*) have branches in all but the smallest towns, and a few are prepared to change travellers' cheques – though stick to major brands to avoid refusal. Banking hours are Monday–Friday 8.30am–2pm, Saturday 8.30am–1pm (except June–Sept when banks close on Sat). In heavily touristed areas, such as the Catalan or Basque coasts, you may find **exchange booths** (*casas de cambio*), with more convenient hours (though "no commission charged" often means a poor exchange rate).

Travellers' cheques are next to useless in the Pyrenees; readers have reported even euro-denominated, name-brand ones almost impossible to cash. UK-based travellers may have better luck with International Postal **Giro Cheques**, which work like ordinary bank cheques except that you cash them at post offices.

A possible compromise between travellers' cheques and plastic is **Visa TravelMoney**,

> Spain, France and Andorra use the European Union currency, the euro (€). For the most up-to-date **exchange rates** of the US dollar, the pound sterling or any other currency against the euro, consult the very useful currency speculators' website, ⓦwww.oanda.com. Euro notes exist in denominations of 5, 10, 20, 50, 100, 200 and 500 euros, and coins in denominations of 1, 2, 5, 10, 20 and 50 cents and 1 and 2 euros.

a pre-paid debit card linked to a PIN, which works with all ATMs and merchants accepting Visa cards. The main disadvantage with them is that merchants may refuse a transaction if they detect that your balance is insufficient; the cards are, however, reloadable. For full information, consult Ⓦusa.visa.com/personal/cards/index.html.

Swimming pools

The *piscine municipale* (French), or *piscina municipal* (Castilian) is a feature of most Pyrenean towns, and is reasonably priced (€2.50–3.50 for a swim). They're a lifesaver in high summer and an excellent way to get the kinks out of muscles fatigued from trekking, though the water is almost never heated.

Time

Both France and Spain are always one hour ahead of Britain, both Greenwich or Daylight Saving Time. Except for a few weeks in March and November, both countries are six hours ahead of US Eastern Standard Time, nine ahead of US Pacific Standard Time.

Toilets

Toilets are called *les toilettes* or *WC* (pronounced "vay say") in France, but variously *los servicios* (*servei* in Catalan), *baños*, *aseos*, *retretes* or *sanitarios* in Spain. On both sides of the range they're apt to be averagely clean, with paper not guaranteed and the squat-type hole-in-the-ground not unknown. Incidentally, *lavabo* means wash basin in both Castilian and French. In France, toilets are usually found downstairs or upstairs in bars or restaurants; in Spain they tend to be on the same floor as the *comedor/menjador*. Bar-restaurant and museum toilets are usually free, though keep a few coins handy for ones in train/bus stations.

Visas and entry requirements

EU or EEA citizens have no problems moving around the Pyrenees, since the range straddles two member nations, France and Spain (whilst Andorra has no visa requirements). But you still need to carry a passport or other authoritative ID, since hotels and refuges often demand identification – especially in Spain, where guests must fill out a registration card at every lodging. Citizens of Canada, the US, New Zealand and Australia do not need visas beforehand to enter France, Spain or Andorra; South Africans should check current requirements.

Both France and Spain allow non-EU/EEA nationality tourists **ninety days' cumulative stay in any period of 180 days**. There are no longer any border-control posts between France and Spain, and non-EU/EEA arrivals will only be stamped in at the region's various airports.

French embassies in non-EU Countries include: Australia ⓣ02/6216 0100; Canada ⓣ613/789-1795; New Zealand ⓣ04/802 7787; US ⓣ202/944-6000.

Spanish embassies in non-EU Countries include: Australia ⓣ02/6273 3555; Canada ⓣ613/747-2252; US ⓣ202/452-0100.

Vegetarians and vegans

Vegetarians will have a fairly hard time of it dining out on either side of the Pyrenees; **vegans** should probably forget altogether about restaurants and stick to self-catering. In the larger foothill towns you'll find a bare handful of vegetarian and non-European restaurants that serve vegetable dishes, and very occasionally elsewhere you'll encounter a vegetarian *menu*; otherwise crêperies and pizzerias can be good fallbacks. You may well tire of eggs and omelettes (in Spain, *tortilla francesa* is a plain omelette, *con champiñones* with mushrooms). In France, the magic words are *je suis végétarien(ne); est-ce qu'il y a des plats sans viande ou poisson?* (I'm a vegetarian; are there any dishes without meat or fish?). In Spain, it's *Soy vegetariano. Hay algo sin carne?* (I'm a vegetarian. Is there anything without meat?). You may have to add *y sin mariscos* (and without seafood) *y sin jamón* (and without ham) to cover all the bases, since Spaniards don't seem to regard these as "real" meat, often adding them to vegetable dishes to "spice them up". For example, *ensalada ilustrada* consists of lettuce, eggs, olives, asparagus spears, tomato wedges – plus a few chunks of ham that you'll have to flick aside.

Guide

Guide

The Eastern Pyrenees

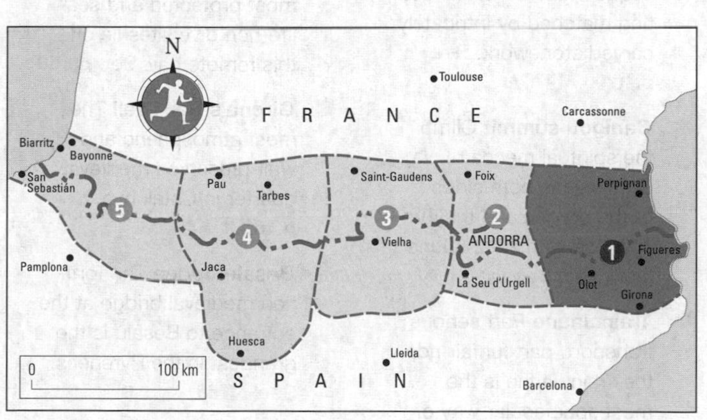

CHAPTER 1

Highlights

* **Château de Peyrepertuse** The largest and most intricate of the so-called Cathar castles evokes medieval border wars. See p.95
* **Prieuré de Serrabona** The most exquisite of Roussillon's many Romanesque monuments, its setting matched by intricately carved stonework. See p.101
* **Canigou summit** Climb the spiritual mecca of Catalonians both sides of the border, and maybe coincide with 23–24 June festivities. See p.105
* **Train Jaune** Part serious transport, part funfair ride, the Train Jaune is the most spectacular way of reaching the Cerdagne from Roussillon. See p.112
* **Céret Musée d'Art Moderne** The rich and varied collection here is the envy of many big-city museums. See p.119
* **Scuba near Cala Joncols** Some of the Costa Brava's most protected and sea-life-rich dive sites lie off this remote bay. See p.139
* **Girona's Barri Vell** The most atmospheric and well-preserved medieval quarter in Catalunya. See p.150
* **Besalú bridge** The fortified medieval bridge at the entrance to Besalú is the grandest in the Pyrenees. See p.158

△ Château de Peyrepertuse

1

The Eastern Pyrenees

The **Eastern Pyrenees**, despite their comparatively modest height, are among the best-loved and most visited areas of the range. This is partly due to convenient airports at Perpignan and Carcassonne in France, plus Girona in Spain, though the ocean-tempered climate, Mediterranean light and alluring scenery certainly help. Landscapes encompass sculpted coastline, arid scrub, foothill orchards and alpine forests. There's a correspondingly wide variety of wildlife: waterfowl and birds of prey stipple the skies, while the terrain supports a surprising number of mammals, small and large, not yet eradicated by local hunters.

Running along the crest of the easternmost Albères/Albera section of the Pyrenees, the **border** is breached by just four road passes: the coastal **Col dels Balistres**, the **Col du Perthus** in the middle of the chain – supposedly used by Hannibal – the unnamed saddle by **Roc del Bau** and the **Col d'Ares** in the west. There are, of course, numerous other footpaths and jeep tracks across the mountains, for example the **Col de Banyuls**, used by smugglers for centuries and by refugees escaping north during the Spanish Civil War, and then south in World War II.

For the **Catalan people** in both Spain and France, the national border is a fiction – even more so since the European Union did away with customs controls in 1995. Locals regularly cross back and forth on foot or by vehicle, as they always have done with their flocks and contraband. But while Catalan (*Catalá*) is the official language of Spanish Catalonia (*Catalunya*), it's no more than an option in the schools of Roussillon or French Catalonia; there is scarcely any interest in a politically unified, cross-border Catalan state, notwithstanding the universal presence of *els quatre barres* (the red-and-yellow Catalan pennant) and the increasing citation of Catalan place-names in France. The whole of Catalonia was last under one ruler in the mid-seventeenth century, and the glories of the early medieval Catalan-Aragonese kingdoms are an even more distant memory.

Artificial though the border may be, it's useful to consider the Eastern Pyrenees as three distinct parts: the **French valleys**, draining predominantly northeast from the main Pyrenean crest between the Cerdagne and the sea; the **Mediterranean coast**, shared between the two parts of Catalonia; and the more uniformly south-facing **Spanish valleys**.

Perpignan is the only substantial town on the French side and the inevitable transport hub for the French valleys; most visitors head southwest up the parallel valleys of the **Tech** and **Têt**, where congenial towns like **Céret**, **Arles-sur-Tech**, **Prats-de-Molló** and **Prades** serve as handy forward bases. Monumental interest is lent by medieval fortifications at **Mont-Louis** and **Villefranche-de-Conflent**, defending the Têt approaches to Perpignan, and by compelling Romanesque foothill monasteries like the **Prieuré de Serrabona**, **Saint-Michel-de-Cuixà** and

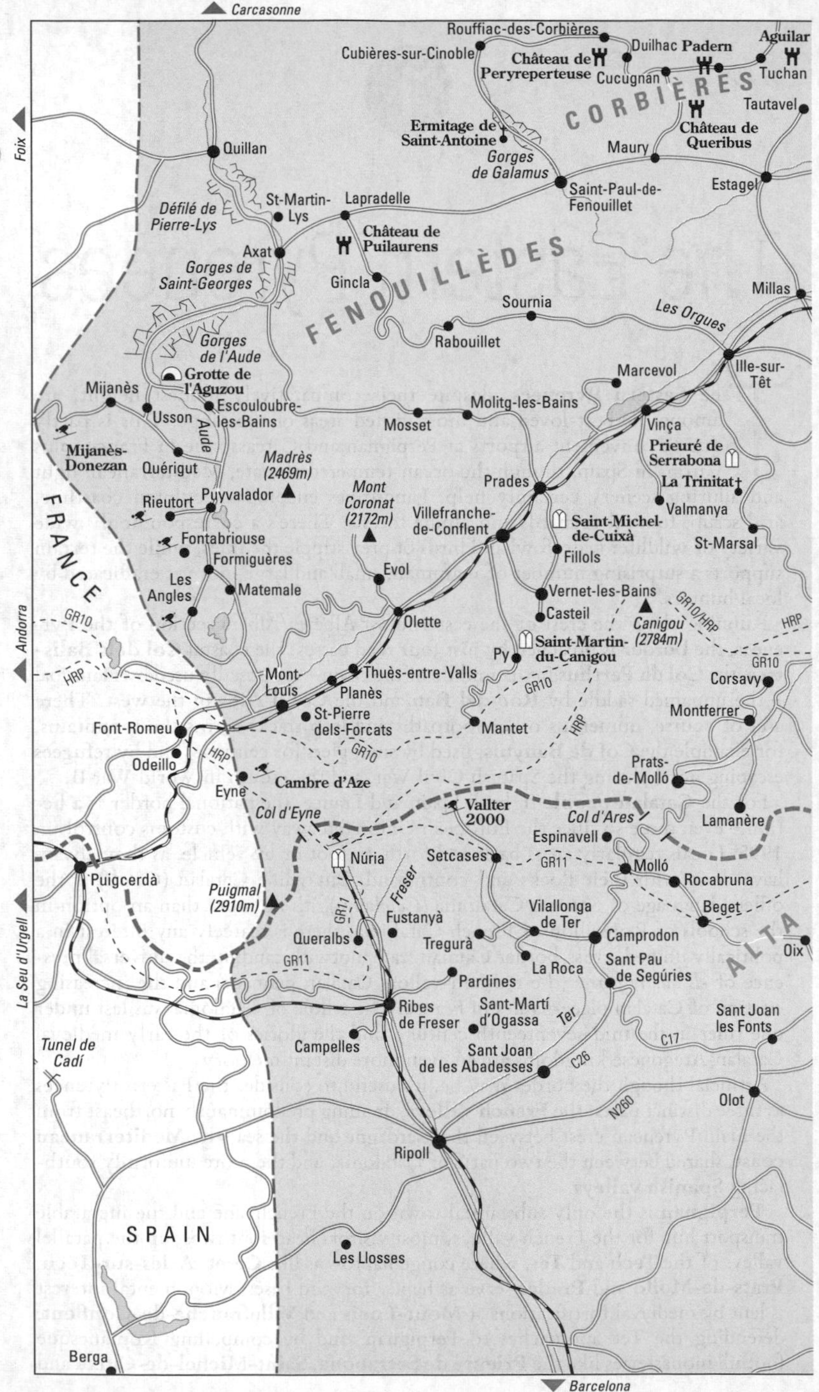
Carcasonne
Foix
Andorra
La Seu d'Urgell
Barcelona
Rouffiac-des-Corbières
Cubières-sur-Cinoble
Château de Peryreperteuse
Duilhac
Padern
Aguilar
Cucugnan
Tuchan
CORBIÈRES
Tautavel
Ermitage de Saint-Antoine
Château de Queribus
Quillan
Gorges de Galamus
Maury
Estagel
Saint-Paul-de-Fenouillet
Défilé de Pierre-Lys
St-Martin-Lys
Lapradelle
Château de Puilaurens
Axat
Gorges de Saint-Georges
Gincla
FENOUILLÈDES
Millas
Sournia
Les Orgues
Rabouillet
Gorges de l'Aude
Ille-sur-Têt
Grotte de l'Aguzou
Marcevol
Mijanès
Escouloubre-les-Bains
Usson
Molitg-les-Bains
Mosset
Vinça
Aude
Mijanès-Donezan
Quérigut
Madrès (2469m)
Prieuré de Serrabona
Prades
La Trinitat
Mont Coronat (2172m)
Puyvalador
Valmanya
Rieutort
Villefranche-de-Conflent
Saint-Michel-de-Cuixà
FRANCE
Fontabriouse
Fillols
St-Marsal
Formiguères
Evol
Les Angles
Matemale
Vernet-les-Bains
Casteil
Olette
Canigou (2784m)
GR10
GR10/HRP
HRP
Saint-Martin-du-Canigou
Py
Mont-Louis
Thuès-entre-Valls
Corsavy
Planès
Montferrer
Font-Romeu
St-Pierre dels-Forcats
Mantet
Odeillo
Prats-de-Molló
Eyne
Cambre d'Aze
Col d'Eyne
Vallter 2000
Col d'Ares
Lamanère
Espinavell
Núria
Setcases
GR11
Molló
Puigcerdà
Freser
Rocabruna
Puigmal (2910m)
Fustanyà
Vilallonga de Ter
Beget
Queralbs
Treguràr
Camprodon
ALTA
Oix
La Roca
Sant Pau de Segúries
Pardines
Ribes de Freser
Sant-Martí d'Ogassa
Ter
Sant Joan les Fonts
Tunel de Cadí
Campelles
C17
Sant Joan de les Abadesses
C26
Olot
N260
Ripoll
SPAIN
Les Llosses
Berga

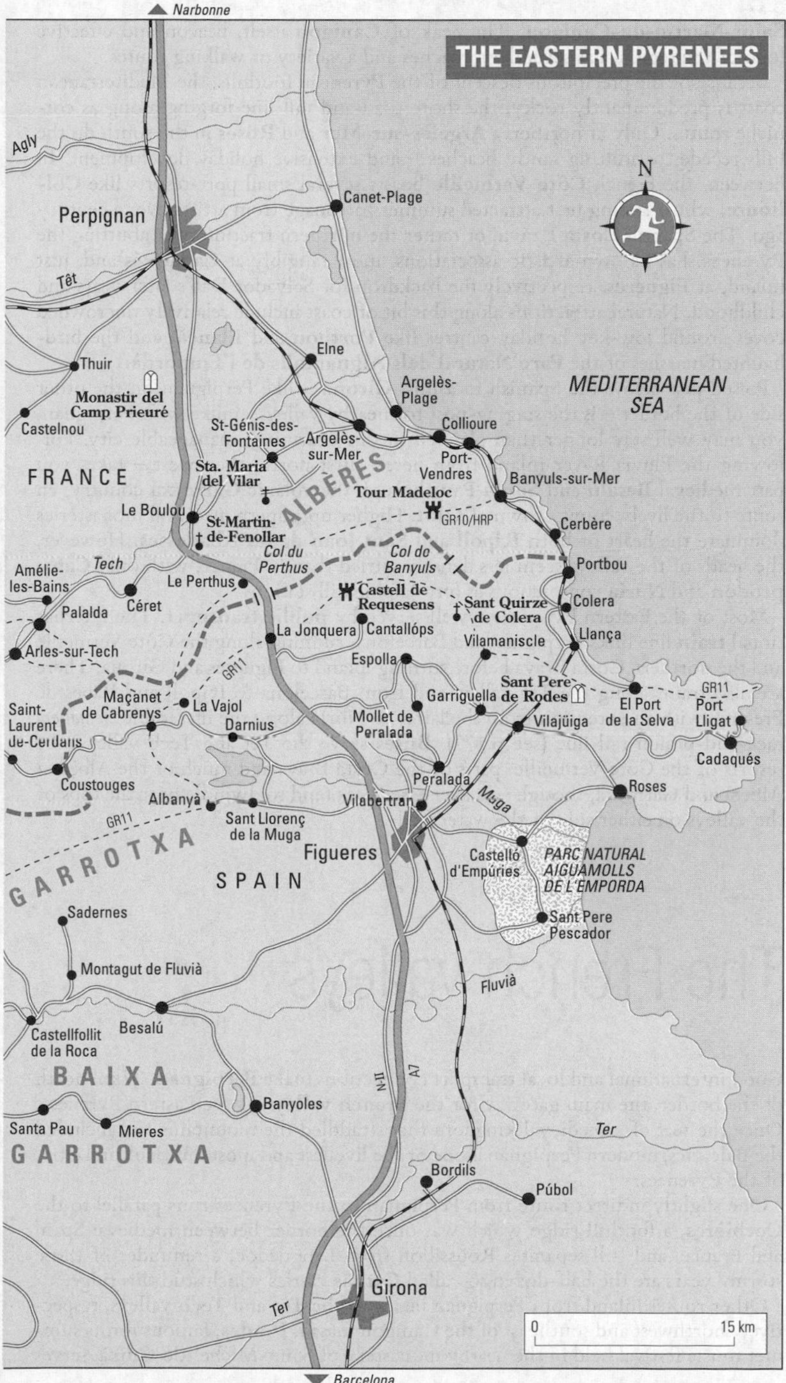
THE EASTERN PYRENEES
Narbonne
Barcelona
Perpignan
Canet-Plage
Agly
Têt
Thuir
Elne
Argelès-Plage
Monastir del Camp Prieuré
Castelnou
St-Génis-des-Fontaines
Argelès-sur-Mer
Collioure
Port-Vendres
Banyuls-sur-Mer
MEDITERRANEAN SEA
FRANCE
Sta. Maria del Vilar
ALBÈRES
Tour Madeloc
GR10/HRP
Le Boulou
St-Martin-de-Fenollar
Cerbère
Portbou
Col du Perthus
Col de Banyuls
Amélie-les-Bains
Tech
Le Perthus
Céret
Palalda
Castell de Requesens
Sant Quirze de Colera
Colera
Arles-sur-Tech
La Jonquera
Cantallóps
Llança
Vilamaniscle
Espolla
GR11
Sant Pere de Rodes
Maçanet de Cabrenys
La Vajol
Garriguella
El Port de la Selva
Port Lligat
Cadaqués
Saint-Laurent-de-Cerdans
Darnius
Mollet de Peralada
Vilajüiga
Coustouges
Peralada
Roses
Albanya
Sant Llorenç de la Muga
Vilabertran
Muga
Figueres
Castelló d'Empúries
PARC NATURAL AIGUAMOLLS DE L'EMPORDA
GARROTXA
SPAIN
Sadernes
Sant Pere Pescador
Montagut de Fluvià
Fluvià
Besalú
Castellfollit de la Roca
BAIXA
N-II
A7
Banyoles
Santa Pau
Mieres
Ter
GARROTXA
Bordils
Púbol
Girona
Ter
0
15 km
N

Saint-Martin-du-Canigou. The peak of **Canigou** itself, beacon and effective logo of the region, has several approaches and a variety of walking routes.

Because of the precipitous descent of the Pyrenean foothills, the Mediterranean coast is predominantly rocky, the shore road and rail line forging along as corniche routes. Only at northerly **Argelès-sur-Mer** and **Roses** in the south do the hills recede, permitting sandy beaches – and extensive holiday development. In between, the French **Côte Vermeille** boasts several small port-resorts like **Collioure**, whose setting first attracted summer patronage from artists over a century ago. The Spanish **Costa Brava**, or rather the northern fraction of it abutting the Pyrenees, has its own artistic associations, most tangibly at **Cadaqués** and, just inland, at **Figueres**, respectively the backdrop for Salvador Dalí's later years and childhood. Natural attractions along this bit of coast include relatively uncrowded coves around low-key holiday centres like **Portbou** and **Llançà**, and the bird-haunted marshes of the **Parc Natural dels Aiguamolls de l'Empordà**.

Poised just below the Spanish foothills, **Girona** – like Perpignan on the other side of the border – is the staging-post for nearby valleys; unlike with Perpignan, you may well stay longer than planned in this charming, manageable city. Following the Fluvià River inland from here – first north, then west – takes you past medieval **Besalú** and **Santa Pau** through the volanic **Garrotxa** country, en route to the lively county town of **Olot**. Higher up, superb medieval monasteries dominate the heart of both **Ripoll** and **Sant Joan de les Abadesses**. However, the heads of the valleys seem less densely settled than in France, with only **Camprodon** and **Núria** conspicuous as (pre-)alpine hill stations.

Most of the Eastern Pyrenees is well served by **public transport**. The international **train** line links Perpignan and Barcelona, running along the Côte Vermeille and the northern Costa Brava before turning inland to Figueres and Girona. There are also trains along the Têt valley, and from Barcelona to Ripoll and Ribes de Freser – with an extension from the latter to Núria along the incredible *cremallera* rack-and-pinion rail line (see p.177). **Buses** serve the Têt and Tech valleys, the resorts of the Côte Vermeille, parts of the Costa Brava and much of the Albères/ Albera and Garrotxa, though – as ever – services tend to dwindle near the tops of the valleys on either side of the watershed.

The French valleys

Good international and local transport connections make **Perpignan**, 27km north of the border, the main gateway for the **French valleys** of the Eastern Pyrenees. Once the seat of a medieval kingdom that straddled the mountains and included the Balearics, modern Perpignan is one of the liveliest and most multicultural cities of the Pyrenees.

One slightly indirect route from Perpignan to the Pyrenees runs parallel to the **Corbières**, a foothill ridge which was once the border between medieval Spain and France, and still separates Roussillon from Languedoc; a reminder of those stormy years are the half-dozen so-called **Cathar** castles which stud this ridge.

Other routes inland from Perpignan lie along the **Têt** and **Tech** valleys, respectively northwest and southeast of the Canigou massif. **Prades**, famous for its summer music festival held in the nearby monastery of Saint-Michel-de-Cuixà, serves effectively as the "capital" of the Têt, whose other principal attractions are the fortified towns of **Villefranche-de-Conflent** and **Mont-Louis**, linked by the **Train Jaune** – a narrow-gauge, electrically powered train service which spectacularly negotiates the river valley. **Céret**, with its unmissable modern art collection, forms an attractive introduction to the Tech watershed, while the monastery-graced **Arles-sur-Tech** and appealingly walled **Prats-de-Molló** beckon up-valley.

Higher up, an ascent of **Canigou** is essential to any exploration of the Eastern Pyrenees. It's effectively the sacred mountain of Catalonia, and though far from the highest, the beauty of the summit approaches is impeccable, as are the views from the top.

Perpignan

PERPIGNAN (Perpinyà in Catalan), the capital of Roussillon or French Catalonia, is the most ethnically diverse city in the Pyrenees. A substantial fraction of its population is descended from Spanish Catalans who poured across the border in the final days of the Spanish Civil War, fleeing reprisals at the hands of Franco's Castilian and Moroccan troops. There's also a sizeable Romany contingent, and a growing student population. Certain suburbs were settled by French colonists fleeing the Algerian independence movement of 1954–62. More recently, Arab and Berber immigrants from Morocco as well as Algeria have occupied a run-down district in the centre of town.

Perpignan's melting-pot atmosphere has prevented the emergence of a distinctly Catalan atmosphere, though townspeople set themselves apart from the rest of France by promoting this identity – even if their own spoken Catalan is limited to a few phrases. Unfortunately, Perpignan is far from a model of tolerance – the racist Front National party and its derivatives typically do well here at the polls.

All told, the city won't necessarily make a good first impression; street life ranges from the lively – flamenco buskers and such – to downright dirty and shabby, with numerous boarded-up business premises evidence of hard contemporary times. Few will want to stay more than a day or two before using the good public transport links in every direction; if you've your own transport, you may prefer to base yourself somewhere in the surrounding area.

Arrival, information and local transport

The small **airport**, Perpignan-Rivesaltes, 6km north of town sees daily flights from London Stansted with Ryanair; the airport **shuttle bus** (€5) makes the twenty-minute trip up to six times daily – rather tightly timed for the flights – stopping at the gare routière, the gare SNCF and Place de Catalogne; a taxi into the centre will cost around three times the bus fare.

Perpignan's **gare SNCF**, towards the west end of avenue Général-de-Gaulle, was once dubbed the centre of the world by Salvador Dalí; the milestone which once read "Centre du Monde: 0.0km" has been removed, and the station is now topped by a large statue of the artist, apparently falling over onto his backside or reaching out to embrace the heavens, depending on your interpretation. To get to the city centre from here, walk along the avenue, through place de Catalogne, and cross the River Basse at **place Arago** – a twenty-minute hike – or take one of the frequent #2 city buses from avenue Général-de-Gaulle to the "Castillet" stop. If you arrive by long-distance bus, you'll be dropped at the **gare routière**, just off avenue du Général-Leclerc near Pont Arago, a short distance northwest of place de la Résistance.

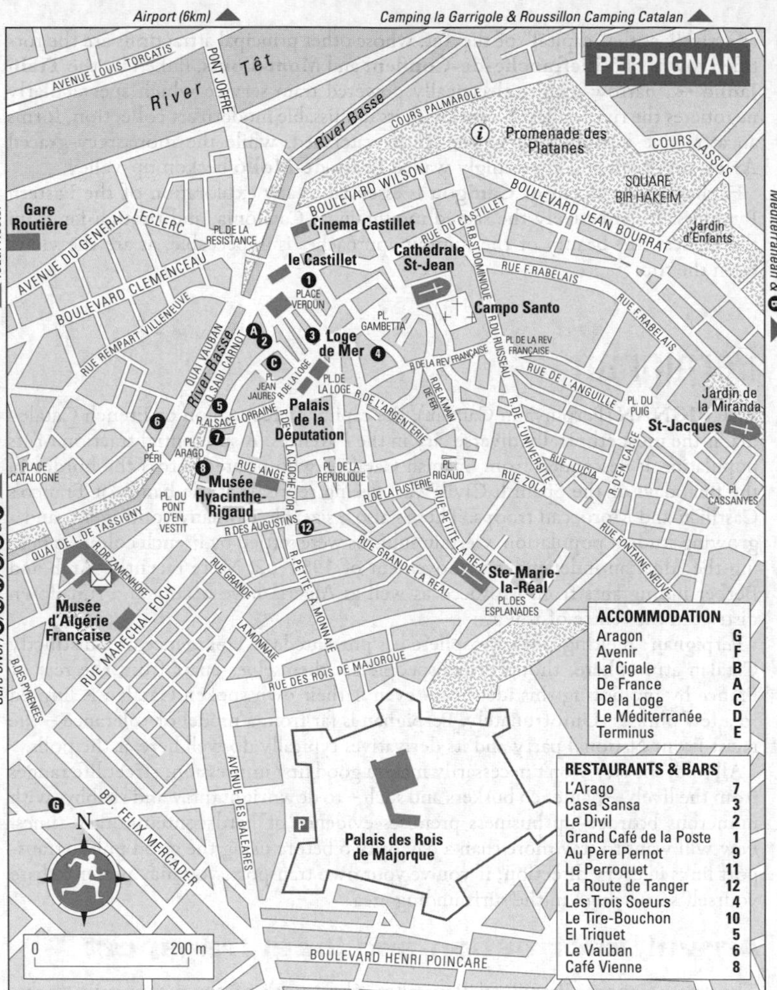

Driving in or around Perpignan is a nuisance, the bypass road involving a maddening series of roundabouts. For the old town, drive straight in along the "Route National" and follow signs for "Centre". There are some enclosed fee-garages, but also free and metered street **parking** on most roads outside of the central pedestrian area. The open car park in front of the Palais des Rois de Majorque is a good option; avoid leaving your car in the seedier areas of the old town.

The **municipal tourist office** (mid-June to mid-Sept Mon–Sat 9am–7pm, Sun 10am–4pm; mid-Sept to mid-June Mon–Sat 9am–6pm, Sun 9am–noon; Ⓣ04.68.66.30.30, Ⓦwww.perpignantourisme.com) is in the Palais des Congrès, on the leafy Promenade des Platanes; they can supply you with the free *Perpignan Mag* (monthly in summer, otherwise quarterly), which will keep you abreast of cultural events in the city. There's also a **departmental tourist office** (Mon–Fri 9am–12.30pm & 1.30–6pm; Ⓣ04.68.51.52.53, Ⓦwww.cg66.com) at 16 av des Palmiers, just off boulevard Georges-Clemenceau.

Your feet are the best option for city **transport** – you can cross from Castillet to the Palais des Rois de Majorque in twenty minutes, or you can rent a **bike** (see "Listings", p.93). Otherwise, **city buses** are run by CTP; visit their kiosk in place Péri for information and tickets (Mon–Sat 9am–noon & 1.45–6.15pm).

Accommodation

Accommodation is adequate in Perpignan in all price and comfort ranges, although the most common establishments are small, few-frills **hotels**. Cheaper places tend to cluster along noisy avenue Général-de-Gaulle near the train station, but they're a long way from the sights – central lodgings are more convenient and comfortable.

The well-run **youth hostel** (ⓣ04.68.34.63.32; closed late Dec to late Jan) abuts a noisy main road between the train and bus stations in Parc de la Pépinière near Pont Arago (entry from avenue de Grande-Bretagne). The two closest **campsites**, both with a swimming pool, are well-equipped *Roussillon Catalan* on route de Bompas 8km north of town (ⓣ04.68.63.16.92; March–Oct), out of bus range, and the smaller, more basic but shady *La Garrigole*, 5km northwest of town at 2 rue Maurice-Lévy, reachable by bus #19 (ⓣ04.68.54.66.10).

Near the station

Avenir 11 rue de l'Avenir ⓣ04.68.34.20.30, ⓦwww.avenirhotel.com. Unprepossessing, simple comfort on a relatively quiet side street, with a wide range of rooms from singles to a family quad; also has secure parking (extra fee). ❶

Le Méditerranée 62bis av Général-de-Gaulle ⓣ04.68.34.87.48, ⓦwww.hotel.mediterranee.com. Trendy hotel that's popular with the backpacking crowd. The building isn't stellar and service is rather lax, but a bar, cybercafé and laid-back atmosphere compensate. ❷

Terminus 2 av Général-de-Gaulle, right opposite the gare SNCF ⓣ04.68.34.32.54. Probably the best standard available amongst the train station hotels. ❶

In the centre

La Cigale 78 bd Jean-Bourrat ⓣ04.68.50.20.14, ⓦwww.hotel-cigale-perpignan.com. Modernized, comfortable hotel at the far end of the Promenade des Platanes, near the church of St Jacques. Good facilities include parking and small terrace. Closed mid-Dec to mid-Jan. ❸

De France 16 Quai Sadi Carnot ⓣ04.68.34.92.81, ⓔfrancehotel@wanadoo.fr. Beautifully appointed nineteenth-century hotel perfectly located on the edge of the old town, overlooking the canalized Basse River. Rooms have a/c. ❸

De la Loge 1 rue Fabriques-Nabot ⓣ04.68.34.41.02, ⓦwww.hoteldelaloge.fr. Sensitively renovated medieval mansion with a central fountain-courtyard, on a quiet alley in the old quarter. Good value for two-star facilities; a/c and minibar in most rooms. Closed Christmas to Epiphany. ❷

Aragon 17 av Gilbert-Brutus ⓣ04.68.54.04.46, ⓔhotel.aragon@wanadoo.fr. Managed by an ex-language teacher who encourages guests to bone up on their French, this simple but clean and convenient hotel has a/c and balconies for many rooms. ❷

The City

Demolished in the early 1900s to allow expansion, Perpignan's medieval walls were replaced by wide boulevards which maintain the separation of the city's older districts – where most monuments and museums are – from the new ones. The

Discounted admissions

If you're planning to visit more than a few monuments and museums in Rousillon, consider purchasing a **Pass Inter-site**, available for €4 at main tourist offices or at any of the 38 participating attractions in the **département of Pyrénées-Orientales**. The card (valid one year) gives €1 off adult admission and free child tickets to (among others) the priory of Serrabona, the abbey of St-Michel-de-Cuixà, the Palais des Rois de Majorque, the art museum in Céret and the cloister at Elne.

△ Palais des Rois de Majorque, Perpignan

Mediterranean is perceptible to the east, the River Têt skirts the town to the north, while the narrow, canalized River Basse threads through the centre, dispensing welcome greenery along its banks. The pedestrianized old quarter is defined by place de la Loge, place de Verdun and place Gambetta.

The place de la Loge and around

The marble-paved **place de la Loge** has been the city's forum for eight centuries; however, the square itself is so small and narrow that you may not realize you've reached it until you spot the voluptuous statue of Venus by Aristide Maillol (see box on p.128) in the centre. The *place*'s principal landmark, the 1397-vintage Gothic **Loge de Mer**, was once the city's stock exchange and headquarters for maritime trade (symbolized by the ship-shaped weathervane); the fast-food restaurant which for years defaced the ground floor has, after public outcry, been replaced with a café-restaurant more in keeping with the lacy balustrades, lancet windows and gargoyles adorning the upper storeys. Side by side next door stand the sixteenth-century **Hôtel de Ville** (with a second Maillol bronze, *La Méditerranée*, in the courtyard, visible through wrought-iron gates) and the fifteenth-century **Palais de la Députation**, once the Roussillon parliament. Place de la Loge long served as the scene of grisly executions, notably during the seventhteenth-century Catalan revolt against newly imposed French rule. During World War II, the busy pavement cafés were the place to meet *passeurs*, the men – and sometimes women – who guided refugees across the Pyrenees into Spain.

To the north of place de la Loge rises the fourteenth-century, red-brick **Le Castillet**, the emblem of the city, a surviving fragment of the medieval walls later used as a prison. The adjoining **Porte Notre-Dame** was added in 1478 by Louis XI as the main entrance to the town through its now mostly vanished walls. The whole building, with its massive nail-studded doors and spiral stone staircase, is now home to the **Casa Païral** (Wed–Mon: May–Sept 10am–7pm; Oct–April 11am–5.30pm; €4), a beautifully designed museum celebrating Roussillonaise rural culture and the anti-French rebellions of 1661–74, when the tower held captured Catalan insurgents. Nearby, at 1 bd Wilson, stands the splendidly ornate

Cinéma Castillet, the oldest (1911) cinema in France, now converted into an eight-screen complex.

A couple of minutes' walk to the southwest of place de la Loge at 16 rue de l'Ange is the **Musée Hyacinthe-Rigaud** (Wed–Mon: May–Sept noon–7pm; Oct–April 11am–5.30pm; €4), housed in a seventeenth-century palace, originally the workshop of local artist Hyacinthe Rigaud (born 1659), a favourite of Louis XIV. Later it served as a studio and living space for Picasso, Dufy and Cocteau; today it holds a good collection of modern art, including works by Maillol, Alechinsky and the aforementioned artists.

The cathedral and medieval Perpignan

East of place de la Loge and place Gambetta – the latter scene of the town's open-air market for centuries – stands the **Cathédrale Saint-Jean** (Mon & Wed–Sat 10am–noon & 2–5pm, Tues & Sun 2–5pm; free). It was commissioned in 1324 by Sancho, king of Mallorca, and elevated to cathedral status in 1602 when the diocese was transferred here from Elne. Adjacent stands the Romanesque St-Jean-le-Vieux (closed), the two churches joined by mammoth buttresses. The cathedral's striking exterior sports bands of polished river stones sandwiched by brick, while inside there's a majestic, columned nave, whose side chapels retain some elaborate sixteenth- and seventeenth-century retables. The best of these is the fourteenth-century polychrome Crucifixion known as the *Dévôt Christ*; it's in the fifth side chapel along the north wall, of Rhenish origin and probably brought from the Low Countries by a travelling merchant. Out the south door a few steps, on the left, is the entrance to the **Campo Santo**, a vast enclosure that's one of France's oldest cemeteries, now the main venue for the Estivales summer festival (otherwise Oct–April Tues–Sun 11am–5pm, May & Sept Tues–Sun noon–7pm).

On the far side of Campo Santo, rue de la Revolution Française leads to rue de l'Anguille which forges through the slums of old Perpignan, as far as **place Cassanyes**, venue for a daily market. Inhabited almost exclusively by recent arrivals from North Africa, with a Roma enclave centred on **place du Puig** (pronounced "pooch"), this can seem an intimidating district, its refuse piles and hung-out washing stereotypical images of immigrant poverty. Just north of place Cassanyes stands the fourteenth-century **church of St-Jacques** (Tues–Sun 11am–5pm), the nucleus of Perpignan's oldest parish, originally founded a hundred years earlier by Jaume I of Aragón and Valencia in honour of his patron saint. Since then it

The caganer and cagatió

Among the Catalan folkloric customs that have survived centuries of French domination are two rather strange ones associated with **Christmas**. The Catalans are known for their elaborate Nativity scenes (**pessebres**), populated by hordes of figurines. But looking carefully at the local version, among the various shepherds, angels and wise men you'll notice a small figure, usually dressed in peasant garb and a traditional Catalan red cap. This is the **caganer**, or "shitter": a crouching man, poised with pants around his ankles, in the act of defecation. Similarly, although Catalan children customarily receive presents on Three Kings Day (Jan 6), the **cagatió** (the "shitting log") ensures that they don't go completely empty-handed at Christmas. This consists of a log with a painted-on face, draped with a red cloth at its posterior end. As children gather round the **cagatió**, beating it with sticks and singing a song invoking bowel movements, the cloth is removed to reveal the sweets that it has apparently "excreted". You can purchase your own **caganers** (which now come in various guises including policemen, football referees and political figures) and **cagatiós** at Perpignan's Christmas market, held in front of the cathedral during the four weeks of Advent.

has been the seat of the Confraternitat de la Sanch ("blood" in old Catalan), dedicated to the Holy Blood of Christ; each Maundy Thursday, its members process as penitents from the church through town, barefoot and anonymously hooded in red or black (so as not to take pride in their piety), carrying heavy candles or crosses. Behind the church the secluded **Jardin de la Miranda** (daily: June–Sept 8–11.45am & 2–5.45pm; Oct–May 8–11am & 3.30–6pm), occupies a section of the city's old fortifications and provides an airy respite for the inhabitants of this quarter.

The Palais des Rois de Majorque

Perpignan's most famous sight, and the kernel around which it grew, is the massive **Palais des Rois de Majorque** (daily: June–Sept 10am–6pm; Oct–May 9am–5pm; €4) on the southern fringes of the old city; the entrance is on the west side of the complex in rue des Archers, around fifteen minutes' walk from place de la Loge, or slightly longer from the church of St-Jacques.

The history of Perpignan is more or less synonymous with that of the palace, originally built in the late thirteenth century as a residence for Jaume I of Mallorca, son of Jaume I of Aragón and Valencia ("The Conqueror"), who captured Muslim Mallorca. At his death the king divided his kingdom between his two sons: to the elder, Pere II, went the titles of Count of Barcelona and King of Aragón and Valencia, along with the greater portion of the realm; the remainder, including Roussillon and Mallorca, went to the younger Jaume II, who ruled from here and from Montpelier. The two branches of the family were immediately at each other's throats, and stayed that way until Roussillon was reunited with Aragón and Catalonia, governed from Barcelona, in 1349 by the powerful Pere III. After three more centuries of see-saw sovereignty, Perpignan changed hands for the last time in 1642, a couple of years after France had occupied Roussillon when all Catalonia revolted against the Habsburg rulers of Madrid. In September of that year, after a siege at times commanded personally by Louis XIII and Cardinal Richelieu, Perpignan fell. Vauban, military engineer to Louis XIV, constructed the palace's imposing outer walls as part of the fortification campaign that followed confirmation of French sovereignty by the 1659 Treaty of the Pyrenees.

After ascending a broad zigzagging ramp designed to accommodate cavalry, you enter a grassy park, with the square, deceptively plain **castle** ahead of you. Passing into the splendid **courtyard**, surrounded by two storeys of dissimilar, part-Gothic, part-Moorish arches, you ascend the stairs to the former king's apartments, now a wine boutique. Opposite you'll find the unsullied but sparsely furnished queen's apartments, which have delicately vaulted period ceilings and windows. Between the two sets of royal quarters are the so-called king's and queen's **chapels**, one on the upper floor and one on the lower, both retaining interesting Gothic details including carved corbels and fading frescoes. The palace frequently holds temporary exhibitions on local history and culture, as well as hosting summer musical events.

Eating and drinking

Full-service restaurants are thin on the ground in central Perpignan; there are rather more bistros or brasseries, including (besides those listed below) *Café Vienne* on palm-shaded place Arago, the Art Deco *Brasserie le Vauban* across the River Basse at 29 quai Vauban, and a pair of obvious ones on place de la Loge. For a fix of North African food, head for the eastern side of the old town, particularly rue Llucia, where very modest establishments serve couscous/tajine dishes – you'll find food like this in very few other places along the Pyrenees.

L'Arago place Arago. Generous portions of above-average-quality standard brasserie platters, and thus always busy. Open daily noon until late.
Casa Sansa 3 rue Fabriques-Couvertes. Founded in 1846, this serves traditional Catalan cuisine amidst a decor of bullfight posters and old photos. Wheelchair-accessible. *Menus* €19–29.
Le Divil 9 rue Fabriques-Nebot. Swish designer restaurant tucked away in a little alley near the *loge*. The speciality is wood-grilled meats, including succulent shoulder of lamb. *Menus* €12–32. Closed Sun.
Grand Café de la Poste place Verdun. Slightly pricey for drinks, but an unrivalled people-watching spot – including performances of the *sardana* apt to take place spontaneously of a summer evening.
Au Père Pernot 16 av Général-de-Gaulle. Locally respected Catalan cooking featuring a variety of meat and fish dishes, as well as an array of homemade soups. *Menus* €12–30. All-you-can-eat pancake brunch Sat noon–4pm. Closed Sun.
Le Perroquet 1 av Général-de-Gaulle. By the station on the north side of the street, with a good choice of Catalan specialities. Supper *menus* from €20. Closed Wed Sept–April.
La Route de Tanger 1 rue du Four St-Jean. Welcoming Moroccan restaurant with the usual tajines and couscous as well as more adventurous fusion recipes. *Menu* €12. Closed Sun & Mon lunch.
Le Tire-Bouchon 20 av Général-de-Gaulle ⓣ04.68.34.31.91. Small family-run brasserie, the best of those in the vicinity of the station. *Menu* at €13, although an à la carte meal for two can easily run over €50. Closed Wed eve, all Sun & Mon.
El Triquet 9 rue Lazare ⓣ04.68.35.19.18. Friendly Spanish-run eatery specializing in Catalan cuisine as well as *tapas*. *Plats* from €8. Closed Sun & Mon.

Nightlife and entertainment

The most reliable central **bar** is *Les Trois Soeurs*, 2 rue Fontfroide, with . to nibble on during novelty acts and dedicated evenings (eg Sunday "tea dance" at 6.30pm, Wednesday jazz night, "hen nights" with male live acts). Overall, Perpignan is not a great city for **nightlife**, but in July the town comes alive with the *Estivales* (ⓦwww.estivales.com) theatre, music and dance events, mostly in the Campo Santo, succeeded in August with Thursday-night street performers and live music. The Palais des Rois de Majorque is the venue for the *Trobades* festival (22–24 June), plus **jazz** concerts every Friday in July. Besides the Castillet **cinema**, there's the Rive Gauche four-plex at 29 quai Vauban, with some VO screenings.

Listings

Airlines Ryanair ⓣ08.92.55.56.66, ⓦwww.ryanair.com
Airport Aéroport de Perpignan Rivesaltes ⓣ04.68.52.60.70
Bicycle rental Véloland, 95 av Mal Juin ⓣ04.68.08.19.99; Cycles Mercier, 20 av Gilbert Brutus ⓣ04.68.85.02.71.
Car rental Avis, 13 bd du Conflent ⓣ04.68.34.26.71; Budget, 9 av Général-de-Gaulle ⓣ04.68.56.95.95; Citer, ⓣ04.68.51.09.09; Europcar, 28 av Général-de-Gaulle ⓣ04.68.52.95.29; Hertz, ⓣ04.68.51.37.40; Leclerc, 27 av Général-de-Gaulle ⓣ04.68.34.77.74; Sixt, 48 av Général-de-Gaulle ⓣ04.68.35.62.84.
Hospital Centre Hospitalier, av du Languedoc ⓣ04.68.61.66.33, on the north side of the city, reached via av Maréchal-Joffre.
Laundry Laverie Foch, 23 rue Maréchal-Foch (daily 9am–7pm); Laverie St-Jean, 3 rue Cité E. Bartisol, near Campo Santo (daily 7.30am–7pm).
Markets General market in place de la République (Mon 7am–1pm, Tues–Sat 7am–12.30pm & 4.30–7.30pm); antiques in Allées Maillol (Sat 8am–6pm); organic food in place Rigaud (Sat 8am–noon). The most colourful market takes place on Saturday and Sunday mornings in the tree-shaded place Cassanyes, where French, Arab and African traders sell cheap clothes, crafts and all sorts of local produce.
Police av de Grande-Bretagne ⓣ04.68.35.70.00, and allée Marc-Pierre ⓣ04.68.66.30.70.
Swimming pool Champs de Mars, rue Paul-Valéry (Mon & Sat 12.15–1.30pm, Tues, Thurs & Fri 6.30–8pm; €3).
Taxis There are taxi stands near place de Verdun, at the train station and on place Arago.

The Cathar castles

The romantically ruined medieval fortresses which perch atop the arid, herb-scented **Corbières** hills to the west and north of Perpignan have become known as the **Cathar castles**, though in fact most were built well before the Cathar era (see p.240), and in one case after. **Walking** is the most direct way to experience them; the **GR36**, crossing from Carcassonne to Saint-Paul-de-Fenouillet (and beyond), plus the **Sentier Cathare**, crossing east to west from Port La-Nouvelle to Foix, together pass most of the sites. The Sentier Cathare is divided into twelve stages, described in the *Sentier Cathare Topoguide* (Rando Editions).

Without your own transport or walking boots, the best way to approach the castles is from the south, from the **Quillan–Perpignan road**. This route is served by bus, but a pleasanter option is the narrow-gauge **Train du Pays Cathare et du Fenouillèdes** (Ⓣ & Ⓕ 04.68.59.96.18, Ⓦ www.tpcf.fr) which runs from Rivesaltes, just north of Perpignan, to Axat, stopping at the main towns along the way. The service (sometimes only Saint-Paul-de-Fenouillet to Axat) runs on weekends in May, June, September and October, daily in July & Aug (adult fares €8–17 depending on direction & distance).

Quéribus, Cucugnan and Duilhac

A pre-1659 mansucript characterized the citadel of Carcassonne as the "mother" castle, and the **Château de Quéribus** (Jan: Sat, Sun & school hols 10am–5pm; Feb: daily 10am–5.30pm; March, Nov & Dec: daily 10am–6pm; April–June & Sept: daily 9.30am–7pm; July & Aug: daily 9am–8pm; Oct daily 10am–6.30pm; €5) as one of her five "sons". Spectacularly situated above the Grau de Maury pass 6km north of the D117 road, about 30km in total from Rivesaltes, Quéribus balances on a storm-battered pillar of rock above sheer cliffs – access is forbidden in bad weather.

Because of the cramped topography, the space within the walls is stepped in terraces, linked by a single stairway and dominated by the polygonal keep. High point, in all senses, is the so-called **Salle de Palmier**, whose vaulted ceiling is supported by a graceful pillar sprouting a canopy of intersecting ribs; currently it's off-limits for works, but you can see everything from the top of the steps leading down to the chamber. More steep stairs lead to the roof and fantastic views in every direction, including northwest to the next Cathar castle, Peyrepertuse, actually in Languedoc.

Quéribus was built at the end of the tenth century, belonging successively to the counts of Barcelona, the kings of Aragón and the counts of Fenouillèdes, the area just south of the D117. After the fall of Montségur (see p.243), it became the last Cathar stronghold, holding out until 1255 or 1256; never reduced by siege, its sanctuary role ended with the capture of local lord and Cathar champion Chabert de Barbaira by Louis IX's forces, who obliged him to cede this and other castles as ransom. Unlike at Montségur, however, the garrison escaped to Spain.

A convenient base for visiting Quéribus (and Peyrepertuse) is the small village of **CUCUGNAN**, in the valley halfway between the two; its popularity is such that in season you must **park** vehicles at the outskirts. There's ample **accommodation**, including *Chambres d'Hôtes L'écuri de Cucugnan* at 10 rue Achille-Mir (Ⓣ 04.68.33.37.42, Ⓔ ecurie.cucugnan@wanadoo.fr; ❸ B&B); fully fledged hotels include the central *Auberge du Vigneron* at 2 rue Achille-Mir (Ⓣ 04.68.45.03.00, Ⓔ auberge.vigneron@ataraxie.fr; ❸; restaurant, menus from €19, closed Sun eve & Mon, also mid-Nov to March), and the *Auberge de Cucugnan* (Ⓣ 04.68.45.40.84, Ⓕ 04.68.45.01.52; closed Wed & Jan to mid-March; ❸), downhill from the church (which supposedly contains a statue of a pregnant Virgin), with a restaurant known for its hearty servings of game (from €16; closed on Wed Sept–June). The nearest other rooms are in **DUILHAC**, about 4km away just below Peyrepertuse (see below), at the unstaffed *Auberge du Vieux Moulin-de la Source* (contact as for *Auberge du Vigneron*).

Peyrepertuse, Rouffiac and Aguilar

If you only have time for one Cathar castle, let it be the **Château de Peyrepertuse** (Nov to early Jan & Feb–March 10am–5pm; April–June & Sept daily 10am–7pm, later closing Easter week; July–Aug daily 9am–8.30pm; Oct daily 10am–6pm; closed 3 weeks in Jan; €5), not only for its unbeatable site and stunning views, but also because the complex is unusually well preserved, staying in use until 1789. The 3.5-km access road starts in Duilhac, or alternatively you can walk up from Rouffiac-des-Corbières village to the north via the GR36 – a tough, hot climb of over an hour. But either way the effort is rewarded, for Peyrepertuse is one of the most awe-inspiring castles anywhere in Europe, draped the length of a jagged rock-spine with sheer drops at most points. As signs warn, access is banned during fierce summer thunderstorms, when (as at Quéribus) the ridge makes an ideal lightning target.

Tickets are sold by the southerly car-park, but you then walk fifteen minutes through thickets of box to the entrance on the north side. The bulkiest fortifications enclose the lower, eastern end of the ridge, with a keep and barbican controlling the main gate. Things get increasingly airier as you progress west along the ridge past and through various cisterns, chapels and bastions, culminating in a stairway of over a hundred steps carved into the living rock, which leads to a keep, tower and **chapel of San Jordi** at the summit. The views – some of the most sweeping in southern France – are as you'd expect; the castle was obtained by treaty with the Kingdom of Aragón in 1258, and most of the existing fortifications were built afterwards.

In **ROUFFIAC-DES-CORBIÈRES**, 3km north, there's a **hotel**, the *Auberge de Peyrepertuse* (Ⓣ04.68.45.40.40; closed Dec 15–Jan 15, & Tues; ❷), with a hearty restaurant (menus €14 & €18) and well-appointed en-suite rooms. For hikers, there's a rudimentary shop; the Sentier Cathare heads west-southwest towards Puilaurens, or generally east via Quéribus, Padern and Aguilar.

Drivers and cyclists going east from Rouffiac also pass the castle at **Padern** village to arrive at the fine, isolated **Château d'Aguilar** (April to mid-June & mid-Sept to mid-Nov 11am–5pm, mid-June to mid-Sept 11am–7pm, closed mid-Nov to March; €3.50), a hexagonal thirteenth-century citadel with six towers just east of Tuchan, overlooking the slopes of the Côtes de Roussillon-Villages wine domaine.

Gorges de Galamus and Saint-Paul-de-Fenouillet

Moving west from Rouffiac by car or bike, you can return to St-Paul-de-Fenouillet, initially via the villages of Soulatgé and Cubières-sur-Cinoble, through the **Gorges de Galamus**, a short but impressive limestone defile worn through the ridge by the River Agly. From Cubières, the perilously narrow corniche D10 road threads the gorge, with a limited number of turnouts and car-parks, from one of which stairs through a rock-tunnel lead down to the bottom via the eagle's-nest **Ermitage de Saint-Antoine** (daily 10am–6pm) on the east flank of the ravine. This is a popular canyoning venue, though most visitors just swim in the river-pools below the *ermitage*.

Some 30km from Rivesaltes, **SAINT-PAUL-DE-FENOUILLET** itself, despite proximity to all these attractions, is no tourist mecca, being riven by the D117. There is, however, one decent central **hotel**, *Le Relais des Corbières* (☎04.68.59.23.89; closed Jan; ③), at 10 av Jean Moulin.

Château de Puilaurens and around

Lapradelle, 6km before Axat, is the closest point on the D117 to the **Château de Puilaurens** (daily: April–June & Sept 10am–5.30pm; July & Aug 9am–7.30pm; Oct–March 10am–4.30pm, but closed Nov 16–Jan 31 & weekdays Feb/March; €3.50), perched majestically on a seven-hundred-metre-high ridge of the forested Fenouillèdes hills. Without wheeled transport, the castle is just under an hour's walk distant: 2km along the D22 to Puilaurens hamlet, then about a thirty-minute climb up a marked path. With a car, there's a 1500-metre access road beginning 500m south of the hamlet.

Built originally by the Visigoths, Puilaurens was enlarged by the kings of Aragón not long before it, like Quéribus (see p.94), was surrendered to the French crown as part of Chabert de Barbaira's ransom. You enter from the west, via a stepped maze of chicanes or staggered low walls; much of the interior is dilapidated, but be sure to catch the view east from outside the **southeast postern gate**, and the point on the **western donjon** complex where you're allowed briefly on the curtain wall for an eyeful in the opposite direction. Nearby, on the parapet, are

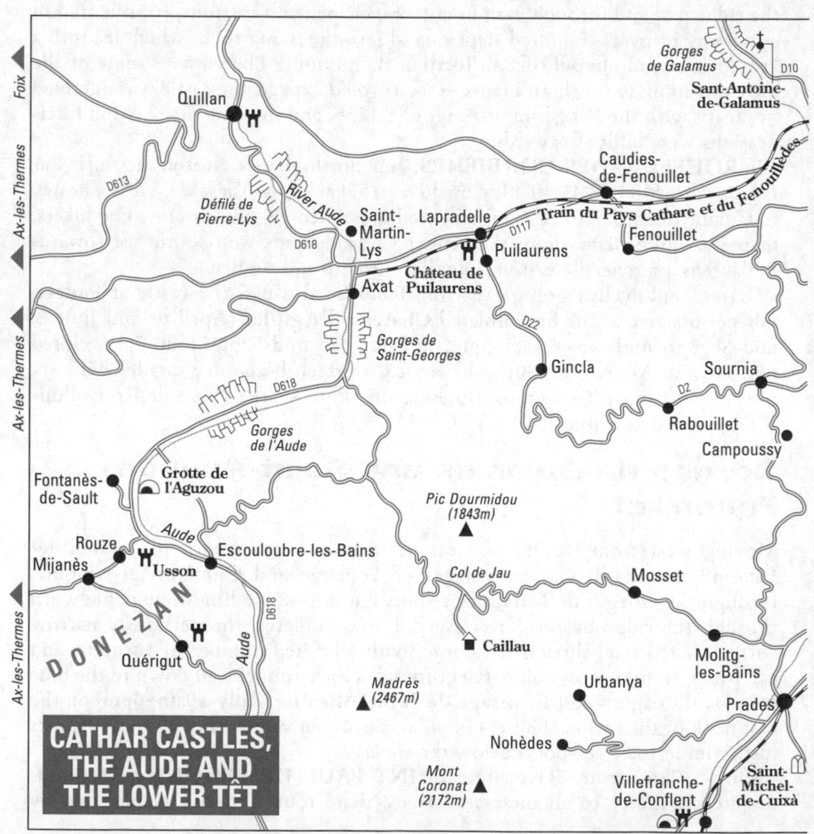

machicolations which apparently doubled as latrines, and the so-called **Tour de la Dame Blanche**, with rib vaulting and a *porte-voix* wormhole for communication between different storeys of the tower.

Back at **LAPRADELLE**, the *Hôtel Viaduc* – named after the rail viaduct opposite – has better food than its appearance suggests (*menus* from €14) and will do for an overnight stay (Ⓣ04.58.20.53.01; ❷). There are also *chambres d'hôtes* in Puilaurens hamlet, beyond which the next closest facility to the castle is 6km south in the middle of dozy **GINCLA**, where the *Hostellerie du Grand Duc* (Ⓣ04.68.20.55.02, Ⓦwww.host-du-grand-duc.com; closed Nov–March; ❹), a converted manor house with an equally pricey restaurant, also manage *chambres d'hôtes* (❸).

The upper Aude valley

The dramatic, short-lived **Aude** is one of the great rivers of the French Pyrenees, matched in the east of the range only by the Ariège. Rising on the east side of the Carlit Massif, it is restrained briefly by the dams of Matemale and Puyvalador, then allowed to hurtle through several gorges to **Quillan**. Just upstream from the

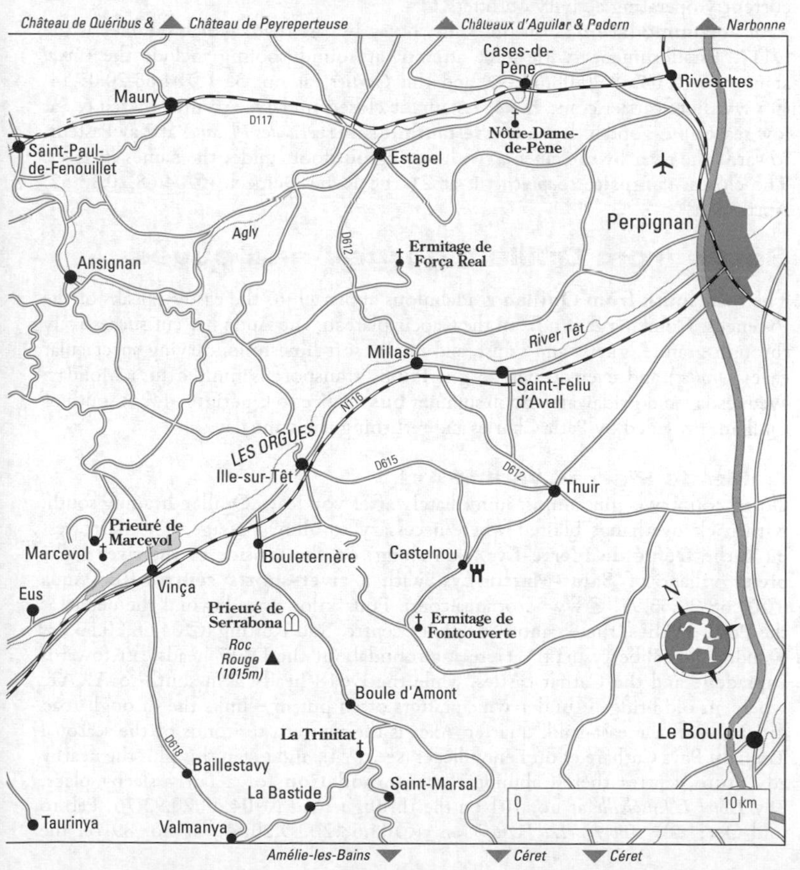

gorges, around **Quérigut**, sprawl vast forests of beech and pine interspersed with lush meadows. This is the **Donezan**, a scenic – but poor and neglected – corner of the Ariège. From Quillan, the Aude flows north to Carcassonne, then east to the sea between Narbonne and Béziers.

❶ Quillan

Clustered on the west bank of the Aude about halfway between its sources and Carcassonne, **QUILLAN** makes a handy stopover on the way to the high Pyrenees. The main attraction of this formerly industrialized place – it used to manufacture hats – is the river itself, running right past the town and (further upstream) furnishing ample opportunity for canoeing and rafting. The only monument is the ruined **castle** on the east bank of the Aude just across the Pont Vieux. It was burned by Huguenots in 1575 and partly dismantled in the eighteenth century, but the remnants are still worth a scramble.

The **gare SNCF** and **halte routière** sit together on the main bypass road, whilst the **tourist office** (June–Sept Mon–Sat 8am–noon & 2–7pm, Sun 9am–noon; Oct–May Mon–Fri 9am–noon & 2–6pm, Sat 9am–1pm; ⓣ04.68.20.07.78, ⓦwww.ville-quillan.com) stands opposite in the former Art Deco public baths; they can help with Grotte de l'Aguzou reservations (see opposite) and contacts for currently operating activity outfitters.

All **accommodation** is on this same, noisy bypass road, which doubles as the D117. Establishments with some attempt at soundproofing include the *Canal* at no. 36 (ⓣ04.68.20.08.62; ❷) and the *Cartier*, at no. 31 (ⓣ04.68.20.05.14, ⓦwww.hotelcartier.com; ❷–❸; restaurant closed mid-Dec to mid-March & Sat low season). A good independent **restaurant** is *Pizzeria des Platanes* at 2 av Pasteur, towards the river by the cinema, with seating outdoors under the namesake trees. The closest **campsite**, *Sapinette*, is at 21 rue René-Delpech (ⓣ04.68.20.13.52; April–Oct).

South from Quillan: gorges and caves

The road **south from Quillan** is a fabulous approach to the eastern peaks of the Pyrenees. Coursing down from the Capcir plateau, the Aude has cut successively through granite, gneiss and schist, and finally soft limestone, carving spectacular caves (*grottes*) and ever-deeper gorges. Public transport is limited to a Monday, Wednesday and Friday afternoon summer **bus** service to Quérigut, 44km south of Quillan, provided by Petit Charles and returning the same day.

Défilé de Pierre-Lys and Axat

Gorge country begins almost immediately after you leave Quillan heading south, with rock overhangs blasted where necessary to allow passage. The narrowest bit is the **Défilé de Pierre-Lys**, 8km along; on the far side of the river is the pretty village of **Saint-Martin-Lys**, with a **river-sports centre**, Roc Aqua (ⓣ04.68.20.53.97, ⓦwww.rocaqua.com). Four kilometres beyond the defile, at the **Pont d'Aliès**, there's another activity centre, Sud Rafting (ⓣ04.68.20.53.73, ⓔsudrafting@libertysurf.fr). Here at a roundabout the D117 heads east towards Lapradelle and the Cathar castles, while the D618 heads 1km south to **AXAT**, where an old bridge – under which rafters often put in – links the through-road district with the east-bank quarter. Axat is the western terminus of the seasonal Train du Pays Cathare et du Fenouillèdes (see p.94), and given this plus the nearby adventure centres there's abundant **accommodation** for a fairly sleepy place. Try *Hôtel L'Ensoleillé* at no. 101 on the through road (ⓣ04.68.20.93.76; Feb to mid-Oct; ❷); *Auberge La Petite Ourse* (ⓣ04.68.20.59.20;❸), at no. 89 on the main highway; or the spotless *gîte d'étape Le Saint Roch* at 20 rue du 19 Mars 1962 (ⓣ04.68.20.65.71, ⓔlesaintroch@wanadoo.fr; Easter–Sept; 10 places).

Grotte de l'Aguzou

If you have time, try to visit the **Grotte de l'Aguzou**, 15km southwest of Axat towards the upstream end of the Gorges de l'Aude. The guided tour of this magnificent complex is as close as a non-specialist can get to real speleology, and is thus very popular, so during summer book well in advance (contact Philippe Moreno, ⓣ04.68.20.45.38, ⓔgrotte.aguzou@wanadoo.fr). Equipped with overalls, helmet and lamp, groups of four to ten (€60 full day, €30 half-day) are taken into the unlit cave system at 9am, and through the *grandes salles* of stalactites, stalagmites and draperies, some of them 20m high. Lunch (bring your own) is taken 600m underground – then it's on to the "gardens of crystals": some grow in long needles from the rock, some like pine cones dusted by hoarfrost, and others clear and convoluted like the accidents of a Venetian glass-blower.

The closest place to stay, most easily accessible with a car or bike, is 8km up the valley at **ESCOULOUBRE-LES-BAINS**, where *Chambres d'Hôtes Maison Roquelaure* (ⓣ04.68.20.47.29, ⓔdaniel.bilot@wanadoo.fr; ❷), in the old thermal establishment, makes evening meals for hikers and cyclists, and still has an on-site hot spring.

The Donezan

In the twelfth century the **Donezan** region and its then-capital **USSON** – in the southern neck of the Gorges de l'Aude – became a sort of forerunner to Andorra: separated from the rest of the Ariège by the **Col de Pailhères** (2001m), it was granted financial privileges on account of its inaccessibility. Today Usson and the region's eight other villages are severely depopulated; the spa of Usson-les-Bains 1km downstream is boarded up and for sale, while the dry-stone walls around the fields are as dilapidated as the **château** (May, June & early Oct weekends 2–6pm; July & Aug daily 10am–1pm & 3–7pm; most Sept, Easter & winter school hols daily 2–6pm; €3.50), supposedly the first refuge for the four Cathars who escaped the massacre at Montségur (see p.243). Dating back at least to the eleventh century, the castle was mostly in the hands of the counts of Foix from the thirteenth to the sixteenth century.

Just above Usson, 3km along the D25 to Ax-les-Thermes, **MIJANÈS** is an immensely attractive stone-built village, where you may **stay** and **eat** year-round at the simple but perfectly adequate *Relais de Pailhères* (ⓣ04.68.20.46.97; ❷), with good-sized, wood-floored rooms. This should be reserved at weekends as it's the only facility in the area comparable in quality to *Maison Roquelaure*, with people coming from some distance to patronize it.

Some 13km west, on north-facing slopes near the Col de Pailhéres, the tiny, nine-run **Mijanès-Donezan** downhill ski station (just four drag lifts) is only usable during snowy winters (the top point is just 2000m). Cross-country skiers are probably better served by the 36km of prepared trails in the area.

These days, **QUÉRIGUT**, 8km up-valley from Mijanès, is the capital of the region. It stands at the head of a slope of neglected terraces, notable only for the stump of the **Château de Donezan**, last stronghold of the Cathar leaders, who held out here eleven years after the fall of Montségur. **Accommodation** is either at the central, simple *Hôtel du Donezan* (ⓣ04.68.20.42.40, ⓦwww.hoteldonezan.com; closed mid-Nov to mid-Dec; ❷), uphill from the church opposite the fountain (it also has the town's only **restaurant**), or at the *Auberge du Cabanas* **gîte** (ⓣ04.68.20.47.03; 17 bunks) out at the Col des Hares.

The lower Têt

From Perpignan, the Têt valley (also known as the Conflent) provides a fast if initially not very scenic route southwest into the Pyrenees. The **lower Têt valley** skims the base of Canigou peak, with its most interesting parts some 30km southwest of Perpignan, where **Ille-sur-Têt** provides access to the spectacular rock formations of **Les Orgues** to the north. Just west, the narrow Boulès gorge climbs south to the region of **Les Aspres**, within whose wooded isolation you'll find the magnificent Romanesque **Prieuré de Serrabona**.

Further upstream along the Têt valley, you'll come first to the turning for the recently restored **Prieuré de Marcevol**, and then to **Prades**, an attractive town and classic access point for the Canigou Massif. Skirting the north side of the famous massif, you reach **Villefranche-de-Conflent**, which marks the transition to the upper Têt (see on p.109).

Upstream towards Prades

From Saint Feliu d'Avall on the N116, a six-kilometre detour southeast (or 13km directly southwest from Perpignan on the D612a) brings you to **THUIR** (Tuïr), known chiefly as the main producer of the red aperitif wine called Byrrh (pronounced "beer"). You can visit the winery at 6 bd Violet (daily: April–June & Sept–Oct 9–11.45am & 2.30–5.45pm; July–Aug 10–11.45am & 2–6.45pm; €1.70) and taste the sweet ferment, aged in a cathedral-like gallery of enormous oak vats.

From Thuir head directly to Ille-sur-Têt (13km) along the D615, or detour slightly via **CASTELNOU**, an atmospheric, fortified stone village capping a hilltop 5.5km west from Thuir. Besides a gate and perimeter walls, you'll find a proper tenth-century **castle** (daily: late March to late June & late Sept to late Dec 11am–6pm; late June to late Sept 10am–7pm; late Dec to late March 11am–5pm; closed latter 3 weeks Jan; €4.50), with good views. On Tuesdays, a local **market** (June–Sept) breathes extra life into the place. You can **eat** well at *Le Patio* (closed part Oct & part Jan; ⓣ04.68.53.23.30), offering Catalan cuisine in an intimate atmosphere from €20; it's just up the street from Castelnou's old gate.

Ille-sur-Têt and around

ILLE-SUR-TÊT (Illa) has an attractive medieval quarter of narrow alleys, within which the **Centre d'Interpretation du Patrimoine Catalan** (Feb–March & Nov 2–6pm Mon & Wed–Fri; April–June & Oct daily except Tues 2–6pm; mid-June to Sept Mon–Fri 10am–noon & 2–7pm, Sat 2–7pm; €3.50) occupies the seventeenth-century Hospici d'Illa – local headquarters of the medieval Knights Hospitallers – with extensive, changing exhibitions of local religious art. More remarkable are the clay cliffs just across the River Têt, a kilometre or so along the road north towards Bélesta, which the elements have eroded into extraordinary formations known as **Les Orgues** ("the Organs"), so called because of their resemblance to the pipes of that instrument. Rising dramatically from a deep tributary of the Têt, they can be explored by a series of footpaths (daily: April–June & Sept daily 10am–6.30pm; July & Aug 9.30am–8pm; Oct & Feb–March Mon–Fri 10am–12.30pm & 2–5.30/6pm; Nov–Jan 2–5pm; €3.50).

Some 2km beyond Vinça (see opposite) at Marquixanes is the signed detour for the **Prieuré de Marcevol**, 8km distant via Arboussols village. This fortified, twelfth-century monastic church (April–June & Oct–Nov Tues–Sun 10.30am–12.30pm & 2.30–6pm; July–Sept daily 10.30am–12.30pm & 2.30–7pm; Dec–March by arrangement; €3) has a rose-marble west portal and iron-studded door, plus superb views south to Canigou; the austrere interior is enlivened only by an engagingly primitive fresco, in the southerly apse, of Christ in Glory attended by angels.

Practicalities

Ille's **train station** is a five-minute walk south of the centre and the town's **tourist office** (Mon–Fri 9am–noon & 2–6/7pm, Sat & Sun 9am–noon & 2–6pm; not Sat pm or Sun Sept–June; Ⓣ04.68.84.02.62, Ⓦwww.ille-sur-tet.com). For **accommodation**, you must continue 8km upstream, beyond the fortified village of Bouleternère, to **VINÇA**, where you can stay (simply) and eat (well; *menus* €16–39) at *La Petite Auberge* (Ⓣ04.68.05.81.47; closed Sun pm, Tues pm, Wed; ❷), in the very centre. Vinça's old town is atmospheric, with running fountains everywhere; the nearby reservoir provides good swimming, windsurfing and canoeing.

Les Aspres: Serrabona and La Trinitat

The gentle hills of **Les Aspres**, with their alternating hillside meadows and thick woods, are entered by turning south at Bouleternère and continuing through the gorge of the River Boulès. About 8km along the D618, the steeply winding D84 leads 4km west up to the most celebrated Romanesque monument in Roussillon, the **Prieuré de Serrabona** (formerly Serrabonne; daily except public hols 10am–6pm; €3), whose square belfry is visible from afar. The bluff-top setting with a sheer drop behind is impressive, and the monastic cultivation terraces have been partly adapted to support a well-labelled botanical garden of local flora.

Local schist slabs cover most of the plain exterior, and only the ornate column capitals of the unused north portal anticipate the richness inside. Halfway along the almost windowless nave (consecrated in 1151), against starkly bare walls, stands a rib-vaulted tribune of rose marble, in effect an interior cloister reminiscent of some Spanish Mozarabic churches. The prevailing austerity makes its column-capitals even more striking: lions, centaurs, griffins and human figures with Asiatic faces and hair-styles – motifs brought back from the Crusades – executed in pink marble from Villefranche-de-Conflent. The pillars and equally elaborate capitals of the cloister to the south are carved from the same stone.

Continuing south 14km along the D618, through the village of Boule d'Amont, brings you to the chapel of **La Trinitat** (aka Trinité), beside the tiny *mairie* of Prunet-Bolpuig. Inside (usually open) is a fine, serene *Majestat*, the particularly Catalan wood-carved Crucifixions of the eleventh or twelfth centuries – not as large as the one in Beget (see p.68) but more likely to be viewable.

From the Col Xatard just beyond, the D618 drops south into the Tech valley at Amélie-les-Bains, 22.5km away (44km total from Bouleternère). Some 3km beyond the col is the only amenity en route, in the tiny village of **SAINT-MARSAL** with its broad vistas: *Hôtel Auberge de Saint-Marsal* (Ⓣ04.68.39.42.68, Ⓦwww.saintmarsal.net; ❷), a converted *mas*. Another attractive option for drivers is to complete a loop back to the Têt valley at Vinça along the D13 from the Col Xatard. This road goes via the tiny villages of La Bastide, Valmanya and Baillestavy (see "The Canigou Massif", p.105).

Prades and Saint-Michel-de-Cuixà

Halfway up the Tét valley, **PRADES** (Prada in Catalan), with its distinctively pink marble masonry and pavements, is by far the valley's largest town. It is also the birthplace (in 1915) of Thomas Merton, the American Catholic mystic and author of *The Seven Storey Mountain*, who eventually settled in a Trappist monastery in Kentucky. But Prades is best known for its late-July to mid-August **chamber music festival**

(Ⓦ www.prades-festival-casals.com), instituted in 1950 by the Catalan cellist **Pablo Casals** (Pau Casals in Catalan; 1876–1973). In exile here from Franco's Spain, Casals composed such works as the oratorio *The Crib* and the popular *Song of the Birds*, after which he named his house. The church of **Saint-Pierre**, in the main place de la République, contains a huge and sumptuous seventeenth-century retable (with Peter enthroned) by the Catalan sculptor Josep Sunyer, plus a huge organ at the west end. Prades is indeed ardently Catalan, hosting a mid-August Catalan language course and the first Catalan-language primary school in France.

Much of the music festival takes place at the originally eleventh-century Benedictine monastery of **Saint-Michel-de-Cuixà** (May–Sept Mon–Sat 9.30–11.50am & 2–6pm, Sun 2–6pm; Oct–April Mon–Sat 9.30–11.50am & 2–5pm, Sun 2–5pm; €4), whose single crenellated belfry (its mate collapsed in early 1839) suddenly appears above a copse of trees 3km south of town, juxtaposed against Canigou. Closed and abandoned in 1790, much of Saint-Michel's stonework was pillaged thereafter, and the place was only recently re-tenanted by a small community of Spanish Benedictines. Since 1937, the premises have been restored in stages, replacing where possible original masonry retrieved from surrounding villages.

You enter via the labyrinthine, vaulted crypt, with a round central chamber, before proceeding to the church with its strange Visigothic-style "keyhole" arches. But the glory of the place is the **cloister with its twelfth-century column capitals**. Although most of the north and east bays were taken to the Cloisters Museum in New York early in the twentieth century, the remaining west and south series rival Serrabona and Elne for virtuosity. Executed in the same rose-tinted marble used at Serrabona, they depict highly stylized figures strongly reminiscent of Sumerian or Assyrian relief art: often monsters, either alone or being grappled by human keepers displaying an array of Asiatic beards, headgear and corpulent anatomies.

Practicalities

The **train station** is at the southern edge of Prades, about ten minutes' walk from the centre; **buses** set you down on at a small terminal on avenue Général-de-Gaulle, the main thorough road. The **tourist office** is at 4 rue des Marchands (July

△ Saint-Michel-de-Cuixà with Mt Canigou

& Aug Mon–Sat 9am–12.30pm & 2–7pm, Sun 9am–noon; Sept–June Mon–Fri 9am–noon & 2–6pm; ⓣ04.68.05.41.02, ⓦwww.prades-tourisme.com), and can help with booking a 4WD taxi up Canigou.

For **accommodation**, there are two central hotels, but both have seen better days, and currently the best option lies just west of town on Chemin de la Llitera: *Chambres d'Hôtes Castell Rose* (ⓣ04.68.96.07.57, ⓦwww.castellrose-prades.com; ❺–❻), in a converted manor house set in extensive grounds with a pool and tennis court. (With transport, consider also as a base Molitg-les-Bains, below.) The beautifully sited municipal **campsite** (ⓣ04.68.96.29.83; April–Sept), by the river northeast of the town centre off chemin du Gaz, also has chalets (for 5) for rent.

In terms of non-hotel **restaurants**, the newest, most interesting entry on the scene is *La Meridienne* at 20 rue des Marchands, with a properly trained chef and *menus/formules* at €12 and €15. Alternatives include *Le Jardin d'Aymeric* at 3 av du Général-de-Gaulle by the bus station, with a regularly changing regional *menu* (closed Sun eve & Mon); and upscale *L'Hostal de Nougarols* in adjacent Codalet hamlet (closed Tues), serving wood-oven pizzas and Catalan specialities (*minceur menu* from €20) in a pleasant environment looking out to a garden. On place de la République, *Casa Nostra* is the favourite **bar-café** for a tipple, especially after the Tuesday and Saturday markets, though the food's unmemorable.

West from Prades: Molitg-les-Bains and Mosset

The D14, first north then west out Prades, is a quiet and beautiful way of travelling **west to the Aude valley**. The first community reached is gorge-set **MOLITG-LES-BAINS** (Molig els Banys), a spa 7km away across the river. **Accommodation** here includes the delightful, welcoming *Hôtel St Joseph* (ⓣ04.68.05.02.11, ⓔgerard.pommerol6yahoo.fr; all year; rooms ❷, studios €40), which has an excellent restaurant (copious *table d'hôte* suppers €12). If they're full, try the nearby *Hôtel Oasis* (ⓣ04.68.05.00.92, ⓦwww.welcome.to/h_oasis; April–Nov; ❷), also with a competent restaurant. If money's no object, burn it at the *Grand Hotel Thermal* (ⓣ04.68.06.00.50, ⓦwww.chainethermale.fr; ❺), with a marble-clad on-site spa and equally pricey restaurant.

The road climbs 5km from Molitg to **MOSSET**, an atmospheric, fortified and gated old village whose life and times are described engagingly by Rosemary Bailey (see p.564 in "Books"). Here you'll find the *Ferme-Auberge Mas Líuganas* (ⓣ04.68.05.00.37; ❷ B&B) with rustic accommodation in the farmhouse 2km before the village, and a single restaurant in Mosset itself. The road then goes over the **Col de Jau** (1513m) before dropping 18km through fir forests to join the Aude 4km above Axat – or with a slight deviation, 25km to Escouloubre-les-Bains.

Villefranche-de-Conflent

Some 6km beyond Prades the Têt valley narrows dramatically into a gorge, where the high walls of **VILLEFRANCHE-DE-CONFLENT** almost block the way. As there's almost no construction outside the walls, the town looks much as it did three hundred years ago (especially from a distance): an elongated, two-street place squeezed between the palisade just to the south and the river. Within the ramparts, alas, it's an out-and-out tourist trap, though the medieval past can be glimpsed around thirteenth-century **Saint-Pierre** and the belfried twelfth-century church of **Saint-Jacques**. More interesting, perhaps, are the vast cave complexes (see p.104) that riddle the strata below and around the town.

Villefranche (Vilafranca) dates from 1092, when Guillaume Raymond, count of Cerdagne, granted the charter for the foundation of "Villa Libéra" as a strategic counter to the counts of Roussillon. His seat was at Corneilla, just up the valley of the Cady, and the logical site for a stronghold was here, at the confluence of the

Cady and the Têt. Some remnants from that period still stand, notably the **Tour d'en Solenell** on the little **Placette** square. In 1654 Villefranche – then controlled by Spain – was besieged by Louis XIV's troops, and fell after eight days. After the Treaty of the Pyrenees annexed Roussillon, the ubiquitous Vauban rebuilt the Spanish fortifications.

As you walk the maze-like **ramparts** (daily: Feb–May & Oct–Dec 10.30am–12.30pm & 2–5/6pm; June & Sept 10am–7pm; July & Aug 10am–8pm; closed Jan; €4.50), their vulnerability to attack from above is obvious – a defensive weakness that Vauban remedied in 1681 by building the upper stronghold now known as **Château-Fort Libéria** (daily: June–Sept 9am–8pm; Oct–May 10am–6pm; €5.80), high above the main town on the steep northern bank of the Têt, and frequently used as a prison. Inmates have included a group of seventeenth-century Versailles noblewomen, confined in isolation and silence for over thirty years, on charges of witchcraft and poisoning, as well as German POWs during World War I. Getting up there involves taking the free minibus leaving from near the town's main gate; you can return to Villefranche by descending a subterranean stairway of a thousand steps, which debouches at the end of rue St-Pierre.

The caves

The most notable incident in Villefranche's history was the 1674 revolt against French rule, which culminated in the betrayal of **Charles de Llar** and his co-conspirators by Llar's daughter Inès. The tale was melodramatized by Louis Bertrand in his novel *L'Infante*, published in 1930. Llar's hiding place was the Cova Bastéra, now known as the **Grottes de la Préhistoire** (daily: July & Aug 10am–8pm; Sept–June 10am–noon & 2–6pm; €5), a cave that he could enter and exit from within the walls of the town; today's entrance is just west of the walls. Consider buying a combined ticket, also good for the limestone **Grottes des Canalettes** (April–Sept 10am–6.30pm; off-season call Ⓣ04.68.05.20.76; 45min guided tour; €6), 1km along the road south towards Vernet-les-Bains. The most spectacular caves, however, are the adjoining **Grottes des Grandes Canalettes**, which demand a separate ticket (April–June 15 & Sept 16–Oct daily 10am–6pm; June 16–Sept 15 daily 10am–6.30pm; Nov–March Sun & school hols 2–5pm; Ⓦwww.grotte-grandes-canalettes.com; 1hr guided tour; €7). Entry is via a 160-metre passageway, hollowed out by water over 400 million years. Beyond a door you enter a succession of huge, fancifully named chambers crammed with stalactites, stalagmites, pillars and tiny, feathery formations. Beyond the "Dôme Rouge" lies the "Gouffre sans Fond" (The Bottomless Pit), stretching for several kilometres and the domain of speleologists only.

Practicalities

Main-line **trains** from Perpignan terminate in Villefranche, at the **station** 400m north of the town; for *Train Jaune* services further up the Têt (see box on p.112) simply change platforms. Buses to Vernet-les-Bains stop at the *gare SNCF* and just outside the Porte de France. The **tourist office** (Feb–Dec daily 10am–12.30pm & 2–5.30pm; Ⓣ04.68.96.22.96, Ⓦwww.conflent.com) is in place d'Église.

The only **hotel** here is the magnificent old *Auberge du Cédre* (Ⓣ & Ⓕ04.68.96.05.05, Ⓦfr.federal-hotel.com; ❹), situated just north of the old walls, near the *gare SNCF*, though there are welcoming, comfortable **chambres d'hôtes** with a swimming pool, *Chez Mireille Pena* (Ⓣ04.68.96.52.35, Ⓔmpebafain@aol.com; ❸), located off the same lane. The best-value local **restaurant**, in the old town at 31 rue St-Jean, is *La Casa de la Nine* (closed Sun eve & Mon, Oct–March also closed Tues & all eves except Fri/Sat, all Feb) English-run but well respected by locals.

The Canigou Massif

Rising in splendid isolation to 2784m between the Tech and Têt valleys, the **Pic du Canigou** (Canigó in Catalan) is the great landmark of Catalonia, visible across the coastal plains from both the French and Spanish Mediterranean coast. Though well inside French territory, the mountain became a symbol for lost Catalan independence and enduring cultural unity during the nineteenth-century literary renaissance, endorsed today by the small Catalan flags and other patriotic paraphernalia festooned from its summit cross. Before modern topographic surveys took place, Canigou was thought erroneously to be the Pyrenees' highest peak – a curious conceit, given the handful of 2800-metre-plus frontier peaks visible just southwest between Mantet and Núria.

There are essentially only two ways of reaching the top of Canigou – via the **Chalet des Cortalets** (2150m) on the northern slopes, or via the **Refuge Grand Mariailles** (1718m) to the southwest. The various approaches to these shelters are detailed below. Routes from the Tech valley on the south are longer and therefore not specifically recommended for climbing Canigou – although you might use them to move from the Tech to the Têt, taking in Canigou along the way. When not clouded over, the peak affords breathtaking views. Autumn is generally the best time to bag the **summit**, when it's snow-free (unlike in late spring); conditions are not optimal in summer, owing to the heat and reduced visibility.

If you're serious about exploring the massif – which is a partly protected natural reserve, good for several days' trekking – either Rando Éditions' 1:50,000 "Canigou/Vallespir/Fenouillèdes" *carte de randonnées*, or the TOP 25 1:25,000 **map** no. 2349ET "Massif du Canigou", is a mandatory investment, available in all surrounding villages. Editorial Alpina's 1:40,000 "Massís del Canigó" may also be of interest, not least for giving all place names in Catalan.

Northern approaches to Canigou

The northeasterly route up Canigou is the quiet and impressively steep (but not difficult) approach from **Valmanya**. To its northwest, a 4WD track from near **Prades** is the scenic but busy alternative.

The Valmanya route

From Vinça in the Têt valley, the D13 follows the River Lentilla south along the eastern flanks of Canigou, past Finestret (4km). From here the **GR36** cuts through the wooded western slopes and fields of the valley, rejoining the road at Baillestavy (12km from Vinça). As the russet streaks on nearby rocks suggest, the Canigou massif is rich in iron ore; there's a mine above the village and traces of a Roman forge by the river.

The Resistance stronghold of **VALMANYA** (Vallmanyà), another 5km by road or GR trail, was destroyed by the Germans in 1944 – some of the houses were reduced to rubble, others set ablaze. Despite rebuilding and the magnificent setting at 874m, there's a lingering sadness to the place; on the plus side, it has a 24-bunk *gîte d'étape*, *Le Roc de l'Ours* (Ⓣ04.68.05.93.99; mostly triples and quads), well placed to end a day's march from Vinça.

From Valmanya, the **GR36** climbs sharply west through woods to **Ras del Prat Cabrera** (1739m), where it meets a track from Villerach, near Prades, and more attractively the **GR10**, which traverses a bit higher via la Tartère to the *Chalet des Cortalets*. Alternatively, minor trails head south from Valmanya to intersect the GR10 at the forestry hut at **Estanyol** or the **Abri du Pinatell**. You could just about make the return trip from Valmanya to Canigou's summit in a day, but it's more manageable with a night at or near *Chalet des Cortalets*.

The Prades route

The gentlest ascent to *Chalet des Cortalets* is the one used by the 4WD taxis (roughly €25 per person) from Prades. If you're driving, take the D35 out the south side of Prades to Villerach (8km; signposted as "Clara-Villerach"), where a dirt track rises to the chalet 20km away – an hour's drive. (If you're on foot, there are much better hiking approaches – read on.) This is a superb route, often shadowing the River Llech, each turn revealing a new arrangement of rock, water, sky and forest. An ordinary car can easily get as far as the ruined hut at Prat Cabrera (1650m), an hour's walk from the *Chalet des Cortalets*, and – with extra care and ideal conditions – all the way to Cortalets.

Northwestern approaches: Vernet-les-Bains and around

More direct footpaths from the northwestern side begin from Fillols and Casteil, both above Vernet-les-Bains, the closest proper town to the massif. The D116 leads 6.5km south from Villefranche to the pleasant spa of **VERNET-LES-BAINS** (Vernet dels Banys), its springs first exploited in 1377. English visitors like Rudyard Kipling made the place fashionable during the nineteenth century, and a waterfall, 3km out of town on a well-marked path, is even called the **Cascade des Anglaises**. The often-overlooked old quarter is capped by the ninth-century but much-restored double church of **Nôtre-Dame-del-Puig/Saint-Saturnin**, which incorporates remaining bits of a castle.

The **tourist office** is on place de la Mairie (Mon–Fri 9am–noon & 2–6pm; Ⓣ04.68.05.55.35, Ⓦwww.ot-vernet-les-bains.fr). **Jeep-taxis** up Canigou (same price as from Prades) can be arranged through Garage Villaceque (Ⓣ04.68.05.66.58) or Jean-Paul Bouzan (Ⓣ04.68.05.62.28). Vernet has a *gîte d'étape* (Ⓣ04.68.05.51.30; 32 bunks; closed Nov) in chemin St-Saturnin, on the left bank of the Cady next to the municipal pool. Several two-star **hotels** offer a range of amenities; two of the best-value ones are the spa hotel itself, *Les Sources* (Ⓣ04.68.05.52.84, Ⓦwww.thermes-vernet.com; closed Dec to mid-March; ❷), and Logis de France affiliate *Princess*, rue de Lavandiers (Ⓣ04.68.05.56.22, Ⓦwww.hotel-princess.com; closed Nov to mid-March; €50–53). . Nearest **campsites** are *Les Cerisiers* (Ⓣ04.68.05.60.38; mid-May to Sept), on the same side of the river as the *gîte*, and *Dels Bosc*, 1km north on the Villefranche road (Ⓣ04.68.05.51.62; April–Sept). For a **meal**, try roast-meat specialist *Le Cortal* (closed Oct–Nov & Mon, also Tues–Wed low season), at the top of the old quarter behind the church, by the upper car park.

The Fillols routes

The standard **walking ascent** from Vernet is by a footpath that begins 700m northeast along the D27, towards the tiny village of Fillols. This climbs within three hours to the derelict **Refuge de Bonneaigue** (Bonaigua; 1741m) and the **GR10**, along which the *Chalet des Cortalets* is another ninety minutes' walk.

For those with a 4WD or a very sturdy car, a track begins some 5km from Vernet, just past Fillols; this route is also used by taxis from the two villages – you can book one at the dead-central *Café de l'Union* in **FILLOLS** (Ⓣ04.68.05.63.06), as well as get a meal. The track rises gradually at first, past *Les Sauterelles* **campsite** (Ⓣ04.68.05.63.72; June–Sept), then with dramatic steepness in a series of tight hairpins to the large **Refuge de Balatg** (1610m), the derelict *Cabane des Cortalets* (1975m) and finally the chalet itself. This isn't as pretty a route as that from Prades – and the poorer surface makes it inadvisable for conventional cars – but more open topography produces awesome views.

Casteil and Saint-Martin-du-Canigou

From Vernet-les-Bains the paved road leads 2500m south to **CASTEIL** (Castell), where you can **eat** and **stay** at either the basic *Relais St-Martin* (Ⓣ04.68.05.56.76; ❷), at the top of the village by the start of the path to St-Martin, with a wonderful terrace, or two-star *Le Molière* (Ⓣ04.68.05.50.97, Ⓦwww.lemoliere.com; ❷), with garden-view front rooms and a friendly summer restaurant under the mulberries (great country cuisine from €20). There's also a **campsite**, *Domaine St-Martin* (Ⓣ04.98.05.52.09; April–Sept), with a swimming pool. Casteil is an appealing, quiet hamlet, well placed for Canigou and the GR10, the latter less than an hour away on the **Col de Jou**, accessible by a delightful short trail that shortcuts the road. On the ridge just east stands the restored twelfth-century **Tour de Goa**, reached by another path from the *col*, which eventually drops to the spa at Vernet.

Saint-Martin-du-Canigou

You're most likely to visit Casteil for the nearby monastery of **Saint-Martin-du-Canigou**, whose image is ubiquitous, celebrated on local book covers, postcards and posters. Access is only by a thirty-minute climb up the path from Casteill, which helps protect the place from the worst tour-bus excesses – as does its continued use by an active religious community.

Built from tan stone and roofed with grey slates, the monastery ranks as one of the most striking monuments in the Eastern Pyrenees, and the surrounding woods of sweet chestnut, beech and aspen contrast with the pinnacle of rock on which it stands. It was founded in 1001 by Count Guifred de Cerdagne, who retired with his second wife Elisabeth to the monastery in 1035; you can see their purported **sarcophagi** at the base of the tower. Severely damaged by an earthquake in the fifteenth century – the tower lost a storey – and thoroughly pillaged after abandonment during the Revolution, Saint-Martin (Sant Martí in Catalan) was restored in two phases (1902–32 and 1952–82), initially through the efforts of the bishop of Perpignan. The glory of the place resides in its **cloister capitals**, retrieved by the good cleric from a particularly wide dispersal.

The monastery is now occupied by an unusual mixed order of monks and nuns, called the "Beatitudes", with a sprinkling of lay workers. Ordinarily, visitors are allowed only on French-language **guided tours** (year-round Mon–Sat 10am, 11am, 2pm, 3pm, 4pm; also noon & 5pm June–Sept; Sun/hols 10am & 12.30pm rather than 10am, 11am, noon; closed Jan & Mon low season; €4). The "Beatitudes" sponsor extended retreats by individuals (contact the abbey at Ⓔvisitezabbayestmartin@wanadoo.fr, or phone Ⓣ04.68.05.50.03).

Descending from the rear of the complex, you can take an alternative marked footpath for half an hour back to Casteil via the entrance to the **Gorges du Cady**, where the river falls 500m over a distance of 3km, making this a popular spot for canyoning.

Saint-Martin to Mariailles or Cortalets

At the rear of the monastery grounds another path leads up to a signposted viewpoint. You can continue on the path, an excruciatingly steep but shady, beautiful and well-marked route, for just under three hours to the **Col de Segalès** (2040m, spring 5min away) on the GR10. Despite the grade, this provides the most direct all-trail access from the Vernet area to the staffed *Refuge Grand Mariailles* (see p.108), another ninety minutes of up-and-down trekking, south of the *col* by a roundabout route. The three-hour traverse north to *Cortalets* is quite scenic and a bit more direct, but again there is a fair bit of roller-coastering and a short stretch of track-walking. Many people do the Saint-Martin-to-Cortalets leg in reverse, as part of an east–west traverse of the massif, beginning from Valmanya or Batère (for which see pp.105 & 121).

Cortalets to the summit

A *maquisard* hideout in the last war, and consequently heavily shelled by occupation forces, the restored, CAF-run **Chalet des Cortalets** (2150m; ⓣ04.68.96.36.19; 111 places; mid-May to late Oct) offers double rooms as well as made-up beds in the **dormitories**; **meals** in the bar-restaurant cost about €13. Be warned that despite its capacity the refuge can fill, and the tracks bring up cars full of revellers – as opposed to walkers – at weekends to picnic at the tables around the little lake, ten minutes' walk west of the refuge. **Tents** are tolerated on the lake shore, and next to another smaller pond closer to *Cortalets*.

The summit

The normal, well-marked approach to the **summit** goes past the larger lake, with its fine view up into the summit cirque, then climbs south along the ridge leading from **Pic Joffre**, which often teems with isards at sunset. It takes a little over ninety minutes and provides only a slight sense of exposure as you reach the wrought-iron summit cross and *table d'orientation*. In clear weather, the views taking in everything from Andorra to the sea are as hoped for.

At midsummer (observed in Catalonia on the eve of June 23–24, the *Festa de Sant Joan*), the refuge and the peak are spots to avoid or to gravitate towards,descends for merrymaking and the lighting of the traditional bonfire, torches from which are then relayed to ignite numerous others in Catalan villages on both sides of the frontier. Even at other times, a patriotic Catalan or two is prepared to bivouac the night beside the peak's highest cairn.

There is an alternate, less frequented and even more dramatic route, climbing south from *Chalet des Cortalets* along the **Crête de Barbet** to the **Porteille de Valmanya** (2591m), a beautiful ridge-walk. Beyond the *porteille*, follow the ridge a bit below it to the left – the sharp drop northeast is alarming – before clambering up a boulder-gully to the summit (2hr 30min). The Pic Joffre and Barbet routes can, of course, be combined to make a circuit.

Southwestern approaches: the Rotja valley

To tackle ascents of Canigou **from the southwest**, take a bus from Prades or Villefranche (Mon–Sat 1–2 daily) along the **Rotja valley** to **SAHORRE** (Saorra). This has an ancient church plus an excellent, admirably set **hotel**, *La Châtaigneraie* (ⓣ04.68.05.51.04; ⓦwww.hotel-lachataigneraie.com; ❸), with a pool and good **restaurant**.

PY (Pi del Conflent), 6km upstream, remains a traditional mountain village – certainly compared to more-visited Casteil or Mantet – but even here there is second-home occupation. So far the only concessions to tourism are a *gîte d'étape* (ⓣ04.68.05.58.38; 13 dorm bunks; June to mid-Sept) and a combination café-restaurant-*épicerie*.

The usual approach to Canigou from Py is to follow the **GR10** northeast to the **Col de Jou** (1125m), then descend into the ravine upstream from Casteil, short-cutting the dirt road most of the way to the large, comfortable **Refuge Grand Mariailles** (1718m; ⓣ04.68.92.22.90 or 04.68.04.49.86; 55 bunks; open late May to early Oct), three hours on foot from Py. After a night at *Mariailles*, take the GR10 east into the forest via the **Col Vert**, then into the Cady valley. From Jasse de Cady the footpath heads west to the Col de Segalès and continues to the *Chalet des Cortalets* (route described on p.107).

The direct way to the **summit** from Jasse de Cady, though, is to continue east-northeast along the Cady valley, past the basic, unstaffed Refuge Arago, to the **Porteille de Valmanya** (2591m), then up to the summit as described opposite.

Mantet

From Py the paved road climbs steeply southwest through countless hairpins, many of which are bypassed on the GR10, though it's a dull, steep hike. When you reach the **Col de Mantet** (1761m), two-plus hours' walking from Py, Mantet village is still invisible, clinging to the slope 200m below the *col*, while further south spreads the beautiful pine-covered Alemany valley; its far end, where the **Porteille/Portella de Mantet** (2412m) leads into Spain, is a *réserve naturelle*.

The inhabitants of **MANTET** (Mentet) were expelled by the Nazis towards the end of World War II, and the village was resettled only in the 1960s. It's since been expensively restored for holiday homes, and despite having only twenty or so permanent inhabitants, Mantet supports a 22-place *gîte* as part of the local horse-riding centre, *La Cavale* (Ⓣ04.68.05.57.59, Ⓦwww.la-cavale.fr), with four comfortable doubles (❷) as well as en-suite quads and evening meals. On the road below is the *Auberge Bouf'tic* (Ⓣ04.68.05.51.76; ❹ HB only), its good **restaurant** open to others with advance notice.

Walks from Mantet

From the Col de Mantet a spectacular **route up Canigou** involves climbing through the woods southeast to the **Pla Ségala**, and then along the ridge to **Roc Colom** (2507m). Here, pick up the **HRP** and follow it along the line of rock teeth known as Les Esquerdes de Rotja to **Collade des Roques Blanches** (2252m) and then **Pla Guillem** (2277m), where there is a simple, unstaffed refuge. It's already a long day but if you still have daylight and strength, the *Refuge Grand Mariailles* – an hour-plus descent further – is much more congenial.

Canigou aside, this is a great walking, riding (and in winter, snow-shoeing) area. The **GR10** climbs from the Alemany valley west over the **Coll del Pal** (2294m) into the **Carança valley** and the *Refuge Ras de Carança* (4hr 30min from Mantet; see p.112).

The upper Têt

The lower Têt ends at Villefranche-de-Conflent, above which the shaggy flanks of the **upper Têt** close dramatically around the *Train Jaune* line and the N116; these forge separately along the river to Mont-Louis, at the top of the Têt. En route there are a number of small villages, on the valley floor or perched just above, which make serviceable bases for excursions into the hills. Of these, the hot springs and no-nonsense **Carança gorge** near **Thuès**, and the **Mont Coronat** area north of **Olette**, are the most rewarding goals.

Many **abandoned villages and farmsteads** on the Têt valley slopes have become home to colonies of ageing hippies and more punkified "travellers". The presence of these mainly non-French interlopers in an isolated and conservative mountain society still causes tension, but most locals have grown accustomed to their flamboyant appearance and accepted them in a live-and-let-live spirit. At any rate, these settlers, frequently seen operating market stalls in lower-altitude centres, are here to stay – after more than twenty years of continuous habitation they have acquired legally binding "squatter's rights" and cannot be evicted from the hamlets, many of which still lack utilities or any other municipal services.

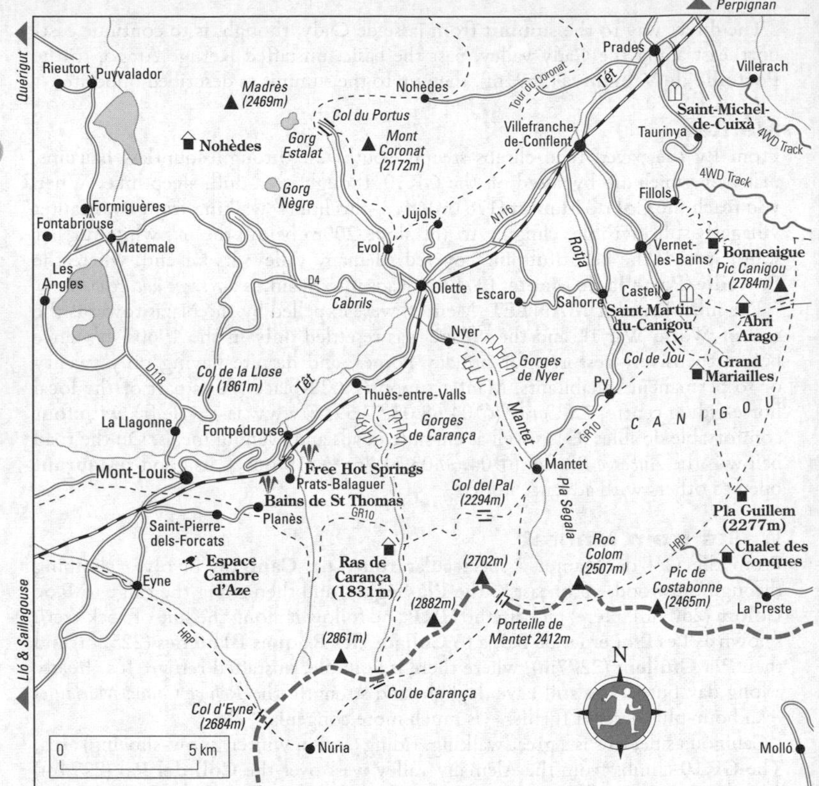

Excursions north of the Têt

Most of the villages along the Têt valley aren't really worth leaving the train for, but some give access to marvellous hikes just north. At **OLETTE** (Oleta), much the biggest place between Villefranche and Mont-Louis (with the only proper shops en route), you can **stay** comfortably at *La Fontaine* (ⓣ 04.68.97.03.67, ⓔ hotel.restaurant.la.fontaine@wanadoo.fr; closed Jan, Tues eve & Wed low season; ❸), on the main street, though its restaurant is humdrum. From Olette, a path and road lead 2.5km north to **EVOL**, where the church of **Saint André** contains a splendid painted retable by the so-called Maître du Roussillon, dating from 1428. The massive ruined **château**, just above Evol on the onward road to the Col de Portus, was built in 1260. Between Olette and Evol the D4 peels off into the tranquil **Cabrils valley**, a longer, steeper (1861m at the Col de la Llose/Coll de la Llosa) but more attractive road to Mont-Louis than the Têt route.

The Tour du Coronat

From Olette it's also 4.5km by road northeast to **JUJOLS**, usual start of the four-stage, waymarked **Tour du Coronat** around the **Mont Coronat** massif. There's a good *gîte d'étape* in Jujols, *Les Cardabeilles* (ⓣ 04.68.97.02.40; 25 places), and fancy *chambres de hôtes* in **NOHÈDES**, *Le Presbytère*, (ⓣ 04.68.05.62.59, ⓦ www.gite-

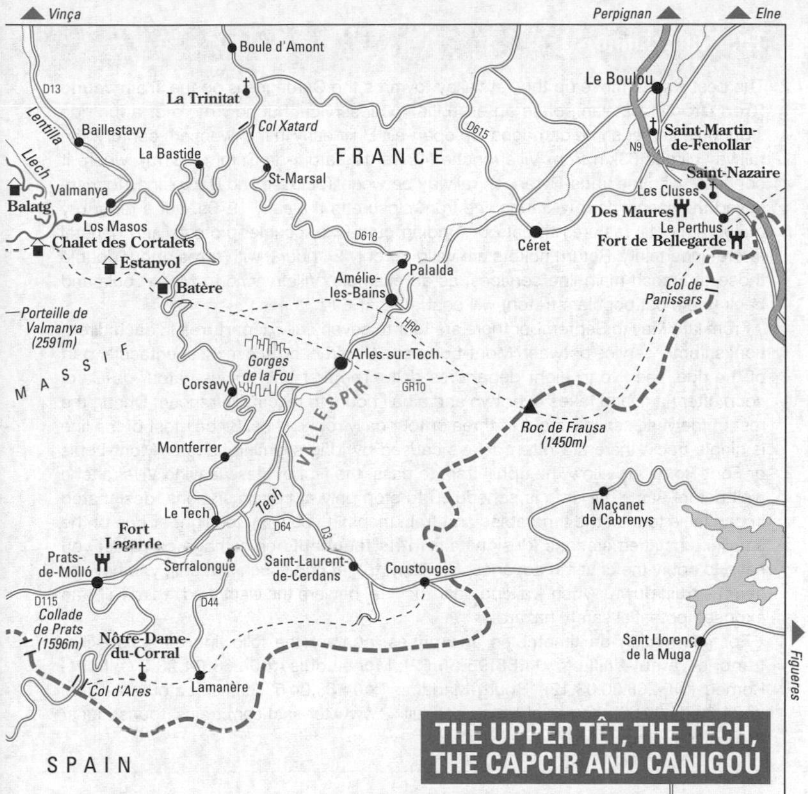

roussillon.com; ④), but you'll still need to camp out one night. The highlight of the tour is actually slightly off its western extension, the **Col de Pertus/Coll de Portos** (1736m), from where you climb 300m to the lakes of **Gorg Estelat** and **Gorg Nègre** at the foot of the gentle **Pic Madrès** (2469m).

The Carança gorge area

A few minutes past Olette on the *Train Jaune* at **NYER**, the road south from the station through the village climbs into the impressive **Gorges de Nyer** en route to Mantet. However, you're better off staying on the train until Thuès-Carança station, four minutes above the small spa of Thuès-les-Bains and gateway to the even more spectacular Gorges de Carança. The nearby village of **THUÈS-ENTRE-VALLS** is home to Luk and Micheline Peters' unsigned **gîte**, *Mas de Bordes* (ⓣ04.68.97.05.00), next to the church up the lane up from the train stop or the main road (N116). Choose between dorms, en-suite doubles (②) or self-catering suites. This restored *mas* is part of an eighty-hectare property that includes its own outdoor hot springs (40°C, 25min walk distant), a remote log cabin and a meadow for pitching tents. Good *table d'hôte* dinners are provided for about €13; the closest **restaurant** is the Antillean-flavoured *Pyrénéen*, 4km upvalley at **FONTPÉDROUSE**.

The Train Jaune

The best way to move up the Têt valley towards the Cerdagne is on the **Train Jaune** (**Tren Groc** in Catalan), once an essential local service, but now more of a fun ride – during summer some carriages are open-air. Built early in the twentieth century, the railway climbs 63km from Villefranche (427m) to Latour-de-Carol (1231m), where it connects with the trans-Pyrenean railway between Toulouse and Barcelona. Tourism saved the scenic narrow-gauge line from closure in the early 1970s, but a repertory melodrama still features threats of funding cutbacks, counter-protests and general future uncertainty. Return tickets are valid for only 24 hours, with **fares** about double those of French main-line services; as an example, Villefranche to Mont-Louis and back (the most popular stretch) will cost at least €17.

From late May to September there are four to seven daily **departures** in each direction; summer service between Mont-Louis and Villefranche, the most spectacular part of the ride, see five to eight departures daily. The first train leaves Latour-de-Carol soon after 8am, and takes over two and a half hours to reach Villefranche. During the rest of the year, service is cut to three or four daily round-trips. Since most of the line is single track, there are often delays caused by long shunting halts at Mont-Louis or Font-Romeu to allow the uphill train to pass, the first of these leaving Villefranche well before 8am. The train is scheduled to stop only at certain stations, designated in capital letters on the timetables and train maps; if you want to alight at one of the smaller, unstaffed stations (designated **arrêts facultatifs** on carriage placards) you have to notify the driver in advance. Similarly, to get on at such stations, you have to flag the train down. When walking near the line, beware the electrified "third rail", an exposed potential safety hazard.

For information on timetables and prices, contact the following stations: Villefranche-Vernet-Fuilla (ⓣ04.68.96.56.62); Mont-Louis (ⓣ04.68.04.23.27); Font-Romeu (ⓣ04.68.30.03.12); Bourg-Madame (ⓣ04.68.04.53.29); or Latour-de-Carol (ⓣ04.68.04.80.62). You might also consult ⓦwww.ter-sncf.com/trains_touristiques/train_jaune.htm.

The Gorges de Carança

The **Gorges de Carança** are clearly signposted from Thuès' *halte facultatif* and from the N116, while more notices at its mouth (over which the *Train Jaune* clatters on a bridge) advise that you enter at your own risk. Shortly beyond the car park, the path divides: the left-hand trail (signposted for Roc Madrieu) climbs steeply up the wooded side of the valley, while the right-hand path (over a small bridge) follows the more spectacular corniche route; the two converge at the *pont des singes* (suspension bridge). The first ninety minutes of corniche walkway are the most amazing, poised over sheer four-hundred-metre drops – not for the vertigo-prone. Next are a series of nerve-wracking catwalks, ladders and wobbly metal suspension bridges, the latter not advisable for heavily laden walkers.

Yet the overall elevation gain towards the border is gentle, so the canyon makes a popular outing: it's best to start off early to beat the crowds and the heat. Beyond the narrows, the route becomes a shady, streamside trail on the west bank; the countryside opens out, and you reach **Ras de Carança** (1831m) in about three and a half hours. The rather basic **refuge** here (ⓣ04.68.04.13.18; 19 places; staffed June–Sept 15) offers equally simple meals, and there's plenty of camping space nearby. Reaching the first of a series of lakes – the easternmost along the main Pyrenees crest – requires another ninety minutes, while the border at Coll de Carança, and the GR11 towards Núria, is at least three hours distant and thus beyond the scope of a day trip from Thuès.

Hot springs – and Planès

If you're a fan of **hot springs**, leave the train at **Fontpédrouse** (Fontpedrosa) station, the stop above Thuès-Carança, and follow the twisty road up towards **Prats-Balaguer** village on the south slope. From the second hairpin, a path leads east down to a trio of undeveloped **thermal pools** on the far side of the valley. Alternatively, stay on the road for 3km to the renovated **Bains de Saint-Thomas** (daily 10am–7.40pm, last admission 8.40pm July/Aug; closed Nov 14–Dec 5; €4–€4.50), with open-air pools at a pleasant 37–38°C, ideal for a hot dip or hammam after skiing or hiking.

Just before Planès, the *Train Jaune* passes over the 150-metre-long **Pont Gisclard** suspension bridge, which carries the track 80m above the river. It was designed by mathematician and engineer Albert Gisclard, who was tragically killed by a runaway train on the day of the official bridge trial in 1909. The peculiar triangular church at **PLANÈS** was once thought to be an adapted Muslim structure, but the bell tower is typically Cerdagnois, and the array of domes has close parallels throughout the region. Near Planès, there's a 24-place *gîte d'étape*, *Le Malaza* (Ⓣ & Ⓕ 04.68.04.83.79, Ⓦ www.lemalaza.com), with two dorms, a handful of doubles (❷) and evening meals (€12).

Mont-Louis and around

The next *Train Jaune* station – **La Cabanasse** – serves fortified **MONT-LOUIS**, at 1600m the highest town on the Têt, lying 14km southeast of the river's source, the Lac des Bouillouses. Known as the gateway to the Cerdagne, Mont-Louis (10min walk northeast of the station) is another **Vauban** masterpiece, built quickly but solidly between 1679 and 1682. In contrast to the high, fragile walls of Villefranche, the moated **ramparts** (all year Mon–Sat, also Sun summer, 10am–noon & 4–5/6pm; €4.50) of Mont-Louis are massive and low to maximize resistance to artillery fire. Even Vauban admitted that the fortifications might fail in their intended function; indeed, throughout the eighteenth century hostile armies entered France through the Cerdagne, bypassing the citadel.

Though promoted as a resort, Mont-Louis is still essentially a garrison town, with French commandos occupying its citadel and training on surrounding slopes. Apart from the ramparts, Mont-Louis' only other attraction is the world's first **solar oven** (*four solaire)*, built in 1949 (daily except Dec 1–15 9.30am–12.30pm & 2–5/6pm; €5.50); the huge mirror for the oven stands in the moat, just left of the main gate (Porte de France). There's another, bigger *four solaire* in nearby Odeillo (see p.221).

There is a **tourist office** in rue du Marché (July & Aug 9.30am–noon & 2–7pm; Sept–June Tues–Sat 10am–noon & 2–6pm; Ⓣ 04.68.04.21.97, Ⓦ www.mont-louis.net). The most comfortable **accommodation** is *chambres d'hôtes La Volute* (Ⓣ 04.68.04.27.21, Ⓦ www.lavolute.monsite.wanadoo.fr; ❹), set in the seventeenth-century former governor's mansion, with a lawn-garden atop a section of the ramparts, and the attractively furnished *Hotel La Taverne*, 10 rue Victor Hugo (Ⓣ 04.68.04.23.67, Ⓦ www.latavernebernagie.fr; ❸), with *menus* from €16. The only independent **restaurant**, just below the car park, is *La Dagobert*, pricey once off the €15 menu. The closest **campsite**, *Pla de Barres* (Ⓣ 04.68.04.21.18; mid-June to mid-Sept), lies 3km west along the road towards Lac des Bouillouses, beautifully set under the pines by a stream.

The Eyne area: skiing and walking

The road from Mont-Louis to Planès passes through **SAINT-PIERRE-DELS-**

FORCATS, one of the base villages for the amalgamated ski zones known as the **ESPACE CAMBRE D'AZE** (Cambra d'Ase), after the eponymous peak overhead (2711m), cloven by a quarry-like cirque. Heading right at the fork above Saint-Pierre takes you to **EYNE** (Eina), the other base village (the *Train Jaune* stop is Bolquère-Eyne). The 25 runs, served almost entirely by drag lifts, are biased towards beginners and intermediates, though some are quite long and end scenically amidst the pines. Espace Cambre d'Aze is north-facing, with respectable top points of 2400m/2300m for the two sectors (where the few advanced pistes start), but snow can be unreliable this close to the Mediterranean – 257 snow canons help combat any deficit.

Saint-Pierre has no short-term accommodation, but at the ski station you can stay at the two-star *Le Roc Blanc* (Ⓣ04.68.04.72.72; closed Sept–Nov; ❹), or below in Eyne at the **gîte/chambres d'hôtes** *Cai Pai* (Ⓣ04.68.04.06.96; 30 places) by the church, which serves up excellent country-style meals for under €20.

Southeast of Eyne lies the **Col d'Eyne** (or **Coll de Núria**; 2684m), the second most important bird migration corridor in the Pyrenees, after the Col Organbidexka in the Basque country; autumn migrators include honey buzzards, kites and falcons, as well as bee-eaters and other rarities. A signposted path about 300m west of Eyne village, part of the HRP, runs up to the *col* through a forested valley, blessed with a peculiar microclimate and thus a wealth of flowers and herbs in its meadows. After three-plus hours the HRP attains the *col*, then follows the ridge east (soon in tandem with the GR11) until the head of the Carança valley.

The Capcir

Between the upper Têt valley and the gorges of the upper Aude spreads the sedimentary plateau called the **Capcir** (Ⓦwww.capcir-pyrenees.com). Bare and extremely flat – traits accentuated by the large artificial lakes of Matemale and Puyvalador – it's cradled by densely wooded slopes that sweep up to Pic Madrès and the Carlit Massif, with only the **ski-resort** pistes interrupting the trees. One of the harshest winter climates in southern France makes this excellent cross-country ski terrain, while summer promises easy walking, with several refuges or *gîtes d'étape*, plus hotels in a number of villages.

Capcir ski resorts

All of the Capcir **ski resorts** lie on, or just off, the D118 road served by the taxi-bus, and all share a pass scheme amongst themselves (and the nearby Cerdagne resorts). Nearest to Mont-Louis, northeast-facing **LES ANGLES** is also the area's largest and most advanced centre, with 32 pistes, more than half of them red-rated, totalling over 40km. Two *télécabines* and a chair-lift get you up from the base station and village (1650m) to a plateau at 1900–2000m, where there's another chair-lift to the secondary top station, 2325-metre **Roc d'Aude**; from here two drag lifts give access to the true summit at **Mont Llaret** (2377m). Numerous drag lifts and 255 snow canons fill any gaps in coverage. Chalets rather than high-rises predominate, but the old village has still been almost completely swamped. **Accommodation** is in five hotels, best value being *Le Coq d'Or*, place du Coq d'Or (Ⓣ04.68.04.42.17, Ⓦwww.hotel-lecoqdor.com; ❸) and *Llaret*, 12 av de Balcère (closed April–June & Sept–Dec; Ⓣ04.68.30.90.90, Ⓕ04.68.30.91.66; ❸). There are also two local high-quality **gîtes d'étape**: *L'AziMut*, at 1-bis rue des Pics-Verts (Ⓣ04.68.30.93.03, Ⓦwww.gite-azimut.com; 22 places, mostly triples/quads; HB only), and *Equisud* on Route de la Forêt (Ⓣ04.68.04.43.62, Ⓦwww.equisud.com; 24 places), doubling as a **horse-riding** centre, geared up for one-week packages.

Formiguères and Matemale

FORMIGUÈRES, 6km further north, is far more attractive, with its shops (some selling outdoor gear), cafés and *crêperies* giving it the feel of a county town. Its **church of Sainte-Marie** features an unusual triangular facade culminating in a *clocher-mur*; inside is a masterful, if late (seventeenth-century) *Majestat*. The seventeen downhill runs (total 20km), through the conifers between 2350m and 1700m, are pitched at strong intermediates, but more interesting perhaps are the over 100km of local **cross-country skiing** trails.

On the southeast corner of the church square there's a helpful **tourist office** (July & Aug 8.30am–12.30pm & 2.30–6.30pm; Sept–June 9am–noon & 4–6.30pm Ⓣ04.68.04.47.35, Ⓦwww.formigueres.net). Formiguères has two **hotels**: the one-star *Picheyre* behind the church (Ⓣ04.68.04.40.07, Ⓔhotel-picheyre@wanadoo.fr; ❸; closed April & Nov–Dec) and the less characterful *Auberge de la Tutte*, at the southeast outskirts (Ⓣ04.68.04.40.21, Ⓔlatutte@laposte.net; ❷). There's a 20-place *gîte d'étape* in an old barn, with a few doubles and meals offered, at **ESPOUSOUILLE** (Ⓣ04.68.04.45.37), a kilometre or two up through the trees by footpath – but 6km by road. The **restaurant** in the *Picheyre* has had a much-needed refit and boasts a new chef; *menus* start at €20.

If Formiguères doesn't suit, the *Auberge de la Belle Aude* (Ⓣ04.68.04.40.11, Ⓕ04.68.04.39.89; ❸) in **MATEMALE**, a deceptively large village tucked in a hollow by the Aude 4km south, has more comfortable accommodation and traditional Catalan *menus*, which include typical dishes such as *boules de picoulat*, starting at €18; they've even managed to squeeze in a tiny pool under a conservatory for rare *capcinoise* hot days, plus there's a sauna/hammam for the ski season.

Puyvalador and Rieutort

The ski station at **PUYVALADOR**, at the north end of the Capcir plateau, is 5km west of its namesake reservoir and village (which has no amenities). It's the smallest of the Cerdagne ski resorts, with just sixteen east- or north-facing runs between 2382m (the **Pic du Ginèvre**) and 1700m, with more here for beginners or weak intermediates than at Formiguères. The only tourist facilities at this end of the plateau, outside the ski station, are at **RIEUTORT**, 2km west of Puyvalador village. Here you can **stay** at *Gîte le Moulin* (Ⓣ04.68.30.97.37); some fifty paces above the square, *Al Cortal* (Ⓣ04.68.04.45.00; open supper only during ski season; lunch and dinner in summer; weekends only otherwise), offers pricey four-course *menus* from €25.

Hiking: the Tour du Capcir

The Capcir woodlands are eminently suitable hiking territory for novices. Randonnées Pyrénéennes issues maps and booklets describing the **Tour du Capcir**, a four-day circuit (easy to pick up at Espousouille, Puyvalador or Matemale) that runs along both sides of the valley as well as taking in **Pic Madrès** (2469m) to the east. You can make use of the *gîte d'étape* at Espousouille, the hotel at Matemale plus the staffed refuges at Bouillouses (see p.225) and Camporells, with one night either camping out or staying in the unstaffed *Refuge de Nohèdes*, a little to the southeast of Madrès summit. The *Refuge de Camporells* (2240m; Ⓣ06.82.12.99.22; 19 places; open mid-June to mid-Sept), by the cluster of eponymous lakes on the western leg of the *tour*, is wonderfully set in an area rich in wildlife, also partly accessible by the chair-lift that operates even in summer at Formiguères (45min walk from the top of the lift to the refuge).

The Tour du Capcir grazes the Tour du Carlit on the west and the Tour du Coronat on the east, making it possible to add portions of either of these to your itinerary.

The Tech valley and the Albères

The **Tech valley** (or Vallespir, El Tec in Catalan) is the southernmost in France, and its exceptional sunshine (300 days a year) and relatively low rainfall nurture subtropical flora lower down – as well as dense forest on the higher slopes. Proximity to the border made the Tech a major escape route from occupied France during World War II. The easiest mid-elevation pass into Spain, the Col d'Ares, was so heavily patrolled that *passeurs* had to use remoter routes along the main **Albères** ridge. Fugitives assembled at **Céret** or **Le Boulou** would be led out over one of two *cols*, either Lly or Llosa; from **Amélie-les-Bains** there was a tough ascent past the 1450-metre Roc de Frausa. From **Arles-sur-Tech**, further up the valley, the route led to **Saint-Laurent-de-Cerdans** and the Col des Massanes into Alto Garrotxa, or **Coustouges** and along the Riou Majou into Alt Empordà. From the tiny spa of **La Preste** and the walled town of **Prats-de-Molló**, escapees fled along the ancient paths of the *contrabandiers*, through the Col del Pal or the Collade de Prats.

The solitude of the **Albères** ridge from Saint-Laurent-de-Cerdans in the west to the Mediterranean at Banyuls-sur-Mer, which still appeals to casual walkers, is intruded on east of the Tech only at **Le Perthus**, little better than a border shopping mall and truck-stop. Besides the crossing at Le Perthus, the D115 road up the Tech valley slips into Spain at the **Col d'Ares**, a scenic and almost equally popular driving route. Between the Tech and the Mediterranean coast is a cluster of **rural Romanesque churches**, some frescoed and others with carved relief art, easily accessible to cyclists or drivers in relatively flat country. Much the most impressive Romanesque monument, however, is found at **Elne**, near the mouth of the Tech, early medieval capital of Roussillon.

Elne

Standing on a hill just 6km from the sea on the north bank of the Tech, astride the main train and bus lines between Perpignan and Argelès, the ancient fortified town of **ELNE** (Elna in Catalan) was once the capital of Roussillon. It was only eclipsed by Perpignan, 13km northwest, when the latter became the seat of the kings of Mallorca; Elne's decline accelerated in 1602 when the bishopric moved to Perpignan. It began life as the Gaulic Illibéris, and was then the Castrum Helenae of the Romans, seeing Hannibal camping here en route to Rome.

Elne's one great attraction, inside its remaining sixteenth-century ramparts, is the fortified, partly Romanesque **monastery of Sainte-Eulalie** (daily: April & May 9.30am–5.45pm; June–Sept 9.30am–6.45pm; Oct 9.30am–12.30pm & 2–5.45pm; Nov–March 9.30am–12.30pm & 2–4.45pm; €4). The ten massive free-standing piers of the ex-cathedral, which dates from 1069, lean slightly outward to bear the stress of the vault; the town was besieged by the French crown in 1285, and the entire population slaughtered in the church where they had taken refuge. But the **cloister**, fashioned in light Céret marble, is the clear highlight: its four colonnades ably demonstrate a gradual transition from Romanesque to

Gothic styles as you proceed clockwise from the south bay (twelfth century) to the east bay (fourteenth). The capitals are intricately carved with biblical and secular scenes (including the creation of Adam and Eve), plus mythical creatures such as dragons and mermaids. A museum, in the vaulted subterranean cisterns, covers regional archeology from Neolithic times to the Romans.

Practicalities

The **tourist office** is at 2 rue du Docteur-Bolte (June–Sept Mon–Fri 9.30am–noon & 2–5/6pm, Sat 9.30am–noon; Oct–May Mon–Fri 9.30am–noon & 2–5pm; ⓣ04.68.22.05.07, ⓦwww.ot-elne.fr). Of two **hotels**, the 2006-renovated *Cara Sol* (ⓣ04.68.22.10.42, ⓦwww.hotelcarasol.com; ❺), bd Illibéris 10 at the edge of the old town, offers air con, DVD players and plasma TV, with great views over the Tech valley and the Albères; their somewhat more reasonable, competent restaurant has seating on the ramparts outside. The other option is *Le Weekend*, 29 av Paul Reig (ⓣ04.68.22.06.68, ⓦwww.perso.libertysurf.fr/hotel.weekend; closed Christmas–New Year; ❷), just off the Argelès road, with a celebrated garden **restaurant** (*menus* from €16). Among a few *chambres d'hôtes*, try *Au Remp'arts*, 3 place Colonel-Roger just in from bd Illibéris (ⓣ04.68.22.31.95, ⓦwww.remparts.fr; ❹), also with an on-site restaurant and tea house.

Le Boulou and around

LE BOULOU (El Voló), a traffic-clogged little spa town situated just off the autoroute 20km south of Perpignan, is the **champagne-cork** capital of France. At the beginning of the 1900s vast groves of cork oaks were planted as a substitute for grapevines recently destroyed by phylloxera. The plantations shrank after World War II, eclipsed by less expensive Portuguese cork, but their extent is up again since the advent of regular wildfires, as cork oak is flame-resistant and thus more viable than combustible crops like olives.

In town, it's worth pausing at the **Église Sainte-Marie**, whose portal features a fine Romanesque tympanum frieze; more works by the same anonymous artist – "Le Maître de Cabestany" – can be found at the eleventh-to-fourteenth-century, fortified **Monastir del Camp Prieuré** with its Gothic cloister (guided tours only July–Aug daily except Thurs on the hour 10–11am & 3–6pm; Sept–June on the hour 10–11am 3–4pm, also 5pm June & Sept; €4), 11km north, between Passa and Villemolaque.

South of Le Boulou, just beyond the River Tech and the local spa, stands the remarkable ninth-century **chapel of Saint-Martin-de-Fenollar** (June 15–Sept 15 daily 10.30am–noon & 3.30–7pm; Sept 15–June 15 daily except Tues 2–5pm; €3). Its twelfth-century frescoes – including a rare image of the Virgin reclining in bed after the Nativity – rank as the best Romanesque wall paintings in Roussillon, and their clarity and simplicity may have influenced Picasso and Braque, who sometimes stayed in nearby Céret.

A stretch of the non-toll N9 follows the line of the Roman Via Domitia, and 4km south of Saint-Martin the route's antiquity is borne out by a pair of **ruined Roman forts** on the steep outcrops flanking the road. The nearby tenth-century **church of Saint-Nazaire** contains a fresco reminiscent of those at Saint-Martin, and possibly by the same painter (key available from the *mairie* in Les Cluses village).

Practicalities

Le Boulou's **tourist office** (Mon–Fri 9am–noon & 2–6pm, Sun 9am–noon; ⓣ04.68.87.50.95, ⓦwww.ot-leboulou.fr) is on the central place de la Mairie. Local **accommodation** might come in handy during high season: *Le Grillon d'Or* (ⓣ04.68.83.03.60, ⓦwww.grillon-dor.com; ❸) at 40 rue de la République, with a pool and restaurant, or elegantly rustic *Le Relais des Chartreuses* (Ⓣ04.68.83.15.88, Ⓔrelais.des.chartreuses@wanadoo.fr; closed mid-Nov to Jan; ❹), occupying an old Catalan *mas* at 106 av d'En Carbonner.

Le Perthus and the frontier zone

On February 5, 1939, a column of 20,000 Spanish Republicans arrived at the border post of **LE PERTHUS** (El Portús, Castilian; Els Límits, Catalan), 4km beyond Les Cluses, to seek sanctuary in France. The main shopping street is French on one side, Spanish on the other, and ranks of French consumer armies still descend to take advantage of the lower Spanish VAT rate for booze, tobacco, food and petrol. Nipping into Spain by car, a small toll for the *autoroute* will likely save you an hour's delay in nasty, bottle-necked Le Perthus. If you're on a GR10 traverse and need **accommodation**, your best choice is *Chez Grand-Mère* at the summit of the main road (Ⓣ04.68.83.60.96; closed Christmas–March; ❷).

The Roman Via Domitia crossed the Albères 800m southwest at the **Col de Panissars**, also probably the way Hannibal came in 218 BC. When Pompey returned victorious from Spain 150 years later, he ordered a triumphal monument to be built at the *col*; the excavated base of this remains visible. On a nearby French hill rises the **Fort de Bellegarde** (June–Sept daily 10.30am–6.30pm; €3). Constructed in the sixteenth century and later reinforced by Vauban, it contains changing art exhibits and the deepest (63m) well in Europe within mighty walls, giving superb views south into Spain and north across Roussillon. Both fort and monumental base are reached by a narrow dirt road doubling as a section of the GR10 (20min walk from Le Perthus).

The **GR10** and the **HRP**, here combined, pass through Le Perthus on their east–west route along the summits of the Albères. Banyuls-sur-Mer, on the Côte Vermeille (see p.127), lies nine hours east of Le Perthus along the GR10. There's just one facility en route: the *Chalet de l'Albère* (Ⓣ04.68.83.62.20), two and a half hours distant at the **Col de l'Ouillat**, a twenty-place *gîte d'étape* with **restaurant** aimed also at those arriving by car on the D71. Heading west on the GR10/HRP, the nearest amenities are at **LAS ILLAS**, about four hours away and the first spot to divide the twelve-hour stage to Arles-sur-Tech. Choose between the well-run *gîte d'étape* (Ⓣ04.68.83.23.93; April–Sept; 19 places; no meals), or the *Hostal des Trabucayres* (Ⓣ04.68.83.07.56; ❹) just up the road, with a decent **restaurant** open to all.

Other Albères Romanesque monuments

Aside from the churches around Le Boulou, the **Albères** are well sown with other **Romanesque churches and monasteries**, which can be visited by bicycle, scooter or car in a single day – a stimulating break from the beach-side hedonism of the Mediterranean coast. Buses serve the D618 between Le Boulou and Argelès only sporadically; non-suicidal cyclists can avoid much of this busy road by using older, quieter, parallel routes.

Just over 6km northeast of Le Boulou, a side road leads south to Vilalonga (Villelonge)-dels-Monts. From here a steep and winding road, intermittently signposted for the "Prieuré", leads 2.5km up to the former Augustinian priory of **Santa Maria del Vilar**, in a lovely bucolic setting alive with the sound of birds and running water. This is an ancient site, with a nearly intact **Roman nympheum** which contained a fish oracle behind the existing church, founded in 1083, though the refectory and entry portal are Carolingian. Disestablished long before the Revolution (in 1525), Santa Maria served as a farm until 1942 and was then abandoned to dereliction until being restored by a private foundation in 1993–94. Today a young, educated Romanian resident monk offers an exhaustive one-hour tour (daily 2.30–6pm;

€4), the only permitted access. The church's main attraction, besides column capitals by the portal carved as bats, are gorgeous apsidal **frescoes** with human, animal and geometric motifs; given superb acoustics, it's also the venue for a well-reputed *Festival Lyrique*, featuring Gregorian chant and troubadour songs (July & Aug each Sat 9pm; €16; reserve on ⓣ04.68.89.68.35 or 04.68.89.64.61).

From Vilalonga bear east on the D11 to Laroque-des-Albères, and then descend 3km to **SAINT-GÉNIS-DES-FONTAINES**, its centre dominated by the eponymous Benedictine **monastic abbey-church**. The two-metre lintel over the church doorway is the earliest (1019–20) known Romanesque relief in France – an engagingly primitive Ascension, with Christ in a mandorla, attended by angels and watched by six apostles. Inside (June 16–Sept Mon–Fri 10am–noon & 3–7pm, Sat & Sun 9am–noon & 3–7pm; Oct–June 15 daily 9.30am–noon & 2–5/6pm; €2), the church is crammed full of Baroque polychrome images, but the highlight is the thirteenth-century **cloister**, meticulously restored in 1987–94 after the colonnade had been dismantled and sold in 1924. All but a few of the original elements have been recovered, and column capitals in varicoloured marble feature mermaids, local fauna and vignettes of medieval life.

Some 4.5km further east on the D618, you'll reach **SAINT-ANDRÉ**, where the eleventh- to twelfth-century **abbey-church of Sant Andreu** has another fine lintel over the west portal, with Christ in Glory flanked by angels and apostles. The nearby **Musée Transfrontalier d'Art Roman** (June 15–Sept 15 Tues–Sun 10am–noon & 2.30–7pm; Sept 16–Nov 15 & March 16–June 14 Tues–Sat 10am–noon & 3–6pm; €2) tries gamely to make sense of Catalan Romanesque, but with its French-only labelled dioramas and strictly reproduction art it isn't really worth the admission.

Céret

The cherry orchards of **CÉRET**, 8km upstream from Le Boulou, are the basis of its prosperity, yielding around 4000 tonnes of fruit in early summer. Like Prades on the Têt, Céret was a sanctuary for Catalan refugees from Franco's regime, and one of the first Roussillonais towns to adopt bilingual street nomenclature. It's a friendly, bustling place with a wonderfully shady old quarter overhung by huge plane trees; narrow, winding streets open onto small squares like **plaça dels Nou Raigs** (Nine Spouts), named after its central fountain. The best time to visit is during one of the town's mid-July taurine festivals – both *corridas* and Pamplona-style bull-running – but you'll have to book accommodation well in advance; other popular events include a notable Easter Sunday procession, and an August *sardana* competition. The year-round Saturday **market** spills out of place Pablo-Picasso into the main avenue d'Espagne, where two remnants of the medieval walls, the **Porte de France** and **Porte d'Espagne**, are obvious, though many houses are incorporated into the fortification walls themselves.

According to legend the multi-arched **Pont du Diable**, spanning the Tech north of Céret, was built with diabolic assistance in 1321 in return for the soul of the first *Céretian* to cross. The engineer who made the bargain duly sent a cat over first, but the trick backfired as no local would then risk Satan's vengeance by using the bridge themselves. Other minor attractions include a small **archeological museum** (July–Aug daily 10am–noon & 1–6pm, Sept–Jun Mon–Fri 10am–noon & 2–5pm; €2.50) on place Pablo-Picasso, the **war memorial** by Aristide Maillol in the old town and the **monument** to the composer Déodat de Sévérac by the Catalan sculptor Manolo near the tourist office.

Musée d'Art Moderne

Céret's indisputably prime sight, however, is the remarkable **Musée d'Art Moderne** (July to mid-Sept daily: 10am–7pm; rest of year daily except Tues 10am–6pm; ⓦwww.musee-ceret.com; €5.50), just off bd Maréchal-Joffre. Long before the Spanish Civil War – from 1910 to about 1935, with peak arrivals during 1913–19 – the town served as a temporary residence for avant-garde artists such as Pablo Picasso, Henri Matisse, Marc Chagall, Raoul Dufy, Joan Miró, the sculptor Manolo and lesser-known Catalan, Russian-Jewish and French artists, including Pierre Brune, who in 1950 founded the museum.

The varied exhibits – with many items specifically donated by artists – do ample justice to the Fauvists, Cubists and Surrealists. Even since a much-needed gallery expansion, space is dwarfed by the stored collection, but highlights on display are likely to include Chagall gouaches (eg *Les Gens du Voyage*), portrait sketches and statuettes by Manolo (eg *La Llobera*), Pignon's portrait of Pablo Neruda and Miró's ink and crayon work. Most famous (and a permanent fixture) is Picasso's marvellous series of ceramic bowls illustrating bullfighting scenes, executed over just five days in April 1953. The top floor hosts excellent temporary exhibits of even more contemporary art, such as works by Antoní Tapiès.

Practicalities

Buses from Perpignan stop 250m north of the old quarter at the bottom of avenue Clemenceau. The **tourist office** (July & Aug Mon–Sat 9.30am–12.30pm & 2–7pm; Sept–May Mon–Fri 9am–noon & 2–5pm, Sat 9.30am–12.30pm; ⓣ04.68.87.00.53, ⓦwww.ceret.fr) is at the top of avenue Clemenceau, corner boulevard Maréchal-Joffre. Among several central **hotels**, much the best is friendly *Hôtel Vidal* at 4 place Soutine (ⓣ04.68.87.00.85, ⓦwww.hotelvidalceret.com; closed Nov; ❷), a tastefully converted episcopal palace with variable-sized but salubrious en-suite rooms. Opposite stands the modern *Des Arcades* (ⓣ04.68.87.12.30, ⓦwww.hotel-arcades-ceret.com; all year; ❸), with parking, and you might also try the *Pyrénées* at 7 rue de la République (ⓣ04.68.87.11.02, ⓔericlegentil@wanadoo.fr; March–Dec; ❷).

Full-service **restaurant** options aren't abundant but include the *Vidal*'s very own *El Bisbe* (closed Tues & Wed low season), with gourmet if *minceur menus* at €28; on closure days, their *tapas* bar (*El Tall*) operates at street level. Otherwise, try *Pizzeria Quattrocento* on Plaça dels Nou Reigs, or *Le P'tit Grill* at 47 rue St-Ferréol down from the museum, exactly as described, economical and thus hugely popular, lively and smoky (closed Sun noon; reserve on ⓣ06.13.56.73.35).

Arles-sur-Tech

ARLES-SUR-TECH, 12km further along the valley, is arrayed around the **Abbaye de Sainte-Marie** (Sept–June Mon–Sat 9am–noon & 2–6pm; July–Aug 9am–7pm; also Sun April–Oct 2–5pm; €3.50), whose Carolingian origins are thought to account for its unusual back-to-front alignment of altar at the west end and entrance at the east. Entry is now via the thirteenth-century cloister, pleasant enough though it can hardly compare in merit to Elne's or St-Michel-de-Cuixà's; its late vintage explains its Gothic tendencies, though not the complete absence of decorated column capitals. The unique and compelling feature of the massive church interior (consecrated 1046) is a band of still-vividly coloured twelfth-century **fresco** high up in the apse of the eastern antichapel dedicated to St Michael, appropriately featuring the archangel. Outside, next to the east façade – surmounted by an impressive Romanesque **relief** of Christ and the Tetramorphs – stands a very ancient (fourth- or fifth-century) sarcophagus. This is **La Sainte-Tomb**, formerly a reliquary for the bones of Abdon and Senen, two obscure early martyrs, and now focus of a phenomenon that has resisted scientific explanation. Since the saintly bones were removed, this sacrophagus has produced over 500 litres of very pure water annually, drawn off and distributed to the faithful after Mass on July 30.

Arles is most famous, however, for its **Fête de l'Ours** (2 weeks before Carnival), a pagan holdover claimed to be among the oldest observances in Europe. Traditionally, bears were said to interrupt their hibernation at the February new moon, terrorizing the villagers, who devised the ploy of luring the boldest animal with a local girl as bait, before chaining the bear down and then shaving it. There being a contemporary shortage of bears, these days a young man is dressed in a bear skin and blackface, hunted down by the crowds, captured and stripped, after which a communal meal is served.

Practicalities

The **tourist office** (Mon–Sat 9am–noon & 2–6pm, Sun 2–6pm; ⓣ04.68.39.11.99, ⓦwww.villes-arles-sur-tech.fr) also serves as the abbey ticket office. **Accommodation** is limited to the *Hôtel les Glycines* on rue du Jeu-de-Paume (ⓣ04.68.39.10.09, ⓔhotelglycines@wanadoo.fr; closed Nov 15–Feb; ❸), with a terrace **restaurant** (from €18), the best of three in town; and *chambres d'hôtes La Couvent Sana* (ⓣ04.68.83.92.90; ❸), on the edge of town. There's also a **campsite**, *Riuferrer* (ⓣ04.68.39.11.06), on the west side of town, of most interest to those on a GR10 traverse.

The Gorges de la Fou

Just west of Arles, on the Prats-de-Molló road, is the entrance to the **Gorges de la Fou** (April–Nov daily 10am–6pm, weather permitting – phone ⓣ04.68.39.16.21 if in doubt; €5), one of the great – if touristy, with car park and snack stalls outside – spectacles of the Eastern Pyrenees. You need at least an hour to cover the 1500m of metal walkway to the end and back, squeezing between 250-metre-high walls, so close together that they have trapped falling rocks. In places, water erosion has made the walls as smooth as plaster, and on occasion the storm-swollen torrent has swept part of the walk away. If you can't make it to the Gorges de Kakouetta in the French Basque country (see p.469), these are a respectable consolation prize.

Walking out of Arles: to the Albères or Canigou

The GR10 climbs **southeast** from town through the Arles forest some five and a half hours to the summit ridge of the Albères, just below Roc de Frausa (1450m). The only facility en route, and a better overnight choice for trekkers than anything in Arles, is about two hours along: cosy *gîte d'étape Moulin de la Palette* (ⓣ04.68.39.12.01; 20 places), part of a honey-producing farm. The next facility beyond this point is the *gîte* at Las Illas (see p.118), five hours' trek away – an hour less if you use a non-GR trail which avoids the drop to and climb out of Montalba d'Amélie hamlet.

Heading **northwest**, you could do the **Arles-to-Cortalets** leg in a single day with an early enough start, but it's an arduous trek of over nine hours, beyond the capabilities of most walkers. From Arles, it's wisest to forego the first, unsightly section of the GR10 in favour of the blue-dot-marked "Dolmen 1hr 30min" path, which leaves the road towards the campsite, just above the town swimming pool. You can break the trek four hours along at the *Auberge de Batère* (ⓣ04.68.39.12.01; April–Oct; all year; 32 places, dorms and 5 doubles at €30) installed in the old miners' hostel at **BATÈRE**, which has an excellent bistro. The ironworks are evident as an ugly scar resulting from open-cast extraction between the twelfth and seventeenth centuries. If you're in a group, you can save yourself some rather tedious trekking by taking a **taxi** up to this *gîte*, along the paved D43 side road, which begins from the west end of Arles.

Alpine Canigou truly begins just west of the *gîte* at the **Col de le Cirère** (1731m), beyond which unfurls the section of corniche trail that is dubbed the **Balcon du**

Canigou for its sweeping views. Two hours beyond Batère, the forestry hut at Estanyol (potable spring) fits eight at a pinch, or you can camp adjacent; the *Chalet des Cortalets* (p.105) is still almost three hours away along the GR10.

Minor upper Tech villages

Accessible along the D54 from the main valley floor, **MONTFERRER**, 6km from Arles, is – with its ruined castle and Romanesque church – one of the most attractive settlements in the upper Tech. Set amongst dense forest and crags, with sweeping views east to the opposite side of the valley, it's the truffle capital of Roussillon; the village can also muster a good campsite with a swimming pool.

Some 6km beyond Arles-sur-Tech, the D3 side-road ascends south from the main D115 through chestnut forests to the village of **SAINT-LAURENT-DE-CERDANS** (Sant Llorens de Cerdans; 9km from the junction). During World War II the local clergy oversaw the passage of refugees southwest towards Mont Nègre, crossing the frontier by the Col des Massanes (1126m) or up to Coustouges for the Riou Majou trail. Nowadays, marked variants of the HRP trace the border.

Passeurs normally asked their clients to wear espadrilles – quieter than ordinary shoes and providing good traction on rock; Saint-Laurent was once a major producer of *bigatanes*, the special Catalan rope-soled espadrille. You learn how espadrilles were made from esparto grass in the **Musée d'Arts et Traditions Populaires** (May, June & Sept daily 10am–noon & 3–6pm, July & Aug 10am–noon & 2–7pm; Oct–April Mon–Fri 10am–noon & 3–6pm; €2.50). In Saint-Laurent there's just a seasonal **restaurant** and a **campsite** beside the Laurent stream. The nearest **hotel** is the very comfortable *Domaine de Falgos*, a three-star resort complete with eighteen-hole golf course and small thermal spa, off the road to Coustouges (Ⓣ04.68.39.51.42; closed Jan–Feb; ❼ but substantial Internet discounts findable).

From Saint-Laurent, the road climbs 5km further east to **COUSTOUGES** (Costojas), from where the spine of the Albères rises northeast to the highest point of the chain at **Roc de Frausa** (1450m). The twelfth-century church, built in pink sandstone and granite, sports a richly carved portal and landmark belfry visible from afar if you're approaching from the Spanish side; an excellent road, not shown on many maps, continues over the frontier saddle just below Roc de Bau towards Maçanet de Cabrenys (see p.147).

You can vary the road-return to the Tech valley by detouring along the D64 to **SERRALONGUE** (Serralonga), which offers a fine eleventh-century **church** with an elevated pavillion used by priests of old to ward off destructive storms (another such structure is found at Son; see p.260). The D44 from the Tech valley floor continues up to delightfully secluded **LAMANÈRE** (La Manera), the most southerly village in France, also reached by path west from Coustouges. The closest facility to Lamanère is a 45-place *gîte d'étape* an hour's walk west, at the fifteenth-century Ermitage de Nôtre-Dame-du-Coral (Ⓣ04.68.39.75.00).

Prats-de-Molló

From Arles, the D115 climbs 19km to the medieval town of **PRATS-DE-MOLLÓ**, end of the bus line. The present road follows the path of a former railway (the old station houses can be seen en route); the old road was washed away by disastrous floods during October 1940. After the 1659 Treaty of the Pyrenees subjected this area to Louis XIV's onerous taxation, Prats-de-Molló and a number of other Tech communities revolted. Living at the far end of what was then a densely wooded valley, the rebels probably thought they could get away with murdering the king's tax collectors. Indeed, they held off two battalions before the forces of Maréchal de Noailles made a surprise attack over the western flanks of Canigou to put down the insurrection. **Fort Lagarde** (April–June & Sept–Oct Tues–Sun 2–5.30pm; July & Aug daily 11am–1pm & 5–7pm; €3.50), which dominates the town, was built in 1680 under Vauban, as much to subdue the local population as to keep the Spanish out; the walls of the old town, raised on fourteenth-century foundations, are another Vauban project. Easiest access is from the footpath starting from behind the old church; the fort itself has been beautifully restored, with great views from the ramparts. An extra seasonal attraction is the **Animation Historique** (daily mid-July to mid-Aug 1–5pm; €7), when horsemen dressed as cavaliers re-create eighteenth-century cavalry exercises, with stunt riding, sword-fights and the firing of period weaponry.

Sandwiched between Canigou and the young Tech, Prats is the last French town before the Spanish frontier, but has none of the usual malaise of border towns and is much the most attractive place in the valley since Céret. Hub of the newer quarter is **El Firal**, the huge square in use for markets since 1308; the walled and gated **ville haute** just south makes for a great wander, with steep cobbled streets and a weathered grey church with marvellous ironwork on the door under the porch.

Practicalities

The well-stocked **tourist office** in place du Firal (Jan–March, Nov & Dec Mon–Fri 9am–noon & 2–6pm; April, May, Sept & Oct Mon–Sat 9am–noon & 2–6pm; July & Aug daily 9am–12.30pm & 1.30–6.30pm; Ⓣ04.68.39.70.83, Ⓦwww.pratsdemollolapreste.com). There's plenty of quality **accommodation**, which makes Prats a good base or transit stopover; in the walled quarter, go for *Hostellerie Le Relais* at 3 place Josep de la Trinxeria (Ⓣ04.68.39.71.30, Ⓦwwwhostellerie-le-relais.com; ❷–❸), with cheerful pastel-hued rooms and a south-facing garden restaurant. Just outside, overlooking El Firal, is *Hôtel Le Bellevue* (Ⓣ04.68.39.72.48, Ⓦwww.lebellevue.fr.st; closed Dec to mid-Feb; ❸), with more old-fashioned rooms but a creditable restaurant (menu from €19). The (relatively) budget option, at 6 place du Foiral, is *Le Costabonne* (Ⓣ04.68.39.70.24, Ⓦwww.lecostabonne.free.fr; all year; ❷), though the restaurant, while popular, can't compare to its neighbours. Alternatively, pamper yourself with affordable luxury 8km west at **La Preste spa** and its associated *Grand Hôtel Thermal* (Ⓣ04.68.87.55.00, Ⓦwww.sante-eau.com; April to early Nov; ❸). Local **campsites** with the longest seasons are *St Martin* (Ⓣ04.68.39.77.40; closed Dec) and *Can Nadal* (Ⓣ04.68.39.77.89; April–Nov), 1km along the road towards La Preste.

Onward routes above Arles-sur-Tech

From Prats, the road climbs 14km to the **Spanish border** at **Col d'Ares**, dropping on the other side to Camprodon (see p.173). Roughly halfway to the border, just beyond the Col de la Seille on the left, you'll find the *Ferme-Auberge La Costa de Dalt* (Ⓣ04.68.39.74.40), a working farm with spotless two-bedroom cottages (by the week only) and excellent restaurant (summer open Wed–Sun, winter weekends only), near the terminus of the path and track coming west from Lamanère.

The easiest of the former escape trails is the one west to the **Collade de Prats** (1596m) from the south bank of the Tech, just south of Arles. The route passes the ruined **Tour de Mir**, one of the signal towers built by Jaume of Mallorca in the late thirteenth century, like the Tour Madeloc above the Côte Vermeille (see p.127); allow two and a half hours to the pass and the HRP.

Prats-de-Molló can also be used as a base for ascending Canigou from the south. Take the road to **La Preste** (1130m), then the track up north to the Collade des Roques Blanches and the Pla Guillem area (see p.109 for these, and onward directions to the peak). The only facility, about halfway along, is the *Chalet de Conques* (1600m; Ⓣ04.68.39.23.49; all year; 12 places in quads), with meals offered.

The Mediterranean coast

The Pyrenees meet the Mediterranean with magnificent abruptness. Approaching from the north, the flat strands of the Côte Radieuse end at Argelès-Plage, succeeded by the rocky coves and low foothills of the **Côte Vermeille**. This vivid clash of land and water has long attracted artists, especially the group of early twentieth-century French painters known as the **Fauves** (Wild Beasts) for their ebullient use of colour and form, and who spent their summers at **Collioure**, immediately southeast of Argelès.

Continuing along the coast, the N114 traces a tortuous course as a corniche road to the easternmost point of the French Pyrenees, **Cap Cerbère**. Here the sea floor drops precipitously to a depth of 40m, a habitat protected since 1974 by the *réserve marine* between **Banyuls-sur-Mer** and **Cerbère**. Once the most elegant resort of the Côte Vermeille, Banyuls was the home of sculptor Aristide Maillol (see box on p.128); it also marks one end of the **GR10** and the **HRP** trails, which both cross to the Atlantic coast, 400km away.

Beyond the border at **Portbou**, the orderly vineyards of France give way to more dishevelled ones behind the Spanish **Costa Brava**, ravaged during the nineteenth century by phylloxera. The **Serra de l'Albera** – as the Albères are called on this

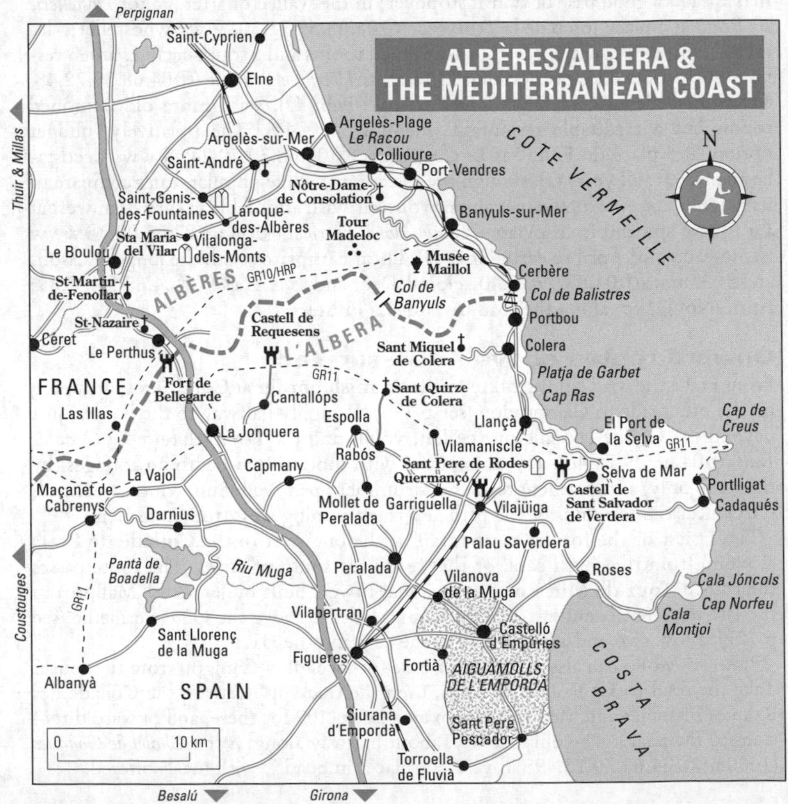

side – is once again a major wine producer, and at harbours like **Llança** and **El Port de la Selva**, fishing is still important and the coastline remains relatively unknown to non-Catalans. The major – if grossly overrated – local sight is the pre-Romanesque monastery of **Sant Pere de Rodes**, in the hills above El Port de la Selva.

At **Cap de Creus** the Spanish Pyrenees reach the sea, as does Spain's trans-Pyrenean footpath, the **GR11**. The rugged landscape continues around the cape to **Cadaqués** and **Portlligat**, both pregnant with the memory of Surrealist artist Salvador Dalí, who lived here for decades. Beyond atmospheric **Castelló d'Empuriés** and the **Aiguamolls de l'Empordà** sanctuary, you're back to broad sandy beaches and mass-market resorts; just inland, the county town of **Figueres** is most remarkable for its Teatre-Museu Dalí.

Public transport is generally adequate, with frequent buses and trains between Perpignan and every resort of the Côte Vermeille. On the Spanish side trains and buses are nearly as good as long as you stick to the main N260 between Figueres and the frontier and the C260 linking Figueres to Cadaqués, but connections into the Serra de l'Albera can be problematic.

The Côte Vermeille

When the Fauves discovered the **Côte Vermeille**, which extends southeast from Collioure to the Spanish border, they took natural inspiration for their revolutionary use of colour: the sunsets (from which the coast earned its name) are a gentle red, the sea is turquoise and, as Matisse wrote, "no sky is more blue than that at Collioure". The beauty of this stretch of coastline has inevitably been exploited, but in the hills behind you'll often be on your own.

Collioure

About 13km east of Elne, **COLLIOURE** (Cotlliure) to a certain extent still banks on its maritime and artistic past. Established as a trading port by the Phoenicians and ancient Greeks, Collioure was later occupied by the Romans, Visigoths and Arabs. Since then, the place has been the focus of a dozen territorial disputes, including four invasions by the French and two by the Spanish. The thirteenth-century **Fort Sainte-Elme** (privately owned), overlooking the town from the south, and the seventeenth-century **Fort Miradou** immediately above to the northwest (still a military zone), are reminders of this turbulent past.

Starting in 1905, invaders of a different sort appeared: the painters – including Henri Matisse and André Derain – known as **Les Fauves** made Collioure their summer residence. You can follow Collioure's *Chemin du Fauvisme*, a trail of twenty reproductions of their paintings placed on the sites where they were painted (map available from the tourist office). The local artistic tradition survives today, albeit with less distinction: the forest of easels that occupies the promenade all summer produces tame souvenirs, and the small permanent collection at Collioure's **Musée d'Art Moderne** (daily 10am–noon & 2–6pm; closed Tues Sept–June; €2) at the eastern edge of town is decidedly disappointing. On a different note, the historical novelist Patrick O'Brian, whose *Master and Commander* was lavishly filmed in 2003, lived as a recluse just outside the town from 1949 almost until his death in 2000.

The town and its beaches

Colliloure's old quarter, the **Mouré**, forms a warren of steep, narrow streets lined by pastel-tinted houses and assorted shops, galleries and cafés. A bare handful of

△ Collioure

lateen-rigged fishing boats – all that remains of the traditional fleet in use until the 1960s – might be moored in the **old harbour** bounding the Mouré, mostly restored as pleasure vessels by their new owners. The working fleet – distinguished by bow-lamps – brings in the famous local catch of *boquerons* (salt-cured anchovies, an important component in local cookery) and sardines (grilled fresh). The south side of the harbour is dominated by the imposing **Château-Royal** (daily: June–Sept 10am–6/7pm; Oct–May 9am–5pm; €4), founded by the Templars in the twelfth century, rebuilt for use as a part-time residence by the kings of Mallorca and Aragón two hundred years later, and modernized by Vauban after 1659. However impressive from afar, the castle scarcely merits a visit except to attend a concert in the courtyard; inside, bare rooms have a few mediocre, unlabelled exhibitions.

More worthwhile are the two palm-lined, sand-and-pebble **beaches** which bracket the castle to either side: **Plage de Port d'Avall** on the east, and **Plage Boramar** across the harbour mouth. Just north of Plage Boramar, the seventeenth-century **Église Nôtre-Dame-des-Anges** was a replacement for the ancient Sainte-Marie, razed on the orders of Vauban. The distinctive round belfry – once the lighthouse – onto which it was grafted has been damaged many times by storm and war, and is thus a pastiche of the thirteenth (base) to nineteenth (top) centuries. The church interior (daily 9am–noon & 2–6pm) houses a magnificent gilt three-level retable by seventeenth-century Catalan sculptor Josep Sunyer. Beyond the church, tiny **Chapelle-Saint-Vincent** overlooks the sea on a rocky peninsula which was once an islet; the spit joining it to the mainland shelters south-facing **Plage Saint Vincent** and naturist **Plage Nord** on the other side, from where a concrete walkway leads west 1500m to **Le Racou** bay.

Practicalities

Collioure's **train station** is under ten minutes' walk west of the centre, along avenue Aristide-Maillol; **buses** stop at the central car park, between avenue Général-de-Gaulle and the Château Royal. On-street **parking** is a nightmare even off-season; you'll probably end up using the fee car park by the bus stop. The **tourist office** is north of the harbour in place du 18 Juin (July & Aug daily 9am–8pm; Sept–June Tues–Sat 9am–noon & 2–6.30pm; ⓣ04.68.82.15.47, ⓦwww.collioure.net).

The most central place to **stay**, in the Mouré, is atmospheric *Hostellerie des Templiers* (Ⓣ04.68.98.31.10, Ⓦwww.hotel-templiers.com; closed Jan; ❸ annexes, ❹ main building) at 12 av Camille-Pelletan, which houses any overflow in various, less attractive annexes. The common areas and individually decorated rooms of the main building were once crammed with original Fauvist art, but security considerations now mean that many items are careful reproductions. Just up the paved creek which forms the head of the harbour is Collioure's plushest option, courtyarded *Casa Païral* in impasse des Palmiers (Ⓣ04.68.82.05.81, Ⓦwww.hotel-casa-pairal.com; closed Nov–March; ❼), a garden-set converted mansion with pool. With a car and/or desire for a sea view, opt instead for *Hôtel Triton* at the east end of Port d'Avall (Ⓣ04.68.98.39.39, Ⓔhoteltriton@wanadoo.fr; all year; ❷) or the remoter *Hôtel Caranques* (Ⓣ04.68.82.06.68, Ⓔles-caranques@little-france.com; closed Nov–March; ❷) at the east side of the bay on route de Port-Vendres, somewhat overpriced but very friendly and with direct access to a lido from the terraced gardens. The best **campsite** is seaside, caravan-free *La Girelle* (Ⓣ04.68.81.25.56; April–Sept), at Plage d'Ouille, west of town on the coastal path to Le Racou.

In the Mouré, rue Camille-Pelletan and its perpendicular lanes have various outwardly tempting **cafés** and **restaurants** – for example the ground-floor café of *Hostellerie des Templiers*, filled with (mostly reproduction) drawings and paintings donated by avant-garde painters in exchange for bed and board. But, except at *Crêperie Bretonne* at 8 rue Camille-Pelletan, you'll fork out well over the odds for listless grub; get what you pay for at *Amphytrion* on Port d'Avall, crowded even off-season for the sake of good-sized seafood-based *menus* from €20.

Walks south from Collioure

For an easy walk out of Collioure, take rue de la République from the harbour, cross the main road and follow signs for the old **Ermitage Notre-Dame-de-Consolation**, reached by lane and track within ninety minutes and much loved locally for its barbecue and *boules* area. To fill a half-day's hiking, continue, mostly on path, to **Tour Madeloc** on the crest of a ridge (360m), descending to Banyuls-sur-Mer (4hr 30min from Collioure), the final distance on the GR10 and HRP footpaths. The tower, also accessible by paved road from Banyuls, was built by Jaume II of Mallorca at the end of the thirteenth century as one of a chain of such signal stations.

Port-Vendres

PORT-VENDRES, 3km east of Collioure along the minor D914 (the main highway bypasses it), is by contrast a functional place, with no special sights. But for a genuine **fishing port** with nets and other paraphernalia piled along the harbour wall, this is your best (indeed only) choice on the Côte Vermeille. You won't want to stay longer than it takes to tuck into a seafood meal at one of the quayside **restaurants**, before or after watching the fish auctions held at the far end of the quay when the sardine and tuna trawlers arrive with their catch (Mon–Fri 4.30–6pm).

This was the Roman *Portus Veneris* (Port of Venus); its medieval significance diminished as neighbouring Collioure's increased, but by the eighteenth century it began to revive through the business of shipping Roussillon wines. In 1830 Port-Vendres became the primary port for dispatching soldiers and supplies to the French North African colonies, a link that lasted for more than a century.

Banyuls-sur-Mer to the frontier

As the highway crosses the Col du Père Carnère and drops towards the Plage des Elmes, the once-elegant wine town of **BANYULS-SUR-MER** (Banyuls de la

Aristide Maillol (1861–1944) and his museum

Sculptor **Aristide Maillol**, the Banyuls boy made good, started out as a painter and tapestry designer; recognition came only in his forties, after he had devoted himself to sculpture and returned to Banyuls-sur-Mer from Marly-Roi, outside Paris.

In 1904 Parisian admirers introduced him to **Count Harry Kessler**, who became Maillol's patron and confidant over the next three decades. The two could hardly have been more different: Kessler, son of a wealthy Prussian industrialist, dubbed the "Red Count" for his political leanings, his repressed homosexuality sublimated into art collecting and generous sponsorship; Maillol, an incorrigible Catalan peasant, never picking up the tab for anything, apolitical at best, accused of pro-Falange or pro-Nazi sympathies on occasion. Yet the collaboration between them endured almost until 1937, when Kessler, exiled from Germany since 1933, died impoverished in Paris.

Maillol initially had no taste for the **male nude**, and found it difficult to find obliging local models; Kessler, with his contacts among athletes, dancers and labourers, solved the problem. Kessler saw Maillol's work as classicism in embryo, and accordingly in 1922 took Maillol on a surprisingly productive trip to Greece. There was not a great distance between Maillol's vision and the ancient masterpieces, nor between Kessler's tastes and the Greek youths.

In the best tradition of bohemian artisits, Maillol's long, unhappy marriage to the suitably jealous Clotilde was punctuated by dalliances with female models in his old age. But it was his next and last model-mistress, **Dina Vierny**, who definitively eclipsed Clotilde. Maillol met Vierny in 1935, and by 1938, aged just 19, she was living next door to him in Banyuls, and spending most days with the sculptor up in the hills at his retreat. After the Nazi occupation of northern France, Vierny – of Russian-Jewish background, and a Communist sympathizer – joined the Comité de Secours Américain pour Intellectuels Antifascistes, and helped smuggle a number of Jews, dissidents and other anti-Nazis over the border. Apparently Maillol, whatever his political views, taught her the best route into Spain.

When the Vichy regime learned of this, Vierny was confined to house arrest in Banyuls, and then detained by the Gestapo when she escaped to Paris in early 1943. Maillol appealed to his old acquaintance **Arno Breker**, the official Third Reich sculptor then resident in Paris, to secure her release. A little flattery of Breker and the Nazi elite's reciprocal admiration of Maillol – thus the accusations of collaboration – did the trick. Vierny was saved from deportation to a concentration camp in October 1943, and warned to stay out of trouble, but after a brief period at Banyuls, she returned to Paris and never saw Maillol again. In September 1944 Maillol died in a car crash – having made Vierny, and his son Lucien by Clotilde, joint heirs and executors.

Upon Clotilde's death in 1952, Lucien made Vierny sole executor, and between 1964 and 1996 she honoured Maillol's memory by founding three **museums** dedicated to his work: two in Paris and one at Maillol's farmhouse retreat (for directions see "West of Banyuls"), La Métairie, where he is buried in a tomb topped by his **La Pensée**. The **Musée Maillol** (daily: May–Sept 10am–noon & 4–7pm; Oct–April 10am–noon & 2–5pm; Ⓦwww.museemaillol.com; €3.50), installed in the rooms where he lived and worked, displays nearly forty bronze and clay statues, large and small, along with his paintings, lithographs and photos of work elsewhere; curiously, there are only a handful of Vierny poses. In his recreated cellar-kitchen (despite his penny-pinching, Maillol was a good host and fine cook), some of his early tapestries can be seen. Back in Banyuls itself, there's only a sculpture behind the **mairie**, visible through the back gate. Maillol's birthplace is at 6 rue du Puig del Mas.

Merenda), 7km from Port-Vendres, comes into view, with dry-stone walls and neat terraces of vines stretching inland. Besides being the Mediterranean terminus of the GR10, Banyuls is famous for its eponymous dessert wine, which the French tend to drink as an aperitif (but the Spanish Catalans after meals). One of the largest vinters, the **Cellier des Templiers** on route du Mas-Reig, can be visited (April to early Nov daily 10am–7.30pm; early Nov to March Mon–Sat 10am–1pm & 2.30–6.30pm; group tours €2 each).

Less fashionable than Collioure, Banyuls remains a popular seaside resort, albeit marred by the busy seafront road. The stony main beach is less attractive than some smaller bays to the north and south, but the whole town – especially the promenade cafés and restaurants – comes alive in the evenings.

Besides the local Maillol museum (see opposite), the main sight is the **Laboratoire Arago**, the large white building overlooking the port, part of the Sorbonne's marine biology faculty. Its **aquarium** (daily: July & Aug 9am–1pm & 2–9pm; Sept–June 9am–noon & 2–6.30pm; €4) tanks contain a comprehensive collection of the region's fish and invertebrate submarine life. The nearby coastal waters of this area, rich in marine life due to the steep drop-off, were the first *réserve marine* declared in the Mediterranean. They can be explored with local **scuba outfitters**, for example CMAS-affiliated Aqua Blue Plongée at the port (ⓣ04.68.88.17.35, ⓕ04.68.88.05.93; all year).

Practicalities

The **train station** lies at the western edge of town, while **buses** stop on the coastal boulevard. The **tourist office** stands diagonally opposite the *mairie* on the seafront (July & Aug daily 9.30am–12.30pm & 2.30–7pm; Sept–June Mon–Sat 9am–noon & 2–7pm; ⓣ04.68.88.31.58, ⓦwww.banyuls-sur-mer.com). Of the less expensive **hotels**, best is *Le Manoir*, 20 rue de Maréchal-Joffre (ⓣ04.68.88.32.98; closed Nov–March; ❷); with a bit more to spend, try *Al-Fanal* (ⓣ04.68.88.00.81, ⓦwww.al-fanal.com; all year; ❸) overlooking the yacht port. A remoter option is comfortable, well-appointed *Les Elmes* (ⓣ04.68.88.03.12, ⓦwww.hotel-des-elmes.com; closed mid-Nov to Dec; ❸), north of town at the eponymous beach. **Camping** is 1km south of town at *Camping Municipal La Pinède* on route du Mas-Reig (ⓣ04.68.88.32.13; March–Nov).

Banyuls has a range of seafood **restaurants**, the priciest – with real table nappery and live lobster tanks – lining the seafront. One of the more affordable is *Les Canadells*, just off this boulevard at 4 av du Général-de-Gaulle, with excellent lunch-only *menus* at €17 (closed Sun eve, & Mon Oct–March). The hotels *Al-Fanal* and *Les Elmes* both have well-regarded eateries, especially the latter's *La Littorine*, but perhaps the best value in town – on an otherwise touristy street – is provided by 🏃 *La Casa Miguel* at 3 rue St-Pierre, purveying abundant, savoury *tapas*; inside are displayed original Maillol lithographs and photos of old Banyuls.

West of Banyuls: Musée Maillol and Col de Banyuls

The four-kilometre trip from Banyuls to the **Musée Maillol** makes a pleasant excursion, though better with a vehicle or bicycle than walking along the busy road. Pass the PTT going along avenue Général-de-Gaulle; immediately after the rail viaduct, where the road curves to the right, bear left, following signs for "Vallée de Roume/Musée Maillol".

Keen hikers could continue from the museum to the **Col de Banyuls** (357m; also drivable with care) and into Spain. Once over the pass you can continue to Espolla via Sant Quirze de Colera, or follow the GR11 to Llança; either of these options requires a fairly long day.

Cerbère

The Côte Vermeille comes to an end at **CERBÈRE**. The harbour is quite pretty and the mountain backdrop impressive, but the beach negligible. Depending on

△ Statue at the Musee Maillol

the service, train passengers change either here or on the Spanish side at Portbou (see opposite), where the rail line changes track size: a deliberate manoeuvre by the Spaniards during the late nineteenth century to hamper any possible invasion from Europe. In Cerbère, you can **stay** and **eat** at *La Dorade* on the harbour (Ⓣ 04.68.88.41.93, Ⓦ www.hotel-ladorade.com; closed Oct–March; ❸).

The Costa Brava

The **Costa Brava**, synonymous with the first – and worst – stirrings of postwar package tourism, extends from the border to just north of Barcelona. Yet despite rampant commercialization, it's still possible to find quiet stretches of shoreline, graced by the dramatic cliffs, pine-fringed coves and pebble beaches that prompted all the development in the first place. This is more likely in the northern portion of the Costa Brava, near the Mediterranean terminus of the GR11 trail at Cap de Creus; accordingly our coverage is restricted to smaller, more human-scale resorts north of the Golf de Roses, where tired hill-walkers will appreciate a few days by the sea.

Upon crossing the border with its abandoned customs posts at the **Col dels Balistres/Col des Balitres**, you'll notice an abrupt change from the tidy viniculture of the French hillsides to the shaggier Spanish slopes. The effects of the phylloxera plague during the late nineteenth century were compounded by a killing frost in 1956 which interrupted commercial olive production. There have been continual brush- and forest-fires in the region ever since, which have left the Cap de Creus in particular 85 percent deforested; pockets of pines survive only at southerly coves, around villages or in folds of hillsides where the flames have skipped over them.

This deterioration of the agricultural economy has been accelerated through migration to Barcelona and beyond, and by the exponential growth of tourism. The northernmost resorts – **Portbou**, **Colera**, **Llançà** and **El Port de la Selva** – are still very much for Catalans and passing French motorists, with little of the internationally pitched development that has blighted the *costa* further down. In season, **Cadaqués** is more cosmopolitan and, thanks to Dalí, has a palpably arty feel. You'll never find complete tranquillity nearby in summer, but if you're willing to walk a bit there are some relatively empty beaches on the **Cap de Creus** peninsula, as well as inland sites like the clumsily restored Benedictine monastery of **Sant Pere de Rodes** or the wildlife reserve at **Aiguamolls de l'Empordà**. As a base for the latter, medieval **Castelló d'Empuries** is far preferable to tatty Roses.

Portbou

PORTBOU, just 3km below the border, is the northernmost settlement of the Costa Brava, isolation and good anchorage formerly making it a smugglers' haven. The village is arrayed around a superbly protected bay in the green foothills of the Albera, amidst the sort of scenery that moved Catalan poet Fernando Agulló to bestow the epithet *brava* (rugged) on what had before been merely the *Costa de Llevant* (East Coast). Besides the main, stony harbour-beach, small, clean coves flank the harbour on either side, accessible by paths threading over the rocks – **Tres Platgetes** and **Platja del Pi** (part-nudist) to the north are the most popular. The road in from the south climbs vertiginously up to the 202-metre **Col de Frere** before dropping into town – though a tunnel is slowly being completed.

Portbou's main claim to fame is as the terminus of the Barcelona rail line: the **massive station**, built in 1872, is – with its shunting sidings – nearly as large as the town. For more than a century, Portbou lived from border traffic and the disparity in luxury-goods prices between France and Spain; since the advent of the European single market, and the closure of eighty-plus customs agencies, the place is struggling to reinvent itself as a holiday destination – already a large marina has been built.

Historically, the most illustrious – and ill-fated – visitor was German-Jewish Marxist philosopher **Walter Benjamin**, who arrived here on September 26, 1940, as a refugee from the Nazis. When it appeared that the Spanish would deny him entry and deport him back to certain death – he was near the top of the Gestapo's "wanted" list – Benjamin committed suicide by ingesting an overdose of morphine. Ironically, it appears that crypto-Republicans amongst the border police were in fact disposed to admit Benjamin the next day, as they did his travelling companions. Today he is honoured locally by a plaque on the wall of the well-signed cemetery, where he was interred for five years before his bones were tossed in a common ossuary, and by Israeli sculptor Dani Karavan's 3D art installation *Passagem*, a rectangular metal tunnel leading down towards the sea, open to the sky only for the last few steps before a glass barrier above the roiling surf, and its five-language inscription quoting Benjamin: "It is more arduous to honour the memory of the nameless than that of the renowned. Historical construction is devoted to the memory of the nameless."

Practicalities

There's a range of somewhat overpriced **accommodation**, most of it open only in summer; one all-year option is cheerful *La Masia* at Passeig Lluis Companys 1 (Ⓣ972 390 372; ④) with balconies overlooking the beach. Most **restaurants** on the seafront *passeig* are poor value; best bet is *L'Ancora*, offering excellent seafood paella and beer in large steins. The *Art in Café*, c/Mercat 11 (daily 8am–1am), serves tasty crêpes, salads and juices while you surf the **Internet** or await a train.

Colera and Platja de Garbet

Some 10km from the border, **COLERA** – signposted as "Sant Miquel", its official name – is a shabby, down-at-heel place, with high-rise blocks crammed into the narrow gulch draining to the coarse-pebble bay, and marred further by the giant rail viaduct that splits Colera in two. It's frequented mainly by Spanish holiday-makers, who splash about in water rather cleaner than the town's off-putting name implies. **Accommodation** is limited to the overpriced *Hotel La Gambina* on the harbour front (Ⓣ972 389 172; ⑤), with the main **restaurant**, and *Hostal Mont-Mercé* at Passeig del Mar 107 (Ⓣ972 389 126; ④).

For a better beach and cheaper lodging head south 2km to **Platja de Garbet**, where the en-suite *Pensió Garbet* (Ⓣ972 389 001; April–Oct; ②) is perfectly adequate, with a reasonable attached restaurant facing the scenic, gravel-and-sand bay.

Llançà

The rail line leaves the coast at **LLANÇÀ**, set back from its port to preclude the attentions of pirates. The port lies 2.5km from the **train station** (some buses stop in the port too), but the (not very) old town (**Vila**) is much closer, just off to the right as you emerge. Once prosperous thanks to its marble industry, Vila does not have a great deal to commend it, except for an attractive, café-ringed **Plaça Major** with the **Arbe de la Llibertat**, a huge tree planted in 1870. This is flanked by an outsize fifteenth-century episcopal palace attached to an eighteenth-century parish church, as well as the renovated fourteenth-century **Torre Romàntica**, which should house a museum once renovation is complete.

At first glance the **port** seems to be dominated by its yacht marina, a coarse-sand beach backed by the concreted Passeig Maritim and a **car park**; the fish depot and commercial anchorage lie around the corner, under the landmark headland of **Es Castellar** which everyone climbs to get sweeping views.

For better, more secluded **beaches**, you'll need to head 2–3km north to **Cap Ras**, a promontory covered by a forested nature reserve criss-crossed by trails. First you'll pass the strand of **Grifeu**, but it's best to continue to the cape itself, where north-facing **Borró** is the main sandy bay near the parking area. Beyond Borró, accessible by path only, lie more protected coves popular with nudists.

Practicalities

The **Turisme** lies halfway along Avgda d'Europa (July & Aug Mon–Sat 9.30am–9pm; Sept–June Mon–Fri 9.30am–2pm & 4.30–8pm, Sat 10am–1pm & 5–7pm; ⓣ972 380 855, ⓦwww.llanca.net), the road linking Vila with Port. The most durable local **scuba outfit** is Centre d'Immersió Cap de Creus (ⓣ972 120 000, ⓦwww.cicapcreus.com), c/Martínez Lozano 9.

For **accommodation**, there are a few choices in Vila such as *Pensió Can Pau* at c/Puig d'Esquer 4 (ⓣ972 380 270; ❷) or *Hotel Carbonell* on c/Major 19 (ⓣ972 380 209; ❸). Alternatively, stay down in Port at *Hotel La Goleta*, two blocks inland at the corner of c/Pintor Torroella and c/Roger de Flor (ⓣ072 380 125, ⓕ972 120 686; ❹), with antique-furnished, air-con rooms; or out at the pink, slightly kitsch *Hotel Grifeu* (ⓣ972 380 050; April–Sept; ❹), behind Grifeu beach.

Reliable, affordable **restaurants** amongst a somewhat tacky bunch include *La Brasa*, two blocks inland at Plaça de Catalunya 6 (*menú* €13, *carta* €34 and up), specializing in grilled meat and fish, and the nearby *Can Quim* on c/Lepanto.

El Port de la Selva and around

From Llançà, it's 8km along the coastal road (regular buses in summer) to El Port de la Selva; you can **walk** part-way, via **Platja de la Gola** and **Cau del Llop**, as far as the Punta de S'Arenella promontory and its lighthouse, on the **Camí to Ronda**, a not entirely continuous shoreline trail designated as the **GR92**.

Occupying the eastern side of a large bay formed by the promontory of Cap de Creus, whitewashed **EL PORT DE LA SELVA** is primarily a locals' family resort, but also the first place, heading south, that you'll see other foreigners in any numbers. It's not extravagantly picturesque (though rather more so than Llança), but makes a good base for the Cap de Creus *parc natural* just northeast. Though the pleasure-craft marina is now larger, the **fishing fleet** still plays a major role: unless the *tramontana* is blowing, boats venture forth most days to set their nets.

Buses stop on the seafront, near the giant, free municipal **car park**. A **Turisme** operates near the fishing port (June–Sept daily 8am–10pm; Oct–May Mon–Fri 8am–3pm, Sat 9am–1pm; ⓣ972 387 025). Weekend flats and villas for Catalans – especially on the western shore of the bay – predominate, so short-term **accommodation** choices are somewhat limited. The preferable of two local **campsites** is gigantic *Port de la Vall* at the far western edge of town (ⓣ972 387 186; April–Oct), sloping down to its own patch of beach. Top-end quarters are *Hotel Porto Cristo*, c/Major 59 (ⓣ972 387 062, ⓦwww.hotelportocristo.com; closed Nov–Feb; ❻), a converted mansion with luxuriously appointed units in four grades. *Pensió Sol y Sombra*, one quiet block inland from the water at c/Nou 8 (ⓣ972 387 060, ⓔsolisombra@teleline.net; ❸), is by a hair the cheapest option, the pricier rooms en-suite and balconied; the nearest alternative is the large-roomed *Hostal La Tina* at c/Major 15 (ⓣ972 387 149, ⓦwww.hostallatina.com; ❹), which also offers studios and houses. You might take up their offers of half-board – *La Tina*'s *menjador* is good and popular, if pricey – as there are few recommendable independent **restaurants** here, other than expensive *Ca L'Herminda*, seafood specialists at c/Illa 7.

Nightlife, while hardly cutting-edge, is more varied: *Cal Sereno* (7pm–3am), at c/Cantó dels Pescadors 4 near *Sol y Sombra*, is a subterranean premises with a nautical past, *Café Espanya* at c/Illa 1 functions seventeen hours a day, with a waterside terrace and mixed clientele, while *Gus Bar* at the north end of the esplanade doubles as an **Internet** café. The town's **scuba centre** is French-run *CIPS*, at c/Platja 9 (ⓣ972 126 584, ⓦwww.cips-dive.com).

Beaches

Platja Gran, at the southwestern edge of town, is popular despite exposure to the wind and steep shelving. The shore road heading north ends after a couple of kilometres at **Cala Tamariua**, a sheltered, part-nudist pebble cove. An obvious path leads 25 minutes further to the narrow pebble inlet of **Cala Fornells**, guarded by an ancient lime kiln. Beyond this point, the trail becomes faint, and sea-going excursions are more rewarding.

Selva de Mar

Medieval parent of El Port de la Selva, the tranquil oasis-village of **SELVA DE MAR**, 2km inland, is an atmospheric, semi-fortified place right under the Castell de Sant Salvador de Verdera. Little round towers pop up here and there along the lanes that converge on the stepped Plaça Camp de l'Obra. Walkers' signposts point up the stream valley to a **watermill** (El Molí del Salt del Aigua), assorted fountains, and up to the twelfth-century **church** of San Sebastià, now the cemetery chapel.

You can **stay** at *Fonda Felip* on the *plaça* (Ⓣ972 387 271; June–Sept; ❷), which, being good value, generally requires pre-booking. They also do **meals**, as does *Ca L'Elvira* on the lower perimeter road. Opposite *Fonda Felip*, **bar** *El Celler de la Selva*, a former haunt of Dalí, has occasional live music sessions in summer.

Sant Pere de Rodes

Just below the summit of the Serra de Roda stands the Benedictine monastery of **Sant Pere de Rodes** (Tues–Sun: June–Sept 10am–7.30pm; Oct–May 10am–5pm; €3.60, plus €1.20 per car; Tues free). It's 8km up the paved **road** from El Port; if you're approaching **by foot**, rather than follow the GR11 – which is forced repeatedly onto the access road – use the marked trail through the Vall de Santa Creu, beginning at Molí de la Vall, just past *Port de la Vall* campsite. Count on ninety minutes from Port de la Selva, emerging just below the monastery at the spring which possibly prompted the founding of the monastery in the first place.

According to legend, when Rome was threatened by barbarians, seventh-century Pope Boniface IV ordered the Church's most valuable relics – including **St Peter's head** – to be hidden, and he dispatched three monks to find a safe refuge. The monks eventually dropped anchor at Armen Rodes (now El Port de la Selva), where they stashed their treasures in a cave on the remote cape. Subsequently unable to relocate the hiding place, the trio founded Sant Pere rather than return to face the pope's wrath. In any case, the monastery was probably built over a pagan temple dedicated to the Pyrenean Venus, Afrodita Pyrene – a theory bolstered by the discovery of fragments of pagan sculptures and Corinthian capitals in the area.

The first reference to Sant Pere dates from 879; by the late tenth century it was the wealthiest and most powerful foundation in the region. Inevitably the monastery aroused local jealousy, and fortified itself against attacks by nearby feudal lords. After four hundred years of splendour, physical and moral decline set in, and by 1789 the last discredited monks had departed and the buildings were abandoned to the elements and to plunderers.

Sant Pere used to be one of the most romantic ruins in Catalonia, but since a brutal 1990s restoration with abundant civil engineering and concrete (and not much sensitivity) in evidence, the monastery now ranks as a textbook tourist-trap. No original columns or capitals remain in the cloister; only the lofty **church** retains its mystery and original stonework from the tenth to fourteenth centuries, including column capitals carved with wolves' and dogs' heads. The crypt also remains as it was, while a steep spiral staircase leads up to tiny Sant Miquel chapel, then to the *girolla* (ambulatory) above the apse, which retains a few Romanesque fresco fragments. It's most worthwhile showing up for the annual series of July piano concerts (8pm each Sun, some Wed).

Castell de Sant Salvador de Verdera

From the monastery a steep, narrow path climbs 25 minutes more to the mountaintop (670m) and the severely ruined **Castell de Sant Salvador de Verdera**, contemporary with Sant Pere and another possible site of the temple of Venus. Its views south across the bay of Roses and the now-drained marshlands of the Empordà plain made it the perfect watchpoint against frequent invasions (French or Moorish), normally from the sea. Take extreme care once atop the walls – there are no barriers between you and many sheer drops.

Dolmens – and Vilajuïga

A road snakes between Sant Pere and Vilajuïga, 9km west on the Barcelona–Portbou train line and served by bus to Cadaqués, Roses and Figueres. Small signs along the way indicate paths to **dolmens** at **Vinyes Mortes**, dating from 4000 BC. Particularly impressive is a pair of tombs left of the road, under 3km from the monastery car park (near which there are more signposted *dolmens*). The marked **path** down to Vilajuïga shortcuts a considerable amount of the curvy road.

VILAJUÏGA can offer the ruined Visigothic **Castell de Quermançó** just north, guarding a pass on the N-II highway (a minor, signposted road goes right by), and an eleventh/twelfth-century **synagogue** in the centre. Cool, damp and barrel-vaulted, this now serves as the antechamber to the hideous late-medieval **Església de Sant Feliu**. Vilajuïga has a single, rather drab *hostal* and a few restaurants; you'll find better facilities 3.5km west in Garriguella (see p.145).

Cadaqués and Portlligat

CADAQUÉS is the most pleasant base on the Pyrenean Costa Brava, reached only by a single, winding road over the bare hills behind Port de la Selva, and thus retaining an air of isolation. Bougainvillea-draped, whitewashed houses lining narrow, cobbled streets, a tree-lined promenade and craggy headlands to either side of a picturesque harbour make it irresistable.

Already by the 1920s and 1930s the place had begun to attract the likes of Utrillo, Picasso, Chagall, Man Ray, García Lorca, Buñuel, Thomas Mann and Einstein. But Cadaqués really "arrived" as an **artistic-literary colony** after World War II when Surrealist painter Salvador Dalí and his wife Gala settled at nearby Portlligat, attracting for some years a floating bohemian community. The impecunious hippie crowd that flocked here during the 1960s and 1970s has been largely supplanted by a relatively well-heeled trendy set, albeit (especially after dark) a youthful and unpretentious one. Outside peak season Cadaqués can be great and even in midsummer – despite the crowds and high prices – you'll probably have fun.

The extravagantly large landmark **Església de Santa Maria** – conspicuous whether you approach by sea or land – has guided generations of seafarers past the rocks and reefs at the harbour entrance. It might have been better sited less conspicuously: the village suffered numerous pirate raids, the worst in 1543 at the hands of the Ottoman "admiral" Barbarossa, who sacked the town and burnt the original church. The present edifice was built in the seventeenth century and has a remarkable Baroque altarpiece carved by Pedro Costa – including a gilded relief of Atlas supporting the world (the figure at the bottom right). Every summer, the church hosts a **classical music festival** (late July to late Aug) – rather tamer, perhaps, than the traditional saint's-day rites where local fishermen used to tether live lobsters to the altar. The early-September festival is mostly for the benefit of visitors; the locals themselves have their "private" *festa* on December 16–18, in honour of Nuestra Senyora de Esperança.

West of and below the church, the **Museu de Cadaqués** at c/Narcís Monturiol 15 (10.30am–1.30pm & 4–7pm, closed Wed; €3) features changing exhibits of local artists and displays relating to aspects of Dalí's work.

Local **beaches** are all tiny and pebbly, but lie within walking distance along either shore of the southeast-facing harbour. The best, on the southwest shore, are **Platja Sa Conca**, and – 45 minutes from centre quay, partly on the Camí de Ronda – isolated **Cala Nans**.

Practicalities

Buses (several daily from Figueres, two a day from El Port de la Selva) arrive at the little SARFA office on c/La Riera de Sant Vicenç, on the edge of town, from where it's less than ten minutes' walk to the central beachside Plaça Frederic Rahola. Having a **car** is a distinct liability here – you're usually forced to use the large fee car **park** near the bus stop, though there are free spaces on the coast road south and at the Rec de Palau lot (follow signs to hotels *Rocamar* and *Llané Petit*). The **Turisme** is just in from the beachside square at c/des Cotxes 2 (July–Sept Mon–Sat 9am–9pm, Sun 10.30am–1pm; Oct–June Mon–Sat 9am–1pm & 3–6pm; ⓣ972 258 315, ⓦwww.cadaques.org).

Accommodation

Finding **rooms** is likely to be a big problem unless you arrive outside peak season; the area's dozen hotels and hostals predictably trade on the arty reputation, charging well over the odds. For those finishing a GR11 traverse, the noisy *Camping Cadaqués* (ⓣ972 258 126; April–Sept) beckons, 1km along the road to Portlligat.

Calina Portlligat beach ⓣ972 258 851, ⓦwww.hotelcalina.com. Closed early Jan to late March. Two-storey apart-hotel with a large pool, parking, and a variety of units ranging from simple doubles (❹) to spacious studios (❻).

Cristina c/La Riera de Sant Vicenç 1 ⓣ972 258 138. Open all year. Friendly budget *hostal* with mostly en-suite, cheerful, tile-floored rooms; those with bath have good-sized ones, with tubs, and many rooms have tiny balconies. No breakfast given off season, but you can park out front then. ❸

La Fonda c/Tórtora 64 ⓣ972 258 019. Rooms here overlook a vegetable patch, with parking just conceivable nearby. ❸

Llané Petit shore road 1km south of town ⓣ972 251 020, ⓦwww.llanepetit.com. Closed Jan–Feb. Friendly, relaxing hotel by a small beach; all rooms have cable TV and a/c, most have terraces with sea views. ❼

Misty Ctra Portlligat ⓣ972 258 962, ⓦwww.hotel-misty.com Closed Jan–Feb. Hacienda-style hotel arrayed around a garden and swimming pool on the edge of town. Extras include small pool, tennis court and limited parking. ❹

Playa Sol Platja Pianc 5 ⓣ972 258 100, ⓦwww.playasol.com. Closed Jan–March. Set in a curve of the northeast seafront, this quiet hotel offers simply furnished but comfortable rooms with TV, a/c and balconies affording superb views of the town or over tranquil gardens. ❼

Marina c/La Riera de Sant Vicenç 3 ⓣ972 258 199. Closed part of May. Slightly plusher *hostal* than its neighbour the *Cristina*, with balconies for the front rooms. ❹

Eating, drinking and nightlife

The seafront drive Riba Nemsi Llorens, between Plaça des Portitxó and much-painted (and -photographed) Platja Portdoguer is lined with fairly indistinguishable **restaurants** – a notable exception being *Casa Nun* on Plaça des Portitxo, with good if small-portioned food (lunch *menú* €16) and a popular outdoor terrace – and some more memorable bars. Poking around the backstreets for a meal can be more rewarding, though the only real budget spots are Italianate *Celeste* at c/Nou 1–2, just inland from Platja Portdoguer, where €16 will see you to antipasti, chicken or pasta and a dessert; or *Sa Grota* at no. 11, with *tapas*, seafood and a

€12.50 lunch *menú*. For more upmarket seafood, try *La Sirena* on c/Es Call, with pebble-court seating, a sensibly limited fish list, creative desserts and *a la carta* bills of €27–30. Last but not least, *Casa Anita* at c/Miquel Rosset 16 (dinner only; closed Mon & late Jan to late Feb) is a long-running, obligatorily sociable institution where diners are seated together at long tables; there are only 72 seats upstairs and down, so you need to book in person on the day. The food – no printed menu, strong on local seafood – is good if not especially cheap at €50–55 for two with house wine.

Miquel Rosset, one block inland from the port and perpendicular to main artery Avgda Caritat Serinyana, is also home to much of Cadaqués' **nightlife** – eg *Tropical* at no. 19, where a candlelit garden leads to an appropriately surreal interior with marine decor and Antillean soundtrack. Other worthy venues are scattered along the waterfront. *L'Hostal*, behind Portitxó beach and the Dalí statue, opened in 1901, became a favourite haunt of the great man plus other luminaries, and has live music many nights. There may be more live acoustic sounds after 11pm at Cuban-themed *Café de la Habana*, towards the south end of town at Punta d'en Pampà, while *S7T* just past Platja Portdoguer sees patrons spilling out from the tiny bar onto the seawall for a nightcap. For less strictly alcoholic indulgence, *Rosa Azul* on the tiny shaded *plaça* behind Portdoguer does ice cream as well as drinks, while the enduringly popular, normally priced and municipally run *Casino Societat de l'Amistat* on Es Portal beachfront operates long hours and contains the town's most reliable **Internet** café.

Portlligat and Cap de Creus

From Cadaqués a paved road serpentines 1.5km north over the ridge to **PORTLLIGAT**, with views over a striking seascape as you descend. For five decades Salvador Dalí lived here with his wife and muse, Gala, having from 1930 onwards gradually converted a series of waterside fishermen's cottages into a labyrinthine home that has all the quirks you would expect. It now operates as the **Casa-Museu Salvador Dalí** (mid-March to mid-June & mid-Sept to 6 Jan Tues–Sun 10.30am–6pm; mid-June to mid-Sept daily 10.30am–9pm; closed early Jan to mid-March; reservations mandatory peak season on ⓣ972 251 015 or ⓦwww.salvador-dali

△ Casa-Museu Salvador Dalí, Portlligat

.org; €8), and despite the strictly controlled access (maximum eight people per group), it's worth it to see first-hand how the bizarre couple lived until Gala's death in 1982. Wall-art is reproduction – the originals are in the museum at Figueres (see p.142) – but all the furnishings actually belonged to Dalí and Gala.

Tours begin at the **Hall of the Bear**, the first hut acquired and named after its stuffed beast; next you take in the **winter kitchen** with its set of miniature chairs, the **library** with stuffed herons, the master's **studio** much as he left it, the exotically draped **model's room** and the so-called **Yellow Room** with its large windows and giant snail clock. Above this are the couple's **bedroom** with a cricket cage and a mirror placed to deflect the sunrise up from the Yellow Room to the couple's separate beds. In the adjacent vestuary, Gala made the **photo-montage** of celebrity acquaintances and press-cuttings; beyond opens out the domed **Oval Room**, Gala's sitting room which boasts stunning acoustics. Finally you're taken outside to the highest level and the **summer diner**, the **garden** topped by egg forms and the phallic **swimming pool** flanked by a Pirelli tyre shrine; the couple entertained guests at the bar, underneath a giant soft-toy snake.

From Portlligat, a spectacular road goes 6km through a desolate landscape to **Cap de Creus**, the easternmost point on the Iberian peninsula. Without your own **transport**, you can take a minibus from Cadaqués, use the seasonal fake train from Portitxó cove (10am–6pm) or **walk** from Portlligat along a particularly demanding section of the Camí de Ronda. Following this path gets you, after twenty minutes, to partly nudist **Platja de San Lluís**, best of the **beaches** en route; just before the headland there's a pair of wilder coves, **L'Infern** and **Cala Jugadora**. At Cap de Creus proper, you'll find the terminus of the GR11, an 1853-vintage **lighthouse** (the 1971 film *The Light at the End of the World* was filmed here) and, housed in an old barracks, *Bar-Restaurant Cap de Creus* (Easter & June–Sept 11am–1am, low season Fri–Sun 11am–midnight, Mon–Thurs noon–8pm), with pricey Indian dishes as well as Catalan fare; booking (Ⓣ972 199 005) is advisable in season.

Roses

ROSES, 17km from Cadaqués on the south flank of the peninsula, was founded by Greek colonists in the eighth century BC, who named it Rhodes after their original home. By the eleventh century AD the town's fine natural harbour had effectively supplanted that of nearby Castelló d'Empúries, by then silting up. After Barbarossa's 1543 raid, Carlos I of Spain built the star-shaped fortress of **La Ciutadella**, slighted by the French during the Peninsular War but now home to the **Museu de la Ciutadella** (Tues–Sun: April–Sept 10am–8pm (9pm July–Aug); Oct–March 10am–6pm; €2.50).

The fortress and four kilometres of fringing beach are the extent of interest; Roses is principally engaged in flogging cheap, high-rise flats to Spaniards and foreigners, now that package tourism in the area has levelled off. Some sources make much of its palm-fringed esplanade, but overall the town is extremely grim.

Practicalities

Buses stop near the corner of c/Gran Vía Pau Casals, the inland ring road, and Rambla Ginjolers. On the seafront promenade there's a **Turisme** (Mon–Fri 9am–7pm, Sat 10am–6pm, Sun 10am–1pm; Ⓣ972 257 331). The only characterful **accommodation** in the immediate area is just outside the satellite resort of Santa Margarida, right off the road linking it with Palau-Saverdera: *Mas la Torre* (Ⓣ972 151 185, Ⓔperefplanas@terra.es; open all year by arrangement; ④), a *turisme rural* based in an isolated cattle ranch. The en-suite rooms – some balconied, those in the medieval tower of the name with vaulted ceilings – are comfortable, the common areas pleasant. Near the roundabout shunting traffic towards Palau, in Canals de Santa Margarida, a **bar-restaurant**, *El Rancho*, is most remarkable for its extended hours (7pm–3am) in a country where constrained meal times are increasingly the rule. The rodeo-kitsch interior is popular with locals and foreigners, plus there's an outdoor terrace. Fare is limited to grills and salads, and portions are small, but so are prices, and quality is decent.

The coast to Cala Jóncols

From the eastern edge of Roses, signs direct you towards the paved road for Cala Montjoi and Cala Jóncols, 13km distant. **Walkers** (in spring or autumn only) will take a full day to cover the distance to Cadaqués on the Camí de Ronda/GR92. En route, you pass a succession of unshaded sand-and-pebble coves, or at least the side roads to them: the lovely horseshoe-shaped **Cala Murtra** and the pine-fringed **Cala Rostella**, both part-naturist, are the first you'd want to stop for. **Cala Monjoi**, 6km along, is the home of *El Bullí* **restaurant**, one of the most famous in Spain, sporting three Michelin stars (Ⓣ972 150 457, Ⓦwww.elbulli.com; supper only except some Sun, closed Oct–March, & Mon & Tues April–June); you usually have to book months in advance, and you will part with a minimum of €100 per person. Just beyond, the pavement gives out in the vicinity of scenic **Cala Calitja** and **Cala Pelosa**, after which the track skirts the base of the Cap de Norfeu headland before dropping bumpily to **Cala Jóncols** (even jeeps should not attempt to proceed further towards Cadaqués).

Here there's an excellent if pricey seafood **restaurant**, *El Chiringuito*, just behind the beach, and further inland in lovely poolside grounds, the rustic *Hotel Cala Jóncols* (Ⓣ972 253 970, Ⓦwww.calajoncols.com; Easter–Oct; ④). This, with both doubles and top-floor family suites, is largely the province of Euro Divers **scuba school** (Ⓔcalajoncols@euro-divers.com), which does two escorted dives daily (at 10am and 4pm), plus a weekly night dive. The protected bay between Cabo Figueres and Cabo Norfeu is among the best on the Costa Brava for red corals, invertebrates and walls, with nearly a score of sites visited in repertory, according to conditions.

Castelló d'Empúries

The delightful medieval town of **CASTELLÓ D'EMPÚRIES**, halfway between Roses and Figueres on the Riu Muga, is intrinsically worthwhile in itself, and as a base for exploring the nearby wildlife sanctuary at Aiguamolls de l'Emporda. A five-minute walk from the outskirts takes you into a medieval precinct that's lost little charm despite being so close to the beach resorts; arcaded **Plaça dels Homes**, with its cafés, is the de facto hub of modern life. Formerly the capital of the counts of Empúries, the town has narrow streets lined with well-preserved Gothic buildings, including a thirteenth-century would-be cathedral. This, the **Església de Santa Maria**, on terraced Plaça Mossèn Cinto Verdaguer, was intended to be the seat of a bishopric, but opposition from rival Girona meant this never happened, and Castelló was left with a church vastly surplus to requirements. The elaborate portal features carved figures of the apostles, including (on the far right) Judas Thaddeus, a copy of the original image (now in the museum inside the church; daily 10am–1pm & 4–8pm; €2), which was defaced by medieval townspeople in the mistaken belief it was Judas Iscariot. Beyond the pair of **belfries** flanking the facade (the right one unfinished), there's an earlier one on the north side, overlooking the **Lonja del Mar**, still used as a covered market.

Practicalities

Buses halt at the south edge of town; **cars** should also be parked nearby unless you're patronizing the recommended hotels, which have private space. The **Turisme** (summer daily 10am–2pm & 3–7pm; winter Mon–Sat 10am–2pm & 4–6pm, Sun 10am–1pm; ⓣ972 156 233, ⓦwww.castellodempuries.org) occupies the same premises as the **Presó i Cúria**, a medieval prison (same times; €1) on Plaça Jaume I, with graffiti scratched by prisoners visible on the walls. The best of several places to **stay** is the two-star *Hotel Canet* (ⓣ972 250 340, ⓦwww.hotelcanet.com; ❹) at Plaça Joc de la Pilota 2 in the old quarter; they've a luxury annexe in a restored medieval palace around the corner, *Hotel de la Moneda* (ⓣ972 158 602, ⓦwww.hoteldelamoneda), with three grades of rooms (❺–❼) and a pool/gym/spa used by both hotels.

Connoisseurs of **cases rurals** will want to consider three nearby offerings. The first is *Ca La Caputxeta*, just across the river and C260 from Castelló and accessed via the "Castelló Nou" exit from the roundabout (ⓣ972 250 310, ⓦwww.caputxeta.com; ❹ B&B), with spotless, tiled-floor rooms (shared baths), a self-catering kitchen and a choice of continental or traditional Catalan breakfast; despite being sited by a commercial park and golf course, it's not at all claustrophobic, with a garden and parking. In **FORTIÀ** village, 4km south from the next junction west on the C260, *Can Bayre* on Plaça de l'Església (ⓣ972 534 324, ⓦwww.canbayre.com; ❺) is state-of-the-art if somewhat glumly managed, with painted-tile floors for the rooms, including some famly suites, occupying a sensitively converted sixteenth-century manor house. **SIURANA D'EMPORDÀ**, 18km away beyond the C31, can offer *El Molí* (ⓣ972 525 139, ⓦwww.girsoft.com/elmoli; ❹), also with family quads and half-board available; though it's a working cattle ranch, and more Scandinavian than Iberian in feel, *El Molí* remains popular and must be reserved two months in advance. Overpriced, over-hyped *Can Navata* in the same village is, by contrast, worth avoiding.

Among local **restaurants**, top honours go to the ever-popular *menjador* of the *Canet*, where a Baroque church façade, lit up at night, overlooks the dining terrace; the €20 *menú* is, unusually for this price, interesting, while *a la carta* (endives, sole, dessert, drinks) won't go much over €30. Behind Santa Maria church and the Lonja del Mar, *Portal de la Gallarda* is a tad cheaper for simple fare, stressing grilled game and meat. At the southern outskirts, on the corner of Avinguda Generalitat and c/Santa Clara, *Hostal Ca L'Anton* – while not brilliant as lodgings – has a popular, traditional *menjador*; and 3km northwest in Vilanova de la Muga, affordable *La Resclosa* (ⓣ972 507 526; closed Mon) is celebrated for its cod and duck recipes.

Parc Natural dels Aiguamolls de l'Empordà

Southeast of Castelló lies the **Parc Natural dels Aiguamolls de l'Empordà** (daily; free), an important wetland reserve created by the Catalan government in 1983 to save the remaining Empordà marshes, much reduced from their original extent by decades of agricultural and tourist enterprise. The wetlands and local rice paddies attract a wonderful selection of birds, as well as less-promoted mammals like water voles, otters and red foxes; avian sightings are most frequent in the morning and evening during migration periods (March–May & Aug–Oct).

To reach the heart of the park from Castelló d'Empúries, take the road south towards Sant Pere Pescador. After about 4km, you'll see a sign on the left for the **visitors' centre** at El Cortalet (daily: April–Sept 9.30am–2pm & 4.30–7pm; Oct–March 9.30am–2pm & 3.30–6pm; ⓣ972 454 222, ⓦmediambient.gencat.net/), where there's ample parking, a free map of walking routes, binoculars for rent and (arranged in advance) guided tours by staff ornithologists. The more popular of two principal **marked paths** is shaded **La Massona** (2hr round trip to the beach and back), with a series of **hides** along the way; nos. 5 and 7 will be most rewarding

The sardana

The main difference between the **sardana** – the national dance of Catalonia – and most other folk dances is that it's performed by the entire community, rather than just specialists. However, this doesn't mean that you can simply barge in and have a go. It's a very complex dance, and etiquette requires that you join a circle of dancers of your own ability. Following the arm movements isn't too challenging, as every dancer holds hands with his or her neighbours in the circle – consequently, your limbs will be hauled up and down at the appropriate moments. But the footwork is fiendishly difficult, with the step changing mid-bar and the beat changing mid-step. Musical accompaniment is provided by a **cobla** band, comprising five wind instruments, five brass horns, a double bass and percussion. The rite-like intensity, the linking of hands and the upright posture suggest that the **sardana** may have originated with ancient Greek settlers on the Empordan coast (though cynics claim it was artificially resuscitated during the nineteenth century as part of the resurgence in Catalan national feeling).

On summer Sundays and festival days the **sardana** is danced all along the Costa Brava (and on the Côte Vermeille too), as well as at many inland towns and villages – particularly on **La Diada** (National Day), September 11.

in summer, as the adjacent waterholes rarely dry up. A converted rice silo nearby functions as an aerial **observatory** – you'll need a good head for heights.

Figueres

FIGUERES is the capital of **Alt Empordà** county – the alluvial plain (and coast) formed by the rivers Muga and Fluvià, and the foothills to the north. For most visitors its chief appeal lies in the fact that **Salvador Dalí** was born, began his career and died here, yet if you linger after touring the museum devoted to his work, you'll discover a pleasant provincial town with a busy, café-lined *rambla*, other museums and adequate food and lodging.

Arrival and information

The **train station** lies 600m directly east of the centre; the **bus station**, across the same *plaça*, issues tickets for both local (mostly SARFA and TEISA) and international buses; there are also two car-rental franchises on the square. The focal point of Figueres – the *rambla*– is reached from the stations by walking west along c/Sant Llàtzer and then turning right at c/Nou. **Parking** a car is nearly impossible in the centre; either pay to use designated car parks or resign yourself to walking in from the outskirts.

There's a small **information booth** just outside the bus station (July 1–Sept 15 Mon–Sat 9.30am–1.30pm & 4.30–7pm); the helpful central **Turisme** is at Plaça del Sol (July–Sept Mon–Sat 8.30/9am–8/9pm, Sun 9am–3pm, not Sun Sept; Nov–June Mon–Fri 8.30am–3pm & 4.30–8pm, Sat 9.30am–1.30pm & 3.30-6.30pm, not Sat or eves Nov–Easter; Ⓣ972 503 155, Ⓦwww.figueresciutat.net). Both can provide a town map and current timetables for onward transport.

Accommodation

Accommodation options range from basic to upmarket, with several adequate central choices, though many of the better hotels (with ample parking) lie on main roads out of town. Acceptable budget options include *Pensió Bartis*,

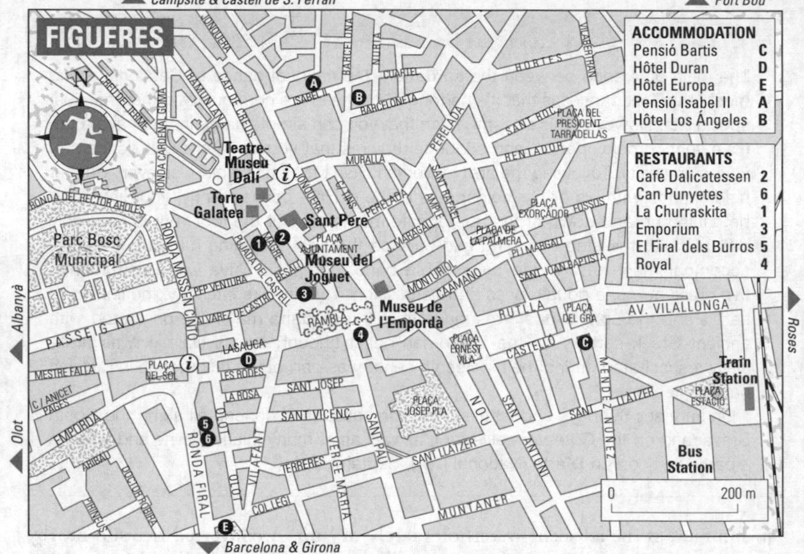

c/Mendez Nunyez 2 (Ⓣ972 501 473; ❷), near the bus and train stations; and *Pensió Isabel II*, c/Isabel II 16 (enquire at Muralla 12; Ⓣ972 504 735; ❷), where airy bathrooms compensate for small, air-con rooms. For two-star comfort, quiet but slightly overpriced *Hotel Los Ángeles* at c/Barceloneta 10 (Ⓣ972 510 661, Ⓦwww.hotelangeles.com; ❸), has bathrooms the same size as the smallish bedrooms, done up in vulgar-Spanish-Modern (off-street parking costs extra), or the better-value *Hotel Europa* at Ronda Firal 18 (Ⓣ972 500 744, Ⓕ972 671 117; ❸). Top standard downtown is at the three-star *Duran* on c/Lasauca 5 (Ⓣ972 501 250, Ⓦwww.hotelduran.com; ❻), originally a carters' inn dating from 1855, with comfortable if slightly dark rooms.

Figueres has a **campsite** about 3km out on the N-II northwest towards France: smallish, shady *Pous* (Ⓣ972 675 496; April–Oct).

The Teatre-Museu Dalí

Figueres' **Teatre-Museu Dalí** (July–Sept daily 9am–7.45pm; Oct–June Tues–Sun 10.30am–5.45pm; €10; Ⓦwww.salvador-dali.org) is the most visited museum in Spain after Madrid's Prado and Bilbao's Guggenheim, but it's as much an absurdist theatrical fantasy as it is a conventional art collection. Appropriately enough, before destruction at the end of the Spanish Civil War, the building *was* the municipal theatre and the venue for Dalí's first exhibition of paintings in 1918 (when he was 14). Upon reconstruction in 1974, the artist set about fashioning it into a repository for some of his most bizarre works. Having moved to the adjacent Torre Galatea in 1984, Dalí died there on January 23, 1989; his body, against his wishes, now lies behind a simple granite slab in a basement gallery of the museum.

The **building**, on Plaça Gala i Salvador Dalí, was designed as an exhibit itself. Three-cornered imitation bread rolls speckle the exterior walls, one of which is painted terra-cotta pink; topped by a huge metallic-glass dome, the roof line is studded with giant eggs and faceless bronze mannequins preparing to dive from the heights. In the courtyard, the "**Rainy Cadillac**" contains three vine- and snail-infested mannequins, with a statue of a buxom biblical queen on the bonnet, while overhead a totem pole of tyres supports Gala's rowboat, from which hang pendulous blobs of resin, made using condoms as moulds. Inside, steps from the stage area under the dome lead to the **Mae West Room**, where a carefully manipulated viewing of some draperies and a labial red sofa converge into a portrait of the actress. The **Palau de Vent** on the first floor is dominated by the ceiling painting of Gala and Dalí ascending to heaven, their grubby feet dangling in the viewer's face.

All the pranks and optical illusions can distract from the reality that there's far more "serious" art here than generally credited, both by Dalí and other artists of his choosing. Lesser-known "conventional" canvases from the 1920s (*Portrait of His Sister*) are juxtaposed with more stereotypically surreal later material like *Soft Self-Portrait with Bacon* and *Portrait of Picasso*, while *The Spectre of Sex Appeal* seems the epitome of Dalí's shame-ridden pathology. Featuring Gala *Atomic Leda* and *Galatea of the Spheres* are two of many portraits of his muse, culminating in the Portlligat-set *Dalí from the Back Painting Gala from the Back* (1972–73), though there are some of friends too, such as *Laurence Olivier as Richard III*.

The rest of town

The oft-overlooked **Museu de l'Empordà** at Rambla 1 (July–Sept Tues–Sat 11am–9pm, Sun & public holidays 11am–2pm; Oct–June Tues–Sat 11am–7pm, Sun & public holidays 11am–2pm; €2 or same ticket as Teatre-Museu Dalí), hosts a serious collection, albeit labelled in Catalan only, bolstered by donations from the Prado and wealthy Figuerans. The first floor combines Greek and Roman ceramics with medieval polychrome wood Virgins, while upstairs there's a gallery of Empordan sculptors and painters, of which the "modern" division of local landscapes and portraits is best. The third floor, devoted to abstract and figurative depiction of the region, is enlivened with works by Dalí, Joan Miró, Ramon Reig and Antoni Tàpies among others, though these holdings are occasionally removed for temporary exhibits. The **Museu del Joguet** (June–Sept Mon–Sat 10am–1pm & 4–7pm, Sun 11am–1.30pm & 5–7.30pm; Oct–May same hours but closed Sun pm & Mon; €4.50), housed in a beautiful old hotel in the *rambla*, above *Café Emporium*, houses over four thousand toys from all over Catalunya. The statue at the bottom of the *rambla* honours Narcís Monturiol, a local who distinguished himself by inventing the submarine.

The only other sight is the huge **Castell de Sant Ferran** (daily: July–Sept 10.30am–7pm; Oct–June 10.30am–2pm; €5.50), 1km northwest of town – follow Pujada del Castell from just beyond the Dalí museum. Built in 1753 to defend against French invasion – and failing signally in that role twice during the Napoleonic Wars – it remains one of the vastest citadels in Europe. Sant Ferran served as the last bastion of the Republicans in the Civil War, when Figueres became their capital for a week in February 1939 after the fall of Barcelona. Earlier in the war, it had been used as a barracks for newly arrived members of the International Brigades before they moved on to the front; more recently, it was used as a prison for Colonel Tejero after his failed coup attempt in 1981. The outer circuit of star-shaped **walls** exceeds 3km, so you might consider shelling out another €7 for a three-hour tour which includes a jeep ride around the perimeter, and then a dinghy trip through the cathedral-like **water cisterns** under the parade ground, engineering marvels sufficient to outlast a year's siege.

Eating and drinking

The gaggle of touristy **restaurants** flanking the narrow streets around the Dalí museum are generally worth avoiding in favour of less obvious prospects. An exception here is *La Churraskita* at c/Magre, which purveys Argentine-style grills, pizzas and pasta. Ronda Firal has more late-serving, budget choices: *El Firal dels Burros* at no. 15, a *bodega* where cheese and paté accompanies wine, or *Can Punyetes* at no. 25, doing more carniverous fare in a rustic environment. For a bit more outlay, the *menjador* of the *Hotel Duran* does generously proportioned regional dishes like duck with pears that come with a modern flair (€15 *menú*, €25-plus *a la carta*).

Classic **cafés** on the *rambla*, which doubles as a busy traffic circle, include *Emporium* at no. 10, with snacks and tables inside or out, and the *Royal* opposite at no. 28, with *modernista* tiled walls and *orxata* served as it should be. Among the more tourist-pitched places on Plaça Ajuntament near the Dalí museum, *Café Dalicatessen* at c/Sant Pere 17–19 offers good juices, pots of Earl Grey tea and fresh croissants. Figueres used to be fairly comatose **at night**, with local youth making a beeline for the coast, but lately there has been a cluster of changeable bars/clubs on the north side of Plaça del Sol.

North and west of Figueres

During World War II, the region **north of Figueres** was essentially unguarded between the **Castell de Requesens** and Portbou, which made the **Serra de l'Albera** ridge a favoured escape route from France. The stretch between **Garriguella** in the east and **Cantallóps** in the west remains relatively unfrequented, with semi-abandoned villages tucked between vineyards, olive groves and cork-oak plantations. Since the 1980s, many foreigners have moved in to convert crumbling local farms, and Catalan day-trippers scour the countryside at weekends, replenishing their cellars at the many wineries that dot the area, especially around Capmany. Below the foothills, places like **Peralada**, **Mollet de Peralada** and **Vilabertran** have always been more going concerns than the isolated Alberan hamlets.

The most interesting outings **west from Figueres** visit the large villages of **Maçanet de Cabrenys**, **Darnius** and **Sant Llorenç de la Muga** either side of the forest-fringed **Pantà (Reservoir) de Boadella**, less impressive than it seems on the map, especially after dry winters, but still attracting watersports enthusiasts.

Vilabertran, Peralada and Mollet de Peralada

Easily overlooked, quiet **VILABERTRAN**, 2km northeast of Figueres, has two claims on your attention: a former Augustinian monastery and an excellent restaurant. The **Canònica de Santa Maria de Vilabertran** (Tues–Sat 10am–1.30pm & 3–5.30/6.30pm, Sun 10am–1.30pm, not Sun Oct–May; €2.50, Tues free), with its fine Lombard belfry pierced by three tiers of arcaded windows, dominates the village. The late eleventh-century monastic **church**, now the venue of a respected late August/early September Schubert festival, was carefully chosen for the 1322 Christmas Day marriage of Jaume II of Aragón and Catalan queen Elisenda de Montcada. Hosting a royal wedding bestowed tax-free status on Vilabertran, but as it was (and is) a tiny place, this hardly affected the royal coffers. Pride of the church is an ornate **silver crucifix** in the northerly Capella dels Dolors; the cloister is disappointing, its column capitals bare of relief art. Try and schedule a **meal** at *L'Hostalet d'en Lons* (closed Mon), a vaulted former wine warehouse at the northwest edge of town; there's no *menú*, but a huge *panaché de verduras*, savoury *xipirones* with parsley and garlic and a *flan de coca*, washed down by the light house rosé, will come to just over €20.

Some 5km further northeast, you reach fortified **PERALADA**, a medieval town centred on its arcaded *plaça*. The main sight is the moated **castle**, which contains a casino, a wine factory and the stage and seating for a prestigious **summer festival** (jazz, classical, opera and dance; mid-July to mid-Aug; Ⓦwww.festivalperalada.com). Local **restaurants** are generally expensive, but *Cal Sagristà* at c/Rodona 2 (closed Mon) does moderately priced home-style dishes. Even better, head 6.5km further north to eat hearty country fare at *Ca La Maria* (closed Sun night, Mon night, Tues all day), another cavernous former wine warehouse in the very centre of **MOLLET DE PERALADA**. Under €30 gets you generous starters of salami and olives, *bacalla amb xamfaina* (cod in tomato sauce), stir-fried artichoke hearts and pear tart washed down with a *porró* of Banyuls dessert wine. Despite over-stretched service, it's an Alt Empordà institution and highly recommended.

The Serra de l'Albera

The **Serra de l'Albera** is better for car-touring and cycling than walking; narrow but paved country roads link well-spaced hamlets and wine-tasting bodegas, while wide dirt tracks lead to remote *dolmens* and churches. Gateway to the region is **GARRIGUELLA**, reached by a different seven-kilometre road from Peralada and itself distributed to either side of the GI603 road. The village lies mainly north of the highway, but prime **accommodation** in the *turisme rural* scheme is in a little neighbourhood to the south: plain *Can Coll* at no. 3 on the Peralada road (Ⓣ972 530 116; ❸ B&B) and the more sumptuous *Can Garriga* a little further south at c/Figueres 1–3 (Ⓣ972 530 184, Ⓦwww.cangarriga.net; ❺ B&B), a lovely walled compound with a grassy front garden and vaulted ground-floor rooms that fill quickly. On Plaça de Baix, near both of these, you can **eat** well at *Can Battle*, as you also can at *La Plaça*, by the church in the northern district.

ESPOLLA, 9km northwest of Garriguella on the GI603, is home, at the east edge of town, to the **Centre d'Informació** (May–Oct daily 10am–2pm & 4–6pm, Nov–April weekends only; Ⓣ972 545 039) for the **Paratge Natural d'Interès Nacional de l'Albera**, created all around here in 1986 to help protect the local environment and its distinctive fauna, which includes tortoises and a species of dwarf wild cow. Otherwise this is a typical Alt Empordà wine village, its shuttered houses crammed into a labyrinth of streets that come to life each year during the grape harvest. **Accommodation** is at *Can Salas*, a *casa de pagès* on c/Figueres 11–13 (Ⓣ972 563 376; ❸).

Prehistorians will delight in two local Neolithic **dolmens**, lying either side of Espolla. Take the GI602 southwest towards Sant Climent Sescebes; at a rising bend 1km along, turn right onto a dirt track for another 700m to the eerie **Cabana Arqueta**, standing alone in the shade of oaks. Harder to find is **Dolmen del Barranc**, the only carved tomb in the area: it lies 3km from the village off the track leading north towards the frontier Col de Banyuls.

Sleepy **RABÓS D'EMPORDÀ**, 4km southeast of Espolla, is crowned by a superb fortified church – the apse is the tower – and can muster a good local **restaurant** at the village entrance, *Can Tomas* (closed Wed). From Rabós, a road (2km paved, thereafter 4km rough track) leads up to the fortified Benedictine **Monastir de Sant Quirze de Colera**, off-limits for interminable restoration, though the three-aisled, tenth-century church appears startlingly impressive in its wild setting. Adjacent is a handy, reasonable **restaurant**, *Corral de Sant Quirze* (lunch daily except Wed, supper also in summer), occupying the former monastic stables. The **GR11** passes through, and camping is possible if the monastery's spring hasn't dried up, but you're well advised to avoid summer walking in the often shadeless Albera.

From Espolla, 23km of roundabout driving leads to appealing **CANTALLÓPS**, though there's also a sporadic bus service from Figueres. Cantallóps has a single **pensió** at the outskirts if you get stuck, *Can Pau* (☎972 554 881; ❷), and a **restaurant** in the village, but you're really here to continue on 7km of wide, well-signposted dirt track to the **Castell de Requesens** (Recasens; July 15–Sept 15 daily 11am–7pm, rest of year 11am–5pm Sat/Sun/hols only; €2), set amidst a marvellous countryside of cork oaks (their harvested bark stacked for collection) and a few cedars. Originally ninth-century, the castle might best remain admired from afar by purists; after a chequered history, it spent two decades from 1942 as a Guardia Civil barracks, whose tenants vandalized the place to a deplorable extent, their alterations wrecking its fabric. The masonry gets older and less spoiled as you climb the various levels of labyrinthine cisterns, vaulted halls, kitchens, latrines and parapets; though you're denied access to the highest towers, the views are superb.

Sant Llorenç de la Muga and Albanyà

There are three weekly **buses** from Figueres to these settlements; **driving** yourself, follow signs out of town for the N-II (currently being widened, straightened and tunnelled) to La Jonquera, and keep an eye peeled for the poorly marked turning for Llers, and then to **SANT LLORENÇ DE LA MUGA**, about 17km west of the town. Without there being much specific to see, this large, fortified village, nestled in pines along the upper Riu Muga, makes an excellent destination; it's linked to Maçanet de Cabrenys (see opposite) by a marked but rough track (hikers, bikes or jeeps only; 9.5km) skirting wetlands on the reservoir's west shore. The medieval stone houses form much of the defensive perimeter, but there are two portcullised thirteenth-century gates – one on the west, the other opening onto an old *camí* to Girona – and stout towers at scattered points, for example behind the twelfth-century parish church. Entering Sant Llorenç from the north, you pass a lovely, massive fourteenth-century **bridge** – like Besalú's (see p.158) in miniature – and a millrace leading down to a dilapidated **mill**; the only **place to eat** is *Sa Muga* on the central *rambla*, and you can **drink** at either *El Lluro* on Plaça Baixa, or the municipally run *Societat La Fraternitat* on the *rambla*. Thus far, the only **accommodation** is *Hostal Can Toni*, a modern place on the outskirts (☎972 569 225; ❸), though you'll also find a small-scale, tent-friendly **campsite**, *La Fradera* (☎972 542 054; Easter–Oct), 1.5km west.

By contrast, **ALBANYÀ**, 7km upstream from Sant Llorenç, is nothing special, though it too has a minuscule medieval core with an arched gate giving onto the old *camí* to Sant Llorenç. If you're on a **GR11** traverse you'll necessarily pass through, as Albanyà lies between the **Col de Bassegoda** – 11km west and the boundary of Alta Garrotxa *comarca* – and Maçanet de Cabrenys (20km or 4hr walk north). Since Albanyà's single hotel-restaurant has closed, east-bound trekkers might prefer to continue towards *Camping La Fradera* after perhaps replenishing supplies at the single **shop**. The closest indoor **accommodation**, 1.5km beyond Albanyà, is *Can Carreras* (☎972 569 199; ❹ B&B), off by itself near the river, though it's a working pig farm, with all the attendant noise and aromas.

Darnius, Maçanet de Cabrenys and La Vajol

North of the Pantà de Boadella – accessible from the Muga valley by a link road below the dam, or directly off the N-II on a road widened in 2006 – lies **DARNIUS**, linked weekdays by bus to Figueres with the company David i Manel. It's not exactly a thriving place, though it does have two good **accommodation** options nearby. Closest is a *casa de pagès* at the south edge of town, near the stoplights: massive, vaulted *Can Massot* (ⓣ972 535 193, ⓦwww.canmassot.com; ❹ B&B), with extensive common areas including a lovely breakfast room and self-catering kitchens. More luxurious and unusual is *Hotel La Central* (ⓣ972 535 053, ⓦwww.hlacentral.com; ❺), 6km southwest along a well-marked and -graded dirt track. This *modernista* chalet in idyllic streamside surroundings bills itself as a "*Centre de Salut i Esport*", with a full spa and activity programme; the rooms, in three grades, are irreproachable – the tower suites the most distinctive. The in-house **restaurant** with its waterfall-wall out the rear window excels at seafood; monkfish, *escalivada*, lemon mousse and drinks will come to about €30 *a la carta*.

You may prefer to carry on from Darnius through dense cork-oak groves to livelier and more atmospheric **MAÇANET DE CABRENYS**, 26km from Figueres. The **bus** stops just south of this densely built, oval-shaped medieval ensemble, next to a **Turisme** (summer only Mon–Fri 10am–1pm & 4–8pm; ⓣ972 544 297). Sole place in the old town to **stay** and **eat** is welcoming Casa Fonda affiliate *Hostal La Quadra* on the northwest edge of the fortifications (ⓣ972 544 032, ⓦwww.laquadra.com; closed 2 weeks in June and Jan, also Tues off season; ❹ B&B), with a variety of rooms, private parking and a sustaining basement **restaurant** where *a la carta* won't top €18. The only specific local "sight" is **O Pedra Dreta**, a menhir dating from around 3000 BC and standing 2m high on the western fringe of the village, just beyond Mas Pitxo. There's also a useful **cross-border road**, paved and broad despite some map depictions, to Coustouges in France (see p.122), via Tapis hamlet.

Under your own steam, you can vary a return to Figueres or the N-II by looping north (7km from Maçanet) via the compact knolltop village of **LA VAJOL**, famous for its sweeping views of Alt Empordà. Plaça Major is a popular venue for **eating**, at either the superior *Hostal La Vajol* or *Casa Comaulis* (closed Mon). Though the GR11 skims by, there's **no accommodation**.

The Spanish valleys

The higher valleys of the Spanish Eastern Pyrenees begin well away from the Mediterranean coast. Easiest access to the mountains is via **Girona**, 40km south of Figueres, an ancient capital with ample cultural appeal; it also has Catalunya's largest airport outside Barcelona, handling year-round flights from Britain. From Girona, head northwest through lakeside **Banyoles** to the exquisite medieval town of **Besalú**, then west into the heart of the volcanic **Garrotxa** region, centred on the town of **Olot**. Continuing in the same direction brings you to **Ripoll** and its famous monastery, or to **Sant Joan de les Abadesses**, with another monastic cathedral. Just northeast of here, **Camprodon** is the first town truly enclosed by foothills, but for a more dramatic introduction to the Spanish Catalan Pyrenees, the upper **Freser valley** awaits just north of Ripoll, with its popular narrow-gauge train and grandiose Marian shrine at **Núria**.

Public transport connections from Girona towards the hills are initially excellent, with numerous daily bus departures as far as Olot, via Banyoles and Besalú, from where onward links to Camprodon and Ripoll are spotty. Frequent train and bus departures serve Figueres and the coastal resorts northeast of Girona.

Girona

The obvious gateway to any eastern approach to the Spanish Pyrenees, **GIRONA** spills down a fortified hill above the occasionally stagnant but carp-clogged Riu Onyar, just before it joins the Ter. Like Perpignan – the equivalent gateway city on the French side – it has a distinctly Arab flavour, but here the influence dates from the Moorish conquest, retained in the architecture and narrow streets of its old quarter. You're likely to spend more time here than planned, and at least two nights are recommended; although the place now gets plenty of attention from day-trippers, calm returns to the old town after dark, when Girona's abiding character reasserts itself.

So-called "City of a Thousand Sieges", Girona has been fought over in almost every century since it was the Roman fortress of Gerunda on the Via Augusta. In the eighth century it became the seat of a Carolingian earldom; the Muslims stayed for over 200 years, a fact apparent in the web of narrow central lanes, and there was also a continuous Jewish presence through six centuries. By the eighteenth century Girona had been besieged 21 times, and during 1808–09 it earned the nickname "Immortal" for withstanding two sustained assaults by Napoleon's forces. Each occupier left their mark on the town, and connoisseurs can identify a succession of architectural styles from Romanesque to *modernisme*. But as palpable as any monumental interest is the feel of a confident, young (thanks to the university) and prosperous place that has recovered from years of neglect and repression under the Franco dictatorship.

Arrival, transport and information

Girona's **airport**, 13km south of the city, now has a daily scheduled service from the UK year-round. The small arrivals hall has three car-rental booths (Avis, Hertz and one other), as well as a ticket booth for the almost hourly **bus service** to both Girona train/bus stations (€1.75) and Barcelona; a taxi into town costs around €18. The **train station** (Ⓣ972 207 093) is off Crta Barcelona in the modern, western part of the city; the **bus station** – also serving international arrivals – is behind the same building on Plaça d'Espanya. Both are a mere fifteen-minute walk southwest from the old quarter. You're more likely to use a **taxi** – the handiest ranks are at the train station, Plaça Catalunya and the old-town end of the Pont de Pedra – than the city bus lines.

Girona is sandwiched by the toll *autopista* A7 (west of town) and the free N-II highway (east). If you **drive** in, you'll find **parking** generally nightmarish: the old town especially is a controlled-access zone for residents only, so you'll be fined or towed unless your lodgings provide parking. Use the fee car park at Plaça Catalunya, or compete for free spaces in the lot by Pont Pedret or up on Passeig Fora Muralla, just outside the medieval walls near the university campus (difficult during term time).

The main **Turisme** (April–Sept Mon–Fri 8am–8pm, Sat 8am–2pm & 4–8pm, Sun 9am–2pm; Oct–March Mon–Sat 9am–5pm, Sun–9am–2pm; Ⓣ972 226 575, Ⓦwww.ajuntament.gi) is at Rambla de la Llibertat 1, the tree-lined promenade one block behind the river; this has English-speaking staff and stocks useful maps and brochures, accommodation lists and local transport timetables. There's also a **municipal office** at the river end of c/Berenguer Carnicer (Mon–Fri 10am–5pm).

Accommodation

There are more than twenty officially classified *pensions*, *hostals* and hotels on both sides of the river, so with few exceptions (indicated below) you shouldn't need to

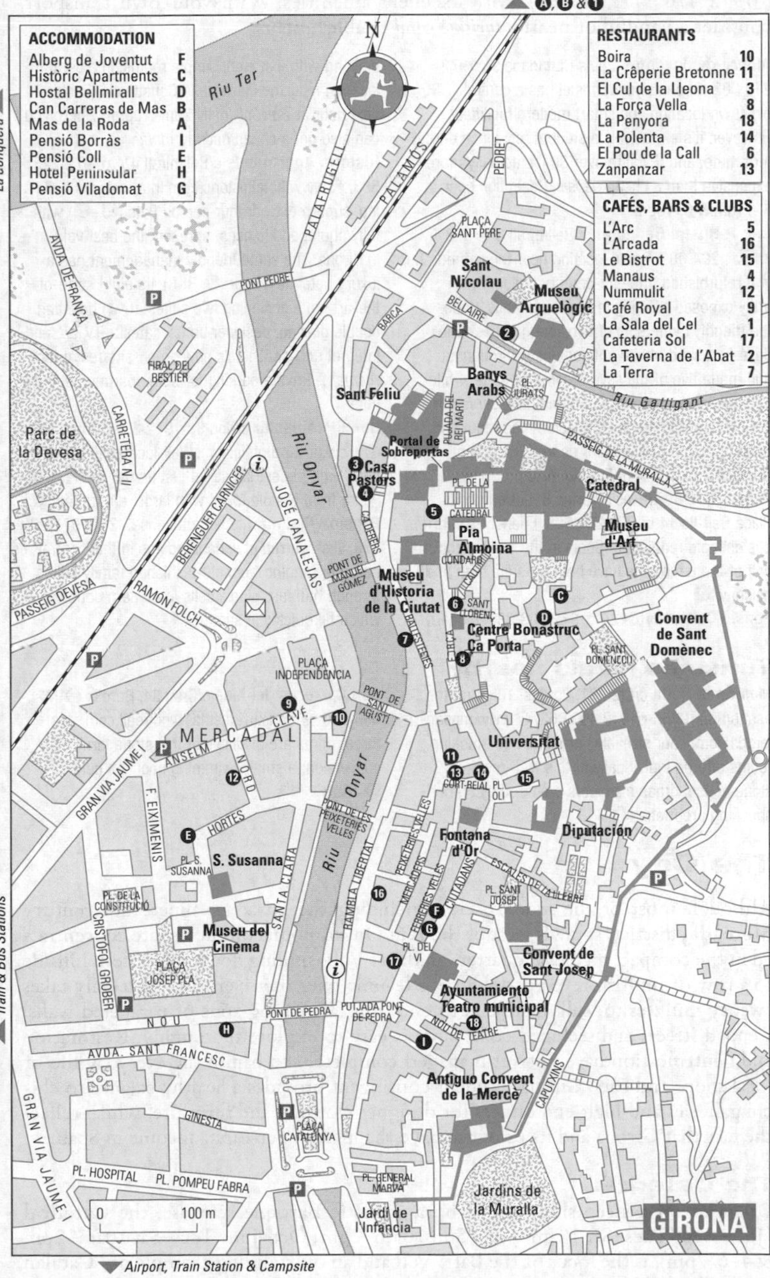
ACCOMMODATION
Alberg de Joventut F
Històric Apartments C
Hostal Bellmirall D
Can Carreras de Mas B
Mas de la Roda A
Pensió Borràs I
Pensió Coll E
Hotel Peninsular H
Pensió Viladomat G
RESTAURANTS
Boira 10
La Crêperie Bretonne 11
El Cul de la Lleona 3
La Força Vella 8
La Penyora 18
La Polenta 14
El Pou de la Call 6
Zanpanzar 13
CAFÉS, BARS & CLUBS
L'Arc 5
L'Arcada 16
Le Bistrot 15
Manaus 4
Nummulit 12
Café Royal 9
La Sala del Cel 1
Cafeteria Sol 17
La Taverna de l'Abat 2
La Terra 7
A, B & 1
La Jonquera
Train & Bus Stations
Airport, Train Station & Campsite
Riu Ter
Riu Onyar
Riu Galligant
Parc de la Devesa
Sant Nicolau
Museu Arqueològic
Sant Feliu
Banys Arabs
Portal de Sobreportas
Casa Pastors
Catedral
Museu d'Art
Pia Almoina
Museu d'Historia de la Ciutat
Centre Bonastruc Ça Porta
Convent de Sant Domènec
Universitat
Fontana d'Or
Diputación
S. Susanna
Museu del Cinema
Convent de Sant Josep
Ayuntamiento
Teatro municipal
Antiguo Convent de la Mercè
Jardins de la Muralla
Jardí de l'Infancia
MERCADAL
PLAÇA INDEPENDÈNCIA
PLAÇA JOSEP PLA
PLAÇA CATALUNYA
PLAÇA SANT PERE
FIRAL DEL BESTIER
0
100 m
GIRONA

book ahead. The nearest **campsite** is *Can Toni*, 8km south at Fornells de la Selva (☎972 476 117; all year), with excellent amenities. With your own transport, consider a handful of nearby *turisme rural* establishments.

Alberg de Joventut c/dels Ciutadans 9 ☎972 218 003. Girona's youth hostel has a central old-town location and smart modern facilities. However, it's exclusively a student residence during term time, and if you're over 30 it's actually more expensive than a cheap *pensió*. Reception open 8–11am & 6–10pm.

Hostal Bellmirall c/Bellmirall 3 ☎972 204 009. Prime location near the cathedral, in a refurbished fifteenth-century building with artily exposed pointing in the stone walls. Under the friendly ownership of two young ladies, who have furnished it with antique decor throughout and made five of the seven rooms en suite, while maintaining famously good breakfasts, served in the courtyard in summer. Reservations required; parking permit provided for nearby Plaça Sant Domènec; closed Jan–Feb. ❹ B&B

Pensió Borràs Travesia Auriga 6, but enquiries Plaça Bell-lloc 4 ☎972 224 008. Friendly, salubrious cheapie redolent of Spain in the 1980s; about half of the ten rooms have both en-suite bath and balcony. ❷

Pensió Coll c/Hortes 24 ☎972 203 086. Modern building with just eight simple rooms, in a central location near the Plaça de la Constitució. Enquire next door at *Bar Coll* (daily 7am–10pm), where you can also get a cheap midday *menú*. ❷

Històric Apartments c/Bellmirall 4/A ☎972 223 583, ⓦwww.hotelhistoric.com In a restored building, superb two- or four-person flats (❺–❻) with fully equipped kitchens represent the best value in Girona. The same friendly management has a luxury hotel next door (❼ B&B), its eight state-of-the-art units (including two suites at ❼) boasting double glazing, designer baths, satellite TV, a/c and Internet access. There's now an on-site restaurant, *Alemany*. Private parking for both apartments and hotel.

Hotel Peninsular c/Nou 3 ☎972 203 800, ⓦwww.novarahotels.com. Well-located, if bland, hotel on a pedestrian street just across the Pont de Pedra from the old town, with large, a/c rooms. ❹

Pensió Viladomat c/de Ciutadans 5, 2º ☎972 203 176. Vast warren of variable rooms in this central building, ranging from old-fashioned family suites through bathless single cells to modern doubles which fill quickly in summer. ❷

Turismes rurals nearby

Mas de la Roda c/Creu 31, Bordils, 10km northeast on the C255 ☎972 490 052, ⓦwww.masdelaroda.com. Four sizeable, en-suite, non-smoking rooms offered individually at this well-restored stone house; organic suppers prepared by French-speaking proprietor. ❹ B&B

Can Carreras del Mas c/Creu 34, Bordils ☎972 490 276, ⓔcancarrerasmas@hotmail.com. Just three rooms are available at this stone farm conversion; a small swimming pool is a bonus. ❹ B&B

The City

Although most of the modern city, including the attractive nineteenth-century **Mercadal** district, sprawls west of the Riu Onyar, points of interest are concentrated in the compact medieval quarter, or **Barri Vell**, spilling down the eastern hillside to a row of multistoreyed pastel houses leaning over the riverbank. As it only takes twenty minutes to walk from end to end, this fascinating zone of parapeted walls, stepped streets and secluded courtyards is easy to explore thoroughly. Restoration and gentrification have not yet managed completely to banish the everyday life of local shops and bars. Girona's student contingent provides a healthy balance to chichi galleries and high-end outlets for designer clothing and furniture, which reflect the fact that Girona and its province have the highest per-capita income in Spain.

The Catedral

Balanced on a steep slope scaled by a majestic Baroque staircase, the **Catedral** (July–Sept Tues–Sat 10am–8pm, Sun 10am–2pm; Oct–June Tues–Sat 10am–2pm & 4–6/7pm), is the focus of the Barri Vell and an outstanding example of "Catalan Gothic". There has been a place of worship here since Roman times, and a mosque stood on the site before the foundation of the cathedral in 1038. Most of the building dates from the fifteenth century, though parts are 400 years older, notably the five-storey **Torre de Carlemany** and the Romanesque **cloisters**.

The main Rococco **facade**, remodelled in the eighteenth century, writhes with exuberant ornamentation: floral motifs, coats-of-arms and niche statues (most of them 1960s copies) in three tiers. Inside, the aisle-less cathedral overwhelms you with its single **nave** spanning 22.5m, the second-widest Gothic vault in the world after St Peter's in Rome. Contemporary sceptics deemed the proposed design unsafe, and the vault was raised in 1417 only after an appeal by the architect, Guillermo Bofill, to an independent panel of architects. The walls rise to stained-glass windows, the single object interrupting the sweep of space being an enormous organ installed late in the nineteenth century.

From the main body of the cathedral, you emerge into the irregularly shaped **cloisters** (1180–1210), which feature minutely carved figures and scenes on double columns. Finally, the tour route leads to the **Tresor Capitular** (Chapter Treasury), four overstuffed rooms of religious art whose highlights include Beatus' *Commentary on the Apocalypse*, illuminated in 975 by Mozarabic miniaturists, and (in the last room) a magnificent eleventh-century, Italian *Tapestry of the Creation*, the finest surviving specimen of Romanesque textile, depicting in strong colours the forces of light and darkness, the Creation and seasonal rural activities.

Museu d'Art and Sant Feliu

Girona's **Museu d'Art** (March–Sept Tues–Sat 10am–7pm, Sun 10am–2pm, Oct–Feb Tues–Sat 10am–6pm, Sun 10am–2pm; €2), in a well-restored episcopal palace, has galleries arranged chronologically as you climb through five floors. Early wings highlight Romanesque and Gothic art, particularly rare manuscripts, such as an eleventh-century copy of Bede and an amazing martyrology from the monastery of Poblet, and impressive *Majestats* (wooden images of the crucified Christ garbed in a tunic). The top two floors progress through Renaissance works to the collection of nineteenth- and twentieth-century Catalan art, including a selection of pieces by the "Olot School" (see p.160), depictions of the French siege and some entertaining pieces of *modernista* sculpture.

One of Girona's best-known landmarks is the blunt tower of the **Església de Sant Feliu**, nicely framed as you descend the cathedral steps. Shortened by a lightning strike in 1581 and never repaired, the belfry tops a hemmed-in church that happily combines Romanesque, Gothic and Baroque styles. The north transept contains the **tomb of Sant Narcís**, patron of the city, while some elegantly sculpted Roman and early Christian **sarcophagi** are embedded in the wall either side of the high altar.

The Banys Arabs

Very near the cathedral, reached by going through the **Portal de Sobreportas** (fourteenth-century but built on visible Roman foundations), and then turning right, stand the so-called **Banys Arabs** (April–June & Sept Mon–Sat 10am–7pm; July & Aug Mon–Sat 10am–8pm; Oct–March Mon–Sat 10am–2pm; Sun & hols all year 10am–2pm; €1.60), probably designed by Moorish craftsmen around 1194 and rebuilt a century later. Closed down in the fifteenth century, supposedly to protect public morals, the building was appropriated by a Capuchin convent in 1617. After years of dereliction, the baths were restored by local architects Rafael Masó and Emili Blanc in 1929, and subsequently opened to the public as a museum. The finest of their type in Spain outside Granada, they have the usual under-floor heating system in the *caldarium* (steam room) and the Roman-derived layout of four principal rooms. The *apodyterium* (changing room) is the most

△ Banys Arabs, Girona

interesting; there are niches for one's clothes and a stone bench for relaxation after bathing, while the room is unusually lit by a central vaulted skylight supported by an octagon of columns.

The Museu Arqueològic and the city walls

From the Banys Arabs, it's a short downhill stroll, over the usually dry Riu Galligants, to the **Museu Arqueològic** (June–Sept Tues–Sat 10.30am–1.30pm &

4–7pm; Oct–May Tues–Sat 10am–2pm & 4–6pm; Sun 10am–2pm all year; €1.80), housed in the former Benedictine monastery of **Sant Pere Galligants**. The twelfth-century **church** itself contains Roman artefacts, including a vivid mosaic showing a chariot race, unearthed in 1876 at a nearby Roman villa. Extensive galleries above the cloisters methodically outline the region's history from Paleolithic to Roman times, but unless you read Catalan or Spanish, or pay €2 for the English-language guidebook, you'll get little out of these exhibits.

Near the museum you can gain access to the nearby **Passeig de la Muralla**, with steps through landscaped grounds beside the Banys Arabs leading up onto the **city walls**, from where there are fine views over Girona and the Ter valley. Once onto the ramparts (daily 8am–10pm; free), you can walk right round their perimeter, with intermediate exits near the Museu d'Art, behind the Sant Domènec convent and at the gate of the university, before the final descent to Plaça Catalunya, at the south end of the old town. Some detours are worth taking, for example steps down to the shaded gardens of the **Jardins dels Alemanys**, with ruined seventeenth-century barracks where German mercenaries were billeted. Further on is the rubble-strewn site of the **Torre Gironella**, where Jewish citizens were locked up for their protection during anti-Semitic riots in 1391 and which was finally destroyed by Napoleon's troops during the 1809 siege.

The Call or Aljama

Heading south instead of north from the Portal de Sobreportas, c/de la Força leads past the **Call**, considered the best-preserved Jewish quarter in Western Europe. A **Jewish community** of 25 families was well established in Girona by the late ninth century, with an initial settlement near the cathedral later shifting up to **Carrer de la Força**, which follows the course of the Roman Via Augusta. With a population of over three hundred at its peak, the new quarter became known as the Call or the **Aljama,** forming an autonomous municipality within Girona, under royal protection in exchange for payment of tribute. Cabbalistic scholarship thrived here under the leadership of **Rabbi Moisés Ben Nahman** (born 1194; Nahmánides or Bonastruc ça Porta in Catalan), and members of the community excelled in the professions – commerce, property speculation and banking – reserved for them. But from the thirteenth century onwards, Gironan Jews suffered systematic and escalating physical persecution; in 1391 a mob stormed the Call and killed forty of its residents, after which the neighbourhood became a restrictive ghetto like those of northern Europe, until the expulsion of the Jews from Spain in 1492.

The Aljama wasn't allowed to open windows, or more than one door, onto c/de la Força, so the inmates created a maze-like, multi-level complex of rooms, stairways and all-important courtyards, which in the final century of Jewish life here contained the synagogue, kosher slaughterhouse and communal baths. The **Centre Bonastruc Ça Porta** at c/de la Força 8 comprises much of this, plus a café, small bookshop and the **Museu d'Història dels Jueus** (June–Oct Mon–Sat 10am–8pm; Nov–May Mon–Sat 10am–6pm; all year Sun 10am–3pm; €2). This, disappointingly, is long on speculative archeology and short on substantive exhibits, these being principally a room full of enormous **grave stelae** inscribed in Hebrew, originally from the Bou d'Or cemetery on Montjuïc hill northeast of town, their fervent inscriptions the most definitive legacy of Jewish life here. Temporary expositions are likely to be more compelling.

The Museu d'Historia de la Ciutat

Housed in the eighteenth-century Capuchin monastery of Sant Antoni at c/de la Força 27, the **Museu d'Historia de la Ciutat** (Tues–Sat 10am–2pm & 5–7pm, Sun 10am–2pm; €2) completes the Barri Vell's complement of museums, and despite Catalan-only labelling, is likely to prove the most rewarding one – and certainly the most eclectic. A portion of the monastic catacombs is on the right as you enter, with niches for the (vanished) deceased. The entire ground floor is devoted to the development of local industry and technology, with an antique dealer's bonanza (salvaged from around the province) of ancient phones, typewriters, printing presses, dynamos and even an arc-lamp cine projector. The first floor covers the history of broadcasting in Catalunya – complete with some magnificent old radio sets – and Roman Gerunda, featuring a rather crude mosaic from a villa on the surrounding plain. On the top floor you'll find a modern art exhibition, plus material on the evolution of the *sardana*.

Museu del Cinema

Tucked away on the west bank of the Onyar at c/Sèquia 1, the **Museu del Cinema** (May–Sept Tues–Sun 10am–8pm; Oct–April Tues–Fri 10am–6pm, Sat 10am–8pm, Sun 11am–3pm; €4) is a fascinating museum detailing the history of the cinema from the first moving images to the present. Based on the private collection of award-winning local director Tomàs Mallol, the museum has a good mix of interactive exhibits and informative displays to please kids and adults alike. Most interesting are some surprisingly sophisticated early attempts by diverse cultures to create animated images; the ground-floor shop stocks a full complement of cinematic memorabilia.

Eating, drinking and nightlife

Most of Girona's more adventurous **restaurants** and **bars** (plus some obvious tourist-traps) are grouped along and just off c/de la Força, or on c/Ballesteries, while outdoor daytime **cafés** cluster on or around the Rambla de la Llibertat, and on the parallel Plaça del Vi. **Nightlife** is varied, with venues scattered across the Barri Vell, Mercadal and the former tradesmen's quarter of Pedret, about 700m north of the old quarter between the rail line and the riverbank. Formal events and **concerts** by foreign guest artists tend to take place in one of three venues: the Teatre de Sant Domènec, the Auditoria de la Mercé or Sala la Planeta. The Turisme has current details.

Restaurants

Boira Plaça de la Independencia 17. The best food on the square, very popular with locals and visitors alike, with a cafe open 7.30am–1.30am and smart restaurant for lunch and dinner. Local Girona classics such as grilled veal and other *plats del dia* for €7–15.

La Crêperie Bretonne c/Cort Reial 14. Savoury and sweet crêpes, prepared by a French ex-pat, plus salads and Breton cider, form the basis of good-value *menús*. Vast, striking interior belies narrow street frontage, which is dominated by a converted minibus (part of the pantry). Summer tables in the street. Closed all Sun plus Wed lunch time in winter.

El Cul de la Lleona c/Calderers 8. Cosy if potentially pricey bistro specializing in Moroccan dishes; three courses (including house wine and lovely Catalan or North African sweets) can run to €30. Also a much cheaper "local" *menú* at lunch time, plus summer tables on the nearby fountain-*plaça*. Closed Sun & Mon.

La Força Vella c/de la Força 4. *Menús* (€12) served in the stone-clad area in front of the bar; fare encompasses snails, sausage, rabbit and squid. Open until 4pm for lunch, 11pm for dinner.

La Penyora c/Nou del Teatre 3. Catalan *nouvelle cuisine* in suitably minimalist surroundings; ordering platters such as *carpaccio de filet de vidella* nets *a la carta* bills in excess of €30, though there's a much cheaper lunch *menú*. Closed Tues.

La Polenta c/Cort Reial 6 ⓣ972 209 374. Tiny, generally busy (best to reserve) vegetarian restaurant serving delicious organic fare (*menú* €11). Open weekdays 8.30–10.30pm, Sat also 1–3.30pm, Sun lunch only; closed Thurs.

El Pou de la Call c/de la Força 14. More elaborate than usual recipes and ingredients in exceptionally pleasant surroundings right next to the Call; *menús* (€13–25, drink extra) comprise three courses such as vegetarian *terrina*, squid rings with parsley and garlic, plus baked apple with custard, but *a la carta* (allow €30) is more varied. No outdoor seating, but a/c premises.

Zanpanzar c/Cort Reial 10–12. Started life to great acclaim as a *tapas* bar doing Basque-style *pintxos* like *bacalao* and Gernika pimientos (€5 & up); there's now also an attached full-on restaurant (*menú* €10; allow €25 *a la carta*). Closed Mon.

Bars, clubs and cafés

L'Arc Plaça de la Catedral 9. The only café in Girona with a cathedral on the terrace. During the day it's a pleasant spot for coffee or *orxata*, while at night it becomes a secluded hideaway.

L'Arcada Rambla de la Llibertat 38. Bar-café tucked under the arcades, with designer-minimalist interior and sought-after outdoor tables, serving good breakfast pastries, pasta and pizza. Also *tapas* and an Italian-flavoured lunch *menú* (€11). Daily 7.30am–12.30am.

Le Bistrot Pujada de Sant Domènec 4. Stylish, Belle Époque tile-floored surroundings inside, massively popular tables on the steps outside. Evening meals, however, don't quite live up to the stylish surroundings; best stick to the better-value €12 lunch-time *menú* or a drink.

Manaus c/Calderers 6. Tropical fruit juices and nothing but, served in summer on the nearby fountain-*plaça*.

Nummulit c/Nord 7, Mercadal. Very lively bar near Plaça Independencia, where half Girona's young seems to fetch up after midnight. Daily 10pm–3am.

Café Royal Plaça Independencia 1. Pleasant corner spot that's equally good for breakfast, juices or a tipple from late afternoon onwards.

La Sala del Cel c/Pedret 118 ⓦwww.lasaldelcel.cat. Vast, multi-level club (including chill-out rooms and terraces) whose visiting and resident DJs draw crowds from across the province. Fri–Sat 11pm–6am.

Cafeteria Sol Plaça del Vi. No-nonsense bar that's good for breakfast or *plats combinats* under the arcade.

La Terra c/Ballesteries 23 (tiny sign on door). Popular student hangout, open from 6pm until late: a wonderfully cavernous space, with glazed tiles everywhere and river-view windows. Serving juices, foreign beers, coffees, cakes and teas in a pot. Daily 6pm–2am.

La Taverna de l'Abat c/Galligants, opposite Museu Arquelògic. Occupying a sixteenth-century episcopal manor, this atmospheric bar also offers light snacks and live music, plus tango and jazz nights. Closed Mon.

Listings

Books and maps Ulyssus, c/Ballesteries 29, is an excellent travel-book specialist with lots of Spanish- and Catalan-language guides to Catalunya, plus all Editorial Alpina and Catalan government ICC maps.

Buses The most important companies are TEISA (ⓦwww.teisa-bus.com), handling all services northwest through the Garrotxa to Olot, with onward connections to Ripoll and the Cerdanya, and SARFA (ⓦwww.sarfa.com), which handles most departures northeast towards Figueres and the northern Costa Brava.

Car rental Most agencies are in or near the train station – for example, Avis (ⓣ972 224 664) and Hertz (ⓣ972 210 108). Otherwise, pick cars up at the airport.

Hospital Dr Josep Trueta, Avgda França 60 (ⓣ972 202 700), at the northern outskirts of town, is best for emergencies; urban bus #2 gets you there.

Internet access Try *Communica-T Net* at c/Peralta 4 (Mon–Sat 10.30am–10.30pm, Sun 4–10.30pm) or *La Lli-Breria* at c/Ferreries Velles 16, a cafe and bookshop (daily 9am–1am, Sun 9am–10.30pm).

Newspapers English-language papers are available at the kiosks on Plaça de Independencia and along Rambla de la Llibertat.

Police Policia Municipal at c/Bacià 4 ⓣ972 419 092; Mossos d'Esquadra (Catalan gendarerie: ⓣ972 213 450).

Pubol: Casa-Museu Castell Gala Dalí

Especially if you've been to, or plan to visit, the other two Dalí museums in Alt Empordà, you'll want to make the journey (easiest with your own transport) 22km from Girona to attractive **PÚBOL** village, site of the small medieval castle which Dalí bought and restored for his wife Gala in 1970. Now open to the public as the **Casa-Museu Castell Gala Dalí** (March 16–June 14 & Sept 16–Dec Tues–Sun 10.30am–5.15pm; June 15–Sept 15 daily 10.30am–7.15pm; closed Jan–March 15; €6), it contains a lurid mix of precious artworks and Baroque kitsch which the pair bought or made, for example a suitably surreal bronze chess set Dalí created in honour of Marcel Duchamp. The castle itself, while perhaps not as wacky as their dwelling at Portlligat, has its quirks as well, such as the womb-shaped fireplace off the kitchen, and the crypt (formerly a tithe warehouse for grain) where Gala is entombed. There's plenty of biographical material on display, in particular photos of Dalí in his 1930s–40s prime, and a fascinating album devoted to Gala (1894–1982), née Elena Dimitrievna Diakonova. Her collection of *haute couture* dresses is on the top floor, while her Cadillac is still parked in the garage.

Dalí's innate snobbery was stoked considerably when, in 1982 (the year of Gala's death), he was awarded the title of Marqués de Dalí de Púbol by King Juan Carlos. He lived permanently at the castle thereafter, writing extensively and painting his last authenticated work (*Kite's Tale and Guitar*) until a fire broke out in 1984, severely injuring Dalí and obliging him to move to Figueres.

The Fluvià valley and the Garrotxa

Northwest of Girona lies the lush, humid Garrotxa region, watered by the Riu Fluvià and its various tributaries. South of the Fluvià extends the volcanic **Baixa Garrotxa**, where eleven millennia of erosion have moulded dormant cinder cones into rounded and fertile hills. The more northerly **Alta Garrotxa** is an area of deserted farms set amidst low chunky limestone mountains, the highest of which – 1558-metre Puig de Comanegra – straddles the frontier.

The easiest route through the area – served by buses – involves following the C150 from just north of Girona, through lakeside **Banyoles**, to the junction of the N260 at resolutely medieval **Besalú**. West of there, a brash stretch of the short A26 motorway past **Castellfollit de la Roca**, whose houses peer over a sheer basalt cliff, comes as a shock. For a glimpse of back-country Garrotxa, especially with your own vehicle, use the narrower C524 from **Banyoles** to **Olot**, capital of the Garrotxa region, via atmospheric **Santa Pau**. Near Santa Pau, there's easy, scenic walking in the **Parc Natural de la Zona Volcanica**, set aside to protect the best of the Garrotxa, including the surviving beech forest known as **La Fageda d'en Jordà**.

Banyoles

BANYOLES, 21km from Girona, makes a moderately pleasant place to pass a few hours on the way to Besalú or Santa Pau. The town's distinction is its **Estany** (lake), fed by underground springs and 75m at its deepest point.

Arrival and information

All **buses** stop on Passeig de la Indústria, with the ticket office nearby at the intersection with c/Àlvarez de Castro, the road in from Girona. Plaça Major lies 200m northeast of here, while the **Turisme**, which gives out a town plan, is at Passeig de la Indústria 25 (June–Aug Mon–Sat 10am–2pm & 5–7pm, Sun 10am–1pm; Sept–May Mon–Fri 10am–2pm & 5–7pm, Sat 10am–1pm; Ⓣ972 575 573, Ⓦwww.banyoles.org); there's also a summer-only wooden annexe on lakeside Passeig Darder.

Accommodation

With Girona and Besalú so near, few will choose to stay in Banyoles, though there's **accommodation** in all price ranges. Two pleasant, modern budget *pensions* sit just a couple of blocks back from the water: *Fonda La Paz* (Ⓣ972 570 432; ③)

at c/Ponent 18 and *Can Xabanet* (Ⓣ972 570 375, Ⓕ570 252; ❸) around the corner on Plaça del Carmé 24–27. There are two lakeside establishments, including *Hotel l'Ast* (Ⓣ & Ⓕ972 570 414; ❺) on Passeig Dalmau 63, with a pool, though room views are of trees rather than the water. The best campsite is lakeshore *El Llac* (Ⓣ972 570 305), on the way to Porqueres, just below and before the church.

With your own transport, three local **turismes rurals** may appeal. *Can Ribes* (Ⓣ972 573 211, Ⓦwww.canribes.com; ❹ B&B), 6km south of Banyoles beyond the hamlet of Camós (also reached from Girona via the Palol de Revardit exit from the N-II) is geared for resident Spanish-language courses, but welcomes all comers with a grassy garden and superb views east, a fridge full of cold drinks and savoury Catalan breakfast. The downsides are somewhat primitive furnishings (it was one of the first such inns established, with not all rooms en suite) and less than brilliant suppers. More universally popular, 14km east of Banyoles just off the N-II, is *Mas Alba* in Terradelles village (Ⓣ972 560 488, Ⓦwww.masalba.com; ❺ B&B), with riding stables and organic-produce dinners. About halfway to Besalú on the C150, just off the highway in Serinyà, thirteenth-century *Can Solanas* (Ⓣ972 593 199, Ⓦwww.cansolanas.com; ❺ B&B) is well kept, with a pool and multi-lingual management.

The Town

Around the lake, cruises, rowing boats and pedaloes are on offer, while private waterside *pesqueres* (fishing gazebos) further domesticate the *estany*, a process completed by its hosting of the 1992 Olympic rowing events. An eight-kilometre walking or cycling circuit of the lake passes through tiny **Porqueres** hamlet, whose twelfth-century church of **Santa Maria** has unusual column capitals flanking the entrance.

Back in the somewhat drab town, the arcaded **Plaça Major**, studded with plane trees and with a few bars tucked under the arches, has hosted a Wednesday market since the thirteenth century. From here, it's 200m northeast to the **Museu Arqueològic Comarcal** (Tues–Sat: July & Aug 10.30am–1.30pm & 4–7.30pm; Sept–June 10.30am–1.30pm & 4–6.30pm; Sun 10.30am–2pm all year; €1.80; Catalan labelling only but English crib sheet provided). Installed in a thirteenth-century almshouse on Plaça de la Font, the collection used to contain the famous jawbone of a pre-Neanderthal woman found in the nearby Serinyà caves, but nowadays a replica is displayed; authentic specimens include Paleolithic tools and Pleiocene/Pleistocene bison, rhino and elephant bones, all found in local quarry works. Galleries of historical eras feature three bronze figures of the Roman deities Lar, Fortuna and Mercury, remounted in a *lararium*, or household shrine, that would have graced local villas from the first to seventh centuries, as well as medieval painted plates, found in a dry well in the almshouse.

Eating and drinking

Taking lunch or supper at one of the town's many **restaurants** makes more sense, and indeed Banyoles is something of a foodie's destination. A few designer-interior ones are on, or just off, the Plaça Major, for example *Brasseria El Capitell*, at no. 14 (closed Tues eve & Weds), specializing in cod and meat, or *La Cisterna* at c/Àlvarez de Castro 36 (open Mon–Sat lunch, also Sat eve), which takes minimalist decor to the point of clinical sterility, but is always packed at lunch thanks to a good-value €12 *menú*. More traditional but salubrious *menjadors* are those of *Fonda La Paz* (€9–12 lunch *menús*, €10 dinner, €26 *a la carta*) and equally popular *Can Xabanet*, where the €8–12 *menús* are a bit limited, but €22 is well spent *a la carta* on such dishes as shellfish-stuffed peppers or duck with prunes, plus dessert, served in leisurely fashion by bow-tied waiters.

Besalú

From the road, the imposing eleventh-century **fortified bridge** by the confluence of the Fluvià and Capellada rivers is the only sign of anything remarkable about **BESALÚ**, 16km from Banyoles. But pass under the portcullis in the bridge's central toll-house and you'll enter a medieval settlement that's been a preserved historical monument since 1966. Steep narrow streets, sunbaked squares and cave-like arcaded shops bear silent witness to an illustrious history out of proportion to its current humble status. Besalú was an important town before the medieval period – Roman, Visigothic, Frankish and Muslim despots came and went – but all the surviving monuments date from the tenth to twelfth centuries, when it briefly became the seat of a small, independent principality under the dynasty of Guillem el Pilós.

Christian intolerance drove the Jews from Besalú, and their **Miqvé** (ritual bath-house) was later turned into a dyeworks. Originally attached to a synagogue, now excavated above, the Miqvé (may be open, otherwise 5 daily visits Mon–Fri, 2 Sat–Sun; €1.25; enquire at the Turisme) hides inconspicuously down by the river, at the end of signposted Baixada de Mikwè, underneath the bridge-viewing platform. It proves to be a high, single-vaulted chamber, with steps leading down into the former plunge pool.

Continuing in the same direction, you'll reach the porticoed **Plaça de la Llibertat**, site of the Tuesday market and enveloped by medieval buildings such as the thirteenth-century Casa de la Vila, now home to the *ajuntament* and the tourist office. Majestically arcaded c/Tallaferro leads uphill to the ruined shell of **Santa Maria** (4 tours Fri only; €5; ask at Turisme), which for just two years (1018–20) was the cathedral of the bishopric of Besalú; political union with Barcelona ended this short-lived episcopal independence.

Further west, you emerge onto a vast, fan-shaped *plaça*, the Prat de Sant Pere, dominated by the Benedictine monastic **Església de Sant Pere**. The barrel-vaulted interior is impressive enough, with a fine colonnaded ambulatory preserving four carved column capitals with monsters and human figures, but the church's most distinctive feature is the arched Gothic window of the west facade, flanked by a pair of grotesque stone lions; it's best admired from a pair of bar-cafés diagonally opposite.

Working your way up c/Ganganell brings you to extensively rebuilt twelfth- to fourteenth-century **Sant Vicenç**, where arches and capitals flanking the Gothic side entrance bear intricately carved mythical monsters; this church, too, has a Gothic rose window, high up on its southwest facade, while the little landscaped square faces tables set out by the nearby restaurant (see opposite).

Practicalities

Buses stop on the main road, from where it's a short walk south to the central Plaça de la Llibertat and the **Turisme** (daily 10am–2pm & 4–7pm; ⓣ972 591 240, ⓦwww.besalu.net), which keeps the expected stock of brochures, as well as keys to locked monuments. **Parking** is best on the far side of the old bridge, near where the *turístic* **fake train** commences its to-ings and fro-ings.

Staying overnight is highly recommended, since Besalú's character changes completely once the daily quota of trippers has departed. The pin-neat, en-suite *Fonda Venència* at c/Major 6 (ⓣ972 591 257; ❷) represents excellent value; *Habitacions-Residència Marià*, Plaça de la Llibertat 7 (ⓣ972 590 106; ❸), is a more atmospheric, rambling old building, also with heated en-suite rooms. For more comfort, try three-star *Hotel Comte Tallaferro* (ⓣ972 591 609, ⓦwww.grupcalparent.com; ❹) at c/Ganganell 2, with a small roof terrace and rear patio. The rooms

△ Arcaded street, Besalú

themselves, four of them facing Prat de Sant Pere, range from "standard" doubles to galleried family quads to skylit top-floor suites, with some disabled facilities. The most unusual accommodation, however, is *Hotel Els Jardins de la Martana*, a three-storey mansion from 1910 at the far end of the bridge (Ⓣ972 590 009, Ⓦwww.lamartana.com; ❻ B&B). The large rooms all have balconies, antique-tile floors, fridges and state-of-the-art bathrooms; common areas include a panelled library with fireplace and gardens dropping in two levels to the river.

There's also an excellent **casa rural** about 10km northeast. Take the minor road 5km north to Beuda village, then swing east to continue a similar distance to **Segueró**, where *Can Felicià* (Ⓣ972 590 523; ❺) occupies the old schoolhouse next to the church. Homely rooms transcend the former institutional status, there's a plunge-pool on the lawn and meals are provided. The closest **campsite** to Besalú lies just off the N260, about 5km towards Figueres: *Masia Can Coromines* (Ⓣ972 591 108; April–Oct), centred on an ancient farmhouse doubling as a well-regarded pizzeria. This is Spanish camping as it should be: 45 spaces predominantly for tents, a nice big pool with a grassy verge and a lively bar.

The best food in Besalú is found at *Cal Parent*, a Cuina Volcànica-affiliated (see p.163) **restaurant** up on the main road (closed Mon Nov–Easter; *menús* €9–14 or pricier *a la carta*). Another good-value option is *Can Quiei* (shut Wed) on Plaça Sant Vicenç, with two *menús*, *a la carta* and some outdoor tables.

Castellfollit de la Roca

CASTELLFOLLIT DE LA ROCA, 14km west of Besalú, promises great things, as its church and houses perch atop a sixty-metre precipice overlooking the Riu Fluvià. Arrival is most impressive by night, when spotlights play on the natural basalt columns underpinning the village. But as the road curls around and up, Castellfollit proves disappointing, its main street lined by tightly packed rows of grubby buildings giving no hint of the extraordinary palisade. Despite the opening of the four-lane bypass tunnelling around the village in 2003, Castellfollit still hasn't recovered from being threaded by the main road for so long.

You might leave your vehicle, however, to sample the view from the cliff: head south from the prominent clock tower to the church and the banistered viewing platform behind. On the main street, 100m downhill from the clock tower, Castellfollit's **Museum of Sausages** (Mon–Sat 9.30am–1.30pm & 4–8pm, Sun 9.30am–2pm & 4.30–8pm), run by the Sala family to celebrate a century and a half in the skin-stuffing business, is almost certainly unique, as claimed. Pungent with the aroma of sausages, it's mainly an excuse to sell them; the exhibits consist mostly of antique production machinery.

The only **accommodation** is *Pensió Cala Paula*, next to the clock tower at Plaça de Sant Roc 3 (Ⓣ972 294 032, Ⓔcalapaula@terra.es; ❸), surprisingly comfortable, with a decent, popular ground-floor **bar-restaurant** and off-street parking.

Olot

Capital of the Garrotxa *comarca*, **OLOT** is more rewarding than its sprawling, anonymous outskirts suggest. Today, most of the centre of Olot consists of eighteenth- and nineteenth-century buildings, a consequence of devastating earthquakes in 1427–28, which levelled the medieval settlement. But follow any of the narrow lanes north into the *barri vell* from the through road, and the scene changes to one of intimate squares, elegant shops, a pleasant *rambla* and convivial bars. It's also one of the most cosmopolitan places in the Pyrenees, with noticeable Chinese, Senegalese and Sikh communities.

The town's original prosperity was based on its crafts tradition. Religious-images manufacture began here in 1880, remaining a major industry until the 1950s. Cotton-milling also flourished during the late eighteenth century, alongside workshops printing patterned textiles; the latter were instrumental in the formation of the Escola Pública de Dibuix (Public School of Drawing) in 1783. Joaquim Vayreda i Vila (1843–94), a founder of the "Olot School" of painters, was a pupil at the drawing school, but an 1871 trip to Paris brought him under the spell of Millet's rural painting and exposed him to the Impressionists. From these influences, and the Garrotxa scenery, sprang the distinctive style of the Olot artists.

Olot lies between three (dormant) volcanic cones easily accessible without long treks or drives; bare-topped **Volcà de Montsacopa** in particular, with its picturesque summit chapel of Sant Francesc, is worth the walk up on local "Itinerari 17". Frequent bus connections and a fair choice in food and lodging (some of this just out of town) make Olot a likely base for touring the Garrotxa.

Arrival and information

All buses use the central **bus station** at the east end of c/Bisbe Lorenzana. Arriving by **car**, you can usually find **parking** spaces, both fee-paying and free, near the post office; otherwise it's best to use the two central enclosed car parks shown on the map. There are **taxi** ranks at Plaça Clarà and the bus station.

The **Turisme** (Mon–Fri 9am–2pm & 5–7pm, Sat 10am–2pm & 5–7pm, Sun 11am–2pm; Ⓣ972 260 141, Ⓦwww.olot.org) is just inside the entrance of the Museu Comarcal, stocking the all-important schematic map (inside the "Parc Natural de la Zona Volcànica" folding brochure) of designated walking routes through the Garrotxa. At the southeast end of Passeig d'en Blay, with its whimsical Teatre Principal, the Drac **bookshop** on the ground floor of another *modernista* building sells commercial maps and guides (in Spanish or Catalan) for the area.

Accommodation

Good-value in-town lodgings are limited; if you've got transport you're well advised to cast your net a bit wider to include *turismes rurals* in neighbouring hamlets. The nearest **campsite** is well-arrayed *La Fageda* (Ⓣ972 271 239), 4km distant on the minor road to Santa Pau, with its own pool. Olot's **youth hostel**, *Alberg Torre Malagrida*, Passeig de Barcelona 15 (Ⓣ972 264 200; closed Sept), lies

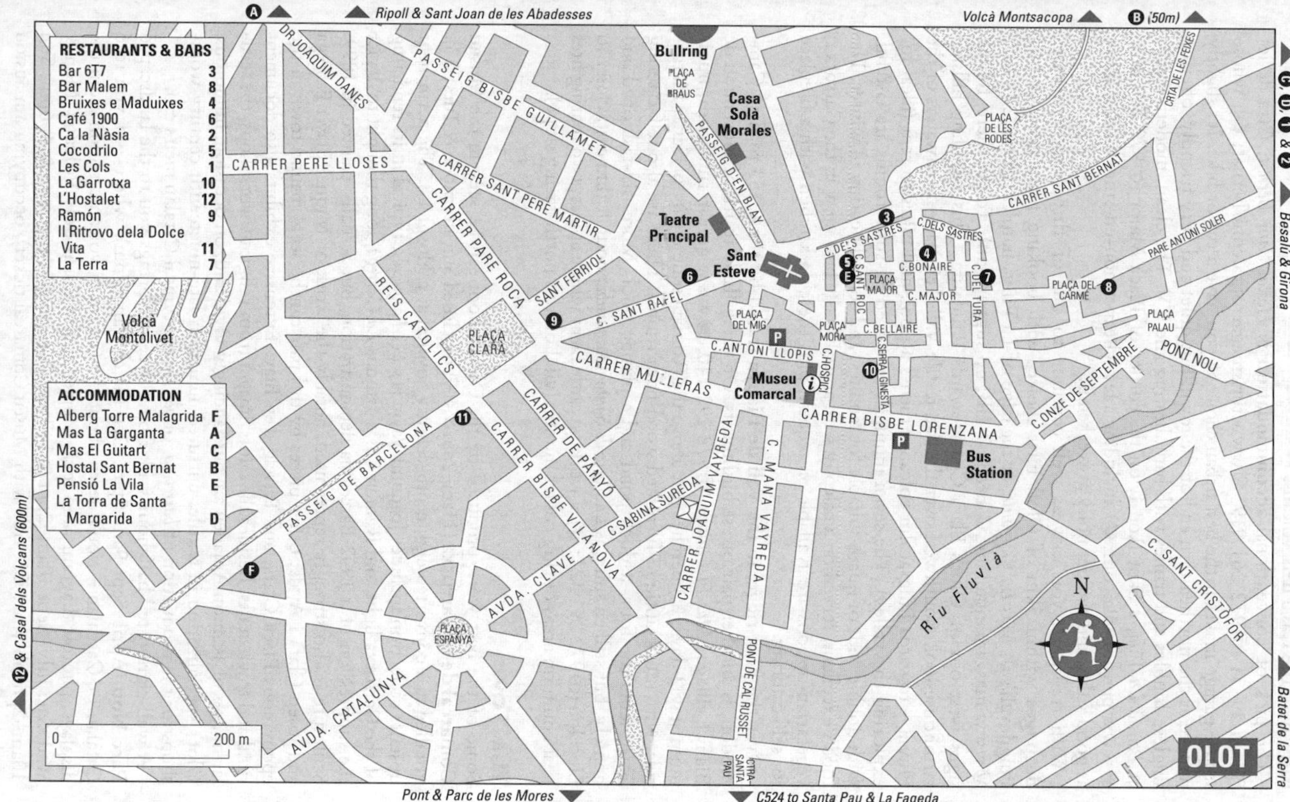
OLOT
A
Ripoll & Sant Joan de les Abadesses
Volcà Montsacopa
B (50m)
C, D, 1 & 2
Besalú & Girona
Batet de la Serra
Pont & Parc de les Mores
C524 to Santa Pau & La Fageda
12 & Casal dels Volcans (600m)
RESTAURANTS & BARS
Bar 6T7 3
Bar Malem 8
Bruixes e Maduixes 4
Café 1900 6
Ca la Nàsia 2
Cocodrilo 5
Les Cols 1
La Garrotxa 10
L'Hostalet 12
Ramón 9
Il Ritrovo dela Dolce
Vita 11
La Terra 7
ACCOMMODATION
Alberg Torre Malagrida F
Mas La Garganta A
Mas El Guitart C
Hostal Sant Bernat B
Pensió La Vila E
La Torra de Santa
Margarida D
Volcà Montolivet
0
200 m
Bullring
Casa Solà Morales
Teatre Principal
Sant Esteve
Museu Comarcal
Bus Station
Riu Fluvià
N
CARRER PERE LLOSES
PASSEIG BISBE GUILLAMET
CARRER SANT PERE MARTIR
CARRER PARE ROCA
REIS CATOLICS
PASSEIG DE BARCELONA
AVDA. CATALUNYA
AVDA. CLAVE
CARRER BISBE VILANOVA
CARRER DE PANYO
CARRER MULLERAS
CARRER JOAQUIM VAYREDA
C. MANA VAYREDA
CARRER BISBE LORENZANA
C. ANTONI LLOPIS
C. SANT RAFEL
SANT FERRIOL
PASSEIG D'EN BLAY
CARRER SANT BERNAT
PARE ANTONI SOLER
CRTA DE LES FEIXES
DR JOAQUIM DANES
C. SANT CRISTOFOR
C. ONZE DE SETEMBRE
PONT NOU
PONT DE CAL RUSSET
CTRA SANTA PAU
PLAÇA PALAU
PLAÇA DEL CARME
PLAÇA DE LES RODES
PLAÇA DE BRAUS
PLAÇA DEL MIG
PLAÇA MORA
PLAÇA MAJOR
PLAÇA CLARA
PLAÇA ESPANYA
C. DELS SASTRES
C. DEL TURA
C. BONAIRE
C. MAJOR
C. BELLAIRE
C. SERRA I GINESTA
C. SANT ROC
C. HOSPICI
C. SABINA SUREDA

well southwest of the centre, in an adapted 1920s villa overlooking the river, about halfway to the Casal dels Volcans.

The pick of conventional **accommodation** is *Hostal Sant Bernat*, Ctra de les Feixes 29–31 (Ⓣ972 261 919, Ⓦwww.turismegarrotxa.com/bernat; ❸), whose secure garage makes it the best urban choice if you have a car or bike. It's slightly remote at the northeastern end of the town, but quiet and very friendly, offering singles, doubles and triples with bath, heating and TV. The clean, modern rooms at *Pensió La Vila*, c/Sant Roc 1, on the corner of Plaça Major (Ⓣ972 269 807, Ⓦwww.pensiolavila.com; ❷), including a few cheaper non-en-suite singles, aren't as good value and can get noisy at weekends.

With transport, you may as well continue to one of three excellent **cases de pagès** within 5km of Olot. First choice, with booking mandatory, is Inès Puigdevall's *Mas La Garganta*, at the edge of La Pinya hamlet (Ⓣ972 271 289; Ⓦwww.masgarganta.com; ❺ B&B, ❻ HB; no supper Sun). To get there, follow signs west out of Olot's Plaça Clarà towards Riudaura. This rambling hillside farmhouse looks southwest over the flat, fertile Vall d'en Bas – headwaters of the Fluvià – towards Puigsacalm volcano; there's a pool, and bikes to rent (ideal for exploring the valley). The seven minimally restored en-suite rooms are tasteful, with double beds or quads suitable for families, and central heating in winter. The food's excellent, served on a balcony with arguably the best view in the Garrotxa; vegetarian options are available on request, plus there's a kitchen with a fireplace for self-catering.

Over the next ridge, in the **Vall de Bianya** traced by the C153 road to Camprodon, is another pair of establishments. On the hillside south of Hostalnou de Bianya village, *Mas El Guitart* (Ⓣ972 292 140, Ⓦwww.guitartrural.com; minimum stay 2 days; ❸) perches just above the Romanesque *ermita* of Santa Margarida, with mock-antique-furnished wood-floor rooms. There are also self-catering apartments for four, a duck pond and a plunge pool. More old-fashioned and homely, but still en suite, is *La Torre de Santa Margarida* about 1.5km east, closer to Llocalou (Ⓣ972 291 321; ❸), a working cattle farm where at least two roaring fires heat common areas during colder months (vital on this north-facing slope).

The Town

Some of the best work produced by the Olot School can be seen in the **Museu Comarcal de la Garrotxa** (11am–2pm & 4–7pm, closed Sun afternoon & Tues; €3), installed in a converted eighteenth-century hospital at c/Hospici 8. The permanent upstairs collection includes Joaquim Vayreda's *Les Falgueres*, typical in its rendering of the Garrotxa light, and Ramon Casas' famous *La Càrrega*, long thought to depict the suppression of a 1902 Barcelona demonstration, but actually painted in 1899. Sculpture is also strongly represented, notably the work of Miquel Blay i Fabrega and Josep Clarà i Ayals; other pieces by this pair can be seen around town in the eponymous Plaça Clarà, and Passeig d'en Blay. Extensive exhibits also document rural and town crafts. Besides the saints' images from religious workshops, the secular figures of Ramon Amadeu are outstandingly vivid and, on occasion, humorous. Olot's specialization in textiles nurtured numerous late-nineteenth-century workshops for the production of *barretinas* or *gores* – the typical Catalan men's cap.

A well-signposted half-hour walk from the centre brings you to the landscaped **Parc Nou** (April–Sept 9am–9pm; Oct–March 9am–7pm), where – if you read Catalan or Castilian – you'll learn about the Garrotxa volcanic region from the displays, photos, diagrams and rock samples in the **Casal dels Volcans** (Mon & Wed–Sat: July–Sept 10am–2pm & 5–7pm; Oct–June 10am–2pm & 4–6pm; Sun 10am–2pm all year; €3, free with Museu Comarcal ticket), occupying a mansion in the park.

Eating and drinking

Olot in particular and the Garrotxa generally is the focus of the **Cuina Volcànica** group, whose restauranteur members undertake to use eleven core local ingredients – including beans, boar and truffles – in their recipes. That said, outstanding city-centre choices are few, and with transport and a fuller wallet, you'll do better on the outskirts, or just out of town.

Ca la Nàsia 1km west of La Canya suburb in Llocalou hamlet ☏972 290 200. Fancy spot specializing in *faisà a la terra* (pheasant cooked with raisins in a clay pot), game and wild mushrooms. Reservations advised. Closed Mon & late July.

Les Cols northern outskirts of town on Crta de la Canya, towards the C153 ☏972 269 209. The typical *masia* exterior belies an ultra-modern interior where excellent *cuina de mercat* (seasonal ingredients) prevails. Reservations suggested. Lunch till 3.30pm, supper to 11pm. Closed eves Sun–Tues & mid-July to mid-Aug.

La Garrotxa c/Serra i Ginesta 14. Don't be put off by the institutional decor of this self-service Cuina Volcànica restaurant near the museum. A changing list of specials (€9 *menú* or *a la carta*) – fish soup, pork cheek, grilled quails, potatoes stuffed with sardines – represents excellent value, if not always flawless execution. Open daily for lunch, also Sat eve April–Sept.

L'Hostalet in Les Hostalets d'en Bas, 10km from Olot on the C152, less from La Pinya ☏972 690 006. The best of three restaurants in the very attractive village of Les Hostalets d'en Bas, this Cuina Volcànica affiliate offers three courses for around €22 *a la carta*, including own-made desserts. Reserve in advance. Closed Sun eve, Tues & a random month in summer.

Ramón Plaça Clarà 11. Bar serving mid-priced Catalan *tapas*, seafood *plats combinats*, plus an economical *menú*; its under-arcade seating also makes a good vantage point if you just want a drink. Shut Sun eve.

Il Ritrovo dela Dolce Vita Passeig de Barcelona 1. Smart and trendy *trattoria* serving the best pizzas in town for €8–9; also salads plus meat and pasta dishes, pricey wine list but normal beers. Open Sun eve also, unusually for Olot.

La Terra c/Bonaire 22. Fashionable macrobiotic veggie restaurant that does a decent lunch-time *menú* for under €10. Lunch Tues–Sat, also dinner Tues & Sat.

Nightlife and entertainment

More than a dozen **bars** and **cafés** are scattered between the bullring and Plaça Verge del Carmé at the eastern end of the *barri*. Aside from a few on Passeig d'en

Flora and fauna of the Garrotxa region

The lower slopes of the Garrotxa region's distinctive hills nurture **forests** of evergreen oak (*Quercus mediterraneo-montanum*), yielding further up to deciduous oak and beech woods, with subalpine meadows and pastures at even higher altitudes. More than 1500 species of **vascular plant** have been recorded within the park, ranging from typical forest-floor dwellers like snowdrops, yellow wood anemones and rue-leaved isopyrum, to alpine specialities like ramonda and Pyrenean saxifrage. In addition, the Garrotxa contains a number of endemics, found nowhere else: the white-flowered *Allium pyrenaicum*, typical of rocky limestone cliffs; Pyrenean milkwort (*Polygala vayredae*), a woody species with large pinkish-purple flowers; and shrubby gromwell (*Aithodora oleifolia*), a climbing plant with pale pink flowers that turn blue with age.

A phenomenal 143 species of **bird** have been observed in the region. Since three-quarters of the park is covered with forest, goshawks, tawny owls, short-toed treecreepers, great spotted woodpeckers and nuthatches are common. Flocks of bramblings and hawfinches take refuge in the beech woods during winter, while the more barren volcanic summits support alpine choughs and alpine accentors. Summer visitors include short-toed eagles, hobbies, wrynecks, red-backed shrikes and Bonelli's warblers, along with Mediterranean species such as subalpine warblers, golden orioles and bee-eaters.

Forest-dwelling **mammals** include beech martens, wildcats, genets, badgers and acorn-loving wild boar, as well as a number of small insectivores – common, pygmy and Etruscan shrews – and the noctural oak dormouse, characterized by its "Lone Ranger" mask and long, black-tufted tail. Otters are also occasionally sighted along the rivers.

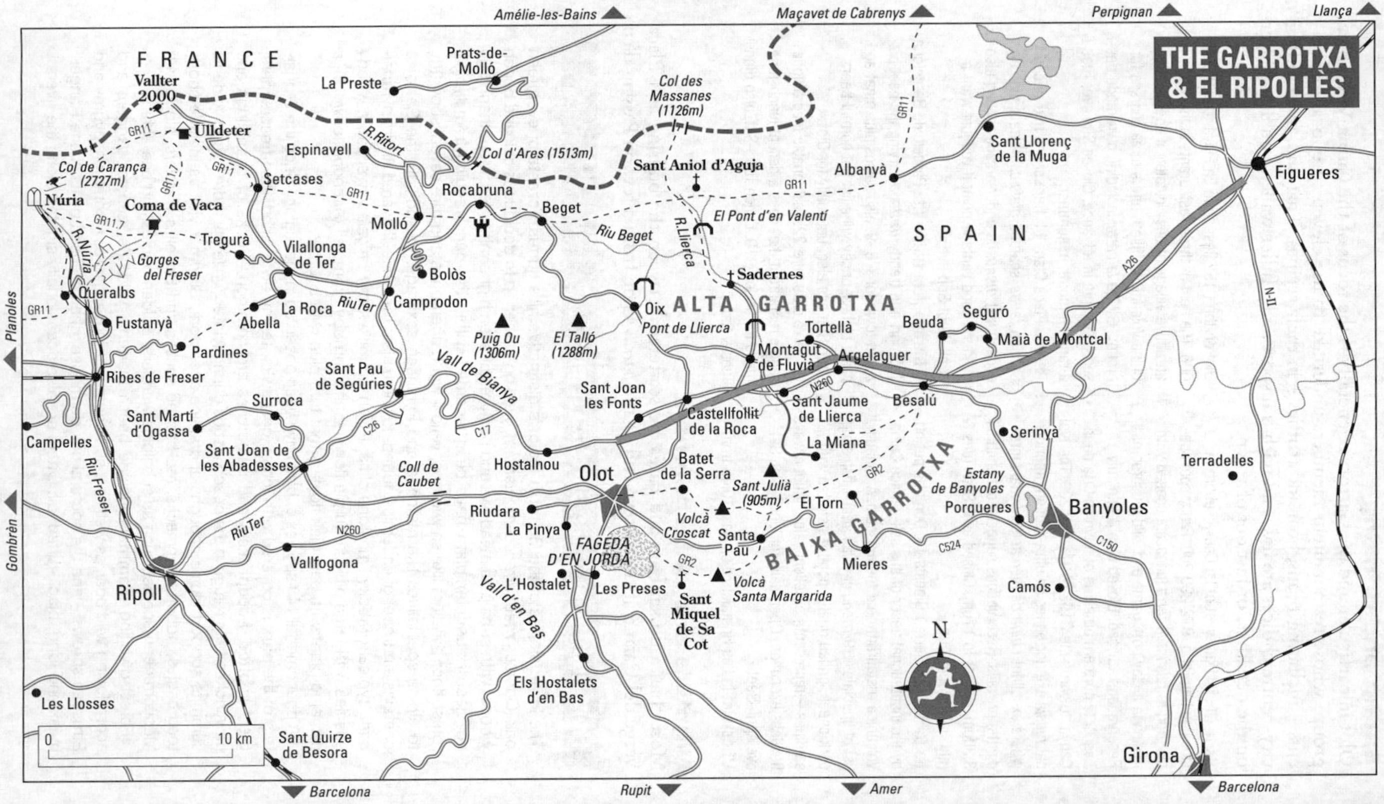

THE GARROTXA & EL RIPOLLÈS

Llança
Perpignan
Maçavet de Cabrenys
Amélie-les-Bains
Planoles
Gombrèn
Barcelona
Rupit
Amer
Barcelona
FRANCE
SPAIN
ALTA GARROTXA
BAIXA GARROTXA
Figueres
Sant Llorenç de la Muga
Albanyà
Sant Aniol d'Aguja
Col des Massanes (1126m)
Col d'Ares (1513m)
Prats-de-Molló
La Preste
Vallter 2000
Ulldeter
Col de Carança (2727m)
Núria
Coma de Vaca
Espinavell
R.Ritort
Setcases
Rocabruna
Beget
Molló
Tregurà
Vilallonga de Ter
Gorges del Freser
R. Núria
Queralbs
Fustanyà
Abella
La Roca
Riu Ter
Camprodon
Bolòs
Pardines
Ribes de Freser
Sant Pau de Segúries
Vall de Bianya
Puig Ou (1306m)
El Talló (1288m)
Riu Beget
R.Llierca
El Pont d'en Valentí
Sadernes
Oix
Pont de Llierca
Tortellà
Beuda
Seguró
Maià de Montcal
Montagut de Fluvià
Argelaguer
Besalú
Sant Jaume de Llierca
Castellfollit de la Roca
Sant Joan les Fonts
La Miana
Serinyà
Terradelles
Campelles
Surroca
Sant Martí d'Ogassa
Sant Joan de les Abadesses
Riu Freser
Coll de Caubet
Hostalnou
Olot
Batet de la Serra
Sant Julià (905m)
El Torn
Estany de Banyoles
Porqueres
Banyoles
Riudara
La Pinya
Volcà Croscat
Santa Pau
FAGEDA D'EN JORDÀ
Ripoll
Vallfogona
L'Hostalet
Les Preses
Sant Miquel de Sa Cot
Volcà Santa Margarida
Mieres
Camós
Vall d'en Bas
Els Hostalets d'en Bas
Les Llosses
Sant Quirze de Besora
Girona
N
0 10 km
N-II
A26
N260
C26
C17
C524
C150
GR11
GR11.7
GR2

Blay (the only places for an outdoor drink), two to pick out are arty, genteel *Cocodrilo* on c/Sant Roc (until 2.30am), and galleried *Café 1900* at c/San Rafel 18, offering herb teas or stronger stuff. More youthful, alternative choices include all-day *Bar 6T7* at c/dels Sastres 35; *Bruixes e Maduixes* at c/Bonaire 11, with German beer on tap; and Senegalese-run *Bar Malem*, c/Pare Antoni Soler 6, a spacious, converted clothing factory decorated with original artwork.

Two **cinemas** screen first-run fare: the Colom on Passeig d'en Blay and the Núria at Verge del Carmé 8, off the *plaça*. Most concerts and other events of the **summer festival** take place in Plaça del Mig, near Sant Esteve church.

The Baixa Garrotxa volcanic zone

In 1985 the Catalan parliament designated much of the **Baixa Garrotxa**, a 120-square-kilometre area extending southeast of Olot, as the **Parc Natural de la Zona Volcànica de la Garrotxa**. Since most of it is private property, this means less than one might think. The volcanic cones and the **Fageda d'en Jordà** beech wood between the cones and Olot gained some necessary protection, but cinder-quarrying (for building materials) had already spoiled some of the proposed park.

The Baixa Garrotxa is not a zone of belching steam and molten lava. It's been nearly twelve thousand years since the last eruption, during which time the ash and lava have weathered into a fertile soil whose luxuriant vegetation – including extensive fields of corn, beans (the tiny local white *fegolets* are especially esteemed) and various grains – masks the contours of the dormant volcanoes. There are thirty cones in all, the largest of them around 160m higher than their surroundings and 1500m wide at the base.

Santa Pau

The central village of the volcanic zone, medieval **SANTA PAU**, 9km southeast of Olot, presents to the outside world a defensive perimeter of continuous and almost windowless house walls. Slightly less discovered than Besalú, it's even more atmospheric, though verging on the twee. At the very least, it's a mandatory meal stop, and would make a good base for exploring the park's network of signposted paths and tracks.

Buses on the minor Olot–Mieres–Banyoles route call daily (often at uncivil hours). With a **car**, you're obliged to park in the lot on the southern outskirts; otherwise a pair of well-engineered paths take you into the old quarter from the west. Santa Pau's outer archways open onto dark, ancient buildings, many sympathetically converted into business premises and homes. The core of the village is the engagingly sloping thirteenth-century **Firal dels Bous** (Cattle Market; also known as Plaça Major), with arcaded shops, the **Turisme** (Mon & Wed–Sat noon–6pm, Sun noon–3pm; ⓣ972 680 349) and the restored Gothic church of **Santa Maria** with its fine interior rib-vaulting. At no. 6 of the adjacent Plaçeta dels Balls, overlooked by the three-storeyed tower of the Balls family, you'll find pricey but tasty **meals** at Cuina Volcànica member *Cal Sastre* (closed Sun night & Mon, open Fri & Sat only in winter), though several other normally priced restaurants have sprung up on the approaches to the old quarter.

In terms of **accommodation**, best value is *Can Menció* at Plaça Major 17 (ⓣ972 680 014 or 616 669 6880, ⓦwww.garrotxa.com/canmencio; closed 15–30 Sept & Mon; ❸), with seven very sweet en-suite wood-trimmed rooms, some with balcony and all with designer baths; there's a rear-facing lounge with self-service bar, and up front the village's liveliest proper café-bar, with ringside seats on the *plaça*. For self-catering, *Can Marfany* (ⓣ972 680 518 ⓦwww.canmarfany.com; ❺; minimum stay 2 nights), Plaça Major 4, offers three small but comfortable apartments with full kitchen, living area and bedroom. Of two local **campsites**, *Masia Can Patxet*, 2km east (☎972 680 066), is compact, calm and tent-friendly.

Loop walks long and short

One way to get acquainted with the Baixa Garrotxa is to take a **loop walk** out of Olot (or Santa Pau), largely avoiding paved roads and easily completable in a single day. Various numbered and signposted itineraries prepared by the park authorities are often just out-and-back or forked; this route combines the virtues of several.

From the Pont and Parc de les Mores at the southern edge of Olot, follow the signposts for "Itinerari 3" across the Riu Fluvià, from where it's an hour south along surfaced country lanes – equally suited to mountain-biking (as is most of this circuit) – to the **Fageda d'en Jordà**. Although much reduced, this beech forest is still a treat in the autumn when the leaves are turning; within half an hour more you emerge on the far side of the spooky, maze-like groves, deserted except for the tourist *carruatges* (horse-carts) visiting from Santa Pau.

Turn left when you meet the **GR2** long-distance trail, then right when you encounter the track ("Itinerari 1") to Sa Cot. Stay on the GR2, which soon becomes a proper path as it heads east for thirty minutes to the medieval chapel of **Sant Miquel de Sa Cot**, a popular picnic spot. The **Volcà Santa Margarida** is visible just behind the chapel, and within forty minutes you should be up on its rim and then down in its grassy caldera, where another tiny *ermita* (country chapel) sits at the bottom; allow at least an extra hour for this side trip. From the turn-off to Santa Margarida – just fifteen minutes from Sant Miquel – you resume progress on part of "Itinerari 4", and descend to the **Font de Can Roure**, source of the only water en route, before skirting Roca Negra with its disused quarry and entering Santa Pau: 45 minutes from the shoulder of Santa Margarida, and some three hours from Olot (not counting the detour to the caldera).

Rather than follow the onward GR2 east, bear west at **Can Masnou** and approach Volcà Croscat via the *Lava* campsite. You skirt the northeast flank of Croscat, badly scarred by quarrying; from the campsite it's another hour, along a progressively narrowing track to the high (720m) plateau of **Batet de la Serra**, scattered with handsome farms.

Here you meet a marked path-and-track coming west from the Serra de Sant Julià del Mont, turning west yourself to follow this route briefly before taking the beautiful, well-marked *camí*, partly cobbled in basalt, which passes the hamlet of **Santa Maria de Batet** on its way down to Olot at "Itinerari 8". It takes just under another hour of downhill progress, or a total of something less than seven hours on the day, to emerge at the top of c/Sant Cristòfor, which crosses the river into central Olot at the Pont de Santa Magdalena.

If you're not committed to such a long day, you can drive or ride a bus to the parking area for Volcà de Santa Margarida; here you're directly on the circular "Itinerari 1", which takes in the Fageda d'en Jordà, Sant Miquel de Sa Cot and the cones of Santa Margarida and Croscat in a **two- to three-hour tour**. There are *centres d'informació* en route at Can Serra (Fageda d'en Jordà) and Can Passavent (Croscat) where you can find all the information you might need.

La Miana

From Santa Pau, the GR2 continues briefly north towards the scenic Serra de Sant Julià del Mont, then veers east away from "Itinerari 6" down a valley to Besalú. East of the summit and accessible by a 45-minute spur trail from the streamside hamlet of El Torn are a group of excellent *turismes rurals* at **La Miana**, which can also be reached by a signposted, 6.5-kilometre dirt track from Sant Jaume de Llierca on the old Besalú–Olot road, just off the A26. The proprietors have indicated the side path in from El Torn, as well as down from the summit of Sant Julià, itself reachable by using itineraries 6 and 8. They have also signposted onward, non-GR trails to Sant Ferriol and Besalú (3hr).

Can Jou (Ⓣ972 190 263 or 660 656 633, Ⓦwww.canjou.com; ❺ B&B, ❻ HB), co-managed by the helpful Michael Peters, has capacity for fifteen in modernized, en-suite rooms and sits right on the Coll de Jou with views south and west, especially from the idyllic pool just above the *masia*. Michael and assistants also run the area's best **horse-riding** programme, with half-day rides around the mountain, full-day excursions to Santa Pau and longer trips to the coast on request. That said, there's a good mix of nationalities, and horsey, hiking and sedentary dispositions among the clientele. Just 300m east is the amazing *Rectoria de la Miana* (Ⓣ972 190 190, Ⓔrectoriadelamiana@yahoo.es; ❺ HB, vegetarian on request), run by Franz Engelhard, a medieval manor house complete with crumbling twelfth-century Romanesque chapel adjacent used for musical workshops. Every room – most with its own bath – is unique and antique-furnished, meals being served in the arcaded ground-floor hall. Both places enjoy incredible tranquillity in the middle of forested nowhere and are thus massively popular; reserve rather than showing up on spec.

If you come up empty at La Miana, there's one more *casa rural* in the immediate vicinity: *El Turrós* (Ⓣ972 687 350, Ⓦwww.elturros.com; ❸ B&B), its steep, one-kilometre access drive signposted just under 4km north down the dirt track towards Sant Jaume de Llierca. Though falling within the muncipality of Argelaguer, the nearest village on the main highway, this is the *only* road access in. This rambling country manor has mostly triples and is thus particularly good for families, though not so convenient for walkers as *Can Jou* or *Rectoria de la Miana*.

The Alta Garrotxa

The Alta Garrotxa stretches north from the main Besalú–Olot road as far as the frontier summits. Unlike the lower Garrotxa, the rock strata here are mostly limestone, riddled with numerous caves. For walkers or mountain-bikers it's a rewarding area as well, especially in spring or late autumn when the highest Pyrenees are inaccessible. Editorial Alpina's 1:40,000 "Garrotxa" map is a useful – though as ever far from infallible – aid; the ICC's 1:50,000 Mapa Comarcal is better.

North to France: the Llierca valley

From a point 2km east of Castellfollit de la Roca, a paved but one-lane road past Montagut de Fluvià traces the Llierca up to Sadernes. Continuing on the main Llierca valley route brings you after 5km to the wonderfully photogenic **Pont de Llierca**, a medieval bridge with one of the greatest drops to the water in the Pyrenees. You can swim in the river-pools below, but don't imitate the local youth diving from the span – one was knocked unconscious and drowned in 2003. Also, use the designated car park – wardens patrol assiduously, citing violators (or even having them towed).

The asphalt gives out just below **SADERNES**, which notwithstanding depiction on maps, is barely a hamlet, let alone a village. This has as a focus the sparely handsome tenth-century church of **Santa Cecília**, sacked by the Republicans in 1936, subsequently restored and now usually locked; surviving interior treasures have in any case been whisked away to museums in Girona and Barcelona. One of the few other buildings here is the popular *Hostal de Sadernes*, despite its name offering **meals** only (open Oct–June Fri pm to Sun pm, plus hols; July–Sept daily, but drink only Wed); the food is hearty country fare – *mongetes amb ventresca*, mixed grill, dessert (€19 for three courses, drink extra) – served on the arcaded ground floor of an old farmhouse. There's a convenient if basic adjacent **campsite**, *Sadernes* (Ⓣ972 687 536; closed Dec 15–Jan 15), staked out by semi-permanent caravans but with some tent space.

Just past the church, the road is seasonally barred (July–Sept 15 10am–5pm), with parking space provided just before. Upstream from Sadernes, the dirt track steadily worsens as you begin to thread the scenic gorge of the Llierca; after 2.5km you reach the short side path to **El Pont d'en Valentí**, a medieval bridge much used by smugglers of old, with a ruined mill on the far side (and swimming opportunities in the stream). Beyond this point vehicles are banned all year – there's another barrier, and parking proves nearly impossible anyway along this stretch. From the bridge it's ninety minutes on foot, first on the track and then by trail veering off to the ninth-century **Ermita de Sant Aniol d'Aguja**, a landmark, rather squat chapel astride the GR11. Dedicated to an obscure third-century local saint, this has a charming legend attached to it. Aniol, fleeing Roman persecutions in Gaul, slept on this spot but was roused by two persistent oxen. Taking this as a sign from God (the ox being the Evangelist Matthew's symbol for the self-sacrifice of Christ), Aniol returned to his homeland and was promptly martyred in 208 AD. Yearly on Ascension Day there occurs here the **Aplec dels Francesas**, a pilgrimage festival attended by various Alta Garrotxa folk and the inhabitants of Sant Llorenç (Saint Laurent) de Cerdans, the closest large village on the French side of the border (see "The upper Tech", pp.122). This, or higher, smaller Coustouges can be reached by continuing northeast on the footpath from the refuge towards the much-used **Col des Massanes** (1126m) on the frontier.

Northwest to El Ripollès: Oix, Beget and Rocabruna

Staying in Spain, a more populated route heads **northwest** towards El Ripollès. From just below Castellfollit de la Roca, take the paved but one-lane road 10km northwest to **OIX**, which dominates a bowl-shaped, intensely cultivated valley. The attractive village, surrounded by huge modern barns, features the Romanesque **church** of Sant Llorenç and a small but graceful medieval **bridge** just 1km east. Right opposite the church on Plaça Major, you can **stay** at the *Hostal de la Rovira* (Ⓣ & Ⓕ972 294 347; ❹ B&B), a restored mansion, whose rooms – all different – have tubs in the bathrooms and pastel decor, plus a ground-floor **restaurant**. There's a single **campsite** 1km west, shady *Els Alous* (Ⓣ972 294 173; April–Oct), with a pool.

Beget

The easiest-to-find onward road passes the old bridge. Paved as well as wide, it leads northwest 18km, passing little other than the high hamlet of Sant Miquel de Pera and ambling cattle, to the showcase village of **BEGET**, done up by lowlanders as a weekend retreat verging on the embalmed. Two slender bridges link three neighbourhoods separated by the confluence of two streams, and the graceful twelfth-century church of **Sant Cristòfor**, standing at the entrance to the village, is celebrated for its particularly solemn and serene *Majestat*. All but a dozen or so of these Catalan wooden images of a fully dressed Christ were destroyed in 1936; this example, perhaps as old as the (usually closed) church itself, is one of the very few that can be seen in its intended context (keys available at house no. 7; donation expected). Beget has three **restaurants**, two with **accommodation**: *Can Joanic*, by the church (Ⓣ972 741 241; ❷), which has rooms (including singles) sharing bathrooms above a fair-value *menjador* with a riverside terrace, and the pricier *El Forn* (Ⓣ972 741 231; ❹ B&B) near the top of the village, where en-suite, heated rooms and the outdoor terrace have commanding views. The food here is slightly more ambitious – rabbit with figs, trotters with chestnuts – and sustaining rather

Pyrenean food and drink

Throughout the Pyrenees, the best food is based on what's available locally, and often seasonally. This might encompass fresh trout, forest mushrooms, medium-hot peppers, sheep's and goats' cheese and wild berries or game such as wild boar, rabbit, chamois and pigeon. Pastoral pursuits, as opposed to conventional agriculture, still survive; the only AOC lamb in the Pyrenees, wild-grass-and-herb-fed, is from the Barèges area and is prized by Michelin-starred restaurants. The Mediterranean and Atlantic provide a continual supply of fish and seafood, which feature strongly in the Basque country. Indeed Basque cooking, either side of the frontier, is acknowledged as the finest in these mountains.

▶ Peppers drying, Ezpeleta

Festivals and the cider season

Food is an integral part of many Pyrenean **festivals** – at Céret's late-spring cherry feast, the autumn wine celebrations of Banyuls-sur-Mer, the bash in honour of Ezpeleta's famous red peppers and (most vividly) the *tamborrada* of San Sebastián on 19–20 January. There, members of the city's gastronomic societies honour the city's patron saint by re-enacting an event from the Napoleonic wars; they engage in raucous drumming duels while dressed as soldiers and chefs, growing increasingly tipsy as onlookers ply them with drink.

From January through May, when last year's apple-pressing has matured, **cider houses** (*sagardotegiak*) flourish across the Basque province of Gipuzkoa. Amidst general conviviality – the *bertsolariak* tradition of oral poetry originated in these places – beef, salt cod and sausage are washed down with cider served straight from the barrel. Cloudy, strong and on the sour side, it's a world away from typical British pub fare.

Basque cuisine

Basque cuisine, especially along the coast, is likely to be a highlight of your visit. The locals are prodigious eaters, and you'll encounter them tucking into enormous spreads at rural eateries throughout the region. Basque mariners brought back various crops from the New World which Europeans now take for granted – corn, several bean varieties, peppers – and these enliven signature dishes such as *pil-pil* (salt cod sautéed with olive oil, garlic and peppers) or *alubias de tolosa* (red bean stew). The sea yields hake (*merluza*), squid (*txipirones*), the scrawny spider crab (*txangurro*), invariably served stuffed back into its own shell, and baby eels (*angulas*), an increasingly rare and expensive delicacy.

▶ Seafood for sale at Biarritz

Basque pintxos

Pintxos is the Spanish Basque word for what's known elsewhere as *tapas*. On a local bar counter, this means two bite-sized morsels, usually freshly prepared and excellent, either traditional (seafood or meat titbits on a bread base) or *nouvelle* with more bizarre, unpredictable combinations such as flower petals, Asian condiments and vegetables. San Sebastián (as seen on the front page of this colour section) and to a lesser extent Hondarribia are the best venues for sampling *pintxos*.

Unique to the Basque country are **gastronomic societies** (*txokos*); first founded in the mid-nineteenth century, they originated as places where craftsmen could socialize. Female membership has traditionally been banned (though there are now some "family" clubs) and all cooking is still done by men who pay a token subscription for the facilities. Members, who usually inherit their status, are often keen hunters or fishermen who prepare elaborate dishes to perfection as a hobby, and traditional Basque cookery has largely retreated to these societies. Outsiders can only attend by member invitation, so most visitors will instead get acquainted with the avant garde *Nueva Cocina Vasca* (New Basque Cookery), which dominates better restaurant menus.

Ham, salami and sausage

Cured meats have high status everywhere in the Pyrenees; they're mostly eaten raw, as *tapas/pintxos*, for a restaurant appetizer or as the centrepiece of a salad. Each valley seems to have its own **salami**, usually made from domestic pork or duck, though at higher altitudes you'll find varieties based on wild boar, venison or goat. The Spanish Pyrenees even has its very own version of haggis, called *chireta* or *xireta* – stuffed with rice and blood pudding or lamb offal. On the French side, **jambon de Bayonne** – which despite the name is specific to a broad zone southwest of the Adour – is the most noted, salted and then hung to age for seven to ten months.

▲ Salamis in a Seix storefront

Pa amb tomaquet

The quintessential Catalan snack or breakfast dish is **pa amb tomaquet**, "bread with tomato". Order it and you'll be supplied with all the basic ingredients on a cutting board. Slice the country-style loaf, and drizzle some olive oil on the slices. Next, cut the garlic cloves crossways (not lengthwise), and rub the exposed surface vigorously into the bread slices. Finally, halve a tomato – the riper the better – and mash it onto the surface (but don't eat the bruised vegetable remains). Enjoy.

▲ State-of-the-art winery near Barbastro

Drinking

The Pyrenees are far from the stereotypical Spain of sherry and sangria (though you can certainly find sherry on sale in any Spanish Pyrenean bar), and equidistant from the France of *pastis* and champagne. Local production centres on quality **wines** from recognized *domaines* and AOCs (see p.54). On the Spanish side, both the Catalunyan and Aragonese foothills have vineyards and vintners which dominate local restaurant offerings; the Somontano region near Babastro is, with its twenty-odd wineries, one of the biggest and most respected *domaines* in Spain. And of course Catalunya is home to *cava*, the Spanish "champagne". On the French slopes, the AOCs of Côtes de Roussillon and Corbières have international cachet, but the central Pyrenees around Pau and Tarbes also produce highly characteristic – if limited – wines, while the only Basque AOC is at Irouléguy. Among a handful of fortified **dessert wines**, the most famous is *Banyuls* from the Mediterranean coast. Besides widely available commercial **liqueurs** like Izarra and *patxaran*, central Pyrenean valleys produce even more exotic infusions of herbs like *génépi*.

Chocolate in Bayonne

Hernan Cortés brought cocoa beans and some useful recipes employing them from Mexico to Spain in 1528, and the Portuguese brought the knowledge of chocolate from Brazil to Portugal shortly afterwards. Jews expelled from Spain by the Inquisition went to Portugal during the sixteenth century and learnt the secrets of chocolate manufacture; ejected from Portugal, they took their skills with them into exile at Saint-Espirit, the township opposite Bayonne on the north bank of the Adour. Iberia's loss was the Pays Basques' gain; though the Spanish Basques still cook game and rabbit in a chocolate sauce based on Mexican *mole*, it was from Bayonne that chocolate confection spread across Europe. Once the emancipation of the French Revolution dissolved the Jewish ghetto in Saint-Espirit, the chocolate trade moved across the Adour. Today several *confisseries* in central Bayonne serve the highest-quality chocolate in every conceivable form, from fondant to ice cream to hot cocoa.

▲ Chocolates, Bayonne

than elegant; budget over €30 with drink. The GR11 passes through Beget, and these are the only places to stay on the stretch of trail between Rocabruna and Albanyà.

Rocabruna

Some 7km west on either the GR11 or the now-much-narrower road, **ROCABRUNA**, with its ruined castle and stubby but handsome Romanesque church, stands just below the watershed traditionally dividing the Garrotxa from El Ripollès, the county of Ripoll (though the modern administrative boundary is between Beget and Oix). The onward C38 road remains unnervingly narrow along the 7km more to the Camprodon–Molló highway. The only **accommodation**, 2km west on the main road and then 1km down a dirt track, but almost astride the GR11, is the friendly, English-speaking *turisme rural Casa Etxalde* (Ⓣ972 130 317, Ⓦwww.etxalde.net). This offers three en-suite doubles (❹ B&B) plus a pair of two-bedroom apartments, as well as a tiny self-catering kitchen. Perhaps surprisingly for such a tiny place, Rocabruna has two independent **restaurants** good enough to draw crowds on weekend nights from far away. *Can Pluja* (Ⓣ972 741 064; lunch Thurs–Tues, also supper Fri–Sun) has tables on two levels and honest, straightforward mountain food like goat chops and blackberry sorbet; allow €24 *a la carta* with drink. At *Can Po* (Ⓣ972 741 045), reckoned one of the best eateries in the region, a meal of cold lentil and smoked fish salad, duck *confit*, prunes in armagnac and house wine runs to nearly €30, but you can easily drop €50 a head by sampling the premium wine list.

El Ripollès

Moving towards Cerdanya and Andorra from the Costa Brava, you really begin to feel among high mountains in the *comarca* (county) of **El Ripollès**. The N260 climbs west from Olot through densely tree-clad foothills to the Coll de Caubet, then drops to the county town of **Ripoll** along the scenic Vallfogona valley. You can also approach less directly along the C17 from Olot to Sant Pau de Seguries, a route made much easier by tunnels under the Coll de Capsacosta.

From Ripoll, the C26 heads northeast via **Sant Joan de les Abadesses** and **Camprodon**, both – like Ripoll – graced with fine Romanesque monuments – until the frontier and road crossing at the Col d'Ares/Aras (1513m); winter sportsfolk head northwest to the ski station of **Vallter 2000**.

Due north of Ripoll, road and rail climb gently to **Ribes de Freser** and then more sharply west out of the *comarca* via the Collada de Toses. At Ribes, there's the option of riding the dramatic, narrow-gauge *cremallera* railway up the gorge to **Queralbs** and **Núria**, a combined pilgrimage shrine and all-year resort below the summit of 2910-metre **Puigmal**. Walkers can link the valleys of Ter and Núria by hiking between Setcases and Queralbs, via two staffed refuges and the marvellous Riu Freser.

Ripoll is the **public transport** hub, with trains heading north to Puigcerdà and the French border, while the most regular bus lines head east to Olot and northeast to Sant Joan and Camprodon.

Ripoll

RIPOLL occupies so prominent a place in Catalunya's history that it's impossible not to be initially disappointed by this rather shabby place, buzzing with traffic and divided by the manifestly polluted Riu Ter. The inhabitants seem to agree, resigned to working here but deserting it in droves on Saturday afternoon when Ripoll assumes the air of a ghost town until Monday. But just ten minutes' walk from the southeast corner of town – where trains and buses stop – stands one of the most remarkable monuments in the Catalan Pyrenees, the Monestir de Santa Maria, founded in 888 by **Guifré el Pilós** (Wilfred the Hairy) to spur Christian resettlement of the surrounding valleys following their wresting from Muslim rule.

Arrival and information

The **train and bus stations** stand within sight of each other, just a ten-minute walk from the heart of town, over the Pont d'Olot to the Plaça de l'Ajuntament. Under the sundial on Plaça d'Abat Oliba, the **Turisme** (Easter, June, July & Sept daily 9.30am–1.30pm & 4–7pm; Aug daily 10am–2pm & 4–8pm; Oct–May Mon–Sat 9.30am–1.30pm & 4–7pm, Sun 10am–2pm; ⓣ972 702 351) dispenses plenty of maps, pamphlets and local transport timetables.

Accommodation

Accommodation in Ripoll tends to be overpriced and uninspiring, making it highly advisable to base yourself elsewhere and make a flying visit. If you do decide to stay, the least expensive option is en-suite *Habitacions Paula*, Plaça de l'Abat Arnulf 6 (ⓣ972 700 011; ❷), 70m west of the Turisme. *Hostal del Ripollès*, on Plaça Nova (ⓣ972 700 215; ❹), entered through its ground-floor pizzeria, and *Pensió La Trobada*, across the river at Passeig Honorat Vilamanyà 4 (ⓣ972 714 353; ❹), are more comfortable if somewhat overpriced alternatives. If you have transport, opt for one of the two **cases de pagès** adhering to the *turisme rural* programme, 18–23km distant on the road to Berga, near the hamlet of **Les Llosses**. Some 6km north of the road stands isolated *La Riba* (ⓣ972 198 092; ❸ B&B, ❺ HB), a huge sixteenth-centry *mas* with individually let rooms, a pool and ample common areas. A bit west, in equally remote **Palmerola** hamlet, high-standard *Mas Moreta* (ⓣ972 198 095, ⓦwww.masmoreta; ❺ B&B, ❻ HB) is also worth considering.

The Town

Following an 1835 fire, the Benedictine **Monastir de Santa Maria** lay in ruins; today's barrel-vaulted nave (daily 10am–1pm & 3–7pm; €2) is a copy of the original structure erected over Guifré's tomb by Abbot Oliba in the early eleventh century. (Oliba and his immediate successors created an important library here, instrumental in the preservation of Islamic scholarship.) The magnificent Romanesque **west portal**, however, survived the fire, and is now protected against the elements by a glass conservatory – and from the over-curious by a low iron barrier. Erected in the twelfth century, and now the main entrance, this portal squirms with carvings of religious and astrological subjects: the Apocalypse (across the top), the Book of Kings (to the left), Exodus (to the right), scenes from the lives of David, St Peter and St Paul (at the bottom), and the months of the year (around the inner side of the pillars).

The adjacent, double-columned **cloister** (daily 10am–1pm & 3–7pm; same ticket as nave), far less damaged in the succession of earthquakes, sackings and fires visited on the monastery, is particularly beautiful. The **capitals** on the lower of two colonnades, dating from the twelfth-century Romanesque "Golden Age", portray monks and nuns, beasts mundane and mythical, plus secular characters of the period. Across the Plaça Abat Oliba from Santa Maria, the fourteenth-century church of **Sant Pere** is open only when it serves as a venue for Ripoll's **music festival**, staged on successive weekends during July and August.

Apart from the monastery there's little to detain you, though down in the

△ Ripoll monastery

modern district, two *modernista* buildings may claim your attention: the spouting stone flourishes of **Can Bonada**, c/del Progés 14, on the way to the bus and train stations, and the tiny church of **Sant Miquel de la Roqueta** (1912), a couple of blocks up the hill, looking like a pixie's house with a witch's cap on top – and designed by Antoni Gaudí's contemporary Joan Rubió.

Eating and **drinking** options in Ripoll are far from plentiful. *Pizzeria Piazetta* on the ground floor of the *Hostal del Ripollès* is reasonable priced and appetizing, as is *Canaules* next door. These are the only notable full-service restaurants in the centre.

Sant Joan de les Abadesses

The small town of **SANT JOAN DE LES ABADESSES**, 11km northeast of Ripoll, owes its existence to the eponymous **monastery** (daily: May, June & Sept 10am–2pm & 4–7pm; March–April & Oct 10am–2pm & 4–6pm; July & Aug 10am–7pm; Nov–Feb 10am–2pm, also 4–6pm weekends; €2) founded in 887 by Guifré el Pilós, apparently for the benefit of his daughter Emma, the first abbess. The institution was closed temporarily in 1017 by Pope Benedict III as a result of politically motivated accusations of immorality (see box below) by Comte (Count) Bernat Tallaferro, to whom devolved – not coincidentally – all the prior feudal privileges of the convent. The present church, consecrated in 1150, is a single-nave structure of impressive austerity, built to a Latin-cross plan with five apses, and housing a curious thirteenth-century wooden sculpture depicting Christ's Deposition, the *Santíssim Misteri*, in the central apse. Admission to the monastery also includes entry to the Gothic **cloisters** and the **Museu del Monestir**, whose well-presented exhibits include superb choir-stall partitions with (for example) a fox carrying off a hen and a wild boar playing the bagpipes, as well as a fine series of late medieval altarpieces and polychrome images.

Other than the monastery, there are few specific sights in Sant Joan, but the old quarter boasts a fair-sized grid of ancient houses lining streets almost shorter than their names, all leading to a small but appealingly arcaded **Plaça Major**. The slender twelfth-century bridge down in the well-tilled valley was only restored in the 1970s, after being destroyed in fierce fighting in February 1939, during the final Republican retreat of the Civil War. Having scared the pigeons from the abandoned shell of **Sant Pol** church in the centre, you've pretty much exhausted the potential of the town.

The legend of Comte Arnau

The monastery at Sant Joan des Abadesses is inextricably linked with numerous legends concerning one **Comte (Count) Arnau**, a quasi-historical feudal lord of the eleventh century, notorious for parsimony towards his serfs. More sensationally, he is immortalized in local folk-song and poetry as a Ripollès Don-Juan equivalent, renowned for his lust and fecklessness in various amorous adventures. Arnau even managed to secure the affections of Sant Joan's incumbent abbess, Engelberga, whom he visited at night on horseback by means of a long tunnel from his lands between Gombrèn and Campdevànol, some 15km west. Her death hardly curtailed his ardour or his appearances, as in the meantime he had managed to seduce a fair number of the lower-ranking nuns; the new abbess attempted to secure all the orifices of the convent, so to speak, but Arnau had concluded a pact with the Devil and used his new-found satanic powers to filter through the very walls.

However, unlike Don Juan, the count eventually fell genuinely, abjectly in love with a young local lass, who understandably failed to return such sentiments, given his rather chequered history. To escape his continued advances, she enrolled as a novice at the nunnery; after a humbling vigil at the gates, Arnau managed to gain entrance by conventional methods, only to find the object of his affections recently dead. As he approached the bier, she returned to life just long enough to denounce his various misdemeanours in an other-worldly voice. Filled with terror and remorse, Comte Arnau fled back to his feudal estates, condemned both before and after death to eternally wander the hills above. On stormy nights he has also been seen as a mournful ghost in the cloister of the monastery itself, but the favoured venue for his hauntings remains the vicinity of Gombrèn, where the count supposedly appears as a baleful apparition on horseback, accompanied by spectral packs of hunting dogs in full howl.

Practicalities

Buses arrive at a shelter behind the monastery church apse; the well-stocked **Turisme** (Mon–Sat 10am–2pm & 4–7pm, Sun 10am–2pm; ⓣ972 720 599) occupies the cloistered, fifteenth-century **Palau de Abadia** (Episcopal Palace), just fifty paces left of the Museu del Monestir's entrance.

In theory Sant Joan would make a far more pleasant base than Ripoll, with frequent bus links in each direction; in practice, there's just one reliable accommodation option in the newer district near the bus stop: *Pensió Can Janpere* at c/del Mestre Josep Andreu 3 (ⓣ972 720 077; ④), which offers comfortable en-suite rooms with heating and TV. Preferable, if you have a car, is the **turisme rural** *Mas Mitjavila*, 10.5km northwest of Sant Joan in the hamlet of **SANT MARTÍ D'OGASSA** (ⓣ972 722 020, ⓔmasmitjavila@tiscali.es; ⑤ B&B). From the north side of the new bridge, follow the asphalt road 4.2km to the old iron-miners' village of **Surroca**, and then continue the remaining distance on a cement driveway. With the adjacent tenth-century church of Sant Martí, *Mas Mitjavila* was once a dependency of the monastery of Sant Joan; it enjoys a superb eyrie-like setting 1350m up, overlooking the valleys of Ripoll. Non-identical rooms are rustic but with all mod cons, including kitchens; some are more like suites, sleeping up to six. Supper (served in the converted sheep barn) and own-farm produce are both available.

Back in town, the main full-service **restaurant** is *Can Janpere*, with a €10 *menú* and a slightly more adventurous *carta* featuring such dishes as seafood-stuffed squash; except during high season it's shut at lunch, when your alternatives are *Brasseria Gil* at c/Major 6 in the old town, or *plats combinats* at the pleasant cafés on the main *rambla* Passeig Comte Guifré.

Camprodon

As you follow the lively Riu Ter upstream from Sant Joan, the first place with any mountain-town character is **CAMPRODON** (950m), a fact exploited during the late nineteenth century by the Catalan bourgeoisie who arrived by a (now defunct) rail line from Ripoll to spend summer in the hills. The tracks' former course is now a marked cycling route, **La Ruta del Ferro**. Camprodon, 14km from Sant Joan, still retains the prosperous air of former times, with shops full of leather goods, outdoor gear, cheese and sausages. Ornate villas front a *rambla* (Passeig de la Font Nova) clogged with towering trees, and other town houses are occasionally embellished with *modernista* flourishes.

Like Ripoll, Camprodon straddles the confluence of two rivers, here the Ter and the Ritort, and is knit together by little bridges. The principal one, the sixteenth-century **Pont Nou**, still has a defensive tower. From here you can follow the narrow main commercial street east to the restored Romanesque monastic church of **Sant Pere** (consecrated in 904), near the northeast end of town next to the larger parish church of Santa Maria. There is also a small castle overhead, easiest reached by crossing the Pont Nou and then climbing the narrow lanes on the far side.

Camprodon was the birthplace of the composer **Isaac Albéniz** (1860–1909), a fact which neither the town nor the region made much of until recently – probably because there is little distinctively Catalan in the music he produced during wanderings which took him to London (1890–93), Paris, Nice and finally Cambo-les-Bains in the Basque country. (His most celebrated work, for piano or guitar, is entitled *Iberia*.) However, the great man now has a street named after him, a bust near Sant Pere, an eponymous July/August **music festival** in his honour and a less worthwhile **museum** near Pont Nou commemorating his life and times (daily 11am–2pm & 4–7pm; €2.50).

Practicalities

Buses from Ripoll stop 300m south of the main Plaça d'Espanya, where you'll find the **Turisme** (all year Tues–Sat 10am–2pm & 4–7pm, Sun 10am–2pm; Ⓣ972 740 010) in the *ajuntament* building.

Accommodation tends to be expensive, given the town's role as a minor ski resort, with advance reservations advisable in peak seasons. On often noisy c/ Josep Morer there's Casa Fonda member *Can Ganasi* at no. 9 (Ⓣ972 740 134; ❸); quieter *Pensió La Placeta* (Ⓣ972 740 807; ❹) overlooks Plaça del Carmé, just east of c/Josep Morer and the first square you reach as you come into town from Sant Joan. For a splurge, try the *modernista Hotel de Camprodon* at Plaça del Dr. Robert 3 opposite the cinema (Ⓣ972 740 013, Ⓕ740 716; ❺), with particularly elegant common areas.

Can Ganansi's **restaurant** offers at least two different *menús* plus local dishes such as duck and trout, while *Pensió La Placeta* also has an attached *menjador* (dinner only). Alternatively, *Bar-Restaurant Núria*, at Plaça d'Espanya 11, is a characterful place and features a rather basic lunch *menú* (at night it's *a la carta* only, including frog's legs). *El Pont 9* (closed Mon low season) has views to the river bridge and a more appealing *menú* priced a bit higher than *Núria*'s.

Beyond Camprodon: the Ter and Ritort valleys

Beyond Camprodon you're increasingly dependent on your own transport and ultimately your own legs; just one daily **bus** daily from Camprodon goes as far up as Setcases (see below). The majority of people who venture this way are either hikers, or skiers driving northwest up the **Ter valley** to the runs of Vallter 2000, or moving northeast up the **Ritort** bound for France. The construction of holiday flats for lowlanders now reigns supreme, but you still catch a glimpse of the area's former agricultural economy in the herds of grazing horses, and cattle ambling home at dusk.

The first settlement that might prompt a stop is rather low-key **VILALLONGA DE TER**, 5km from Camprodon. Opposite the standard-issue Romanesque church of **San Martí** on the main *plaça* are two **accommodation** possibilities: Casa Fonda affiliate *Hostal Pastoret* (Ⓣ & Ⓕ972 740 319; ❺ HB) at c/Constitució 9, and *Hostal Cal Mestre* around the corner at c/del Pou 1 (reception at c/Major 3; Ⓣ972 740 407; ❸).

Immediately south of Vilallonga, on the far side of the valley, the hamlet of **LA ROCA** huddles strikingly under its unmissable namesake monolith; there are two restaurants here and another at road's end 4km west in **ABELLA**. Despite tempting depictions on some maps, the track beyond to Pardines (see p.177), over the Coll de Pal, is nearly impossible even for jeeps.

Alternatively, bear left 1km past Vilallonga for the steep detour to **TREGURÀ**, 5km from the main road; perched on a sunny hillside at 1400m, with sweeping views east over the valley, the upper part of this double village has a church dating from about 980. There are also two places to **stay**, the better being welcoming *Fonda Rigà* (Ⓣ972 136 000, Ⓦwww.fondariga.com; ❺ HB; also apartments), with its massively popular and reasonable **restaurant** (allow €19 plus drink).

Setcases

Back in the Ter valley, **SETCASES**, 6km northwest of Vilallonga, has been completely gentrified since the 1980s. Once an important agricultural village, it was almost totally abandoned until the nearby ski station began to attract hoteliers, chalet developers and second-home owners. The ski trade ensures that some short-term beds and food are relatively pricey; Setcases straddles the GR11, a half-day's march west from Molló or two hours east from the Refugi d'Ulldeter (see below). If you need to **stay**, the most affordable accommodation is on the lane just in from the riverside bypass road, at *Can Tiranda* (Ⓣ972 136 037; ❸), though you may be required to take half-board – as you definitely are in the village centre at *Hostal El Molí* (Ⓣ972 136 049; ❺ HB). At those rates, the relative luxury of *Hotel La Coma* (Ⓣ972 136 073; ❺ B&B), at the entrance to the village, might be worth considering. Local trippers flock here to eat at weekends, most notably at the one independent **restaurant** *Can Jepet* (reserve on Ⓣ972 136 104, Ⓦwww.restaurantcanjepet.com; closed Thurs Oct–June). The food – well-presented salads, grilled quail with artichoke and roast peppers, home-made *flan* – is excellent value at under €22 a head.

Vallter 2000

Situated at the head of the valley, below the frontier summits of Bastiments (2883m) and Pic de la Dona (2704m), compact **VALLTER 2000** is the easternmost downhill ski resort in the Pyrenees. Although south-facing, the glacial bowl here has a chilly microclimate that lets snow linger into April most years – though the twelve pistes remain heavily dependent on canons. Weak intermediates will find plenty of challenge in the two-kilometre blue (Jordi Pujol) or easy red (El Clot) runs from the top station of 2535m (served by chair-lift). But only strong intermediates should attempt the five-kilometre Riu-Xalet joint piste, nominally blue but ending in a narrow, strongly red drop to the low point at 1910m, from where a bubble-lift returns to the resort centre (equipment rental, restaurant) at 2184m. In short, enough to keep you interested for the duration of a weekend, when Barcelonans flood the place; certain Camprodon and Ter valley hotels offer advantageous all-in packages of half-board and lift pass.

Hiking west: the GR11 and GR11.7

From Setcases, you can follow the GR11 and then the GR11.7 to a pair of useful refuges, though you're obliged to road-walk towards Valleter 2000 for the first hour or so of the GR11. Some three hours along, you arrive at the well-managed CEC **Refugi d'Ulldeter** (2235m elevation; Ⓣ972 192 004, Ⓦwww.ulldeter.net; 52 places; open daily Christmas/Easter weeks, late June to mid-Sept & weekends all year), just south of the Vallter ski resort. Its restaurant is open to all, and the three-storey stone chalet makes a particularly good halt coming east on the GR11/HRP from Núria. Otherwise, the GR11.7 diverges south from the Coll de la Marrana (2529m) overhead, threading the scenic Coma de Freser en route, to reach the 1999-built **Refugi Coma de Vaca** at the top of the Gorges del Freser within three hours – a popular snow-shoeing or skiing route in winter. This FEEC refuge, run by the welcoming Xavier and Yolanda (2020m; 42 places; staffed Easter, mid-June to mid-Sept, or off-season by arrangement; Ⓣ649 229 012, Ⓦww.comadevaca.com), offers above-average meals, hot showers and a full activities programme, including rock-climbing and winter mountaineering. Summer weekends the refuge is booked solid, but quiet otherwise except for the numerous bells on the grazing cows of the name. You can also get here from Núria (see p.178), or from Tregurà via the Coll dels Tres Pics (2396m) in about four hours, but that approach involves mostly track-trudging up to the pass.

Along the Ritort

From Camprodon, the road up to the **Col d'Ares** (1513m) and down into France initially follows the relatively treeless **Ritort valley**. The main, slight attractions of **MOLLÓ**, 8km from Camprodon (bus on Sat only), are the Romanesque church of Santa Cecília, with its four-storey bell tower, and *El Costabona* **restaurant** on the central *plaça*. The best place to **stay** in the village is *Hotel Restaurant Calitxó*, a modern structure on the outskirts (ⓣ972 740 386, ⓦwww.hotelcalitxo.com; ❼); the rooms are of good standard, with balconies, wood trim everywhere and tubs in the baths, but it's rather overpriced except in low season (❹). Especially if on a GR11 traverse, you may prefer a **casa de pagès** 3km north in Ginestosa district, *Can Illa* (ⓣ972 740 512; ❷), accessible by road or a half-hour, yellow-and-white-marked spur path. A working cattle ranch with sweeping views, *Can Illa* has mostly en-suite rooms, double beds, self-catering kitchen, a lounge with wood stove and a refuge-type dorm for groups. Your final chance of food and a place to stay before the border is the well-kept *Habitacions El Quintà* (ⓣ972 741 374; ❸) with balconied rooms at the base of attractive hillside **ESPINAVELL**, 2.2km northeast of the main road (4.2km in total from Molló; turn off before Ginestosa); half-board is available through the *Restaurant Les Planes* next door.

Another option, a little east of the Ritort valley, just off the start of the road up to Rocabruna, is a *casa de pagès* best suited for connoisseurs of the middle of nowhere: *Mas Tubert* (ⓣ972 130 327, ⓦwww.mastubert.com; ❹ B&B). It's 7km by rough track from the *urbanizació* of Font Rubí, itself about 6km from either Camprodon or Molló. Rooms are medium-sized if rustic, evening meals *nouvelle* verging on the precious (miniature frozen-liver lollies, and so on).

The upper Freser valley

From Ripoll, the **Freser valley** rises to Ribes de Freser and then climbs more steeply to Queralbs, where it swings eastwards through a gorge of remarkable beauty. Just above Queralbs, to the north, the Riu Núria has scoured out a second gorge, beyond which lie the ski station and valley sanctuary of Núria itself (1967m), the usual point of access to Puigmal (2910m) and other frontier peaks.

Ribes de Freser

Generally bypassed in the rush up to Núria, dull but unobjectionable **RIBES DE FRESER** offers little to the traveller except accommodation – better value than anything in Ripoll – and, out of season, its integrity as a real town. Local shops sell sacks of grain, seeds, oils and other agricultural and domestic paraphernalia in wonderfully random juxtapositions, plus there's a lively weekly market. More organized diversions consist of a much-used *petanca* court in the centre, and an annual sheepdog contest every September.

Alight from any regular **train** on the Barcelona–Puigcerdà line at "Ribes de Freser-RENFE" for the ten-minute walk into town, or just cross the platform to "Ribes-Enllaç" and take the *cremallera* (see box opposite), which makes another stop in the town centre (Ribes-Vila) before trundling off into the mountains.

Pick of the budget **accommodation** is *Mas Ventaiola* (ⓣ972 727 948), a *casa de pagès* 1km north of Ribes-Vila station, reached via the cemetery track taking off from the Pardines road. Perched on the hillside and refurbished in exemplary taste, this offers en-suite rooms (❷), a few quad apartments, plus common and self-catering areas. Otherwise, in the town itself, near Ribes-Vila station, the quietest choices are *Hotel Caçadors,* c/Balandrau 24–26 (ⓣ972 727 006, ⓦwww.hotelsderibes.com; ❸), offering four grades of en-suites in two separate premises, or the plainer rooms at *Hostal Porta de Núria* just around the corner at c/Nostra Senyora de Gràcia 3 (ⓣ972 727 137; ❸). If you're still stuck, there's a helpful **Turisme** on Plaça de l'Ajuntament (Tues–Sat 10am–2pm & 5–8pm, Sun 11am–1pm; ⓣ972 727 728) by the post-1936-rebuilt church of Santa Maria, or repair to the **campsite** *Vall de Ribes*, 800m from Ribes-Vila station on the Pardines road (Ⓣ972 728 820; all year); it's basic but pleasant, with tents welcome on the lower terraces, plus a few bungalows (❷). **Eating** out, the restaurant at the *Caçadors* is pleasant, reliable and much better value if used on a half-board basis; also a *menú* is available at weekday lunch times.

Pardines and Campelles

If you still come up empty – a possibility in midsummer or during the ski season – two outlying villages, each 6km from Ribes in opposite directions, have more **accommodation** and **eating** possibilities. **PARDINES** (1250m), reached via a two-lane road east, enjoys a wonderful hilltop setting only slightly marred by sprouting apartments; the medieval core, whose Romanesque church of **Sant Esteve** sports a round, thirteenth-century fortified belfry, remains atmospheric and reassuringly livestock-patrolled. Flanking the main square with its vaulted fountain is *Pensió Can Serra* (Ⓣ972 728 078; ❸ B&B), also serving meals. **CAMPELLES**, to the southwest at a similar altitude, is less compact and more gentrified, and offers at the outskirts the *Hotel Terralta* (Ⓣ972 727 350, Ⓦwww.hotelterralta.com; ❹). Near the centre is the good and popular if erratically open village **restaurant**, *Cal Marxened* (allow €22 *a la carta*; always open Fri pm to Sun noon, always shut Tues pm & Wed, ring Ⓣ972 729 237 for other days).

Queralbs and Fustanyà

The only intermediate stop on the *cremallera*, **QUERALBS** (1220m) is an attractive, stone-built village, though now being dwarfed by apartment complexes on its outskirts, and suffering from the attentions of too many tourists at peak season. Near the highest point, close to where the GR11 passes through, stands the twelfth-century church of **Sant Jaume**, adorned with a fine colonnaded porch with sculpted column capitals; inside there's a painted wooden altar with scenes from the Life of Christ. Reasonable en-suite **accommodation** is provided by *Hostal L'Avet*, on the main street 80m in from the car park (Ⓣ972 727 377; open daily 24 June to mid-Oct, weekends only at other times; ❺ HB only). *Table d'hôte* fare at the attached *Ca La Mary* restaurant is very good (allow €19 each), though opening hours can be idiosyncratic. More reliable is *El Restaurant de la Plaça* (closed Tues), where a similar amount gives you the run of a *carta* with delights such as cèpe soup and sausages.

The cremallera railway

The **cremallera** ("Zipper" in Catalan) railway, built in 1931, is the last rack-and-pinion line operating in Catalunya, a miniature – though rather more daring – version of the *Train Jaune* just over the border. After a leisurely start through the lower valley, the blue-and-white, two-car conveyance lurches up into the mountains relying on its third rail, following the river between great crags before starting to climb high above both valley and forests.

Services **depart** Ribes-Enllaç daily year-round except during November. "Low season" (weekdays Dec–June except Christmas, New Year and Easter, plus Oct) sees seven daily departures between 7.30am and 5.40pm, plus two extra departures between 6.40 and 8.40 pm on Fridays. "High season" (winter holidays, plus July–Sept) features a minimum of twelve daily trains from about 7.30am until 5.45pm, plus extra departures on holidays. The day's first train always starts at Ribes-Vila (where there's a weather report posted), six minutes down the line from Ribes-Enllaç. The **journey time** up or down is nominally 35 minutes; return adult **tickets** to Núria from Ribes cost €15.25 (or €9.55 one-way). No rail passes are valid. For current information phone Ⓣ972 732 020, or consult Ⓦwww.valldenuria.com/valldenuria/crem.htm.

For year-round board and lodging, head 3km out of Queralbs to well-signposted *Mas La Casanova* on the opposite side of the valley (☎972 198 077; ❸ B&B, or ❹ HB), in **FUSTANYÀ** hamlet, by its church of **Sant Sadurní**, the oldest in the region. This en-suite *casa de pagès* is a superbly restored farmhouse with a literary pedigree: the classic Catalan play *Terra Baixa* had as main characters the former inhabitants. The outgoing managing family provides *table d'hôte* suppers, and there are also large family suites; the only drawback is that the predominantly wood construction amplifies sounds between floors.

Núria

Beyond Queralbs, the *cremallera* railway hauls itself up the precipitous valley to **NÚRIA**, twenty minutes further on. Once the train passes the entrance to the Gorges del Freser, seen tantalizingly to the right, and enters the Gorges de Núria, the views are dramatic – when you're not passing through a sequence of tunnels.

Having cleared the final tunnel, you emerge into a south-facing bowl, with a small, dam-augmented lake at the bottom and – at the far end – the hideously monolithic, *café-au-lait*-coloured **Santuari de Nuestra Senyora de Núria** (1964m), founded in the eleventh century on the spot where an image of the Virgin was miraculously found. Local shepherds actually revere **Sant Gil** (Sept 1), an eighth-century Benedictine abbot who crossed over from France, set up shop in this valley, and attempted to proselytize the then-pagan herdsmen. The Virgin of Núria, of more general appeal, is believed to bestow fertility on female pilgrims, and many Catalan girls – presumably the result of successful supernatural intervention – are named after her.

The sanctuary building combines a dull church, tourist office (which posts weather reports), bar, restaurants, ski centre and **hotel** all in one. Rates at the *Husa Vall de Núria* (☎972 732 000, Ⓦwww.valdenuria.com; 2 nights min stay; ❻ obligatory HB) vary according to season – winter is cheaper – and its **restaurant** is equally pricey. The only indoor budget lodging is the youth hostel *Pic de L'Àliga* (☎972 732 048), marvellously poised at the top of the ski centre's cable-car line (often not running in summer). **Camping** is permitted only at a designated area behind the sanctuary complex.

Besides the hotel, **eating** options include *La Cabana dels Pastors*, behind the complex, sporadically offering expensive bistro fare at midday only; the *Bar Finestrelles*, downstairs in the sanctuary building, with typical bar snacks; and, best value of all, the lunch time-only *Autoservei* self-service restaurant in the west wing, where you can eat reasonably well for under €20. Summer activities in the valley include an archery range, pony-riding programme and boating on the lake.

Winter activities

Downhill **skiing** at Núria is surprisingly popular, given that the lift and piste system is very limited; the chair-lift only reaches 2252m, and the maximum altitude difference is a paltry 288m. The blue Les Creus run from the top station, is only 1800m long, while red-rated Mulleres traces just over a kilometre down from Point 2262, so Núria is best for beginners and weak intermediates.

Off-piste, the summits of **Pic/Puig de Finestrelles** (2829m) and **Puigmal** (2910m) are fairly easy to conquer. Each ascent takes three to five hours, depending on conditions and skill; crampons may be required. It's possible to take in both peaks as a full day's outing, passing between them along the frontier ridge; otherwise resort guides take clients on ten-peaks-in-a-day winter itineraries.

Walking

Summer **walkers** can follow similar routes detailed on Editorial Alpina's 1:25,000 "Puigmal-Vall de Núria-Ulldeter" map and accompanying booklet, most notably east along the **GR11**, which attains its greatest altitude following the frontier ridge and the HRP for a few hours – risky in poor visibility – en route to the Refugi d'Ulldeter. At the Coll de Carança, you have the option of descending into France to Ras de Carança (see p.112); the area's three staffed refuges promote a figure-of-eight-shaped "**Three Refuges Traverse**", using well-defined paths and taking four to five days.

A **return to Queralbs** on foot along the river gorge is perhaps the most popular hike out of Núria. The GR11 threads the gorge on a high-quality, well-marked path, but you'll still want sturdy boots and a water bottle (there are a few drinkable torrents and springs en route). You'll need two to two and a half hours descending, depending on load and stops, three to three and a half hours going up. The trail generally adopts the opposite side of the gorge to the *cremallera* tracks, giving you the opportunity to watch the little train at work; the valley begins to open out below Sallent del Sastre, and after crossing back to the west bank for good at the Pont de Cremal, you'll see the Freser gorge yawning to the east.

The two gorges walk

A more challenging, **five-hour descent**, traced correctly on the recommended Alpina map, gives you the best of **both local gorges**. This route starts alongside the cable car to Núria's youth hostel, with an initial ten minutes up the Camí de les Creus to a Via Crucis, where the onward GR11.7 is signed as the **Camí dels Enginyers** (Engineer's Trail), named after the engineers who came after 1945 to make a feasibility study for a dam in the valleys here – luckily it wasn't profitable. As you proceed, past the first announcement for Coma de Vaca, spectacular views open south and the terrain becomes more rugged, the path more of a corniche. While there's little net altitude change between Núria and the Coma de Vaca refuge, roller-coaster progress means you need to be fit; there's occasional scrambling over boulder falls and little metal ladders, with a cable and pegs about two hours along to get you over some steep patches, hazardous if wet. The *camí* attains its high point a few minutes further at the **Coll dels Homes**, and the hut appears suddenly at the base of a slope two-and-a-half hours from Núria.

After lunch here (recommended; see p.175), resume course on the **Camí de les Gorgues del Riu Freser**, marked only with red dots. Head initially southeast from the refuge, then bear right after ten minutes; once over the rocky promontory, descend on gentle, well-graded switchbacks. An hour below Coma de Vaca, you're in forest, with the river close by on the right. Next, cross the Freser on a plank bridge, and remain on the right bank thereafter: first in open meadow, then following a corniche path, with intermittent cobbling, high above the gorge. Pass the **Salt del Grill** stream, and just under two hours along, the wood bridge and signage for the Central Electric of Daió de Baix, where the Núria and Freser streams unite. The only boring bit involves following a cement drive out to the main road, and a final haul up the asphalt to the Queralbs *cremallera* car park (2hr 20min from the refuge).

Hard cases can instead head from the refuge up the Coma de Vaca itself (red-dot markings) to the Coll de Carança, and thence down to Núria, for a five-hour trajectory; it's best to do this only with an early start during late June/July, and on a Friday or Saturday when there's a late train downhill.

Travel Details

Trains

French trains

NB SNCF buses may substitute for trains on these lines; services are reduced Sun/hols.

Perpignan to: Banyuls-sur-Mer (8–12 daily; 30min); Cerbère (8–12 daily; 40min); Collioure (8–12 daily; 25min); Elne (8–12 daily; 10min); Ille-sur-Têt (8 daily; 25–30min); Prades (4–6 daily; 45min); Villefranche-de-Conflent (4–6 daily; 50min).

Quillan to: Carcassonne (4–6 daily; 55min–1hr 15min).

Villefranche-de-Conflent to: Latour-de-Carol (4–7 daily; 2hr 45min); Mont-Louis (5–8 daily; 1hr 35min). **NB** These are *Train Jaune* (see p.112) departures.

Spanish trains

Figueres to: Colera (9 daily; 25min); Girona (21 daily; 30min); Portbou (12 daily; 30min).

Girona to: Barcelona (21 daily; 1hr 10min–1hr 30min); Llançà (12 daily; 1hr); Portbou (14 daily; 1hr 10min).

Ripoll to: Barcelona (8–12 daily; 2hr 20min–2hr 40min); Puigcerdà (5–6 daily; 1hr 10min–1hr 30min; 4 continue 7min more to French station of Latour-de-Carol).

Buses

French buses

Arles-sur-Tech to: Coustouges (2–3 daily; 40min); Prats-de-Molló (6 daily; 15min); St-Laurent-de-Cerdans (2–3 daily; 30min).

La Cabanasse/Mont-Louis to: Puyvalador via Les Angles, Matemale and Formiguères (2 daily in summer and ski season at 10.35am and 6pm, returns mid-afternoon and dawn; 50min).

Perpignan to: Arles-sur-Tech (6 daily; 1hr 15min); Axat (1 daily; 1hr 40min); Banyuls-sur-Mer (3 daily; 1hr 10min); Cerbère (3 daily; 1hr 15min); Céret (14 daily; 55min); Collioure (3 daily; 45min); Elne (3 daily; 35min); Font-Romeu (2–3 daily; 2hr 30min); Ille-sur-Têt (11 daily; 35min); Latour-de-Carol (2–3 daily; 3hr); Le Boulou (12 daily; 20min); Le Perthus (6 daily; 45min); Mont-Louis (4 daily; 2hr 15min); Port-Vendres (3–6 daily; 55min); Prades (7 daily; 1hr); Prats-de-Molló (6 daily; 1hr 40min); La Preste (3 daily; 2hr); Saint-Génis (4 daily; 45min); Saint-Laurent-de-Cerdans (3 daily Mon–Sat, 2 Sun; 1hr 45min); Thuir (3–5 daily; 25min); Vernet-les-Bains (4 daily; 1hr 25min); Villefranche-de-Conflent (7 daily; 1hr 15min).

Prades to: Molitg-les-Bains (4–5 daily Mon–Sat, 1 Sun; 10min).

Quillan to: Axat (2 daily; 20min); Carcassonne (2 daily; 1hr 20min); Comus (1–2 daily; 1hr 5min); Perpignan (1 daily; 1hr 30min); Quérigut (3 weekly in summer; 1hr 30min).

Villefranche-de-Conflent to: Casteil (3–4 daily; 15min); Prades (14 daily Mon–Sat, 7 Sun; 10min); Sahorre (1–2 daily Mon–Sat; 15min); Vernet-les-Bains (12 daily Mon–Sat, 7 Sun; 10min).

Spanish buses

Camprodon to: Molló (Mon–Sat 1 daily; 15min); Setcases (Mon–Sat 1 daily; 30min).

Figueres to: Cadaqués (3 daily Mon–Fri, 4 Sat–Sun; 1hr 10min); Castelló d'Empúries (hourly; 15min); Espolla (1 daily Mon–Sat; 35min); Girona (4–8 daily Mon–Sat, 3 Sun; 1hr); Llançà (2 daily; 25min); Maçanet de Cabrenys via Darnius (1–2 daily Mon–Sat; 45–55min); Roses (every 30min; 40min); Vilajuïga (1 daily; 50min).

Girona to: Banyoles (11–15 daily Mon–Sat, 6 Sun; 30min); Cadaqués (1 daily Mon–Fri in eve; 50min); Figueres (8 daily Mon–Sat, 3 Sun; 50min); Olot (10 daily Mon–Sat, 3 Sun; 1hr 20min).

Olot to: Banyoles via Besalú (6–7 daily Mon–Sat, 4 Sun; 40min); Banyoles via Mieres (3 weekly; 1hr); Besalú (8 daily Mon–Sat, 6 Sun; 30min); Camprodon (1–2 daily; 45min); Figueres (2–3 daily; 1hr); Ripoll (1–2 daily; 50min); Santa Pau (Wed & Sat am, plus 2 Mon; 15min); Sant Joan de les Abadesses (1–2 daily; 30min); Vall d'en Bas (12 daily; 15min).

Ripoll to: Camprodon (6 daily; 45min); Guardiola de Berguedà (1 daily Mon–Fri at 5.25pm; 2hr); La Pobla de Lillet (1 daily Mon–Fri at 5.25pm; 1hr 45min); Sant Joan de les Abadesses (6 daily; 20min).

2

Andorra and around

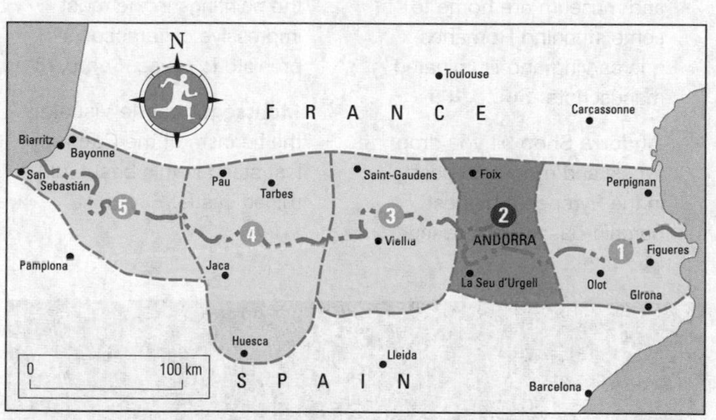

CHAPTER 2

Highlights

* **Alp 2500** Ski at the oldest and one of the largest and longest alpine-sports regions in the world. See p.187

* **Ascent of Pedraforca** Climb to the top of Catalunya's most sculpted peak. See p.197

* **La Seu d'Urgell** Its cloister and museum are home to some stunning Romanesque carving and illuminated manuscripts. See p.199

* **Andorra** Shop till you drop for ski and mountain gear in the Pyrenees' biggest bargain-basement bazaar. See p.202

* **The thermal spa of Dorres** Have a soak at one of the Cerdagne's rare outdoor hot pools. See p.222

* **Carlit Massif** Hike through, around or over the easternmost high-mountain region of the range. See p.224

* **Grotte de Niaux** Marvel at the paintings in the most impressive of Tarascon's prehistoric caves. See p.231

* **Montségur castle** Visualize the heroism of the Cathars' last stand in this beautiful ruined castle. See p.243

△ Cloister, La Seu d'Urgell

2

Andorra and around

Approaching the principality of Andorra from the Mediterranean, you begin to encounter concentrations of glacial lakes and permanent snow on the highest summits. On the Spanish side, the best appetizer for the main range en route to Andorra is the **Parc Natural del Cadí-Moixeró**, featuring the distinctively cloven **Pedraforca**. In 1906 Pablo Picasso spent a summer in Gósol at the foot of this quintessential Catalan peak, and much of what he experienced still exists: unspoilt, vividly coloured scenery, raptors soaring overhead and herds of isards.

La Seu d'Urgell, capital of the Spanish *comarca* (county) of **Alt Urgell**, north and west of the Cadí, is one of the main gateways to Andorra, and pivotal to its history. La Seu's bishops controlled the principality with the nobility of Foix in a unique feudal power-sharing arrangement which endured, more or less peacefully, for over seven centuries, until Andorra opted for independence in 1993. There are just two ways of entering **Andorra** by road: along the Valira valley from La Seu d'Urgell, or from the Ariège valley in France. At each frontier, and for a considerable distance beyond, duty-free megastores peddling cut-price consumer goods line streets congested with shoppers' cars. But the remotest corners of Andorra remain untrammelled, and on foot you can traverse the principality (almost) without touching asphalt or seeing a single shop.

Like Catalonia in general, the mountain-ringed plateau of **Cerdanya**, southeast of Andorra, was partitioned by the 1659 Treaty of the Pyrenees, a division that left **Llívia** as an island of Spanish territory surrounded by the **Cerdagne**, the French part of this formerly unified territory. **Puigcerdà** on the Spanish side, once capital of the entire district, is now a kilometre or so from the border. To the north rises the **Carlit Massif**, the easternmost high-alpine region in the Pyrenees.

The **Ariège valley**, north of Andorra, makes an excellent choice if you have time for only one other region near the principality. The caves around **Tarascon** include stunning prehistoric paintings at **Niaux**, and a magnificent forest of stalactites and stalagmites at **Lombrives**, the largest cave open to the public in Europe. For walkers, **Ax-les-Thermes** is the most attractive place to stay, with a trio of long-distance footpaths – the **HRP**, **GR10** and **GR7** – within easy reach. Further down the valley, historic **Foix** banks on its legacy as the seat of an early medieval mini-state.

North of the Ariège lies the isolated **Pays de Sault**, an area inseparable from the tragic history of Catharism, a religion persecuted out of existence by the kings of France and the Catholic Church. At **Montségur**, the last leading figures of the Cathar sect were besieged in a 1244 crusade that ended with the immolation of over two hundred members of this community (see box on pp.240–241).

Public transport in the region is scarce except along the main north–south valleys. Buses from the south run up the corridor from Lleida to La Seu d'Urgell and Andorra,

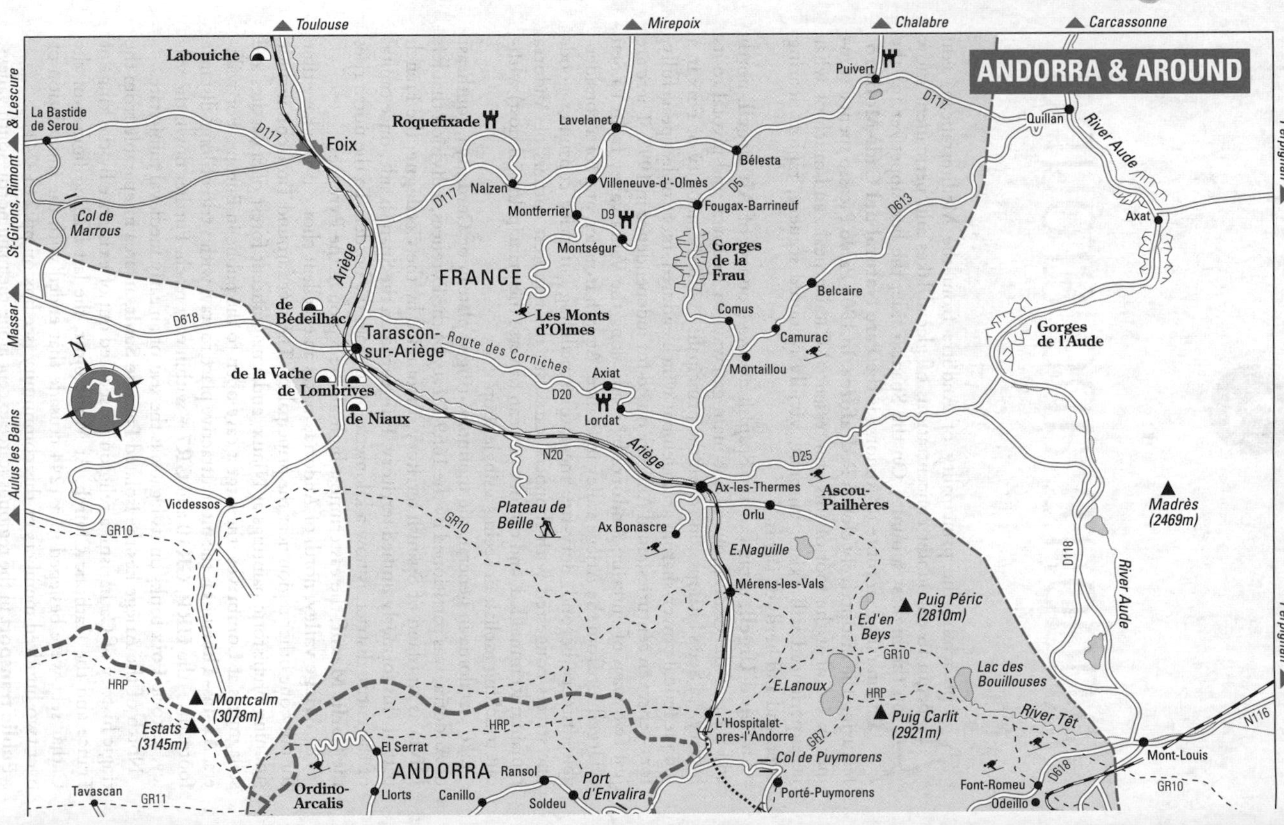
ANDORRA & AROUND
Toulouse
Mirepoix
Chalabre
Carcassonne
Perpignan
Perpignan
St-Girons, Rimont & Lescure
Massar
Aulus les Bains
Labouiche
Roquefixade
Puivert
Quillan
River Aude
Axat
La Bastide de Serou
Foix
D117
Lavelanet
Bélesta
Villeneuve-d'-Olmès
Nalzen
Montferrier
D9
D5
Fougax-Barrineuf
D613
Col de Marrous
Ariège
Montségur
Gorges de la Frau
FRANCE
Gorges de l'Aude
de Bédeilhac
D618
Tarascon-sur-Ariège
Route des Corniches
Les Monts d'Olmes
Comus
Belcaire
Camurac
Montaillou
de la Vache
de Lombrives
de Niaux
Axiat
D20
Lordat
N20
D25
Ax-les-Thermes
Ascou-Pailhères
Orlu
Madrès (2469m)
Vicdessos
GR10
Plateau de Beille
Ax Bonascre
E.Naguille
D118
Mérens-les-Vals
Puig Péric (2810m)
E.d'en Beys
Lac des Bouillouses
HRP
E.Lanoux
Puig Carlit (2921m)
River Têt
Montcalm (3078m)
Estats (3145m)
L'Hospitalet-pres-l'Andorre
GR7
N116
Mont-Louis
El Serrat
Col de Puymorens
ANDORRA
Ransol
Port d'Envalira
Ordino-Arcalis
Llorts
Canillo
Soldeu
Porté-Puymorens
Font-Romeu
Odeillo
Tavascan
GR11

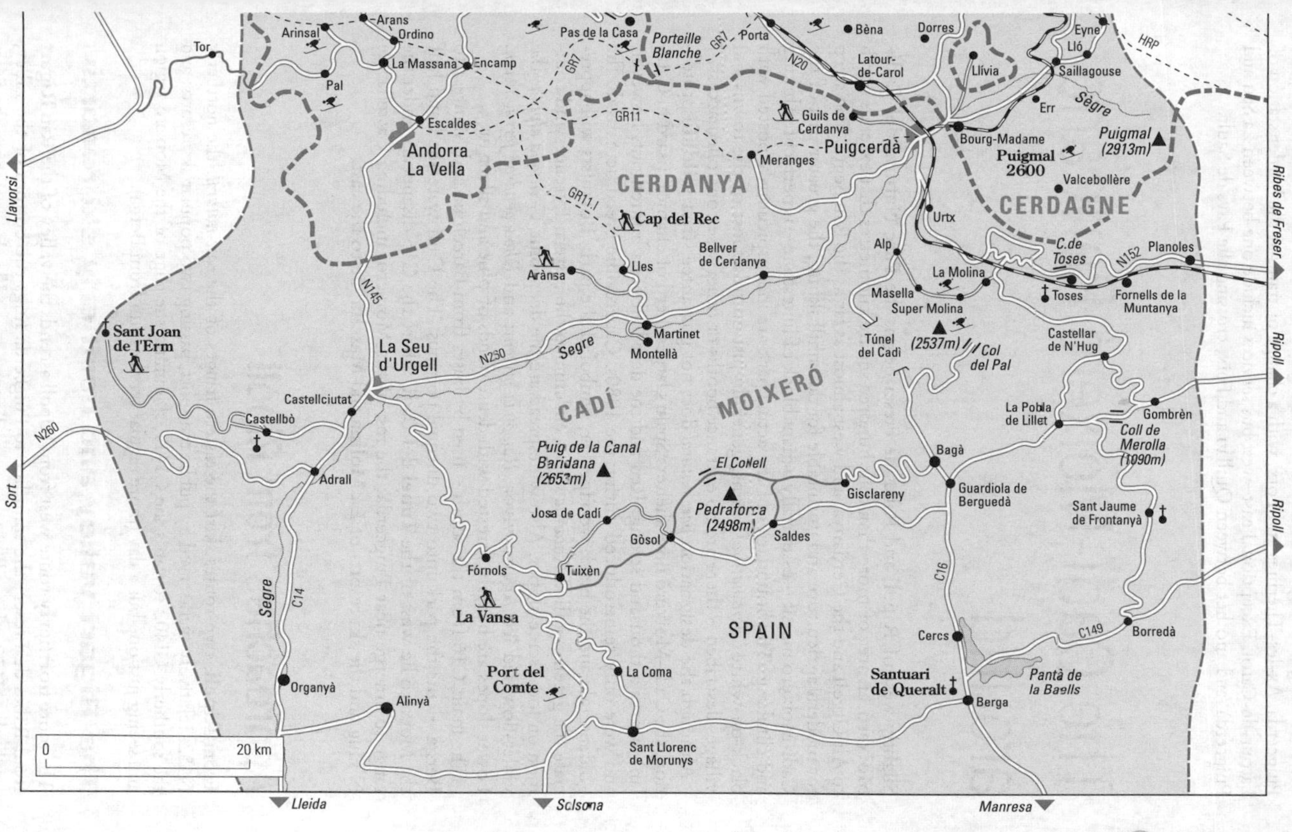

Arans
Arinsal
Ordino
Tor
La Massana
Encamp
Pal
Escaldes
Andorra La Vella
Pas de la Casa
Porteille Blanche
GR7
Porta
N20
Bèna
Dorres
Latour-de-Carol
Llívia
Eyne
Lló
Saillagouse
HRP
Err
Sègre
GR11
Guils de Cerdanya
Puigcerdà
Meranges
Bourg-Madame
Puigmal 2600
Puigmal (2913m)
Valcebollère
CERDANYA
CERDAGNE
GR11.1
Cap del Rec
Urtx
Alp
C.de Toses
N152
Planoles
Aránsa
Lles
Bellver de Cerdanya
La Molina
Masella
Super Molina
Toses
Fornells de la Muntanya
N145
Martinet
Montellà
Sant Joan de l'Erm
La Seu d'Urgell
N260
Segre
Túnel del Cadí
(2537m)
Col del Pal
Castellar de N'Hug
Castellciutat
CADÍ
MOIXERÓ
Castellbò
La Pobla de Lillet
Gombrèn
Coll de Merolla (1090m)
Puig de la Canal Baridana (2653m)
El Collell
Bagà
Adrall
Pedraforca (2498m)
Gisclareny
Guardiola de Berguedà
Josa de Cadí
Sant Jaume de Frontanyà
Gósol
Saldes
Fórnols
Tuixèn
C16
La Vansa
Segre
C14
SPAIN
Cercs
C149
Borredà
Port del Comte
La Coma
Santuari de Queralt
Pantà de la Baells
Organyà
Alinyà
Berga
0
20 km
Sant Llorenc de Morunys
Llavorsi
Sort
Lleida
Solsona
Manresa
Ribes de Freser
Ripoll
Ripoll

and from Berga to Puigcerdà. The last surviving trans-Pyrenean rail line links Ripoll, Puigcerdà, Ax-les-Thermes and Foix, with a change of trains at the border station of Latour-de-Carol. Exceptional east–west bus services include one between La Seu and Puigcerdà, and another between Quillan and Foix, crossing the Pays de Sault.

The Cadí-Moixeró Park and around

Slightly west of Ripoll and Ribes de Freser begins the **Parc Natural del Cadí-Moixeró**, an area of more than four hundred square kilometres that extends north to Alt Urgell and the Cerdanya, and west almost as far as the Riu Segre. Too steep for modern agriculture and unsuitable for downhill skiing, the greater part of the Cadí-Moixeró massif – essentially a giant block of limestone – is perfect for hiking and climbing. The boundaries of the actual park are inconspicuously posted with black-on-white "*parc natural*" signs, generally just outside most of the towns and villages described – there are no entrance booths or otherwise controlled access.

Although the designation *parc natural* does not guarantee strict **wildlife** protection, the Cadí-Moixeró now shelters Spain's largest herd of chamois (isard in Catalan), nearly a thousand strong. Red and roe deer had been hunted out, however, and were only reintroduced during the 1980s. Capercaillie breed here, as do the golden eagle and the black woodpecker, symbol of the park. Botanists will appreciate the green-petalled *Xatardia scabra*, endemic to the eastern Pyrenees and common on local scree slopes. Also widespread are the deep-blue *Gentiana alpina*; the violet-flowered Ice Age survivor, *Ramonda myconi*; and *Rhododendron ferrugineum*. Lower slopes are heavily forested with dense stands of pine and silver fir.

The main C16 from the south – used by buses from Barcelona and Manresa to **Berga** – cuts the park into two unequal portions. The Cadí watershed and half the Moixeró lie west of the **Túnel del Cadí**, where the C16 disappears under the range to emerge near Puigcerdà; the rest of the Moixeró, including Castellar de N'Hug and the ski resorts of **La Molina** and **Masella**, lie to the east.

Approaches from Ripoll

From Ripoll, two routes skirt the eastern fringes of the *parc natural*: the northerly N152, relatively well served by public transport, passing two popular ski resorts; and the southerly GI402 towards the C1411, skimming the edge of the Moixeró region and seeing just one bus a day (more regular services run from Berga).

The Rigart valley and northerly ski resorts

The more **northerly** route west from Ripoll ascends the valley of the **Riu Rigart** from Ribes de Freser; the train line to Puigcerdà hugs the bottom of the valley, while the N152 takes a higher course, allowing a good look south over the Serra

Montgrony. Beyond the Collada de Toses, technically in the Cerdanya, the ski resort of **Alp 2500** is the easternmost really serious winter-sports area in the Catalan Pyrenees.

Planoles, Fornells and Toses

PLANOLES village, 7km from Ribes on a south-facing slope, is nothing extraordinary, but it straddles the GR11 and makes a good base for the ski slopes to the west. Most local **accommodation** is of the second-home variety, but there's an outstanding *casa de pagès*, *Mas Cal Sadurní* (Ⓣ972 736 135; ❺ HB only), unimprovably set on a natural terrace just uphill from the train station. This offers doubles and family-size quads, mostly en suite, in a superbly restored farmhouse. It's packed out most weekends, when the pricey *carta* restaurant is open to those not staying (other days *menú*-format for guests only); breakfast is served in a separate, medieval refectory.

The hamlet of **FORNELLS DE LA MUNTANYA**, 8.5km beyond Planoles, has another **casa de pagès**, the blandly modern, en-suite *Cal Pastor* (Ⓣ972 736 163; ❹). Fornells is really noteworthy for its single, friendly **restaurant**, *Can Casanova* (closed Mon eve & Tues), serving large portions of hearty mountain cuisine from a limited menu. It's good value at under €23 per person, including a strong, ruby house wine, and (unusually) serves lunch until 4.30pm (but supper only Fri/Sat low season), so reservations are suggested (Ⓣ972 736 075).

TOSES, 3.5km beyond Fornells, is the last village in the Rigart valley and, at 1450m, is one of the highest permanently inhabited villages in Spain. It enjoys views east towards El Ripollès and 4km west to the **Collada de Toses** (1800m), which closes off the horizon. The only **accommodation** option, 100m from the train, is pricey *Cal Santpare* (Ⓣ972 736 226; ❹ B&B, ❻ HB). Food at the ground-floor restaurant is basic but sustaining, the en-suite rooms heated and comfortable.

The glory of Toses is its tenth- to twelfth-century church of **San Cristófol**, at the highest, southeast end of the village, with a simple barrel-vaulted nave and a rectangular, gable-roofed "Lombard" belfry. The ancient, hard-to-work key (obtain from *Cal Pep* on the square – their nearby affiliate *Les Forques d'en Pep* is a good independent **restaurant**) allows you inside to study the apsidal **frescoes**, skilful copies of originals in the Museu d'Art de Catalunya in Barcelona. The main theme, Christ's Ascension, is half-destroyed, but well preserved around the lancet window is an image of a lad hefting a sheep – highly apt for this pastoral community.

Beyond Toses, road and train enter Cerdanya over and under the Collada de Toses – the railway by the amazing **Cargol tunnel**, where the line executes a complete spiral to gain altitude. The pass affords excellent views west, the bare rolling mountains of the Montgrony range relieved by swathes of deep-green forest.

Skiing Alp 2500 – and Alp village

LA MOLINA, its lifts scattered 4–7km from the pass on the north flank of 2409-metre Puigllançada, ranks as the oldest ski resort in Spain, inaugurated in 1909. From 1922, special Sunday return trains from Barcelona catered to enthusiasts, though for some years the line only ran to Toses, from where intrepid skiers had to proceed through an unfinished rail tunnel by torchlight, then trudge up the slopes to begin their runs – there were no lifts until 1943. Local villagers derived great amusement from these pioneer skiers with their clumsy wooden gear – "Throw them on the fire and get some benefit from them!" was a typical comment. Needless to say, the sport took off, and in 1967 another resort opened at **MASELLA**, 4.5km west of La Molina, on the slopes of 2536-metre Tosa d'Alp.

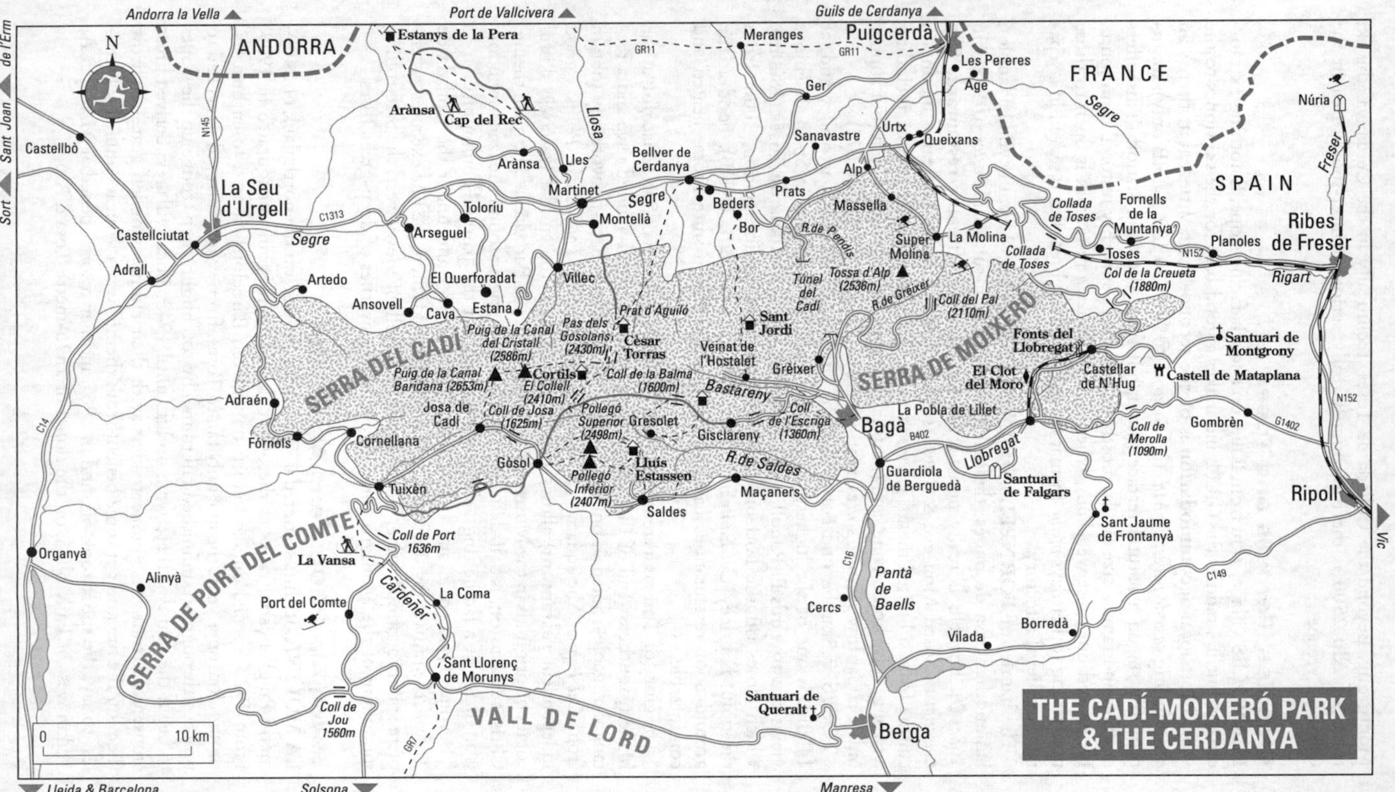
THE CADÍ-MOIXERÓ PARK
& THE CERDANYA
Andorra la Vella
Port de Vallcivera
Guils de Cerdanya
de l'Erm
Sant Joan
Sort
Lleida & Barcelona
Solsona
Manresa
Vic
ANDORRA
FRANCE
SPAIN
Estanys de la Pera
Arànsa
Cap del Rec
Llosa
Meranges
Puigcerdà
Les Pereres
Age
Ger
Segre
Núria
Fresser
Castellbò
La Seu d'Urgell
Arànsa
Lles
Bellver de Cerdanya
Sanavastre
Urtx
Queixans
Alp
Martinet
Prats
Beders
Massella
Collada de Toses
Fornells de la Muntanya
Ribes de Freser
Castellciutat
C1313
Segre
Toloríu
Arseguel
Montellà
Bor
R.de Pendís
Super Molina
La Molina
Toses
Planoles
Adrall
Artedo
El Querforadat
Villec
Túnel del Cadí
Tossa d'Alp (2536m)
Collada de Toses
Col de la Creueta (1880m)
Rigart
Ansovell
Cava
Estana
Prat d'Aguiló
Sant Jordi
R.de Greixer
Coll del Pal (2110m)
Santuari de Montgrony
Puig de la Canal del Cristall (2586m)
Pas dels Gosolans (2430m)
César Torras
Veïnat de l'Hostalet
SERRA DE MOIXERÓ
Fonts del Llobregat
Castell de Mataplana
SERRA DEL CADÍ
Puig de la Canal Baridana (2653m)
Cortils
El Collell (2410m)
Coll de la Balma (1600m)
Grèixer
El Clot del Moro
Castellar de N'Hug
Bastareny
N152
Adraén
Josa de Cadí
Coll de Josa (1625m)
Pollegó Superior (2498m)
Gresolet
Coll de l'Escriga (1360m)
La Pobla de Lillet
Gombrèn
G1402
C14
Fórnols
Cornellana
Gisclareny
Bagà
B402
Coll de Merolla (1090m)
Gòsol
Lluís Estassen
R.de Saldes
Guardiola de Berguedà
Llobregat
Santuari de Falgars
Tuixèn
Pollegó Inferior (2407m)
Maçaners
Saldes
Ripoll
SERRA DE PORT DEL COMTE
Coll de Port 1636m
Sant Jaume de Frontanyà
Organyà
La Vansa
C16
Alinyà
Cardener
La Coma
Pantà de Baells
C149
Port del Comte
Cercs
Borredà
Vilada
Sant Llorenç de Morunys
Coll de Jou 1560m
GR7
GR11
Santuari de Queralt
VALL DE LORD
Berga
0
10 km
N145
N

Both La Molina and Masella have their own websites (Ⓦwww.lamolina.com and Ⓦwww.masella.com), though they're marketed together as "Alp 2500". By Spanish Pyrenean standards the skiing is impressive: the two resorts, sharing a lift pass, are linked via chair-/bubble-lifts and runs focused on Tosa d'Alp, forming one of the largest ski area in the Pyrenees. La Molina is publicly owned by the Catalan government, and probably better suited for beginners; slightly larger Masella has passed into private hands, and is considered the better managed of the two. Certainly it has the edge in scenic appeal, provision of strategic chair-lifts and length of runs, including seven kilometres of consecutive blue and red runs from Tosa d'Alp summit to Pla de Masella at 1600m, the second greatest altitude drop in the range. Despite northerly orientation and forest cover, both resorts rely heavily on snow canons and may close early in the day during spring – though it works the longest season in Cerdanya/Cerdagne.

Getting to the slopes, it's best to have your own car, though there is a bus service between La Molina-Vila RENFE station and the so-called Pista Larga of La Molina resort (every 20min 8.30–10.15am, hourly 10.15am–4pm, every 20min 4–6.30pm).

With few exceptions, **accommodation** at the foot of the slopes is overpriced, sterile and beset in high season by what Spaniards call *mucho follón* – hassle, noise, congestion. A departure from the norm is the wood and stone chalet *Niu dels Falcons* on c/Font Moreu 10 in La Molina (Ⓣ972 892 073; Ⓦwww.niudelsfalcons-xalet.com; ❼ HB only). Generally, though, you're far better off staying downhill to the north in the villages of the Cerdanya (see pp.215–218). Closest is **ALP**, 6.5km northwest, where the old quarter up on the hillside is well disguised by *avant-* and *après*-ski facilities, plus vast phalanxes of weekend chalets. The best of three hotels here is friendly Casa Fonda affiliate *Aero Hotel Cerdanya*, Passeig Agnès Fabra 4, on the northeast edge of town (Ⓣ972 890 033, Ⓔhotelrestaurant@caleudald.com; ❹), popular with families. The wood-floored rooms have mildly kitsch decor, wall art adorns the common areas, and there's a competitively priced gourmet **restaurant** in the basement, *Ca l'Eudald* (*menú* from €15, *a la carta* €30).

Gombrèn, Montgrony and La Pobla de Lillet

The **southerly route** from Ripoll aims right at the heart of the Cadí-Moixeró region. Beginning just north of Ripoll, at Campdevànol, this minor road crosses the Riu Freser and heads 8km west to the foothill village of Gombrèn, served by a single weekday evening (Mir company) bus from Ripoll. If you get stranded at **GOMBRÈN**, a sleepy spot where the church clock tolls the hours twice, you needn't worry (other than about sundry hauntings from Comte Arnau; see box p.172): the village offers reasonable **accommodation** in the form of *La Fonda Xesc* (Ⓣ972 730 404, Ⓦwww.fondaxesc.com; ❸ B&B). Its **restaurant** (Oct–June closed all day Mon & Tues, Wed pm, Sun pm) draws crowds from afar for the sake of its elegant new-wave cuisine (*yuca* crisps, cold courgette soup, lamb cooked in peach-hazelnut sauce, creative sorbets); budget €30 per person, with wine. Rooms by contrast are on the spartan side, but all common areas were overhauled in 2003. If it's full or doesn't suit, try *Masia la Canal* (Ⓣ972 712 131; ❸ B&B), a *casa de pagès* some 4km out of "town", offering rustic en-suite doubles and triples.

Less than 3km beyond Gombrèn, a paved road on the right leads north to the **Santuari de Montgrony** (Mon–Fri 9am–6pm, Sat–Sun 9am–8pm), worth the 5.5-kilometre detour for its spectacular setting. Steep steps lead to the tiny shrine itself, tucked swallow's-nest fashion into the side of a cliff and focused on an equally diminutive wooden image of the Virgin and seated Child; a path leads ten minutes more over the hillside to the cruciform, Romanesque church of **Sant**

Pere. Part of the shrine is now an agreeable old **inn** (Ⓣ972 198 022, Ⓦwww.montgrony.net; ❹ B&B, ❻ HB; closed Mon & Tues Oct –June), with a well-respected, beamed-ceiling **restaurant** (closed Tues). With your own transport you can continue another 10km from the *santuari* to Castellar de N'Hug (see p.191), passing the tiny, ruined **Castell de Mataplana**.

The main GI402 road west continues 16km from Gombrèn to the **Coll de Merolla** (1090m) – with some weird rock formations to the southwest and excruciating curves each side of the watershed – then drops as the B402 to **LA POBLA DE LILLET**, 28km from Ripoll. Here, two ancient bridges arching over the infant Llobregat River and the old districts on either side make for a pleasant half-hour stroll, but the main local attractions lie just outside the town: the *carrilet* or **narrow-gauge railway** from here up to Castellar de N'Hug, which makes a stop 2km along at the **Jardins Artigas** (July–Sept daily 10am–7pm, Oct–June Sat–Sun 10am–5pm, guided visits only weekdays; €3), designed by Antoni Gaudí in 1901 for local industrialist Joan Artigas. Straddling the Riu Llobregat near a pungent-smelling paper mill, the gardens constitute an enjoyable ensemble of walkways, bridges, sculpted planter boxes, sculpted railings and belvederes.

△ El Clot de Moro

La Pobla has a **Turisme** (daily Easter & June–Sept 10am–2pm & 5–8pm) by the smaller bridge. **Accommodation** and **dining** are restricted to the central *Hostal Can Pericas*, c/Furrioles Altes 3 (Ⓣ938 236 162; ❹), with average food and slow service, the slightly shabbier *Hostal Cerdanya* at Plaça del Fort 5 (Ⓣ938 236 083; ❸) and (for meals only) *El Verger* in the old centre.

El Clot de Moro, Fonts de Llobregat and Castellar de N'Hug

From La Pobla there's a steady ascent by road (11km) northeast towards Castellar de N'Hug, a distance covered by evening **bus** (daily except Sun) up from Berga via La Pobla. Alternatively, take the **carrilet** noted above (daily summer, weekends only spring/autumn). Three kilometres out of La Pobla on the left (the *carrilet* stops) stands **El Clot de Moro**, a flamboyant *modernista* building designed by Rafael Guastavino in 1901 as a cement factory; today it functions as the **Museu del Ciment Asland** (daily July to mid-Sept 10am–2pm & 4–7pm; rest of year weekends only 10am–3pm; €3), with exhibits on the industry.

Approaching Castellar, you'll pass the **Fonts del Llobregat**, source of the river that divides Spanish Catalunya in two. Numerous jets of water burst from the rock of a densely wooded ravine, the most powerful forming a broad, photogenic waterfall. Catalans come here as if on pilgrimage – summer droughts reduce many of Catalunya's rivers to nothing, so there's great pride in any durable water source, and this one has never stopped in living memory. Coming uphill, the main access is by a signposted turning leading past the giant *Hostal Les Fonts* to a car park, snack bar, souvenir stall and old water mill, a few minutes' walk from the cascades. You can also get here via a fifteen-minute stepped path from the bottom of Castellar de N'Hug.

Heaped up against the ridge of the Serra de Montgrony, **CASTELLAR DE N'HUG** (1400m) makes a good if slightly touristy base for the Moixeró section of the park, or (in winter) for Alp 2500 (see p.187); high seasons are September–October, when people hunt mushrooms in surrounding forests, and the main ski period of January–February. There's a fair amount of reasonable **accommodation**: top choices are the friendly *Hostal Fonda La Muntanya* (Ⓣ938 257 065; ❹ B&B, ❺ HB; all year except part June) at Plaça Major 4, with excellent, copious dinners, 2005-redone rooms on site plus remoter apartments, or the *Pensió Fanxicó* (Ⓣ938 257 015; ❺) across the way. An airy fallback, at the start of the road towards the Santuari de Montgrony and La Molina, is *Hostal Alt Llobregat* (Ⓣ938 257 074; ❹ B&B, ❹ HB), with very plain though balconied rooms.

North from Castellar, the paved, bleakly scenic BV4031, sporadically snowploughed in winter, continues 15.5km over the range to La Molina and the Collada de Toses via the **Coll de la Creueta** (1880m).

Sant Jaume de Frontanyà and beyond

The eleventh-century church at **SANT JAUME DE FRONTANYÀ**, the most imposing Romanesque church in the region, lies just 12km southeast of La Pobla, easily accessible by a paved road, though many older maps may not show it as such. The turning south from the B402, 2km east of La Pobla, is well marked.

Built in the shape of a Latin cross with three apses, this Augustinian foundation has an engaging setting at the foot of a naturally terraced cliff. The twelve-sided, squinch-supported lantern was unique in Catalunya until the restoration of the monastery at Ripoll. Inside, the church is chilly and bare, though evocative in its emptiness.

The surrounding hamlet, all of a dozen stone houses, offers two excellent, characterful **restaurants**, *Cal Eloi* and *Fonda Cal Marxandó*, the latter with inexpensive, shared-bath **rooms** (Ⓣ938 239 002; ❷ B&B) above its beam-ceilinged *menjador*. *Cal Eloi* (shut Mon) offers a hearty three-course *menú* including wine for under €20; *Cal Marxandó* (closed Mon eve & Tues) has slightly more elaborate dishes at around €22 *a la carta*.

From Sant Jaume the road continues 9km south to nondescript **BORREDÀ** on the C26, where small lumber mills on the outskirts slowly process the lush surrounding forest. Amenities comprise just the *Baix Pirineu* **restaurant** on the main street, with rooms suitable for emergencies. It's another 21km southwest to Berga past the **Pantà de la Baells**, a reservoir on the Llobregat, where at low water local boaters claim you can see the cupola and crumbled walls of a submerged monastic church.

Berga and around

From the south, the major public-transport approach to the Cadí is the twice-daily bus from Barcelona to **BERGA**, where the Pyrenees rear up with startling abruptness. The town itself is fairly dull, bearing ample traces of its long history as an industrial centre, but it does offer a ruined castle, a well-preserved, part-pedestrianized medieval core and – as capital of Berguedà – onward connections to higher settlements in the county, provided by the ATSA bus company at the top of Passeig de la Pau.

The other main reason to come to Berga is for the town's **Festa de la Patum** at Corpus Christi, one of Catalunya's most famous festivals. For three days in June, huge figures of giants and dwarfs process to hornpipe music along streets packed with red-hatted Catalans intent on a good time. A dragon attacks onlookers in the course of a symbolic battle between good and evil, firecrackers blazing from its mouth, while the climax comes on the Saturday night, with a dance performed by masked men covered in grass.

The helpful **Turisme** is in the heart of the old town at c/dels Àngels 7 (Ⓣ938 211 384; Ⓦwww.ajberga.es; closed Sun–Mon). Not surprisingly, **accommodation** is impossible to find during the festival unless you've booked weeks in advance; at other times you should have few problems. Among seven places to stay, try the small but well-appointed *Hotel Passasserres*, Passeig Abeuradors (Ⓣ938 210 645, Ⓦwww.passasserres@telefonica.mnet; ❹), with sauna, gym and off-street parking; or *Pensió del Guiu* on Ctra de Queralt, en route to the eponymous shrine (Ⓣ938 210 315; ❷). The most famous local **restaurant** is *Sala* at Passeig de la Pau 27 (closed Sun dinner & Mon) – count on over €50, either *carta* or *menú*, for a gourmet meal. If your budget won't stretch that far, the *menjador* of the *Pensió del Guiu* offers regional specialities, while *Bar La Barana* at the heart of the old town on Plaça Sant Pere offers economical four-course *menús*.

West of Berga: Sant Llorenç de Morunys

Just one **bus** a day serves the magnificent, scenic but twisty BV4241 skirting the southern rim of the Pyrenean foothills for 32km to Sant Llorenç de Morunys. There's little to stop for along this route other than the panoramic, eighteenth-century **Santuari de Queralt** (4km west of Berga), which houses a far older image of the Virgin and marks one end of the GR107 trail (see p.68).

The chief appeal of **SANT LLORENÇ DE MORUNYS** lies in its setting near the head of the Vall de Lord, but the ancient city walls enclosing a defensive huddle of houses, and steep, narrow streets leading to several portals, will reward a half-hour stroll. The eleventh-century monastic **church** – venue for a summer music festival – has a beguilingly odd interior, one of its two chapels being overwhelmed by Baroque gilt work, the altar by a huge fifteenth-century retable. By contrast the cloisters, with plain-capitalled columns, are understated.

Sant Llorenç has an adequate amount of **accommodation** (except perhaps during the ski season), though none is in the old quarter. If travelling by public transport you should plan on spending the night, as the daily bus from Berga arrives in the evening. The best options are the *Hostal La Catalana*, Plaça del Dr Ferran 1 (Ⓣ973 492 272; ❸), its rooms with large baths but no balconies, and breakfast at the separately managed namesake bar downstairs, or the *Hostal Piteus* (Ⓣ973 492 340; ❸), opposite on the through road, which also has pricier penthouse apartments. There's a **campsite**, too, *Morunys* (Ⓣ973 492 213; July–Sept), 2km north of town, just off the side road to La Pedra hamlet. There are a few **restaurants** in the old walled town, for example *Cal Tecu* on Plaça Major.

Onwards from Sant Llorenç

The views are startling in whichever direction you leave Sant Llorenç, though it's best to have a car or bike as there's no public transport. If you hitch, don't accept partial rides, as traffic to the west especially is sparse.

To the **west** the road climbs 8km to the **Coll de Jou** (1560m), then briefly along a corniche before dropping through a tunnelled gorge to join the C14, 44km further along, in the Segre river valley near Organyà. Along this paved one-lane road, now the L401, there's little but farming hamlets, each individual house signposted.

To the **north** of Sant Llorenç looms the ski resort of **PORT DEL COMTE** (Ⓦwww.portdelcomte.net), reached via the village of La Coma, 5km from Sant Llorenç near the sources of the Cardener, or by a more direct road that climbs from the Coll de Jou. The scenic, part-forested ski domain, which is making valiant efforts to stay competitive with new chair-lifts, has a decent snow record (especially in the Bòfia sector) despite modest top points of under 2200m; with its red runs on the blueish side, blues of the greenish persuasion and fairly well linked zones it's fine for a day's intermediate skiing, a weekend at a stretch.

Accommodation at the slopes is restricted to two pricey hotels and the *Refugi del Bages* (Ⓣ973 492 000). More attractive options are in **LA COMA**, 11km east and downhill, at the simple *Hostal Casa Nin* (Ⓣ973 492 354; ❸), in the village centre by the church, or the fancier *Hotel Fonts del Cardener* (Ⓣ973 492 377, Ⓦwww.hotelfontsdelcardener.com; ❹ B&B), also offering apartments, 1km north of the village on the highway. The latter has an excellent **restaurant** with an emphasis on mushrooms (in season) and local sausages.

The **GR7** heads north from Sant Llorenç via La Coma to the 1636-metre **Coll de Port**, then on to Tuixén – a day's march – but the marked route is so often track or asphalt rather than path that you'll be better off arranging a ride along the paved road. At Tuixén (see p.196) you're at the very edge of the Cadí park.

North of Berga: Bagà

Settlements along the Llobregat and Grèixer valleys **north of Berga** were once centres of a flourishing smuggling trade with Andorra, protected from law-enforcing pursuers by the Serra del Cadí. Nowadays the C16 cuts under that mountainous screen via the Túnel del Cadí, and there's no longer a whiff of illicit activity. Strung out grimly along the old course of the C16 (a new bypass avoids the town) 17km from Berga, Guardiola de Berguedà is on the bus route to La Pobla de Lillet.

However there are no longer any facilities here, and the occasional bus from Berga to Saldes and Gósol (see p.196) turns at the junction 1500m south of the town.

BAGÀ, 5km further north and the second largest town in the county after Berga, has considerably more going for it in a tiny old quarter with an arcaded *plaça* (La Porxada), a hybrid Romanesque-Gothic church and three **accommodation** options. First choice is *Hotel Fonda Ca L'Amagat* (T 938 244 032; W www.hotel-calamagat.com; closed part May, part Oct, Dec 24–Jan 6; 4 B&B), a Casa Fonda member, quietly placed in the heart of the old quarter at c/Clota 4, and meticulously refurbished to top standards in 2005; during high season, half-board (5), taken in the barn-like *menjador* under the roof, is obligatory. At the southeastern outskirts of town on c/Raval, *Hostal Cal Batista* (T 938 244 126; 3) occupies two unexciting modern buildings, but it's popular for the sake of its pool, lawn-garden and private parking; the restaurant's *menú*, alas, also part of half-board rates, is not good value. The central **park information office** at c/La Vinya 1 (T 938 244 151; daily 9am–1.30pm, also Mon–Fri 3.30–7pm, Sat 4–6.30pm) stocks a full line of maps and literature for sale.

Continuing north through the five-kilometre **Túnel del Cadí** (which charges an exorbitant €11 per saloon car; no pedestrians or bicycles) brings you into the Cerdanya, for which see p.214. To the west of Bagà runs the GR107, "El Camí de les Bonnes Hommes", which begins in France and is allegedly the route used by fleeing Cathars (see pp.240–241); locally it links Bagà with Gósol (see p.196) via Gisclareny.

The Serra del Cadí

The western part of the Cadí-Moixeró park – the karstic **Serra del Cadí** – offers three or four days' trekking through wild, lonely areas. Numerous tracks and paths cross the range, though the favourite excursion for most visitors remains the ascent of **Pedraforca**. As in other limestone massifs, finding fresh **water** can be problematic, and that – combined with the intense summer heat at this relatively low altitude – means that peak (non-winter) visitor seasons are May to June and September. The Cadí supports several fairly well-placed, seasonally staffed **refuges**, accessible from a number of foothill villages, which are in turn served poorly or not at all by bus, so you may have to walk or use other means of transport from the valley towns. Extended explorations of this region require possession of the Editorial Alpina 1:25,000 "Serra del Cadí-Pedraforca" and "Moixeró" **maps** and guide booklets.

From the Llobregat valley north of Berga there are two main ways west into the Cadí. **From Bagà**, an initially paved track follows the Riu Bastareny to the hamlet of Gisclareny. A much busier paved road begins just south of **Guardiola de Berguedà** and leads to Gósol, via Saldes.

From Bagà: via the Bastareny valley

The fourteen-kilometre vehicle route up the **Bastareny valley** begins at a riverside campsite on the west side of Bagà: from there the road crosses the river, passes through a tunnel, then climbs steeply through dense forest to naked white cliffs on the south side of the **Coll de l'Escriga** (1360m). The views over the Saldes valley are superb, the river glinting far below, with range upon range of mountain unfurling south.

GISCLARENY, 3km beyond the pass at pavement's end, is little more than a handful of spread-out farms (total population 31) and two **campsites**, one of which – *Cal Tesconet* (T 608 493 317 or 937 441 016), 1500m west of the hamlet centre

△ Serra del Cadí ridgeline in spring

– also operates a **refuge** (24 places). Beyond Gisclareny, the track continues through **Coll de la Balma** (1600m), where it divides left (southwest) in a sharp down-and-up to the village of Saldes via the lushly forested **Gresolet valley**, and right (west) in a more level if less interesting trajectory via El Collel. The former route takes about three hours on foot, the latter at least five. The Gresolet area also has **accommodation** at *Refugi del Gresolet* (1280m; Ⓣ600 605 530, Ⓦwww.refugidelgresolet.com; 43 places), though the track access as described is closed by snow mid-winter.

The twisty road up the Bastareny valley can be negotiated on mountain bike or by 4WD; if on foot, you might do better to skip it for the direct Bagà–Gisclareny **path**, shown on the Editorial Alpina "Moixeró" map. From the *Cal Tesconet* refuge (where you'll need to confirm directions), a path drops down into the beeches and silver firs of Gresolet en route to Saldes, two hours shorter – assuming you don't lose the way – than the roundabout track option.

Traverses of the Moixeró

By staying with the Bastareny valley-bottom track rather than going through the Bastareny tunnel, you'll reach a cluster of farms at **VEINAT DE L'HOSTALET**, from where a good trail (marked as the PR125) leads up via the Gorge dels Empredats to the staffed FEEC *Refugi de Sant Jordi* (1640m; Ⓣ919 239 860 or 933 322 381; 48 places; daily Easter & late June to early Sept), four hours' walk from Bagà. Once over the Coll de Pendis (1800m), just above the refuge, you have to dodge – and briefly use – an unsightly 4WD track, but mostly it's marked path (now part of the GR107) for a further four hours to Pedre in the Segre valley, linked by paved road to Bellver de la Cerdanya. From the refuge you can also ridge-walk east along the Moixeró watershed – as the GR150.1 – all the way to Masella, also a popular route in winter for cross-country skiers.

From Guardiola: via the Saldes valley

The minor road from just south of **Guardiola to Saldes** and Gósol is spectacular, with steep drops into the Riera de Saldes giving way to brilliant views of Pedraforca beyond the hamlet of Maçaners (Massanés). Campsites and accommodation are spaced at intervals along the road. Best of each type is *Repòs del Pedraforca* (Ⓣ938

258 044) 13.5km from the turning, a campsite offering a pool and bungalows, and (about 12.5km along) *Hostal Pedraforca* (Ⓣ938 258 021, Ⓦwww.pedraforca.com; ❹, HB ❺), no architectural marvel but friendly and enviably set in a wood with unbeatable views of Pedraforca.

Saldes and Gósol

SALDES, a small village 18km from Guardiola, set dramatically at the foot of Pedraforca, is the usual starting point for explorations of the peak, despite a relative dearth of facilities. Here you'll find a Turisme with haphazard hours (Sat–Sun 11am–2pm, also Sat 5–7pm), a shop or two with trekking provisions, and not much else – **accommodation** is restricted to *Cal Xic* (Ⓣ938 258 081; ❷, HB ❹), a *casa de pagès* 1.5km west of the village in Cardina hamlet, at the start of the road up towards Pedraforca. Although the building is characterless, the en-suite rooms are clean and cheerful, and the *desayuno salado* comprises ham, sausages, cheese and a *porrón* to wash it all down with. The old stone village of **GÓSOL** (1430m), 10km beyond Saldes, is an altogether more substantial place, spilling appealingly from a castellated hill. Pablo Picasso came here during the summer of 1906 and stayed several weeks in fairly primitive conditions, inspired to paint by the striking countryside; one of the streets off the Plaça Major is named after him. Well established by the ninth century, the original village now lies in ruins, a fifteen-minute walk above the present one; the twelfth-century castle commands sweeping views of the valley, and the less spectacular rear flank of Pedraforca.

Gósol probably makes a better base than Saldes for explorations of the entire Cadí; the GR107 goes through here, linking with the saddle of El Collell to the north (see p.198), and the PR123 loops over and around the peak as a day hike. There are two basic **hostals**, both with decent attached restaurants: *Cal Franciscó* (Ⓣ & Ⓕ 973 370 075; ❷, HB ❹), on the little roundabout as you come into town, or the smaller central *Can Triuet*, Plaça Major 4 (Ⓣ973 370 072; ❷ B&B, ❹ HB). The best independent **restaurant** is *El Forn*, near *Triuet* (lunch most days, also supper weekends). There's also a **campsite**, *Cadí* (Ⓣ973 370 134; open all year), southwest of the village, reached off the lower road to Tuixén.

West of Gósol: Josa de Cadí and Tuixén

To skirt the Cadí by vehicle, keep on the main, paved road west to Josa de Cadí, and thence to Tuixén. Alternatively, you can follow a more direct (17km) road to Tuixén, beginning from the roundabout at the edge of Gósol and signed for Molí and El Vert. The Josa-bound track climbs in two long hairpins to the **Coll de Josa** (1625m), 5km from Gosól, where there are superb views north, with the 2648-metre summit of Cadí ahead; from here you drop through Scots pine to the Riu Josa.

JOSA DE CADÍ, 6km beyond the pass on a church-capped hill with one slope plunging to a ravine, is one of the most picturesquely set villages in Catalunya. Since the paving of the road in, its role as a second-home venue for urban Catalans has grown – the traditional dwellings with windows outlined in chalky blue paint and ancient wooden doors are fast disappearing, replaced by modern conversions. With just a single, pricey restaurant here, you'll probably elect to proceed another 8km southwest to **TUIXÉN (TUIXENT)**, one of the more touristically equipped of the Cadí villages. Dominated by the hilltop Romanesque church of Sant Esteve with its square tower, it's an attractive and relatively lively place set at the edge of a gently sloping valley. Tuixén has a combination **local museum/Turisme** (Ⓣ973 370 039; Easter week, Christmas week, July 15–Sept 15, weekends all year 10am–2pm & 5–8pm), just off the main square that doubles as a car park. All **accommodation** is found on one or other of the two streets leading off the parking area. Best are *Can Farratgetes*, at c/Coll 7 (Ⓣ973 370 034; ❹ HB only), its dining room available to all; *Cal Gabriel* (ⓣ973 370 142; ❷) at no. 5 of the other lane; and English-speaking *Pensió Can Custodi*, c/de la Riba 1, corner c/Coll and Plaça Major (ⓣ973 370 033; ❷ B&B, ❹ HB), with en-suite rooms and the best local **restaurant**, featuring sustaining four-course *menús*. Tuixén can fill in winter, as it's the closest settlement to the excellent cross-country skiing centre of **LA VANSA** a few kilometres southwest, which has 35km of marked trails between 1660m and 2135m. This is accessed by a steep road rising 8m to the Coll de Port with its bar-restaurant and the side road for La Vansa (the main road continues 22km more to Sant Llorenç de Morunys).

In the opposite direction, another road threads through the villages of Cornellana (9km), Fórnols de Cadí (12km) and Adraén (19km), their houses largely renovated as summer homes. **FÓRNOLS** has the most facilities, with a **restaurant** in the village centre and, in the valley below, a **campsite**, *El Molí de Fórnols* (ⓣ973 370 021), which also keeps an eponymous *casa de pagès* (❷). From Fórnols, a side road ascends the Congost de la Vansa for 3km and then climbs a like distance to **PADRINÀS**, location of the plushest *casa de pagès* in the region: *Cal Paller* (ⓣ973 298 260, ⓦwww.calpaller.com; ❺ B&B, ❼ HB), a bluff-top complex of interlinked stone buildings outside the hamlet.

Walks and climbs on Pedraforca

Pedraforca is for Catalunya what Canigou is to Roussillon: the logo and mascot of the region, and accordingly much loved. The name means "stone pitchfork", supposedly the Devil's, and indeed from afar the mountain does look like an upended goat's hoof. The distinctive two-pronged summit – **Pollegó Superior** (2498m) and **Pollegó Inferior** (2407m) – is divided by a gentler saddle, **l'Enforcadura** (2348m). In medieval times, local witches' covens met here, and it's still a popular place to camp on the evening before 24 June, *El Dia de Sant Joan*, when some personality from the Catalan "alternative" world generally organizes an after-dark, summer-solstice event.

From 1500m west of Saldes, a paved road winds just under 5km to within fifteen minutes' walk of the well-signed, FEEC-owned **Refugi Lluís Estassen** (1668m; ⓣ608 315 312; 100 places). It offers hot showers and evening meals, and is open all year, though the peak seasons are spring and autumn, especially at weekends, when big-wall climbers come to tackle the sheer north face of Pedraforca. The refuge sits just above the car park and **Mirador de Gresolet**, which looks down into the Gresolet valley. Hikers beginning in Saldes should use instead the PR124 trail.

The ascent

Despite appearances, a **walking ascent** of the peak is strenuous but not technically difficult, and well documented by the Alpina "Serra del Cadí-Pedraforca" map. From the refuge you have a choice of a relatively dull but easy out-and-back walk from the east, or a more challenging and exciting loop over the mountain, beginning north of the summit. In either case a dawn start is advisable, or you'll be baked against the bare rock by the summer sun.

For the **simpler approach**, head south forty minutes from the refuge fountain along a narrow but well-trodden path (now marked as part of the PR123) through pine and box, to the base of the giant scree gully leading up to l'Enforcadura. Turning sharply west up this gully, guided by a few paint splodges, brings you to the saddle in just under two hours from the refuge, after a very slippery, mostly trailless climb. At l'Enforcadura, you'll glimpse Gósol to the west – and a gentler, distinct trail slithering up the **Tartera de Gósol** (*tartera* means scree-gully in Catalan). From l'Enforcadura it's another 25 minutes north up a reasonable, obvious trail to the top of Pollegó Superior, with its assorted Catalan flags, "mailbox" for dedications and the expected views. Return is by the same route, for a total outing of just under five hours.

The **more difficult** circuit starts west from the *Refugi Lluís Estassen* along a trail shaded in the morning, then climbs sharply up to the **Collada de Verdet** (2244m; 2hr), where you meet another path coming up from Gósol. From this pass you turn south, then east, creeping along the spine of Pedraforca towards Pollegó Superior; a rope and a partner are suggested if you suffer from vertigo, and it will soon be obvious why you can't use this section going downhill. You descend to l'Enforcadura and return to the refuge as in the first itinerary, after a six-hour-plus day.

A south-to-north traverse of the Cadí

From the south, the peaks of the Cadí appear as a chain of rounded summits separated by shallow saddles, but seen from the north they form a wall of sheer, bare rock, dropping 500m in places. A one- to two-day **traverse from south to north** takes in all aspects of the Cadí, coming down into the Cerdanya to intercept the Puigcerdà–La Seu d'Urgell road.

For traverses, Gósol is a slightly better starting point than Saldes; from its centre, take the GR107, which soon dwindles to a path heading northeast through jagged rock teeth to the strategic pass known as **El Collell** (1845m; 2hr 15min), with fine views east over Gresolet and west towards Josa de Cadí. El Collell is also accessible in about an hour from *Refugi Lluís Estassen*, a rather unexciting if shady track walk. No motorized vehicles are allowed on the mountain slopes north of the pass, though they may continue east.

Stay with the track coming up from the refuge as it curls east towards Gisclareny for another kilometre, then take the zigzagging, obvious path on your left (north) – part of the PR124 – towards the watershed of the Cadí. The ascent to the **Pas dels Gosolans** (2430m; 3hr from El Collell) is not easy and takes longer than expected, owing to the up-and-down, limestone-dell topography and the necessity of clearing the minor Serra Pedragosa.

At the pass – essentially a slight notch in the watershed – you're near the roof of the Cadí, with awesome views west along the crest and north across the Segre valley. Plainly visible below, the *Refugi Cèsar Torras* at **Prat d'Aguiló** (2037m; Ⓣ639 714 087 or 973 250 135; 30 places; staffed daily in summer, weekends most of the year) is an hour's descent along a steep path negotiating a convenient spur. From the refuge and its spring, the PR124 continues down to Olià hamlet, 2km southwest of Bellver de Cerdanya (see p.215); alternatively you might arrange a ride along the 15km of track north via Montellà to Martinet, on the main valley road linking La Seu d'Urgell with Puigcerdà.

A more advanced **ridge-walking** option veers west just before the Pas dels Gosolans; two conspicuous paths head to the top of the Cortils canyon, where you'll find a rare spring and a former shepherds' cottage to shelter. You should overnight here before completing a long day west cross-country (though marked as the GR150.1) along most of the Cadí summits, taking in **Puig de Canal Baridana** and **Puig de la Canal del Cristall** (both 2648m), highest in the range. But the nearest *canals* ("ravines" in local dialect) draining from the peak line are trailless and savagely steep – choked by snow or scree according to season – making a descent to the north highly problematic, though the PR121 does so from the vicinity of Canal del Cristall, ending up in Estana village.

West of the Cadí: routes to Alt Urgell

Daily buses from Barcelona and Lleida, bound for La Seu d'Urgell, head into the *comarca* of **Alt Urgell** along the C14 road, which threads the impressive gorge of

Tresponts as it follows the Riu Segre upstream. Exciting as the scenery is, only two spots merit a brief stop en route with your own transport; if you get stranded after alighting from a bus, there is affordable accommodation in each. **COLL DE NARGÓ** offers one of the earliest (11th–12th century) – and strangest – Romanesque churches in Catalunya, Sant Climent, with a bizarre tapering belfry at the west edge of town. At **ORGANYÀ**, 6km further, a small, round building (summer Mon–Sat 10am–2pm & 6–9pm, Sun 10am–2pm; winter Mon–Sat 11am–2pm & 5–7pm, Sun 11am–2pm) just off the main road contains both the local **Turisme** (Ⓣ973 382 002) and what is possibly the oldest document in the Catalan language, the twelfth-century *Homilies d'Organyà* – annotations to some Latin sermons, discovered in a local presbytery at the beginning of the twentieth century.

La Seu d'Urgell and around

The capital of Alt Urgell, **LA SEU D'URGELL** (pronounced "*Sodurjell*"), beside the Riu Segre 23km upstream from Organyà, was for years a rather sleepy place, overshadowed by the excesses of nearby Andorra. But now housing prices in the principality are such that La Seu has become a popular dormitory community for both Andorrans and Spaniards with jobs in Andorra, spurring a recent apartment-

building boom. Nevertheless its medieval core and decent canoeing facilities on the Segre (a legacy of the 1992 Olympics) constitute enduring attractions.

Arrival and information

The **bus station** is on c/Joan Garriga Massó, just north of the old town; local services include Alsina Graells buses to Puigcerdà, and frequent La Hispano-Andorrana departures to Andorra (for details, see box on p.204). The friendly, well-stocked **Turisme** (Mon–Sat 10am–2pm & 4/5–6/8pm summer/winter; ⓣ973 351 511; ⓦwww.turismeseu.com) is on Avinguda de les Valls d'Andorra, the main road into town from the north. Drivers should use the handy free **parking** area signposted about 200m east of the cathedral.

Accommodation

In the wake of the Olympic facelift, little **budget accommodation** remains in La Seu. The standard seems set by *Pensió Palomares*, c/dels Canonges 38–40 (ⓣ973 352 178; ❷), a warren of windowless chipboard closets, tolerable only if you can obtain one of the multi-bedded front rooms with balcony. Just around the corner, *Pensió Jové* is a tad more comfortable (ⓣ973 350 260; ❷). The colossal **campsite**, *En Valira* (ⓣ973 351 035; all year), is 300m northeast of the hostel, at Avgda del Valira 10.

You're possibly better off at one of the **hotels** on the main roads through town. Best placed and most characterful of these is the *Andria*, Passeig Joan Brudieu 24 (ⓣ973 350 300, ⓦwww.hotelandria.com; ❺ B&B), an elegant, historic establishment which has benefited from multi-phased renovation which so far has yielded antique-furnished rooms with terracotta floors, independent temperature control and huge bathrooms; four suites are planned. Top of the heap is the exclusive *El Castell de Ciutat* (ⓣ973 350 000; ❼), now reinvented as a "wellness and anti-stress" spa, incorporated within the castle, as the name implies. Also in Castellciutat, with a pool and restaurant, *Hostal La Glorieta* (ⓣ973 351 045, ⓔglorietavalirasl@tiscali.es; ❹), perches above the river on the road up to the village.

The Town

Named after the imposing cathedral (La Seu) at the end of c/Major, the town has always had a dual function as episcopal seat and commercial centre; there's a street farmers' market each Tuesday and Saturday, attracting vendors from throughout the *comarca*. By 820 this was already the seat of a bishopric – there's still an episcopal palace and active seminary here – with all the parishes of Andorra belonging to the counts of Urgell. But in the wake of the Moorish retreat this nobility headed south, and by the early twelfth century La Seu's bishops had acquired these possessions. Ambiguities of jurisdiction eventually led to a conflict between the bishops and the French nobility of Foix, settled in the 1278 Act of Paréatge, which allowed for joint control of Andorra.

The original cathedral and city, on the hill where Castellciutat now stands, was destroyed in the eighth century by Muslim invaders. The present **Cathedral** (June–Sept Mon–Sat 10am–1pm & 4–7pm, Sun 10am–1pm; Oct–May Mon–Fri noon–1pm, Sat & Sun 11am–1pm) was consecrated in 839 but completely rebuilt in 1175, and restored several times since. Nonetheless, it retains some graceful interior decoration and fine cloisters with droll carved capitals, which you can see by buying an inclusive ticket at the cloister portal; €2.50 gets you into the cloisters, the adjacent eleventh-century chapel of Sant Miquel and the **Museu Diocesà** (same hours as the cathedral), containing an illuminated tenth-century Mozarabic manuscript with miniatures, the *Beatus*, a commentary on Revelation. To see only the cloister and chapel costs €1.50.

Other than these few sights, time is most agreeably spent strolling the dark, cobbled and arcaded streets west of the cathedral. A strong medieval feel is accentuated by the fine buildings lining c/dels Canonges (parallel to c/Major); the town's fourteenth-century stone corn-measures still stand under the arcade on c/Major.

Eating and drinking

Traditional **tapas bars** are dying out in La Seu's old town, with *Bar Eugenio* at c/Major 20 being the most reliable survivor, flanked by the sort of modern bar-cafés – *Café dels Escoberts* at no.24, and *El Cafetó* at no.6 – which have displaced their rivals. For good-value **restaurant** meals, *Cal Pacho* (closed Sun), in a quiet corner on c/la Font (at the southern end of c/Major, then east), has a reasonable lunch *menú*, and *a la carta* dishes in the evening – cod-stuffed peppers and roast goat will set you back around €18, dessert and drink extra.

In the new town, *Les Tres Portes* at c/Joan Garriga Massó 7 (closed Tues & Wed) offers nouvelle *a la carta* fare (allow €28–33) in a chalet-style house with a patio. The *Hotel Andria's menjador* also serves gourmet *a la carta* dishes at similar prices (or *menú* at €20), featuring home-reared chicken and mushrooms in season.

Around Town: Castellciutat

Comprehensive views over the Segre valley can be enjoyed from the village of **CASTELLCIUTAT**, just 1km west of town, and its nearby ruined castle (now a luxury hotel). Follow c/Sant Ermengol across the river and up to the village; there's still some farming on the slopes below the tiny stone church, and a couple of comfortable accommodation options, making the village a nice retreat from La Seu. You can vary your route to Castellciutat or back by following the walkways through the pleasant riverside **Valira** park, with its modern cloister made from pink stone. Salvador Dalí, Pablo Casals, Albert Einstein, Winston Churchill and Groucho Marx are among the famous twentieth-century characters (mainly men) whose heads decorate the capitals; one reproduces a fragment of Picasso's *Guernica* in 3D, alongside posturing Francoist figures. From La Seu, head west from Avinguda de Pau Claris (north of c/Sant Ot) to intercept it.

West of La Seu: Castellbò and Sant Joan de l'Erm

Four kilometres southwest of La Seu a minor road climbs west along the River Solanell, between cornfields and then over successively more scrubby rises, to the village of **CASTELLBÒ**, 14km from La Seu. This was the seat of Arnau de Castellbó, whose marriage to Arnalda de d'Isarn de Caboet was a key event in Andorran history (see p.202). The only thing to see now is the thirteenth-century church of **Santa María**, an example of Romanesque-Gothic transitional style with pointed arches and Romanesque ironwork.

Beyond Castellbò, the road climbs to the *Refugi Pla de la Basseta* (Ⓣ973 298 015; 83 places; open all year) at **SANT JOAN DE L'ERM**, a superb **cross-country ski** resort with 150km of trails between 1600 and 2150m. Westward progress is by 4WD and mountain-bike tracks, which emerge just below the downhill ski centre of Port-Ainé (see p.255). Those without transport can take the twice-daily minibus along 47km of paved road west from **ADRALL**, 7km south of La Seu, to Sort in the Noguera Pallaresa. Adrall itself has a single **casa de pagès** (*Cal Xico*; Ⓣ973 387 055; ❷) and a clutch of **restaurants** on the through road, more country-style than anything in La Seu – *Can Pere* comes recommended for good food and an entertaining proprietor.

Andorra

After seven hundred years of feudalism, modernity finally forced itself upon the **PRINCIPALITY OF ANDORRA**, 450 square kilometres of precipitously mountainous land between France and Spain. A referendum held on March 14, 1993 (henceforth the big national holiday) produced an overwhelming vote in favour of a democratic constitution, replacing a system in effect since 1278, when the bishops of La Seu d'Urgell and the counts of Foix settled a longstanding quarrel by granting Andorra semi-autonomous status under joint sovereignty. In 1185 the marriage of Arnalda d'Isarn de Caboet and Arnau de Castellbò united the Andorran possessions granted to these families by La Seu's bishops. Their only daughter Ermensende later married Roger-Bernard II, count of Foix, who claimed sole rights to Andorra when Arnau died without male issue. The bishops of La Seu contested this, claiming that sovereignty reverted to them with the cession of the male line of Castellbó. This dispute ended with the 1278 Act of Paréatge, through which La Seu d'Urgell and Foix became *co-seigneurs* of Andorra. (Incidentally, the Act also forbade the building of castles in Andorra, which explains their absence.)

Despite the counts' sovereignty passing to the French king and later to the French president, the principality largely managed to maintain its independence

over the centuries. The Spanish and French *co-seigneurs* appointed regents who took little interest in Andorra's day-to-day life. The country was instead run by the Consell General de les Valls (General Council of the Valleys), made up of representatives from Andorra's seven valley communes, who ensured that the principality remained well out of the European mainstream – it even managed to stay neutral during the Spanish Civil War and World War II.

During these conflicts, Andorra began its meteoric economic rise, as locals first smuggled goods from France into Spain during the Civil War and, a few years later, goods from Spain into German-occupied France. After World War II, this was replaced by duty-free trade in alcohol, tobacco, sporting goods, petrol and electronics, plus the huge demand for winter skiing. Much of the principality became an unsightly drive-in megastore, the main through road clogged with French and Spanish "shopping tourists". Seasoned Spain-watcher John Hooper has called Andorra "a kind of cross between Shangri-La and Heathrow Duty-Free", while the Spanish daily broadsheet *El Pais* once dismissed it as a "high-altitude Kuwait".

Ironically, though, this **tax-free status** contained the seeds of Andorra's belated conversion to democracy. Although the inhabitants enjoyed one of Europe's highest standards of living, twelve million visitors a year began to cause serious logistical problems: infrastructure was sorely stretched and the valleys increasingly blighted by speculators' building sites, while budget deficits grew alarmingly since little entrepreneurial wealth went towards the public sector. Spanish entry to the EU in 1986 only exacerbated the situation, reducing the difference in price of imported goods between Spain and Andorra to the current twenty percent. However, the damage has long since been done; Andorra's commercial growth has pretty much killed off trade in the nearest French/Spanish towns, though ironically is sparking a boom in residential properties just over the border for Andorran workers who can no longer afford to live in the principality.

The 1993 referendum was an attempt to come to terms with contemporary Europe's economic realities. Or rather, some of them, since nobody involved in the debate seriously proposed the introduction of direct taxation: there is still no income tax in Andorra, and barely any indirect tax either (other than 4% VAT). Instead the strategy has been to transform Andorra into a kind of "offshore" banking centre, to rival the likes of Gibraltar, Lichtenstein and the Caymans, with the slight whiff of unsavouriness that attaches to such places.

Following the referendum, the state's first **election** was held in December 1993. Only the 10,000 native Andorrans were entitled to vote (out of a total population then of 60,000) for the new 28-seat parliament, dominated then and since by centre-right parties. Since then, Andorran citizens (those born here, or who have lived here over twenty years) can vote and join trade unions or political parties, while their government runs its own foreign policy and judicial system. The country has also become a full member of the United Nations and the Council of Europe – but not the EU.

Given all this, it's useful to remember that as recently as 1950 Andorra was all but cut off from the rest of the world – an archaic region which, romantically, happened also to be a separate country. There are still no planes or trains, but for many visitors that is the full extent of any attractive quaintness. For much of the year it can take an hour in bumper-to-bumper traffic to drive the few kilometres from La Seu d'Urgell to Andorra la Vella, the capital. Surprisingly, the main crop here, which you see on either side of the road and in every available space up to 1600m altitude, is tobacco. In the higher valleys, large-scale ski resorts have already monopolized the most attractive corners of the state, with further enlargements mooted.

Andorra practicalities

Getting there

From Spain, there are hourly services (Mon–Sat 7am–8pm; Sun 5 daily between 7.45am and 6.30pm) from **La Seu d'Urgell** on La Hispano-Andorrana, taking a minimum forty minutes to reach the capital of Andorra la Vella, and a further five minutes to Escaldes.

From France, daily buses co-run by Hispano-Andorrana and Pujol Huguet leave **L'Hospitalet** at 7.35am and 7.45pm, arriving at Pas de la Casa 25 minutes later; from **Latour-de-Carol** there are departures at 10.45am and 1.15pm, taking 45 minutes to reach Pas de la Casa. During July and August, there is an additional service from **Ax-les-Thermes** at 4.20pm. From Pas de la Casa the onward bus journey to Andorra la Vella takes an hour.

Even if you're **driving**, consider leaving the car behind and taking the bus – in high season (summer or winter) the traffic is so bad that the bus isn't much slower, and parking in Andorra la Vella is an ordeal. Drivers are well advised to use the giant car parks provided in the largest towns, or kerbside meters – traffic police and tow-trucks are both very industrious. On the plus side, petrol is famously cheap – 12–15 percent less than in Spain, 20 percent savings compared to France – so fill up before leaving.

Leaving Andorra

Buses back **to La Seu d'Urgell** leave from Plaça Guillemó in Andorra la Vella, parallel to the main road, though the service originates in Escaldes (Mon–Sat 14 daily between 8.05am and 9.05pm; Sun 5 daily between 8.20am and 7.20pm). **To France**, La Hispano-Andorrana (Ⓦwww.hispanoandorrana) and Pujol Huguet (Ⓣ376 821 372) run two buses a day from Andorra la Vella to Pas de la Casa at 5.45am and 5pm, with services at 7.30am and 10.30am to Latour-de-Carol. During July and August, there's an additional departure at 1.30pm to Ax-les-Thermes.

Getting around

Internal **bus services**, arranged in six lines (Ⓦwww.andorrabus.com), are cheap and frequent. The following routes run every 20 minutes during daylight hours: Escaldes–Sant Julià de Lòria, Andorra la Vella–Escaldes–La Massana–Ordino, Andorra la Vella–Escaldes–Encamp. Less frequent services ply Andorra la Vella–Canillo–Soldeu–Pas de la Casa (with an extra direct line to Soldeu in winter) and Andorra la Vella–La Massana–Arinsal. Buses leave from Plaça Guillemó.

But it's worth leaving the capital and main developments behind to see some of the scenery that attracted early visitors. Although the highest point (Alt de Coma Pedrosa on the western border) reaches just 2946m, there is still wilderness aplenty here. Scots pine is endemic, and the mountain pines *Pinus uncinata* or *Pinus mugo* thrive at altitudes up to 2200m, or even 2400m on south-facing slopes; moisture-craving silver fir grows on north-facing slopes between 1600 and 2000m. Wild boar, golden eagles and griffon vultures are native species, but – last seen in 1978 – bears aren't any longer.

Through Andorra by road

The main through road – consecutively the CG1 from the Spanish frontier to Andorra la Vella, and then the CG2 from the latter to the French border – runs 38km north, then east, through the main valley draining Andorra. The CG3 heads northwest to the dead-end, and therefore quieter, Valira del Nord.

Customs

French, Spanish and Andorran police may board buses looking for faces that don't fit, and ask luggage bays to be opened, as a check against illegal immigrants. Inspections of goods when entering are nonexistent, but on leaving, the Spanish police are very interested in just how many consumer durables all EU nationals have acquired – the French guards 2km below Pas de la Casa seem much less active, running only spot-checks.

Currency, mail and phones

Andorra never had its own money, and the euro is now its common **currency**. There's a shared **postal system**, with both a French and Spanish post office in Andorra la Vella and Canillo, for example. Andorra has its own phone system and **phone code** – ⓣ376 – applicable to the whole republic. A single **mobile** network, MobileAnd/STA, provides surprisingly good coverage even in the deepest valleys.

Population and language

The **population** of Andorra is currently around seventy thousand, of whom about twelve thousand are native Andorrans; the rest are mainly Portuguese, Spanish and French "guest workers" or permanent residents, with a smattering of other nationalities. Catalan is the official **language**, but Spanish and, to a slightly lesser extent, French are widely understood.

Skiing and ski passes

Downhill skiing is one of the principality's main money-spinners (though there's also a tiny nordic skiing area at La Rabassa in the far south, comprising just 15km of pistes). Since the late 1990s, about 100 million euro have been invested in state-of-the-art lift systems – something reflected in the **pass prices** (minimum €32/day), which now nearly equal those of the French Alps (food and lodging are also expensive). The various ski domains are aggregated into marketing groups, with shared passes; El Tarter, Soldeu, Grau Roig and Pas de la Casa are amalgamated as ⓦwww.grandvalira.com, with passes priced at €37 per day, or €34.50 to choose just one area. Vall Nord (ⓦwww.vallnord.com) encompasses the linked Pal and Arinsal domains, and remote Arcalis: costs there run €32 per day or a more attractive €144 for six non-consecutive days. There's also a Ski Andorra pass, valid country-wide, getting you five non-consecutive days for €162.

Andorra la Vella

With its stone church of **Sant Esteve** and appealing riverside setting amidst crags and green slopes, the capital **ANDORRA LA VELLA** must once have been an attractive little town. Today the main street, Avda Princep Benlloch/Avda Meritxell, is a seething mass of tourist restaurants (specializing in six-language menus), tacky bars and brightly lit shops crammed with every item imaginable.

There's some respite in the narrow streets of the *barri antic* (old quarter), above the Riu Valira and south of the main street. Besides the church, its sole monument is the sixteenth-century **Casa de la Vall** in c/de la Vall (free guided tours Mon–Sat 10am–1pm & 3–7pm); it now houses the Sala de Sessions of Andorra's parliament and the chief courtroom (Tribunal de Corts). Between Sant Esteve and the town hall, Rambla Molines leads to raised Plaça del Poble, laid out as a spacious pedestrian square with stone benches, sculptures, flower beds, fountains and a covered picnic place. The church of **Santa Coloma**, over 1km west of the centre in the namesake suburb, merits a look for the oddity of its round tower – nearly all Romanesque churches have square ones.

Practicalities

Buses leave passengers on Avda Princep Benlloch, near the church of Sant Esteve. For drivers, there are about half a dozen open-air **car parks** scattered around town; the huge, covered Planta de la Creu car park, right under the Turisme, usually has space. The **Turisme**, on c/Dr Vilanova (Mon–Sat 9am–1pm & 3–7pm, Sun 10am–1pm; ⓣ376 820 214), east of the old quarter, has lists of accommodation, restaurants and bus timetables, and also sells a good topographical map of Andorra.

There are several reasonable places to **stay**: the friendly, basic *Hostal del Sol* at Plaça Guillemó 3 (ⓣ376 823 701; ❶); the 2004-renovated, three-star *Hotel Florida* (ⓣ376 820 105, ⓦwww.hotelflorida.ad; ❺) with balconied rooms nearby at c/La Llacuna 13; and the *Hotel Racó d'en Joan*, in the old quarter at c/de la Vall 20 (ⓣ376 820 811; ❷), which also has an attached restaurant.

You're probably better off, though, lingering just long enough for something to **eat**; intense competition fosters (for Andorra) low prices. Best value in the *barri antic* is *Minim's* (*Casa Leon*), tucked away in the tiny Placeta de la Consorcia (closed Wed Oct–June), a small, stylish place with French-cuisine *menús*. Another fairly central and characterful place is the basic *Restaurant Macary*, c/Mossèn Tremosa 6, just northeast of the Plaça Princep Benlloch, serving Spanish rather than Catalan dishes. The favourite spot for a cake and a drink is the *Granja Pastisseria del Barri*, opposite the church of Sant Esteve.

Evening entertainment includes two **cinemas** (Modern Triplex at Avda Meritxell 26, and Principat at Avda Meritxell 44) and *Àngel Blau*, a live jazz **club** in c/de la Borda.

Escaldes-Engordany

Andorra la Vella merges seamlessly with **ESCALDES-ENGORDANY,** in effect a suburb named in part after the local hot springs. The ultramodern thermal baths of **Caldea**, with their landmark glass pyramid and indoor/outdoor lagoons, provide the latest in hydrotherapy and luxury beauty treatments (daily 10am–11pm, last admission 9pm; ⓣ376 828 600, ⓦwww.caldea.ad). Cultural interest is provided by the work of Catalan sculptor Josep Viladomat i Maçanes (1899–1989), 250 of whose pieces are on display at the **Museu Viladomat** on c/Josep Viladomat (Mon–Fri 10am–1pm & 4–8pm, Sat 10am–1pm; €2); his stylistic affinities lie with Miquel Blay and Josep Clarà of Olot (see p.162).

The twelfth-century church of **Sant Miquel d'Engolasters**, one of the most attractive Romanesque churches in the area, stands on a plateau east of Escaldes. Its original frescoes have been appropriated by the Museu Nacional d'Art de Catalunya in Barcelona, leaving just reproductions inside. The quickest way there is via the road climbing to the Engolasters reservoir, which passes the church after 4km. To make a day of it, follow the **GR7** from the main street in Escaldes for two hours to just beyond the hamlet of Ramio, where you take the marked footpath towards Encamp (see p.209) for another hour.

There's an abundance of **accommodation** in Escaldes, though most is aimed at the free-spending ski crowd. The few basic, budget options include *Residència Pont de la Tosca* at Avda Miquel Mateu 6 (ⓣ376 821 938; ❷); *Residència Astòria* at Avda de les Escoles 16 (ⓣ376 820 515; ❶); and the Residència *Núria* at c/Santa Anna 11 (ⓣ376 821 572; ❷). The most reasonable **eating** is found at two Italian specialists: *Restaurant Bon Profit*, Avda Carlemany 53, and *Pizzeria Roma*, on the same street at no.95, both offering Italian meals from €20.

The Valira del Nord

For more peace and quiet you can head up the **Valira del Nord** (also known as Valira d'Ordino) from Escaldes, but you'll have to wait until you get past dreary

La Massana, 7km northwest, for it to begin. **LA MASSANA** has a useful central **Turisme** in a wooden booth (Mon–Sat 9am–1pm & 3–7pm, Sun closes 6pm; ⓣ376 835 693).

Arinsal and Pal

The left-hand (northwesterly) CG4 road at La Massana climbs 4km to the popular, mushrooming and fairly hideous ski village of **ARINSAL**. Starting in Arinsal's centre, a bubble-lift gets you up to Point 1551m (as does the bus), where there's a chair-lift to Point 1950m, base for most of the 23 runs. These tend to be short and sharp except for a number of wide blue pistes that can be taken in sequence for a long descent from near the resort's top point of 2560m, just this side of the Spanish border. Overall, in conjunction with Pal (see below), it's a good venue for beginners and weak intermediates.

Much of the **accommodation** is British-package-self-catering, but you could always try one of the more modest establishments within a few paces of the *télécabine*: the basic *Hotel Pobladó* (ⓣ376 835 122, ⓔhospoblado@andornet.ad; ③); *Hotel Comapedrosa* (ⓣ376 737 950; ④); and *Hotel Micolau* (ⓣ376 835 052, ⓔhmicolau@arinsal.com; ⑤). Owing to large numbers of self-catering apartments there are essentially no independent **restaurants** – you'll have to descend 1km to **ERTS**, where *La Cuina d'en Joan* and Aragonese-style grill *L'Hort de Casa* stand adjacent opposite the turning for Pal (dull *menú* at either, allow €27–31 for *a la carta*).

About 6km south of Arinsal, up yet another side valley, **PAL** is very attractive by Andorran standards, a stone-built village with its fine belfried Romanesque church of Sant Climent but unfortunately no short-term accommodation, though the single **restaurant**, *L'Eulari*, is excellent (shut Mon eve & Tues; *menú* from €16). Some 5km further on you reach the **Pal ski centre**, 200m lower than Arinsal and thus heavily dependent on snow canons and likely to close by late March or early April. That said, the skiing is challenging enough with most runs red-rated, though several blue ones are found in the Setúria zone; the chair-lift from Els Fontanells at 1810m gets you up to the 2358-metre summit of Pic de Cubil and the best pistes. The road carries on 24km out of Els Fontanells to the village of Alins in Spain (see p.257), via the 2300-metre Port de Cabús (passable only in summer) and the hamlet of Tor.

Ordino to Llorts

Back at La Massana, the right-hand (northeasterly) CG3 road leads 3km on to **ORDINO**, a relatively agreeable but increasingly built-up place with a handful of old stone edifices surrounded by new chalets and apartment buildings. The only **car park** is just downhill from the edge-of-town **Turisme** (Mon–Sat 8.30am–1.30pm & 3–6pm, Sun 9am–1pm; ⓣ376 737 080, ⓦwww.ordino.ad). The best places **to eat** are either *Topic*, a central restaurant-café-pizzeria-bar which serves supper until 10.30pm, or the more traditional *Armengol-Casa Leon*, opposite the French **post office**. *Hotel Santa Barbara* on the *plaça* (ⓣ376 837 100, ⓔsanta-barbara@andorra.ad; ④) is an agreeable place to **stay**. Just 2km beyond Ordino, there's a pleasant riverside campsite at **SORNÀS**, the *Borda d'Ansalonga* (ⓣ376 850 374; closed May & Oct). Just before the campsite there's another late-opening **eatery**, *La Farga/Les Fargues*, a good-value grill where the *menú*, including grilled rabbit, costs under €15.

As you proceed up the Valira del Nord proper, along the 8km or so north of Ordino, the landscape becomes more appealing, with fewer tower-cranes and chalet developments. About 2.5km north of Ordino at **LA CORTINADA**, the partly Romanesque church of **Sant Martí de la Cortinada** (July & Aug daily 10am–1pm & 3–7pm; free) contains original apsidal twelfth-century frescoes, uncovered in

△ Skiing in Andorra

1968, showing scenes of hunting, harvesting, music-making and fantastic animals as well as the patron saint. During the sixteenth century, the church was curiously reoriented northwards, with subsequent additions of a carillon, a women's gallery and convertible pews that could be inverted for social chats after services.

Reasonable **accommodation** en route includes the stone-clad *Hotel Cal Daina* (Ⓣ376 850 988, Ⓦwww.hotelcaldaina.com; ④) in La Cortinada and *Pensió Vilaró* (Ⓣ376 850 225; ②; rooms with shared bath only), slightly isolated just below the village of **LLORTS**, some 5km from Ordino. Llorts also offers one of the better rural **restaurants** in Andorra, *L'Era del Jaume* (closed Sun pm; book on ⓣ376 850 667), by the church. It specializes in grills as well as vegetable-based dishes; stick to the house wine and lunchtime *menú* if on a budget, otherwise you're looking at €30 *a la carta* for small portions.

El Serrat and Ordino-Arcalis

At the head of the valley, 18km from Andorra la Vella, stands **EL SERRAT**, astride the HRP and graced by tumbling waterfalls and horse-riding stables. There are also four hotels, the last **accommodation** before the ski centre (see below), including the *Hotel Tristaina* (ⓣ376 850 081, ⓕ850 730; ❹), and the fancier *Hotel Ahotels El Serrat* (ⓣ376 735 735, ⓦwww.ahotels.com; ❼ HB only).

From El Serrat the CG3 climbs steeply 5km more to the ski resort of **ORDINO-ARCALIS**, which owing to high points of over 2600m and a chilly microclimate retains the best-quality Andorran snow well into April. It's also probably the most aesthetic intermediate place to ski in the principality, with a mostly local clientele, plus appealing views north over the Tristaina lakes (see below) and border ridge beyond. Ordino-Arcalis is good for intermediate to advanced skiers, with five well-placed chair-lifts to the top of mostly blue and red runs ranging from 1km to over 2km in length. The resort has two focuses: **La Coma** at (the summer-only) road's end (2200m, 27km from Andorra la Vella), with a good **restaurant** open for lunch year-round except May and November (allow €13 for self-service, €24 upstairs at the full service), and **Les Hortells** at about 1940m. Some six to twelve times daily, a "Bus Neu" plies between La Massana and Les Hortells. In summer, the base of the La Coma lift is the starting point for easy hikes north into the cirque containing the three attractive **Tristaina lakes**. Around and between them all, paths are waymarked in a variety of colour schemes; allow an hour and a half for a full circuit.

The Valira del Orient

It's around 35km from Escaldes to the French border at Pas de la Casa (7km less by the toll tunnel) along the **Valira del Orient**, a route served as far as Soldeu by regular buses from the capital. You're unlikely to be tempted to get off anywhere for casual touring, although those with a car or with skiing in mind have several possibilities.

Encamp and Meritxell

ENCAMP, 6km from Escaldes, is the first tolerable place to stay. In the centre, among old stone houses and concrete high-rises, the modern town hall stands out like a giant video screen. For a pleasant stroll, follow the riverside walkway north along the west bank to the unspoilt village of **Les Bons**, with its tiny twelfth-century Romanesque chapel of **Sant Romà** (daily July–Aug 10am–1pm & 3–7pm; free) with reproduction frescoes and a four-storey defensive tower standing nearby. The local **turisme** is on Plaça del Consell General, ⓦwww.encamp.ad, ⓣ376 731 000). There's abundant, affordable two-star **accommodation**, including *La Mola* at Avda Coprincep Episcopal 62 (ⓣ376 831 181, ⓦwww.hotellamol.com; ❸) and the *Montecarlo* at no. 104 of the same street (ⓣ376 731 116, ⓦwww.hotelmontecarloandorra.com; ❸); the only budget options are the balconied *Pensió Benito* at Avda Coprincep Episcopal 51 (ⓣ376 831 226; ❷), and the stone-clad *Residència Relax* at c/Bellavista 8–14 (ⓣ376 834 777; ❷). An ambitious funicular, the **Funicamp**, transports skiers up to the runs of El Tarter (see p.210).

Some 3km past Encamp, a small road climbs south to the **Santuari de Meritxell** (daily except Tues 9am–1pm & 3–6pm), the ugly shrine designed by Barcelona

Olympics architect Ricardo Bofill to replace a Romanesque building that burnt down in 1972. The fire also destroyed the ancient carving of Our Lady of Meritxell; a replica stands in her place. The local September 8 festival is one of the four main national holidays, when most things in Andorra shut down.

Canillo

CANILLO (1562m), beautifully situated 6km beyond Encamp, makes one of the best compromise bases in Andorra: along the main road (and bus route) between Andorra la Vella and the nearby ski resort of Soldeu-El Tarter, but far enough away to retain some dignity and character. On the eastern fringe of town, the belfried Romanesque church of **Sant Joan de Caselles** (July & Aug daily 10am–1pm & 3–7pm; free) is largely eleventh century; inside highlights include a 3D stucco *Crucifixion*, with personified Sun and Moon, plus lance-wielding Romans, and an exquisite sixteenth-century altarpiece, portraying the life and martyrdom of John the Evangelist. The big recreational attraction is the **Palau de Gel** (daily 10am–11pm, though some facilities close at 10pm), with an ice rink, indoor pool, gym, sauna and squash courts. Prices start at €5.70 for a gym-sauna session, up to €13 including skate rental for a session on the ice. When snow levels are sufficient, a bubble-lift rises to **El Forn**, part of the Grand Valira ski domain. Incidentally, the direct road to Ordino via the **Coll d'Ordino** is scenic but slow going – allow forty minutes by car for the 19km.

The local **Turisme** is on central Avda Sant Joan de Caselles (Ⓣ376 751 090; Ⓦwww.vdc.ad; Mon–Sat 9am–1pm & 3–7pm, Sun 8am–4pm). **Hotels** line the main through road, c/General, with the last surviving budget choice being the rock-bottom *Comerç* (Ⓣ376 851 020; ❷). Affordable comfort can be had at *Les Terres* on the uphill side of town (Ⓣ376 851 550, Ⓕ376 851 461; ❸) or *Aparthotel Montarto* (Ⓣ376 853 008, Ⓦwww.hotelmontarto.com; ❺ for up to 4 persons) on c/Prats. Among several local **campsites**, best is tree-shaded *Camping Santa Creu* (Ⓣ376 851 462; mid-June to Sept), near the centre on the south bank of the river. The **restaurant** at the *Comerç* offers French-style *table d'hôte*; alternatively, try the *Molí del Peano* (closed mid-May to mid-June & mid-Oct to mid-Nov), where €28 will get you grilled duck, goat's cheese salad, home made mousse and a beer or two (they also have much cheaper *menús*).

Soldeu-El Tarter

Development at **SOLDEU** village, at the head of the valley 19km from the capital, is surprisingly restrained, considering that over half the ski pistes in Andorra are nearby. It's the most attractive, all-round ski resort in Andorra, with English-speaking instruction widely available, and ample nightlife for all age brackets.

Most of the **hotels** line the boulevard, and while the British package industry tends to get first crack at them, it's worth trying the *Bruxelles* (Ⓣ376 851 010, Ⓦwww.hotelbruxelles.ad; ❷) or the chalet-like *Roc de Sant Miquel* (Ⓣ376 851 079, Ⓦwww.hotel-roc.com; ❹). From **EL TARTER** just below Soldeu – where there's little affordable accommodation – a narrow road heads north up the lovely **Vall d'Incles**. There's an inexpensive, beautifully set if basic **campsite**, *Camping Font de Ferosins* (Ⓣ376 851 341; mid-June to mid-Sept), at the far end of the valley, well placed for the HRP – allow an hour's walk from the main road.

Restaurants and **bars** not affiliated with Soldeu's hotels are limited and Brit-oriented. *Aspen* is the most popular pub, serving Tex-Mex food through co-owned *Colorado* next door, while on the upper lane, *Fat Albert's* and grilled-meat specialist *Cort del Popaire* (closed May & Nov) are both good for salubrious local cuisine.

The Soldeu-El Tarter **ski centre** ranks as the most extensive in the principality, with ample skiing for all ability levels amongst its 52 runs – it's the best place in

Andorra for beginners, and is frequented mainly by British and Spanish families. Chair-lifts are numerous, runs well planned, and the views north to the French border ridge magnificent. You're pampered with an initial bubble-lift from the Soldeu rental centre to **Pla dels Espiolets** (2250m), the novice's area, with some very long green runs (Os, Duc, Gall de Bosc). Gall de Bosc in particular offers a tranquil descent – 8km if you take it all the way from 2560-metre Tossal de la Llosada – through the trees right back to the bubble-lift building. Intermediate and advanced skiers will find the **Pla Riba Excorxada** zone at 2100m (main restaurant) more suitable, with chair-lifts up to **Tosa dels Espiolets** (*c.* 2400m) and **Cap de Clots** (2388m) giving access to more challenging red and blue runs. From Cap, two drag-lifts ascend **Tossal de la Llossada**, from where virtually all the runs are accessible, including the easterly Solana del Forn area, with its 2600-metre top point and blue/red runs served by two more chair-lifts.

Pas de la Casa

Once over the **Port d'Envalira** (or under most of it via the 2004-opened **tunnel**, €5.70 toll well worth paying in blizzard or mist conditions), you're deposited in the ghastly, high-rise border-town of **PAS DE LA CASA**, "Ibiza-on-Snow" for hordes of young *Toulousains* and Brits in search of snow, sex and sangria (as the Ski Club of Great Britain memorably put it), plus a car-full of duty-free goodies. After a hard night at the bars, the "yoof" in question enjoy advanced skiing between points at 2600m and 2050m. Runs are linked to those of **Grau Roig** in the next valley, with 29 lifts serving 53 runs (mostly red), as well as (eventually) to Soldeu-El Tarter.

Among Pas de la Casa's predominantly pricey **hotels**, three-star *Hotel Casado*, close to the ski slopes at c/Catalunya 23 (Ⓣ376 855 219, Ⓔhotelcasado@andorra.ad; ❻), stands out as helpful, clean and good value. Cheaper options slightly further from the ski lifts include the faded but central *Hotel La Muntanya*, c/Catalunya 12 (Ⓣ376 855 318; ❺), and *Hotel El Chat*, c/La Solana (Ⓣ376 855 545; ❺ HB only), just uphill from the two main chairlifts.

Through Andorra on foot

To cross Andorra on foot, the main routes are the **GR7**, which skirts the south-eastern mountains; the **GR11**, which cuts more or less through the middle; and the **HRP**, which keeps to the northern fringes of the principality. Most of the alpine shelters en route are small, unattended and pretty basic. The best **maps** are the Catalan Mapa Excursionista no.21 "Andorra-Cadí"; the Randonnées Pyrénéennes 1:50,000 no.7 "Haute-Ariège-Andorre"; and the Editorial Alpina 1:40,000 "Andorra". The eastern half of Andorra is also shown on the French IGN 1:50,000 "Cerdagne-Capcir" sheet.

Southwest from the Porteille Blanche: the GR7

Many walks into and around Andorra follow the old paths of the smugglers who carried heavy parcels of Andorran tobacco and other contraband across the border. Porta (see p.223 for access details), at the top of the Carol valley in France, was one of the great smuggling villages in the Pyrenees, on account of its link with Andorra along the Campcardos (Campquerdós) valley, now the route of the **GR7**.

A three-hour climb up the valley from Porta brings you to the **Porteille Blanche** (Portella Blanca; 2517m). The meeting of borders here allowed *paquetaires* in trouble to step quickly into France, Andorra or Spain according to who was pursuing them. From here, veer northwest towards **Pic Negre d'Envalira** (2825m), just south of the source of the Ariège; the summit has views into the valley of the Valira del Orient to the northwest. West of Pic Negre, the GR7 descends to the Grau Roig ski station, and finally to **BORDES D'EN VALIRA**, 3km north, where you'll find **accommodation** at the *Hotel Confort* (ⓣ376 852 288; ④) or the barracks-like *Hotel Peretol* (ⓣ376 851 264; ⓦwww.hotel-peretol.com; ③).

Next day, continue via the lake-spangled **Circ dels Pessons** to the **Clots (Ponds) de la Gargantillar**, where there is a large refuge at **Estany l'Illa**. The next one – a more logical choice for an overnight – is the tiny *Refugi del Riu dels Orris* at **Pla de l'Ingla**, at the head of the beautiful **Madriu** valley. Here you can continue on the GR7 along the valley to Escaldes, or cut through the **Coll de la Maïana** to the west, reaching the Andorra la Vella–La Seu d'Urgell road near Santa Coloma.

West from the Ariège: the GR10/HRP

The routes **west** from the top of the Ariège into the Incles valley are beautiful approaches to the best Andorran landscape. From the train station at **Hospitalet-Près-l'Andorre**, the **HRP** variant initially climbs the Siscar valley, then switches to the Baldarques, going past the **Étang de Pedourrès** to the **Étang de Couart**, where it joins a path from Mérens-les-Vals.

Coming from **Mérens-les-Vals**, you can take the **GR10** southwest up the more inspiring **Mourgouillou valley**. After a little under two hours, the GR climbs west and to the right for a steepish climb of another ninety minutes to the modern, staffed *Refuge de Rulhe* (2185m; ⓣ05.61.65.65.01, ⓦwww.rulhe.com; 53 places; June–Sept). For Andorra, go straight on, past the **Étang de Comte**, through the defile and over the chaos of boulders to link up with the HRP at the Étang de Couart. From the lake, amid bleak, rocky terrain, the HRP cuts through the Port de Juclars between the double **Estanys de Juclar (Juclà)** – just inside Andorra, with an unstaffed *refugi* (2315m; 50 places) – and then down to the head of the **Vall d'Incles**, where you can stay overnight at the recommended campsite.

To avoid going down to Soldeu and the main road along the Valira del Orient, continue on the HRP to El Serrat, near the head of the Valira d'Ordino, and finally into France via the **Port de l'Abeille/Abella** or the **Port de Rat**. There are three ways to do this, more or less parallel to each other.

The easiest route is the most southerly, climbing west from the head of the Incles valley, dropping down into the head of the **Ransol valley** and up to the **Coll de la Mina**. A more difficult route passes the small *Refugi Cabana Sorda* (2295m; 20 places) on **Estany de Cabana Sorda**, then runs parallel to the base of the frontier peaks to Coll de la Mina. The hardest and wildest route goes north from Incles through the **Port de Fontargente** to the two Fontargente lakes, then curves west to re-enter Andorra through the **Port de Soulanet/Solaneta**.

Whichever one you choose, you can use the unstaffed **Refugi Sorteny** (1965m; 25 places) towards the end of the trek. From here it's a ten-minute walk to the top of the 4WD track 5km up from El Serrat. Fit walkers will manage the Incles–El Serrat hike in eight hours; the main caveat is to take plenty of water for this stretch, as springs are not always reliable.

West from the Cerdanya: the GR11

From Spanish Cerdanya, the logical starting points are the villages of Meranges (see p.216) just south of the GR11, and Lles (see p.215), further west and well inside Lleida province. Either route occupies a fairly leisurely two days, but the Meranges-based one is of better quality.

From Meranges, a rough track leads up to the *Refugi de Malniu* (2200m; ⓣ938 257 104 or 616 855 535; 32 places; open sporadic weekends year-round, Easter week, & late June to late Sept). The half-hour walk from the Malniu hut to its namesake lakes is the most popular family outing, but trekkers prefer the 2.5-hour jaunt northwest along the **GR11** to the FEEC-run *Refugi J Folch i Girona* (2400m; ⓣ934 120 777; same opening periods as Malniu hut), below the cluster of lakes in the Circ d'Engorgs. From the Engorgs area, the route heads west into Lleida province, across the Llosa valley and past the crude **Cabana dels Esparvers**, entering Andorra and the Madriu valley via the **Port de Vallcivera** (2519m).

The less challenging route **from Lles** actually starts from the Cap del Rec cross-country ski area (see p.215), 6km north and above the village. From here, **GR11.10** heads west-northwest for 2hr 45min to the scenic lakes and FEEC-managed *Refugi Estanys de la Pera* (2333m; ⓣ973 293 108 or 679 410 492; 38 bunks; staffed late June to late Sept), though the surface en route is entirely 4WD track (closed to cars Nov–May).

From Arànsa (see p.215), any car can reach the parking area and tarn at **Les Pollineres**, from where it's forty minutes on the poorly marked GR11.10 (now path) up to the refuge, a popular lunch stop for trippers doing this day hike. Beyond the lake the path slips north over the **Port de Perafita** (2587m), then down into the eponymous Andorran cirque, before rejoining the main GR11 near the bottom of the Madriu valley. The route then veers north-northeast, skimming above the Engolasters dam, to arrive at Encamp.

West out of Andorra: the HRP and GR11

There are several trails **west out of Andorra** towards the Montcalm-Estats Massif on the Franco-Spanish border; the main ones are the HRP from near El Serrat, initially into France, and the easier GR11 from Encamp directly to Spain.

The classic option begins at the ski station of Ordino-Arcalis, from which a clear trail – part of the HRP – climbs the short distance to **Port de Rat** (2542m) on the French frontier. From there you drop sharply to the track running south from the Soulcem dam, then climb equally steeply on the far side to the **Port de Bouet** (2520m) on the Spanish border. Descend on the path west until you meet a track at the **Pla de Bouet/Boet** (camping possible); the *Refugi de Vall Ferrera* (see p.257) lies a few minutes' walk north. Even with a lift to the trailhead at Ordino-Arcalis, it's a challenging day of about seven walking hours; if you have to hoof it from El Serrat, add two hours more.

The **GR11** from Encamp passes through more developed areas, and has its fair share of roller-coastering, but facilities en route mean you can do without a tent if you make arrangements in advance. Allow just under two hours from Encamp to reach the **Coll d'Ordino** (1979m) on the minor Canillo-Ordino road; a non-GR path about 1.5km south of Canillo also gives access to the pass. Descend west along the Segudet stream valley, then veer northwest away from Ordino through La Cortinada village, nearly five hours into the day. You can use the recommended accommodation here (see p.208), or the *Mitxeu* **campsite** in nearby Llorts (ⓣ376 324 557; July to mid-Sept) if you don't fancy the sharp ascent up to the **Coll de les Cases** (1964m) the same day, with a gentler drop to Arinsal – just over seven hours' walking from Encamp.

From Arinsal, you climb west into the valley of **Aigües Juntes**, in the shadow of 2946-metre Alt de Coma Pedrosa, reaching after a couple of hours the *Refugi de Coma Pedrosa* (2265m; ⓣ376 327 955; 60 places; June–Oct), Andorra's only staffed refuge, with food and hot showers, five minutes' walk from the attractive Estany de les Truites. From the refuge you climb sharply northeast through the Circ de Coma Pedrosa, past Estany Negre, and then negotiate the **Port de Baiau** (2796m) where snow often remains until July. Once on the Spanish side, you face a steep, scree-laden descent to the lake and simple, unstaffed *Refugi Josep Maria Montfort* (2500m; 12 places) at the head of the **Baiau valley**, along which the GR11 bears northwest to intersect briefly with the HRP below the Port de Bouet, en route to the *Refugi de Vall Ferrera*.

Cerdanya/Cerdagne

The fertile, gently rolling upland of the **Cerdanya** (Catalan) or **Cerdagne** (French) – about one-fifth of the way west along the Pyrenean watershed – has never quite been able to decide whether it is French or Spanish. Essentially the mountain-ringed basin of a huge prehistoric lake, this region's lack of natural frontiers fostered an ambiguous identity. The 1659 Treaty of the Pyrenees imposed nominal allegiances, which arbitrarily divided an area that considered itself Catalan in language and culture. Yet development of overt French or Spanish national consciousness and a hardening of the notoriously porous frontier were a long time coming. The French and Spanish languages didn't acquire official status here until the early 1800s, following the French Revolution, a 1793–95 border war and the Napoleonic campaigns. A formal boundary was marked for the first time only by the supplementary Treaty of Bayonne in 1866.

Given its former military significance, good **roads** have long converged here. Mont-Louis, on the eastern fringe of the French Cerdagne, had a road – now the **N116** – in from Villefranche-de-Conflent as early as the seventeenth century, while Napoleon ordered the construction of the original **N20** from the north, terminating at Bourg-Madame. Spanish development lagged behind, but during the 1950s the **N260** was sealed from La Seu d'Urgell, west of the Spanish Cerdanya, as was the **C16** from points south, both meeting at **Puigcerdà**, the geographical centre of the region.

Because of its gentle terrain, the Cerdanya/Cerdagne hosted the first – and now last surviving – trans-Pyrenean **rail line**, between Barcelona and Toulouse via Puigcerdà and Latour-de-Carol. Threatened abolition of service between Puigcerdà and Ripoll was only averted in 1985 by a massive Cerdan letter-writing campaign to Spanish Premier Felipe Gonzalez, coupled with half-serious threats by local authorities to request renegotiation of the Treaty of the Pyrenees and secession to France.

The Cerdanya

The name **Cerdanya** applies to the Spanish portion of the upper Segre valley (a high plateau which continues on the French side as far as Mont-Louis). On its north, mountains rise up to the Andorran frontier, their slopes dotted with tiny villages near the tops of tributary streams to the Riu Segre. On the southern side, the Serra del Cadí forms an impressive barrier, with more sleepy settlements tucked away at the base of the range. **Puigcerdà** at the frontier is connected by 6km of road to anomalous **Llívia**, former capital of the region and now a Spanish enclave in French territory. The Cerdanya was already a popular summer holiday area for wealthy Barcelonans in the nineteenth century; lately this trend has accelerated, with blocks of holiday flats mushrooming at the edge of – and dwarfing – nearly every village. Skiing, both downhill and cross-country, provides the main impetus for construction; but golf, horse-riding, plus even gliding and hot-air ballooning grow in popularity, the gently rolling countryside being ideal for such activities.

Martinet and cross-country skiing resorts

Climbing from La Seu along the N260, which follows the Riu Segre upstream, the first roadside place of any significance, 13km along, is **ELS BANYS DE SANT VICENÇ**, a recently rejuvenated spa; the **hotel** here (Ⓣ973 384 010, Ⓦwww.hotelsantvicenc.com; ❺ B&B) also has a well-regarded **restaurant** (closed Sun eve, Mon, Tues; *menú* €20). The first actual village, 10km further, is **MARTINET**, where the Cadí traverse described on p.198 emerges. Martinet is mostly strung uninspiringly along the through road, c/El Segre, but if you need to **stay** there's the quiet *Hostal Miravet*, north of the highway at c/de les Arenes 2 (Ⓣ973 515 016; ❸), with views across a little stream. The best local **meal** option is *Pluvinet* on Martinet's through road (*a la carta* only, allow €20; closed Mon & Tues low season).

Lles and Cap del Rec

From the western edge of Martinet a narrow paved road climbs steeply north to two villages, each the gateway to their respective cross-country skiing centres. It's 9km, bearing right at the fork just below it, to the somewhat higgledy-piggledy village of **LLES** (often "Lles de Cerdanya"; 1471m), a good base for the popular ski centre 6km further on. The most reliable and comfortable **accommodation** and **eating** is at *Ca L'Abel* (Ⓣ973 515 048, Ⓦwww.restaurantcalabel.com; ❹ B&B), with high-ceiling, airy upstairs units and a competent country-style restaurant (slightly pricey *a la carta* but cheapish *menú*) adjacent. Otherwise, *Fonda Domingo*, near the top of the village (Ⓣ973 515 087, Ⓦwww.fondadomingo.com; ❹), has equally good views and another pricey restaurant.

Exposed to the full glare of the sun at 1942m, the **CAP DEL REC** cross-country ski resort at the road's end, has 29km of marked runs. Here there is the *Refugi Eduard Jornet I Esteve* (Ⓣ973 293 049; 60 places) and a restaurant, both of which remain open in summer, with a local horse-riding centre and rental mountain bikes providing the means for exploring the myriad local tracks.

Arànsa

Returning to the fork 1.5km below Lles and then heading 4.5km northwest brings you to **ARÀNSA** (Arànser), much more of a piece architecturally than Lles, and set on a spur of land gazing at the Cadí's north wall. Near the village entrance you'll find the best **accommodation** and **eating** choices: *Hostal Restaurant Pas de la Pera* (Ⓣ973 515 001; ❸) and *Cal Sandic* (Ⓣ973 515 193, Ⓦwww.agroturisme.org/sandic.htm; ❺ HB only), whose restaurant is open to all. The road continues to Les Pollineres trailhead for the Estanys de la Pera, via the Arànsa **cross-country ski station**, 6km along, with 32km of marked pistes between 1850m and 2150m. At the ski station, a kind family runs *El Fornell* **restaurant** (lunch only; open ski season, also late July & Aug), serving grill-based *menús*.

Bellver de Cerdanya

Eight kilometres east from Martinet, **BELLVER DE CERDANYA** sits on the bank of the trout-laden Segre, 18km west of Puigcerdà, astride the GR107. Its semi-fortified hilltop old town, with its arcaded Plaça Major and a massive church at the summit, merits a stop, despite the overpowering telecom antenna. A short stroll south of town, the Romanesque church of **Santa María de Talló** is a plain twelfth-century building, with a wooden statue of the Virgin as old as the building itself.

The **Turisme** occupies an old chapel at Plaça Sant Roc 9 (Easter, Christmas, June 15–Sept 15 Mon–Sat 11am–1pm & 6–8pm, Sun 11am–1pm; ⓣ973 510 229), while the best **accommodation** by far is Casa Fonda member *Fonda Biayna*, c/Sant Roc 11 (ⓣ973 510 475, ⓦwww.biayna.com; ❺ B&B), an atmospheric, rambling old mansion working as an inn since 1880. The listing, wooden-floored rooms all have compact bathrooms, wall art, antique furnishings and a preponderance of double beds. The downstairs *menjador* with its swirling fans lays on an excellent supper for €16; specials such as wild mushrooms attract supplements. The adjacent lively locals' bar has a summer terrace which hosts Saturday-night films and live music. For lovers of solitutde, the same management has the *Ermitatge de Quadres* about 5km northeast (ⓣ618 550 183; ❻ dbl, €160 quad, B&B), five state-of-the-art apartments and a restaurant built next to a thirteenth-century *ermita* on a minor branch of the Santiago pilgrimage route. On the outskirts of Bellver, there's a riverside **campsite**, *Solana del Segre* (ⓣ973 510 310), offering pleasant plots for tents.

Meranges and Guils Fontanera

From Ger, about halfway between Bellver and Puigcerdà, a narrow road leads 10km northwest past hayfields, hamlets and copses of silver birch and maple to **MERANGES** (1539m). Once a crucial outpost in the smuggling trade, the village is an idyllic spot below the Malniu lakes at the foot of **Pic Farinós** and **Puig Pedrós**. The only **accommodation** here is prestigious *Hotel Can Borrell* (ⓣ972 880 033, ⓦwww.canborrell.com; daily except Wed–Sun Nov, Fri–Sun Dec–Easter; ❼), a converted farmhouse with rustic decor and a well-regarded restaurant. The alternative for **dining** is basic but inexpensive *Cal Joan* (closed Tues) in the village centre.

Just before Puigcerdà, another minor road heads northwest to **GUILS DE CERDANYA**, home to the newest and most ambitious **cross-country ski resort** in the Cerdanya: **Guils Fontanera**, with 45km of marked pistes.

Puigcerdà

Although founded by King Alfonso I of Aragón in 1177 as a new capital for then-unified Cerdanya, **PUIGCERDÀ** (pronounced "*Poocherda*") retains no compelling medieval monuments, partly owing to heavy bombing during the Civil War. The church of Santa María was one of the casualties, but its forty-metre-high **bell tower** still stands in the namesake *plaça*. The east end of town, around pleasant, tree-lined Passeig Deu d'Abril, escaped more lightly; here medieval murals adorn the gloomy parish church of **Sant Domènec**. Dwelling morbidly on the saint's martyrdom, surviving fragments show Dominic's head being cloven in two by a sabre – he's already been run through by a sword.

The town's greatest attraction is its atmosphere: if you've just arrived from France, the streets and squares, with busy pavement cafés and well-stocked shops, present a marked contrast to moribund Bourg-Madame. Allow at least enough time for a meal or an evening in a bar, though Puigcerdà does not offer much good-value accommodation. Enjoyable outdoor cafés line the merged *plaças* of Santa María and dels Herois; between drinks, you can explore the old quarter between Plaça de l'Ajuntament and Passeig Deu d'Abril, or amble five minutes north to a small recreational lake.

Arrival and information

Puigcerdà is on the Barcelona–Latour-de-Carol rail line; from Latour, several daily trains or SNCF coaches have instant connections for Toulouse. From Puigcerdà's **train station** (outside which **buses** also stop) in Plaça de l'Estació, wearyingly steep steps lead up to Plaça de l'Ajuntament in the heart of town, with views west over the Cerdanya. At the top of the steps, to the right, stands the **Casa de la Vila**, a replacement for the Gothic original destroyed in the Civil War, with the municipal **Turisme** alongside at c/Querol 1 (June to mid-Sept daily 9am–2pm & 3–8pm; mid-Sept to May Mon 9am–1pm, Tues–Sat 10am–1pm & 4–7pm; ⓣ 972 880 542). The giant **regional branch** (June to mid-Sept daily 9am–2pm & 3–8pm; mid-Sept to May Mon–Sat 9am–1pm & 4–7pm, Sun 10am–2pm; ⓣ 972 140 665), 1500m southwest of town near the *Puigcerdà Park Hotel*, is well stocked with leaflets and more convenient with your own transport.

Accommodation

There's not a great selection of **accommodation** in town, and you should consider various alternatives in the villages around Puigcerdà (see p.218). Budget options in town include central, friendly *Hostal Alfonso*, c/d'Espanya 5 (ⓣ 972 880 246; ③), with superior upper-storey rooms; *Hostal Residència Rita Belvedere* at c/Carmelites 6–8 (ⓣ 972 880 356 or 608 088 085), offering excellent views, private parking and a choice of old-style (②) or more expensive modern rooms (③), though it's only open daily July 25–September 30, plus holidays and weekends from Christmas to Easter; or *Fonda Cerdanya* at c/Ramon Cosp 7 (Ⓣ972 880 010; ❸), with half-board (❺) usually obligatory at the ground-floor restaurant (open to all). For a splurge, there's none better than popular *Hotel del Lago*, Avda Dr Puiguillém 7 (Ⓣ972 881 000, Ⓦwww.hotellago.com; ❺), with a breakfast gazebo in the garden, a fair-sized pool and parking.

Eating, drinking and entertainment

French day-trippers are partly responsible for the high prices and bland menus prevalent in Puigcerdà, but there are still a few reasonable places to **eat**. At the budget end of things, *Sant Remo* at c/Ramon Cosp 9 has a pleasant upstairs *menjador* offering copious *menús* at €10–12; the *Fonda Cerdanya* opposite is more upmarket. For a jump in standards (and prices), head for *La Cachimba* at c/Beates 12. The best wood-oven pizzas (around €12 each) in town are at *Pizzeria del Reg*, on Plaça del Reg.

The **bars** with outdoor seating on Plaça de Santa María are to be preferred to the more touristy ones on Plaça dels Herois. Just round the corner at c/Major 46, fare at *Petit Café* ranges from desserts and crêpes to mojitos and caipirinhas. *Cerveseria Claude*, on arcaded Plaça Cabrinetty, specializes in international beers: you can sit indoors or out, tippling your way around the world's breweries.

Finally, Puigcerdà has the only **cinemas** in the Cerdanya: the Avinguda, c/Major 53, and the Caretà in the old casino on Plaça Barcelona, also the venue for a late-July **music festival**.

Villages around Puigcerdà

You'll find better-value **accommodation**, and often food, in the hamlets and villages south of Puigcerdà, home to some of the more distinguished members of Girona's *turisme rural* scheme. Top billing goes to the superb *Residència Sant Marc*, 1.5km south of town on the road to **Les Pereres** hamlet (Ⓣ972 880 007, Ⓦwww.santmarc.galeon.com; ❻ HB only; advance booking recommended). Accommodation at this 150-hectare stud farm is based in a 1913 Belle Époque mansion with huge, elegant common areas and old-fashioned but unmusty rooms decorated with antique furniture, wood floors, and artistic tiles in the large bathrooms. Equestrian holidays are also offered in the centre of **AGE**, 2km east of Les Pereres and 3km southeast of Puigcerdà, at *Cal Marrufès/Hipica Age* (Ⓣ972 141 174, Ⓦwww.calmarrufes.com; ❹ B&B; also family quads), a tasteful restoration of an old stone-built farm.

Sleepy **URTX** 5km south of Puigcerdà, has yet to be disfigured by too many new chalet-apartments, and is home to *Cal Mateu* (Ⓣ972 890 495; ❸ B&B), a working dairy farm by the church, offering good-value en-suite rooms with full-sized bathtubs. Decor is bland modern rather than rustic, but there are self-catering facilities next to the common-room-with-fireplace, and the managing couple is disarmingly friendly. Urtx proper hasn't any other facilities; the closest decent **food** is 1500m downhill inside the semi-converted Queixans RENFE station, where *L'Estació* (closed Wed) offers two lunch *menús* as well as *a la carta*. Portions of *escalibada* and *botifarra amb mongetes* aren't huge, but the ingredients are fresh and the presentation exemplary.

Finally, in resolutely rural **SANAVASTRE**, accessible only from the Alp–Prats road (not from the main highway to La Seu), *Can Simó* (Ⓣ972 890 240; all year; ❸) is an engagingly rustic dairy farm which hasn't been overly restored, though most units are en suite: it's at the edge of the village, tucked in a hollow just beyond the airstrip runway. Nearby, in **PRATS** village, *Cal Furné* (Ⓣ972 890 565, Ⓕ141 484; ❸ B&B, ❺ HB) sits at the narrowest point of the through road, with a wood-beamed *menjador* and secure parking.

Llívia

The Spanish town of **LLÍVIA**, 6km from Puigcerdà but totally surrounded by French territory, is a curious place indeed, worth visiting not least so you can say you've been there. There are several **buses** daily from Puigcerdà (the Alsina Graells coach stops in front of the train station and in Plaça Barcelona). Under your own power, bear left at the junction 1km outside town, just before the border at Bourg-Madame, and keep to the main road. From French territory, the turn-off to Llívia is completely unmarked; your only clue is the highway overpass above the *Train Jaune* tracks.

French **history** books claim that Llívia's anomalous status resulted from an oversight. According to the traditional version of events, in the exchanges that followed the Treaty of the Pyrenees, the French delegates insisted on possession of 33 Cerdan villages between the Ariège and newly acquired Roussillon. The Spanish agreed, then pointed out that Llívia was technically a town not a village, and thus excluded under the terms of the handover. Llívia had in fact been capital of the valley before Puigcerdà, and Spain had every intention of retaining it at the negotiations, held in Llívia itself.

The Romans were perhaps the first to recognize the strategic value of their settlement here, named Julia Livia, though its castle was destroyed on the orders of Louis XI in 1479. Despite a manic chalet-building programme, there's a lingering medieval feel to the town centre, not least in the fifteenth-century fortified **church** (June–Sept daily 10am–1pm & 3–7pm; Oct–May Tues–Sun 10am–1pm & 3–6pm). Inside is a beautiful gilt altarpiece, delicately carved and painted with cherubs and scenes from the Nativity, and (in the third side chapel on the north) a polychrome wood triptych showing Christ between John the Baptist and St Peter, a fine example of the Romanesque-Gothic transitional style. On August weekends, a popular **music festival** takes place in and around the church.

Opposite the church, the unusual **Museu Municipal** (April–June Tues–Sat 10am–6pm, Sun 10am–2pm; July & Aug daily 10am–7pm; Sept Tues–Sun 10am–7pm; Oct–March Tues–Sat 10am–4.30pm, Sun 10am–2pm; €2) contains the oldest pharmacy in Europe, functioning in Llívia from 1594 until 1918. Displays emphasize apothecarial pots and hand-painted boxes of herbs, as well as local Bronze Age relics, old maps and even the eighteenth-century bell mechanism from the church.

Practicalities

Most visitors just stay long enough for a **meal** – not a bad idea given the limited choice of short-term accommodation. The most reasonable of several eateries around Plaça Major are *Cal Cofa* at c/Frederic Bernades 1, where €25–28 nets hearty country fare, and *Bar Alea* at no. 6 on the *plaça*, with pricey *tapas* but an economical weekday *menú*. At c/Frederic Bernades 7, sample what are claimed to be Catalunya's top "artesanal" pizzas for €25–30, at *Pizzeria Taller*.

The Cerdagne

The **Cerdagne** is the sunniest area in the French Pyrenees; the tawny colours of summer grain and hay on treeless slopes reinforce this impression. It is bracketed by Bourg-Madame on the southwest, opposite Spanish Puigcerdà, and by Mont-Louis to the northeast at the head of the Têt valley, the usual entry corridor from the French side. To the southeast rises **Puigmal**, one source of the River Sègre, while it's flanked to the northwest by the mountains of the **Carlit Massif**, principal source of the River Têt and venue for some excellent walks.

The *Train Jaune* (see p.112) continues from Mont-Louis as far as **Latour-de-Carol**, from where regular **train** services run north into the Ariège under the **Col de Puymorens**. The **road**, which snaked solely over this pass until 1995, now has a counterpart running through the Tunnel de Puymorens.

Font-Romeu and around

Sprawling at the foot of Roc de la Calma, at the southeast corner of the Carlit Massif, **FONT-ROMEU** has a reputation representing a triumph of marketing over reality, since the vaunted *Cité Préolympique* was merely an altitude training

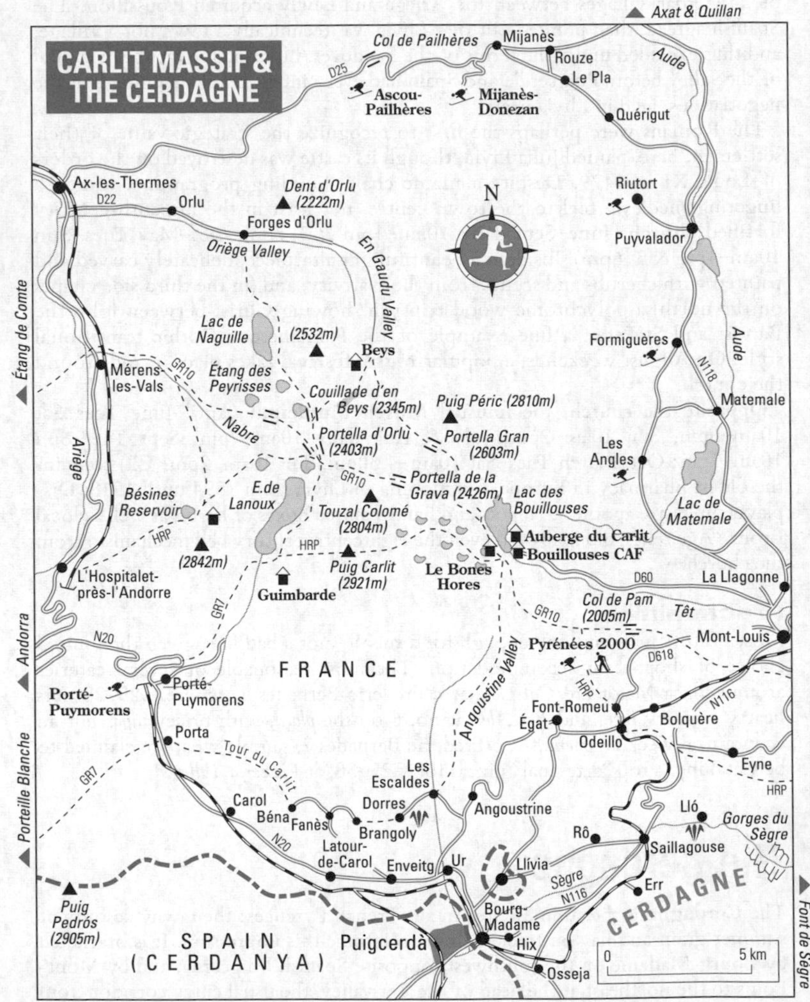

centre for the 1968 Mexico City Olympics. Its high point is a mere 2204m, the maximum vertical descent just 500m; adjacent and barely higher is the ugly purpose-built resort of **PYRÉNÉES 2000**. The two linked resorts have forty pistes between them, but drag-lifts predominate; the majority of the runs are for beginners or intermediates, and only a handful are north-facing – hence 460 snow canons (the most in Europe). It does, however, have 90km of marked cross-country skiing trails – the second biggest extent in the French Pyrenees.

The Ermitage

Font-Romeu is Catalan for "pilgrim's spring", named after a legendary cowherd who uncovered a buried figure of the Virgin and a source of pure water, having been led to the spot by a bull. The holy image has been installed in the barracks-like **Ermitage**, off avenue Emmanuel Brousse (daily early July to early Sept 10am–noon & 3–6pm), a seventeenth-century enlargement of the original fourteenth-century shrine. Catalan artist Josep Sunyer sculpted the retable in 1707, and five years later created a sumptuous "bedroom" for the Virgin, known as the *camaril*.

On September 8 the Virgin is taken down the hill to **ODEILLO**, returning on Trinity Sunday. Odeillo has the only other "sight" in the immediate area – the **Four Solaire**, or solar power station (daily 10am–12.30pm & 2–6pm, July & Aug 10am–7.30pm; €5.50). It no longer functions as a generator, but rather as a museum and PR exercise, with full-moon-powered demonstrations on summer evenings.

Practicalities

From the **train station** (Odeillo/Via) it's a fairly steep walk 2km north to Font-Romeu, passing Odeillo about halfway. **Accommodation** in Font-Romeu tends to be expensive, but with 18,000 beds you should find something; the **tourist office**, near the top of avenue Emmanuel Brousse (daily 9am–12.30pm & 2–6.30pm; Ⓣ04.68.30.68.30, Ⓦwww.font-romeu.fr) has lists of apartments. The best budget option is the **gîte** *Les Cariolettes*, 1 rue de Fontanilles (Ⓣ04.68.30.25.48, Ⓦwww.gite-cariolettes.com; 24 places; HB only), a renovated old house offering doubles, triples and one quad. Good-value **hotels** include summer-only *L'Oustalet*, in rue des Viollettes (Ⓣ04.68.30.11.32, Ⓕ04.68.30.31.89; ❸), with an outdoor swimming pool; old-fashioned *Cara Sol* on avenue Emmanuel Brousse (Ⓣ04 68 30 08 11, Ⓦwww.font-romeu.com/carasol; all year; ❸); and the plusher *Y Sem Bé* west of town at 5 rue des Écureuils (Ⓣ04.68.30.00.54, Ⓦwww.hotel-ysembe.com; closed May & mid-Oct to mid-Nov; ❺), enjoying views over much of the Cerdagne. Over in **BOLQUÈRE** village – a bit handier for those on a GR10 traverse, if a characterless agglomeration of chalets – there are two more good-value **hotels**: central *L'Ancienne Auberge* (Ⓣ04.68.30.09/51; closed May, Nov & Dec; ❷) by the church, and modern *Lassus* nearby at 14 place de la Mairie (Ⓣ04 68 30 09 75; closed April; ❷).

Southwest to Latour-de-Carol

Beyond Odeillo, the *Train Jaune* winds its way across the open plain to **SAILLAGOUSE** (Sallagosa in Catalan; 1302m) with its attractive old quarter and excellent **hotel**, the dead-central 🏃 *Planotel* (Ⓣ04.68.04.72.08, Ⓦwww.planotel.fr), which offers rooms in the 1895-built *vieille maison* (❸) or in a nearby modern annexe (❹) with a pool, and excellent-value meals either in its brasserie (from €14) or the full-on restaurant adjacent.

From Saillagouse you can move southeast through the **Gorges du Sègre** to picturesque **LLÓ** and its renovated spa, the **Bains de Llo**, in the gorge at the bottom of the village (daily 10am–7.15pm except closed Nov 2–Dec 16; water 33–37°C; €7.50). The village itself has **accommodation** at a quality *gîte d'étape*, *Cal Miquel* (ⓣ04.68.04.19.68, ⓦwww.calmiquel.com; 19 places in doubles, quads & a triple). Beyond Lló a dirt track climbs through the gorge, past a car park and vehicle barrier, to a point where the track becomes a path to the **Col de Finestrelles** (2604m), above Núria in Spanish Catalonia (see p.178). From the *col*, you can either drop back southwest via the **Font de Sègre** to Err on another path or carry on into Spain or pick up the **HRP** along the crests.

Err and Puigmal 2600

The next *Train Jaune* stop serves **ERR** at the foot of heavily wooded Puigmal – and another place with a "found Virgin" legend. The twelfth-century effigy is housed in the **Chapelle de la Vierge**, considerably enlarged in the eighteenth century, facing the equally venerable church of **Saint-Genis** across the cemetery. The only **accommodation** at Err is its *gîte d'étape* (ⓣ04.68.04.74.20; 17 places; dorms only), though there's also a **campsite**, *Las Closas*, off place Saint-Genis (ⓣ04.68.04.71.42).

Some 7km southeast of Err, on the north slopes of 2913-metre Puigmal, lies **PUIGMAL 2600**, one of the Cerdagne's smaller ski stations. But the top point is as cited, and its 25 runs, the majority red and black, end most of their descents scenically amongst the pines. There are few snow canons, so check conditions before setting out.

Valcebollère, Bourg-Madame and Hix

Osséja (no notable facilities) is the next *Train Jaune* stop, and the start of the paved road 5km east-southeast up another valley to the secluded, unspoilt village of **VALCEBOLLÈRE**, at the centre of which is a superior rustic hotel, *Auberge Les Ecureuils* (ⓣ04.68.04.52.03; ⓦwww.aubergeecureuils.com; all year; ❺ B&B, ❼ HB), with impeccably done-up rooms, on-site spa, gym and pool, plus all manner of activities (especially cross-country skiing and horse-riding) at the doorstep.

The *Train Jaune* reaches the border at **BOURG-MADAME**, from where Puigcerdà is plainly visible on its hill; it's quicker (and cheaper) to get off the *Train Jaune* here and walk across the border. In 1815 Bourg-Madame changed its name from Les Guinguettes d'Hix to honour the wife of the duc d'Angoulême, and prospered briefly as a competitor to Puigcerdà. But it hasn't amounted to much since then, and as the EU negates national borders, Bourg-Madame is visibly depressed and fading, its vitality sapped by more favoured Puigcerdà – you probably won't want or need to use either of its two modest hotels. Just 1km east, **HIX** hamlet, now virtually part of Bourg-Madame, has a delicate eleventh-century chapel, one of the oldest Romanesque structures in the area.

Angoustrine and Dorres

The next train stop beyond Bourg-Madame, Ur-les-Escaldes – or if you're travelling by road, the N20 – leaves you in the middle of Ur village (no amenities), from which it's 3.5km along the D618 to pretty **ANGOUSTRINE**, with its single **hotel-restaurant**, the *Relais du Belloch* (ⓣ04.68.30.07.24; closed Nov–Christmas; ❸). Just before Angoustrine, a minor road heads off past an ugly modern spa – the "Escaldes" of the rail station – en route to well-positioned, stone-built **DORRES**, which offers the characterful *Hotel-Restaurant Marty* (ⓣ04.68.30.07.52; ❸) in the very centre. But the big draw here, with its own car park well below the village centre, are the so-called **Bains Romans** (daily 8.30am–8.15pm; €3.90), whose open-air granite pools (39–40° C) are at their best in ski season – a welcome change from the sterile regimentation of so many spas. The paved route dwindles to a jeep track just before the Romanesque hilltop shrine of **Santa Maria Belloch**, beyond Dorres.

Latour-de-Carol and Bena

The *Train Jaune* ends seven minutes beyond Ur at the Gare Internationale of Latour-de-Carol, the **vast interchange for trains** south to Barcelona and north for Toulouse. Several daily cross the border **into Spain**. Despite its official name, the station lies closer to the village of Enveitg (no notable facilities). **LATOUR-DE-CAROL** itself, 1km northwest, has a fine old quarter for strolling, and an excellent **hotel** on the main road, *L'Auberge Catalane* (Ⓣ04.68.04.80.66, Ⓦwww.auberge-catalane.fr; ❸), going since 1929, with soundproofed rooms and a well-attended **restaurant** where the menus encompass fish, *foie gras*, *gesiers* and *boudin noir*. If you can't get a table, *Peyroch* on place du Mairie (shut Sun eve to Tues) is an acceptable, almost-as-popular alternative (*menu* at €20). Some forty minutes' walk uphill and north is **BENA**, a delightful hamlet with an equally wonderful *gîte d'étape* (Ⓣ04.68.04.81.64, Ⓔgiteauberge@bena.org; 40 places, mostly doubles and quads) in a restored Catalan farmhouse.

Northwest to the Col de Puymorens

After years of controversy, the tunnel beneath the **Col de Puymorens** (1920m; Pimorent in Catalan) northwest of Latour was completed in 1995 and the rapid toll road (cars €5.50 single, €8.70 ten-day return) – like the railway – now disappears under the pass to reappear in the Ariège. In fine weather, though, many motorists prefer the scenic *col* road.

Porta

On the way up to the pass you'll see the much-photographed but seldom-visited towers at Querol, all that's left of a castle built to defend the Cerdagne from Foix. Near the top of the climb, 13km from Latour, the village of **PORTA** has a pretty old quarter slightly uphill, though its single amenity is on the main highway: *Auberge du Campcardos* (Ⓣ04.68.04.82.26; ❸), with a restaurant (*menus* €15–26). Hikers should come supplied, as there's no shop.

Porté-Puymorens

The nearby ski station above the village of **PORTÉ-PUYMORENS** (Ⓦwww.porte-puymorens.net) is one of the best the French Catalan Pyrenees has to offer. While the Col de Puymorens marks the shift from the arid Cerdagne to the damp Ariège, lots of snow often falls on the Cerdan side and stays there, protected from the worst wind. The 17 runs here are fairly evenly distributed amongst all ability levels, with high points at a respectable 2400m and 2500m, and four well-placed chair-lifts. There are also 25km of trails for *ski de fond* up on the *col*.

The village below has a nice valley setting, off the main highway, though the only facility is the central **gîte**, *Ferme d'en Garcie* (Ⓣ04.68.04.95.44, Ⓔnathalie.komaroff@wanadoo.fr; 31 places, including 6 doubles), which also operates the local **horse-riding** centre.

The **GR7** east into the Carlit Massif from Porté provides the gentlest grade into the Carlit, but is also the most spoilt western approach, what with overhead cable cars, various damworks and the generally dull topography. For an alternate trailhead for Carlit, consider L'Hospitalet (for the HRP) or Mérens-le-Vals (for the GR10), both slightly north on the Latour–Toulouse rail line.

The Carlit Massif

The granite ridges of the lake-spangled **Carlit Massif** occupy a compact area just north of the Cerdanya/Cerdagne, the easternmost truly alpine region of the Pyrenees – Canigou notwithstanding, only foothills undulate on the horizon towards the Mediterranean. Being easily accessible, these mountains are popular; the lakes – even when not dammed – can seem a little overly manicured. The massif's upland marshes have been disrupted by EDF dams which manipulate water levels, most notably at Lac des Bouillouses and several other reservoirs. There are still some relatively unspoiled corners, however, and ample scope for several days of trekking or scrambling.

The ascent of **Puig Carlit** (2921m) lies within the capabilities of any reasonably fit person, especially from Lac des Bouillouses on its eastern slopes. Three major walking routes – the **HRP**, the north–south **GR7** and the trans-Pyrenean **GR10** – as well as marked secondary trails cross the massif, while segments of the GR7 and GR10 comprise sections of the less demanding **Tour du Carlit**. For all of these explorations you'll want either the IGN 1:50,000 *Carte de Randonnées* no. 8, "Cerdagne-Capcir", or the IGN TOP 25 no. 2249 ET.

Traverses and alpine loops

The three western **trailhead villages** are Mérens-les-Vals (p.226), L'Hospitalet-près-l'Andorre (p.226) and Porté (p.223). Each of the suggested routes converge near the centre of the range, close to the focal Porteille d'Orlu.

From Porté, the GR7 leaves the village at the first hairpin, climbing gradually east and then north towards the grey concrete wall of the **Lanoux** dam, four hours from Porté – not a particularly aesthetic trip. Just beyond, at the entrance to the Fourats valley, the decrepit, three-person *Abri de la Guimbarde* overlooking the reservoir, is useful only in dire emergencies. Most people prefer to camp on the grass below or to get an early enough start from Porté to finish the day at a more exciting spot. The GR7 continues northeast for another ninety minutes above the lakeshore, initially quite steeply, before joining the GR10 which cuts roughly east-west across the top of the lake from the easy pass of Porteille de la Grave.

From Mérens-les-Vals, the GR10 climbs sharply up the **Nabre valley** to reach the staffed CAF **Refuge des Bésines** (2104m; ⓣ05.61.05.22.44, ⓦwww.besines.free.fr; 55 places) next to the Bésines reservoir in something over five hours; the HRP **from L'Hospitalet-près-l'Andorre** gets you there in roughly half the time. There are no other refuges east of Bésines towards the GR10/GR7 intersection, only a limited number of **campsites** at the north end of Lanoux.

From Lanoux, the climb up the south grade of the **Porteille d'Orlu** (2403m) is deceptively easy, but, once up, the Carlit reveals its other uncompromising face in the view north: granite spires, giant boulder falls and drifting cloud. It's vital to keep west here for the grassy route skirting the **Étang de Feury**, avoiding the deadly rocks. At Feury, a nameless variant heads west via the **Porteille de Madides** (2.5km) to shortcut the GR10, joining the latter at Courals de la Présasse and allowing rapid descent to Mérens-les-Vals.

Even if the mist doesn't close in, you'll still need about three hours to descend northeast from the Porteille d'Orlu along the GR7 to **Étang d'en Beys** (1980m), a natural lake surrounded by scree, pasture and clumps of rhododendron. Here the useful **refuge** managed by the Orlu municipality (ⓣ05.61.64.24.24; 49 places; staffed late May–late Sept) is strategically located below the intersection of several traverse routes.

From the lake, it's about two hours down to the end of the road tracing the **Oriège valley**, or three hours coming uphill, but it's strongly suggested that you elect another way to finish a traverse or circuit. Particularly if you have left a vehicle at Lac des Bouillouses, which lies one day's reasonable march via the Porteille de la Grave, you can return as follows. Some twenty minutes below the lake, part company with the GR7 and adopt a cairned and paint-splodged (but unnamed) route which curls around through the **Portella Gran** (2603m), before descending through a lake-speckled valley enclosed by 2810-metre **Puig Péric** to Bouillouses, all within six hours.

If you're going to finish a traverse in the Oriège valley (see p.229), you might reduce the amount of road-tramping by following yet another anonymous but marked route up to the easy **Couillade d'en Beys** (2345m), then descend past the easterly **Peyrisses** lake to the **Naguille reservoir**, finally dropping by track to the Forges d'Orlu in about five hours.

Climbing the peak

If you're merely intent on bagging the summit of Puig Carlit, a quick approach can be made from Mont-Louis **on the east** side, up the very narrow but paved D60 road. During peak season, private cars are banned from the 13km of access road up to **Lac des Bouillouses (La Bollosa)** – you must park near the bottom and take a *navette* most of the way. For purist hikers who don't mind a long slog, the **GR10** out of Bolquère climbs gently through woods to the **Col del Pam** (2000m), where it links with the HRP coming from Font-Romeu; both continue past ski lifts and pistes to Lac des Bouillouses (4hr from either town).

There's plenty of **accommodation** and **food** at the Bouillouses lake, actually a huge reservoir dating from the early 1900s. The CAF-run *Refuge des Bouillouses* (Ⓣ04.68.04.20.76; 42 places; dorms and doubles) is the cheapest option, east of the dam wall at just under 2000m. Tucked inconspicuously behind this is the smallish, privately managed *Auberge du Carlit* (Ⓣ04.68.04.22.23; all year) with rooms (❹ HB) and a 32-bunk *gîte* in a separate building, as well as meals. Just above the west end of the dam at 2050m looms the gigantic *Refuge Le Bones Hores* (Ⓣ04.68.04.24.22), popular with families.

Beside *Le Bones Hores*, you adopt the **HRP**, whose course is scantily marked with faded paint splodges but deeply grooved into the terrain and sometimes cairned. You arc up gently through the woods, between **Étang Negre** and **Étang del Viver**, twenty minutes along; the next natural lake, **de les Dugues**, is just 45 minutes above the dam, and thus a hugely popular outing. The crowds will thin out as you press on past the necklace of smaller lakes – Castellá, Trebens and Sobirà – under the shadow of **Touzal Colomé** (2804m), and finally up the ridge that leads to the summit from the east. This is a superb climb, the tarns glinting in the sun, the grass green in June but a faded ochre by August, and the scree-strewn pyramid of Carlit overhead. There and back from Lac des Bouillouses is at most six and a half hours, an easy day's walk in good conditions – though rather ominously there are green sheds by most of the lakes, placed there as to shelter from the foul weather which frequently appears without warning. If you just want to take in the lakes, it's only a three-hour round-trip from the dam to the highest one, Sobirà, at 2310m.

From the west, the ascent of Carlit is a little more difficult, a good four hours one way starting in the vicinity of the *Abri de la Guimbarde*, close to the Lanoux dam (see opposite). Again using HRP cairns and blazes, follow the **Fourats valley** east to its tiny lake and then keep going straight to the summit, or if that looks too formidable, bear away towards the *col* on the south and approach the summit along the line of the ridge, dropping a little way down the eastern slope when the ridge gets narrow.

The Ariège Valley and the Pays de Sault

Draining north from the Col du Puymorens, the **Ariège valley** is one of the most depressed areas of France, with low income levels and high unemployment. Coming directly from the Cerdanya, where the disposable incomes of Barcelonans and Gironans have made a striking impact on the landscape, a visitor could be mistaken for thinking Spain the wealthier country. Unsurprisingly, perhaps, the Ariège has long been a stronghold for nonconformists and anti-royalists, and, in more recent times, the political Left. This political affiliation is owed more to resentment of neglect by Paris than any deeply held Marxist convictions.

The Ariège is a much-frequented corner of the Pyrenees, the local tourist industry being one of the region's few going concerns. Natural attractions such as the **Oriège** tributary valley and the bear-sheltering forests west of the river are enhanced by the prehistoric painted caves around **Tarascon**. On the main valley floor, **Mérens-les-Vals** and **Ax-les-Thermes** are serviceable bases for excursions into the surrounding mountains, including the severe fastness of the Carlit. Further downriver, the showcase town of **Foix** is almost in the flatlands, but allows access to the gorge-furrowed, Cathar-haunted **Pays de Sault**, an eerie tableland extending between the Ariège and the Aude valley to the east. Here, the Cathars began the local tradition of rebelling against Church and State eight centuries ago, antecedents which the modern *Ariègeois* acknowledge with pride.

The upper Ariège

Both train line and highway from the Cerdagne emerge from their respective tunnels at or just above minuscule **L'HOSPITALET-PRÈS-L'ANDORRE**, while a variant of the GR107 goes through here as well. There's a basic, unremarkable one-star **hotel** – *Puymorens* (Ⓣ05.61.64.23.03; ❷) – plus the preferable *Gîte Hospitalité* (Ⓣ & Ⓕ05.61.05.23.14, Ⓔgitedetape.lhospitalet@libertysurf.fr; closed Nov; double, triples, quads) and a municipal **campsite** (Ⓣ05.61.05.20.04; June–Oct). Heading into the Carlit Massif, the **GR107C** gets you quickly to grips with the mountains, offering the shortest approach from the west as it climbs unusually gently to the dam and the refuge at Bésines, where you link up with the GR10.

Mérens-les-Vals

The reputation of **MÉRENS-LES-VALS** (Merenç-de-las-Vals in Occitan), 10km further north, rests on the stocky **Mérenguais horse**, a breed which – thanks in part to the Niaux cave paintings (see p.231) – is considered the closest thing in Europe to the wild horse of prehistory. Nowadays there are more specimens outside the area than here, but the village remains a point of reference for horse-

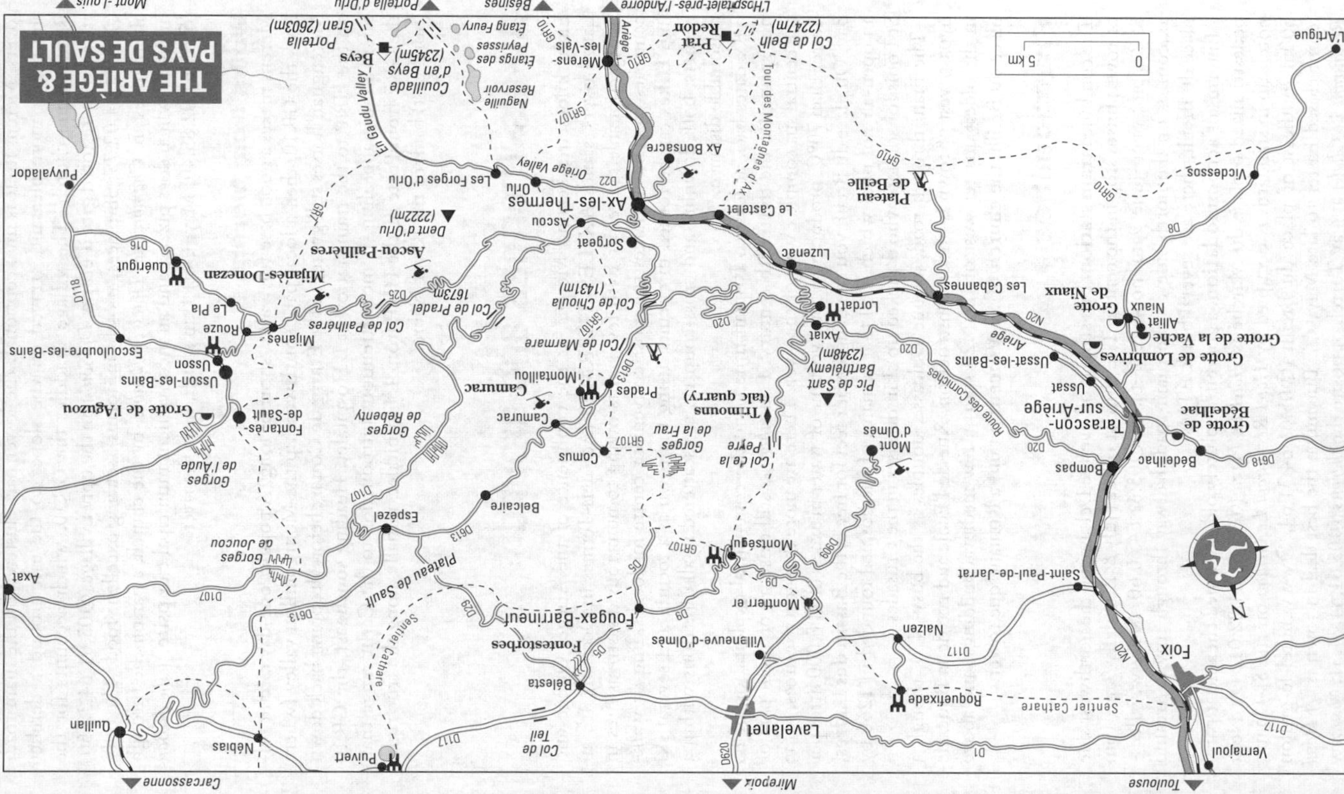
THE ARIÈGE & PAYS DE SAULT
Perpignan
Carcassonne
Mirepoix
Toulouse
St-Girons
St-Girons
Massat
L'Hospitalet-près-l'Andorre
Bésines
Portella d'Orlu
Mont-Louis
Axat
Quillan
Nébias
Puivert
Col de Teil
Lavelanet
Bélesta
Fontestorbes
Fougax-Barrineuf
Plateau de Sault
Sentier Cathare
Villeneuve-d'Olmès
Montferrier
Montségur
Roquefixade
Nalzen
Saint-Paul-de-Jarrat
Foix
Vernajoul
Sentier Cathare
Bédeilhac
Grotte de Bédeilhac
Bompas
Tarascon-sur-Ariège
Ussat
Ussat-les-Bains
Route des Corniches
Grotte de Lombrives
Grotte de la Vache
Alliat
Niaux
Grotte de Niaux
Vicdessos
L'Artigue
Les Cabanes
Plateau de Beille
Lordat
Axiat
Luzenac
Le Castelet
Ax Bonsacre
Tour des Montagnes d'Ax
Col de Belh (2247m)
Prat Redon
Mérens-les-Vals
Ax-les-Thermes
Orlu
Orlu Valley
Les Forges d'Orlu
Naguille Reservoir
Étangs des Peyrisses
Étang Feury
Couillade d'en Beys (2345m)
Beys
Portella Gran (2603m)
En Gaudu Valley
Dent d'Orlu (2222m)
Ascou
Sorgeat
Ascou-Pailhères
Col de Pailhères
Col de Pradel 1673m
Col de Chioula (1431m)
Col de Marmare
Prades
Montaillou
Camurac
Comus
Gorges de la Frau
Col de la Peyre
Trimouns (talc quarry)
Mont d'Olmès
Pic de Sant Barthélemy (2348m)
Belcaire
Espézel
Gorges de Rebenty
Gorges de Joucou
Gorges de l'Aude
Fontanès-de-Sault
Grotte de l'Aguzou
Usson-les-Bains
Usson
Escouloubre-les-Bains
Rouze
Le Pla
Mijanès
Mijanès-Donezan
Quérigut
Puyvalador
Ariège
0 5 km
N
D117
D620
D613
D107
D118
D16
D25
D29
D5
D9
D909
D20
D618
D8
D22
N20
D1
GR10
GR107
GR7

lovers. Mérens itself is unexceptional: the lower part clustered on the main road, the other, more pleasant, arrayed on the slopes to the east around a derelict Romanesque church. The village straddles the GR10, which accounts for the attractively restored **gîte d'étape**, *Du Soula*, in the upper village (Ⓣ05.61.64.32.50, Ⓕ05.61.04.02.75; 38 places, mostly in dorms), serving excellent food. The only alternatives are *Chambres des Hótes Du Nabre*, by the church, a bar on the through highway which does pizzas, and an inconvenient municipal **campsite**, *Ville de Bau* (Ⓣ05.61.02.85.40; May–Oct) 1km south, near the river.

Walks from Mérens

Mérens makes a good base for **walks**, short or long. A popular one-day circuit follows the GR10, then a local path **southwest** up the Mourgouillou valley (where Mérenguais horses still graze) to the **Étang de Couart** before dropping back down on the HRP to the train station at L'Hospitalet. Heading **southeast**, the GR10 offers a more appealing, if more strenuous introduction to the Carlit range than the GR7 from Porté or the HRP from L'Hospitalet, initially along the true right (northeast) bank of the River Nabre.

Ax-les-Thermes and around

Eight kilometres beyond Mérens, at the confluence of the Ariège, Oriège and Lauze rivers, stands **AX-LES-THERMES** (Acs-dels-Tèrmes in Occitan). It's an unobjectionable spa resort with few sights owing to numerous disastrous fires in centuries past, but it makes the most convenient centre for local skiing or walking. **Hikes** can be routed in circuits, using the town as a focum, and several **ski resorts**, both downhill and cross-country, are scattered in all directions within a reasonable distance.

Ax dates back at least to Roman times, and the commercial exploitation of its hot springs to the thirteenth century. Four *thermes* still exist, all of them part of the central spa complex west of the river. There are more than forty sources, some hotter than 70°C, producing a total volume of water in excess of 600,000 litres per day. On place du Breilh you can dangle your feet for free in the **Bassin des Ladres,** an open-air hot pool which is all that remains of the hospital founded in 1260 by St Louis for soldiers who'd picked up skin diseases in the Crusades.

The main through road, avenue Delcassé, doubles as the busy N20, though a bypass west of town is under construction. Rue de l'École and rue de la Boucarie in the oldest quarter west of the N20 sport a few medieval buildings, and above place du Breilh, the **church of St-Vincent** retains a Romanesque tower.

Practicalities

The combined **train station/bus stop** is off avenue Delcassé on the northwest side of town; **buses** stop in the centre. The **tourist office** (July & Aug daily 9am–1pm & 2–7pm; Sept–June 9am–noon & 2–6pm; Ⓣ05.61.64.60.60, Ⓦwww.vallees-ax.com) is on the north side of the main road, halfway through town. Around place du Breilh, there are several **bank** ATMs.

In terms of **accommodation**, a good if resolutely old-fashioned cheapie at part-pedestrianized 6 place du Marché is *Hôtel Le Plaza* (Ⓣ05.61.64.22.01; ❸). Next notch up in standards is occupied by *Hôtel Restaurant Le Grillon* on rue St-Udaut, 300m southeast of place du Breilh (Ⓣ05.61.64.31.64, Ⓦwww.hotel-le-grillon.com; closed Easter to late May; ❸). But much the best deal in town is *Hôtel Restaurant Le Chalet* at 4 av Turrel, opposite the *thermes* (Ⓣ05.61.64.24.31, Ⓦwww

.le-chalet.fr; ❸), managed by a friendly, energetic young couple and thoroughly overhauled in 2006. No two of the airy rooms distributed over two wings are alike, but all have parquet floors and plasma TV, and most have balconies overlooking the river. The municipal **campsite**, *Malazéou* (Ⓣ05.61.64.69.14; closed Nov), is beside the Ariège, 500m downstream from the train station.

Eating out, you'll do best for full meals at *Le Grillon* (€18 weekday menu, otherwise à la carte), or at the riverside diner of *Le Chalet* (*menus* €16–40). However there's more of a buzz to **drinking** at *Le Grand Café*, on avenue Delcassé, and *Brasserie Le Club*, on place Roussel, which occasionally hosts live jazz.

The Oriège valley

Extending east from Ax, the damp, leafy **Oriège valley** allows access to both the Carlit peaks and the **Réserve Nationale d'Orlu**, created south of the road in 1975. Under the shadow of the distinctive Dent d'Orlu, a favourite of technical climbers, the D22 heads up the valley to **ORLU**, where there's camping at the *Municipal* (Ⓣ05.61.64.30.09) and a popular *gîte d'étape* aimed at walkers, the *Relais Montagnard* (Ⓣ05.61.64.61.88; 34 places). A path from **Les Forges d'Orlu** further up the valley permits a link-up with the Tour des Montagnes d'Ax, via a climb from near the power station to the dam at **Naguille**.

At a popular picnic area some 12km from Ax, the asphalt ends and all private cars are banned from further progress along a track which climbs south into the *réserve* through the **En Gaudu valley**, meeting the GR7 below the Étang d'en Beys with its refuge. If you prefer to approach the Carlit via the Oriège, it's worth paying for a taxi to the picnic grounds: the walk is tedious and steep, with little chance of a lift in either direction.

Walking: the Tour des Montagnes d'Ax

The tourist office sells a *topoguide* of 23 short walks out of fifteen local villages; among longer treks, the five-day, four-night **Tour des Montagnes d'Ax** is recommended. You can begin at **Le Castelet**, on the main road 5km northwest of Ax, climbing south for a day to link up with the GR10 at the **Col de Belh** (2247m), near the *Refuge de Rulhe* (described p.212). The route then heads east to cross the Ariège valley at Mérens-les-Vals, your second overnight stop. From there you stick with the GR10, and later the GR7, all the way to the *Refuge d'en Beys* (see p.224), which will be your third night out after a very long day, unless you take the Porteille de Madides shortcut (see p.224) – or you could insert an extra overnight stay at the *Refuge des Bésines* (see p.224), at the junction of the two trails. From this refuge, you've a shorter day up to the gentle Couillade d'en Beys and then on to the Oriège valley floor as described on p.225.

Skiing around Ax-les-Thermes

The nearest ski station to Ax is **AX-TROIS-DOMAINES**, 8km south up the D820; in winter there are ski-bus services from the town to the base station at Bonascre (1400m), or a *télécabine* from Ax. The action begins with another *télécabine* ride up to the beginners' area on **Plateau du Saquet** (2040m), and then a chair-lift to **Tute de l'Ours** (2255m), where serious skiing commences. The snow record is good, there are 70km of pistes (mostly red-rated, some over 3km long) and the top point is 2305m – with the beautiful Andorran frontier peaks as a backdrop.

Three valleys west, the **Plateau de Beille** rivals Font-Romeu for cross-country skiing; 60km of pistes range in length from one to twenty kilometres, at just under 2000m – which should ensure adequate snow. The plateau is reached by a sixteen-kilometre *route forestière* from the village of Les Cabannes, 15km down the main N20 road.

North of Ax on the D613 there's potentially good cross-country skiing to be had around the **Col de Chioula** (1431m), with 60km of trails; be wary of the low altitude, though, and check conditions before setting out. The nearby *Refuge du Chioula* (1600m; ⓣ05.61.64.06.97, ⓦwww.refugeduchioula.free.fr) is open summer also as a stage on the GR107, renting out skis and snowshoes during winter.

A pretty drive 13km east of Ax leads to tiny **ASCOU-PAILHÈRES**, which offers just sixteen downhill runs, totalling 20km, and a top point of 2030m. The closest desirable **accommodation** is about 8km down towards Ax at the *Auberge-Gîte La Forge d'Ascou* (ⓣ05.61.03.67.95; dorms, or doubles ③ B&B), in the eponymous hamlet overlooking the Lac de Goulours.

The Route des Corniches

A scenic alternative to the N20 along the floor of the Ariège valley is the **Route des Corniches** or D20 west from Bestiac, which you can access via the D2 from Luzenac through **UNAC**, which has a superb twelfth-century **church** with an earlier clock tower-belfry, once the seat of a priory. It's particularly recommended for cyclists, who thus avoid the dangerous race-track of the main highway. Just before Bestiac is the side turning for the **talc quarry up at Trimouns** (regular tours mid-May to mid-Oct), one of the world's largest sources of the mineral, though now probably three-quarters exhausted. While it lasts, the raw talc is sent down by cable car to a plant at Luzenac for final processing; the workers conducting the tours are usually immigrants, who also sell semi-precious stones to visitors.

The first village beyond the cable-car lines is **LORDAT**, guarded by an eleventh-century castle of the counts of Foix which was also a Cathar place of refuge. It escaped dismantling during the sixteenth-century Wars of Religion, apparently because it was too big; but even though the perimeter walls and gatehouse are intact, all structures inside have been razed, save for the highest keep. Immediately around this are the caged and chained inmates (owls, vultures, eagles) of the **Château de Lordat** (April–June & Sept–Nov Tues–Sun 2.30–4.30pm; daily July–Aug 10.30am–12.30pm & 2–6pm; €6), who are allowed free flight only in one to three daily spectacles (reliably at 3pm).

Some 2km further stands **AXIAT** and its highly photogenic Romanesque church, with a distinctively chunky bell tower, a double series of arches decorating each face. More sleepy, enjoyable villages succeed each other – one rejoicing in the name of Appy – until the corniche at Bompas, 3km north of Tarascon on the N20.

Tarascon-sur-Ariège and its caves

A small, utilitarian ex-iron-mining centre on river's east bank, **TARASCON-SUR-ARIÈGE** is mainly a base for visiting the unrivalled cluster of **prehistoric caves** nearby, famous for their **Paleolithic paintings and artefacts**. There are four main sites, all accessible in one day with your own transport. Yet the town itself is more rewarding than first impressions suggest, and worth a brief stroll. From the east bank of the Ariège, where riverside cafés provide pleasant vantage points, narrow **rue de Barri** leads up through the old quarter to the church of St-Michel, presiding over a partly arcaded square. Surviving bits of the mostly razed medieval walls include the **Tour Saint-Michel**, and the **Porte d'Espagne** with a fountain inside. From the gate, a short hike past walled orchards up to the **Tour**

du Castella, now a clock tower, is worthwhile for the views over the five valleys that converge here.

Practicalities

The combined **train station/bus stop** is a few minutes' walk north from the centre, on the west bank of the Ariège. The **tourist office** is also just west of the bridge in the unmissable Centre Multimédia François Mitterrand (Mon–Sat 9am–1pm & 2–6pm, also Sun 9.30am–1pm peak summer/ski season; Ⓣ05.61.05.94.94, Ⓦwww.paysdetarascon.com).

One quiet and attractive central **hotel** is the *Confort* on riverside quai Armand-Sylvestre (Ⓣ & Ⓕ05.61.05.61.90; closed Jan; ❷), with some rooms facing a courtyard. For rooms facing the river and a cosy fireside lounge, try *Hostellerie de la Poste*, (Ⓣ05.61.05.60.41, Ⓦwww.hostellerieposte.com; all year; ❷), three doors down from the **post office** on the main street, very close to the free **central car park**. This hotel also has the best **restaurant** (closed Nov 15–Dec 15) in town, with summer seating facing a lawn-garden and four *menus* (including one vegetarian) at €14–35; a mid-range one features *auzinat*, a rich hotpot of cabbage, potato, sausage and game. There's also a **campsite**, *Pré Lombard* (Ⓣ05.61.05.61.94), on the left bank of the river, ten minutes' walk upstream from the bridge.

The caves

The high concentration of **caves** here is due to the abundant local limestone, a rock ideally suited to the millennial work of seeping water that creates caverns. What served as shelters and places of ritual for early humans later came in handy as hideouts for religious dissidents during the Christian era.

Grotte de Niaux

Unquestionably the finest of the Pyrenean prehistoric caves is the **Grotte de Niaux**, 2km southwest of Tarascon, which can only be viewed on a twenty-person, 45-minute guided tour (daily: July & Aug 9.15am–5.30pm, English tours at 9.30am & 1pm; Sept 10am–5.30pm, tour at 1pm; Oct–June Tues–Sun tours at 11am, 2.30pm & 4pm; €9.40; reservations mandatory; Ⓣ05.61.05.88.37, Ⓦwww.sesta.org).

The 1968-bored artificial entrance to Niaux is near the low and narrow natural opening under an enormous rock overhang. Using flashlights for illumination, you penetrate 900m (from a total 4km of galleries) to see some of the famous black outlines of horse and bison, minimally shaded yet capturing every nuance. Studies have shown that these drawings, and those of ibex and stag in the recess further back, were produced around 10,800 BC with a "crayon" made of bison fat and manganese oxide. A line of footprints left by the young artists can be seen in a part of the cave that was opened up in 1970, while primitive graffiti are represented by dots and bunches of lines on the wall of the main cavity.

NIAUX village itself, between the cave and Tarascon, has a small, private **Musée Pyrénéen** (July & Aug daily 9am–8pm; Sept–June 10am–noon & 2–6pm; €8), which displays tools, furnishings and archival photos illustrating the vanished traditions of the Ariège. Exhibits also explain local Pyrenean architecture, specifically its use of *lauzes* (stone slabs), *ardoise* (slate) and occasionally *chaume* (thatch) for roofing.

Grotte de la Vache

The **Grotte de la Vache** at Alliat (90min guided tours: April, May, June, Sept & school hols 2.30–4pm; July & Aug daily 10am–5.30pm; otherwise by arrangement; Ⓣ05.61.05.95.06 or Ⓦwww.grotte-de-la-vache.org; €9) is well worth the

Cave art

The **painted caves** of the Pyrenees were created by (semi-) nomadic communities of Ice Age hunters during the Late Paleolithic period, 27,000 to 10,000 years ago. Pyrenean cave art marvellously conjures shape and movement from **minimal line and colour**, often exploiting the very **contours of the rock**. Niaux contains an excellent example of such artistic opportunism: a bison carved on the clay floor around holes caused by dripping water, which now function as an eye and wound marks. Early artists were, in effect, "helping" pre-existing animals to emerge from the rock. Besides the **Tarascon group**, the major Pyrenean cave is **Gargas**, with its array of hand prints, many with apparently missing fingers (see p.315).

Various theories, none definitive, have been expounded as to the purpose and origin of cave-painting. According to pioneering French paleo-anthropologist **Abbé Breuil** (1877–1961), the "Pope of Prehistory," this art served a **magical function**, ensuring "that the game should be plentiful and that sufficient should be killed". The frequent appearance of ibex, wild boar, reindeer and bison images makes this notion initially attractive, but animal remains found in the caves indicate that the species depicted were not the main food supply. Moreover, while about fifteen percent of the animals are shown wounded by arrows, the rest are not.

André Leroi-Gourhan (1911–86) and **Annette Laming-Emperaire** (1917–77) maintained that cave art was arranged in a **predictable layout**, much like the decorative schemes of frescoed Christian churches. Their surveys of 62 caves revealed that hand outlines occurred only at the entrance to caves or in the centre, and that mammoths and bison were confined to the centre. They suggested a **sexual polarity**, with bison symbolizing the female element and horses the male. Others have argued that the weak illumination available – grease and a wick, or wooden torches – would not have allowed cave denizens to see cave decorations as a unity. Nevertheless, there seemed to be some **pattern**: bison and horses, for example, are thirty times more likely to occur in cave centres than are deer.

The first cogent attempt at refuting these early theories was published in 1996 by **Jean Clottes**, a French prehistorian and cave-art expert, and **David Lewis-Williams**, a South African archeologist specializing in the art and beliefs of the Kalahari Bushmen, one of the last surviving hunter-gatherer societies, strongly reminiscent of European Paleolithic culture. Their *Les Chamanes de la Préhistoire* (Éditions Seuil) hypothesized that many of the images were created by **shamans** in a trance or other altered state, and that "the paintings and engravings do not represent real animals hunted for food in an actual landscape; rather they are visions drawn from the subterranean world of spirits because of their supernatural powers and ability to help the shamans."

In 2006 **R. Dale Guthrie**, a specialist in paleozoology, entered the fray with *The Nature of Paleolithic Art* (U of Chicago Press). Rejecting the notion that cave art formed part of any ritual schema, he established that most of the handprints were not of mutilated anatomies, but those of adolescent boys too young to hunt. They were responsible for much of the cruder, unfinished animal outlines, the graffiti-like sequences of dots, dashes and arrows, as well as doodles of female human genitalia – exactly what young males would be obsessed with. Older male hunters executed the more masterful pictures purely for fun, and to celebrate the beauty of their prey. Historian **William McNeill**, in a response to Guthrie, suggested that the best, unwounded animal portraits were meant to serve as symbolic, placatory homes for the spirits of slain beasts – an animistic, rather than organized-religious theory.

Paleolithic art will undoubtedly continue to stimulate polemics. Similarities between image style and subject in widely separated caves suggests some coherent "school" of artistic development – even if just the effect of teenage hormones, assuming Guthrie is at least partly correct – or simply the universality of animism in early human experience.

short journey across the valley from Niaux. Excavations have revealed remains of ten millennia of habitation (including hearths) from 12,500 BC to the Bronze Age. Around 30,000 flint fragments were unearthed here, plus over 6,000 complete tools, mainly for embossing bones; some pieces are displayed in the cave.

Grotte de Bédeilhac

To reach the **Grotte de Bédeilhac** (same tour length and schedule as de la Vache, plus every Sun at 3pm; ⓣ05.61.05.95.06, ⓦwww.grotte-de-bedeilhac.org; €8) above the eponymous village, you have to return to Tarascon and cover 5km along the D618 towards Saurat. This cave, a hollow in the ridge of Soudour, contains examples of every known technique of Paleolithic art, including polychrome painting (now faded to monochrome). The imposing entrance yawns 35m wide by 20m high, making it easy for the Germans to adapt the cavern as an aircraft hangar during World War II. Although the art inside is not as immediately powerful as at Niaux, its diversity – including modelled stalagmites and mud reliefs of beasts as well as painting – compensates.

In the village below, you can **stay** at the *Relais d'Étape* (ⓣ05.61.05.15.56; ❷) and **eat** at the adjacent *Auberge de la Grotte*, on the through road next to the *mairie* and the post office.

Grotte de Lombrives

The **Grotte de Lombrives** (hopelessly complicated schedule viewable on ⓦwww.cathares.org/lombrives.html; ⓣ05.61.05.98.40; €1.50–7 depending on tour chosen), 3km south of Tarascon along the N20, near Ussat-les-Bains, may disappoint if you've already seen Niaux, Vache and Bédeilhac. Access by underground train (€1.50 extra) gives it the atmosphere of an amusement park – as do the *spectacles* regularly staged here – but the stalagmite formations are superb, and the sheer size of the complex is impressive. It is, in fact, the largest cavern in western Europe open to tourists, and would take five days' walking to see entirely. Groups can arrange three- or five-hour walks (€17 & €35 respectively) around the cave, daily in July and August, Wednesday, Saturday or Sunday otherwise.

Lombrives was inhabited around 4000 BC, but all finds now rest in museums elsewhere. Its later history is embellished by utterly spurious legends of Cathars walled up inside in 1328, and of 250 soldiers subsequently disappearing without trace, victims of troglodytic bandits.

Foix

FOIX, 16km downstream from Tarascon, is the smallest *départmental* capital in France, and the most agreeable base in the valley if you don't mind catching a train or bus to get into the mountains. A nonindustrial livelihood based on bureaucracy and tourism has helped Foix preserve its old town of narrow alleys in the triangle between the Ariège and the Arget rivers, where some overhanging houses date from the fourteenth to sixteenth centuries; especially attractive are place Pyrène and place Saint-Vincent with their fountains, though many junctions in the old town sport some sort of water-quirk.

Arrival, information and accommodation

The **train and bus stations** are together on avenue de la Gare, off the N20 on the right bank of the Ariège, though a few short-haul bus services call at the car parks on cours Gabriel-Fauré. **Car rental** can be arranged though ADA, 59 av du Général Leclerc (ⓣ05.61.68.38.38), Europcar, Route d'Espagne (ⓣ05.61.02.32.74), or Hertz, RN20 Peysales (ⓣ05.61.65.15.99). The **tourist office** is on rue Théophile-Delcasse (July & Aug Mon–Sat 9am–7pm, Sun 10am–noon & 2–6pm; Sept–June Mon–Sat 9am–noon & 2–6pm; ⓣ05.61.65.12.12, ⓦwww.ot-foix.fr).

Most **accommodation** is in the old town, on the west bank of the Ariège, though little of it is inspiring. The quietest and most comfortable option is three-star *Hôtel Lons*, at 6 place Duthil, near the Pont-Vieux (ⓣ05.61.65.52.44, ⓔhotel-lons-foix@wanadoo.fr; ❸; closed late Dec to early Jan), with a respected restaurant. The *Eychenne* at 11 rue Noël-Peyrevidal (ⓣ05.61.65.00.04; ⓕ05.61.65.56.63; ❸) has been upgraded to fully en-suite status, with a busy ground-floor café (but no restaurant). Opposite at no. 16, the *Auberge Léo Lagrange* (ⓣ05.61.65.09.04, ⓔleolagrange-foix@wanadoo.fr) offers hostel-style accommodation (72 bunks in doubles or quads), plus economical weekday lunches in its downstairs *foyer*. *L'Echauguette* at 1 rue Paul Laffont (ⓣ05.61.2.88.88, ⓕ05.61.65.29.49; ❷) is another mid-range option, though noisier than other choices. The municipal **campsite,** *Lac de Labarre* (ⓣ05.61.65.11.58; all year), is 3km down the N20 towards Toulouse.

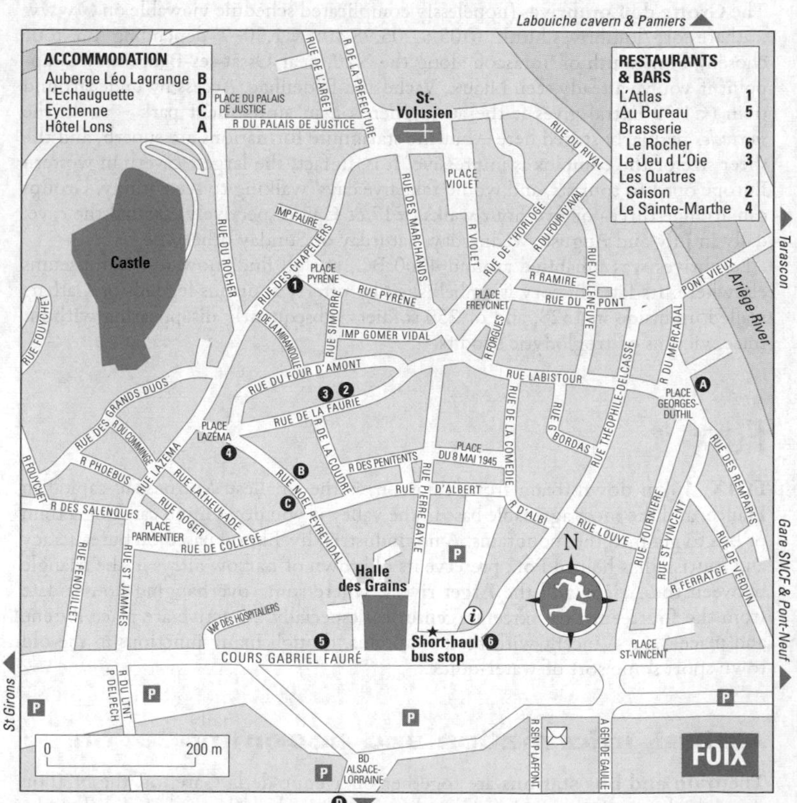

△ Foix town and castle

The Town

All the old town's lanes seem to lead eventually to the conspicuously large church of **Saint-Volusien** in the north of the old town, originally Romanesque but almost completely reconstructed after being razed during the Wars of Religion. Its eponymous square, along with the Halles aux Grains just off cours Gabriel-Fauré, hosts lively Wednesday and Friday **markets**: produce and plants are sold at place

Saint-Volusien, but meat, cheese, savouries and pastries at the metal-roofed *halles*, which serves as a prime drinking venue other days.

Presiding over everything is the hilltop **Château des Comtes de Foix** (May, June & Sept daily 9.45am–noon & 2–6pm; July & Aug daily 9.30am–6.30pm; Oct–April Wed–Sun 10.30am–noon & 2–5.30pm; €4.20), not so much a single fortification as three magnificent, dissimilar towers from different eras, dramatic when viewed from any angle. The best part of a castle-visit is clambering up worn stairs in the southern and central towers for startling views across the valley. The interior, by contrast, houses a determinedly dull handful of themed exhibits on medieval history, society and crafts.

From 1012, this castle was the seat of the counts of Foix, whose association with the Cathar faith led to its being besieged unsuccessfully four times by Simon de Montfort (though he did capture the town in 1211). Count Roger-Bernard II – known as *Le Grand* – was a determined opponent of the anti-Cathar crusade, but made his most lasting contribution to history by marrying Ermensende of Castellbò early in the thirteenth century, thereby linking the fortunes of Foix and Andorra (see p.202). In 1290 the counts married into the house of Béarn and transferred their court to Orthex a few decades later; that dynasty ended illustri-

Gaston Fébus

Across the central Pyrenees, you'll encounter the name of local hero **Gaston Fébus** (or Phébus), Count of Foix and Viscount of Béarn. Although ultimately frustrated in his plans, he is still celebrated for his struggle towards regional independence and his character, which epitomized the chivalric ideals of the Middle Ages – as well as for his invention of *hypocras*, a spiced-wine drink still enjoyed around Foix. Poet, soldier and provincial aristocrat, Gaston was born in 1331 and died sixty years later, but it is difficult to disentangle verified events of his life from the myths – many self-promoted – that sprung up around him. The troubadour poets acknowledged him as a friend and embellished his deeds in their lyrics, while Jean Froissart – chronicler of the Hundred Years' War – was invited by Fébus to write his biography. Gaston was a poet himself and the author of a book on hunting – an example of many "self-help" books for image-conscious nobles of the era. His surname, Fébus, was his own invention, derived from the Occitan for sun and celebrating his long, golden hair. Although an autocratic ruler, who abolished the legislative councils of town-dwellers and set himself up as the highest judicial authority in his realms, he cultivated a reputation as a fair-minded and dauntless soldier, always leading his men into battle with the cry *Fébus avan* (Fébus at the front).

His great ambition was to create an autonomous kingdom of the Pyrenees, adding by conquest the regions of Bigorre and Soule to his inherited domains of Nébouzan (around Saint-Gaudens), Béarn and Foix. This goal was made impossible by the continuing Hundred Years' War, which divided the loyalties of his subjects; Gascony on the west was ruled by the English Crown – in particular the Black Prince (in direct control 1362–71), while to the east lay Languedoc, subject to France. In addition, feuding between the leading families of the area kept him occupied; one of his most significant victories came in 1362, when he crushed his Gascon arch-enemies, the English-allied Armagnacs. In time he lost the appetite to pursue his grand plan, by most accounts after 1380, when it seems Fébus that killed his only son on discovering the son's role in a plot to assassinate him.

Thereafter, determined that his enemies should not succeed where he apparently had failed, Fébus dedicated himself to campaigning for a strong, united France, pledging his lands to the French Crown by inheritance. Yet this was not to happen until 1589, with the accession to the Parisian throne of Henri III of Foix-Béarn and Navarre, a descendant of Fébus' fierce rivals, the d'Albrets.

ously with Henri III of Foix-Béarn and Navarre, who annexed what had become a Pyrenean mini-state to the Crown when he became Henri IV of France. But the biggest name in Foix is that of the fair-haired knight Gaston III, known as Gaston Fébus (see box opposite).

Eating and drinking

A prime area for **eating** is rue de la Faurie, the old blacksmiths' bazaar at the heart of the old town, still home to crafts and antique shops. At no. 17, *Le Jeu de l'Oie* does classic French country-bistro fare – *cassoulet*, duck dishes, *terrines*, offal, good desserts – at friendly prices (*formules* from under €10), which guarantees a lunch-time crush – though service doesn't suffer unduly. Also popular is *Les Quatres Saisons* at no. 11 (*menus* from €13.50–16; closed Sun–Thurs eve low season), whose speciality is *pierrade* – fish and meat grilled on hot ceramic plates at your table. A pricier but worthwhile option is *Le Sainte-Marthe*, at 21 rue Noël-Peyrevidal (Ⓣ05.61.02.87.87; closed Wed off-season, Tues eve & part Feb), with a street-side terrace and a range of specialities, including *cassoulet* (*menus* €23–34). *L'Atlas* on place Pyrène (closed Mon) serves up authentic if expensive Moroccan cuisine (€19–28).

Either side of the Halle aux Grains on cours Gabriel-Fauré are a few café-brasseries which occasionally double as **music-bars**. *Brasserie Le Rocher* and *Pub Au Bureau* are two to try here.

West of Foix: Labouiche and the road to Saint-Girons

Some 6km along the Vernajoul road northwest from the centre of Foix lies the subterranean **river-cavern of Labouiche** (April–June & Sept daily 10–11.15am & 2–5.15pm; July & Aug daily 9.30am–5.15pm; Oct–Nov 11 weekends/hols 10am–11.15 & 2–4.30pm, expect a 15 min wait; €7.50), which claims to be the longest navigable subterranean stream in western Europe. It appears never to have been inhabited, and indeed high water levels in winter completely block access. The amusement-park atmosphere of Lombrives (see p.233) prevails here also: twelve-person boats give 75-minute rides along the 1500m of galleries open to the public. Highlights are the waterfall and a small chamber full of formations, both at the upstream end of the river. These and other curiosities are described by guides who do their best to keep up a witty patter while hauling the craft along using ceiling-mounted cables.

The D117 main road west from Foix climbs rapidly to the **Col de Bouich** (599m) before descending through the Aujole and Baup valleys to arrive at Saint-Girons and Saint-Lizier (see p.301). There's little to detain you en route, although you might stop at **La Bastide de Serou**, just under halfway, for a drink in the square outside its old market building.

Two unusual English-run **chambres d'hôtes** along the D117 are best suited for those with transport. At **RIMONT**, 34km from Foix, excellent accommodation is offered at *Le Guerrat*, a working organic farm (open mid-May to mid-Oct; Ⓣ05.61.96.37.03, Ⓔleguerrat@aol.com; ❷), with strict vegan meals available. At **LESCURE**, 4km further on, hilltop *La Baquette* (Ⓣ & Ⓕ05.61.96.37.67; April to mid-Oct ❷) can arrange guided walks and tours of the local wildlife and flora. Heading south from La Bastide de Serou towards Massat, you'll find one of the better **hotels** in this area at the **Col des Marrous** (also accessible by a minor road 18km direct from Foix): *Auberge les Myrtilles* (Ⓣ05.61.65.16.46; ❹; closed Nov–Jan & Mon, also Tues–Wed low season) a rustically decorated hotel with amenities such as an indoor pool and Jacuzzi, as well as a fine country restaurant (*menus* €16–24).

The Pays de Sault

If you haven't got a car or a bike, the magnificent **Pays de Sault** – the upland area bounded by the Aude, the Ariège and the main road from Quillan to Foix – can be crossed in a few days on foot, making occasional use of sporadic public transport. A network of **walking itineraries** – especially the Tour du Pays de Sault and the GR107 – provide ways of exploring. The most famous route is the **Sentier Cathare**, which begins at Foix and arrives at Montségur in two stages via **Roquefixade**, then continues to the Mediterranean; it's easy walking much of the year (though avoid midwinter and midsummer), with strategically placed accommodation in *gîtes d'étape*.

Regular **bus services** cross the Pays de Sault: one links the train station in Quillan with the one in Foix, via **Puivert** and **Lavelanet**, 10km north of Montségur; the other runs from Quillan via Belcaire and Camurac to **Comus**, 12km southeast, from where Montségur can be reached through the Gorges de la Frau. Because departures are slightly more frequent from the east, the two routes described below approach the area from Quillan.

Much of the Pays de Sault is a spacious agricultural plateau, famous for its potatoes, but it contains more vertiginous terrain, too. At the southeast edge, the dramatic D107 road from Axat to Ax-les-Thermes runs through the **Gorges de Rebenty** and over the **Col du Pradel** (1673m), a tough but wonderful cycling route. Further west beyond the heart of the Sault looms the clifftop castle of **Montségur**, the greatest stronghold of the Cathars.

The sprawling highlands are composed primarily of limestone, and thus riddled with caves and ravines such as the spectacular **Gorges de la Frau**. Above ground, agriculture has changed little since Cathar times; pesticides have yet to infiltrate the region's ecosystem, so the silhouettes of birds of prey are fixtures in the sky.

Neither of the region's downhill **ski stations** is worth much effort. **Les Monts d'Olmes** resort, southwest of Montségur, is focused on a seedy apartment development at the base of twenty runs which, though north-facing, barely reach 2000m elevation. **Camurac**, due north of Ax-les-Thermes along the D613 near Camurac village, is even dinkier and lower (1800m), failing to operate in many years.

Puivert

Although it's just a twenty-minute drive out of Quillan, the countryside around **PUIVERT** feels quite different, a vast upland planted with corn and sunflowers, buzzed by amateur pilots using the small airport near the middle. The village itself offers only a **gîte d'étape** *Le Relais des Marionnettes* (Ⓣ04.68.20.80.69; 22 places); less than a kilometre south of the village is a small lake with a **campsite** (Ⓣ04.68.20.00.58; May–Sept) and swimming area (daily except Mon), a welcome sight whether you've been cycling, driving or hiking.

The **Musée du Quercorb** in the centre (daily: April 3–July 14 & Sept 10am–12.30pm & 2–6pm; July 15–Aug 31 10am–7pm; Oct 2–5pm; €4), with its small crafts exhibition and eight casts of the original musician reliefs from Puivert's château – each sculpted in the form of a figure playing a different period instrument – is paltry compensation for the fact that the **castle** itself, standing like a cardboard cut-out atop a gently rounded hill about 1km east of the village, is now sadly closed to the public.

The northern approach to Montségur

From Puivert the D117 heads west over the Col de Teil, the divide between the Aude and the Ariège, and the Pyrenean watershed: east of it, rivers flow to the Mediterranean, while on the west they empty into the Atlantic. You can walk from Puivert to Montségur along the **Sentier Cathare**, a long but not difficult day of some 25km, mostly through dense fir forests.

The next stop on the bus route is 11km west of Puivert at pleasant **BÉLESTA**; if you get stranded there are shops, a bank and **accommodation** at *Le Troubador* (ⓣ05.61.01.60.57; ❷) on the through road near the main *place*, erratically open but with good food at its restaurant, and **camping** on the east side of the village at *Le Val d'Amour* (June–Sept).

Attractions begin almost immediately south: some 1500m out of Bélesta, the D5 toward Montségur passes **Fontestorbes**, a rare intermittent spring (*source intermittente*) under a rock overhang. For most of the year this spring flows constantly, but during the three to five driest months, it adopts a schedule of between 30 and 45 minutes of flow, alternating with 30 to 45 minutes of quiescence.

The D5 continues through the double village of **FOUGAX-ET-BARRINEUF**, 2km southwest, which has excellent **accommodation** in *chambres d'hôtes* opposite the post office: English/Canadian-run *Tindleys* (ⓣ05.61.01.34.87, ⓦwww.tindleys.com; ❸ B&B), with three restored rooms, a copious breakfast and supper on request. There's also a decent independent **restaurant**, *Les Cinque Fours* (open May–Sept); portions aren't huge, but the *menu* is quite adequate as a four-course lunch. The building was once a **bone-comb** factory, formerly an important local industry, established by Protestants between the sixteenth and eighteenth centuries; the last local bone-crafts workshop is discreetly signed José da Fonseca, on the highway between Bélesta and L'Aigullon.

LAVELANET, 8km west of Bélesta on the D117, has little to offer other than onward bus connections and its **tourist office** on the central roundabout (July & Aug Mon–Sat 9am–noon & 2–7pm, Sun 9am–noon; Sept–June Mon–Sat 9am–noon & 2–7pm; ⓣ05.61.01.22.20).

The southern approach to Montségur

From Monday to Friday there are two late-afternoon buses from Quillan to Comus, some 40km southwest. The only **hotel** in the region is at **BELCAIRE**, at the top corner of the Plateau de Sault: the roadside *Bayle* (ⓣ04.68.20.31.05; ❷), with a garden and restaurant. **CAMURAC** 6km beyond, with **accommodation** at central *Gîte La Marmite* (ⓣ04.68.20.73.31) and a **campsite**, *Les Sapins* (ⓣ04.68.20.38.11; summer only), is equidistant (2.5km) from either Montaillou or Comus.

MONTAILLOU (Montelhó in Occitan), defended by a tiny, now ruinous **castle**, subscribed to the Cathar heresy long after the fall of Montségur, until the Inquisition, directed by the bishop of Pamiers, arrived here in 1308 and again in 1320–24. The inquisitors' records were so precise that Emmanuel Le Roy Ladurie, in his classic work *Montaillou*, and René Weis in his later *The Yellow Cross*, were able to re-create every aspect of the villagers' lives. While there are growing numbers of new and restored summer homes, fewer than twenty people live here permanently now, all of them descendants of the Cathars, as you can see by comparing their surnames with those on the headstones in the ancient graveyard.

COMUS isn't much bigger than Montaillou, but it does have an excellent **gîte d'étape**, the *Gîtes et Loisirs de Montagne* (ⓣ04.68.20.33.69, ⓦwww.gites-comus.com; 38 places, mostly quads, some doubles ❶), in the former school at the village centre, with supper served in the attic diner. Montségur is 13km away, through

The Cathars

Catharism was essentially a form of **Manicheism**, a dualistic Middle Eastern doctrine condemning the material world as an eclipse of the world of Light by the powers of Darkness. It was first espoused in Europe among the tenth-century Bogomils of the Balkans, who – following long persecution – mostly converted to Islam under the Ottomans. By the twelfth century a version of this belief, introduced by returning Crusaders as well as refugee Bogomils, had taken root in southern France, especially around Albi where the first disputation between these dualists and the Church took place in 1165 – hence the alias of **Albigeois** (or Albigenses) for the Cathars. In the Pyrenees, the sect was especially strong in the Fenouillèdes, Aude, Donezan and Ariège regions.

According to Cathar thinking, God reigned over the spiritual world and the Devil created the material world; Christ was God's messenger, an apparently physical manifestation of paradise, into which souls could attain release rather than being reincarnated repeatedly. In line with their **antimaterialism**, the most ardent believers shunned milk and meat (though they ate fish), and considered procreation evil. Cathars relied heavily on the Gospel of John and the Lord's Prayer, but denied the doctrine of the Virgin Birth, transubstantiation, infant baptism (converts had to be at least 12 – preferably 18 – years old) and the mystery of Christ's mixed human and divine nature, while insisting that Catholics, in worshipping any Creator of matter, were actually revering the Devil. Asceticism was seen as the only route to redemption, so believers had no need for the Church's sumptuous buildings or trappings. They were initially **pacifists**, and condemned the Crusades, an important method of increasing papal and aristocratic fortunes. Moreover, the austere spirituality of Cathar leaders – the *parfaits* and *parfaites* (also known as *bons hommes* and *bonnes femmes*) – was a constant rebuke to the dissolute clergy of the Church, as was their meeting the spiritual needs of common folk habitually ignored by Catholic institutions. Moreover, Cathar conviction that they were exempt from feudal allegiances made the sect attractive to a nascent town-dwelling bourgeoisie – and anathema to distant, centralizing powers.

Upon assuming the papacy in 1198, Innocent III spent a decade trying peacefully to convince the heretical clergy to recant. His patience exhausted, he formally declared a crusade in 1208, persuading the previously reluctant Parisian king Philippe Auguste, to provide troops. Ranged against the papal forces (including the local bishops) were the *seigneurs* of Languedoc, many of whose subjects had become adherents of Catharism. The first target was **Raymond VI of Toulouse**, excommunicated by Innocent in 1207 for his tacit approval of Catharism (and employment of Jews). Early the following year Raymond got papal legate Pierre de Castelnau to lift the excommunication, but the next day the legate was murdered by a never-identified assailant, providing Raymond's enemies with a pretext for action.

In July 1209 an army led by the archbishop of Narbonne **Arnaud Amaury** invaded Languedoc with the aid of English mercenaries. Béziers was besieged, taken suprisingly quickly and its entire population of 20,000 massacred for refusing to surrender a score of Cathars in their midst. When asked how to distinguish Catholic citizens from heretics, Amaury supposedly replied: "Kill them all, God will recognize His own." Apocryphal utterance or not, this effectively became the motto of a campaign distinguished even by medieval standards for its brutality. After stiffer resistance, Carcassonne fell, soon handed over – like Béziers – to professional Anglo-Norman crusader **Simon de Montfort**. For a few years Raymond VI played a double game to survive and have his excommunication finally revoked, even occasionally marching with the crusaders. But by 1213 the inexorable de Montfort, terrorizing the popula-

the **Gorges de la Frau**, which begins 3.5km down a signed lane between fields, part of the GR107 (formerly the GR7B). The lane becomes rough, steep track as the initially broad gorge narrows to a defile carved out by the river Hers, where

tion with his atrocities and having crushed a Cathar army at Muret, controlled most of Languedoc, forcing Raymond VI and his son to flee to the English court of King John. When the two Raymonds returned in 1216, they confronted de Montfort at the siege of Toulouse, where the latter finally was killed in June 1218.

This respite was fairly short-lived; although Raymond VII regained lost territory after succeeding his father in 1222, a scorched-earth campaign unleashed in 1226 by fanatical Parisian king **Louis VIII** forced Raymond VII to sue for peace in 1229. Though remaining count of Tolouse, he had to submit to public humiliations, the razing of the city walls of Toulouse, extensive territorial losses, indemnities to the Catholic Church and the marriage of his only daughter to the younger brother of the new Parisian king, underage Louis IX. Raymond, who died in 1249, was never again able to provide the Cathar community with significant protection; indeed in order to prove his sincere recantation and stave off repeated excommunication attempts, Raymond voluntarily denounced and burnt heretics.

After the first wave of crusades, the Cathar heresy was still far from eradicated, especially in the Pyrenean foothills. In 1233 the new pope Gregory IX authorized the creation of the infamous **Inquisition**, supervised by Dominican and Franciscan monks. The Dominicans had been founded in 1206 by Domingo de Guzmán (later **St Dominic**), a Castilian proselytizer who came specially to the Cathar heartland to combat the heresy. His preferred strategies were strenuous disputations with Cathar theologians, imitation of their austere habits and the founding of a convent for Cathar women who recanted their beliefs. But the inquisitors of the late 1230s who visited Languedoc employed the harsher methods for which they became notorious, provoking such resistance that the pope temporarily suspended their activities in 1237.

Inquisitorial convictions, imprisonment, burnings at the stake and confiscation of the property of sympathizers resumed in 1240, and the Cathars still at liberty reacted in a manner which sealed their doom. In May 1242 85 knights from Montségur, led by **Pierre-Roger de Mirepoix**, hacked the eleven chief inquisitors to death as they slept in Avignonet. The retaliatory assault on Montségur, by a force of almost ten thousand men, began in May 1243, and continued through the winter. On March 2, 1244, de Mirepoix, despairing of relief, agreed terms: non-Cathar soldiers within the citadel could leave unmolested, but after two weeks' truce the Cathars themselves were to abjure their faith or submit to immolation. One night before March 16, in contravention of the terms, four Cathars climbed down the cliffs, escaped over the Col de la Peyre, recovered the Cathar "treasure" from a cave and then vanished. (Recent crackpot theories, from Nazi to New Age, indentified this treasure as the Holy Grail, and the Cathars themselves as proto-Aryan pagans untainted by Mosaic Law, their castles ingenious solar temples.) The next day Montségur surrendered, and the 225 surviving Cathar civilians who refused to recant were burned on a mass pyre.

Catharism ceased to exist as a significant force in France after the holocaust at Montségur, though two of the four escapees later appeared in Lombardy, where proceeds from the "treasure" supported a refugee Cathar community there. When Raymond VII's daughter died childless in 1271, all of Languedoc passed to the French Crown. From then on, Catharism persisted mainly as an underground network, with safe houses and escape routes extending across the mountains into Aragón and Spanish Catalunya, where it was more openly practised until the Inquisition arrived there during the fifteenth century. The last significant Cathar *parfait*, Guilhem Bélibaste, was executed in 1321, lured into a trap by an undercover agent, while the last Lombard *bons hommes* were unmasked by the Inquisition in 1412.

thousand-metre cliffs admit sun only at midday. The canyon bottom is densely wooded with beech, ash, cornelian and fir, though it is in fact a major pastoral-migratory route; each mid-October hundreds of cattle who've summered on the

Sault plateau are driven down en masse one fine dawn. The gorge widens again as you meet the D5 coming south from Fougax-et-Barrineuf, just below Pelail hamlet. Continue west to Montségur along the Sentier Cathare from near Pelail, for a total walking time from Comus of four hours.

△ Montségur village and castle

Montségur

The ruined castle of **MONTSÉGUR** lives up to the promise of its distant view, its plain stone walls poised emphatically above the straggling, eponymous village on a 1207-metre-high *pog* (from the Occitan *puèg*, "peak"). The original fortifications were built by Guillaume "Short-Nose", duke of Aquitaine, but between 1204 and 1232 it was reconstructed as a bastion of the Cathars under the direction of Guilhabert de Castres, leader of the sect. Drastically eroded into naked vertical faces and gullies, the *pog* would have been a formidable defence. Only on the southern side can you walk up to the summit (about 30min) through the *prat dels cremats* where the surviving Cathars were burned alive after the castle fell (a stone memorial pays tribute to them); see box on p.240–244.

The natural beauty of **the site** (daily: Feb 10.30am–4pm; March 10am–5pm; April, Sept & Oct 9.30am–6pm; May–Aug 9am–7.30pm; Nov 10am–5.30pm; Dec 10.30am–4.30pm; €4) impresses you first, since the original walls were reduced by half after the siege, and all internal structures are gone except the simple keep, now open to the sky. Then you begin to wonder how that last Cathar community of five hundred could have held out so long in such a small area. Although some lived in now-vanished houses at the foot of the walls on the north and west faces, there was still a sizeable garrison here, together with local aristocrats dispossessed by the crusade against Catharism. What's left of it takes no more than a few minutes to view – disappointingly, you're no longer allowed to climb up on the walls, merely to traverse the keep to visit the west *donjon*. But it's not so much what you see at Montségur that makes the trip unforgettable, as what you re-imagine from its remnants.

Down in the village, 1km below, a one-room **museum** (daily: May–Sept 10am–noon & 2–7pm, Oct–April 2–5pm; free) displays artefacts excavated at the original village up beside the walls, from both pre- and post-Cathar periods – mostly food bones, personal effects, tools and surviving fragments of houses.

Practicalities

Despite its small size, Montségur village has a seasonal **tourist office** (July–Sept daily 10am–1pm & 2–6pm; ⓣ05.61.03.03.03, ⓦwww.citaenet.com/montsegur), of most use for information on the GR107; check also the local *topoguide*, which they occasionally stock. Several **accommodation** options fill quickly in (and out of) season; least expensive is the old-fashioned, partly en-suite *Hôtel Café Couquet* (ⓣ05.61.01.10.28; ❷), a rambling *pension* fronted by pollarded lime trees and with an unsigned restaurant on the first floor (three-course *table d'hôte* supper with wine €15). An even homelier option is *Maison d'Hôtes L'Oustal* at the north end of the village (ⓣ05.61.02.80.70, ⓔserge.germa@wanadoo.fr; ❷), where extroverted hosts Serge and Annick lay on a superb, four-course supper (€16); the four rooms, mostly triples/quads, share baths but there are extensive common areas. The fancier *Costes* (ⓣ05.61.01.10.24; closed mid-Nov to April; ❹) also manages a **gîte d'étape**.

Roquefixade

Approximately 7km west of Lavelanet on the D117, the minor side road D9a gives the most direct access to **ROQUEFIXADE**, the westernmost Cathar castle and last stop on the Sentier Cathare before Foix. A two-kilometre journey leads up to the village of Roquefixade, rebuilt after the Cathar crusades as a *bastide*. From the high end of the village it's a twenty-minute climb to the eleventh-century castle (free), which takes its name (originally *roca fissada*) from the vast natural fissures augmenting its defences. Perched at the western end of a long ridge, it's larger than it appears from below but utterly ruined; your main reward is the view over the valley below with its clustered villages, and south (weather permitting) to the high Pyrenean ridge.

A **gîte d'étape** (☎05.61.03.01.36; all year; 15 places, including doubles ❶) stands by the base of the path up to the castle, providing drinks and meals as well. **Accommodation** is also available at the *Relais des Pogs* (☎05.61.01.14.50), 1km west at the edge of Cazals hamlet.

Travel details

Trains

French trains

NB Some services on these lines are on SNCF buses.

Foix to: Ax-les-Thermes (11–13 daily; 55min); L'Hospitalet-près-l'Andorre (7 daily; 1hr 30min); Tarascon-sur-Ariège (11–13 daily; 15min–20min); Toulouse (11–13 daily; 1hr 20min–1hr 45min).

Latour-de-Carol to: Ax-les-Thermes (7 daily; 55min); Bourg-Madame (5 daily; 15min); Foix (7 daily; 1hr 40min–2hr); L'Hospitalet-près-l'Andorre (7 daily; 25min); Mont-Louis (4–7 daily; 1hr–1hr 25min); Puigcerdà (5 daily; 7–11min); Tarascon-sur-Ariège (7 daily; 1hr 25min); Toulouse (6 daily; 3hr–3hr 45min); Villefranche-de-Conflent (4–7 daily; 2hr 45min).

Spanish trains

Puigcerdà to: Barcelona (6 daily; 3hr 10min); Ripoll (6 daily; 1hr 15min).

La Pobla de Lillet to: Castellar de n'Hug (9 *carrilet* trains daily Easter & late June to early Sept, 8.30/9.30am–6/7pm; Fri–Sun only April to late June & early Sept to early Nov; 40min).

Buses

French buses

Ax-les-Thermes to: Foix (2 daily; 1hr); Pas de la Casa (July–Aug only 1 daily; 1hr 10min); Tarascon-sur-Ariège (2 daily; 30min).

Comus to: Quillan (1–2 daily Mon–Fri; 1hr 5min).

Foix to: Lavelanet (2–3 daily; 35min); Quillan (Mon–Sat 1 daily in afternoon; 1hr 30min); Saint-Girons (4 daily; 45min).

L'Hospitalet-près-l'Andorre to: Andorra la Vella (2 daily; 1hr 15min–1hr 35min); Pas de la Casa (2 daily; 25–35min).

Spanish buses

Berga to: Barcelona (4–5 daily; 2hr); Borredà (1 daily Mon–Sat afternoon, returns next morning; 30min); Castellar de N'Hug (1 daily Mon–Sat late afternoon, returns next morning; 1hr 20min); Gósol via Saldes (3–5 weekly Mon–Fri late afternoon, returns next morning; 1hr); La Pobla de Lillet (2–4 daily; 1hr); Ripoll (1 daily; 1hr 20min); Sant Llorenç de Morunys (1 daily Mon–Fri late afternoon, returns next morning; 1hr).

Puigcerdà to: Alp (4 daily; 10min); Bagà (4 daily; 35min); Berga (4 daily; 1hr); Llívia (5 daily; 5min); La Molina (1 daily in ski season; 30min); La Seu d'Urgell (3 daily; 1hr).

La Seu d'Urgell to: Andorra la Vella (14 daily Mon–Sat, 5 Sun; 40min); Barcelona (4 daily; 3hr 40min); Lleida (2 daily; 2hr 20min).

Andorra: domestic buses

Andorra la Vella to: Arinsal (8 daily; 30min); Encamp (every 20min 7.30am–9.30pm; 15min); Escaldes-Engordany (every 20min 7am–9.30pm; 8min); Ordino (every 30min 7am–9pm; 20min); Pas de la Casa (4 daily 8.30am–7pm; 1hr 15min); Soldeu (hourly winter only 8am–8pm; 45min).

La Massana to: El Serrat/Arcalis (6–12 daily in ski season; 35min)

Andorra: international buses

Andorra la Vella to: Ax-les Thermes (July/Aug only; 2hr 15min); L'Hospitalet-près-l'Andorre (2 daily; 1hr 30min); Latour-de-Carol (2 daily; 2hr).

3

The Val d'Aran region

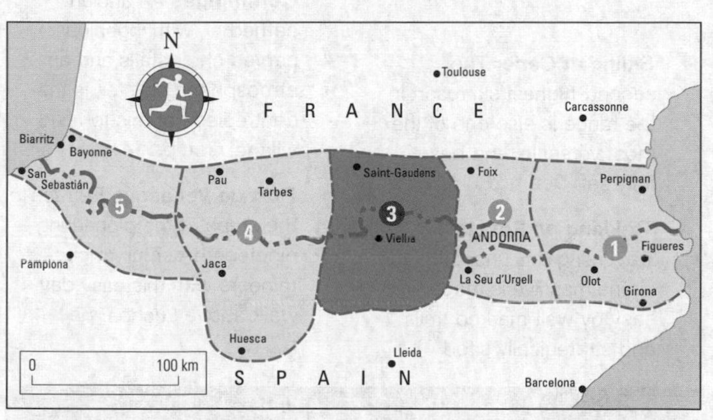

CHAPTER 3

Highlights

* **Rafting on the Noguera Pallaresa** The most boisterous river in the Pyrenees attracts novices and experts alike. See p.256
* **The Vall de Boí** Home to a remarkable concentration of eleventh-century Romanesque churches with improbable belfries. See p.277
* **Skiing at Cerler** The second-highest ski resort in the range is also one of the most versatile, and beautifully set. See p.289
* **Trekking on Posets** Traversing this unspoilt alpine massive is made easy by well-marked trails and strategically sited refuges. See p.294
* **Notre-Dame de Tramezaygues** The fourteenth-century portico frescoes in this little church are the most impressive sacred art in the region. See p.309
* **Saint-Bertrand-de-Comminges** An ancient cathedral, with ingenious carved choir stalls and an atmospheric cloister, is the centrepiece of this fortified village. See p.314
* **Port de Vénasque** Retrace the steps of the pioneering nineteenth-century mountaineers with this easy day walk above Luchon. See p.319

△ Saint-Bertrand-de-Comminges choir stalls

3

The Val d'Aran region

Isolated from Spain and draining towards France, the **Val d'Aran** ranks as a curiosity: the frontier here is displaced so far north that both sources of the Garonne, one of southern France's major rivers, lie in Spanish territory. With easy access from both Spain and France, the Val d'Aran makes an obvious starting point into the surrounding mountains, though it's heavily developed for skiers and summer weekenders from lowland cities.

The popular notion of the Pyrenees as two separate mountain chains, overlapping for 70km at the Val d'Aran, is widespread but erroneous. Authoritative geomorphological maps demonstrate that the watershed is merely distorted here: a spur off the main ridge is deflected east–west rather than the usual north–south, giving the illusion of separate peak lines. In fact, only some low hills in the Basque country are tectonically separate from the main Pyrenean chain.

Between Aran and Andorra, the easternmost of the Pyrenean "three-thousanders" – **Montcalm** and **Estats** – loom over remote valleys on either side of the border. Their approaches see few visitors, except along the banks of the **Noguera Pallaresa**, one of the great Pyrenean rivers which flows from just east of Aran south to Lleida. South of Aran, and also accessible from the Noguera Pallaresa valley, spreads the only national park in the Catalan Pyrenees, the **Parc Nacional d'Aigüestortes i Estany de Sant Maurici**, a wonderland of crags, tarns and dense forest, delighting hikers, alpine skiers and naturalists alike.

Maladeta – the great massif southwest of Aran, in Alto Aragón – was erroneously translated from the Aragonese *Mala Eta* ("The Highest Point") as "The Accursed" by early French climbers, thanks to the lethal glaciers that once dominated this the range. Their fearful crevasses delayed the first successful ascent of **Aneto** – the 3404-metre roof of the Pyrenees – until 1842, using a long and convoluted route avoiding the ice. Owing to global warming, today's glaciers are scant vestiges of those that once covered the slopes, while modern equipment further reduces this terrain's power to intimidate.

Immediately west of Maladeta looms the comparatively unsung massif of **Posets**, second highest in the Pyrenees and equally beloved by alpine aficionados. Together these two great mountains form a vast region far easier seen and crossed on foot or skis than by vehicle, so the comfortable town of **Benasque**, mountaineering capital of eastern Aragón, at the bottom of the Ésera valley separating the two peaks, comes as a welcome surprise. There's no other appreciable settlement until you reach the villages of the **Valle de Chistau**, on Poset's western flank.

If Spain has the region's most spectacular high-mountain scenery, France boasts the finest man-made attractions. Two millennia of settlement have left their traces at **Saint-Bertrand-de-Comminges**, near the Garonne, and a similar air of antiquity pervades **Saint-Lizier**, originally founded by the Romans. Long before, the

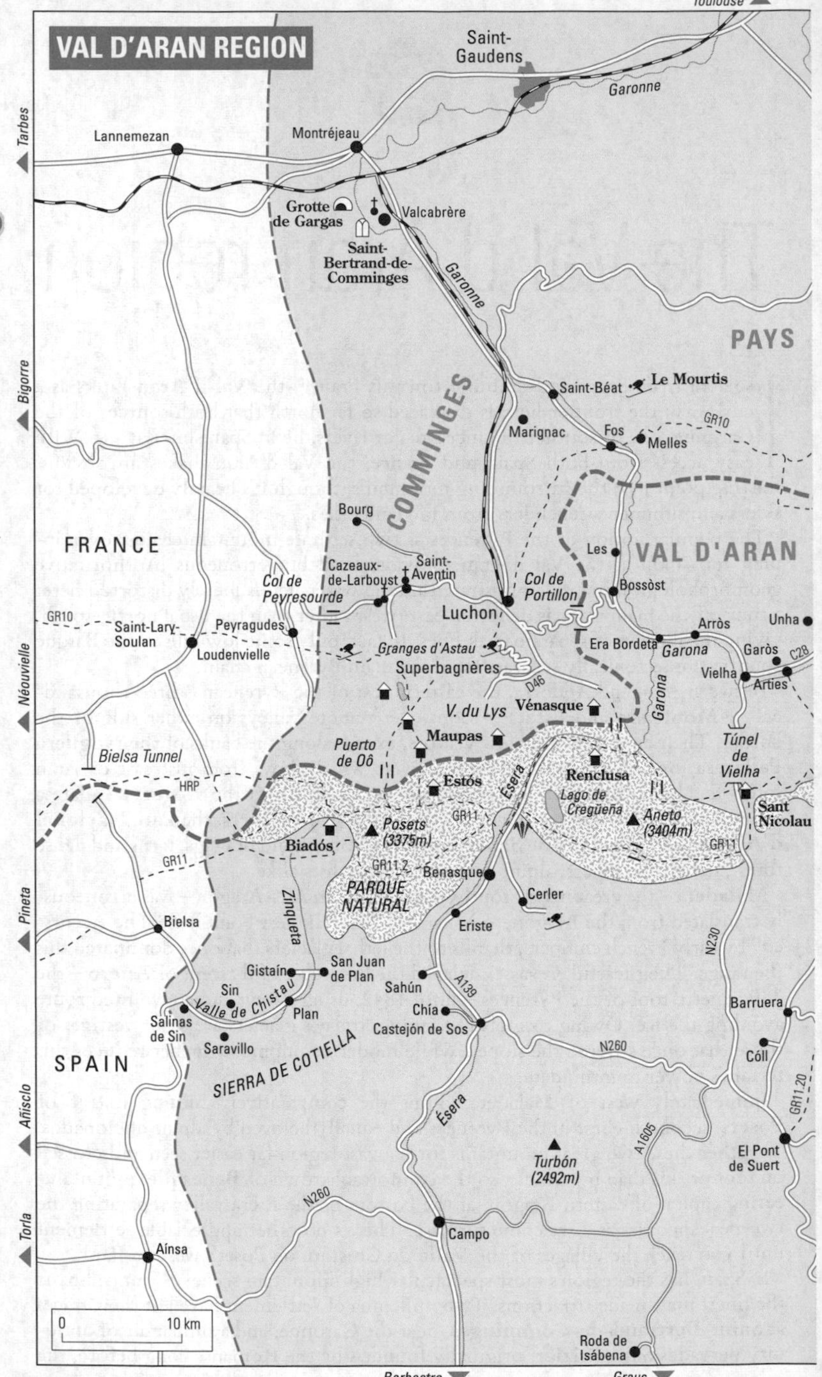
VAL D'ARAN REGION
Toulouse
Saint-Gaudens
Garonne
Tarbes
Lannemezan
Montréjeau
Grotte de Gargas
Valcabrère
Saint-Bertrand-de-Comminges
Garonne
PAYS
COMMINGES
Bigorre
Saint-Béat
Le Mourtis
Marignac
Fos
Melles
GR10
Bourg
Les
VAL D'ARAN
FRANCE
Cazeaux-de-Larboust
Saint-Aventin
Col de Peyresourde
Col de Portillon
Bossòst
Luchon
GR10
Saint-Lary-Soulan
Peyragudes
Loudenvielle
Granges d'Astau
Era Bordeta
Arròs
Unha
Garona
Garòs
C28
Vielha
Arties
Néouvielle
Superbagnères
Garona
D46
V. du Lys
Vénasque
Maupas
Puerto de Oô
Túnel de Vielha
Bielsa Tunnel
Renclusa
HRP
Estós
Ésera
Lago de Cregüeña
Sant Nicolau
Aneto (3404m)
Posets (3375m)
GR11
Biadós
GR11
GR11
GR11.2
Benasque
PARQUE NATURAL
Zinqueta
Cerler
Pineta
Eriste
Bielsa
N230
Gistaín
San Juan de Plan
Sin
Sahún
A139
Valle de Chistau
Plan
Barruera
Chía
Salinas de Sin
Castejón de Sos
N260
Saravillo
Còll
SPAIN
SIERRA DE COTIELLA
GR11.20
Añisclo
Ésera
A1605
Turbón (2492m)
El Pont de Suert
N260
Torla
Campo
Aínsa
0
10 km
Roda de Isábena
Barbastro
Graus

Mas d'Azil
Lavelanet
Ax-les-Thermes
Puigcerdà
Lleida & Congost de Mont-rebei
Talarn, Santa Engràcia & San Salvador de Toló
Lleida
FRANCE
SPAIN
ANDORRA
DE COUSERANS
Salat
Saint-Barthélemy
Lescure
Ségalas
La-Bastide-de-Serou
Foix
Saint-Lizier
Saint-Girons
Tarascon-sur-Ariege
Ariège
Massat
Argein
Audressein
Castillon-en-Couserans
Oust
Seix
Ercé
Miglos
Bonac
Vallée de Bethmale
Sentein
Pont de la Taule
Trein d'Ustou
Aulus-les-Bains
Auzat
Vicdessos
Goulier
GR10
Estagnous
Mont Valier (2838m)
Saint-Lizier-d'Ustou
Guzet-Neige
Eylie
HRP
Couflens
C. de Cagateille
Cascade d'Ars
Salau
Certascan (2840m)
Mounicou
Santuari de Montgarri
Bonabé
Mont Roig (2864m)
Certascan
Montcalm (3077m)
Baguerge
Baqueira-Beret
Alòs d'Isil
Vall d'Isil
Pleta de Prat
Noarre
Planell de Boavi
Estats (3143m)
El Serrat
Salardú
Isil
Barrage de Soulcem
Tredòs
Port de la Bonaigua (2072m)
Tavascan
GR11
Vall Ferrera
València d'Àneu
Esterri d'Àneu
Colomèrs
Gerdar
Son del Pi
Estaón
Àreu
Pla de la Font
Val de Cardós
Ribera de Cardós
Tor
Saborèdo
La Guingueta d'Àneu
Restanca
Espot
Alins
ANDORRA LA VELLA
Ventosa-Calvell
Parc Nacional
Espot Esquí
Vall Ferrera
Punta Alta (3015m)
Caldes de Boí
Peguera (2983m)
GR11.20
C13
Noguera Pallaresa
Virós-Vallferrera
Llavorsí
Colomina
Erill la Vall
Boí
Taüll
Roní
Capdella
Llessui
Rialp
Espui
Port-Ainé
Sort
Boí-Täull
Durro
La Seu d'Urgell
Torre de Capdella
Coll de Cantó (1725m)
Adrall
Baro
Mare de Déu d'Arbolo
La Pobleta de Bellveí
N260
Gerri de la Sal
Senterada
E. de Montcortès
Desfiladero de Collegats
N
La Pobla de Segur

Paleolithic hunting culture left mysterious hand outlines inside the **Grotte de Gargas** near Saint-Bertrand.

Depopulation is severe across this French region, particularly in the Pays de Couserans extending south from Saint-Girons to the Val d'Aran; its isolation meant that traditional customs, costumes and occupations persisted into the early twentieth century. The only major signs of modern development on either side of the frontier are unsightly **hydroelectric schemes** that occupy almost every canyon. Neither the sites – often still littered with construction debris – nor the pylons marching away from them were conceived with much consideration for aesthetics, wildlife preservation or the wishes of local residents.

Public transport is fairly sketchy on the French side; in Spain, bus services are hardly more frequent, again a consequence of rural depopulation. **Trains** from the south (once the line has been repaired) stop at La Pobla de Segur, while in the north there is a foothill rail (or rail-bus) service only on the spur line from Montréjeau to Luchon, and from Boussens to Saint-Girons. By contrast, the busy main highway between Vielha and La Pobla, threading the entire length of Aran and passing close to Aigüestortes, has fairly regular **buses**, as does the road which heads south from Vielha, capital of Aran, to Lleida. Away from this central hub, Benasque in the west has adequate bus services, as does much of the Couserans, with all connections through its regional capital of Saint-Girons.

The Montcalm-Estats Massif and around

The joint massif of French **Montcalm** (3077m) and border-straddling **Estats** (3143m), the highest mountain in Catalonia, tucked into a remote fold of land where the Spanish and French borders meet the westernmost corner of Andorra, is one of the least-known areas of the Pyrenees. It's also one of the least accessible; public transport on both the French and Spanish sides stops about 20km distant, from which point it's a day's walk to the flanks of the mountain.

There are three usual approaches: by road from the **Vicdessos valley** in the Ariège; by track, then trail, from the Spanish valleys of Cardós and Ferrera, themselves reached from the larger **Noguera Pallaresa** downstream; or by footpath **from Andorra** (a route covered on pp.213–214). The two **summits** are connected by a ridge-walk that crosses the border; to the west a particularly beautiful but challenging section of the HRP zigzags along the frontier towards Aran.

The Vicdessos valley

Steep-sided, damp and thick with deciduous forest, the **Vicdessos valley** is a sunless, uncomfortable place to live in winter. But it does have intrinsic interest – specifically castles at **Miglos** and **Montréal de Sos** – aside from being the most convenient French corridor to Montcalm.

There are several weekly late afternoon buses from Tarascon-sur-Ariège up the valley as far as Auzat, which leaves you about 9km short of Marc, and the Pinet alpine hut just above it, the usual Montcalm base-camp, and a similar distance shy of the trailhead for the Refuge du Fourcat, serving the HRP.

Miglos and around

Heading up-valley along the D8, you might stop briefly at the ruined thirteenth-century château of **Miglos** (unrestricted access), perched atop a rocky outcrop a couple of kilometres upstream from Niaux. It was originally built by a family of Cathar sympathizers; the château was later razed by Cardinal Richelieu, though the towers – best seen from the northerly approach road – remain intact.

If you have your own transport you could detour down the dead-end D24 to **SIGUER**, where the three-storey, brick-and-timber **Maison des Comptes de Foix** just off the square (closed for restoration) is a splendid Renaissance hunting lodge used by Gaston Fébus, and another 3km to **LERCOUL**, a tiny hamlet clinging to the top of a near-vertical cliff. The GR10 passes through both villages as it comes west from Mérens-les-Vals, then continues over the Col de Lercoul to the village of **GOULIER**, above Vicdessos. Goulier has two **gîtes d'étape**: *Relais de L'Endron* (ⓣ05.61.03.87.72; 40 places), on the outskirts, pitched as an outdoor-activity-coordinating centre with a few rooms (❷) as well as a dorm, and the central *Al Cantou* (ⓣ05.61.64.81.84; 12 places). Both offer half-board rates, useful as Goulier village has no shop.

Vicdessos and Auzat

VICDESSOS, 9km beyond Capoulet, and its close neighbour **AUZAT** are the southernmost outposts of civilization in the valley. Important foundry centres in decades past, neither has much to recommend them now, though Auzat is pleasant enough, with a little stream coursing through between rows of plane trees, while Vicdessos has a Thursday street market.

At nearby **Montréal de Sos**, a ruined Templar château stands on a mound above the tiny hamlet of Olbier; it's reached by footpath from the east bank of the river just past Auzat, or by track beginning halfway along the road connecting Vicdessos and Goulier. The Templars were responsible for many pilgrims' hospices in the Pyrenees, but became too rich for the liking of the Catholic Church and its allies, who in 1307 accused them of corruption, heresy and sexual depravity, tortured their leaders and finally burnt them to death. The view from the ruin is fabulous, marred only by the aluminium works at Auzat, the last significant source of local employment.

Practicalities

There's an **Office du Tourisme** in the centre of Vicdessos (ⓣ05.61.64.87.53). The better of two local **hotels** is one-star *Hotel Hivert* in Vicdessos (ⓣ05.61.64.88.17, ⓦwww.hotelhivert.com; ❷), on the through road, with an attached **restaurant**; Auzat has another, *La Bonne Auberge* (ⓣ05.61.03.80.99), serving well-priced *menus*. Each village has a **campsite**: the large *La Bexanelle* at Vicdessos (ⓣ05.61.64.82.22; all year) and *La Verniere* at Auzat (ⓣ05.61.64.84.46; all year). Organized local activities are limited, though you can ride horses at the Centre Equestre in Ournac, 2km south of Auzat (ⓣ05.61.64.84.66, ⓦwww.centre-equestre-ariege.com).

The ascent of Montcalm

Around 9km south of Auzat is the village of **MARC**, situated on both the GR10 and a northerly variant of the HRP. It has only a *gîte d'étape*, *Marc et Montmija* (ⓣ05.61.64.88.54; 18 places; closed Nov–March) and two *chambres* *d'hôte*; ⓣ05.61.64.83.86; ❷ B&B). If you've arrived early enough in the day, you might prefer to walk uphill for three hours to the modern *Refuge de Pinet* (2246m; ⓣ05.61.64.80.81, ⓦwww.refuge.pinet.free.fr; 55 places; daily June–Sept, by arrangement otherwise). Staying there makes the **ascent of Montcalm** a more manageable five- to six-hour round-trip. Alternatively, in seven to eight hours you can just trek one way from Pinet to the *Refugi de Vall Ferrera* (see p.257) in Spain – a beautiful and popular traverse, though you'll need crampons early in the season. The requisite IGN 1:25,000 **maps** are TOP 25 2148OT "Montcalm-Estats" or Editorial Alpina's "Pica d'Estats/Mont-roig", though you could manage with Rando Éditions' Carte de Randonnées no. 7, "Haute-Ariège/Andorre".

From Marc, follow the side road west towards L'Artigue for about thirty minutes to a car park at road's end, from where a path waymarked with yellow paint leads to the Pinet refuge. Montcalm looks formidable from here, its summit looming almost 1000m overhead, the bare rock sunless above the grass and trees. The easy going lies all behind you, and the only emergency campsite is beside the **Étang de Montcalm**. Next, you scramble over scree and rock – with one very steep section – to the **Tables de Montcalm**, a sort of gangway rising south, then clamber up rocks to the right, finally reaching a relatively easy shoulder of the summit. The walk along the ridge up to Estats takes another forty minutes. To descend, either retrace your steps or reverse the instructions from the Vall Ferrera (see p.257).

Trekking west of Marc

At Marc, the **GR10** runs up onto the hillsides above the west bank of the River Vicdessos to the hamlet of Hérout. There it bears northwest, climbing very steeply to the dammed lakes of Escales and Bassiès and up again to Étang d'Alate, from where you descend to the **Port de Saleix** (1794m) and then west through forest to Aulus-les-Bains (p.308) – eight hours' walking in total. You can break this sector at the *Refuge des Étangs de Bassiès* (1660m; ⓣ06.89.40.65.00; staffed daily June–Sept, by arrangement otherwise; 49 places), above the higher and smaller natural lake.

Beyond Marc, the **HRP** leaves L'Artigue car park, then climbs west-southwest to the **Port de l'Artigue** (2481m; 4hr) on the Spanish frontier. From the pass you drop to a cluster of lakes in the Spanish **Guiló valley**, threading northwest among them to the **Port de Colatx/Port de Couillac** (2418m). The first day's goal, the **Étang de la Hillette** (1797m), lies two hours below, magnificently situated above the Cirque de Cagateille (total 8–9hr from Marc). There are plans to build a staffed refuge here, but until then there's only the crude *Cabane de la Hillette*.

Instead of climbing to the Port de Colatx, you can follow the Spanish variant of the HRP, which next intersects the French route at the Port de Salau (see p.307); your first shelter is the *Refugi de Certascan* (see p.259). Staying on the French side, beyond La Hillette the HRP grazes the border just below the **Port de Marterat/Materet** (2217m) before veering northwest towards the Col de Crusous (2300m) on the shoulder of Cap de Ruhous, prelude to a steady descent to Salau (8hr from La Hillette).

If either you or the weather are not up to this, opt for the beautiful half-day ramble from La Hillette down the **Cirque de Cagateille** (see p.307 for more details), through the woods and along the Cors stream, reaching the D38 and the GR10 at Saint-Lizier d'Ustou, with Trein d'Ustou 3km further (see p.307 for these).

Vallon d'Artiès and Refuge du Fourcat

East of Marc, the GR10 executes a couple of leisurely S-bends, dictated by the terrain, en route to Goulier. A more exciting prospect, with an initial road-stretch from Auzat, is the six-hour walk up the **Vallon d'Artiès**, via dammed Étang d'Izourt, to the **Refuge du Fourcat** (2445m; ⓣ05.61.65.43.15, ⓦwww.fourcat.free.fr; 37 places; July 1–Sept 15), the highest hut in the Ariège, beside its namesake *étang*. This is an important staging post on the HRP; it straddles the routes into Andorra at the Tristaina lakes (see p.209), and could be the starting point for various lake-loops and peak-climbs in the immediate vicinity.

Up the Noguera Pallaresa

The **Noguera Pallaresa**, the most powerful river in the Spanish Pyrenees, was once used to float logs down to the sawmills at **La Pobla de Segur**, a job now done by truck. This is the river every visiting rafter wants to tackle, but if you're not of that persuasion, the valley is primarily a way of reaching the mountains to either side, or arriving in the Val d'Aran. To ascend Estats or Montcalm, you leave the Noguera Pallaresa at Llavorsí, heading northeast along the valleys of **Cardós** and **Ferrera**; for Aran, the busier C13 road continues northwest, via the **Vall d'Àneu**, up to the seasonally open **Port de Bonaigua**. Much of the territory east of the river now benefits from some statutory protection as part of the **Parc Natural de l'Alt Pirineu**, with the usual severe restrictions on camping, vehicle traffic, dogs and campfires.

Access from the east

Access to the valley is easiest via La Pobla de Segur, which has public transport connections in three directions. Coming into the Noguera Pallaresa **from the east**, twice-daily minibuses are available in either direction – book seats on the phone numbers in "Travel Details" on p.324. Otherwise, drive along the 47-kilometre road from Adrall (near La Seu d'Urgell) to Sort, or take one of a number of mountain-biking routes. The 4WD track from Sant Joan de l'Erm, west of La Seu, drops into the Noguera Pallaresa between Rialp and Llavorsí, near the Port-Ainé downhill ski resort. There's also a track from Ars, just outside Andorra's extreme southwest corner, coming down to Tirvia near Llavorsí. From inside Andorra there's another track – passable to most cars in summer – from Pal over the Port de Cabús, descending into Spain at the head of the Tor valley; from there you move into the Vall Ferrera valley at Alins and finally into the Cardós valley, not far from Llavorsí.

La Pobla de Segur and around

LA POBLA DE SEGUR has intrinsically little to offer; you only come here for onward connections. Besides buses further north along the Noguera Pallaresa (and seasonally beyond to Vielha in the Val d'Aran), local services journey west to El Pont de Suert, Boí and Capdella for entering the Aigüestortes region.

La Pobla is served year-round by three daily Alsina Graells **buses** from Barcelona (departing from Plaça de la Universitat) and by three daily **trains** from Lleida which terminate here; by a royal Spanish decree dating to 1892, the railway is supposed to extend into France by tunnel under the Port de Salau, but this seems less likely with every passing decade. All bus services continue up the Noguera Pallaresa through Sort and Llavorsí as far as Esterri d'Anèu, passing the side road for the Cardós and Ferrera valleys, and within 7km of Espot, a major entry point to the Aigüestortes national park (see p.273). From July to mid-September, one of these buses continues over the pass into the Val d'Aran. Morning bus services from Lleida, Tremp or Barcelona all connect with services up the Noguera Pallaresa – or indeed *are* the same coach.

Trains – once track repairs have been completed by 2008 – arrive in the new town's station, from where you walk 200m north up the road and then over the bridge to a kiosk-shelter, terminal for the Alsina Graells company; current schedules are posted. Don't get stranded: there is **nowhere to stay** in La Pobla, and little to recommend for refreshment other than the *Raiers* **bar** for *tapas* and beer, on Avgda Madrid, at the western edge of town past the post office.

Talarn, Santa Engràcia and San Salvador de Toló

The closest spots to **stay** and **eat** lie outside **Tremp**, 13km downriver from La Pobla, just beyond the giant **Sant Antoní reservoir**. The large, fortified hill town of **TALARN**, 2km northwest of Tremp, proves to be a gem, its houses (plus a few ad hoc towers) forming a defensive perimeter, with an old church at the low end of the maze of interior lanes. Just inside from the car-park plaza at c/Soldevila 2, *Casa Lola* shines as a beacon of country cuisine, attracting clientele from near and far; €21–24 *a la carta* gets wild mushroom salad, *girella* (tasty lamb-and-rice haggis) or venison with chocolate and bacon and a choice from the most extravagant dessert list in the region, with excellent local red wine. Proprietress "Lola" (Florita) is a character, giving free *pa amb tomaquet*-making lessons to the uninitiated; she also has ten spotless, air-con studio apartments upstairs, a few with terraces (ⓣ973 650 814, ⓦwww.casalola.info; ❹).

Just below Talarn a narrow but paved ten-kilometre road heads west to **SANTA ENGRÀCIA**, surely the most spectacularly set village in Catalunya, tumbling off the south flank of a rock monolith offering 270-degree views. This was the limit of the Cretaceous-era sea, and the entire region is a geologist's paradise of stacked sedimentary rock and exposed fossils. Here Richard and Sandra Loder manage *Casa Guilla* (ⓣ973 252 080 or 620 911 935, ⓦwww.casaguilla.com; ❺ B&B, ❻ HB; closed Dec–Feb), a restored, rambling farmhouse poised like the prow of a ship at the monolith's east end, with sweeping views. En-suite accommodation consists of a suite/quadruple upstairs and three doubles plus there's a lovely mineral-water pool, basement bar, generous continental breakfast and group evening *table d'hôte* meals. The area is a mecca for birders, botanists and geologists alike, so reservations are mandatory. If they're full, an alternative lies 26km southeast of Tremp, 6km outside **SAN SALVADOR DE TOLÓ**: *Casa Pete y Lou* (ⓣ973 252 309, ⓦwww.casapeteylou.com; closed Dec–Feb; ❸ B&B). This is a completely isolated hilltop farmhouse, with just three non-en-suite rooms; breakfast (and by arrangement, supper) relies largely on own-made/grown bread and produce.

Gerri de la Sal and around

From La Pobla de Segur the C13 road threads through the **Congost de Collegats**, an impressive gorge hewn by the Noguera Pallaresa through three-hundred-metre-high cliffs. Unfortunately, since a series of tunnels was blasted through much of the defile, drivers see little of it, though the narrow, abandoned old road is still open to cyclists and pedestrians. The Catalan intelligentsia have been coming to admire the scenery here since the 1880s, and the portion of the canyon labelled **L'Argenteria**, with its sculpted, papier-mâché-like rockface streaked with rivulets, supposedly inspired Antoní Gaudí's La Pedrera apartment building in Barcelona.

As the canyon opens out, you emerge at the rickety village of **GERRI DE LA SAL** – "de la Sal" because of the local salt-making industry. Salt pans are still in use by the riverside, but more obvious is the Benedictine monastery of **Santa Maria**, founded in 807. The present twelfth-century structure, with its huge and dilapidated bell-wall, faces the village on the far side of a beautiful old bridge. The church interior (Easter & June–Sept 11am–1pm & 4.30–7.30pm; rest of year phone ⓣ973 662 068; €1.50) is a three-aisled basilica, with soaring barrel-vaulting upheld by four fluted columns. An unusual arched hay-loft runs along the south side of the building's exterior. From the old bridge, you can also follow a clear path 25 minutes north along the east bank to the late twelfth-century **Santuari de la Mare de Déu d'Arboló**, photogenically perched high above the river, near a road tunnel.

Gerri has two **restaurants** and a bar; 4km north in tiny **BARO**, *Cal Mariano* (ⓣ973 662 077; ❷) offers rooms and food and there's a large, riverbank **campsite**, the *Pallars Sobirà* (ⓣ973 662 033).

West to La Pobleta de Bellveí: the Estany de Montcortès

The minor road from Gerri de la Sal to La Pobleta de Bellveí, 17km west, makes a pristine, tranquil run through rolling uplands speckled with picturesque villages. It's ideal for mountain-biking or driving, but not suitable for hitching or walking: there's little traffic and the initial punishing climb up to Peramea is unshaded. This road, incidentally, is wrongly shown on both recommended touring maps – it's not a dead-end, and is paved all the way. From Bretui, 10km along, you peer into the gorge of Cortscastells, a tributary of Collegats, but the high point of the route is idyllic little **Estany de Montcortès** (1065m), just west of the eponymous village. Though warm and reed-fringed, this attractive karstic lake drops suddenly to thirty-metre depths, so there's no bottom muck to contend with – several wooden jetties allow instant access to deep water. Beyond lies a sharp, featureless descent to La Pobleta de Bellveí in the Vall Fosca (see p.276).

Sort to Port-Ainé

SORT, 30km north of La Pobla, retains an old core of tall, narrow houses plus a tiny castle, now overwhelmed by ranks of apartment buildings. This development is due to the area's reputation as one of the premier springtime river-running spots in Europe. Every year, during late June or early July, valley communities stage the *Raiers* (Rafters) festival, re-enacting the exploits of the old-time timber pilots.

Because of an upmarket clientele, Sort prices itself out of casual trade, and in any case it's not a place to linger unless you're here for the action (which can be exhilarating; see box on p.256). Its main street is exclusively devoted to rafting and adventure shops; among these, Rubber River (ⓣ973 620 220, ⓦwww.rubber-river.com) is reputable, with its own garden-set **hotel**, the two-star *Florido* (ⓣ973 620 337; ❺). There's a **Turisme** (summer Mon–Fri 9am–2pm & 5–9pm, Sat 10am–1pm & 5–8pm ⓣ973 621 002) on the main street, while **buses** stop at Plaça Catalina Albert, at the north end of town where the two through roads meet. **RIALP**, 3km north, is a marginally more appealing mix of old houses and new boutiques; its bus stop is at the bar under the *Hotel Victor*.

Skiing: Port-Ainé

Though still shown on most maps, the Llessuí ski station, 16km west of Sort, closed long ago. **PORT-AINÉ**, 14km northeast of Rialp, has filled the breach, offering some of the best beginners' and intermediates' skiing in the Catalan Pyrenees on 33 longish runs in a glorious setting. Much money and effort has gone into transforming the formerly eccentric logistics of the place; there are now large car parks and ticket windows at both Points 1650 and 2000, and equipment rental at Points 2000 and 2100. From the beginners' runs around Point 2100 there's a short drop to a chair-lift mounting 2440-metre Pic de l'Orri, the start of most pistes. These include the aptly named 4300-metre Bella Vista green run along the

Rafting on the Noguera Pallaresa

The main **rafting season** on the Noguera Pallaresa lasts from April until September, though some organizations offer programmes in March and October if snowmelt (and the power company) are amenable.

The original rafts for the journey to the sawmills of La Pobla de Segur were logs lashed together ten-wide, controlled by a long, stern-mounted oar. Today's water-sport versions are reinforced inflatables, up to 6.5m long and weighing around 100kg. If you sign up for a trip – which guarantees a soaking and as much excitement as any well-balanced person could want – you'll usually share a **boat** with seven others, including your guide/pilot, who sits in the rear. Standard **gear** includes crash helmet, buoyancy jacket (*chaleca*), wet suits (water temperature in April is a bracing 8°C) and lightweight paddles, but *not* gloves. You need bare fingers to keep hold of the T-grip at the end of the oar (*remo*), of which you should never let go – even on the calmer stretches a sudden bump could catapult it from your hands and knock your neighbour's teeth out.

Everyone keeps one foot in stirrups, but it's certain that you'll **go overboard** – the more mischievous skippers make sure everyone takes a spill during the first moments of easy paddling, so that you lose your fear of the water. When you get pitched in, just "go with the flow", floating on your back feet first with your knees slightly bent to brace for impact against submerged rocks; crewed boats float faster downstream than you do, but you'll be thrown a fifteen-metre line if necessary.

Since groups are mostly local, it's worth knowing a few Spanish **commands**: *adelante* (row forward), *atrás* (paddle backward), *alto* (stop rowing), *contrapeso derecho/izquierda* (throw your weight to the right/left, when entering a rapid).

The twelve-kilometre stretch of river between Llavorsí and Rialp is the easiest and most commonly rafted, while the 26km from Sort through the Congost de Collegats is advanced and even more scenic. Daily **departures** are typically at 11am and noon; in the former case you'll be in the water by 11.20am, and clambering into the return shuttle van at Rialp by 12.40pm. **Prices** for rafting range from about €31 for a two-hour, Llavorsí–Rialp trip, up to €70 for the entire 42-kilometre distance (a full afternoon's outing, packed lunch included).

ridge and through the pines, and the 2300-metre Les Pilones red run to the base of the Pic de l'Orri lift. Piste colour-coding is overrated – blues are rather greenish, reds blueish – but the north-facing valley generally enjoys powdery snow, even in spring. A large three-star **hotel** stands at Point 2000 (Ⓣ973 627 627, Ⓦwww.port-aine.com; ❻); otherwise the closest **accommodation** are two *cases de pagès*: *Casa Macià* (Ⓣ973 620 837; ❷) and *Casa Millet* (Ⓣ973 623 125; ❷) in the village of **RONÍ**, 9km downhill on the road in.

Llavorsí

The most attractive place to stay along this stretch of the valley is **LLAVORSÍ**, 10km above Rialp. Despite extensive modernization, a rash of bar/restaurants and rafting outfitters on the main road, plus a mammoth power substation across the way, this huddle of stone-built houses and slate roofs at the confluence of the Noguera Pallaresa and Cardós rivers still retains some character. There are two good riverside **campsites**, both with pools and bars: the *Aigües Braves* 1km north of town (Ⓣ973 622 153; March–Sept), and the smaller, municipally run *Riberies* east of the centre, basic but tent-friendly (Ⓣ973 622 151; mid-June to mid-Sept). **Accommodation** catering for the river trade, while abundant, should be reserved in advance during the rafting season. Try the *Hotel de Rei* (Ⓣ973 622 011, Ⓦwww.hotelderei.com; ❸) on the riverfront, or the welcoming *Hostal Noguera*

(Ⓣ973 622 012, Ⓔnoguerahostal@wanadoo.es; ❸) on the opposite bank, with many balconied rooms overlooking the water. Their restaurant also has river-view seating and a reasonable if rather limited *menú*.

Established local **activity outfitters** offering rafting, canyoning, kayaking, hydrospeed, mountain-biking and rock-climbing include Roc Roi at Plaça Nostra Senyora de Biuse (Ⓣ973 622 035, Ⓦwww.rocroi.com); Yeti Emotions (Ⓣ973 622 201, Ⓦwww.yetiemotions.com), some 500m south of Llavorsí, on the west bank of the river opposite a road tunnel; and the central Rafting Llavorsi (Ⓣ973 622 158, Ⓦwww.raftingllavorsi.com).

The Vall Ferrera

From Llavorsí, the initially paved L510 road up to the *Refugi de Vall Ferrera* – base for the ascent of Estats and Montcalm – ambles through an underpopulated area of pastures, and hayfields scythed in July; get a taxi (Ⓣ973 624 411 or 973 624 353) if you're without a vehicle. The first part of the route follows the Cardós valley (see p.258) from Llavorsí; after about 4km, you turn off east along the **Vall Ferrera**, which, as the name suggests, traditionally lived from iron-mining and -smelting. At **ALINS**, 13.5km from Llavorsí, there's a choice of en-suite **accommodation**: the plush *Hotel Salòria* (Ⓣ973 624 341; ❹ B&B), offering full savoury breakfasts and balconied rooms, and the *Hostal Muntanya* (Ⓣ973 624 358, Ⓕ973 624 411; ❸), with a respected, family-run restaurant on the first floor. If Alins is full or too busy for your taste, *Casa Gabatxó* (Ⓣ973 624 322; ❸), in **ARAÓS** 6km downstream back towards Llavorsí, is the most highly regarded of the valley's dozen-plus *cases de pagès*, offering half-board as well. Araós is also the start-point for the dirt track (winter jeep transfer offered) up to the **Bosc Virós** cross-country skiing centre, with 28km of pistes between 1550m and 2200m and lodging or meals at the *Refugi Gall Fer* (25 places). All activities here are run by Yeti Emotions (contact details above).

Another 5km beyond Alins along the main valley lies the tiny village of **ÀREU**, the last settlement before Estats, and on the GR11. The local iron industry required copious timber for charcoal; accordingly the local **Museu de la Fusta** (Lumber Museum) showcases a working hydro-powered *serradora*, or sawmill (July–Sept only; Ⓣ973 624 355 to summon custodians; €2). Àreu has a small shop, a pleasant, tent-friendly **campsite**, *Pica d'Estats* (Ⓣ973 624 347; Easter & June–Sept), and a muncipal pool. The most obvious indoor **accommodation** is the rambling *Hotel Vall Ferrera* (Ⓣ973 624 343; ❺ HB); they also have the main village **restaurant**.

The route up the mountain continues, first via dirt track and then, 3.5km above Àreu, along the marked east-bank trail "Camí Vell del Port de Boet/Pla de Boet", routed in common with the GR11, to just below the **Refugi de Vall Ferrera** (1940m; Ⓣ973 624 378; 30 places; open and staffed June–Sept), nearly four hours from Àreu. The stretch of river here, though short (4km), presents some of the best, and least commercialized, kayaking in the Catalan Pyrenees.

Next day, allow four to five hours to **climb Estats**. Follow the marked TRF (*transfrontalier*) path north through the Sottlo valley and past the photogenic lakes of Sottlo and Estats, then up into the Port de Sottlo (2893m); from here a short ridge walk east leads to the summit. You can then either retrace your steps, or continue to the Pinet refuge (see p.252).

Other onward routes from Vall Ferrera

Southeast of the *Vall Ferrera* refuge, the HRP variant/TRF and GR11 lead into Andorra by different sets of passes – described on p.213; the GR11 is easier, not exceeding 2517m elevation en route, at the small unstaffed refuge of Baiau just before the frontier. Northwards, then **westwards**, you can make the traverse to Tavascan (9hr; below), initially via the Sotllo lake, where you should bear west over the 2618-metre Coll de Barborte to the **Baborte** lake (3hr 30min from *Refugi Vall Ferrera*; unlocked 8-person refuge adjacent) and **Planell de Boavi** (7hr), a beautiful but occasionally over-subscribed wilderness camping area among birches and firs.

The Vall de Cardós

If you keep to the L504 road up the broader, more developed **Vall de Cardós** instead of taking a right into the Vall Ferrera, you'll pass through **RIBERA DE CARDÓS** (10km from Llavorsí), a sizeable and attractive village with a twelfth-century, squat-belfried church and a giant active sawmill, last vestige of the valley's wood-cutting industry. For **accommodation**, there's just the well-equipped *Hostal Sol i Neu* (Ⓣ973 623 137; open March–Oct; ❹), by the river at the south entry to the village.

Tavascan

The road continues past other steeple-crowned hamlets surrounded by hayfields and grazing sheep to **TAVASCAN** (often "Tabascan"), 20km from Llavorsí, where the single high street is a solid mass of accommodation. This recent gentrification is due largely to the tiny **ski station** at **Pleta de Prat** (Ⓦwww.centrealpitavascan.com), 11km northwest past Noarre hamlet, with just 17km of cross-country pistes and a few downhill runs. Yet Tavascan is a larger, more traditional village than it appears from the through road, with an old bridge over the Riu Tavascan above the church, and the last shop before the wilderness; the **GR11** slips over the bridge and through lanes of old houses on the west bank.

Of three **hotels**, simplest is the friendly, low-key *Marxant* (Ⓣ973 623 151, Ⓔmarxant@autovia.com; ❹ HB), something of a trekkers' haven despite its plain, well-worn 1970s en-suite rooms. For more comfort at similar prices, the adjacent, wood-floored *Hotel Llacs de Cardós* (Ⓣ973 623 178, Ⓦwww.llacscardos.com; ❸ B&B, or ❹ HB) is arguably better value, sharing a restaurant with co-managed *Hotel Estanys Blaus* opposite (same contact details; ❹ B&B, ❺ HB), best for a splurge, with gym, sauna, wi-fi and rear rooms overlooking the river. The sole budget option is the rather ordinary, non-en-suite *Pensió Feliu* (Ⓣ973 623 163; ❹ HB). One **campsite**, *Bordes de Graus* (Ⓣ973 623 246; April–Oct), lies 5km up towards the ski centre, but it's pleasant, friendly and caravan-free. Another site, *Serra* (Ⓣ973 623 117; July–Sept), 4km south in Lladorre village, lies just off the GR11.

Hikes out of the Vall de Cardós

If you're traversing along the **HRP** (see p.259), it's advisable to skip Tavascan altogether, since you have to lose and regain a lot of altitude to get there. As noted, however, the **GR11** goes through Tavascan, and for the less committed hiker forms the partial basis of a six-hour **loop-walk**, dubbed the "Itinerari Panoràmic per l'Alt Cardós", which takes in several villages clinging to the side of the upper valley, using sections of the GR11 plus local PR paths for lateral links. The route, shown on a placard beside the *Hotel Marxant*, heads south from Tavascan to the villages of Aineto and Lleret on the GR11, crosses to the east bank of the valley at Lladorre, then climbs up to Boldís Jussà and Boldís Sobirà to rejoin the GR11 for a northerly descent to Tavascan.

Above Tavascan, there's a choice of access to the high peaks: the more easterly dirt track, towards Planell de Boavi, is the direct route to Pic de Certascan

(2853m); the paved road northwest, beyond the power station, connects at Noarre with the HRP towards the Val d'Aran. Both lead to delightful wildernesses of long valleys and tarn-spangled cirques up against the border.

For the **Certascan area**, take a turn-off at the Montalto dam 6km beyond Tavascan on the rough track towards Boavi, and climb steeply up the Sierra Marinera past the western shore of the superb **Estany de Naorte**, with the summit of Estats just visible above the low, rounded hills and sparse pines on the opposite bank. Some three and a half hours from Tavascan you reach the **Llac de Certascan**, star of many a postcard; over 100m deep and 1200m long, it's supposedly the largest natural lake in the Pyrenees. (With a 4WD vehicle, you can drive to within 20min of the lake.) At the south end stands the *Refugi de Certascan* (2240m; Ⓣ973 623 230, Ⓦwww.certascan.com; 40 places; staffed mid-June to Sept), with hot showers, meals and cooking facilities; from here the **Pic de Certascan** is an easy half-day, round-trip ascent.

The HRP and GR11

From the refuge, it's possible to follow the **HRP** west for six hours to the hamlet of **Noarre** (no facilities), but this is a tough section with lots of cross-country route-finding, only feasible in good conditions. From Noarre, or from **Pleta Palomera** with its unstaffed refuge another hour upstream, you can continue west to Salardú in Aran. This involves two or three days' walking on the HRP or one of its variants; the quickest heads due west for Alòs d'Isil, about ten hours away via a necklace of lakes at the base of 2864-metre **Mont Roig**. The only facility en route, under two hours west of Pleta de l'Arenal, is the unstaffed *Refugi Mont Roig-Enric Pujol* (2290m; 18 places), an ambitious target for a day's trek west from Certascan, but well placed for exploring the lakes, as well as the peak.

Alternatively, the Cardós valley is linked to both the Vall Ferrera and the Vall d'Àneu (see below) by the easier though less dramatic **GR11**. From just above Àreu in the Vall Ferrera, the route cuts over Montarenyo ridge via the Coll de Tudela to Boldís and Tavascan, then bears sharply southwest over another 2500-metre spur to La Guingueta d'Àneu via **ESTAON** and Lleret. The Àreu–Tavascan sector makes for an easy day's walking of about six hours; Tavascan–La Guingueta is getting on for nine hours, with a *casa de pagès* in Lleret and the *Refugi GR11-Estaon* (Ⓣ973 623 287, Ⓦwww.refugigr-11estaon.com; all year) the only amenities en route.

The Vall d'Àneu

From Llavorsí, the main C13 continues upstream along the Noguera Pallaresa, past the Espot turning (see p.273) and the placid Pantà de la Torrasa, to **LA GUINGUETA D'ÀNEU** at the head of the reservoir. This is the first of three villages incorporating the name of the local valley, **Vall d'Àneu**, offering a small cluster of roadside **accommodation**. The best option is the *Hotel Poldo* (Ⓣ973 626 080; ❸), with a pool and decent restaurant emphasizing spit-grilled meats (*carta* only; allow €20 plus drink); opposite stands the more economical *Hostal Orteu* (Ⓣ973 626 086; ❷).

Esterri d'Àneu

ESTERRI D'ÀNEU, 4km further beyond the lake, has morphed from sleepy farming community to chic resort. The few huddled old houses between the road and the river, an arched bridge and slender-towered Sant Vicenç church form as graceful an ensemble as you'll see in the Catalan Pyrenees, but the new apartment buildings and fancy hotels to the south are another matter. The 2003–04 expansion of the Baqueira-Beret ski domain to a point accessible all year from the Vall d'Àneu has set off another spasm of construction.

The best-value place to **stay** and **eat** is the friendly *Fonda Agustí* (ⓣ973 626 034; ❸ B&B, ❸ HB), in a quiet location behind the church at Plaça de l'Església 6, with an old-fashioned, popular *menjador*; there's only a four-course *menú* with wine offered, plainly presented to the point of austerity, but at €12 you can't complain. Alternatively, try *Pensió La Creu* at c/Major 3 (ⓣ973 626 437, ⓦwww.pensiolacreu.com; ❸), some of its rooms with river view. The closest **campsite**, *La Presalla* (ⓣ973 626 263; April–Sept), is 1.5km south of the village.

The Vall d'Isil

From the centre of Esterri d'Àneu, a narrow, paved road leads up the **Vall d'Isil**, its atmospheric villages little visited and effectively abandoned, some of them (like Àrreu) squatted by "alternative" types. The highlight, 11km along just before **ISIL** (alias Gil), is the engaging Romanesque church of Sant Joan, with its fine south portal, two Gothic windows retaining some tracery, its apse just about in the river and pairs of strange carved figures studding the roofline. **Accommodation** comprises just a single *casa de pagès* on the west bank, *Casa Fuster* (ⓣ973 626 196; ❷). **ALÒS D'ISIL**, 12km from Esterri at the end of the paved route and with another tiny medieval bridge, has **accommodation** 4km north of the village – *Xalet-Refugi el Fornet* (ⓣ973 626 520; 40 places) – a welcome sight if you're trekking along the HRP.

València d'Àneu

Three kilometres further up the main road (now the C28), **VALÈNCIA D'ÀNEU**'s core of traditional stone houses and small Romanesque church is now well enveloped by modern chalet development spurred by the expansion of Baqueira-Beret onto this side of the Bonaigua pass. València was once much more important than its current profile suggests. An ongoing archeological dig on the outskirts has revealed foundations of a tenth-century **castle**, apparently the power base of counts who ruled over many of the surrounding valleys.

An excellent choice for **accommodation** is the good-value *Hotel La Morera* (ⓣ973 626 124, ⓦwww.hotel-lamorera.com; closed Nov, Feb–March; ❹ B&B), with variable balconied rooms, a valley-side pool and good breakfasts; supper is also excellent as long as you dine *a la carta* and shun the relatively dull half-board *table d'hôte*. Honourable mention goes to the smaller *Hotel Lo Paller* (ⓣ973 626 129; ❺ HB only) on c/Major, in the old quarter off the highway, with interior rustic decor belying a harsh exterior, and a pleasant rear garden. On or just off the same street are two *cases de pagès*: *Casa Campane* (ⓣ973 626 251; ❸), and *Casa Sala* facing the church (ⓣ973 626 254; ❸). Another worthwhile **restaurant**– certainly the chalet construction crews favour it – a few paces down from *Lo Paller*, is *Felip*, with *menú* or an ample *carta*.

Son (del Pi) and the Port de la Bonaigua

About 1km beyond València d'Aneu, then 4km south following signs for Estaís, is **SON (DEL PI)**, remarkable for its eleventh- to twelfth-century fortified church of **Sants Just i Pastor** (daily summer only 10am–2pm & 5–8pm; €1). This has a four-storey Lombard-type belfry with a pyramidal roof, while a sixteenth-century *retable* and carved stone font (previously a Visigothic sarcophagus) grace the interior. But its most unusual feature is the round tower by the gate, the *Comunidor*, which the local priest used to climb and, sacred Host in hand, cast spells against destructive storms and avalanches. The village is a beauty as well, with the chalet-style *Restaurant-Refugi Casa Masover* opposite the church (ⓣ973 626 383); if it's shut, the nearest comparable facility is the **Refugi Pla de la Font**, poised between here and Espot, and accessible by 8km of good dirt track (ⓣ619 930 771; 23 places; open mid-June to late Sept plus Dec–May weekends/hols).

The sources of the Garona/Garonne

The river draining the Val d'Aran begins life as the **Garona**, then in France becomes the **Garonne**, swinging northeast through Saint-Gaudens and Toulouse, and then northwest to the Atlantic at Bordeaux. The river has two commonly accepted sources: the Ruda stream at the east end of the valley, fed by the Saborèdo lakes, and the Joeu, in the west beyond Vielha, up against the French frontier.

Contrary to what was believed until 1931, the **Joeu** doesn't rise in Aran at all, but in the Maladeta-Aneto Massif to the southwest, on the opposite side of the watershed from the Val d'Aran. In that year, French speleologist Norbert Casteret (see box on p.313) proved that the Joeu was a resurgence by emptying 55 kilos of dye into the **Forau dels Aigualluts**, the sinkhole for the Aneto glacier's meltwater. In Casteret's own words: "Next day, the Garonne revealed its secret. For twenty-seven hours a million cubic yards of bright green water poured down the Val d'Aran and for over fifty miles into France."

Beyond València and the turning for Son, the road quits the Noguera Pallaresa and climbs above the quilt of fields around Esterri. The Riu de la Bonaigua takes over as the roadside stream, lined by forests of silver birch, pine and fir. Views get ever more impressive as you approach the treeline, above which is perched the **restaurant-bar** *Les Ares* (daily 9am–6pm), next to the Ermita de la Mare de Déu de les Ares, with a good-value lunch *menú*..

Three hairpins above the *ermita*, next to the base of the La Peülla chair-lift, you'll notice the seasonally busy car park and trailhead for the path up into the Vall Gerber (see p.268 for this route). Near the top of the bleak **Port de la Bonaigua** (2072m; usually kept open in winter for the ski trade), half-wild horses graze and you get simultaneous panoramas of the valleys you've just left and the Val d'Aran to come.

The Val d'Aran

Though undeniably on the French side of the Pyrenean watershed, the **Val d'Aran** has long been under Spanish sovereignty. This oddity seems even more pronounced when you consider that Andorra, while opening towards Spain, was long semi-autonomous (and opted for full independence in 1993), and that the Cerdanya/Cerdagne, despite a lack of pronounced natural demarcations, is divided between the two countries. However, in June 1990 a special law of the Catalan Generalitat restored a degree of self-rule to the valley.

Cut off from the outside world for centuries, the Val d'Aran evolved its own language – **Aranès** – which is only spoken and written here. It's based largely on medieval Gascon, plus elements of Catalan and a generous sprinkling of Basque vocabulary. The valley's name, for example, is not Aranès but pure Basque, and "Val" is technically redundant – *aran* means "valley" in Euskera. (From here westwards, Basque place names are commonly encountered, tide-markers of the former extent of a people now restricted to the west end of the range.) The Aranès **spelling of local place names** is now exclusively used on local road signs and tourist literature (if not yet on internationally published maps), so is given preference in the following account, with Castilian or Catalan in parentheses.

Aran was a source of Franco-Hispanic conflict as long ago as 1192, when it passed from the counts of Comminges to the kings of Aragón. In 1808 Napoleon announced its annexation, sending in 2500 French troops. Only a thousand reached the Val d'Aran – the rest deserted – but they sufficed to briefly expel the Spanish. The valley was a stronghold of Republicanism during the Spanish Civil War and a refuge for the defeated afterwards, safe behind passes snowed up half the year. It was invaded once again by Franco's Nationalists in 1944, in particular his greatly feared Moroccan auxiliaries who brutally suppressed opposition by massacring the population of several villages. The isolation of Aran was finally relieved by the boring of the **Túnel de Vielha** between 1948 and 1953 (using the slave labour of Republican POWs), allowing the N230 road to link the valley with the provincial capital of Lleida.

Since Franco's passing, life in the valley has changed dramatically. At peak skiing times – **two million-plus visitors** to Aran are recorded in a good winter – the tunnel can no longer cope, and a second one (estimated completion date 2008) is now being bored to double car capacity. Scythe-wielding summer hay-reapers have been replaced by Massey-Ferguson balers, the hayfields themselves overlooked by holiday chalets that have sprouted at the edge of every village. Ever-greater numbers of restaurants and sports shops, and the constant year-round traffic on the C28 valley-floor road, make the Val d'Aran one of the most expensive, overdeveloped and (unless you're skiing) overrated corners of the Spanish Pyrenees. With the Spanish royal family setting its imprimatur on the Baqueira-Beret ski centre, and members of the "commoner" government regularly holidaying here too, the sky's the limit for prices.

All that said, if you leave the main route in favour of side valleys like the Ruda or the Unhòla, you get an inkling of the region as it used to be. But don't expect superlative wilderness walking: Aran is best viewed as a comfortable rest stop on Pyrenean traverses, rather than a target in its own right.

Nautaran

Nautaran, "High Valley" in Aranés, is the more scenic eastern part of the region, and a good start- or end-point for walks in the Aigüestortes park. From almost any elevated point in Nautaran you'll have full-on views of snowy Maladeta, hovering like a ghost to the west. The local architecture resembles very much that of French Gascony, utterly unlike that of the Spanish valleys to the east and south. Sturdy Nautaranese houses are traditionally stone with slate roofs, so there's surprisingly little to distinguish a 400-year-old home from a four-year-old one. Many display dates on the lintels – not of the same vintage as the local Romanesque churches, though some date back to the sixteenth century.

Baqueira-Beret

The road descent west from Port de la Bonaigua isn't for the acrophobic or those with dodgy brakes, given its hairpins and sharp drop into the Ruda valley. The first place below the pass is **BAQUEIRA-BERET** (Ⓦ www.baqueira.es), a huge skiing development frequented by French and Catalan enthusiasts, and the primary engine of change in the region; the road linking the resort core at Baqueira to Tanau (at 1700m) and the Beret sector serpentines through the chalet apartments and four- or five-star hotels comprising the modern, posey *urbanizació*. But it's no trouble to stay nearby at Salardú or Tredòs (see opposite p.264) and show up for some of the best **skiing** in these mountains – with one important caveat. Most runs face west or south, and the snow, especially after February, can deteriorate quickly, closing slopes by 3pm. The most reliable, north-facing runs in the Baqueira sector descend to **Orri** (1850m), with its own car park and lifts, and also the link to the **Beret** (1850–2516m) and east-facing **Beret-Blanhibllar** (1850–2338m) sectors, most suitable for beginners and weak intermediates, though you'll need your own transport to reach it by road. More advanced skiers can use chair-lifts from Points 1500 and 1700 in the Baqueira *urbanizació* to reach 2500-metre **Cap de Baqueira**, start of numerous, mostly red-rated pistes in open bowls above the trees. The south-facing **Bonaigua** sector, either side of the pass, has mostly intermediate runs and at un-snowploughed times may have automobile access only from the Noguera Pallaresa. Lift passes are the priciest in the Pyrenees at about €40 per day, but you are being pampered with a preponderance of chair-lifts (21 of 26), groomed, wide pistes, a first-class accident recovery service and an interlinked domain of over seventy runs.

Salardú

SALARDÚ, a few kilometres further west, is the largest of a local cluster of villages, notional capital of Nautaran and a logical base for explorations: large enough to offer a reasonable choice of accommodation and food, but small enough to feel pleasantly remote (except during August or peak ski season). Staying gives you the opportunity to visit surrounding villages, all centred on beautiful **Romanesque churches**. Salardú's is the spacious, thirteenth-century **Sant Andreu**, set in its own pleasant grounds and surrounded by characterful houses with steeply pitched roofs. The church doors, usually open, are flanked by the most elaborate portal in the valley, its carved column capitals featuring birds feeding their young and four eerie little human faces. Once inside, you can enjoy some fine restored sixteenth-century fresco patches, including *Christ Enthroned*, the *Assumption*, various saints and smudged panels of the Four Virtues. The only jarring note is sounded by the octagonal fifteenth-century belfry, whose clock tolls with an electronic tone (silenced between midnight and 7am) instead of a bell.

Practicalities

There's an unreliable, summer-only wooden **Turisme** hut (theoretically June–Sept daily 10am–1.30pm & 4.30–8pm) just off the main road at the central **car park**. The single **bank** has an ATM; there's also a **swimming pool** (mid-June to Aug daily 11am–7pm).

Even at the height of the summer you should find a **bed** (if not necessarily a room) in Salardú. Dependable options aimed at **hikers** include the *Refugi Rosti*, Plaça Major 1 (Ⓣ973 645 308, Ⓦwww.refugirosti.com; closed May, June, Oct & Nov; ❺ HB in non-en-suite doubles; also dorms), in a rambling, 300-year-old building on the main square, and *Refugi Juli Soler i Santaló* (Ⓣ973 645 016; dorms or four-bunk en-suite rooms), 200m east of the car park next to the pool

For conventional, central **accommodation**, try *Pensió Casat* (Ⓣ973 645 056; ❹) at c/Major 6, or for heated, en-suite rooms try *Residència Aiguamòg* (Ⓣ973 645 996; ❹ B&B) on c/Sant Andreu 12. More upmarket choices include the *Hotel deth Pais* in Plaça dera Pica (Ⓣ973 645 836, Ⓕ644 500; closed May & Nov; ❹ B&B), with underfloor heating and a few balconies; and, top of the heap for Salardú, the *Hotel Colomers* near the bank at c/dera Mola 8 (Ⓣ973 644 556, Ⓕ644 170; ❻ B&B), has designer rooms and a few luxury attic suites (❼).

For **meals**, non-guests can enjoy excellent *menús* at the *Refugi Juli Soler i Santaló*, or spend about €26 *a la carta* across the river at *Prat Aloy*, linked to the *Hotel deth Pais*. Alternatives are scarce, since the handful of independent village restaurants are overpriced and suffer frequent management changes. While the restaurant at the *Refugi Rosti* is decent enough (€18 *menú*), its main appeal is its **bar**, the best in town: *Delicatesen*.

Villages around Salardú

UNHA (Unya), 700m up the hill into the Unhòla valley, has a church of the same age as that in Salardú, though you're more likely to be interested in the several **restaurants** and *vinacotecas* (wine-bars) here, the most economical and consistently open being *Es de Don Joan* (game and Aranese local cuisine) and *Casa Restaurante Perez*, the latter offering **accommodation** at *Casa Benito* (Ⓣ973 645 752; ❸).

BAGERGUE, 2km higher up the road (or reached via the GR211 path from Unha and Garòs) remains the most countrified (and at 1419m, the highest) of the Nautaran settlements, and offers yet another handsome church – plus several **restaurants**. Most famous is *Casa Peru* (Mon, Tues, Thurs, Fri eves, lunch also Sat–Sun; closed May–June & Oct–Nov, Wed all year; reserve on Ⓣ973 645 437), which deserves the plaudits adorning its entrance thanks to offerings like *olha aranesa* (hot-pot) to die for, venison meatballs in wild mushroom sauce, wild-fruit flan with meringue plus good house wine, all for €30 – far less than more pretentious equivalents in Salardú, Vilha or Arties. Bagergue also has excellent **accommodation** at *Hotel Seixes* (Ⓣ973 645 406, Ⓦwww.seixes.com), which fills quickly at weekends; it's at the entrance to the village, with relatively easy parking. Choose between wood-trimmed rooms in the original hostal wing (❹ B&B), or the newer hotel wing (❺ B&B) featuring south-facing balconied rooms or attic suites.

Tredòs

Across the river from Salardú, and about twenty minutes' walk upstream along the signposted *Camin Reiau* (King's Road), **TREDÒS** – once the prettiest of the Nautaran villages – has had its old core overlaid by a rash of new ski chalets. However it retains a massive twelfth-century church – one of whose murals is now at the Cloisters Museum in New York – with freestanding belfry. In the centre is a find: *Restaurante Saburedo*, where the construction crews for all those apartments **eat**. The food's hearty rather than *haute*, with four courses (giant salad, onion soup, a meat dish, stewed pears) for €12 on weekdays (*carta* at weekends, €17–20). If you're taken with the village, they also have **rooms** (Ⓣ973 645 089; ❹), as does *Casa Micalot* (Ⓣ973 645 326; ❹) on the same lane. The palatial *Hotel De Tredòs*, on the outskirts of the village (Ⓣ973 644 014, Ⓦwww.hoteldetredos.com; ❺–❻ B&B), can arrange one-week ski packages, and has chalet-style units.

Arties and Garòs

ARTIES, 3km west and downstream from Salardú, has the usual complement of recent holiday homes, with more under construction. However, if you're driving and/or Salardú is full, Arties has considerable appeal, particularly high-quality food and lodging, and the old village core straddling the Garona River. There are two **churches**: the central, ninth- to fourteenth-century Santa María, with Templar fortifications, and the deconsecrated Sant Joan on the main road, now home to a sporadically open **museum** of changing exhibits.

The best budget **accommodation** is the quiet, good-value *Pensió Barrie*, alias *Casa Portolá* (Ⓣ973 640 828; ❸) at c/Mayor 21 – three floors of wood-and-tile decor ensuite rooms with bathtubs, the top two storeys very alpine with skylights and dormer windows. A considerable notch up in price is the *Hotel Besiberri* by the stream at c/Deth Fòrt 4 (Ⓣ973 640 829, Ⓕ973 642 696; ❹–❻ B&B; closed Nov & May–June). Rooms (except for the rambling attic suite) are smallish but well appointed; lovely common areas and savoury Catalan breakfasts are further pluses.

Arties' ten or so **restaurants** are usually of higher standard and better value for money than those in Salardú, though many hike up their prices during ski season. Tried and tested options include *Montagut* (closed Sun eve) up on the highway, with two *menús*, the pricier one featuring French paté, carrots in mustard, duck *confit* and dessert; and Zimbabwean-run *El Pollo Loco* (closed May–June & Oct–Nov), in the same building, which offers four *menús* under €23 (including a vegetarian one) featuring the chicken of the name, all washed down by organic cider. For something more upmarket, try *Sidreria Iñaki* across the road for Basque-style grills, dishes and *tapas* like *alubias de Tolosa* and *bacalao*; or *Restaurant Urtau*, on the eponymous *plaça* in the old quarter, which does *a la carta* only for about €30. On, or just above, Plaça Urtau are four musical **bar-clubs**, at least one of which should be operating summer or winter.

The village of **GARÒS**, 3km west, is the lowest-altitude community of Nautaran, completely ringed with new, stone-built holiday cottages. Yet its old core, focused on the twelfth-century church of San Julian, retains some charm, and offers quality **accommodation** at *Garòs Ostau* (Ⓣ973 642 378, Ⓦwww.aran.org/ostaugaros; closed early July & early Sept) en route to the church at the (current) edge of the village. Choose between larger, woodsy rooms with views of the church and meadow (❺ B&B) or much smaller village-view units (❹ B&B). There's also a central **cake-and-pie** salon, *La Tarteria* (open 4.30–8pm), with all fare made on the premises; this includes fresh juices, scones, crumbles, sweet and savoury tarts, brownies and English teas; they've also opened a longer-hours branch in Arties (9am–1pm & 3.30–9.30pm), with good **breakfasts**.

Mijaran and Baixaran

West of Nautaran lies **Mijaran** (Mid-Valley) and the major town of **Vielha**, capital of the entire region, served by two long-distance bus routes: one seasonally from Barcelona via La Pobla de Segur, the other year-round from Lleida via El Pont de Suert, culminating in the 5300-metre **Túnel de Vielha**. You emerge from the tunnel mouth just above the town at the southwest corner of the valley, close to the old but still-used pilgrims' and drovers' track descending from the 2442-metre Port de Vielha, which used to guarantee Vielha's isolation. The N230 road then heads north to the French border just 28km away, through **Baixaran**, the lower part of the valley.

Vielha

The ride towards **VIELHA** (Viella) from either direction is more memorable than the town itself, and there's little reason to stay if you have your own transport or can make a bus connection. A sort of mini-Andorra-la-Vella (without duty-free bargains), Vielha offers numerous supermarkets, boutiques and restaurants. The demise of La Tuca ski resort just south hasn't slowed growth; urban density expands yearly, leaving little open space in the centre, except for a pedestrian walkway along the Garona. Amongst all this glitz, members of Spain's crack alpine warfare squad occupy barracks just east of the centre.

If you have time to kill, pop into the parish church of **Sant Miquèu**, right in the centre on the east bank of the Riu Nere. Its twelfth-century wooden bust, the *Crist de Mijaran* – probably part of a *Descent from the Cross* – is one of the finest specimens of Romanesque art hereabouts. The **Museu dera Val d'Aran**, c/Major 26 (Tues–Sat 10am–1pm & 5–8pm, Sun 11am–2pm; €1.50), across the river, merits a look for its coverage of Aranese history and folklore. The only other diversion is the mammoth **Palai de Gèu** (Ice Palace) across the river, with a swimming pool, ice rink and gym (pool, gym, sauna: Mon–Fri 8.30am–9.30pm, Sat & Sun 11am–2pm & 4.30–9pm; ice rink: Mon–Fri 5.30–8.45pm, Sat 4.30–9pm, Sun noon–2pm & 4.30–9pm; €12.70 for all facilities including skate hire).

Practicalities

Buses stop at two marquees opposite each other (with schedules posted), just downhill from the major roundabout at the west end of town; tickets are sold on the bus. The **Turisme** (daily all year 9am–9pm; ⓣ973 640 110), offering maps and valley accommodation lists, is beside the **post office** at c/Sarriulera 6, by the church square. There's **Internet** access at imaginatively named Cyber Café (daily 10am–midnight) on Plaza Coto Marzo behind the church.

There's no shortage of **accommodation** in Vielha, but most is aimed at ski clientele, with little of outstanding value. Heading north from the church, you'll find the best of the inexpensive places by turning left along the main street and then right down the lane just across the bridge, towards the main **car park**. At Plaça Sant Orenç 3, there's the *Hotel El Ciervo* (ⓣ973 640 165; ❹), while tiny en-suite *Pension Casa Vicenta* is at c/Camin Reiau 3 (ⓣ973 640 819; ❸). For more comfort, try the *Hotel Turrull* at c/Camin Reiau 7 (ⓣ973 640 058; ❹), which encourages half-board at its ground-floor restaurant.

Vielha's best-value independent **restaurant** is *Basteret*, c/Major 6b, where ham-stuffed trout, cheese salad, blueberry cheesecake and house wine costs around €23. For something a bit more upmarket, head for *Deth Gorman* (closed Tues & June) above the church, strong on game and fish for €23–28 each, or consider the two-kilometre detour east to Escunhau hamlet, where *Casa Turnay* in the centre (closed May & June, Sun) features Aranese-style game, fish and elaborate vegetable dishes for a similar amount.

Baixaran

You can continue down the Garona through **ARRÒS** (6km) and **ERA BORDETA** (Es Bòrdes; 9km), both of which play a key role in Aranese architecture. Era Bordeta supplies the granite for the walls and Arròs the slates for the slightly concave roofs that planners require in Nautaran and Mijaran. Arròs itself, though, is almost in the **Baixaran** (Low Valley) region; its balconied houses around an octagonal belfry have rendered white walls and red-tiled roofs. There are two big summer-only **campsites** at Arròs: the *Artigané* (ⓣ973 640 189) and the *Verneda* (ⓣ973 641 024).

Baixaran is "low" indeed at 800m and fully exposed to the mists which habitually drift up the Pyrenean north slope. Its focus is **BOSSÒST**, 16km from Vielha, where houses are strung out along the main road and on both sides of the river, alternating with tacky shops. Its twelfth-century Romanesque church has a carved tympanum and three apses with raised Lombard brickwork. Apart from the church, there's no reason to stop (except for petrol, much cheaper than in France), and it's only 4km more to **LES**, with a spa (daily 11am–2pm & 5–9pm; closed Nov & Sun eve low season) and affordable **accommodation** and **meals** at *Hotel Europa* (ⓣ973 648 016; ❸), offering four copious if not exactly elegant *menús* at €20 or under; on the east side of the stream bridge stands the *Hotel Talbart* (ⓣ973 648 011; ❷), also with a popular, similarly priced *menjador* and better, balconied rooms. Les is home to an unusual **Saint John's eve festival** centred on the burning of the **haro** pole, split and studded with shorter wood bits; a new one is erected on June 29, remaining up until the following year.

From Les, it's a further 5km to the French border and bus terminus at Eth Pònt de Rei (Pont de Rei), and 18km to the first significant French town, Saint-Béat. An alternative road out of Bossòst into France, the N141 from just south of the village, climbs through dense woods to the French border at **Coll deth Portilhon** (Col du Portillon; open March–Dec), then descends sharply to Luchon.

Walking and biking from the Val d'Aran

Numerous tracks and rather fewer footpaths allow you to walk or mountain-bike from the valley in every direction. Editorial Alpina publishes a 1:40,000 "Val d'Aran" map of the whole area, but if you stray outside its coverage you'll need adjacent 1:25,000 sheets as well: "Montgarri" if you're going east; either Alpina's or the official Catalan 1:25,000 map for the national park to the south; "La Ribagorça" together with "Maladeta/Aneto" if you're headed west. The French Cartes des Randonnées "Couserans-Cap d'Aran" (1:50,000 sheet no. 6) is the most useful for trans-border treks north from Aran.

East to Montgarri and the Vall d'Isil

An easy excursion takes you along the sources of the Noguera Pallaresa, which flows initially northeast before curling south. Make an early start **from Salardú or Bagergue** to join the asphalt road from Baqueira into the Noguera Pallaresa valley; keep on it, past the first trickle of the river, until the surface becomes dirt track just past the last ski lifts. You're now on the broad **Plan de Beret**, with grass and cows in the foreground and a tangle of frontier peaks in the far distance. Four walking hours (15km) out of Salardú – half that time on a mountain bike – you reach the twelfth-century **Santuari de Montgarri**, next to which are two refuges, the more established being *Refugi Amics de Montgarri* (1657m; ⓣ973 645 064; 50 places), also open in winter for cross-country skiers. You can either overnight here or continue for the same distance again to Alòs d'Isil (see p.260), with its refuge. Although the track makes for dull walking, it's an attractive route with sweeping views from the plateau, especially beyond Montgarri. From Alòs, you can reverse the itinerary described on p.259 to arrive in the Vall de Cardós, or descend to Esterri d'Àneu.

North towards France

To head **into France** from the upper Noguera Pallaresa, follow an HRP variant east from Montgarri or north from Alòs through the Port de Salau, or a less-used route over the Coll de la Pala/Col de la Pale (2522m) to the *Refuge des Estagnous* (see p.310), on the west side of **Mont Valier** (2838m); the Salau route is much lower and easier.

It's also possible to enter France at a more westerly point using the initially dreary, rutted track up the **Unhòla valley** from Bagergue, passable in its lower reaches by 4WD and mountain bike. Beyond some abandoned mines, the landscape and the trail improve before reaching **Estany de Liat** (4–5hr). Here you can link with another section of the HRP, climbing due north from the lake through the **Portilhon d'Albi** (2457m) on the frontier, with the tiny Albi tarns scattered on both sides. Once through the pass you drop down over scree towards the French Albi tarn; from there, head north, contouring along the ridge behind, then northeast to the **Col de la Serre d'Araing**, where you pick up the GR10. After that, simply follow the GR down to the northeast corner of the **Étang d'Araing** reservoir, under the bare pyramid of **Pic de Crabère** (2630m), where there is a **refuge** (9–10hr from Salardú; see p.263). This is three hours on foot from Eylie, the roadhead to Sentein and Saint-Girons.

South to Aigüestortes

South of Nautaran, two lengths of part-paved road, a track-then-trail and a narrow path run towards the beautiful Aigüestortes region. Only the latter two approaches make for enticing walking, and are described first.

Via Saborèdo

The approach to Saborèdo begins on the south side of the river at Tredòs as a sparsely waymarked track, before curling past the edge of Baqueira and along the west bank of the **Riu de Ruda**. Although you can hear traffic descending from Bonaigua overhead, you'll see little other than wide green pasture until you sight the **Circ de Saborèdo** and the jumble of shattered granite peaks along the north edge of the Aigüestortes park. Some two-and-a-half hours from Salardú the track crosses the Ruda; then the grade stiffens, the surface underfoot becomes coarse pebbles, and a proper path begins some three-and-a-half hours along. After another hour's climb you reach the basic but friendly *Refugi de Saborèdo* (2310m; ⓣ973 253 015; 21 places; staffed Feb & March on request; Easter & mid-June to Sept). The next refuge is a further three hours' walking, through the easy **Port de Ratèra** (2530m), to the *Refugi d'Amitges* (2380m; ⓣ973 250 109, ⓦwww.amitges.com; 66 places; staffed Feb & March on demand, Easter week, mid-June to Sept & hols), inside the park by Estany Gran.

Via Gerber

A quicker if more challenging route to the Amitges refuge takes off from a popular car park and information placard 2.5km southeast of the Port de la Bonaigua. Take the obvious, green-and-orange-marked trail, initially next to a ski lift, south along the **Vall Gerber** past the swimmable **Estanyola de Gerber** (2020m; 30min), the trout-stocked **Estany Petit** (2120m; 50min) and the magnificent **Estany Gerber** (2165m; 1hr). Now the crowds thin out as the trail worsens and steepens en route to **Estany de l'Illa** (1hr 45min with day-pack, 2hr 30min with full pack) and its simple *Refugi de Mataró* (2460m; 8 places). Continue south into the park proper, negotiating the **Coll d'Amitges** (2740m), between Tuc de Saborèdo and Pic d'Amitges, before descending steeply to the Amitges refuge (see above). This could be problematic after a snowy winter, requiring crampons and ice-axe on the north flank – allow three hours from Mataró with a full pack.

The **Col de Gerber** (2587m), half-hour west of *Refugi de Mataró* on the route to Amitges, provides great views over Estany Glaçat towards Maladeta, and also allows access to the Circ de Saborèdo. The path becomes faint beyond the Estany de l'Illa, and almost nonexistent as you round Glaçat high above its north shore, with some tricky scrambling at one point before dropping to its outlet (2hr 30min from the car park). The going's easier to the dammed **Lac Major de Saborèdo** (2340m; 3hr); follow the outflow to the staffed hut (3hr 15min), which makes an excellent lunch stop.

You're now poised to complete a popular **one-day circuit** combining the two approaches detailed above. After 25 minutes further down the path from the refuge to the start of the rough track, continue perhaps another forty minutes, clear of the forest, to a grassy hillside (1850m) studded with boulders, and cairns marking the way back to the car park (if you reach the bridge over the Riu Ruda, you've gone too far). After a thirty-minute zig-zag climb, hot work even in late afternoon, the grade slackens as you contour around the hillside to cross a service track to assorted hilltop antennae, some five hours into the day. The trail, now broad, was the major route down from the Bonaigua pass in pre-highway days; drop east, following the left-hand (northerly) set of high-tension cables to arrive at your starting point. Though it's a five-and-a-half-hour walk at a brisk pace, allow an eight-hour day out, with rests and lunch stop.

Via Aiguamotx

From Tredòs, a partly paved road ascends steeply up the attractive **Vall d'Aiguamotx** (Aiguamoth) towards the exquisite **Circ de Colomèrs**; walking the steep road is neither attractive nor exquisite, so arrange a ride if possible. The potholed road finishes after about 8km at the luxury *Banys/Banhs de Tredòs* hotel, leaving another ninety minutes on dirt track, then path to the 2006-rebuilt *Refugi de Colomèrs* (2130m; ⓣ973 253 008; 60 places; staffed weekends Feb & March, Easter week, mid-June to late Sept & major hols).

The refuge stands by a reservoir, but there are dozens of natural lakes and tarns in the cirque, set among stands of black pine. A sketch map of day circuits varying from two hours to four hours is available from the warden. Full-pack treks from Colomèrs include the five-hour hike south, then west via the **Port de Colomèrs** (2604m) to the popular *Refugi Ventosa i Calvell* (see p.282). Alternatively, four hours' walk west along the joint HRP/GR11.18 takes you via the easier **Port de Caldes** (2567m) and the **Port d'Oelhacrestada** (2474m) to the *Refugi de la Restanca*. En route you skirt the foot of **Montardo d'Aran** (sometimes Montarto; 2830m) – an easy ascent with fabulous views over Aran.

Via Valarties

The friendly **Refugi de la Restanca** (2010m; ⓣ608 036 559; 80 places; open weekends most of the year, plus daily Easter week and mid-June to late Sept) can be reached directly from Arties via a road threading up the **Valarties**. However, there's little chance of hitching it, and the way up on foot, dotted by day-trippers' parked cars and illicitly placed tents, is even less inspiring than the Aiguamotx slog, if shorter. After 5km, asphalt yields to dirt, ending 3km later at the bottom of a short, sharp climb to the *Restanca* refuge near the eastern end of the reservoir dam.

West to Maladeta

The *Restanca* refuge permits the quickest access from the Aran to the **Maladeta** Massif, via the refuges and camping spots near the south end of the Túnel de Vielha. You have the choice from **Lac dera Restanca** of the longer, more difficult HRP – around **Lac de Mar** and **Lac Tort de Rius** (6hr) – or the GR11, which makes an easy, direct and well-marked traverse past **Lac de Rius** (4hr 30min). The HRP is recommended if you're an experienced, lightly laden trekker, since Mar is one of the area's most impressive lakes: a bare island hunkers in the middle, with a chaos of huge grey boulders on the shore, and Besiberri Nord peak looming to the south.

The HRP and GR11 rejoin briefly at the **Refugi Sant Nicolau** (aka *Er Ospitau de Vielha*), rebuilt on the site of a medieval pilgrims' hospice (1650m; ⓣ973 697 052; 70 places; open year-round except May, Nov & Dec 24–Jan 7). Though just above the main highway and paired tunnel mouths, it's the only amenity for miles around, and a welcome sight. Hosts Sebas and Juani provide reasonable meals to all comers (not Sun eve mid-Sept to June; not Sat lunch in summer), though there's no shop.

Approaches from the Noguera Ribagorçana

The Noguera Ribagorçana has its source near the tunnel; crossing it you forsake Catalunya for Aragón and face three different approaches to Maladeta and beyond.

The **HRP** takes the classic route west via the Molières valley and the **Coret de Molières** (Coll de Mulleres; 2935m; crampons/ice-axe often necessary) – a gruelling but spectacular traverse, which can be split by overnighting at the simple, metal-shed *Refugi Mulleres* (2360m; 8 places; always open), above a chain of tarns just below the pass. The **Cap deth Hòro/Cap de Tòro** (2969m), a fifteen-minute scramble up the north side of the saddle, gives a magnificent view over Maladeta's northeast glacier – where one branch of the Garona rises – and into the Joeu valley, where the infant river emerges after 4km underground.

The **GR11** continues south from Refugi Sant Nicolau to the head of the **Senet (Basserca) reservoir**, where it crosses the road at Pont de les Salenques and dips into the mouth of the **Salenques valley**, keeping to the south (true right) bank. Fairly well marked at first, the route (as well as the stream valley) divides about an hour along.

The inconspicuous right-hand option crosses the stream, then labours northwest through rhododendron-cloaked boulders prior to an exhausting slog up through scree and usually snow to the **Coll de les Salenques** (2807m); camping is possible two-thirds of the way in meadows at the base of the sharpest climb. There's an easier gradient down the other side to the **Plan dels Aigualluts**, one of the best wild campsites in the Pyrenees, also easily accessible from the Coret de Molières.

The waymarked, left-hand bearing is the **official GR11**, which threads through the lake-speckled **Vall d'Anglòs**, then over the easy **Coll de Ballibierna** (2728m), affording spectacular views of Maladeta's southwest face. Passing more lakes on the descent, the GR11 meets the track coming up the **Ball de Ballibierna**, and follows it down to Benasque – again a long day out of the Noguera Ribagorçana, best broken with a night out on either side of the pass, and/or an evening bus ride down to Benasque (see p.287). There's a tiny, wooden shepherds' shelter at 2220m, beside the easterly Ibón de Anglòs.

Approach via the Joeu valley

The easiest, though nowadays least used, approach to the Maladeta region starts from Era Bordeta, 9km west of Vielha on the N230 road. From here you walk (or taxi) south down the **Joeu valley** as far as the **Pla de l'Artiga** (8km; 1465m; simple unstaffed refuge) and the resurgence of waters from the Forau dels Aigualluts. From here a path climbs west to the **Pòrt dera Picada/Port de la Picada** (2470m; 3hr from the Pla), through which you descend gently to either follow the Ésera valley in front of you downstream.

The Aigüestortes-Sant Maurici region

Water is the salient feature of the **Parc Nacional d'Aigüestortes i Estany de Sant Maurici**, with its streams and waterfalls, nearly four hundred lakes reflecting harsh granite peaks, and reed-fringed upland marshes. Rain or snow falls on these mountains – some reaching 3000 metres – almost half the days of the year. The name *Aigüestortes* ("Twisted Waters") has something of an unintentional subtext, as local streams have been diverted through enormous galleries into the mountainsides, and the lakes and reservoirs, thus tapped (Sant Maurici among them), intermittently become mud-bowls. The region has been exploited in this way since 1914, when Swiss- and German-designed hydroelectric works were first undertaken to power the rapidly industrializing cities of Catalunya.

The park, bounded by the Val d'Aran, the Noguera Pallaresa and the Noguera Ribagorçana, was established in 1955 during the hydroelectric schemes' expansion, no conflict being apparent to the Francoist government. By the rules of the International Union for the Conservation of Nature, no hydroelectric exploitation is permitted in such a reserve, but since this is still Catalunya's only fully fledged national park, the authorities proudly brandish the title despite a continuing lack of international recognition. The arrogance of the bureaucrats of the era was epitomized in a 1970s pamphlet which reads: "Some changes have occurred recently with the construction of hydroelectrical installations which the country needs, and Nature has had to pay her tribute to man, The King."

But attitudes are slowly changing, and park authorities wage constant battle with FECSA-ENHER (the power corporation) in an attempt to limit their depredations. The park's western area increased considerably during 1986 through the cession of lands by the Boí municipality, then again in 1996, when a huge area north of Caldes de Boí was incorporated. Some 140 square kilometres now enjoy full protection, though further expansion is unlikely given the spiralling costs of compensating FECSA-ENHER and other private landowners. It's easy to steer clear of the dams, and recommended **hiking routes** keep to the wilder corners as far as possible.

There's something for walkers of all abilities, from the simple mid-altitude track-jaunt across the park east to west, to gruelling climbs over jagged passes requiring snow equipment, by way of several popular trekkers' traverses using the GR11 or its variants. The **Sant Nicolau valley** and its tributaries (in the west) have many glacially formed lakes and cirques, as well as the water-meadows of Aigüestortes. Eastern-sector highlights include the Peguera valley around the Josep María Blanc refuge, as well as the Estany de Sant Maurici itself, at the head of the Escrita valley. Just outside the park, in the 27,000-hectare so-called "peripheral zone of protection" (augmented a bit in 2006), are more lake-spangled cirques, particularly towards the Val d'Aran.

Flora and fauna

The most common **trees** in Aigüestortes-Sant Maurici are fir and Scotch pine, plus silver birch and beech, especially on north-facing slopes. There's an abundance of **flowers** in spring and early summer, with blooms present until August above 2000m.

Isards are the most conspicuous **mammals**, easily seen in winter when harsh weather drives them downhill, but staying on the high summits in summer. Perhaps the most curious animal of this region is the long-nosed, mole-sized **desman**, which lives in holes along the stream banks, feeding on aquatic insects; its timidity and nocturnal habits make it almost invisible. This species' western European territory is now confined to the Pyrenees and the Picos d'Europa. The **otter** is also elusive; **wild boar**, **fox** and **hare** less so. Outside its spring display-time, the **capercaillie** is glimpsed only when flushed out by chance; **ptarmigan** are similarly shy, and **black woodpeckers** are more likely to be heard than sighted. You will almost certainly see spectacular **birds of prey**: **golden eagles** soaring with open-V wings; **griffon vultures** floating high above like huge tasselled scarves; and **kestrels** hovering, tails fanned with wings pumping to maintain altitude.

Approaches to Aigüestortes

There are four chief **bases** from which to explore the Aigüestortes park and environs. Access to the Sant Maurici and Monestero areas is from the village of **Espot**, just beyond the eastern fringe of the park and within 7km of the La Pobla

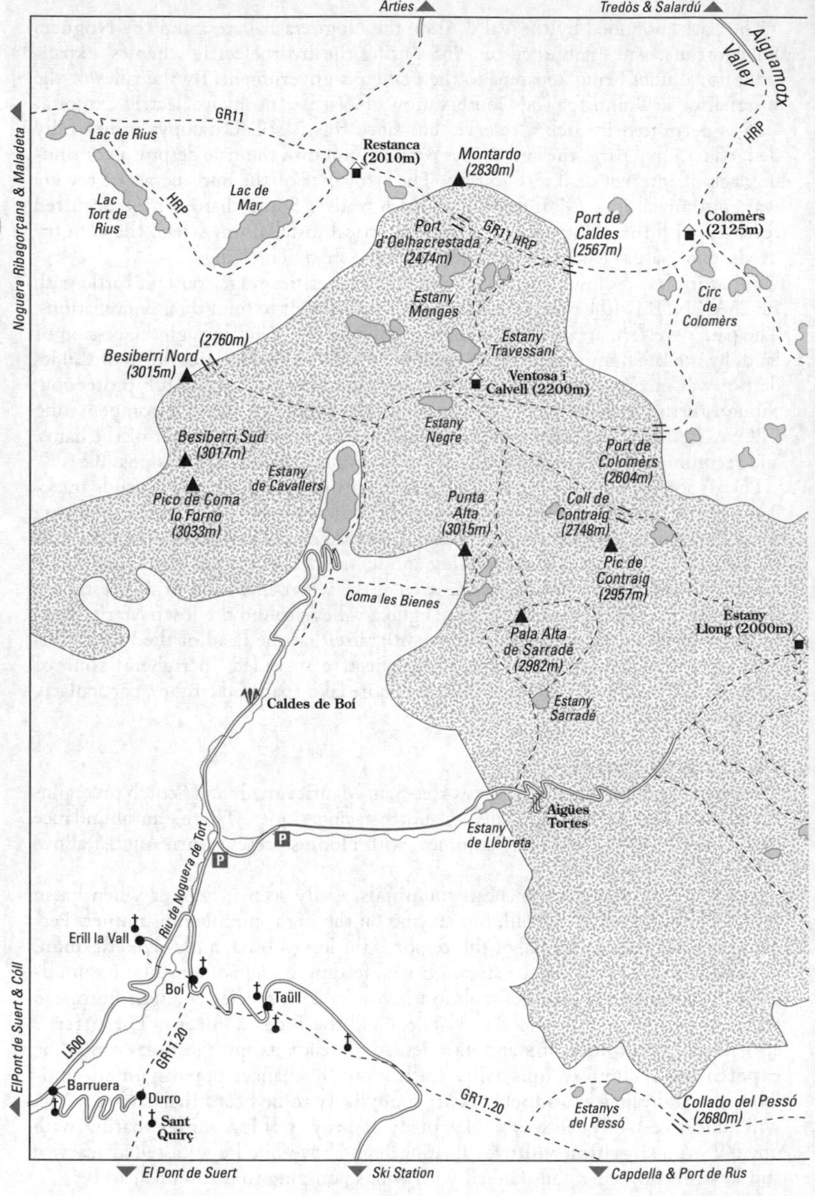

de Segur–Val d'Aran bus route. Possible approaches from the Val d'Aran are covered on p.268–269. Quickest access to the high, remote peaks around the Circ de Saburó is via **Capdella**, at the head of the **Vall Fosca**, one valley west of the Noguera Pallaresa and served by occasional bus from La Pobla de Segur. Finally, for the western Aigüestortes zone, or the many lakes below Besiberri peak, the usual entry is from **Boí** or **Taüll**, the former served by bus from La Pobla via El Pont de Suert, which is also on a bus route from Vielha.

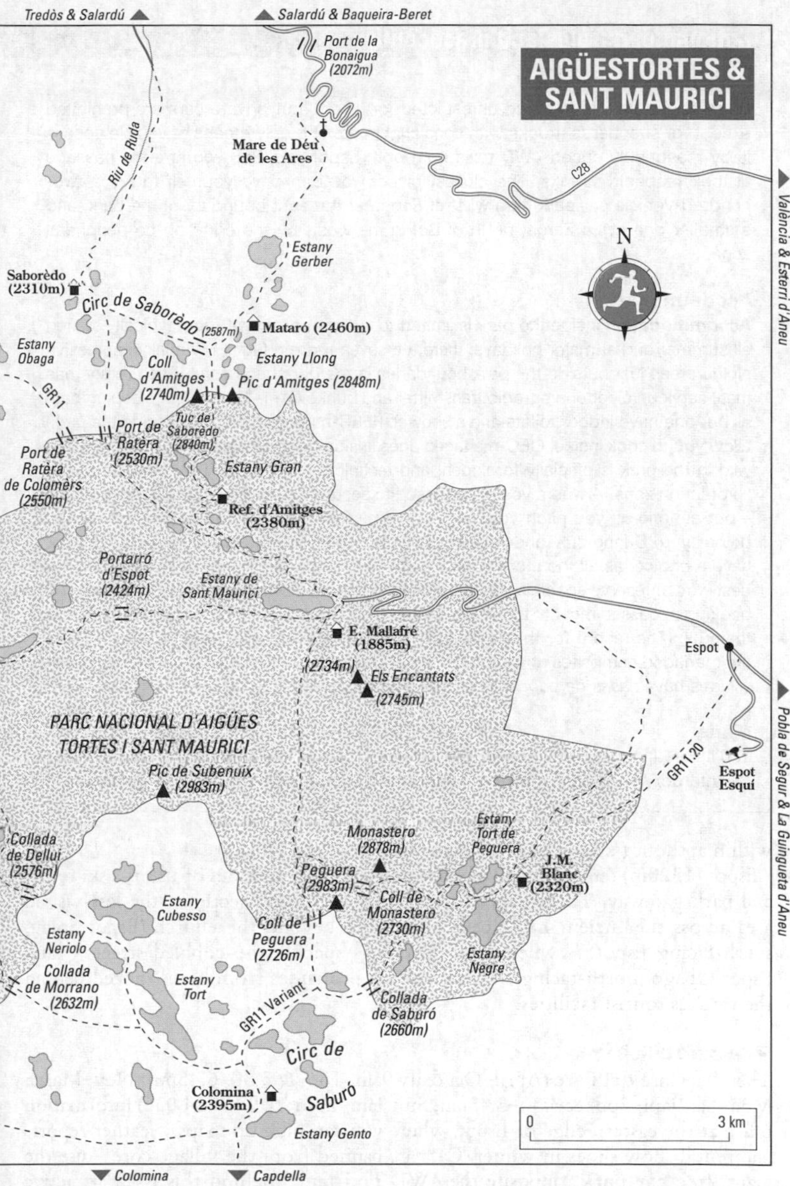

Espot

The main disadvantage of a public-transport approach through **ESPOT** is the probability that you'll have to road-walk the very steep 7km from the turning (and petrol-station forecourt) on the C13 highway where the Barcelona–Vielha bus drops you, and a similar distance beyond the village to the usual park entrance. Take a **4WD taxi** if there's one waiting at the turn-off; if not, one should appear

National park rules and practicalities

Park entry

Entry to the park is free and unrestricted for hikers, but private cars are prohibited except for shepherds' trucks with special permits. The only means of vehicle access is by reasonably priced 4WD taxis from both Espot and Boí; you arrange passage at their respective ranks. The closest places you can drive yourself to are a two-hundred-vehicle car park 4km west of Espot, at the east boundary of the park, and a smaller one at La Farga, north of Boí in the west, by the edge of the peripheral zone.

Accommodation

Accommodation inside the park is limited to five **mountain refuges**, typically staffed all summer and at major holidays; there are seven more refuges in equally impressive alpine areas just outside the park boundaries in the peripheral zone. Each refuge has meal service, telephone or radio transmitter and bunks (€11–12) for your sleeping bag; all but one have indoor toilets and a shower. FEEC-managed places (outside the park) allow you to cook inside; CEC-managed ones (inside the boundaries) do not. **Camping** wild in the park is officially forbidden, and technically restricted within the peripheral "protection zone" – where you're supposed to secure a permit from the nearest village – but as long as you pitch your tent well away from refuges and paths, nobody will bother you. During July and August (plus weekends in June and Sept) you may not have a choice, as all the more popular park-centre refuges fill weeks in advance. The best way to reserve space is via the website Ⓦwww.carrosdefoc.com, which gives you booking access to most of the area's refuges – and also details the loop itinerary linking them all. (The record for this is 10hr 35min; most mortals take about a week.) There are managed campsites at Taüll in the west, and at Espot to the east. All the approach villages have *cases de pagès*, *hostals* and hotels.

Maps

You'll need current editions of the Editorial Alpina 1:25,000 "Sant Maurici" and "Montardo/Vall de Boí" **map-booklets**; these are easily available in all gateway vil-

within an hour (€5 per person for the trip up to the village).

Espot (1320m) remains relatively unspoiled, despite decades of use as a ski resort and park gateway. The village is split into two distinct sections: the less-visited area across the ancient La Capella bridge and beyond the church (Espot Solau, south-facing Espot) – where goat droppings speckle the cobbled streets – and Espot Obago (north-facing), where hay still protrudes from barns tucked behind the various tourist facilities.

Practicalities

There's a **Casa del Parc** (April–Oct daily 9am–1pm & 3.30–6.45pm; Nov–March Mon–Sat 9am–2pm & 3.30–5.45pm, Sun 9am–2pm; Ⓣ973 624 036) information office at the eastern edge of Espot, where you can pick up maps, weather reports and rental snow shoes in winter. Cars are banned from the village core – use the giant, free **car park**, opposite the 4WD **taxi** rank. Behind this is an attractive municipal **pool**, while nearby there's a **bank** ATM.

The best-value **accommodation** in Espot Obago is *Residència Felip* (Ⓣ973 624 093; ❷), simple but spotless with most rooms en suite, plus laundry service and a small front garden. Also worth trying are the adjacent *Pensió La Palmira* (Ⓣ973 624 072; ❷) and the plush *Hotel Roya* (Ⓣ973 624 040, Ⓕ624 041; ❹ B&B). There are three **campsites** close by: the smallish *Sol i Neu* (Ⓣ973 624 001; June–Sept), just a few hundred metres from the village, has excellent facilities including a pool; *De*

lages except Capdella. If you're willing to forego the included pamphlet (text only in Castilian or Catalan), you can buy a two-for-the-price-of-one map-only packet, entitled "Parc Nacional d'Aigüestortes i Estany de Sant Maurici". The Catalan Generalitat's Mapa Topogràfic de Catalunya 1:25,000 folding map no. 1 is much more accurate, with 20-metre contour intervals, but a bit difficult to read. If you intend to approach from the north, you'll also need the 1:40,000 "Val d'Aran" Alpina, and if you're moving west towards Maladeta the 1:25,000 "La Ribagorça" makes a good investment. Sketched handouts at the various park information offices prove insufficient for route-finding – get a proper commercial map if you intend to leave the most popular paths.

Weather and route conditions

Be aware of, and prepared for, bad **weather**, which as everywhere in the Pyrenees can arrive rapidly and without warning. In midsummer many rivers are passable which at other times are not, but temperature contrasts between day and night are still very marked. Local climatic patterns in recent years have alternated between daily rain showers throughout July and August, or prolonged drought, with a general trend towards warmer, drier summers. The best time to see the wonderful colour contrasts of the vegetation is autumn or early summer. Many passes, even those mapped with a bona fide trail, will be difficult or impossible after a harsh winter owing to snowpack. If you're doing an unusual traverse, tell the warden of the refuge you'll be leaving, who should be able to give current **route pointers** and, if there's any cause for concern, phone your estimated time of arrival to your destination.

Skiing

In winter, the park is excellent for cross-country and high-mountain **skiing**, though there are no marked routes. Many of the refuges open for a week or two around Christmas and Easter, and selected weekends and school holidays in between. There are currently two downhill ski resorts on the fringes of the park – Boí-Taüll in the west and Espot Esquí in the east – with another under construction on the slopes of Pic

La Mola, 2km further down the hill (Ⓣ973 624 024; July–Sept), also has a pool. At the far (upstream) edge of Espot beyond the old bridge, the tiny but grassy *Solau* (Ⓣ973 624 068) also rents out rooms at *Casa Peret de Peretó* (❷), a good fallback if the village centre is full.

Quality **eating** opportunies are limited to the vine-shrouded *Ju Quim* (closed Mon) in the centre, which gets jammed at lunch thanks to its good-value *menú*, and the *menjador* of the *Pensió La Palmira*. Two well-stocked **supermarkets** and another shop sell maps, camping-gas cartridges and the like

Espot Esquí

Two kilometres above the village, parts of the **ESPOT ESQUÍ** ski centre (formerly Super Espot; Ⓦwww.espotesqui.com) edge into the park's peripheral protection zone. Its 31 runs are laid out with two chair-lifts from Point 1500 (very limited gear rental and lift tickets) to Point 2000, and further lifts to the tops of mostly intermediate pistes at 2300m, or more advanced runs from 2500m. Despite a northeasterly orientation, its snow record can't match most neighbouring resorts; by late March many runs may close.

Into the park

The road divides in the middle of the village. The left-hand bearing leads up to **Espot Esquí**; right takes you west into the park. It's 3.5km to its boundary and

△ Estany de Sant Maurici

the designated car park at **Prat de Pierró**, and 7km to the end of the asphalt at **Estany de Sant Maurici**. The GR11 trail avoids most of the road, or local 4WD taxis provide an inexpensive (€4.40) way to avoid dull track-walking.

Once at the lake, there is a classic postcard view to the south, dominated by the 2700-metre spires of **Els Encantats** ("The Enchanted Ones"). In legend, these were once two hunters and their dog, who snuck off hunting instead of attending church on the day of the patron saint's festival. Lured heavenward by a spectral stag, the trio were turned to stone by a divine lightning bolt.

Another enticing trail leads southwest from Espot Obago in just under four hours to the **Refugi Josep Maria Blanc** (Ⓣ973 250 108, Ⓦwww.jmblanc.com; 2350m; 40 places; open Easter & mid-June to late Sept), inside the park boundary on **Estany Tort de Peguera**. You can then continue another four hours to the Colomina shelter (see opposite), over the 2680-metre **Collada de Saburó**; the entire way from Espot is a well-travelled route, marked as the variant GR11.20.

Vall Fosca

The half-dozen villages of the narrow **Vall Fosca** are mostly tucked away, out of sight, up the slopes. What you see on the valley floor are the harbingers of the future Interllacs ski station: a widened road to the half-built chalets, apart-hotels and a golf course at **ESPUI**, already home to the volubly friendly *Hotel Monseny* (Ⓣ973 663 079; ❺ HB, suites ❻; Easter–Nov), a Casa Fonda affiliate with a pool and a well-regarded restaurant. Bus service from La Pobla de Segur has dwindled to three a week (Mon, Wed & Fri at 5.15pm), and terminates 800m beyond Espui in the lower quarter of **CAPDELLA** (30km from La Pobla), beside the Central (de Energia), the oldest hydroelectric generator in these mountains. In the upper quarter, the excellent *Refugio Tacita* (1300m; Ⓣ973 663 121; Ⓦwww.tacitahostel.com; July–Sept or by arrangement; 23 places) is run by a welcoming couple who may offer pick-up service from the bus stop in La Pobla de Segur. Apart from the *menjador* of the *Hostal Leo* at the Central (no accommodation offered), the closest independent **restaurant**, is in **LA POBLETA DE BELLVEÍ**, 17km south and

3km up from Senterada, where the Vall Fosca and its Riu Flamisell join the main highway. Here popular *L'Era del Marxant* (booking required on ⓣ973 661 735; lunch daily, also Fri & Sat eves) specializes in grills (€12 *menú*, €20–23 *a la carta*).

Into the park

From Capdella, a half-day trek past the ugly Sallente dam takes you to the wonderful **Refugi Colomina** (2395m; ⓣ973 252 000; 40 places; staffed early Feb, mid-March to mid-April & mid-June to mid-Sept), an old wooden chalet ceded to mountaineers by FECSA-ENHER and set among the alpine lakes of the **Circ de Saburó**, just south of the park boundary. You can skip the steepest hiking by taking the *teléferic* (July–Sept; daily upward departures at 9am & 3pm, down at 1pm & 6pm) from the road's end at the back of the Sallente reservoir to within 45 minutes' walk of the refuge. The immediate surroundings of the refuge have a few two- to three-hour walks, most notably the circuit of the Circ de Saburó.

El Pont de Suert

The route into the southwestern area of Aigüestortes begins just past **EL PONT DE SUERT**, a small town 41km northwest of La Pobla de Segur; **buses** stop at a roadside terminal at the southeast edge of town. El Pont de Suert's most remarkable, central sight is an unmissably hideous **modern church**, with a baptistry like a vertical egg and a brick belfry resembling the head of Spielberg's ET. It was designed by engineer Eduardo Torroja and architect J. Rodríguez Millares in 1955 as a bizarre homage to the Romanesque churches further up the valley (see below). The "egg" and the vaulting of the Nissen-hut-like nave are made entirely from curved, prestressed concrete panels, considered a daring technique back then but now looking thoroughly dated.

El Pont de Suert is pleasant enough if you need to spend the night before catching the early afternoon bus north up the Valle de Boí, but you shouldn't need to because midday departures from Vielha, Lleida and La Pobla all connect with this service. The old town, a small maze of arcaded streets, compensates for the grim buildings lining the highway, but it's not exactly a tourist hot-spot, with only two **accommodation** options: *Hotel Can Mestre* at Plaça Major 8 (ⓣ973 690 306; ④) and *Hostal Cotori* (ⓣ973 690 096; ③) on the next plaza north, with a pleasant river-view **restaurant**.

Vall de Boí

Some 2km northwest of El Pont de Suert, a good road threads north (right) along the **Vall de Boí**, following the Noguera de Tor towards Caldes de Boí, and passing several villages on the way. It's an area crammed with **Romanesque churches** dating from the eleventh and twelfth centuries, when the area was more populous and wealthy than at any time since, and could hire master-masons from Lombardy. As a happy result, these churches have never been rebuilt, and rank as the finest in Catalunya. All were constructed with astonishing detail and elegance from hand-split chunks of local stone, roofed by slates and graced by literally over-the-top belfries. Unfortunately most of the frescoes on view today are reproductions, the originals having long since been whisked away to the Museu d'Art de Catalunya in Barcelona. The entire valley was declared a UNESCO heritage site in 2001, which may slow the growth of modern chalets at Boí and Taüll. All the churches detailed share the same **visiting hours and admission** (summer daily 10am–2pm & 4–8pm, winter Mon–Sat 10.30am–2pm & 4–7pm, Sun 10.30am–2pm; €1.20), except where otherwise stated.

Cóll and Barruera

Some 8km upstream there's a turn-off left to the hillside village of **CÓLL**, with the twelfth-century church of **Santa María de l'Assumpció**; its west portal and masonry are particularly fine, but the grounds are usually locked. You're more likely to detour for *Hotel Casa Peiró* (Ⓣ973 297 002, Ⓦwww.casapeirocoll.com; ④), with somewhat bland en-suite rooms: wood floors, TV, pastel colours. But its **restaurant** is regarded as one of the best in the area – not cheap at €35–40 a head, but worth it, especially the starters.

BARRUERA, 5km further on and much larger, has several places to **stay**, best value being *Casa Coll* (Ⓣ973 694 005; ②), an echoing old mansion near the top of c/Major in the old town. The salubrious rooms (some en-suite) are on the top floor, with a kitchen on the ground floor and common areas stuffed with antiques. For a more conventional alternative, try the high-quality, modern *Hotel Farre d'Avall* (Ⓣ973 694 029, Ⓔhotel@farredavall.com; ④), also in the old quarter, with limited parking and a restaurant. Opposite the petrol station stands the **Turisme** for the entire valley (Mon–Sat 9am–2pm & 5–7pm, Sun 10am–2pm; Ⓣ973 694 000, Ⓦwww.vallboicom); also on main thoroughfare Passeig Sant Feliu is a recommended guides' bureau, Cara Sur (Ⓣ973 694 132, Ⓔcarasur@yahoo.es), which organizes canyoning, caving and snowshoe expeditions. Near the filling station stands Barruera's Romanesque church, the riverside **Sant Feliu**, with its engaging thirteenth-century portal and creaking interior.

Durro and Erill La Vall

Another fine Romanesque church graces **DURRO**, 3km away on the hillside to the east, reached by a steep side road. The bell tower of **La Nativitat de la Mare de Déu** is the thickest in the valley, its raised brickwork contrasting with crude masonry and a stark southern portal. Durro is situated on the variant GR11.20 linking El Pont de Suert with Boí, Taüll and the Colomina refuge (see p.277). Coming from Boí, the well-signed path starts just over the little bridge behind the old district, climbs forty-five minutes to a shrine, then drops to Durro fifteen minutes later. Another fifteen minutes along the GR11.20 brings you to the twelfth-century *ermita* of **Sant Quirç**, prominent on the ridge opposite. The most reliable facility is central *Hostal Aude* (Ⓣ973 694 139, Ⓦwww.hostalaude.com; ③–⑤ B&B), with somewhat clinical, parquet-veneer-floored rooms and a ground-floor **restaurant**.

Further on, just before the turn-off for Boí, a 1km side road leads west to **ERILL LA VALL**, also linked to a Boí by a useful non-GR path (30min). Erill's twelfth-century church of **Santa Eulàlia** has an unusual arcaded porch and a climbable, six-storey belfry which rivals Sant Climent's in Taüll (see p.280); the interior holds a museum of religious folk art, dominated by a replica of a carved, seven-figure twelfth- or thirteenth-century *Deposition*, complete with the two Thieves. In high season Erill is more likely to have a vacancy than Boí or Taüll; **accommodation** includes *Hostal La Plaça*, opposite the belfry (Ⓣ973 696 026, Ⓦwww.hostal-laplaza.com; ④), with comfortable rooms and galleried family suites. Alternatively, the nearby *Hostal L'Aüt* (Ⓣ973 696 048, Ⓔlauteril@wanadoo.es; ④) has plain rooms but the village's best **restaurant**, whose simple but abundant fare attracts diners from the whole valley: €18 *a la carta* for mushroom sautée, grilled quail, dessert and a beer. If you can't get a table, *La Granja d'Erill* at the village entrance opposite the car park is your other choice, with plain if good-value daily *menús* for €12.

Boí

BOÍ stands 1km above the main road, which continues up to Caldes de Boí (see opposite); however the bus service comes this way. On arrival, the village proves something of an anticlimax: a tiny medieval core huddled around a crag, swamped by car parks, modern buildings and old houses defaced with new brick repairs. Even the twelfth-century church of **Sant Joan** has been extensively renovated, the only original parts being the squat belfry and part of the apse; a cycle of reproduction frescoes in the spandrels of the north aisle feature animals symbolic of the Christian virtues (eg, the camel for submission and humility).

Practicalities

The **Casa del Parc information office**, tucked under an arch in the old quarter (April–Oct daily 9am–1pm & 3.30–6.45pm, Nov–March Mon–Sat 9am–2pm & 3.30–5.45pm, Sun 9am–2pm; ⓣ973 696 189), sells local maps at a slight mark-up. The 4WD-taxis have a rank and ticket office on the central Plaça Treio (summer only; book space on ⓣ973 696 314 or 629 205 489). The lone **bank** on the main through road has an ATM – the only one beyond Barruera.

If you need to **stay** in Boí, a good budget choice is *Hostal Pascual*, down by the junction and bridge, halfway to Erill (ⓣ973 696 014, ⓦwww.hostalpascual.com; ❸ B&B; open Christmas, New Year, Easter week, June–Sept), with helpful owners, wood-trimmed, tiled-floor rooms and a pleasant terrace atop one of the two *menjadors*. In the village itself, try the central *Hostal Pey* (ⓣ973 696 036; ❹), with a popular terrace overlooking Plaça del Treio. There are also clean if partly non-en-suite **rooms** in *Casa Tenda* (ⓣ973 696 034; ❷) just through the stone archway in the old quarter – follow the *habitacions* sign.

Eating out, you'll not do better than *Casa Higinio*, 200m up the road to Taüll, above the village centre. Its wood-fired range produces excellent meat dishes, or try the fine *escudella* (minestrone soup) and trout. A big *menú* accompanied by local wine comes to around €14.

Into the park – and Caldes de Boí

It's 3.5km from Boí to the national park entrance, and another 3.5km to the scenic waterfalls of **Aigüestortes**, tumbling from water-meadows to feed the reedy **Estany de Llebreta**, where half-wild horses roam. One final kilometre above the falls – passed closely by both road and trail #5, the "Ruta de la Nutria/Llúdriga" – is a summer-only park information booth; an adjacent map placard suggests day hikes, with corresponding time estimates. The most popular stroll, about an hour one-way, leads east from the information post to Estany Llong.

The 4WD taxis from Boí (€4.40 each way) take you as far as the booth. Vehicles wait to depart until they're full; last return from Aigüestortes is at 7pm in midsummer. The closest you can get to the park boundary in your own vehicle is the car park at La Farga, or there's another smaller one 1.5km east, right at the boundary. If you leave your car at either, and arrange to meet a taxi to take you further uphill, at day's end you can follow the trail signed for the "Aparcament" from the info booth which shortcuts the road by 45 minutes.

Alternatively, you can flag down the one midday bus from the junction of the Boí side road up to the large **spa** complex of **CALDES DE BOÍ** (June 1–Oct 15 only), 6km upstream. The four-star *Hotel Manantial* here is beyond the financial reach of most travellers, but the adjacent two-star *Caldes* (ⓣ973 696 230; June 15 Sept 30; ❺), a renovated old building with plush, non-fusty rooms, constitutes reasonable-value spa **accommodation**, with every imaginable hydrotherapy.

From Caldes de Boí, it's 4km to a large car park below the high dam at the south end of Estany de Cavallers. The dam itself marks the trailhead for walks towards the beautiful natural lakes northwest of the park, just below the Besiberri and Montardo peaks.

Taüll

TAÜLL – 3km above Boí by road or forty minutes on a fairly steep but well-marked section of the GR11.20 – had been a much larger medieval village before an avalanche divided it into two districts. More recently, it has been massively affected by the ski resort of Boí-Taüll (see opposite) on the mountainside a few kilometres southeast. There's an enormous holiday complex 1500m beyond the village at Pla de l'Ermita (terminus of the bus line) en route to the ski station, and even in summer Taüll is targeted by tour coaches and family cars in search of panoramic picnic spots. Yet away from the peripheral ski chalets, the old core retains considerable character, and is certainly preferable to Boí as a base.

Two of the best local Romanesque churches stand in the village, consecrated on successive days in 1123. Of the pair, **Sant Climent de Taüll** is more immediately impressive by virtue of its six-storey belfry and original triple apse. The stark interior, doubling now as a museum of religious artefacts, retains copies of vivid murals showing Christ, saints and apostles, plus scenes from the New Testament and the Apocalypse. These, however, are outshone by a sixteenth-century retable of St Anne, the Virgin and Christ as a seated group, and a fine thirteenth-century polychrome wood statue of Christ Enthroned. Climb the rickety wooden steps to the top of the bell tower, and you're rewarded with sweeping views through delicately arched windows.

At the heart of the upper quarter, **Santa María** (daily 10am–8pm; free) is similar in design, though its belfry has only four storeys. After a millennium of subsidence, there's not one right angle remaining in the building, with the tower in particular at an engaging list. The mural (again a reproduction), soberly coloured in reddish brown, yellow and blue, depicts the Adoration of the Virgin and Child by the Three Kings.

Practicalities

Budget **accommodation** options include *Pensió Sant Climent* at the village entrance (Ⓣ973 696 052; ❷), with en-suite rooms, cosy attic apartments sleeping four and limited parking, while *Casa Plano Minguero* (Ⓣ973 696 117; ❹), is well located in the upper part of the village, again with parking. *Ca de Corral* (Ⓣ973 696 176; ❸), run by the sister of the *Bar Mallador* management (see below), offers en-suite rooms on the top floor of an old house well situated in the lower part of the village. For something smarter, try *Pensió Santa María* (Ⓣ973 696 170; Ⓔsantamaria@taull.com), a lovingly restored old house in the upper quarter with self-catering garden studios (❹) and tastefully rustic upstairs rooms (❺ B&B), or the welcoming, wood-trimmed *El Xalet de Taüll* (Ⓣ973 696 095, Ⓦwww.elxaletdetaull.com; ❺ B&B), whose big strength is the attic breakfast room and library with panoramic plate-glass windows – the easiest way of recognizing the building from below. A **campsite** (Ⓣ973 696 082), also with bungalows, spreads attractively on the grassy slope below Sant Climent.

Sant Climent's **restaurant** is justly popular for filling, no-nonsense feeds (*menús* with drink at €10 and €15) – reserve in season. *El Caliu*, at the top of Taüll in a modern apartment building, is well regarded for more careful cooking, and is still affordable at €14 for the weekday *menú*; allow €26 *a la carta*. Last but not least, beside Sant Climent, David and Consell's *Mallador* (closed May–early June & mid Oct–Nov) combines the virtues of being the most popular village **bar** (garden seating in summer), with full meal service (three courses including grills), eclectic taste in music, **Internet** access and a Romanesque-theme gift shop upstairs.

Day-hike to the Estanys del Pessó

The two **Estanys del Pessó**, just northwest of the eponymous pass, are a favourite day-hike destination from Taüll. The trailhead for the eastbound GR11.20 is 4km up from the village, at a bend in the road to the ski station; you can drive another

600m to a disused quarry, but it's hardly worth it. Just over half an hour along, turn up and left onto a minor trail initially marked with yellow-topped stakes – the way is steep but fairly well defined. It's 1hr 15min from the road-bend to the lower lake, and another fifteen minutes to the upper lake (2492m), swimmable on a warm day. You're just outside the park, but the (likely) solitude and the line of often storm-lashed peaks to the northeast is as good as anything in it. Allow 1hr 20min for the return trip down to the road.

Skiing: Boí-Taüll

The ski centre at **Boí-Taüll** (Ⓦ www.boitaullresort.es), some 11km southeast of Taüll, is the newest in the Catalan Pyrenees and the only rival to Baqueira-Beret, with 46 pistes, more than half red-rated, and 16 lifts, mostly drag-type. It's not the best resort for beginners or weak intermediates, as their runs tend to be short, but advanced skiers can tackle the six-kilometre off-piste descent of the Vall de Moró, typically an hour to drop the 1000m. Boí-Taüll has the highest lift-top in the range (2750m), start of a four-kilometre advanced run, and the snow quality is good in the glacial bowl facing north to Besiberri and other peaks beyond the Cavallers reservoir. With a 2020-metre bottom point at Pla de Vaques, the centre will probably survive global warming, unlike many other Pyrenean resorts, though early closures are common on spring days, and plans to expand have been stalled by environmental considerations. Lift passes and on-site gear rental are pricey; Taüll or Barruera offer better rental rates.

Walking in Aigüestortes

Initial stretches of trail or track into Aigüestortes are detailed in the sections "Approaches to Aigüestortes" (see p.271) and "South to Aigüestortes" (see p.268). Moving deeper into the region, the clearly signposted **GR11** path skims the northern margins of the park, linking Espot with the Túnel de Vielha; variant **GR11.20** connects Espot and the Vall de Boí. There are also numerous waymarked (but unnumbered) lateral paths which permit any number of circuits and traverses in the best of the park and peripheral zone, including the so-called *Carros de Foc* (Chariots of Fire) itinerary linking most of the refuges. Less exciting, and sometimes over-subscribed because of its ease, is the east–west track crossing the park from Estany de Sant Maurici to the springs of Aigüestortes.

If you want solitude and wilderness, stick to the more difficult south–north trails, which run perpendicular to most hiker traffic. Map, altimeter and compass are essential when departing from more travelled routes – it's easy to get lost amongst the hundreds of lakes and lookalike granite whalebacks dividing them, especially in cloudy conditions.

Traverses

Three good traverses of the park start from the *Refugi Colomina* (see p.277), in addition to the one to/from Espot via the *Refugi Josep Maria Blanc* (see p.276).

North to Refugi Ernest Mallafré via Monestero valley

Heading north through the often snow-clogged, steep **Coll de Peguera** (2726m) and down the beautiful **Monestero valley**, it's a six-hour hike to the **Refugi Ernest Mallafré**, near the dam and roadhead at Sant Maurici (1885m; Ⓣ 973 250 118; 24 places; mid-June to Sept). If it's full, you'll need to reserve enough energy and daylight to continue ninety minutes to the more comfortable **Refugi-Xalet d'Amitges** (see p.268). Next day you could leave the park via the gentle **Port de Ratèra de Colomèrs**, finishing this less strenuous leg at the *Refugi de Colomèrs* (see p.269), where you're poised to continue along the routes described on pp.268–269.

Northwest to Refugis d'Estany Llong, Ventosa i Calvell and Restanca

A more adventurous route heads northwest from *Refugi Colomina* through the easy trekkers' passes **Collada de Dellui** (2576m) or **Collada de Morrano** (2632m) to the **Refugi d'Estany Llong** (2000m; ⓣ973 299 545 or 629 374 652; 36 places; open Easter week & June to mid-Oct) beside the eponymous lake. If it's full, the nearby, unstaffed *Refugi de la Centraleta* (8 bunks, fireplace) will be home for the night. The Dellui route descends through the valley of that name, speckled with natural lakes, additionally (with a slight detour) past the scenic Corticelles tarns.

On the following day, climb for three and a half hours to the cirque-bound Estany de Contraig, with two very sharp grades on route. This lies just below the **Coll de Contraix** (2748m) another hour along, with stunning views but requiring snow equipment after a heavy winter. From here you must drop along the nastily steep north side (self-arrest device always required) to the very popular **Refugi Ventosa i Calvell** (2200m; ⓣ973 297 090; 80 places; open select winter weekends & mid-June to Oct), 2hr 15min below the pass beside **Estany Negre**, where again you're near the heart of a lake-rich glacial basin. From here, you can walk an easy four hours to the *Refugi de la Restanca* (p.269) in the peripheral zone.

West to Taüll

From *Colomina*, it's possible to head west through deserted country along the GR11.20 **to Taüll**, a long nine-hour day, via one of two passes. The easy **Port de Rus** carries both the variant and the old spa patrons' *camí* from Capdella, but it's more exciting to maintain altitude by the park boundary, via a series of lakes and the inconspicuous **Collado del Pessó** (2760m), testing your cross-country skills.

Sant Maurici to Aigüestortes

If you're not fully committed to alpine trekking, but are in reasonable physical condition, stick to the broad *camí* **between Sant Maurici and Aigüestortes**. Take a 4WD taxi to/from one or both ends of the fifteen-kilometre traverse, which can be walked in six hours. You definitely won't be alone, and will mostly look up at the peaks rather than down from them. The exceptional moments come either side of the **Portarró d'Espot** (2424m), where you can detour for moderate ridge-touring. The main track took its present form early in 1953, when in a typical pharaonic gesture General Franco commanded that it be widened with hand tools so that his private jeep could be driven through that summer. Much of the poor labourers' work has since reverted to nature – 4WD vehicles can no longer pass – though keen walkers regard the route as far too easy for serious consideration. Still, if you spread it over two days with an overnight at *Estany Llong* (see above), there are some excellent day treks to be enjoyed from the refuge.

Peak ascents

Featured on countless posters, postcards, window-stickers and T-shirts, the spikey profile of **Els Encantats** is the park's de facto logo. Like the Agulles d'Amitges near the *Refugi Amitges*, the pinnacles are a favourite of technical climbers, but experienced mountain-walkers equipped with a rope can reach the top of **Encantat Gran** (2745m) in about five hours from the *Ernest Mallafré* refuge, via the gully separating the twin summits.

The second-highest peak inside the park, **Pala Alta de Sarradé** (Serrader on some maps; 2982m), is a much easier goal, reached from Boí by the track to the park entrance, then via Estany Sarradé and a gully to the summit – a 4WD taxi cuts journeys from five to three and a half hours one-way. Its neighbour and highest park summit, **Punta Alta** (3015m), is usually climbed from the Cavallers dam, via a path up the vale and tarns of **Coma les Bienes** and then scrambling.

The third-highest summit, **Pic de Peguera** (2983m), is a nontechnical ascent if tackled from the Coll de Monestero, half an hour to the east; this pass is less than two hours from the *Josep Maria Blanc* hut (see p.276) and three from *Ernest Mallafré* (see p.281). From the *coll* a cairned route leads southwest to the top in 45 minutes; however the final scramble up (or especially down) a steep couloir can be daunting.

Maladeta and Posets

The trough-like **Ésera valley** drains the Pyrenees' high mountain wilderness, with Aneto peak (3404m) crowning the **Maladeta Massif** to the east, and **Posets** (3375m) looming on the west. Since the creation of the **Parque Natural Posets-Maladeta** in 1994, both ranges have enjoyed some protection from development. **Benasque** is the pivotal point, a valley-bottom town that lives for alpine tourism but has managed to retain some rural Aragonese character, not least in a vigorous campaign to promote renewed use of the **regional language**. Aragonese town names are noted below in parentheses following the Castillian, since you still see the latter on city-limits and road signs; the convention is reversed for place names in the mountains, since on most hiking maps – including Editorial Alpina's – Aragonese now takes precedence.

Accompanying the resurgence of regional feeling, efforts have been made throughout Alto Aragón to improve the quality of tourist services and information – especially trail guides and maps – to match Catalan standards. Aragonese Pyreneans feel, with some justice, that the Catalans benefit disproportionately from tourism, and have misrepresented regional history and linguistics. Local advocates point out that Catalunya was long subsumed within the kingdom of Aragón, and that the yellow-and-red Catalan flag is based on the original, horizontal Aragonese version.

Not scaled until 1842, **Aneto** was long visited by mountaineers rather than walkers, not so much for any technical difficulty – though the climb does have vertiginous final moments – as for its inaccessibility. The former approach from France through the Portillón de Benasque was superseded in the 1970s with the extension of the A139 from Benasque to within a short walk of both the Portillón de Benasque, just northwest, and the *Refugio de la Renclusa* (south of the road's end), the standard base for the conquest of Aneto.

The most momentous day at the **Portillón de Benasque/Port de Vénasque** – the historic route across the watershed – was April 1, 1938, when thousands of Spanish Republicans fled from a Nationalist advance that had trapped them in the Ésera cul-de-sac. Many others didn't make it after being caught in a snowstorm the next day. Towards the end of World War II, numerous surviving Republicans met their deaths when they returned to contest Franco's rule in Spain.

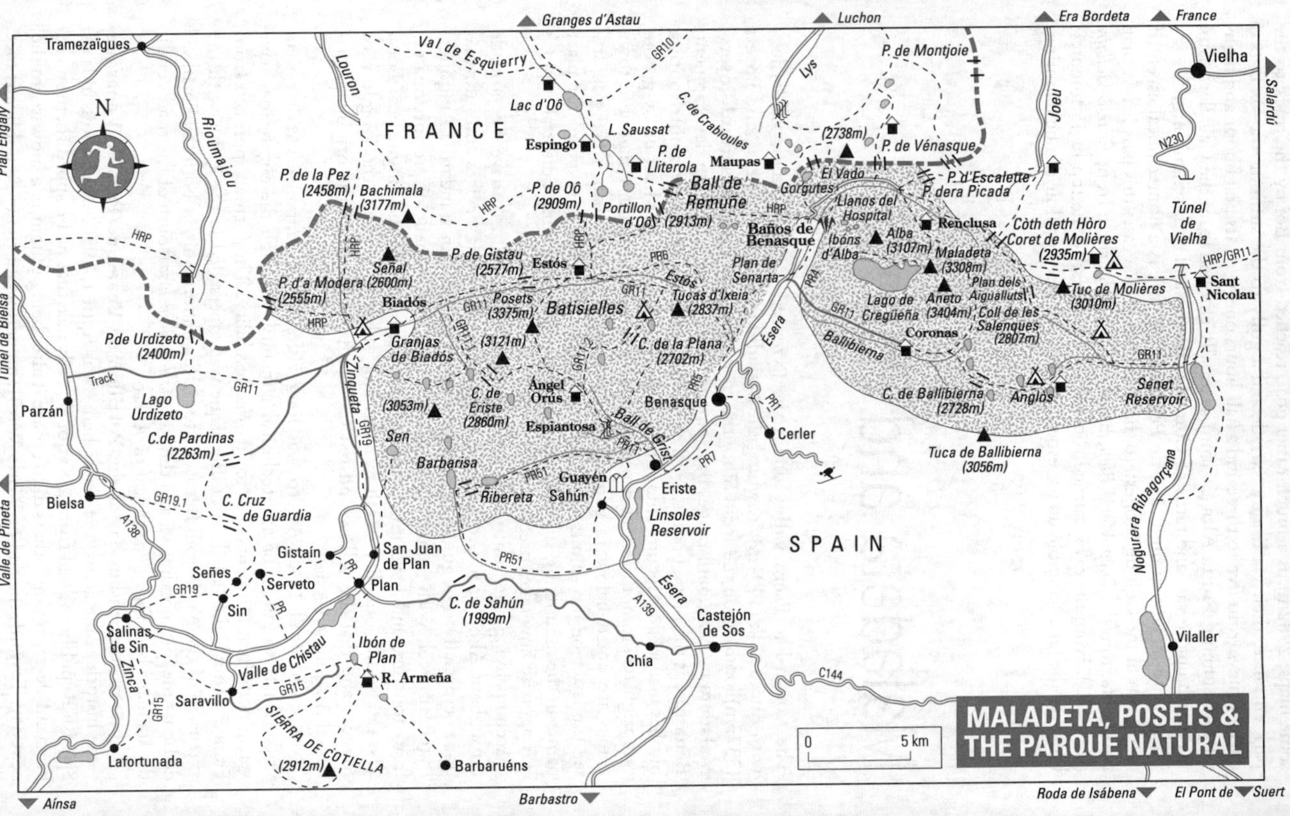
MALADETA, POSETS & THE PARQUE NATURAL
0 5 km
FRANCE
SPAIN
N
Granges d'Astau
Luchon
Era Bordeta
France
Vielha
Salardú
Tramezaïgues
Piau Engaly
Túnel de Bielsa
Valle de Pineta
Aínsa
Barbastro
Roda de Isábena
El Pont de Suert
Val de Esquierry
Louron
Rioumajou
Lac d'Oô
L. Saussat
Espingo
P. de Lliterola
C. de Crabioules
Maupas
Lys
P. de Montjoie
(2738m)
P. de Vénasque
El Vado
Gorgutes
Joeu
N230
P. d'Escalette
P. dera Picada
Túnel de Vielha
HRP/GR11
Sant Nicolau
P. de la Pez (2458m)
Bachimala (3177m)
P. de Oô (2909m)
Portillon d'Oô (2913m)
Ball de Remuñe
Llanos del Hospital
Baños de Benasque
Renclusa
Còth deth Hòro
Coret de Molières (2935m)
Señal
P. d'a Modera (2600m)
(2555m)
P. de Gistau (2577m)
Estós
Plan de Senarta
Ibóns d'Alba
Alba (3107m)
Maladeta (3308m)
Plan dels Aiguallluts
Tuc de Molières (3010m)
Biadós
Posets (3375m)
Batisielles
Tucas d'Ixeia (2837m)
Lago de Cregüeña
Aneto (3404m)
Coll de les Salenques (2807m)
Coronas
Ballibierna
Granjas de Biadós
(3121m)
C. de la Plana (2702m)
P.de Urdizeto (2400m)
Track
Zinqueta
Ángel Orús
C. de Eriste (2860m)
Benasque
Ésera
Cerler
C. de Ballibierna (2728m)
Anglós
Senet Reservoir
Parzán
Lago Urdizeto
(3053m)
Espiantosa
Ball de Grist
Sen
C.de Pardinas (2263m)
Barbarisa
Tuca de Ballibierna (3056m)
Guayén
Sahún
Ribereta
Eriste
Linsoles Reservoir
Bielsa
C. Cruz de Guardia
Noguera Ribagorçana
Gistaín
San Juan de Plan
Señes
Serveto
Plan
C. de Sahún (1999m)
Sin
Castejón de Sos
Salinas de Sin
Chía
Vilaller
Ibón de Plan
Valle de Chistau
R. Armeña
C144
Zinca
Saravillo
SIERRA DE COTIELLA
(2912m)
Barbaruéns
Lafortunada
A138
A139
GR10
GR11
GR11.1
GR11.2
GR15
GR19
GR19.1
HRP
PR
PR1
PR4
PR5
PR6
PR7
PR11
PR51

Though marginally lower than Aneto, and thus less known, the sculpted **Posets Massif** with its paradisical valleys is popular with the Spanish, and has more staffed refuges than any other major Pyrenean peak. If you don't want to bag the summit, a westward traverse or half-circuit is the best and most scenic passage west – otherwise you have to detour way south on the bus to Barbastro before heading up the Cinca valley, a route poorly covered by public transport.

The Ésera valley

The **Ésera valley** remains for the moment a dead end for cars, and since the area's inclusion in the local *parque natural* further restrictions on private traffic have come into effect (see p.290). Park status has not, however, ended perennial proposals for a tunnel through the frontier ridge to Luchon in France, for which many locals on both sides of the frontier have campaigned since the 1980s.

Coming from the **south** you can reach the Ésera valley by bus from Barbastro (in turn served frequently from Huesca or Lleida), a three-hour journey to Benasque. From El Pont de Suert and the Noguera Ribagorçana valley to the **east**, along a lonely 41-kilometre stretch of the N260 to Castejón de Sos, you're dependent on your own vehicle or bike; hitching this route can be very slow. En route, you'll notice road signs "edited" by Catalan nationalists – this is part of **La Franja**, a transition zone between Aragón and Catalunya inhabited by Catalan-speakers. The only public transport towards Aragón from El Pont de Suert is the daily bus southwest to Graus, via the cathedral outpost of Roda de Isábena.

Roda de Isábena

Attractive hill villages are ten-a-penny in Aragón, but **RODA DE ISÁBENA**, 32km south of the N260 in the middle of nowhere just above the A1605 road between El Pont de Suert and Graus, is unique for its superb Romanesque **cathedral** at the heart of town. Originally a tenth- to eleventh-century monastic church, it has three aisles, Lombard apses and an eighteenth-century octagonal belfry visible from afar, but there ends any conformity to the norm. The ornate entrance portal, with six series of capitalled columns inside a Renaissance portico, breaches the south wall, since the west end of the nave is occupied by a carved choir and a fine organ, claimed to be one of the best in Europe. Mass is celebrated on the now-authenticated sarcophagus of San Ramón, squirming with twelfth-century carvings of the Nativity and the Flight into Egypt. Immediately below the raised altar is a vast triple crypt (currently shut for restoration), the central section with worn column capitals but the northerly one graced by brilliant Romanesque frescoes of the Baptism, St Michael weighing the souls of the dead and Christ in Glory surrounded by the four symbols of the Evangelists. Admission is only by guided visit (6 times daily 11.15am–6pm; €2.50), though you can see the twelfth-century cloister and its colonnade (eroded like the crypt's) by patronizing the excellent restaurant in the former refectory. Apart from that, there's little to do but wander the attractive streets and take in 360-degree views from the *mirador* behind the refectory, where it's easy to see why the medieval counts of Ribagorça chose Roda as their capital and citadel.

Practicalities

Most visitors arrive in their own vehicle; besides the A1605 highway from the N260, a paved but narrow road runs 22km east from Campo in the Ésera valley, emerging on the A1605 7km north of Roda. Unless you're staying the night, you must use the **car park** on the outskirts of town. Roda is a popular Spanish weekend retreat, and booking **accommodation** is necessary all year. Top choices include the excellent-value *Hospedaría de Roda*, right on the central plaza (Ⓣ974 544 554, Ⓕ974 544 500; ❸), whose rooms have views and all mod cons, or the friendly, English-speaking *Casa Simón* (Ⓣ974 544 528 or enquire at *Bar Mesón de Roda*), with en-suite rooms (❷) and larger apartments.

The *Mesón de Roda* on the plaza serves decent meals and breakfasts with a ring-side seat for people-watching, but the best **restaurant** by far is the *Hospedería*

△ Roda de Isábena Cathedral

La Catedral (reservations usually necessary on ⓣ974 544 545). Its *carta* has plenty of vegetable-based *entrantes*, meat and game for seconds, homemade desserts and a local wine list, and proves so reasonable (€17–20 for 3 courses) that there's little point in taking the *menú*.

Castejón de Sos and Sahún

The N260 meets the Ésera at **CASTEJÓN DE SOS** (Castilló de Sos), 14km south of Benasque. If you've come up from Barbastro, it's the first place you'll see with much mountain character, at least in the tiny, fortified old quarter north of the highway. The unique local topography has made it a mecca for **paragliders**, with two international competitions here annually; TándemTeam (ⓣ974 553 447, ⓦwww.tandemteam.org) is one of the better-established outfits. Moderately priced **accommodation** lies on or just off the through road, c/El Real. Top choices include the well-kept, en-suite *Hotel Plaza*, central but quiet at Plaza El Pilar 2 (ⓣ974 553 050, ⓦwww.aneto.com/hostalplaza; ❸); the *Hostal Sositana* towards the east end of town on the north side of c/El Real (ⓣ974 553 094; ❷), with a bar and *comedor*; and the partly en-suite *Casa Miranda* opposite (ⓣ974 553 222; ❷). There's also a central *albergue*, affiliated with a *parapente* school: *Pájaro Loco* at c/El Real 48 (ⓣ974 553 516, ⓦwww.aneto.com/pajaroloco; six-bunk dorms).

Sahún

If you have your own vehicle, the relatively unspoilt hillside village of **SAHÚN** (Saunc), 7km up the valley on the west slope, makes a more atmospheric base, especially in high season. There are several places to **stay**, including the *Hostal Casa Lacreu* on Plaza Mayor (ⓣ974 551 335, ⓦwww.casalacreu.com; ❸), a restored manor house with en-suite rooms, arcaded bar and cheery, good-value *comedor*. Most accommodation in the village consists of *casas rurales*; of these, *Casa Alquesera*, at the north end of town next to the church belfry (ⓣ974 551 396; ❹), offers high-standard apartments, while the single, centrally heated apartment at *Casa Colás* (no sign), 70m from the church door, downhill, then right (ⓣ974 551 398) sleeps six at ❺ per day and boasts a full kitchen with dishwasher.

Prime outings from Sahún are the **all-day hikes** along locally marked *caminos*. One leg of the trip heads north past the deconsecrated Guayén (Guayente) monastery (now a tourism school), then west along the Aigüeta de la Ball to a series of lakes at about 2400m. Another potential start goes west, then north along the Aigüeta de Llisat stream to the scattered *ibones* of Barbarisa at 2360m. Both are designed for moderately fit walkers, and get a fraction of the patronage of the "classic" walks up-valley (see pp.290–294); these routes can be linked via the 2538-metre Collado de la Ribereta to form a loop, now designated as the **PR51**.

Benasque and Cerler

Surrounded by hayfields in a wide part of the Ésera valley, **BENASQUE** (Benás) strikes most people as an agreeable place, combining modern amenities with old stone houses, some built as summer homes for the Aragonese nobility in the seventeenth century. The town was once a seat of the counts of Ribagorça, who provided a castle and perimeter walls, both razed during the Napoleonic wars. The surviving old quarter, with its thirteenth-century church of **San Marcial** and fifteenth-century **Torre Juste**, is still atmospheric and fairly homogeneous.

Despite murmurings of despoliation, modern Benasque and its nearby ski annexe of Cerler aren't nearly as obtrusive as the new developments in the Val d'Aran – and, before or after the rigours of Aneto or Posets, you'll welcome the chance to indulge in a little luxury. Benasque attracts younger Barcelonans intent on a good time indoors or out – and so has a bit of nightlife as well.

Arrival and information

Buses from Barbastro stop on the main Avenida de los Tilos, a little south of the compact old quarter. The not terribly helpful **Turismo** (daily: summer 9am–2pm 4.30–9pm; winter 10am–2pm & 5–9pm; ⓣ974 551 289, ⓦwww.turismobenasque.com) can be found at the southeast edge of the old town, and has a single coin-op **Internet** terminal; there's longer-hours Internet access at Cyber Café, c/los Huertos 5 (10am–midnight). Several **banks** have ATMs – the only ones you'll see for some distance, trekking east or west – plus there's a **laundry** on the bypass road, Ctra Francia, east of the Torre Juste.

Accommodation

Budget **accommodation** in and around the old town is restricted to the somewhat shabby, unstaffed *Hostal Salvaguardia* at c/San Marcial 5 (ⓣ974 551 733; ❶), by the church.

For more comfort, try the plush, wood-interior *Hotel Aragüells* (ⓣ974 551 619, ⓦwww.hotelaraguells.com; ❹) at Avda de los Tilos 1, the main commercial street, or the mountaineer-friendly *Hotel Avenida* next door at no. 3 (ⓣ974 551 126, ⓦwww.h-avenida.com; ❹), with good half-board deals. Otherwise, the Valero Llanas family own five variable hotels and *hostales;* consult ⓦwww.hoteles-valero.com, or call in at the conspicuous *Hotel Aneto*, just south of the A139 skirting town on the Anciles road (ⓣ974 551 061; ❹), which has a pool, tennis courts, gym, sauna and parking facilities. Less institutional is one of Benasque's three-star facilities, *Aparthotel San Marsial* at the north end of town at Ctra. Francia 77 (ⓣ974 551 616, ⓦwww.hotelsanmarsial.com; ❺).

The closest authorized **campsites** begin 4km upstream along the Ésera valley, conveniently near the GR11 junction: caravan-clogged *Aneto* (ⓣ974 551 141; year-round), *Chuise* (ⓣ974 552 121; summer only) and *Ixeia* (ⓣ974 552 129; June–Sept). Of the three, the *Chuise*, at the mouth of the Estós valley, is the most basic and tent-friendly.

Eating and drinking

Competition means relatively affordable fare at several local **restaurants**. Carnivores should head for *Asador Restaurante Bardanca* at c/Las Plazas 6 (reserve at busy seasons on ⓣ974 551 360 as seating is limited), where meat platters go by weight – up to a kilo if you wish, or to *Asador Ixarso*, behind the *Turismo* (*a la carta* only €21–25). The tiny *comedor* of the 🏃 *Hotel Avenida* has sustaining, excellent-value grub, with €14.50 *menús* encompassing *escudella* stew and mocha pannacota. For a splurge, *La Parilla* on Ctra Francia serves nouvelle Aragonese cooking – stuffed vegetables and creative puddings – as a *menú* (€15) or *a la carta* (from €28).

Among **bars**, *Bar Sayó* at c/Mayor 13 as a decent *menú* but is probably better for *tapas* and affordable tipples; *Bar Plaza* on Plaza Mayor is a tad cheaper for the same items, and its outdoor tables are a favourite sundown rendezvous point.

Activities and equipment

Everything in Benasque revolves around the great outdoors, evident from the number of people strolling about in brightly coloured Gore-Tex. Three rival **guiding centres** – Ilorcha, Avda de Los Tilos (ⓣ974 552 094), Equipo Barrabés (ⓣ974 551 056, ⓦwww.barrabes.com) and Compañia de Guías Valle de Benasque (ⓣ974 551 336, ⓦwww.guiasbenasque.com) on Avenida de Luchon organize climbing, alpine-skiing, canyoning, rafting and trekking expeditions, including both nearby summits in five days. The lower reaches of the rivers in the Estós and Ballibierna valleys offer some of the best **kayaking** in the Spanish Pyrenees; more sedately, you can paddle out on the Linsoles reservoir with Grist Kayak in Eriste (Ⓣ974 551 692). Of the **mountaineering equipment shops**, one of the biggest in Spain, if not Europe, is Galleria Barrabés, near the corner of the A139 and Avenida. de los Tilos: four floors of outdoor gear, with an annexe across the road. There's also Deportes Aigualluts/Casa de la Montaña, with three outlets on Avenida de los Tilos.

Most useful of the local guidebooks on sale is *Senderos PR Señalizados: Valle de Benasque*, issued jointly by PRAMES and the Aragonese mountain club together with an invaluable map, worthwhile even if you don't read Spanish. If you're unsure about tackling high-mountain walks, these yellow-and-white- or blue-and-white-blazed *pequeño recorrido* (PR) **short-haul paths** make an ideal introduction. The PR itineraries, routed to avoid roads as much as possible, lead to surrounding villages, lower-altitude alpine attractions and also to all three local refuges.

Cerler: ski centre and village

CERLER (Sarllé), a small dependency of Benasque reached by 6km of driving or the one-hour PR1 path, ranks as the highest (1540m) village in Aragón. It's an attractive enough if slightly twee place, worth considering as a base if you've a car, though the old quarter is now engulfed by straggly, low-density modern chalets which come to life in winter courtesy of the adjacent **ski centre** (Ⓦwww.cerler.com). A top point of 2630m, second only to Boí-Taüll, plus massive government investment in snow canons and a well-linked system of high-speed chair-lifts have made this an excellent intermediate resort, with fifteen red and fifteen blue runs among its 45 pistes. There are two sectors, separated by conical Pic de Cerler: Ampriu to the northeast, reached by an eight-kilometre road, with more advanced runs from 2630m down to 1900m (good restaurant), and Cerler proper, with longer, easier runs (including a lovely green through trees) north from 2372-metre Cogulla peak. The Coll d'Ampriu (2260m) is the main link between the two sectors, with most of action centred around Cota 2000 (where there's another decent restaurant).

The best **accommodation** in the old village is at *Casa Cornel*, c/Obispo 11 (Ⓣ974 551 102, Ⓦwww.casacornel.com), a converted twelfth-century manor house with good-standard *hostal* rooms facing a courtyard (❹ B&B), and a newer wing opposite of large, well-heated parquet-floored rooms with solid-wood furniture and free wi-fi access (❺ B&B). Ample parking and frequent discount periods are further attractions; the restaurant is adequate, but best patronized *a la carta* rather than on half-board basis. *Casas rurales* include the en-suite *Casa Llorgodo*, c/La Fuente, above the church plaza (Ⓣ974 551 067; ❷), or, abutting the church at the top of the path up from Benasque, *Casa La Abadia* (Ⓣ974 551 641; ❸), with good views. There are three independent **bar-restaurants** on the main through lane: high-quality *La Picada*, serving snails and mushrooms in season plus the usual grills, though portions could be bigger; *La Borda del Mastín*, specializing in *carnes a la brasa*; and *Bar Rincon*, near the church.

Into the Parque Natural Posets-Maladeta from Benasque

Benasque offers the only road access to the **Parque Natural Posets-Maladeta**, which extends from the Noguera Ribagorçana in the east to the Valle de Chistau in the west, but excludes the lower reaches of the Ésera valley up to the Baños de Benasque, an old *balneario* (spa) 10km from Benasque (see p.290). **Private vehicle**

traffic into the park is restricted between June 30 and September 10. The track east into the Ballibierna (Vallhiverna) valley, 6km above Benasque, is normally completely closed for entry. The A139 splits some 11.5km north of Benasque; the right-hand option leads after 1500m to a small, over-subscribed car park at **El Vado**, beyond which passage is generally forbidden. Guards tend the barriers; the only exceptions are for those continuing about 400m from El Vado to the car park of the Hospital de Benasque (see below). Between June 30 and September 10, there's a **shuttle-bus service** (8am–9.15pm mid-summer, plus two pre-dawn departures) from here to La Besurta, road's end (16km from Benasque) and start of the paths to the *Refugio de la Renclusa* and the Forau dels Aigualluts. Other routes covered by the same company (Alarsa) include Benasque to **La Besurta**, via Plan de Senarta and Baños de Benasque (6 daily 4.30am–6pm; €6.50 one way) and Benasque–Senarta–Puente de Coronas in the Valle de Ballibierna (3 daily at 5am, 7am & 3pm; €11), which spares you a considerable, dull track-section of the GR11. A **jeep-taxi** service is also provided by Benasque-based Angel Lledo (Ⓣ608 930 450).

Camping within the *parque natural* had been forbidden since the park opened; however a more recent law permits a one-night tent-stay at all points above 2000m – legalizing this previously widespread practice.

Baños de Benasque and Ibons d'Alba walk

The **Baños de Benasque** (Bañs de Benás), part of the Valero **hotel** empire (Ⓣ974 344 000; mid-June to early Oct; ❸), presents itself as a contemporary spa with full hydrotherapy and massage programmes. The premises however, remain old-fashioned overall, with a slightly funky plunge-pool (37°C water) downstairs and a popular bar above it, where terrace tables are at a premium on fair days.

From the baths, the best **hike** heads east up the Ball d'Alba to its cluster of glacial lakes. Start out along the old *camino* (marked as "Sendero de las Fuens de Alba") northeast towards the Hospital de Benasque; within ten minutes veer east onto a fainter, yellow-dotted side trail which climbs sharply along the true left (not right, as Alpina claims) bank of the Turonet gully to a saddle at 1975m (40min along). After a momentary dip, the ascent continues past the last hardy black pines, the way now only cairned; within another forty minutes you should arrive at the largest and lowest (2260m) of the three **Ibons d'Alba**, cradled in its own steep-flanked cirque on the west flank of Maladeta, just below 3107-metre Pico de Alba.

The Alpina map is wrong again concerning the continuation to the upper lakes. The proper, cairned way goes west, then southeast past a boulder-slide swarming (as the whole valley does) with marmots, to the first of the upper *ibones* (2359m; 30min more); from there use your map, compass and nous for twenty minutes more to the highest, little-visited lake (2452m) at the base of the Cresta de Alba and its non-pedestrian *brecha*, again marked misleadingly with a trail on Alpina's map. Return is thus the same way, for a walking day of at least four hours – best allow six with lunch and stops.

Llanos del Hospital and nearby walks

The old pilgrims' hospice of **Hospital de Benasque** (13km from Benasque), a Templar foundation of the twelfth century, has been revamped and enlarged by an activities group as an eponymous, three-star **hotel** (Ⓣ974 552 012, Ⓦwww.llanosdelhospital.com; all year). It offers state-of-the-art lodging in two grades of room: standard (❺) and superior (❼). It's also the focus of the popular **Llanos del Hospital cross-country skiing** centre, whose routes extend up-valley to La Besurta; in winter you're obliged to take half-board, multi-day "packages". On the ground floor are a convivial **bar** and a highly regarded **restaurant**, its €21 *menú* featuring regional dishes such as *recao*, a chickpea-with-greens hotpot.

One popular summer excursion near *Llanos del Hospital* is the easy two-and-a-half-hour round-trip **hike** to two small tarns and one sizeable lake to the north, just on the Spanish side of the frontier ridge. The least complicated trailhead, with parking available year-round, is at the abrupt end of the left-hand fork in the A139, west of El Vado. The path, shown pretty accurately on the Alpina "Maladeta/Aneto" map, waymarked with green paint-stripes, climbs north to cross the Torrente de Gorgutes, then veers briefly east to skim above the two well-hidden **Ibones de la Solana de Gorgutes** (de la Montañeta), the smaller being shallow and warm enough to swim in. The route then curls west to the **Ibón de Gorgutes**, with the 2367-metre **Puerto de la Glera** just behind, an easy pedestrian route into France.

A slightly meatier but equally popular hike west up the gorgeous **Ball de Remuñe** starts from a different trailhead off the same road; the path along the main valley is marked with double red paint-dashes. About an hour and a quarter along, you'll arrive at the water-meadows beside the Ibonet de Remuñe, currently much smaller than as shown on the Alpina map, as – alas – are the ice-fields on the west. Do not enter the Aigüeta narrows just ahead, but head up and south, crossing the stream on a plank-bridge, to the smaller of the two **Ibons de Remuñe** (2240m); hardy walkers can swim here with the frog-spawn. It's twelve minutes more, bearing east-south-east, to the biggest and most visited lake at 2200m. The proper path which resumes along the outflow of this joins the main valley trail just over twenty minutes below at another saggy plank-bridge, with the trailhead an hour below the larger lake.

Maladeta climbs and walks

Despite its forbidding appearance from a distance, the **Maladeta Massif** offers scope for day hikes, traverses and circuits of various grades, as well as alpine ascents. The main logistical drawback is that there's only one staffed refuge, better positioned for peak-climbers than long-distance trekkers. For other extended forays you'd do well to have a **tent**. The relevant **maps** are either Editorial Alpina

△ Aneto massif from the Ball de Remuñe

1:25,000 "Maladeta/Aneto", or Rando Editions 1:50,000 Mapa Excursionista no. 23, "Aneto-Posets".

The ascent of Aneto

The **ascent of Aneto** typically begins at the **Refugio de la Renclusa** (2160m; ⓣ974 552 106; 44 places; staffed Christmas, Easter, Sat & Sun Easter–June, daily July–Sept), located well north of the summit. The final stop of the summertime shuttle-bus from El Vado at the La Besurta parking area is 45 minutes' hike below *Renclusa*. Unless you're incredibly fit and experienced, plan for a full day to the summit and back with necessary stops, starting before sunrise. Walking equipment must include **crampons**, **ice-axe** and a **rope**. For less experienced climbers, the ascent is the most commonly offered guided excursion in Benasque.

Routes – and their history

There are two basic routes on the northeast face, which can be combined as a circuit. The standard itinerary heads south from the refuge, climbing steeply towards the pass known as **Portillón Inferior** (2742m). Before the top, bear southwest to the next pass along, **Portillón Superior** (2870m), which you should reach in about three hours.

Now you have your first good view of Aneto, with the secondary peak of **Maladeta** (3308m) to your right. The guide Pierre Barrau – who had made the first recorded ascent of Maladeta with Frédéric Parrot on September 29, 1817 – was killed when he fell unroped into a crevasse on the Maladeta glacier in 1824. The accident postponed conquest of Aneto itself by two decades, and Barrau's body was only recovered when it emerged from the ice over a century later.

A gully descends on the far side of Portillón Superior to a saddle, beyond which extends the Aneto glacier. During summer months, a "path" will have been worn across it, a little whiter than the grit-stained glacier to either side. It should be perfectly safe but rope up if there is any doubt. You now traverse 2500m south-southeast to the **Collado de Coronas** (3196m; 4hr 30min from the refuge), just below which a summertime lake forms every few years.

Climb east beyond the *collado*, possibly with crampons and ice-axe, to the broad jumble of rocks known as the **Puente de Mahoma**. Negotiated on all fours, this represents 50m of sheer terror for the inexperienced, especially if iced up (its name refers to "Mohammed's rope", the Islamic bridge over Hell to Paradise). On the other side of the bridge the **Aneto summit** (3404m) is staked by a large cross and what looks like a small rocket, but turns out to be a Virgin and Child on a metal pedestal. Savour your triumph, but don't linger, especially if clouds close in – climbers have been killed by lightning in the mid-afternoon.

The first to stand here, on July 20, 1842, were the Russian Platon de Tchihatcheff, the French count Albert de Franqueville and their guides, Bernard Ursule, Pierre Redonet, Jean Argarot and Pierre Sanio. However, they did not use the route described, avoiding the formidable northerly glacier in favour of the smaller Coronas glacier on the southwest side of the ridge. Today all of Aneto's glaciers – like most in the Pyrenees – are a third (or less) the size they were in the nineteenth century; the main northerly one is the biggest, at just under ninety hectares.

To make a **circuit**, descend to Collado de Coronas and then bear right on another path east across the glacier to the Plan dels Aigualluts (described on p.270) and the **Forau dels Aigualluts/Trou du Toro** – a pit of grey, splintered rock into which cascading waters of the Aneto glacier disappear before re-emerging in the Joeu valley. Beside a green shed-refuge, upstream from the sinkhole, an initially very faint path leads directly west back to the *Refugio de la Renclusa*.

Walks around Maladeta

If you don't want to stay at the *Renclusa* shelter, or if it's full, wilderness **camping** at the Plan dels Aigualluts is highly recommended. You've reached the 2000-metre camping limit, though if you stay more than one night you're supposed to dismount your tent between 8am and dusk. The *plan* is your destination coming west from the Noguera Ribagorçana over either the Coll de Salenques or the Coret de Molières – approaches detailed in "West to Maladeta" on p.269. Using **Plan dels Aigualluts (de Aiguallut)** as a base, you're also well positioned for rewarding, not overly strenuous **day hikes**; there are four relatively gentle passes on crests to the northeast, and the paths through them can be combined into circuits. Otherwise, starting **from Benasque**, two other day-hike targets are slightly beyond the scope of the local PR excursions in length and effort.

Itineraries around Plan dels Aigualluts

The way up from Plan dels Aigualluts towards the Coret de Molières along the **Valleta de la Escaleta** brings you to the **Còth deth Hòro/Coll de Tòro** (2236m) and, shortly after, the **Còth deth Aranesi/Coll dels Aranesos** (2446m). Both passes overlook lakes and have sharp but scenic descents – largely cross-country – to the Pla de l'Artiga in the Val d'Aran. You can return to the Aragonese side of the crest via a well-trodden trail up the Pomèro valley, leading to the **Pòrt dera Picada** (Puerto de la Picada; 2477m), where the boundaries of Aragón, Catalunya and France meet.

The **Portillón de Benás/Port de Vénasque** (2445m), the age-old route to Luchon in France, is the next pass west of Picada, an easy two-and-a-half hours' walk by well-trodden paths from either *Refugio de la Renclusa* or Plan dels Aigualluts. Even if you're not bound for France, this notch in the ridge is a worthwhile goal for the opportunity to visit **Tuca de Salbaguarda/Pic de Sauvegarde** (2738m), 45 minutes' climb west of the pass. The views in every direction are among the best in the Pyrenees, especially south over Maladeta, a giant reef of dark rock striped by patches of snow and ice. Less than an hour north is the friendly *Refuge de Vénasque*, well placed for a lunch stop (see p.319).

Itineraries from Benasque

The first, longer hike from Benasque is the steep trek up to **Lago de Cregüeña** (2657m), third-largest body of water in the Pyrenees, trapped in a deep cirque southwest of Maladeta. To reach the lake, turn off the PR4 at the fountain and waterfall of **San Ferrer** (San Farré), about ninety minutes' walk above Benasque (limited parking at trailhead). The path up the Ball de Cregüeña is distinct and cairned; allow at least six hours return (the sign says three and a half hours uphill). Misleadingly optimistic routes shown on the Alpina map over the 2905-metre pass southeast into the Ball de Coronas, or northwest over the 2646-metre Brecha d'Alba, are both technical climbing exercises and should not be attempted by casual, unequipped hikers.

About half an hour before San Ferrer, at the **Puente de Ballibierna** by the Paso Nuevo reservoir, you can also leave the PR4 to explore the **Ball de Ballibierna** (Valle de Vallhiverna), an idyllic tributary forested in black pine, fir and birch, by following the eastbound GR11 – unfortunately forced onto a 4WD track for much of the way. There's no private vehicle traffic during summer, but still you're best off saving your stamina for higher altitudes by using the seasonal shuttle-bus service as far as **Puente de Coronas**. Whichever way you arrive, you'll find a permanently open, ten-person **refuge** for use if you're traversing rather than day hiking; camping is theoretically forbidden, as Coronas lies just under the 2000-metre legal limit.

From Puente de Coronas, you can either tackle Aneto via the valley and glacier of Coronas or, more likely, continue east **along the GR11** into the Anglòs (Angliós) valley on the Noguera Ribagorçana side, via the lakes and **Coll de Ballibierna** (2728m). Even with help from the shuttle-bus, it's a long (8hr) day to the *Refugi Sant Nicolau* at the Vielha tunnel mouth; camping is unlikely to cause problems given the remoteness of the countryside.

Posets climbs and walks

Seen from Aneto, the magnificent dark granite mass of **Posets** (3375m), topped by an almost complete circle of low schist ridges, looks like a giant's fort. From the west it seems even more formidable, a huge free-standing lump deeply etched by gullies and false trails. An ascent requires ice-axe, crampons and rope, and perhaps a helmet against falling rocks.

For both day-hikers and long-haul trekkers, Posets is more user-friendly than Maladeta, with three well-sited, staffed refuges, a host of places to camp and options for circuits and traverses of varying length. From Benasque there are two main approaches for climbs and traverses. You're likely to exit the region via the Valle de Chistau to the west, well poised for hikes further into Aragón. The relevant **map** is Editorial Alpina 1:25,000 "Posets"; if you intend walking in or out via the *Viadós* refuge and the Valle de Chistau, take the 1:25,000 "Bachimala/Bal de Chistau" sheet too. Rando Editions Mapa Excursionista no. 23 "Aneto-Posets" is also useful.

The approach from Estós

More pastorally attractive and unspoilt than the Ésera, the **Estós valley** curls around Posets to the northeast. Although the track's lower reaches can be driven, private cars are banned except for the jeep belonging to the warden of the modern three-storey *Refugio de Estós* (1890m; ☎974 551 483; 115 places; all year). The staff can be curt and unhelpful, so you may prefer to omit this refuge from your overnight plans.

To reach valley and refuge, follow the PR5 path from Benasque, then a bit of the PR4, to the medieval **Cuera (San Jaime) bridge** 45 minutes above town, then switch to the GR11 going northwest over the bridge. After another hour or so, the PR6 peels off from the GR11 and adopts the opposite bank of the valley stream, rejoining it shortly before the *Estós* refuge – though the GR11 track isn't objectionable. Whichever route you take, count on four hours total from Benasque to the shelter.

The ascent of the peak

The *Estós* refuge marks the start of the easiest and most popular six-hour hiking **ascent of Posets**. Drop down to cross the bridge and follow the path west along the stream's right (south) bank, soon leaving this to climb into the Coma de la Paúl. This leads to the **Glaciar de la Paúl**, beyond which you reach the **Collado de la Paúl** (3062m). Once on its south side, cross the **Glaciar de Posets** – normally by a clearly trodden path in the ice – to the east face of the summit. A scramble up a narrow gully brings you to the top, known locally as **Llardana**.

The approach from Eriste (Grist)

The much less frequented **Ball de Grist** forges into the alpine heart of Posets from the southeast. Near the top stands the *Refugio Ángel Orús (Forcau)*, the alternative base camp for a Posets climb (2095m; ☎974 344 044; 98 places; all year). To get there, follow the PR7 path from Benasque to Eriste (Grist) village, then the PR11 up the narrow wild canyon, cloaked in foothill vegetation thanks to a mild microclimate. After two hours, mostly on track, you come to the bridge and waterfalls of **Espiantosa**, where there's a fair-sized car park – the five-kilometre track up from Eriste is passable to ordinary cars (or jeep-taxis). From here it's ninety minutes' walk on the PR11 to the refuge, nearly four-and-a-half hours in total from Benasque. If *Refugio Ángel Orús* is full, you can **camp** an hour to the north, in or around the simple Cabaña de Llardaneta.

From the *Ángel Orús* refuge, the best approach to the summit is along the **Ball de Llardaneta**, up the **Canal Fonda** between the outcrops of Tuca Alta and Diente de Llardana at the end of the *canal*, then straight up to the summit – a total of five hours one way (nine hours return).

Traverses and circuits

The following **traverses and partial circuits** – except for the day loop out of Viadós – can be combined into a giant loop around the massif, so that with three or four days at your disposal you trek through the best of Posets. Outside peak season – when bunk space is hard to come by and a tent is mandatory equipment – you can find on-spec vacancies in the well-spaced refuges.

Traverse via Batisielles

A superb traverse from the vicinity of the *Ángel Orús* refuge to the Estós valley, mostly relying on the variant GR11.2, enters the **Ball d'es Ibóns** northeast of Llardaneta and then, just below the Lago de les Alforches, ascends east to the **Collado de la Plana** (or Piana; 2702m). On the other side, a marked but non-GR, essentially cross-country route descends more sharply into the **Ball de Perramó**, with the *ibón* of the same name huddled at the base of the photogenic Tucas d'Ixeia (2837m). The route swings north again to the Escarpinosa lake, where a clearly trodden path leads down to the meadows of **Batisielles** (1900m). The GR11.2 veers northeast from the pass, taking in the Ibón de l'Agüeta de Batisielles and the Ibón Grán de Batisielles (camping possible) before dropping to the meadows – a wonderful (if insect-plagued) place to camp, which you may have to do since it's six to seven hours from *Ángel Orús* to here. Without a tent, you might use the little *cabaña* here, or press on for another ninety minutes along the GR11.2 through meadow and woods to the *Estós* refuge.

The Posets half-circuit

The most popular Posets activity for non-climbers is the **half-circuit** of the massif which follows the main GR11 west, skirting the mountain's north and west flanks. From the *Estós* refuge continue along the valley, climbing to the **Puerto de Chistau** (2577m; 2hr 15min), before descending the other side to the head of the **Zinqueta de Añes Cruzes**. As you amble down this progressively more hospitable valley, you're treated to impressive views of the mountain's forbidding west flank before arriving at **Granjas de Biadós** (Viadós), a dozen or so scattered barns amongst summer hayfields, and one of the most beautiful spots in the Spanish Pyrenees, awash with purple irises in July. You can do the entire walk in five to six hours, with plenty of daylight left for the worthwhile hop up to **Señal de Biadós** (2600m), which has the best possible view east to Posets and west over the Zinqueta valley.

Biadós – and back to Benasque

At Granjas de Biadós, the welcoming **Refugio de Biadós** (ex-Viadós; 1740m; ⓣ974 506 163; 70 places; open Easter and weekends to June 25, thereafter daily to Sept 25, winter by arrangement) is privately run by Joaquín Cazcarra and family.

The refuge is accessible by road, meaning that its meals and bunks are cheaper than the Pyrenean norm. The Cazcarra family also runs a **campsite**, *El Forcallo* (same phone number; open Easter, July & Aug), fifteen minutes' walk below at 1580m elevation. Free camping in the meadow beside the refuge, at the *parque natural* boundary, is no longer permitted.

It's possible, and highly recommended, to loop **back to Benasque** by one of two demanding but nontechnical routes, which cut through the much-admired Posets crest. You'll need extra water, crampons and an axe after a severe winter. From the *Refugio de Biadós*, follow the instructions for the start of the day loop given next section, climbing up the Bal de Millars to just below and north from the eponymous lake. Here the GR11.2 guides you steeply up a stable slope to a false pass, then after a slight dip to the true **Collado de Eriste** (2860m), flanked by the peaks La Forqueta (3007m) and Diente Royo (3010m), three hours from the refuge. Great striated bands of tawny orange and purplish serpentine loom above this pedestrian pass over the Posets flank, busy on a summer's day. From Collado de Eriste, descend east to the vicinity of the Ibón de Llardaneta, then down its valley to the *Ángel Orús* hut (5hr 30min–6hr from Biadós).

Alternatively, you can continue up to the Ibón d'es Millars for a more challenging route. There's no path up from this lake, with only a few cairns guiding you over the rock-girt **Collado de Millares** (2831m), three and a half hours along. The descent southeast calls for more cross-country work through a moonscape of tortured granite before you reach the upper **Bagüeña lake**. Then simply follow the **Vall de Bagüeña** down to Sahún or Eriste, with a good path (part of the PR51) once you're below the lower Ibón de Bagüeña (allow eight hours plus).

Lake circuit from Biadós

Of the various day hikes out of Granjas de Biadós that Joaquín Cazcarra recommends, the loop taking in a chaplet of lakes and tarns tucked into Posets' southwest flank is the most beautiful, but (in its trail-less stages) the most arduous. Follow the main GR11 back towards the Puerto de Chistau, then turn right downhill just past the last *granja* or barn towards a plank bridge. A *parque natural* sign points the way, with estimated time-courses to the most popular destinations: "Ibón d'es Millars, 2hr", "Ibón d'es Lerners, 2hr 30min", and so forth. Red-and-white waymarks are painted over older lime-green-and-turquoise ones, as this is now officially the GR11.2 variant. From here, there's a steady climb along the northeast (true right) bank of the *barranco* through pines. At about 2300m, or some 1hr 45min with a day-pack, the official GR11.2 goes up left towards the Collado de Eriste. Following the older waymarks, it's just over two hours to the **Ibón d'es Millars** (or Millás; 2350m) augmented by a rock dam, with a few turfy patches for a picnic, and where you can join the frogs for a swim in August. Continue another half-hour, the path only cairned now, to the **Ibón d'es Leners** (or Lenés; 2530m), wedged into even more severe terrain beneath the hulking Bagüeñola peaks.

Beyond here there's no more trail, but cairns help you up the 2600-metre ridge dividing Leners from the **Ibón d'es Luceros** (aka Ibón de la Solana), your next goal. As ever, some cairns are misleading; don't veer south, but rather north to overlook Luceros, with an enormous barrel-cairn at the lowest point of the descending ridge. There are magnificent views of the frontier peaks before you begin the only safe way down to the lake, using turfy patches in the slope below the barrel-cairn. Without getting lost, allow an hour from lake to lake; circle anticlockwise around Luceros to its western shore to find the stream gully feeding the **Ibón del Pixón** (just visible). Descend the right bank of this ravine, keeping to the grassy bits or stable granite, avoiding the cavities created by the alpenrose; it's another hour's attentive downhill trekking to scenic del Pixón, with just enough flat ground at the upstream end for an emergency bivouac.

Exit the lake basin, where forest resumes, via the north bank to a tiny pass – the start of another hour's nasty descent along the right bank of the Barranco Pixón. There's still no real path, only cairns and hacked-out blazes on pine trees to guide you – the best general advice is to keep well right, away from the bed of the *barranco*. At one point you'll have briefly to slither over forested hillside at a forty-five-degree angle towards a vast sloping meadow, its higher side at about 1850m. At the far end, nearly half an hour later, pick up the resumption of the trail (red paint dots mark it) and broach a little saddle on the shoulder of El Castellazo hill (1728m). It's another twenty minutes, or just under two hours from Ibón del Pixón, to the junction with the GR19 and a cheerful sign (appropriately disparaged by irate walkers' graffiti) predicting 1hr 30min uphill to the first lake. Follow the GR19 north another 25min to the refuge, making the **total time** nearly seven hours. A reverse itinerary is inadvisable – you'd never find your way uphill to Ibón del Pixón.

Onwards from Posets

From Posets you may head north **into France** via several passes of varying difficulty in the border ridge, or continue west and south deeper **into Aragón**.

Into France

If you're walking north from Posets into France, two fairly difficult but spectacular routes lead to the popular **Lac d'Oô** on the GR10 (see p.321). From the *Estós* refuge, ascend north up the **Ball de Gías**, past three tarns and into France via the **Puerto d'Oô** (pronounced "oh"; 2909m). It's an exhausting four-hour climb, much of it through a forbidding boulder field with no real path in the screes for some distance either side of the pass. From here it's another ninety minutes' (easier) trek down along the HRP to the *Refuge du Portillon* (see p.321), via the **Lac du Port d'Oô** (shown on many French maps as the *Lac Glacé* after its permanent ice floes).

Alternatively, bear east from the Gías trail about a third of the way up, through the **Collada de Molseret** (2520m), to the frontier pass of **Portillón d'Oô** (2913m; 4hr 30min). The *portillón* is guarded by permanent ice and might require crampons, but the refuge at **Lac du Portillon** is just an hour away. The next refuge, *Espingo*, is two hours down-valley via **Lac Saussat**. An hour below *Espingo* is the Lac de Oô, a favourite picnic spot, not far above the roadhead at **Granges d'Astau**. All these areas are covered in detail under "Walks from Luchon", pp.319–21, at the end of this chapter.

Two easier ways into France depart from the *Refugio de Biadós*: up the Zinqueta de la Pez to the **Puerto de la Pez** (2458m), giving access to Pont du Prat (see p.337); or through the even easier **Puerto de Urdizeto** (2405m) north of its lake, where a variant of the HRP leads down to the Rioumajou valley (see p.341). Neither route can compare to the Oô itineraries; slightly more exciting is a third itinerary (an HRP variant), again starting along Zinqueta de la Pez, then veering west over the **Puerto d'a Madera** (2555m) to descend along the Couarère stream to the main Rioumajou drainage. All these routes require a full day's walk to reach the next permanent habitation or suitable camping spot.

Further into Aragón

From the *Refugio de Biadós*, the main treks west and south into Aragón follow the GR11 or the GR19 trails; both begin with a sharp descent to the valley of the **Zinqueta** stream.

The GR11 stays with the vehicle track until turning right onto another track at **La Sargueta**, which shortly reaches a junction. Heading up and right puts you on the main GR11 branch to **Lago Urdizeto** (Ordiceto; 2377m) – popular with picnickers despite its unsightly dam – from where another 4WD track descends 11km to the main road at Parzán (see p.407), 4.5km north of Bielsa. It's best to come here only as a day walk from *Biadós*, or to enter the French Rioumajou valley. The track in from La Sargueta has been extended up to the 1900-metre contour, further reducing the appeal of this section of the GR11.

From the ruined **Espital de Chistau**, fifteen minutes southwest of La Sargueta, another 4WD track leads ninety minutes up to the shallow **Collada de Pardinas** (2263m). From there you should contour southwest to intercept the old *camino* from Gistaín and the Collada de la Cruz de Guardia to Bielsa in the Zinca (Cinca) valley, now waymarked as the GR19.1. Part of the old, mid-altitude shepherds' route west from Biadós, this follows the Barranco de Montillo down to Bielsa within three hours.

The GR19 forest *camino* spares you about an hour of trudging down the main track along the Zinqueta, but it's not brilliant walking so arrange a lift if you can along the main dirt road, either 10km from the refuge car park down to the asphalt and turning for Gistaín, or the full 13.5km to Plan, "capital" of the valley described below.

The Valle de Chistau

Renowned throughout Spain as a repository of medieval Aragonese folk culture, the **Valle de Chistau** (alias Gistau or Xistau) makes a worthwhile rest-stop if you're trekking between Posets and the Ordesa region. Tourism came late to the area, but facilities are improving and remain excellent value as (so far) there's no local ski industry to drive prices up.

The valley was the focus of national attention in March 1985 when many of its bachelors placed a lonely-hearts ad in the press, one of the consequences of Aragonese rural depopulation. Mountain women were (and still are) unwilling to marry those not inclined to relocate to more prosperous towns. The bachelors threw a magnificent three-day *fiesta* to welcome the **caravana de mujeres/ "women's caravan"** (as it was dubbed), and a surprising number of the visitors ended up marrying and settling down here. Given such success, the event was repeated annually until 1989.

By car, the valley can be reached during snow-free months from the east, starting at **Chía** (4km off the A139) in the Ésera valley, via a 25.5-kilometre signposted forest track over the 1999-metre Puerto de Saunc/Collado de Sahún. The dirt surface (except for a kilometre of cement either side of the pass) requires an hour of driving, in first or second gear most of the way, but the countryside's superb, with views northwest to numerous frontier peaks. The usual approach from the west is along the paved side road beginning at **Salinas de Sin**, home to a well-stocked Turismo booth (mid-June to mid-Sept daily except Thurs 10am–1pm & 4.30–8pm; ⓣ974 504 089). The road threads past the turn-offs for Saravillo and Sin (see p.300), and then through a series of dramatic tunnels downstream from the local dam on the Río Zinqueta. Before the tunnels were built, the valley's isolation was instrumental in preserving its culture; bus service remains sparse (see "Travel Details").

Plan, San Juan and Gistaín

A trio of villages, linked by a mesh of PR (plus a few GR) trails on the Benasque model, nestles at the head of the valley, and together they offer most of the area's facilities. Their outskirts were long free of the *urbanizaciones* disfiguring so many Spanish Pyrenean communities – but lately some have appeared around Plan and San Juan.

Plan

With about three hundred inhabitants, broad lanes and imposing architectural detail such as carved lintels and window frames, **PLAN** is the de facto valley "capital". Its main attraction is an eighth- to eleventh-century **church** (usually open), harmoniously blending Visigothic and Romanesque elements. Two side aisles are set off from the main one by arcaded colonnades, all with vaulted ceilings. The nave is slightly asymmetrical at the rear, a consequence of the existing church being built around an older tower.

There's a small Turismo near the church (Tues–Sun 10am–1.30pm & 4.30–7pm). Plan's top **accommodation** is the *Hotel Mediodía* (Ⓣ974 506 006, Ⓦwww.hotelmediodia.com; ❸), with easy parking and balconied rooms. Local *casas rurales* include en-suite rooms at *Casa Ignacio* on Plaza Mayor (Ⓣ974 506 051; ❶). The best places to **eat** are the *comedor* of the *Mediodía* or at *Casa Ruché* on the bypass road, where €12 will get decent vegetable *platos primeros*, a grilled main course and house wine; it's a popular local hangout, where the forestry wardens lunch. Local amenities include shops, an **ATM** and the Guías del Ball de Chistau (Ⓣ974 506 178), offering the usual range of caving, climbing, canyoning and trekking activities.

San Juan de Plan

SAN JUAN DE PLAN (San Chuan de Plan), 2km upstream, is smaller still, but famous for its lively Lenten *Carnaval*. Visitors can enjoy some of the best-value **accommodation** and **food** in the valley, at welcoming, dead-central *Hostal Casa la Plaza* (Ⓣ974 506 052; ❸), with tasteful, wood-decor en-suite rooms, and an excellent, mountain-style *menú* featuring *chireta* (like a haggis made with rice and *morcilla*) and a range of sweets – though they only serve dinner. For lunch, repair to nearby *Casa Sanches* on the same plaza, with a good-value €12 *menú*, tucked into by passing tourists and local construction crews alike; the *comedor* is smoky but there's a small summer terrace out front.

Gistaín

Well perched on the north flank of the valley, with superb views south to the Cotiella Massif, **GISTAÍN** (Chistén) has three prominent **medieval towers** visible from afar. One rises from the church, while the other two were built by feuding families during the seventeenth century. Close up, the village is a little disappointing, with a hotchpotch of half-timbered and modern brick walls, and roofs fashioned from asbestos or tin sheet as often as traditional slate. That said, it's a self-sufficient mountain settlement where rural pursuits remain dominant over tourism – no imported fertilizer is used, as there's plenty of animal manure about.

The most central **accommodation** is opposite the church at *Pensión Casa Elvira* (Ⓣ974 506 078; ❶); en-suite rooms here are spartan but adequate, with TV and some valley views. Downstairs is the only independent restaurant in the village – good value for fare like *acielgas* (chard) and *trucha a la navarra*, especially if taken on half-board basis. Otherwise, Gistaín has most of the *casas rurales* in the valley, a dozen in all; the best can be taken up for days on end by Spaniards, so it's wise to reserve in advance. An excellent if non-en-suite cheapie is volubly friendly Carolina Bruned's *Casa Zueras* (Ⓣ974 506 038; ❶), in an old-fashioned but salubrious half-timbered house near the village entrance, with huge breakfasts extra. On the lower central plaza, en-suite facilities are available at adjacent, 200-year-old *Casa Guillén* (Ⓣ974 506 067; ❷) and *Casa Palacín* (Ⓣ974 506 295; ❷), the latter offering meals.

West to the Zinca valley

The sparse bus services to/from the Valle de Chistau are not that useful. Heading west, instead of hitching 12km to the main road at Salinas de Sin, it's better to take either the **GR19** track-and-trail from Gistaín via Serveto and Sin, the **GR19.1** to Bielsa from Serveto or the wilder **GR15** along the valley's south slope, easily picked up from Plan.

The GR19 leads high along the north flank of the valley through the quiet village of **SERVETO** (Serbeto; 1hr 30min from Gistain), from where a scenic PR curls around Peña San Martín back to Plan. After passing the side track to Señes hamlet and the actual start of the GR19.1, it reaches **SIN** (2hr), with a sixteenth-century grain mill and a municipal *albergue* permanently filled with school groups. Two hours west from Sin, the GR19 leads through dense forest to **SALINAS DE SIN** in the Zinca valley, where you'll find the *Caserio San Marcial* (Ⓣ974 504 010, Ⓦwww.lospirineos.com/caseriosanmarcial; all year), a manor house built around a twelfth-century *ermita*. This offers *table d'hôte* meals (€13), en-suite rooms (❶), a four-person apartment (❺) and a grassy, tent-friendly if basic **campsite** (April–Oct). It's uphill on the west side of the highway, just south of the road junction, conveniently below the onward GR19 into the southeasterly sector of the Ordesa national park (see p.418–419). The **PR137** to Bielsa, veering off the GR19, is a spectacular corniche with occasional galleries, hacked out with hand tools early in the 1900s to service a hydroelectric canal linking the Pineta valley and Lafortunada.

From Sin you can descend south by road to **SARAVILLO** (Sarabillo), near the mouth of the valley. There is a large **campsite**, *Los Vivés* (Ⓣ974 506 171; Easter & June–Sept), slightly west in the valley floor. One kilometre up the south slope in the village itself there's **accommodation** and **meals** at *Albergue Borda Miguela* (Ⓣ974 506 218; all year; six-bunk dorms) and *Casa Cazcarreta* (Ⓣ974 506 273; ❶) and a **horse-riding** centre (Ⓣ692 974 949). Saravillo sits on the **GR15** trail, which heads west then south to Lafortunada in just over two pleasant hours, the quality of the route improving after an initial stretch of track.

The Sierra de Cotiella

Saravillo is also a popular starting point for excursions southeast to the two celebrated lakes and *refugio* (oldest in the Spanish Pyrenees) of the evocatively shaped **Sierra de Cotiella**, once among the least visited corners of the Spanish Pyrenees but now well frequented; Editorial Alpina's 1:25,000 "Cotiella" map-pamphlet is the most useful aid.

Drivers should follow the dirt track heading out of Saravillo and, 2km along, take the left fork towards "Lavasar", then make another left 1.5km further on. The track expires 13.5km from Saravillo at the Collado del Ibón (1928m) parking area and the locked refuge at **Lavasar**. Here you pick up the GR15, which has toiled uphill from Saravillo, and follow it twenty minutes southeast to the picturesque **Ibón de Plan** in its own conifer-flecked cirque at 1910m. Its alias, *Basa de la Mora*, stems from a charming local legend: if you rise at dawn on Midsummer's Day (June 24) and wash your face in the waters, you'll see a long-lost Moorish princess (*mora* in Castilian) dancing on the surface of the lake. Be warned, however, that *Basa* means "seasonal pond": this one's not more than 4m deep at best, shrinking after June to a reedy frog-pool ringed by muddy flats.

Southeast from Ibón de Plan, the GR15 effects another two-hour traverse via two moderate passes to the unstaffed but well-equipped *Refugio de Armeña* (1860m; 20 places) at the entrance to the Circo de Armeña and half an hour from the **Ibón de Armeña**, the massif's other natural lake. The onward path, eventually a track, emerges at Barbaruéns village (no facilities), high up the western flank of the Ésera valley, between Castejón de Sos and Campo.

The Couserans and the Comminges

North of the Val d'Aran sprawls a neglected, isolated corner of France, slashed by eighteen large and small valleys tilting in every direction. This is the **Couserans,** an eerily remote landscape of unkempt pastures, abandoned terraces and ruined barns. Most of the local mines – principally for iron – have been worked out, and the small farms have been unviable since World War I. The population has halved since the 1890s, yet unemployment remains high. Traditionally marginal livelihoods included gold-panning, itinerant peddling, bear-training and acting as wet-nurses for city families. Nowadays the main rural products are hay, cheese and honey, the latter two on sale everywhere. That said, thousands of sheep, hundreds of cattle and rather fewer goats and Merens horses are still grazed in the highlands on a transhumant basis: up in early June, down in early October – you can track the migrations of the flocks on Ⓦwww.transhcouserans.com.

Saint-Girons, 44km west of Foix and capital of the Couserans, is not particularly interesting, but you'll come here to visit the adjacent charming old town of **Saint-Lizier**, and for bus services which make it the hub of all local exploration. Heading south into the "Empty Quarter" extending towards the border and the Val d'Aran, one has bus connections to the old spa-resort of **Aulus-les-Bains** via **Seix**, an important canoeing centre on the River Salat. Buses also run via **Castillon-en-Couserans** to **Sentein**, near the local stretch of the GR10. The River Lez between these two towns traces the misty **Vallée de Biros**, where you'll see *Toulousains* based in their holiday homes, and walkers bound for **Mont Valier** – an easy, beautiful and popular ascent.

Just west, straddling the Garonne, is the slightly more prosperous **Comminges** region. Since 1790, it has belonged to a different administrative *département* (Haute-Garonne), yet the Couserans have always had a deeper connection to it – both areas being Catholic and Gascon-speaking – than with historically Protestant and Occitan-speaking Ariège, now in the same *département*. There are relatively few tourist facilities or conventional attractions in the southern Couserans and the easterly Comminges, the most mountainous part of Haute-Garonne. This changes once you reach the busy road and rail line between **Saint-Gaudens**, functional capital of the Comminges, and **Luchon**, an old-fashioned spa revelling in its new role as a ski resort and hikers' centre. Southwest of Saint-Gaudens, the magnificent cathedral at **Saint-Bertrand-de-Comminges** is a highlight, along with the **Grotte de Gargas** and its outlines of prehistoric hands.

Saint-Girons and Saint-Lizier

Well-connected **SAINT-GIRONS**, known for its mostly vanished cigarette-paper industry – one pulp plant survives at the outskirts – will possibly be your first taste of the Couserans. It's a pleasant if sleepy town straddling the River Salat, with an old bridge, and reddish-pink marble paving-stones on many sidewalks, but little else of note other than a lively July **music festival**.

The simplest orientation point is the sixteenth-century **Pont-Vieux**, just below picturesque rapids on the river; the bridge leads into the old commercial centre on

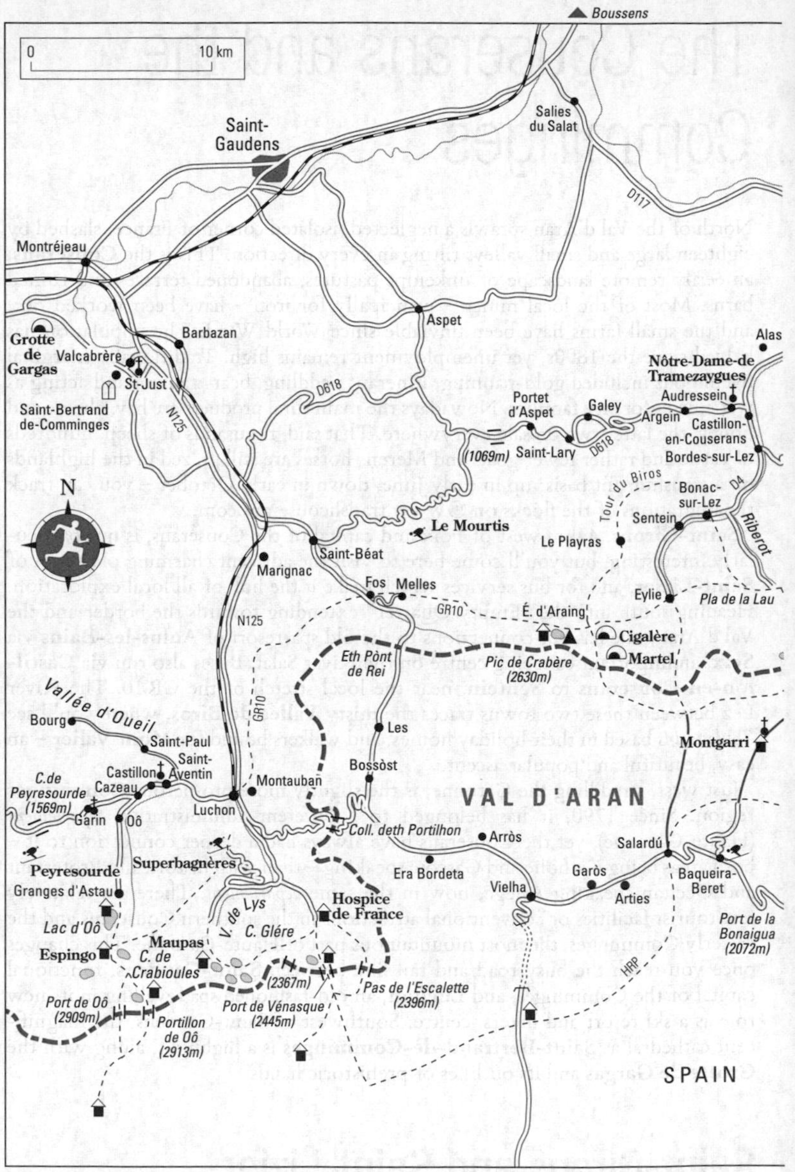

the right bank, whose old-fashioned shops have alas largely succumbed to modern competitors. Upstream, past the tiny cathedral, lies the typically provincial **place des Poilus**, ringed by elegantly faded period-pieces. Beyond this square, along the river, the asphalted **Champ de Mars** – shaded by plane trees – hosts **markets** on the second and fourth Mondays of every month, plus every Saturday morning: herbs, honey, clothes, produce and Africana.

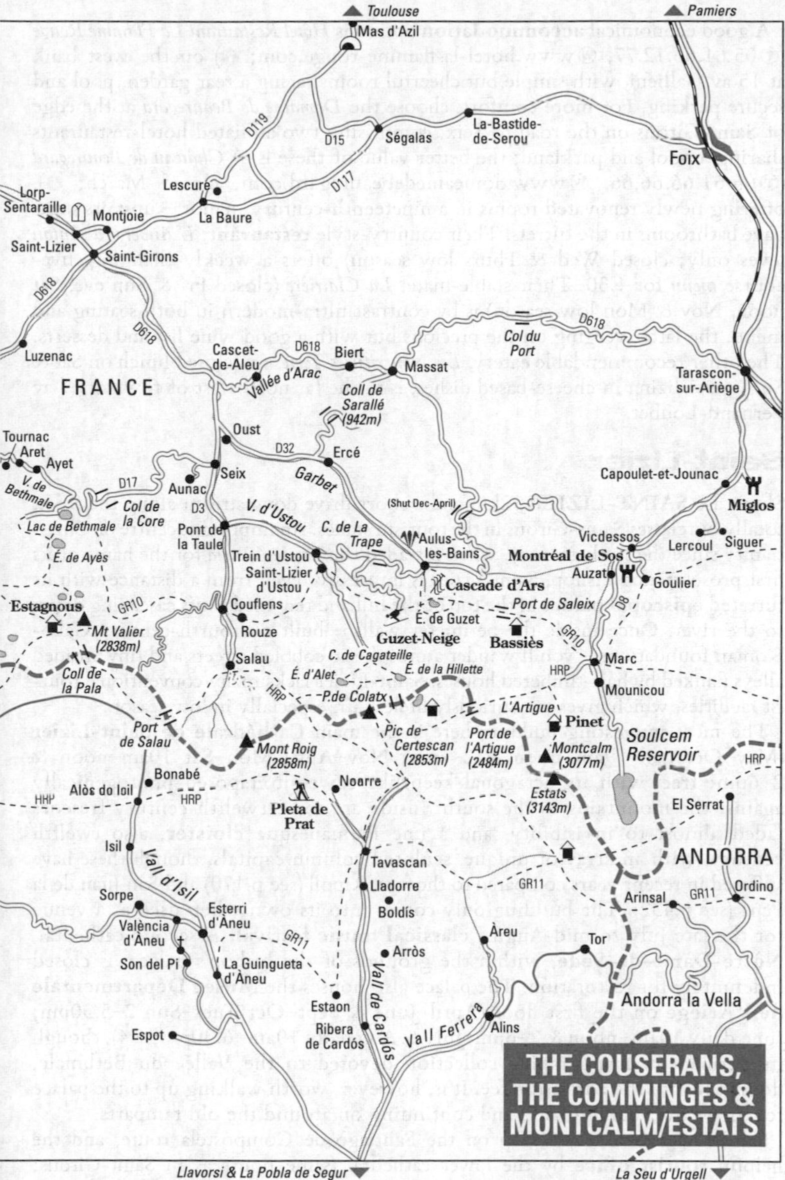

Practicalities

Buses, both private and SNCF, arrive at place des Capots on the left bank of the river, close to the Pont-Vieux. The well-stocked **tourist office** occupies the Maison de Couserans (July & Aug Mon–Sat 9am–7pm, Sun 10am–1pm; Sept–June Mon–Sat 9am–noon & 2–6pm; ⓣ05.61.96.26.60, ⓦwww.ville-st-girons.fr), on the right bank, just downriver from the cathedral.

A good economical **accommodation** option is *Hôtel Restaurant La Flamme Rouge* (Ⓣ05.61.66.12.77, Ⓦwww.hotel-la-flamme-rouge.com; ❷) on the west bank at 15 av Galliéni, with simple but cheerful rooms facing a rear garden, pool and secure parking. For more comfort, choose the *Domaine de Beauregard* at the edge of Saint-Girons on the road to Seix, comprising two affiliated hotel-restaurants sharing a pool and parkland; the better value of these is *Château de Beauregard* (Ⓣ05.61.66.66.66, Ⓦwww.domaineedebeauregard.com; closed March; ❹), offering newly renovated rooms in a nineteenth-century manor – upstairs units have bathrooms in the turrets. Their country-style **restaurant**, *L'Auberge d'Antan* (eves only; closed Wed & Thurs low season) offers a weekly-changing, five-course *menu* for €30. Their stable-mate, *La Clairière* (closed Fri & Sun eve, Sat noon, Nov & Mon low season) is by contrast ultra-modern in both seating and menu, the latter verging on the precious but with a good wine list and desserts. The other recommendable eatery, *Les Nourritures Terrestres* (closed lunch on Sat & Sun) specializing in cheese-based dishes, is in the far northwest of town at 17 av Fernand-Loubet.

Saint-Lizier

Showcase **SAINT-LIZIER**, 2km and a short drive downstream along the Salat, totally outclasses Saint-Girons in the tourism stakes. An important centre of Christianity since the sixth century, when it traded the Latin *Austria* for the name of its first proselytizing bishop, Saint-Lizier is impressive even from a distance with its turreted **episcopal palace** at the top of the hill and red-tiled roofs cascading down to the river. Once inside the perimeter walls – built on fourth-century Gallo-Roman foundations – you'll wander atmospheric cobbled streets and tiny arcaded alleys flanked by half-timbered houses. Saint-Lizier lacks many conventional tourist facilities, which gives it a curiously lifeless air, especially in low season.

The most interesting building here is the main **Cathédrale de Saint-Lizier** (May–Oct daily 9am–noon & 2–7pm; Nov–April Mon–Sat 10am–noon & 2–6pm; free) with its octagonal keep-like tower juxtaposed photogenically against the mountains to the south. Inside are some twelfth-century frescoes faded almost to invisibility, and a fine Romanesque **cloister**, also twelfth century, with an array of unique, sculpted column capitals, though these have suffered in recent years compared to those at Ripoll (see p.170) and San Juan de la Peña (see p.432). The building only comes into its own when used as a venue for the late July to mid-August **classical music festival**. A second cathedral, **Nôtre-Dame-de-Sède**, within the grounds of the bishop's palace, is closed indefinitely for restoration. The palace also houses the **Musée Départmentale de l'Ariège** on the first floor (April–June & Sept–Oct Tues–Sun 2–5.30pm; June daily 10am–noon & 2–6pm; July & Aug daily 10am–6.30pm; €4), though its permanent ethnographic collection devoted to the Vallée du Bethmale, doesn't justify the admission fee. It is, however, worth walking up to the palace for views over Saint-Lizier, and continuing on around the old ramparts.

Saint-Lizier is a major stop on the Santiago de Compostela route, and the helpful **tourist office** by the lower cathedral (same hours as in Saint-Girons; Ⓣ05.61.96.77.77, Ⓔot.saintlizier@wanadoo.fr) lodges bona fide pilgrims in its tiny, three-bunk **hostel**. Non-pilgrim **accommodation** is available at *Hôtel de la Tour* (Ⓣ05.61.66.38.02, Ⓔhoteldelatour09@wanadoo.fr; ❷), in a remodelled old building down by the River Salat on rue du Pont, with the pricier rooms overlooking the water. The on-site **restaurant** has four seafood-strong *menus*, but reports indicate quality varies. You'll have a consistently better feed 600m northwest, just over the municipal boundary in **LORP-SENTARAILLE**, at *La Petite Maison* (closed Mon–Tues; *menus* €16–46) on the main road, whose blank façade belies pleasant garden seating; the cuisine is *minceur* but highly creative.

South of Saint-Girons: the Pays Couserans

A limited bus service – often running only on demand – serves the **Pays Couserans** between Saint-Girons and the Spanish border: some services go southeast to Oust, Seix, Ustou and Aulus-les-Bains, others southwest to Castillon-en-Couserans. These routes can be used to access the **GR10** or its variant, which pass through Aulus, Couflens, Seix and various villages south of Castillon. The upper Lez valley is the focus of the **Tour du Biros**, which skims the flanks of **Mont Valier**, served by both the GR10 and the HRP, as well as a staffed refuge. Between Seix and Aulus, you can detour south at Trein d'Ustou to take in the **Cirque de Cagateille** (see p.307), second largest in the range after the Cirque de Gavarnie, but with a fraction of the crowds. The route east from **Massat** towards Tarascon has no public transport, but under your own steam makes an effective corridor between the Ariège and the Couserans. All these places, if a bit depressed and depopulated, have tourist facilities and some interest in the form of ancient churches or rickety houses.

Seix and Oust

SEIX, the county town of the lower Salat valley, forms a congenial jumble of old, galleried houses strewn by the river, culminating in a vine-draped fifteenth-century **castle**, now home to the Centre d'Interprétation des Valées du Haut-Salat (hours in flux; open Easter & June–Sept), as well as Les Accompagnateurs en Montagne du Couserans (Ⓣ05.34.14.07.64, Ⓦwww.am-couserans.com), organizing walking or snowshoeing by season. The seventeenth-century riverside **church** has an elaborate *clocher-mur*, illuminated by night, while the old market hall a few paces north sees lively use on the second and fourth Wednesday of the month. Seix is also the region's main **canoeing and kayaking** centre, with Haut Couserans Kayak Club (Ⓣ05.61.66.62.76), 2km south upriver being the principal operator on the Salat.

All **buses** to and from Saint-Girons stop virtually adjacent to the **tourist office** in a small booth on the Place de l'Allée on the east bank (summer daily 9am–1pm & 3–7pm; winter Mon–Sat 9am–1pm; Ⓣ05.61.96.00.01, Ⓦwww.haut-couserans.com), which sells hiking guides and maps, and has bus timetables. On the same *place* is Seix's only **hotel**, *Auberge du Haut Salat* (Ⓣ05.61.66.88.03, Ⓦwww.ariege.com/hautsalat; closed mid-Nov to mid-Dec; ❷); two doors west on the corner of the main road is the best independent **restaurant**, *La Gourmandine* (€13–23; closed Sun eve & Mon, part March & Nov–Dec 25), with local dishes.

Some 4km southwest (and 300m above) in the hamlet of **AUNAC**, *Pyrénées-Ânes* (Ⓣ05.61.66.82.15, Ⓦwww.Pyrenees-Anes.com) has both dorms and quads and serves copious gourmet **meals** with locally sourced ingredients. As the name suggests, this *gîte* specialize in **donkey-trekking**. Alternatively, in **OUST**, 2km north of Seix, the central *Hostellerie de la Poste* (Ⓣ05.61.66.86.33; Ⓕ05.61.66.77.08; ❸; closed Nov–Easter; ❸) has been in the same family for five generations, with a pool-garden and a well-regarded restaurant. Despite its position at the junction of roads and the rivers Salat and Garbet, the village itself is dead compared to Seix, turning its back on the Garbet bounding it to the north.

Vallée d'Arac: Massat to Castet d'Aleu

Some 21km north, then east of Oust along the **Vallée d'Arac** and the D618 – the Tour de France passes here sometimes – **MASSAT** does not exactly hum with activity, being among the doziest places in a generally sleepy region, a hangout for alternative types. Its former role as a chief town of a *canton* left a legacy of a large, draughty fifteenth-century **church**, a fair number of old-fashioned shopfronts and houses, plus an open-air market held on the second and fourth Thursdays of every month. There's a **tourist office** below the church (Tues–Sat 10am–1pm & 2–6pm; Ⓣ05.61.96.92.76). Of two surviving **hotels**, the most congenial is *Hostellerie des Trois Seigneurs* on the Saint-Girons road (Ⓣ05.61.04.90.52, Ⓕ05.61.04.94.18; closed Nov–Palm Sunday; ❷), with modern en-suites in an annexe and an excellent **restaurant**.

Otherwise, *Auberge du Gypaète Barbu*, 3km west in pretty **BIERT**, right opposite the church (Ⓣ05.61.04.89.92; ❷; closed mid-Dec to mid-Jan, Sun eve & Mon), has 2005-redone rooms and a trio of *menus* at €17–25. Cyclists especially might prefer, 9km west in **CASTET D'ALEU**, the *Auberge de l'Arac* (Ⓣ05.61.96.87.15, Ⓦwww.ariege.com/aubergedelarac), high-quality English-run *chambres d'hôtes* in a former creamery; half the six rooms are fully en suite (❷), plus there are three river-view studios in an annexe (3–7 days' minimum rental), ideal for groups of three to four. The **restaurant** in the annexe is open to all for supper (€14).

The Vallée de Bethmale

Seix is also the eastern entry, via the D17 over the Col de la Core or the GR10, to the **Vallée de Bethmale**, celebrated for its vivid, almost Balkan female costumes and gold-nailed wooden *sabots* (clogs) for both sexes, though these have long vanished except for their appearance on a few feast days. What remains is an exceptionally beautiful valley – and exceptionally high depopulation, even by local standards. On the heights there's little specifically to see other than abandoned *granges*, or **barns**, traditionally used to store hay but increasingly restored as summer quarters by lowlanders. A little west of the Col de la Core (1395m; closed Dec–April), on both D17 and GR10, the tranquil green **Lac de Bethmale**, ringed by beech trees, is a popular picnic or fishing spot.

In the valley floor, which drains west-northwest towards Bordes-sur-Lez in the Vallée du Biros (see p.311), huddle six half-empty hamlets graced by eighteenth-century architecture. **ARÊT** has the last **sabot-making workshop** in the valley; the curvy-pointed clogs were traditionally exchanged as tokens of betrothal between the newly engaged.

Excursion to the Étang d'Ayès

The Lac de Bethmale marks the start of the most popular excursion from the valley, to the **Étang d'Ayès**, an ideal sampler of the mountains hereabouts if you're not committed to full-pack treks. Without a car, you'll have to hike the whole distance along the GR10 (2hr 30min one way). With a car, you can avoid much of the climb by driving fifteen minutes along the *piste forestière* marked "Mont Ner/Noir" up to a barred gate and car park. Here a yellow-marked path, the old GR10, toils for forty minutes up to the Col d'Auédole and junction with the new GR10. Turn right here (southeast), and continue another twenty minutes on the GR10 to the sizable glacial tarn, just above treeline at 1694m, and hemmed in by crags to the south but marvellously open to the north. With such easy access, Étang d'Ayès is understandably a popular picnic and camping spot, just about swimmable on a hot day. The return route is the same, and takes as long owing to a steep grade just above the parking area.

The upper Salat

Upstream and south from Seix, the D3 follows the Salat almost to its source, passing a few hamlets that make tranquil bases and start-points for forays on the GR10 or HRP. **PONT DE LA TAULE**, where the D8 veers up the Vallée d'Ustou (see below) 4km south of Seix, offers the Dutch-run **hotel-restaurant** *Auberge des Deux Rivières* (Ⓣ05.61.66.83.57, Ⓦariege.com/auberge2rivieres; closed mid-Nov to late Jan, plus Sun eve & Mon in low season; ❷), where for €20 you can enjoy regional treats at its river-terrace restaurant. Rooms are all en suite, though the best ones are the dormer units with skylights.

COUFLENS, 6km up the still-paved but narrowed D3, is a deceptively substantial village along the river, hemmed in by shaggy hillsides. There's no shop here and the local *gîte d'étape* (Ⓣ05.61.66.95.45; 14 places), doubling as a cheese farm, is 1km – a steep forty-minute walk – east at Rouze.

The highest village and end of the line for most traffic (plus the occasional bus), **SALAU** is even bigger, with various amenities (but again no shop) on the single high street. Like Couflens, the place once lived off nearby, long-abandoned tungsten mines. The Knights Hospitallers formerly had a hospice overhead, now crumbled, though the large village church clearly shows their influence. Salau's single **hotel-restaurant** is Dutch-run *Auberge des Myrtilles* (Ⓣ05.61.66.82.58, Ⓦwww.aubergelesmyrtilles.com; ❶; closed Nov, restaurant closed Wed), renovated in 2006 though most tile-floored rooms have showers and sinks but not toilets. The standard breakfasts (€5) are excellent with eggs and yoghurt (€7 gets you *charcuterie* as well). Other meals are relatively simple (€14–22); drinks are served out on the riverside terrace.

The HRP skims just above Salau, heading west to the ruined frontier hospice at **Port de Salau**, site of a big solidarity festival (*La Pujada*) between Occitans and Catalans on the first Sunday in August. If you're not interested in a long-haul traverse, the HRP is the partial basis for the two-day **Tour des Montagnes de Salau**, shown on the Carte de Randonnées no. 6 and taking in the border peak of Mont Rouch/Roig (2858m).

The Vallée d'Ustou and the Cirque de Cagateille

From Pont de la Taule, the D8 heads southeast up the sunnier and more generously proportioned **Vallé d'Ustou**, gateway to the Cirque de Cagateille. The main places en route are **TREIN D'USTOU**, home to the comfortable *Auberge des Ormeaux* (Ⓣ05.61.96.53.22, Ⓔormeaux.ustou@libertysurf.fr; ❷), with the most reliable **restaurant** in the valley (menu €20; closed Tues eve, Wed lunch), and **SAINT-LIZIER D'USTOU** 1km south, astride the GR10. Saint-Lizier has only a *camping municipal* with a pool; the closest indoor accommodation is 2km south by road or along the GR10 in **BIDOUS**, where the 30-place *Gîte L'Escolan* (Ⓣ05.61.96.58.72) also has a handful of doubles (❷).

The road ends above the last farms, 7.5km above Trein d'Ustou, at a car park (1000m) with trailheads for the **Étang d'Alet** (3hr one way; 1900m) and the underrated, forest-girt **Cirque de Cagateille** (35min to its base at 1250m), where several cascades garland the wall during springtime snowmelt. The Cagateille path, sporadically blazed in yellow and red but often faint and rough, continues to **Étang de la Hillette** (2hr 30min; 1800m), tucked into a hanging glacial valley above the cirque. Rather than crossing the frontier to Certascan at the 2416-metre **Port de Couillac**, you can make a satisfying circuit by continuing west to Alet, then down to the car park, on sporadically maintained paths. It's a seven- to eight-hour walking day, harder and less travelled than the nearby Cascade d'Ars loop (see below): a placard at the car park details all possible hikes.

Aulus-les-Bains

Thirty minutes southeast by bus from Seix along the Vallée d'Ustou and over the Col de Latrape, the remote spa-village of **AULUS-LES-BAINS** has, on a clear day, one of the most stunning locations in the Pyrenees. Dense forests and dramatic peaks rise steeply on either side, while rock walls channel water into numerous lakes and into the River Ars with its waterfalls. If you're driving or cycling, it's much easier to arrive on the D32 threading the **Vallée du Garbet**, via Ercé. Once famous for its bear-trainers, Aulus is now a sleepy, faded place with numerous defunct hotels and little to do other than enjoy (and walk through) the scenery, though many old houses are being renovated and new recreational facilities are planned. The centrally placed **thermal baths** (early May to early Oct Mon–Sat 8.30am–noon & 4–8pm; rest of year Sat–Sun only same hours; daily winter hols & Easter) are undergoing phased renovation but remain open – just the thing for trekkers' or skiers' aches and pains.

For summer bike rental and information on other activities, consult the **tourist office** in the allée des Thermes (daily: July & Aug 10am–1pm & 2–7pm; Sept–June 10am–noon & 2–6pm; Ⓣ05.61.96.01.79, Ⓔtourisme@haut-couserans.com). Among surviving **accommodations**, two friendly, good-value choices are *Hôtel L'Oustalet* (Ⓣ05.61.96.00.90, Ⓦwww.hotel-ariege-loustalet.com; ❶–❷), its **restaurant** in particular a tasty slice of old-fashioned France (weekday lunch *menu*; €12 gets four hearty courses plus wine; otherwise €15–23.50; closed Sun eve & Mon, & Nov), and turreted *Les Oussaillès* (Ⓣ05.61.96.03.68, Ⓔjcharrue@free.fr; all year; ❸), with more modern rooms, English-speaking staff who keep a binder of local walks, and a competent restaurant (by arrangement in winter), with menus from €14 and wider choice of local and vegetarian platters in summer. The better of two **gîtes d'étape**, at the rear of the old casino, is *La Goulue* (Ⓣ05.61.66.53.01; all year; 16 places, some doubles ❶), offering good suppers and bike storage. *Le Couledous* (Ⓣ05.61.96.02.26; all year), 500m west towards Ercé along the river, is the local **campsite**.

The Cascade d'Ars and Étang de Guzet

South of Aulus-les-Bains, the famous Cascade d'Ars and the Étang de Guzet are favourite walking destinations, easily combined in a five-hour loop. You are less likely to get lost on an anticlockwise circuit, described as follows: start from the road curve above town, where a sign indicates a non-GR trail for Plan de Souliou and the Étang de Guzet. Climb for one hour through beeches to the junction with the GR10, just past the bracken-covered *plan*, a clearing with great views of the ridges surrounding Aulus. It's another half-hour, with firs now on par with the beeches, to the **Étang de Guzet** (1425m), an idyllic clear pool just west below the GR10 via side trails. Most of the climbing is over; the trail proceeds another hour as a corniche route along the hillside to a meadow and bridge – the **Passerelle d'Ars** (1485m), just above the falls. During the next half an hour the path curls around and under the famous **Cascade d'Ars**, with the best views just before the trail disappears into forest again. The cascades plunge 110m in three stages, though during spring melt it can be just one long drop. From the falls it's another ninety minutes back to Aulus, following the river, mostly by path on the left bank. Cross the **Pont de la Mouline** over the Garbet, turn left, then left again when you meet the asphalt, and you're at the edge of town.

Guzet-Neige

A half-hour road journey from Aulus-les-Bains to **GUZET-NEIGE** during winter is worthwhile for the view alone. Located on a high shoulder 13km from Aulus, it looks northwest along the Vallée d'Ustou and (from higher points) south to frontier peaks. Ski-season **buses** climb first into the **Col de la Trape** (1111m), then up to the resort itself at 1390m.

The 27 shortish **runs** are fairly evenly divided as to green, blue and red ratings, and well linked by fourteen **lifts** (four chairs), making Guzet a fair beginners' or intermediates' resort. However, with a top point of just 2100m on the Pic de Freychet, and the westerly orientation of the pistes, Guzet typically operates only from mid-December to late March, despite the efforts of snow canons. If you show up for just an afternoon's skiing – not a bad idea given the limits of the resort – best eat lunch first in Aulus, as the deceptively numerous snack bars and restaurants are poor quality and poor value.

Mont Valier and around

Pyramidal **Mont Valier** (2838m), the most famous mountain of the Couserans, was long mistaken as the highest Pyrenean peak. It's named after a fifth-century bishop, Valerius, who – crucifix in hand – supposedly made the first ascent. Lying entirely in France, this beacon and mascot of the valleys conceals five lakes in its folds. The mines in Mont Valier's foothills may be long defunct, but timber is still a viable enterprise – if you're driving the narrow roads, beware of slow-moving **lumber trucks**. Mont Valier is accessible from both the GR10 and the HRP, the former skirting it to the east, north and west, the latter to the south. If you're not following either trail, the D618 from Saint-Girons forges southwest along the River Lez to various **gateway villages**.

Castillon, Bordes, Audressein and Alas

It's just under 14km from Saint-Girons to **CASTILLON-EN-COUSERANS**, its houses topped by the fortified twelfth-century chapel – another important halt on the Chemin de Saint-Jacques – which is all that Cardinal Richelieu left standing of the château. A regional **tourist office** occupies Castillon's disused train station at the north edge of town (March–Oct Mon–Sat 10am–12.30pm & 2.30–6.30pm, Sun 9.30am–12.30pm, summer also Sun 10am–noon; ⓣ05.61.96.72.64, ⓦwww.ot-castillon-en-couserans.fr). The only **accommodation** is Jonathan and Myriam Peat's *Le Clos Enchanté* (ⓣ05.61.04.64.47, ⓦwww.jonathanstours.com; ④ B&B), a superb *chambres d'hôtes* in a refurbished Napoleonic mansion at 58 rue Noël Peyrevidal (the through road). The spacious, wood-floored rooms are all en-suite, most with period furnishings, and the vast garden stretches down to the local river. The "tours" of the website encompass summer treks and winter snowshoeing expeditions led by certified mountain guide Jonathan. There are no **restaurants** in Castillons – the closest is 2km south in **BORDES-SUR-LEZ** with its **ancient bridge**, where *Le P'tit Resto*, installed in the local *salle de fêtes*, has garnered a reputation for affordable but savoury *menus* (€16–22) such that you need to reserve Friday and Saturday nights (ⓣ05.61.66.98.63; closed Sat lunch, Sun eve, Wed).

The pride of **AUDRESSEIN**, 1km north of Castillons, is the engaging medieval **church of Notre-Dame de Tramezaygues**, built at the confluence of the rivers Lez and Bouigane. Its highlight is an unrivalled collection of well-restored fourteenth-century **frescoes**, adorning the arcade of the west porch (always open; commentaries posted in French). Two pairs of angels in noble period dress play the flute and rebec, and harp and lute; there are ex voto cartoons of a penitent murderer, a freed prisoner, a recovered invalid and a curiously bare-arsed youth (presumably saved from harm) falling from a tree. A panel of St Jacques du Compstelle (St James the Great) confirms this as a halt on the pilgrim route to Spain, while another of St Jean Baptiste (St John the Baptiste) shows him dressed in a bearskin (complete with head), so appropriate for the Ariège.

In the village itself, there's **accommodation** at *Les Relay des Deux Rivières* (Ⓣ05.61.04.76.32, Ⓦwww.lerelay.com; ❷), with three modern en-suite rooms. Alternatively, head 3km north to peaceful **ALAS**, on the left bank of the Lez at the mouth of the Blaguères valley, where *Les Silènes* (Ⓣ05.61.66.09.75, Ⓦwww.les-silenes.com; ❷) comprises five *chambres d'hôtes* occupying a former school; the three river-view rooms succeed best in transcending the building's institutional past.

Circuit via Refuge des Estagnous

Getting to grips with the Mont Valier country means proceeding 4.5km upstream from Castillon to the **Riberot valley** turning on the left, and then 6.6km up this side road to the parking area and trailhead for assorted trails (including the GR10) at **Pla de la Lau** (ca. 950m), where a **refuge and visitors' centre** are under construction (estimated completion 2009). From here it's just under an hour's easy daypack-hiking to the **Cascade de Nerèch**, a double waterfall, after which the grade stiffens considerably en route to (at 2hr 45min) your first glimpse of **Étang Rond**, which stays in view the rest of the way (3hr 30min) to the **Refuge des Estagnous** (2240m; Ⓣ05.61.96.76.22, Ⓦwww.ariege.com/refuge-estagnous; 70 places; staffed June–Sept, also weekends May & Oct), from which **Étang Long** (above Rond) is also visible.

From Estagnous, Mont Valier looming overhead is just a couple of hours away (you'll need to overnight at the refuge if you bag the peak). Walk southeast on the clear path to **Col du Faustin** (2643m), then northeast by path to the **summit**. The views south are terrific – Montcalm and Estats on your left, the Val d'Aran and Aigüestortes in the middle, the Maladeta Massif to your right.

Otherwise, you can enjoyably vary the return to Pla de la Lau by executing a **loop** along a yellow-blazed trail heading north, dubbed "Muscadet" on the refuge's promo pamphlet. You've a forty-minute climb to the **Col de Pouech** (*c.*

△ Étang Rond and Mont Valier

2450m) before dropping – often with poor waymarking – to the lower end of tranquil **Étang de Milouga** (1959m), an hour below the *col*; camping is possible at the top of the lake. (Two higher lakes, **Cruzous** and **Araouech**, are normally visited by a separate, hard-to-find route from Col de Pouech.) Beyond Milouga, the path improves noticeably as it progresses levelly to the **Cabane de Tous** (*c.* 1900m; sleeps six, spring adjacent), with fine views west en route; ten minutes later you join the GR10 at Cap de Lauzes (1892m). After an initially sharp, zigzagging descent over bare hillside, the grade slackens as you enter a stream canyon thick with beech and reach Pla de la Lau some ninety minutes below Cap de Lauzes. Allow at least eight walking hours, plus stops, for the entire circuit.

The Tour and Vallée du Biros

The popular **Tour du Biros** will occupy four to five days and is clearly marked on the Carte de Randonnées 1:50,000 no. 6 "Couserans–Cap d'Aran" map.

From Pla de la Lau in the Riberot valley, take the GR10 west. After three hours' steep climbing, followed by an equally severe one-hour descent into the Besset forest, you're on the Tour, waymarked in red-and-yellow stripes and briefly in tandem with the GR10. There's a well-sited twenty-bunk *gîte d'étape* (Ⓣ05.61.96.14.00; Ⓦwww.ariege.com/gite.eylie; meal service June–Sept) at the former mining hamlet of **EYLIE** another four to five hours ahead, at the top of the **Vallée de Biros**. If you've reached Eylie by car, you'll finally feel you're in the mountains, with barns and rivulets clinging to the steep slopes all around. As a major trailhead, it has ample signposting to various points of hiking interest.

Next day, the joint Tour/GR10 climbs past the old lead and zinc mines at Bentaillou, and close by the **Gouffre Martel** and the **Grotte de la Cigalère**, discovered by Norbert Casteret (see box on p.313). Four hours from Eylie you reach **Étang d'Araing**, with the **Pic de Crabère** (2629m) reflected in its waters and the friendly *Refuge de l'Étang d'Araing* beside it (1965m; Ⓣ05.61.96.73.73, Ⓦwww.araing.free.fr; 52 places; staffed June–Sept, by arrangement otherwise). The remainder of the day can be spent scaling Crabère, a three-hour round-trip.

The Tour now diverges from the GR10, swinging back northeast on an easier day through beech forests, via abandoned **Le Playra**, then along the north flank of the valley to just outside **BONAC-SUR-LEZ**. This has an excellent *gîte d'étape* by the church, *Le Relais Montagnard* (Ⓣ05.61.04.97.57; 25 places in quads; all year) with evening meals likely to feature couscous or tajine (proprietress Fatima is of Algerian descent). If this is full, it's just 2km west to Sentein. The final, less frequented leg of the Tour heads south from near Bonac along the east flank of the Orle valley to meet the GR10 again at Besset within six hours, from where one finishes a long day descending to Pla de la Lau.

The "capital" of the Vallée du Biros, **SENTEIN**, is dominated by a curious fortified fifteenth-century church with three towers (originally there were four) and some surviving interior frescoes. It also has a shop, a **tourist office** (summer Mon–Sat 10am–noon & 3–7pm, Sun 11am–1pm & 5–7pm, winter Sat 9am–noon; Ⓣ05.61.96.10.90, Ⓦwww.otbiros.free.fr), a **camping municipal** (*La Grange*; Ⓣ05.61.96.18.74) and indoor **accommodation**, best being *La Maison du Rabada* (Ⓣ05.61.96.80.38, Ⓦwww.ariege.com/maison-du-rabada; two-night minimum; closed Jan; ❸ B&B), just three wood-floored rooms in a restored house opposite the church.

West: the GR10 to Fos and Melles

Following the **GR10 west** from the Étang d'Araing requires six hours, the last third on asphalt, to **FOS**, a moribund village on the main road between Vielha (in Spain) and Saint-Béat. There's a *gîte d'étape* on place du Sarramoulin

(Ⓣ05.61.94.98.59; 17 places) with excellent food, as well as a *camping municipal* – but no public transport in any direction.

You might call it quits 40min east of Fos at **MELLES**, a surprisingly substantial, once-wealthy village with excellent-value **accommodation** and **meals** at the *Auberge du Crabère* (Ⓣ05.61.79.21.99, Ⓔpatrick.beauchet@wanadoo.fr; ❹ HB only; closed Tues eve & Wed from Sept–June, also Dec 1–15). Chef Patrick's food – duck breast in green-peppercorn sauce, crayfish hotpot, patisserie – is very good, and the €24 menu gives you the run of most specialities, though wine is pricey; reservations are needed in season.

West: the road to the Comminges

With your own transport, the D618 west from Audressein towards the Col de Portet d'Aspet is the quickest and most scenic way from the Couserans into the Comminges (see below), following the Chemin de Saint-Jacques. En route, there are two excellent places to **eat** and (in one case) **stay**. Opposite the church in **GALEY**, some 10km along (the last distance on the D304 up from Orgibet), *Chez Monique et Stéphane* (Ⓣ05.61.96.71.52; closed Wed low season) offers top value for menus (€15 four courses, €20 five courses) dominated by game and local meat: frogs' legs, wild boar, venison, lamb. Some 2km west, following the D304 loop back to the D618, the equally attractive village of **SAINT-LARY** offers the *Auberge de L'Isard* (Ⓣ05.61.96.72.83, Ⓔaubergeisard@aol.com; ❸), which combines the virtues of local bar, restaurant and shop selling local products with its hotel function. En-suite rooms in the old wing are bang up-to-date if a bit on the cosy side, with several family units; the restaurant is in a newer building across the little stream (*menus* €17–27), while breakfast is self-service in the old wing, a boon for early risers.

Once past the Col de Portet d'Aspet (1069m), just over the provincial boundary, forsake the D618 at a fork in favour of the narrower D44 south, which brings you to the Col de Menté (1349m) and the side road serving the little ski station of **LE MOURTIS** (Ⓦwww.boutx-le-mourtis.com). Despite an exceedingly modest top point of 1860m on the Tuc de l'Étang, the snow record (until late March) is reasonable for twenty shortish, beginner-to-intermediate pistes; scenic runs through the forest are the main appeal, along with 15km of cross-country tracks. At the resort core of **Front de Neige**, *Hôtel La Grange* (Ⓣ05.61.79.41.08; ❹ B&B; open most of year) offers far better fare in its **restaurant** than the usual foot-of-the-slopes snacks. From Le Mourtis, it's 11km further to Saint-Béat on the main N125.

The Comminges

The **Comminges** is an ancient feudal county which, lacking the prestige or power of neighbouring Foix or Bigorre, was absorbed into a unifying France in 1454. Haute-Garonne, the modern successor *département* that approximates the traditional boundaries, is drained by the **Garonne** and its tributary the **Pique**. On public transport, the quickest way from the Couserans to the Comminges is by bus from Saint-Girons to **Boussens**, from where frequent trains run fifteen minutes west along the river to **Saint-Gaudens**. This is chiefly of note as a transport hub for visiting the adjacent great attractions, **Saint-Bertrand-de-Comminges** and the **Grotte de Gargas**.

Saint-Gaudens to Valcabrère

Although capital of the Comminges, **SAINT-GAUDENS** is essentially a way-station rather than a place to linger, its character epitomized by a lively Thursday

Norbert Casteret

Norbert Casteret (1897–1987), who was born and lived at Saint-Martory, 4km outside Saint-Gaudens, was one of the first professional speleologists, earning his living from his books and from survey work for hydroelectric companies. His first big coup came in 1922 with the penetration of Montespan, a cave on the south bank of the Garonne halfway between Saint-Gaudens and Salies-du-Salat. Casteret's account captures the moment of discovery:

"We entered a gallery which I had neglected to explore on the former occasion, and stopped in amazement before the statue of a bear modelled in clay. Further on lay more of these figures: two felines walking single file, and some horses. The following day we came upon some curious tracks; the cave had undoubtedly been used as a shelter or hiding-place by prehistoric people. We were the first men to enter that chamber since the cave-folk dwelt there several thousand years ago. On the muddy floor there were imprints of their naked feet, and also some stone weapons. The walls had been ornamented with the aid of sharpened flints, and we gazed in wonder upon the fauna of far distant ages: mammoth, reindeer, horses, bison, chamois . . .The clay figures of Montespan . . . date from the beginning of the Magdalenian era, say about 20,000 years ago, and are therefore the oldest known statues in the world."

In 1926, with his wife Elisabeth, Casteret discovered the Grotte Casteret (see p.372) on Mont Perdu/Monte Perdido, the highest known ice-cave in the world. Four years later came the discovery of animal engravings at Labastide, west of Saint-Gaudens in the Baronnies. The following year Castaret's dye test – described in the box on p.261 – proved that the Garonne sprang in part from the Aneto glacier, and he also explored the Grotte de la Cigalère, near Mont Valier. In 1952, as part of a team plumbing the depths of Gouffre de la Pierre Saint-Martin in the Western Pyrenees, Casteret broke his own cavern-descent mark set two decades previously, at the 303-metre-deep Gouffre Martel near Cigalère. This record of cave exploration in the Pyrenees has no equal, and it's unlikely that anyone will ever surpass his tally of "firsts" in these mountains.

Note: Montespan, Labastide, la Cigalère and la Pierre Saint-Martin are accessible only to experienced speleologists.

market – and a cellulose plant across the river, spewing pungent white smoke. A small, part-pedestrianized old quarter huddles on an escarpment looking southeast over the Garonne; two *café-brasseries* on place Napoléon exploit the view. The only sights are the massive church of **Saint-Pierre** on the same *place*, originally eleventh- to sixteenth-century but over-restored, and a **Musée Municipal**, in the Place Mas-St-Pierre east of the church and the main Place National Jean Jaurès (Tues–Sat 9am–noon & 2–6pm; €3), displaying prehistoric finds and Gallo-Roman ceramics.

The **tourist office** is at 2 rue Thiers (Mon–Sat 9am–noon & 1.30–6pm; Ⓣ05.61.94.77.61), and the town's most pleasant **hotel**, the *Esplanade* (Ⓣ05.61.89.15.90; ❸), with some south-facing rooms, stands by the museum. The *Pedussaut*, 9 av de Boulogne north of the through road (Ⓣ05.61.89.15.70; ❷), foregoes the view but has parking and a decent **restaurant** (*menus* €17–42). More meals are available at *Les Comminges* next to the *Esplanade* (€22 *menu*), or *Restaurant de l'Abattoir*, 2km away on bd Leconte-de-Lisle, beyond the *gare* opposite the livestock market (lunch only Mon–Sat, plus evenings Thurs–Sat) with impeccably fresh cuts of meat.

Valcabrère

With its rough stone barns and open lofts full of drying hay in June or July, **VALCABRÈRE** lies a short distance south of Montréjeau, itself on the main

Bayonne–Toulouse rail line. It can be reached by SNCF bus (direction "Luchon") to the hamlet of Labroquère, by the Garonne, and then a 500-metre stroll across the river. Standing among cypresses at the village graveyard south of Valcabrère, is the jewel-box-like twelfth-century Romanesque church of **Saint-Just** (daily 9am–noon & 2–7pm; €2). Saint-Just was built largely of stone from the local Roman city Lugdunum Conventarum, founded by Pompey in 72 BC. Inside the elegantly sculpted north portal, showing Christ borne heavenward by angels and flanked by the four Evangelists clutching their symbols, there's ample evidence of recycled masonry: marble in the altar floor, a wall inscription dated 347 AD and several columns augmenting the six massive stone piers upholding the nave. Between the altar and the triple apse with its blind arches towers a carved Gothic freestanding shrine, and a sarcophagus which presumably once contained the saint's relics. The soaring vaulted ceiling creates splendid acoustics, and Saint-Just is a major music venue for the summer Festival du Comminges.

A little further on, protruding from grass at each side of the crossroads, are the foundations of **Lugdunum Conventarum** (closed for excavations), a former town of 60,000 and one of the most important in Roman Aquitaine. According to the first-century Jewish historian Josephus, the town was the place of exile for Herod Antipas – who'd executed John the Baptist and received Christ from Pontius Pilate – and his wife Herodias around 39 AD. It was at its height during the first and second centuries AD, but survived well into the Christian era despite destructive barbarian raids.

Saint-Bertrand-de-Comminges

This part of the French Pyrenees harbours few monuments, but one of the finest stands at **SAINT-BERTRAND-DE-COMMINGES** – a magnificent fortified cathedral reflecting three distinct eras of architecture, commanding the fields of grain and hay beyond Valcabrère.

Roman Lugdunum stretched up the hill to where Saint-Bertrand now stands. The lower part was destroyed by the Vandals in 409 AD, and the more protected walled upper part – where a Christian church had since been built – was wrecked in 585 by King Gontran of Burgundy. For five centuries the site lay deserted, until Gascon aristocrat Bertrand de l'Isle – made bishop of Comminges in 1073 and canonized in 1218 – began to rebuild. Bertrand's Romanesque church was enlarged during the early fourteenth century in Gothic style by the future Clement V (first of the Avignon popes), and remodelled inside during Renaissance times by another bishop, Jean de Mauléon.

The village and cathedral

The handsome walled and gated village of Saint-Bertrand-de-Comminges, its half-timbered-and-brick houses dating from the fifteenth and sixteenth centuries, clusters tightly around the **Cathedral** (Nov–Jan Mon–Sat 10am–noon & 2–5pm, Sun 2–5pm; Oct & Feb–April Mon–Sat 10am–noon & 2–6pm, Sun 2–6pm; May Mon–Sat 9am–6pm, Sun 2–6pm; June–Sept Mon–Sat 9am–7pm, Sun 2–7pm; admission to cloister and choir €4). Dedicated to the Virgin (not to St Bertrand as you'd expect), its plain white-veined facade and ponderous buttressing give no hint of the treasures within. Right of the west door, a twelfth-century Romanesque **cloister** with engagingly carved capitals looks south towards the foothills, haunt of resistance fighters during World War II. In the aisleless interior, the church's great attraction is the central **choir**, built by *toulousain* craftsmen and installed 1523–35. The 66 elaborately carved stalls, each one the work of a different master, are a feast of virtuosity, mingling piety, irony and malicious satire – though sadly roped off-limits and difficult to see in detail even from a metre away. Each of the gangways dividing the misericords has a representation of a cardinal sin on top of the end partition. By the middle gangway on the south side, for example, Envy is represented by two monks, faces contorted with hate, fighting over the abbot's baton of office, pushing against each other foot to foot in a furious tug-of-war. The armrest south of the (locked) rood-screen entrance depicts the abbot birching a monk, while the bishop's throne has a particularly fine back panel in marquetry, depicting St Bertrand himself and St John. In the **ambulatory**, a fifteenth-century shrine depicts scenes from St Bertrand's life, with the church and village visible in the background of the top right panel; the saint's marble tomb, still venerated by pilgrims, is here too. Up a stairway on the south side of the nave is a small **treasury**, featuring gold-embroidered tapestries and chasubles.

Practicalities

The former peak-season ban on **cars** in the village appears to have been suspended, but **parking** is restricted to two areas at the south and southwest outskirts. During July and August the cathedral and St-Just in Valcabrère (see opposite) co-host the musical **Festival du Comminges** (ⓦwww.festival-du-comminges.com for details). The **tourist office** is installed in the nineteenth-century Olivétain chapel and monastery on the cathedral square (Mon–Sat 10/11am–5/6/7pm, ⓣ05.61.88.32.00 or ⓣ05.61.98.45.35, ⓔolivetains@wanadoo.fr;), and also doubles as an adjunct festival box office.

Staying overnight is an attractive proposition, at least outside peak season. Opposite the cathedral, the friendly *Hôtel du Comminges* (ⓣ05.61.88.31.43, ⓕ05.61.94.98.22; April–Sept; ❷) makes a fine, if slightly old-fashioned option, though only breakfast is served (outside in fine weather). The *Hôtel L'Oppidum* (ⓣ05.61.88.33.50, ⓕ05.61.95.94.04; mid-March to mid-Nov; ❸), north of the cathedral on rue de la Poste, has engaging en-suite rooms ranging from cave-like to mansarded-attic, though if you're not staying you're made to feel distinctly unwelcome at their restaurant (*menus* €16–21). Other **eating** options in and around Saint-Bertrand aren't up to much, so if you have transport it's advisable to strike out 6km east to **BARBAZAN**, where *Hôtel Restaurant Le Rocher* (ⓣ05.61.89.58.56, ⓦwww.hoteldurocher.com; closed Wed eve; ❷) offers better value (*menu* from €17) and less snootiness. The nearest campsite is *Es Pibous* (ⓣ05.61.94.98.20; May–Sept), north of the road to Saint-Just.

Grotte de Gargas

About 6km from Saint-Bertrand in the direction of Saint-Laurent, lies the **Grotte de Gargas** (45-minute guided tours daily, max group twenty people: July & Aug 10am–12.30 & 2.30–7pm; rest of year by prior arrangement, but reservations almost always necessary; last tour 45min before stated closing time; ⓣ05.62.39.72.39, ⓦwww.gargas.org; €7). Although it also has engravings and finger-tracings of mammoths, horses, bison and deer, Gargas is unique in the Pyrenees for its 231 Paleolithic painted **hand-prints** (though only a fraction are available for viewing). It's debatable whether these images, in black, red, yellow or white, are genuine outlines – perhaps created by spraying pigment from a reed – or free drawings. If true outlines, the hands placed on the cave walls may have been ritually mutilated, or deformed by leprosy or frostbite, though recent theories have cast doubt on these hypotheses. French prehistorian André Leroi-Gourhan has proposed that the hands are deliberately stylized, code symbols like those used by Kalahari Bushmen for silent communication when hunting. American paleozoologist R. Dale Guthrie has argued (see p.232) that most such hand-drawings are realistic, not damaged but that of (pre-) adolescent youths.

The upper Comminges

Upstream from Valcabrère and Saint-Bertrand extends the highest portion of the Comminges. **Luchon** – formerly known as Bagnères-de-Luchon – is a versatile spa resort at the end of most public transport lines, a staging post for numerous classic walking itineraries and slightly less rewarding ski runs. There's also a notable collection of Romanesque churches in the vicinity.

Luchon

Along with Gavarnie, **LUCHON** – where the rivers One and Pique join – was one of the classic lodestars for Pyrenean explorers. The spa re-entered history in the eighteenth century, when Jacques Barrau and Baron Antoine d'Étigny revived the thermal baths built by Roman emperor Tiberius. They persuaded Louis Richelieu, governor of Gascony and great-nephew of Cardinal Richelieu, to endorse the *thermes* – and the fashionable set from Paris duly descended for the waters and salons. After the peak-climbing expeditions of Ramond de Carbonnières in the late eighteenth and early nineteenth century, Luchon became a base of choice for serious climbers and also attracted numerous Romantic literati.

Arrival, information and accommodation

From the **train station** on avenue de Toulouse (where **buses** also stop), it's a fifteen-minute walk southwest across the River One to the **tourist office** at allées d'Etigny 18 (daily: July–Aug & peak ski season 8.30am–7pm, rest of year same hours but closes for variable lunch; ⓣ05.61.79.21.21, ⓦwww.luchon.com). Several **banks** have ATMs, the first or last you'll see a few trekking days to either side.

There's plenty of **accommodation** in and around Luchon, though you should avoid the obvious establishments on the allées d'Étigny in favour of quieter side streets, or the hamlets immediately around. For longer stays, the tourist office has a noticeboard of apartments to rent. There's no local *gîte* or hostel, but there are eight **campsites** in the vicinity, including two on avenue de Vénasque, the continuation of cours de Quinconces. The least cramped and best-equipped is *Camping La Lanette* (ⓣ05.61.79.00.38), 1.5km east over the Pique (down rue Lamartine) near the village of Montauban-de-Luchon.

L'Auberge de Castelh Vielh 2.5km south on the D125, en route to Superbagnères ⓣ05.61.79.36.79, ⓔLespinasse.Michel@wanadoo.fr. Just three wooden-trim, en-suite rooms (two with balcony), in a lovely forested setting at this fine country restaurant (see p.318). The *castelh vielh* in question is a nearby hilltop signal tower, originally Celto-Roman but last used during World War II. Open daily April–Oct, weekends only in winter. ❷–❸

Hôtel des Deux Nations 5 rue Victor-Hugo ⓣ05.61.79.01.71, ⓦwww.hotel-des2nations.com. Popular, well-kept one-star with a busy ground-floor restaurant (closed Sun eve & Mon) and a range of rooms: two lower floors are modernized and en suite (❷), while the top-storey rooms (❶) are pokier. Limited nearby parking, lift, small garden opposite; open all year.

Hôtel Le Jardin des Cascades above the church in Montauban-de-Luchon, 2km east ⓣ05.61.79.83.09, ⓕ05.61.79.79.16. Six peaceful, wood-decor rooms (some en suite) in a lovely spot backed by a wild, hilly garden nurtured by the falls. Drivers, however, must park well below and hump their luggage in. Well-regarded restaurant (see p.318); open late April to early Oct. ❷

Hôtel Lamartine 48 rue Lamartine ⓣ05.61.79.02.68, ⓕ05.61.79.60.26. An unassuming facade conceals clean, quiet, pink-decor rooms at this well-priced two-star, with bathrooms including hair-dryers. Ground-floor restaurant; closed Nov. ❷

Papilio route Subercarrère, Montauban-de-Luchon, right on boundary with Juzet ⓣ05.61.89.29.82, ⓦwww.papilio-luchon.com. Five superior wood-floored *chambres d'hôtes* installed in a renovated farmhouse that once doubled as a pilgrims' hostel; the attic units have most character. Co-proprietor Rolfe is a certified mouuntain guide and can arrange or take you on any local activity. Supper by arrangement. ❸ B&B

Hôtel la Petite Auberge 15 rue Lamartine ⓣ05.61.79.02.88, ⓕ05.61.79.30.03. Installed in a fine Belle Époque manse set well back from the street, this is the best value amongst the one-stars, often full with a repeat French clientele. Ample parking, all rooms en suite and a decent restaurant doing *table d'hôte* meals; closed Nov–Dec & March. ❶

Hôtel La Rencluse 4 av de Gascogne, Saint-Mamet ⓣ05.61.79.02.81, ⓦwww.hotel-larencluse.com. Well-sited two-star by the river, just outside Luchon municipality, that offers excellent value and off-street parking. Their restaurant's €14 lunch menu is understandably popular. Open May–Oct plus winter holidays. ❸

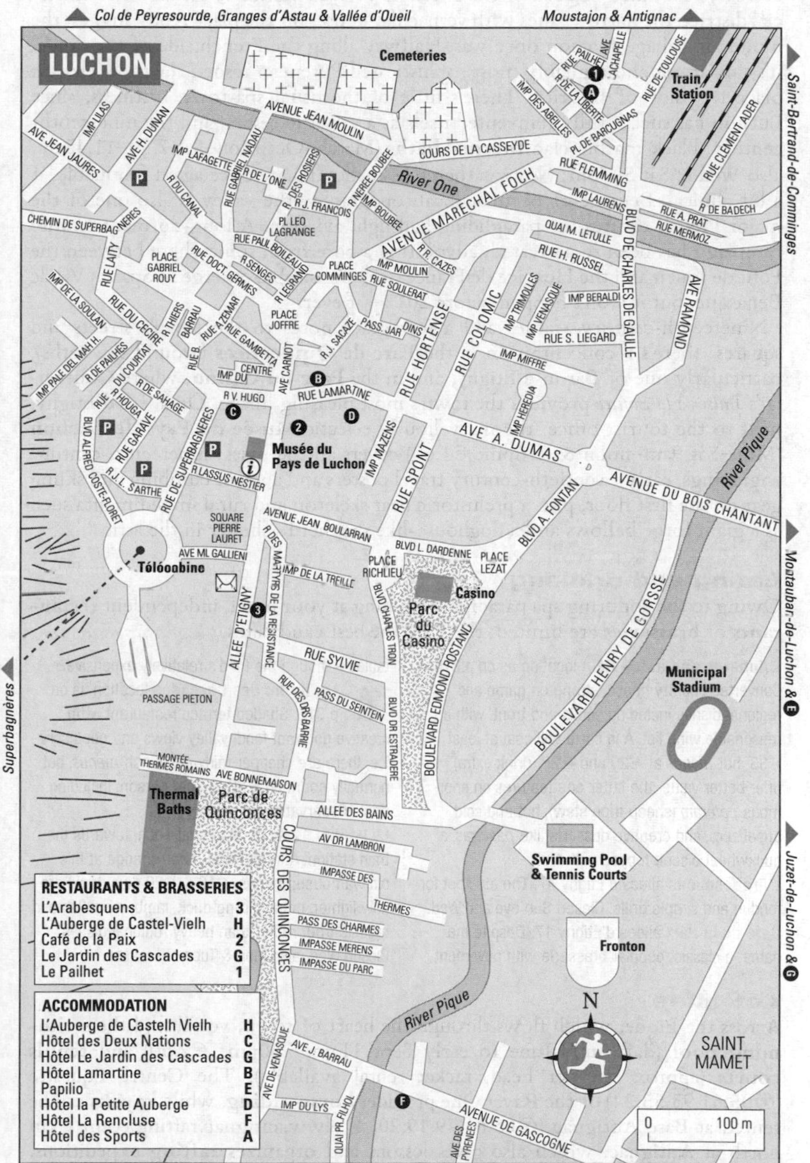

Hôtel des Sports 12 av Maréchal Foch. ⓣ05.61.79.97.80, ⓦwww.hotel-des-sports.net. A bit remote, but quiet and with fairly easy street parking; all rooms en suite and (unusually) non-smoking throughout. Ground-floor restaurant and a secure bike garage; open all year. ❷

The Town

East of **allées d'Etigny**, the main thoroughfare, Luchon's glory days have left a huge neighbourhood of sumptuous villas, which partly justifies the town's self-bestowed moniker "Queen of the Pyrenees". If you venture west of the commercial district, the narrow lanes with vernacular houses off the place Rouy suggest the mountain village Luchon once was. Halfway along the French side of the range, it's the largest and arguably most sophisticated Pyrenean resort, the most elegant place this side of Biarritz. There's little of the usual spa-town fustiness, since Luchon has successfully reinvented itself as a versatile resort, and the nineteenth-century, black-marble-clad **thermal baths** (March–Oct Mon–Sat 7.30–11.45am, also Wed & Sat 5–7pm; ⓦwww.theremes-luchon.fr) are once again fasionable, if a bit clinical. Because of peculiar local topography, the valley is also one of the major French centres for paragliding and light aviation. A long-dormant **tunnel** campaign has been re-activated, advocating a bore from somewhere between the Pont de Jouéu and the Hospice de France (see opposite) to emerge in Spain's Val de Benasque, but it won't happen before 2012 – if ever.

Nineteenth-century statues add a few grace notes to the town's streets and squares: there's a concentration in the **Parc de Quinconces** (around the baths), particularly one of Baron d'Étigny, and in the **Parc du Casino**, where Coutheilai's *Baiser à la Source* provides the town's most pleasing image. On allées d'Étigny, next to the tourist office, the marvellously eclectic **Musée du Pays de Luchon** (Mon–Sat 9am–noon & 2–6pm; €1.60) covers all the bases: nineteenth-century engravings, early twentieth-century travel posters and ancient climbing and skiing gear on the first floor, plus a prehistoric bear skeleton and rural impedimenta such as a giant forge bellows and a doghouse-like shepherd's shelter in the attic.

Eating and drinking

Owing to the enduring spa paradigm of dining at your hotel, independent **restaurants** or **brasseries** are limited; these are the best candidates.

L'Auberge de Castel-Vielh location as on p.316. Converted country house, strong on game and regional dishes including snails and trout, with a reasonable wine list. À la carte will cost at least €33, but *menus* at €20 and €28 (drink extra) offer better value; the latter one features an enormous *pétéram* (sheep tripe stew), hot and cold appetizers, and creative desserts like *pastéras*, a buckwheat biscuit topped with fruit.

L'Arabesquens allées d'Etigny 47. The top spot for fondue and simple grills. Closed Sun eve and Wed.

Café de la Paix allées d'Etigny 17. Despite the name, a classic, popular brasserie with pavement tables – though the food's relatively expensive.

Le Jardin des Cascades location as on p.316. Shaded terrace restaurant, with creative gourmet food, valley views and good service; there are cheaper midweek lunch *menus*, but normally count on €32–37 per person, including drink. Reservations mandatory.

Le Pailhet 12 av du Maréchal-Foch, towards the train station. A format and *menu* change at this old warhouse; *menus* (€16 & €20 plus drink) are now lighter, emphasizing duck, lamb, monkfish and organic trout rather than heavy regional dishes. Closed Wed, also Mon & Tues off-season.

Activities

Across the Pique, which flows through the heart of town, you'll find the **swimming pool** (daily mid-June to early Sept 11am–6.30pm; €2.50) and **tennis courts** (approx €6 per head, racket rental available). The Centre Équestre (ⓣ05.61.95.55.34) of the River One provides **horse-riding**, while **kayaks** can be rented at Base Antignac (ⓣ05.61.79.19.20, ⓦwww.antignac.rafting.com), 3km north at Antignac, which also gives lessons and organizes **rafting** expeditions.

You can get **airborne** in a biplane (€70 for 30min; two passengers) or a glider (€55 for 30min) at Aéroclub de Luchon (ⓣ05.61.79.00.48, closed Wed & Thurs) or learn to **parapente** (flights start at €60) from certified instructors at Freddy Sutra (ⓣ06.87.34.20.54) or Soaring, 29 rue Sylvie (ⓣ05.61.79.29.23). Arapaho at 4 place du Comminges, off avenue du Maréchal Foch, offers a bit of everything, including **mountain-bike rental** and **adventure expeditions** (from €30/day). For the more sedentary, the **télécabine** is the easy way up the 2666-metre distance to Superbagnères (see p.321), with some superb views en route (April daily 1.30–5pm; May to mid-June & Sept to mid-Oct Sat & Sun 1.30–5pm; mid-June to Aug daily 9.45am–12.15pm & 1.30–6pm; €7 one-way, €11 return). It's frequently used by paragliders heading up to a launch-pad, and is also a popular way for trekkers to cut out a 1200-metre climb on the westbound GR10. In winter (Dec–March), the ascent is included in the general ski pass.

Walks from Luchon

There's enough walking **around Luchon** to keep you occupied for a week or so, mostly amongst the frontier peaks and over the border in the Maladeta and Posets massifs. The tourist office sells booklets of recommended short walks: *Sentiers Balisés du Pays de Luchon*, and *Spécial Rando Facile: La 14 Plus Belle Promenades*, which are fine as far as they go – but since waymarking sometimes leaves a bit to be desired, a good IGN map is essential.

Southeast towards Maladeta from Hospice de France

Even if you're not up for the classic approach from Luchon to **Maladeta**, try to do the section between **Hospice de France** (1386m) and the **Port de Vénasque** (2445m) on the frontier. The roadhead for Port de Vénasque is 11km south of Luchon, with the narrow road restricted in summer: cars go uphill only until 11.30am and from 2–4.30pm; downhill from noon–1.30pm and after 5pm. There's ample parking beside the abandoned hospice, built into a wooded hollow by the Knights of St John in the fourteenth century.

The way up to the pass – appearing U-shaped against the sky at first but culminating in a narrow passage when you actually reach it – lies initially through a steep stream valley, the grade not deterring a steady procession of dogs and five-year-olds en route. Some two hours along (2hr 30min with a full pack), you reach the four clear, turquoise tarns known as the **Boums du Port** or **Lacs de Boum**, brimming with trout and the occasional hardy swimmer. Beside the highest and largest lake stands the CAF *Refuge de Vénasque* (2249m; ⓣ05.61.79.26.46; late May to early Oct; 15 places) where a new generation of wardens from the same family serve excellent four-course lunches (including homemade dessert) until late afternoon, as well as supper to overnighters. Suitably fortified, you can now tackle the thirty- to forty-minute trail-climb to the Port de Vénasque (3hr total from Hospice de France), where the entire crestline of Maladeta is literally in your face. If you're continuing south, the just-visible *Renclusa* refuge is another two and a half hours along well-trodden paths, while the *Hospital de Benasque* refuge-restaurant is just over half as far, on the floor of the Ésera valley (see p.390).

Otherwise, complete a satisfying circuit by taking the distinct trail labelled as "23" to the left and east, just beyond the Port de Vénasque, leading in 45 minutes to the **Pòrt dera Picada** (2477m) in Spain. Beyond this you descend gradually for about twenty minutes to the peak and pass of Espelette, with half-wild horses grazing nearby. You can slip north through the frontier again via the "23" trail through the **Pas d'Escalette** (2398m; *Còth de Lunfèrn* on some Spanish maps), but staying close to the border until drawing even with the **Pas de Montjoie**, from where you descend through open country and then the woods of the Frêche valley back to the Hospice de France, completing a seven-hour walking circuit.

Alternatively, shorten the day to six hours by plunging down to the **Étangs de Fréche**, the higher one visible from the cement cairn on the frontier ridge a few moments west of the Pas d'Escalette. This route is cairned, though initially there's no path; it's half an hour down to the top tarn at 2200m, and another twenty minutes to the lower, banana-shaped lake (2100m). Here the maintained "24" trail kicks in, taking you back to the Hospice de France after ninety minutes, passing riotous growths of wildflowers on bare slopes near the lakes, with the final stretch through beech and fir.

South of Luchon: the Vallée du Lys and lake circuit

The **Vallée du Lys**, south of Luchon, provides another corridor to serious walking. The D46, then D46a, road up is initially more impressive than the route to Hospice de France, with the broad glacial valley dominated by the **Cirque de Crabioules** overhead, and the lower slopes dotted with holiday chalets. The asphalt ends after 10km at a giant car park (1132m) and the **Cascade d'Enfer**, a spectacular waterfall dropping 40m in two stages through a cleft in the cliff, though the effect is spoilt a bit by EDF's adjacent dynamo building and disused *téléphérique*.

A large sign details local **day hikes** on marked and numbered paths. The best can be combined into the suggested seven-hour loop itinerary below, taking in the most spectacular low-alpine lakes and a staffed refuge. First you have a forty-minute stiff climb through fir and beech along trail "40", following a stream up to a sloping meadow at the treeline and the junction right (ignore it) for trail "42" to the Gouffre d'Enfer. At the next junction, 1hr 15min from the car park, turn left towards Lac Vert ("1hr, 2000m") rather than right on "41" to the Refuge de Maupas and Lac Bleu. It's a further 1hr 15min (2hr 30min from the car park) to this lake (ignore a left towards the Col de Pinata and Cirque de la Glère), via a glacial basin where springs well up vigorously beyond the Lac des Grauès, really just a tiny tarn. **Lac Vert**, multi-lobed and green, is a popular family destination and just about warm enough for swimming.

You can continue fairly easily to Lac Bleu just overhead, but the following route is the only safe one. Proceed along the north shore of Lac Vert, forsaking trail "40" for the ridge at the far end; there's no path, but cross-country progress is initially easy over turf, with no scree. Then you face a sharper climb to link up with the path to **Lac Bleu** just west of its dam, conveniently in sight much of the way (allow 3hr 15min to here). The dam is an eyesore, but the cirque and bare crags overhead, with streamers of water feeding the lake, are magnificent.

From Lac Bleu, the path goes east around the shoulder of the Pic de Grauès, with modest altitude changes, to visit **Lac Charles** and **Lac Célinda** (allow 3hr extra return). In the opposite direction there's a half-hour descent to the junction with the main trail "41", and then fifteen minutes' climb back up to the rather elderly **Refuge Maupas** (2430m; ☎05.61.79.16.07; 30 places; staffed mid-June to mid-Sept), at the top of the *téléphérique*; if you time it right you can have lunch here.

From *Maupas*, descend again on the EDF-engineered path, following the rusty funicular pylons, to **Prat Long** (1940m; 1hr below), where neither rough camping in the hummocky terrain nor a crude, Nissen-type hut is likely to appeal. Another 40min along path "41" returns you to trail "40"; when you reach the meadow at the treeline, vary your return by taking the scenic path "42", which passes above the Cascade d'Enfer, then loops around the far side of the valley before dropping to the car park (2hr 45min from *Maupas*).

The Vallée du Lys and the Hospice de France areas are linked by a good, half-day path, veering off from trail "40" below Lac des Grauès. This threads the Col de

Pinata (2152m) and the Col de Sacroux (2034m) en route to the lakeless **Cirque de la Glère** before descending sharply towards the hospice. From the cirque, another path climbs southwest to the easy **Port de la Glère/Puerto de la Glera** (2367m), giving access to Spain at the Ibón de Gorgutes (see p.291).

Southwest to Posets

For **Posets**, take the GR10 steeply south from Luchon up through the Sahage woods to Superbagnères (3hr), then west five hours to the *Refuge Espingo*, situated just south of the GR10, above its namesake lake (see below).

As an alternative you could drive, or take one of the regular daily shuttles (early July to early Sept; three daily), to **Granges d'Astau** (1139m), essentially the parking area for **Lac d'Oô**. Here also you'll find the *Auberge d'Astau* (Ⓣ05.61.79.35.63, Ⓦwww.astau-pyrenees.com; May–Sept), which offers a *gîte d'étape* (16 places), inn (❷) and restaurant, though many hikers prefer *Le Mailh d'Astau* next door for meals. From the roadhead, a crowded section of GR10, initially on broad track, climbs for an hour to the dammed lake (1504m), where the privately run *Refuge-Auberge du Lac d'Oô* (1504m; Ⓣ05.61.79.12.29, Ⓦwww.refuge-lac-oo.com; 26 places; May–Oct) perches beyond the west end of the dam, its shoreline tables enjoying views of the superb three-hundred-metre waterfall opposite. The onward path skims the east shore as it mounts to the Col d'Espingo, where the GR10 bears northeast towards Luchon, but most hikers press on to the CAF *Refuge d'Espingo* just below the pass, exactly an hour above Oô. The hut here (1967m; Ⓣ05.61.79.20.01; 70 places; staffed May 1–Oct 15) overlooks the beautiful, undammed **Lac d'Espingo**, and the frontier ridge; limited midday snacks and drinks are served to passers-by.

Power lines, and most day-trippers with their toddlers and poodles in tow, stop here; beyond lies serious high-mountain country. The path continues south from the refuge past **Lac Saussat**, on whose shores tents sprout in summer. A short way above, there are two possible routes into Spain, both partly visible from Saussat: directly via the **Port d'Oô** (*Puerto de Oô*), or by an easterly route via the **Lac du Portillon.** The path for the latter, like much of the Oô–Espingo section, is paved with stone slabs, relics of the construction of the Portillon dam in the 1930s.

The reportedly unwelcoming CAF *Refuge du Portillon*, an ex-construction workers' hut at the foot of the dam (2571m; Ⓣ05.61.79.38.15; 70 places; staffed May–Oct), lies on the HRP, two hours from Espingo. On a sunny summer's day the lake appears cobalt blue against the surrounding grey rock and scree, occasional patches of shoreline grass dotted with saxifrage and gentian. Onward routes into Spain are tricky and require proper equipment and experience on glaciers. The *Hospital de Benasque* hotel or the *Refugio de la Renclusa* on Maladeta lie a full day's trekking east through the **Col de Litérole/Collado de Lliterola** (3049m), while the most direct route to the *Estós* refuge in the Ésera valley slips south through the **Portillon d'Oô**, high above the lake, and then southwest – at first over permanent ice – to join the alternative path descending from the Port d'Oô/Puerto d'Oô. Count on four to five hard-slogging hours via either pass to *Estós*.

Skiing around Luchon

Despite its proximity to the highest peaks in the Pyrenees, **SUPERBAGNÈRES** (15km from Luchon by the D125/D46; regular ski-season bus, or the *télécabine*) is low and exposed to the sun on an east-facing shoulder at 1800m. Most green and blue runs (about half of the 24 pistes) descend from here – bad news that snow canons can't really ameliorate. It's still a good beginner-to-intermediate resort, whose main appeal is 360° views, including 10km of watershed ridge – and on clear winter days, a few *parapentistes*. The *télécabine* drops you just below the main car park and nineteenth-century *Grand Hotel*; there's equipment rental here, but more choice in Luchon. The only full-service restaurant is *La Plete*, not too overpriced, though it struggles to cope at weekends. The longest, most challenging and wildest runs are in the north-facing Céciré sector (2260m), served by the two-stage Hount chair-lift from the Lac d'Arbesquens (1450m).

When snow cover at Superbagnères is thin and mushy, keen skiers almost always find better conditions at **LES AGUDES** and **PEYRESOURDE** ("*Peyragudes*" in tourist-board-ese; Ⓦwww.peyragudes.com), overlooking each approach to the Col de Peyresourde 15km west of Luchon. Although the top is still only 2400m, the east-, west- and north-facing slopes on each side of the ridge up from the *col* act as snow-traps. The developments are fairly ugly but the skiing is serious, with seventeen lifts and 43 unusually wide pistes descending to the two low points at 1600m. With a preponderance of blue and red runs, it's a deservedly popular intermediate-to-advanced centre; the views of the frontier summits from up top surpass Superbagnères', and more chair-lifts (plus two more runs) are promised in future.

West to the Col de Peyresourde

Along the road west from Luchon over the **Col de Peyresourde** (1569m) you can only hitch, cycle or drive – there's no bus beyond the turning to Granges d'Astau. Along the way, three **churches** are worth more than a cursory look. Most famous is twelfth-century **Saint-Aventin**, perched in the namesake village on a very steep slope some 5km from Luchon. Its two Romanesque towers were immaculately renovated in the nineteenth century, and ample **relief decoration** remains on the exterior. Above the south door, the carved tympanum shows Christ in Majesty, borne heavenward in his mandorla by angels, and flanked by the symbols of the Evangelists; on the right is an excellent *Virgin and Child*. The column capitals flanking the door are finely worked as well, depicting the Washing of the Feet (left), as well as a bear. The hermit Aventin was the local patron of bears, who would approach him to have thorns removed from their paws. To the right, Aventin is beheaded by the Moors (in 813), and further along on the wall a bullock paws at the ground to reveal the saint's buried body. Inside (key from the *mairie* Mon–Fri 9am–noon & 2–5pm), there are more carvings near his tomb showing Aventin helping a bear, and carrying his detached head around, as well as some twelfth-century frescoes.

Two kilometres further on, just above the highway, the parish **church** (usually open daylight hours July–Aug) of **CAZEAUX-DE-LARBOUST** has a superb, well-preserved series of late fifteenth-century **frescoes** in sombre shades of ochre and red. Opposite the door, a particularly lurid Last Judgement confronts you; also in the vaulting left of the nave are rarely seen panels of St John the Baptist preaching, and (below this) being led to prison. In the apse, just above the altar, angels just to the right of the Nativity give the glad tidings to the shepherds, one of whom plays bagpipes. Just above this in the conch of the apse, Christ reigns in Glory, while the Virgin, on a crescent-shaped throne, is borne heavenward by more angels. In the vaulting to the right of the nave are Old Testament scenes, including Adam sleeping through the Creation of Eve. After another 2km, the squat, barn-like **Saint-Pé-de-la-Moraine** just west of the village of Garin is a rarity, a pre-Romanesque edifice from the ninth century, cobbled together from Roman masonry.

For **staying** locally, you won't do better than *La Ferme d'Espiau* (Ⓣ05.61.79.69.69, Ⓕ05.61.95.38.92; closed mid-Oct to mid-Dec; ❷), 2.5km west of Saint-Aventin in the centre of **BILLIÈRE**. There something for all tastes and pocketbooks (5 *menus*) at their country-style restaurant which excels at local

△ Column capital, Saint-Aventin church

meat, game and *foie gras* served amidst antique-rustic decor (closed Mon–Wed low season; reservations suggested). The budget-minded can opt instead for the appealing riverside village of **OÔ**, 3km southwest, with its simple but en-suite *Hôtel Les Spijeoles* (Ⓣ05.61.79.06.05, Ⓔauberge.lesspijeoles@wanadoo.fr; all year; ❷), with a sustaining if no-frills restaurant (*menu* €15) doubling as the village bar; the same minor road continues 4km further to Granges d'Astau (see p.321).

The Vallée d'Oueil

Just east of Saint-Aventin, a minor road heads northwest for 10km along the little-visited **Vallée d'Oueil** and its unspoilt villages, most with noteworthy medieval churches. The ski centre at the top of the valley is tiny, overpriced and virtually useless; the best summer activity is the day-hike loop from Bourg taking in the Lac de Bareilles and Mont Né (2147m). There are two worthwhile places to **stay** and **eat** in the valley. At road's end in **BOURG**, 15km from Luchon, *Le Sapin Fleuri* (Ⓣ05.61.79.21.90, Ⓦwww.hotel-sapin-fleuri.com; closed mid-Oct to Christmas; ❹), is a chalet-style hotel with views of a forested slope, and a respected restaurant. Near the centre of **SAINT-PAUL D'OUEIL**, 3km up from the D618, *Maison Jeanne* (Ⓣ05.61.79.81.63, Ⓦwww.maison-jeanne-luchon.com; all year; ❹ B&B) offers superior *chambres d'hôtes* in a lovely old house with garden where breakfast is served in fine weather. There are just two large doubles, and an impeccable attic suite; snacks are provided 1–6pm, but not supper.

Travel Details

Trains

Luchon to: Montréjeau (5–6 daily, all but 1 on SNCF coach; 45–55min).
La Pobla de Segur to: Lleida (3 daily; 2hr 10min).
Montréjeau to: Boussens (6–10 daily Mon–Sat, 7 on Sun; 25min); Lourdes (6–8 daily; 1hr); Pau (4–6 daily; 1hr 30min); Saint-Gaudens (6–10 daily Mon–Sat, 7 Sun; 10min); Tarbes (8–10 daily Mon–Sat, 6 daily Sun; 40min); Toulouse (6–10 daily Mon–Sat, 7 Sun; 1hr 15min).

Buses

Spanish buses

Benasque to: Barbastro (daily 3pm, also Mon–Sat 6.45pm; uphill 11am, plus Mon–Sat 5.20pm; 2hr). Service provided by Alarsa (Ⓦwww.alosa.es).
Plan to: Aínsa (Mon, Wed, Fri at 5.45am, returns 8.45pm).
La Pobla de Segur to: Barcelona (2–3 daily; 4hr); Capdella (daily Mon–Fri Oct–May at 6pm; 1hr; June–Sept Mon, Wed, Fri only at 6.45pm; returns next day at 8am); Lleida (Mon–Sat 1 daily, at 6.30am, returns 4.30pm; 2hr); El Pont de Suert (1 daily, at 9.30am, returns 2.45pm; 1hr); Esterri de Àneu (daily at noon, also Mon–Fri 2.15pm, Mon–Sat 6.30pm; 1hr 10min); Vielha via Bonaigua (1 daily July 1–Sept 15, at 11.45am; 3hr). All services except Capdella provided by Alsina Graells (Ⓦwww.alsinagraells.es).
El Pont de Suert to: Taüll (all year 1 daily, at 1.45am, returns next day 8.55am; 30min). Provided by Alsina Graells.
Roda de Isábena to: El Pont de Suert (1 daily Mon–Fri at 4.37pm, returns next day at 6.15 am; 1 hr); Graus (1 daily at 7.18am, returns at 4pm; 40min).
Sort to: La Seu d'Urgell (2 daily by minibus, 8am & 5.30pm; returns 10.30am & 7.30pm; 1hr 15min; reserve day before on Ⓣ973 620 733 or 689 495 777 (am service), Ⓣ973 620 802 or 610 477 157 (pm service).
Vielha to: Les (3 daily; 35min); French border (2 daily; 40min); Lleida via Túnel de Vielha (2 daily at 5.30–6am & 1.30pm; 3hr 30min); La Pobla de Segur via Salardú and Bonaigua (1 daily, July 1–Sept 15, at 11.45am; 3hr 15min); El Pont de Suert (2 daily, at 5.30am & 1.30pm; 1hr). Provided by Alsina Graells.

French buses

Auzat to: Tarascon-sur-Ariège (in term time, 1 daily at 6.40am, not Tues, Sat, Sun; returns 5.30pm; all year, Fri at noon, returns 5.30pm; 35min).
Saint-Girons to: Aulus-les-Bains (1 daily; 45min); Boussens (7–10 daily Mon–Sat, 5 Sun on SNCF

coach, 3 Mon–Sat, 2 Sun on private coach; 40min); Castillon-en-Couserans (Mon–Sat 1–2 daily; 20min); Foix (4 daily; 1hr); Guzet-Neige (1 daily; 1hr 30min); Massat (daily term time at 5.25pm, otherwise 3 weekly evenings by arrangement on ⓣ05.61.66.08.77; 35min); Seix (Mon–Sat 1–2 daily between noon & 5.30pm; 25–50min; by request only night before on ⓣ05.61.66.08.77); Ustou villages (Mon–Fri 12.20pm, by request only night before on ⓣ05.61.66.08.77).

4

Around the national parks

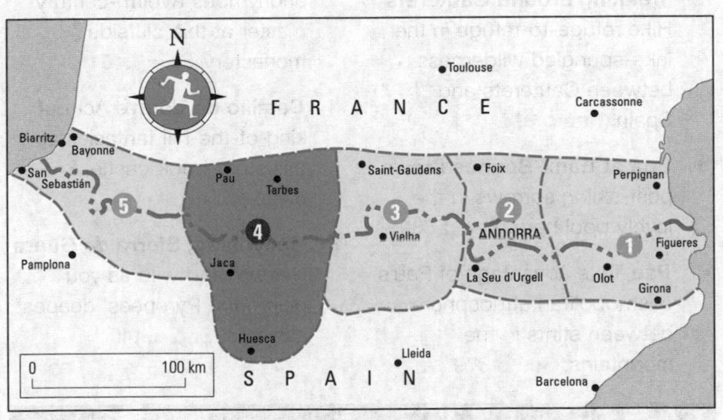

CHAPTER 4

Highlights

* **Skiing at La Mongie-Barèges** This joint domaine is the largest (and often snowiest) in the range. See p.366

* **Cirque de Gavarnie** Don crampons and ice-axe for the ascent to the evocative Brèche de Roland. See p.369

* **Trekking around Cauterets** Hike refuge-to-refuge in the lake-spangled wilderness between Cauterets and Spain. See p.376

* **Spa at Eaux-Bonnes** Drown post-skiing sorrows in the lovely pool here. See p.389

* **Pau** Take advantage of Pau's cosmopolitan atmosphere between stints in the mountains. See p.379

* **Ordesa National Park** Trace the gorges and *fajas* of this spectacular limestone landscape. See p.414

* **Pirineos Sur Festival** Rock until late with top-name world musicians. See p.426

* **San Juan de la Peña** Marvel at relief carvings by an anonymous twelfth-century master at this cliffside monastery. See p.431

* **Castillo de Loarre** Act out king-of-the-hill fantasies at this story-book castle. See p.436

* **Canyoning, Sierra de Guara** Get wet and wild as you plumb the Pyrenees' deepest canyons. See p.440

△ Cirque de Gavarnie

Around the national parks

The allure of the Pyrenees' two largest national parks – the French **Parc National des Pyrénées** and the Spanish **Parque Nacional de Ordesa y Monte Perdido** – remains unmatched by any other part of the range. They contain the landscapes that inspired the gentleman-explorers who pioneered numerous Pyrenean ascents from the late eighteenth century onwards, and it was here that many Romantic literati came to brood. While the exaltation that Ramond de Carbonnières felt standing on the summit of Monte Perdido in 1802 was partly due to his mistaken belief that this was the highest point of the range, he had already explored Aneto – the true high point – without feeling the same delight. So great was the devotion of the eccentric Count Henry Russell that he had caves cut near the summit of Vignemale, highest point of the French Pyrenees, from which he and his guests could watch the changing colours on the frontier peaks.

Nobody can walk through the **Brèche de Roland**, the natural gateway through the **Cirque de Gavarnie**, without being profoundly impressed: in one direction you look down over the mighty palisades of Gavarnie, in the other you gaze out towards the thousand-metre-high walls of the Ordesa canyon. In the two adjoining high-altitude parks, you will almost certainly see Europe's rarest bird of prey, the **lammergeier**, while **griffon vultures**, **golden eagles**, **isards** and **marmots**, reintroduced in 1948, are also fairly easy to spot.

The standard approaches to the Gavarnie area **from the north** are along the **Gave de Pau**, the river valley named after **Pau**, the elegant, relatively cosmopolitan capital of the *département* of Pyrénées-Atlantiques. Near the top, this *gave* frays into several others: the **Gave de Cauterets**, the **Vallée de Bastan** draining from the **Réserve Naturelle de Néouvielle**, an annnexe of the national park, and the Gave de Gavarnie itself. As in the Comminges and Couserans to the east, depopulation and seasonal employment are major issues.

On the other side of the border, in **Alto Aragón**, depopulation is even more pronounced, having been accelerated by the effects of the Spanish Civil War and subsequent Falangist policies. **From the south**, heading up either the **Ara** or **Zinca** river valleys towards the Parque Nacional de Ordesa, you'll encounter the highest proportion of abandoned villages in rural Spain. Only where tourism can guarantee a living – as at **Torla**, **Sarvise** or **Broto**, gateways to the park, or **Aínsa**, **Bielsa**, **Biescas** or **Sallent de Gállego** on main routes to France – are there signs of life. The one sizeable foothill town of any real interest, thanks to its position

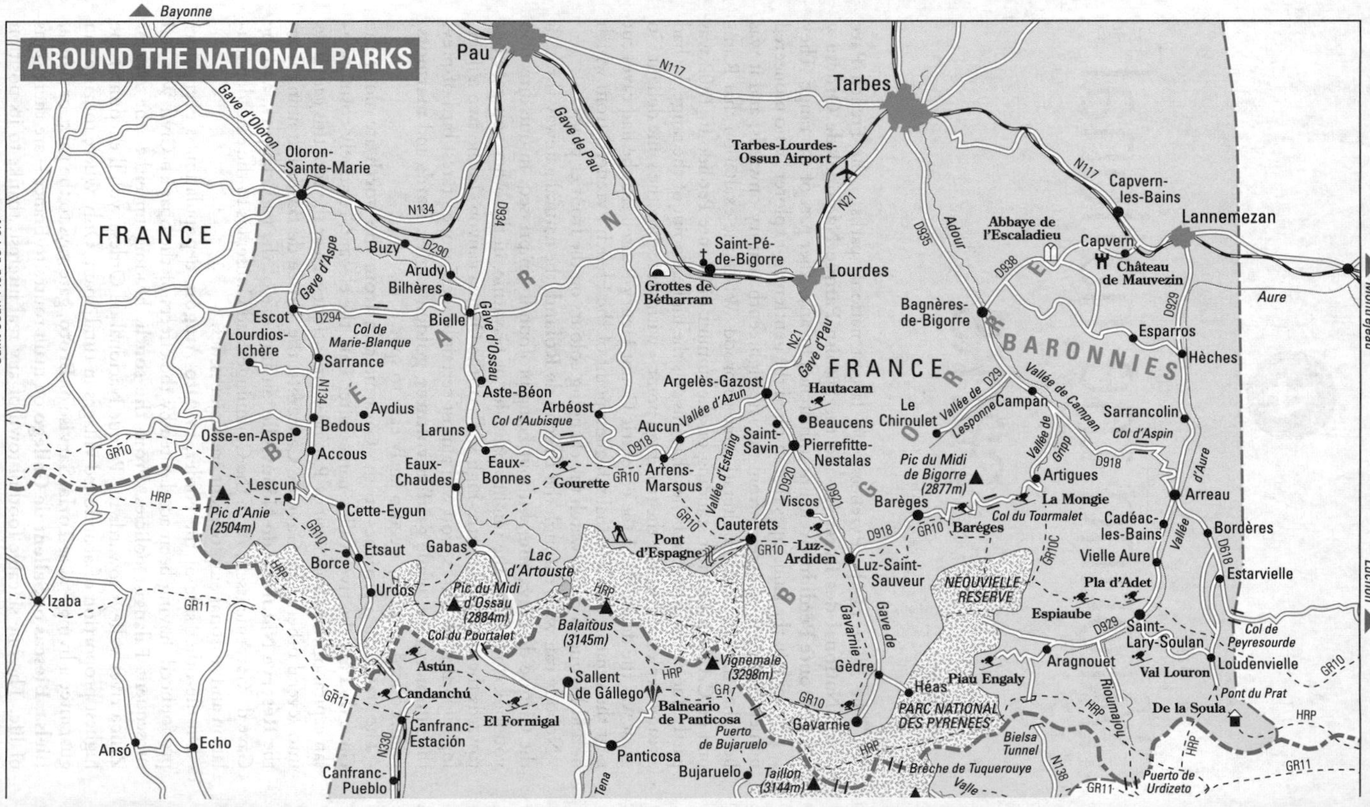
AROUND THE NATIONAL PARKS
Bayonne
Saint-Jean-Pied-de-Port
Montréjeau
Luchon
FRANCE
FRANCE
B É A R N
B I G O R R E
BARONNIES
Pau
Tarbes
Tarbes-Lourdes-Ossun Airport
Lannemezan
Capvern-les-Bains
Capvern
Château de Mauvezin
Abbaye de l'Escaladieu
Oloron-Sainte-Marie
Gave d'Oloron
Gave de Pau
Gave d'Aspe
Gave d'Ossau
Buzy
Arudy
Bilhères
Bielle
Escot
Lourdios-Ichère
Col de Marie-Blanque
Sarrance
Bedous
Aydius
Osse-en-Aspe
Accous
Lescun
Pic d'Anie (2504m)
Cette-Eygun
Etsaut
Borce
Urdos
Izaba
Ansó
Echo
Aste-Béon
Laruns
Eaux-Chaudes
Eaux-Bonnes
Gabas
Arbéost
Col d'Aubisque
Gourette
Lac d'Artouste
Pic du Midi d'Ossau (2884m)
Col du Pourtalet
Astún
Candanchú
El Formigal
Canfranc-Estación
Canfranc-Pueblo
Sallent de Gállego
Balaitous (3145m)
Panticosa
Balneario de Panticosa
Puerto de Bujaruelo
Bujaruelo
Taillon (3144m)
Tena
Saint-Pé-de-Bigorre
Grottes de Bétharram
Lourdes
Argelès-Gazost
Aucun
Vallée d'Azun
Arrens-Marsous
Vallée d'Estaing
Saint-Savin
Pierrefitte-Nestalas
Beaucens
Hautacam
Cauterets
Pont d'Espagne
Vignemale (3298m)
Viscos
Luz-Ardiden
Luz-Saint-Sauveur
Gave de Gavarnie
Gèdre
Gavarnie
Héas
Piau Engaly
PARC NATIONAL DES PYRENEES
Brèche de Tuquerouye
Bielsa Tunnel
Barèges
Col du Tourmalet
La Mongie
Pic du Midi de Bigorre (2877m)
Le Chiroulet
Vallée de Lesponne
Campan
Vallée de Campan
Vallée de Gripp
Artigues
Bagnères-de-Bigorre
Adour
Esparros
Hèches
Aure
Sarrancolin
Col d'Aspin
Arreau
Vallée d'Aure
Cadéac-les-Bains
Vielle Aure
Bordères
Estarvielle
NÉOUVIELLE RESERVE
Pla d'Adet
Espiaube
Saint-Lary-Soulan
Aragnouet
Val Louron
Loudenvielle
Col de Peyresourde
Pont du Prat
De la Soula
Rioumajou
Puerto de Urdizeto
Valle
N117
N134
N21
N330
N138
D934
D935
D938
D929
D290
D294
D918
D920
D921
D29
D618
GR10
GR10C
GR11
HRP

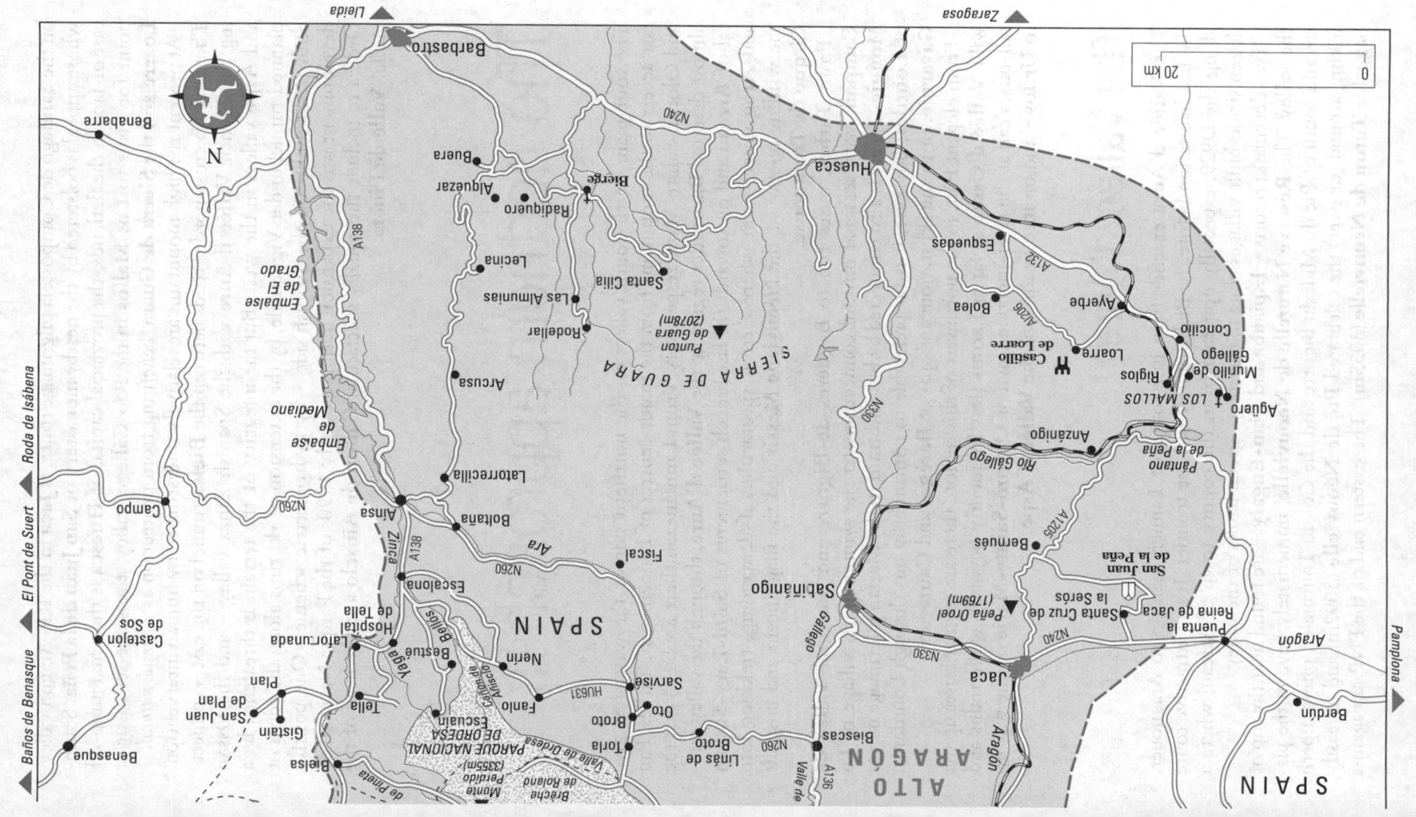
Baños de Benasque
El Pont de Suert
Roda de Isábena
Lleida
Zaragosa
Pamplona
SPAIN
ALTO ARAGÓN
SIERRA DE GUARA
Benasque
Castejón de Sos
Campo
Benabarre
San Juan de Plan
Gistaín
Plan
Bielsa
Tella
Laforunada
Hospital de Tella
Yaga
Bestué
Escuain
Bellós
Escalona
Zinca
A138
Aínsa
Embalse de Mediano
Embalse de El Grado
N260
Boltaña
Latorrecilla
Arcusa
Lecina
Alquézar
Buera
Radiquero
Barbastro
N240
Las Almunias
Rodellar
Bierge
Santa Cilia
Punton de Guara (2078m)
Huesca
Monte Perdido (3355m)
PARQUE NACIONAL DE ORDESA
Brèche de Roland
Valle de Ordesa
de Pineta
Cañón de Añisclo
Fanlo
Nerín
HU631
Torla
Broto
Oto
Sarvisé
Fiscal
Ara
Linás de Broto
Biescas
A136
Valle de
Gállego
Sabiñánigo
N330
Jaca
Aragón
Peña Oroel (1769m)
Santa Cruz de la Serós
San Juan de la Peña
Puente la Reina de Jaca
Berdún
Bernués
A1205
Río Gállego
Anzánigo
Pantano de la Peña
Agüero
LOS MALLOS
Murillo de Gállego
Riglos
Concilio
Loarre
Castillo de Loarre
Ayerbe
A1206
Bolea
Esquedas
A132
N
0
20 km

on the Santiago de Compostela pilgrimage route, is **Jaca** in the Río Aragón valley, whose appeal is bolstered by the nearby monastery of **San Juan de la Peña**. Southeast of Jaca in the flatlands, the provincial capital of **Huesca** is the usual jump-off point for visits to **Los Mallos** in the Río Gállego valley, the stage-set castle at **Loarre** and the **Sierra de Guara**, benefiting from protection as a *parque natural*.

At present the high mountains are relatively undisturbed by human intervention. There are no cross-border roads between the **Bielsa** tunnel on the east – connecting the French **Vallée d'Aure** with the Spanish Zinca valley – and the **Ossau** and **Aspe** valleys in the west. But the integrity of the terrain is threatened by a planned tunnel under Vignemale, by the extension of ski runs along the edges of both parks and – on the Spanish side – by hydroelectric schemes. One positive development was the expansion during the early 1990s of the Parque Nacional de Ordesa to include the equally spectacular **Cañon de Añisclo** and the head of the glacial **Valle de Pineta**.

The northern approaches

The four main north–south valleys on the northern side of the watershed give fast access to the mountains from the major centres of Lannemezan, Tarbes, Pau and Oloron-Sainte-Marie respectively. From Lannemezan there are buses past the almost deserted **Baronnies** region up the **Vallée d'Aure**, through the valley capital of **Arreau** and on towards the last French settlements of **Saint-Lary-Soulan** and **Aragnouet**, from where there is spectacular, if demanding, trekking into the wildlife reserve of the **Néouvielle Massif** and the magnificent and unspoilt **Cirque de Troumouse**.

From **Tarbes**, buses run to **Bagnères-de-Bigorre** and the rural **Vallée de Campan**, with seasonal onward connections to the winter-sports village of **La Mongie**. Tarbes is also connected by bus and train to the Marian pilgrimage mecca of **Lourdes**; however, it is far preferable to continue by bus through Lourdes to **Gavarnie**, or to the ski stations and spas of **Barèges** and **Cauterets**.

From elegant **Pau**, in the northwest of this region, there are regular buses up the wild **Vallée d'Ossau** as far as **Laruns** (less frequently beyond), while trains and rail-buses call at the river-junction town of **Oloron-Sainte-Marie** on the way up to **Urdos** – and on into Spain – via the **Vallée d'Aspe**.

The Vallée d'Aure

The **Vallée d'Aure** extends from just south of Lannemezan up to Aragnouet, the last habitation before the Bielsa tunnel and the frontier. It's an attractive route along the D929, especially upstream from the county town of Arreau, where a dozen stone-built villages cling to the steep, green banks of the valley.

Two decent ski resorts – **Espiaube** and **Piau-Engaly** – are found near the top of the valley. The **Réserve Naturelle de Néouvielle**, immediately beyond the pistes and south of Pic du Midi du Bigorre and the Col du Tourmalet, offers superb hiking around (or over) the celebrated **Pic de Néouvielle** (3092m) and up easily baggable **Turon de Néouvielle** (3035m). The eastern end of the PNP, up against

The Parc National des Pyrénées

The French **Parc National des Pyrénées** (PNP) was a long time coming, meeting such strong local resistance to its establishment in 1967 that it was limited to a thin ribbon of territory along the border. It has real girth only around **Pic du Midi d'Ossau**, between **Cauterets** and **Vignemale**, and where it adjoins the older **Réserve Naturelle de Néouvielle**; in places – for example, near the Col du Somport – it measures barely 1500m across.

The traditional independence of and competition between 87 different mountain *communes* locally means the park isn't as extensive as it should be. Already by medieval times the mountains were carved up between local families, the Catholic Church and a few semi-autonomous valleys, all grouped into two huge feudal counties: **Béarn**, created in 820 and not absorbed by the French Crown until 1589, and **Bigorre**, which kept out of Parisian clutches until 1607. Following the unification of France, and the subsequent Revolution, territory was administratively re arranged into *commissions syndicales*, *syndicats de communes* and *copropriétaires*. However, rivalry between these bodies created complications nearly as numerous as during the feudal era. Right up until 1967 the *communes* – and local hunting clubs – fiercely resisted any abrogation of their privileges regarding the mountain environment, often guaranteed by ancient charters and treaties.

Given such a background, creating a park was inevitably time-consuming, with the compromise result limited in scope, and pleasing no one entirely. The PNP is too easy for vehicles to reach, and not big enough; the paltry number of (re introduced) Pyrenean bears, which the park failed signally to protect, live largely outside its boundaries. Indeed, the plight of the native bears is a convenient stick used by critics to beat park administrators, who retort that their hands are more than full with the task of protecting other, less high-profile species – as well as having to accommodate rural livelihoods and repair the damage caused by tourism.

From the visitor's point of view, the most obvious effects of the PNP's establishment are a system of **trails** amounting to over 400km, including – but not limited to – the GR and HRP routes, and a number of staffed **refuges**, either CAF-affiliated or private. The paths are marked by red or green lettering on yellow **signs**, though the walking times quoted are usually overestimated by between a quarter and a third. Park **boundaries** are marked by red-and-white signs with an isard's head in silhouette; within these limits there is not supposed to be any permanent habitation or obtrusive man-made structures other than alpine refuges. The following activities are banned: making fires, para gliding, mountain-biking, driving any motorized vehicle, hunting and of course littering or flower-picking. Camping is limited to emergency bivouacs, though swimming is allowed, as is fishing (with a permit).

the border, is a tougher proposition but with its own rewards, including a high-mountain approach to the **Cirque de Troumouse**.

The bus ride along the Vallée d'Aure towards the PNP begins at Lannemezan train station on the Pau–Toulouse line. Although the journey provides a geography lesson on glaciation and mountain agriculture – grazing on denuded south-facing slopes, firs on the north-facing hillsides – there's little to justify leaving the bus or your car until the village of **SARRANCOLIN**, 19km from Lannemezan, known for its Romanesque **church of Saint-Ebons**, built to a Greek-cross plan. Inside (usually open) you can view the gilded and enamelled copper casket for the saint's relics, though the carved stalls in the choir (locked) aren't a patch on Saint-Bertrand's (see p.314). **Eat** at roadside *Café Bar Restaurant de France* (*Chez Bruno*), with an excellent €11 lunch *formule* and three *menus* under €24; it's a lively spot favoured by locals, and open most of the year, when other establishments up-valley are shut.

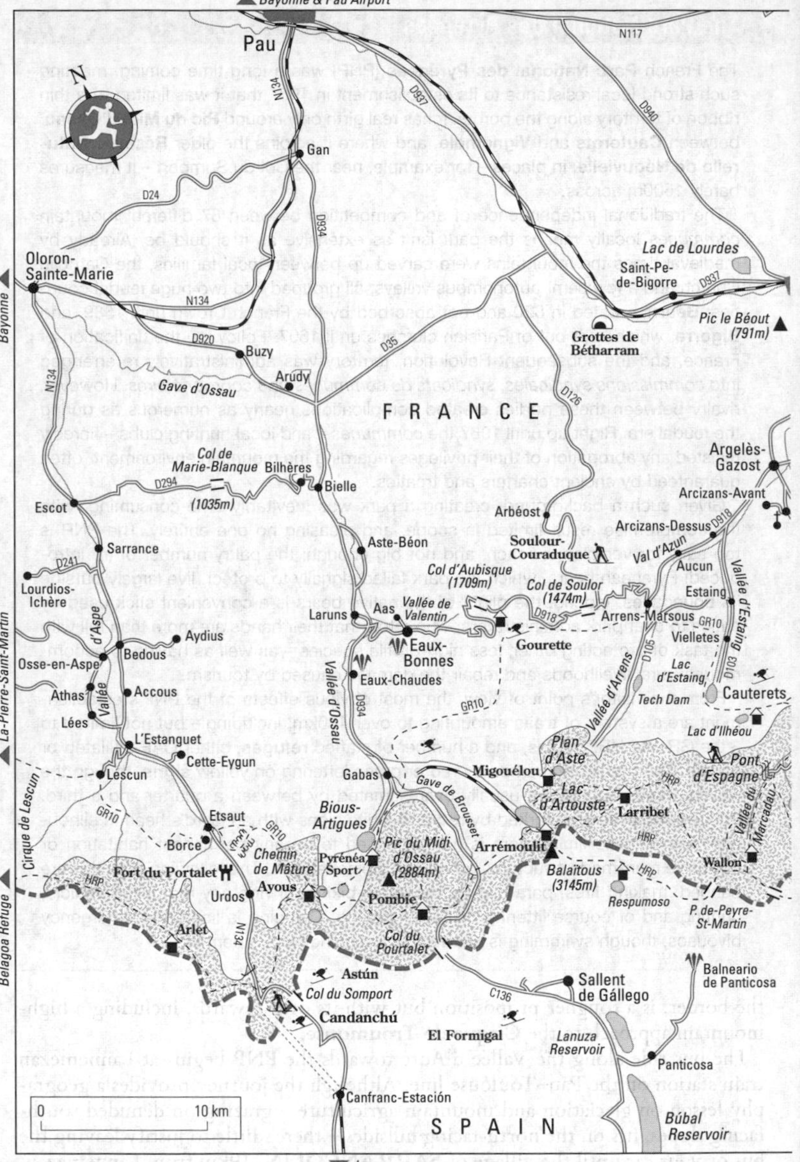

Arreau

ARREAU, 27km from Lannemezan, sits at the confluence of the Louron, Lastie and Aure rivers, a strategic position that first made it capital of the ancient Comté d'Aure under the kings of Aragón. Later it formed the heart of the Pays de Quatre Vallées, finally absorbed by France in 1475. Arreau enjoys an almost rainless microclimate, lying as it does in the shadow of Pic l'Arbizon to the southwest.

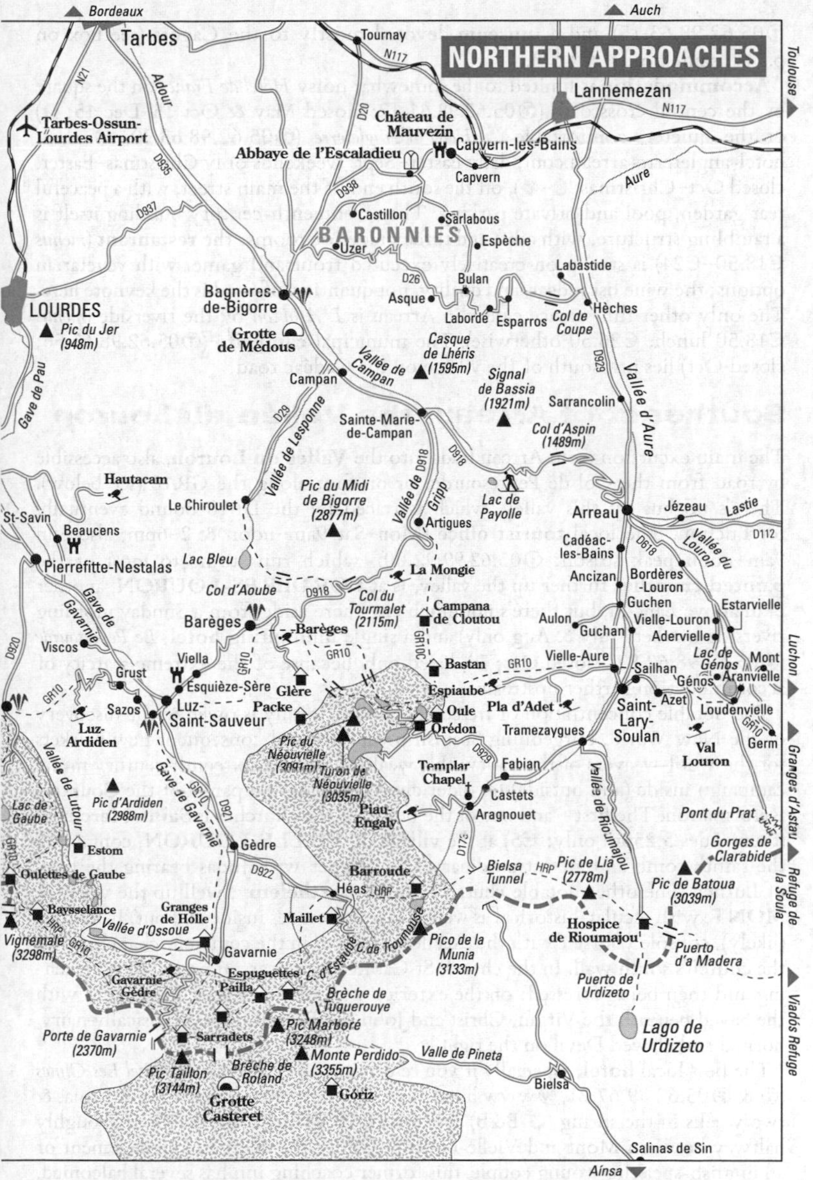

Almost a small town, its tone is set by the medieval **market** building and some half-timbered houses with their *fleur-de-lys* motifs and flower-boxes (especially the Maison des Lys opposite the market). On the east bank of the river, the **Chapelle Saint-Exupère** by the post office merits a look for its flamboyant Gothic nave and eroded Romanesque portal. The tenth-century **Château des Nestes** now houses both the **tourist office** (summer Mon–Sat 9.30am–12.30pm & 1.30–7pm, Sun 9.30am–12.30pm; winter Mon–Fri 9am–noon & 2–6pm;

ⓣ05.62.98.63.15) and a **museum** devoted mostly to the Cagots (see box on p.349; same hours; €1.50).

Accommodation is limited to the somewhat noisy *Hôtel de France* on the square by the central crossroads (ⓣ05.62.98.61.12; closed May & Oct 15–Dec 15; ❷) or the quieter, comfortable *Hôtel d'Angleterre* (ⓣ05.62.98.63.30, ⓦwww.hotel-angleterre-arreau.com; daily Easter–Sept, weekends only Christmas–Easter, closed Oct–Christmas; ❸–❺), off the south end of the main street, with a peaceful rear garden, pool and private parking. The seventeenth-century building itself is a rambling structure, with a lift and three grades of rooms; the **restaurant** (*menus* €18.50–€24) is strong on creatively executed trout and game, with vegetarian options; the wine list is dear, and quality, not quantity, of food is the keynote here. The only other full-service eatery in Arreau is *L'Arbizon* by the riverside (*menus* €18.50 lunch, €26.50 otherwise). The municipal **campsite** (ⓣ05.62.98.65.56; closed Oct) lies just south of the village on the Cadéac road.

Southeast of Arreau: the Vallée du Louron

The main excursion from Arreau leads into the **Vallée du Louron**, also accessible by road from the Col de Peyresourde, or on foot along the GR10 (see below). There's no bus up this valley, which is traced by the D618 bound eventually for Luchon. The local **tourist office** (Mon–Sat 9am–noon & 2–6pm, also Sun 9am–noon peak season; ⓣ05.62.99.92.00), which runs tours to most of the **painted churches** further up the valley, is at **BORDÈRES-LOURON**, another 2km above Lançon, but there's not much else there aside from a Sunday morning riverside market (July & Aug only) and a single uninspiring **hotel**, *Le Peyresourde* (ⓣ05.62.98.62.87; closed Oct; ❸), listed only because of the extreme scarcity of accommodation further upstream.

The notable concentration of frescoed churches locally is owed to the discovery of the New World, burgeoning Spanish prosperity and consequent new markets for the wool-weavers of the valley; this wealth funded a sixteenth-century mural campaign inside (and outside) far older churches, part and parcel of the Counter-Reformation. The first – and one of the best – of the churches is **Saint-Mercurial** (tours Tues 5.25pm only; €5) at the village of **VIELLE-LOURON**, containing the saint's tomb and an extraordinary Last Supper with Judas bearing the head of Luther. The other notable church is **Saint-Barthélemy**, well up the valley at **MONT**, with secular-historical as well as sacred frescoes inside and out. If it's shut (likely), console yourself with the excellent frescoes in the cemetery chapel and on the church's south wall. In the chapel, St Catherine appears in period dress, teaching and then being arrested; on the exterior wall, there's a Last Judgement with the Saved beneath the Virgin, Christ and John the Baptist, plus a classically hairy, horned and clawed Devil on the right.

The best local **hotel**, especially if you're driving or cycling, is *Hôtel Les Cimes* (ⓣ & ⓕ05.62.99.67.21, ⓦwww.hotel-les-cimes.net; closed Sept 15–Christmas & two weeks in the spring; ❷ B&B) above **ESTARVIELLE** on the D618, roughly halfway between Mont and Vielle-Louron. Under the energetic management of an English-speaking young couple, this former coaching inn has several balconied, en-suite rooms with valley views (plus cheaper ones) and excellent, abundant fare in the **restaurant**. The *garbure*-focused €22 *menu* is the basis of advantageous half-board rates; you must reserve a table if you're not staying there.

Approach from the east: the GR10

The GR10 heads west from **Granges d'Astau** to the **Vallée du Louron**. Initially the way lies west along the **Val d'Esquierry**, south of the ski development of

Les Agudes-Peyresourde, over the **Couret d'Esquierry** (2131m; 2hr 30min) and then briefly along the **Val d'Aube** into the Louron valley before turning north to the hamlet of **GERM**, high up on the east flank of the valley (1339m; 2hr 30min from the pass). It's another three-plus hours to the next indoor accommodation, so many will call it a day here after five hours of trekking, and will **stay** and **eat** at one of two establishments: the *Auberge de Germ* (Ⓣ05.62.99.90.86, Ⓦwww.auberge-de-germ.com; ❷), one of the southernmost buildings in the village, and the group-oriented *Centre de Montagne* (Ⓣ05.62.99.65.27, Ⓦwww.germ-louron.com), with a huge restaurant, pool and choice of dorms (five- or ten-person) and family quads in the new wing.

The GR10 continues downhill to the southeast shore of the artificial Lac de Génos-Loudenvielle, and the village of **LOUDENVIELLE**, 45 minutes by foot from Germ. Unfortunately, all its accommodation has closed; the only facilities are a **campsite**, *Pène Blanche* (Ⓣ05.62.99.68.85), a shop and a bank ATM. However, beyond the village at the edge of the lake stands **Balnéa**, an ambitious *centre thermoludique* (Ⓦwww.balnea2000.com; all year except last half Nov; open variable hours, minimum 3–8pm). The stone and wood architecture of the combination lagoon-with-waterfalls, sauna and oriental hammam is stunning, but for the stiff entry fee (€12–14.50, better value in combination with Peyragudes ski pass) you'd hope the pools were kept rather hotter than they are. **GÉNOS**, on the northwest shore, has the only other local "sight": a small, thirteenth-century **castle** (locked). Come up for the view over the lake to the snowcapped peaks, not for the stubby fortifications themselves.

From Loudenvielle the GR10 climbs, mostly on track parallel to the paved, two-lane D25, towards the Col d'Azet (1580m) before dropping to the wonderfully set, tranquil village of **AZET**. Much the best of three places to **stay** here is *La Bergerie* (Ⓣ05.62.39.49.49, Ⓦwww.la-bergerie.net; ❸ B&B, ❹ HB), an old stone house with a south-facing lawn garden; runner-up, on the same lane by the church, is *Auberge du Col* (Ⓣ05.62.39.43.97; ❷ B&B, ❹ HB), another old-house inn. From here you've less than an hour's walk down to the main N129 road at Vielle-Aure, with the comforts of Saint-Lary-Soulan (see p.339) 2km south.

Skiing and parapente: Val Louron

The local ski station of **VAL LOURON** perches southwest of, and high above, the Lac de Génos-Loudenvielle. Although it's across the valley from the runs at Peyresourde (see p.322), Val Louron can't compare, with a top point of 2150m (descending to 1450m) and just two chair-lifts – all in all a tiny centre, which despite a northerly orientation is apt to lose its snowpack quickly to wind and the low altitude. In summer, it's a popular site for **parapente**, with schools based at Génos and Adervielle.

Walking in the Vallée du Louron

At the top of the Vallée du Louron lie a number of eminently scenic lakes and secluded tributary valleys which get a fraction of the **hiking** traffic above neighbouring Luchon. Equip yourself if possible with the excellent, French-only **booklet**, *Randonnées et Ascensions dans la Vallée du Louron* by Jean-François Rouys, published and sold by the tourist office in Bordères-Louron, detailing thirty itineraries and meant to be used in conjunction with the IGN 1:25,000 **map** 1848 OT. The best recommended routes start from the **Pont du Prat** car park (1229m), at road's end 6km south of Loudienville, and involve a traverse of the spectacular **Gorges de Clarabide**; after an initial steep climb through forest – via either *raid* (straight up) or *lacet* (switchback) trails – you emerge onto a superb corniche path, originally built to serve hydroelectric works, along the canyon, with interesting placards (in French/Spanish) on local topics. After ninety minutes (all times logged with a day-pack) you reach friendly *Refuge la Soula* (1690m; ⓣ06.16.85.68.66, ⓦwww.refugelasoula.com; 60 places; June–Sept), designed to serve the HRP and rather dwarfed by an adjacent power-dynamo building.

From *La Soula*, one cairned branch of the **HRP** goes east to dammed **Lac Caillauas** (2171m; 1hr 15min further), not very scenic with its dam and fluctuating water levels. Better things beckon as the onward path toils up the slope south of Caillauas to arrive within another hour at the north shore of **Lac des Isclots** opposite its famous islet (2398m), pictured on the cover of the suggested guide-booklet, lowest of the three **Gourgs Blancs** (misnamed as they are green rather than white) and an idyllic picnic spot. From there it's just a quarter-hour to the **Lac du Milieu** (ie the mid-most of the Gourgs Blancs), where the distinct path ends; allow another twenty minutes of rock-hopping to reach **Gourg Supérieur** (2560m; not labelled on the 1848 OT map).

This is as far as you can comfortably reach and return to Pont du Prat in a day. During summer, long-distance trekkers continue to traverse the **Col des Gourgs Blancs** (2877m; ice-axe and crampons usually needed) just under the eponymous peak (3129m), descending past Lac Glacé to the Lac and Refuge du Portillon. Day-trippers should retrace their steps or more excitingly, with an early start in July, clamber strenuously over the Col de Pouchergues (2718m) southwest of Gourg Supérieur to reach half-frozen **Lac de Clarabide** (2650m; 1hr 30min), nestling under its namesake frontier summit. From there, it's more cross country down to **Lac de Pouchergues** (2111m; 3hr from Supérieur), where a choice of two proper trails – the corniche Chemin de Quartau, or a valley-bottom route along the Neste de Clarabide – bring you back to *Refuge La Soula*. The main HRP *variante* west proceeds from the Neste de Clarabide at the ruined Cabane de Clarabide to the **Lacs et Vallon d'Aygues Tortes** (2280m; 1hr 45min from La Soula), another popular day-trip target.

The most popular walk from the **Pont des Chèvres** (1103m) 1.5km south of Loudenvielle, initially uses the **GR10** east along the Val d'Aube to the vicinity of the Couret d'Esquierry. From there a spur path heads south to the two **Lacs de Nère** (2430m; 4hr) dominated by Pic de Hourgade (2984m), in high, wild territory; return is the same way.

South of Arreau: the upper Aure

Continuing up the Aure from Arreau along the D929, after 2km vehicles pass under the rock arch that is the porch of Notre-Dame-de-Pène-Taillade at **CADÉAC-LES-BAINS**, another possible base. Here two-star Logis de France affiliate *Hôtel Restaurant du Val d'Aure* (ⓣ05.62.98.60.63, ⓦwww.hotel-valdaure.com; closed April–May & late Sept to Christmas, weekdays all winter; restaurant open late May to late Sept; ❸; HB only July–Aug), is nicely set in its own park on the riverbank with a pool and tennis courts. In the vaulted, ground-floor billiards rooms a cold sulphur spring remains from the spa established here in Roman times. The restaurant's three *menus* (€17–25) feature own-raised trout and meat, but if you intend to lunch here, phone ahead.

Alternatively, 8km southwest of Cadéac along the D30 side road from Guchen lies **AULON** (1230m), a strikingly handsome old village in the middle of nowhere at the base of L'Arbizon and Bastan d'Aulon peaks. Since the closure of most facilities serving the **GR10** in Vielle-Aure, Aulon – just 25 minutes off the trail by spur path – makes a good goal, and you can **stay** at the excellent, central *Hôtellerie de Montagne Le Pic Noir* (ⓣ05.62.39.94.83, ⓦwww.lepicnoir.free.fr; closed Nov; six-bunk dorms, plus six doubles ❷, ❹ HB), with good *table d'hôte* suppers. You

△ Lac du Milieu, Vallée du Louron

can also **eat** well at nearby *Auberge des Aryelets* (closed Sun eves to Tues low season, also Nov 15–Dec 15; reserve on ⓣ05.62.39.95.59) with hearty cuisine featuring duck, meat, *foie gras*, snails and the like; there are *menus* at €17–35, but allow plenty extra for the wine list.

VIELLE-AURE, 9km south of Arreau on the D929 and just before Saint-Lary (see below) is the last semi-traditional village before the ski-related developments, its older quarter scattered mostly along the west bank. The central **tourist office** (ⓣ05.62.39.56.90, ⓦwww.vielleaure.com; Mon–Sat 10am–12.30pm & 2–6.30pm; ⓣ05.62.39.50.00) can help with accommodation, mostly *chambres d'hôte* since the two local *gîtes* closed down. However, a single, friendly **hotel** survives, two-star Logis de France member *Aurelia*, 400m south of town on the old road to Saint-Lary-Soulan (ⓣ05.62.39.56.90, ⓦwww.hotel-aurelia.com; closed late Sept to mid-Dec; ❸ B&B), with a decent restaurant and small pool. The closest **campsite**, 1.5km downstream in Agos suburb on the west bank of the Neste d'Aure, is large, grassy *Le Lustou* (ⓣ05.62.39.40.64).

Saint-Lary-Soulan and Sailhan

SAINT-LARY-SOULAN, 12km south of Arreau, was one of the first Pyrenean resorts to be featured by foreign package-tour operators; though they've since departed, its rustic core is now enveloped by highly forgettable modern development. The **tourist office** opposite the fountain *rond-point* (daily 9am–7pm, closed lunch low season; ⓣ05.62.39.50.81) can help with accommodation in *résidences* (apartments by the week). Saint-Lary also has a **Maison du Parc National** (ⓣ05.62.39.40.91; June–Sept & Dec–April Mon–Sat 9am–noon & 2–6.30pm, also Sun July & Aug; variable hours otherwise), providing guides and general information on the local flora and fauna. Saint-Lary also has the last **bank** ATMs before the Spanish frontier. The Office des Sports de Montagne just north of the *rond-point* (ⓣ05.52.39.42.92, ⓦwww.office-sports-montagne.com) is your one-stop outfitter for **summertime outdoor activities**, including canyoning, rafting and *parapente*.

Budget **accommodation** includes *Gîte Le Refuge* (ⓣ05.62.39.46.81; all year; 46 places) at the southern edge of town, as well as a *camping municipal*, *La Lanne*

(Ⓣ05.62.39.41.58). There are nearly a dozen **hotels** in Saint-Lary, with more at the pair of ski centres overhead, but they're usually booked out by French families. Worth trying on spec are two-star *Pons Le Dahu* on rue de Coudères, a quiet street east of the centre (Ⓣ05.62.39.43.66; ❻ HB only); and the two-star *La Pergola* at rue Principale 25 (Ⓣ05.62.39.40.46, Ⓔjeanpierre.mir@wanadoo.fr; ❹ B&B, ❺ HB), set back from the street, with a well-regarded **restaurant**. Choices for eating outside the hotels aren't brilliant, though the *Crêperie La Flambée Auroise* at 20 bis rue des Fougères, beside the Maison du Parc, has wholegrain bread and a good range of beers or juices, while *La Grange* on route d'Autun just outside of town, run by the son and daughter of the *Hôtel d'Angleterre* management in Arreau, has an excellent reputation (allow €25–30 plus drink). With transport, head up to the village of **SAILHAN**, 2km northeast, where *Chez Lulu* (Ⓣ05.62.39.40.89; closed Mon) offers filling **meals** (*menus* €9–21) at outdoor tables, with *garbure* evenings and fireplace-grilled meat. There's also a high-quality *chambres d'hôtes* south of the church, *Le Relais de l'Empereur* (Ⓣ05.62.40.09.18; ❸).

The Saint-Lary ski stations

The adjacent complexes of **PLA D'ADET** and **ESPIAUBE**, just west of Saint-Lary, have a reasonably linked piste system, with the highest of the thirty lifts (nearly half of them chair or *télécabine*) reaching 2450m, and 43 runs, facing various directions, divided into eight green, twelve blue, thirteen red and three black. The Espiaube sector starts at 1590m, an unobjectionable development of rental shops, eateries and chalets; there's still a hamlet of old barns below – plus a small **hotel**, *La Sapinière* (Ⓣ05.62.98.44.04; ❹), often full in ski season. The shuttle-bus from Saint-Lary passes Espiaube on its way to Pla d'Adet (1700m), its development by contrast a monstrosity; this also receives the direct *téléphérique* up from Saint-Lary. Piste plans confusingly dub Pla d'Adet as "Saint-Lary 1700", and Espiaube as "Saint-Lary 1900", though they're essentially the same altitude (*c.* 1600m); "Saint-Lary 2400" encompasses the entire La Soumaye-La Tourette-Point 2450 area.

The nursery slopes, and a preponderance of drag lifts, are at and above Pla d'Adet; other skiers should instead take the Portet *télécabine* from Espiaube over the Col du Portet (2215m) to La Tourette summit (2320m), or the Mousades and Soumaye chair-lifts to Pic La Somaye (2370m), focuses of most serious skiing. The 2450-metre top point is served by the tough Corneblanque drag lift, but Arrouyes adjacent is accessible to most skiers, and allows superb vantages south descending from the edges of the Néouvielle country. At **lunch time**, those who know go to the *Chalet-Hôtel de l'Oule* (meals noon–3pm), where you eat well indeed for under €22; it's accessible either via a red-piste descent or the bi-directional Lac chair-lift. Similarly, at day's end you can take the bubble-lift down to Espiaube or descend 3km of twisty and narrow blue run – it's the Col du Portet-bound road in summer. The two domains are linked by the Lita and Tortes chair-lifts and their associated blue pistes.

Piau-Engaly

PIAU-ENGALY (Ⓦwww.piau-engaly.com), the last stop on the valley bus route (in winter anyway), 20km above Saint-Lary, is arguably the most futuristic ski resort in Europe, and the newest in the Pyrenees. Some love the architecture while others hate it, but Piau-Engaly has undeniable advantages: illuminated night-skiing (7–10pm), a reasonable snow record owing to a 2500-metre top height and nine chair-lifts among 21 lifts in total. The ring-shaped accommodation units are at 1850m, allowing doorstep access to 37 north-facing pistes, which include eight black, eight red and fourteen blue – in short a good intermediate to advanced centre.

The Vallée du Rioumajou

Above Saint-Lary, the main river drainage begins to curl west and fray into half a dozen tributaries. The most scenic of these is the **Vallée du Rioumajou**, which joins the Aure just over 3km upstream from Saint-Lary. The hamlet of **TRAMEZAYGUES** (meaning "between both waters") stands dramatically at the river confluence, overlooked by the ruins of an eleventh-century **castle with church** and by steep rock walls that exclude the sun most of the winter. Bears used to live in the dense surrounding forest, but only after they were hunted out locally did the Rioumajou valley become a *site classé* (protected area) – meaning no fires, (usually) no camping and no driving 9pm–7am.

A narrow twelve-kilometre road snakes up the valley; 6.7km along, *L'Escalette* (July–Sept only; *menus* €13–22), overlooking a tiny reservoir, does competent if leisurely lunches and suppers, either outside on grassy terraces or in the woodsy interior of this converted barn. The paved road ends at "Km8", where the enormous, and enormously popular, **Frédançon** riverside picnic meadows under the firs attract half of the tourists in the Vallée d'Aure on any given summer weekend. The other half continue along the final 4km of rough track to the renovated **Hospice de Rioumajou** (1560m; aka *Rieumajou*), a traditional halt on one branch of the Santiago pilgrimage trail, and before that a stage of a Roman trade route. It's open early July to early September for drinks and light snacks from 11am to 5pm, but owing to lack of electricity and the nocturnal driving ban there's no supper or accommodation. Tenting down in the vast green meadows here – an authorised *aire bivouac* – will go unremarked upon, however.

The environs of the hospice are a major crossroads of the **HRP** and its variants: you can continue south across the frontier via the **Port d'Ourdissetou/Puerto de Urdizeto** (2403m; 2hr 30min–3hr) for access to Bielsa; hike east over the **Port de Madère/Puerto d'a Madera** (2560m) to the refuge at Biadós; or go west via **Pic de Lia** (2778m) and continue along the frontier to the *Refuge de Barroude* (see below) in a very long day.

Into the Parc National des Pyrénées

The approach to the **Parc National des Pyrénées** from the Vallée d'Aure is a classic alpine walk enlivened at the end by the superb Cirque de Troumouse. Just after the side road for Piau-Engaly goes off to the right, there's a car park and trailhead at the first sharp bend in the main road. From here you take the footpath up the **Vallon de la Géla**, crossing the boundary of the park almost immediately before joining the **HRP** north of the *Refuge de Barroude* (2377m; ⓣ05.62.39.61.10; 30 places; staffed June 15–Sept 15), perched magnificently in a namesake cirque, between two lakes.

It's only a half-day hike up, and thus a popular day excursion, but it's best to spend the night at the refuge, retracing your steps for half an hour next morning to the main HRP. This continues northwest on a path around the base of Pic de la Géla (2851m), via the two passes of **Hourquette de Chermentas** (2439m) and the **Hourquette d'Héas** (2608m). Descending from the second *hourquette*, often snowed up early in the summer, you find yourself in the upper reaches of the **Cirque de Troumouse**; follow the Aguila stream steeply down into the Héas valley, reached some five and a half hours out of the *Refuge de Barroude*. From the valley floor the cirque reveals itself in all its glory; for a description see "The Gavarnie region", p.367.

A Templar chapel and the Túnel de Bielsa

Beyond several hamlets which comprise the *commune* of **ARAGNOUET (tourist office** in **Fabian** hamlet), just north of the road, stands an intriguing twelfth-century Templar chapel (usually locked). Its almost windowless and plain exterior gives nothing away, though the jagged perpendicular edge of its tall *clocher-mur* suggests that there was once a large hospice here, at the base of the pedestrian route over 2429-metre Port de Bielsa. Today, most people **cross the frontier** by car, via the three-kilometre **Túnel de Bielsa** (daily: April–Sept 24hr; Oct–March 8am–midnight; free). For safety reasons, red lights keep passenger cars out when lorries are passing through.

The Réserve Naturelle de Néouvielle

France's first protected area, created in 1935, the **Réserve Naturelle de Néouvielle** forms a lake-rich "annexe" at the very eastern tip of the far larger Parc National des Pyrénées. It encloses some of Europe's highest forests of mountain pine, with substantial stands reaching 2400m and isolated specimens even growing at 2600m. This is due to a predominantly southern exposure, unusual for the French Pyrenees, which also encourages a riot of smaller **flora**.

Néouvielle – *Neoubieh* or *Neu Bielha* in local languages – means "old snow", perhaps a reference to the vestigial glaciers on certain peaks here. It feels similar to the Aigüestortes-Sant Maurici park in Catalunya: day-trippers and dams at the lower elevations, granite walls, tarns and trekkers' passes higher up. And similar rules apply: no camping except in designated areas, no overnighting in caravans, no mountain-biking and a ban from July 1 to Sept 15 (9.30am–6pm) on private car passage along the single road into the *réserve*. Between these hours a **navette** (€4 return, €2.50 single) operates from the **car park** (€5 per day) at Lac d'Orédon on the south side of the *réserve* up to another car park at Lac d'Aubert. During unrestricted hours, drivers can get as far as Lac d'Aubert by means of the "**Route des Lacs**" (toll at Orédon), which as the D929 climbs 14km up from Fabian in the Aure valley; but as ever in the Pyrenees it's more rewarding to do most of your exploration on foot. **Trails** through the *réserve*, often the GR10 or a variant, are accordingly well signposted; either the 1:50,000 Carte de Randonées no. 4 "Bigorre" or 1:25,000 IGN 1748 ET **map** is invaluable.

Lac d'Orédon loop hike

If you're not keen on a full-pack traverse, the following popular three-hour loop, using a small portion of the GR10, gives a good sample of the *réserve*. The starting point is the 2004-refurbished *Chalet du Lac d'Orédon* (1900m; ⓣ06.23.05.72.60, ⓦwww.chalet-neouvielle.com; 80 places; open end May to end Sept; HB obligatory) just above the Orédon dam, with facilities ranging from dorms to doubles and family quads; you'll have to pay a local toll or parking fee to access it by car. A bit of road-walking en route to Lac d'Aubert is unavoidable; head 1km up towards Lac d'Aubert, and then bear left onto the trail marked "**Les Laquettes**", three natural, photogenic tarns below the Aubert dam. Also just below Aubert is one of the few legal bivouac sites in Néouvielle. Next, the route swings east past the car park and a defunct refuge overlooking the natural **Lac d'Aumar**. You then pick up the GR10 along a crest, affording fine views over the three southerly reservoirs of Cap de Long, Orédon and Oule, before descending back to the chalet from the **Col d'Estoudou** (2260m) on an unnumbered trail.

Vielle-Aure to Artigues

Without your own transport, the best way to begin a traverse of the Néouvielle country is to take the **GR10** west from Vielle-Aure, climbing past and through the Saint-Lary pistes and then over the Col de Portet (2215m). After about six hours you reach the rustic, unstaffed Cabane de Bastan, where you have the choice of the variant **GR10C** towards Artigues or the main Barèges route.

For **Artigues**, hike north from the *cabane* and spend your first night at the lakeside *Refuge du Bastan(et)* (2250m; ⓣ05.62.98.48.80; 24 places; staffed June–Sept), one hour further, beyond a series of small lakes. Next day, you first climb the scree slopes up to the **Col de Bastanet** (2507m), then descend between several lakes for lunch at the *Refuge de Campana de Cloutou* (2200m; ⓣ05.62.91.87.47; 27 places; staffed June–Sept), before tackling a three-hour afternoon stage to Artigues through the wide Garet valley, which culminates in some waterfalls. Minuscule Artigues, on the D918 some 10km northwest of the scenic Col du Tourmalet, has no facilities; you must road-walk 2km further to Gripp (see p.351).

Bastan to Barèges

For **Barèges**, follow the generally westward trail from the Cabane de Bastan, which skims along the eastern, then southern boundaries of the *réserve*, and spend the night at the *Chalet-Hôtel de l'Oule* (1820m; ⓣ05.62.98.48.62, ⓕ05.62.39.55.38; 28 places; open & staffed early June to mid-Sept, & ski season; dorms or doubles), 45 minutes away at the dammed south end of Lac de l'Oule, or at the *Chalet du Lac d'Orédon* (see opposite), just under two hours further. The only problem is that both are easily accessible by the D929 road – the Lac de l'Oule hut in the final instance via a 45-minute path from the **Artigousse** parking area, 6km along – and therefore highly popular. After a night at one of these refuges, follow the GR10 or the "Les Laquettes" trail (see opposite) into the heart of the *réserve* as far as the adjacent lakes of **Aumar** and **Aubert**, where there's a choice of two onward routes north.

For the first route, you climb along the GR10 to the **Col de Madamète** (2509m), where you leave *réserve* territory, drop to the basic Cabane d'Aygues-Cluses, and then follow the idyllic Aygues-Cluses valley to join the D918 road at Pont de la Gaubie, seven hours from Orédon.

Alternatively, use an equally distinct, signposted but unnumbered trail departing northwest from the Lac d'Aubert, which negotiates the **Horquette d'Aubert** (2498m) before descending past half a dozen medium-sized lakes before rejoining the GR10 half an hour before the Pont de la Gaubie. The time course is the same as for the all-GR10 itinerary. Once there, you're about 5km above Barèges, discussed in detail on p.365.

A Néouvielle circuit

If you have a car to leave at a trailhead, it's recommended that you make a two- or three-day **circuit**, starting from the Lac d'Aubert or the Pont de la Gaubie. Walking instructions for the sectors between the southerly lakes and the D918 are identical to those previously described; what makes a loop feasible is a minor trail heading east from the Cabane d'Aygues-Cluses, over the **Horquette Nère** (2465m), and then southeast to the *Refuge du Bastan* (see above) – it's seven to eight hours from Pont de la Gaubie to the refuge.

Traverse via Pic du Néouvielle

It's possible to make a more advanced traverse to Barèges via the summit of **Pic du Néouvielle** (3091m), at the western limit of the *réserve naturelle*. Although the ascent of the peak requires no technical climbing skills, it's long and tough, with crampons and ice-axe mandatory. Allowing for stops, plan on twelve hours to the first attended refuge on the far side, from where Barèges is another three hours further on track.

Follow the clearly marked path from the car park at Lac d'Aubert westwards towards the summit, then swing north to cross the bottom of the ridge known as the Crête de Barris d'Aubert. Once over, the path peters out; ascend west again, keeping the ridge to the left, then gradually bear away northeast towards the

Brèche de Chausenque (2790m). Before you get to the *brèche*, you swing back southwards into a wide, snow-filled valley, making your way up among huge boulders until a simple chimney takes you onto the final ridge, from which the **summit** is a short walk south (4hr from Lac d'Aubert).

To continue to Barèges, retrace your steps towards the *brèche*, climb through it this time and descend the steep slope on the other side west to the tiny **Lacs Verts**. Swing north along the shelf and gradually descend towards **Lac det Mail**, one of a succession of other lakes below to the left. Pass around its northeast shore then follow the stream down towards **Lac de la Glère** where you reach the *Refuge de la Glère* (2140m; ⓣ06.80.01.25.64; 70 places; closed May) in about six hours from the summit. From the refuge, which was razed and totally rebuilt in 2006, Barèges is 10km along a track to the north; try to have the warden arrange a lift for you.

The Baronnies

One of the emptiest areas of the Pyrenees, the **Baronnies** – drained by the River Arros – lie between the lower valleys of the Adour and Aure, bounded to the north by the D938 Capvern–Bagnères-de-Bigorre road, and to the south by the D918 linking Sainte-Marie-de-Campan with Arreau. The landscape's too undulating for large-scale agriculture (though you do see the odd tractor or mechanized harrow), too low for skiing and too rounded for technical climbing. For the casual walker and naturalist, however, the Baronnies are excellent: dense forests of beech and pine, lush, little-used pastures and a range of wildlife. Monumental interest, besides old crumbling farms, is lent by the château at Mauvezin and the abbey of Escaladieu, within a few kilometres of each other on the D938.

Public transport for this region is inevitably sparse. From the heart of the Baronnies, it's around 20km to the train station at Capvern, with Lannemezan and Bagnères-de-Bigorre slightly further. The Minibus des Baronnies company operates out of Lannemezan on Wednesdays and out of Bagnères on Saturdays, while André Pene runs a taxi service (ⓣ05.62.39.01.14) from Esparros, a village near the centre of the region.

Otherwise you'll have to walk, hitch, cycle or drive. Entering the Baronnies from the east is the most straightforward method, using the D26 from just north of Hèches in the Aure valley, 13km south of Lannemmezan. It's 3km uphill to the **Col de Coupe** (720m), from where the view west into the Baronnies is all-encompassing: emerald pasture, forest and rolling hills.

Esparros and around

About 2.5km beyond the Col de Coupe, **ESPARROS** was the seat of an ancient *baronnie* of four parishes – hence the name of the region. Like all the villages of the Baronnies, its population has fallen dramatically since the nineteenth century: 844 inhabitants in 1851, but under 200 today. Hilltop Laborde, just west, is currently more of a going concern. Norbert Casteret discovered the local **Gouffre d'Esparros** in 1938, its walls gleaming with a "hoar-frost" of white aragonite flowers. You can view these crystal formations, as well as a bat colony, on one-hour guided visits (ⓦwww.gouffre-esparros.com; daily June–Sept 10am–noon & 1.30–6pm; winter holiday weeks, plus Sat–Sun 10am–noon & 1.30–5.30pm; otherwise only sporadic Wed, Sat, Sun pm; closed early Nov to Christmas, Mon–Tues Oct 1–March 31; €7; reserve on ⓣ05.62.39.11.80).

The Baronnies has two official information points: a **tourist office** in Laborde (ⓣ05.62.39.03.42), 3km west of Esparros, and **La Maison des Baronnies** at Sarlabous, 8km north (summer 9am–noon & 2–5.30pm; ⓣ05.62.39.05.14). The most central **gîtes** are *Jean Colomes* at Esparros (ⓣ05.62.39.05.96; all year), or the *Moulin des Baronnies* on the River Arros just below Sarlabous (ⓣ & ⓕ05.62.39.05.14; all year), also with tenting space. There are also a few simple **inns** hereabouts, specializing in regional food: tiny *Le Relais d'Esparros* (ⓣ05.62.39.02.43; closed Wed except July & Aug; ❷) at Esparros; *La Ferme de Mamette* (ⓣ05.62.39.18.59; open all year; ❹) at Laborde; and the magnificently landscaped *Le Petit Château* (ⓣ05.62.40.90.16, ⓕ05.62.40.90.18; all year; ❹), at the edge of Laborde. The only **campsite** apart from *Moulin des Baronnies* is *Le Randonneur* at Esparros (ⓣ05.62.39.19.34; mid-June to mid-Sept), well laid out and with a pool.

Walking: the Tour des Baronnies

Walking in the Baronnies, while not technically difficult, can present tricky situations. Rain is frequent, mists often dense (some valley bottoms are essentially temperate rainforest) and vistas often devoid of any sign of habitation, except for the occasional herd of livestock tended by solitary shepherds. So you'll need a compass and detailed map, as well as rain gear and possibly waterproof boots.

The **Tour des Baronnies**, marked on the Carte de Randonnées 1:50,000 "Luchon" map, is a lopsided figure-of-eight itinerary with its focus at **ASQUE**, 7km west of Laborde: it takes about three days, generally along tracks. Just outside Asque, at Couret, there's an excellent **gîte** in an old farmhouse, *La Source Loubetas* (ⓣ05.62.40.98.57, ⓦwww.lasourcepyrenees.com; six-bunk dorms, also doubles & independent studios), which organizes special events. The longer loop leaves Asque towards the flat-topped mountain of Casque de Lhéris, then sweeps around towards Uzer, Castillon and Sarlabous; the shorter arc links Asque with Espèche, Esparros and the **Col de Couradabat**.

Mauvezin and Escaladieu

The two great historical sites of this region, the château of Mauvezin and the abbey of Escaladieu, are situated conveniently close enough to each other to be seen in a single visit. If you're reliant on public transport you'll have to take the train to Capvern, from where it's a five-kilometre walk to Mauvezin, and thence a further three-kilometre walk to the abbey.

Mauvezin

The **château** (ⓦwww.chateaudemauvezin.com; daily: April 15–Oct 15 10am–7pm; Oct 16–April 15 1.30–5.30pm; €5) stands on the edge of **MAUVEZIN**, atop a 567-metre-high hill that was first fortified by the Romans. Between the thirteenth and fifteenth centuries it changed hands several times in the wake of protracted hostilities between the English and the French, finally passing after 1373 to Gaston Fébus (see box on p.236).

Built of grey stone, and with a crenellated tower, the square castle is particularly appealing from the outside. Inside, you're left to wander as you please, with the aid of an informative brochure. The now-grassy courtyard was once lined with buildings, the roofs of which funnelled rainwater into the giant cistern, built as an emergency reserve; only once was it drunk dry – during the siege of 1373. On the inside of the cistern it's possible to read the graffito *Dieu seul sera adoré et l'Antéchrist de Rome abisme* ("God alone will be adored and the Antichrist in Rome [cast into the] abyss"), carved by an imprisoned Huguenot in the sixteenth century.

The current tenant is the Escòla Gaston Fébus, a conservation group that promotes Gascon and Occitan culture. The restored tower has been turned into a museum, crammed with various exhibits: sculptures, paintings, photos and bits of armour. More dynamically, on summer Sunday afternoons, there are medieval-themed events, concerts, *spectacles* and markets organized within the castle.

The Abbaye de l'Escaladieu

Three kilometres southwest and downhill from Mauvezin in the valley bottom, towards Bagnères-de-Bigorre, you'll find the **Abbaye de l'Escaladieu** (May–Sept daily 9.30am–12.30pm & 1.30–6.30pm; rest of year daily except Tues 9.30am–12.30pm & 1.30–5pm; free), the first Cistercian monastery in the southwest of France. Founded in 1142, Escaladieu flourished for just a couple of centuries, the monks earning a living by cultivating the Baronnies, a fertile and profitable region before mechanization favoured flat fields. The monastery was burnt and plundered by Protestant forces during the Wars of Religion, and early conservationists began restoring the buildings in the seventeenth and eighteenth centuries.

Since 1997 under the control of the Hautes-Pyrénées *département* – who've assumed responsibility for renovations – the abbey now hosts cinema, seminars, theatre and concerts of various musics from late June to late September, for which the abbey makes a wonderful setting.

The showpiece of the ongoing restoration is the twelfth- to thirteenth-century vaulted **chapter house**, opening onto a leafy inner courtyard through the sparse remnants of a cloister, all but two columns of which was shipped to California during the nineteenth century. The rest, by contrast, is typically Cistercian in its plainness, the long, white eastern facade devoid of decoration, and the enormous, echoing abbey church as bare as possible.

There's an unstarred but perfectly tolerable **hotel-restaurant** in **ESCALADIEU** village at the junction with the D14 south, the *Auberge de l'Arros* (Ⓣ05.62.39.05.05; all year; ❷), with three inexpensive *menus* – the only reliable facility at either Escaladieu or Mauvezin.

Bagnères-de-Bigorre

BAGNÈRES-DE-BIGORRE, 21km southeast of Tarbes along the D935 in the Adour valley, has managed to burnish its somewhat faded image with **Aquensis** (daily: school hols 10.30am–9pm, otherwise Tues & Sun 1pm–8pm, other days 10.30am–8pm; Ⓦwww.aquensis-bagneres.com), perhaps the most striking thermal **spa** in the Pyrenees with its central pool overarched by a forest of cantilevered wood beams. Descended from the Roman Vicus Aquensis, Bagnères opened its Grands Thermes in 1823, to be patronized by the likes of George Sand, Gioacchino Rossini, Gustave Flaubert and Wilfred Owen. From the 1830s, Bagnères' British community was second in size only to Pau's, many having stayed on after the Peninsular War.

The Town

Beside Aquensis stands the ornate **Musée Salies** (July–Aug daily 3–7pm; May–June & Sept–Nov Tues–Sun 3–6pm; €4). Mostly pedestrian landscapes hang on its pink walls, but more surprising artists are represented, including John Jongkind, a Dutch precursor of Impressionism, and Francis Picabia, a major figure of the Dada movement. The same admission ticket also covers the **Musée du Vieux Moulin** (Tues–Fri 10am–noon & 3–6pm), ten minutes' walk away across the Adour in rue Hount-Blanque, just over rue Général-de-Gaulle; it's a typical and well-designed folk museum, with exhibits of local furniture, agricultural tools and *Bigourdan* crafts.

The area's main tourist attraction is the **Grottes de Médous** (daily: April–June & Sept–Oct 15 8.30–11.30am & 2–5.30pm; July–Aug 9am–noon & 2–6pm; €5.50; Ⓣ05.62.91.78.46 for off-season tours), 2km south of the centre on the main road. The twelve-people-minimum-per-tour rule can mean hanging about on a slow day, but it's worth waiting to see the Salle d'Orchidée (Orchid House), rated by Norbert Casteret as one of the great limestone formations of the Pyrenees. The caves were only discovered in 1948, and thus escaped the vandalism suffered by others.

Practicalities

The heart of town lies 500m south along rue de la République from the train station on avenue de Belgique where SNCF **buses** from Tarbes stop – though ticket windows function normally, and coaches continue into the centre for a final halt by the fifteenth-century church of Saint-Vincent, within sight of place Lafayette. Other buses up the Vallée de Campan as far as Payolle (see p.348) depart from next to the **tourist office** at 3 allée Tournefort (July & Aug Mon–Sat 9am–12.30pm & 2–7pm, Sun 9am–noon & 2–6pm; rest of year Mon–Sat 9am–noon & 2–6pm; Ⓣ05.62.95.50.71, Ⓦwww.hautebigorre.com), south of the *place*. From the tourist office, it's a short walk northwest to the leafy **allée des Coustous**, home to many cafés and the post office, west of which is pedestrianized **place de Strasbourg** and the covered market occupying **place Ramond**. Drivers should beware the fairly comprehensive pay-and-display **parking** scheme (Mon–Sat 9am–noon & 2–7pm).

Hotels facing the spa tend to be overpriced and musty, catering for a rather sedentary clientele. Better-value central choices include, just north of the *halles* on rue de l'Horloge 3bis, old-fashioned *Hôtel l'Horloge* (Ⓣ05.62.91.00.20; closed Dec–Feb; ❶), named after the clock in the Tour du Jacobins, the last remnant but one of a convent destroyed during the Revolution (a portal also remains on rue Saint-Jean), or the well-kept *Hôtel de la Paix* (Ⓣ05.62.95.20.60, Ⓦwww.hotel-delapaix.com; closed mid-Dec to Jan; ❸), with a decent restaurant and room facing away from the noisy avenue. Central but set back from the busy street at 24 place André-Fourcade is well-kept *Hôtel Commerce* (Ⓣ05.62.95.07.33; closed mid-Nov to Dec; ❷) north of Saint-Vincent church, again with creditable meals. Drivers especially will be interested in the rambling *Hôtel Tivoli* (Ⓣ05.62.91.07.13, Ⓕ05.62.91.15.20; all year; ❷), in its own grounds southwest of the centre on avenue du Salut; rooms can be a bit ramshackle, but the en-suite ones have modern bathrooms, and rear units have small balconies.

Independent **restaurants** aren't Bagnères' strong point; among the few are *Nhu-Y*, affordable Chinese fare on place Lafayette, and *La Fontaine Saint-Blaise*, on rue Saint-Blaise, corner of rue du Pont d'Arras, near Aquensis (closed Mon eve summer, Wed eve winter), a resolutely old-fashioned place (*menus* €16.50–23). The town's top choice, *Le Bigourdan* (closed Sun & Mon) occupies two upper storeys at 14 rue Victor-Hugo; with a €25 supper *menu* (plus drink) encompassing *cèpes*, monkfish and varied desserts – though portions are on the small side. Next door at no. 12, cheap-and-cheerful *Crêperie de l'Horloge* (closed Nov & Sun–Tues low season, Mon summer) has more pleasant interior seating than its sidewalk tables and is better for sweet or savoury crêpes, salads and cider than the perfunctory *plats du jour*.

Bagnères has a **music festival** every year, normally from mid-August to mid-September, but a more original musical tradition is the male choir, Chanteurs Montagnards, founded in the 1840s and still performing at most civic functions.

Bagnères is easy to reach, but it's harder to move on from – only two buses daily go south past the Grottes de Médous to Sainte-Marie-de-Campan (see p.349). From July to September this service covers the extra 15km southeast along the

D918 to Lac de Payolle (see p.350); during summer buses go southwest on the D918 only as far as Gripp hamlet, though in winter this line extends all the way to La Mongie.

Upstream from Bagnères

South of Bagnères-de-Bigorre, the valley sides of the Haute-Adour rise steeply into the Baronnies and the **Casque du Lhéris** on the northeast, and towards **Pic du Midi de Bigorre** to the southwest, with the Néouvielle Massif rising ahead to the south. Subsidies, high rainfall and fertile soil keep the thatched farmhouses in business, three crops a year being common. Away from the main Adour valley and its extension, the **Vallée de Campan**, two tributaries can be explored: the lush **Vallée de Lesponne**, with much-visited Lac Bleu at its head; and the **Vallée de Gripp**, at the top of which is **La Mongie**, one of the best Pyrenean ski resorts, and the strategically perched observatory on **Pic du Midi de Bigorre**.

The Vallée de Lesponne

The countryside just north of Barèges, at the head of the **Vallée de Lesponne**, is well worth a day or two. From Beaudéan, 5km along the D935, the D29 side road (no public transport) heads 10.5km to its end at **LE CHIROULET** (1062m). This tiny hamlet supports a **hôtel-restaurant**, the four-room *La Vieille Auberge* (Ⓣ05.62.91.71.70; ❷). If it's full, alternatives 5.5km down-valley at **LESPONNE** hamlet include rustic *Chez Gabrielle* (Ⓣ05.62.91.28.81, Ⓦwww.aventures-en-pyrenees.com; closed Nov 15–Dec 15; ❷, also dorm), or the plusher *Domaine de Ramonjuan* (Ⓣ05.62.91.75.75, Ⓦwww.ramonjuan.com; all year; ❷–❹), with a good restaurant, on-site horse-riding centre, tennis courts, sauna and Jacuzzi.

From Le Chiroulet, a popular path rises steeply for nearly three hours to **Lac Bleu** (1950m), set in a peak-ringed cirque, or to **Lac d'Ourrec** in about two hours; a loop walk, shown clearly on the "Bigorre" Carte des Randonnées, takes in both. The Col du Tourmalet (see p.352) can be reached by climbing around the eastern side of 120-metre-deep Lac Bleu – the path in places cut into the rock – and then heading due east to the **Col d'Aoube** (2389m), from where a faint path continues down to the D918 a short distance from Tourmalet, four hours beyond Lac Bleu.

The Vallée de Campan

Upstream from Beaudéan lies the **Vallée de Campan**, whose east flank edges into the Baronnies. Below woods of spruce, pine and beech, the gentle valley's meadows are speckled with farms arrayed in south-facing ranks. House and barn are built as a unit, with the balconied living quarters always to the right as you face the sun. The valley is also known for the local craft tradition of **mounaques** or giant rag dolls; of both genders and variously costumed, these are often propped up on pavements, windowsills or even house gables for summer-long display.

It's indicative of the tenuous nature of tolerance early in the Age of the Enlightenment that when the church of **Saint-Jean-Baptiste** at **CAMPAN** (6km from Bagnères) was rebuilt after a fire in 1694, a separate Cagot door (see box opposite) was inserted at the west end; the Cagot ghetto here was on the right bank of the Adour, in the part known as the *Quartier Charpentier* after their habitual trade. The church's personality is now defined by the ornate white-and-gilt *retable* by the local

The Cagots

Numerous towns in the western half of the Pyrenees – including Saint-Savin, Luz-Saint-Sauveur, Cauterets and Saint-Jean-Pied-de-Port – once had sizeable populations of a mysterious people known as **Cagots**, of whom little is known for certain other than that they were persecuted. First mentioned in thirteenth-century manuscripts, Cagots were forbidden to live in the centre of towns, to kiss the Cross, to walk barefoot, to have sexual relations outside the Cagot community or to enter a mill (in case they contaminated the grain). They had to wear a distinguishing symbol on their clothes, variously described as a crow's or a duck's foot, and live in a separate ghetto at the edge of villages. Cagots had their own baptismal fonts – sometimes even their own churches – and were buried in separate graveyards.

In compensation, Cagots were exempt from feudal duties and taxes, were subject only to ecclesiastical courts and were not expected to bear arms, except for work. Prohibited also from owning land, many therefore became skilled woodworkers in particular, and Gaston Fébus apparently insisted on Cagot carpenters for his fortress at Montaner. But Cagots were excluded from all normal social life, and despite appeals to the pope and the secular authorities, discrimination continued for centuries. The Cagots themselves began agitating for equal rights as early as 1479, but social consciousness lagged behind legal rulings in their favour. It was not until 1789 and the Revolution that their second-class status was officially, and definitely, ended. The measures taken against them sound like those taken against lepers, and indeed one of the many alternative names for the Cagots – *crestianas* – is almost certainly derived from *cristianaria*, the places reserved for "white" lepers – those considered infected but not contagious, and whom modern medicine would probably recognize as afflicted by some minor skin disease.

So the Cagots may have been lepers or the descendants of lepers, but it also seems plausible that they were racially distinct. Some linguists derive "Cagot" from *can goth* or "dog of the Visigoths", implying a descent from the Visigoths who fled into this area after their defeat by Clovis in 507. Furthermore, the architecture of many Basque country churches – with their low "Cagot windows" through which services could be watched, and proportionally low "Cagot doors" – suggests to some that Cagots were a group of less-than-average stature. However, it's not even certain that these architectural features had anything to do with the Cagots. The mystery will probably never be solved; the subject was already steeped in confusion by the fourteenth century, when contemporary accounts variously described Cagots as tall, fair and blue-eyed, or short, dark and Moorish-looking.

brothers, the Ferrérers of Asté; the fifteenth-century wooden image of Christ, originally at L'Escaladieu, is a cruder but more moving statement of faith. The village itself, with its slate-roofed houses, is attractive; for **accommodation**, the one-star *Hôtel Beauséjour* (Ⓣ05.62.91.75.30; closed Oct 15–Dec 15; ❷), opposite the colonnaded, sixteenth-century market hall, represents fair value. There's also the *Camping de Layris*, on the northwest side of town, and the main **tourist office** for the valley (Mon–Sat 9am–noon & 2.30–6/7pm, also Sun 9am–noon peak season; Ⓣ05.62.91.70.36).

At **SAINTE-MARIE-DE-CAMPAN**, another 6km southeast, there's more **accommodation** at either *Gîte L'Ardoisière* (Ⓣ05.62.91.88.88, Ⓔardoisiere@wanadoo.fr; closed Nov–Christmas; dorms, or doubles ❷, ❹ HB), or the more conventional *Hôtel Les Deux Cols* (Ⓣ05.62.91.85.60, Ⓕ05.62.91.85.31; closed Oct 15–Dec 15; ❶), with *menus* at €12–22, a small private car park and rear rooms overlooking the valley. Both cater to cyclists, and are on the main through road (as is the entire town), which as it divides is designated the D918 in either direction.

To the right, this climbs southwest to La Mongie (see p.352), via Gripp and

Artigues. The southeasterly (leftward) fork attains the **Col d'Aspin** (1489m) – where half-tame horses and cows gambol, causing traffic jams – before dropping into the Vallée d'Aure at Arreau. Just the Campan side of this pass (closed in winter), 25km shy of Arreau, the environs of **Lac de Payolle** offer a respectable 50km of marked cross-country skiing pistes between 1100 and 1450m; during summer, picnickers throng the lakeshore.

The Tour de France

Every July the **Tour de France** passes through the Pyrenees in a stage of 180–200 kilometres, on its way either to or from the Alps. Most years the riders tackle the savage haul up to the Col du Tourmalet, before or after having climbed a selection from amongst the *cols* of de Menté, Portet d'Aspet, Core, Peyresourde, d'Aspin, Aubisque and Soulor. First incorporated into the route in 1910, Tourmalet has now been included in almost fifty contests, forming a particularly gruelling (and often wet and freezing) episode in what is one of the toughest days of the three-week race.

Enormous entourages of back-up teams, television crews and journalists occupy every hotel room in the vicinity of each day's finishing line, but **accommodation** is not the only problem – even **seeing the riders** at the crucial points can be tricky. Prudent spectators take up position at any of the major passes at least three hours before the bikes are due – when the leaders come over the pass, the crowds will be twenty deep. The most ardent devotees position themselves under the banner marking the crest of the *col*, armed with sheafs of **newspapers** – not to fill in the wait reading, but to help the cyclists. As the riders appear, the newspapers are held out for the cyclists, who tuck them under their shirts to provide added insulation for the freezing descent, on which the bikes reach speeds of up to 100km per hour.

Although between 180 and 200 riders start each Tour, only a dozen have the all-round ability needed to win the champion's yellow jersey. Within the main race, there's another contest going on in the Pyrenees (and the Alps) – for the title "**King of the Mountains**", awarded to the rider who records the best results in the alpine stages. Winning this competition – whose leader wears a white shirt with red polka dots – secures a reputation only marginally less illustrious than the overall winner's. The favourites for the yellow jersey of course feature strongly in the "King of the Mountains" tussle – any rider with hopes of winning overall has to finish each mountain stage near the front – but most teams also have a specialist climber.

The reticent Spaniard **Miguel Indurain** (aka "The Colossus of Roads" or "The Sphinx") was the first rider to win five consecutive Tours in 1991–95 (though others had won five separated contests since the 1960s). Yet his mountain stages didn't show him at his best, and from 1994 to 1997 Frenchman **Richard Virenque** rode off with the "King of the Mountains" jersey. After finishing a disappointing eleventh in the 1996 Tour, Indurain announced his retirement; it was the end of an era, with no single cyclist then looking set to dominate the competition, despite German **Jan Ullrich** pedalling to victory in 1997.

Tainted by lurid **drug scandals**, the "Tour de Farce" (as many dubbed it) of **1998** cast a long shadow over the sport. France's Festina Watches team, with Virenque as captain, was disqualified when a huge stock of prohibited doping substances was found in their trainer's car. Arrests and prosecutions of various team managers and trainers followed, as all Spanish teams were withdrawn. After initial protestations of innocence, and allegations that Festina was being made a scapegoat, scores of riders admitted using performance-boosting supplements since at least the 1980s. Eventually seven of the 21 teams were banned, and by the end of the Tour hardly anyone noticed that **Marco Patani** had triumphed, the first Italian victor in 33 years

Up the Vallée de Gripp: La Mongie, Tourmalet and Pic du Midi

The D918 road to La Mongie from Sainte-Marie-de-Campan rises steadily along the **Gripp valley** past **GRIPP** itself, where there's a comfortable two-star **hotel** in a converted old house, *La Maison d'Hoursentut* (Ⓣ05.62.91.89.42, Ⓦwww

(ironically, he too later fell prey to drug abuse and died, a recluse, of an apparent overdose in 2004).

At this first nadir of the race's fortunes, the Tour needed a wholesome, against-the-odds saga to restore its image – and got it. American **Lance Armstrong**, favoured to do well in both the 1996 Tour and the Atlanta Olympics, had bombed mysteriously in both. A few weeks later, he diagnosed with cancer that had spread from his testicles to his lungs. Few expected him to live, let alone ever cycle again. But after surgery and chemotherapy, 1999 saw him power through the mountain stages en route to overall victory as head of the US Post Office team. In 2000 he repeated this feat, overtaking Patani, Ullrich and Virenque in a miserably cold, sodden Pyrenean stage on his way to a second yellow jersey. When Armstrong got his third overall title in 2001, commentators speculated about a possible successor to Indurain, and the public's faith in the romance of the Tour de France was partly restored. In 2002 Armstrong recovered from a crash which lost him 27 seconds for his fourth triumph. 2003 saw Armstrong suffer dehydration during torrid initial stages, and then crash again, before outduelling Ullrich in a rainy finale, with the latter skidding out of contention on a wet road. It was the most accident-prone Tour ever, but Armstrong had matched Indurain's five back-to-back triumphs. After a rainy first week in 2004, Armstrong edged out all rivals – including Italian Ivan Basso and an undertrained, overweight Ullrich – though his record sixth consecutive win was marred by a libel vendetta between himself and Italian contender Filippo Simeoni which ended up in court. Basso and Ullrich again played second and third fiddle respectively to Armstrong's final, unprecedented seventh 2005 Tour win, as much tactical and psychological as physical, after which he announced, aged 33, the end of his 14-year professional cycling career.

Doping returned to haunt the Tour with a vengeance in 2006, throwing the race – and the sport – into the disrepute it had wallowed in after the 1998 Tour. A Spanish connection figured again as a Madrid-based system of blood-doping – whereby blood is withdrawn from athletes and replaced some months later, after which time the body has made good the loss in oxygen-carrying red blood cells – was uncovered, with the result that Ullrich, Basso and several other post-Armstrong-era favourites were forced out of competition. With the field decapitated, no obvious favourite emerged until American **Floyd Landis** narrowly won – or so it seemed – the race by just 57 seconds, coming from well behind with a nearly incredible final mountain stage. Not just "nearly" according to two separate post-Tour test results, which showed excess levels of testosterone – another common doping substance – in his system on the day of his Alps triumph. The Tour organizers promptly stripped Landis of his title – the first winner disqualified in the race's 103-year history – but could not yet award it to second-place finisher Spaniard Oscar Pereiro until an official arbitration hearing, scheduled for some time in mid-2007. Meanwhile, both Landis and Jan Ullrich have hired high-powered legal and media professionals in attempts to clear their names. But as numerous racers' confessions attest, doping of some kind has been indulged in since the 1960s; even notionally squeaky-clean Armstrong fell under suspicion of banned-chemical use, a charge he vehemently denied. Given sponsor and audience expectations of ever-greater performance, the temptation to resort to artificial "enhancements" seems ineradicable.

.maison-hoursentut.com; all year; ❹–❺ B&B, ❻ HB). Facility-less Artigues, 2km higher, is a popular start- or end-point for hiking in the Réserve Naturelle de Néouvielle (see p.342) and there are short walks to the nearby Cascades de l'Arises and Cascade du Garet.

La Mongie

The ski centre of **LA MONGIE**, 8km above Gripp – together with Barèges on the opposite side of the Col du Tourmalet – constitutes the largest skiing area in the Pyrenees, with 34 pistes totalling 60km on the La Mongie side alone. Once you're away from the unsightly high-rise resort at 1800m it's beautiful, with a combination of open bowls, runs through trees and some exciting off-piste itineraries. There are only three short black runs, but it's an eminently suitable place for beginners to intermediates. By taking the Porteilh *télécabine* and then the Quatre Termes chair-lift, you access the top point of 2500m and a reddish blue run descending 3km, with eyefuls of the Pic du Midi the whole way; the easy and intermediate runs dropping east from the Espade and Béarnais chair-lifts are even longer, but can get mushy in the afternoon.

The Col du Tourmalet and the Pic du Midi de Bigorre

The **Col du Tourmalet** (2115m), 4km beyond La Mongie, ranks as the highest driveable pass in the French Pyrenees, usually playing a tormenting role in the Tour de France and almost always closed between late October and the end of April. The name literally means "the bad detour", a title bestowed by the carriers of the sedan chairs that used to taxi the wealthy between the spas of Bagnères and Barèges by this long, cold road. Wheeled transport first used the *col* in 1788, when the road along the Luz valley was blocked by floods; from the La Mongie side of the pass you can still see the faint trace of the old route. The perennially windy pass itself is dominated by "**Le Géant du Tourmalet**", a sleeker replacement for a lumpy, anatomically correct statue of a nude cyclist, which commemorated the Tour de France's first passage here in 1910. Opposite stands a stone-clad restaurant which is much the best of several high-altitude eateries for skiers; in summer either this or another eatery east of the pass will operate. Drivers should beware livestock – and manic cyclists.

From the *col*, a service track leads up towards the summit of **Pic du Midi de Bigorre** (2877m), bristling with antennae, radio masts and a famous observatory; views from the terrace extend west as far as Balaïtous, south into the Néouvielle country and east as far as Andorra. But there's little point in the two-hour walk up, as you'll still have to pay full admission anyway (read on).

Opened in 1878, and still the fourth highest in Europe after a trio in Spain and the Canaries, the **observatory** (Ⓦ www.picdumidi.com) has been continuously staffed since, even when cut off for months at a time by storms and snow, with all provisions and equipment carted up by man or mule for the first 66 years. Despite the observatory's distinguished history of lunar, solar and planetary observation, plus its ongoing role as a weather station, most French investment has been switched to even larger installations in Hawaii, Chile and Tenerife.

For years the observatory's dozen or so resident scientists resisted plans to develop it as a tourist attraction, but in 2000 they bowed to the inevitable, with the opening of an initially mediocre visitors' centre on the premises, subsequently transformed into a more worthwhile **museum**. This is accessible only by means of a two-stage **téléphérique** from La Mongie (Jan, May & Oct Wed–Mon 10am–3.30pm, last descent 5.30pm; daily Feb–April 10am–3.30pm, last descent 5.30pm; daily June–Sept 9am–4.30pm, last descent 7pm; closed early Nov to early Dec and part April; €23–25, or €60–64 family rate, includes museum).

The *pic* was also opened to recreational **ski descents** in early 2003, a great half-day out. Groups of up to six need to be of strong intermediate competence or superior, and must be accompanied by a winter mountaineering guide or an ESF instructor.

Tarbes

If you're heading towards the Central Pyrenees from the northeast you'll almost certainly pass through **TARBES**, capital of medieval Bigorre and the contemporary, far larger *département* of Hautes-Pyrénées. A medium-sized, unobjectionable if dull place, it will mainly appeal if you have an interest in things military. Destroyed by the Normans, then ruined during the Wars of Religion, Tarbes retains little evidence of any past prior to the eighteenth century. An overall view gives a general impression of functional and graceless white apartment and office blocks; more inspiring architectural efforts include the futuristic National Music School and the Parvis Cultural Centre. Arms manufacture has long been Tarbes' primary industry, but it now employs just a few hundred people (compared to sixteen thousand at the end of World War I), with most remaining jobs threatened by automation.

The Town

Tarbes' few specific attractions lie within walking distance of each other. Off rue Massey sprawls the tranquil, peacock-patrolled **Jardin Massey** (daily dawn to dusk; free), designed by Tarbes-born Placide Massey (1777–1853), who also managed the Parc du Trianon at Versailles. This carefully landscaped botanical collection has specimens – both local and exotic – informatively labelled and discussed in French. Architectural interest is supplied by the partially reconstructed Gothic cloister from the abbey of Saint-Sever-de-Rustan, with vivid, if slightly eroded column capitals: swans attacking a bear, and a sword-brandishing angel expelling Adam and Eve from Eden.

The **Musée Massey**, housed in a rather eclectic nineteenth-century building in the middle of the *jardin*, is closed indefinitely while its section on the Hussars regiment (based in Tarbes), from its fifteenth-century Hungarian origins to today's parachutists, is rehoused elsewhere. When the gallery reopens, it should more generously highlight its other two themes: fine arts and local archeology.

Some 300m southwest of the Jardin Massey, at 2 rue de la Victoire, is the **birthplace of Maréchal Foch** (guided tours only Thurs–Mon: June–Sept 9am–noon & 2–6.30pm; Oct–May 9am–noon & 2–5pm; €3.50), supreme Allied commander on the western front during World War I. A traditional pitched-roof *Bigourdan* town house, it contains two floors of photos, medals and other memorabilia from the field marshal's life – including, a little morbidly, the armchair in which he died.

Tarbes' renowned stud farm, **Les Haras**, lies a couple more blocks south on rue Mauhourat (ⓣ05.62.56.30.80, ⓦwww.haras-nationaux.fr; 1hr guided visits only, tours depart Mon–Fri year-round 10am, 11am, 2pm, 3pm, 4pm plus last Sun of month 2.30pm & 4pm; €6). Founded in 1806 by Napoleon, Les Haras is best known for its *cheval Tarbais*, a cavalry breed produced by crossing English, Basque and Arabian stock. Despite its urban location, the farm is set in acres of beautiful grounds. The immaculately groomed horses are best seen at exercise drill, usually held at about 3pm (except Feb–July when most of the horses are out to stud). Highpoint of the year is the Equestria dressage festival during the last week of July (ⓦwww.festivalequestria.com).

Practicalities

Near the SNCF **train station** on avenue Maréchal-Joffre there's a choice of **car rental**, with Budget right opposite the station (Ⓣ05.62.93.61.15) and Hertz a few steps west. The **gare routière** on place au Bois, off rue Larrey, has services to Bagnères-de-Bigorre, Lannemezan and Pau. **Tarbes-Ossun-Lourdes airport**, 9km southwest of town, for the moment only has pilgrim charters, with no bus or train links. **Drivers** will find a certain amount of free, relatively abundant **parking** around the Jardin Massey; elsewhere it is metered or otherwise controlled. The **tourist office** is just off the central place de Verdun at 3 cours Gambetta (Mon–Sat 9am–12.30pm & 2–7pm; Ⓣ05.62.51.30.31; Ⓦwww.tarbes.com).

Tarbes has a few reasonable **hotels** in the vicinity of the train station, including friendly, helpful *Hôtel de l'Avenue*, 80 av Bertrand-Barère (Ⓣ05.62.93.06.36; ❷), and the remoter, more comfortable *Hôtel L'Isard*, 70 av Maréchal Joffre (Ⓣ05.62.93.06.69, Ⓕ05.62.93.99.55; ❷), with a decent restaurant.

In terms of **restaurants**, *Le Petit Gourmand* (closed Sat noon, Sun eve & Mon) at 62 rue Bertrand-Barère is a popular lunch spot (*menu* €18), while if you're craving something exotic, *Thanh Thúy* across the street at no. 53 does passable Vietnamese dishes. Other eateries include classic *Chez Patrick*, 6 rue Adolphe-d'Eichtal (closed Sat eve & Sun), on the corner of rue Saint-Jean, a cheery, welcoming, working-class institution that fills by 12.30pm with a regular clientele come for the €10 *menu* that sees them to *potage*, charcuterie, steak and *frites*, a choice of dessert, house wine and coffee. For haute cuisine, head for 48 rue Abbé Torné near the Préfecture, where Christine and Daniel Labarrère's *L'Ambroisie* (Ⓣ05.62.93.09.34; closed Sun–Mon) is the *département*'s only Michelin-starred restaurant, with seating in the rooms of an old house or out back in the orchard on fine days. There's an affordable €36 lunch *menu*, but you'll easily spend €85 à la carte.

Lourdes and around

LOURDES, 20km south of Tarbes on the N21, is difficult to avoid, as it sits squarely astride the direct route up to Argelès-Gazost, Cauterets and Luz-Saint-Sauveur; even if it weren't so pivotal, the town would be an unmissable detour. East of the main street, Lourdes seems superficially like many other small French foothill communities. But the western part, around the *cité religieuse* on the banks of the Gave (River) de Pau, is another world – shut down in winter, and in summer seething with the pilgrims who constitute its *raison d'être*. The huge crowds attending the Masses and the grotto make an overwhelming spectacle: over seven million people come each year to this town of fewer than eighteen thousand inhabitants. Lourdes' nod to high culture comes in the week or so after Good Friday, when an **International Festival of Sacred Music** is held.

The cult of Lourdes

The unwitting instigator of the cult of Lourdes was **Bernadette Soubirous**, 14-year-old daughter of a poor local miller. On February 11, 1858 she was collecting firewood near the Grotte de Massabielle when she had a vision, who spoke to her in *Bigourdan* dialect, asking her to return regularly to the cave. At the penultimate of seventeen subsequent visitations, the Virgin Mary revealed her identity (as the "Immaculate Conception") to Bernadette, and commanded the girl to dig at the ground with her hands, thus releasing a spring whose water would supposedly prove to have curative powers. Bernadette's apparition also demanded that she notify the local priests, have a chapel built and organize devotional processions to the spot.

These visions were authenticated by the Church authorities in 1862, and eleven years later the first nationwide pilgrimage took place, organized by the **Assomptionistes**. This was an ultra-conservative Catholic movement founded in 1845 in response to the reigning positivism, republicanism and atheism of the era. Its ranks swelled by reaction to the short-lived Paris Commune of 1871, the *Assomptionistes* effectively took over the town of Lourdes, supplanting the local clergy and running the pilgrimages as a going concern. Not coincidentally, from this coup dates the proliferation of hotels in Lourdes (more than 350, the second most in France after Paris), and shops devoted to the sale of unbelievable (in all senses) religious kitsch: Bernadette and/or the Virgin emblazoned on key rings, candles, candy-bars, thermometers and illuminated plastic grottoes.

With each miraculous cure – of which there were a number – the pilgrimage to Lourdes gained momentum. Among early rich and famous visitors were Napoléon III and Empress Eugénie, making the trip on behalf of their sick son (ironically, the emperor had closed the grotto a few years earlier, fearing public disorder). Bernadette herself had been hustled into a convent in 1866, ostensibly for her own safety, where she died of a degenerative bone disease thirteen years later.

No matter how cynical you may be about contemporary pilgrimage "management", you cannot fail to be moved by the thousands of pilgrims themselves, many crippled or quite obviously ill, who converge here to give their faith a chance to cure them. You see them everywhere, being wheeled about by *brancardières* – young volunteers, many foreign and not even Catholic, each assigned a sick or handicapped pilgrim to push along for the duration of their stay. They're interspersed with legions of nuns, priests and a surprisingly heavy police presence (not least to dispense citations to those parked illegally). What impresses next is the international mix of the crowds: Madagascans and *Réunionais*, Africans, Spanish, Italians, Poles, Germans, Dutch and quite a few Anglophones.

The flamboyant, gargantuan double **Basilique du Rosaire et de l'Immaculée Conception**, built between 1871 and 1883 in "Romano-Byzantine" and Gothic styles, was no longer large enough by the centenary of the apparitions; hence the construction of the underground **Basilique Saint-Pie X** dominating the Esplanade des Processions, which can hold a further twenty thousand, with overflow capacity of forty thousand more. Just across the river, sectioned by paths, is an enormous grassy meadow, the **Prairie**, also used for religious events when needed. But the heart of this Catholic Disney World is the **Grotte de Massabielle**, site of Bernadette's visions, for unbelievers merely a small, dark cavity beneath a rock overhang beside the river, below the Basilique du Rosaire. On high stands a marble statue of the holy apparition, which Bernadette herself denounced as a mockery of her precise description to the sculptor. Neither the shoddy likeness nor the modest dimensions of the grotto concern the pilgrims who, queuing beside signs demanding silence (in the main obeyed), circumambulate the cave clockwise, stroking the wall with their left hand. To the right of the grotto stand *bruloirs* or rows of braziers holding enormous **votive candles** (700 tonnes of wax consumed annually) left to prolong one's prayer, and bathhouses for immersing the sick. On the left, right under the basilica, is a row of taps channelled from the **spring**, for the collection of holy water in containers of every shape, size and material, sold in the souvenir shops and embossed with medallions depicting the Virgin and Bernadette.

The rest of the town

The Bernadette story is not the only one about Lourdes. Another tale tells how, during a siege of the Muslim-occupied city by Charlemagne, an eagle let drop an enormous trout into the famine-stricken town. Mirat, the Muslim chief, threw it over the walls, tricking Charlemagne into believing that the Muslims still had plenty to eat; he duly lift the siege. As with all good Christian moral parables, this one ends with Mirat being converted from his Mohammedan ways; he took the name Lorus, which in turn, subtly modified, was given to the city that now bears a giant trout on its coat-of-arms.

Lourdes' only secular attraction is its **château**, poised on a rocky bluff on the east bank of the Gave de Pau and entered from rue du Bourg. Briefly an English stronghold in the late fourteenth century, it later became a French state prison, detaining among others Lord Elgin (he of the Parthenon marbles) on his troubled way back to Britain from Ottoman territory. Today it contains the **Musée Pyrénéen** (1hr guided visits daily: April to mid-July & mid-Aug to Sept 9am–noon & 1.30–6.30pm; mid-July to mid-Aug 9am–6.30pm; Oct–March 9am–noon & 2–5/6pm; last tour 1hr before closing; €5). For the dedicated mountaineer, the primitive axes, crampons and other expedition necessities of the pioneer *Pyrénéistes* are particularly intriguing. On show, too, are magnificently detailed maps by Franz Schrader, who first came to the Pyrenees in 1873 on a cartographic mission; he also executed paintings and drawings of the high peaks (one now named in his honour). Other exhibits cover local folklore, flora and fauna, mostly presented in tableau form. The museum has an excellent library (which you can use with permission), containing first-edition books such as Charles Packe's *Guide to the Pyrenees*, documents such as the 99-year lease of Vignemale granted to Henry Russell (see box on p.373) and hundreds of rare photographs.

Practicalities

The **train station** lies on the far north side of Lourdes, about ten minutes' walk from the centre; the **gare routière** is in the central place Capdevielle, behind the Palais des Congrès. There's a not particularly helpful, if well-stocked, **tourist office** in a futuristic glass building on place Peyramale (Easter to mid-Oct Mon–Sat 9am–6.30/7pm, Sun 10am–6pm; mid-Oct to Easter Mon–Sat 9am–noon & 2–6pm; ⓣ05.62.42.77.40, ⓦwww.lourdes-infotourisme.com). **Parking** is strictly controlled almost everywhere, and having a car here is a distinct liability; for a quick visit, the best strategy is to leave vehicles on unrestricted route de Pau, between the Prairie and the rail line, and walk the 200m across the Prairie and river-bridges to the *grotte*.

There's abundant, fairly indistinguishable **accommodation** in Lourdes – some two hundred two- and three-star hotels, concentrated in the small central streets close to the castle. Establishment names like *Christ Roi*, *Golgotha* and *Calvaire* hint at the usual clientele; devout Catholic Hilaire Belloc, writing in 1909, asserted sourly that "honestly one cannot say that any one hotel at Lourdes is better than another...avoid the hotels that have Holy names to them, they are usually frauds." That said, more upmarket choices in the "normal" part of town, both Logis de France members, include two-star *Hôtel d'Albret* at 21 place du Champs-Commun, (ⓣ05.62.94.75.00, ⓔalbret.taverne.lourdes@libertysurf.fr; ❸), with the co-managed *Taverne de Bigorre* on the ground floor offering a range of *menus* (❶), and slightly noisier three-star *Hótel de Nevers* at 13 av Maransin (ⓣ05.62.94.90.88, ⓔhotel.nevers@wanadoo.fr; ❸), housed in a former convent, with secure private parking and another decent restaurant. A good budget option is *Hôtel Relais des Crêtes*, at 72 av Alexandre-Marqui on the Tarbes side of town (ⓣ05.62.42.18.56; closed mid-Nov to mid-March; ❶), more of a guesthouse with simple rooms overlooking a courtyard. Most hotels require half-board, so there are few decent independent eateries in town.

Excursions around Lourdes

There are a number of **excursions** to be made around the town, albeit expensive and overcrowded ones. For good views with minimum effort, take the funicular up 948-metre **Pic du Jer** (Easter–Oct daily 10am–7pm; Ⓦwww.picdujer.info), going since 1900, to an excellent panoramic view; you can easily walk down, following a well-marked trail. For a short trip out of town, head 4km west to **Lac de Lourdes**, a pretty though somewhat over-subscribed picnic spot; there are local buses along the main D937 to Pau. Twelve kilometres further you come to the **Grottes de Bétharram** (Feb 6–March 25 Mon–Fri tours 2.30 & 4pm only, reserved on Ⓣ05.62.41.80.04; March 25–Oct 25 daily 9am–noon & 1.30–5.30pm, July–Aug 9am–6pm; Ⓦwww.grottes-de-bethrarram.com; €8), where barges and trains take you through 5km of underground galleries. The cave's name derives from the Bigourdan phrase *Bét Arram*, meaning "beautiful branch": legend has it that the Virgin Mary saved a young girl from drowning here in the Gave de Pau by throwing a branch to her.

Close to the caves are two **accommodation** choices calmer than anything in Lourdes – and they could just about serve as a base for visiting Pau. The ridgetop *Ferme Campseissillou* (Ⓣ05.62.41.80.92, Ⓦwww.ferme-campseissillou.com; ❷ B&B), 4km by narrow mountain lane north of **SAINT-PÉ-DE-BIGORRE**, offers five modernized, en-suite rooms in a converted barn on this working farm with sweeping views, a warm welcome, plus good breakfasts and *table d'hôte* suppers. In the centre of Saint-Pé, *Le Grand Cèdre*, 6 rue du Barry (Ⓣ05.62.41.82.04, Ⓦwww.grandcedre.com; ❹) is the total opposite of the preceding listing: a seventeenth-century mansion combining original floors and slightly cluttered furnishings with modern bathrooms in its large suites. There's a garden, with the monumental cedar of the name, a Jacuzzi and *table d'hôte* suppers (€23). Saint-Pé itself, though a major canoeing/kayaking centre, is sleepy, with an aptly named central place des Arcades.

The upper Gave de Pau

The upper **Gave de Pau**, paralleled by the N21, offers a number of potential stops, such as Argelès-Gazost, the abbey-village of Saint-Savin and an aviary of raptors at Beaucens. Both road and river split in the vicinity of these attractions; the most rewarding side trip is from Argelès itself, up the joint **Vallées d'Azun, d'Arrens** and **d'Étaing**.

Argelès-Gazost and around

ARGELÈS-GAZOST, 13km south of Lourdes, is an innocuously dull if rather congested spa that makes a possible base for the lower Gave de Pau. The town itself extends from the valley floor, quite broad here, up to the busy medieval core on a terrace to the west. The **tourist office** (Mon–Sat 9am–noon & 2–6.30pm, Sun 9am–noon; Ⓣ05.62.97.00.25, Ⓦwww.argele-gazost.com) is in the principal place de la République (aka Grande-Terrasse), three minutes south of the church. There are a number of old-fashioned **hotels** in and around Argelès, most with attached (and good-value) restaurants. Best and quietest is Logis de France affiliate *Beau Site* at 10 rue Capitaine-Digoy, 100m north of the tourist office (Ⓣ05.62.97.08.63, Ⓦwww.hotel-beausite-argeles.com; closed Nov–Dec 15; ❸ B&B), a classic French country inn with the privileged pink rooms (and restaurant – supper only, by reservation) overlooking an immense, tumbling garden. For lunch-time eating, repair to *La Grange* just uphill from Beau Site, with wooden terrace seating.

The Traversée Centrale des Pyrénées (TCP)

Since World War II, planners on both sides of the border have been obsessed with a notional **Traversée Centrale des Pyrénées** (TCP), piercing the range with two or more broad tunnels near its centre, augmenting inadequate ones at Vielha and Bielsa. This strategy has been advocated with ever-increasing fervency by Spain especially, keen to export heavy and/or perishable goods – paving stones, manufactured items, farm produce – as quickly and cheaply as possible to northern Europe. Besides the now-completed Tunnel du Somport (see p.394), other links – Luchon to Benasque (road), a rail tunnel linking French Arreau and Aragonese Monzón via Bielsa, or another train-only bore between Seix (Ariège) and La Pobla de Segur (Catalunya) – have been mooted, but all were rejected due to steep gradients or prohibitive costs. The latest candidate is a pharaonic 48-kilometre tunnel under Vignemale between Biescas in Spain and Argelès-Gazost in the Gave de Pau, to accommodate a high-capacity rail service for trucks and ordinary vehicles, along the lines of the Channel tunnel. Unlike their peers in the Vallée d'Aspe, local mayors know which side (tourism) their bread is buttered on and thus vehemently oppose the project. Passage of time is the most effective enemy of the TCP, as the lower-wage economies of the EU's newest central European members will soon render Spanish exports uneconomical in comparison. The most likely outcome may instead be massive expansion of port facilities around Perpignan and Bayonne at each end of the range, to take pressure off the hopelessly lorry-congested motorways there. For the current status of opposition to the Vignemale project, consult Ⓦwww.actival.org.

Nearby **ARCIZANS-AVANT**, 2km southwest by a minor road, can offer the privately run, rather bogus **Château of the Black Prince** (July–Sept daily 10am–noon & 2.30–7pm), most of it later than Edward's time; that said, it has four atmospheric en-suite *chambres d'hôtes*, some for families (Ⓣ05.62.97.02.79, Ⓦprince.noir.free.fr/chambres_presentation.htm; closed Dec; ❷ B&B). Below the church is the en-suite *Auberge Le Cabaliros* (Ⓣ05.62.97.04.31, Ⓦwww.auberge-cabaliros.com; closed mid-Oct to mid-Dec, & Jan; ❸), with views south over the valley to high peaks from the outdoor seats of the *cuisine regionelle* restaurant (closed Tues eves & Wed; menus €20–32); the quirkiest rooms are under the mansard roof.

Saint-Savin

The twelfth-century **Romanesque abbey** at **SAINT-SAVIN**, 4km south of Argelès-Gazost, is worth visiting partly for its unusual fortifications – fourteenth-century gun slits and an octagonal tower – and for its connection with the persecuted Cagots.

Monastic fortifications hereabouts generally served a double function: aiding enforcement of the *Trêves de Dieu*, the church-imposed truce days between feuding *seigneurs*, and acting as a defence against Aragonese raiders. At Saint-Savin, defence from irate locals may have become paramount, the abbey having grown rich, unpopular and embroiled in lawsuits stemming from its business ventures. A monastic community existed as far back as the eighth century, and the monks quickly established a virtual mini-state here and in adjacent valleys, along with a reputation for luxury and ungodliness. The contemporary feel of the main church – perhaps the least numinous in the entire range, with little evidence of continued sacred use – reflects this.

There was once a large local Cagot community, and the low opening, now blocked, to the left of the west portal is possibly where they listened to Mass from outside; scholars have concluded that the two granite figures supporting the water stoup in the south transept are Cagots. The organ cabinet (1557) is carved with grotesque faces whose eyes and tongues moved as the instrument was played, said to be the grimacing visages of damned souls unable to endure heavenly music. St Savin himself, an obscure local seventh-century hermit, is supposedly entombed in the choir. The vaulted chapter house north of the **church** (daily 9am–7pm) now serves as the entry to a **treasury** (June–Oct daily 10am–noon & 3.30–6.30pm; €2) whose main highlights are various twelfth-century statuettes of the Virgin.

Many visitors prefer the little **chapel of Notre-Dame-de-Piétat** (daily June–Sept, unpredictable hours; free), which adorns a hill amongst hay meadows 1km south of the village. Its glory is an elaborately painted ceiling, where birds perch on floral motifs covering every available space of the simple vault; you can examine them at close range from the wooden gallery.

Saint-Savin has two **hôtel-restaurants**, the more congenial being friendly English-managed *Les Rochers* (Ⓣ05.62.97.09.52, Ⓦwww.lesrochers.co.uk; closed early April, late Oct to Christmas; ❸, ❺ HB) at the top of the village, peacefully set in its own garden, with easy parking and high-standard, en-suite rooms (half-board encouraged).

Beaucens and around

On the opposite side of the valley to Saint-Savin, there's a chance to see birds of prey in captivity at **Le Donjon des Aigles**, the ruined eleventh-century keep of the château at **BEAUCENS** (Ⓦwww.donjondesaigles.fr; daily Easter–Sept 10am–noon & 2.30–6.30pm; flying displays 3.30pm & 5pm, but Aug 3pm, 4.30pm & 6pm; €10). To reach the *donjon* by public transport, alight at **PIERREFITTE-NESTALAS**, where SNCF buses veer off for Cauterets; cross the bridge and walk the well-signposted 2km. Pierrefitte-Nestalas itself, with its belching chemical plant, has little to detain you, except for a small aquarium, **Le Marinarium** (daily except Sun am & Mon am 9.30am–noon & 2–6pm; €7), 50m from the bus stop, incongruously dedicated to tropical fish.

East of Pierrefitte – though the most direct road access is from Argelès – the dinky beginners' ski station of **HAUTACAM** struggles most years to operate, with a top point for its fourteen downhill pistes (drag lifts only) at just 1800m; 15km of cross-country routes are more worthwhile.

Vallée d'Estaing, Val d'Azun and Vallée d'Arrens

The D918 southwest from Argelès initially follows the Val d'Azun, with a turn-off after 4km south up the D103, which serves the silky-green and gentle-sided **Vallée d'Estaing**. There are some good places to **stay** and **eat** along this latter valley, many aimed at GR10 trekkers, beyond **ESTAING** village; **campsites** include *Le Vieux Moulin* (Ⓣ05.62.97.43.23), with a pool, or the more basic *La Pose* (Ⓣ05.62.97.43.10), while there's a *gîte d'étape* (Ⓣ05.62.97.14.37; 22 places; four- to ten-bunk dorms; all year) at **VIELLETTES** hamlet. Last but not least, just below the Lac d'Estaing, the cuisine at *Hôtel Restaurant du Lac* (Ⓣ05.62.97.06.25; open May–Oct 15; ❸), draws customers from far afield. Unusually for a rural eatery, lunch is provided until 2.30pm; skip the humdrum *menus* in favour of the *carte* which features crayfish in various guises, goose, duck, decent bread and elaborate desserts, most defying translation. At road's end, the natural **Lac d'Estaing** is rather too popular for its own good with weekenders who rent pedaloes and patronize a pony-ride outfit. The lake is also an important **trailhead** for the GR10 (which sticks mostly to road and track on its way over from Arrens-Marsous), leading southeast to the Ilhéou refuge (4hr), and for an unnumbered path going south to the numerous tarns around Pene d'Estradère (2593m) and beyond to the Col de Portet and its lake.

Val d'Azun

The main **Val d'Azun** has two fair-sized villages with facilities and points of interest. At **AUCUN**, 9km above Argelès-Gazost, the **Musée Montagnard du Lavédan** (daily during school holidays 5pm tour only; otherwise by appointment on ⓣ05.62.97.12.03; €3) has a private collection of traditional Bigourdan agricultural and household items. The uncluttered village church of **Saint-Pierre** is also worth a glance for its apsidal south transept (the oldest, eleventh-century bit), a baptismal font with musicians and hunters carved in relief, the two-level gallery and sixteenth-century *retable*. Quality **accommodation** is available at two-star *Hôtel le Picors* (ⓣ05.62.97.40.90, ⓦwww.hotel-picors.com; all year; ❸), with a conservatory pool and buffet breakfast. Aucun is also home to the valley's main **parapente** school, Comme un Oiseau (ⓣ05.62.97.47.63, ⓦwww.commeuneoiseau.com).

More places to stay are 3km up-valley at **ARRENS–MARSOUS**, where the excellent **gîte d'étape**, *Auberge Camélat* (ⓣ05.62.97.40.94, ⓦwww.gite-camelat.com; all year), occupies a fine, rambling old house just off the central *place*, with dorms plus twelve doubles (❸ B&B) in the main building or annexe, and saunas laid on some evenings. Off-season, the cheerful restaurant (*menus* €15–21) is the only reliable one in the area, especially at lunch time; otherwise, **eating** in Arrens is limited to *Mille et Une Epices*, with couscous nights. The **Maison du Val d'Azun et du Parc National** (Mon–Sat 9am–12.30pm & 2–6/7pm, also July–Aug Sun 9am–noon & 3–6pm; ⓣ05.62.97.49.49, ⓦwww.valdazun.com) sells farm products and doubles as the tourist office.

From Arrens, the D918 snakes west over the beautiful *cols* de Soulor and d'Aubisque (both closed winter) into the Ossau valley at Eaux-Bonnes (see p.389); a very minor road also links the village with Estaing village in the Vallée d'Estaing, via the Col des Bordères, a route also followed by the GR10. The only facility en route is *La Grange du Pic de Pan* at Col des Bordères, a working Angora goat ranch doubling as a **restaurant**.

Skiing – and the Tour du Val d'Azun

The environs of the Col du Soulor (1474m) are home to the **Soulor-Couraduque** cross-country skiing network, largest in the Pyrenees with 110km of marked trails extending northeast to the Col du Couraduque, at 1350–1600m elevation. For drivers, Soulor marks the start of the D126 north, an attractive if initially slow shortcut down to the main road between Saint-Pé-de-Bigorre and Pau. After 9km, you intersect the walkers' **Tour du Val d'Azun** at **ARBÉOST**, clinging prettily to the flanks of the Val d'Ouzoum; there's a *gîte d'étape*, *Petite Jeanne* (ⓣ05.59.71.42.50, ⓦwww.gite-lapetitejeanne) by the church. Other *gîtes*, well spaced to the east on the same Tour, are the *Haugarou*, near the Col de Couraduque (ⓣ05.62.97.25.04; 16 places; no meals Mon–Tues low season) and *La Ribère* (ⓣ05.62.97.09.11; 15 places) at **ARCIZANS-DESSUS**, 3km east of Aucun. The full Tour, which requires at least three days, is clearly shown on Carte de Randonnées no. 3, "Béarn".

Vallée d'Arrens: into the PNP

The most popular excursions, however, involve the **Vallée d'Arrens**, which extends southwest of Arrens-Marsous, threaded by the D105. Some 10km upstream along the road, passing the Tech dam, you reach road's end (no public transport) at **Plan d'Aste** (1470m), right at the PNP boundary, with limited parking for several trailheads serving the park. The paths link up with the nearby HRP, or go to a trio of refuges, and can be enjoyably combined into short trekking loops of a few days' duration. Trails from either the Tech dam or Plan d'Aste converge on privately run *Refuge de Migouélou* to the west on its lakeshore (2278m; ⓣ05.62.97.44.92, ⓦmigouelou.free.fr/; 40 places; April 15–Oct); it's indicated "2hr 45min" up from Plan d'Aste, though as ever the PNP signboards are pessimistic, and especially with a day-pack you'll shave 20min off that. Another path heads south past little Lac de Suyen (20min) to the *Refuge Ledormeur* (1917m; 12 places; unstaffed), "2hr 15min" distant, and to the staffed *Refuge de Larribet* (2065m; ⓣ05.62.97.25.39, ⓦrefugelarribet.waika9.com; 62 places; April–Oct, otherwise by arrangement), "2hr 45min" away to the southwest. At either hut you're on the HRP as it threads along between the Lac d'Artouste and the Vallée du Marcadau (see p.392 & p.377); the easiest and most obvious hike circuit, using the HRP and link trails, is Plan d'Aste–Migouélou–Artouste–Arrémoulit–Larribet–Plan d'Aste, which would enjoyably occupy two very long days (best allow three).

Luz-Saint-Sauveur and around

The double spa-village of **LUZ-SAINT-SAUVEUR**, with two distinct quarters straddling the confluence of the Gavarnie and Bastan rivers, lies 12km south of Pierrefitte-Nestalas. It makes a practical base if you have a car or are content to make day trips by public transport – though with your own transport, the handsome settlement of **Viscos** is the most congenial rural headquarters, while various other villages either side of Luz, such as **Sazos**, **Grust** and **Viella**, have facilities suited for **GR10** trekkers. For the serious walker, however, Luz is still a bit too distant from the Gavarnie cirque – the goal of any expedition up this valley – to be ideal, despite notional situation on the northerly *variante* of the GR10. **Skiing** is more promising, with Luz-Ardiden resort just to the west, and much better ones at Barèges further east. The Gave de Gavarnie, upstream from here as far as Gèdre, also provides exciting **kayaking**.

The Town

The oldest, most attractive part of Luz is its upper quarter, whose narrow lanes, hosting a Monday market, radiate from the fortified church of **Saint-André**. Surrounding houses make it difficult to get a good look at the church, a classic of medieval military architecture with its crenellated outer wall, stout, machicolated towers and gun slits below the roof. It was built in the twelfth century by the Knights Templars and further modified in the fourteenth by the Knights of St John, who appropriated all of the Templars' strongholds after their suppression. A fine carved Christ in Majesty, flanked by the symbols of the Evangelists, floats on the tympanum over the north portal, and a *clocher-mur* dominates the roofline. The church interior proves disappointing and rather cluttered with three huge confessionals, but in the creaky side chapel there's a **museum** (daily May 15–Sept 30 3–6pm; €2) of sacred artefacts dating back to the twelfth century, including a manuscript on procedures for exorcisms.

The **Saint-Sauveur** quarter to the west consists of startlingly elegant *thermes* buildings and slightly pretentious hotels on the left bank of the Gave de Gavarnie. The spa itself, immaculately redone in 2000, features a kidney-shaped pool and huge windows overlooking the gorge. According to local legend, Napoléon III authorized the superfluous **Pont Napoléon** (built 1861), spanning the canyon, to commemorate his illicit conception at nearby Gavarnie; today, with its 90-metre height, it's a favourite venue for bungy-jumping (*saut à l'élastique* in French). He also funded the Chapelle Solférino, on a hilltop south of the village.

You can cross the river bridge to visit the prominent, thirteenth- to fourteenth-century **Château Sainte-Marie** (unenclosed, free), just 1km northeast in the adjoining village of Esquièze-Sère. Although the surviving pair of round and square towers don't fulfil their promise as glimpsed from afar, the château provides unrivalled views over the town; it's a popular picnic spot, with a spring, and serves as an occasional venue for concerts.

Practicalities

SNCF buses from Lourdes drop you in place du Huit-Mai, hub of the lower part of the village, beside the helpful **tourist office** (summer Mon–Sat 9am–7.30pm, Sun 9am–12.30pm; also Sun 4.30–7.30pm peak season; ⓣ05.62.92.30.30, ⓦwww.luz.org), which can provide lists of long-term apartments for rent. Off place St-Clément, hub of the Monday market, there's a **Maison du Vallée** (July–Aug Mon–Fri 9am–noon & 2–7pm, Sat 4–7pm; ⓣ05.62.92.38.38), which keeps an exhibition of local flora and fauna, hosts films and live musical events on certain evenings and also provides Internet access. Outdoor outfitters include Luz Aventure, for all extreme and not-so-extreme sports (ⓣ05.62.92.33.47), and the town has several well-stocked equipment shops if you're missing an essential piece of gear.

Two central budget **hotels**, both under new management in 2006, are fully en suite *Les Templiers* (ⓣ05.62.92.81.52, ⓦwww.hotellestempliers.com; may close April or May; ❷), opposite the church with English-speaking management, half-board offered and some rooms with views and partly en-suite *Les Cimes* (ⓣ05.62.92.83.03; ❷), 70m downhill on the same lane. If you want to savour the spa atmosphere, and don't mind a short walk into town, stay at two-star *Ardiden* in Saint-Sauveur (ⓣ05.62.92.81.80, ⓦwww.hotelardiden.com; closed Easter–June 1 & mid-Oct to early Dec; ❸), with gorge views from many rooms. The well-run **youth hostel**, *Auberge Les Cascades* (ⓣ05.62.92.94.14; all year), with a few doubles (❶) and a good restaurant, is in the southern neighbourhood, at 17 rue Sainte-Barbe, diagonally opposite more informal *Gîte d'Étape Le Piolet* (ⓣ05.62.92.92.67; 29 places), in an old house. The best local **campsite** for trekkers is central *Le Toy* (ⓣ05.62.92.86.85; Jan–April & June–Sept), right by place du Huit-Mai.

Outside the hotels, **restaurants** are limited. Two reliable choices are *La Tasca* on place St-Clément, tops for Spanish *tapas* and seafood, and *Chez Christine* (closed late autumn & early spring) near the post office, specializing in own-made pasta and desserts plus locally sourced meat and trout. The busiest **bar** is neon-garish *Le Txoko* on the main road north, tripling as a bowling alley and brasserie, claiming to serve "non-stop" from noon to 11pm (though after 10pm only pizza and *entrecôte* are available), with outdoor tables.

Along the GR10 – and Viscos

If none of this appeals, you might retreat to the hamlet of **VIELLA**, 2km east, astride the GR10 and above the D918, where you can **stay** at *Gîte La Grange au Bois* (ⓣ05.62.92.82.76, ⓦwww.lagrangeaubois.com; all year; 33 places in four- to six-bed dorms, some doubles ❷), run by a mountain/ski guide, and **eat** either there or at the *Auberge de Viella*, strong on locally sourced lamb duck and *garbure*.

In the opposite direction out of Luz, initially northwest along a northerly variant of the **GR10**, it's a moderate, six-and-a-half-hour day to Cauterets via the Col de Riou (1949m). The first four hours, confined initially to paved road surface and then dodging ski paraphernalia at Luz-Ardiden, is less than inspiring, but especially coming the other way from Cauterets there are some halts to consider en route. **SAZOS**, half an hour above Saint-Sauveur, can offer the excellent *Gîte La Maisonée* (Ⓣ05.62.92.96.90, Ⓦwww.gitelamaisonnee.com; 40 places including 3 doubles; HB mandatory), while **GRUST**, forty minutes beyond, supports the rambling, old-fashioned *Auberge les Bruyères* (Ⓣ05.62.92.83.03; ❷, ❹ HB) with a view-terrace restaurant (*menus* €11–30).

But some of the best rural facilities around Luz-Saint-Sauveur are at quiet, stone-built **VISCOS**, 6.5km northwest up the mountainside; the turning's 4km north along the D921. Locals and visitors alike make this detour for the sake of *La Grange aux Marmottes*, much the best **restaurant** in the valley; the €25 *menu* (drink extra) of the four usually offered gives you access to much of the *carte*, though certain week nights there are €19 theme *menus* (*soirée fondues*, *menu gascon*, etc). Reservations in season are generally needed (Ⓣ05.62.92.91.13, Ⓦwww.grangeauxmarmottes.com), as they usually are for two affiliated **hotels**: *La Grange aux Marmottes* (❹) and *Les Campanules* (❸), both offering fully modernized facilities in restored buildings, and sharing a terrace-pool – though management style is decidedly hands-off.

Skiing: Luz-Ardiden

The associated ski development of **LUZ-ARDIDEN**, nearly 1000m higher than Luz itself, is reached by 12km of off-putting hairpins on the D12 heading northwest; there are two or three daily *navettes* from the main bus stop in Luz-Saint-Sauveur. Essentially a small, east-facing bowl, the resort musters fourteen lifts (including six well-placed chairs) – to a high point of 2450m – and 26 pistes, over half of them red-rated; the paltry number and length of the blues and greens mean this isn't a good beginners' resort, and the predominantly easterly orientation means the snow is usually ruined after noon.

Paragliding (Parapente) around Barèges

There are five permitted **launch sites** for paragliding around Barèges, with four more around Luz-Saint Sauveur; when the weather is bad this side of the Gave de Pau, local outfitters take to the Val d'Auzun. Most of the Barèges sites cluster around the car park at **Tournaboup meadows** (1450m; 3km east of Barèges), with launchings from the Capet ridge just north (1900–2000m), the Caoubère ridge just east (1900–2000m) and even the Col du Tourmalet itself. Some of the busiest **schools** in France operate most days from Tournaboup: Air Aventure Pyrénées (Ⓣ05.62.92.91.60, Ⓦwww.air.aventure.pyrenee.free.fr; open all year, weather and demand allowing), with English-speaking instructors; the sound-alike Air Aventures Pyrénées (Ⓣ05.62.92.28.19 or 06.81.50.86.50, Ⓦwww.ecole-parapente-pyrenees.com) and Henri Nogue (Ⓣ05.62.92.69.73 or 06.80.73.07.00). Beginners' *biplace* (tandem) **introductory flights** – *baptêmes de l'air* – typically last about twenty minutes before landing at Tournaboup, though competition-level experts can stay airborne for at least 45 minutes. On a two-seater flight, the instructor sits behind you, and controls the rig, exploiting passive (thermal) lift and creating dynamic lift by changing the air-foil's shape through tugging skilfully on various cord-pulls. Your main task is to run like hell at take-off when the glider begins to fill, offsetting its tendency to drag you backwards; then you just sit back and enjoy, if you can – some folk never get beyond the guaranteed initial minute of sheer terror. Thermal lift conditions are invariably better later in the day, so higher **rates** are charged for afternoon flights; be warned that it's an expensive sport if you get hooked. Introductory tandem *baptêmes* cost €45 for two hours from Capet or Caoubère, €80 from Tourmalet or for a "long-duration" flight. Pupils typically need two and a half days of intensive instruction, both practical and theoretical, before their **initial solo flight**.

Barèges and around

The two-street village of **BARÈGES**, 8km northeast of Luz-Saint-Sauveur about halfway along the **Vallée de Bastan** towards the Col du Tourmalet, is among the most congenial bases around the Gave de Pau, if you're willing to forego instant access to the Cirque de Gavarnie. It pitches itself as a one-stop sports centre, with opportunities for bike rental (touring and mountain), riding, rafting, squash, walking, snowshoeing, skiing and, especially, **paragliding**.

Should you be so unlucky as to break a bone paragliding or skiing, Barèges is not a bad place to do it. It became a fashionable health resort after visits in 1677 by the Duc de Maine, the sickly son of Louis XIV, and the waters were considered particularly efficacious for gunshot wounds – a military hospital was established in 1744, and Napoleon made it one of five military *thermes*. The **military** connection endures: there's an army R&R facility in the village centre, with a mountain-warfare school for the Armée de Terre just opposite – the Vallée de Bastan's strong similarity to conditions in Bosnia-Herzegovina made it a major training venue for the French contingent during the 1991–95 Yugoslav wars.

Perhaps the spa's most significant guest was **Ramond de Carbonnières**, whose passion for these mountains can be traced to Barèges, where he came in 1787 as the confidant of the disgraced Cardinal de Rohan. Today the **baths** (May–Oct Mon–Sat unpredictable am hours, & 4–7pm; Christmas–Easter daily 4–8pm) themselves occupy a lovely Palladian building in the centre of Barèges, and have been enthusiastically incorporated into both *après*-trek and *après*-ski routines. The waters, 38°C and sulphurous, are delivered three ways: communal pool plunge, private *hydroxeur* tub (basically a Jacuzzi), and combination jet-dousing and massage.

Practicalities

The central **tourist office** (July & Aug Mon–Sat 9am–12.30pm & 2–7pm, Sun 10am–noon & 4–6pm; rest of year Mon–Sat 9am–noon & 2–6.30pm; Ⓣ05.62.92.16.00, Ⓦwww.bareges.com) can supply all conceivable accommodation lists and ski-lift plans. Year round, Barèges is the end of the line for many daily SNCF or SALT **buses** from Lourdes train station; car **parking** at designated lots is thus far free, but in short supply at peak times. There are a handful of **bank** ATMs – the last you'll see heading east until the Vallée de Campan or Vallée d'Aure – and a **post office**. Recreational facilities include an open-air **swimming pool** (daily July & Aug 12.30–7pm), **squash courts** (daily all year) and tennis (daily 9am–8pm) at the municipal Hélios leisure centre. A couple of outdoor-goods stores can supply most needs, though Luz has a much wider stock.

Especially if you're traversing the GR10, a top choice for **accommodation** would be the welcoming, Anglo-French-run *Gîte d'Étape l'Oasis*, in a handsome old building just behind the spa (Ⓣ05.62.92.69.47, Ⓦwww.gite-oasis.com; 45 places, mostly in quads), with showers in the rooms, sinks in the dorm and transfers to Pont de la Gaubie offered. Alternatively, there's *L'Hospitalet* (Ⓣ05.62.92.68.08, Ⓔhospitalet.bareges@wanadoo.fr; dorms, family quads, doubles), another high-quality *gîte* at the south upper edge of town, a vast, somewhat institutional structure owing to its past as a military hospital, with original art on the walls and a ping-pong table in the old chapel. Both offer evening meals and reasonable half-board rates, and tend to close Oct 15–Nov 30 and April 15–May 15. The first of two recommendable **B&Bs** is Rob and Rachel's *Les Sorbiers* on the main street (Ⓣ05.62.92.86.68, Ⓦwww.lessorbiers.co.uk; closed Oct–Nov & late April to mid-May; ❸); all rooms have shower, some are fully en-suite. Half-board is encouraged for excellent suppers (vegetarian on request) nightly except

Wednesday, and *Mountain Bug* (Ⓣ05.62.92.16.39, Ⓦwww.mountainbug.com; ❹ B&B), behind the butcher's, is a superbly restored eighteenth-century farmhouse with modern bathrooms and tasteful wood-floored common areas; proprietors Robert and Emma are certified guides offering local walking holidays.

The main through road, rue Ramond, is lined with eight gracefully ageing **hotels**, with fairly similar opening seasons (May–Oct & mid-Dec to early April). The most modest is no-star but en-suite *Castets d'Ayré* (Ⓣ05.62.92.68.17, Ⓔjean-claude.cueff@wanadoo.fr; ❷), near the lower end of town; among plusher choices, *Le Central* (Ⓣ05.62.92.68.05, Ⓦwww.central-tourmalet.com; ❸ B&B) has a garden, outdoor pool and wi-fi throughout, while *La Montagne Fleurie* (Ⓣ05.62.92.68.50, Ⓦwww.utaf.com/lamontagnefleurie; ❸ B&B) was thoroughly renovated in 2002 without losing its charm or repeat clientele. Barèges has just one **campsite**, the high-standard *La Ribère* (Ⓣ05.62.92.69.01; closed Oct 15–Dec 15), at the downhill end of town.

Independent **restaurants** in central Barèges are scarce; the best is friendly *La Rozell*, opposite the lift-pass vendors: pricey (€23 *menu*) but well-presented crêpes, *galettes*, meat and fish dishes, with booking recommended (Ⓣ05.62.92.67.61). The closest "out-of-town" choices are *Auberge la Couquelle*, by the roadside just below Tournaboup, with fairly pricey à la carte grills but a good-value, four-course €19 *menu*, or friendly *Auberge du Lienz* (aka *Chez Louisette*; closed early May & Nov), a venerable institution serving hearty *menus* from €23, typically four courses with *garbure*; duck, pigeon, boar or fish as mains; a cheese platter and a tart. Weather permitting, they set outdoor tables year-round near the end of various ski runs. To get there in summer, head first 2.5km northeast towards Tourmalet, then 1.5km southwest on the paved road up to the wooded Plateau du Lienz. Local **nightlife** is modest, comprising the occasional cinema showing and a few bars along Barèges' high street, of which the cosiest is Basque-run *La Bodeguita* next to *Les Sorbiers*, with *pintxos*.

Beyond Barèges, the D918 snakes up to the **Col du Tourmalet**, before dropping to La Mongie, Campan and Bagnères-de-Bigorre. At Pont de la Gaubie, 4km from town, is the **Jardin Botanique du Tourmalet** (May 15–Sept 15 daily 10am–7pm; €4), which has assembled most of the wild flora of the Pyrenees in a single two-hectare site. You can **eat** buckwheat crêpes and light snacks nearby at *Auberge de la Gaubie* (lunch June–Sept only), which flanks the onward trailhead for the GR10.

Walking and snowshoeing from Barèges

The **GR10** passes through Barèges, heading southeast on an interesting traverse through the Réserve Naturelle de Néouvielle to Vielle-Aure, which is described in reverse sense on pp.342–343. (Owing to forestry works, the path from Luz to Barèges is diverted to the north side of the Vallée de Bastan until further notice.) You can sample the high points of this as a **popular day hike from Pont de la Gaubie** (where parking is extremely limited – arrive early). Adapt the directions given for the full traverse under "Bastan to Barèges" as follows: upon arrival at the Col de Madamète, rather than lose unnecessary altitude by dropping to the lakes of Aumar and Aubert and then regaining it up to the Hourquette d'Aubert, traverse carefully cross-country along the north base of Pic de Madamète, descending west from the col just before Pic de Tracens to reach Lac Nère. Here you meet the descending non-GR trail, following it past Lac de Coubous to rejoin the GR10 just above Gaubie for a seven-hour walking day.

In winter, the valley terrain lends itself to circuits on *raquettes* or **snowshoes**; the best two begin from beside the *Gîte L'Hospitalet* and the intermediate station of the defunct Funiculaire de l'Ayré; you may end up doing both routes from the bottom as a figure-of-eight.

Skiing around Barèges

In a snowy year Barèges has some of the best skiing in the Pyrenees, owing to its affiliation with La Mongie (joint pass) and some enjoyable off-piste itineraries; recent winters have seen it with a better snow record than many spots in the Alps. It is in fact the second oldest ski resort in France after Chamonix, and hosted the 1926 Winter Olympics. Barèges had a military-run ski school as early as 1922 and a famous civilian ski club, Société L'Avalanche, whose members have included French slalom champion François Vignole (1929–1935) and Annie Famose (1968 Olympic multiple medallist). The combined resort (ⓦ www.tourmalet.fr) has seventy pistes totalling 125km; on its own, Barèges has about 60km distributed over 32 runs – 11 green, 10 blue, 10 red and 1 black.

Since 2001 considerable investment has brought most of the ski domain up to date: five new high-speed, high-capacity chair-lifts on both sides of Tourmalet, many more snow canons, redesigned pistes and a revamped beginners' area at Tournaboup. The remaining missing link is a bubble-lift replacement for the derelict Funiculaire de l'Ayré from Barèges village to the Plateau de Lienz, with a high-speed chair-lift thence to La Laquette. Until and unless it's built, you have to use the frequent shuttle-bus (included in lift passes) up to Tournaboup and (usually) Tourmalet-West, also known as "the bunker" after the architecture of its restaurant.

Beginning from **Tournaboup** (1450m; parking), the eponymous chair-lift gets you up to the Laquette sector, with higher intermediate runs accessed by drag lifts and blue/green-piste descents through the trees. The link with the Tourmalet-West sector is effected by a high-speed six-seater to Caoubère (2106m) and the blue Bastan run down from there to the "bunker" (1750m; more parking). When the snow level is low enough, it's even possible for strong beginners to ski all the way back down to the village over two consecutive, monstrously long blue-green runs. Otherwise, at **Tourmalet-West** another high-speed lift gets you to the pass proper, and the link with La Mongie's **Tourmalet-East** sector, which – sheltered from frequent warm southwest winds – holds snow better. The other main highlights of La Mongie are profiled on p.352.

The Gavarnie region

South of Luz-Saint-Sauveur, the D921 follows the Gave de Gavarnie 20km upstream to its source – the superlative-laden **Cirque de Gavarnie**, a glacial bowl which first sparked tourist interest in the Pyrenees. Its heyday began in the late nineteenth century, after enraptured Romantics like Victor Hugo lauded it in almost self-parodying prose – "It's the most mysterious of buildings, by the most mysterious of architects; it's Nature's Colosseum!" – and hyperbole, estimating its height as "ten miles" and length as "ten leagues". Such publicity drew increasing crowds to the area, reaching a record two million visitors during 1958. Since then, annual visitor numbers have fallen 75 percent, thanks partly to the boom in overseas travel; the cirque and its environs have thus gained a bit of breathing space, while the creation of the national park has been the occasion for tidying up both the mountainside and **Gavarnie village**.

It's also possible to stay 9km below Gavarnie, in somewhat calmer **Gèdre**. From there you have easy road-access to two other cirques: wide and ethereal **Troumouse** and lonely **Estaubé**. Most people head straight for Gavarnie, but anyone with a couple of days to spare can traverse all three cirques, one of the finest hiking experiences in the Pyrenees. Alternatively, two of the cirques provide access to the Ordesa region in Spain – via the **Brèche de Roland** from Gavarnie and the **Brèche de Tuquerouye** from Estaubé. Gavarnie village is also the base camp for approaches to Vignemale peak on the more-used, higher, southerly variant of the GR10, which then curves north towards Cauterets. For any such explorations you'll at least want the 1:50,000 Carte de Randonnées map no. 4, "Bigorre", if not the 1:25,000 IGN 1748 OT "Gavarnie".

Gèdre and its cirques

Purists can walk from Luz to Gavarnie in a day along the GR10, but since it's mostly within sight of the D921 road you may as well take the bus at least as far as **GÈDRE** (12km). Living largely from nearby electricity-generating installations, tiny Gèdre has no great attraction other than convenience as a base for visiting the nearby Troumouse and Estaubé cirques, but it figures in Pyrenean history as the home of Henri Cazaux and Bernard Guillembet, the guides who in 1837 first climbed Vignemale. At the **Central de Pragnères** 4km downstream, the **turbine hall** – largest in these mountains – is open for **visits** (July–Aug daily 9am–noon & 1.30–5.30pm, guided tours only roughly hourly; Sept–June by arrangement on ⓣ05.62.92.46.66).

Gèdre has a combined **tourist office/Bureau des Guides** (summer daily 9am–1pm & 2.30–7pm, Sun 9am–noon; winter 8.30am–12.30pm & 2.30–6.30pm, Sun 8.30am–1pm; ⓣ05.62.92.48.05 tourism, ⓣ05.62.92.47.37 guides). If you want to **stay**, choose between *Hôtel Les Pyrénées* (ⓣ05.62.92.48.51, ⓕ05.62.92.49.64; closed Nov 1–Dec 15 & Christmas–April; ❸) in the village centre, and the characterful, walnut-wood-furnished Logis de France member *Hôtel La Brêche de Roland* (ⓣ05.62.92.48.54, ⓦwww.pyrenees-hotel-breche.com; open May–Sept & winter weekends/hols; ❺ HB only), its restaurant open to all. There are five **campsites** of varying standards above and below the village, plus a pair of **gîtes d'étape** on the outskirts: *Le Saugué* (ⓣ05.62.92.48.73; closed Nov–April; 25 places), and *L'Escapade* (ⓣ05.69.92.49.37, ⓦwww.gite-escapade.com; all year; 28 places in dorms). As for independent **restaurants**, *La Grotte* at a bend in the road just above *Hôtel La Brêche de Roland* might look like a tourist trap, but lays on a decent buffet lunch for €14, serves until 3pm and has outdoor seating with a view of the cascade and grotto of the name.

Héas and the Cirque de Troumouse

For the **Cirque de Troumouse**, 15km from Gèdre, take the minor D922 to the east, which starts just south of the village. After 8km you reach the hamlet of **HÉAS**, a collection of farmsteads around a pilgrimage chapel. Until the road was opened in the 1950s – and a branch of the HRP was routed through here from Barroude and Gavarnie – this must have been a lonely spot indeed; it's still one of the highest (1500m) permanently inhabited places in the Pyrenees.

Chambres d'hôte and simple meals are available at the en-suite *Auberge de la Munia*, in Héas by the church (ⓣ05.62.92.48.39; closed Oct 15–Dec 15; ❹ HB only). Beyond the toll post (€4 per car; staffed 9am–5pm), the road climbs steeply in hairpins 4km to the *Auberge de Maillet* (ⓣ05.62.92.48.97; May 15–Oct 12; dorm, plus doubles ❸ B&B), ending 3km later at an enormous car park, still not big enough to accommodate everyone on a summer's day. Walkers avoid both toll and tarmac by using a clear path up the easterly Touyères ravine starting near the *Snack Bar La Refuge*, by the toll booth.

The desolate, wild cirque stretches 10km from end to end, not as high-walled but much bigger than Gavarnie's and, in bad weather, rather intimidating. In better conditions it's a magical spot early or late in the day, when the day-trippers have gone – and even more so in late winter, when you arrive on snowshoes or skis and probably have it to yourself.

Beneath the eastern walls of the cirque are scattered a half-dozen glacial tarns, the **Lacs des Aires**; a marked path describes a circuit of them from Héas (2hr up) or the top car park (30min away), snaking through the pastures spangled with wildflowers (ranunculus, gentian and colchicum in particular) and divided by rivulets. The air is full of small alpine birds, and the turf, despite national-park status, is grazed by hundreds of cows and sheep as in centuries past. A 2138-metre knoll topped by a nineteenth-century statue of the Virgin, some fifteen minutes' walk northeast of the parking lot, affords the best view of the place.

The Cirque d'Estaubé – and hiking to Gavarnie

The relatively small **Cirque d'Estaubé** lies at the head of the next valley west of Troumouse. You can walk there within two hours from the *Auberge de Maillet*, but the easiest way of reaching it involves backtracking 2km from Héas to the mouth of the Estaubé valley, and then climbing the D176 side road up to the **Barrage des Gloriettes**. From its car park, the cirque is two hours further south along a narrow, cliff-lined glen, remote and little visited except by hikers on the HRP which goes through here, linking Gavarnie and Héas. An ice-choked gully – approached by an easier side trail from the HRP – leads finally to the **Brèche de Tuquerouye/Brecha de Tucarroya**, at the top of the cirque at its western end (see p.372 for more on this).

Continuing west, the **HRP** – just below the cirque and marked by a few cairns – climbs sharply in zigzags to the notch-like **Hourquette d'Alans** (2430m), from where the *Refuge des Espuguettes* can be glimpsed below (see "The Cirque de Gavarnie", p.370); to reach it (under an hour), the path first descends slowly north, then steeply westwards in more zigzags, completing a relatively easy trekking day.

Gavarnie

At first glance **GAVARNIE**, 8km upstream from Gèdre, is little more than a tacky collection of ramshackle souvenir kiosks and snack bars, besieged in summer by hordes scarcely less numerous than at Lourdes. The prevailing commercialization is reflected in a €4 fee (8am–5pm) levied on all entering vehicles, whether they park in a huge, earth-surface, high-season car park at the entrance to the village, or along the start of the road bound for the local ski station; traffic is banned within the village from 10am to 6pm. Once the trippers have departed in their cars or swarming tour coaches, Gavarnie's pavements roll up promptly, allowing full realization that it's barely a hamlet; the only exception is during eleven evenings in July, when the **Festival de Gavarnie** takes place, with the nocturnal staging of a classic play or musical extravaganza.

Yet almost every house and (older) hotel here has some connection with two centuries of Pyrenean exploration. For example, the **Hôtel des Voyageurs** counted among its guests Henry Russell, Charles Packe and Francis Swan, as well as George Sand, Gustave Flaubert, Victor Hugo and his mistress Juliette Drouet. Hortense de Beauharnais purportedly conceived the future Napoléon III in one of its bedrooms on the night of August 24, 1807 – the father a Gavarnie shepherd. Alas, this illustrious history failed to save the *Voyageurs* from hard times and closure in 2001 pending conversion to apartments. Beside the Romanesque church, last prayer stop for pilgrims along this minor branch of the Santiago route before crossing into Spain, are buried great early climbers such as Jean Arlaud and the Passet family of guides.

Practicalities

The **tourist office** has premises at the entrance to the village (daily: 9am–12.30pm & 2–7pm; ⓣ05.62.92.49.10, ⓦwww.gavarnie.com); the central **Maison du Parc** (term time Tues–Sat 9.30am–noon & 1.30–6pm; school hols Mon–Sat 9am–noon & 1.30–6.30pm, Sun 10am–noon & 1.30–6.30pm; ⓣ05.62.92.42.48) next door has a more overtly educational function. **Walks and climbs** (€25/day) are organized by certified guide Yuan (ⓣ06.85.09.80.44 or Mon–Sat 6.30–7pm in the tourist office). For **snow and weather conditions**, ask the CRS mountain rescue unit opposite *La Bergerie*. There's a Crédit Agricole (but *no* ATM) beside the Maison du Parc, and a **post office** nearby.

Currently the best value among six surviving **hotels** is offered by Logis de France affiliate *Le Marboré* (ⓣ05.62.92.40.40, ⓦwww.lemarbore.com; closed Nov 15–Dec 20 & late April; ❹) at the north end of the main street, or the small but well-placed *Compostelle* by the church (ⓣ05.62.92.49.43, ⓦwww.compostellehotel.com; closed Oct–Christmas; ❷), where most rooms face the cirque, with skylights in the top-floor ones. Modern, less characterful *Le Taillon* (ⓣ05.62.92.48.20, ⓦwww.letaillon.com; closed Nov 7–Dec 15; ❷) offers easy parking (inbound access 6pm–10am) and hearty breakfasts.

Chambres d'hôte (both non-en-suite) include *La Chaumière*, 500m from the village centre on the way to the cirque (ⓣ05.62.92.48.08; closed Nov–Christmas; ❷), with an attractive brasserie/breakfast bar overlooking the river; and *Jeanine Fernandes*, on the opposite (northern) outskirts, situated up on a knoll (ⓣ05.62.92.47.41; April–Nov; ❶). **Hostels** include *Le Gypaète* (ⓣ05.62.92.40.61; all year; 45 places in 7 dorms), a fancy *gîte d'étape* near the tourist office, and the CAF refuge *Les Granges de Holle* (ⓣ05.62.92.48.77, ⓔjoseph.thirant@wanadoo.fr; closed Oct 1–Dec 18), 2km out on the road towards the ski station. The closest **campsite** is *La Bergerie* (ⓣ05.62.92.48.41; May–Oct) on the east bank of the river 600m above the village; facilities are exceedingly basic, and the ground sloping, but there are unbeatable views up into the cirque, and a breakfast bar. The other local site, *Le Pain de Sucre* (ⓣ05.62.92.47.55; June–Sept & Dec 15–Easter), is marginally more comfortable (hot water costs extra) but inconvenient, 3.5km north of the village.

The only independent full-service **restaurants** in Gavarnie village are *Le P'tit Toy* (closed Nov 15–Dec 15) just behind *Hôtel Taillon*, with panoramic upstairs seating and two *menus* below €19, and *Les Cascades* by the Maison du Parc.

Skiing: Gavarnie-Gèdre

Although it doesn't compare with Barèges-La Mongie, **Gavarnie-Gèdre** rates highly on account of its snow record and wonderful situation. The resort gets its weather from the south, so has plenty of snowpack when the rest of the French Pyrenees has little or none (though the reverse is also true). Owing to its exposure, this is an exceptionally cold spot, with high winds often halting the lifts. But when you get off the top lift and ski out from behind the concealing summit of 2400-metre Pic des Tentes, you have spellbinding views towards the cirque; this peak also marks the start of some fine *ski-randonnées* along (and over) the frontier ridge.

Otherwise, Gavarnie-Gèdre is a good beginners' and intermediates' downhill resort; three of the green runs are longish and descend from the high slopes, though five blue runs are less satisfactory. Seven red and two black pistes, out of a total of 24, plus three high-speed lifts complete the tally of facilities (there's no ski hire, so come equipped).

The Cirque de Gavarnie

Approaching from the north along the D921, your first glimpse of the **Cirque de Gavarnie** occurs just above Gèdre, from where the Brèche de Roland – the famous gap on the west side – is clearly visible. Closer up, the stupendous cirque doesn't disappoint, scoured by glaciation into an almost perfect semicircle, 1500m from top to bottom and 900m across. Despite appearances, the palisades are neither completely vertical nor uniform, actually rising in three stages – a layer of granite sandwiched between two limestone beds – separated by sloping terraces, banked by snow and ice. A main **waterfall** – a straight drop during spring, two or three separate cataracts later in the year – plus numerous smaller ones embellish the great wall. It has been classified as a UNESCO World Heritage Site, hopefully ensuring that the meadows between Gavarnie and the cirque (a distance of 4km) remain unspoiled.

Visiting the cirque

The *muletiers* who were long noted for taking patrons up into the cirque on mule- or horseback have recently dwindled considerably in numbers, as has the amount of animal ordure speckling Gavarnie's streets – the ride up is mostly a kiddie attraction these days. You'll most likely ascend to the cirque on foot, best done late in the afternoon on a long summer's day when the crowds have departed. The broad, well-trodden east-bank trail (a harder-to-find path traces the west bank also) climbs first to the *jardin botanique*, where there are more graves of *Pyrénéistes* – Louis Le Bondider and Franz Schrader – and then to the **Plateau de la Prade**, a beautiful area of streams and forest, now graced by an open-air theatre used during the annual late-July festival. Beyond the plateau, another short, steepish climb brings you to the *Hôtel du Cirque et de la Cascade* (1580m; 45min from Gavarnie) – once a famous meeting place for mountaineers, nowadays a heavily subscribed restaurant with suprisingly reasonable meals and drinks. It's situated just within the bowl of the cirque, and should you be there during an electric storm (quite probable on summer afternoons) you're unlikely ever to forget the echoes of the thunderclaps.

From the *hôtel* (closes at dusk; no beds), an increasingly strenuous climb takes you, in just under half an hour, to the base of the **Grande Cascade**, the source of the Gave de Gavarnie (and ultimately the Gave de Pau) and, at 423m, the longest falls in Europe. On a late July afternoon, the rainbowed stream catches the last rays of the sun, showering spectators as the plumes waver in gusts of wind. Above you, the three-banded walls rise to a summit-ridge of nine 3000-metre-plus peaks, curving over 5km between **Astazou** (3017m) in the east and **Le Casque/El Casco** (3006m) in the west. The ridge – the border between Spain and France – is festooned by the severely shrunken remnants of the glaciers that formed the amphitheatre. Inaccessible though it may seem, the cirque is traced by **climbing routes**, both summer and winter.

Alternate return route

Rather than retrace your steps, the most pleasant way back to Gavarnie, starting just behind and above the *Hôtel du Cirque*, is via the marked path up to the meadow-set *Refuge de Pailla* (1760m; only snacks available, overnights reserved for private members; open July 1–Oct 15), along a 45-minute corniche route through fir and black pine, with dripping rock overhangs, grotto-springs and fine views.

Just beyond the Pailla meadow, there's a fork in the path. Left and down leads in sharp zigzags, initially beside a stream, within 45 minutes more to Gavarnie, but most prefer to head right and east a similar time uphill to the popular *Refuge des Espuguettes*, 1hr 30min–2hr from the cirque (2030m; ⓣ05.62.92.40.63; 60 places; weekends Easter & Oct, daily May–Sept), huge, grey and isolated above the tree line. Lupins and crocus are abundant on the way up, and the detour is amply rewarded by sweeping views west along the frontier crest from Marboré to Vignemale and beyond. With a day-pack, allow an hour and a half for the total return to Gavarnie from the refuge. From *Espuguettes* you can also continue east in less than a full day to Héas, via the Barrage des Gloriettes (see p.368).

The Brèche de Roland

Most Gavarnie hikers want to get to – and through – the **Brèche de Roland/Brecha de Roldán**, a curious, nearly vertical frontier gap at the top of the cirque, so in summer you'll have company of all ages, nationalities and walking abilities. Such popularity has one big advantage – a lone traveller can risk the climb knowing there's no chance of a mishap going unaided. The glaciers guarding the final approach are especially dangerous when no snow covers the treacherous ice, while an ice-axe and crampons will be a major aid at any time. If you're able to stay at the *Refuge de la Brèche de Roland* just below, you'll have the opportunity to ascend various peaks flanking it, or visit some famous ice caves just over on the Spanish side. Done as a day expedition from Gavarnie, count on a minimum of ten hours there and back.

According to legend, the 100m-by-60m gap was hacked out by the dying Roland, nephew of Charlemagne, as he attempted to smash his magic sword Durandal to prevent it falling into the hands of the Muslims. The twelfth-century *Chanson de Roland* describes how:

> Count Roland smites upon the marble stone;
> I cannot tell you how he hewed and smote;
> Yet neither does it break nor splinter,
> Though groans the sword,
> And rebounds heavenwards.

The battle in which Roland died supposedly took place nearly 100km to the west near Roncesvalles (see p.480), so the tale is pretty thin, and the startling views from the top need no legend to augment them.

Approaches to the Brèche

There are three **approaches** to the *brèche*, all converging on the *Refuge de la Brèche de Roland*. The lazy way involves driving up to the **Port de Gavarnie/Puerto de Bujaruelo** (Port de Boucharo on some maps), at the end of the road to the ski station (13km); from there a clear path climbs east under the north face of **Taillon/Tallón**, rising gradually until a gully just over an hour along, where it joins a footpath coming directly up from Gavarnie. This trail – the next easiest way to the *brèche* – begins by the village's Romanesque church, climbs steadily but manageably on the western flank of the valley, turns into the small plateau of Pouey d'Aspé and, after a time, climbs steeply again in zigzags to join the footpath from the Port de Gavarnie (2hr 45min).

Following either of these approaches, you continue on up through the Col des Sarradets to the **Refuge de la Brèche de Roland** (aka *Refuge des Sarradets*; 2557m; ⓣ06.83.38.13.24; 60 places; June–Sept), reached in under an hour from the junction of the paths. Situated in full view of the *brèche* and just 220m below it, the refuge is understandably packed in summer, when an average of ninety walkers a night fight for places.

The third and most challenging route, the **Échelle des Sarradets**, takes between four and five hours from Gavarnie. Having reached the *Hôtel du Cirque* you carry on south a short distance, cross a bridge, then bear southwest on a well-trodden path to the west wall of the lower cirque, below which flourish clusters of Pyrenean irises in midsummer. For the non-climber the next hundred-metre section requires a lot of teeth-gritting and not too much looking down – it's not technically difficult (steps have been cut in places), but it is rather exposed, and inadvisable going downhill. The final section follows the steep Sarradets valley to the refuge.

From its namesake refuge, the **Brèche de Roland** is about forty minutes' stiff climb away, ending with the glacier crossing. Often, on an apparently windless day, you'll be almost bowled over as you step through the rock "doorway", while flocks of calling choughs circle easily and endlessly in the gale. Looking into Spain, a high-altitude scree-desert forms the summer foreground, followed by the top of the Ordesa canyon walls and then, receding into the distance, dense blue-green forest, turning pink, red, then purple at sunset. Looking back towards France, you'll find the summits barer and more jagged, the light more yellow.

Climbs from the Brèche

To the west of the Brèche de Roland, towards Taillon, the rock rampart known as **Pic Bazillac** (2975m) ends at the so-called **Fausse Brèche** with its menhir-like finger of rock. For the ascent of **Taillon** (3144m), continue on the path beyond the Fausse Brèche and climb along the east ridge. This is one of the easiest Pyrenean three-thousanders but the views are no less exciting for that.

The **Casque/Casco** (3006m) forms the eastern part of the *brèche* and is a slightly trickier climb than Taillon. Pass through to the Spanish side and follow the path that runs hard left, keeping close to the rock wall. A steel cable gives moral and physical support over a difficult section, beyond which you bear left to the slopes that separate Le Casque and **Tour/Torre** (3009m) – next peak of the cirque – and then left again to scramble up to the summit.

The Grotte Casteret

Standing in the *brèche* and looking southeast into Spanish territory, you can see a curious dome-shaped rock about a kilometre (and nearly an hour's hike) away. This is the entrance to **Grotte Casteret**, the most spectacular of 32 known ice-caves on the Marboré/Monte Perdido Massif and the highest such caverns in the world, discovered by Norbert Casteret in 1926. The outer chamber requires no special equipment just to look in; but for the magnificent lower chamber, with its "*Niagara de Glace*" ice-column, you'll need crampons, rope and head lamp.

South of the Brèche: into Ordesa

Once through the *brèche* you're in the Spanish **Parque Nacional de Ordesa** (see pp.418–419). If you want to explore further its higher altitudes, you should head for the *Refugio de Góriz*, two to three hours away to the east-southeast. The terrain is bleak, exposed karst, with no potable water sources, but anyone who can reach the Brèche de Roland can easily get to this shelter. Keeping the bare **Pico del Descargador** (2627m) to your right and the back of the Gavarnie cirque on the left, cross the **Plana de San Ferlús** and follow the valley draining from the **Cuello de Millaris** (2457m). The only difficulty is at the **Circo de Góriz**, just before the refuge, easily negotiated by a path on the north side; if you miss it you'll be confronted by an impassable succession of vertical descents. For outings from the *Refugio de Góriz*, see p.420.

Via the Brèche de Tuquerouye

An alternative access from Gavarnie to Ordesa lies via the tougher, much less frequented **Brèche de Tuquerouye/Brecha de Tucarroya** (2660m). The first part of the approach partially reverses the itinerary from the **Cirque d'Estaubé** to Gavarnie (described on p.368), climbing from Gavarnie village to the *Refuge des Espuguettes* and the Hourquette d'Alans. Once through the pass, the route drops eastwards in zigzags towards the floor of Estaubé, then veers south-southeast, more or less along the 2200-metre contour, to the foot of the gully that leads up to the *brèche*. It's a

Henry Russell

Beyond any doubt, Comte Henri Patrick Marie Russell-Killough – known usually as **Henry Russell** (1834–1909) – was the most original mountaineer of all time. God, wrote the devoutly Catholic Russell, is a *présence palpable* in the Pyrenees, and he went to extraordinary lengths to achieve a communion with the spirit of the mountains. One August night in 1880, for instance, he had two guides cover him with scree on the summit of Vignemale, with only his head protruding above the blanket of stone.

Russell was an elegant eccentric who threw great parties and did the full social season in Pau most winters, yet who spoke of Vignemale as his wife and enjoyed nothing more than a seventy-kilometre stroll between Luchon and Bagnères-de-Bigorre. Despite a youthful period of travel in America, Siberia, India, China, Australia and New Zealand, he seemed more than content to come home and explore the nearer wildernesses of the Pyrenees. In 1863, aged 29, he bagged the highest peak of the range, Aneto. In the years that followed he made sixteen first ascents, including a climb of Vignemale in 1869 that was the first winter ascent of a major European summit. The bravery and the flamboyance of the man comes through in his fascinating *Souvenirs d'un Montagnard/Recuerdos de un Montañero*: completely impressionist and untechnical, it contrasts strongly with the writings of his friend and fellow *Pyrénéiste*, Charles Packe, who made precise observations on everything from geology to botany.

Vignemale was Russell's greatest obsession; his statue in Gavarnie (a replacement for one melted down by the Nazis) gazes west up the Ossoue valley towards his beloved mountain. Russell climbed it 33 times – his last ascent aged 70 – and his passion led him to dig several cave-homes on the peak. In 1882 work began on a set of three caves close to the head of the Ossoue glacier, which soon were joined by two others; a huge party with fine wines and dishes set on damask tablecloths, marked their completion. Within five years these caves had been made uninhabitable by the shifting glacier, so Russell moved lower, carving out the Grottes Bellevue in 1888. The position didn't satisfy him, and in 1893 his seventh and final cave, Paradis, was hollowed out by explosives only 18m below the peak. By then the commune of Barèges had granted him a 99-year lease on the summit.

Russell spent extended periods in his mountain homes, sometimes entertaining lavishly; he insisted on guests getting up at dawn in order to witness sunrise, rewarding them with punch at 11am. He tempted people away from the comfortable valley resorts and into the mountains themselves, a relatively new experience for the time. His activities also boosted local commerce, especially for the hotels and guides of Gavarnie, then a poor, pastoral village. But, despite his commemorative statue in the village, the caves that Russell constructed are now completely neglected – or worse, used as public conveniences. And Russell is no doubt spinning in his grave at proposals to bore a rail tunnel under Vignemale (see box on p.358).

steep (80-percent grade) ascent for which crampons and axe are invariably essential; if you're not up to it, the contour path continues to and through an easier pedestrian pass on the east, **Port Neuf de Pinède** (2466m). Sandwiched between the rock walls of the Brèche de Tuquerouye itself, looking like a twinned Nissen hut, stands the oldest hut in the Pyrenees, the unstaffed *Refuge de Tuquerouye* (2660m; 12 places), opened – with a lavish banquet – by the Club Alpin Français in 1890. Thoroughly overhauled in 1999 and fitted with a heating stove, kitchen and solar-powered emergency phone, the hut further justifies an overnight stay by its setting and views south to glacier-hung Monte Perdido. If you have a tent or bivvy sac, you could descend on the other side to the camping area around the **Lago de Marboré**, 80m lower in elevation and the first reliable water since the base of the gully.

West of Gavarnie: Vignemale and Russell's caves

The problem with visiting **Vignemale** from the east (or any direction, for that matter) is that the approach is long. With a car you can drive on road and track along the Gave d'Ossoue as far as the **Barrage d'Ossoue**, but on foot the GR10 from Gavarnie takes over three hours. It's a wonderful hike, though, first under spectacular cliffs where lammergeiers nest, and then across pasture where marmots whistle and isards are a frequent sight. From the dam, the path runs along the eastern shore to a concrete bridge over the Ossoue stream. Beyond the bridge the landscape gets even more interesting, the path zigzagging across a short section of permanent ice at one point in the climb.

About three hours above the lake you reach the dilapidated, smelly but aptly named **Grottes Bellevue**, where Russell spent some summers (see box on p.373), with fine views south. Another fifteen minute's walk brings you to the 2003-renovated *Refuge Baysselance* (2651m; ☎05.62.92.40.25; 60 places; June to Sept), traditional base camp for the **ascent of Vignemale**.

Make an early start next morning, dropping back down the path towards the Grottes Bellevue, then cutting off west-southwest just above them to the moraine at the foot of the **Ossoue glacier**, the largest remaining one in the Pyrenees. This is grubby-looking in summer, with huge and thankfully obvious crevasses; the trodden path runs a little right of the centre. You'll need crampons and ice-axe, and you should rope up. At the top end of the glacier is another of Russell's summer homes, the **Grotte du Paradis**, just 18m below the summit of **Pique Longue** (3289m), an easy final scramble (4hr in total from the refuge). There are several loftier peaks in Spain, but this is the highest Pyrenean point actually on the frontier.

From the *Refuge Baysselance* you can continue on the GR10 over the **Hourquette d'Ossoue** (2734m) to the *Refuge des Oulettes de Gaube* (2hr 30min further; see p.378) and thence to Cauterets.

△ Terraced building, Cauterets

Cauterets and around

Unlike towns along the *gaves* de Pau and de Gavarnie, the spa and mountain-sports mecca of **CAUTERETS** – 30km south of Lourdes and 10km up the D920 from Pierrefitte-Nestalas – features colonnaded, iron-balconied Neoclassical buildings in its western quarter, especially on boulevard Latapie-Flurin, facing the more traditional part on the east bank of the Gave de Cauterets. A long and narrow village, its surprisingly tall buildings prompted by the lack of flat ground, Cauterets wears a general air of elegance gone to seed; Belle Époque follies lie abandoned or fitted out with cinemas, slot machines or bowling alleys, while hotels now superfluous to requirements are constantly converted to studios or *résidences* available only by the week or the month. This all contrasts markedly with the idyllic alpine setting, and "endorsements" by numerous notables in centuries past.

The place owes its existence to Count Raymond de Bigorre, who in 945 gave land and money to the monks of Saint-Savin, enabling them to establish the baths. The lush countryside around Cauterets positively haemorrhages with waterfalls and no fewer than eleven **hot springs**; in town two *thermes* still operate, those of César (daily 7am–12.30pm & 2/3–5pm) and Rocher (Mon–Sat 7am–12.30pm).

National fame came in the sixteenth century when Marguerite d'Angoulême (see "Pau" p.379) became a regular client, reputedly penning her *Heptameron*, the French equivalent of the *Decameron*, while here. In 1807 Louis Napoléon and his wife Hortense stayed for several months after the death of their first son; subsequently George Sand, Gustave Flaubert, Châteaubriand and Victor Hugo spent time in Cauterets, as did Alfred Tennyson, who with Arthur Hallam arrived in 1831 carrying funds for a revolutionary group plotting against the king of Spain. Later, Baudelaire, Debussy, Sarah Bernhardt and Edward VII of England added their names to the illustrious guest list.

Cauterets' reputation as a winter *après*-ski resort is probably overshadowed by its summer hiking profile. Most of the best walks depart from the massive PNP gatehouse at Pont d'Espagne, 6km southwest: you might explore the valley of the Marcadau further in the same direction to the border ridge and beyond, or fashion an enjoyable loop through the valleys of Gaube and Latour. The Vallée de Marcadau is also a top cross-country skiing venue, for which the Cauterets area is perhaps a better bet than for downhill snow sports.

Practicalities

The town is small enough that you should have no trouble finding your way around. **SNCF buses** from Lourdes arrive at the *fin-de-siècle* wooden train station at the north edge of the centre; the adjacent **Maison du Parc** (summer daily 9.30am–noon & 3.30–6.30/7pm; ⓣ05.62.92.52.56) has a small wildlife display plus film shows on Wednesday and Saturday evenings in season. The **tourist office** on place Maréchal-Foch (Mon–Sat: July & Aug 9am–12.30pm & 2–7pm; Sept–June 9am–noon & 2–6pm; ⓣ05.62.92.50.50, ⓦwww.cauterets.com), sells a useful guide to local short walks; the Bureau des Guides, 5 place Clemenceau (mid-June to mid-Sept daily 10am–noon & 4.30–7.30pm; ⓣ05.62.92.62.02, ⓦwww.guides-cauterets.com) has the weather report plus current information on the condition of mountain paths and climbs, and also organizes the usual range of outdoor activities. Cauterets is an excellent place to stock up for a long-haul trek; there's a fruit and vegetable **market**, several supermarkets and bakeries, a laundry at rue Richelieu 19, plus several outdoor-gear shops.

Cauterets has a baker's dozen of surviving **hotels**, pinpointed on a placard at the north end of town. Budget options beside the *gîtes* listed below include one-star *Le Grum* at 4 rue Victor Hugo, off rue de la Raillère (ⓣ05.62.92.53.01,

Ⓕ05.62.92.64.99; closed mid-Oct to mid-Dec; ❷), with a mix of rooms both en suite and not. For something more upmarket, try old-fashioned but well-kept *Lion d'Or* at 12 rue Richelieu (Ⓣ05.62.92.52.87, Ⓦwww.hotel-lion-dor.net; closed Oct–Christmas & part May; ❷–❺) or the more basic *César* (Ⓣ05.62.92.52.57, Ⓦwww.cesarhotel.com; closed May 1–24 & Oct 1–24; ❷) at 3 rue César near the eponymous *thermes*. However, superior comfort at similar prices can be had at *Asterides-Sacca*, 11 bd Latapie-Flurin (Ⓣ05.62.92.50.02, Ⓦwww.perso.wanadoo.fr/hotel.le.sacca; ❷), at the end of a Belle Époque terrace, with a few balconied rooms and far and away the best restaurant in Cauterets (*menus* €16.50–42).

There are two quality **gîtes d'étape**: hillside *Beau Soleil* at 25 rue Maréchal-Joffre (Ⓣ05.62.92.53.52, Ⓔgite.beau.soleil@wanadoo.fr; closed Oct 15–Dec 1; 38 places), with en-suite, one- to five-bunk rooms, and less regimented *Le Pas de L'Ours,* 21 rue de la Raillère (Ⓣ05.62.92.58.07, Ⓦwww.lepasdelours.com; all year; 12 places), with a one-star hotel annexe (❸) offering basic but en-suite rooms and copious buffet breakfasts. On the way into Cauterets from the north, there are several **campsites**, the most tent-friendly being quiet *Les Bergeronnettes* (Ⓣ05.62.92.50.69; June–Sept) and *La Prairie* (Ⓣ05.62.92.54.28; June–Sept), fairly close to town and shaded.

Eating outside of the hotels (which often require half-board in season) is sharply limited. Latin flavours include *Pizzeria Giovanni* at 5 rue de la Raillère and *Casa Bodega Manolo* at no. 11 of the same street, with *tapas* and a *menu*. It's worth driving up to *La Ferme Basque* (closed unpredictable periods low season; Ⓣ05.62.92.54.32), 3km west of town on the road to the ski station; managing couple Léon and Chantal purvey country fare (black pudding, wild-spinach *garbure* by special order, lamb, homemade desserts) in their €17–22 *menus*, though it's fine to just have a coffee and admire the sweeping view – or pick up a can of their own-made *foie gras*, pork paté or duck-based concoctions (Ⓦwww.fermebasque.com). They're also the closest decent restaurant to the Courbet-Lys skiing domain (see p.379).

Walking around Cauterets

There is magnificent walking around Cauterets, which lies just at the edge of PNP territory extending immediately southwest. The most useful **map** for local treks is the 1:50,000 Carte de Randonnées no. 4, "Bigorre", though if you're not interested in linking up with the Gavarnie area, no. 3, "Béarn", or IGN 1647 OT "Vignemale Ossau" will do. Most worthwhile itineraries depart from the **Pont d'Espagne**, a scenic old stone bridge high over the confluence of the foaming *gaves* du Marcadau and du Gaube, and an important landmark on the historic route across the mountains to Spain. For those with their own car, there are 1350 spaces (€4 summer, free for winter skiers) in the **Puntas car park** at the end of the D920, 7km above Cauterets, in front of the giant PNP visitors' centre. Except for the refuges' service vans, vehicles of any sort are not allowed beyond this point. Otherwise *navettes* from Cauterets up the Val de Jéret (summer 6 daily 8am–6pm uphill, 9am–7pm downhill; winter 2–3 daily, 9am–noon up, 2–5pm down; €4 one way, €6 return) leave you at the centre. Purists can walk there from **La Raillère**, a satellite spa building with clustered snack/souvenir stalls 3km south of Cauterets, along a fine streamside section of the GR10, pressed into double service as a park trail; it's about ninety minutes uphill along this *Sentier des Cascades*, under fine woods of beech and pine.

Next to the bridge itself, just five minutes from the Puntas car park, stands the *Hôtel de Pont de Espagne* (Ⓣ05.62.92.54.10, Ⓕ05.62.92.51.72; closed Oct

15–Christmas; ②), with perfunctory rooms, and meals served; some fifteen minutes above here, past the *télésiège* to Gaube (see p.378), the privately run, youth-oriented *Chalet du Clot* (1581m; 40 places; open Dec–Easter & May–Oct; ⓣ05.62.92.61.27, ⓔchaletduclot@wanadoo.fr) on the broad **Plateau du Clot** offers simple meals and overnighting, with doorstep cross-country skiing.

Refuge Wallon and the Pont du Cayan loop walk

From Plateau du Clot, signs for the **Vallée du Marcadau** and the *Refuge Wallon* point southwest towards sparkling streams, meadows and tall pines. When the valley narrows sharply at the **Pont du Cayan**, some forty minutes beyond via either bank of the main stream, the path climbs left through forest to the **Pont d'Estaloungué**, and then rises more steeply to the rambling, old-fashioned **Refuge Wallon** (1866m; ⓣ05.62.92.64.28; 115 places; daily May–Oct & selected winter hols). Although it's barely two hours from the Puntas car park, you get a real sense of the surrounding mountains, which are ideal for walks and light scrambles of all sorts, rather than technical climbing. Owing to the mild climate, Scots and black pines, some several hundred years old, flourish up to 2000m elevation hereabouts.

Rather than retrace your steps to Cauterets, loop back to **Pont du Cayan** along the marked footpath that heads initially northwest. After an hour, you reach rock-girt **Lac Nère** (2320m), and after twenty minutes further through a chaos of boulders, you arrive at the even more lunar **Lac du Pourtet** (2420m), a sawtooth ridge bounding it on the north. At a small notch on the lake's east shore you turn down and eastwards, passing three turf-fringed tarns called the **Lacs de l'Embarrat** (as well as a marked side trail for the Lac d'Ilhéou – see p.378); just over ninety minutes from the highest lake you should be back at the Pont du Cayan. This circuit does involve a stiff climb, and you should count on six hours' walking time return from the Puntas car park – as opposed to four if you backtrack entirely along the Vallée du Marcadau from *Wallon*. But this is one of the more representative – and deservedly popular – day walks you can do around Cauterets; the lakes are all dissimilar, and wildlife surprisingly conspicuous for such a relatively accessible route.

Treks above Refuge Wallon

Above and beyond *Refuge Wallon*, there's a choice of routes in several directions, the most exciting of them along the HRP or its *variante sud*. You can follow the **HRP** west towards the important frontier peak of Balaïtous, using the Lac Nère approach for about 25min, then veering away west-northwest up the Gave de Cambalès, through bare terrain strewn with a dozen lakes, to the **Col de Cambalès** (2706m; 3hr from the refuge). The HRP drops southwest on the other side to the very easy **Port de la Peyre-Saint-Martin/Cuello d'a Piedra de San Martin** (2295m) on the border, then goes north down the Arrens valley to the *Refuge Ledormeur* (see p.361 for details), a six-hour day from the *Refuge Wallon*.

If you have the time and energy, press on for another ninety minutes to the more comfortable *Refuge de Larribet* (see p.361) – to reach it drop northwards to the junctions of the Arrens and Larribet valleys, then curl back south along the latter. From either refuge you can descend if necessary to Arrens-Marsous (see p.360).

The **HRP variante sud** skirts Balaïtous (3146m) to the south on a generally westward course to the next staffed French alpine hut at Arrémoulit – a minimum eight-hour trekking day. It runs initially southwest from the *Refuge Wallon* along the Port du Marcadau stream, then climbs westwards to **Col de la Fache/Cuello da Facha** (2664m); once through this you're in Spain, dropping down to the north shore of the huge **Respumoso** reservoir with its staffed refuge (see p.425). From

Respumoso, you head back into France via the **Arriel** lakes and the **Col du Palas/Cuello de Pallas** (2517m) to the *Refuge d'Arrémoulit* (Ⓣ05.59.05.31.79; 2305m; 30 places; staffed July–Sept) between the lakes of the same name, just beyond the southern end of Lac d'Artouste. (For more on Lac d'Artouste and Balaïtous, see p.392.)

Southeast from *Refuge Wallon*, the marked HRP trail begins five minutes below the shelter at a bridge, up the Gave d'Arratille and its lake to the **Col d'Arratille** (2528m; 2hr 45min from the refuge). From there either continue into the Spanish Ara valley, which drains towards the Ordesa region, or head east for a couple of hours – dropping briefly into the top of the Ara valley and then over the **Col des Mulets/Puerto de los Mulos** (2591m), always on the **HRP** – to the *Refuge des Oulettes de Gaube* (see below). This is a fairly meaty but short, well-marked traverse of five hours from *Wallon*.

Loop via the Gaube and Lutour valleys

The head of the **Vallée du Gaube** is more usually approached directly from the Pont d'Espagne, as part of the deservedly popular, two- to three-day **loop** back to Cauterets, which also takes in the **Vallée de Lutour**. To accomplish it anticlockwise, you first head up the Gave du Gaube for an hour as far as the popular **Lac de Gaube**, with the restaurant *Hôtellerie du Lac de Gaube* at the north end of the lake. If you're heavily laden, a small *télésiège* (daily summer 8.30am–6.30pm up, 9am–7.30pm down; €4.70 one way, €6.70 return) spares you most of the climb. Done as a day trip, the lake is another "poodle walk" for the French, though dogs must be kept on a lead and are banned beyond the *hôtellerie*.

From the top of the lift, continue south two hours to the 2005-refurbished *Refuge des Oulettes de Gaube* (2151m; Ⓣ05.62.92.62.97; 120 places; staffed daily May 15–Oct, by arrangement winter), poised to contemplate the gaunt north face of Vignemale. You'd need an extra overnight to tackle the peak from here; casual walkers continue east steeply over the **Col d'Arraillé** (2583m), which permits passage to the far less crowded Vallée de Lutour at the boundary of PNP territory.

The next suggested overnight stop is *Refuge d'Estom* (1804m; Ⓣ05.62.92.74.86; 30 places; staffed June–Sept), perched by its lake; staying an extra night here you can explore the half-dozen sizeable **Soubiran lakes** hiding under the crags defining the head of Lutour. The main itinerary carries on north along the valley for a very easy half-day back towards Cauterets, joining the Val de Jéret at La Raillère; about forty minutes before the latter you meet the end of the narrow but paved road in at *Hôtel La Fruitière* (Ⓣ05.62.92.52.04, Ⓕ05.62.92.06.12; open April–Nov 15; ❷). The rooms here will do in an emergency but the restaurant abuses its monopoly, being twenty percent overpriced for average food.

Traverse to Lac d'Estaing via the GR10

One exception to the pattern of walks arrayed around the Pont d'Espagne is the day-long traverse from Cauterets to **Lac d'Estaing** in the eponymous valley via the Lac d'Ilhéou, following the main **GR10**. Taking the **Télécabine du Lys** from just above boulevard B. Dulau in Cauterets up to the Cirque du Lys at 1850m (July–Aug about every 30min 9am–12.15pm & 1.45–5.45pm; €5 single, €7.50 return) spares you the sharp initial climb, while continuing on the ski area's **Grand Barbat** chair-lift (approx same schedule; €8/9.50 for a combined one-way/return ticket with the Télécabine du Lys) brings you to the Crêtes du Lys, actually 500m higher than the Lac d'Ilhéou, with 45min on foot separating you from the refuge there (see opposite). Without any assistance from mechanical lifts, it will take you the better part of three hours, heading up the Vallée du Cambasque, to draw level with the **Lac d'Ilhéou**, best seen in June when ice floes drift on its calm surface and the surrounding peaks such as Grand Barbat (2813m) are still frosted with snow. The modern, PNP-built *Refuge d'Ilhéou* (1988m; ⓣ05.62.92.52.38; 32 places) at the northeast end of the lake is staffed all summer and also offers pricey meals and drinks on its outdoor terrace. From here the GR10 bears northwest out of the *parc national*, over the grassy **Col d'Ilhéou** (2242m), dropping down to Lac d'Estaing, with its hotel and campsite, after four more hours.

Skiing around Cauterets

With 36km of **cross-country** pistes (mostly red-rated), the **Plateau du Clot** area makes an excellent place to indulge, or you could embark on a **ski-touring** ascent (369m elevation change over 7km) of the the Marcadau valley to *Refuge Wallon* (sporadically staffed in winter), which should take around three to four hours for beginners; count on half that to descend.

Beyond the refuge, there are possible itineraries into Spain via the **Col de la Fache/Cuello da Faxa** and the **Port du Marcadau/Puerto de Panticosa** into the Panticosa region, or the **Col d'Arratille** into the Ara valley, but these are for experts only, despite their relative ease as summer walking passes.

Downhill skiing: Lys-Courbet

Cauterets' reputation for **downhill skiing** is perhaps inflated, but by Pyrenean standards it has a good snow record, and conditions aren't too bad despite the sunny, easterly exposure at the principal area of **Lys-Courbet** at the top of the Vallée de Cambasque. It's accessible either by 6km of road from Cauterets, or the *télécabine* described above (included in the lift *forfait*). There's no ski rental at the **Cambasque** car park (1350m), and often no *navette* from Cauterets, so non-drivers should take the *télécabine* all way up from town; drivers use the "egg-shell" Télécabine Courbet to the base of the **Cirque du Lys** (1850m; rental, snack bar). From there, five chair-lifts (top point 2500m) climb to strategic points on the ridge leading off 2657-metre Soum de Grum – the long, aptly named "Crêtes" run yields great views, though "Gentiane" and "Dryade" are more challenging – but the piste network isn't extensive, and most of the 21 runs descend to Point 1850. Nonetheless, it's a good place to hone intermediate skills, with a preponderance of blue and red runs, though they're often poorly marked, so it's easy to stray onto the wrong piste – or off piste, for which there's plenty of (intentional) scope.

Pau

Once capital of the medieval viscounty of Béarn, and now of the modern *département* of Pyrénées-Atlantiques, the pleasant, surprisingly cosmopolitan city of **PAU** lies some 40km west of Tarbes. From this major stop on the main east–west rail line along the base of the French Pyrenees, you can move on to Bayonne and the Basque country, or directly south to the PNP through the Vallée d'Ossau. You may well prefer to use Pau, rather than Lourdes, as a base for heading into the mountains: transport is no problem and Pau is a far more amenable place.

The city first rose to prominence in 1464, when it became capital of Béarn (and Navarre) under Jean d'Albret and his wife Catherine of Navarre. In 1567 their descendant Henri d'Albret married the sister of the French king François I, Marguerite d'Angoulême, a writer of some gifts who turned the local court into a focus of the arts. Her daughter, Jeanne d'Albret, was by contrast a Protestant

△ Bridge and castle, Pau

philistine, bringing ruin to Pau and its environs during the Wars of Religion, when her armies and those of Charles IX rivalled each other in atrocities committed. Temporary peace was restored upon the accession of her son Henri IV to the French throne in 1589, but Béarn itself was not formally annexed by Paris until 1620 by Henri IV's son Louis XIII.

Pau entered the spotlight once more with the arrival of Wellington and his troops in 1814, following their defeat of Maréchal Soult at nearby Orthez. So taken were they by the place that many officers returned in retirement, inaugurating an English colony which would endure for a century. By the early 1860s fifteen percent of the city's population was English, encouraged by the tireless (and ultimately wrong-headed) promotion of Pau's climate as especially curative for tuberculosis patients, by a certain Dr Alexander Taylor. Enduring legacies of the English include the continuing pursuit of horse-racing, fox-hunting, polo, cricket, golf (the first eighteen-hole course in Europe was here), rugby and a few surviving tearooms. When the train line reached Pau in 1866, the French intelligentsia came too, including Victor Hugo, Stendhal and Lamartine.

Although the city has mere 212m elevation, it's the only one this side of the Pyrenees with any palpable mountain identity. From the escarpment of **boulevard des Pyrénées** which bounds downtown Pau on the south, you can see a hundred-kilometre stretch of peaks, including Pic du Midi de Bigorre and Pic d'Anie, all identified on a handy *table d'orientation*. In the time of Henry Russell – buried in Pau – the boulevard provided the finest vantage point for the north face of the Pyrenees, overlooking eighty peaks including Vignemale. Now the view is diminished by new construction and frequent air pollution, but on a clear day it's still an evocative introduction to the mountains.

Pau's atmosphere (in all senses) changed substantially in the 1950s when natural gas was discovered just northwest at Lacq, creating new jobs, suburbs and spin-off industries – plus massive air pollution, subsequently reduced by filtration and the steady depletion of the gas deposits. With the end in sight for that industry, Pau has assumed new identities – most obviously as a student town, courtesy of the 1972-opened University of Pau, whose 15,000-strong student body support a lively events schedule – and a research and technology hub. High-end designer shops downtown are juxtaposed somewhat jarringly with large African and Asian immigrant communities in the northern suburbs, as marginalized as they are elsewhere in France.

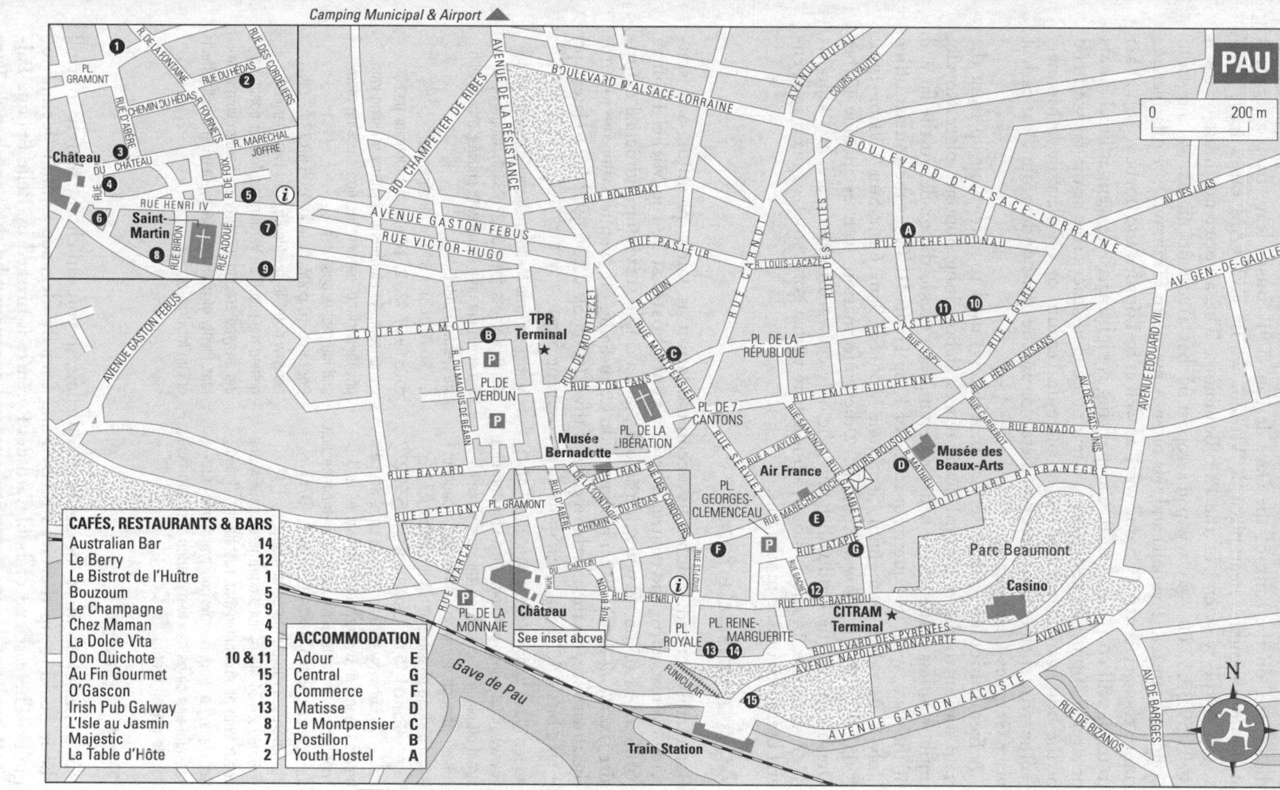
PAU
0 200 m
Camping Municipal & Airport
Tarbes
Oloron-Sainte-Marie
Lourdes
N
BOULEVARD D'ALSACE-LORRAINE
AVENUE DE LA RÉSISTANCE
BD. CHAMPETIER DE RIBES
AVENUE GASTON FEBUS
RUE VICTOR-HUGO
RUE BOURBAKI
RUE PASTEUR
RUE CARNOT
RUE DES ALLIÉS
RUE MICHEL HOUNAU
AV. DES LILAS
AV. GEN.-DE-GAULLE
AVENUE EDOUARD VII
AV. DES ÉTATS UNIS
AVENUE DUFAU
COURS LYAUTEY
COURS CAMOU
TPR Terminal
PL. DE VERDUN
R. DU MAQUIS DE BÉARN
RUE DE MONTPEZET
RUE D'ORLÉANS
RUE MONTPENSIER
PL. DE LA RÉPUBLIQUE
RUE CASTETNAU
RUE E. GARET
RUE HENRI FAISANS
RUE LESPY
RUE EMILE GUICHENNÉ
PL. DE 7 CANTONS
PL. DE LA LIBÉRATION
Musée Bernadotte
RUE SERVIEZ
RUE SAMONZAT
RUE A. TAYLOR
Air France
COURS BOSQUET
RUE CARREROT
RUE BONADO
Musée des Beaux-Arts
R. MATHIEU
BOULEVARD BARBANÈGRE
RUE BAYARD
RUE TRAN
RUE DES CORDELIERS
PL. GEORGES-CLEMENCEAU
RUE MARECHAL FOCH
RUE GAMBETTA
RUE D'ÉTIGNY
PL. GRAMONT
RUE D'ABÈRE
CHEMIN DU HÉDAS
RUE LATAPIE
Parc Beaumont
Casino
RUE ST-LOUIS
RUE GACHET
RUE LOUIS-BARTHOU
CITRAM Terminal
RUE MARCA
PL. DE LA MONNAIE
Château
RUE DU CHÂTEAU
RUE BIRON
RUE HENRI IV
See inset above
PL. ROYALE
PL. REINE-MARGUERITE
BOULEVARD DES PYRÉNÉES
AVENUE NAPOLÉON BONAPARTE
AVENUE L SAY
FUNICULAR
Gave de Pau
Train Station
AVENUE GASTON LACOSTE
RUE DE BIZANOS
AV. DE BARÈGES
R. DE LA FONTAINE
RUE DU HÉDAS
R. FOURNETS
R. MARECHAL JOFFRE
R. DE FOIX
RUE ADOUE
Saint-Martin
CAFÉS, RESTAURANTS & BARS
Australian Bar 14
Le Berry 12
Le Bistrot de l'Huître 1
Bouzoum 5
Le Champagne 9
Chez Maman 4
La Dolce Vita 6
Don Quichote 10 & 11
Au Fin Gourmet 15
O'Gascon 3
Irish Pub Galway 13
L'Isle au Jasmin 8
Majestic 7
La Table d'Hôte 2
ACCOMMODATION
Adour E
Central G
Commerce F
Matisse D
Le Montpensier C
Postillon B
Youth Hostel A

Arrival and information

The **train station** (and terminal for SNCF buses) lies at the southern edge of the centre, on the bank of the Gave de Pau. TPR **buses** leave from a terminal at 4 rue Lapouble, near place de Verdun, whilst CITRAM buses leave from a stop at the west end of the Parc Beaumont. The **airport** northeast of town (Ⓣ05.59.33.33.00, Ⓦwww.pau.aeroport.fr) has frequent flights to and from London Stansted (Ryanair) and less often Amsterdam (Transavia); regular *navettes* run to the city centre (€5 one way), as well as to Lourdes and Tarbes (€6); a taxi to town will cost about €20. **Car-parking** is nightmarish (except at lunch hours or after 6.30pm); there are often a few unmetered spaces free at the far west end of the boulevard des Pyrénées, on place de Verdun, or on place de la Monnaie – otherwise shell out for kerbside meters or use the giant underground car park at place Georges-Clemenceau.

A **free funicular** (out of service indefinitely) used to carry you up from the train station to the boulevard des Pyrénées, debouching opposite place Royale; until or unless it's repaired, pedestrian rampways tackle the grade. At the far end of the *place*, with its equestrian statue of King Henri III/IV, is the **tourist office** (July & Aug daily 9am–6pm; Sept–June Mon–Sat 9am–6pm, Sun 9.30am–1pm; Ⓣ05.59.27.27.08, Ⓦwww.pau.fr). Other information sources include Cyber Dreams, 9–11 rue Emil Guichenné, the only central **Internet** café, and Librairie des Pyrénées at 14 rue St-Louis, a **bookstore** with a good stock of maps and general literature on the mountains.

Accommodation

Reasonably priced, salubrious **accommodation** is fairly plentiful, and scattered evenly across the centre. There's a **youth hostel** at 30 rue Michel-Hounau (Ⓣ05.59.11.05.05, Ⓦwww.ldjpau.org), and a single surviving municipal **campsite**, *La Plaine des Sports* on boulevard du Cami-Salié, off avenue Sallenave towards the autoroute, on the northern edge of town (Ⓣ05.59.02.30.49; May to late Sept) – take bus #4, "Palais des Sports", to cover the 5km.

Adour 10 rue Valéry-Meunier Ⓣ05.59.27.47.41, Ⓦwww.hotel-adour-pau.com. On a little-travelled street off place Clemenceau, this has some en-suites – though alarming pink decor throughout – and parking possible at night outside. ❸

Central 15 rue Léon-Daran Ⓣ05.59.27.72.75, Ⓦwww.hotelcentralpau.com. Soundproofed rooms in two grades ("*economie*" and "*confort*"), with tasteful rooms and wi-fi connection throughout; parking nearby is difficult. ❷/❹

Commerce 9 rue du Maréchal-Joffre Ⓣ05.59.27.24.40, Ⓔhotel.commerce.pau@wanadoo.fr. With all amenities (bar, restaurant, closed Sun) facing a long, narrow courtyard, this caravanserai-like place has two grades of comfortable, double-glazed rooms. ❸/❹

Matisse 17 rue Mathieu-Lalanne, opposite Musée des Beaux Arts Ⓣ05.59.27.73.80. Rooms here are smart enough, some with shower, others with shower and toilet. ❷

Le Montpensier 36 rue Montpensier Ⓣ05.59.27.42.72, Ⓔhotel.montpensier-pau@wanadoo.fr. An eighteenth-century building with private parking, garden, lift, non-smoking rooms and internet access. ❸

Postillon 10 cours Camou Ⓣ05.59.72.83.00, Ⓦwww.hotel-le-postilon.fr. This two-star just behind the place de Verdun is a former coaching inn arrayed around a courtyard-garden with fountain. Plenty of parking nearby, making this the best option for drivers. ❸

The Town

Pau possesses no must-see sights or museums, so you can choose merely to stroll about, soaking up the city's relaxed and friendly elegance without feeling too guilty. The east end of boulevard des Pyrénées is marked by Belle Époque **Palais Beaumont**, now a convention centre, surrounded by the English-style **Parc**

Beaumont. At the opposite end of the boulevard, the landmark **Château** (exterior gardens free & unenclosed) overlooks the bridge over the Gave de Pau on the vital Bordeaux–Zaragoza route. The first castle here was built by Gaston Fébus as part of his strategy to create a unified Pyrenean kingdom; more importantly, Henri III of Foix-Béarn, king of Navarre and later **Henri IV of France**, was born in the castle in 1553.

An adroit politician, Henri renounced his Protestant faith to assume the French throne, quipping that "Paris is worth a Mass" and then appeasing the regional sensibilities of his Béarnais subjects by announcing that he was giving France to Béarn rather than Béarn to France. (Like other Pyrenean feudal counties, it retained separatist leanings centuries after incorporation into France, and many Béarnais still speak their dialect of Gascon along with French – and Gascon-language street signs are making their appearance here.) Pau's most famous son, Henri had a suitably colourful reputation. He was baptized in traditional Béarnais style with the local Jurançon wine, while his infant lips were rubbed with garlic; by adulthood he was known as the *vert-galant* for his romantic prowess. He also gave France one of its more famous recipes, *poulet au pot* – chicken stuffed and boiled with vegetables – legendarily saying that he wished no one in his realm so poor as not to be able to afford a *poulet* in the pot once a week.

At the time of Henri's birth the castle was somewhat neglected, only Gaston Fébus' original brick keep remaining in an otherwise grey monolith. The d'Albrets added some sophisticated touches, like the Renaissance windows and doorways, but the most substantial alterations – including the addition of an arcade and tower close to the entrance – were carried out during the nineteenth century, first by Louis-Philippe and then by Napoléon III and Eugénie.

Inside the castle, the **Musée National** (daily: mid-June to mid-Sept 9am–12.15pm & 1.30–5.45pm; mid-Sept to mid-June 9.30–11.45am & 2–5pm; €5 except €3.50 Sun) consists essentially of Napoléon III's and Eugénie's nineteenth century apartments, with stellar vaulting, coffered ceilings hung with chandeliers, statuary, huge fireplaces and marble-relief lintels. These are expatiated on in minute detail during the skull-thumpingly boring one-hour guided visit (French only but summary sheet provided), the only way also to take in some vivid eighteenth-century tapestries with their wonderfully observed scenes of hunting, sheep-shearing, card-playing, harvesting and picnicking. The career of Henri IV is followed in portraits from various stages of his life, plus the legendary giant tortoise shell which allegedly served as his cradle in the top-floor room of his birth.

Just north of the castle, defined by ravine-bottom chemin du Hédas, is the **quartier du Hédas**, what remains of medieval Pau (except for some houses by place de Monnaie south of the château). At the base of the descending **rue René-Fournets** is a small square with an ancient fountain – the only source of water before the Revolution. The main farmers' market takes place around the *halles* on nearby place de la République each Saturday morning.

Immediately north of Hédas, at 6 rue Tran, the mildly interesting **Musée Bernadotte** (Tues–Sun 10am–noon & 2–6pm; €3) occupies the birthplace of the man who, having served as a commander under Napoleon, went on to become Charles XIV of Sweden in 1818. The house contains fine traditional Béarnaise furniture and some valuable works of art collected over his lifetime. At the west end of rue Tran, the arcaded **place Gramont** with its active fountains is more compelling for most, despite its use as a parking area.

Pau's final museum, the **Musée des Beaux Arts** (daily except Tues 10am–noon & 2–6pm; €3), well east on rue Mathieu-Lalanne, houses an eclectic collection of (sometimes deservedly) obscure works from various European schools spanning the fourteenth to twentieth centuries. It's strong on locally born painters such as Eugène Devéria or Victor Galos – two of the few artists to have discovered the Pyrenean landscape – and Alfred de Richemont, with his intimate *The Sacrifice* (two women burning love letters). But the only really world-class items are Rubens' *The Last Judgement* (ground floor) and Degas' famous *The Cotton Exchange* (upstairs), a slice of finely observed Belle Époque New Orleans.

Eating, drinking and nightlife

Pau has a fair quantity of affordable, varied places to eat and drink, concentrated in the pleasant pedestrian lanes around the château (slightly touristy), place Royale, and the quartier du Hédas (less so). If you've exotic cravings, this is a relatively good place for Moroccan, Indian or Indochinese cuisine. Bars and cafés on boulevard de Pyrénées are at their liveliest during the hours either side of sunset; later the crowds tend to go to the student pubs or pricey clubs around the Hédas multiplex cinema, near the *Hôtel Commerce*. In terms of **formal entertainment**, the municipal theatre on rue Saint-Louis and the church of Saint-Martin around the corner host various events.

Restaurants

Le Berry rue Gachet, near corner rue Louis-Barthou. Less than brilliant siting by the "rabbit hole" of a subterranean car park, which detracts from outdoor seating, but compensated for by excellent brasserie grub (*magret de canard*, Chateaubriand steaks). Expect a wait for interior tables; service until 11pm; budget €20–28 à la carte.

Le Bistrot de l'Huître rue Tran, corner place Gramont. As it says – and pricey, but there are attractive lunch specials (eg €14 for a dozen oysters plus two other platters), salads and other seafood. The pleasant interior is more inviting than sidewalk seating.

Le Champagne 5 place Royale. Newish, popular, upscale brasserie with *carte* or five *formules* at €11–22; there's a lovely interior with swirling fans, or eat out on the *place* in fine weather. Service barely copes with the crush, however.

Chez Maman 6 rue de Château. Simple but palatable *crêperie/cidrerie* overlooking the castle, which doesn't unduly abuse its unbeatable position. A good option for vegetarians, with big salads – for two courses and a bit of cider you'll have change from a 20-euro note. Open Tues–Sun 11am–midnight.

La Dolce Vita 13 rue du Moulin. Salads, good pizzas and pasta dishes, a few grills and Italian wines at €18–20 (à la carte) make this the most popular pizzeria in this area.

Don Quichote 30 & 38 rue Castetnau (two premises). Convenient for the youth hostel, this has authentic Spanish fare (paella, chorizo, parillada, zarzuela) at budget prices – eat and drink for little more than a (euro) tenner each. Closed Sat & Mon noon, all Sun.

Au Fin Gourmet, 24 av Gaston-Lacoste, opposite train station. Trim, modern place with a few game-oriented lunch *menus* (pigeon, rabbit) from €17, but best allow €35-plus à la carte. Closed Sun eve & Mon, plus 2 weeks mid-summer.

O'Gascon 13 rue du Château. The most popular and reasonable of the four non-pizzerias on this little *place*; their €27 *menu tradition* – big salad, stuffed quail, free dessert choice – is excellent. Supper Mon–Sat plus Sun lunch.

Majestic 9 place Royal. Cutting-edge cooking (pigeon with cèpes, confit canneloni) at affordable prices: somewhat dull lunch *menu* €17, more exciting at €26–35. Lovely outdoor seating on the place in fine weather; closed Sun eve & all Mon.

La Table d'Hôte 1 rue du Hédas. Elegant restaurant in a bare-brick-walled former warehouse, one of the first to colonize this trendy area and relying on the backbone of traditional French cooking: duck, pork, *foie gras*, lamb. Affordable *menus* at €23–29; service can be leisurely. Closed all Sun, Mon lunch.

Bars, cafés and tea rooms

Australian Bar 20 bd des Pyrénées. Pretty much as it says, with decor and TV fare to match.

Bouzoum 6 rue Henri IV. The most prestigious of the surviving tearooms, with a wide range of patisserie; indoor seating only.

Irish Pub Galway 22 bd des Pyrénées. No comment on authenticity, but it is packed from late afternoon onwards.

L'Isle au Jasmin 28 bd des Pyrénées. Tea (dozens of varieties) served outside on chaise longues facing the view. Daily except Wed 10am–7pm.

The Ossau and Aspe valleys

The parallel north–south valleys of the **Ossau** and **Aspe**, beginning about 20km south-southwest of Pau, are the French Pyrenees at their most *sauvage*, though this hasn't prevented the complete extinction of the native **brown bears** that used to roam locally (see p.386). The Aspe valley is less developed because inappropriate topography and unreliable snow conditions have precluded ski-resort construction – but what tourism has failed to do, a major road-building scheme threatens to achieve (see box on pp.394–395). Even before this, both valleys were major arteries into Spain. Along these main roads – the D934 through Ossau, the N134 along the Aspe – the steep, densely forested sides obscure everything other than the valley-bottom rivers and the villages directly on their banks. To see the best of the region, you need to walk perpendicular to the line of the valleys.

Currently French train service ceases at **Oloron-Sainte-Marie**, though the reopening of the transborder service is being debated. Coming from Pau, you bypass Oloron completely en route to the Vallée d'Ossau, which has most to offer near the border: surprisingly good skiing at **Gourette**, the touristic train ride up to **Lac d'Artouste**, tough climbing on **Balaïtous** peak and easier, classic rambles around the **Pic du Midi d'Ossau**. Highlight of the Vallée d'Aspe, and likely to remain undisturbed by any road-widening project, is the **Cirque de Lescun**: not so grand as Gavarnie's, but infinitely satisfying by virtue of its unexpectedness in a much gentler landscape.

Oloron-Sainte-Marie

The Ossau and the Aspe valleys join 33km southwest of Pau at **OLORON-SAINTE-MARIE**, a small town reverberating with the roar of the mingling rivers – and even more so, the roar of traffic converging from three directions. It's the traditional centre for manufacturing the Béarn woollen **beret**, once standard headgear for all French men but now seldom seen. Nowadays, the single surviving factory has diversified into fashion hats for both sexes, though they still make berets for armed forces worldwide. Overall it's a tolerable, if rather sprawling place, older Oloron poised opposite board-flat Sainte-Marie.

Oloron grew from Celto-Iberian/Roman Iluro, founded on a hill just south of the river confluence, where today's Sainte-Croix quarter is located. When barbarians threatened to take the settlement, the inhabitants crossed the Gave d'Ossau and founded Sainte-Marie, which later became the episcopal seat, while Sainte-Croix evolved into a commercial and military centre.

The town's two churches are the sole points of interest. Hilltop **Sainte-Croix**, one of the oldest Romanesque structures in Béarn, has unusual interior vaulting, created by thirteenth-century Spanish stonemasons in imitation of the Great Mosque at Córdoba; upheld by six massive piers, it dominates the two-aisled interior, extremely austere except for a few ornate capitals near the apse.

The Romanesque-Gothic cathedral of **Sainte-Marie** across the Gave d'Aspe glories in an ornately sculpted portal that has escaped damage by religious vandals – even during the Revolution – thanks to the extremely durable Pyrenean marble from which it is constructed. In the upper arch, the elders of the Apocalypse play violins and rebecs, while in the second arch scenes from medieval life – hunting wild boar and fishing for salmon – are represented. Above the left-hand door, the Persecution of the Church is balanced by the Triumph of the Church over the opposite door. The gallant knight on horseback over the outer column on the right is Gaston IV, count of Béarn, who commissioned the portal on his return from the first Crusade at the beginning of the twelfth century – hence the inclusion of

The "Pyrenean" brown bear

Compared to the American grizzly or the bears of Siberia, the Pyrenean brown bear – *Ursos arctos* – is **small and timid**, its diet largely herbivorous, which restricts it to forested terrain below 1800m. (A full-grown male can attain 300kg and females 200kg, but average much less.) The bear was long **exploited as a symbol** by various factions in the Vallée d'Aspe. Lobbyists opposed to the Tunnel de Somport scheme (see box on pp.394–395) used the presumed fate of the bear as ammunition to slow, though ultimately not stop, the project. Trail signposting for the Vallée d'Aspe still depicts a cute cub clutching a flower, giving the misleading impression that the beasts are as common and loved as in North America's Yellowstone Park.

The **decline of the native bear population** in the Pyrenees was startlingly rapid. In 1937 there were still an estimated 150–200 in the French Pyrenees. By 1954 numbers were down to about 70; by 1960 they had declined to 40, and following the shooting of the last autochtonous bear in November 2004, there are none left.

Such facts seem incontrovertible; what sparks heated debate is just why the bears disappeared. Majority opinion credits the age-old hostility of pastoral communities to the animals, who occasionally bag stray livestock. In the past this led to instant **bounty-hunting,** which has been illegal since 1962, and the animal livestock has been absolutely protected since 1981; today the government pays prompt, ample compensation for such losses. Rural activities such as wood-cutting, berry-picking, bee-keeping and grazing are also blamed for disturbing the animals. In parts of the Ossau and Aspe valleys such endeavours are severely restricted or banned, much to local annoyance; until 1993 national policymakers mooted setting aside of large tracts of land as off-limits to humans.

This conventional wisdom was challenged by scientists who asserted that bears actually thrive in proximity to humans. Their habitat is also not as restricted as previously thought – paw-prints have been sighted as low as 400m, and a den was detected near a roadworks site at 350m, proving tolerance of noisy human activity. These experts considered **depopulation** to be the main reason for declining bear numbers, citing as an example the nearby Ariège, abandoned simultaneously by people and bears alike. Such revisionists maintained that bears and country-dwellers should sort themselves out by whatever means, barring shotgun massacres – by stoutly fencing berry-patches and beehives, and provision of fiercer guard-dogs to shepherds, rather than banning humans from traditional mountain livelihoods. Unfortunately the truth of competing arguments was not established before native bears, for whatever reason, disappeared.

"**Restocking**" programmes with "immigrants" have had decidedly mixed results, but are now the only option. Three Slovenian bears released during 1996–98 at Melles in the Ariège promptly sired seven offspring who all left the area, shunning feeding sites in favour of sheep-bagging. Nearly eighty dead animals resulted before local shepherds shot the main offender, leaving her two cubs orphaned. Though Slovenian bears are less afraid of humans and more aggressive, the *ariégois* practice of leaving sheep unsupervised did not help. In Aspe-Ossau, where sheep are milked regularly and closely looked after by shepherds and dogs, just 27 sheep were killed by bears during 2000; throughout the Pyrenees in 2001, just 330 sheep were lost to bears, far fewer than those dying from accidents or attacks by stray dogs. A minority of shepherds – the dedicated ones who actually guard their sheep, rather than turning them loose all summer and collecting subsidies – accepts that coexistence of wild bears and pastoralism is a price worth paying in terms of an enhanced public image of the Pyrenees.

There are now between 14 and 18 bears in the entire Pyrenees, all descendants of "restocked" specimens, but there are too many males; accordingly four Slovenian females and one male were set loose during mid-2006 near Luchon and Bagnères-de-Bigorre, among other amenable spots. Localities vary considerably in their receptivity to release schemes; while much of the Ariège is speckled with hostile 'OURS NON' or 'OURS = DANGER' graffiti, the approaches to Luchon have stencilled bear-paw silhouettes with a succinct 'OUI'.

Saracens in chains amongst the sculptures supporting the portal. Inside the church, well away from the main area of worship, stands a Cagot stoup, a stark reminder of the long persecution and segregation of this mysterious group (see box on p.349).

Practicalities

The **train station** lies 200m west of the river confluence; CITRAM and SNCF **buses** from Pau arrive in place de la Gare out front. The **tourist office** (July & Aug Mon–Sat 9am–7pm, Sun 10am–1pm; Sept–June Mon–Sat 9am–12.30pm & 2–6.30pm; ⓣ05.59.39.98.00, ⓦwww.ot-oloron-ste-marie.fr) is on the west bank of the Aspe, housed in the Villa Bourdeu, amidst vast car parks which **drivers** should use.

It's unlikely that you'll need, or want, to stay the night in Oloron; that said, **accommodation** nearby includes the Hôtel Bristol at 9 rue Carréot (ⓣ05.59.39.43.78, ⓕ05.59.39.08.19; ❷) with a restaurant (*menus* from €18; closed Sun lunch), or the 2004-refurbished *Hôtel de la Paix* at 24 av Sadi-Carnot opposite the train station (ⓣ05.59.39.02.63; ❸), quiet despite the location and with easier parking. Of higher standard than either of these is the British-run *Château d'Agnos*, 2km south of town via Bidos (ⓣ05.59.36.12.52, ⓦperso.orange.fr/chateaudagnos; ❹–❻ B&B), a sixteenth-century hunting lodge with period furnishings, run as a *chambres d'hôtes* (there are also self-catering studios in outbuildings, ❹). Closest **campsite** is tree-shaded *Camping du Stade* on the D919 heading southwest towards Arette (ⓣ05.59.39.11.26; May–Sept). **Restaurant** choice is limited; try *Le Biscondau* (shut Sun eve, Mon) on rue de la Filature, overlooking the Ossau; cheap and cheerful *La Cour des Miracles* at 13 place de la Cathédral, with a view of the Romanesque facade; and a Moroccan, *Samia*, in Oloron on place Amédée Gabe.

Transport up the valleys

Since the closure of the international rail link through the Aspe valley to Spain, Oloron-Sainte-Marie has been the end of the line for **trains** from Pau. Connecting SNCF **buses** run daily south up the Vallée d'Aspe to Urdos (a few of these going on to Canfranc in Spain), and several daily SNCF services, beginning as a Pau–Buzy train, head from the latter up the Vallée d'Ossau to Laruns, supplemented by CITRAM buses from Pau to Gourette, east of Laruns. On July and August weekdays only, Pic Bus offers service all the way up to the frontier at Col du Pourtalet, via Gabas and the Fabrèges dam, with occasional diversions to the car park below the Lac de Bious.

Along the lower Ossau

Along the **lower Ossau** between Oloron and Laruns, there are really only two places worth stopping. At **ARUDY**, the **Maison d'Ossau** (July & Aug daily 10am–noon & 3–6pm; Sept–June Mon 10am–noon, Tues, Thurs & Sat 2.30–5pm, Sun 3–6pm; €3), housed in the village church, offers a comprehensive account of the prehistoric Pyrenees and an exhibition of the flora and fauna of the *parc national*. **ASTE-BÉON**, a few kilometres further up-valley, is home to **La Falaise aux Vautours** (ⓦwww.falaise-aux-vautours.com; May & Sept 2–6pm; daily: June–Aug 10.30am–12.30pm & 2–6.30pm; school hols 2–5pm; €6), a highly worthwhile vulture-breeding and -viewing centre, where images of vulture families going about their business are transmitted to a giant viewing screen by cameras trained on nests. Telescopes and binoculars are also available for more low-tech viewing, and staff lead walking safaris to pastures where the vultures feed.

If you have transport, a more alluring route into the Ossau starts in the Aspe valley at Escot, from where you cut across over the **Col de Marie-Blanque** (1035m) – through thick beech forests and uplands where more vultures wheel overhead – before descending again through pines to the Ossau valley at Bielle, some 7km north of Laruns. All along the lower Ossau, the influence of the Atlantic is strong, the fields an Irish green and the forests deciduous. Although it's still some way from the Basque country, many of the villages have a *frontón*, the court used for the Basque game of *pelote*.

Laruns

The best time to visit **LARUNS**, 4km upstream from Aste-Béon, is indisputably at the main August 15 festival when young people kitted in traditional red and black costumes dance to a one-man band of three-holed flute and tambourine. Otherwise it's undistinguished but pleasant, and the last place to buy provisions before heading up to the PNP. The tourist office on the main place de la Mairie (Mon–Sat 9am–12.30pm & 2–6.30pm, Sun 9am–noon & 2–6pm; ⓣ05.59.05.31.41, ⓦwww.valleedossau-tourisme.com) stands back-to-back with a **Maison du Parc** (mid-June to mid-Sept daily 10am–1pm & 2–6.30pm; ⓣ05.59.05.41.59). **Accommodation** includes the central *Hôtel d'Ossau* (ⓣ05.59.05.30.14; ❸), with a restaurant out front, or the characterful Hôtel de France, at the eastern end of town opposite the disused *gare SNCF* (ⓣ05.59.05.33.71; ❸). There's also *Chalet-Refuge L'Embaradère* (ⓣ05.59.05.41.88; 28 places; closed Mon–Tues low season), diagonally opposite the *Hôtel de France*, offering inexpensive meals. The nearest all-year campsites are *Ayguebere* (ⓣ05.59.05.38.55) and *Pont Lauguère* (ⓣ05.59.05.35.99), both in Le Pon quarter near the old train station.

Two of the town's few independent **restaurants** are found on rue du Bourguet off the square: *L'Arrégalet* at no. 37 (closed lunch Mon & Tues), strong on local recipes such as *poule au pot* and the namesake dish – garlic-bread crumbs sautéed in goose grease – washed down with a strictly local wine list, and *Auberge Bellevue* at no. 55 (closed Mon eve & all Tues low season), with three varied *menus* encompassing *cèpes*, pigeon or crayfish, and brasserie grub available between main-meal hours.

△ Horses, lower Lac d'Ayous

Eaux-Bonnes and the Vallée du Valentin

East of Laruns, the D918 heads up the tributary **Vallée du Valentin** to the spa of Eaux-Bonnes (4km) and the ski station of Gourette (10km), last stop (after Laruns) for most CITRAM buses out of Pau, from July to mid-September and again during ski season. **EAUX-BONNES**, yet another Second Empire watering-hole, has been tidied up, though its elegant central square remains a traffic hippodrome. A seasonal **tourist office** (summer Mon–Sat 9am–12.30pm & 1.30–6pm, Sun 10am–noon & 3–6pm; ⓣ05.59.05.33.08) occupies a gazebo on the Jardin Darralde, the landscaped, inclined core of the "race track". Best of three surviving **hotels** is Logis de France member *De La Poste* (ⓣ05.59.05.33.06, ⓦwww.hotel-dela-poste.com; ❸) in the centre, with well-appointed if old-style rooms arrayed around a four-storey atrium; take half-board as the four-course *table d'hôte* supper is excellent value. Like many spas near ski resorts, the **thermal baths** at Eaux-Bonnes stay open in peak ski season (daily 5–7pm), with one of the nicer group pools in the Pyrenees; hours otherwise can be erratic.

Gourette

GOURETTE is where the *Palois* ski, and the crush at peak times is such that cars are halted at a lower parking area 1.5km before the resort, and their passengers shuttled up in a free *navette*. The high-rise development at 1350m is dense and unsightly, and the altitude means that the half-dozen lowest of 28 runs are often unusable, and the bottom where everyone finishes is always a chewed-up mess. The good news is that most runs face north, so the higher slopes are usually in good shape; moreover Gourette's predominantly red runs are definitely of the blue-ish persuasion, making the entire domain accessible to any reasonably competent skier, with eight well-placed chairs or *télécabines* among nineteen lifts in total. Serious skiing begins from Point 2124m (served by the Cotch and Fontaines de Cotch chairs), and Point 2400m, accessed by two successive bubble-lifts. The Pène Blanque run from Point 2400 feels wild and alpine as it threads through a slightly spooky mixed forest; continuing onto the L'Amoulat and Les Bosses runs yields a nice long descent to the base of the Fontaines chair, and thence back into the marginally less difficult Cotch sector. There's a better than usual range of eateries overlooking the upper car park at 1350m, but far more aesthetic and perfectly acceptable are two on-piste restaurants.

Among several **hotels**, the two least obtrusive and most economical are chalet-style *L'Amoulat* (ⓣ05.59.05.12.06, ❷ summer, ❹ winter) on the road out of "town", with a good restaurant, and *Le Glacier* on the resort's main drag (ⓣ05.59.05.10.18, ⓦwww.leglacier.fr.st; ❸), both open most of the year. In **summer** Gourette's position on the GR10 attracts a walking clientele, who stay in one of two **refuges**: either the *Club Pyrénéa Sport* (staffed July–Sept & Dec 15–April 30; ⓣ05.59.05.12.42; 60 places in dorms or quads), on the main through road, or the CAF *Chalet de Gourette* (ⓣ05.59.05.10.56; all year except late spring/late autumn; 40 places, some quads). There's also a well-stocked outdoor-equipment shop.

The Col d'Aubisque and beyond

East of Gourette, the D918 (and usually the Tour de France) toils up to the **Col d'Aubisque** (1709m, 17km from Laruns) with its summertime café, from which it's another 18km via the Cirque du Litor and the Col de Soulor to Arrens-Marsous. The only other facility en route, 2km above Gourette, is the no-star *Hôtel Les Crêtes Blanches* (ⓣ05.59.05.10.03; ❶), with shared bathrooms and a *table d'hôte* restaurant, which would be more appealing to trekkers if it weren't slightly off the GR10.

The **GR10** east from Gourette actually shortcuts most of the road on its six-hour way to Arrens-Marsous, but there's still too much narrow, dangerous tarmac for it to be a really popular stretch of the "trail". East of Aubisque, the road becomes a dramatic corniche route, threading a few drippy tunnels as it winds over bleak, heather-studded moorland where cattle, sheep and horses graze freely. It's best to enjoy the views over the moorland from your own car, or join the ranks of Tour de France wannabes who pedal between the various local passes.

The upper Ossau

South of Laruns, the Gave d'Ossau narrows drastically as the D934 enters its upper reaches at **EAUX-CHAUDES**, a dozy, rather gloomy nineteenth-century spa whose main bright spot is the excellent *Auberge La Caverne* (ⓣ05.59.05.36.40, ⓦauberge.lacaverne.free.fr; all year), run by a hard-working couple who offer both dorms and doubles (❶) in an atmospheric old building, with constant improvements undertaken (top-floor rooms are best). They also serve very salubrious *table d'hôte* meals (€12 includes house wine and coffee), unusually available all day. The *gave* here also provides some excellent **kayaking** (subject to EDF water-level manipulations).

Gabas

GABAS, 13km south of Laruns, is a one-street hamlet whose pastoral livelihood has long since been outstripped by its role as an important gateway to the PNP. **Accommodation** fills quickly in summer (and at ski season); the most comfortable option, near the south end of "town", is *Hôtel Le Chalet des Pyrénées* (ⓣ05.59.05.30.51, ⓕ05.59.05.33.64; closed Nov; ❸), with vast common areas including a lawn garden, tennis court and restaurant, with the best small but en-suite rooms facing the river. At Gabas' north entrance, *Hôtel Chez Vignau* (ⓣ05.59.05.34.06, ⓕ05.59.05.46.12; all year; ❷) has basic, non-smoking rooms with toilets down the hall, but a good restaurant across the road, featuring delicacies such as eels *persillade*, blueberry pie and *cèpes* rather than chips with everything (*menus* €16–24). The only independent **restaurant** is cheaper, atmospheric *Du Pic du Midi* up the road (*menus* €12–22), where you down suppers of trout and lamb watched over by enormous but docile Pyrenean sheepdogs. There's also the well-run CAF **Chalet-Refuge** (ⓣ05.59.05.33.14; 46 places in dorms; open June–Sept & winter weekends except mid-Oct to mid-Nov) 700m above Gabas, with unusually good food.

Around the Pic du Midi d'Ossau

An undisputed Pyrenean classic despite its modest height (2884m), the handsome, double-tipped **Pic du Midi d'Ossau** rears up in magnificent isolation above the Vallée d'Ossau, its distinctive mitten shape recognizable from a great distance. This is one of those summits, like Canigou and Pedraforca in Catalonia, which inspire an affection bordering on reverence; nicknamed "Jean-Pierre" by the locals, it's essentially the logo of high Béarn.

The first recorded ascent of originally volcanic Pic du Midi was by an anonymous shepherd in 1787, who erected a summit cairn confirming his success. Today the peak remains a tough scramble at the very least, and is more of a mecca for rock-climbers, but two loop-hikes, designed to be completed in a single summer's day, give walkers ever-changing perspectives on the peak. A mandatory **map** investment is either the 1:50,000 Carte de Randonnées no. 3, the IGN 1547 OT or the PNP 1:25,000 no. 1 "Aspe Ossau".

Gabas has the closest conventional accommodation to the Pic du Midi region, but – disregarding the westbound GR10 which adheres to the cited road – the closest real **trailhead** is 4.5km southwest up the minor D231 beside the artificial **Lac de Bious-**

Artigues, so named because it inundated the *artigue*, or high meadow, that formerly existed beside the infant *gave*. There's one daily morning bus uphill, sparing trekkers some dull, steep asphalt-trudging; drivers will be directed by PNP wardens to one of two car-parks, the higher one just above the dam. There are no longer any facilities of note here (though a refuge will supposedly be built in 2008), so come prepared.

The Tour – or Ascent – du Pic du Midi

The classic, anticlockwise **Tour du Pic du Midi** takes seven hours from Lac de Bious-Artigues, beginning on the **GR10** along the eastern shore. About 1000m beyond the southern tip of the lake, or roughly an hour from the car park, the trails divide; take the left-hand path, crossing the **Pont de Bious** and entering the PNP. Continue upstream on the true right bank, across flat, wet terrain until a sign reading "Pombie par Peyreget" directs you left (south). It's a steepish, zigzagging climb along a section of the HRP to the tiny **Lac de Peyreget**, reached just under three hours into the day. Next, slip over the **Col de Peyreget** (2322m), between Pic Peyreget (2487m) and the southern spur of Pic du Midi, and then down past the **Lac de Pombie** to the CAF *Refuge de Pombie* (2031m; ⓣ05.59.05.31.78; 2031m; 50 places; staffed June–Sept, plus weekends May & Oct), well placed for a lunch stop some four hours along – and a mandatory overnight or two if you're planning on bagging the peak.

From the refuge you return to Bious-Artigues within two hours or so via the onward trail north through the **Col de Suzon** (2127m) and **Col de Moundelhs**, bearing west for the final descent over the **Col Long de Magnabaigt** (1655m).

The standard **ascent** of the peak – a fairly easy climb, but busy in summer and plagued by loose-rock falls – begins with a turning west from the Col de Suzon. Once the initial approach is done, things get more serious with moveable iron pegs in one section to make matters more accessible to inexperienced climbers. Occasional cairns mark the easiest course, and you'll reach the wide summit in about four hours from the *col*.

West to the Vallée d'Aspe

To traverse **west** from the Pic du Midi d'Ossau region to the Vallée d'Aspe, start out on the **GR10** as described for the Tour du Pic du Midi, but don't cross the Pont de Bious; instead, keep right at the fork, following a sign reading "Lac d'Ayous 1.30", and continue climbing westwards, initially through forest, to three successive lakes, each larger than the preceding. You arrive at the 2002-rebuilt, PNP-managed *Refuge d'Ayous* (1982m; ⓣ05.59.05.37.00; 47 places; staffed June 15–Sept 15), well under two hours' walk from Bious-Artigues. Staying the night here – you'll likely camp by Lac Gentau below, as the refuge is often full – is rewarded by the best available vantage point for experiencing spectacular sunrises over the Pic du Midi, reflected in Lac Gentau.

The GR10 heads west through the **Col d'Ayous**, then curves away northwards through the **Col de la Hourquette de Larry**, then down through forest and along the spectacular Chemin de la Mâture to Etsaut in the Aspe valley (3hr; see p.397).

The Tour des Lacs

If you're not confident about tackling the longer Tour du Pic du Midi, the **Tour des Lacs**, a lake-rich circuit of about four hours (plus stops) from the Bious-Artigues car park, makes a fine alternative, actually giving better (if more distant) views of "Jean-Pierre". It uses the *Refuge d'Ayous* as a fulcrum and probable lunch halt, and can be combined with the best of the other local *tour* for a longer loop (though you'll need to overnight at one or other of the refuges).

Begin as for the Tour du Pic du Midi at the **Pont de Bious**, where a sign "Lacs d'Ayous 2.30" hints at what you're about to do. Cross the flat meadow on the far side, full of crocuses and grazing livestock in July; veer right (southwest) at the Houn de Peyreget instead of left, and fifteen minutes from Pont de Bious, bear left onto a minor path to avoid continuing along the cow-herders' recent jeep-track, the latter not shown on the recommended 1:50,000 "Béarn" map. Just under an hour from the car park, you'll pass the Cabane de Cap du Pount, then cross the **Gave de Bious** below the Cabanes de la Hosse, where the track ends. The trail now climbs sharply to scenic **Lac Casterau** (1hr 30min) under the eponymous peak (2227m); beyond it you quickly attain a gentle pass (*c.* 2150m) on the west flank of Pic Casterau, high point of the *tour* in all senses. From here there are great views south to the border ridge, beyond Pic d'Astu to Foratata in Spain; on the north, at your feet, lies **Lac Bersau**, presided over by 2400-metre-plus Hourquette and Larry peaks and irresistible for a midday swim or picnic. Next there's a short descent to *Refuge d'Ayous* (2hr 30min); the downhill return to the upper car park will take another 1hr 15min from the refuge, allowing an extra quarter hour for reaching the lower car park.

East or south from Refuge de Pombie

You can trek to or from the *Refuge de Pombie* towards the east or south, without calling at Gabas or the Lac de Bious-Artigues. Heading **east**, descend by path along the Pombie stream, changing banks as necessary, until arriving after ninety minutes at the **Caillou de Soques** car park/trailhead on the D934 road 9km north of the frontier, or 7km south of Gabas. From here you continue across the Gave de Brousset northeast on the clear **HRP** trail to Lac d'Artouste (see below), a steep but scenic four-hour climb via the Col d'Arrious, or directly to *Refuge d'Arrémoulit* from the *col* via Lac d'Arrious and the somewhat vertiginous, exposed ledge-path (steel safety cables fitted) called the Passage d'Orteig.

Leaving Pombie towards the **south**, you shun the Col de Peyreget route in favour of another marked trail leading in one hour to the **Col de Soum** (*c.* 2100m), from where it's as long again via a heavily used path to a car-parking area 1500m north of the border at **Col du Pourtalet/Puerto de Portalet** (1794m). The transborder road is now kept snowploughed all winter, to facilitate French patronage of El Formigal ski resort, 8km southeast. If you get stuck here, there's a small, simple **hotel**, the *Col du Pourtalet* (Ⓣ05.59.05.32.00; ❷), opposite a cluster of *ventas* and *supermercados* on the Spanish side, still exploiting price differences between the two countries for certain items.

Around Balaïtous and Lac d'Artouste

Balaïtous, almost directly east of Pic du Midi d'Ossau across the Gave de Brousset, is, at 3145m, the most westerly Pyrenean summit to surpass the magic figure of 3000m, and one of the remotest. It was first climbed in 1825 by the military surveyors Peytier and Hossard, but they failed to divulge their route. Charles Packe, nearly forty years later, had to find his own way up. After a failed 1862 attempt, Packe made a second try in 1864 with the guide Jean-Pierre Gaspard, and after a week's search discovered a route to the summit.

A miniature train – and skiing

In Packe's day, of course, there was no *télécabine* from the giant car park and mammoth ski-chalet complex (1250m) at the north end of **Lac de Fabrèges** 6.5km southeast of Gabas, with the final access drive along this reservoir's east shore. Neither was there a miniature **tourist train** of rust-red, open carriages running 10km southeast from the top of the lift (1900m) on Pic de la Sagette (2031m) to just shy of **Lac d'Artouste**. Built in 1924 to serve a hydroelectric project which

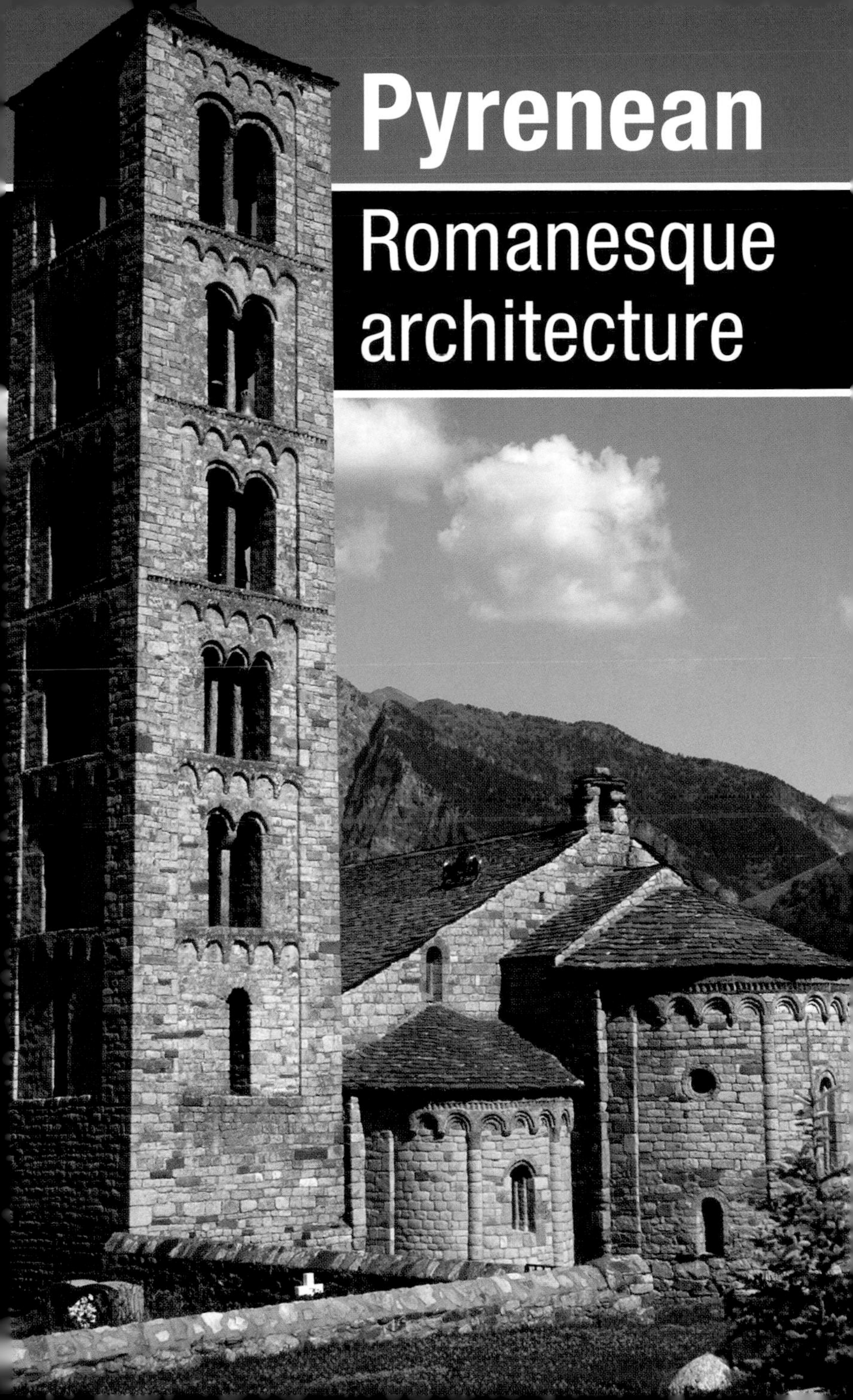
Pyrenean
Romanesque
architecture

"Romanesque" is the term describing the exquisite architecture and art of sacred Pyrenean buildings between the mid-ninth and late thirteenth centuries. Most surviving monuments date from the eleventh or twelfth centuries, a period which coincided with a surge in popularity of the **pilgrimage** to Santiago de Compostela. Monasteries and churches sprang up to meet the needs of pilgrims along the four main routes across France and over the Pyrenees; many were located in the remotest valleys of already sparsely inhabited countryside. This isolation, and later depopulation, of the foothills mean that many original features, which would have elsewhere been remodelled beyond recognition in Gothic or Baroque styles, have survived intact.

▲ Eleventh-century Romanesque church, Senta hamlet, Haute Soule

The Romanesque Church: form and function

Romanesque churches, especially major monastic ones, have a consistent **sacred geography**, with every part of the building carrying theological significance. The west–east axis of the nave and flanking aisles, inherited from pagan temples and basilicas, pointed to the sun of righteousness. Peaceful, usually square cloisters to one side of the nave were derived from the atrium of the Roman house and symbolized paradise for ruminating monks. The western wall was considered the side of a church most vulnerable to ungodly powers, and thus often fortified or elaborately worked with **relief carvings** demonstrating the triumph of the Church over its enemies. By contrast, minor countryside chapels were typically

▲ Relief carving, Saint Andreu church, Roussillon

plain, compact and low-slung, with few windows and a single, barrel-vaulted nave.

Decorative art, whether painted or carved, was also predictably placed according to doctrine. The Virgin always appeared in the apse, Christ could be there or over the main portal, with the Apocalypse inside the west wall. Relief art on the west facades was an outgrowth of Classical sarcophagi-carving and Roman triumphal arches – but instead of the emperor, Christ and other sacred personages were glorified.

In the Pyrenees, main portals were often placed on the south or north side of the nave, not necessarily to the west. During the full twelfth-century flowering of Romanesque, portals were rounded (as opposed to the subsequent pointed Gothic arch) and flanked by recessed or stepped columns or carvings. Architectural elements just overhead were used opportunistically for relief decoration, which first appeared early in the eleventh century. Lintels were ideal for linear

▲ Clocher-mur, Santa Maria church, Gerri de la Sal

▲ Carved column capital, Sant Jaume church, Queralbs

Carved column-capitals

Romanesque cloisters were defined by colonnades, and their columns – whether single or multiple – always had **capitals** on top. Originating as simple unworked elements modelled on the ancient Ionic style, merely serving as the base for springing arches, capitals had evolved by the twelfth century into showcases of virtuosity for **stonecarving**. While one usually finds the expected Old and New Testament scenes, there is often – especially at Saint-Michel-de-Cuixà, Ripoll and Serrabona – a preponderance of contemporary figures and events, familiar domestic animals, acrobats and mythical beings in a range of grotesque or droll poses. These flamboyant intrusions into sacred narrative have spawned various interpretations. The theological explanation is that acrobatics represent the mental contortions of those caught in theological error, while monsters are said to illustrate the horrors of damnation. The psychological answer is that aggressive or menacing figures, especially flanking main doorways, acted to repel the unworthy. But it's equally possible that, in an age of increasing urbanization, pilgrimage and crusading to the Orient with its exotic art and pride in one's workmanship, the craftsmen involved were testing the limits of the permissible and having a bit of secular fun. Such capitals were already controversial in their own time – **Bernard of Clairvaux**, founder of the Cistercians, fulminated against them, after which the appearance of fantastic creatures steadily waned.

compositions such as Christ flanked by Apostles or angels, while the semicircular area (tympanum) just above was more suited to busier, two-dimensional scenes like the Nativity or Christ in Majesty.

The prevalence of pilgrimage – to the Holy Land as well as to Santiago – spread **building styles**. For example, itinerant masons from Lombardy brought engagingly lofty belfries with open arcades to Catalunya's Vall de Boí early in the 1200s, plus so-called Lombard banding – a series of blind arcades just under a cornice. The logistics of pilgrimage dictated internal church features too: ambulatories around the altar-shrine developed to allow pilgrims to revere saints' relics kept in tiny, multiple chapels in the apse, without disturbing monks at their devotions. Crypts under the altar, originally the place of martyrdom or burial for saints, also symbolized the inner contemplative life.

The **Cistercian monastic order**, founded in the mid-twelfth century, was a reaction against the prevailing clerical luxury and ostentation, and the example of its famously austere churches and cloisters inevitably affected Romanesque architecture and ornamentation. But undiluted Romanesque flourished in its strongholds in Italy and southern France and Spain – including the Pyrenees – well into the thirteenth century, long after the style had been overtaken by Gothic in northern Europe.

▲ Twelfth-century fresco, San Cristòfol chapel, Toses, Catalunya

Frescoes

Romanesque frescoes developed directly from Roman villa-murals and catacomb paintings. As a much more fragile medium than column-capitals, few unretouched **frescoes** survive in the Pyrenees. The earliest examples, such as those in the lower chapel at San Juan de la Peña, are of ninth- or tenth-century vintage and restrict themselves to floral or geometric patterns. Only after 825 and Charlemagne's ecclesiastical **Synod of Paris**, which reversed iconoclastic strictures imported from Byzantium, did it gradually become permissible to depict human and divine figures. Whether as single figures or episodic "cartoon strips", frescoes served to illustrate biblical scenes and doctrinal essentials for illiterate parishioners. By far the most popular subjects, in the conch of the apse, were Christ in Majesty and the Virgin Enthroned, though archangels, the symbols of the Evangelists and even historical figures and animals appear. Most visible images date from the eleventh and early twelfth centuries, the local heyday of this craft, executed on both sides of the range by predominantly **Catalan artists**. Their unmistakeable style, with elongated faces and striking use of rust-red, ochre, greyish-green and powder-blue pigments, supposedly reflects Arab influence.

raised the lake level 25m, the train was later converted for tourist purposes. Weather permitting, the train begins operations in late May (guaranteed daily June & Sept 10am–3pm, July & Aug 9am–5pm; reserve on ⓣ05.59.05.36.99 or ⓦwww.train-artouste.com); at peak season you may have a fixed return time on your ticket from the *billeterie* well concealed amongst the chalets – allow also a half-hour for the *télécabine* (first departure 8.30am–9.30am). Fares for the combined lift and subsequent train ride start at €18 depending on season; walkers will be interested in either the *télécabine* fares (single/return €4.90/6.20), or the *Train Montagnard* fare (€25; up 8.30am, return 7.15pm), which allows a full day out in the mountains. It's a fifty-minute trip along the Gave de Soussouéou to the end of the line, where the train waits for 1hr 20min while passengers walk down to and around the lake before heading back. Some 45 minutes above the south end of Lac d'Artouste, nearly twice that far from the dam, sits the *Refuge d'Arrémoulit* (see p.378).

In **winter** the same *télécabine* gives access to the small beginner- to intermediate downhill **ski centre** – thirteen runs and nine lifts – on the northeast side of Col de la Sagette. The resort is about half the size of nearby Gourette, and with a top point of barely 2100m isn't reckoned very serious; there's one ski-bus daily, in the morning, from Laruns.

The ascent of Balaïtous and traverse east to Larribet

The **ascent of Balaïtous** from *Refuge d'Arrémoulit* takes almost nine hours (return), and as this is tough country, you should have the IGN 1647 OT **map** or PNP 1:25,000 map no. 2 "Balaïtous". Ascend east an hour to the **Col du Palas/Cuello de Pallàs** (2517m) on the frontier, descending southeast on the Spanish side to skirt the **Arriel** lakes and the tarn of **Gourg Glacé/Gorg Helada** (a likely lunch stop). Next follow a line of cairns to the primitive *Abri Michaud* shelter (2698m); the gully above it – full of loose, dangerous rock – leads to the western ridge and then, via more gullies, to the **summit** (3146m). From the top you appreciate how opposite in character Balaïtous is from Pic du Midi d'Ossau: the latter showcased by a parkland of lakes and grassy turf, your present vantage concealed by savage, lunar crags in every direction, with nothing to soften the landscape.

The HRP also continues **eastwards** from *Refuge d'Arrémoulit* to *Refuge de Larribet*; this is a short (3–4hr) but strenuous outing, intended for lightly laden trekkers experienced in traversing such terrain cross-country, and assuming passes relatively free of snow. From the Col du Palas, cross the head of the Spanish Arriel valley to the **Port du/Puerto de Lavedan** (2615m), dropping down on the far side to the tiny **Micoulaou** lakes; from there go northeast with a clearer path past the **Batcrabère** lakes, and finally through the **Brèche de la Garénère** (2189m) to descend on *Refuge de Larribet* (described p.361). If you've been hiking westwards from Gavarnie or Cauterets, simply reverse all of the foregoing directions to move on from the Balaïtous area to the Vallée d'Ossau.

Along the Aspe

The **Vallée d'Aspe** between Oloron-Sainte-Marie and the Col du Somport has long been an important corridor between France and Spain; the Romans had a road through it, the Saracens conducted raids along it, and lately the valley has again become embroiled in controversy over its role in north–south travel (see box on pp.394–395). In 1659, during the Wars of Religion, all the local villages but one got burnt to the ground by Protestant forces; early in the next century these settlements were reconstructed simultaneously, and – never having been altered since – now present a pleasingly homogeneous spectacle.

The Battle for the Vallée d'Aspe

Since 1990 the **Vallée d'Aspe** has been the focus of bitter controversy over a road-widening scheme from Oloron-Sainte-Mairie to the Col du Somport, and the boring of an 8600-metre-long road-tunnel under the *col*. Such proposals had been debated for years, but received additional impetus following Spain's joining the EU in 1986. Aragón in particular, long annoyed by the closure of the rail line between Oloron and Canfranc, embraced the plans as a remedy for its perceived isolation.

As originally envisaged, the project would facilitate the passage of heavy lorries by upgrading the N134 between Oloron and the new tunnel to expressway status as part of the trans-European E7. This meant concreting the banks of the Gave d'Aspe, blasting away sections of mountainside and farmland, and placing the tunnel mouth within PNP territory. Only token provision for a restored rail link was made, and there was no consideration of environmental impact on endemic fauna, including brown bears. Besides Parisian technocrats and the Aragonese, the vast majority of valley-dwellers favoured the scheme, seeing improved north–south communications as their last chance of rescuing the Aspe from stagnation and depopulation, especially by young people.

Opposition crystallized quickly in the form of the **Coordination pour la Sauvegarde Active de la Vallée d'Aspe** (**CSAVA**), based at an "alternative" *gîte d'étape* in the disused Cette-Eygun train station and headed by **Eric Pétetin**, who eventually came to be loathed, dismissed as a misguided idealist or respected – in equal measure – by locals. He and CSAVA managed to delay the project for three years by persuading the EU to halt its funding temporarily, claiming that the rail line could be reopened to carry both passengers and trucks at a **cost** one-tenth that of the projected road works. Activists predicted massive **environmental degradation** through an estimated four thousand vehicles per day transiting the tunnel, and also deplored the tunnel's siting within the PNP. Throughout 1991 and 1992 CSAVA, its ranks swelled by foreign activists from Belgium and Holland (where the Pyrenees have many avid aficionados), organized **civil disobedience** campaigns ranging from roadblocks to extensive work-site vandalism. For his pains Pétetin was arrested 35 times, on the final occasion being sentenced to long imprisonment.

The French Environment Ministry attempted to placate CSAVA by moving the tunnel-mouth to the park boundary; unmollified, CSAVA sued to overturn the August 1992 **DUP** (*déclaration de utilité publique*), or go-ahead decree, for works. A revised one – coinciding with Pétetin's pardon and early release from jail – was issued in July 1993, including provisions for bear-crossings and rehabilitation of the abandoned

Sarrance to Cette-Eygun

The upper valley begins in earnest just south of Escot, 15km from Oloron, where a narrow eponynmous defile encloses both road and river. Upstream from the gorge, along the N134, the attractive village of **SARRANCE** has strangely unexploited associations with Marguerite d'Angoulême, who stayed and wrote here when the weather in Cauterets turned bad. The village straggles up to the ancient monastic church of **Notre-Dame-de-la-Pierre**, with a fine organ perched in the gallery and a wonderfully rustic cloister with strange pyramidal turrets. Opposite stands the main premises of the **Ecomusée de la Vallée d'Aspe** (daily July–Sept 10am–noon & 2–7pm, rest of year except Dec 25–Jan 31 Sat, Sun or hols 2–6pm; Ⓦwww.vallee-aspe.com/eco-musee/; €4), devoted to valley history, natural and otherwise.

The closest reliable facilities lie 7km south of Sarrance at **BEDOUS**, were you'll also find a fine church, an arcaded *mairie* and the miniature, eighteenth-century **Château Lassalle** on the quiet place de l'Église east of the through road. On the same *place* is a **gîte d'étape**, *Le Mandragot* (Ⓣ05.59.34.59.33); the only other accommodation is *Chez Michel* on the through road (Ⓣ05.59.34.72.47; 45 ❸), with a full-service **restaurant**. If you're driving, note that Bedous has the highest

rail line. Work on the French side began early in 1994; with far less opposition, the Spanish had already completed boring from their side, plus an approach road across Aragón of the necessary standard.

For many *Aspois*, the eco-activists were just carpetbaggers who would decamp to the next fashionable cause were the issue decided in their favour, leaving the locals with the consequences. Post-DUP tactics, organized by Greenpeace and the WWF, saw thousands of activists (including future Environment Minister, Green Party member Dominique Voynet) buying tiny plots of land along the proposed course of the approach highway, to put a spanner in the process of compulsory land-purchase.

In March 1998 municipalities and interested individuals in France and Spain elaborated the **Pacte de Somport**, which endorsed the tunnel, subject to provision of a dual right of way: a reopened rail line for passengers and heavy freight, plus a reduced-width highway for local traffic and light vehicles. Since the Mont Blanc tunnel disaster, a ban on monster vehicles in the Tunnel du Somport is under consideration – which would undermine any justification for a multi-lane highway. EU-funded rehabilitation of the railway was approved "in principle" in 2000, though to date this has had no effect on the French side.

By the millennium, CSAVA had run its course, with the Cette-Eygun *gîte* abandoned, and Eric Pétetin confined to a psychiatric institution. But ironically, increasing numbers of valley residents have since adopted most of CSAVA's positions; the impending prospect of six traffic lanes has concentrated minds, and opposition is now gentrified, as SAUVE NÔTRE VALLÉE and NON AU BÉTON graffiti are complemented by bumper stickers – on cars belonging to second-home owners – showing a terse NON with a truck silhouette lodged in the 'O'.

The tunnel itself **opened** two years late in January 2003, with more of a whimper than a bang; local mayors boycotted the ceremony, miffed that (except at Etsaut) no bypass road for their villages was provided to keep lorries at bay. Highway widening won't be finished anytime soon, owing partly to the Portalet narrows and difficult rocks at Urdos, but more importantly to spiralling costs which may eventually quash the project. The roadworks to date have brought neither the degree of revitalization to the area that its advocates envisioned, nor quite the environmental damage feared by opponents. But one enduring legacy of the long 'anti' campaign has been to subject decision-making to public scrutiny in what has always been an overly secretive and centralized nation.

petrol pump in the valley – there's nothing else until Canfranc-Pueblo in Spain. On the road between Bedous and Aydius to the east, the **Moulin d'Orcun**, the last stone-grinding flour mill in the valley, functions as a museum (July–Aug daily tours at 11am, 3pm, 4–6pm; otherwise by arrangement on ⓣ05.59.34.74.91).

Villages around Bedous offer further amenities. There's a *gîte* 1500m southwest in **OSSE-EN-ASPE**, *Les Amis de Chaneu* (ⓣ05.59.34.73.23; 28 places), and another, better one in **ACCOUS** 3km south of Bedous, Maison Despourrins (ⓣ05.59.34.53.50, ⓦwww.maison-despourrins.vallee-aspe.com; 23 places in 2-to-4-bed rooms). Accous also offers the unusually salubrious two-star *Hôtel Le Permayou* (ⓣ05.59.34.72.15, ⓕ05.59.34.72.68; closed Oct; ③) between the main road and village centre, with fully en-suite rooms and an affordable restaurant.

Some 3km beyond Accous at **L'ESTANGUET** hamlet, the *Auberge Cavalière* perches high above the highway (ⓣ05.59.34.72.30, ⓦwww.auberge-cavaliere.com; April–Oct), specializing in horse-riding and walking packages (though walk-ins welcome); the stables (ⓣ05.59.34.78.55) are on the premises, near the well-regarded in-house restaurant. Accommodation is either at the *auberge*'s attached hotel (④ HB only) or at its *gîte*-style *Chalet des Ecuyers* up the hill, accessible by 4WD track.

About 4km southeast from the *Auberge Cavalière* turning, another side road snakes 2km east up the slope to engagingly unspoilt **CETTE** village (part of **CETTE-EYGUN**), where a fortified twelfth-century manor has been sympathetically converted to the valley's most distinctive **accommodation**, *Au Château d'Arance* (Ⓣ05.59.34.75.50, Ⓦwww.auchateaudarance.com; ❹). Eight modern, wood-floored, pastel-tinted rooms are excellent value, with TV, wi-fi Internet access and amazing sunsets; most have full baths, except for the tower unit. The competent terrace restaurant (shut Tues low season) has the best views in the valley, the most leisurely breakfast in the Pyrenees (7.30–11am) and slightly pricey meals (*menus* €18–26). Success has engendered a nearby annexe of five spotless rooms (❸) in an old house, with a lawn and pool. If they're full, your alternative is *Chambres d'Hôtes La Grande Volière* by the church (Ⓣ05.59.34.57.12, Ⓦwww.la-grande-voliere.vallee-aspe.com; ❸ B&B), also with family suites.

Lescun and its cirque

Certainly the highlight of a trip along the Aspe valley is the grey-limestone **Cirque de Lescun**, more intimate than Gavarnie's, contrasting sharply with the pastures and dense forest at its foot. Pyramidal and often marbled with snow, the toothy peaks forming the cirque – such as the two Billare summits, the Aigulles de Ansabère and storm-lashed Pic d'Anie (2504m) – rise as a semicircular screen from the quiltwork of fields laid out by generations of farmers.

The substantial stone houses of **LESCUN** village, wonderfully sited on a sunny south-facing slope, lend photogenic balance in the foreground. Six steep kilometres along the minor D239 above and west of the valley floor, the village is no longer really a going concern, despite two sales outlets for sheep's-cheese; two-thirds of its houses are holiday homes or abandoned altogether, and winter desolation is the rule. That said, Lescun makes an excellent base for a walking tour of the cirque. **Accommodation** is at the comfortable, antique-furnished *Hôtel du Pic d'Anie* (Ⓣ05.59.34.71.54, Ⓕ05.59.34.53.22; April–Sept; ❷), which has the village's main full-service **restaurant** with decent, hearty fare (though it's only for hotel guests). Lescun also has two *gîtes d'étape*: a sixteen-place one run by the hotel, just opposite, and the *Maison de la Montagne* a bit north (Ⓣ05.59.34.79.14; 25 places in four- to 6-bed rooms), with drinks served on the lawn but meals through the *Bar de Berger*. There's a medium-sized, grassy, well-equipped and incomparably sited **campsite**, *Le Lauzart* (Ⓣ05.59.34.51.77; May–Sept) south of and below the village.

South of Lescun: the head of the Aspe

Once past the Lescun turning, the N134 carries on through Etsaut and passes just below attractive Borce. In the disused train station of **ETSAUT** (signposted in Gascon as "Eth Saut") you'll find the most westerly **Maison du Parc** (daily May to mid-Sept 10am–noon & 1–6pm; Ⓣ05.59.34.88.30). There's a *gîte d'étape* at lane's end beyond the church, *Auberge La Garbure* (Ⓣ05.59.34.88.98, Ⓦwww.garbure.net; some doubles/quads), and a hotel on the square, *Des Pyrénées* (Ⓣ05.59.34.88.62, Ⓕ05.59.34.86.96; ❶–❷; closed Dec 20–Jan 15) with a restaurant (three *menus*), though you may find the welcome warmer across the *place* at *Bar Tabac Le Randonneur*, which does *plats du jour* in the bar or full meals in the attractive diner upstairs, as well as offering **wi-fi Internet** access (€1 donation). For the laptop-less, the **post office** has computers with Internet access for slightly higher rates.

BORCE, poised above the valley floor on the west bank, is a medieval showcase, the one place to escape the warfare of 1659 and still graced by sumptuous fifteenth-century mansions. It also offers the **Espace Animalier** (daily: April–May & Oct 2–6pm; June–Sept 9.30am–7pm; €7.50), a ten-hectare site with a variety of Pyrenean fauna, both wild and domestic, roaming in semi-liberty. For GR10 trekkers and pilgrims, there are two *gîte*-style places to **stay**: *La Communal*, upstairs from the central bar-*épicerie* (ⓣ05.59.34.86.40; 18 places), or the cosier *Hospice de Borce* (ⓣ05.59.34.89.65; 6 places) at the north outskirts, intended for bona fide pilgrims, with a self-catering kitchen.

Chemin de la Mâture and Fort du Portalet

Both Etsaut and Borce lie on the **GR10**, which en route southeast to Lac d'Ayous negotiates the spectacular **Chemin de la Mâture**, about 3km south of Etsaut. An eighteenth-century corniche route originally hacked out of the sheer flank of the

△ Hikers on the Chemin de la Mâture

Sescoué ravine by convict labour to facilitate removal of tree-trunks for the French navy's masts, this path has an exaggeratedly fearsome reputation; in reality there is little danger in dry weather, and families with toddlers routinely tackle it. The corniche section itself is a sun-trap – get there early or late in the day – though you're often in forest-shade thereafter.

If you're not up for a point-to-point traverse, you can experience the two-metre-wide *chemin* as a loop-walk, shown clearly on the 1:50,000 "Béarn" map (and on locally placed placards). At **Pont de Cebers**, 1.5km south, there is a car park; some 2.4km south of Etsaut along the minor side road up from the bridge, there's another parking area at a sharp bend (740m), though both tend to fill on busy summer days. The GR10 proper resumes here, entering the gorge within a few minutes; from the bend in the road it's 45 minutes to **Grange de Perry**, where many people turn around. Beyond Perry the way levels off, even drops a bit until, just over an hour along, you hairpin left off the GR10 to adopt a yellow-blazed path climbing to the **Col d'Arras** (1hr 20min; 1300m), really just a grassy hillside pasture with sweeping views and a potable trough spring, the only water en route. From here the trail, now marked in yellow and red, drops sharply through beeches to emerge on the minor side road near some farms (2hr), from where it's ten minutes down to the upper car park and GR10 trailhead.

The grim **Fort du Portalet** (privately owned, restoration as a tourist attraction planned) commands a steep slope just east of the N134, just south of the Chemin de la Mâture. It acquired some notoriety during the 1940s as a political prison, where the Vichy government detained Léon Blum, Socialist French premier of the 1930s; later Marshal Pétain himself was held here by the Allies.

Urdos and Col du Somport

Shortly after the Fort du Portalet, **URDOS** is the last village on the French side of the Col du Somport, and arguably worth a special trip for the co-managed *Hôtel des Voyageurs/Le Somport* (T 05.59.34.88.05, E hotel.voyageurs.urdos@wanadoo.fr; 2), a former post house that's been in the same family for seven generations. Eulogized fulsomely by Hilaire Belloc in 1909, it still deserves that praise, its rooms managing to retain character without being musty – try for those in the *Somport* annexe facing west over the river; they also manage a cheap *gîte* (10 bunks) for Santiago pilgrims. The *Voyageurs'* **restaurant** is superb, offering the best value in the valley – the sort of place where the local *gendarmerie* and firemen hold their Saturday-evening do next to bemused skiers and *voyageurs*; the €26 *menu* gets you vegetarian *garbure*, a fish plate such as *lotte* in squid sauce, a meat/game dish (boned duck breast or shank in green peppercorn sauce), and dessert. There are no longer any shops, petrol pumps or banks in Urdos, though the lanes west of the high street provide a pleasant amble.

Beyond Urdos, several daily well-spaced SNCF buses continue on through the new tunnel under the 1632-metre **Col du Somport/Puerto de Somport**, and beyond to Canfranc, the terminus for trains from Jaca in Aragón. The twisty old road, recommended for the views, accesses the cross-country ski centre of **Somport-Candanchú**, 34km of marked trails (9km on the Spanish side), presumably dodging the numerous ventilation silos for the tunnel; that said, it's one of the best such centres in the Pyrenees, and at this altitude one of the last to close in spring. At the pass there are a few snack bars, a snowplough station and the abandoned customs post; just below, you turn left for Astún, right for the main onward road and Candanchú (see p.434).

Walks from Lescun

There are any number of walks for all levels of commitment in the fantastic limestone scenery south and west of Lescun, ranging from day-trips and brief circuits to long-haul traverses. Public transport on either side of the border – which these peaks form – is almost nonexistent; water can be a problem in these rock strata, so top up bottles wherever possible. The best **maps** for the area are the IGN 1:25,000 1547 OT or the PNP 1:25,000 map no. 1, "Aspe Ossau".

West: the GR10, HRP and Pic d'Anie

The **GR10** to La-Pierre-Saint-Martin is the most northerly route, an easy day's walking of under six hours. It follows a six-kilometre road – no short-cuts possible – for ninety minutes northwest of Lescun as far as the closed-down *Refuge de L'Abérouat* (1442m), eye-to-eye with 2300-metre Billare peak. This is as far as cars can go; a huge car park hosts those who've forgone the boring road-tramp up. Next, the route – briefly track, then path and cross-country – enters beech forest under the striking organ-pipe formations of **Orgues de Camplong** before emerging above treeline at the basic *Cabane d'Ardinet* hut. From here the GR10 climbs to another shepherd's *cabane* – last reliable water for the day, cheese for sale when occupied – at Cap de la Baigt, and then steeply northwards into the **Pas d'Azuns** (1873m; 3hr from Lescun). After dropping into a slight bowl the path climbs again to the **Pas de l'Osque** (1922m), after which the GR10 crosses karst desert en route to La-Pierre-Saint-Martin (see p.466), two hours due west.

For an **ascent of Pic d'Anie** (**Auñamendi** in Euskera; 2504m), the most westerly summit over 2000m on the French side, head south from Cap de la Baigt, curving under Pic du Soum Couy and up into the **Col des Anies** (2030m). The main HRP carries on westwards from here to La-Pierre-Saint-Martin; for Pic d'Anie, follow the easy marked path southwards. From the summit (2hr from the *col*; 4hr 30min from Lescun) you can return to Lescun in rather less than four and a half hours, making this a popular day outing from the village.

The best traverse route, though, is the **HRP variante**, which aims for the currently defunct *Refugio Belagoa* in Spain. From Lescun, you head west on road, then track towards Pic de la Breque, reaching the Plateau de Sanchèse at about 1100m. A good trail climbs steeply from here past a potable stream (fill up) to the **Col d'Anaye** (2052m; 3hr 30min), on the south flank of Pic d'Anie. On the other side of this pass you enter the twisted karst dells of Spain's *Parque Natural Pirenaico*; the site of Belagoa lies three hours further west.

Tour of the border peaks

Using Lescun or Borce as a starting point, a worthwhile three-day, two-night **tour of the border peaks** satisfactorily covers the terrain south of the preceding hikes. Beginning in Lescun, head southwest through the Bois de Landrosque, up the *gave* draining from the **Aigulles d'Ansabère**. At the base of the lesser pinnacle (2271m) are a few shepherds' huts, near some all-important springs and potential camping spots. But since these are only about three hours along, you'll probably continue due south up to the frontier. Cross this via a nameless saddle (2030m) above tiny **Lac d'Ansabère**, and then descend slightly to **Ibón de Acherito** (1870m; 5hr from Lescun; see p.459 for full description), just inside Spain and the best possibility for water and camping.

From here, the topography dictates a wide skirting of the border ridge to its south before crossing back into France via the **Col de Pau/Puerto de Palo** (2019m; 90min from Acherito). Back on the French side, within the final westerly extension of the PNP, an increasingly good path, as the HRP, hugs the ridge – except for a diversion north over the **Col de Saoubathou** to avoid **Pic Rouge/Pico Rojo** – to deposit you within five hours from Ibón de Acherito at the relaxed *Refuge d'Arlet* (Ⓣ05.59.36.00.99; 2000m; 43 places; staffed June 15–Sept 15), beside **Lac d'Arlet**.

The most scenic way of returning to the Aspe valley involves heading east along the HRP to the small **La Banasse** cirque with its spring, and then descending north, initially via the **Gave de Baralet**, and then over the Col de Lagréou to the **Gave de Bélonce**, which quits PNP territory on a good if steep path into Borce (5hr from Arlet).

The southern approaches

South of the border in the region of **Alto Aragón**, depopulation is even more pronounced than in the French Pyrenees, as a glance at the map with its isolated villages will confirm. Just Jaca and the provincial capital Huesca muster over ten thousand inhabitants, while more than four hundred mountain villages languish all but abandoned – the highest such concentration in Spain – occupied only in summer by older people with flocks to graze, plus a few city-dwellers restoring ruins as holiday homes or "alternative" enterprises. This desolation is owed largely to the late Generalissimo Franco and his policies. Determined to punish the *altoaragoneses* for their staunch support of the Republican cause, his regime withheld vital services, ignored the ravages wrought by natural disasters and dammed numerous arable valleys, leaving the villagers little alternative but to migrate to the cities. In the seven thousand square kilometres of Alto Aragón there are now fewer than fifty thousand inhabitants, an average density of seven per square kilometre.

The salient geographical features in the east of this region are impressive valleys and strange, wedding-cake-like mountains, both eroded from the same banded limestone. The **Valle de Ordesa** – heart of the **Parque Nacional de Ordesa y Monte Perdido**, and the most popular approach for an ascent of **Monte Perdido**, linchpin of the canyons – was first publicized by French journalist and adventurer Lucien Briet, who over eight consecutive summers after 1904 traced a route from Gavarnie to Torla. (Some of his photographs can be seen at the Lourdes museum, and a Torla inn has been named in his honour.) Nowadays this landscape needs no advertisement; during holiday periods, the riverside paths of Ordesa and all approach roads from the west or south are packed to the gills, while the gateway villages become increasingly commercialized with each successive year.

Other canyons east or southeast of the Valle de Ordesa, wholly or partly within the park, are nearly as impressive but receive far fewer visitors. The absence of public transport to trailheads and limited accommodation here could be both cause and consequence of this neglect, but the extra effort required to visit is amply rewarded. Despite having a road through it, the forbiddingly steep and snow-fringed walls of the **Valle de Pineta**, draining east from Monte Perdido, discourage casual acquaintance with its heights. The **Garganta de Escuaín**, in the **Valle de Tella** south of Pineta, is best appreciated on foot or as part of a canyoning expedition. Continuing clockwise southeast brings you to the bottom of the **Valle de Añisclo**, which gets almost as crowded as Ordesa in high season, but once clear of its lower reaches you'll have only a few long-distance walkers for company.

The main bases for exploring these canyons are **Bielsa**, at the mouth of the Valle de Pineta; **Aínsa**, a public transport terminus within striking distance of the Añisclo and Tella canyons; and **Torla**, the enduringly popular western gateway to the Ordesa country. All of these villages have an ample range of facilities for both trekkers and those more solicitous of their own comfort. Southwest of the park, **Jaca**, ancient capital of the Aragonese kingdom, the nearby monastery of **San Juan de la Peña** and the **Castillo de Loarre** present the only man-made attractions rivalling the mountains. **Huesca** and the wine town of **Barbastro** are ignored by most in favour of the range above them, the **Sierra de Guara**, protected as a *parque natural* and Spain's prime venue for canyoning.

Like almost everywhere south of the Pyrenean watershed, the landscape of Alto Aragón is predominantly drier and less vegetated than that of French Bigorre, but towards the west, in the **Tena** and **Canfranc** valleys, the climate becomes more humid. Numerous lakes reappear above **Panticosa**, and in winter the nearby skiing centres of **El Formigal**, **Candanchú** and **Astún** do thriving business.

Transport and accommodation

Twice as remote as the French approaches in terms of distances from major cities, and twice as deserted, the Spanish side consequently has relatively deficient **public transport**. Of the foothill villages described in this section, only those on the Sabiñánigo–Biescas–Torla–Sarvisé axis see more than one daily summertime bus service, and many have none; careful planning is vital to make necessary connections. You'll gain considerable advantages by renting a car, bringing your own or by trekking along the GR paths which run perpendicular to most of the north–south roads. **Accommodation** can be a serious problem in peak summer or winter seasons if you haven't reserved well in advance – even campsites can fill – but with a vehicle you can simply drive on until you happen upon a vacancy.

The eastern valleys

Heading west from Posets and the Valle de Gistau **on foot**, you're well poised to tackle any of the three major easterly valleys draining out of the national park. The GR11 or its variant leads from Biadós to **Bielsa** and the **Valle de Pineta**, while the GR19 or GR15 link the Valle de Gistau with the **Valle de Tella** with its tiny, photogenic villages perched either side of the **Garganta de Escuaín**. The **Valle de Añisclo** (or Cañon de Añisclo) is easiest visited by car from the valley of the **Río Zinca**, but can also be reached by trail from Pineta or Escuaín. Moving from south to north, there is sporadic **public transport** north of Aínsa to Bielsa, or more regularly west up the **Ribera de Fiscal**.

Aínsa

Sited above the confluence of the Ara and Zinca rivers, **AÍNSA** (*L'Aínsa* in Aragonese) is the natural gateway to the region, with an exceedingly attractive hilltop **old quarter**, focused on a vast, arcaded **Plaza Mayor**, which every first Sunday of September in odd-numbered years hosts the *La Morisima* rite, commemorating a victory of Christians over Moors in 742. The old town has been prettified with boutiques and stone walkways to cash in on some of the cross-border traffic pouring down from the Bielsa tunnel, but it's all in fairly good taste; much of the year, traffic is banned and cars directed to a fee car park on the west. Just off the plaza stands the exceptional Romanesque church of **Santa María**, with a triangular cloister dictated by the sloping topography, and an ancient crypt with a forest of magnificently capitalled columns under the apse. For €1 you can climb the belfry for splendid views over the river valley, the town, *plaza* and fifteenth- to sixteenth-century **Castillo** to the west. Slowly being restored, this is the main venue for the late-July world-music **Festival del Castillo l'Aínsa** (Ⓦwww.festivales.aragon.es), attracting big names such as Tarika, Clannad, Altan and Mariza, as well as

Oloron-Sainte-Marie
Argelès-Gazost
Eaux-Chaudes
Cauterets
GR10
D934
Gabas
Ledormeur
Larribet
Balaïtous
(3145m)
Arrémoulit
Pombie
Oulettes
Wallon
Ayous
Pic du Midi
d'Ossau
(2884m)
HRP
Bayssellance
Respumoso
Col d'Arratille
Puerto
de los
Mulos
GR11
Bachimaña
Vigemale
(3289m)
Puerto de
Portalet
(1794m)
Picos del Infierno
(3076m)
Balneario de
Panticosa
Batanes
Río Ara
Astún
Argualas
(3046m)
Embalse de
Lanuza
Brazato
Lakes
El Formigal
Sallent
de Gállego
Lanuza
Candanchú
Izas
GR11 Var
Escarrilla
Caldarés
SPAIN
Sandiniés
Panticosa
Canfranc-Estación
Partacua
Tramacastilla
Embalse de
Búbal
Piedrafita de Jaca
Río Aragón
Canfranc-Pueblo
Linás de Broto
N330
Villanúa
A136
Biescas
N260
Valle de Tena
Río Gállego
Vallée d'Aspe
Selva de Oza
San Juan de la Peña
Jaca
N330
Sabiñánigo
A1205
Peña Oroel
(1769m)
Puerto de
Oroel
Los Mallos, Ayerbe & Huesca
Huesca & Sierra de Guara

SOUTHERN APPROACHES

Argelès-Gazost
Barèges
Arreau
Luz Saint-Sauveur
D929
GR10
FRANCE
Gèdre
PARC NATIONAL DES PYRENEES
Piau Engaly
D173
Bielsa Tunnel
HRP
Héas
Barroude
Cirque de Troumouse
HRP
Gavarnie
Cirque d'Estaubé
HRP GR10
Puerto de Bujaruelo (2270m)
Espuguettes
Lagos de la Munia
GR11
San Nicolás
Cirque de Gavarnie
Chisagüés
Parzán
A138
Sarradets
Marboré (3253m)
Lago de Marboré
Cilindro (3328m)
Balcón de Pineta
Valle de Pineta
Taillon (3144m)
Brecha de Roldán
Monte Perdido (3355m)
GR11
Bujaruelo
Collado de Añisclo (2470m)
Cinca
Bielsa
PARQUE NACIONAL DE ORDESA Y MONTE PERDIDO
Góriz
Collado S. de Góriz (2343m)
C. de Soaso
Cuello Viceto (2002m)
GR11
Valle de Ordesa
Valle de Añisclo
Valle
Salinas de Sin
Arazas
Faja de Pelay
San Vicenda
GR19
Valle de Gistau
A135
GR15.2
C. de Diazas
Revilla
Escuaín
de Tella
Arinzué
Estaronillo
Torla
Desfiladero de las Gloces
Castillo Mayor (2014m)
Tella
GR15
Valle de Broto
Vaga
GR15/19
Broto
Fanlo
Valle de Vió
Nerín
SESTRALES
Bestué
Lafortunada
Oto
Buesa
Buisán
Sercué
GR15
Puértolas
Hospital de Tella
Badaín
Sarvisé
San Úrbez
HU631
GR15.1
GR19
Vió
Desfiladero de las Cambras
Bellós
Laspuña
Buerba
Asín de Broto
Puyarruego
Peña Montañesa (2291m)
Escalona
Yeba
Río Yesa
Ribera de Fiscal
A138
Río Zinca
San Victorian
Campo & Castejón de Sos
Lardiés
N260
Los Molinos
Fiscal
Jánovas
Río Ara
Boltaña
Aínsa
Guaso
0 10 km
Sierra de Guara
Barbastro

lesser-known Spanish acts. If you've time to fill, either the **Eco-Museo** at one corner of the castle (daily summer 10.30am–2pm & 5–9pm; free), with exhibits on local fauna and a "recuperation centre" for hunter-wounded animals, or the **Museo de Oficios y Artes Tradicionales/Museum of Trades and Traditional Arts** (Tues–Sun: July 1–Sept 15 10am–2pm & 4.30–9.30pm; spring & autumn 10am–2pm & 5–8pm; €2.50) on Plaza de San Salvador merit a few minutes. The latter resembles a well-lit antique shop, labelled in Spanish only, highlighting ironwork, carpentry, basketry and so forth.

Practicalities

The county **tourist office** is lodged in a corner of the castle parade ground (daily 10am–2pm & 4.30–8pm; ⓣ974 500 512). **Accommodation** in the old quarter includes *Casa El Hospital* (ⓣ974 500 750, ⓦwww.caselhospital.com; ❸), a *turismo rural* by the church or, for a splurge, the slightly kitsch *Hotel Posada Royal* at Plaza Mayor 6 (ⓣ974 500 977, ⓦwww.posadareal.com; ❻), or 2006-opened *Hotel Los Siete Reyes* opposite (ⓣ974 500 681, ⓦwww.lossietereyes.com; ❻), most of whose designer rooms have French windows overlooking the square. There's ample scope for **eating** and **drinking** on or near Plaza Mayor: *Bodegas del Sobrarbe* (closed Nov–March), at no. 2, is the most renowned (€32 *a la carta*, €20 *menú*), while *Bodegón de Mallacán* is fine for a coffee under the arches. East of the square, local hangout *Bar Restaurante Fes* at c/Mayor 22 offers affordable *menús* (€12) and a much more interesting *carta* (allow €21); no-frills cuisine comes in fair-sized portions, and the cavernous, stone-walled interior is bigger than it looks from outside. *Bar Bodega L'Alfil*, c/Travesera s/n near the church, purveys somewhat pricey *raciones*, cider and herbal liqueurs.

The unsightly, traffic-plagued **new quarter** below has six *hoteles* and *hostales*, used mostly by clients of several local adventure-sport outfitters; there are also a couple surviving outdoor-equipment shops along Aínsa's single high street. Aínsa is the last stop for the **bus** line plying the C138 road southeast from Torla, overlapping partly with the Barbastro-Boltaña line.

The Ribera de Fiscal: the lower Ara valley

The Río Ara is the major tributary of the Zinca from the west, but the lower reaches of its valley are known as the **Ribera de Fiscal** after its most important village. By Aragonese standards the valley is wide and relatively fertile, yet strangely deserted; nearly a dozen ghost villages between Fiscal and Aínsa, within sight of the road, are sporadically squatted by Spanish anarchists and alternative types. There's a roadside placard above the site of a half-built dam, which would disrupt the flow of the last undammed river in the Spanish Pyrenees, detailing its whole sorry history (see box opposite). Although it seems the dam will never be built, plans are afoot to bulldoze a mega-highway direct from Fiscal to Sabiñánigo through virgin mountainside.

Boltaña

BOLTAÑA, 8km west of Aínsa along the N260, divides like its near-neighbour into two parts: the ugly roadside development on the through highway, and the atmospheric hill quarter. Here the *plaza* is virtually filled by the sixteenth-century **Colegiata de San Pedro Apostol**, with its rib-vaulted ceiling, sturdy piers and carved choir stalls at the rear. Just downhill in a cul-de-sac, *Casa Coronel* does just two things in its **bar-restaurante**, but does them well: salads and grills, served indoors or with mountain views in the courtyard. Much the best **accommodation** nearby is English-Brazilian run ✱ *Casa de San Martín* (ⓣ974 503 105,

Dams in Alto Aragón

The reason behind the lower Ara valley's desolation is the long-mooted **Jánovas dam**, at a critical set of narrows 6km west of Boltaña. The process of compulsory expropriation of property to be inundated began in 1959, targeting Jánovas, Lacort and Lavelilla villages. By today's standards, risible sums were offered as compensation; by 1964 most stubborn resisters had been evicted through the combined threats of Franco's Guardia Civil and privately hired thugs. Residents who sold up had their houses dynamited (thus accounting for the ruinous appearance of the three named villages), while "subtler" methods of persuasion such as blocking all water supplies and staving in the door of the Jánovas school with the children still inside were employed *pour encourager les autres*. Just one brave couple – **Emilio and Francisca Garcés** – insisted on staying in Jánovas, holding out in primitive conditions until 1984, when they too gave up and moved out.

Yet this dam **never materialized**, beyond an earthen dyke half-obstructing the riverbed. Two binding **deadlines** for phase completion came and went, while **Iberduero**, the dam contractor, went bankrupt and re-formed, insisting that it would complete the project in the face of sustained opposition. The dam promoters' position was that the valley residents were paid full and **final settlement** in 1960, and having departed (or rather, been made to) lost all further recourse. The displaced and their partisans argued that this took place under conditions of dictatorship, with scarcely realistic compensation; furthermore, that by failing to complete the project by stipulated deadlines, Iberduero and its successor **voided the original contract** and, upon repurchase of their property (at the original rates, of course), the villagers have a clear case to return unhindered.

The prevailing uncertainty also caused a wave of abandonment in adjacent Javierre, Santa Oloria and Ligüerre de Ara, eventually affecting seven hundred persons in a total of seventeen villages. But despite the hydro-honchos' bluster, an actual dam became less likely with each passing year. It would have to have been substantially **enlarged** to make it economically viable, and the upstream villages affected wised up, demanding hefty sums for their land. Finally, on February 10, 2001, the proposed dam was officially **pronounced dead**, "inappropriate for reasons of adverse environmental impact".

One valley west, in the Río Tena basin, **Lanuza** village was forcibly evacuated and token payouts made when most of its lands, and some houses, were submerged by the namesake dam in 1975. Since then, half the original owners – those 5m or more above the mean water line – have **bought back** their old homes and rehabilitated them. But while attempting to retrieve their beloved 700-kilo bronze **church bells** "Elena" and "Quiteria" (patron saints of Lanuza), they could only find one, concealed in Torla. The local bishop, wanting no nostalgic rearguard action, had removed them and filed their names off – a nice illustration of the collusion by all establishment organs in Franco's state.

Ⓦwww.casadesanmartin.com; ❼), a three-star restored-manor hotel superbly perched in the middle of nowhere, specifically the tiny hamlet of **SAN MARTÍN DE LA SOLANA**, 14km west (the last 5km on dirt track), with gourmet evening meals provided.

Fiscal

FISCAL, 20km upriver from Boltaña, is the next inhabited place, with a genuine country feel: tended kitchen gardens, hay in barns, ambling livestock, though a new *urbanización* looms at the outskirts. Despite falling some distance short of Ordesa it's worth considering as a base, its tourist facilities including shops and two **banks**, the only ones hereabouts. Accommodation includes, 200m before the church, the somewhat eccentrically run *Casa del Arco* (Ⓣ974 503 042; ❷ B&B)

offering lovely antique- (and textile-) furnished, en-suite rooms in a slate-floored, eighteenth-century mansion. Somewhat higher standards are offered by luxurious *Hostal Casa Cadena*, another restored 1780s farmhouse near the top of the village (Ⓣ & Ⓕ974 503 077; ④); rooms are modern but each is different, with central heating. Downstairs is a wine, ham and cheese bar-*mesón* (eves only). Fiscal's other bar is inside the local **albergue** in a Belle Époque mansion opposite the church, *Saltamontes* (Ⓣ974 503 113; 52 places). There are two all-year **campsites** just upriver, the cosier being *El Jabalí Blanco* (Ⓣ & Ⓕ974 503 074) with its own pool.

The Zinca valley

In the valley of the **Río Zinca** above Aínsa, the first spots worth a stop or considering as bases are Escalona and Lapuña, 9km north on opposite sides of the river known in former eras for its timber-rafting (*nabata*) tradition. **ESCALONA** has abundant **accommodation**; best of this is the newish three-star *Hotel Arnal* (Ⓣ974 505 206, Ⓦwww.hotelarnal.com; ③) with *comedor menús* at €12–18, though the village is essentially a roadside strip. Hillside **LASPUÑA** has more character. with its tiny old quarter, though short-term facilities are limited to *Pensión Sidora* at Barrio Viejo 5 (Ⓣ974 505 007; ①), with meals offered.

Hospital de Tella and Lafortunada

HOSPITAL DE TELLA, 6km north of Escalona on the A138, is even tinier than Escalona but does offer a valuable amenity for walkers in the Valle de Tella (see p.409): the roadside **pension-restaurante** *Casa Quino* (Ⓣ974 504 055; ②). An alternative base 3km east is **LAFORTUNADA**, again not the most prepossessing of villages, but with more comfortable if somewhat overpriced **accommodation** at *Hotel Badain* (Ⓣ974 504 000, Ⓦwww.hotelbadain.com; ⑤), though its **restaurant** has creditable three-course *menús* (€15). The hotel is named after the hamlet of **BADAÍN**, 500m southeast, graced by a severe eleventh-century church with a round staircase tacked onto its square belfry. The church's nave a bit over-restored, but it retains its Gothic stellar vaulting and a finely carved gallery. Both the GR19 and GR15 pass the church: the former on its rather humdrum way along the Río Zinca to Laspuña, the GR15 more excitingly east through the mountains towards Saravillo and the Valle de Gistau (see p.298), or north, then west around the Valle de Tella to Añisclo.

Bielsa and Parzán

Near the top of the Río Zinca's course, at the entrance to the Pineta valley, **BIELSA** hung on as a Republican stronghold – the so-called *bolsa* – long after much of Alto Aragón had been overrun by the Nationalists; when the place finally fell in June 1938, most of it had been bombarded by Franco's air force and then burnt by the defeated. Today it's a prime summertime target for more pacific armies of French (and Spanish) day-trippers, and could be further affected if a planned nearby ski resort becomes reality. Nonetheless, traces of its past as a traditional mountain county-town persist in its old river bridge and porticoed *ayuntamiento*, with magnificently framed first-floor windows, on the Plaza Mayor. Walkers heading towards the Valle de Pineta from the Posets Massif are pretty much obliged to stop in here, since it's the only place en route with supplies and accommodation. Bielsa is also renowned for its lively **Carnival**; material related to this, and the civil war, is displayed in the **Museo del Valle de Bielsa** (July–Sept Tues–Sun 5–9pm; €3), housed in the *ayuntamiento*. On the ground floor of the same building is the local **tourist office** (summer daily 10am–2pm & 4–8pm; ⓣ974 501 127, ⓦwww.bielsa.com).

Practicalities

Bielsa gets daily summer **bus** services **from Aínsa**, less often out of season; if driving, you'd best use the free car parks on the southern outskirts and walk in the short distance. Coming **from France**, the Vallée d'Aure bus only reaches Aragnouet-le-Plan; rather than attempting to hitch through the tunnel (no pedestrians allowed), a better plan would be to trek southeast four-plus hours from the *Refuge de Barroude* (see p.341) on an HRP variant to **PARZÁN** village, 4km north of Bielsa on the A138 and GR11. Sleepy Parzán has a small shop on the main highway, near friendly *Hostal la Fuen* (ⓣ974 501 047, ⓦwww.monteperdido.com/lafuen; ❷), which offers decent en-suite rooms and an adequate *menú* in the pleasant ground-floor *comedor*. There's also a **turismo rural** in the village centre, non-en-suite *Casa Marión* (ⓣ974 501 190; ❶).

However, Bielsa, with its **banks** and shops, is a better supply point for trekkers than Parzán. Central **accommodation** includes the spotless *Hostal Vidaller* (ⓣ974 501 004; ❷), just west of the *plaza* (info in ground-floor café); the old-fashioned but en-suite *Hostal Pirineos Méliz* (ⓣ974 501 015; ❷, ❹ HB), quietly set uphill from the *plaza*, with a ground-floor *comedor*, or the much plusher *Hotel Valle de Pineta* (ⓣ974 501 010, ⓦwww.hotelvalledepineta.com; ❷, ❹ HB) off the southeast corner, with spacious, wood-floored rooms and balconies on the south side of the building overlooking the Zinca valley. The welcoming *Hostal Pañart*, out on the A138 highway (ⓣ & ⓕ974 501 116; ❷), also has a well-regarded *comedor*. About the only independent **restaurant** is the *Pineta* on Plaza Mayor, with a wide-ranging €14 *menú*. You can cobble together regional *tapas* and *raciones* – including *sesina* sausage made from horse, beef or goat – at idiosyncratic *Bar El Chinchecle*, one block downhill northeast from the *plaza*, washed down by homemade nut and flower liqueurs or sherry and attended by a folk-music soundtrack from across the globe.

The Valle de Pineta

A glacial trough scoured into sheer, stepped rock walls, the **Valle de Pineta** extends 15km west-northwest of Bielsa, terminating in the majestic **Circo de Pineta**; just above the *circo* looms **Monte Perdido** (3355m), one of the more celebrated Pyrenean summits. The idyllic valley floor, where reeds and birches fringe the white, boulder-flecked infant Río Zinca, broadened lower down by a dam, contrasts with the awesome cliffs of the Sierra de Espierba to the north and the even more fantastic **Sierra de las Tucas** to the south. At first glance you'll doubt that ascents of either the Circo de Pineta or the Sierra de las Tucas are possible; however, they are, the rewards commensurate with the effort.

The valley's flanking palisades attract legions of technical climbers, but there are a few steep, strenuous **walks** here, too. The classic hikes – up to the Balcón de Pineta, a shelf 1200m higher than the valley floor at the top of the Circo de Pineta, and the GR11 route climbing a similar height over the Collado de Añisclo – both lead into the northeast corner of the *parque nacional*. For all outings, you'll need the Editorial Alpina 1:40,000 "Ordesa Vignemale Monte Perdido" map.

Valley **accommodation** is limited. There are two **campsites**: the well-equipped *Pineta* at "Km 7" (ⓣ & ⓕ974 501 089; April–Oct) and the basic *Acampada Libre Canguro* (ⓣ974 501 041; Easter & June–Aug) in a meadow at "Km 14". The comfortable *Parador Nacional de Monte Perdido* (ⓣ974 501 011, ⓔbielsa@parador.es; ❼), at the base of the Circo de Pineta, has a **restaurant**, or the *Refugio de*

Pineta, prosaically set nearby on the left bank of the river (1220m; ⓣ974 501 203; 71 places) is often overrun with school groups, but serves sustaining meals to all.

Balcón de Pineta and beyond

For the **Balcón de Pineta**, take the path going left (west) just opposite the Ermita de Nuestra Señora de Pineta by the *parador*, which shortly arrives at El Felqueral bridge (1400m) and the foot of the cliffs. A subsequent series of tight zigzags gives progressively more unnerving views, as you climb through loose rock to the *balcón* (2530m; 3hr 45min from *parador*). The ascent is particularly steep in the final stages and shouldn't be attempted early in summer without crampons and ice-axe.

Twenty minutes to the northwest, a one-night tent bivouac is permitted at **Lago de Marboré** (2595m) which, on a sunny day, is a welcoming blue against the hard grey rock. But most eyes will be on the mass of Monte Perdido to the south, its savage northeast wall aproned by its huge glacier. Just north of the lake, the frontier pass of **Brecha de Tucarroya/Brèche de Tuquerouye** (2660m), with its historic hut, gives access to the Estaubé cirque and the HRP down to Gavarnie (see p.372). West of the lake, it's a ninety-minute climb through snowfields and across scree to **Cuello de Astazú/Col d'Astazou** for a magnificent view over the Cirque de Gavarnie.

Finally, you can head south from the lake over the **Cuello del Cilindro** (3074m; 3hr); this is rather more difficult than the much-lower Brèche de Roland, requiring year-round full snow-climbing gear and preferably some prior experience in this sort of terrain. From this pass it takes around three hours more to descend to the *Refugio de Góriz* (see p.420); in theory you could get there in one long July day from the Valle de Pineta, but it's highly advisable to break the journey with an overnight at Lago de Marboré.

The GR11: Parzán to Añisclo

The **GR11** west from Parzán is initially not very exciting: first on a narrow paved road for 3.6km to **Chisagüés** hamlet, then 6.6km more up the valley of the **Río Real** as far as the spring of **Petramula** (1940m), just north of the eponymous peak. With care, an ordinary car can make it this far – if not, leave it by the pastoral hut and broad parking area 2km before; there are usually knots of them parked here below a sharp hairpin curve, as this is also the trailhead for visiting the Munia lakes (see opposite). If you don't have a car, try to arrange a lift to spare you three hours of fairly dull tramping. A proper GR11 path resumes at the bend, and from the obvious saddle (*c.* 2160m) west of Petramula peak you have fine views of the Valle de Pineta before a steady but not gruelling descent (except in the final moments) to an *ermita* by the *parador* (2hr 30min more).

From the vicinity of the *parador* (*c.* 1300m), the GR11 then climbs southwest up what appear to be the impossibly sheer palisades of **Las Fayetas**, through the **Collado de Añisclo** (2453m) and beyond. This is a tough walk, like the Balcón route impossible without crampons and ice-axe until late June, and highly dangerous in early spring because of avalanches, which have gradually felled most of the trees on these slopes. But during summer it offers marvellous scenery close to hand and a bird's-eye view over the valley.

The start of this gruelling four-hour climb is signposted near the *ermita*, and again from the track serving the *Canguro* campsite. This is the most reliable river crossing; if you try from the refuge downstream, you're in for a mud-wallow and impenetrable riverbank thickets at the very least. Once over on the far side there are no further trail ambiguities until you're up on the *collado*. Beyond this saddle, the main GR11 was rerouted during 1989 in response to walkers' complaints. If inexperienced, or laden with a heavy pack, you should *not* use the *variante* heading northwest, since this inches perilously for 400m along the sheer face of **Pico de Añisclo** at the 2500m contour, with only a short cable to help you over a particularly nasty stretch always slippery with snowmelt. Instead, descend south for 1hr 45min along the main GR11 to a crude, unattended shelter at the head of the **Añisclo canyon**; there is plenty of turf and water nearby if you prefer or need to camp.

Otherwise, continue west-northwest along the GR11 up the Barranco Arablo (Fon Blanca) – the last reliable water being the vigorous waterfall of **Fon (Fuén) Blanca** at its mouth – where the occasionally scree-laden trail worms its way up along grassy terraces to the **Collado Superior de Góriz** (aka Arrablo; 2343m; 2hr 20min from Fon Blanca). Here you're treated to great views of Monte Perdido, Pico de Añisclo and Sum de Ramond; beyond the *collado*, the *Refugio de Góriz* is 40min away, for a total of eight and a half hours' walking from the Valle de Pineta.

Lagos de la Munia

One of the best half-day outings in the Pineta region is the hike from the Petramula road bend to the border-hugging **Lagos de la Munia**, sometimes called the Lagos de la Larri, nestled in the Circo de la Munia. The cairned path there begins from the high side of the hairpin, *not* from the onward, initially descending GR11; it's well grooved into the landscape the whole way, keeping to the hillside west of Barranco del Clot. Within an hour you attain the Collado de las Puertas (2533m), and a few moments later have your first glimpse of the lower lake; it's another twenty minutes to the shore of the upper lake (2526m), with surprisingly warm water for the altitude and a few campable, turfy spots on the far shore. Pale, bald pyramidal **Peña Blanca/Pène Blanque** (2906m) on the northwest is the most striking of the frontier peaks here, while 2787-metre Chinipro dominates to the south.

The descent (just over an hour from the upper lake to the road-bend) is enlivened by eyefuls of the Valle de Pineta's south ramparts and the more distant Cotiella Massif. It's not possible to continue into France from the upper lake; the only trekkers' route is west, down the Barranco de Fuensanta draining the lower lake, then south along the Río de la Larri, joining up with the GR11 shortly before reaching the Pineta *parador* – allow two and a half hours going downhill.

The Valle de Tella

The **Valle de Tella**, through which flows the Río Yaga, opens northwest roughly halfway between Aínsa and Bielsa, at Hospital de Tella. Though its praises are little sung in conventional tourist annals, it has long been one of the favourite **canyoning** venues on the flanks of Monte Perdido. At the head of the valley, just inside *parque nacional* territory, plunges the **Garganta de Escuaín**, a series of waterfalls, smooth chutes and pools where properly equipped devotees abseil, slide and swim.

This is great walking country too, especially when the terrain closer to Monte Perdido is snowed up. The **GR15** and **GR19** overlap briefly near Tella village, on the valley's east flank, and an onward PR path completes a tour of most highlights. Scenically, the eight local villages are overshadowed, in all senses, by a landscape dappled by the interaction of soothing vegetation and dazzlingly bare rock. Green, lush scrub – much of it *boj* (box), made into souvenir utensils – blends into low alpine forest, with two-thousand-metre **Castillo Mayor** presiding on the west, and remoter **Peña Montañesa** (2301m) – logo of this part of Aragón – dominating the skyline to the southeast.

Car access – and canyoning

The top of the valley is easily accessible by ordinary car: paved roads lead to Revilla on the east bank and to the village of Escuaín on the west. The **Revilla turning** leaves the main road at Hospital de Tella, from where it's 8km in total to the end. As the road climbs to the hamlet of Cortalaviña there are wonderful views east to the distinctively tilted lump of Peña Montañesa; then, 2km beyond Cortalaviña, the road divides. The right-hand option climbs to Tella (see below), while the left-hand road continues along a ridge to Revilla, where it ends.

The **Barranco de Consusa** just below Revilla is one of the six main canyoning courses of the area, and includes a three-hundred-metre-long "staircase" with four thirty-metre chutes and countless smaller drops. It'll take four to six hours to cover the full length of the stream, and at the bottom it's about 45 minutes' walk back to either Revilla or Escuaín.

The **turning for Escuaín** begins at the north edge of Escalona, west along the minor HU631 towards Añisclo. After 1km on this, take the paved road on the right (north) signposted to Escuaín (via Belsierre and Puértolas), 15km in total from the A138. (Some maps mistakenly indicate a nonexistent access road from Hospital de Tella.) From Escuaín a track to the northwest (barred to vehicles at the park boundary) affords access to the main canyoning area in the *garganta*.

Walking in the Valle de Tella

If you don't have transport, the quickest way into canyon country is along the joint **GR15/19** trail, well signposted 200m north of the church in Lafortunada. This climbs initially northwest within two hours to the picturesque village of **TELLA**, bigger than it looks from afar and restored for seasonal use. There's a park **information office** (April–Nov daily 9am–2pm & 4–7pm), an all-important fountain and **meals** or *bocadillos* at the *Bar Tella*. As well as the imposing parish church of San Martín, a trio of remoter *ermitas* just west, which can be visited on the signposted **Ruta de las Ermitas** loop-walk (45min). The remotest, with a tiny crypt, is eleventh-century **Juan y Pablo** at the base of an intriguing pinnacle, where the numerous local witches held their medieval covens; on the leg back to Tella you pass between sixteenth-century **Virgen de Fajanillas** and thirteenth-century **Virgen de la Peña**.

Just north of Tella, the GR19 and GR15 part company. The former heads east to Salinas, or north as the GR19.1 (Camino del Portiello) to Bielsa. The GR15 descends to a picnic area and **dolmen**, threads through the hamlet of **ARINZUÉ** and drops to the river at **ESTARONILLO** hamlet (1hr 15min from Tella). The final track approach to Estaronillo is often jammed with cars belonging to French rafters, who delight in running the **Garganta de Marval** of the Yaga just downstream.

From Estaronillo, the GR15 climbs another hour or so through thick woods to **ESCUAÍN**, a mostly abandoned settlement taken over in summer by strolling cows and rough campers, usually enthusiasts exploring the **Garganta de Escuaín**, which lies just upstream. You might pause at the park **information office** (same hours as Tella's) before continuing along paths into the water-sculpted ravine.

From Escuaín, a very steep trail drops in twenty minutes to the Río Yaga, then continues on the far bank past a derelict mill, crosses the outflow of the Barranco de Consusa and climbs from the river. Ninety minutes out of Escuaín, five minutes shy of the road up from Tella, be extra observant: here you can veer south on the fairly clear, marked **PR39** trail down to Estaronillo or north along an overgrown twenty-minute path to **REVILLA**. Even more desolate than Escuaín, with just a few houses modernized as vacation retreats, the hamlet is well camouflaged by the orange and grey cliff immediately behind. From just west of Revilla, a path leads 45 minutes to a *mirador* of the **Barranco de Angonés**.

If you opt instead for the PR39 south, you continue past Estaronillo and then along a shelf of land wedged between the Garganta de Marval and Castillo Mayor, finishing after two and a half hours in total at **Hospital de Tella** on the A138. It's possible to complete the entire figure-of-eight itinerary of Lafortunada–Tella–Ruta de las Ermitas–Escuaín–Revilla–Estaronillo–Hospital in a single, long summer's day, taking in the best this limestone region has to offer.

Escuaín to Añisclo

Escuaín itself is a good jumping-off point for walking further **into the parque nacional**, specifically the **Valle de Añisclo**. Head northwest, high up on the right (southwest) bank of the Yaga, at first on track (signposted as "Surgencia del Yaga") and then on path, until you reach the **Cuello Viceto** (2002m; 3hr). From here a wide path curves south down into Añisclo, pausing at a shelf on which are the spring and unstaffed refuge of **San Vicenda** (4hr 30min along), beside one of the park's few permitted camping areas.

From San Vicenda, the best trail drops north into the bottom of the canyon past **Fuente de Foradiello**, and then crosses the main Añisclo watercourse just downstream from the mouth of the Capradizas ravine. Once on the far bank, you can head north to Fon Blanca and the GR11 (see p.409), or follow the main Añisclo canyon trail south for three and a half hours to the **Ermita de San Úrbez**, at the entrance to the Añisclo canyon (see below).

More simply, you can also follow the **GR15 southwest** from Escuaín to the *ermita* in about six hours, leaving you enough daylight to reach accommodation in Nerín or Buerba. The trail initially heads west over the **Cuello Ratón** on the shoulder of Castillo Mayor, and then veers south, mostly on track, to the village of **BESTUÉ**. This has one of the best views southeast in Alto Aragón, with the banded Sestrales ridge on the west separating you from Añisclo; unfortunately there are no longer any facilities here. Beyond Bestué on the GR15, you're on scenic path again for three hours to San Úrbez, involving a roller-coaster course over the Sestrales, rewarded by views into Añisclo from the top.

The Valle de Añisclo

The uninhabited **Valle (Cañon) de Añisclo**, forging due south from the Collado de Añisclo, is on a far grander scale than the Valle de Tella and accordingly more visited. It's a beguiling spot, more intimate and wild than its other rival Ordesa; neither is the path running through it, parallel to the Río Vellos (Bellós), a pram-pushing stroll, given its often sharp grades and drop-offs from unguarded edges.

If you have transport, you can reach Añisclo on the minor but paved HU631 road heading west from just north of Escalona on the A138. Once past a large **campsite** 2km along, *Valle de Añisclo* (☎974 505 096; Easter–Oct 15) below Puyarruego village – your last chance to swim in the Río Vellos, forbidden further upstream – you enter the *parque nacional* at the dramatic **Desfiladero de las Cambras**. Here the road is confined to a shelf blasted out of the rock wall, too narrow for excursion buses, and is designated one-way westbound (eastbound traffic heads to Escalona along a purpose-built detour via Buerba – see p.413). At the west end of the gorge, 12km from the main highway, knots of parked cars announce the mouth of Añisclo just to the north. If you're approaching from the west (ie Nerín or Sarvise), the one-way system forces you to park 1600m above the canyon (a link path descends to it).

The canyon walk

From the parking areas, two broad paths – equally valid, as they form a loop around the confluence of the Vellos and Aso rivers – lead north into the canyon. The right-hand path crosses a delicate, vertiginous **medieval bridge** high above the joint streams, then follows a ledge where a cave has been converted into the **Ermita de San Úrbez**, honouring a fifth-century wonder-working hermit, master of wild beasts plus patron of rain and shepherds. Some fifteen minutes past the *ermita* you change to the west bank and climb to meet the GR15 trail coming east from Nerín on its way to Bestué. Soon you're passing through box thickets and beech woods,

△ Valle de Añisclo

with the occasional conifer or yew, the locality damp and shady except at midday. The river's flashing cascades and tempting green pools glimmer far below you on the right, tantalizingly out of reach except for a few points when the trail draws level with the water, and perhaps just as well, since you're not allowed to bathe. High, sheer walls amplifying the roar of the torrent culminate in the **Sestrales crest** to the east, here interrupted by an uncanny keyhole-shaped cleft.

Progress upstream is not steady – the path roller-coasters constantly, with a particularly notable climb and hairpins away from the river about two hours along, at the top of which you have the best views possible into the lower canyon. The most spectacular section finishes at the grassy expanse of **La Ripareta** (1400m), only about 500m higher than San Úrbez but, because of the nature of the trail, nearly three hours distant. Here, you're level with the river again, but camping is not permitted until 1800m elevation; otherwise it's a good spot for a picnic, or watching the sky for birds of prey.

From La Ripareta there's a choice of onward routes on which you'll have more solitude, since the gradient stiffens and the trails become fainter. About 40min north you can cross the main river and follow a path up to the authorized bivouac area and shelter at **San Vicenda**. Continuing on the west bank from La Ripareta for about ninety minutes, you'll reach the Fon Blanca cascade at the Barranco Arrablo (see p.409), which funnels the **GR11** west to the *Refugio de Góriz*. In the opposite direction the GR11 leads over the Collado de Añisclo to the Valle de Pineta; you'll want a fairly early start from San Úrbez to finish either of these traverses in a single day (the *Refugio de Góriz* is a more reasonable goal).

West from Añisclo: the Valle de Vió

West from the mouth of the Añisclo canyon, the road follows the **Valle de Vió**, a deserted district particularly affected by the exodus to the lowland towns; the half-dozen or so local villages have just a handful of residents, and one is completely abandoned. But unlike in the Valle de Tella, the villages with their eleventh- to thirteenth-century churches are far more interesting than the valley itself, sun-scorched and overgrazed to barrenness on the north, though still heavily wooded on its south slope.

Buerba and around

The namesake village of **VIÓ**, 5km south of the Añisclo gorge car parks, is the one place hereabouts where (in summer at least) there are still more tractors than tourists, trundling through the surrounding hayfields, though it's deserted in winter. Not so at **BUERBA**, 2km further at the end of the paved road, always packed with canyoners plumbing the secrets of the **Río Yesa** to the south. For non-canyoners, the best outing from here is the two-hour **walk** on an unmarked path to very attractive Yeba village, crossing the river. The GR15.1, a short *variante* path, links Buerba via Vió with the GR15 at San Úrbez, while another leg of the GR15.1 goes to Fanlo via Buisán, making a good day-loop possible.

In terms of **food** and **accommodation**, relaxed en-suite *Casa Marina* (Ⓣ608 714 450, Ⓦwww.ordesa.net/casa-marina/; all year; ❸ B&B), the first building on the right as you enter Buerba, with young, English-speaking management and home-cooked meals (vegetarian on request), is more homely than the slick and somewhat sterile *Casa Lisa* (Ⓣ974 337 215; ❷), with variable rooms and meals for guests only (bar open to all).

Nerín

If you're without transport and only committed to day walks in Añisclo, you'll have to stay either at Buerba or **NERÍN**, an hour's walk west of the canyon on the GR15, via the forlorn, utterly deserted hamlet of Sercué. By road from San Úrbez (not recommended for pedestrians) it's 5km away. Nerín is blessed with an incomparable setting, gazing east to Peña Montañesa, plus a reliable spring and an exceptionally fine Romanesque church. What's locally billed as the "Fanlo" **cross-country skiing area** (22km of pistes at 1975–2100m) is actually accessed from Nerín – but the track in requires a 4WD vehicle.

Short-stay tourism and the renovation of a dozen or so buildings as holiday homes have somewhat revived what was once another dying hamlet. The *Añisclo Albergue* (Ⓣ974 489 010, all year; 36 places), with its front garden and ravishing view, serves meals to guests only, and requires reservations, as does the *Pensión El Turista* (Ⓣ974 489 016; ❷), with its panoramic *comedor*. Top standard for some distance around is offered by chalet-style *Hotel Palazio* (Ⓣ974 489 002, Ⓦwww.hotelpalazio.com; ❹), three floors' worth of plush, loft-style rooms, ski or snow-shoe rental and a popular ground-floor restaurant.

Fanlo

The GR15 carries on west to Fanlo, curling through effectively abandoned, though beautifully sited Buisán, whose hilltop houses have also been restored for seasonal use. **FANLO**, 6km beyond Nerín by the more direct paved road, and again engagingly sited, is the biggest place hereabouts, with a unique, turreted manor house and an equally photogenic communal laundry just south of it juxtaposed uneasily with a huge, unfinished hotel just downhill. The few **turismes rurales** here are rented entire as self-catering houses, though *Casa Pedro y Lourdes* at c/Las Fuentes 29 (Ⓣ974 314 156, Ⓦwww.pedroylourdesturismorural.com; ❹) is good value, hosting up to seven guests. For **meals**, there's just a sandwich bar (*Las Eras*), unimprovably perched amongst the hilltop grain barns and threshing grounds west of the village.

Just northwest of Fanlo yawns the **Desfiladero de las Gloces**, a congenial beginners' canyoning venue – a fact not lost on the French who throng the place. From the high point of the road, west of Las Eras, a path runs north for half an hour through abandoned fields, woods and scrub to the stony riverbed. The first obstacle, a ten-metre chute, presents no problems if you've ever been to a water park, and subsequent drops are easy by comparison. Two to three hours later you emerge a bit southwest of Fanlo, well below the road.

Moving on

West of Fanlo, 12km of steep, lightly travelled road bring you down to Sarvisé on the N260 (see opposite). The **GR15** also emerges on the asphalt an hour out of Fanlo, but, following a much-needed rerouting, soon leaves it to adopt approximately the 1300-metre contour west on its way to Buesa village, via the **Ermita de la Virgen de Bun**. Alternatively, you can use a track, a bit higher than the Desfiladero de las Gloces path, heading northwest within three hours to the **Cuello de Diazas** (2133m), which overlooks the Valle de Ordesa. Once there, you've a choice of paths and tracks, either north into the valley or west to Torla, the latter easily reached after another two and a half hours.

The Valle de Ordesa and around

Carved out first by glaciers and later enlarged by the fast-flowing Río Arazas, the eight-hundred-metre-deep trough of the majestic **Valle de Ordesa**, in the north of Alto Aragón, deservedly draws hundreds of thousands of visitors a year. It forms the core of the **Parque Nacional de Ordesa y Monte Perdido**, which takes the second part of its name from the imposing limestone massif lying at the centre of park territory.

The two usual road approaches to the *parque nacional*, both served by **public transport**, are via either Sabiñánigo and Biescas (see p.423) to the west, or from Aínsa (see p.401) to the southeast, along the N260 following the Río Ara, which has headwaters close to Vignemale and merges with the Zinca some 60km later at Aínsa. Along the first half of its course, before curling east, the Ara flows south through the **Valle de Broto**, where villages like **Sarvisé**, **Oto** and **Broto** have been rescued by tourism from the desolation that has befallen those further downstream. **Torla**, 45km upstream from Aínsa and 39km northeast of Sabiñánigo, is much the busiest of these settlements, being closest to the Valle de Ordesa, though surprisingly lifeless in winter as there's no ski centre nearby.

North of Torla, beyond the confluence of the Ara and the Arazas, there are just the campsites and refuge at **Bujaruelo**, beyond which lies a wilderness not included in the park. Coming from the strategic *Refugio de Góriz* below Monte Perdido, the **GR11** threads through the Ordesa canyon, follows the Ara north almost to its source, then crosses west to Panticosa. Alternatively you can hike **into France** through a number of passes: the Brecha de Roldán/Brèche de Roland towards Gavarnie, or two others at the top of the Ara into the Cauterets basin.

The Valle de Broto

Travelling upstream from Fiscal (see p.405), the N260 turns north past gradually more forested slopes to reach **SARVISÉ**, the lowest village of the **Valle de Broto**, 38km from Aínsa. In high season you could be compelled to stay in Sarvisé, rather than further north, but **accommodation** here is of a high standard. Best by some way is the *Hotel Casa Frauca* (Ⓣ974 486 353, Ⓕ974 486 789; Ⓦwww.casafrauca.com; closed 6 Jan–March; ❸) on the N260, with cosy, custom-furnished, wood-floored rooms in a variety of formats, including attic suites with painted beams; eight new annexe units are due to open in 2008 behind the original building, a 1904-vintage mansion. Their two famous ground-floor *comedores* draw crowds from near and far (€17 *menú*, €26–30 *a la carta*; reservations required) for the sake of daily-changing gourmet fare – baked fish, quail with onions, leek mousse, creative desserts – in medium-sized portions. Otherwise, go for the stone-built, quiet *Casa Puyuelo* (Ⓣ974 486 140, Ⓔcasapuyuelo@staragon.com; ❷), with small but sweet, pastel-toned rooms, an attic lounge and broad front lawn, or the 2006-enlarged *Hotel Viña Olivan*, by itself at the edge of town on the Fanlo road (Ⓣ & Ⓕ974 486 358; ❷). Sarvisé is also a major **horse-riding** centre, with two stables: Sarvise (Ⓦwww.caballossarviseadolfo.com), and Casa Blas (Ⓦwww.caballoscasablas.com).

Perched 4.5km away by road on the hillside northeast of Sarvisé (or reached more directly from a PR trail from the north edge of Sarvisé), beautiful, secluded **BUESA** consists of two sleepy *barrios* flanking a wooded vale – rural Aragón as it was until the 1980s. Grilled suppers are available at *Bar Merendero Balcón del Pirineo*, and there are rather basic rooms with self-catering kitchen at *Casa Pleto* up by the church (Ⓣ974 486 175; ❶) – no palace, but a potential lifesaver in August. Another useful fallback is the handsome village of **ASÍN DE BROTO**, 5km south of Sarvisé and then 600m east up the slope, which offers the enormous *Hostal Albergue Casa Notario* (Ⓣ974 337 209, Ⓦwww.ordesa.net/casa-notario; all year), with doubles (❷), dorms and apartments under one roof, ideal for self-catering groups.

Broto, Oto and Linás de Broto

BROTO itself, 4km north of Sarvisé, is the valley's "capital"; a **Turismo booth** (summer only Tues–Sun 10am–2pm & 4.30–8.30pm; Ⓣ974 486 002) advises on

accommodation vacancies. It's a noisy, teeming place in summer, the old quarter hemmed by traffic and a massive *urbanización*, a plight symbolized by the collapsed Romanesque bridge just upriver, destroyed during the Civil War. Beside this is the quietest place to stay, and one of the last to fill: *Casa O'Puente* (Ⓣ974 486 072; ❷). Other accommodation includes the one-star *Hotel Gabarre* at no. 6 onthe through road (Ⓣ974 486 432; ❸) and the good-value *Hotel La Posada* on c/Los Arcos (Ⓣ974 486 336, Ⓦwww.hotel-laposada.com; ❸), with a quiet riverside setting downstream from the bridge. Casteret Grupo Explora (Ⓣ974 486 432, Ⓦwww.grupoexplora.com), at c/Santa Cruz 18 downhill from the *Gabarre*, is the local guides' bureau, specializing in canyoning, caving and especially **rafting** – the stretch of the Río Ara from Puente de los Navarros (see opposite) and Broto is particularly appropriate. Broto also has two **bank** ATMs and the only **fuel** between Aínsa, Biescas and Torla.

Alternatively, head for the more attractive village of **OTO**, 1.5km south, which features homogeneous architecture and two notable medieval towers: one on the church, the other on a fifteenth-century baronial mansion. More or less opposite each other in the centre are two modern, sterile but spotless **turismos rurales** – *Casa Herrero* (Ⓣ974 486 093; ❷), above the bar, and *Casa Pueyo* (Ⓣ974 486 075; ❷), which also manages the large campsite, *Oto* (April 1–Oct 15), 500m beyond the village.

LINÁS DE BROTO, a tiny, stone-built hamlet 10km west of Broto on the N260 towards Biescas and Sabiñánigo, would also be a reasonable spot to fetch up, as long as you have a car, with its fine position and clutch of **places to stay** along the through road. These include the co-managed *Hotel Las Nieves* (Ⓣ974 486 109, Ⓦwww.hotellasnieves.net; ❸) and *Hostal Cazcarro* (❷) and an *albergue*, *El Último Bucardo* (Ⓣ974 486 323, Ⓦwww.elultimobucardo.com; 82 places in four- to six-bunk rooms). Without a car, you may prefer to trust to luck in Torla; a well-trodden *camino*, part of the **GR15.2**, leads there in 45 minutes from Broto's ruined bridge.

Torla

The brazenly commercialized village of **TORLA** is the principal gateway to the park, just over 8km away by road, and besides Broto or Sarvisé is the only feasible base if you don't have transport. A mushrooming of concrete construction on the outskirts has obscured the village's profile, though the medieval core remains intact and attractive, despite the conversion of every second building for tourist purposes.

Buses stop at the southern edge of town, by the large **car park** where all visitors to Ordesa must leave their vehicles in high season and use the onward shuttle-bus (see box on pp.418–419). The **Turismo** (late June to mid-Sept Tues–Sun 9am–1.30pm & 5–9pm; Ⓣ974 229 804) is on Plaza Nueva, while a new **visitors' centre** (Centro de Visitantes) for the national park is under construction beside the car-park (tentative hours July–Oct 10am–1pm & 4–8.30pm). The village also has a **bank** (with ATM), a **post office** and several shops stocking basic foods and mountain gear. One of the latter doubles as the HQ of Compañia Guías de Torla (Ⓣ974 486 422, Ⓦwww.guiasdetorla.com), organizing rafting, canyoning and climbing expeditions.

During July and August you'll need to book **accommodation** in Torla well in advance; at other times, it's rarely a problem, though from October to Easter most establishments shut from Monday to Thursday. Top mid-range choices are friendly *Hostal Alto Aragón* (Ⓣ & Ⓕ974 486 172; ❷) and the co-managed *Hotel Ballarín* (Ⓣ & Ⓕ974 486 155; ❸), opposite at c/Capuvita 11, with tile-floor rooms and views of the village rooftops; the home-style food at the *Ballarín*'s *comedor* is filling and good value. Among five fancier hotels, the most professionally run is the ★ *Villa de Torla* on the main square (Ⓣ974 486 156, Ⓦwww.villadetorla.com; ❹) which, though not exactly cosy, understands what foreigners want; try for the superior top-floor rooms. It has a pool in the terrace garden, limited parking out front and a creditable restaurant with game occasionally on the menu. Also worth considering if you have a car is the three-star *Abetos* (Ⓣ974 486 448; Ⓔhotelabetos@torla.com; ❹), 2km out towards the national park on the river side of the road, with comfortable rooms and generous breakfast offsetting slightly kitsch common areas.

For budget lodgings, there are two **turismos rurales** on c/Fatás, next to the Turismo – *Casa Laly* (Ⓣ974 486 168; ❷) and *Casa Borruel* (Ⓣ974 486 067; ❶) – or a pair of **albergues**: cramped *L'Atalaya* (Ⓣ974 486 022; 21 places in dorms; April–Oct 15) with a downstairs restaurant, or the friendlier, higher-standard *Lucien Briet* (Ⓣ974 486 221, Ⓦwww.refugiolucienbret.com; 43 places in seven-bunk dorms or smaller rooms), managed by the *Bar Brecha*, which serves good meals (*menú* €13) in its upstairs *comedor*. **Restaurants** independent of lodgings are scarce and not great value except for *A'Borda Samper*, just off the high street – also a *tapas* **bar** – and nearby *El Duende* on c/La Iglesia, with pricey *a la carta* but a €17 *menú*.

Finally, three **campsites** (all April–Oct) line the road to Ordesa. Hikers will prefer either *Río Ara* by the river (Ⓣ974 486 248), 2km from Torla on the east bank, or the smaller, more basic *San Antón* (Ⓣ974 486 063), 3.5km out of town on a terrace above the road.

Into the park from Torla

From Torla the **shuttle-bus** service rolls 4km northwest by the paved A135 road to the boundary of the **Parque Nacional de Ordesa y Monte Perdido**, at the Puente de los Navarros, at which point the road swings east for just over another 4km, where the bus leaves you at the car-parking area (open low season only to private vehicles), well inside the **Valle de Ordesa**. The closest **drivers** can get in summer is a small car park about 1.5km before Puente de los Navarros; from here a marked PR path goes down to Puente de la Ereta and thence into the park.

On foot, you should definitely shun the tarmac in favour of the *camino* marked as part of the GR15.2. This begins in Torla next to the *Hostal Bella Vista* (marked as "Ordesa por Senda Peatonal"), crosses the Río Ara on a cement-and-masonry bridge, then turns sharply left (north) to join the Camino de Turieto at the posted park boundary, 45 minutes from Torla. It's an easy and beautiful hike, two hours in total from the village, signposted all the way and taking you high above the river past some voluminous waterfalls. The path, like the road, eventually leads to the car park at **Pradera de Ordesa**, where there are toilets and a restaurant, predictably world-weary but offering a reasonable midday menu. There is no shop, so come prepared with provisions if you're intent on trekking or picnicking.

Walks in the Valle de Ordesa

Most valley walks begin from the vicinity of **Pradera de Ordesa**, specifically at the **Puente de los Cazadores** a little way upstream. There are dozens of possibilities, encompassing all levels of enthusiasm and expertise: the following are just a selection. Be aware that some of the "paths" marked on maps are actually technical climbing routes, and don't underestimate the time and difficulty of the more conventional pedestrian itineraries. Once you're out of the shady valley floor, the sun can be taxing, and drinking water is usually unavailable – take plenty with you, as the various waterfalls are contaminated.

The most accurate **map** of the Valle de Ordesa is the 1:50,000 Mapa Excursionista/Carte de Randonnées no. 24 "Gavarnie-Ordesa" sheet, which also covers a fair chunk of the French side, though cheaper ones such as the Editorial Alpina

The Parque Nacional de Ordesa y Monte Perdido

The **Parque Nacional de Ordesa y Monte Perdido** was Spain's first protected area, established in 1918 as a reserve of 21 square kilometres encompassing the showcase Valle de Ordesa, immediately south of France's Cirque de Gavarnie. In 1982 the *parque nacional* was extended to 156 square kilometres, incorporating half a dozen three-thousand-metre-plus summits and the entire Valle de Añisclo, plus the headwaters of the Tella and the Circo de Pineta. This made the Spanish park contiguous with France's *Parc National des Pyrénées*; since the late 1980s the two park administrations have undertaken joint policy formulation and management – a sensible strategy given the huge numbers of mountaineers who surge back and forth between the two.

Geomorphology

From the Ara river valley on the west to well past the Zinca drainage in the east, the Pyrenees incorporate a great mass of **karstic limestone**, heaved up from the sea floor about fifty million years ago, its beds first tilted and folded, then diligently sculpted by glaciers into a startling backdrop of peaks, cliffs and gorges. The process continues today on a smaller scale as dozens of seasonal waterfalls pour off the *circos* of the Ordesa and Pineta valleys in particular.

Monte Perdido, roughly in the centre of the park, ranks as the highest limestone peak in Europe, and the third highest summit in the Pyrenees. This mountain dominates the heads of the four major valleys – **Ordesa**, **Pineta**, **Añisclo** and **Tella** – which drain away from it; a glacier still survives on its forbidding northeast face. Invisible to most visitors' eyes, but no less dramatic, are the hundreds of sinkholes and caves riddling the rock strata here, especially in the karst dells between the French frontier and the *Refugio de Góriz*. Bleak uplands surrounding the Valle de Ordesa on all sides, though parched and cheerless in midsummer, delight alpine skiers during the winter.

Flora and fauna

Owing to a 2600-metre difference between the highest and lowest points in the park, and the consequent variation in climate, there's a broad spectrum of **flora**. Beech, birch and poplar forests thrive in the moist Valle de Ordesa; in the drier Valle de Pineta pine predominates; while at the mouths of the lower, warmer Añisclo and Tella valleys, an almost Mediterranean vegetation of oak, yew, box, ash and maple prevails, coexisting at slightly higher elevations with fir and black pine. Above the treeline sprawl vast moors of specially adapted pincushion-type plants, with the genus *Festuca* well represented, but tucked among all of this are nearly 1500 species of small flowering plants, scores of them endemics marooned here by the glaciers and found nowhere else.

Fauna around the *parque nacional* – including golden eagles, lammergeiers, griffon and Egyptian vultures and isards (*sarrios* in Aragonese) – is much the same as on the

---

1:40,000 "Ordesa y Monte Perdido" are adequate if you stick to popular, signed paths.

Valley traverse to the Circo de Soaso

This is one of the most popular – certainly in midsummer – and rewarding of the short-distance treks. It's not especially difficult: a steep, 7.5-kilometre, three-hour traverse of the entire Valle de Ordesa, along a signposted path from Puente de los Cazadores, to the **Circo de Soaso**, which is also the beginning of the route to the *Refugio de Góriz* (see p.420). From wonderful beech forest, the trail climbs past the *mirador* for the **Cascada del Abanico**, 3000m from Pradera de Ordesa, to emerge into the upper valley, with the *circo* at its head and to your left – fanning out over a cliff – the famous **Cola de Caballo** (Horse's Tail) waterfall.

French side, with the isards so prolific that at times hunters are allowed to cull the surplus. By contrast, the last native **ibex** died in January 2000; introduced specimens failed to survive.

Climate and seasons

Weather in the park is notoriously fickle: during some summers there's not a cloud in the sky for days on end, but in other years there's thunder and hail every afternoon. When venturing out of the valley bottoms, always go prepared. In winter the park lies under one to two metres of snow, which can persist in the popular Valle de Ordesa – not to mention higher elevations – until early June. Autumn features the spectacle of turning leaves on the beech and poplar trees, yet the weather remains relatively stable, if cool, and the park is far less crowded. Unless you're equipped for snow, the ideal visiting season is June to October.

Rules and regulations

Given ever-increasing tourist numbers, the park is at risk of being loved to death, so a few of the **rules** are worth elaborating. **Camping is prohibited** within the confines of the park except for a few specified areas, namely the Balcón de Pineta (above 2500m); at San Vicenda and Fon Blanca in the Valle de Añisclo (above 1800m); beside Escuaín village; and around the *Refugio de Góriz* when it's full (above 2100m). Even at these places, you must dismount tents and leave them lying flat during the day – if you don't, park employees or the hut warden may do so in your absence. The small **stone huts** marked on most maps are intended for daytime use only, as shelter from storms; the sole staffed **refuge** is the *Refugio de Góriz*, roughly at the centre of park territory. In addition to the expected bans on disturbing plant or animal life, no **fires** are allowed anywhere, even in the emergency hut hearths, and **no washing or swimming** is permitted in the rivers (most of them are too cold to get in anyway except in August). As at Aigüestortes in Catalunya, there's a **peripheral zone** of varying width to the south and east of the main *parque nacional* where development is controlled but few of the above prohibitions apply – you are allowed to swim, for instance, between Torla and the park boundary.

Motorized vehicles are not admitted beyond the chained gates at various points on the park periphery, and private-car approach from Torla along the paved access road is banned completely during Easter week and from July 1 to September 1. The Pradera de Ordesa car park is closed during those periods; the only vehicles allowed in are the **shuttle-buses** (departs 6.00, 7.00, 7.30 & 8am, then 15min intervals to 7pm; €3.30 return fare only) from the fee car park (€6.60/day) at the southern outskirts of Torla. A control booth at the road fork near Puente de los Navarros ensures that all private traffic goes north towards Bujaruelo during the restricted periods.

Return via Faja de Pelay

Looking downstream from the *circo*, you have a clear view of one of the artificial-looking but entirely natural ledges known as *fajas*: a standard feature of banded-limestone terrain, they are formed where a layer of softer calcareous rock has been exploded loose by repeated cycles of freezing and thawing. The ledge running along the south side of the canyon – the **Faja de Pelay** – is negotiated along its entire length by an easy path that can be followed back to the car park. Along the way you get more solitude than is possible in the valley bottom, and an aerial view of the canyon; opposite looms a succession of remote peaks and features – most conspicuously the Brecha de Roldán and the peaks of Cilindro and Monte Perdido.

The route is almost level at first, then drops gently to the *mirador* and stone shelter at **Calcilarruego**. From there, you descend fiercely along the **Senda de**

los Cazadores (Hunters' Path) by a long series of tight zigzags, finally crossing the Puente de los Cazadores to return to the bus stop. The total walk back from the Circo de Soaso is four and a half hours; there's no reliable water source until just before Calcilarruego, so you must carry your own supply the whole way. You might consider doing this loop in reverse: fewer crowds on the way back, and the stiff climb up the Senda de los Cazadores (2hr 30min) in morning shade.

Onward to the Refugio de Góriz

To ascend from the Circo de Soaso to the *Refugio de Góriz*, you have the choice of a gently zigzagging path to the right, or the direct assault up the cliff aided by *clavijas* (pegs and chains). The *clavijas* aren't as bad as they look, but if you've got a heavy pack, or the rocks are wet, take the path. Once past this point, follow the marked trail north to the **Refugio de Góriz**, 90min from the *circo* (2200m; ⓣ974 341 201; 96 places; all year; reservations advisable), sometimes known as *Delgado Úbeda*, where you can stay cheaply and eat expensively. The refuge, despite its regimentation and famously abrupt staff, is extremely popular and at peak times floor-space, and even food, might run out. When this happens camping is allowed nearby, but often the immediately adjacent area becomes revoltingly unsavoury – budget extra hiking time to reach better sites further east, towards the Collado Superior de Góriz (Arrablo).

Ascent of Monte Perdido

The standard expedition from the refuge is the **ascent of Monte Perdido**, done mostly for the views, since the southwest flank of the mountain – facing the top of the Valle de Ordesa – is the least impressive. It's more of a walk and scramble than a climb, but Monte Perdido can kill, so take advice from the refuge wardens. Most importantly, get an early start, since thunderstorms can break in the afternoon. Follow the path climbing steeply north up the east bank of the **Barranco de Góriz**, where cairns show the way through alternating tracts of grass and boulders. After two tough hours you reach the 3000-metre contour and the small frozen **Lago Helado**, in the shadow of **Cilindro**, Perdido's sister summit.

From the lake you almost double back for the final approach, climbing steeply southeast, often over snow and ice, the grade slackening only a little just before the summit (5hr from the refuge). From the top you can gaze down the Pineta valley to the east; over the Tella and Añisclo canyons to the south; across Lago de Marboré to the Brecha de Tucarroya to the north; and towards distant Vignemale to the west.

Once back down at Lago Helado, you don't have to return to the *Refugio de Góriz*, but can execute a traverse. This implies an extra early start, as you'll not only be climbing Monte Perdido, but negotiating the Cuello del Cilindro, dropping along the snowfields on the far side to Lago Marboré and – if you don't camp there – descending to the Valle de Pineta via the steep *balcón* trail.

To move on **west** from the *Refugio de Góriz,* trace the north side of the valley past the **Circo de Góriz** to the Breche de Roldán, the Cirque de Gavarnie and the *Refuge de la Brèche de Roland* (see p.371).

To the Cascada de Cotatuero and beyond

A popular side trip from the valley bottom goes up to the impressive **Cascada de Cotatuero**. Starting from the wayside shrine of the Virgen de Ordesa several hundred metres beyond the Puente de los Cazadores, the Cotatuero route takes you steeply but easily through the woods to a vantage point below the waterfall within an hour.

If you have a head for heights, you can continue on from here into France. With the help of more *clavijas*, you climb above the falls (2hr 30min) to reach the Gruta de Casteret and the Brecha de Roldán (4hr from the Puente de los Cazadores), for access to Gavarnie.

Alternatively, you can ford the stream beside the collapsed bridge here and adopt the un-signposted **Senda Canarrellos**, which roller-coasters up to about the 1800-metre contour on its way southeast, across the lips of hanging valleys and under rock overhangs, to a junction (3hr 30min into the day) with the main valley-bottom track at **Bosque de Haya**. This is just above the **Cascada de la Cueva**, from where the Puente de los Cazadores is about an hour downhill. However, the Senda Canarrellos is now unmaintained, with lots of tree-fall and boulder slides, though the path isn't formally closed and shouldn't present problems to experienced hikers. It's certainly the wildest and, after the Faja de Pelay route, the most impressive of the trails in the canyon, and it's a bit easier and quicker if done in reverse from the Bosque de Haya junction (which is still signposted); coming anticlockwise around the flank of Monte Arruebo, you get impressive views of the falls. Going clockwise, allow four and a half hours for this loop; anticlockwise, slightly less.

To the Cascada de Carriata and the Faja de las Flores

Another route signposted from the former car park leads to the **Cascada de Carriata**, pouring out of the **Circo de Salarons**. You head north into the trees, fork left and begin a steep zigzag up to the falls, which are most impressive in late spring when melted snow keeps them flowing.

If you want to continue into the *circo*, the left-hand route (at a fork on the open mountainside ninety minutes above the visitors' centre) ascends via a series of thirteen *clavijas*, not nearly as intimidating as those on the Cotatuero route and feasible for any reasonably fit walker; once on top you can carry on to the Brecha de Roldán.

The right-hand fork quickly becomes a nail-biting corniche trail along the **Faja de las Flores**. Nowhere wider than a mere 7m, this terrace runs for about 3000m horizontally along the 2100-metre contour of the valley's north wall, with an immense drop to the south. If you haven't got a head for heights you'll either have acquired one by the end, or be whimpering on your hands and knees. If you cover the entire distance, you meet up with the ascending path for the Circo de Cotatuero in about ninety minutes; reckon on an hour to descend to the Puente de los Cazadores.

Walks from the upper Ara valley

To reach the **upper Ara valley** on foot from Torla, head up the GR15.2 for just under an hour, as far as the junction with the Camino de Turieto and then, instead of continuing east into Ordesa, take the **GR11** northwest. This crosses the Arazas at the **Puente de la Ereta**, an anticlimactic cement aqueduct with some icy pools beneath it. Half an hour later the GR11 meets the access road for the *parque nacional* at the **Puente de los Navarros**, and then runs north along the Río Ara: first along the very rough dirt road, and then after the Puente de Santa Elena, as an east-bank trail. About 1km above that bridge, on the road, you'll find *Camping Valle de Bujaruelo* (☎974 486 348; April–Oct 15, also with bungalows), where there's a shop for supplies – the highest one in the valley – and a restaurant (reservations suggested): maybe not worth a detour, but great if you're on a trek, where the €12 *menú* might consist of lentil soup, lamb chops and apple mousse.

Staying instead with the east-bank trail, you'll arrive (1hr 30min or 7km from Puente de los Navarros) at the wide riverside meadow of **San Nicolás de Bujaruelo**, graced with the ruined eleventh to twelfth-century **church** of that name – and some contemporaneous hospice buildings originally built by the

Knights of St John to succour pilgrims. These now operate as an **albergue**, the *Meson de Bujaruelo* (1338m; ⓣ974 486 412, ⓦwww.mesondebujaruelo.com; 48 places in dorms & quads). Though clients of an affiliated activity centre seem to get first crack at the pastel-coloured rooms, the *albergue* offers lunch to all comers, and also manages the basic adjacent **campsite**. From the church, there are a number of possible trekking routes out of the Ara basin, all traced on the Editorial Alpina 1:30,000 "Vignemale Bujaruelo" map. You can, incidentally, proceed no further up-valley by vehicle – there's a locked barrier just past the hospice buildings.

Trekking into France

For the **Gavarnie** basin, take the path that crosses the Ara over a beautiful Romanesque **bridge** (currently scaffolded) and then zigzags quite steeply east to the frontier at **Puerto de Bujaruelo/Port de Gavarnie** (2270m); at the pass you pick up the HRP trail to the *Refuge de la Brèche de Roland*. Work on the dirt road which the Spanish were bulldozing up to the pass appears to have ceased, the project deemed incompatible with the aims of the two national parks.

For the **Cauterets** area, hike northwest upstream beside the Ara along the **GR11**, but at the point – four hours beyond San Nicolás – where the GR climbs west towards Panticosa, continue instead to the head of the valley, where you pick up the **HRP** west through the **Col d'Arratille**, reaching the *Refuge Wallon* (see p.377) after ten hours. You can also use the **HRP** east through the **Puerto de los Mulos** (2591m) to arrive at the *Refuge des Oulettes* in somewhat less time.

Trekking to Panticosa: the GR11

For **Balneario de Panticosa**, start out as for Cauterets but stay on the GR11. From the Ara valley floor, the route veers west-southwest up the **Barranco de Batanes** to the **Cuello de Brazato** (2578m; 6hr from San Nicolás) before dropping quite sharply to Balneario de Panticosa (see p.424) – a spectacular if full trekking day of seven and a half hours. The small tarns in the Batanes valley, plus the larger Brazato lakes, make this route a choice strategy for moving west; as part of a day-hike out of Panticosa, it's covered in detail on pp.425–426. In any event don't make the mistake of following the **old GR11** up the Valle de Otal, still marked as a *variante*. This might seem easier – the Collado de Tendeñera at the top is only 2327m – but it's longer and, as the GR marking committee concurred, pretty tedious.

The Valle de Tena and around

The next major north–south valley west of the Ordesa region, the **Valle de Tena**, wins few beauty prizes in the judgement of many travellers. The **Rio Gállego** which waters it, starting near the Puerto de Portalet/Col du Pourtalet and the ski complex of **El Formigal**, has been extensively dammed, with the usual pipelines and high-tension lines in attendance. At **Lanuza** reservoir, many houses in the namesake village stand poignantly half-submerged, as they have since 1975. Recently, though, owners have had some success in reclaiming their properties (see box on p.405), and Lanuza now co-hosts a summer music festival (see box on p.426), with an excellent, informal atmosphere.

At other times, you'll want a sound pretext to head upstream along the A136 road. This is furnished by the westernmost concentration of three-thousand-metre **peaks** and **glacial lakes** in the Spanish Pyrenees, northeast of the Valle de Tena, reached either from **Sallent de Gállego**, near El Formigal, or the side valley of the Río Caldarés, which flows past **Panticosa** village from **Balneario de Panticosa**.

Biescas

Some 25km west of Torla, by the intersection of the N260 and A136, the small town of **BIESCAS** dominates the lower end of the Valle de Tena, with a Templar-built church gracing the medieval upper quarter on the east bank of the Gállego. Biescas comes to life on August 14–17, when consecutive festivities in honour of San Roque and La Virgen de la Assunción feature a procession of giant papier-mâché effigies.

At other times of the year you might schedule a lunch stop at the **hotel-restaurant** *Casa Ruba*, c/Esperanza 18 (Ⓣ & Ⓕ974 485 001; ❸) on the east bank of the river. This has been in the same family for three generations, with a lively, authentic bar for *tapas* and breakfast. The *comedor* offers only *a la carta* supper, featuring lots of game and fish, though lunch *menús* are dull. Otherwise, in the west-bank quarter, there's *Hotel La Rambla* (Ⓣ974 485 177; ❸) and *Pensión Las Heras*, an old stone house at Agustina de Aragón 35 (Ⓣ974 485 027; ❶ sink-only, ❷ en-suite), a quiet cul-de-sac near the Guardia Civil barracks. If you get stranded here of an evening, one of these establishments will certainly come in handy – and Biescas is a more appealing place to spend the night than Sabiñánigo. There's also a **tourist office** by the southerly bridge (most of year: Mon–Sat 10am–2pm & 6–8pm, Sun 10am–2pm; Ⓣ974 485 002).

Sabiñánigo – and its museum

Unabashedly industrial **SABIÑÁNIGO**, 14km south of Biescas on the A136 and 18km east of Jaca, persuades few to linger, but almost everybody passes through at some point on their way to or from Ordesa, because there's an inevitable change here of buses, or from train to bus. The **train station** lies at the northwest edge of town on the Jaca road, right next to the **bus terminal**. Few will need, or choose, to stay overnight.

If you've your own transport, make an effort to visit the **Museo Ángel Orensanz y Artes de Serrablo** (April–June & Sept Tues–Sun 10.30am–1.30pm & 4–7pm; July & Aug daily 10.30am–1.30pm & 5–9pm; Oct–March Tues–Sat 10.30am–1.30pm & 3.30–6.30pm, Sun 10.30am–1.30pm & 4–7pm; Ⓦwww.orensanz.org/museum/; €2), installed in an eighteenth-century farmhouse (plus a modern annexe) at the extreme southern edge of town by Puente Sardás. Besides changing exhibits of cutting-edge contemporary art, it's justly reckoned the best ethnological museum in Aragón, with themed displays (musical instruments, religious art, wooden tools, etc). There are also fascinating archival photos and the original kitchen, axis of winter life, with its cooking implements and massive chimney hood. What little English labelling there is, is eccentric, but two interrelated truths are worth translating. Until the early twentieth century, the eldest son inherited the entire estate in rural Aragón, and alone would marry; his bachelor brothers, the *tiones*, became the family handymen or even itinerant craftsmen, and to them are owed the wealth of displays here. The items on show have been gathered from the 46 deserted villages of the Serrablo, the zone around Sabiñánigo, which in 1910 had a population of 77; its growth during the 1950–70 industrialization period depopulated three-quarters of the Serrablo and, by giving them homes in town, finally allowed younger brothers to marry.

Panticosa: skiing, village, spa

Fifteen kilometres upstream from Biescas, buses detour briefly at the far end of the **Embalse de Búbal** for the three-kilometre run northeast to **PANTICOSA** (Pandicosa) village, before continuing towards Sallent de Gállego. With its stucco exteriors and ornate windows on some remaining older buildings, Panticosa makes a tolerable – if pricey – base, especially in winter. The small local **ski complex** has prompted a mushrooming of chalet growth at the village outskirts; former patronage by Brits has left a legacy of English-language signage. With antiquated equipment and a poor natural snow record, the station nearly closed during the early 1990s, but has been rescued (for now) by massive investment in snow canons, new lifts and a new hub at 1900m. A state-of-the-art, eight-seater *telecabina* ferries clients from a vast car park at the bottom of the village (1150m) up to Petrosos (1900m), and from there the Sabocos chair-lift – one of six – continues to Valle de Sabocos, focus of the meatier runs, with access to the top point of 2200m. Of 38 pistes, fourteen are blue and fifteen red, making this a good beginner-intermediate resort (Ⓦwww.panticosa-loslagos.com), but runs below Petrosos are seldom usable. In **summer**, the *telecabina* and Sabocos lift take mountain-bikers and walkers to two lakes around the **Valle de Sabocos** (daily 10am–6pm; €10 return).

Accommodation in the village centre is heavily subscribed at peak times; top-value choices are the one-star *Vicente* up on the road to Balneario de Panticosa (Ⓣ974 487 022, Ⓦwww.hotelvicente.com; ❸), offering sweeping views across the valley, a restaurant and private parking, or the two-star *Escalar* at the village entrance (Ⓣ974 487 098; Ⓦwww.hotelescalar.com; ❹), with plusher rooms, a pool and again a *comedor* plus off-street parking. The central *Hotel Navarro* (Ⓣ974 487 181, Ⓦwww.hotelnavarro.com; ❸) on Plaza de la Iglesia has variable rooms – the best ones better than *Vicente* standards – but eccentric management and noise from poor insulation; its *comedor* is basic, with a restrictive *menú*. Central *Mesón Sampietro* on c/La Parra is the better of just two independent **restaurants**, and where the locals go. You can buy trekking provisions in Panticosa, and there are three **banks** with ATMs.

Balneario de Panticosa

From Panticosa, a narrow road (and summer-only bus) forges upstream along the Río Caldarés through the narrow **Garganta del Escalar**, where the sun seldom penetrates and waterfalls spray the road. **BALNEARIO DE PANTICOSA**, 10km beyond the village, is another one of those places claiming to be the highest (1636m) permanently inhabited spot in the Pyrenees. The emperor Tiberius supposedly visited Panticosa – the main baths are named in his honour – and there are, in fact, traces of Roman occupation in the vicinity, as well as an imposing Belle Époque casino, the only Spanish one comparing to its opposite numbers on the French side of the range. Between 2002 and 2004 this somewhat dated spa was turned upside down: the resulting five-star *Gran Hotel* (Ⓣ974 487 161, Ⓦwww.panticosa.com; ❼) offers all creature comforts (including three upscale restaurants and every sort of therapy) – though Internet searches on generic sites may shave a few tens of euros off rates. Sitting somewhat uneasily with all this glitz is an FAM **refuge** in the northwest corner of the resort, *Casa de Piedra* (Ⓣ974 487 571; 98 places; all year), sited to serve the GR11 which passes through here. In future years the refuge may be shut down and re-established up at the lower Bachimaña lake (see opposite); in winter a small **cross-country ski** facility operates around the spa.

Walking from Balneario de Panticosa

You're well poised at Balneario de Panticosa for treks of all durations and difficulties: either the long day-traverse to Sallent de Gállego along the GR11 (best broken with an overnight en route), or the equally extended loop east using a GR11 variant. The appropriate Editorial Alpina map is the 1:25,000 "Panticosa Formigal", plus the 1:30,000 "Vignemale Bujaruelo" for the easterly loop.

Traverse west via the GR11

For the moment, the westbound **GR11** trailhead in Balneario is easiest found from the *Refugio Casa de Piedra*. Some fifteen minutes along, there's a T-junction just above an avalanche weir: right for Brazato ("2 oras"), left for Bachimaña ("1.15"). These timings are overly brisk – even with a day-pack, it's 80 minutes from here to the lower Bachimaña dam, and 35 minutes more to reach another T-junction at the water-meadows by the inflow of the upper **Ibón Bachimaña** (2hr 15 minimum from Balneario). Here you've the option of going north through the Puerto de Panticosa/Port du Marcadau (2540m) for the *Refuge Wallon*, a short trekking day of about six hours (see p.377). To continue on the GR11, you swing west over gently rising ground to the upper **Ibón Azul** (3hr from Balneario), where there's good camping.

Next, you climb steeply to the double pass of **Cuello d'o Infierno** (2721m) and **Collado de Tebarray** (2782m), problematic after snowy winters; once through this, it's all downhill past the **Ibón de Llena Cantal** (another wonderful campsite) to the **Respumoso (Respomoso) reservoir** (2150m; 3hr from Ibón Azul). This is about as far as you'd comfortably get with a full pack in one day from Balneario; on the north shore stands the *Refugio Respomoso* (Ⓣ974 490 203; 2200m; 105 places; open all year). If they're full, or the brusque wardens put you off, there's ample grass for camping on the south shore (the antiquated Alfonso XIII hut, still shown on all maps, is now kept locked). The view north to **Balaitus/Balaïtous** and east to the triple pyramids of **Cambales** (2968m), **Petite Fache** (2947m) and **Grande Fache/Gran Facha** (3005m), more than compensates for the ugly concrete dam and construction debris at the western end of Respumoso. (For climbing Balaïtous or heading into France on the HRP, see "Around Balaïtous and Lac d'Artouste", p.392.)

To continue on the GR11, drop down the skilfully engineered path west from the lake, following the curving Aguas Limpias stream to Sallent de Gállego village (2hr 30min), the last half-hour or so beyond the **Embalse de la Sarra** on asphalt road. If you've made an early start after staying at Respumoso, it's possible and recommended to lengthen this final stage with a side trip north, on a cairned minor trail, to the **Arriel lakes** just below the HRP.

Loop east via Circo de Bramatuero

For this scenic circuit – with none of the potential shuttling problems of arriving in Sallent, if you've left a car at Balneario – begin as for the westerly GR11 traverse. But when you reach the junction at the water-meadows by the upper Bachimaña reservoir, turn right instead of left, following a sign to the lower **Bramatuero dam** ("35" – really 40min), bearing right and slightly down at the next fork to avoid going up to the Puerto de Panticosa and *Wallon*. From the lower to the upper Bramatuero lake (2500m) it's 1hr 15min (4hr 15min from Balneario), on a fair trail through more water-meadows and past natural tarns. Gentians are out in profusion during early summer, with a few black-and-white bar-blazes mixed with cairns as waymarks. At the upper dam, the path fizzles out; cairned isard-traces lead above the north shore to natural **Ibón Letrero** (2540m; 5hr) at the top of the **Circo de Bramatuero**, a fine lunch spot where snow lingers into July.

From Letrero, it's a deceptively easy twenty minutes more up to the **Collado de Letrero** (2680m), with magic views of the Ordesa *fajas* and Vignemale. The 45-minute descent to the upper **Ibón de los Batanes** (2380m) is along a nasty couloir, with a scree slope to negotiate towards the bottom. It's another hour, via the equally scenic lower lake, to the junction with the main GR11 (6hr 45min), avoiding unnecessary altitude loss. Looking north, you glimpse frontier pinnacles comprising the **Circo de Ara**, and probably wisps of cloud in the late afternoon, while at the trail junction (turn west) there's the sound of three mingling streams in spate.

You will take 45 minutes up the confusingly named Barranco de Batanes to the first tarn (2350m); marmots shriek all around from boulder piles, and a broad meadow just below is popular with campers. The Alpina map tracing is not precise – the good trail spends as much time on the true right bank as the left. Within 35 minutes more, you attain the **Cuello de Brazato** (2578m), where herds of isards are often seen. If you're overtaken by nightfall, camping is congenial at the natural lake just below the pass, but it's only an hour and three quarters more (almost 10hr for the day) to the Balneario. You need stamina and a long June/July day to accomplish this without spending a night out.

The upper Tena valley

Regular buses ply the **upper Tena valley** along the main road as far as Sallent de Gállego; with your own transport, you can easily explore a handful of villages clinging to the slopes just west of the Bubal dam. The southernmost, **PIEDRAFITA DE JACA**, is attractive, with both an *albergue* (ⓣ974 487 627; 20 places in two dorms) and the *Refugio Telera* (ⓣ974 487 061; 14 places in four- to 6-bunk rooms) catering to patrons of the nearby cross-country ski centre at **Partacua**. Claiming to be the largest in Alto Aragón with 45km of prepared routes (though only about half the extent is likely to be open), Partacua is actually between the villages of **TRAMACASTILLA DE TENA** – largely overrun by *urbanizaciones*, but offering the luxurious four-star **spa-hotel** *Privilegio de Tena* (ⓣ974 487 206; ⓦwww.elprivelgio.com; ❼) in a converted monastery – and more unspoilt **SANDINIÉS**, which offers another excellent **hotel-restaurant**, *Casa Pelentos* (ⓣ974 487 500, ⓦwww.pirineo.com/casapelentos; ❹), with award-winning country

Pirineos Sur – some tips

Pirineos Sur (ⓦwww.pirineos-sur.es), established in 1992 and now a fixture of the latter half of July, has evolved into one of Europe's best **world music** bashes, typically attracting the likes of Manu Dibango, Khaled, Esma Redzepova, Fanfare Ciocârlia and Alpha Blondy, among others. Besides the main evening events at a **floating stage** in Lanuza on the shore of the reservoir, there are specialist **workshops** and a *mercado del mundo* (crafts and food) in the centre of Sallent de Gállego.

The **ticket** booth in Sallent has very limited hours; **advance sales** (*venta anticipada*) are easier at Cocodisk, c/Villahermosa 3, Huesca; in France at FNAC Pau; or French Carrefour or Géant supermarkets. Irritatingly, there is no sales point in Jaca. You can also buy online through Ibercaja (ⓦwww.ibercaja.es) or Tick Tack Ticket (ⓦwww.ticktackticket.com), but all agencies outside Sallent or Lanuza levy a stiff commission on top of the already substantial **admission** charge (also, twelve percent extra on the door). If you're planning to attend more than five events, consider the season ticket offered.

On the evening of events, a giant **anticlockwise traffic system** around the reservoir is instituted; drivers can only approach from the south, over the dam. **Parked** cars eventually line the entire road from Lanuza village back to the dam – it's a very long walk in if you arrive late (after 9.30pm for 10pm nominal start times which invariably end up being 10.30pm). **Eat** at the *mercado del mundo* beforehand, since at Lanuza there's only beer for sale. No cameras, VCRs or water bottles are allowed; bring warm clothing as it gets cold onstage towards midnight. **Accommodation** in the Valle de Tena is of course sorely stretched at festival time, but camping rough along the approach road – as hundreds do – is not recommended unless you have a self-sufficient caravan, as there's no water or sanitation.

fare. From Sandiniés you can descend briefly to **ESCARRILLA**, 500m north of the side road to Panticosa, marred by tower-blocks of holiday flats, though with ample facilities. **Accommodation** is available at the *Hotel Sarao* (Ⓣ974 487 065, Ⓦwww.hotelsarao.com; ❸), with preferred attic rooms and a popular **restaurant** (*menús* €13–15, or at the more luxurious *Hotel Ibón Azul* (Ⓣ974 487 211; ❺), both on the main through road.

Sallent de Gállego

Once past the **Embalse de Lanuza**, a right turn at a bridge over the Gállego takes you into **SALLENT DE GÁLLEGO** (Sallén de Galligo), a sizeable old village 21km from Biescas, at the confluence of the Gállego and the Aguas Limpias. In the centre, there's another fine old bridge across the Gállego and a fortified hilltop church – though the nearby ski resort is spurring steady expansion west and north-east along the riverbanks. Sallent plays a dual role as a winter-sports and summer mountaineering centre, as well as co-hosting (with Lanuza) the *Pirineos Sur* **festival** the lattter half of July (see box opposite).

Accommodation is fairly abundant and pitched with an eye to the French. Working your way from east to west along the single high street, c/de Francia, you encounter *Hostal El Centro* (Ⓣ974 488 019, Ⓦwww.valledetena.com/centro; ❸), whose rear rooms face the stream and the peaks, and a decent if simple *menú* with wine served in the tiny *comedor*; *Hotel Familiar Maximina*, tucked away on a side street at c/La Iglesia 3 (Ⓣ & Ⓕ974 488 436, Ⓦwww.valledetena.com/maximina; ❸), with family suites for the price; *Hostal Faure* (Ⓣ974 488 007; ❷), in a courtyard off the main road, the best budget choice, again with a *comedor*; and last but not least, the atmospheric, creaky-floored, originally eighteenth-century *Hotel Balaitus* (Ⓣ & Ⓕ974 488 059, Ⓦwww.hotelbalaitus.com; ❹), with private parking and smallish but well-equipped rooms. For the truly impecunious, the friendly, non-smoking *Albergue Foratata* stands near the west end of c/de Francia (Ⓣ974 488 112, Ⓦwww.foratata.com; 100 places), with an inexpensive canteen on the ground floor.

There's a good range of independent **restaurants** around the central plaza. *El Rincón de Mariano* is a reliable and popular locals' choice, with *menús* from €16 but pricier game and grills *a la carta*, while *Casa Martón* is pleasant, though with a dull *menú*, so splurge on *a la carta*. *Granja Casa Bernet* has a range of imported beers and homemade pastries, becoming a lively nocturnal **bar**. On c/del Vico, going uphill from the *Faure* & *Maximina*, there's the inexpensive but pleasant *Restaurante El Sarrio* at no. 3. Sallent also has two **banks** (ATMs) and three shops for trekking supplies, plus daily buses to Jaca.

El Formigal

The uphill road from Sallent, with views of striking Peña Foratata on the north, weaves for almost 5km to **EL FORMIGAL** (Ⓦwww.formigal.com). Neither twee nor chic, it's a more serious ski resort than Panticosa, expanded several times before 1997, with further (and controversial) growth planned in the Valle de Izas. Mostly north-facing runs are scattered on a vast, treeless slope across the valley from the chalets, between 1500m and 2200m; as at Panticosa, a *telecabina* gets you up to the hub of the action at 1800m. In total, 22 other lifts (one-third chairs) serve 34 pistes, mostly red-rated – this isn't a great beginners' resort.

Except for the pleasant, small two-star *Hotel Tirol* at the edge of the *urbanización* (Ⓣ974 490 377, Ⓦwww.hoteltirol.org; ❼ HB only) with good views, **accommodation** in El Formigal is overpriced; beds are hard to find anyway, so you'll appreciate Sallent and lower villages as useful fallbacks.

Jaca and around

JACA (Chaca), 18km west of Sabiñánigo on the N330, is approached through featureless, traffic-choked suburbs of ski chalets and apartments: an unpromising introduction to this early capital of Aragón, from which the kingdom was recaptured from the Muslims. The old centre, however, is a lot more characterful, overlooked by a huge star-shaped citadel and endowed with a superb Romanesque **cathedral**. This, and the monastery of **San Juan de la Peña** 20km southeast, are the major local sights, while in winter the proximity of **Candanchú** and **Astún**, westernmost ski resorts in the Spanish Pyrenees, provides an added bonus. Rail enthusiasts may be tempted by the train trip to **Canfranc**, almost at the French border and a good place to pick up the GR11 trail.

After a spell in the mountains, Jaca's (relatively) "big town" feel and facilities may well be an equal attraction. It's enlivened by cadets of the mountain-warfare

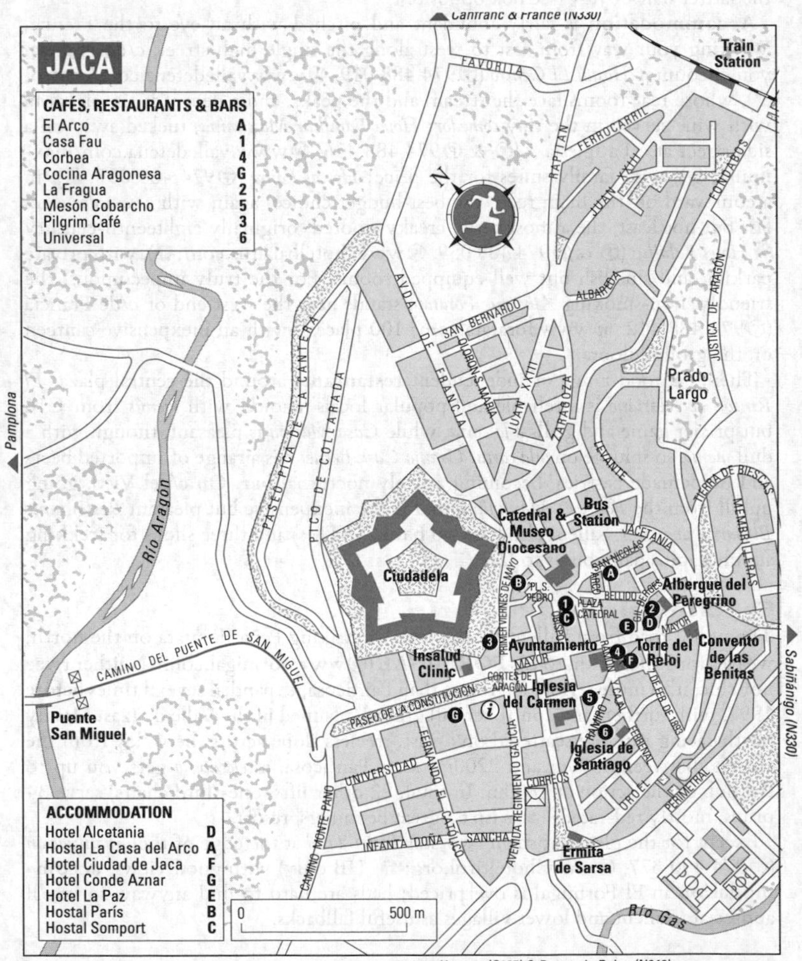

battalion based here and students attending a summer English-language university, while boisterous festivals punctuate the spring and summer months, especially on August 14–15 and during the early-August folklore festival, held odd-numbered years.

Arrival and information

The central **old town** divides into a somewhat dingy northeastern side – home to most of the budget accommodation and the noisier student bars – and the smarter southwestern quarter, abutting Avenida Regimiento Galicia, with its sidewalk cafés, more obvious restaurants and banks.

The **train station** (ticket office open 9am–1pm & 4–8pm) is a fair walk from the centre, so take urban bus #3 from the closest stop outside to the **bus station** on Avenida Jacetania, around the back of the cathedral. Useful long-distance coaches (rare on Sun) include those for Pamplona, Biescas via Sabiñánigo and Echo/Anso, as well as even more frequent services to Zaragoza and Huesca. **Drivers** will find parking easiest in the less congested district around the far end of, and side streets off, the Paseo de la Constitución, though look out for pay-and-display zones; a new underground car park is being built next to the bus station.

The helpful **Turismo** on Avenida Regimiento Galicia (summer Mon–Sat 9am–1.30pm & 4.30–7.30pm; winter Mon–Fri 9am–1.30pm & 4.30–7pm, Sat 10am–1pm & 5–7pm; ⓣ974 360 098, ⓦwww.aytojaca.es) stocks a range of free leaflets. For commercial products, see "Maps" under "Listings".

Accommodation

Although 820m up, Jaca counts as a Pyrenean resort; as such its accommodation fills up in August or during peak ski season, so advance booking is prudent. The youth hostel has closed, and just one **campsite** survives nearby: *Camping Victoria*, 1500m out of town on the Pamplona road (ⓣ974 360 323; all year), basic, shady and with a *bar-restaurante* on site.

Hotel Alcetania c/Mayor 45 ⓣ974 360 030, ⓕ356 073. Most rooms have balconies in this 1995-refurbished building; the alternate entry from c/Condo Aznar leads to a cheap and salubrious *comedor*. ❸

Hostal La Casa del Arco c/San Nicolás 4 ⓣ974 364 448, ⓦwww.lacasadelarco.net. Just five well-restored, stone-walled rooms (doubles and triples), above the handy eponymous bar and restaurant. ❷

Hotel Ciudad de Jaca c/Siete de Febrero 8 ⓣ974 364 311, ⓕ364 395. Centrally located but quiet place with good en-suite rooms in a modern building. ❸

Hotel Conde Aznar Paseo de la Constitución 3 ⓣ974 361 050, ⓔconde_aznar@jaca.com. An attractive old family-run hotel, with well-renovated rooms and off-street parking. ❺

Hotel La Paz c/Mayor 41 ⓣ974 360 700, ⓕ360 400. Large, somewhat airless en-suite rooms with heating in winter. ❹

Hostal París Plaza de San Pedro 5 ⓣ974 361 020. Best budget *hostal* in town, across from the cathedral, offering clean, spacious rooms with washbasin (no en-suites). ❷

Hostal Somport c/Echegaray 11 ⓣ & ⓕ 974 363 410. Jaca's most affordable en-suite digs, in another renovated old building; attractive ground-floor bar-restaurant. ❸

The Town

Sited at the foot of Peña Oroel, on a broad plain where the Río Aragón suddenly twists westwards into the Canal de Berdún, Jaca is a venerable place, called *Iacca* by the Romans after the local Iaccitani tribe. The Muslims occupied Jaca briefly from 715 to 760, when the Christians reconquered the town and (save for a brief spell) held it thereafter. The battle of **Las Tiendas** (4km west of Jaca), in 795, in which a Moorish army was repulsed mostly by the local women, is still commemorated on the first Friday in May by a mock all-female battle between Christians and Moors.

Within two centuries an embryonic democracy had emerged among the Aragonese nobility, whose comprehensive customary rights (*fueros*) – confirmed by King **Sancho Ramírez** in 1077 – limited royal power. Jaca itself reached its zenith during the three decades after 1035, when **Ramiro I**, Sancho's father, established the Aragonese court here and began work on the present cathedral.

The Catedral

The **Catedral** (daily 8am–2pm & 4–8pm; free) is the main legacy of Jaca's years as the seat of the young Aragonese kingdom, and ranks as one of the Pyrenees' most architecturally important monuments. Rebuilt on old foundations during the eleventh century, it was the first cathedral in Spain to adopt French Romanesque architecture, and thus exerted considerable stylistic influence on other churches along the Camino de Santiago.

Ramiro's endowment of the cathedral was undoubtedly intended to confirm Jaca's role as a Christian capital in what was still an overwhelmingly Muslim Iberia. Its design saw the introduction of the classic three-aisled basilica, though unhappily the original Romanesque simplicity has been much obscured by florid decoration in the intervening centuries. It retains some of the original sculpture, however, including realistic carving on the capitals and doorway – a later, Baroque statue of Santiago looks down from the portal. Inside, the main treasure is the silver shrine of Santa Orosía, Jaca's patron saint; a Czech noble, married into the Aragonese royal family, she was martyred by Muslims for refusing to renounce her faith.

Installed in the cloisters is an unusually good **Museo Diocesano**, closed indefinitely for renovations. If and when it reopens, it will feature frescoes and wooden religious sculpture gathered from village churches in the area and from higher up in the Pyrenees. Highlights should still include an eerily modern Pantocrator fresco from a church in Ruesta, a walnut crucified Christ, and the *Flight into Egypt* and *Adoration of the Magi* from Navasa, all of twelfth-century vintage.

The Ciudadela and Puente San Miguel

The **Ciudadela** (aka Castillo de San Pedro), a redoubtable sixteenth-century fort built to the French pentagonal-star-shaped ground-plan then prevalent, is still partly occupied by the Spanish army. You can visit part of the interior (daily: April–June & Sept–Oct 11am–noon & 5–6pm; July–Aug 11am–noon & 6–8pm; Nov–March 11am–noon & 4–5pm; €4) by forty-minute guided tour only. Its walls offer good views of the surrounding peaks, and of the wooded countryside around.

Below the citadel, reached along a steep dirt road from the end of the Paseo de la Constitución, lies a remarkable medieval bridge, the three-arched **Puente de San Miguel**. It was across this bridge over the Río Aragón that pilgrims on Camino Aragonés – a branch of the **Camino de Santiago** – entered Jaca. It must have been a welcome sight, marking the end of the arduous Pyrenean stage for pilgrims following this route from Provence into Spain over the Puerto de Somport. From Jaca, the pilgrims headed on westwards, through Puente la Reina de Jaca, towards Navarra, where they joined up with the more popular route from Roncesvalles. This Aragón section of the Camino de Santiago – like other branches of the route – has experienced quite a revival since the early 1990s and is marked as the **GR65.3**, though it's constantly threatened by inundation by dams or covering over by building projects. In Jaca, there's an **Albergue del Peregrino** (pilgrims' hostel) in the partly medieval hospital on c/Conde Aznar (64 bunks; ⓣ974 355 758; reception daily 3–10.15pm).

Eating and drinking

Jaca has a selection of fairly reasonably priced **restaurants** and **bars** concentrated in the old town, and even in the rowdier northeastern quarter there's a wholesome after-dark atmosphere.

El Arco c/San Nicolás 4. That rare Spanish breed: a vegetarian, no-smoking restaurant (though wine is served). Fresh, filling, international dishes and inexpensive *menús* at €10–12, with juices, teas and alcohol in the equally cheap adjoining bar. Closed Sun in winter.

Casa Fau Plaza de la Catedral 4. Classic *tapas* bar, with a few tables under the arches, more inside and notoriously rude staff. All the usual platters, plus *ciervo* (venison) sausage, *boletus* (wild mushrooms) and quiche.

Cocina Aragonesa Paseo de la Constitución 3. The *comedor* of the *Conde Aznar* hotel is reckoned to be one of the best eateries in town. There is a choice of unusually interesting *menús* for about €15, while *a la carta* won't much exceed €23 (booze extra).

Corbea c/Mayor corner c/Ramón y Cajal. Seriously good Basque-style *pintxos* at this small bar opposite the *ayuntamiento*; downside is that it's got about as much atmosphere as the usual bus-station *mostrador*.

La Fragua c/Gil Berges 4. Generous, reasonably priced grills without any airs or graces; no *menú*, budget €25–30 *a la carta*. Closed Wed.

Mesón Cobarcho c/Ramiro Primero 2. Don't let the decor – part Gaudí, part Flintstones – distract you from the excellent cooking; the €17 *menú* features both seafood and meat, though *a la carta* is pricey at €27–33.

Pilgrim Café Avda Primer Viernes de Mayo 7. Inevitably a bit touristy, and the fare (burgers, *pintxos*, *platos combinados*, bocadillos, coffees) is nothing exceptional, but this occupies a fine old industrial, wood-floored building with outdoor tables facing the Ciudadela's lawn.

Universal c/Campoy Irigoyen 11. Very popular, self-described "*brasa*-bar" specializing in *cochinillo* (suckling pig), *caracoles* (snails) and other wood-fired, country-style grills at €11–13, though there are cheaper platters if no *menú*. Homestyle desserts, courteous service and a skylit *comedor* are other pluses. Closed Mon.

Listings

Adventure activities Jaca Adventura on Avda Francia 1 (ⓣ974 363 521) and Alcorce-Adventura, opposite the Turismo at Avda Regimiento Galicia 1 (ⓣ974 356 781, ⓦwww.alcorceaventura.com) organize a variety of expeditions; both companies have English-speaking staff.

Hospital In addition to the main one on c/Rapitan, off the map beyond the train station, there's the very central, public Insalud clinic on Paseo de la Constitución, good for minor ailments.

Maps La Unión at c/Mayor 34 and El Siglo at c/Mayor 17 sell all the maps and guides required for the region.

Outdoor gear In the centre, Charli Avda, Regimiento Galicia 3, and Intersport-Piedrafita, Avda de Francia 4, have a limited stock; for a wider selection, go to Forum Sport, in a shopping mall at the far northeastern edge of town. It's a bit tricky to reach; you have to cross the N330 via two underpasses near the RENFE station.

Southwest of Jaca: San Juan de la Peña and Santa Cruz de la Serós

San Juan de la Peña, high in the Sierra de la Peña southwest of Jaca, is the best-known monastery in Aragón. In medieval times an important *variante* of the pilgrim route from Jaca to Pamplona detoured here, as San Juan reputedly held the Holy Grail – actually a Roman chalice which later found its way to Valencia cathedral. These days, most tourists (and there are many) visit for the views and Romanesque cloister.

The most direct **route to the monastery** begins from the Jaca–Pamplona N240 highway. A side road, 11km west of Jaca, leads south 4km to the village of **Santa Cruz de la Serós** with its Romanesque church, from where it's a further 7km by road up to San Juan. There is no public transport, although you could take the afternoon Pamplona-bound bus from Jaca and walk from there – assuming an overnight in Santa Cruz. From Santa Cruz, walkers can take the **old path** up to San Juan in about an hour. The path is waymarked as Variant 2 of the GR65.3.2 and is signposted from near the church (where there is also a map-placard). The **road** takes a more circuitous route around the mountainside, giving wonderful views of the Pyrenean peaks to the north and the distinctive Peña de Oroel to the east – though **parking** near the monastery is subject to restrictions.

Santa Cruz de la Serós

The picturesque village of **SANTA CRUZ DE LA SERÓS**, which comes to life in summer, is dominated by its thick-set but nonetheless stylish Romanesque **church** (daily 10am–2.30pm & 3.30–8pm; €1 or included in San Juan de la Peña admission); inside, a steep stairway leads to a rib-vaulted chapel in the dome, a hiding place in time of danger. The tenth-century sanctuary was once part of a large Benedictine convent which flourished until the sixteenth century; indeed *serós* appears to be a corruption of *sorores* (sisters), after the nuns who once dwelt here. There are a couple of places to **eat** and **drink** in the village: *Casa d'Ojalatero* in the centre, purveying *migas*, *endivias* with roquefort and grills (*menú* €16, or €30 *a la carta*), and the similarly priced *Hostelería Santa Cruz*, also hosting the village bar. The latter also has high-standard **rooms** (Ⓣ974 361 975, Ⓦwww.santacruzdelaseros.com; ❸), four with balconies.

San Juan de la Peña

SAN JUAN DE LA PEÑA actually comprises two monasteries, 2km apart. Approaching from Santa Cruz, you reach the lower (and older) one first. Built into a hollow under an escarpment from which various springs seep and birds of prey soar, the **lower monastery** (summer Tues–Sun 10am–2.30pm & 3.30–8pm; spring & autumn Tues–Sun 10am–2pm & 4–7pm; winter Wed–Sun 11am–2pm; €4.50, €6 includes shuttle-bus) is an unusual and evocative complex, even in its partial state of survival. Entering, you pass first into the **Sala de Concilios** – once the refectory – and the adjacent, double-naved, ninth-century **Mozarabic chapel**. Both retain fragments of Romanesque frescoes – particularly the church arches – and were jointly adapted as the crypt of the main Romanesque **church**, built two centuries later. There, in 1071, Cluniac monks replaced the Mozarabic Mass with the Latin rite – the first such substitution in the Iberian peninsula, made possible by the re-establishment of contact with Rome after centuries of isolation.

Upstairs, alongside the main church, is an open-air **pantheon** of Aragonese and Navarrese nobles; reliefs on the nobles' Gothic tombs show events from the early history of Aragón. An adjacent, closed pantheon for the kings of Aragón was remodelled in a cold, Neoclassical style during the eighteenth century and later sacked by Napoleon's troops.

All these are appetizers, however, for the twelfth-century Romanesque **cloisters**, at the far end of the complex where the rock overhang has been left open to the sky rather than being completely walled off. Only two of the bays survive intact, but the carved capitals are among the greatest examples of Romanesque carving anywhere. All depict scenes from the Old Testament and synoptic Gospels: the most obvious are Cain and Abel, Adam with a fig leaf, an angel warning Joseph to flee to Egypt, two of the Magi, Christ's Entry into Jerusalem, Christ on the Sea of Galilee, meeting Lazarus' sister Martha with the Raising of Lazarus, and the Deposition. They were the artistry of an anonymous, idiosyncratic craftsman who left his mark on a number of churches in the region. He is now known as the Master of San Juan de la Peña, his work easily recognizable by the figures' unnaturally large eyes.

The late-seventeenth-century **upper monastery**, a sizeable complex with a flamboyant Baroque facade, can be seen from the outside only. Facing the monastery is a popular picnic ground in a huge, forest-enclosed meadow; if you arrive by car, this is where you must **park** during high season – a shuttle-bus will take you down to the older monastery. In low season private cars may park in the bus bays at the lower monastery.

North of Jaca: Canfranc, Candanchú and Astún

The Río Aragón drains south from the Puerto de Somport, but its valley – extending directly **north of Jaca** – is known as the **Canfranc**. So too are a pair of settlements along the way: **Canfranc-Pueblo**, 19km out of Jaca on the N330, devastated by fire in 1944 (population 40), and **Canfranc-Estación**, 4km further and (currently) the final stop for northbound trains, as well as being near the south end of the **Somport tunnel** which leads under the watershed into France. A crag-top fortress 2km up the valley, plus the bizarre, round **Torre de Fusileros** south of the tunnel mouth, attest to the age-old military importance of this corridor; just shy of the frontier, 9km beyond Canfranc-Estación along the old road, **Candanchú** and **Astún** ski resorts flank the approaches to the Puerto de Somport.

Canfranc: Pueblo and Estación

Consistent with its depopulation, short-term tourist facilities (other than ski chalets) in the one-street village of **CANFRANC-PUEBLO** are limited, though out on the highway is the first/last filling station since/until some way down the French Aspe valley. Accommodation comprises the *Refugio Sargantgana* (1045m; Ⓣ974 373 217, Ⓦwww.sargantana.org; 100 places; all year), an **albergue** for pilgrims on the Camino de Santiago and two adjacent **bars** for meals and drink, one of which (*La Cabaña*) has two *turismo rural* **rooms** (Ⓣ974 372 119; ❷). **VILLANÚA**, 4km south in a wider part of the valley, is more attractive, but has only a clutch of overpriced hotels and another **albergue**, *Refugio Triton* on Plaza Mediodía (Ⓣ & Ⓕ974 378 281, Ⓦwww.alberguetriton.com; 54 places in four- or eight-bunk dorms); the main independent **restaurant** a block away is *Asador Jose*.

Since the French discontinued their part of the local trans-Pyrenean line, the enormous train station at **CANFRANC-ESTACIÓN** – equipped with the second-longest platforms in Europe – has become a badly vandalized white elephant. It's a sad fate for an elegant spot which saw heads of state attend its inauguration in 1928, and which later served as a location for the film *Doctor Zhivago*. Spanish undercutting of French ski-resort rates (ironically, the Spanish slopes are now pricier) prompted the closure of the line in 1970, though the last straw was the collapse of a bridge on the French side, left unrepaired (along with two others later collapsed at Urdos and Estaut) to this day. EU funding for the rehabilitation of the rail line between Oloron-Sainte-Marie and Canfranc has been approved, and (apparently) the first step was the 2006–07 rehabilitation of Canfranc station as a luxury hotel and conference centre.

The surrounding village, such as it is, was founded to house those made homeless by the 1944 disaster, and now exists primarily to lodge skiers and catch the passing motorist trade (mostly French), with a few souvenir shops and lodgings. **Accommodation**, all on or just off the through highway, includes the high-quality *Albergue Pepito Grillo* (Ⓣ974 373 123, Ⓦwww.pepitogrillo.com; 36 places in six-bunk dorms; all year), serving the GR11 as well as the Camino Aragonés, and the chalet-style *Hotel Villa Anayet*, towards the north end of "town" at Plaza de Aragón 8 (Ⓣ974 373 146; closed mid-April to mid-June & mid-Sept to mid-Dec; ❸), with a pool. There are also two adjacent, somewhat overpriced *casas rurales* on Plaza Aragón: renovated *Casa Marieta* (Ⓣ974 373 365; ❹) and *La Tuca* (Ⓣ974 373

104; ❷). For **meals**, the *Hotel Villa Anayet*'s *comedor* offers good value at €10 for service at white-napery tables by obsequious waiters, though the cooking is more careful and the €13 *menú* wider ranging at either *Borda l'Anglassé*, in the southern sector of town, or at *Casa Marieta* (€17). **Nightlife** is limited to mid-July and mid-August fiestas, as well as a valley-wide **classical and jazz music festival** over much of July.

Though there's no proper train yet, you can travel on **into France** with a few daily **SNCF buses**. Coming **from France**, these buses arrive in Canfranc from Oloron with equal frequencies. **Train** connections for Jaca are awkward; you're more likely to continue south by more frequent **bus**. Consult Canfranc's **Turismo** (June 15–Sept 15 Mon–Sat 9am–1.30pm & 5–8pm; Oct–June Tues–Sat 9am–1.30pm & 4–7pm, closed Nov 1–15; ⓣ974 373 141, ⓦwww.canfranc.com), opposite the station, for schedules and festival info.

Walking from Canfranc: the GR11 east and west

The **main GR11** runs **northeast** from between Canfranc and Candanchú via the **Canal Roya** valley, then curls southeast to the attractive, upper **Ibóns Anayet** (3hr 30min), from where you've fine views of Pic du Midi d'Ossau. From here it's another three hours, mostly on 4WD track through the slopes of El Formigal, to Sallent de Gállego, for an easy hiking day. For the record, a variant goes east directly from Canfranc-Estación along the **Valle de Izas**, the two routes converging at El Formigal, but this is less scenic, and will become even less so if Formigal's expansion into this valley happens.

Heading west from Candanchú itself involves a longer and tougher day's trek hugging the border, enlivened by the **Ibón de Estanés** (2hr 30min), the largest natural lake in these parts. From here – as long as the campsite at **Selva de Oza**, near the top of the **Valle de Echo** fails to reopen – you're best off taking the variant south through the Valle de los Sarrios and Los Puertos pass to *Refugio de Lizara*, from where Echo is an easy stage away (see p.456).

Skiing: Candanchú and Astún

Two of the more advanced Aragonese ski resorts are **CANDANCHÚ** (ⓦwww.candanchu.com) and **ASTÚN** (ⓦwww.astun.com), respectively 8km and 11km north of Canfranc (weekend buses in winter from Sabiñánigo, more frequently from Jaca); a bypass on the east side of the valley takes you directly to Astún. These unaesthetic, functional complexes – recently expanded Astún dating from 1975, Candanchú the first established in these mountains – are just 4km apart, though there's no shared lift pass or physical link. Jaca's failed bid to host the 2010 Winter Olympics (there's another current try for 2014) has, however, ensured pretty decent facilities. Both resorts have extensive north-facing runs in treeless valleys just southeast of the frontier ridge; given Atlantic-influenced climate, their top points of 2300–2400m should ensure good snow.

The fifty pistes at **Astún**, mostly blue- and red-rated, are served by six chair-lifts, though these are prone to closure because of high winds, and only two are high-speed; one, "Truchas", operates in summer, shuttling hikers up to one of several lakes either side of the border. From the top point at La Raca, you have fantastic views northeast to the Pic du Midi and west beyond Candanchú, though runs from here can be hard and icy. Also, liaisons between the sectors are often obscure, and you really need to be of intermediate ability to enjoy this resort. Rank beginners are better off at **Candanchú**, which has a half-dozen nursery slopes among its 51 runs, 29 of them red or black; though only a quarter of 24 lifts here are chair-type, they're well placed to serve most of the meatier runs. Off-piste possibilities at both resorts are considerable, with a half-dozen routes minimally maintained.

Budget **accommodation** in Candanchú is restricted to two good *albergues* encouraging half-board: *El Águila* (Ⓣ974 373 291, Ⓦwww.infobide.com/elaguila; 58 places in four-bed en-suites or six-bed dorms; open Dec–April & July–Aug), and *Aysa* (Ⓣ974 373 023; 38 places). Of three **hotels**, marginally the most economical is wood-chalet, two-star *Hotel Candanchú* (Ⓣ974 373 025, Ⓦwww.hotelcandanchu.com; ❼ B&B winter, ❹ summer). For **eating** out, skiers – and in summer, GR11 trekkers – congregate at friendly *Cafeteria Cristiania*, which despite the name does full meals.

Huesca and around

Huesca, one of Aragón's three provincial capitals, lies 56km due south of Sabiñánigo on the broad, fast N330/E7 – or more circuitously, and scenically, 76km from Jaca via the A1205 southwest through the Puerto de Oroel, and then onto the A132 southeast past the natural wonder of **Los Mallos** and the imposing **Castillo de Loarre**. The rail line out of Sabiñánigo also approximately traces this journey, along the Río Gállego. The next major town east of Huesca is **Barbastro**, smack in the middle of Aragón's most esteemed wine-producing district, just east of the Río Zinca valley, which provides a corridor for the A138 up to Aínsa or beyond. North of the Huesca-Barbastro road, occupying a rectangular territory of roughly 800 square kilometres, looms the low-altitude **Sierra de Guara**, an ever-popular target especially when the higher Pyrenean ranges are still under snow.

Huesca

Despite a big-city feel, with African, Muslim and gypsy communities, **HUESCA** is perhaps the least memorable Aragonese foothill town, and if you're heading towards the mountains you might bypass it altogether. However, to the northeast lies the **Sierra de Guara** with its canyonlands, while northwest of Huesca the striking **Los Mallos** pinnacles and the **Castillo de Loarre** provide worthy pretexts for breaking a journey towards Jaca.

That said, Huesca has a fair-sized **old quarter** (if a bit over-modernized with neo-Iberian brickwork) tucked into a loop of *paseos* and the Río Isuela. Dead centre stands a late Gothic **Catedral**, whose unusual facade combines the thirteenth-century portal of an earlier church with a brick Mudéjar gallery and a pinnacled, Isabelline top section. The great treasure inside (visitable only via the Museo Diocesano except when services are on) is a *retablo* by Damián Forment, a Renaissance masterpiece depicting the Calvary, Crucifixion and the Deposition. Next door, the **Museo Diocesano** (Mon–Sat 10am–1.30pm & 4–6/7.30pm; €2) contains a rather mixed collection, gathered from churches in the surrounding countryside. On Plaza Universidad 1, the **Museo de Huesca** (Tues–Sat 10am–2pm & 5–8pm, Sun 10am–2pm; €2) contains an assortment of archeological and ecclesiastical items from across the province. These apart, there's little to detain you. The liveliest time to visit is during Huesca's big **fiesta** in honour of San Lorenzo, held over the week nearest August 10.

Arrival, information and accommodation

Finding your way around Huesca shouldn't be a problem. The **estación intermodal** (joint train and bus terminals) lies southwest of the centre off c/Zaragoza, a main thoroughfare. The not terribly well-stocked **turismo** (daily 9am–2pm & 4–8pm; Ⓣ974 292 100, Ⓦwww.huescaturismo.com) is on Plaza Luís López Allués. If you need an item of **trekking or adventure equipment**, Tienda Guara-Mascún at c/Vicente Campo 11 is well stocked.

In mid-summer, when trekkers are passing through, and during skiing season, when higher-altitude lodgings fill and the overflow is forced down to Huesca, it's worth booking **accommodation** in advance. Budget digs include *Pensión Augusto*, c/Aínsa 8 (ⓣ974 221 470; ❷), tidy rooms above a bar; *Hostal San Marcos*, c/San Orencio 10 (ⓣ974 222 931; ❸), is a good mid-range en-suite option handy for nightlife clustered in nearby alleys; and *Hostal El Centro*, c/Sancho Ramírez 3 (ⓣ974 226 823, ⓔhcentro@auna.com; ❷), offers well-renovated en-suite rooms, many with a balcony, in a grand old building with a lift. More comfortable choices on Plaza Lizana just downhill from the cathedral include *Hostal Lizana/Lizana 2* (ⓣ974 220 776, ⓦwww.hostal-lizana.com; ❸) at no.6–8, and three-star *Hotel Sancho Abarca* at no. 13 (ⓣ974 220 650, ⓕ974 225 169; ❻), where most rooms have balconies or air con. The **campsite**, *San Jorge* (ⓣ974 227 416), is at the end of c/Ricardo del Arco.

Eating and drinking

Restaurante Marisquería Navas, c/Vicente Campo Palacio 3 (closed Sun pm & Mon) is considered Huesca's top **restaurant** by virtue of delicious fish, game dishes and *artesanal* desserts. The chef's full works will cost about €32 plus drink, but there's also an excellent-value *menú* (€15). Its only serious rival is *Restaurante Las Torres* at c/María Auxiliadora 3 (closed Sun & Aug 20–Sept 3) – a fancy place offering *nouvelle* Aragonese cuisine (try the *menú gastronómico at* €50). A more affordable, trendy choice is *La Bodeguita del Centro* (closed Mon), under the eponymous *hostal*, with a basement restaurant (*menú* €12) and a street-level bar doing *cazuelas*, *raciones* and wines by the glass. For other excellent **tapas bars** and **nightlife** head for the *zona* around c/San Lorenzo and c/Padre Huesca, between the Coso Bajo and the Plaza de Santa Clara, while for *horchata*, cakes, crêpes and real *gelato*, there's *Los Italianos* at Coso Bajo 18.

Castillo de Loarre

The **Castillo de Loarre** (mid-March to mid-Oct 10am–1.30pm & 4–7pm; Oct–March 11am–2pm & 4–5.30pm; closed Mon except June–Aug; free) is Aragón's most spectacular and best-maintained fortress. As you approach across a plain carpeted with almond groves, the castle seems to blend into the hillside but up close assumes a breathtaking grandeur: compact but intricate, its south ramparts are rooted in a sheer palisade at 1100m elevation, commanding the landscape for miles around.

Its builder was Sancho Ramírez, king of Aragón and Navarra (ruled 1063–94), who used it as a base for his resistance to the Moorish occupation. The first structure encountered inside the curtain walls is the **Capilla Real**, consisting of the delicately proportioned Romanesque Iglesia de San Pedro, with capitalled columns adorning blind arches in the apse, and a beehive-domed and vaulted crypt reached either by narrow, claustrophobic stairs from the altar or a conventional door. Elsewhere, the labyrinthine ground plan conforms well to most fantasies of what a castle should be with its dungeons, ruined palace, lancet windows and turrets; accordingly it was used as a location for Ridley Scott's 2003 crusader film *Kingdom of Heaven*. Of a pair of towers, the **Torre de la Reina** has ornate Gothic windows, while the taller **Torre del Homenaje** – climbable to the penultimate storey – is dominated by a massive hooded fireplace.

Practicalities

The castle stands some 30km northwest of Huesca on the most direct route via Bolea (buses pass this way), and 4km beyond the village of Loarre (stiff hike up along the PR105 path). **Bus** timetables conspire against a day trip: Loarre has morning bus service only from Jaca, while Ayerbe has two or three afternoon/evening services from Huesca. Fortunately there are adequate facilities in both sleepy **LOARRE**, graced by a fifteenth-century parish church with an ornate spire, and equally provincial **AYERBE** 7km away, which has the nearest train station. Judging from the ornate fifteenth-century **Palacio de los Urries** and adjacent clock tower on the central *plaza* Santiago Ramón y Cajal (1852–1934), called after the distinguished scientist who spent his childhood here, Ayerbe must once have been a place of some importance.

Closest **accommodation** to the castle is the three-star *Hospedaria de Loarre*, a restored seventeenth-century mansion on the central *plaza* (Ⓣ974 382 706, Ⓦwww.hospedariadeloarre.com; ❺); its bland, non-air-con rooms are rated one star too many, though the **restaurant** (closed Sun) is well respected (€17.50 *menú* or about €30 *a la carta*). Failing this, Loarre has one *casa rural*, *Casa Tolta* (Ⓣ974 382 605; ❷) and Ayerbe a further four, the most characterful being the *Antigua Posada del Pilar* at Plaza Aragón 38 (Ⓣ974 380 052; ❷), with good suppers offered. There's also a quiet **campsite** 1600m out of Ayerbe on the road to Loarre, *La Banera* (Ⓣ974 380 242; all year), and another between Loarre and the castle.

Tested **restaurant** options in Ayerbe include the sustaining *Floresta*, at the start of the Loarre road (*menú* €11), and the fancier *Rincón del Palacio*, next to a medieval manour house on the main Plaza de Ramón y Cajal, where the €23 *menú* gives you access to the best of the *carta*. At no. 11 on the same *plaza*, *Bar El Pozo de Sherea* acquits itself well for *tapas* and drinks.

Los Mallos and its villages

The train line from Huesca to Jaca and the A132 road from Huesca to Puente la Reina de Jaca give views not only of Loarre but of the fantastic, pink-tinged, cylindrical rock formations known as **Los Mallos** ("the Ninepins"), divided into two separate clusters at Riglos and Agüero. Their majesty, however, may not serve to protect them from partial inundation by a **proposed new dam** at Biscarrués on the Río Gallego, augmenting the Pántano de la Peña already existing just

△ Los Mallos pinnacles

upstream. Ubiquitous roadside graffiti – RÍO = VIDA (River = Life), PÁNTANO BISCUARRÉS JAMÁS (Biscuarrés Reservoir Never), BASTA CON INUNDAR (Enough Flooding), PÁNTANO = DESPOBLACIÓN (Reservoir = Depopulation) – leaves you in no doubt as to prevailing local sentiment. For the moment, the pinnacles remain popular with climbers and parapentists, while the river below the existing reservoir swarms with rafters from April to early summer.

Riglos to Murrillo de Gállego

If you're travelling by train and want a closer look, get off at **Riglos** station (just an unattended platform; you must ask the conductor to stop) and walk about 700m up the access drive to **RIGLOS** village, tucked underneath the most impressive stretch of the pinnacles. At Riglos you can **stay** above the *Bar Restaurante El Puro* (aka *Casa Toño*; ⓣ 974 383 176; ❷); Toño himself is a mine of information on climbing routes up the *mallos*. Failing that, there's an en-suite **turismo rural** in the heart of the village, *Casa Escalaretas* (ⓣ974 383 096; ❷). Another superbly restored *casa rural* is at **CONCILIO** village, on the A132 just before the side road to Riglos: *El Corral de Concilio* (ⓣ974 380 898, ⓦwww.elcorraldeconcilio.com; ❺), with meals, sauna and bike rental. Non-climbers can enjoy a cool-season loop-walk along the marked **PR98 trail** from Riglos, which takes in the villages of Escaleta la Peña and Carcavilla, as well as the base of the cliffs, in under four hours.

Otherwise, an alternative local base is **MURILLO DE GÁLLEGO**, another stunning village above the main A132 highway. The main sight here – if you can gain admission – is the twelfth-century church of the **Virgen de la Lliena** just behind the village, with a pebble-mosaic floor, wooden gallery at the rear, delicate arches and excellent fifteenth-century murals. The roadside quarter is pretty much taken over by river enthusiasts in season. No fewer than four outfitters offering rafting, kayak and hydrospeed are based along the busy highway; **canoeing** starts from €34, **rafting** €31, depending on group size and rapids rating. **Accommodation** includes the roadside *Hostal Los Mallos* (ⓣ974 383 026; ❸), which also runs an *albergue*; there's another more comfortable one up in the village at c/La Manga, *Casa Chancabez* (ⓣ974 383 018; 47 places; March–Nov), as well as a partly shaded **campsite** towards the river, *Armalygal* (ⓣ974 383 005; Easter & July–Aug). **Eating** options are limited; you're probably best off sampling the *degustación gastronómica* at the roadside winery *Reino de los Mallos*.

Agüero and its churches

More *mallos* loom behind **AGÜERO**, a completely isolated village 5km off the main road just south of Murillo de Gállego, or a seven-kilometre walk from Concilio station. Agüero itself is characterful and unspoilt, graced by two Romanesque **churches**: the central, eleventh-century San Salvador and the isolated twelfth-century Santiago 700m east, both with superb portal carvings by the Master of San Juan de la Peña (see p.432). **San Salvador's** north tympanum shows Christ in Majesty, attended by the four symbols of the Evangelists; the door itself is flanked by column-capitals carved with imaginary beasts. Triple-apsed **Santiago**, accessed by good dirt track, has a blank western wall and its sole entrance on the south (supposedly the church is unfinished); carvings above the door here show the visit of the Three Kings, with one stooping to kiss the infant Jesus's foot, while Joseph on the right, leaning on his staff and with his right fist dug into his cheek, seems visibly wearied by the august visitors. On the adjacent column-capitals, monsters devour a ram, men playing rebec and psaltery serenade a lady and knights engage in combat.

In Agüero, you may **stay** either at *Hostal La Costera* at the very top of the village (ⓣ 974 380 330, ⓔlacostera.hostal@wanadoo.es; ❷), reached via the cemetery ring-road, with basic, prefab rooms but lovely grounds, a pool and restaurant, or at

Casa Camilo (Ⓣ974 380 121; ❷) in the lane north of the church, providing evening meals. There's also a grassy if not very shady **campsite** at the lowest margins of the village, *Peña Sola* (Ⓣ974 380 533), with a small pool.

Barbastro

BARBASTRO, 51km east-southeast of Huesca and straddling the Río Vero before it joins the Zinca, has considerable historic importance. The union of Aragón and Catalunya was sealed here in 1137 by the marriage of the daughter of Ramiro of Aragón to Ramón Berenguer IV, count of Barcelona. Although it's now just a slightly shabby provincial market town, Barbastro retains a significant old quarter. South of the river, just a few steps from the bus station, the Gothic **Catedral** (Mon–Sat 8.30am–1.30pm & 4–8pm, Sun 10am–noon; optional guided visit to Museo Diocesano €2), on a site once occupied by a mosque, has a *retablo* whose construction began under the supervision of Damián Forment; when he died in 1540 only part of the alabaster relief had been completed, so the remainder was finished by his pupil Liceire, in 1560. The broad, austere nave, staked out by six fluted columns sprouting palmate ribbing into the vault, contrasts sharply with the rococo carved dome of the chapel of San Victorián, on the left as you enter. Just northeast, on the Plaza de la Constitución, the facade of the restored fifteenth-century **Ayuntamiento**, designed by the Moorish chief architect to Fernando el Católico, is also worth a look. Elsewhere, narrow, pedestrianized shopping streets radiating out from the arcaded, central **Plaza del Mercado** are lined by faded-pastel houses piled up with their backs towards the river; tree-lined **Paseo del Coso** at the southwest edge of the old quarter is home to outdoor tables for many of the town's bars and cafés.

But the foregoing is incidental to the town's main present and future prospects: **wine**, wine and more wine. Barbastro lies at the centre of the **Somontano** *denominación de origen* vintage district in Aragón, one of the top dozen in Spain. This may seem peculiar for a place dominated by the abstemious, militant Catholic movement Opus Dei whose power-base is the nearby monastery of Torreciudad, but Opus Dei members are prominent in Spanish industry – including wine-making – raising money to further the faith. Twenty local **wineries** lie within a fifteen-kilometre radius, and many can be toured, preferably with advance notice (the Turismo stocks a booklet listing contacts); the biggest half-dozen – of whom **Bodega Pirineos/Montesierra** (Mon–Fri 10am–2pm & 4–7pm, Sat 10am–2pm) tends to be the most welcoming (and has the best wines) – cluster along the main road towards the Sierra de Guara. Outside visiting hours their retail tasting and purchase boutiques remain open, and there's also a very well-stocked one back in Barbastro, inside the Turismo.

Practicalities

The **bus station** is at the southwest end of the *paseo*, abutting Plaza de Aragón, with regular daily departures for Huesca and to Benasque. The helpful English-speaking **Turismo** (July & Aug daily 9am–2pm & 4.30–8pm; Sept–June Tues–Sat 10am–2pm & 4.30–8pm; Ⓣ974 308 350, Ⓦwww.barbastro-ayto.es) is 200m uphill and south from the station, inside the **Conjunto de San Julián y Santa Lucía**, a restored thirteenth-century hospice.

Appealing budget **accommodation** is scarce, so plump for one of two mid-range establishments on c/Corona de Aragón, running parallel to the river at the northeastern edge of the *casco viejo*: *Hostal Roxi* at no. 21 (Ⓣ974 311 064, Ⓕ312 462; ❷) and the *Hotel Clemente* at no. 5 (Ⓣ974 310 186, Ⓔclemente.3066@cajarural.com; ❸). Several decent **restaurants** have sprung up to take advantage of all that wine sloshing about. The most central is *Cenador de San Julián* (closed Sun pm & Mon), just beside the Turismo in a round, brick-walled *comedor*, considered one of the town's best, though its *menú* includes surprisingly average wine. Further afield in the new quarter, within walking distance of the centre via the Avenida Pirineos bridge, is *Flor* at c/Francisco de Goya 3, with a nouvelle cuisine *menú* at €15 served in slightly kitsch surroundings; allow €35–40 *a la carta*, even more if you crack into the stratospheric wine list. At one corner of Plaza del Mercado, *Bar Restaurante La Braseria* does *raciones* at the bar or a sit-down *menú*.

Sierra de Guara

North of the N240 road linking Huesca and Barbastro sprawls the **Sierra de Guara**, a thinly inhabited region protected as a *parque natural* since 1990. These are definitely Pyrenean foothills – the highest point is 2078-metre Puntón de Guara – with no dramatic peaks and often distinctly scrubby low-altitude vegetation, enlivened by olive and almond groves. The Guara's allure lies in its unrivalled array of sculpted gorges, painted prehistoric caves, early churches and sleepy villages. This is the main venue for **canyoning** in Spain, and arguably all of Europe; it's been known to the French for decades, to the point that French (and Belgian) cars match or outnumber Spanish ones in the popular centres. French-run, too, are many of the adventure outfitters – there's at least one in every village – though the Spanish are clawing back some of the trade. **Walking** opportunities are limited, owing to poor trail-marking and documentation, and hiking is prudently confined to the cooler spring or autumn months. July or August days are best spent in a wetsuit, splashing down a watercourse.

The eastern half of the Guara is more frequented, and covered by the Alpina 1:40,000 **map** "Sierra de Guara II", a must for touring. Owing to massive depopulation, there's **no public transport** except for one summer bus line from Alquézar, though the main access road from Barbastro to Adahuesca has been widened; similarly, the only **fuel** and **bank ATM** are at Alquézar (see below). **Accommodation** tends to be either comfortable hotels or fairly basic, crowded *albergues* and equally packed campsites, with very little in between.

Alquézar and around

At the far southeastern corner of the range and *parque*, 22km from Barbastro, **ALQUÉZAR** (Alquezra) is the Guara's gateway and most developed tourist mecca. Perched on the west bank of the Río Vero, it's a supremely atmospheric village, though packed to the gills most weekends and all summer. Arcaded lanes culminate in the eighth-century Moorish **citadel** on a pinnacle dropping to the river; the Christians took it in 1064, and by the start of the following century the **Colegiata de Santa Maria la Mayor** (closed for restoration until 2008) already existed within the fortifications. Only the cloister, its column-capitals carved with biblical scenes, remains from the Romanesque era; the Gothic-Renaissance church itself dates from the sixteenth and seventeenth centuries. Renovation should not deplete its miscellany of Baroque art, mostly polychrome wood, and a masterly thirteenth-century wooden Crucifixion in the side chapel. The only other specific cultural diversion is the **Museo Etnológico Casa Fabián** at c/Baja 16 (daily except Mon & Wed morning 11am–2pm & 4–8pm; €2), with a working olive press in the cellar.

From the north end of Plaza Mayor begins the path towards the Río Vero and its **Puente de Villacantal**, one of several ancient bridges in the sierra. Just northeast of the village, you ignore a fork northwest towards the Balsas de Basacol, continuing instead over a slight saddle and then sharply down to the river. The

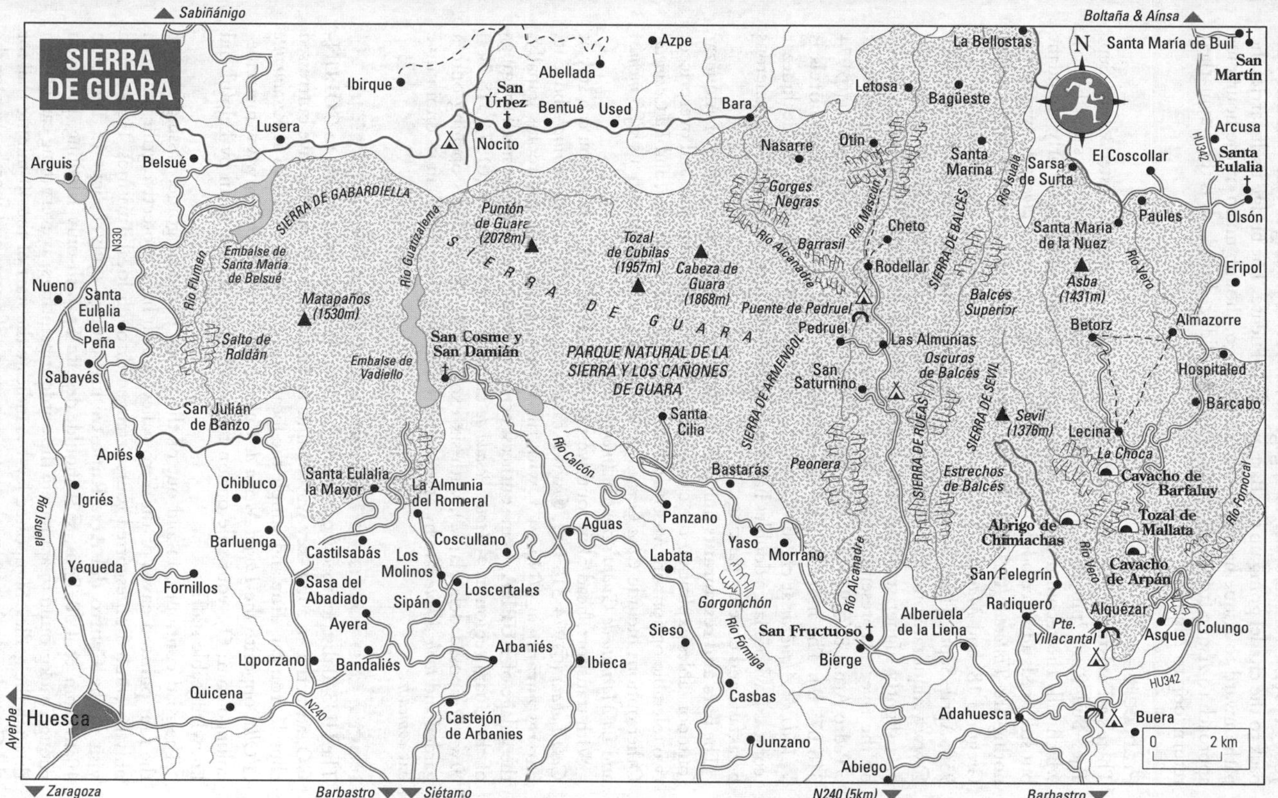

SIERRA DE GUARA
Sabiñánigo
Boltaña & Aínsa
Ayerbe
Zaragoza
Barbastro
Siétamo
N240 (5km)
Barbastro
N
0
2 km
Azpe
Abellada
Ibirque
San Úrbez
Bentué
Used
Bara
Letosa
Bagüeste
La Bellostas
Santa María de Buil
San Martín
Arcusa
Santa Eulalia
HU342
Lusera
Nocito
Nasarre
Otín
Santa Marina
Sarsa de Surta
El Coscollar
Arguis
Belsué
Olsón
Paules
N330
SIERRA DE GABARDIELLA
Gorges Negras
Río Mascún
Río Isuela
Santa María de la Nuez
Puntón de Guara (2078m)
Tozal de Cubilas (1957m)
Cabeza de Guara (1868m)
Río Alcanadre
Barrasil
Cheto
SIERRA DE BALCES
Río Vero
Eripol
Embalse de Santa María de Belsué
Río Flumen
Río Guatizalema
SIERRA DE GUARA
Rodellar
Asba (1431m)
Nueno
Santa Eulalia de la Peña
Matapaños (1530m)
Puente de Pedruel
Balcés Superior
Betorz
Almazorre
Salto de Roldán
Pedruel
Las Almunias
San Cosme y San Damián
PARQUE NATURAL DE LA SIERRA Y LOS CAÑONES DE GUARA
Oscuros de Balcés
Hospitaled
Sabayés
Embalse de Vadiello
San Saturnino
SIERRA DE ARMENGOL
SIERRA DE SEVIL
Bárcabo
San Julián de Banzo
Santa Cilia
SIERRA DE RUEAS
Sevil (1376m)
Lecina
Apiés
Río Calcón
La Choca
Bastarás
Peonera
Estrechos de Balcés
Cavacho de Barfaluy
Santa Eulalia la Mayor
Chibluco
La Almunia del Romeral
Río Fornocal
Igriés
Río Isuela
Panzano
Aguas
Abrigo de Chimiachas
Tozal de Mallata
Barluenga
Coscullano
Yaso
Morrano
Castilsabás
Los Molinos
Labata
Río Vero
Cavacho de Arpán
Yéqueda
Fornillos
Sasa del Abadiado
Loscertales
San Pelegrín
Sipán
Gorgonchón
Río Alcanadre
Alberuela de la Liena
Radiquero
Alquézar
Ayera
Pte. Villacantal
Asque
Colungo
Sieso
San Fructuoso
Río Fórmiga
Arbaniés
Loporzano
Bandaliés
Ibieca
Bierge
HU342
Quicena
N240
Casbas
Adahuesca
Buera
Huesca
Castejón de Arbanies
Junzano
Abiego

double-arched bridge is beautiful and worth the trip, though you'll have to retrace your steps (1hr 15min return) or engage in some river wading to reach another trail back to the citadel going up the Barranco de la Fuente. The bridge itself carries the path onward to Asque hamlet and then Colungo, though much of the hour-plus approach to Asque from Villacantal is along bulldozed track, as is the waymarked return loop to Alquézar.

Practicalities

There's a **Turismo** at the southwest edge of town on c/Arrabal (Easter & July–Sept Tues–Sun 9am–2pm & 4.30–8.30pm; Oct–June weekends only, same hours), which sells the recommended Alpina map. **Accommodation** is fairly abundant but still needs advance booking at busy times. Among several *albergues*, two worth noting are *Tintorero* (Ⓣ974 318 354; April–Sept) in the heart of town at c/San Gregório 18, and *Marmita de Guara* on c/Pilaseras up by the car park (Ⓣ974 318 956; April–Sept). There are also two nearby **campsites**: *Alquézar* (Ⓣ974 318 300, Ⓦwww.alquezar.com; all year), 1km downhill by the petrol pump, and generally of a slightly higher standard than *Río Vero* (Ⓣ974 318 350; Easter–Sept), down by the river. Representative of six *casas rurales* are the friendly *Casa Jabonero* at c/Pedro Arnal 8 (Ⓣ974 318 908; ❷) and *Casa Espartero* at c/San Lucas 20 (Ⓣ974 318 07; ❷). The more helpful and reliably open of two fully fledged **hotels** is *Villa de Alquézar* at c/Pedro Arnal 12 (Ⓣ974 318 416, Ⓦwww.villadealquezar.com; ❸), whose large doubles have castle-view balconies; rates include a generous breakfast, and covered parking.

The **bars and restaurants** lining Plaza Nueva at the southwest edge of Alquézar (outdoor tables exploiting the castle view) are generally mediocre and overpriced; two tolerable options are *Mesón del Vero*, with reasonable *a la carta*, and *La Cocineta*. Other options include *Casa Gervasio* in the centre, with mountainous €25 *menús*, and *La Marmita de Guara*'s *comedor* (*menú* €21).

With transport, head 5km southwest to **ADAHUESCA**, where you can stay at *Casa Labata* (Ⓣ974 318 019, Ⓦwww.casalabata.com; ❷), a *turismo rural* above its **bar-restaurante** at c/Nueva 3, with tile-floored, beam-ceilinged rooms. Finally, the village of **BUERA**, 6km southeast across the river, has the best small lodgings of the Guara region in *Hotel Posada de Lalola* at c/la Fuente 14 (Ⓣ974 318 347, Ⓦwww.laposadadelalola; ❺), with six exquisite designer rooms opening onto a garden and *table d'hôte* fare by appointment for non-guests (€27) in its diminutive bar-*comedor*.

North: the route to Lecina and Santa María de Buil

The HU340 district road from below Alquézar heads northeast 5km to **COLUNGO**, attractive in a low-key way with its arched doorways and massive buttressed church. You can **dine** and sample the locally made *aguardiente de anís* at *Restaurante A'Olla*, opposite the *Hostal Mesón de Colungo* (Ⓣ974 318 195, Ⓦwww.mesondecolungo.com; ❷), your sole option for **staying**, fortunately run by helpful and knowledgeable staff.

The road continues, in and out of the minor Fornocal gorge, passing two of the four **painted caves** of the Vero valley, which have protective grilles and can only be entered on escorted tours arranged through local Turismos. However, a visit to the **Centro del Arte Rupestre** in Colungo (July 1–Sept 15 Tues–Sun 10am–2pm & 4.30–8pm; €2) should, despite Spanish-only labelling, give you enough background to appreciate the outdoor paintings, as everything can be seen through the grilles. Signposted lay-bys indicate the start of the 40-minute trail for the **Covacho de Arpán**, with its striking image of a stag, and shortly after for the half-hour track to the **Tozal de Mallata** (abstract stick-figures); the **Covacho de Barfaluy** (more stick-figures) is accessed by forty-minute trail from Lecina (see below). Visits to the remote **Abrigo de Chimiachas** (conventional-figural art) involve a long 4WD journey, beginning from near Alquézar.

Lecina and Santa María de Buil

LECINA itself, some 16km from Colungo, has some imposing houses – it was one of the wealthier Guara villages – an enormous, **millennial holly-oak** at the outskirts (thus the name, from *La Encina*) and a sense of height, looking northeast as it does to the main Pyrenean peaks. Moreover, there's an excellent mid-range place to **stay** and **eat** here: *La Choca* (Ⓣ 974 343 070 or 659 633 636, Ⓦwww.lachoca; ❷), a restored mansion opposite the church with creditable *table d'hôte* supper (€15–20 daily Easter week & July–Aug; weekends only otherwise, also lunch Sat/Sun; closed Mon–Thurs Dec–March; guests only unless you reserve

Canyoning in the Sierra de Guara

There's a **huge variety** of canyons to explore in the Sierra de Guara, from beginners' outings with no special equipment needed, to highly technical chasms visited only by experts holding special permits. You need to know how to swim, and be in reasonable physical condition, since every body part – especially fingers and forearms – gets a workout. Judging from the number of folk hobbling about with arms in slings and bandaged abrasions, canyoning is a moderately dangerous sport. But don't feel intimidated or excluded: hundreds of people emerge daily in peak season without a scratch, and you see whole families with five-year-olds in tow happily threading the **easier** canyons, such as the Vero near Alquézar, the Peonera just upstream from Bierge and the Barrasil at Rodellar. **Moderate** ravines, with some drops requiring rope or prolonged swims, include Oscuros de Balcés, Estrechos de Balcés and Gorgonchón, all close to Bierge, while **experts-only** abysses above Rodellar include Gorgas Negras, Otín and Mascún Superior, all involving thirty-metre abseilings and strenuous clambering. Organized outings, run daily or by demand from April to October, typically **cost** €36–42 per person, including equipment, with little price difference between easy and difficult canyons. Local *albergues* offer advantageous "packages", such as three nights and two days of expeditions for €180–200, full board.

Since all the most popular canyons lie within the **Parque de la Sierra y los Cañones de Guara**, park authorities have stipulated common-sense **conditions** of access, spelt out in their leaflet "Normativa Sobre el Descenso de Barrancos" (Rules Concerning the Descent of Ravines). If you go with an outfitter, they'll be well aware of the rules, but for those going solo, an English summary follows. The maximum number of persons per group is ten in the Vero, Barrasil, Peonera and Balcés ravines, four in the Gorgonchón and eight in all the others. Groups must enter with a minimum **spacing** between them of ten minutes, and entry in summer must be **no later** than 2pm for Vero, 2.30pm for Peonera via Morrano, noon for Gorgas Negras, 1pm for Mascún and 4pm for Formiga and Oscuros de Balcés. In canyons with permanent water (most of them) you must wear a **neoprene suit**, and any descent involving abseiling means mandatory provision with **harness**, **helmet** and adequate **rope**. Certain canyons have partially or totally restricted access for safety, ecological or archeological reasons. La Choca always requires a special permit from the park authorities, as does Otín between March and June; a number of gorges (eg the Vadiello system) are completely forbidden from December to June. You're not ever to enter the pools of the Canal del Palomo (to protect its rare species). Finally, there are various **general prohibitions**: no fires, rough camping, unnecessary noise, leaving rubbish, molesting flora and fauna, defacing rocks or introducing motor vehicles onto the many barred 4WD tracks.

in advance). There's also a **campsite** down by the river, *Lecina* (Ⓣ974 318 386; June–Sept) which doubles as the closest canyoning outfitter, but this is one of the few Guaran areas where **walkers** are actively catered to.

The local municipality has waymarked sixteen **PR trails**, indicated on a sketch map available from from *La Choca*. A particularly good outing is the three-hour loop Lecina–Almazorre–Betorz–Lecina, combining three of the most unspoilt paths (#5, #9, #6). It's an hour on #5 from Lecina (760m), mostly through shaded woods on a walled *camino* (but also some dreary track), to the bed of the Río Vero (670m) and a disused, combined **grain mill and olive press**; all the workings are still intact. Allow fifteen minutes one-way for the detour up to **Almazorre** village (750m; no facilities), or proceed directly onto trail #9 up a side canyon, first on the left bank, then on the right, through low pines, box and oak to **Betorz** (under 1hr; 970m). This is an attractive, though almost empty, village with a marvellous setting. The descent to Lecina begins with the *camino* starting on the right road-verge just past the lowest houses; there's even some cobbling (plus a stretch of track) along the twenty minutes to a **spring**, your only reliable water en route, feeding a round livestock pool in a shady glen. It's an hour in total (not "40min" as posted) along a gentle grade through baby oaks back to Lecina.

Some 18km north of Lecina on the road to Ainsa, via Bárcabo and Arcusa, is the dirt side road east to **SANTA MARÍA DE BUIL** and its unique eleventh-century **church of San Martín** (usually open), a protected national monument. The three-apsed structure by the central car park gives nothing away from outside, but the pebble-floored interior shelters the most vivid frescoes in the Guara except for San Fructuoso's at Bierge. Spandrels of the soaring arches between the three aisles, the transepts and baptistry walls are decorated with floral motifs, peacocks, the Virgin and Child (the north wall), an entire town of heaped-up buildings (south wall) – well worth braving the 3.5km of bad road in.

Northwest: the route to Rodellar

West of Alquézar and Adahuesca, the next significant village is **BIERGE**, with arguably the most significant religious monument in the Guara: the **Ermita de San Fructuoso**, at the north end of the village (late June to Sept, apply to Turismo booth on bypass road 9.30am–1.30pm & 4.30–7.30pm; €1.20; rest of year, ask for key-keeper in village). The twelfth-century building was adorned with frescoes in two stages during the latter half of the thirteenth century, depicting a Crucifixion, the trial and martyrdom of Fructuoso (an early bishop of Tarragona), the trial of St John the Evangelist (complete with a demon whispering disinformation into the judging king's ear), and – easy to miss inside the arch – two angels blowing the trumpets of the Last Judgement.

Accommodation is limited to a restored-house *casa rural* in the centre, *Casa Rufas* at c/La Cruz 2 (Ⓣ974 318 373; ❷), and a welcoming *albergue* at the southwest outskirts, *Casa Barbara* (Ⓣ974 318 060, Ⓦwww.casabarbara.com; 24 places; Easter–Oct), aimed at canyoners who don't mind being packed eight to a dorm, but the food – including own-baked breads and turnovers – is excellent, and served out in the garden; half-board is encouraged.

North along the ridge-top HU341, the scenery gets grander after some 5km, with canyons yawning either side. Beyond "Km11" you descend through woods to *Expediciones* (Ⓣ974 318 600, Ⓦwww.expediciones.sc.es; June–Sept), the most pleasant **campsite** of three in the Alcanadre valley; they're also about the most switched-on local canyoning operator. **LAS ALMUNIAS**, 2km further, is the first proper village, offering the *Hostal Casa Tejedor* (Ⓣ974 318 686, Ⓕ343 015; March–Oct; ❷) with a restaurant, plus the *Albergue Las Almunias* across the road (Ⓣ974 318 602; 42 places in six-bunk dorms).

△ Fresco, San Fructuoso, Bierge

RODELLAR, some 4km further and 18km from Bierge at the end of the road, looks achingly photogenic draped along a ridge above the Río Mascún, but the reality close up in peak season is likely to be 150 cars parked nose-to-tail and overstretched **accommodation**. This comprises *Casa Arilla* (Ⓣ974 318 343; April–Nov; ❷) and *Casa Ortas* (Ⓣ974 318 364; April–Sept; ❶), while *Bar-Restaurante Florentino* opposite *Casa Arilla* is the only spot to eat or drink. Two **campsites** – *Mascún* at the edge of the village (Ⓣ974 318 367, Ⓦwww.guara-mascun.com; April–Oct) and *El Puente* (Ⓣ974 318 312, Ⓦwww.campingelpuente.com; April–Oct), 1500m south by the river and the medieval **Pedruel bridge** both act as canyoning guide centres. If you're not interested in plumbing the deep gorges, the most popular activity is the two-and-a-half-hour (one-way) **hike** north to the abandoned hamlet of **Otín**, though path-marking is terrible. It's sobering to reflect that before the current canyoning boom, just two families lived in Rodellar (down from forty in 1900), plus a few pioneering French explorers like Pierre Minvielle and Christian Abadie who bought houses here during the 1960s.

Travel details

Trains

French trains

Pau to: Lourdes (8–12 daily; 30min); Oloron-Sainte-Marie (6–9 daily; 35min); Tarbes (8–12 daily; 50min).
Tarbes to: Capvern (2–3 daily, slower service on SNCF bus; 30–55min); Lannemezan (8 daily Mon–Sat, 6 Sun; 25min); Lourdes (14 daily Mon–Sat, 9 daily Sun; 20min).

Spanish trains

Jaca to: Ayerbe (4 daily; 1hr 20min); Canfranc-Estación (2 daily; 35min); Huesca (4 daily; 2hr 15min); Sabiñánigo (4 daily; 18min).

Buses

French buses

Bagnères-de-Bigorre to: Campan (2 daily July–Sept, 1 daily in term time; 20min); Lac de Payolle

(2 daily July–Sept, 1 daily in term time; 45min); Sainte-Marie-de-Campan (2 daily July–Sept, 1 daily in term time; 35min).
Lannemezan to: Arreau (SNCF or Brunet buses; 7 daily year-round; 25min); St-Lary-Soulan (SNCF buses only; 5–6 daily year-round; 50min).
Laruns to: (all services July–Aug only) Bious-Oumette trailhead (1 daily in morning, returns late afternoon; 40min); Col du Pourtalet (2 daily; 1hr 20min); Gabas (2 daily; 25min); Lac de Fabrèges (2 daily, also ski season; 1hr).
Lourdes to: Bagnères-de-Bigorre (2 daily during school term, 3 daily in summer; 45min); Barèges (SNCF or SALT bus; 6–7 daily, may change at Pierrefite; 1hr 10min); Cauterets (SNCF bus; 5–7 daily; 50min); Luz-Saint-Sauveur (SNCF bus; 5–7 daily; 45min); Pau (4–8 daily; 1hr 15min); Tarbes (hourly; 30min).
Luz-Saint-Sauveur to: Gavarnie (July & Aug 2 daily morning and late afternoon; winter 3 weekly; 30–40min).
Oloron-Sainte-Marie to: (all SNCF buses) Bedous (5–7 daily Mon–Sat, 4 Sun; 30min); Cette-Eygun/Lescun junction (5–7 daily Mon–Sat, 4 Sun; 45min); Urdos (5–7 daily Mon–Sat, 4 Sun; 1hr).
Pau to: Bayonne (run by TPR; 3–4 daily Mon–Sat, 2 Sun; 2hr); Eaux-Bonnes (3 daily on CITRAM; 1hr 15min); Gourette (CITRAM; 2 daily; 1hr 30min); Laruns (CITRAM; 3 daily on CITRAM, plus 2–3 on SNCF coach, using train up to Buzy; 1hr–1hr 10min); Lourdes (4 daily; 1hr 15min); Oloron-Sainte-Marie (Mon–Sat 2–3 daily; 1hr); Tarbes (6 daily; 1hr).
Tarbes to: Argelès-Gazost (6 daily; 50min); Arrens-Marsous (Mon–Sat 3–4 daily, change at Argelès; 1hr 15min); Bagnères-de-Bigorre (Mon–Sat 8–9 daily, 3 Sun; 40min); Luz-Saint-Sauveur (5–8 daily on SALT; 1hr).

Spanish buses

NB Almost all services are on Alosa/Alarsa (www.alosa.es) or La Oscense.
Aínsa to: Bielsa (July–Aug Mon–Sat, otherwise Mon, Wed, Fri only at 8.45pm, returns 6.00am next day; 40min); Gistaín (Mon, Wed, Fri at 8.45pm; 45min); Sabiñánigo via Torla (1 daily at 2.30pm; 2hr).
Alquézar to: Fuente de Lecina (Mon–Fri at 9.30am, Sat–Sun 11am; July–Aug only; 45min).
Barbastro to: Boltaña via Aínsa (Mon–Sat year-round at 7.45pm, returns next day 6.45am; July 15–Aug 31 also 11am, returning 3pm; 1hr 10min; Huesca-Barbastro 10am/6.30pm services connect); Benasque (daily 11am, plus Mon–Sat 5.30pm; 2hr).
Huesca to: Ayerbe (3 daily Mon–Fri, 1 Sat; 45min); Barbastro (4–6 daily; 50min); Jaca (2 daily via Sabiñánigo, 1 daily Mon–Fri via Ayerbe; 1hr 15min–1hr 35min); Lleida (7 daily Mon–Sat, 4 Sun; 2hr 15min); Pamplona (2 daily via Jaca, plus 1 extra July–Aug; 3hr).
Jaca to: Astún/Candanchú (2–3 daily in winter; 45min); Ayerbe (1 daily Mon–Fri, 7.15am; 1hr); Biescas (1–2 daily; 55min); Canfranc-Estación (4–5 daily; 45min); El Formigal (1 daily ski season at 10.15am, returns 3.45/5.15pm; 1hr 45min); Loarre (1 daily at 7.15am; 1hr 10min); Panticosa (1 daily 9am, continues up to Balneario July–Aug; returns 4.05pm; 1hr 40min); Sabiñánigo (2 daily Mon–Fri 10.15am, 12.15pm, 5.15pm, 6.15pm; Sat 10.15am, 12.15pm, 6.15pm; Sun 10.15am 5.15pm but daily 5.15pm July–Aug; 25min); Sallent de Gállego (2 daily Mon–Sat 10.15am & 6.15pm, Sun 10.15am only; 1hr 45min).
Sabiñánigo to: Aínsa via Torla (Mon–Sat 1 daily at 11am; 2hr 15min); Biescas (1 daily at 10.45am, plus 1 Mon–Sat 6.30pm, also Sun July–Aug; 25 min); Sallent de Gállego (2 daily Mon–Sat 10.45am & 6.30pm; also 1 Mon–Sat ski season 8.30am (continues to El Formigal); returns 7am & 4pm Mon–Sat, also 5.30pm ski season (starts El Formigal); 1hr); Torla (1 daily at 11am, plus additional service in July & Aug Mon–Sat at 6.30pm up to Sarvisé, rest of year Fri & Sun at 5.30pm; 55min).

International buses

Jaca to: Lourdes via Canfranc, Pau, Tarbes (Sat at 9.45am, Sun at 5.45pm; 4hr 15min for the entire trip).
Oloron-Sainte-Marie to: (SNCF buses) Canfranc via Urdos (3 daily; 1hr 20min).

5

The Western Pyrenees

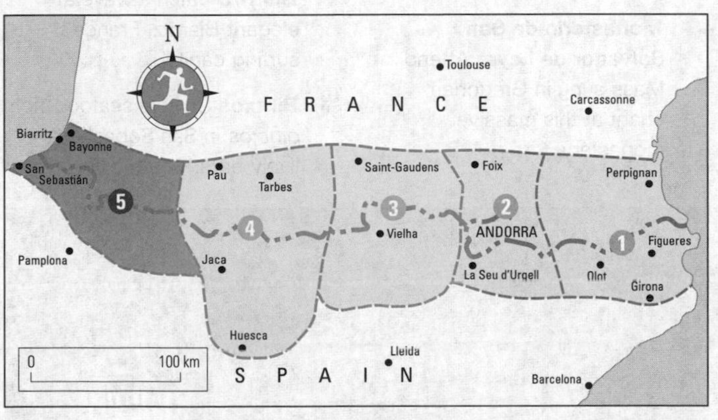

CHAPTER 5 Highlights

* **Ansó and Echo** Marvel at the substantial stone-built architecture of Ansó and Echo, in Aragón's westernmost valleys. See p.455

* **Haute-Soule gorges** Explore the yawning limestone gorges of the Haute-Soule, on the GR10 or local paths. See p.466

* **Monasterio de San Salvador de Leyre** Attend Mass sung in Gregorian chant at this massive monastery. See p.475

* **GR65** Retrace the retreat of legendary Roland and his army along the GR65 across the border. See p.481

* **Crête d'Iparla** Follow the majestic, airy Crête d'Iparla between Baïgorri and Bidarraï, the Pyrenees' best ridge-walk. See p.487

* **Biarritz** Catch a wave at elegant Biarritz, France's surfing capital. See p.500

* **Pintxos** Sample seafood-rich *pintxos* in San Sebastián's lively bars. See p.516

△ Surfing, Biarritz

5

The Western Pyrenees

The widespread notion that the Pyrenees begin or end at Pic d'Anie, 80km from the Atlantic coast, dismisses the range's densest forests, greenest landscape and the most tenaciously retained ethnicity – that of the Basques. The region lacks only lakes and extreme altitude: there's nothing higher between Pic d'Anie and the sea, while beyond Pic d'Orhy/Pico de Ori (2017m) the summits subside markedly.

The **Western Pyrenees** cover an area more extensive than **Euskal Herri**, the Basques' name for their homeland on both sides of the frontier. They also include a corner of Alto Aragón in the **Echo** and **Ansó** valleys, draining the same karst country as the **Haute-Soule** in France and **Valle de Belagoa** in Navarra. The Spanish slopes are often uncharacteristically densely forested below the alpine zones, nowhere more so than in the vast **Irati forest**, which extends some way into French territory. But much of the French Basque country is strongly reminiscent of rural Scotland, especially near **Saint-Jean-Pied-de-Port**, its chief inland tourist attraction.

The west also has a high concentration of small gateway cities for the mountains. **Bayonne** and **San Sebastián** on the Atlantic coast gracefully combine roles as commercial *entrepôts*, resorts and administrative centres, and both – along with the dedicated playground of **Biarritz** – prove livelier than anything along the Mediterranean coast of the Pyrenees.

Public transport is reasonable on the Spanish side of the Pyrenees, but poor in France except on the coast and along the Nive valley. Starting from Jaca, you can take a bus up into the Echo and Ansó valleys, hike west to the Valle de Roncal and then over the border to French attractions such as the Kakouetta gorges. From Roncal or the Valle de Salazar just west there are links with Pamplona, from where you could head straight out to the coast of Gipuzkoa, or inland via Auritz towards Saint-Jean-Pied-de-Port, served by French trains.

The Basques

Nothing is conclusively proved about the **origin of the Basques**. Some consider them to be descended from Europe's **aboriginal** population, a theory supported by early twentieth-century archeological finds. Skull fragments of late Cro-Magnon man tentatively dated to 9000 BC are nearly identical to present-day Basque cranial formation. Anthropological work, largely by Joxe Mikel Barandiaran (who

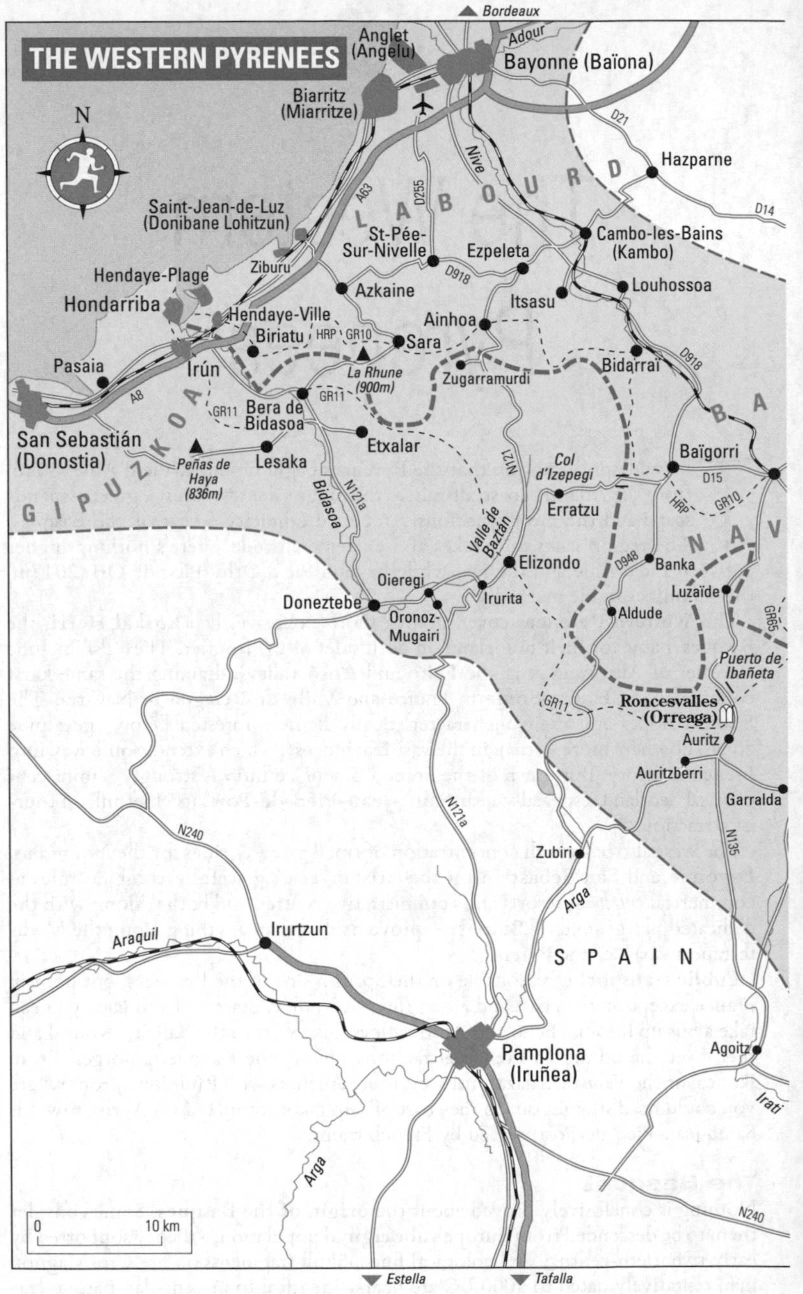
THE WESTERN PYRENEES
N
Bordeaux
Anglet (Angelu)
Adour
Bayonne (Baïona)
Biarritz (Miarritze)
D21
Hazparne
D14
L A B O U R D
A63
D255
Nive
Saint-Jean-de-Luz (Donibane Lohitzun)
St-Pée-Sur-Nivelle
Espeleta
Cambo-les-Bains (Kambo)
Ziburu
D918
Azkaine
Itsasu
Louhossoa
Hendaye-Plage
Hondarriba
Hendaye-Ville
Ainhoa
Biriatu
HRP
GR10
Sara
La Rhune (900m)
Zugarramurdi
Bidarraï
Pasaia
Irún
A8
GR11
Bera de Bidasoa
Etxalar
San Sebastián (Donostia)
Lesaka
Peñas de Haya (836m)
G I P U Z K O A
Bidasoa
N121a
N121
Col d'Izepegi
Erratzu
Valle de Baztán
B A
Baïgorri
D15
N A V
D948
Banka
Elizondo
Oieregi
Irurita
Doneztebe
Oronoz-Mugairi
Aldude
Luzaïde
GR65
Puerto de Ibañeta
Roncesvalles (Orreaga)
Auritz
Auritzberri
Garralda
N240
N135
Zubiri
Arga
Araquil
Irurtzun
S P A I N
Pamplona (Iruñea)
Agoitz
Irati
N240
0
10 km
Estella
Tafalla

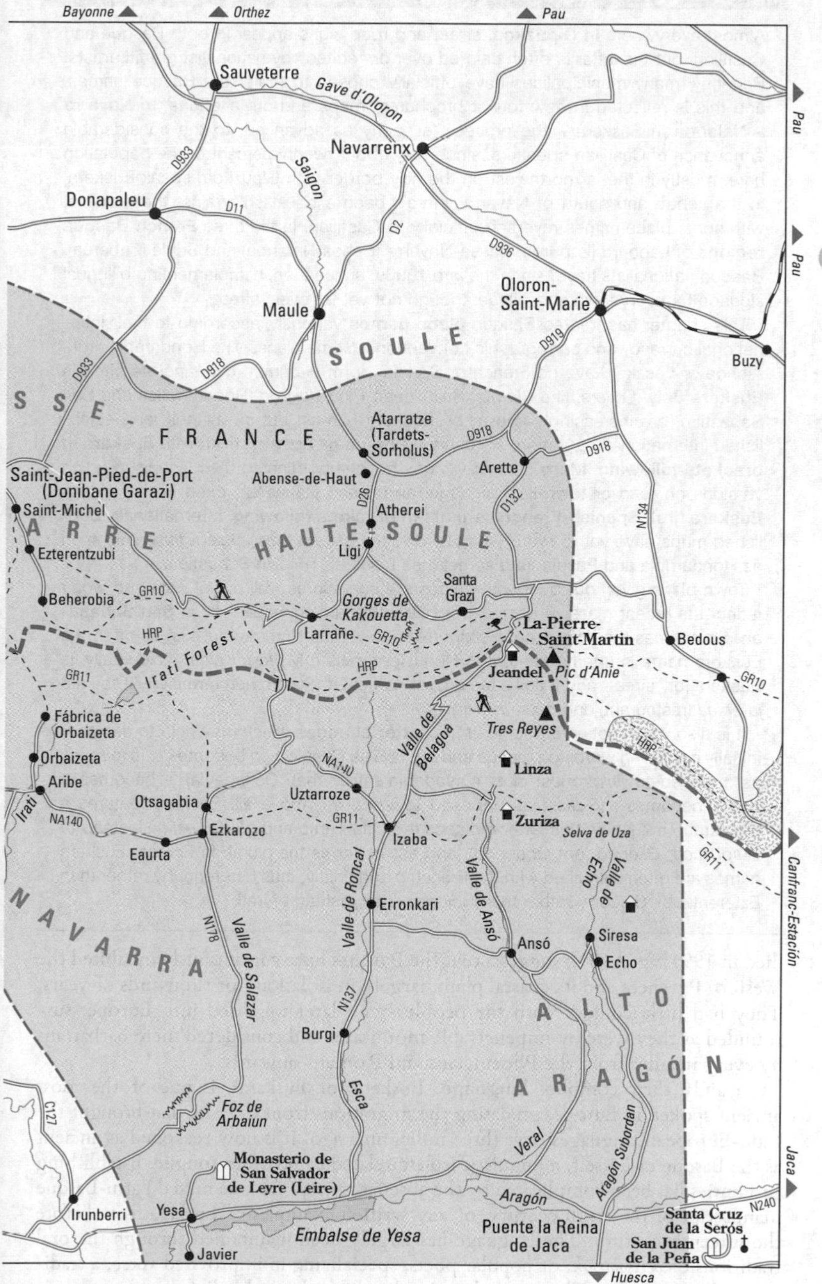
Bayonne
Orthez
Pau
Sauveterre
Gave d'Oloron
Navarrenx
Saigon
D933
Donapaleu
D11
D2
D936
Oloron-
Saint-Marie
Maule
SOULE
D919
D918
Buzy
D933
FRANCE
Atarratze
(Tardets-
Sorholus)
Abense-de-Haut
Arette
D132
N134
Saint-Jean-Pied-de-Port
(Donibane Garazi)
Saint-Michel
Ezterentzubi
HAUTE-SOULE
D26
Atherei
Ligi
Beherobia
GR10
Santa
Grazi
Gorges de
Kakouetta
Larrañe
La-Pierre-
Saint-Martin
Bedous
HRP
Irati Forest
Jeandel
Pic d'Anie
GR11
Fábrica de
Orbaizeta
Orbaizeta
Tres Reyes
Valle de
Belagoa
Linza
Aribe
NA140
Irati
Uztarroze
Otsagabia
Zuriza
Selva de Uza
Ezkarozo
Eaurta
Izaba
Canfranc-Estación
Erronkari
Valle de Ansó
Valle de Echo
Valle de Roncal
Valle de Salazar
N178
NAVARRA
Siresa
Ansó
Echo
N137
ALTO
Burgi
ARAGÓN
Esca
Foz de
Arbaiun
C127
Veral
Aragón Subordan
Monasterio de
San Salvador
de Leyre (Leire)
Jaca
Aragón
N240
Irunberri
Yesa
Santa Cruz
de la Serós
Puente la Reina
de Jaca
Embalse de Yesa
San Juan
de la Peña
Javier
Huesca

Basque place names and street names

Almost everywhere **in Gipuzkoa**, street and road signs appear in both Basque and Castilian, but the latter is often painted over or "edited" by nationalist graffiti artists. Recently, many municipalities have officially chosen to prefer the Basque names, and this is reflected in new tourist brochures, maps and our citations. **In Navarra** – Nafarroa in Euskera – the process is nearly as advanced, to the considerable annoyance of Castilian-speakers, since only about twenty percent of the population here, mostly in the far northwest on the hilly border with Gipuzkoa, speak Euskera; in the centre and south of Navarra, there's been a backlash against the process, with some place names reverting officially to Castilian. In the three **French Basque regions** of Labourd (Lapurdi), Basse-Navarre (Behea Nafarroa) and Soule (Zuberoa), Basque nationalists have, since the late 1990s, succeeded in implementing bilingual signage for every town and village, though not yet for every street.

This chapter has treated Basque **place names** variously, according to their international currency and cartographic conventions. Some places, like Hondarribia, Irún, Ainhoa or Lesaka, have no French or Spanish form in current use, and are cited in **Euskera only**. Others, like Biarritz, Saint-Jean-Pied-de-Port, Roncesvalles and San Sebastián, are increasingly known by Euskera names, but given their long-established international reputation, are cited in **French or Spanish first**, with **Euskera in brackets following**. Many smaller villages have subordinated their Spanish/French versions on road or town-limit signage, and these places are cited in the text as **Euskera first**, **Spanish/French variants in brackets following**. Internationally published maps have yet to switch over to strictly Euskera tags, except for cases such as Hondarribia and Pasaia (and sometimes Donostia for San Sebastián).

Town plans given out by tourist offices are sometimes well out of date and won't reflect the recent massive campaign of street renaming, especially in **San Sebastián**. Sometimes the difference is slight (Narrika versus Narrica), but just as often the Euskera name is utterly different (c/Nagusia versus c/Mayor). *Kalea*, incidentally, is Euskera for "street" and follows the proper name. Other common terms you'll see are *jatetxea* (restaurant) and *ostatua* (bar).

It is also worth noting a couple of key **letter changes** which may help to decipher initially confusing words on menus and signs. The Castilian *ch* becomes *tx* (*txipirones* as opposed to *chipirones*) or *ts* (Otsagabia rather than Ochagavía), *v* becomes *b* and *y* becomes *i* (*Bizkaia* as opposed to *Vizcaya*). Above all, Euskera features a proliferation of *k*s, as this letter replaces the Castilian *c* and *qu* (*Gipuzkoa* instead of *Guipúzcoa; Okendo,* not *Oquendo*), and as *-ak* forms the plural. In France, Euskera names are often disguised with the French ç and final *y*; thus Esterençuby rather than Ezterentzubi, Baïgorry rather than Baïgorri, Iraty instead of Irati.

died in 1991, aged 101), suggests that the Basques have continuously inhabited the Western Pyrenees and its coastal plain, largely in isolation, for thousands of years. They had little contact with the peoples who later migrated into Europe, surrounded as they were by impenetrable mountains and considered mere barbarians by every invader from the Phoenicians and Romans onwards.

Certainly their complex **language**, Euskera (or Euskara), is one of the most ancient spoken in Europe, predating the migrations from the east that brought the Indo-European languages over three millennnia ago. It is now reckoned as ancient as the Basque race itself, a linguistic isolate related to no other tongue. Establishing certainties has been complicated by the absence, except for one mixed Latin-Basque manuscript of the tenth century, of any written examples of Euskera from before the fifteenth century. The language has largely been maintained through the oral traditions of *bertsolariak*, or popular poets, specializing in improvised verse, a tradition still alive today. The vocabulary implies lifestyles and beliefs long pre-dating Christianity, reflected in terms referring to ancient sites such as *dolmens* and cromlechs. Further evidence is an extensive mythology relating to *jentilak*, legendary giants supposedly responsible for building these sites, as well as ancient roads and bridges. Yet crucial though it has been for defining Basque identity, Euskera is nowadays spoken – mostly along the coastal strip – by not more than 500,000 people, roughly twenty percent of the total Basque population in France and Spain.

There are strong dialectal differences in usage, spelling and pronunciation throughout the **seven Basque regions** (four in Spain, three in France), though there's a standardized written form called Batua. It's worth learning to recognize the Basques' term for themselves – Euskaldunak, sometimes Euskualdunak – and their homeland, referred to as Euskadi or Euzkadi in Spain but more generally as Euskal Herri(a). In Spain, the more or less homogeneous autonomous regions of Gipuzkoa and Bizkaia on the coast account for the bulk of Euskera-speakers; Alaba (Araba) and Navarra (Nafarroa), with longer adherence to a unitary Spanish state, experienced – until a recent, conscious revival – a steady decrease in the proportion of Euskera-speakers to as little as ten percent. The weakening of Euskera's hold was accelerated following the rapid industrialization of Bizkaia and Gipuzkoa during the nineteenth century and the resultant immigration of labour from the rest of Spain, a process accelerated under Franco. By 1975 more than half of the working class of the coastal Spanish Basque regions came from other parts of the country, whereas in Navarra the proportion of people from elsewhere in Spain was just eighteen percent. During the 1990s labour agitation in Gipuzkoa and Bizkaia the impulse to protect both a decreasing number of jobs from outsiders – and linguistic purity – neatly coincided.

Architecturally, there's a marked difference between the French and Spanish Basque areas. The genuine Basque dwelling – a solid stone structure that often incorporates overhanging upper storeys – is now rare, though some can be seen around Santa Grazi in Haute-Soule. Today the stereotypical Basque house is a white building with colourful shutters and half-timbering, but this type of construction, originally particular to the Labourd region on the French coast, spread inland comparatively recently, and has been adopted in Spain only along parts of the frontier.

The extended **family** – the word for which, *etxe*, is the same as that for "house" – has always been the basic social unit of Basque life, rather than the village. A farmstead, or *baserri*, was a multifunctional building sheltering up to four generations, plopped in the middle of its fields or pastures. A yearning for this rural idyll probably accounts for the linear, straggled appearance of the smaller Basque hamlets on either side of the border. Property was handed down intact, traditionally from one's paternal aunts, to the oldest son, compelling younger sons to seek their fortunes elsewhere, usually as seamen or emigrants to the Americas.

The karst country and around

Few Pyrenean landscapes have quite the impact of the terrain west of Pic d'Anie. There may be more photogenic glaciers, lakes and wildflowers elsewhere, but nothing so surreal as the **karst** country around **Tres Reyes**, the highest border mountain of the Basque Pyrenees, and along the Atlantic flank of **Pic d'Anie**, the westernmost peak of Béarn. Their upper slopes have been rain-carved into fantastic shapes and sluiced clean of every particle of soil; yet the heights are waterless, the Atlantic precipitation vanishing instantly through waist-deep fissures and bowl-shaped *dolines*, eroding the limestone underneath into a Swiss cheese of potholes and horizontal caverns. Between the two summits lies a zone of shattered boulders, where occasional stunted black pines erupt.

Yet the lower elevations where water reappears courtesy of the numerous subterranean rivers – sometimes weeks later – are almost tropically lush, with dense forest and pastures of brilliant green, a marked contrast to scattered red-tiled barns and light-grey, stone-built villages. These comprise the valleys of **Echo** and **Ansó** in westernmost Alto Aragón, **Roncal** in Navarra, **Sainte-Engrâce** in Haute-Soule and the gorges of **Kakouetta** and **Ehujarré** which open onto the Saint-Engrâce valley.

The French **Parc National des Pyrénées** ends at the border peak of Laraille/Arraya de las Foyas, while the less stringent forestry administration zone beyond only guarantees partial preservation of Pic d'Anie and none at all for the Sainte-Engrâce valley. Navarra has conferred *parque natural* status on the **Larra-Belagoa**

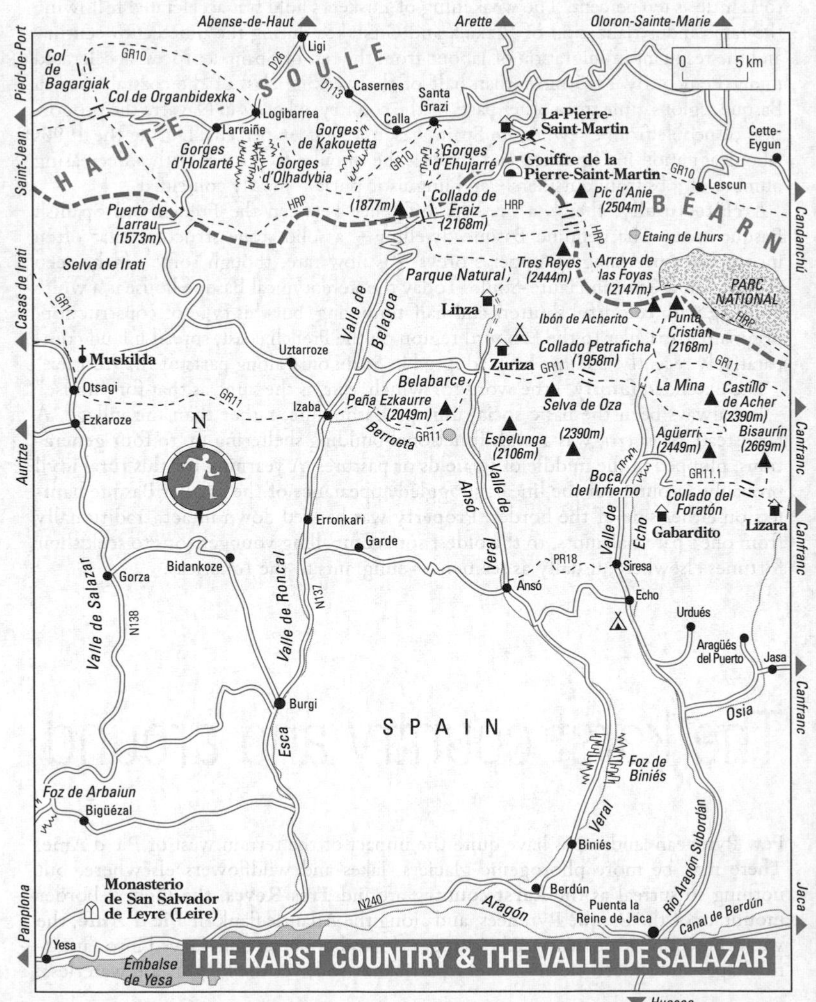

area at the head of the Valle de Roncal, but it needs more to reduce wear and tear on the terrain, increasingly popular with Spanish city-dwellers. Just to the west, the limestone strata nurture the splendid trans-border **Forêt d'Iraty/Selva de Irati**, though it, too, is much diminished from its former extent and devoid of any formal protection regimen.

The Echo and Ansó valleys

The **Valle de Echo** and **Valle de Ansó**, northwest of Jaca, are the westernmost valleys of Alto Aragón and, in their upper reaches, among the most beautiful, watered respectively by the Aragón Subordán and Veral rivers. They communicate over shallow passes between karst summits, with the Haute-Soule region in France to the north and the Spanish Valle de Roncal to the west.

The principal villages – Echo (833m) and Ansó (860m) – once lived (and grew wealthy) from sheep-raising. In modern times, timber-cutting has supplanted livestock, but, despite the modest altitude, good roads in and manifest beauty, seasonal or weekend habitation is now the rule. Echo and Ansó are lonely places in winter, as it's considered too arduous to commute to jobs in the provincial centres. Until recently, both villages felt extremely remote all year round, and Echo preserves an Aragonese dialect known as *Cheso*, widely spoken and taught in the school. Another holdover is the presence of the *espantabrujas*, little hoodoo figures perched atop the domed chimneys or over windows; also found in other parts of Alto Aragón, these were believed to repel witches in the habit of entering houses through such openings.

Lately, Echo and Ansó find themselves squarely on the tourist map, a favourite target for Spanish weekenders. However, in each case the local country shows its best side and only offers worthwhile walking some distance upstream from the villages, though the Valle de Echo makes a more dramatic impression lower down. The big local environmental issue is the pending enlargement of the Yesa reservoir downstream on the Río Aragon – you'll see (rather bizarrely for English speakers) "YESA NO" graffiti everywhere.

Access

There is only one daily **bus service** (Mon–Sat), calling first at Echo, then Siresa, and finally Ansó. This departs **from Jaca** at 6.30pm in summer (may be 1hr earlier winter), reaching Echo at 8.10pm and Ansó 45 minutes later, returning towards Jaca at 6am the next day.

A **bicycle** is a good means of exploring either valley; reckon on around two and a half hours from Jaca to Echo village, turning off the C134/N240 at Puente la Reina de Jaca, or much the same to Ansó village, turning off at Berdún, 7km west of Puente la Reina de Jaca. **BERDÚN** itself is a very atmospheric, bluff-top settlement, its houses arranged in a fortified oval; there's prime accommodation at the southeast base of town, English-run *Casa Sarasa* (Ⓣ609 341 460, Ⓦwww.casasarasa.com; all year; ❹ B&B), with four self-catering units including a two-bedroom cottage, set in the ample grassy grounds of a restored farm; closest **restaurant** is *Rincón de Emilio* in the town centre. The road north from Berdún to Ansó, not served by bus, is particularly spectacular, passing below a privately owned castle at Biniés before threading a narrow course through the Foz de Biniés, carved out by the Río Veral.

The **GR65.3.3** – a very minor variant of the Santiago pilgrimage route – also links Berdún and Biniés with Echo, threading over the hills on a variety of surfaces.

△ Ansó village

Trans-Pyrenean trekkers use the **GR11** to hike into and out of the area, although the trail intersects both valleys a considerable way above the two villages.

Echo and Siresa

ECHO (formerly "Hecho", still thus on old maps), the larger of the two villages, is a splendid old place, though historically less wealthy than Ansó. Arcades ring the main double-plaza, while whitewash outlines the windows and doors on some of the massive houses, the more sumptuous of them built around pebble-mosaic forecourts. Apparently ancient, Echo in its present form is actually less than two centuries old; it and Ansó were burnt to the ground during the Napoleonic wars. Echo can otherwise lay modest claim to fame as the seat of an embryonic Aragonese feudal state under Conde Aznar Galíndez in the ninth century, and as the birthplace of the "warrior king" Alfonso I.

An annual art festival held between 1975 and 1984, the Simposio de Escultura y Pintura Moderna, left a permanent legacy of the **open-air sculpture gallery** on the hillside west of the village. Created by a group of artists led by Pedro Tramullas, the 46 stone or metal pieces are not individually stunning but, taken as a whole, quite compelling. Local resistance to the Simposio's expansion has been overcome, but unfortunately funds are now lacking to resume the project.

Near the enormous central church, there's a more conventional museum, the **Museo Etnológico** (Easter, July & Aug 11am–2pm & 6–9pm; otherwise contact the *ayuntamiento*; €1), with interesting collections on Pyrenean rural life and folklore.

Practicalities

The **Turismo** occupies premises amidst the sculpture garden (daily except Sun eve & Mon am June–Sept 10am–1.30pm & 5.30–8pm; Ⓣ974 375 329). In summer or at weekends reservations for Echo's better **accommodation** are mandatory (the closest alternatives are in Siresa – see p.458). The clear first choices are *Casa Blasquico*, discreetly marked at Plaza Palacio de la Fuente 1 (Ⓣ974 375 007; ❸), next door to the *Bar Subordan*, its five tastefully converted rooms (including one suite) offering all comforts, and the *Casa Chuanet* on the hillside opposite (Ⓣ974 375 033, Ⓦwww.casachuanet.com; ❷), with appealingly decorated en-suite rooms above *Bar Danubio*. A definite fallback, at the north end of the village, is en-suite *Hostal de la Val* (Ⓣ974 375 028; ❸), whose front rooms overlook the village. The closest **campsite**, *Valle de Echo* (Ⓣ974 375 361; all year), lies just south of the village.

By far the most notable **restaurant** in Echo is *Restaurante Gaby* (closed part Sept; reservations essential), on the ground floor of *Casa Blasquico*. Owner-chef Gaby Coarasa was among the first stars of Pyrenean nouvelle cuisine, and the walls of the tiny, six-table *comedor* are lined with awards to prove it. *A la carta* offers ample choice for vegetarians – the mushroom crêpe and cardoon are ace – though these tend to be starters, with game, lamb and duck mains predominating. Bills with Dénominación d'Origen wine, run well over €30 per person; if money's tight, ask about their cheaper *menú* and stick to the adequate house wine. If you can't get in, the *Restaurante Canteré* nearby is nearly as good, doing creative if slightly *minceur* platters such as *hojaldre de espinacas*, game and duck (allow €20–35 each for three courses; *menú* at €14 available). Last but not least, the friendly *Bar Subordán*, next door to *Restaurante Gaby*, purveys superb, inexpensive *raciones* of *longaniza* and *chipirones*, plus good salads and desserts. Local families and visitors alike drink at all hours at the *Subordán*'s outdoor tables; other popular **bars** include *Acher*, *Danubio* and *Borruel*.

Echo has at least one **bank ATM**, the only petrol station in these hills and an **adventure outfitter**: the local Compañia de Guías (Ⓣ974 375 218, Ⓦwww.guiasdehecho.com), offering canyoning, rock-climbing, kayaking, snowshoeing and cross-country skiing depending on the season. Also worth contacting is Alto Aragón (Ⓣ974 371 281 or 974 371 267), which offers both summertime treks and winter activities with English-speaking guides. Echo has no pool; people just swim in a scooped-out area of the river east of town.

Siresa

Some 2km north of Echo stands another beautiful little village, **SIRESA**. Keeping watch over the riverside pastures is a remarkable ninth-century church, **San Pedro** (daily 11am–1pm & 5–8pm; €2). A massive structure built to a cruciform, single-apse plan, austerely plain inside, it was once the core of a monastery and is claimed to be the oldest church in Aragón.

The single **hotel**, the *Castillo d'Acher* (Ⓣ974 375 313, Ⓦwww.castillodacher.com; ❸), has decent rooms (attic ones are newest) with large beds, full bathtubs and tiny balconies; they also operate a reasonable **restaurant**. There's also a YHA-affiliated *Albergue Siresa* (Ⓣ974 375 385, Ⓦwww.alberguesiresa.com), with predictably institutional dorms – it was the old school – but a reliable sales-point for local maps and PR guides.

If you desire more solitude, the *Hotel Usón* (Ⓣ & Ⓕ974 375 358; March 20–Oct; ❺ HB only), 5km north of Siresa, has enthusiastic management, environment-friendly design, plus good Basque-style food (for guests only), served in a conservatory. Rooms are tasteful and colourfully done up, but often fill with UK-based trekking groups, so reservations are mandatory. Immediately across the valley, 3km up the side road to the *Gabardito* refuge, *Camping Borda Bisáltico* (Ⓣ974 375 098; late June to late Sept & Easter) offers clean facilities, including an *albergue* and restaurant.

Walks in the Valle de Echo

Above Siresa, the **Valle de Echo** constitutes a tapestry of pasture and beech forest against a backdrop of towering limestone cliffs and summits, harbingers of the karst country at the border. The most popular **day walks** east of the valley are the ascents of Bisaurín (2669m), Agüerri (2449m) and Castillo de Acher (2390m); best is the climb up Agüerri, the summit of the huge bluff that forms the easternmost side of the Boca del Infierno gorge, beginning 7km north of Siresa.

The usual starting point lies 12km north of Siresa at **Selva de Oza**, where there's just a pleasant rustic bar and a defunct campsite. For any outing the best **map** is the Editorial Alpina 1:40,000 "Ansó-Echo", applicable also to all walks discussed up to and including "The Valle de Roncal and the Parque Natural Pirenaico" section on p.463. Beginning from Echo, avoid dreary road-trudging by taking the GR65.3.3, well signposted as the **Via Romana** some 3km north of Siresa. This "Roman road", unlike many so called in the Pyrenees, actually was built in the time of Augustus, and threads through the Boca del Infierno gorge, continuing beyond Selva de Oza to the Puerto de Palo/Col de Pau on the frontier.

Bisaurín and the Osia valley

For **Bisaurín**, make an early start along the variant GR11.1 that climbs east on the southern slopes of the Agüerri valley – it leaves the main valley 6km north of Echo, across the Puente de Santa Ana, and shortcuts the twisty, narrow paved road past *Camping Borda Bisáltico* to run high above the Agüerri stream. About an hour from the valley road, you reach the *Refugio de Gabardito*, 8km in by road (1360m; 50 places; all year; Ⓣ974 375 387 or 676 850 843), with a range of en-suite rooms, set on a beautiful grassy clearing near the treeline. It's managed by Echo's Compañia de Guías (see p.457), who run the popular cross-country skiing centre at the doorstep here, and who are the contacts for reservations year-round. From *Gabardito*, the path climbs east to the **Collado del Foratón** (2032m), 2hr 30min from the refuge; then it's a stiff two-hour climb further to the summit, rising steeply to the northeast.

You can also use the approach via the Collado del Foratón as a full-pack traverse, finishing 45 minutes southeast of the pass near at the top of the **valley of the Río**

Osia, at the *Refugio Lizara* (1540m; 75 places; ⓣ974 371 473). This sits in the middle of another major cross-country skiing area; in summer you can trek northeast to the main GR11 (see p.460 for directions in reverse), or continue east along the GR11.1 in under a day to Canfranc.

Castillo de Acher and Agüerri

Castillo de Acher and Agüerri can be tackled singly or together in one gruelling day; take plenty of water. Begin along the track that climbs east-southeast from close to the ex-campsite at Selva de Oza; this curves back southwest after crossing the Espata stream and climbs steeply to a simple forest hut (1740m; 2hr), just beyond which the ways divide. The summit of **Castillo de Acher** – from a distance looking exactly like a castle – lies a little north of east, along a fairly easy path (4–5hr from Selva de Oza).

For **Agüerri**, take the right-hand path just beyond the refuge, climbing east along the **Borreguil de Acher** stream and crossing after about half an hour onto a newer path that doubles back on the other side, rising west to a small saddle. Beyond this, the path swings east again, along the **Jardín** stream; at the head of the valley defined by the Collado de Costatiza, climb south for the summit (5hr 30min from Selva de Oza).

Frontier peaks and Ibón de Acherito

North of Selva de Oza, the frontier peaks of **Punta Cristian/Pic Lariste** (2168m) and **Arraya de las Foyas/Pic Laraille** (2147m) make classic targets, with near-identical approaches. Continue on the asphalt road north through dense forest, with the Río Aragón Subordán to the left; some 2km above Selva de Oza, before the end of the pavement, you veer left to cross a bridge onto a side track, beyond which the main track follows the eastward curve of the valley. Once over the Barranco Acherito side-stream via another bridge, the track ends at the locale known as **La Mina** (1230m). Here there's just a large signboard-map beside a small car park; cows graze all around, with scattered buildings for the use of the herders, plus a derelict refuge. This is the junction with the GR11, descending from the west and continuing up the main valley; it's also the trailhead for the popular day outing to both the peaks and the **Ibón de Acherito**, second westernmost glacial lake in the Spanish Pyrenees.

Take the path north along the left (east) bank of the Barranco Las Foyas, switching over to the right bank sooner than indicated on the Editorial Alpina map. In July wild irises abound, and the occasional Egyptian vulture wheels overhead. After 45 minutes' climbing, guided by red-and-white or single-yellow waymarks, you reach the T-junction with the HRP variant.

Bear right on this, and leave it soon after to head north into the cirque (*c.* 1800m; 1hr 30min) under the frontier summits. The routes divide here: Punta Cristian is the summit immediately north, climbed directly in another hour; Arraya looms to the west, reached by a route of similar duration curving to a point just southeast of the summit, then swinging back for the top. From both summits you look north across the idyllic pine forests and fields of the Lescun valley (see p.398) and westwards over the barren karst – an arresting contrast.

To visit **the lake**, bear left along the well-trodden HRP; some ninety minutes out of La Mina, the path grade slackens on a grassy hillside at the base of Arraya, and you get your first eyeful of the limestone cirque to the west. Fifteen minutes further, you round a corner in the landscape and suddenly the Ibón de Acherito is there: one of the most striking in Aragón, with the crests of the frontier peaks as a backdrop and tadpoles in its shallows. Arraya can be climbed equally easily from the lakeshore; allow 45 minutes each way. Camping, while tempting, is difficult – there's a flat meadow, with a spring, just ten minutes east along the HRP.

△Ibón de Acherito and Pic Laraille

To vary the return to La Mina, and include some ridge-walking with views into France, follow the HRP west from the lake along a hogback to a grassy point on the frontier crest at just over 2000m. From here you can glimpse the stagnant pond of **Ibón de Ansabère** at your feet, or gaze over the **Cirque de Lescun**, and to the shattered peaks closing it off on the west. Now descend gently for twenty minutes or so to a rectangular shepherd's shelter, used more from the French side. The obvious continuation along the border ridge would be to the strategic Puerto de Acherito at the top of the cirque, but there is no non-technical way around or over Pic d'Chourique (2084m), which blocks progress. So you must descend, more or less as traced on the Alpina map, steeply cross-country for twenty minutes to the proper trail in the valley bottom, called the **Barranco de Ferrerias**. From the vicinity of an unstaffed, stone-built shelter here, it's about 1hr 20min down to La Mina; the path is unmarked but obvious and gradual.

East or west: the GR11

The GR11 arrives at La Mina from Candanchú to the **east** in a full day's trek along the headwaters of the Río Aragón Subordán, a route enlivened by the large **Ibón de Estanés/Lac d'Estaëns** (2hr out), and the squelchy water-meadow of **Aguas Tuertas** (4hr from Candanchú), with a usable if unstaffed refuge and the best camping possibilities en route. Camping is *not* allowed at La Mina – and plans to restore and staff the refuge here have never passed the talk stage – though you can have a pleasant river-dip just downstream by the end of the asphalt.

The GR11 continues **west** along a much easier traverse to Zuriza in the Valle de Ansó (see p.462). From the upper bridge over the Barranco Acherito described above, the GR11 climbs steeply west into the Collado de Petraficha (1958m; 2hr uphill from Selva de Oza), from where it's all downhill along the Petraficha stream, the last forty minutes of the four-hour hiking day on track.

On to Ansó by road or trail

The daily evening bus from Jaca to Echo continues west to Ansó along 11km of 2006-improved road, climbing over the Sierra de Vedao before dropping into the

Valle de Ansó. Final approaches to the valley from the east are guarded by two strangely shaped rocks known locally as "the Monk and the Nun", just above a tunnel.

If you wish to walk there, shun this still-dangerous road in favour of the very enjoyable **PR18 trail from Siresa to Ansó**, indicated by a sign reading "Fuen d'a Cruz" by the cemetery and stream below Siresa. This, which also doubles hereabouts as the **GR15**, is probably the most useful of the area's dozen PR trails; a descriptive booklet, published by Prames Ediciones, is sold locally.

Starting on the south side of the bridge, the path is initially waymarked by red arrows and purple paint splodges as well as newer PR blazes. Gaining height quickly, you intersect with an unmaintained track at a saddle about 45 minutes along; turning onto this, fifteen minutes later you top out at a T-junction in the track system (1180m), where you bear right (north). After another half-hour along the serpentine track, you'll emerge at a pass affording a first view of Ansó village; the track continues north, but you should plunge down left (southwest) on the resurgence of the old *camino*. Passing a ruined farm, continue dropping steeply into the valley running west to the village, zigzagging to meet the stream bed, on whose right bank you should arrive some two hours out of Siresa. You'll reach a fountain at the eastern outskirts of Ansó about half an hour later. With the exception of the initial climb from Siresa, the route is shown more or less correctly on the Editorial Alpina map.

Ansó

Once a more prosperous village than Echo, **ANSÓ** fell upon hard times during the depopulation of rural Aragón in the 1950s and 1960s. Today, however, there are signs of a small but definite revival, with Jacan and Pamplonan professionals keeping second homes here, plus a growing stream of tourists sampling the village's attractions. Without having many specific landmarks, the village outshines its setting, whose scrubby pine cover gives no hint of the splendours waiting up-valley. The sixteenth-century, wood-floored church of San Pedro houses an interesting **Museo Etnológico** (daily summer only 10.30am–1.30pm & 3.30–8pm; €2), its exhibits including a video and photographic exhibition of Pyrenean wildlife and rural trades.

Practicalities

Ansó's popularity is reflected in several places to **stay**, somewhat less expensive than in Echo but filling equally quickly in summer. Best is the *Posada Magoria* (Ⓣ974 370 049, Ⓔposadamagoria@lospirineos.info; ❹ B&B), installed in a 1920s mansion by the church at c/Milagros, with en-suite rooms, views and a garden. The four dormer rooms have double beds, while the lower-floor units have balconies; they serve excellent communal vegetarian meals (preference given to guests). A worthy alternative, at the northern end of town 200m towards Zuriza on the bypass road, is modern, comfortable *Hostal Kimboa* (Ⓣ974 370 184, Ⓕ370 130; open all year by arrangement; ❹). A less likely option is eccentrically managed *Hostal Aisa*, on central Plaza Domingo Miral 2 (Ⓣ974 370 009; ❶), essentially an Aragonese Fawlty Towers crossed with a Victorian orphanage, its clientele, décor and (to some extent) prices unchanged for decades. A summer-only **campsite** (Ⓣ665 926 149) operates beside the very good (and apparently free) municipal **swimming pool**, at the south end of the village.

Among the very few **restaurants**, *Kimboa*'s is about the best, their cousin's own-raised meat featuring in €15 *menús*, served under the terrace canopy in summer (lunch only, by the fireplace-grill, off-season). But don't overlook the competent restaurant by the swimming pool, with a basic €9 *menú* but more interesting *carta*. Of the many **bars**, liveliest and friendliest is spit-and-sawdust *Zuriza* at the top of c/Mayor. One of Ansó's two **banks** has an ATM.

Going **west from Ansó**, an eighteen-kilometre minor road (the NA176) passing the village of Garde, with a campsite and two restaurants, eventually joins the NA137, which threads through the Valle de Roncal, in Navarra. There's no bus service in this direction, and it's 21km in total to Erronkari village.

Walking in the Valle de Ansó

Other than the path in from Siresa, the lower Ansó valley has little serious trekking potential; walking really starts from Zuriza, 14km north. There's no bus service there, and the paved road up-valley makes for tedious trudging – the green-and-yellow-blazed SV9 path cuts out some, but not all, of this – so arrange a lift if without transport. The scenery improves as you follow the Río Veral upstream, the steep valley sides covered with pine, later giving way to beech. Dotted around are stone-built ex-farmhouses, two of which have become the *comedores* of *Borda Arracona* 7.5km along, an excellent and popular rural restaurant specializing in open-fire grills and Aragonese dishes like *migas*; portions are on the small side but so are prices at about €22 for two full meals with house wine.

After 9km you enter the narrow gorge between **Peña Ezkaurre** (2049m) and **Espelunga** (2106m) where there's a chance of spotting rare black vultures. Eventually the gorge opens into the luxuriantly green basin of **Zuriza** (1227m), less forested than the Selva de Oza. The most obvious amenity is an enormous, somewhat regimented but tent-friendly campsite, *Camping Zuriza* (mid-June to early Sept; also quad bungalows), with an attached *albergue* (Ⓣ974 370 196; all year; dorms plus 10 doubles at ❷), a general store and a decent restaurant. If these are full – a distinct possibility during peak seasons – you'll find another staffed refuge at **Linza** (aka Plano de la Casa), 5km north along the track parallel to the Petrechema stream. Here the friendly, well-run *Refugio de Linza* (1320m; Ⓣ & Ⓕ974 370 112; 100 places; all year) rents out cross-country skis for use on nearby pistes.

Tres Reyes ascent

From Plano de la Casa, you can make a day walk to **Mesa de los Tres Reyes** (*Hiru Erregeen Mahaia* in Euskera), the karst plateau astride the border with France; carry plenty of water, as there's none above the 1900-metre contour. Start by heading a little north of east along the path to the **Collado de Linza** (1906m; 2hr); from this pass the path heads north a short way before resuming its original trajectory, dropping into the shallow Hoya la Solana and then climbing out to the **Collado de Esqueste/Col d'Escoueste** (2114m; 3hr). You're now on the frontier – dramatically delineated by the sharp drop to the French side – amidst unbelievably barren terrain.

Follow the top of the cliffs north into a small *col* that leads to **Tres Reyes summit** (2444m; 4hr); this meeting point of France, Navarra and Aragón is adorned with a bronze statue of St Francis Xavier, the Jesuit evangelist of the Indies. Again there's an amazing contrast between the lush Lescun valley beyond the tarn of Lhurs to the east, and the lunar rock and summits to the north and west, notably pyramidal Pic d'Anie.

West to Belagoa

Rather than return to Zuriza to adopt the GR11, you can partly duplicate the above directions in a mid-altitude traverse to Belagoa (see p.464). Instead of going east from the Hoya La Solana, veer north through the Hoya del Portillo de Larra, over the eponymous pass (1829m), and then west through the Larra karst formations and beech forest; allow six hours.

West to Izaba: the GR11

Zuriza straddles the **GR11**, with Selva de Oza an easy day away to the east (see p.458); heading west for six walking hours towards **Izaba** in the Roncal valley (14km by narrow, paved road), the GR11 was rerouted in the early 1990s. The new itinerary starts from the Puerto Navarra, 700m west of Zuriza, at the border between Aragón and Navarra – where the difference in public-works funding between the two autonomous regions is made graphically apparent by the respective states of the asphalt.

The **new path** heads spectacularly, if strenuously, southwest up the flanks of **Peña Ezkaurre/Ezcaurri** (2049m; 2hr 30min), which though not especially high, impresses with its profile. Just the other side lies its namesake *ibón*, the westernmost natural tarn in the Spanish Pyrenees. Thereafter the GR11, now in Navarra, descends west into the **Berroeta valley**, soon becoming a track along the right bank until the confluence of the Berroeta and Belabarze streams. From here another track leads west to Izaba.

The Valle de Roncal and Parque Natural Pirenaico Larra-Belagoa

The **Parque Natural Pirenaico Larra-Belagoa**, which straddles the road connecting Roncal and La-Pierre-Saint-Martin in France, occupies the head of the **Valle de Belagoa** where landscapes range from karst desert to dense forest, by way of lush pastures. Further downstream, the **Valle de Roncal** – next valley west of Ansó – is famous for the hard, cylindrical *roncalés* cheese, made from sheep's milk and widely available in the two main valley villages of **Erronkari** and **Izaba**.

The area has an evening **bus** service from Pamplona, via the Foz de Arbaiun and Burgui and following the course of the Río Esca up the Valle de Roncal as far as Izaba. Foresters used to float logs down the Esca by lacing them together into a raft, with three or four such rafts linked and controlled by two huge oars; nowadays the rafts are constructed only for fun.

Erronkari and Izaba

Once beyond the low-altitude villages Lumbier and Burgui, the road climbs slowly to **ERRONKARI** (Roncal), capital of the valley. Here you cross to the west bank of the river for the old quarter (including the arcaded town hall). The churchyard (follow signs to "Mausoleo") is worth visiting for the flamboyant tomb of the great opera tenor **Julián Gayarre** (1844–90), whose sarcophagus is surmounted by four sculpted-bronze nymphs, plus an angel, bearing a mock coffin heavenwards. Born into a Roncal shepherd family, Gayarre was regarded by international audiences as the equal of the later Caruso; he died – eerily, from cancer of the vocal cords – just a bit too soon to be captured by the new technology of the gramophone.

Erronkari supports the helpful regional **Turismo** (Mon–Sat 10am–2pm & 4.30–8.30pm, Sun 10am–2pm; ⓣ948 475 136); in the same building a **Centro de Interpretación de la Naturaleza** has exhibits on valley wildlfie. **Accommodation** includes *Hostal Zaltua* on the through road (ⓣ948 475 008; ❷), as well as several *casas rurales*, best of which is en-suite *Casa Villa Pepita* (ⓣ948 475 133;

❷) opposite the *Zaltua* on the west bank, which also provides *table d'hôte* meals at reasonable cost, but you'll have more choice in Izaba.

Izaba

IZABA (Isaba; ⓦwww.isaba.es), 7km north of Roncal, is larger and busier; a small, modern district at the south end of the village (with a small **Turismo** and **bank ATM**) is easily ignored in favour of its old quarter. This sprawls appealingly around a fortified hilltop church, a massive structure with a rib-vaulted nave and ornate *retablo* and organ inside. Izaba is a major year-round touring centre for the Western Pyrenees, descended upon by weekend trippers from nearby cities. Accordingly there's a fair amount of conventional **accommodation**; pick of this, east of the busy through road on narrow c/Mendigatxa, is the sleek and clean *Hostal Lola* (ⓣ & ⓕ948 893 012, ⓦwww.hostal-lola.com; closed Nov; ❹), with limited parking (hopeless elsewhere in Izaba) and the best **restaurant** in town (€16 *menú*, €24 *a la carta*). At the junction of c/Mendigatxa and the high street, en-suite *Pensión Txiki* (ⓣ948 893 118; closed May & Nov; ❸) perches above the simple, namesake *bar-restaurante* (€12 *menú* and good fish soup). Quietest, at c/Isargentea 25bis, is 2005-inaugurated *Hotal Onki Xin* (ⓣ948 893 320, ⓦwww.onkixin.com; ❹ B&B), a tasteful conversion of an old chicken ranch. Izaba has eight *casas rurales* rented by the room (mostly en-suite and ❷), though expect to try several places at busy times. The *Albergue Oxanea* (ⓣ948 893 153; 55 places; HB encouraged) on c/Bormapéa, west of the main street, is an unusually salubrious private **youth hostel**. The **campsite**, *Asolaze* (ⓣ948 893 034), also with bungalows, a few doubles and an *albergue*, lies 6km upstream towards the border, at the edge of the *parque natural*.

The Valle de Belagoa

There's no bus service beyond Izaba, so without transport you'll have to arrange a lift (easily done) up the valley into the **Parque Natural Pirenaico Larra-Belagoa**. The road enters the park along the Río Belagoa, flanked by forests of

The Tributo de las Tres Vacas

Beyond Belagoa the road climbs to the border, crossing close to the frontier cairn which has replaced the original marker of La Piedra de San Martín/La-Pierre-Saint-Martin. Here, every July 13, the people of the Spanish Valle de Roncal and the French Vallée de Barétous gather to enact the **Tributo de las Tres Vacas**, a ceremony stemming from a 1326 treaty on grazing rights, the oldest of several such agreements (*faceries*) still extant. Four representatives of Roncal, dressed in white shirts, black capes and black hats, join hands with four representatives of Barétous *commune*, whose only concession to folklore is sashes in the French national colours. With their hands linked on modern frontier cairn number 262, they chant "Pas aban, pas aban, pas aban" ("Peace above all" in local dialect) while three identical blonde heifers (*las tres vacas*) are handed over to the Roncalese as tribute, securing the right of the French herdsmen to graze cattle in the Spanish valley for another year. Originally such *faceries* and tributes served to prevent violent altercations provoked by illegal bovine immigrants; these days, though, the cows are discreetly returned to the French afterwards. A huge and disparate crowd (up to three thousand strong) of itinerant food-and-drink vendors, French gendarmes, Spanish forestry wardens, journalists, tourists and locals always turn up, even if it's raining, mainly to take part in the *fiesta* afterwards. Be sure to arrive by 11am for the ceremony; shortly after noon it's all over, save for the feasting.

beech and silver fir, until the terrain opens out into flat fields and, just before tight switchbacks in the road, you find the *Venta de Juan Pito* (May–Oct daily, winter weekends only; 1–2pm & 7–8pm outside July & Aug), a **traditional inn** serving hearty meals – including locally concocted milk-based desserts – for under €20.

This is currently the highest facility in the valley, as the decrepit *Refugio de Belagoa* (1428m; 19km from Izaba) has been closed since 2005 owing to lack of wardens and non-compliance with EU standards. This hasn't affected the 25km of **cross-country skiing** routes for all ability levels at 1350–1720m altitude, which begin near *Juan Pito*. In summer the same hillsides become pastures extending to the limestone peaks on the east.

Walking in the Parque Natural

The best way of seeing the eastern side of the park – where all the karst formations are – involves taking the **HRP variant** which links Belagoa with Lescun in France via the frontier Collado de Insolo, also known as the Portillo de Lescun or Col d'Anaye. Don't confuse this pass with the Col des Anies on the north side of Pic d'Anie, well inside French territory, but you can return via the Col des Anies to make a **circuit**. Take ample water; in deteriorating weather, turn back. Navigating through karst badlands, which form natural mazes, is hopeless when visibility is bad – not to mention the possibility of disappearing down one of the numerous caves and deep sinkholes that pepper the terrain.

From the abandoned refuge the path tends slightly south of east, first across pasture and then through beech forest, before arriving in the eerily beautiful Larra region, distinguished by bone-white rock and trees stunted by altitude and lack of soil. Yellow paint splodges then guide you through the boulders, until the **Collado de Insolo** (2052m) is reached in about another two and a half hours.

An ascent of Tres Reyes fills another memorable local day out. The route lies a little south of the HRP; after climbing over **Lapazarra** (1777m; 1hr 20min), the path heads east through the Collado Larrería. This is again typical Larra scenery, littered with boulders and dotted with bonsai-sized trees in repetitious patterns. In autumn the landscape is brightened somewhat by the turning foliage of scattered deciduous specimens.

From Larra, continue up to the frontier ridge at the Col d'Ourtets (2182m), next turning south-southeast along it for the **Tres Reyes summit** (3hr 20min). At this altitude the karst landscape seems more like Sinai than the Pyrenees, but the views emphasize the paradoxes of the area, where high-mountain desert is fringed by lower pasture and forest – so lush precisely because all available water percolates down through fissures in the karst, emerging in quantity below the 1500-metre contour.

Gouffre de la Pierre-Saint-Martin

Just on the Spanish side of the frontier, despite the French name, and close to the NA137 road, yawns the entrance – now grilled over – of the **Gouffre de la Pierre-Saint-Martin**, among the largest underground caverns in the world. It was discovered by chance in 1950, when, on the last, disconsolate night of an apparently unsuccessful expedition led by Norbert Casteret (see box on p.313), a stone was thrown into an opening and clattered audibly down an abyss. In 1953, the year that Everest was conquered, speleologists reached the bottom of this cavern, at 734m the deepest penetration of a cave system until then.

The vertical entrance shaft of 346m remains the longest known, and its largest chamber, the Sala de la Verna (now desecrated by an EDF tunnel), measures 270m by 230m by 180m. Using higher entrances, subsequent 1982 expeditions logged a total depth of 1342m and explored an overall length of interconnecting passages exceeding 50km.

La-Pierre-Saint-Martin

Some 10km beyond the *Refugio de Belagoa* and 3km into French territory from the border by road, **LA-PIERRE-SAINT-MARTIN** (still Arette-la-Pierre on many maps) is a modern **downhill-ski resort**, the westernmost in the entire Pyrenees. Atlantic weather influences generally mean good snow conditions, even in spring, despite a modest top point of only 2153m (descending to 1527m or 1650m). The Basques, both French and Spanish, are well aware of this, and at weekends the antiquated lift system (including five two- or three-seater chairs) can barely cope. Of eighteen pistes in this small centre, most are green- or blue-rated – and red runs are blueish, the blues greenish – so Arette-la-Pierre is essentially a beginner to intermediate resort, with handicapped access to several lifts. That said, the easterly runs are routed through gnarled trees, and reasonably long – there's a three-kilometre red run from the top, two even longer blue "boulevards", Pyrénées and Myrtilles, plus a 1900-metre black piste. The setting is lovely, with views to the ocean on good days, though the concentration of Brutalist-style chalets and *résidences* at 1650m is distinctly unlovely. **Cross-country skiing** is offered in token fashion at **Boucle de Braca**, 1km northeast, and much more substantially at **Issarbe**, 5km northwest.

In **summer** the main thing that counts in La-Pierre's favour for anyone following the **GR10** between Lescun and Santa Grazi is the *Refuge Jeandel* (1670m; Ⓣ05.59.66.14.46 or 06.19.82.41.69; Ⓦwww.refugejeandel.com; May–Sept; 25 places in three- to six-bunk dorms), on a rise at the western edge of the ski pistes. It's a high-quality outfit with hot showers, a fireplace and meal service provided by jolly proprietor Jean Hourticq and his chef-wife, set to have its diner expanded in the future. There's also a self-catering kitchen, and a small stock of trekking groceries for sale, as the *épicerie* in the ski "village" is unreliable – though a single restaurant operates fitfully there in summer. Schedule an extra night here and use the intervening day to bag Pic d'Anie (Auñamendi in Euskera) – a six-hour round trip on sections of the HRP and GR10. You're just inside Béarn at La-Pierre-Saint-Martin, on the border with the Pays-Basque county of Soule.

Gorges of the Haute-Soule

Four gorges, south of the D113/D26 route linking La-Pierre-Saint-Martin in the east and Larraiñe in the west, are the principal reason outsiders visit the district of **Haute-Soule** (Zuberoa), easternmost and remotest corner of the French Pays Basque. Here, vast green pastures and beech groves stretch under an open, vulture-haunted sky; there are far more sheep than people, few tourist facilities and no villages to speak of except Larraiñe, Ligi, Tardets, Abense-de-Haut and (stretching the definition) Santa Grazi.

The **Gorges de Kakouetta** are the best of the managed gorges in the Pyrenees, but if you prefer a completely uncommercialized chasm, visit the adjacent **Gorges d'Ehujarré**. Both are somewhat difficult to reach without your own vehicle, as there's no public transport on the French side, and the scattered "village" of Santa Grazi – at the mouth of Ehujarré – lies four hours' walk northwest of La-Pierre-Saint-Martin, along the GR10 or its variants. The best way of visiting both on foot is from Belagoa, trekking down the Ehujarré to Santa Grazi and then up alongside the Kakouetta.

The other pair of great gorges, 18km west of Kakouetta by road, are the interconnecting **Holzarté** and **Olhadybia** (Olhadubi), crossed at their junction by a long, jiggly and absolutely unmissable – though very touristed – suspension footbridge. By the serpentining GR10, these lie seven hours west of Santa Grazi, with Larraiñe another half-hour or so beyond.

A walking tour of the gorges

Head up the NA137 road from the refuge at Belagoa for a couple of kilometres until the ridge from the summit of Lakhoura – the 1877-metre peak immediately north – subsides at the **Collado de Eraiz**. An HRP variant goes north through this pass onto the Errayzé-Sentolha plateau above the end of the **Gorges d'Ehujarré**, where you quit the HRP and drop into the canyon on another path (see p.468). Palisades rise 400m above you, but it's not a difficult walk, and this route has been used for decades for the movement of sheep from the Sainte-Engrâce valley onto the pastures around Pic Lakhoura.

Three to four hours from the refuge you emerge at the hamlet of Senta, one of three comprising the *commune* of **SANTA GRAZI** (Sainte-Engrâce, Urdaite). Until 1987 this was dubbed locally *le bout du monde*, "the end of the world", approachable by road only from the west and arguably the remotest spot in the French Basque country. The extension of the D113 east to La-Pierre-Saint-Martin was supposed to change that, but, despite increasing traffic, the Santa Grazi valley has retained its rural somnolence, still surrounded by hay-meadows and losing its young to the big cities.

The Santa Grazi hamlets, Ligi and Abense-de-Haut

SENTA has a combination **inn/gîte d'étape**, the *Auberge Elichalt* (☎ 05.59.28.61.63; 30 dorm places, also doubles ❷ B&B), which serves light meals, and has space for a few tents on the rear lawn. If it's shut, the *Café Bar Berriex* above the village serves sandwiches and drinks on its lawn, and may do hot snacks in the evening. The *Elichalt* overlooks the **church**, a strikingly original example of eleventh-century Romanesque architecture, effectively the logo of the Western Pyrenees. It's an engagingly asymmetrical structure, with a sloping-roofed belfry, a lean-to-style nave and a graveyard containing some typically Basque disc-crowned headstones, much in evidence as you move further west. The interior offers graphically carved column-capitals near the altar, some gaudily painted in the 1880s; look carefully and you'll find the *Adoration of the Magi*, lions devouring Christians, Solomon and the Queen of Sheba apparently copulating, and owl-faces peering from the base of some columns. Beside the church, a map-placard outlines a loop-hike – up the

Transhumant shepherds

Like other shepherds in south European or Mediterranean climes, the Basques have always been obliged to take their flocks to high **mountain pastures** in summer for better grazing. They live out on the bare slopes in stone-hut sheepfolds called *cayolars*, with a couple of dogs, milking the ewes twice a day and making cheese, the *fromage de brebis*, whose soft and hard versions are ubiquitous throughout the pastoral Pyrenees. Trekkers are usually welcome to buy small quantities when passing by such huts. Most of the pastures today are accessible by car, at least at the gentler Basque end of the Pyrenees, so a shepherd's life is not as harsh and isolated as it used to be – though there are still areas in the higher mountains accessible only by mule or *pottok* pony. A measure of the traditional pre-eminence of sheep in the local economy is the Basque word for "rich", *aberats*, the literal meaning of which is "he who owns large flocks".

east bank of the Ehujarré gorge, then down its bed – for the benefit of day-trippers based here; full details below. The middle hamlet of **Calla**, about 1500m downstream from Senta, has nothing to offer passers-by. The northwesternmost settlement is **CASERNES**, 4km beyond Calla, with the only **food shop** in the valley, opposite the *mairie*; just below on the riverbank is a friendly, well-placed **campsite**, *Ibarra* (Ⓣ05.59.28.73.59; Easter–Oct),

The closest proper **hotel** is at **LIGI** (Licq-Athéry), 4km north on the D26, where the graceful Pont des Laminaks spans the River Saison at the weir. Just north, rambling, old-fashioned *Des Touristes-Bouchet* (Ⓣ05.59.28.61.01, Ⓕ05.59.28.64.80; closed Dec–Jan; ❸) has its best balconied rooms on the first floor and a grassy camping area down by the river. The **restaurant** is competent but surprisingly pricey; half-board taking in the *menu du soir* eases the pain. Just under 6km north in **ABENSE-DE-HAUT**, *Hôtel Restaurant Ühaltia-Le Pont d'Abense* (Ⓣ05.59.28.54.60, Ⓔuhaltia@wanadoo.fr; closed early Dec & Jan; ❸) offers better value, especially at half-board, with an exceptionally accomplished **restaurant** (reservations needed), strong on wild produce, duck and fish drawing clientele from some distance; the best two rooms have terraces overlooking the valley. The small town of **ATARRATZE** (Tardets-Sorholus), with shops and two **bank ATMs**, lies just 800m north across the Pont d'Abense over the Saison.

Gorges de Ehujarré loop

This suggested itinerary is indicated schematically on a **map-placard** by the church in Senta, with an estimated time-course of six hours, but is also traced with reasonable accuracy on Carte de Randonnées no. 2, "Pays Basque Est". Doing the loop clockwise is advisable, with the climb tackled when fresh, getting you safely down into the gorge by afternoon, when mists tend to obscure the heights. With a car, save yourself another half-hour by parking down at the end of the pavement, in the stream valley by the bridge.

The path begins there, marked with green-and-white paint splodges. The initial grade is sharp, and you tangle repeatedly with 4WD tracks, but there's dense shade (and some deerflies) in the **Bois d'Utzia** beech forest, and trail short-cuts are effective. About 1hr 45min along, the worst climbing is over as you emerge from the forest at the single, tin-roofed hut of **Cayolars d'Utzipia** (1450m). The waymarked route continues up and right (southwest), curling over the brow of the ridge for great views of the Sainte-Engrâce valley, and allowing a glimpse of the Pic d'Anie hovering above the trees to the southeast. The elevation high point of the day (1600m) is reached about 2hr 45min out, as you cross high moorland with heather and sheep; the frontier appears ahead, while the gorge yawns down on the right.

Some 3hr along, you arrive at the **Cayolars d'Utzigagna**, at the edge of the beech/fir woods; there's no reliable water here, despite what the IGN map says. When you meet a dirt track serving an isolated sheep-farm to the left, turn right (west-southwest); some fifteen minutes later, use a ravine-path short-cut to descend right to the **pastures of Errayze**, where herds of *pottok* (Basque ponies) often graze. Another quarter-hour across the turf should see you to the **Fontaine d'Errayze**, a strong spring at the very top of the gorge – and the only drinkable water en route. A distinct trail appears, initially on the left bank, the torrent disappears into the ravine bed, and beech woods resume. About an hour downhill from the spring, the path crosses to the right bank, where it stays for most of the final hour down to the higher of two tin-roofed barns where you rejoin your uphill route, a few minutes above the end of the asphalt. In many ways this is the most low-key of the four gorges – the dense tree cover and sloping scree means you rarely get an eyeful of the canyon walls – but even in summer you won't pass more than half a dozen people all day.

The Gorges de Kakouetta

The entrance to the **Gorges de Kakouetta** (daily March 15–Nov 15 8am–dusk; €4) yawns between Calla and Casernes. Though Kakouetta lies squarely on the tourist trail, don't be put off – the gorge is genuinely dramatic and, outside high summer, not too crowded; allow ninety minutes to two hours for a visit. Except in a part from of July, little light penetrates the gorge midday, so the chilly interior is essentially temperate rainforest; the air hangs heavy with mist produced by dozens of seeps and tiny waterfalls, pampering tenacious ferns, moss and other greenery, all of which festoon vertical walls rising 300m and seldom split more than 5m apart. For an organized attraction the going is often hard – sometimes along a narrow metal catwalk with a safety cable, sometimes on a narrow, slippery path right in the gorge bottom, with the stream almost lapping over your feet – so come with good boots. Helmets against rockfalls are offered to the nervous, with emergency phones at strategic spots; the gorge is also prone to flash-flooding after storms, and there is an alarm system for warning hikers to exit immediately.

Just under an hour along you reach a picnic area, near which pours a twenty-metre waterfall, the accumulated percolation of a winter's precipitation through the karst strata overhead; if you don't mind a spray-bath, you can walk right behind the cascade. About 200m past here, the path ends by a cave (signed as "La Grotte 2km" at the car park), with formations beginning to appear inside. Unfortunately for trekkers, the gorge is a dead end – you'll have to retrace your steps and adopt one or other of the local GR10 variants to get anywhere else.

Gorges d'Olhadybia and Gorges d'Holzarté

From the entrance of the Kakouetta to the entrance of the Holzarté is about four hours' walk using the newer GR10, traced when the Pont d'Olhadybia was temporarily washed out. But if possible it's really preferable to make a slightly longer day of it along the original **GR10**, now rated as a *variante*, which leaves the D113 just west of the Kakouetta entrance. From there it climbs gradually southwest into the **Col d'Anhaou** (3hr), and shortly after begins to curve north, almost level, towards the **Gorges d'Olhadybia** (Olhadubi).

Owing to the steepness of the terrain, the GR handles the final approach in a giant S-bend which drops to the head of the gorge at the **Pont d'Olhadybia** (5hr). It then continues above the west bank for another hour to the intimidating Himalayan-style suspension bridge **Passerelle d'Olhadybia**, which crosses the mouth of the Olhadybia to meet the **Gorges d'Holzarté**, swinging over a drop of 180m. Rebuilt in 1920, the bridge was originally constructed before World War I by an Italian miner to facilitate getting out of the woods for lunch hour at Logibarrea. Penetrating the Holzarté, first achieved in 1933, is for experts only; less demanding **canyoning** is organized locally by Eau Sud (Ⓣ06.03.42.98.71, Ⓦwww.eau-sud.com).

Once over the bridge, continue north on the corniche path along the cliff forming the east bank of the joint gorges; it's sharply graded towards the end, with a safety cable, but within 45 minutes you'll reach the gorge car park at **LOGIBARREA** (Logibar), where there's a good *gîte d'étape* (Ⓣ05.59.28.61.14, Ⓦwww.aubergelogibar.fr.st; all year; 30 places in dorms or quads) with reasonable meal service (not Dec–Feb).

Larraiñe

If there's no room at Logibarrea, leave the GR and follow the D26 west for 2.5km to the village of **LARRAIÑE** (Larrau, Larrañe), where the stucco walls and steeply pitched grey-slate roofs of the houses contrast with the green, north-facing shoulder of land on which they stand, slashed by little rivulets and nestled in

△ Larraiñe village

gardens. The church is nearly as impressive as Santa Grazi's, and despite the modest altitude (630m) it snows heavily – thus the steep roofs and distinctly *béarnais* architecture.

Though Larraiñe is quiet – almost dead – out of season, its two **hotels** are usually busy, for good reason. The rambling, old-fashioned *Hôtel Despouey* (Ⓣ05.59.28.60.82; closed Nov 15–Easter; ❷), the embodiment of *la vieille douce France*, has variable rooms, the local **shop** on the ground floor and a bar/breakfast salon, but no restaurant. Open all year are the *chambres d'hôtes* next to the bakery run by Jeannette Etcheto (Ⓣ05.59.28.63.22; ❷), with suppers available four nights weekly. Otherwise, head across "town" to much fancier *Hôtel Restaurant Etchémaïté* (Ⓣ05.59.28.61.45, Ⓦwww.hotel-etchemaite.fr; closed most Jan & early Dec; ❸, HB advised), whose unusually polished **restaurant** (closed Sun pm & Mon low season) serves assorted creative *terrines*, eel, *cèpes*, pigeon *foie gras*, stuffed artichokes and decadent desserts. Given quality and price (*menus* €18–34, *à la carte* €40, plus expensive wine) – though portions are small – reservations are usually required. The rooms are state of the art, with powerful heating, proper shower stalls and dimmers even on the bedside lamps. There's also a small **campsite**, *Ixtila* (Ⓣ05.59.28.63.09; April to mid-Nov), at the lower, east end of town.

South of Larraiñe, the D26 climbs to the frontier at the **Port/Puerto de Larrau** (1573m; closed in winter), just under **Orhy/Orhi**, the first peak above 2000m as you head east from the Atlantic; on the other side the Spanish NA127 drops down to Otsagi (Otsagabia), 33km away (see p.472).

Forêt d'Iraty/Selva de Irati

Straddling the frontier between the Port de Larrau on the east and the Puerto de Ibañeta on the west, the **Forêt d'Iraty/Selva de Irati** (Iratiko Oihana) is the most extensive broadleaf forest in the Pyrenees. The legions of trees, principally beech but interspersed with oak, fir and ancient yew, have long been exploited by boatyards on the nearby Atlantic, as beech-wood especially makes excellent oars.

Overcutting was already a concern in the 1600s, but only recently has systematic reforestation and controlled logging been implemented – thus, much of what you see is actually second-growth forest, but none the less appealing for that.

From the north, the forest can be reached conveniently from the **Col d'Organbidexka** (1284m), 10km west of Larraiñe along a minor but paved road. During September and October the *col* is the site of amazing bird migrations, well attended by bird-watchers who stand by tripod-mounted telescopes. During this period, millions of wood-pigeons, thousands of honey buzzards, kites and cranes, and hundreds of white storks pass over the Pyrenees, the majority through the Organbidexka pass. After years of controversy and altercations between hunters and conservationists, shooting is no longer allowed from this particular pass.

Access and practicalities

Without transport, the easiest way of reaching the *cols* of Organbidexka and Bagargiak (see below) is along the **old GR10** from Larraiñe, now unmarked, taking three and a half hours, mostly shortcutting the road. The **new routing** from Logibarrea is more attractive but longer, at nearly six hours, a ridge-walk which curls northwest, just above the one-thousand-metre contour, then climbs to 1472m before dropping slightly to the Col de Bagargiak.

Just under 1km west of 1327-metre **Col de Bagargiak** (aka Col d'Irati, Col de Bagargui; snowploughed in winter), itself 500m northwest of the bird-watching grounds, there's a collection of eleven wooden chalets (25 places; doubles, quads, singles) intended primarily for summer walkers or winter users of the 44km of **cross-country skiing/snowshoeing** pistes. The **information office** (Ⓣ05.59.28.51.29; Ⓔinfo@chalets-pays-basque.com) at the *col* handles bookings, while across the car park there's a small shop and a popular, inexpensive view-restaurant (open most of year) which serves forest mushrooms when in season. Some 2km west along the D19, through some of the densest forest, you pass a **campsite** well hidden in the trees near a pond, before emerging temporarily into the open at the **Plateau d'Iraty**, aka the **Plateau des Lacs**. Here there's a small dammed lake, a pair of snack bars and a "free" camping meadow crammed with caravans in season. It's better to continue 1km south on the D18 to the more elegant *Chalet Pedro* (Ⓣ05.59.28.55.98, Ⓦwww.iraty.chaletpedro.com; 5 apartments by weekend or week only, plus eight-bunk, summer-only *gîte*; restaurant open most of year), a local streamside institution offering such delicacies as wild trout, roast pigeon, *cèpe* omelette and eel.

Walking in the forest

There's enough walking here to occupy a few days, in particular the **day hikes** which the information booth at Bagargiak recommends up Pic d'Orhy (5hr return) or the semi-loop ascending Pic des Escaliers to the north (2hr return), both using well-marked sections of the GR10 or HRP.

One way quickly to sample all the region's landscapes is a north-to-south **traverse** of the forest via Casas de Irati on the **GR11**, finishing in Otsagi at the head of the Spanish Valle de Salazar (see p.472). With an early start, and plenty of stamina, you can make it in one long summer's day.

From Col Bagargiak follow the GR10 west, shortcutting the D18, as far as the Plateau d'Iraty. Bear south here onto the D18 and keep going for about twenty minutes – ignoring a right turn to Ezterentzubi – to *Chalet Pedro*. With time to spare, the summit of **Occabé/Okabe** (1456m) is an easy ascent due west along the wide, briefly conjoined GR10/HRP (75min from the plateau). The bare, flat top sports various Iron Age cromlechs, possibly linked with contemporary graves discovered adjacent, and gives views all over the forest and the Sierra de Abodi to the south.

Back at *Chalet Pedro*, the paved road continues south for 2.5km and then becomes track along the Iratiko Erreka (which later becomes the Spanish Río Irati), crossing the frontier after 1km. An hour after that, you reach the tiny white-painted **Ermita de Nuestra Señora de las Nieves** (*romería* on the Sunday before Aug 15) and the nearby derelict huts of **Casas de Irati** (880m). The only "facilities" here are a spring and a seasonal information booth.

From Casas de Irati, Otsagi lies more or less due south. The GR11 climbs steeply over the **Sierra de Abodi** via Harrizabla summit (1496m), with fantastic views over the forest and peaks, then drops more gradually to the village – a minimum four-hour march. Waymarking for the first hour is ambiguous – as on much of the GR11 west of Izaba – so you will certainly lose some time in getting lost. Casas de Irati is also served by a 23-kilometre paved road from Otsagi, and since the *ermita* is a favourite picnic area there's a slight chance of a lift in peak season.

The Navarran valleys

From the lowland Navarran capital Pamplona (outside the scope of this book) roads radiate in all directions; towards the Pyrenees, they follow various river valleys, all served by public transport to varying degrees. Attractive **Otsagi (Otsagabia)** dominates the head of the **Valle de Salazar** in Spain, just below the Selva de Irati; highlights of the lower reaches are the **Foz de Arbaiun** natural reserve and – just south under a ridge overlooking the Río Aragón – the imposing **Monasterio de San Salvador de Leyre**. The traditional pilgrims' route via Auritz and Roncesvalles is described in the next section, while the quiet Arga valley sees few visitors. The main road due north from Pamplona crosses the Cantabrian watershed at the Puerto de Belate (Velate), beyond which all rivers flow into the Atlantic rather than the Mediterranean. A subsequent major junction gives access to the **Valle de Bidasoa**; the latter is busy, being the traditional corridor to the Basque coast in the days before the direct Pamplona–San Sebastián motorway was built.

The Valle de Salazar

The **Valle de Salazar** (Zaraitzu) isn't particularly spectacular, but it does possess a gentle beauty not entirely compromised by the broad NA178 trunk road. The main attractions are at either end: handsome **Otsagi** village near the top, the **Foz de Arbaiun** and the **Monasterio de San Salvador de Leyre** at the bottom. Of particular interest for anyone emerging from the Selva de Irati is the valley's workday bus service, the quickest way south towards Pamplona.

Otsagi

With its white plastered walls, stone-framed windows, wrought-iron balconies and pebble-mosaic courtyards for the grander houses, **OTSAGI** (Ochagavía,

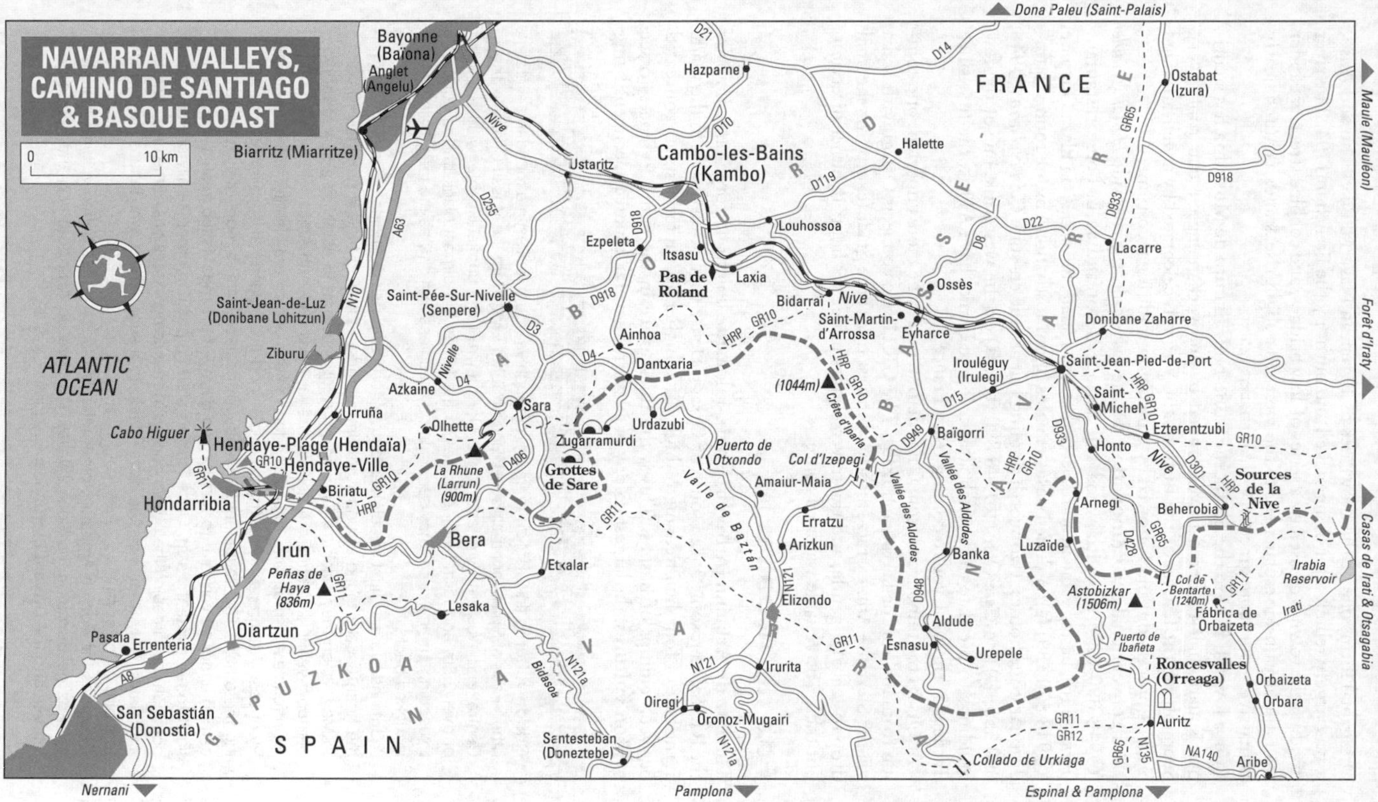

NAVARRAN VALLEYS, CAMINO DE SANTIAGO & BASQUE COAST

0 10 km

Dona Paleu (Saint-Palais)
Maule (Mauléon)
Forêt d'Iraty
Casas de Irati & Otsagabia
Nernani
Pamplona
Espinal & Pamplona

FRANCE
SPAIN
ATLANTIC OCEAN
PAYS BASQUE
NAVARRA
GIPUZKOA
BASSE NAVARRE

Bayonne (Baïona)
Anglet (Angelu)
Biarritz (Miarritze)
Hazparne
Halette
Ostabat (Izura)
Ustaritz
Cambo-les-Bains (Kambo)
Louhossoa
Lacarre
Ezpeleta
Itsasu
Pas de Roland
Laxia
Ossès
Saint-Pée-Sur-Nivelle (Senpere)
Bidarrai
Saint-Martin-d'Arrossa
Eyharce
Donibane Zaharre
Saint-Jean-de-Luz (Donibane Lohitzun)
Ziburu
Ainhoa
Dantxaria
Irouléguy (Irulegi)
Saint-Jean-Pied-de-Port
Saint-Michel
Ezterentzubi
Azkaine
Sara
Urdazubi
Zugarramurdi
Grottes de Sare
Urruña
Olhette
Cabo Higuer
Hendaye-Plage (Hendaïa)
Hendaye-Ville
Biriatu
Hondarribia
La Rhune (Larrun) (900m)
(1044m)
Crête d'Iparla
Puerto de Otxondo
Col d'Izepegi
Baïgorri
Honto
Sources de la Nive
Beherobia
Arnegi
Amaiur-Maia
Valle de Baztán
Vallée des Aldudes
Erratzu
Arizkun
Luzaïde
Banka
Irún
Bera
Etxalar
Peñas de Haya (836m)
Lesaka
Elizondo
Aldude
Astobizkar (1506m)
Col de Bentarte (1240m)
Irabia Reservoir
Irati
Fábrica de Orbaizeta
Oiartzun
Pasaia
Errenteria
Esnasu
Urepele
Puerto de Ibañeta
Roncesvalles (Orreaga)
Orbaizeta
Orbara
Irurita
Bidasoa
San Sebastián (Donostia)
Oiregi
Oronoz-Mugairi
Santesteban (Doneztebe)
Auritz
Collado de Urkiaga
Aribe

Nive
Nivelle
D21 D14 D10 D119 D918 D933 D22 D8 D255 D3 D4 D15 D949 D406 D301 D428 D948 A63 N10 A8 N121 N121a N135 NA140
GR10 GR11 GR12 GR65 HRP

Otsagabia) forms one of the showcases of Pyrenean Navarra. Like Echo and Ansó, it was largely rebuilt after being sacked and burnt by the French in 1794. The river dividing the town is crossed by a series of low bridges, and cobbled streets meander from the streamside esplanades; to the west, on a slight rise, stands a church nearly as massive – but more graceful – than that at Izaba.

On a low hill 5km to the north, the stone-built **Ermita de Muskilda** has a curious, square, half-timbered tower topped by an overhanging circular roof; every September 8 the festival of the Birth of the Virgin is celebrated by a well-attended *romería* (procession) and followed by dancing in traditional costume.

For conventional **accommodation** on the east bank, try riverside *Hostal Urialde* (Ⓣ948 890 027; ❸), with wood and antique decor and an in-house restaurant (*menú* €16), better value in all respects than the *Hostal Auñamendi* on Plaza Gúrpide (Ⓣ948 890 189; ❺). A dozen **casas rurales** offer mostly non-ensuite rooms in traditional stone houses; two worth singling out are the en-suite *Casa Ñabarro* (Ⓣ948 890 355; ❷) and *Casa Osaba* (Ⓣ948 890 011; ❷) on the west bank, one of the few buildings to pre-date the French attack. Three **banks** have ATMs, the first since Tardets-Sorholus if you're coming from France.

At Otsagi the minor road from Casas de Irati meets the more important one coming from the Port de Larrau and Izaba. The **GR11** also connects Otsagi with Izaba via the Sierra de Atuzkarratz, mostly on forest track; the grade (except for the final drop to Izaba) is gentle, and the traverse takes under six hours in either direction, but there's no reliable water en route.

Foz de Arbaiun

The **Foz de Arbaiun** (Arbayún) is a six-kilometre limestone gorge carved out by the Río Salazar, some 35km south of Otsagi. Dense vegetation thrives in the shade at the base of four-hundred-metre-high cliffs; higher up, raptor nests are concealed between clumps of bushes. This is the finest place in the entire Pyrenees to see **griffon vultures**, the largest colony of Navarra's several hundred specimens being

Griffon vultures

Griffon vultures (in Castilian *buitres*, in French *vautours fauves*) are found in several other areas of Spain, but their sole French habitat away from the Massif Central is the Central and Western Pyrenees. In the sky they're fairly unmistakeable, with a span of over 2.5m and fawn leading edges to the wings but almost black trailing edges. Exceeding 1m in length, they seem almost headless in flight, as the long, pale neck is tucked back.

Griffons live and hunt in colonies of four to twelve pairs, ranging up to 60km from the nest, usually found at under 1100m altitude. Hatching time is generally March to May; when they reach maturity young birds move on to establish a new territory, perhaps within kilometres but possibly as far away as North Africa.

Griffons eat carrion only, especially dead sheep, which are plentiful in the Western Pyrenees. When one of the troupe spots food it descends in spirals, thus attracting the others. The troupe seldom lands immediately but is more likely to keep the carrion under surveillance for one or two days – if the meat is too fresh it will be difficult to penetrate the skin. Once feeding starts a pecking order literally prevails, the dominant bird keeping the others back with menacing extensions of the neck, wings and claws. Only when satisfied does it yield to a subordinate, who in turn gives way to a bird of lower rank.

Besides the Foz de Arabaiun, other reliable places to see griffon vultures include the **Foz de Burgui** in the Roncal valley, **Cumbre de Arangoiti** near the Puerto de Ibañeta and the **Crête d'Iparla** near Baïgorri.

protected here by a *reserva natural* of 1200 hectares. You can see the gorge from the viewing platform just to the north of the hamlet of Iso; for the intrepid, very steep trails snake down to the river bed.

The Monasterio de San Salvador de Leyre

From the Foz de Arbaiun, it's 17km to the N240 highway at Venta de Lumbier, where you turn east and proceed another 13km to dull Yesa village and the paved, four-kilometre side road up to the **Monasterio de San Salvador de Leyre** (Leire). Do not be deceived by an apparent short-cut beginning just east of the *foz* from Bigüézal hamlet – this proceeds 4km up, on a single lane, to a radio mast at 1353m in the Sierra de Leyre, and expires at the edge of a precipitous drop.

The monastery contrasts vividly with the hermitages back in the mountains, its massive size underlining its former position as both a political and pilgrimage focus of Navarra – it is still mobbed by locals on Sundays and major holidays. After languishing in ruins for over a century, it was restored and reoccupied by Benedictine monks in 1954 and now basks in an immaculate condition. Although the resolutely institutional monastic buildings are sixteenth to eighteenth century, the **church** is largely Romanesque with thirteenth-century Gothic additions, its tall, severe apses and asymmetrical belfry being particularly impressive. The **west portal**, the Puerta Speciosa, is carved with images of Christ, the Virgin, St Peter, St John and assorted monsters; the **crypt**, with its sturdy little waist-high columns, no two alike, is only visible on a guided tour (Mon–Fri 10.15am–2pm & 3.30–7pm, Sat, Sun & hols 10.15am–2pm & 4–7pm; Spanish-only narration, minimum 15 people, every 45min, €2). Otherwise, you can access the church alone by coinciding with Mass (7 daily 6am–9pm all year). This is well worth doing, since the twenty to thirty white-habited, purple-suppliced monks employ (except for matins) **Gregorian chant** – often in Latin.

The former hospice now operates as a two-star **hotel**, the *Hospedería de Leyre* (Ⓣ948 884 100, Ⓦwww.monasteriodeleyre.com; ④), which, however, actively caters to solo pilgrims of either gender with very advantageous single rates. Even if you don't stay, the restaurant deserves patronizing for the sake of its carefully prepared if limited-choice three-course *menús* (€16; allow €28–36 for *a la carta*). Though this is nominally still an important halt on the Aragonese variant of the Camino de Santiago, today codified as the GR65.3, budget-conscious pilgrims are warned by a large sign at the base of the access road that the closest pilgrims' hostel per se is in Sangüesa, over 20km southwest.

An interesting local excursion is to the free **hot springs** in the Yesa reservoir, which are usually uncovered by falling water levels before the winter rains. Just before Tiermas village, about 7km east of Yesa, a dirt track heads down from the south side of the N240 towards the exposed hot pools at the base of the dam.

The Valle de Baztán

Due north of Pamplona, the heavily travelled N121a climbs over the watershed **Puerto de Belate** (Velate) before descending to **ORONOZ-MUGAIRI**, home to the **Parque Señorio de Bértiz** (daily 10am–2pm & 4–6/7/8pm; €1.50), a former private estate now combining the functions of botanical garden and managed recreational forest. At Oieregi, you fork right onto the N121 for the **Valle de Baztán** (meaning "Rat's Tail" in Euskera) with its succession of villages, beautiful countryside and cave formations.

Elizondo

The "capital" of this most strongly Basque of Navarran valleys is **ELIZONDO**, seat of a municipality composed of fifteen villages. What's visible from the through road leaves a poor impression, but once away from it the town is full of typical Basque Pyrenean architecture, especially along the river with its bridge and weir.

Elizondo's several places to **stay** make it a good base for the valley. A good budget option is the central, en-suite *Pensión Eskisaroi*, c/Jaime Urrutia 40 (Ⓣ948 580 013; ❷), above a recommended restaurant (see below); *Casa Rural Jaén* (Ⓣ948 580 487; €29), with two attic rooms, makes a good second choice. There are also two considerably more expensive places: the three-star *Hotel Baztán* (Ⓣ948 580 050, Ⓦwww.hotelbaztan.com; ❺), on the Pamplona road south of town, an incongruously modern pile complete with garden and huge pool, and in town near the river, a nineteenth-century mansion at c/Braulio Iriarte 16 restored as the *Hostal Trinquete Antxitonea* (Ⓣ948 581 807, Ⓦwww.antxitonea.com; ❹), with a choice of sky-lit attic or balconied rooms, and a small on-site *comedor*.

Among a handful of **restaurants**, the *Txokoto* at c/Braulio Iriarte 25 (west end of the river bridge; closed Wed), run by the same family for three generations, has a cosy, water-view *comedor* and a good line in eminently reasonable seafood and meat. The nearby *Eskisaroi* (address as above) can feed you with creative bean dishes, fish fillets, pear tart and assorted drinks (*a la carta* €21, *menú* €10; closed Thurs winter); it's justly popular, with long waits for tables. Finally, the *Galarza*, at the very northern town limits by the Río Baztan, is strong on seafood (€22 for three courses).

Buses arrive daily from both Pamplona and San Sebastián, but there is no public transport to the smaller villages beyond. Elizondo also lies astride the **GR11**, which heads west out of Auritz (see p.479), then turns north along the border (about 10hr). It's worth getting a dawn start from Auritz and trying to polish off this stretch in a day, as there are no facilities in between. If you have to break the journey, **Puerto de Urkiaga** (912m), about halfway, offers water and the possibility of camping.

Arizkun, Erratzu and Amaiur-Maia

In nearby **ARIZKUN**, beside the minor road to the Izepegi pass on the French border (and beyond to Baïgorri), the seventeenth-century convent of Nuestra Señora de los Angeles flaunts its striking Baroque facade; just beyond the village, there's a typical example of a fortified house (very common hereabouts) where Pedro de Ursua, the leader of an expedition up the Amazon in 1560 in search of El Dorado, was born. You can **stay** in Arizkun at the friendly and well-run (if non-en-suite) *Pensión Etxeberría*, near the western edge of town and the *frontón* at c/Txuputo 43 (Ⓣ948 453 013; ❶), which also functions as a bar, grocery and reasonable, if basic, restaurant. For more comfort try *Casa Gontxea* (Ⓣ948 453 433, Ⓔgontxea@terra.es; ❷).

Some 4km northeast and the last Spanish village before France on this road, **ERRATZU** is another gem, with a few characterful **casas rurales**. *Casa Etxebeltzea* (Ⓣ948 453 157, Ⓦwww.etxebeltzea.com; ❸) is a converted fourteenth-century seigneurial manor at the southern edge of the medieval core. The more isolated *Casa Juanillo* (Ⓣ948 453 356, Ⓦwww.casajuanillo.com; ❷) is a well-converted farmhouse, which also offers evening meals.

AMAIUR-MAIA, 6km north of Arizkun but just off the N121, where the last unsuccessful battle to preserve the independence of Navarra took place, is another unspoilt village worth a stop. The gateway to its single street displays the village shield depicting a red bell – most houses still proudly emblazon their door lintels with this coat-of-arms. **Casas rurales** here include en-suite *Casa Goiz-Argi* (ⓣ948 453 234, ⓦwww.goizargile.com; ❷) and non-en-sute *Casa Miguelenea* (ⓣ948 453 224; ❷).

Urdazubi and Zugarramurdi

Northwest of Amaiur-Maia, the N121 climbs over the **Puerto de Otxondo** at the top of the Valle de Baztán to the villages of Urdazubi and – reached by side road – Zugarramurdi, both potential stopovers between Pamplona and the French Basque coastal towns of Biarritz and Bayonne.

URDAZUBI (Urdax), ringed by hills and guarded by a tiny castle, has three *hostales* and *pensiones*, the most upmarket and central being *Hostal Irigoiena* (ⓣ948 599 267, ⓦwww.irigoienea.com; ❹), in a renovated eighteenth-century farmhouse. If your budget won't stretch to that, try the more modest but en-suite *Pensión Beotxea* on the Zugarramurdi road (ⓣ948 599 114; ❷), or the only *casa rural* here not let by the week, *Dutaria* (ⓣ948 599 237; ❸). For **eating**, the *Koska* at c/San Salvador 3 has reasonable *menús* (closed Sun eve & Mon).

ZUGARRAMURDI, 4km southwest of the border, off the N121, is famous for its **Cueva de las Brujas** (daily: summer 9am–9pm; winter 9am–7.30pm; €3), whose highlight is the giant natural arch through which the *regata de infierno* (Hell's stream) flows. The cavern was supposedly a major centre for medieval witchcraft and consequently the area bore the brunt of an Inquisition campaign in 1609–11. Underneath the arch, *akelarres*, or witches' sabbaths, allegedly took place during the immediately preceding years; these seem to have survived, as a tame derivative, in the *zikiroyate* rite every August 18, which features a "love-feast" of roast meat held in the grotto. The appealing village makes a good base for excursions into surrounding countryside; one possibility is to walk 3km along the track beyond the caves into France to another set of caves, the **Grottes de Sare** (see p.505). The actual frontier divides the village of Dantxarinea/Dantxaria (the latter just inside France) – a fairly shabby place offering little other than cheap Spanish tobacco and petrol, best seen from your rear-view mirror.

Zugarramurdi has two **casas rurales** letting rooms short-term, heavily subscribed at weekends: en-suite *Casa Sueldeguía* (ⓣ948 599 088; ❷) and *Casa Teltxeguia* (ⓣ948 599 167; ❶), both in the village centre.

The Valle de Bidasoa

If at Oieregi you instead bear left to stay with the N121a, you exit Navarra along the scenic **Valle de Bidasoa** towards Irún, Hendaye and Hondarribia. There's a direct bus service between Pamplona and San Sebastián, as well as a considerable amount of other traffic, especially long-distance lorries – so a restful country road it isn't. But en route are a series of villages worth a stop or even an overnight.

Etxalar

ETXALAR is a small, bucolic place, 4km off the main road on the way up to a minor border crossing at the Lizarrieta pass. It's perhaps the best-preserved village of the valley, famous for the impressive array of Basque funerary stelae in the churchyard. There's a central, en-suite **pensión**, *La Basque* (ⓣ948 635 153; ❷), with a *comedor*. Among numerous **casas rurales** here are two good ones doing en-suite rooms for a short **stay**: the central *Casa Tonpalenea* (Ⓣ948 635 166; ❷), and another, *Casa Herri-Gain* (Ⓣ948 635 208, Ⓦwww.herri-gain.com; ❷), perched on a steep hill, with fantastic views of the surrounding area. There are also a couple of restaurants and bars near the giant church.

Lesaka

Slightly down-valley but up a short side road on the opposite side lies **LESAKA**. Despite the large, eyesore factory and lumber depots on the outskirts of town, it's an attractive place dominated by the hilltop parish church in which the pews bear family names tied to local farms. On the banks of the irrigation channel that flows through town is one of the best remaining examples of a *casa torre* (fortified private house) of a design peculiar to the Basque country, dating back to the days when northwestern Navarra was in the hands of a few powerful and constantly feuding families.

Places to **stay** include the helpful *Hostal Ekaitza* at central Plaza Berria 13 (Ⓣ948 627 547, Ⓦwww.ekaitzalesaka.com; ❸), in a converted ancestral home flanking the central car park. The most noteworthy local **casa rural** is *Agiña*, 9km west on the road to Oiartzun (Ⓣ948 387 057; ❸), a spectacularly set hillside inn with non-smoking rooms and evening meals provided. **Restaurant** options in Lesaka proper, other than the *Ekaitza*'s snack bar, are few.

Bera

The last substantial place before the Navarra/Gipuzkoa border, **BERA** (Vera de Bidasoa) offers some of the finest examples of old wood-beamed and traditional stone houses in the region; the brightly painted buildings on Altzarte Kalea and the main plaza are particularly attractive. The **Turismo** (Easter and summer 10am–2pm & 4–7pm; Ⓣ948 631 222) is on the Lizuniaga road, a short walk from the centre, while at the eastern end of the village, Itzea Kalea 24, just past the old customs house, is the former home of the Basque writer Pío Baroja, which should reopen as a museum by 2008. From Bera, border-straddling Larrun (see p.504) is an easy climb.

Options for **staying** include comfortable *Hostal Euskalduna* at the noisy central junction (Ⓣ948 630 392; closed Oct 15–31; ❸), with parking and ground-floor restaurant; three-star *Hotel Churrut*, Foruen Plaza 2 (Ⓣ948 625 540, Ⓦwww.hotelchurrut.com; ❻), occupying a renovated eighteenth-century mansion with antiques; and a large *casa rural*, *Casa Alkeberea* (Ⓣ948 630 540, Ⓦwww.alkeberea.com; ❷), 2km out on the Col de Lizuniaga road, with secure parking and ample common areas.

Walking: the end of the GR11

Heading northwest from Elizondo, the **GR11** finishes its course passing through or very near many of the places above. The tough, penultimate day of a trans-Pyrenean traverse from **Elizondo to Bera** crosses deserted country to skim the frontier between Etxalar and Sara; count on seven hours to reach Bera. The final half-day is more perfunctory, skirting rather than climbing the **Peñas de Haya**, and then unrelentingly urban in character once you enter Irún and Hondarribia. Only at the end is there a bit of drama, as you emerge beyond the beach of Hondarribia onto **Cabo Higuer**, the promontory marking the terminus of both the seven-hundred-kilometre GR route from the Costa Brava, and the Spanish Pyrenees.

Along the Camino de Santiago

Despite the attractions of the other Navarran valleys, the most popular itinerary entails moving northeast along the principal branch of the **Camino de Santiago** into France, via the fabled **Puerto de Ibañeta**. It's a route easily covered by vehicle, mountain bike or – for purists or pilgrims – on foot along the **GR65** long-distance trail.

Auritz, a village on a wide plain at the foot of the frontier peaks, is an obvious and comfortable staging-point. A short distance north, the abbey of **Roncesvalles** has long been a hallowed stop on the pilgrim route to Santiago de Compostela, and occupies a central location in the legend of **Roland**. The famous ambush of Charlemagne's rearguard, supposedly under Roland's command, took place close by – possibly after the Franks emerged from the thick, gloomy beech forest onto the barren expanse of the Puerto de Ibañeta.

This pass notches the main Pyrenean watershed, but an anomalous finger of Spanish territory encompassing **Luzaïde** protrudes north and down halfway to **Saint-Jean-Pied-de-Port**, touristic mecca of the French Pays Basque since its days as a pilgrimage way-station. The main Chemin de Saint-Jacques arrives here from various points northeast; a minor branch of the *chemin* – now paralleled by the modern road and rail line – heads northwest along the River Nive to the attractive cathedral city of Bayonne. This minor branch transects the two westerly historic divisions of the French Basque country, **Basse-Navarre** and **Labourd**.

Auritz

AURITZ (Burguete) is a typically pleasant, one-street Basque Pyrenean settlement, surrounded by fields, cattle barns and wooded ridges on the horizon. It seems not much bigger than in Ernest Hemingway's time – he (and his fictional characters Jake and Bill) used to come trout-fishing nearby, before or after Pamplona's San Fermín festival.

The GR65 and GR11 both pass through here on the same right-of-way just outside Burguete to the west, a fact somewhat confused by lingering, faded waymarks for the old GR11 to the east. The new GR11 traces a very circuitous route north, then east towards Otsagi for two walking days, with little in the way of facilities in between except for the *Albergue Mendilatz* (Ⓣ948 766 088, Ⓦwww.mendilatz.com) near **Fábrica de Orbaizeta**. For short day-strolls along streams and through the woods, with Auritz as a base, the rolling countryside immediately east of the village is still your best bet.

Practicalities

The best value among conventional **accommodation** is *Hostal Burguete* at the north end of the main street (Ⓣ948 760 005; Easter–Dec; ❸), the oldest (1912) establishment here: three echoing storeys of huge, spotless, squeaky-wood-floored, en-suite rooms, with literary cachet to boot. Hemingway stayed here during the early 1920s and immortalized it in his first novel *Fiesta*; the room he occupied, now #25, is still preserved much as he described it, save for discreetly placed photos of the great man (including one with his second wife, Martha Gellhorn). At the south end of the "high street" stands three-star *Hotel Loizu* (ⓣ948 760 008, ⓔloizu@telefonica.net; closed mid-Dec to mid-March; ❺), whose double-glazed rooms had a makeover in 2005. Failing these, try one of the *casas rurales*: en-suite *Casa Pedroarena* (ⓣ948 760 164; ❷), *Casa Loperena* (ⓣ948 760 068; ❶), two rustic rooms sharing a bath above the **bank** (next-to-last one before the frontier), or en-suite *Casa Vergara* ⓣ948 760 044; ❷). A **campsite**, *Urrobi* (ⓣ948 760 200; April–Oct), lies 3km south of the village at Auritzberri (Espinal). When it comes to **eating** out, the *Loizu* has the best restaurant in town, with *menús* for about €16 (though game and regional specialities cost just €23 *a la carta*); otherwise the *Txikipolit* (*menú* €17, *a la carta* €23) probably just pips the *Burguete*'s *comedor* (*menú* €14, *carta* €21) diagonally across the way.

East of Auritz

The afternoon bus from Pamplona first calls at Roncesvalles and then continues 10km east on the NA140 past attractive Garralda to **ARIBE** (Arive), an equally appealing little village on the banks of the Río Irati, with a lovely stone bridge and attic **rooms** at *Casa Txikirrin* (ⓣ948 764 074; ❷). The bus carries on eastwards from Aribe, terminating 18km later at **EAURTA** (Jaurrieta), another attractive village with a good deal of half-timbering, several non-en-suite *casas rurales* and two quality **inn-restaurants** in the centre, the wood-and-stone *Eseverry* (ⓣ98 890 348; ❹) and the *Sario* (ⓣ948 890 187; ❹). With a car or bike, you're just 6km shy of the Valle de Salazar at Ezkaroze (Escaroz), 2km below Otsagi, but road-walking is not suggested – the grade is stiff and the right of way narrow.

Roncesvalles

Contemporary **RONCESVALLES** (Orreaga in Euskera, Roncevaux in French), a hamlet 2.5km north of Burguete on the N135, doesn't quite match the expectations prompted by its semi-legendary history. As you approach from Auritz the impact of its **Colegiata**, an Augustinian abbey founded by Sancho VII el Fuerte (the Strong) of Navarra in 1219, is considerably diminished by the ramshackle associated buildings, topped with sheets of oxidized zinc roofing and overawed by swivelling tower cranes engaged in lengthy renovations.

Sancho was one of the heroes of the battle of Las Navas de Tolosa (1212), a decisive defeat for the Almohadan Moors symbolized by the broken chain – which had guarded the Muslim chieftain's tent – in the Navarran coat-of-arms. Sancho's **tomb** lies in the Sala Capitular of the cloister, topped by a massive 2.25-metre-long effigy of the man, said to be life-size; nearby, safe behind an iron grille, a purported bit of the chain is displayed.

The best of the architecture is the echoing **church** (free), with a thirteenth-century crypt (€1 fee) and a Gothic **cloister**, rebuilt after a fire in 1400. The cloister is visited on the same ticket for a separate, small **museum** (April–Oct daily 10am–1.30pm & 3.30–7pm; Nov–March limited pm hours; €2.30) at the southwest corner of the monastery building, which contains the expected ecclesiastical reliquaries, processional crucifixes, mitres, croziers and chalices, as well as an exquisite eighteenth-century gold cigarette box from Paris, embossed with a swan confronting a fox – possibly a pilgrim's donation. For another €1.60 you can visit the ancient churches of Santiago and Sanctus Spiritus.

The legend of Roland

In 778 the Frankish emperor Charlemagne besieged and demolished the fortifications of Pamplona on his way out of Spain, which he had invaded – the only time he ever crossed the Pyrenees – to assist one faction during an outbreak of inter-Moorish strife. He was continuing homeward, laden with booty from various other raids in the Ebro valley, when on August 15 the rear of his army was ambushed somewhere in the area of the Puerto de Ibañeta by Basques determined to avenge the attack on Pamplona.

The episode hasn't much historical significance, but it achieved international prominence through the myth of Roland, supposedly the greatest of Charlemagne's paladins, who is said to have commanded the rearguard and been killed in the battle. The precise source of the Roland tale is unknowable, but it belongs to the genre of knightly ballads popular at the time of the battle. By the ninth century, *cantilènes* (chanted stories) were being told throughout the Ariège and Andorra about this valiant companion of Charlemagne, and the tale even found its way to Germany and Italy. But it was during the twelfth century that the legend really took off, with the appearance of a mysterious epic called **La Chanson de Roland** (The Song of Roland).

In 1130 the archbishop of Pamplona, Sancho de Rosa, relived the ambush in a dream that placed it at the Puerto de Ibañeta. The vision was well publicized, and it was elaborated in 1170 by an anonymous clerk as the *Chanson de Roland*, the ultimate medieval epic. The Catholic Church eagerly exploited the story, not just as a propaganda device against the infidel – ignoring the minor detail that Roland's final, Basque adversaries were also Christians – but also to promote the sales of souvenirs and relics along the *camino*. Although the factual accuracy of the poem is open to question, its evocation of chivalric valour adds poignancy to a visit to Roncesvalles; the Penguin edition fits easily into a backpack.

Roland's purported martyrdom notwithstanding (see box above), the abbey was primarily a way-station on the Camino de Santiago; its founding – centuries after the battle – was motivated by the need for a strategically placed pilgrims' hospice a day's journey south of Saint-Jean-Pied-de-Port. Had it really been intended as a memorial to Roland, the *colegiata* would have been sited (rather impractically) up on the Puerto de Ibañeta. The tale of the attack merely provided a general endorsement for exemplary defenders of Christianity.

In the years immediately following its establishment, the abbey enjoyed a meteoric success, ranking among the wealthiest and most powerful of the thirteenth century; a pilgrim of the era could supposedly travel from London to Roncesvalles entirely on lands belonging to the *colegiata*. Today the place is more commonly the destination of numerous summer *romerías*, from both the French and Spanish valleys, by virtue of its thirteenth-century image of the **Virgen de Orreaga**, honoured with special fervour on September 8.

Practicalities

Accommodation is fairly abundant, considering there's no real village here. Non-pilgrims should head for the small *Hostal Casa Sabina*, right next to the monastery (ⓣ948 760 012; ❸), or larger *La Posada* (ⓣ948 760 225; ❸), run by the monastery, offering Internet access; both serve **meals**. Bona fide **pilgrims** following the Camino de Santiago can use the spartan **pilgrims' hostel** at the monastery (token donation requested). All this seems a mere echo of the medieval hospice here, which for seven centuries listed its services for the (predominantly male) pilgrims as follows: a bath, haircut, shave and mending of shoes or clothes, performed – as various manuscripts attested – "by women solicitous and far from ugly".

The Transpyrenean Camino de Santiago

A better way to get a sense of the Roland legend is to take the half-hour hike up through the beech woods from the back of the abbey to the **Puerto de Ibañeta** (1057m). According to many scholars, you'll be treading through the site where Roland's defeat occurred. On a misty day – and these are frequent – the pass proves suitably melancholy. An ugly modern chapel stands on the saddle, on the site of the ancient chapel of San Salvador, whose bell used to guide pilgrims in foggy weather. There are also a couple of small medieval stone monuments to Roland and the vestiges of another built by a doctor from Pamplona in 1934.

Thirty-two years after Charlemagne followed approximately this route, his son, Louis le Débonnaire, avoided another Basque ambush by forcing local civilian hostages to accompany his troops through the pass. It was also the site of King of Basse-Navarre Jean d'Albret's crushing defeat at the hands of the Spanish in 1517; Napoleon's troops retreated this way after the Peninsular War; and the defeated Republicans fled in their thousands through here as the Spanish Civil War drew to a close.

The **Camino de Santiago**, marked officially the GR65 with characteristic star-ray yellow-on-blue signs, no longer goes via the Puerto de Ibañeta, but on an initial northeasterly bearing from Roncesvalles, avoiding most major roads. It's at least seven hours to Saint-Jean-Pied-de-Port, much of it on the paved, one-lane D428 but occasionally on medieval cobbles, through beautiful countryside.

From the *colegiata*, it's ninety minutes by path through thick beech woods to the **Collada Lepoeder** (1445m), flanked by the rounded summit of Astobizkar (1506m). You descend slightly, past the ruins of the Elizacharre chapel, to cross the border at the **Col de Bentarte/Collado de Betartea pass** (1337m) – which many insist was the more likely place for the ambush (and an extra justification, perhaps, for rerouting the *camino*). The joint GR11/HRP heads east here, parting company with the GR65, which heads north to meet the D428 for Saint-Jean after about 25 minutes, just below **Pic Urdanarré** (1240m).

From the base of Pic Urdanarré, where sheep are likely to outnumber pilgrims, Saint-Jean is about 16km or 4hr away, with the GR65 providing just a few short-cuts across woods and farmland. There are two good places to break the trek if it looks like you'll be overtaken by darkness. The first, about two hours beyond the frontier, is 2004-built *Refuge-Auberge Orisson* (Ⓣ06.81.49.79.56, Ⓔrefuge.orisson@wanadoo.fr; 18 bunks; April–Oct), offering meals as well. The next, in the tiny hamlet of **HONTO**, are excellent *chambres d'hôtes* at *Ferme Ithurburia* (Ⓣ05.59.37.11.17; year-round; ❷, also dorm), again with suppers offered. Both are popular, so reserve especially during summer.

Luzaïde and Arnegi

Alternatively, you can drive from Roncesvalles – beyond which there's no public transport – along the main road into France down the Luzaïde valley, a narrow salient of Spanish territory jutting north from the usual frontier ridge. **LUZAÏDE** (Valcarlos), 16km below the Ibañeta pass, has a number of **accommodation** options; best of three *hostales* is *Casa Marcelino* on the through road (Ⓣ948 790 186; ❸), a restored manor house, with meals offered. Best of several **casas rurales**, on the Frenchward side of the village, is *Casa Etxezuría* (Ⓣ948 790 011, Ⓦwww.etxezuria.com; ❷) with just two beautifully furnished rooms sharing a bathroom – they also have other properties let by the week. **ARNEGI** (Arnéguy), 3km on, is the first French village, with a Spanish district across the river-bridge offering the last cheap **petrol**.

Saint-Jean-Pied-de-Port

SAINT-JEAN-PIED-DE-PORT (Donibane Garazi), 8km from the border on the young River Nive, is a seasonally overrun tourist attraction, its highly photogenic old quarter enveloped in pink sandstone walls inching up to an imposing fortress. Former capital of Basse-Navarre, Saint-Jean thrived until the sixteenth century on **pilgrim traffic to Santiago de Compostela**, and all over town you'll see the tell-tale, scallop-shell emblem – 25,000 bona fide pilgrims still arrive annually. The three main pilgrim routes across France converge some 20km northeast at Ostabat, from where travellers continue to Saint-Jean, entering by the northerly **Porte de Saint-Jacques** and leaving through the **Porte d'Espagne**, heading up to the Puerto de Ibañeta – hence the suffixed Pied-de-Port, meaning "Foot-of-the-Pass".

The oldest neighbourhood lies on the right bank of the River Nive, inside the medieval fortifications, and consists essentially of a single street. This begins as the rue d'Espagne, heading north from Porte d'Espagne, and lined on both sides with souvenir shops and pastel-painted houses, some with carved lintels dating them to the sixteenth and seventeenth centuries. Crossing the **Vieux-Pont**, which offers the best photo opportunities in town – balconied houses, decked in washing and flowers, handsomely reflected in the placid waters of the Nive – you pass through the well-preserved **Porte Nôtre-Dame** to reach the fourteenth-century, largely Gothic **Notre-Dame-du-Bout-du-Pont** on the right – on the left short rue de l'Église leads through the **Porte de Navarre** and the modern town. But the main thoroughfare becomes cobbled rue de la Citadelle, climbing steeply to the Porte de Saint-Jacques. Above this looms the **Citadelle**, built in 1628 on the orders of Cardinal Richelieu, and redesigned by Vauban in 1685. It's now a college, but the lower, grassy ramparts have unrestricted access, and are worth the climb up for the sweeping views. You can also walk around part of the town's lower walls, though you see little other than people's back gardens.

Practicalities

The **tourist office** (July & Aug Mon–Sat 9am–7pm, Sun 9.30am–1pm & 2.30–5pm; Sept–June Mon–Sat 9am–noon & 2–6pm; ⓣ05.59.37.03.57, ⓦwww.terre-basque.com) is at 14 place du Général-de-Gaulle, in a tile roofed kiosk, while a handful of newsagents and bookshops sell guides and maps. The **train station** is ten minutes' walk away at the end of avenue Renaud, on the northern edge of the centre, while Cycles Garazi at 32bis ave du Jaï Alaï rents everything from bikes up to 600cc motorcycles. **Parking** in the designated lots is unrestricted except during the Monday market on place du Trinquet.

The best **accommodation** possibilities for pilgrims, cyclists and trekkers are helpful *Gîte d'Étape Etchegoin* at 9 rte d'Uhart, on the Bayonne road (ⓣ05.59.37.12.08; 12 bunks), and Dutch-volunteer-run *L'Esprit du Chemin*, 40 rue de la Citadelle (ⓣ05.59.37.24.68, ⓦwww.espritduchemin.org; April–Sept; 14 bunks; 10pm curfew), offering sound advice, meals and moral support to walkers and Santiago pilgrims. The basic *Accueil Saint-Jacques* at 55 rue de Citadelle (ⓣ05.59.37.05.09; Easter–Sept; 20 places) is for certified pilgrims only. En-suite *chambres d'hôtes* on the same street include *E. Bernat* at no. 20 (ⓣ05.59.31.23.10, ⓦwww.ebernat.com; €57), with a pricey restaurant. The municipal campsite *Plaza Berri* (ⓣ05.59.37.11.19; Easter to early November), the more convenient of two, is south of the Nive, just off avenue du Fronton.

Hotels include relatively quiet *Les Remparts*, 16 place Floquet (ⓣ05.59.37.13.79, ⓦwww.touradour.com/hotel-remparts.htm; closed Nov–Dec; ❷), just before you cross the Nive coming into town on the Bayonne road, with parking spaces nearby (a problem here). But with a car to park, you're better off staying at the friendly if restaurant-less *Camou* (ⓣ05.59.37.02.78; closed Dec–Jan; ❸) 600m west of the centre in Uhart-Cize suburb, and walking to the action. More comfortable are the Logis de France affiliate *Ramuntcho*, just inside the city walls at 1 rue de France (ⓣ05.59.37.03.91, ⓕ05.59.37.35.17; closed mid-Nov to mid-Dec, Tues & Wed low season; ❹), with a popular restaurant (*menus* €13–17.50), and the *Central* on place du Général-de-Gaulle (ⓣ05.59.37.00.22, ⓕ05.59.37.27.79; closed Dec–Feb; €73), with marginally quieter river-view rooms and free parking, plus hearty *menus* (€19–42) in its restaurant.

Other eateries tend to be slapdash bistros and "café-snacks" aimed squarely at the day-tripper trade. One exception is splurge-worthy *Chez Arrambide*, the restaurant of the luxury *Hôtel des Pyrénées* at 19 place du Général-de-Gaulle (closed Jan & mid-Nov to mid-Dec, also Tues low season); count on €40–90 (drink extra) for the works, which may include baby rabbit, duck breast in spicy fruit sauce or roast pigeon with mushroom ravioli. Inside the old town, choose between the *Hurrup Eta Klik* at 3 bis rue de la Citadelle (closed Wed) serving Basque specialities washed down by abundant cider; and popular *Paxkal Oillarburu* at 8 rue de l'Église just inside the Porte de Navarre (closed Tues low season; book August on ⓣ05.59.37.06.44), with a small-portioned €20.50 *menu*, but *garbure* or *frites* are refilled free and quality is high.

Southeast: the upper Nive valley

Heading southeast of Saint-Jean, the D301 road provides access to the upper reaches of the **Nive valley**, with its attractive villages and small red- or green-shuttered farmhouses. The GR10 stays well northeast of the river, first paved, then on track and trail along Handiamendi ridge, running roughly parallel to the D301. The road continues almost all the way to the river's source, with a short final approach on foot.

The villages

Sleepy **SAINT-MICHEL** (Eiheralarre), 3km southeast along the D301, may prompt a halt for en-suite *Hôtel Xoko-Goxoa* (ⓣ05.59.37.06.34, ⓦwww.xoko-goxoa.com; all year; ❷, ❹ HB) on the main through road, good value despite rooms with floral wallpaper and mottled carpets. Best are the rear, balconied units overlooking hayfields and a stream valley; the restaurant, equally panoramic, purveys simple but savoury and reasonable fare (*menus* €17–24).

Proceeding 5km further – or three and a half hours' walk from Saint-Jean along the meandering GR10 – brings you to tiny **EZTERENTZUBI** (Esterençuby) with its medieval galleried church and two **accommodation** choices near the *trinquet*. Hikers' hangout *Auberge Carricaburu* (ⓣ05.59.37.09.77; closed Feb, also Tues–Wed low season; ❷), some rooms with river-view, incorporates a streamside restaurant (*menus* €13–18) and the lively village bar, while larger *Hôtel Andreinia-Larramendy* over the bridge (ⓣ05.59.37.09.70, ⓦwww.hotel-andreinia.com; closed mid-Nov to mid-Dec, Wed low season; ❷), has 2005-remodelled bathrooms and a more ambitious restaurant (*menus* €10–29); they also run a twelve-bunk *gîte d'étape*.

The valley-floor **D428** road continues alongside the Nive, now no more than a mountain stream; there's little cultivation in the progressively deepening valley other than vast hay meadows, harvested in early summer, and extensive tracts of bracken fern, prized as animal bedding. Some 4km from Ezterentzubi the road reaches tiny Beherobia before climbing to the border and then looping back to

Saint-Jean-Pied-de-Port: an excellent **cycling loop**, but a low-gear drive of over an hour. It's nearly 14km from Beherobia to the border at Col de Bentarte (see p.482), 31km to Saint-Jean.

At **BEHEROBIA** (Béhérobie), in the valley bottom beside the infant Nive, one of just a few buildings is the *Hôtel des Sources de la Nive* (Ⓣ05.59.37.10.57, Ⓔsource.nive@wanadoo.fr; closed Jan and Tues low season; ❷); frogs'valley's lodgings, the hotel is invariably booked out for the October wood-pigeon shooting season, but otherwise makes a relaxing hideaway; all rooms are en suite, but ask for the quieter, eight-room annexe.

The Sources de la Nive

Just before the bridge at Beherobia, a lane veers left, signposted for the **Sources de la Nive**. With a car, you can drive to the end of the road by another bridge and a few farmhouses, then continue on foot by the dirt track heading left, not the one over the bridge (which carried the old, now-abandoned GR10 from St-Jean, its waymarks obliterated by grey paint). The track soon dwindles to trail along the fifteen-minute walk to the springs, where water percolating a thousand metres down through karstic hillside wells up as surging rapids. Lost in dense beech woods, it's a magical spot in any weather, with a faint mist often rising from the surface of the water.

East: walking the GR10 or driving

The **new GR10** has been re-routed to head from Ezterentzubi to the Forêt d'Iraty via Phagalcette hamlet and Iraukotuturru peak, meeting up with the old, now-unmaintained route at Occabé. **PHALGACETTE**, ninety minutes along, offers an excellent, farm-based *gîte d'étape, Kaskoleta* (Ⓣ05.59.37.09.73; 13 places; all year), worth a stop for lunch even if you don't stay – and overnighting here does better balance out the two stages necessary between Saint-Jean and Iraty. It's nearly six hours in total to *Chalet Pedro* (see p.471), the first two hours a rather dull, stiff climb on paved, one-lane road. But soon you're off this onto farm track and path, dodging wandering herds of healthy-looking horses and ponies, masses of sheep and big, sleek, caramel cows with bells on wooden collars. There are superb places to camp if you've started late, with views west to the revolving beacon of the Biarritz lighthouse visible in the dark.

Drivers should follow the D301 east out of the Nive valley from a junction 3km south of Ezterentzubi, signposted for the Forêt d'Iraty. This is very steep, narrow and full of tight hairpins, frequent oncoming traffic and the ambling livestock noted above; it's to be avoided at night or in misty conditions, is not kept snowploughed in winter, and requires an hour in low gear at the best of times to the junction with the D18 at the Plateau d'Iraty. But there are compensations: as you climb higher around the heads of labyrinthine gullies, ever more spectacular views open beneath you. You look back over the valley of the Nive, St-Jean and the hills beyond. Stands of beech fill the gullies, shadowing electrically green turf juxtaposed with purplish rock outcrops.

Baïgorri and the Vallée des Aldudes

Although **BAÏGORRI** (Saint-Étienne-de-Baïgorry) lies only 11km west of Saint-Jean-Pied-de-Port along the D15, it's a different world, where agriculture rather than tourism is the prime focus of life. Like most other Basque settlements, Baïgorri is divided into quite distinct quarters, more like separate hamlets than a unified village. The town's Euskera name translates as "beautiful view", and from the outlying districts clambering up pastured and vine-clad hills, you do indeed get a marvellous panorama of the gentle lower slopes of the Pyrenees. But there's little specifically to see here, other than a seventeenth-century, barrel-vaulted church with a fine organ over the southwest door besides the usual galleries and altarpiece, plus a hump-backed medieval bridge posing against a backdrop of the romantic **Château de Etxaus** (Etchauz) and distant hills.

Market centre of the **Vallée des Aldudes**, Baïgorri is a prosperous, rather sleek place. The strong local **Irouléguy (Irulegi) wines**, the only *appellation* red, white and rosé produced in the Pays Basque, are worth stocking up on; the vintner's shop 5km east on the D15 road offers *dégustation* and sales. Other local specialities, sold in the village, include ham, sheeps' cheese and preserved mushrooms.

Practicalities

The **tourist office** is opposite the church (May–Sept Mon–Sat 9am–noon & 2–6pm, Sun 10am–1pm; Oct–April Mon–Sat 9am–noon & 2–6pm; ⓣ05.59.37.47.28). For budget **accommodation**, there's only the *Camping Municipal Irouléguy* (ⓣ05.59.37.43.96; April to mid-Dec), opposite the swimming pool on the St-Jean road, plus *Hôtel Restaurant Juantorena* on the through road in Bourg quarter (ⓣ05.59.37.40.78, ⓔrestaurant.juantorena@wanadoo.fr; ❷), with a pleasant terrace and parking at the back. For more comfort at similar prices, head for tranquil, stream-side *Hôtel Maechenea*, 5km north in the hamlet of **Urdos (Urdoze)** (ⓣ05.59.37.41.68, ⓔhotel-manechenea@wanadoo.fr; closed Nov–Feb; ❸), with a decent restaurant (*menu* from €16). Back in central Baïgorri, just over the bridge by the church, *Hôtel Arcé* (ⓣ05.59.37.40.14, ⓦwww.hotel-arce.com; closed Nov–March; ❼) lives up to its three stars with a pool, tennis courts and enormous, wood-floored, antique-furnished rooms attached to modern, well-equipped baths (best are the river-view balcony units); the more reasonable restaurant purveys *menus* at €25–38. The only independent **eatery** in town is friendly *Bar Chez Oronos*, in Bourg district.

The upper Vallée des Aldudes

The villages of the upper **Vallée des Aldudes** are quiet rural spots, beyond the reach of public transport, major hiking routes and most tourism. Although it lies on a fairly major corridor to Pamplona, accommodation and restaurants here are simple and reasonably priced, if limited in number.

The first village, about 8km south of Baïgorri, is **BANKA** (Banca), shoehorned into the steep narrows carved out by the river here. It used to live from mining lead and copper – you can see the ruined works – but now depends on hosting trout fishermen. They stay mostly at the one-star, en-suite *Hôtel-Restaurant Erreguina* above the church (ⓣ & ⓕ05.59.37.40.37; open April–Nov 15; ❷), offering much the highest standard food or lodging in the valley – though the front garden has become a car park. There are three *menus* under €20 served in the cave-like, beam-ceilinged dining room, though going *à la carte* for scarcely more gives a better selection of pigeon, venison and fish both ocean and local.

Some 7km further upstream, the valley opens out considerably, with **ALDUDE** (Les Aldudes) plopped in the middle of the fields. The dead-central, somewhat scuffed *Hôtel Baïllea* (ⓣ05.59.37.57.02; closed Nov 15–March 1; ❷), with equally basic food, is the only facility. For more comfort, follow the main road 1500m towards Spain to **ESNASU** (Esnazu), where the cosier of two hotels is *Auberge Menta* (ⓣ05.59.37.57.58; closed mid-Nov to Easter; ❷), with country-style meals (*menus* €14–17).

Walking around Baïgorri: the Crête d'Iparla

The **GR10** arrives circuitously in Baïgorri from Saint-Jean in about six hours, curling southwest via 1021-metre Monhoa hill, then northeast. It's a rather dull stretch of the route, with a lot of track sectors.

Not so the continuation west towards Bidarraï, by far the more popular and rewarding outing, which begins in Lespars district. A sharp, two-and-a-half-hour climb, first through woods and then along a bare ridge, emerges at the **Col de Buztanzelhay** (843m), at the southern end of the **Crête d'Iparla**, which here forms the border. Iparla offers the classic ridge-walk of the French Pays Basque, and indeed one of the best in the entire Pyrenees.

Once up top, it's hard to get lost: simply follow the ridge due north, as close to the eastern face as is prudent. You're virtually guaranteed close-range sightings of griffon vultures and the occasional black vulture, though they tend to go to ground after midday when the thermal qualities of the air change. Although the highest point, **Pic d'Iparla** (under 3hr from Buztanzelhay), is only 1044m, it's as impressive a walk as you could hope for, with France precipitously below to the east, and a gentler decline towards a much less developed corner of Spain on the west.

You'll need a full eight hours (an hour less with a daypack) to traverse the length of the entire crest to Bidarraï village. Only attempt it in settled conditions; otherwise you won't get its views or vulture sightings, and every year hikers are struck by lighting or fall off the sheer precipice in mist. It's possible to return to your start-point the same day by public transport, a somewhat easier undertaking if you begin the walk from Bidarraï, a common strategy. Consult current SNCF schedule placards before setting out so that you coincide with one of the afternoon **rail-buses** back from Baïgorri to the proper train station of Ossès-St-Martin-d'Arrossa 8km northeast, one stop above Pont-Noblia (Bidarraï).

Starting the walk from Bidarraï, begin following the GR10 markers at *Gîte Arteka* and then bear right at each of two subsequent track junctions. The climb is brutal for the first ninety minutes, then slackens at a jagged crag where your spirits will be further lifted by your first glimpse of the vultures – who seem to have lost most fear of humans. Once around the Pic d'Iparla – about 2hr 45min out of Bidarraï with a daypack at a good pace – you descend to the important **Col de Harrieta** (808m) within another hour.

Immediately to the left (east), a communally maintained path, then tractor track, marked with single yellow paint-dashes, descends within ninety minutes to **Urdos** hamlet, your safety bail-out if the weather has turned nasty. From Urdos, it's two and a half hours back to Bidarraï, mostly on track and road. Diagonally off to the right or southwest from the *col*, a clear trail leads within five minutes to the **only spring** on Iparla, though even this may run low or dry by August. Straight south along the GR10 should get you to Baïgorri, and the last late-afternoon rail-bus, within a further three and a half hours.

Bidarraï

If you've arrived by train, **BIDARRAÏ** (Bidarray) at first sight seems to comprise just a few scattered houses on the riverbank near its medieval, humpbacked **Pont Noblia**, also the name of the SNCF station on schedules. Hikers arriving on the GR10, whether from Ainhoa on the west or Baïgorri to the south, get a truer picture of the upper village, scattered appealingly on a ridge with superb views, around a relatively narrow, modest church with a single gallery. The first building encountered going either direction on the GR10, at the extreme south edge of the village, is *Gîte d'Étape Arteka* (Ⓣ05.59.37.71.34; closed Nov 15–March), consisting of two wings, *Menditarrena* (50 places) and the more comfortable *Etxe*

Zaharria (30 places, some doubles) – though activity groups tend to fill one or other. Further along, the central place de l'Église is flanked by *Hôtel Barberaenea* (Ⓣ05.59.37.74.86, Ⓦwww.hotel-barberaenea.fr; closed mid-Nov to mid-Dec), with three grades of rooms: old-style with sinks (❷) or en-suite (❸); their **restaurant** serves a four-course €22 *menu du terroir* featuring baby trout or cod-stuffed peppers under the plane trees. Lately they've stiff competition from *Auberge Iparla*, next to the shop and *fronton*, with another €22 *menu terroir* served in the wood-

△ Pont d'Enfer, Bidarraï

trim salon or on the shaded terrace. Down in the riverbank quarter, the best choice is welcoming *Hôtel du Pont d'Enfer* (ⓣ05.59.37.70.88, ⓕ05.59.37.76.60; closed Jan–Feb; ❸), better known as *Chez Anny* after the proprietor, with three grades of large, non-musty rooms in the main building and annexe opposite, plus a restaurant serving on a river-view terrace in summer. A bit east, equidistant from upper and riverside quarters, lies tent-only *Camping Errekaldia* (ⓣ05.59.37.72.36).

Through Labourd to the coast

Beyond Baïgorri and Bidarraï, travelling along the Nive by road or train, you enter **Labourd** (Lapurdi), the westernmost of the three traditional French Basque regions which are now gathered into the *département* of Pyrénées-Atlantiques. The spa of **Cambo-les-Bains** is the biggest place between Saint-Jean-Pied-de-Port and Bayonne; here also, with your own vehicle, you can forsake the Bayonne-bound artery for the westerly D918, which passes through or near such tourist-friendly villages as **Ezpeleta** and **Ainhoa** on its way to Saint-Jean-de-Luz.

Itsasu and Laxia

Famous for its dark cherries, the small, spread-out village of **ITSASU** (Itxassou), northwest of Bidarraï in a bowl of wooded hills, makes a good introduction to the region and a great place to hide away (though only one daily train stops here). The seventeenth-century **church of Saint Fructueux** (open daylight hours), 1km south of the centre on the minor D349, retains a significant number of ancient, keyhole-shaped tombstones in its graveyard. Inside you'll find the typical French Basque three-tiered galleries, constructed to deny the Devil mischievous opportunities arising from the mingling of the sexes during Mass: the men sat upstairs, the women down in the nave. Another kilometre southeast along this road, the River Nive loops through a narrow defile at the **Pas de Roland**, yet another element in the Roland legend. Merely a hole in a boulder above the river, it's claimed to have been punched out by the hooves of the great knight's horse.

In terms of local **accommodation** and **eating**, don't bother with any of the obvious central establishments – the best choices are either on the outskirts or in bucolic Laxia hamlet just past the Pas de Roland, where river-bathing is popular. (Laxia can also be reached via a spur trail off the GR10 and Artzamendi peak with its naval-air installation, or by a perilously narrow but paved direct riverbank road from Bidarraï.) The *Hôtel du Chêne* (ⓣ05.59.29.75.01, ⓕ05.59.29.27.39; closed Jan, Feb & Mon, also Tues low season; ❸), opposite Saint Fructueux, represents excellent value in its large, bright, well-kept rooms with full baths; the restaurant is equally creditable, the €22 *menu* getting you *piperade*, salad, game and a simple dessert (decent own-*cuvée* wine extra). At **LAXIA**, the *Hôtel Ondoria* (ⓣ05.59.29.75.39, ⓕ05.59.29.25.99; closed Nov 15–Jan & Mon; ❷, ❺ HB) enjoys an amazing situation within sight and sound of the river gorge, where five-courses *menus* (€25 including parsleyed eel or *cèpe* omelette) can be taken on a wisteria-festooned terrace. About the only other building in the hamlet is non-en-suite *Hôtel Pas de Roland* down the hill (ⓣ05.59.29.75.23; ❷), with a more basic restaurant (closed Tues) and a hikers' *gîte*.

Cambo-les-Bains

Less than 5km north of Itsasu, **CAMBO-LES-BAINS** (Kambo) ranks as one of the largest towns in Labourd, encircled by a lushly rural landscape and an appealing (if slightly stuffy) place to break the journey. Long a magnet for sufferers from respiratory ailments – though Isaac Albeniz (p.173) lived out his last years here before dying of kidney failure – the **spa** establishment is the focal point of the ornate houses and hotels that radiate out along the heights above the Nive. The original town of **Bas Cambo**, typically Basque with its square, whitewashed houses and galleried church, lies down in the valley, beside the river and train station.

The most famous resident was Edmond Rostand, author of *Cyrano de Bergerac*, who from 1903 to 1918 lived in the huge **Villa Arnaga**, 1.5km west of Bas Cambo on the Bayonne road. Today the house is a **museum** (Ⓦ www.arnaga.com; guided visits: March Sat–Sun 2.30–6pm; April–June & Sept 10am–12.30pm & 2.30–7pm; July–Aug 10am–7pm; Oct 2.30–7pm; €5), amidst a bizarre formal garden defined by reflecting pools, with patches of lawn punctuated by blobs, cubes and cones of topiary box, and the boundaries lined by limes and blue cedars. Inside, it's very kitsch, with a minstrels' gallery, fake pilasters, allegorical frescoes, chandeliers, numerous portraits and various memorabilia.

The **tourist office** occupies a purpose-built structure next to the *mairie* (all year Mon–Sat 8.30am–noon & 2–5.30/6.30pm, continuously July–Aug; Sun July–Aug only 10am–12.30pm; Ⓣ 05.59.29.70.25, Ⓔ cambo.les.bains.tourisme@wanadoo.fr). For an overnight **stay**, try the *Auberge de Tante Ursule* (Ⓣ 05.59.29.78.23, Ⓔ chez.tante.ursule@wanadoo.fr; closed Feb 15–March 15 & Tues; ❸), in Bas Cambo by the *pelota* court and convenient only for the train station. The rooms are in a modern annexe with parking, while the excellent **restaurant** in the red-and-white older building offers rich *menus* (€16–35), featuring sweetbreads, black pudding and the like. The nearest **campsite** is *Ur-Hégia* on route des Sept-Chênes (Ⓣ 05.59.29.72.03; March to mid-Dec) in Bas Cambo.

Ezpeleta

From Cambo it's 5km southwest on the D918 (occasional buses) to **EZPELETA** (Espelette), a somewhat busy village, though a recent southerly bypass road has substantially quieted traffic on the main street. Large, dark-red **chilli peppers** are the principal crop here, and during summer and autumn many housefronts are festooned with strings of them hung out to dry; on the last Sunday in October a special Mass is preceded by a Saturday-night party celebrating the various Basque culinary uses of the pepper. The other major event of Ezpeleta's social calendar is the annual fair for trading **pottok** (pronounced *potiok*) ponies, the last Tuesday and Wednesday of January. An ancient, stocky breed of Paleolithic origin, little changed from the horses depicted in Pyrenean cave paintings, *pottoks* were once exported to work in British mines, but are now reared locally for both riding and meat.

The *Hôtel Euzkadi*, on the main street at the northeast edge of the village (Ⓣ 05.59.93.91.88, Ⓦ www.hotel-restaurant-euzkadi.com; ❸), with calmer rear rooms, a pool and tennis courts, also has what is reckoned among the best traditional **restaurants** in Labourd – reservations mandatory – and very reasonable for what you get (*menus* €16–31; closed Mon all year, Tues in low season & Nov–Christmas). The nearby *Hôtel Chilhar* (Ⓣ 05.59.93.90.01, Ⓕ 05.59.93.93.25; ❷), set back slightly from the same road, is cheaper, but its restaurant can't compare.

West to Saint-Jean-de-Luz

The D918 curls west from Ezpeleta via Saint-Pée-sur-Nivelle (Senpere) en route to Saint-Jean, 25km away. You might, however, veer south along the D20 to Ainhoa, 8km from Ezpeleta and just 3km shy of the frontier at Dantxarinea.

Basque sports

The Basque sport of **pelota** (*pelote* in France) is played – and keenly wagered on – all over Spanish Euskadi and the French Pays Basque. Even the smallest village has a *frontón* (open court) or *trinquet* (closed one), and indeed they are found well east into Aragón and Béarn where the sport has also caught on. Over twenty different versions of the game are known, including the most famous and spectacular, *cesta punta*, played in a covered court called *jaï alaï* (now widely confused with the name of the game itself). In essence it resembles a high-risk version of squash, the players smashing the ball against a wall either with bare hands or encased in the merest of leather gloves (the *pasaka*), and with a wooden bat (*pala*) or a *chistera*, a narrow wicker-work "claw" that extends the player's forearm. The largest *chisteras* launch the ball at speeds of around 200km an hour, making *pelota* one of the most dangerous games in the world. The *pelotas* themselves are balls of wool yarn and cotton thread wound tightly around a latex-tape core, all encased in goat leather; tedious to make (only to order), they are phenomenally expensive and sensitive to extremes of temperature and humidity.

Other unique Basque sports, all forming part of the many local fiestas, include *palankaris* (tossing an iron bar), *aizkolaritza* (log-chopping), *harri-jasotzea* (stone-lifting), *soka-tira* (tug-of-war) and *segalaritza* (grass-cutting). The finest exponents of the first three are popular local, sometimes international, heroes; world champion stone-lifter Iñaki Perurena's visit to Japan resulted in the sport being introduced there.

Ainhoa – and the end of the GR10

Yet another showcase village in a region not lacking in them, **AINHOA** gets understandably crowded in season, when tourists fill its single street lined with substantial, mainly seventeenth-century houses, their lintel plaques offering mini-genealogies as well as foundation dates. Take a look at the bulky-towered, two-galleried church with its extravagant Baroque altarpiece of prophets and apostles in niches, framed by gilt-wood Corinthian columns.

There's no budget **accommodation** per se, but Logis de France two-star *Hôtel Oppoca* (Ⓣ05.59.29.90.72, Ⓦwww.oppoca.com; closed mid-Nov to mid-Dec and most Jan; ❸) remains affordable, its restaurant (closed Mon) offering four *menus* (€18–45). *Hôtel Ohantzea* (Ⓣ05.59.29.90.50; ❸), also on the main street, isn't quite as good value, though it too has an attractive back garden. If money's no object, then plump for three-star, *Hôtel Ithurria* (Ⓣ05.59.29.92.11, Ⓦwww.ithurria.com; ❻), a former coaching inn on the pilgrim route, with sauna, pool and gourmet restaurant (*menus* €32–48). **Campers** should head for the basic *Camping Harazpy* (Ⓣ05.59.29.89.38; June–Sept) near the village centre.

Just over the frontier, 3km south at rather dismal **Dantaxarinea** (**Dancharia**) stand several **ventas**, relics of former times when these impromptu Spanish-run inns, essentially the retail outlets of smugglers, did a roaring trade in the many items that were far cheaper in Spain than in France. Today, with EU VAT rates still not uniform, their main stock is booze and cigarettes.

If you've hiked west six hours from Bidarraï on the **GR10**, Ainhoa is a logical stop. From here towards the Atlantic, the GR, meandering over to Sara within three and a half hours, next brings you to the base of La Rhune (see pp.504-05 for both) and finally reaches civilization again at Biriatu, an impossible walking day of nearly eleven hours. Thus it's best to halt six hours from Ainhoa at the isolated *gîte d'étape* at **Olhette** hamlet, *Manttu Baïta* (Ⓣ05.59.54.00.98; 14 places), also with *chambres d'hôtes*. Only purists do the final, urbanized stretch through to Hendaye; for detailed reverse walking directions to La Rhune, see p.507.

The Basque coast

For a region with such a long maritime tradition, the **Basque coast** – *Côte Basque* in French, *Costa Vasca* in Castilian – is surprisingly short and devoid of good natural harbours. It's barely 120km from the mouth of the River Adour, separating Bayonne and Biarritz from the dunes of the Landes on the north, to the Cantabrian border beyond Bilbao in the west. Of that just 50km – between Bayonne and San Sebastián – can be considered to be Pyrenean shoreline, and only at the mouths of the rivers Nivelle, Bidasoa and Oiartzun is there evidence of past Basque prowess in whaling, navigating and piracy.

The all-enveloping carpet of green vegetation, so unlike the Mediterranean coast, reflects a damp, often misty climate without sharp differences between winter and summer temperatures. Yet the sun shines enough in season to attract hordes of holidaymakers, and if you've been up in the hills for some time, the sea comes as a very welcome sight. Unfortunately it is often just for looking: frequently dangerous and wave-lashed, as at **Anglet** and **Hendaye** – to the delight of wet-suited surfers, and ensuring steady employment for lifeguards – and sometimes murky.

Otherwise the Basque coast has all the ingredients for a perfect vacation: excellent food and drink, seductive scenery, characterful architecture and a handful of side trips inland to **Azkaine**, **La Rhune** and **Sara**. The two defining cities of **Bayonne** and **San Sebastián** are the biggest attractions, though the small ports of **Pasaia** and **Saint-Jean-de-Luz**, the historic border town of **Hondarribia** and the period-piece resort of **Biarritz** also have considerable appeal.

Bayonne

Although contiguous with fashionable beachside Biarritz (see p.497), the inland position of **BAYONNE** (Baïona) protected it until recently from significant touristic exploitation. Built astride the confluence of the rivers Adour (navigable) and Nive (less so), 5km from the sea and roughly 60km down the Nive from Saint-Jean, the city has long served as an important port, a status guaranteed by determined 1578 engineering works to fix the wandering mouth of the Adour. Bayonne is both a Gascon city and the capital of the Pays Basque, with trilingual street signage – the third language being Gascon. However, tall, white older houses, their shutters and half-timbering picked out in the distinctively Basque brownish-reds and greens, betray the major influence.

The place was founded as the Roman garrison town of Lapurdum. The name, corrupted to Lapurdi (Euskera) and Labourd (French), later signified the entire westernmost French Basque province; the current Euskera-derived name – Bayonne/Baïona – means "good river". For three centuries until 1453 and the end of the Hundred Years War, it enjoyed prosperity and relative peace under English domination. During the sixteenth century, Sephardic Jews fleeing the Iberian Inquisitions arrived, bringing their knowledge of chocolate manufacturing. The city's heyday came during the eighteenth century, based on the dubious underpinnings of armaments manufacture (*bayonet* derives from the place) and a judicious amount of piracy. After the French Revolution, it lost considerable prestige when Paris merged the three traditional French Basque regions into the single modern *département* of Pyrénées-Atlantiques, governed from Pau.

Just as Perpignan became a refuge for anti-Franco Catalans, so did Bayonne for the Spanish Basques, seeking refuge among their own. For decades until a late 1980s clampdown the Petit Bayonne quarter was a haven for Basque nationalists (especially ETA fugitives). Wall art in the neighbourhood still demands freedom for imprisoned ETA members, or failing that, confinement within the Basque country – and urges *insumisoa* (disobedience) in the face of new repressive measures.

Economically there are also parallels between Bayonne and Perpignan, both dominating increasingly busy truck and train routes between Portugal, northern Spain and Western Europe. New enterprises – mostly aerospace and electronics – only partly compensate for the decline in traditional industries like footwear, clothing and chemical plants, but Bayonne's riverside harbour at Boucau is supposedly the ninth busiest in France.

These issues don't immediately affect a visitor, however, and despite a certain amount of tourist tat on shopfronts, initial impressions of Bayonne as a small-scale, easy-going city will likely stick. Wherever you're headed you'll at least stop in, as it's a major transport hub; you might even consider it as a relatively inexpensive and quiet base, except of course during the festival season when beds are at a premium.

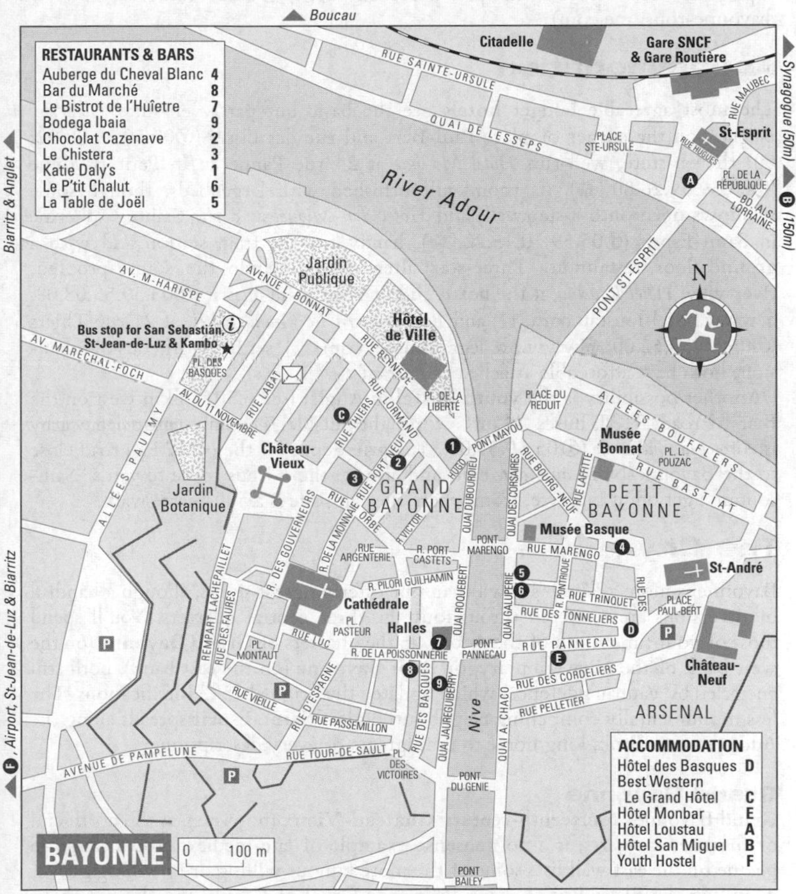

Arrival, transport and information

The **airport**, Biarritz-Anglet-Bayonne/BAB, lies 6km southwest at Parme (general airport info ⓣ05.59.43.83.83, Ryanair ⓣ05.59.43.83.93; #6 or C bus from/to town). The **gare SNCF** and **gare routière** for points in Béarn, Basse-Navarre and Soule are adjacent just off place de la République in the somewhat shabby district of Saint-Esprit on the north bank of the Adour, across the wide Pont Saint-Esprit from the city centre. There is, however, another **bus terminal** on place des Basques on the Adour's south bank, used by STAB (ⓦwww.bus-stab.com) for Biarritz and Anglet, ATCRB to Cambo and Saint-Jean-de-Luz (changing for Hendaye) and Spanish coaches to San Sebastián. In town a free red **navette** executes a complicated route between Porte d'Espagne and Pont de Génie.

If you arrive by car, **parking** – mostly metered – is easiest just south of town, around rue Tour-de-Sault and Pont du Genie. Otherwise, you can **rent cars** from several booths at the airport, or at several outlets near the stations, including Adour Auto Location at 7 rue Hugues (ⓣ05.59.50.70.60). The **tourist office** is also in place des Basques (July–Aug Mon–Sat 9am–7pm, Sun 10am–1pm; Sept–June Mon–Fri 9am–6.30pm, Sat 10am–6pm; ⓣ05.59.46.01.46, ⓦwww.bayonne-tourisme.com).

Accommodation

The most agreeable budget **hotels** are the basic but partly en-suite *Hôtel des Basques*, on the corner of place Paul-Bert and rue des Lisses (ⓣ05.59.59.08.02; ❶); the en-suite, well-run *Hôtel Monbar* at 24 rue Pannecau in Petit Bayonne (ⓣ05.59.59.26.80; ❷), its rooms all furnished with large beds, though some windows open onto a stairwell; and *Hôtel San Miguel* at 8 rue Sainte-Catherine in Saint-Esprit (ⓣ05.59.50.15.22; ❶), handy for the train station and with a ground-floor restaurant. Three-star alternatives include the sound-proofed, river-view *Hôtel Loustau* at the north end of Pont Saint-Esprit (ⓣ05.59.55.08.08, ⓦwww.hotel-loustau.com; ❹) and *Best Western Le Grand Hôtel*, at 21 rue Thiers (ⓣ05.59.59.62.00, ⓦwww.bw-legrandhotel.com; ❹), set in a gorgeous old mansion; both have affordable attached restaurants.

Another possibility is the **youth hostel** in Anglet (see p.501), 6km west on the Biarritz road; STAB buses #4 or C stop right outside. The only **campsite** nearby is *Airotel la Chêneraie* (ⓣ05.59.55.01.31; April–Sept), off the N117 Pau road close to the Bayonne-Nord *autoroute* exit, and also on the #4 bus route towards "Sainsontan"; get off at Navarre, from where the campsite is a 500-metre walk.

The City

Bayonne is more a *flâneur*'s town than one offering great sights, though a handful of diversions are scattered throughout the three central quarters. You'll spend most of your time south of the Adour, in the quarters of **Grand Bayonne** (on the west bank of the Nive tributary) or **Petit Bayonne** (on the east bank), both still encircled by Vauban's defences which updated the original 1523 fortifications. The less monumentally compelling neighbourhood of **Saint-Esprit** spreads along the Adour's north bank, long home to immigrants of every description.

Grand Bayonne

Grand Bayonne's fourteenth-century **Chateau-Vieux** (no visits), at the north end of the later ramparts, is a no-nonsense example of late-medieval fortification; a plaque on the east wall lists some of the more famous willing or unwilling guests, including the Black Prince, King Pedro the Cruel of Castile and the notorious mercenary Bertrand de Guescelin. The **Jardin Botanique** (daily April 15–Oct 15 9am–noon & 2–6pm; free) lies just west of the château – a well-designed, enormous garden with plants labelled in French, Euskera and Latin.

The twin-towered **Cathédrale Sainte-Marie** (Mon–Sat 10–11.45am & 3–5.45pm, Sun 3.30–6pm) on magnolia-shaded place Pasteur at the summit of Grand Bayonne, looks best from a distance, its steeple rising with airy grace above the houses. Up close, the yellowish stone reveals bad weathering, with most of the decorative detail lost to post-Revolutionary vandalism. The interior is more impressive, thanks to the height of the nave and some sixteenth-century stained glass (restored in 2002). Like other southern French Gothic cathedrals of the period (about 1260) it was based on more famous northern models, in this case Soissons and Reims. On the south side is a fourteenth-century **cloister** (daily 9am–12.30pm & 2–5/6pm; free) with a lawn, affording a rather flattering view of the church.

From place Pasteur, **rue de la Monnaie** and its continuation rue du Port-Neuf lead downhill to the main **place de la Liberté**, past various aromatic confiseries purveying **chocolate**, *the* Bayonne speciality, on a par with its famous air-cured hams. Though most of it is still made in the Saint-Esprit quarter, the most prestigious retail outlets are Cazenave and Daranatz, arcade shops at nos. 19 and 15 respectively in **rue du Port-Neuf**, and Atelier du Chocolat on perpendicular 1 rue des Carmes. South and west of the cathedral, along rue des Faures, rue d'Espagne and other streets closest to the ramparts, there's a more Iberian feel, with washing strung out of the windows, ethnic restaurants and quirky bars.

The Nive Quais and Petit Bayonne

East of the cathedral, the **Nive Quais** form a lively and picturesque focus; the **halles** on the Grand Bayonne side host a comprehensive market every workday until 1pm, plus Friday late afternoon. On the right (east) bank, arcaded sixteenth-century houses are reflected appealingly in the placid Nive; one of these, near the end of Pont Marengo, contains a worthwhile ethnographic museum, the **Musée Basque** (Ⓦwww.musee-basque.com; May–Oct Tues–Sun 10am–6.30pm, also Mon July–Aug; Nov–April Tues–Sun 10am–12.30pm & 2–6pm; €5.50, €9 with Musée Bonnat). Several floors of ethnographic and historical exhibits on Basque life through the ages are exhausting as much as exhaustive, with labelling in French, Castilian and Euskera only. Highlights include (on the second floor) collections of eighteenth-century faience pottery and *makilak* – innocent-looking walking sticks, often elaborately carved from medlar wood, but with a concealed steel spear tip at one end, used by pilgrims and shepherds for self-protection. Agricultural artefacts include a solid-wheeled oxcart, wooden ploughs plus a roller to tamp down the field afterwards and wine presses. The seafaring room features a superb rudder-handle carved as a sea-monster, a wooden-hulled fishing boat, plus a model of Bayonne's naval shipyards *c.* 1805; Columbus's skipper was Basque, and another Basque, Juan Sebastián de Elkano, completed the first circumnavigation of the world in 1522.

The painting collection of Bayonne's second museum, the **Musée Bonnat**, at 5 rue Jacques-Laffitte (Ⓦwww.musee-bonnat.com; daily except Tues & hols: May–Oct 10am–6.30pm; Nov–April 10am–12.30pm & 2–6pm; €5.50, €9 with Musée Basque), provides welcome variation from the usual dross of provincial galleries. Thirteenth- and fourteenth-century Italian art is well represented, as are most periods up to (but not including) Impressionism; highlights include Goya's *Self-Portrait* and *Portrait of Don Francisco de Borja*, Rubens' powerful *Apollo and Daphne* and *The Triumph of Venus*, plus works by Murillo, El Greco and Ingres. A whole gallery is devoted to high-society portraits by Léon Bonnat (1833–1922), whose personal collection formed the original core of the museum. Frequent temporary exhibits in an annexe at 9 rue Frédéric-Bastiat (same days, 2–6pm) are well worth catching.

North of the river: Saint-Esprit

Apart from savouring the wide river skies, there is little reason to venture north of the Adour. A deliberately inconspicuous, early nineteenth-century **synagogue** at 33 rue Maubec serves as a reminder that Bayonne's Jewish community first settled here in France on arrival from Portugal early in the sixteenth century. Saint-Esprit became their ghetto after Henri IV's 1602 expulsion order, when Grand Bayonne was consecrated to the Virgin and off-limits to nonbelievers. The **church of Saint-Esprit**, opposite the train station, is all that remains of a hostel that once ministered to the sore feet and other ailments of pilgrims on the Chemin de Saint-Jacques – worth a peek inside for a fifteenth-century wood sculpture of *The Flight into Egypt*, showing Notre-Dame-des-Voyageurs (appropriately, given the nearby train station) seated in voluminous robes on a donkey, holding the Child. Just above the station is Vauban's massive **citadelle**; built in 1680 to defend the town against Spanish attack, it actually saw little action until the Napoleonic wars, when its garrison resisted a siege by Wellington for four months in 1813 before falling the next year.

Eating, drinking and entertainment

The best area for **eating and drinking** is along the right-bank (Petit Bayonne) quay of the Nive and the back streets to either side of the river. Besides the listings below, you'll find other variable possibilities in Petit Bayonne, especially along rue Pannecau, rue des Cordeliers and rue des Tonneliers. For Asian or North African food, try rue Sainte-Catherine in Saint Esprit.

As far as **festivals** go, Bayonne's biggest bash of the year is the Fêtes de Bayonne, which usually starts on the first Wednesday in August and consists of five days and nights of continuous boozing and entertainment. There are *corridas* (bullfights) the last two days, plus a few more in the run-up to August 15. A well-established jazz festival, La Ruee au Jazz, covers four days in mid-July, and every October there's Les Translatines, a Franco-Spanish theatre festival.

If you hear Spanish, French or Basque sounds you'd like to take home, Bayonne has several sizeable **record shops**, including a Virgin Megastore at 27–29 rue Victor-Hugo, and Harmonia Mundi at 5 rue du Port-Neuf. There are two central **cinemas**: L'Autre Cinema at 3 quai Amiral Sala, and L'Atalante at 7 rue Denis Etcheverry, with "art" fare and *voix originelle* screenings.

Restaurants

Auberge du Cheval Blanc 68 rue Bourg-Neuf, Petit Bayonne ⓣ05.59.59.01.33. Durable gourmets' mecca sporting a single Michelin star; despite that, €38 weekday lunch *menus* exist, though you can easily spend €90. Reservations suggested. Closed Mon except Aug, Sun eve & Sat noon all year round.

Le Chistera 42 rue Port-Neuf. *Pelota* decor, as you'd expect with the proprietor, a player in his own right, being the son of a *cesta-punta* champion and trainer. Hearty *bayonnais* specialities based on fish, pork and tripe best ordered off the daily-specials board; budget €15 for the *menu* or €19–25 *à la carte*. Closed Mon, part May & Tues–Wed eves except July & Aug.

La Table de Joël 28 quai Galuperie, Petit Bayonne. Indoor or outdoor seating on a riverside terrace; mostly meat served but a few monkfish and cod dishes, plus creative desserts. *Menu* €17, *à la carte* €28–32. Closed Mon noon & Sun.

Le P'tit Chalut 24 quai Galuperie. Not as upmarket as its neighbour across the street, but a decent venue for seafood under the arcade; two lunch *menus* for under €24.

Bars and cafés

Bar du Marché 39 rue des Basques. This place begins purveying food and drink – including good draught beer – at 5am to a mix of market sellers and bar-flies on their way home to bed, continuing with economical *plats du jour*

at lunchtime, served amidst a decor of posters for Izarra liqueur and the Pamplona bull-running. You can eat very well for €17, plus drink, though there's not much seafood. Closed Sun & all eves.
Le Bistrot de l'Huître corner of *halles* building, facing Pont Pannecau. Mainly Quiberon and Marennes oysters, washed down with Jurançon or Irouléguy wine. Closed Mon.
Bodega Ibaia 49 quai Jauréguiberry. Lively, well-loved *pintxos* bar – reputedly Bayonne's favourite – with a mixed crowd and *plats du jour* for €7–12 at midday. One of several similar here, if you can't squeeze in. Closed Mon, also Sun low season.
Chocolat Cazenave 19 rue du Port-Neuf. Drink a hot cup of local cocoa or scoop an ice cream, either under the arcades or inside the Art Nouveau interior; also every conceivable chocolate goodie to take home.
Katie Daly's 3 place de la Liberté. Passably authentic Irish theme pub, with live music Tues, Fri & Sat, Guinness on tap and major sporting matches on a wide screen. Open nightly.

Biarritz

BIARRITZ (Miarritze), 8km west of Bayonne, makes no secret of its identity as the Atlantic Monte Carlo. Much of this hotch-potch of ocean-liner-style hotels and mock-Gothic châteaux wears a nostalgic air that appeals to more traditional middle-class visitors, while the town's newer neighbourhoods attract a younger, variably prosperous market.

Biarritz burst into prominence during the mid-nineteenth century when Spanish-born Empress Eugénie, wife of Napoléon III – whom she met here – brought the entire entourage of the Second Empire to what had been the favourite seaside watering hole of her childhood. Others soon followed, including Edward VII, who effectively held a second court here, nominating Asquith prime minister in Biarritz in 1908. After World War I destroyed the existing European social order, high fashion moguls like Hermès and Lanvin, film stars like Douglas Fairbanks and Gloria Swanson and various other glitterati replaced the crowned heads and nobility.

Following the next global convulsion, and the rise of the Côte d'Azur during the 1960s, Biarritz went into seemingly terminal decline not unlike that of English coastal resorts. But since the late 1980s, events have rescued the place from crash-landing on the dust-heap of touristic history. Recovery was initially slow, spurred by the town's embrace of golf, conferences and even a small September cinema festival – but the biggest shot in the arm was Biarritz's transformation into **Europe's premier surfing mecca**. That actually began in 1957, when American screenwriter Pieter Viertel, here for the filming of *The Sun Also Rises*, took to the waves with a board and inspired locals to join him. You still can see many of these white-haired old-timers – *Les Tontons Surfeurs* or "Surf Uncles" as they call themselves – bobbing in the waves with kids their grandsons' age. This international surf-bum fraternity (biggest at annual July competitions), and more sedentary Parisian yuppies, coexist fairly harmoniously with a population that's one-third retirees. Against all odds, Biarritz is chic and trendy once more, new money (or no money) rubbing shoulders with old, and without any Côte d'Azur pretensions.

Arrival, information and transport

The **tourist office** occupies a Belle Époque structure abutting the square d'Ixelles (daily: July & Aug 8am–8pm; Sept–June Mon–Sat 10am–6pm, Sun 10am–5pm; Ⓣ05.59.22.37.00, Ⓦwww.biarritz.fr), also selling tickets for local events at a *billeterie*. The **gare SNCF** lies an inconvenient 3km southeast at the end of avenue Foch/avenue Kennedy in La Négresse district (STAB bus #2 or B from square d'Ixelles). Other STAB **buses** may use another stop a block away on avenue

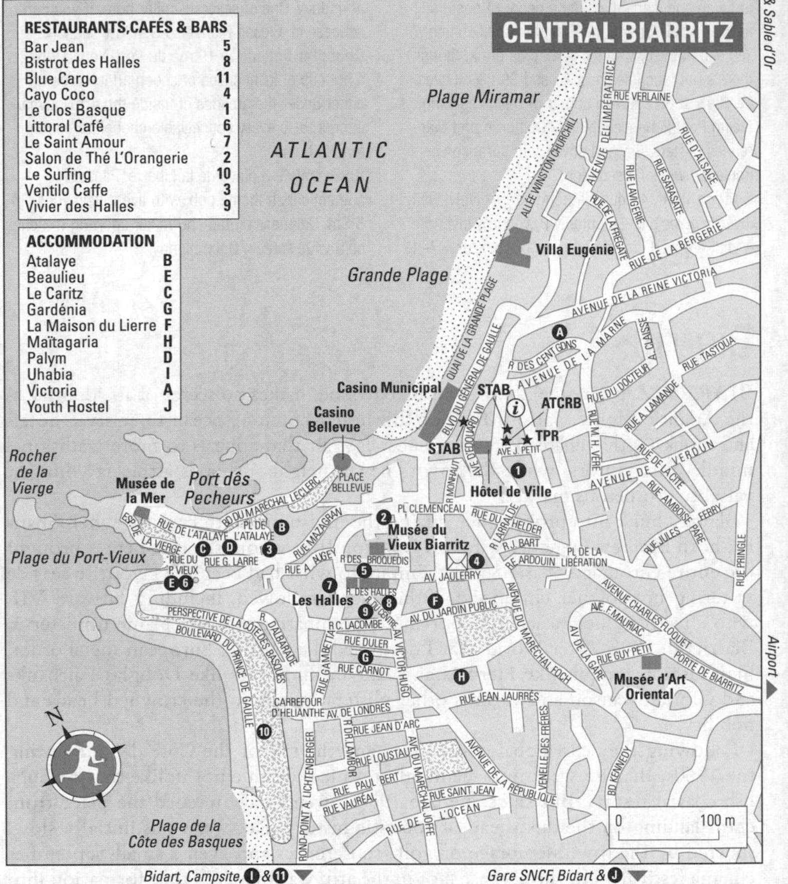

d'Edouard VII, while TPR (from/to Pau) and ATCRB (from/to Saint-Jean-de-Luz and Hendaye) use stops on the south side of the square. Arriving with your own car, you'll find **parking** mayhem year-round. The best strategies are to opt for a €10, one-week ticket (valid for street parking all over the centre), strike out into the uncontrolled streets just south (eg avenue Carnot) or submit yourself to the pricey *parkings couverts*.

Accommodation

Contrary to expectations, Biarritz has a handful of good-value **hotels**, though for July or August advance reservations are mandatory. **Campers** should try *Biarritz Camping*, at 28 route d'Harcet, the inland continuation of avenue de la Plage (☎05.59.23.00.12; mid-May to mid-Oct), behind Plage de la Milady, to the south of town. The nearest official **youth hostel** (☎05.59.41.76.00; 96 places) is 2km southwest of the centre on the shore of Lac Mouriscot, just walkable from the gare SNCF; otherwise get #2 or B bus from the centre to "Bois de Boulogne" stop.

Hotels

Atalaye 6 rue des Goélands ⓣ05.59.24.06.76, ⓦwww.hotelatalaye.com. A bit funky but serviceable and all en-suite, this is better value and quieter than nearby rivals on rue Port–Vieux. The best rooms (including a few tiny singles) have equally small balconies and face the place de l'Atalaye and sea obliquely; parking available on said *place*. ❷

Beaulieu 3 esplanade du Port Vieux ⓣ05.59.24.23.59, ⓦwww.hotelbeaulieu.fr. Unbeatable location, but only worth it if you can get one of the modern, en-suite rooms overlooking said *port* (about half of them) – cheaper rear ones are airless in summer and no quieter. Pleasant breakfast room with partial bay view. Closed Christmas–Feb. ❸

Le Caritz 2006-inaugurated three-star hotel with designer pretensions, and just over half the rooms facing the sea; all are a/c and the suites have Jacuzzis. The ground-floor restaurant is predictably expensive, but the *Café Leffe* section provides an outstanding buffet breakfast (€10), taken up on the terrace and open to all. ❻

Gardénia 19 av Carnot ⓣ05.59.24.10.46, ⓦwww.hotel-gardenia.com. Mix of rooms, some with plumbing down the hall, in this old-fashioned but quiet and well-cared-for non-smoking outfit. Free street parking. Closed mid Nov & mid Jan. ❷

La Maison du Lierre 3 av du Jardin Public ⓣ05.59.24.06.00, ⓦwww.maisondulierre.com. Another old-mansion hotel, under new ownership from 2006 and being renovated in stages. Rooms, some with balcony, are a good size and have wood floors, and a good breakfast is laid on in the pleasant salon; that said it's better value off-season when rates are in the lower price category. ❸

Maïtagaria 34 av Carnot ⓣ05.59.24.26.65, ⓦwww.hotel-maitagaria.com. Smart, updated (2003–05) ooms in a quietly set town house near a landscaped square; pleasant back garden and indoor lounges; fair bit of metered and free parking nearby. ❸

Palym 7 rue du Port-Vieux ⓣ05.59.24.16.56, ⓕ05.59.24.96.12. A welcoming budget choice offering a variety of rooms, with not a right angle remaining in the building. The hot water sometimes runs out on summer evenings, though. Ground-floor bar-restaurant. ❷

Uhabia Bidart, 6.5km south on D911 ⓣ05.59.54.92.39, ⓦwww.hotel-uhabia.com. A good overflow option if Biarritz proper is full, this small hotel with a preponderance of balconied en-suite rooms and a justifiably popular restaurant is right behind the car park for Bidart village's Plage de Centre. Closed Nov–Jan. ❸

Victoria 12 av de la Reine Victoria ⓣ05.59.24.08.21. Worth a mild splurge for the unbeatable location two blocks in from the Grande Plage, private parking and often huge rooms in this Neo-Gothic mansion, with comfortable beds, iron bathtubs and the odd chandelier. ❸

The Town

Most attractions are strung out along the landscaped, clifftop terraces just inland from the promontories and coves around which Biarritz grew. The Art Deco **Casino Municipal**, just behind the Grande Plage, has been restored as an exhibition and conference venue. Inland, the town forms a surprisingly ordinary and workaday sprawl, with the sole points of interest being the welcoming, vibrant **halles**, with separate *poissonerie* and produce/meat sections; the **Musée d'Art Oriental/Asiatica** on 1 rue Guy-Petit (ⓦwww.museeasiatica.com; Mon–Fri 10.30am–6.30pm, Sat & Sun 2–7pm; €7), exhibiting the collection of Indian and Tibetan art specialist Michel Postel; and the **Musée du Vieux Biarritz**, installed in a disused Anglican church on rue Broquedis (Tues–Sat 10am–noon & 2.30–6pm; €3), displaying knick-knacks and documents relating to Belle Époque royalty.

Like several coastal spots hereabouts, Biarritz started life as a whaling centre, which industry collapsed late in the eighteenth century; its only remnants are a whale-spotting tower near place de l'Atalaye and some memorabilia in the **Musée de la Mer** atop the claw-shaped promontory west of town (ⓦwww.museedelamer.com; open all year except mid-Jan & Mon low season; otherwise daily: July–Aug 9.30am–midnight; June & Sept 9.30am–7pm; rest of year 9.30am–12.30pm & 2–6pm; €7.50). Along with exhibitions on local fishing and wildlife, this offers a small aquarium and seal-frolicking section, making it – if not exactly a must – a good place to take the kids. The promotory ends in the **Rocher de la Vierge**, an offshore rock adorned with a white statue of the Virgin, and linked to the mainland by an iron catwalk built by Eiffel, he of the tower. Around it are scattered other rocky islets where the swell heaves and combs; the scenery figured largely in Eric Rohmer's wonderful film *Le Rayon Vert*. Just below is the picturesque **Port des Pêcheurs**, easiest approached by pedestrian lanes zigzagging down through banks of hydrangeas. The professional fishermen have long gone, replaced by pleasure boats, but there are two **scuba outfitters** here (USB ⓣ06.23.41.12.95 and BAB ⓣ05.59.24.80.40) and a few pricey seafood restaurants.

The only inland **streets and squares** really conducive to relaxed strolling are those between the Musée de la Mer and the place Sainte-Eugénie. Both that square and **place de l'Atalaye**, high above the Port des Pêcheurs, can muster a number of whimsically **turreted and balconied hotels and villas**. In recent years numbers of these succumbed to the wrecker's ball, but in 1997, under threat of a fifty-acre development proposed by Gaullist councillors to replace the Casino Municipal, the rest of the council stood down, forcing the resignation of the mayor. He was replaced by a centrist acceptable to conservationists, who immediately slapped a preservation order on the town's surviving 230 follies. Downhill and south from place de l'Atalaye, you can stroll the length of the characterful if now touristified **rue du Port-Vieux**, which links its namesake beach with rue Mazagran.

The beaches

The wave-pounded **beaches** north of the promontory are generously sandy – those south are rockier – and, according to the fickle weather, either carpeted with a mix of beautiful people and middle-class families tanning themselves cheek by jowl, or abandoned to wet-suited surf fanatics. Served by STAB's La Navette des Plages all day during July and August, the municipal strands extend about 5km from the southernmost **Plage de la Milady** to **Pointe Saint-Martin** in the north. The southerly sections are set apart from one another by smaller headlands: **Plage Marbella**; **Côte des Basques**, focus of the annual surf championships and home to four surf schools; and **Plage du Port-Vieux**, the most sheltered and intimate – you'll share it with scuba-divers and kayakers at times – tucked in the lee of the Rocher de la Vièrge.

But most of the action takes place along the contiguous Grande Plage and Plage Miramar, sweeping northeast from the Port des Pêcheurs. The **Grande Plage** was originally dubbed the "Plage des Fous" after the 1850s practice of taking lunatics to bathe here as a primitive form of thalassotherapy; Picasso later used it as the setting for his *Les Baigneuses*. Today it's a highly regimented playground, with separate sections for surfers and bathers, and lifeguards tweeting their whistles or paddling out into the water to shoo people out of danger zones. The **Plage Miramar** just beyond is shadowed by the domes of a Russian Orthodox church dating from 1908, and also overlooked by the former **Villa Eugénie**, a present of Napoléon III to his wife in 1855. Now the luxury *Hôtel du Palais*, it was gutted by fire in 1881 and 1905, so that little remains of the original fabric. Beyond Pointe Saint-Martin and its landmark **lighthouse** (April 15–June Sat & Sun 3–6.30pm; July & Aug Tues–Sat 10am–12.30pm & 2.30–6.45pm; €2), built in 1831, begin the even wilder, broader beaches of Anglet (see opposite).

Eating and drinking

It's possible to **eat** well and affordably in Biarritz, away from the touristy snack bars on rue du Port-Vieux, especially near the *halles* – and until 11pm or so in summer.

Restaurants & bistrots

Le Bistrot des Halles 1 rue du Centre ⓣ05.59.24.21.22. Within sight of the *halles*, this is strong on generously portioned, tasty fish dishes, but except for the lunch-only *menu* count on €32 a head plus service, and a steeply priced wine list. Reservations essential. Closed Sun except school hols.

Blue Cargo Just south of the city limits on the

Plage d'Ilbarritz ☎05.59.23.54.87. Dual premises popular with the *beau monde*: *Café de la Plage* in the beachside terrace, €29 for three courses strong on fish and salads; at the old villa just uphill (eves only), reckon on €35 minimum for a fancier selection – plus stiffly priced wine list. Reservations suggested for the villa.

Le Clos Basque 12 rue Louis-Barthou ☎05.59.24.24.96. A genuine *bistrot* tucked back slightly from the street, this does three meaty traditional French courses for €25 – and is accordingly packed out at supper (less so at lunch). Reservations suggested. Closed Sun eve & Mon.

Le Saint Amour 26 rue Gambetta ☎05.59.24.19.64. Lyonnais-style *bistrot* where a pleasant environment offsets rather startling à la carte prices (€33 for three average courses); beer on tap, or a *pot* of wine also helps, plus there are cheaper lunch *menus* under €18. Large parties can book the quieter room at the back. Closed June, Nov & Sun–Mon low season.

Le Surfing California-style diner-cum-pilgrimage-site for surfers, behind Plage de Côte des Basques, run by Robert Rabagny, organizer of the annual Surf Festival. As much shrine-museum, festooned with antique boards, as purveyor of grills, seafood and *frites*; €23 *menu*.

Le Vivier des Halles 8 rue du Centre. The *vivier* is the fish-tank in the middle with your potential dinner in it – seafood and nothing but. Mains, such as half a lobster with Ezpeleta pepper sprinkles, vary by season; à la carte only will be €28–31. Supper until 11pm; closed Mon.

Cafés and bars

Bar Jean 5 rue des Halles. Popular, semi-subterranean Spanish-theme spot with Latin soundtrack, *tapas* at the bar from €1 per platter, or large-portioned sit-down meals emphasizing seafood for €21 plus drink. Oysters at lunch only.

Cayo Coco 5 rue Jaulerry. Cuban theme bar with free salsa dance lessons Thurs night. Open 11pm–3am.

Littoral Café 3 Esplanade du Port Vieux. Well-presented brasserie grub, strong on *moules*, *galettes*, *crêpes* and big steins of beer. The sidewalk tables with some of the best views in town are unsurprisingly popular.

Salon de Thé L'Orangerie 1 rue Gambetta. This makes a good start to the day, serving all sorts of hot drinks (including forty kinds of tea, novelty coffees) and a standard breakfast. Closed Wed.

Ventilo Caffe rue du Port-Vieux. Nothing special to look at other than wide-screen plasma TV running surf videos, but this is the main local haunt of Parisian thirtysomethings; fresh fruit juices and breakfast offered. Open all year.

Anglet

Sprawling north and east from Biarritz, amorphous **ANGLET** (pronounced *Anglett*, Angelu in Euskera) occupies most of the triangular territory between the Pointe Saint-Martin, the mouth of the Adour and Bayonne. There is nothing here of note except half a dozen excellent beaches, uncrowded compared with those at Biarritz or Saint-Jean-de-Luz – the most famous being **Chambre d'Amour**, so named after two lovers who were trapped and drowned in their trysting place by the rising tide, and the adjacent surfers' meccas of **Sables d'Or** and **Marinella**, with rental boards and instruction available. As the pair's fate indicates, swimming here is generally dangerous owing to treacherous currents and you should heed the warning signs and lifeguards.

Buses C & 9, or the summer Navette des Plages, call here from central Biarritz; you can also walk it in about thirty minutes, along avenues de l'Impératrice and continuation Général-MacCroskey, then second left down to the seaside boulevard des Plages. Anglet offers a spacious, friendly and well-run **youth hostel** in quartier Chiberta at the north end of route des Vignes (☎05.59.58.70.00; 96 places in four- to six-bed dorms; closed Nov–Feb), which offers a full programme of sporting activities – including, of course, surfing. For **eating and drinking**, the most notable seaside establishments are the *Havana Café* overlooking the parking area (and ocean) at Chambre d'Amour, a permanently crowded bar that does *plats du jour* at lunch for under €9, and nearby *Café Bleu*, more of a proper restaurant (*menu* €16; closed Wed during Sept–June). Inland, *La Fleur de Sel* (closed lunch Mon–Wed), off avenue des Plages at 5 av de la Forêt near the Chiberta pine forest and youth hostel, is more *nouvelle Basquaise* but popular (€28.50 *menu*, €33-plus otherwise).

Saint-Jean-de-Luz and around

Just 20km southwest of Biarritz, **SAINT-JEAN-DE-LUZ** (Donibane Loitzun – "St John of the Marshes" – in Euskera) rates as one of the most attractive resorts on the Basque coast, despite being overrun by families at peak season, especially its part-pedestrianized old quarter and broad beach studded with striped beach tents and more numerous volleyball pitches.

Saint-Jean has historically been one of France's busiest fishing ports, initially occupied with pursuing whales and cod. Local sailors travelled as far as Newfoundland, which the Basques claim to have discovered decades before Columbus's voyages. In the seventeenth century, Dutch and English whalers drove them from their habitual ports in Arctic waters, so the enterprising Basques devised a method of boiling down the blubber on board, enabling the ships – essentially the first factory whalers – to stay at sea much longer. Later, the 1713 Treaty of Utrecht put Newfoundland's rich cod-fishing grounds off-limits to local skippers, who avoided ruin by becoming pirates. The more respectable pursuit of anchovies, tuna and sardines, which still feature strongly on local menus, only resumed during the nineteenth century; the commercial port, at the mouth of the River Nivelle, remains crammed with boats, lobster traps and other piscatorial paraphernalia, all the way back to the Pont Charles-de-Gaulle linking Saint-Jean and Ziburu.

Arrival, information and transport

The **gare SNCF** is on the southern edge of the centre, 500m from the beach, while **buses** arrive at the *halte routière* just opposite. The **tourist office** (July–Aug Mon–Sat 9am–7.30pm, Sun 10am–1pm & 3–7pm; Sept–June Mon–Sat 9am–12.30pm & 2–6.30/7pm, Sun 10am–1pm; ⓣ05.59.26.03.16, ⓦwww.saint-jean-de-luz.com) stands just behind place des Corsaires. **Bikes** can be rented at Luz Evasion on place Maurice-Ravel or ADO on avenue Labrouche, as well as at the gare SNCF, where ADA **car rental** (ⓣ05.59.26.26.22) is also based. **Parking** in the centre is a non-starter – leave cars in the suburbs and walk in. *Pelote* matches take place from late June to late August at 9pm on Tuesdays and Fridays, at the *jaï alaï* on avenue Ithurralde, 1km east of the centre; tickets (€8–18 depending on match) are sold through the *billeterie* division of the tourist office, or online at ⓦwww.cestapunta.com.

Accommodation

Opposite the train station, on and around avenue Verdun, are a few inexpensive (for Saint-Jean), if uninspiringly located **hotels** – for example en-suite, well-kept *Hôtel de Paris*, 1 bd du Comandant-Passicot at the corner of avenue Labrouche (ⓣ05.59.85.20.20, ⓦwww.hoteldeparis-stjeandeluz.fr; May–Dec; ❷). Better placed are *Hôtel Ohartzia* (ⓣ05.59.26.00.06, ⓦhww.hotel-ohartzia.com; ❸), just inland from the beach at 28 rue Garat, with rear rooms overlooking the garden where breakfast is served, and front units with balcony; and the *Lafayette* (ⓣ05.59.26.17.74, ⓦwww.hotelpaysbasque.com; ❸) at pedestrianized 18–20 rue de la Republique, bigger than its frontage suggests, the best rooms with balconies. Three-star comfort means either beachfront *Hôtel de la Plage* (ⓣ05.59.51.03.44, ⓦwww.hoteldelaplage.com; ❺–❼; closed mid-Nov to Easter), with its own (paying) car park, wi-fi access and a ground-floor brasserie, or quietly set *Les Goëlands* at 4–6 av d'Etcheverry (ⓣ05.59.26.10.05, ⓦwww

.hotel-lesgoelands.com; ❹; all year) in a hillside district east of the Grande Plage, consisting of two adjacent 2004-renovated Belle Époque villas, with easy parking and a full-service restaurant (April–Oct) in one wing (❼ HB obligatory mid-July to early Sept). Numerous campsites are grouped east of town in Erromardie and Acotz districts, to seaward of the N10 between Saint-Jean and Guéthary.

The Town

Wrecked in a fire set by invading Spanish in 1558, Saint-Jean subsequently developed into an imposing place, its seafaring wealth transmuted into the seventeenth- and eighteenth-century homes of merchants and shipowners. One of these is the so-called **Maison Louis XIV** (guided visits Mon–Sat: June–Sept 10.30am–noon & 2.30–5.30/6.30pm; €5) beside the Hôtel de Ville. It was actually built for the shipowning Lohobiague family in 1635 but served as temporary residence of the Sun King in 1660 when he came to Saint-Jean for his marriage of political convenience to Maria-Teresa, the Infanta of Castile. (Oddly, the couple managed to fall in love, and the widowed king years later remarked that her death was "the only annoyance she ever caused me".) The authentically Basque interior features heavyweight wooden fixtures, some more delicate pieces of furniture and fine examples of tableware and glass. Maria-Teresa lodged in the equally impressive pink Italianate villa known as the **Maison de l'Infante** (June–Sept Tues–Sat 11am–12.30pm & 2.30–6.30pm, Sun & Mon 2.30–6.30pm; €3) overlooking the harbour from the quay of the same name. The corner house on rue Mazarin, nearby, was the Duke of Wellington's HQ during the 1813–14 winter campaign against Maréchal Soult.

The royal couple's extravagant wedding took place in the church of **Saint-Jean-Baptiste** on pedestrianized rue Gambetta. Cardinal Mazarin alone presented the queen with twelve thousand pounds of pearls and diamonds, a gold dinner service and a pair of sumptuous carriages drawn by teams of six horses – all paid for by money made in the service of France. The door through which Louis and Maria-Teresa left the church – on the right of today's entrance – was permanently sealed immediately afterwards. Even without this curiosity, the church deserves a look inside: the largest French Basque church, it has a barn-like nave roofed in wood and lined on three sides with tiers of dark oak galleries reached by wrought-iron staircases. Hanging from the ceiling is an ex-voto model of the Empress Eugénie's paddle-steamer, the *Eagle*, which narrowly escaped running aground near Saint-Jean in 1867.

Eating and drinking

Leading off **place Louis-XIV** – with its cafés, sidewalk artists and free summertime concerts in the bandstand (Tues–Sun 10pm) – rue de la République has several **restaurants**. *Le Kaiku* (supper only) at no. 17 has an excellent reputation for fish and seafood but costs upwards of €40 without drink. Less expensive alternatives on the same lane include cheap and cheerful *La Ruelle* (closed Mon, also Tues low season) at no. 19, with three seafood *menus* (€18–25), though service is "relaxed" and drinks stiffly priced. The next street east, rue Tourasse, offers more possibilities, notably *La Vieille Auberge* at no. 22 (closed Wed, & Tues lunch), offering four *menus*, and *Le Tourasse* at no. 25, another classic for seafood and desserts (*menus* €18–30). Less scenically set but enduringly popular is friendly *Le Buvette des Halles* (lunch only to 3pm, closed Mon off-season), on the corner of the market hall on boulevard Victor-Hugo, serving impeccably fresh tuna, crab and sardines, plus *pipérade*, drink and dessert for around €22 (3 courses), though portions could be more generous. A block or so east at 3 rue Sallagoïty, there's more seafood (plus a comprehensive dessert list) at tiny *Pil-Pil Enea* (closed Sun pm, & Wed; *menu* €25).

Across the river: Ziburu, Zokoa, Urruña

Saint-Jean shares the Nivelle estuary with **ZIBURU** (Ciboure) on its south bank, both *communes* taking maximum advantage of one of the very few sheltered anchorages along the Atlantic coast south of Arcachon. The harbour is closed off by the little fortress of **ZOKOA** (Socoa) village, home to the local sailing/windsurfing club, as well as a scuba school. In summer, a *navette maritime* (€2 one-way) shuttles regularly on a triangular route between the Digue au Chevaux jetty on the Grand Plage, Zokoa and Saint-Jean's port.

By comparison to Saint-Jean, Ziburu is calm, with two beautiful streets opposite the end of the bridge over from Saint-Jean: the waterfront **quai Maurice-Ravel** (a plaque commemorates the composer's birth at no. 12), and the parallel **rue Pocolette** behind. The latter forms an exquisite terrace of wide-fronted, half-timbered, balconied town houses, many built by seventeenth-century traders who did business with the West Indies and the Orient. The octagonal tower peeking above the houses is that of sixteenth-century **Saint-Vincent** church, inside which are particularly good examples of a Pays Basque altarpiece and three-tiered gallery, and yet another dangling model-ship ex-voto.

Ziburu makes a possible base with its two **hotels**: *Bakea* on place Camille Julian, opposite Pont Charles-de-Gaulle (ⓣ05.59.47.34.40, ⓦwww.hotelbakea.com; all year; ④), including a moderately priced seafood **restaurant**, and hillside, cul-de-sac *Agur Deneri* at 14 chemin de Muskoa (ⓣ05.59.47.02.83, ⓦwww.hotel-agur-deneri.com; all year; ⑤), with priciest sea-view units, a garden and private parking.

The area's only formal attraction is the **Château d'Urtubie** (ⓦwww.chateaudurtubie.net; daily March 15–Nov 2, 1hr tours only 10.30am–12.30pm & 2–6.30pm; €6) at **URRUÑA** (Urrugne), 1500m southwest of Ziburu, which has belonged to the same family since its construction as a fortified château in 1341. It was enlarged and gentrified during the sixteenth and eighteenth centuries and provided hospitality for French King Louis XI, as well as for Maréchal Soult and later the Duke of Wellington during the Napoleonic Wars. If you fancy following in their footsteps, it's also a very upmarket hotel (ⓣ05.59.54.31.15, ⓦwww.chateaudurtubie.net; ④–⑦) with dinner preferentially for guests and only by prior arrangement; otherwise just visit and take tea in the salon afterwards for an extra fee.

Inland from Saint-Jean: Azkaine, La Rhune and Sara

Heading southwest from Saint-Jean, perhaps on one of the two or three summer weekday buses (on Le Basque Bondissant) towards Sara from the train station, you reach **AZKAINE** (Ascain) after 7km along the D918. Like so many *labourdan* foothill villages, it's doll's-house cute and thus inevitably a target of the overspill from Saint-Jean in season. There are several moderately affordable **hotels** here, in one of which – *De la Rhune* (ⓣ05.59.54.00.04, ⓔhoteldelarhune@wanadoo.fr; ④) – Pierre Loti stayed while writing *Ramuntcho* (see p.506).

La Rhune

Conical **La Rhune** (Larrun, 900m elevation), straddling the frontier with Spain, is the westernmost skyward thrust of the Pyrenees before they decline into the

Atlantic. *The* landmark of Labourd, in spite of its unsightly multipurpose antennae, it is predictably popular as a vantage point, offering fine vistas way up the Basque coast and east along the Pyrenees. Like nearby Zugarramurdi (see p.477), it was a haunt of witches during medieval times, and the local authorities used to pay a religious hermit to live on top and keep the shady ladies at bay through his sanctity.

To climb La Rhune, you could walk on a marked path from Azkaine in about two and a half hours or stay on the minor D4 road for 4km more until the **Col de Saint-Ignace**, from where you can ride up on the tourist **rack-and-pinion railway** (mid-March to early Nov, minimum two departures daily 9 or 10am & 3pm, extra according to demand and weather conditions; every 35min July/Aug from 8.30am; €12 return; book on ⓣ05.59.54.20.26, ⓦwww.rhune.com). The 4200-metre journey to the top takes just half an hour, but allow two hours round-trip because of the queues – it's a massively popular outing in high season, with long waits and two snack bars near the base station taking advantage of a captive clientele.

Sara and its caves

With or without a bus or your own transport, it's worth going on to **SARA** (Sare), a hilltop village ringed by satellite hamlets in the shadow of La Rhune. This proves to be another perfectly proportioned Basque village graced by a galleried church, a *frontón* with (unusually) five rows of stone seating and tree-shaded streets. Pierre Loti used it, disguised as "Etchezar", for the setting of his 1897 romance *Ramuntcho*. Animal-lovers might avoid the place in autumn, when Sara earns its nickname of *l'enfer des palombes* – "wood-pigeon hell" – as thousands of the creatures are both shot and trapped in nets strung between trees.

You arrive along the **GR10** from the intermediate station below the summit of La Rhune in about an hour and a quarter, or drive 3km from Saint-Ignace in rather less time. Sara's several **hotels** make for a more attractive overnight than Ascain; most central – and poshest – is the three-star *Arraya* on the village square (ⓣ05.59.54.20.46, ⓦwww.arraya.com; April–Oct; ❻), a former hospice on the Santiago pilgrimage route. More affordable are *Pikassaria*, 1.5km south in Lehenbizkai hamlet (ⓣ05.59.54.21.51, ⓕ05.59.54.27.40; ❸, but ❺ HB only summer; closed Jan–March), has a decent restaurant (*menus* €16–28), as does the *Baratxartea* (ⓣ05.59.54.20.48, ⓕ05.59.54.27.40, ⓦwww.hotel-baratxartea.com; closed Dec 15–March 15; ❷), serving big-portioned meals (€16–22). Sara has no *gîte*, but for impecunious GR10-ers there's no-star, non-en-suite *Hôtel de la Poste* opposite the *Arraya* (ⓣ05.59.54.20.06; ❸). The only independent **restaurant** is the popular *Lastiry* next door, offering *nouvelle Basquaise* cuisine under the arcade (*menus* €21–28). The more consistently open of two **campsites** just south of Sara is *La Petite Rhune* (ⓣ05.59.54.23.97; May–Sept), opposite the *Hôtel Pikassaria*.

This lies on the D306 road to the **Grottes de Sare** (ⓦwww.sare.fr; daily sound-and-light programme except Jan: spring & autumn 10am–6pm; July & Aug 10am–7pm; typically winter months 2–5pm; €6), occasionally served by the Saint-Jean-based bus. These were inhabited as long as 47,000 years ago, with a small gallery on site displaying finds from the caves.

The coast to Hendaye

Running parallel, the D912 road and the **Chemin Piétonnier Littoral** footpath follow the cliffs of the remarkably unspoilt "Corniche Basque" 15km southwest from Saint-Jean-de-Luz to Hendaye, the road cutting inland a little only at the Pointe Sainte-Anne. The path transects the Domaine d'Abbadia, a nature reserve around the **Château d'Abbadia** that belonged to the nineteenth-century Dublin-born explorer **Antoine d'Abbadie**, on the headland overlooking Hendaye-Plage (Ⓦwww.academie-sciences.fr/abbadia.htm; Feb–May & Oct to mid-Dec Tues–Sat guided visits only 2–5pm; June to Sept Mon–Fri guided visit 10–11.30am & 2–6pm, without guide 12.30–2pm; Sat–Sun visit without guide 2–6pm; €5.50–6.50). After expeditions in Ethiopia and Egypt, d'Abbadie had the château built between 1860 and 1870; the architect was Eugène Viollet-le-Duc, and the result is a bizarrre Hibernian-Gothic folly with Arabian boudoirs, Ethiopian frescoes and inscriptions over the doors and lintels inside in Irish, Basque, Arabic and Ethiopic. It is also filled with objects collected by d'Abbadie on his travels; he became president of the Académie des Sciences in 1891, to which he donated the château on his death in 1897.

Hendaye

Arrival in **HENDAYE** (Hendaïa) may prove anticlimactic; neither **Hendaye-Ville** nor the coastal annexe of **Hendaye-Plage** have much intrinsic interest despite a significant past. This includes the lengthy residence (and death in 1923) of **Pierre Loti**, author of locally set *Ramuntcho* as well as assorted orientalist romances. Loti was popular in his time for syrupy, exotic novels, their settings – including Istanbul and Tahiti – gleaned from a lifetime of far-flung postings in the service of the French navy. You can see his house (no visits) in rue des Pêcheurs, on the waterfront below boulevard de Gaulle.

The **beach** at Hendaye-Plage (with surf schools) lies just west of the promontory, and is popular with Spaniards especially, who reckon it better than anything on their side until San Sebastián. The N10 inland road and rail line continue a couple more kilometres to dull Hendaye-Ville, set where the Bidassoa widens into the Txingudy estuary. Hendaye-Plage, like Saint-Jean-de-Luz, is palpably a family resort, but unlike Saint-Jean is also a major yachting centre – and essentially a ghost town from October to Easter.

Hendaye-Ville, on the Bordeaux–Irún and Toulouse–Irún rail lines, lies on the estuary of the River Bidassoa (Bidasoa), with the border running down the middle for about 8km at this point. Just upstream from town, the tiny wooded island known as **Île des Faisans,** or Île de la Conférence, is administered jointly by the two countries. It looks insignificant now, but was once used for meetings between their respective monarchs. François I, taken prisoner at the battle of Pavia in 1525, was ransomed here; in 1659 it was the scene of the signature of the **Treaty of the Pyrenees**. The following year the marriage contracts between Louis XIV and the Spanish Infanta Maria-Teresa were signed here; the great painter Velázquez reputedly died of a chill caught while painting the interior of the negotiations room.

Hendaye made history once more, on October 23, 1940, when Spanish General Franco met Hitler in the Hendaye train station. The version promulgated by Franco and his publicists, long believed even by his opponents, has it that "El Caudillo" preserved Spanish neutrality by parrying the Führer's threats to annexe Spain; in fact, Franco, dazzled by Hitler's early victories and the prospect of a greatly enlarged Spanish Morocco at the expense of France, begged to be allowed to fight alongside Germany. But Hitler – mindful of how much assistance the Nationalists had needed to win the Civil War, and aware of Spain's dire economic state – considered the proposed alliance a liability and was having none of it.

Everyone agrees that Hitler was later overheard saying to Mussolini that he would rather have three teeth pulled than meet his potential ally again.

Practicalities

Hendaye's **tourist office** is at 12 rue des Aubépines in Hendaye-Plage (July & Aug Mon–Sat 9am–7.30pm, Sun 10am–1pm; rest of year Mon–Fri 9am–noon & 2–6pm, Sat 9am–noon; ⓣ05.59.20.00.34, ⓦwww.hendaye.com). As for **parking**, only the beachfront is metered; most other places it's uncontrolled. Hendaye-Ville **hotels** are generally pretty grim, with proximity to the train station their only selling point; the most cheerful is *La Palombe Bleue* at 38 rue du Commerce (ⓣ05.59.20.43.80; March–Dec; ❷). Almost everyone stays down in Hendaye-Plage, where affordable, well-set choices include *La Fon* at 99 bd de la Mer (ⓣ05.59.20.04.67; April–Oct; ❹), a rambling, old-fashioned beachfront place with restaurant; *Uhainak* at no. 3 (ⓣ05.59.20.33.63, ⓦwww.hotel-uhainak.com; Feb–Nov; ❹), again with some rooms overlooking the beach; and the friendly *Bergeret-Sport* inland at 4 rue des Clématites (ⓣ05.59.20.00.78, ⓦwww.hotel-bergeret-sport.com; June–Sept except by arrangement; ❸, ❻ HB obligatory July–Aug), with a well-regarded restaurant. Ten local campsites are all found east of Hendaye-Plage, just off the Route de la Corniche; one of the more tent-friendly, and closest to the beach, is *Alturan* (ⓣ05.59.20.04.55; June–Sept), on rue de la Côte.

Independent **restaurants** are overwhelmingly fishy, if not numerous; cheap (because unromantically set by a car park) and popular is *La Petite Marée* at 2 av des Mimosas, while *Battela* around the corner at 5 rue d'Irun, rond-point du Palmier (*menus* from €17), is more creative. For a sea view, head west a few blocks to the yacht and fishing port, where *La Cabane du Pêcheur* (closed Sun eve and Mon, Oct 15–May 31) on quai de la Floride does full seafood meals (*menus* €15–24). Just around the corner, *Le Parc à Huîtres* (closed Tues, also Mon eve low season) at 4 rue des Orangers is a superb oyster bar-cum-takeaway-deli with seating outdoors and in; make a meal of it with salad, assorted *tapas*, desserts and oyster-compatible wines in every conceivable measure.

Walking from Hendaye

The **GR10** and **HRP** both start their trans-Pyrenean course beside the former casino at Hendaye-Plage. The first, two-hour stage to Biriatu is dull and gives no sense of the glories that lie ahead: along avenue Général-Leclerc to Hendaye-Ville, under the rail line via a pedestrian tunnel, across the N10 and finally to the A63 highway. A cattle track passes underneath this and continues to the tiny hilltop village of **BIRIATU** (Biriatou), 7km away, where the walking starts to get interesting, and where many hikers start after a taxi-ride there.

A short, steep section leads to a Basque church with a collection of weather-worn tombstones, next door to the fifteenth-century *Auberge Hirribarren*, a temporary haven for many Allied soldiers during World War II and now an excellent **restaurant**, with meals at €15–26 a head (until 9pm; closed Jan, & Mon low season). It's also possible to overnight near the village, as there are two isolated **hotels**: *Bakea* (ⓣ05.59.20.76.36, ⓦwww.bakea.fr; ❷; closed Jan 20–Feb 15), spread over two premises, with another excellent restaurant (closed Mon–Tues Oct–March, Mon & Tues lunch April–Sept), and *Larretcheko Borda* (ⓣ05.59.20.20.32; all year; ❷), out at the Col de Courlecou. Beyond Biriatu the main footpaths and a number of local variations rise rapidly to semi-isolation, with only the buzzing power lines (soon left behind) and the occasional walker or local jogger to disturb the peace. From Biriatu to the *gîte d'étape* at Olhette (see p.491) it's nearly five hours' trek, and from there to Sara via the base of La Rhune, another 2hr 45min.

Eastern Gipuzkoa

The Spanish Basque coastal province of **Gipuzkoa** abuts the French frontier, and its border town, **Irún**, is one of the major road and rail entry points into Spain. The tiny village of Behobia (Béhobie) – an unsightly collection of truck stops, bottle shops and pumps for cheap petrol – straddles the frontier. There are fast public transport connections to San Sebastián, although if you're travelling in a more leisurely fashion, the fishing ports of **Hondarribia** and **Pasaia** merit a stop. Foot passengers coming from France can bypass Irún altogether by using the *navette*-launch plying between Hendaye-Plage's yacht port and Hondarribia.

Irún

Like most border towns, sprawling, graceless and largely modern **IRÚN**'s chief concern is how to make a quick buck from passing travellers. The main point in its favour is the ease with which you can leave; there are trains to Hendaye in France and to San Sebastián throughout the day, with regular long-distance and international connections. If you're arriving by main-line train at Hendaye, the quickest way across the border involves taking the *Eusko Tren* from the separate platform on the right outside Hendaye's main station; it runs every thirty minutes to Irún station, at Avda de Colón 52, then on to San Sebastián.

In the vicinity of Irún's main train station are several small, reasonably priced **hostales** and **restaurants**, as well as bars, with prices markedly lower than in France, Hondarribia or San Sebastián. There's little to distinguish *Pensión Bidasoa*, Estación 14 (Ⓣ943 619 913; ❷) and *Pensión los Fronterizos*, Estación 7 (Ⓣ943 619 205; ❷); both have reasonably equipped en-suite rooms, but somewhat deficient sound insulation. For a modest outlay, the *Asador Baserri* at Berrotarán 5 (closed Sun evening and Mon), serves Basque, farm-style meat dishes (allow €17).

Hondarribia

The fishing port and fortified stronghold of **HONDARRIBIA**, 6km north of Irún and looking over the Río Bidasoa to Hendaye, is a far more attractive prospect, though the commercial waterfront district of **La Marina** is blandly modern, enlivened with just a few cafés. The town's real appeal lies in main streets running parallel to the front, and the cobbled back streets further inland, where traditional, wood-beamed Basque houses are interspersed with bars offering some of the best seafood and *pintxos* around. During summer, **Playa Hondartza** immediately north of the town is an alternative to the ultra-crowded beaches in San Sebastián.

Hondarribia's picturesque, walled **old town** is traditionally entered via the fifteenth-century **Puerta de Santa María**, carved with the town coat-of-arms and angels paying homage to Our Lady of Guadalupe, who purportedly saved the town during a two-month French siege in 1638. Nagusia Kalea, leading up from the gate to Arma Plaza, has fine examples of wood-beamed houses adorned with wrought-iron balconies and studded doors, some displaying the family coats-of-arms above the entrance. At the end of Nagusia Kalea stands the originally Gothic church of **Santa María**, extensively (and misguidedly) renovated in the seventeenth century. A proxy wedding between Louis XIV and Maria-Teresa took place here in 1660, six days before the official pre-nuptial contract ceremony on the Île des Faisans. The *plaza* itself is dominated by the **Palacio de Carlos Quinto** (now the *parador*), started originally in the tenth century by Sancho el Fuerte of Navarra and subsequently extended by Carlos V in the sixteenth. Slightly uphill and southwest, the smaller, arcaded **Plaza Gipuzkoa** with more wrought-iron railings is also worth seeking out.

Practicalities

The helpful **Turismo** is on Javier Ugarte 6, at the base of the northerly road up the old town (July & Aug Mon–Sat 10am–8pm, Sun 10am–2pm; Sept–June Mon 9.30am–2pm, Tues–Fri 9.30am–2pm & 4–7pm, Sat 10am–2pm; ⓣ943 645 458). There's no train service; buses for San Sebastián leave frequently from stops on Zuloaga Kalea.

There's a fair amount of characterful, if rather pricey, **accommodation** in Hondarribia. On the budget side, try en-suite if somewhat bland *Hotel San Nikolas* on Arma Plaza (ⓣ943 644 278; ④) or the *Txoko-Goxoa* on Marrua Kalea 22 near the Puerta de Santa María (ⓣ943 644 658, ⓦwww.txokogoxoa.com; ④). Pick of the plusher establishments is two-star *Hotel Obispo*, offering modern rooms with balconies in an old stone manor on Plaza del Obispo, birthplace of Ricardo de Sandoval, later bishop of Seville and chaplain to Carlos V (ⓣ943 645 400, ⓕ943 642 386; ⑥), or the *Parador El Emperador Carlos V*, in the fortified *palacio* at Arma Plaza 14 (ⓣ943 645 500, ⓔhondarribia@parador.es; sometimes closed Nov–Feb; ⑦).

△ Plaza Gipuzkoa, Hondarribia

If you have your own transport, some excellent **casas rurales** just outside town offer better value, though they're all very popular and need to be reserved well in advance. The closest, uphill from the airport in Barrio Arkoll-Santiago, is *Iketxe* (T & F 943 644 391; 3), meticulously built in 1988 in traditional style, offering a variety of huge, wood-ceilinged, tile-floored rooms with balconies and good views. Alternatively, 3km from town in Jaizubia hamlet, friendly *Arotz-Enea* (T & F 943 642 319; 3), in a half-timbered medieval farmhouse at the end of a lane, offers particularly good breakfasts. Another is found 5km away on the Jaizkibel uplands, accessed from the roundabout outside the old town walls: *Artzu* (T 943 640 530, W www.euskalnet.net/casartzu/; 2), a converted farmhouse near the top of a sea-cliff at the end of the road, with four baths for six rooms, all with double beds.

A dozen or so **restaurants** and **bars** along parallel Zuloaga, Santiago and San Pedro *kaleak*, three to four short blocks in from the water, are the best hunting ground for **food** and **drink**. For something special, try the *Hermandad de Pescadores* (Confraternity of Fishermen) at Zuloaga Kalea 12 (reservations on T 943 642 738; closed Sun pm & Mon), once strictly the fishermen's clubhouse but now open to all. Every July 25, preceded by a brass band and dressed in holiday finest, the confraternity parades into the place, oars aloft, for a ceremonial meal. Inside, you eat amidst nautical decor at suitably institutional long tables. The cooking's deceptively simple, in ample portions; rapid turnover guarantees freshness, but that said the *menú* is rather dull, so you'll do better choosing from the *a la carta* menu (allow €30). In the upper town, tucked away in a narrow, cobbled alley two streets behind c/Mayor, the *Mamutzar* (closed Tues) serves a good-value €10 *menú*, as does the *Danontzat* at Denda Kalea 6 (*menú* €15, *a la carta* €30).

Mount Jaizkibel

The stretch of coastline from here as far as the port of Pasaia is particularly rugged and has long been a haven for smugglers; it's the sea-washed flank of the sandstone **Jaizkibel** massif, whose vast uplands, a mix of pasture and parkland, are criss-crossed by trails and tracks beloved of joggers, ramblers and other solitude-seeking locals. With your own transport, foresake the busy highway inland in favour of the initially winding minor road G13440, which starts at the roundabout just west of Hondarribia's old town, towards the chapel of **Nuestra Señora de Guadalupe** (5km), venue for a September 8 festival. The road continues climbing more gradually through pine forests to a pass (9km; 455m) just below the 545-metre peak, with wonderful views along the Basque coastline – if the mist hasn't descended to the two-hundred-metre contour, an all-too-common occurrence. You then descend to Pasai Donibane, a total of 18km.

Pasaia

The other place you might consider stopping en route between Hondarribia and San Sebastián is the port of **PASAIA**, the collective name for three separate settlements built around the sheltered mouth of the Río Oiartzun. Pasai Antxo and Pasai Senpere on the south bank, which once started life as whaling ports, are now modern, industrial ports, where cranes steadily pick through heaps of scrap metal. Considered the least problematic anchorage on a stretch of coast known for its difficult swells, it was from here that the French general Marquis de Lafayette sailed to America to fight for the colonists in the War of Independence.

Well-preserved **PASAI DONIBANE** on the north bank, however, retains its charm, especially since vehicles must be left at a car park on the outskirts. From the patron saint's church, a restrained Baroque edifice of the seventeenth century, narrow cobbled Donibane Kalea (Victor Hugo lived briefly in 1843 at no. 65) leads past Plaza de Santiago with its colourful houses, ending almost a kilometre later at the river channel. En route you pass Ontziola, a traditional **boat-building workshop** and educational exhibit (Easter–Sept Tues–Sun 11am–2pm & 4–7pm; Oct–Easter Mon–Sat 10am–2pm & 3–5pm). The village is famous for its waterside **fish restaurants**, slightly less expensive than those in San Sebastían's old quarter. Three to try are *Casa Camara*, Donibane 79, for shellfish (closed Sun pm & Mon low season; *a la carta* €35); *Ziaboga* at no. 91, with more of an emphasis on fish (from €30 *a la carta*); and cheapest of all, *Txulotxo* (lunch *menú* €18, *carta* €24). A **launch** (*txalupa*) runs throughout the day and evening (until at least 11pm; €0.50) across the harbour to Pasai Senpere, from where frequent buses depart to San Sebastián.

San Sebastián (Donostia)

Capital of Gipuzkoa autonomous region, and the undisputed queen of the Basque resorts, **SAN SEBASTIÁN** (increasingly known as **DONOSTIA**) is a picturesque – and expensive – seaside town with good beaches. Since the nineteenth century it's been among Spain's most fashionable places to escape the heat of the southern summers, and in July and August it's packed. Set around the deep, still bay of La Concha and enclosed by rolling low hills, San Sebastián is beautifully situated. The old quarter sits on a promontory between the bay and the Río Urumea which divides the town, its back to the wooded slopes of Monte Urgull; newer development has spread along the banks of the Urumea with its fine Belle Époque architecture, around the edge of the bay to the foot of Monte Igeldo and onto the hills overlooking the bay.

Arrival and information

Most **buses** arrive at Plaza Pío XII, fifteen minutes' walk along the river from the Centro district (the ticket office is around the corner facing the river). To get to the **Parte Vieja** (Old Quarter), further north, take bus #28 to Alameda del Boulevard. Buses from Pasai Sanpere arrive on Okendo Kalea, just below the Parte Vieja, and from the airport, Irún and Hondarribia on nearby Plaza de Gipuzkoa. RENFE's main-line **Estación del Norte** lies across the Río Urumea on Paseo de Francia, although the local *Eusko Tren* from Hendaye, or Bilbao via Zarautz and Zumaia (rail passes not valid), has its terminus in Centro at **Estación de Amara**. The small **airport** (domestic flights from Madrid only) is 22km from the city centre, just outside Hondarribia; an airport bus plies back and forth as necessary (€3).

San Sebastián's helpful **Turismo** is at c/Reina Regente 3 (June–Sept Mon–Sat 8am–8pm, Sun 10am–2pm; Oct–May Mon–Sat 9am–1.30pm & 3.30–7pm, Sun 10am–2pm; Ⓣ943 481 166, Ⓦwww.sansebastianturismo.com), and produces *Donostiaisia*, a very useful free monthly what's-on guide.

Accommodation

Places to **stay**, though plentiful, are pricey and hard to come by in peak seasons – especially during July, August and the September film festival. There's scant difference in rates between the cheapest places in the **Parte Vieja** and elsewhere, although there is more chance of finding space in **Centro** district or across the river

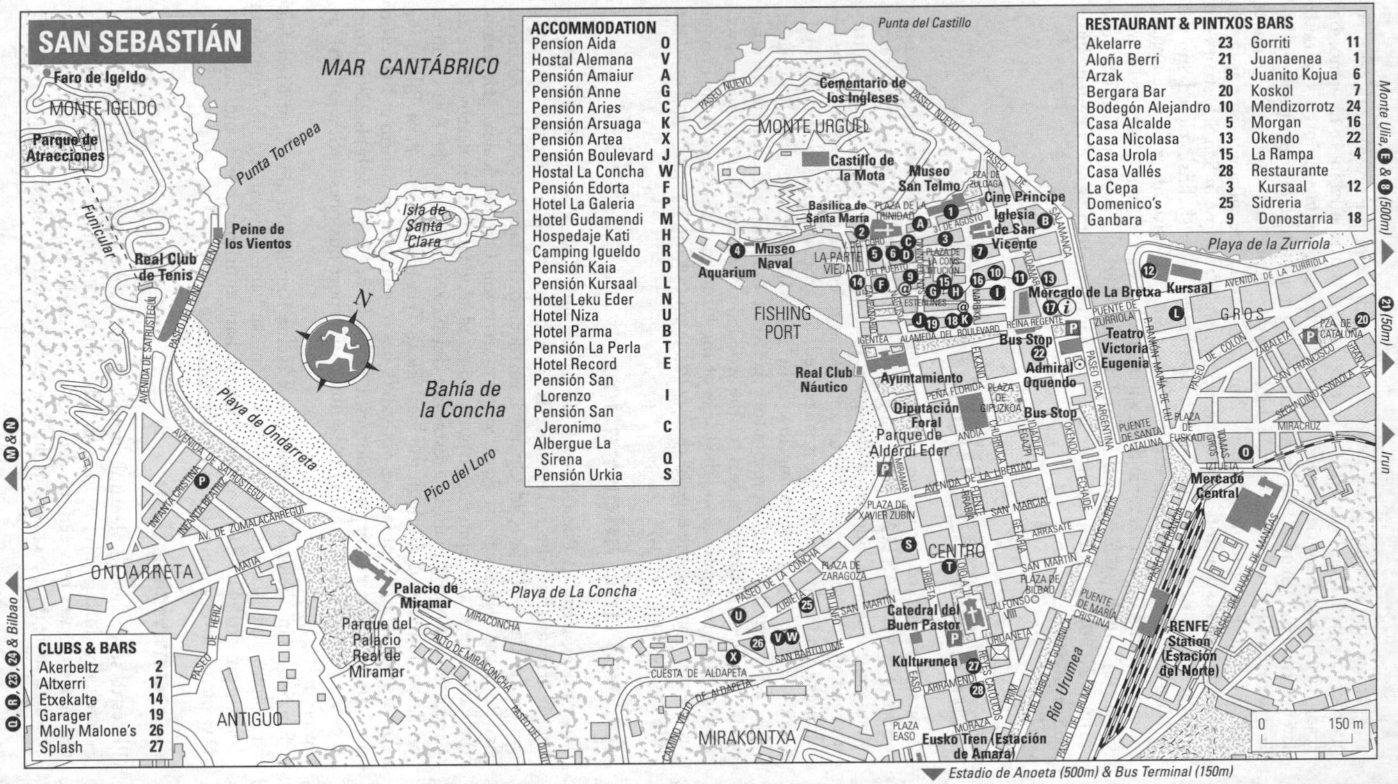

SAN SEBASTIÁN
ACCOMMODATION
Pensíon Aida O
Hostal Alemana V
Pensión Amaiur A
Pensión Anne G
Pensión Aries C
Pensión Arsuaga K
Pensión Artea X
Pensión Boulevard J
Hostal La Concha W
Pensión Edorta F
Hotel La Galeria P
Hotel Gudamendi M
Hospedaje Kati H
Camping Igueldo R
Pensión Kaia D
Pensión Kursaal L
Hotel Leku Eder N
Hotel Niza U
Hotel Parma B
Pensión La Perla T
Hotel Record E
Pensión San Lorenzo I
Pensión San Jeronimo C
Albergue La Sirena Q
Pensión Urkia S
RESTAURANT & PINTXOS BARS
Akelarre 23
Aloña Berri 21
Arzak 8
Bergara Bar 20
Bodegón Alejandro 10
Casa Alcalde 5
Casa Nicolasa 13
Casa Urola 15
Casa Vallés 28
La Cepa 3
Domenico's 25
Ganbara 9
Gorriti 11
Juanaenea 1
Juanito Kojua 6
Koskol 7
Mendizorrotz 24
Morgan 16
Okendo 22
La Rampa 4
Restaurante Kursaal 12
Sidreria Donostarria 18
CLUBS & BARS
Akerbeltz 2
Altxerri 17
Etxekalte 14
Garager 19
Molly Malone's 26
Splash 27
MAR CANTÁBRICO
Bahía de la Concha
Isla de Santa Clara
Punta del Castillo
Punta Torrepea
Pico del Loro
Playa de Ondarreta
Playa de La Concha
Playa de la Zurriola
Río Urumea
Faro de Igeldo
MONTE IGELDO
Parque de Atracciones
Funicular
Peine de los Vientos
Real Club de Tenis
MONTE URGULL
Cementario de los Ingleses
Castillo de la Mota
Museo San Telmo
Basílica de Santa María
Cine Principe
Iglesia de San Vicente
Museo Naval
Aquarium
LA PARTE VIEJA
FISHING PORT
Real Club Náutico
Mercado de La Bretxa
Kursaal
GROS
Teatro Victoria Eugenia
Bus Stop
Admiral Oquendo
Ayuntamiento
Diputación Foral
Parque de Alderdi Eder
CENTRO
Catedral del Buen Pastor
Kulturunea
Mercado Central
RENFE Station (Estación del Norte)
Eusko Tren (Estación de Amara)
Palacio de Miramar
Parque del Palacio Real de Miramar
ONDARRETA
ANTIGUO
MIRAKONTXA
0 150 m
Monte Ulia, E & 8 (500m)
21 (50m)
Irun
Estadio de Anoeta (500m) & Bus Terminal (150m)
O, R, 23, 24 & Bilbao
M & N

in **Gros**. If you're driving and have a bit of cash to spare, you might well consider basing yourself on **Monte Igeldo** west of the beaches, and taking a bus into town rather than pit yourself against its nightmarish parking situation.

Parte Vieja

Pensión Amaiur 31 de Agosto 44, 2° ⓣ943 429 654, ⓦwww.pensionamaiur.com. A justly popular *pensión* in one of the few houses to survive the 1813 fire, with eleven attractive rooms sharing five immaculate tiled bathrooms. Guests have access to Internet and two kitchens with microwave, fridge and free coffee. ③

Pensión Anne Esterlines 15, 2° ⓣ943 421 438, ⓦwww.pensionanne.com. Recently renovated *pensión* with friendly, English-speaking staff. Again, a ratio of two rooms per bathroom. ④

Pensión Aries San Jerónimo 22, 2° ⓣ943 426 855, ⓦwww.infobide.com/pensionaries. Decor in the rooms, many with double beds, is a tad dated but the bathrooms are contemporary and units – some with tiny balconies – all look to the street. ④

Pensión Arsuaga Narrika 3, 3° ⓣ943 420 681. Very friendly *pensión* with simple, spacious doubles with wooden floors and antique feel. There are two shared, nicely tiled bathrooms. Full-board deals are offered at its own restaurant. ③

Pensión Boulevard Alameda del Boulevard 24 1° ⓣ943 429 405, ⓦwww.pensionboulevard.com. Just four comfortable, modernized rooms in an older building, all en suite. ④

Pensión Edorta Puerto 15, 1–2° ⓣ943 423 773, ⓦwww.pensionedorta.com. Attractive, upscale *pensión* in a lovely old mansion, with pointed stone walls, mock-antique furnishings, wooden beams and tiled en-suites – cheaper rooms with shared bathrooms are available. ④

Pensión Kaia Puerto 12, 2° ⓣ943 431 342, ⓦwww.pensionkaia.com. A comfortable two-star *pensión*, with pleasant, brightly painted but smallish modern rooms with bath and TV. Single rates are very good value. ④

Hotel Parma General Jauregi Gudalburuaren 11 ⓣ943 428 893, ⓦwww.hotelparma.com. Nicely located between the Parte Vieja and Paseo Nuevo, this rather characterless modern building offers comfortable rooms with all amenities, the best ones overlooking the sea. ⑥

Pensión San Jerónimo San Jerónimo 25, 2° ⓣ943 420 830, ⓦwww.sanjeronimo.com. Wood-floored, en-suite rooms, some with small balconies, in subdued tones. ④

Pensión San Lorenzo San Lorenzo 2, 1° ⓣ943 425 516, ⓦwww.infonegocio.com/pensionsanlorenzo. Clean, modern *pensión* with just five rooms, bare wood floors, private bathrooms, Internet access and a self-catering kitchen; understandably popular, with phone bookings (9am–1pm) given preference to on-line ones. ③

Centro

Hostal Alemana San Martín 53, 1° ⓣ943 462 544, ⓦwww.hostalalemana.com. Unimprovably located just behind La Concha, this fine Belle Époque two-star offers surprisingly bland if large en-suite rooms with all mod cons, including wi-fi access. Off-street parking charged extra; a bit overpriced at high season rates. ⑤

Pensión Artea San Bartolomé 33 1° ⓣ943 455 100, ⓦwww.pensionartea.com. Somewhat bland but serviceable modern en-suite rooms with wood floors and double glazing. ④

Hostal La Concha San Martín 51 ⓣ943 450 389, ⓦwww.pensionlaconcha.net. Bright if rather characterless en-suite rooms in two grades with TV, work table and Internet access – you're paying for the location, a few steps from La Concha. ⑤ standard, ⑥ suite

Hotel Niza Zubieta 56 ⓣ943 426 663, ⓦwww.hotelniza.com. A stylish modern hotel, right on the beach, in a 1920s building owned by the Chillida family. Rooms – about half with sea view – are simply decorated in modern style, with bare wood floors, bright pastel colours, wi-fi access and TV. In-house Italian restaurant. ⑦

Pensión La Perla Inazio Loiola 10 ⓣ943 428 123, ⓦwww.pensionlaperla.com. An excellent-value *pensión*, near the Buen Pastor cathedral and food market, offering spotless if simply decorated en-suite rooms with TV and, in some cases balconies. ③

Pensión Urkia Urbieta 12, 3° ⓣ943 424 436, ⓦwww.infobidecomunicacion.com/pensionurkia. Run by the sister of the owner of *La Perla*, this *pensión* has six similarly appointed en-suite rooms (including one single). When full, there's another relative in waiting at *Casa Elisa* ⓣ943 453 950. ③

Gros

Pensión Aida Iztueta 9, 1°, Gros ⓣ943 327 800, ⓦwww.pensionesconencanto.com. Friendly, 2001-inaugurated *pensión* in a restored older building with cheerful, pastel decor and en-suite rooms; wi-fi access. ④

Pension Kursaal Peña y Goñi 2, 1°, Gros ⓣ943 292 666, ⓦwww.pensionesconencanto.com. Co-managed with the *Aida*, this enjoys a superb location just a few steps from Zurriola and the Kursaal itself. Large modern rooms and bathrooms, reasonable room-service breakfast and wi-fi Internet access. ❹

Hotel Record Calzada Vieja 35, Gros ⓣ943 271 255, ⓦwww.hotelrecord.com. Inland at the east end of this district and a pleasant alternative to the central bustle; well connected by bus, or fifteen-minutes' walk from the centre, with plenty of free parking. All rooms in this converted 1950s villa are en-suite; the larger ones have terraces, plus there are some sky-lit attic units and one family suite. ❹

Ondarreta & Monte Igeldo

Albergue La Sirena Paseo de Igeldo 25 ⓣ943 310 268. San Sebastián's popular youth hostel is just a few minutes' walk from the end of Ondarreta beach (take bus #5 or #16), and offers en-suite six-bunk rooms. Open all year, with a 2am curfew and 11pm "quiet" rule.

Camping Igueldo Paseo Padre Orkolaga 69, Barrio de Igeldo ⓣ943 214 502, ⓦwww.campingigueldo.com. San Sebastián's pricey campsite is excellent but it's 5km from the centre on the landward side of Monte Igeldo (up a steep hill), reached by bus #16 from the Alameda del Boulevard (every 30min). Open all year.

Hotel La Galeria c/Infanta Cristina 1–3 ⓣ943 317 559, ⓦwww.hotellagaleria.com. Appealing hotel behind Ondarreta beach in a beautifully restored Belle Époque house. Rooms are simply but stylishly decorated, each with a different theme based on a painter such as Picasso, Dali or Miró. Free parking and wi-fi. ❻

Hotel Gudamendi Paseo de Gudamendi, Monte Igeldo ⓣ943 214 000, ⓦwww.hotelgudamendi.com. In a peaceful, park-like cul-de-sac near the top of the mountain, this rambling converted hunting lodge scores for its pleasant pool and common areas, and is popular with the conference and wedding trade. Rooms were completely rebuilt in 2004, emerging with marble-clad baths, carpets and a pastel colour scheme. ❼

Hotel Leku Eder Balenziaga 2, Barrio de Igeldo ⓣ943 210 107, ⓦwww.lekueder.com. Smallish, modern outfit with anodyne decor, but many rooms have great views towards the lighthouse. Pluses include free parking and free wi-fi access. Closed Dec 18–March 9. ❹

The Town

The **Parte Vieja** at the base of Monte Urgull is the town's highlight – cramped and lively streets where crowds congregate in the evenings to wander among numerous bars and shops or sample the shellfish from the street traders down by the fishing port. Much of it was destroyed by a fire in 1813 (set by British troops) but subsequently restored so expertly that you'd never suspect their comparative modernity. The quarter's medieval wall was swept away to allow expansion later the same century; the Alameda del Boulevard marks its former course.

Chief local sights include the elaborate Baroque facade of the eighteenth-century church of **Santa María** (Mon–Sat 8am–2pm & 4–8pm) and the more elegantly restrained sixteenth-century Gothic church of **San Vicente** (or Bizente, somewhat confusingly on Plaza de la Trinidad; Mon–Sat 8.30am–1pm & 6.30–8.30pm). The centre of the old quarter is **La Plaza de la Constitución** (known by the locals simply as *La Consti*) – the numbers on the balconies around the square date from the days when it was used as a bullring. Situated just off Treinta y Uno de Agosto (the only street to survive the great fire of August 31, 1813), behind San Vicente, is the excellent **Museo de San Telmo** (July & Aug Tues–Sat 10.30am–8.30pm, Sun 10.30am–2pm; rest of year Tues–Sat 10.30am–1.30pm & 4–7.30pm, Sun 10.30am–2pm; free). Its displays – around the cloisters of a former convent – include a fine Basque ethnographic exhibition and the largest collection of keyhole-shaped funerary steles in the País Vasco. The convent chapel is decorated with a series of frescoes depicting scenes from Basque life by José Sert.

A stairway off the plaza flanking the museum rises to **Monte Urgull** (daily: May–Sept 8am–9pm; Oct–April 8am–7pm), crisscrossed by winding paths. From the mammoth figure of Christ and and **Castillo de la Mota** (summer 8am–8pm; winter 8am–6pm) on top, there are great views out to sea and back across the bay to the town. On the way down you can stop at the **Cementerio de los Ingleses**, an overgrown but atmospheric patch of ground dedicated to British soldiers killed in the First Carlist War, or the **Aquarium** on the harbour (April–June & Sept Mon–Fri 10am–8pm, Sat & Sun 10am–9pm; July & Aug daily 10am–9pm; Oct–March Mon–Fri 10am–7pm, Sat & Sun 10am–8pm; €10; Ⓦwww.aquariumss.com); it contains the skeleton of a whale caught in the nineteenth century and an extensive history of Basque navigation. Although there aren't many fish, you can walk through the middle of a giant aquarium in a Perspex tube. Close by, at Paseo de Muelle 24, is the **Museo Naval** (Tues–Sat 10am–1.30pm & 4–7.30pm, Sun 11am–2pm; €1.20), with Castillian-only video facilities and exhibits tracing the tradition and history of Basque fishing.

Although its summit is smothered by a tacky amusement park, **Monte Igeldo** around the bay affords still better views: take the #16 bus marked *Igeldo* or walk around the bay to the Real Club de Tenis, from where a 1912-vintage **funicular** (daily: summer 10am–8pm; winter 11am–7pm; every 15min; €1.10) will carry you to the summit. Continuing along the *paseo* past the tennis club you end up at Eduardo Chillida's striking iron **sculpture**, *El Peine de los Vientos* (The Comb of the Winds), looking as if it is trying to grasp the waves in its powerful rusting arms.

The beaches

There are **four beaches** in San Sebastián: Playa de la Concha, Playa de Ondarreta, Playa de la Zurriola and Playa de Gros. **La Concha** is the most central and the most celebrated, a wide crescent of yellow sand extending west from Centro. Despite the almost impenetrable mass of flesh here during much of the summer, this is the best (if most regimented) of the beaches, enlivened by sellers of peeled prawns and cold drinks, and with great swimming out to the diving platforms moored in the bay. Further out sits the small **Isla de Santa Clara**, which makes a good spot for picnics; a boat leaves from the port every half-hour in the summer (daily 10am–8pm; €1.50 round-trip).

La Concha and **Ondarreta** are the best beaches for swimming – the latter is a continuation of the same strand beyond the rocky outcrop which supports the **Palacio de Miramar** (daily 8am–9pm; free), once a summer home of Spain's royal family. You can walk around the pleasant gardens, but the house itself is off limits. Set back from Ondarreta beach are large villas, some of the most expensive properties in Spain, mostly owned by wealthy families from Madrid who holiday here.

Far less crowded, and popular with surfers, are **Playa de la Zurriola** and the adjacent **Playa de Gros**; Pukas at Avda de la Zurriola 24 (Ⓦwww.pukassurf.com) rents boards and offers lessons. A recent addition to the elegant promenade is the giant glass blocks of Rafael Moneo's **Kursaal** (Ⓦwww.kursaal.org; guided tours Fri–Sun 1.30pm; tickets on sale at noon; €2). Besides an auditorium and art gallery, the building houses a pleasant café-restaurant with an outside terrace in summer. One of the best views of the whole town may be had by climbing the steps to the *sidrería* on the side of **Monte Ulia** from the far end of the beach. This walk can easily be extended for about 5km along the coast to the lighthouse overlooking the entrance to Pasaia harbour.

Eating and drinking

San Sebastián has some of the best **restaurants** in Spain, with the highest concentration of Michelin-starred establishments in Europe. There are also plenty of lively **bars**, mostly in the Parte Vieja, but a few in Centro and a growing number in Gros, which is notable for cutting-edge, imaginative *pintxos* (two mouthfuls for €1.30–2.50). Locals head out between 8–10pm on a **txikiteo**, or bar crawl, spending perhaps ten minutes at each place, washing down their signature dish with a *txikito* (small glass) of *txakoli* (a fizzy, dry white Basque wine) or a *zurito* (narrow glass) of beer.

Full meal prices tend to reflect the popularity of the old quarter, but lunchtime *menús* are generally good value. Unless stated otherwise, listed restaurants open between 1 and 4pm, and 8 till 11pm, and close Sunday night and all of Monday, while bars stay open all afternoon. For those on a budget, there are a few worthy Italian and Asian eateries, while the **Mercado de la Bretxa**, a former *pescadería* done up as a mall, houses some affordable snack bars.

Restaurants

Akelarre P° Padre Orkolaga 56 ⓣ943 311 209, ⓦwww.akelarre.net. Located on the far side of Monte Igeldo, *Akelarre* is home of two-Michelin-starred chef Pedro Subijana and a current trend-setter for *nueva cocina vasca*. Enjoy magnificent views, a real fireplace and exquisite seven-course menus strong on seafood and meat – the *foie gras* is especially renowned, and watch out for creations such as roasted mango ice cream. Reckon on €110–130 a head, plus drink, and a taxi if needed (ample parking).

Arzak Alto de Miracruz 21, Monte Ulia ⓣ943 285 593, ⓦwww.arzak.es. A shrine of *nouvelle* Basque cuisine, named after three-Michelin-star winning chef Juan Mari Arzak and his daughter Elena, who with a twenty-strong army of secret recipe-testers evolve a creative menu of up to seventeen monthly changing courses. Seating in an antique dining room with first-class service – expect to pay around €130 per head, plus drink, and a taxi for €6–8. Closed Tues low season, late June & most Nov.

Bodegón Alejandro c/Fermín Calbetón 4. An excellent restaurant from the stable of Michelin-celebrated Basque chef Martin Berasategui, with two pale-yellow dining rooms and an exceptional "tasting" *menú* (€33) which changes every other day, featuring Basque classics such as peppers stuffed with cod, and roast veal.

Domenico's Zubieta 3, Centro ⓣ943 471 537. Smart but affordable Italian restaurant with an emphasis on pasta; budget for €19–26 or choose the weekday *menú*. Very popular, so reservations essential.

Juanito Kojua Puerto 14 ⓣ943 420 180. An exceptional seafood restaurant, off Plaza de la Constitución, with two basic dining areas with wooden beams and traditional decor, behind the bar. Sublime fresh fish from €15, or €25.50 dinner *menú*.

Koskol Iñigo 5. An unpretentious place with a decent spread of *pintxos* (try the tasty omelettes); the cheap *menú* (€8 weekdays, €10 weekends) is a bargain.

Mendizorrotz Barrio Igeldo, at the central *plaza* two stops before end of #16 bus line ⓣ943 212 023. Brief but superbly executed choice of dishes with specialities like *pimientos de padrón* (grilled green peppers) and *pudding de txangurro* (spider-crab mousse). Reckon on €24–32 including local cider and dessert in the tiny *comedor* or have the cheap *menú* (Mon–Fri) at the bar tables. Usually closes one week in March.

Morgan Narrika 7. Bohemian clientele and a jazz soundtrack set the tone for this spot specializing in more affordable *nueva cocina*, emphasizing lighter first courses – stuffed aubergine, venison carpaccio – and creative desserts, rather than the traditional hearty main courses. The bill can quickly mount to €30 a *la carta*, though there is a €12 lunch *menú*. Closed Tues eve & Sun.

Casa Nicolasa Aldamar 4, 1° ⓣ943 421 762. Classic rather than *nouvelle* Basque cookery featuring creative but substantial platters of seafood, game and meat; there's a €60 *menú*, but otherwise the bill can climb to €90. Closed part Jan.

Okendo (Oquendo) Okendo 8. Dark wood trim, ruby-red floors and cinema-festival posters set the tone here, with delicacies such as crab cannelloni, venison and pigeon. The *menu* costs

€22; *a la carta* isn't much more. Good breakfasts too for €7.50.
La Rampa Muelle 30. The best of a string of seafood restaurants on the old fishing harbour, with straightforward, tasty seafood, best sampled in the afternoons with a glass of wine; reckon on around €36 for a meal. Closed Tues eve & Wed.
Restaurante Kursaal Zurriola 1, Kursaal ⓣ943 003 162. Another Berasetegui outlet, the superb restaurant serves a sumptuous weekday *menú* for €16 and dinner from €40, while the simple cafeteria (daily 9am–10pm) offers *pintxos* from €2.

Bars

Aloña Berri Bermingham 24, ⓦwww.alonaberri.com/. One of the most popular and oldest (1986) *tapas* bars in Gros, this is an upscale place with award-winning hot and cold *pintxos* from €2 based on unusual ingredients like pigeon, duck or asparagus, squash or even daisy petals.
Casa Alcalde Mayor 19. A large, elegant bar, over 100 years old with hams hanging from the beams and a vast selection of *pintxos* from €1.35, including thinly sliced ham, cheese and shellfish – a good place for beginners. You can also have full meals in a small restaurant at the back. Daily 10am–4pm & 6–11pm.
Bergara Bar General Artetxe 8. Crammed with drinkers most nights, this swanky bar in Gros has bottles of wine set on the tables and a fabulous array of lavish *pintxos* from €1.50, including *bikote* (marinated anchovies with chillies).
La Cepa 31 de Agosto 7. Inexpensive *raciones* are served amid a decor of bullfighting kitsch and dangling hams. The most celebrated snack is *jamon jabugo*, the most sought-after cured ham in Spain (€4.50), but the grilled squid and salt-cod omelette is also excellent. 11am–midnight, closed Tues.
Ganbara San Jerónimo 21. A small but popular bar with quality (thus pricey) *tapas*, the highlight being mushroom-based ones and the *tartaleta de txangurro* (crab, carrot and onion pie). Tues–Sun 11am–3.15pm & 6–11.45pm, closed Thurs.
Gorriti San Juan, corner Lorenzio Kalea, Parte Vieja. One of the town's best counter-top collections of fresh, seafood-strong *bocadillos* and *pintxos* to be found at this hole-in-the-wall with no seats or *comedor*.
Juanaenea 31 de Agosto 22, Parte Vieja. Under new management since 2004, doing good *pintxos* (from €1.50) like seared *foie gras* and deep-fried *gambas*. Closed Wed.
Casa Urola Fermín Calbetón 20. This is another classic Basque restaurant, but the cosy bar deserves a mention for serving the best *txakoli* in town (€1.50 per glass) – the manager also owns one of the best *bodegas*. Daily 1–4pm & 8–11.30pm.

Sidrerías

If you're in San Sebastián between late January and early May, a visit to one of the many *sidrerías* (*sagardotegiak* in Basque) or cider houses is a must. (Some now stay open all year – check with the Turismo for current lists, or consult ⓦwww.sagardotegiak.com). Cider production is one of the oldest traditions in the Basque country – until the Civil War and the subsequent move towards industrialization, practically every farmhouse in Gipuzkoa produced cider, a valuable, barter-able commodity. Barter remained the main form of exchange in rural communities here until comparatively recently, and the farms were essentially open houses where local people drank cider and socialized.

Cider houses are again flourishing, and for €15–25 a head you can feast on delicious food, drink unlimited quantities of cider from the barrel and enjoy the raucous atmosphere. Of the seventy or so *sidrerías*, some of the most accessible include include *Petritegi* and *Gartziategi*, in Astigarraga 6km from town – take the red Hernani-bound bus from the Alameda del Boulevard or a taxi for about €10. Many of the more rustic and authentic ones, such as *Sarasola* and *Oiarbide*, are on the *ruta de las sidrerías* (cider trail) just beyond Astigarraga. If you're short of time, there's even a decent cider house in San Sebastián's Parte Vieja: *Sidreria Donostiarra*, at c/Embeltrán 5 (€26.50 *menú*, closed Sun eve & Mon).

Basque nationalism

Despite the high-profile activities of **ETA** (*Euskadi ta Askatasuna* – "Homeland and Freedom"), **Basque nationalism** is not a recent phenomenon. Throughout the medieval period, the Basques jealously defended their *fors* or *fueros* – ancient customary privileges guaranteeing effective autonomy – against constant pressure from Paris and Madrid, and guarded the wealth brought by seafaring skills, mineral riches and industrial enterprise. After the Revolution, in 1790, the French Basques' millennium-old *fors* were abolished as part of the centralizing strategy of the Jacobins, and the three traditional French Basque regions were amalgamated with Béarn into a new administrative *département*. In Spain, 1876 and the second, final defeat of the Carlists, whom the Basques supported for sharing their own traditionalist values, saw the victorious Liberals suspend the *fueros* altogether to punish the rebellious Basques.

Although the conservative, traditionalist **Basque National Party** (PNV) emerged towards the end of the nineteenth century under the leadership of racist Catholic extremist **Sabino Arana**, during the 1930s Spanish Basque nationalism became associated with the political Left, in reaction to Franco's regime. Cut off from their Republican allies by predominantly rural Navarra and Alava, which sided with the Nationalists, the urbanized Basque coastal provinces of Gipuzkoa and Vizkaia were conquered in a vicious Civil War campaign that included the infamous German and Italian bombing of **Gernika** (Guernica) on April 26, 1937. Franco's vengeful boot went in hard, and tens of thousands died during his post war attempts to crush the Basques. Public use of Euskera was forbidden, and central control was asserted by force – including covert overseas activities against leading Basque nationalists. But Spanish state violence nurtured new resistance fostered by ETA, which scored its first kill in 1968. Their activities have included scores of bombings and shootings, with almost nine hundred victims to date; their most spectacular success was the 1973 assassination of Franco's right-hand man and probable successor, Admiral Carrero Blanco.

After the **return to democracy**, however, things changed substantially. Today, the Spanish Basque parliament exercises considerable independence (Euskadi is the only autonomous community that collects its own taxes). There's a Basque police force, distinguished by its red berets, while the Basque **language** is flourishing again, taught in most primary schools of the coastal areas. The Basque **flag** (the *ikurriña*, designed by Arana and not particularly ancient) flies everywhere, and street as well as town names are signposted in Euskera across the region.

Since 1978 Spanish Euskadi has been controlled by the centre-right Partido Nacional Vasco. In national governments since 1996, at times when no party has had an absolute majority, the PNV has been able to demand concessions as a condition for participating in coalitions. By contrast **Herri Batasuna** (Popular Unity), ETA's political wing, has had little influence in a Basque parliament dominated by the PNV and the Socialists; their electoral support rarely topped ten percent except in parts of Gipuzkoa and Bizkaia. While wanting increased autonomy, most Basques opposed complete independence. Local economic woes reinforced this stance – Bizkaia in particular was saddled with outdated factories and idle steel foundries and shipyards. Terrorism discourages needed investment, and unemployment remained high. In January 1988 all the Basque parties, except HB, condemned ETA's methods while upholding their goals; in subsequent all-party statements against ETA, HB always conspicuously abstained.

The Spanish government periodically offered **amnesties** to ETA activists who publicly recanted – though the few who did so risked (and in many cases suffered) assassination by their former comrades – and throughout the 1980s engaged in secret negotiations with ETA leaders. But simultaneously a death squad known by the acronym **GAL** liquidated over twenty ETA fellow-travellers during a 1983–88 clandestine "dirty war". Their operations extended into the French Basque regions, while a new extradition treaty with France denied ETA operatives their former refuges across the border. GAL was first thought to consist mainly of rogue Guardia Civil members, but a series of **spectacular trials**, culminating in 1999, saw convictions of former interior minister José Barrionuevo, his deputy, the governor of Gipuzkoa, and a Guardia Civil general.

ETA had a French counterpart, **Iparreterrak**, based in Lapourd. But there was never real desire among ordinary French Basques for an independent, transborder homeland, and any French sympathy for ETA evaporated after Franco's death and the institution of Spanish Basque home rule. While top ETA members still sought refuge in France, the French authorities periodically arrested and tried or extradited leading figures in the organization. After 1994 younger hardliners, including many women, seized control from the historic ETA leadership, mostly exiled in Latin America; by 1998 most recruits were under 25, and far less punctilious about bystander casualties. The extortion of "**revolutionary taxes**" from Basque-run businesses and the kidnapping of VIPs for ransom raised an estimated $8 million annually; funds were laundered in a network of legitimate front businesses, not only in France or Spain, but also in overseas Basque communities.

ETA terror continued, presumably to force a government return to negotiation; in 1996 Premier Aznar narrowly escaped death from an ETA car bomb in Madrid, and that summer saw numerous IEDs – designed more to scare than kill – explode in coastal resorts, a tactic which continued over subsequent years as ETA warned foreign tourists to avoid Spain. But each outrage generated increasing revulsion, especially when PP municipal councillor **Miguel Ángel Blanco** was kidnapped in July 1997 and then killed when ransom demands were ignored. The kidnapping, and funeral, prompted street demonstrations a million strong across Spain. It was, unfortunately, the first of almost monthly **assassinations** by ETA (and counter-demonstrations) until 2001, except for a fourteen-month truce. The hit-men considered fair game anyone who disagreed with their agenda – mostly PP members, but also PNV and PSOE councillors, MPs and a Gipuzkoan ex-governor – as well as symbolic targets in the judiciary and armed forces.

With a clear majority in March 2000 elections, the PP didn't have to make concessions to nationalist coalition partners, and Aznar's government intensified efforts to eradicate ETA. These were indirectly aided by regional Basque election results in May 2001, where PNV and a moderate coalition partner got 43 percent of the vote, and HB was humbled – prior to its mandatory **closure** by Madrid judges and MPs in August 2002, along with various "cultural" front groups. In February 2003 the all-Euskera newspaper *Egunkaria* was shut down for being an ETA mouthpiece, and candidates deemed to be crypto-HB were disqualified from May 2003's Basque elections. The **police** kept busy throughout this war of attrition, arresting top ETA-ites, seizing explosive caches and consequently reducing ETA-caused deaths to just three. In October 2004 French police matched this with the seizure of ETA's alleged top two supremos and a similar stash of arms.

Heavy-handed as some of Madrid's measures were, they wouldn't have been tenable without the effective social marginalization of both HB and ETA on its home turf. Even when confronted by the PP's belligerently intransigent stance, a vast majority of Basques felt that more would be achieved through available democratic channels than by violence. In March 2006 what remained of ETA declared an indefinite ceasefire, and by late June Zapatero's PSOE government, in the face of considerable opposition, announced its intention to negotiate again with ETA – though talks have been temporarily derailed by a huge bomb at Madrid airport at New Year's 2007, attributed to a diehard ETA faction.

Casa Vallés Reyes Católicos 10, Centro. An attractive bar with wooden panels, tables and benches, established in 1942. It tends to stay busier longer than those in the old town mid-week, with *tapas* that are just as good – mainly fresh fish (hake and eel) and ham-based *pintxos* from €1.50. Daily 8.30am–11pm.

Entertainment

In the evenings, you'll find no shortage of action, with numerous **clubs** and **bars**. The two main areas are the Parte Vieja, especially along Fermín Calbetón, Puerto and Juan de Bilbao and in Centro around the intersection of c/Reyes Católicos and c/Larramendi. Most establishments close between 2–3am, later at weekends. **Film** venues include the ten-plex Cine Principe, on the Plaza de Zuloaga by San Telmo, and the Cine Trueba at Secundino Esnaola 2, across the Santa Catalina bridge in Gros, which often shows art and *versión original* movies.

Akerbeltz Virgin de Coro 10. A cosy bar with exposed stone walls and decent beers (Paulaner on tap), usually filled with amicable locals. Daily 11am–3am.
Altxerri Reina Regente 2. A well-established, stylish jazz bar attended by a slightly older crowd. Tues–Thurs & Sun 4pm–2am, Fri & Sat 4pm–3am.
Etxekalte Mari 11. A fashionable bar near the fishing port, with a mix of jazz, fusion and soul, plus live sets most weekends at around midnight. Tues–Thurs & Sun 6pm–4am, Fri & Sat 6pm–5am.
Garager Alameda del Boulevard 22. A large, friendly pub with wood beams, slot machines and assorted Irish or Belgian beers on tap. There's a late-night club upstairs. Daily 10am–2am.
Molly Malone's San Martín 55. One of the best Irish pubs in the city, with decent Guinness and the usual "original" Irish decor.
Splash Sánchez Toca 7. A chic new bar in Centro, with minimalist decor, stylish seating, soft lighting and a mix of garage and hip-hop. Noon–3.30am.

Festivals

Throughout the summer there are constant **fiestas**, many involving Basque sports including the annual rowing (*trainera*) races between the villages along the coast, which culminate in a final regatta on September 9. The **Jazz Festival** (Ⓣ943 440 034, Ⓦwww.jazzaldia.com), held at different locations throughout the town for six days during the latter half of July, invariably attracts top performers as well as hordes of people on their way home from the fiesta in Pamplona. A week around August 15 – known as **Semana Grande** or Aste Nagusia – sees numerous concerts, special events and fireworks laid on. There is also the **Film Festival** (Ⓦwww.sansebastianfestival.com) during the last third of September and frequent theatrical and musical performances throughout the year at the Auditorio del Kursaal or the Teatro Principal.

Listings

Books, maps, recordings Graphos at Nagusia 1 has all conceivable documentation of the Pyrenees and Basque country; Izadi at Usandizaga 18 has more of the same, especially maps; Bilintx, Fermín Calbetón 21, has more books, plus CDs of local music.
Car rental Atesa, Amezketa 7 Ⓣ943 463 013; Avis, Triunfo 2 Ⓣ943 461 527; Europcar, RENFE station, Paseo de Francia Ⓣ943 322 304; Sixt, c/Amezketa 4 Ⓣ943 444 329.
Hospital Hospital Complex Donostia, Dr Begiristain 114 Ⓣ943 007 000.
Internet café Most central are Donosti-Net at Narrika 3; Harkochat at c/Fermín Calbetón 39; and Zar@net at c/San Lorenzo 6.
Taxis Radio-Taxi Donostia Ⓣ943 464 646; Tele-Taxi Vallina Ⓣ943 404 040.

Travel details

Trains

Spanish Trains

San Sebastián to: Bilbao (9 daily; 2hr 30min–3hr); Hendaye, France (every 30min 7am–10pm; 35min); Irún (every 30min 5am–11pm; 30min), on Euskotren.

French trains

Bayonne to: Biarritz (14 daily; 10min); Hendaye (14 daily; 35min); Irún (10 daily; 40min); Lourdes (4–8 daily; 1hr 45min); Pau (7–8 daily; 1hr 15min); Saint-Jean-de-Luz (14 daily; 25min); Tarbes (7–8 daily; 2hr).

Saint-Jean-Pied-de-Port to: Bayonne (4–5 daily; 1hr); Bidarraï (Pont-Noblia, 4–5 daily; 20min); Cambo-les-Bains (4–5 daily; 45min); Itsasu (1 daily; 30min).

Buses

Spanish buses

Ansó/Echo to: Jaca (Mon–Sat 1 daily at 6am, returns 6.30pm; 1hr 40min).

Pamplona to: Auritz (Mon–Sat 1 daily at 5pm; 1hr 30min); Elizondo (Mon–Fri 3 daily, Sat & Sun 1 daily; 2hr); Eaurta (Mon–Sat 1 daily; 2hr 30min); Irún (3 daily; 2hr); Izaba (Mon–Sat 1 daily 5pm, returns 7am; 2hr); Irún (3 daily; 2hr); Otsagi (Mon–Sat 1 daily at 5pm, returns 7am; 1hr 20min); Roncesvalles (Mon–Sat 1 daily; 1hr 35min).

San Sebastián to: Bera de Bidasoa (2 daily; 1hr); Elizondo (2–3 daily; 2hr); Hondarribia (every 20 min; 30min); Lesaka (2 daily; 1hr 15min); Pamplona (6 daily; by *autovía* 1hr, others 3hr).

French buses (including SNCF coaches)

Bayonne to: Biarritz (every 10–20min on STAB urban buses; 15–20min); Cambo-les-Bains (several daily; San Sebastián (2 daily Mon–Sat on PESA; 1hr 45min); St-Jean-de-Luz (5–7 daily summer, 4–6 winter, on ATCRB; 40min).

Baïgorri to: Ossès-St-Martin-d'Arossa rail junction (3–6 daily; 10min).

Biarritz to: Hendaye-Plage & -Ville (5–7 daily by coastal corniche road; 30min).

Saint-Jean-de-Luz to: (all services on ATCRB) Cambo-les-Bains (2–3 daily in summer; 40min); Ezpeleta (2–3 daily in summer; 35min); Hendaye (9–17 daily in summer by coast or inland route, reduced winter frequency; 30min); Sara (2–3 daily in summer; 25min).

Contexts

Contexts

History

The history of the Pyrenees inevitably draws on that of both France and Spain, although the border region has usually found itself well out of the social and political mainstream. The following summary highlights the salient events and trends which directly impinged on the mountains and their people.

Prehistoric habitation

Pyrenean history begins with the bones of a 455,000-year-old man, found in a cave in 1971 near the village of Tautavel in the Fenouillèdes foothills. A gap ensues thereafter until Late Paleolithic times (27,000–10,000 BC), when cave-paintings were left by hunter-gatherers in various parts of the Pyrenees. The most spectacular ones date from the end of this era, at Niaux and Bédeilhac in France. In around 5000 BC **dolmens** appear, either stone burial chambers or seasonal shelters for shepherds, found throughout most of the Pyrenees. No habitations from this period have survived, but perishable huts of some sort were probably erected, and farming had certainly begun by this time.

Early invasions and the Visigoths

Before the start of the **Bronze Age** (around 2000 BC), Pyrenean people began to move into fortified villages, and from then until the thirteenth century AD, when the Muslims were effectively driven out of Spain, the area experienced a succession of **invasions**. First, around 1000 BC, came the **Celtic** "Urnfield People", who settled in Catalonia, and later mingled with the Iberians from the south to become the **Celto-Iberians**. The mysterious **Vascones**, whose origins remain unclear, had probably already occupied what is now the Basque country long before this time.

Later, by 550 BC, the **Greeks** established a trading post at present-day Roses, on the Catalan coast. During the third century BC the **Carthaginians** occupied Catalonia, principally in the future Spanish part, from where their most famous commander, Hannibal, crossed the Pyrenees in 214 BC on his way to Italy. But after the Second Punic War (218–201 BC) the Carthaginians were expelled from the peninsula by the **Romans**, who despite strong resistance from the Celto-Iberian tribes – and never-complete dominance of the Vascones – succeeded in making the Pyrenees, as well as Iberia and Gaul to either side, an integral part of their empire. Although a political backwater, the Pyrenean foothills were endowed by the Romans with a network of roads, bridges, villas and garrison towns; most of the modern highways in the area follow Roman thoroughfares.

Roman rule was slowly eclipsed over several centuries with raids by **Franks** and **Suevi** (Swabians), who overran the Pyrenees between 262 and 276 AD. New invasions by **Alans** and **Vandals** followed two hundred years later, eventually superseded by the fifth-century incursions of the **Visigoths** from Gaul, former allies of Rome who had been pushed out of France by the Franks under King Clovis. The Visigoths established a capital first at Toulouse and then another at Barcelona in 531 AD. By the end of the sixth century, the Visigothic kingdom extended from the Pyrenees to include most of modern Spain and half of modern France, although the Basque region retained its independence. Apparent strength and unity were spurious, however: the Visigothic monarchy was elected, leading to constant factional strife; adherence by many to the Arian heresy forfeited the kingdom support from the Byzantines; and the bulk of the population lived in a state of virtual serfdom.

The "Moors" and the Reconquest

With the Visigothic state in terminal decline, the **Moorish** (or more properly, Muslim North African) **conquest of Spain** was – in contrast to Rome's protracted campaigns – startlingly rapid. In 711, less than a century after Mohammed had left Mecca, the governor of Tangier, Tariq the Berber led a force of seven thousand across the Straits of Gibraltar and defeated King Roderic's Visigothic army. Little effective resistance was mounted elsewhere, and within ten years these Berber clans controlled most of the peninsula, including the foothills of the Pyrenees. By the standards of its time, Muslim administration was remarkably tolerant: effective autonomy was granted to remoter communities on payment of regular tribute, while Jews and Christians were allowed to continue in their faith, these non-converts being dubbed **Mozarabs**.

The Muslims called the area they controlled **al-Andalus**, whose borders expanded and contracted over the next seven-plus centuries. Their authority soon stretched beyond the Pyrenees, a progress only halted at Poitiers in 732 by the Frank **Charles Martel**. A scion of the Merovingian dynasty which then dominated what is now France, he drove the Muslims out of Aquitaine, a fight continued by his son Pepin and his more famous grandson **Charlemagne** (768–814), whose empire at its height effectively included both slopes of the range, most of modern Catalonia and much of Navarra. But Charlemagne endured setbacks, most notably the massacre of his rearguard near Navarran **Roncesvalles** in 778. No reliable account of this event exists, but it seems he had crossed the Pyrenees to assist a Catalan Muslim faction opposed to the Umayyad emir of Córdoba. His putative ally defeated, Charlemagne contented himself with raiding and sacking most of the important towns of the Ebro valley, slighting their fortifications for good measure. By demolishing the walls of Pamplona as well, he antagonized its Basque inhabitants; as his army retreated over the Pyrenees, the Pamplonans retaliated by wiping out part of his army.

After Roncesvalles, Charlemagne switched his attention to the Mediterranean side of the Pyrenees in an attempt to defend his empire against the Moors. He took Girona in 785, and his son Louis le Débonnaire successfully besieged Barcelona in 801. Continued Frankish military success meant that any influence the Muslims had wielded in the Pyrenees waned long before the turning point for the whole peninsula, the battle of **Las Navas de Tolosa** in 1212, won by the united Christian kings of León, Castile, Aragón and Navarra.

To secure recaptured territory, **castles** were built in strategic places south of the Pyrenean crest from Barcelona to the hills of western Aragón. A vassal who held a castle in fief for his lord was variously known as a castellanus, *castlá* or *catlá*, from which is possibly derived the name **Catalonia** (in Catalan, Catalunya). To the west, the Navarran capital of Pamplona and the early Aragonese capital of Jaca remained important strategic towns, and from the ninth century onwards lay astride, or just to one side, of the two main pilgrim routes to the shrine of Santiago de Compostela in Galicia. Protected by the castles and made wealthy by the patronage of kings and pilgrims, **monasteries** flourished throughout the Pyrenees. Beginning in the tenth century, Benedictine monks established themselves in Roussillon, Catalunya, Aragón and the Comminges, taking advantage of grants by local Pyrenean leaders to build on a grand scale. There are also numerous surviving **Romanesque churches** across the range, especially in Catalonia.

Although Islamic influence lingered in Spain until the sixteenth century, when the last **Mudéjars** (Moors living under Christian rule) were expelled from Andalucía, it's unclear whether or how long any remained in the Pyrenees. If they colonized any of the foothills, it was only briefly: by 920 Jaca was out of Muslim hands for the last time, Huesca was reconquered in 1096, and Barbastro returned to Christian rule in 1100. Suggestive toponyms on the French side like Moreau, Serre Mourène and Pouey-Morou are more likely corruptions of the old French word *moreau* (brown) than of "Moor".

Early nation-building

Charlemagne's grandsons divided his empire between themselves after 843, following which the Frankish empire soon fell apart. In the face of destabilizing attacks by Normans and Norsemen during the ninth century, the **Carolingian kings** were forced to delegate more autonomy to provincial governors, whose lands had already acquired strong identities of their own. With the death of the last Carolingian in 987, **Hugues Capet** was elected king of what was left of the empire, founding a dynasty of Paris-based rulers that lasted until 1328.

The **Capetians** were initially no more than first among (un)equals, surrounded by nominal vassals often more powerful than the king. In feudal France, such provincial seigneurs spent their time fighting each other, occasionally besieging each other's castles but more usually destroying crops, stealing cattle and burning villages. Things got so out of hand that the bishops introduced *La Trêve de Dieu* (God's Truce), which banned fighting from Wednesday evening until Monday morning – but they fortified their own monastic churches as a precaution, examples being Saint-Savin and Luz near Lourdes.

The situation began to change when **Eleanor**, daughter of the powerful William VIII, Duke of Aquitaine, married the future Louis VII, thus bringing that duchy under Parisian control. But Eleanor divorced him and in 1152 remarried Henry of Normandy, who shortly became Henry II of England. Thus the English gained control of a huge chunk of what would become modern France, with the vast **Angevin empire** stretching from the Channel to the Pyrenees. The most notorious British personality was **Edward the Black Prince**, whose harsh tactics – hence the epithet – provoked revolts in Bigorre late in the fourteenth century.

At the same time, **Catalunya and Aragón** were also active in "French" territory. In 1137 the betrothal of Count Ramon Berenguer IV of Catalunya to Petronella, the two-year-old daughter of King Ramiro II of Aragón, **united** the two kingdoms. His son Alfonso I added Roussillon and much of southern France to his territories, and fancied himself as the "Emperor of the Pyrenees".

Philippe Auguste (1180–1223) began to reverse the Angevin gains, undermining English rule by exploiting the bitter relations between Henry II and his sons, one of whom was Richard the Lionheart. By the end of his reign, the Capetian royal lands were for the first time more extensive than those of any other French lord, a process assisted by Capetian support for the pope's crusade against the **Cathars**, which began in 1209. The Cathars were a heretical religious group who had rapidly gained ground in Languedoc and the Eastern Pyrenees. By convention, the lands and other property of defeated heretics went to the victors, which explains the enthusiasm of Paris for the venture.

In 1213 **Pere (Pedro) II**, son of Alfonso I and king of Aragón and Catalonia, intervened on the Cathar side, but was killed attacking the English mercenary Simon de Montfort at Muret. His defeat signalled the end of Catalan aspirations north of the Pyrenees: had he won, Languedoc might be Spanish today. The outcome of the crusade was the effective extinction of Catharism and the strengthening of French influence in the Pyrenean foothills. Much of the property of Raymond VII, the defeated count of Toulouse, was forfeited to the Crown, and the walls of Toulouse and other fortified places were razed. Indirectly, the success of the crusade also ended the local nobility's patronage of the **troubadour poets**, and consequently the decline of the *langue d'oc*, the southern French language that they had championed. From this period also date the first **bastides**, some three hundred fortified new towns scattered across the Pyrenean foothills by the victors, built to a grid plan around well-proportioned central squares.

With the death of Pere, **Jaume I of Aragón**, nicknamed "the Conqueror" (1208–76) succeeded to the throne at the age of 5. The 63 years of his reign were a period of concerted expansion for the joint kingdom of Aragón and Catalunya: he drove the Muslims from Mallorca in 1229, took Menorca in 1231 and Ibiza in 1235, and reached Valencia in 1238. Realizing that the Catalan future lay to the south and east, he was less determined north of the Pyrenees and in 1258 signed the **Treaty of Corbeil**, by which he renounced all territorial rights in France (except Montpellier, the Cerdagne and Roussillon), in return for King Louis of France's renunciation of claims on Catalunya.

From the Hundred Years War to the Wars of Religion

The northern Angevin empire was lost by King John in 1204, after which the Capetians steadily undermined English rule in Aquitaine. When the Capetian male line expired in 1328, the French throne went to Philippe VI of Valois, nephew of Philippe the Fair, but this succession was quickly disputed by Edward III of England, Philippe the Fair's grandson. Thus began the **Hundred Years War** (1338–1453), with Paris aiming to take Aquitaine and Gascony – which included much of the western Pyrenees – and the English attempting to recover what John had lost.

Against this background **Gaston Fébus**, count of Foix, contended with the powerful house of Armagnac for the Gascon district of Bigorre. Fébus' defeat of the Armagnacs at the **Battle of Launac** in 1362 was the first step towards the creation of a small **kingdom of the Pyrenees**, and at its zenith the area ruled by Fébus included Foix, Bigorre, Béarn and Soule. However, he died without an heir in 1391, and the chance of an independent north-Pyrenean principality went with him.

Roussillon was taken from an increasingly united Spain by Louis XI of France in 1463, but Perpignan revolted against the French a decade later. Although the city was recaptured in 1474 after a harsh siege followed by brutal repression, Charles VIII – who succeeded Louis in 1483 – decided there were richer pickings to be had in Italy and handed Roussillon back to Spain in 1493.

Despite prevailing in the Hundred Years War, France was eventually forced by the Spanish to relinquish most of its interest in the Pyrenean-straddling kingdom of **Navarra/ Navarre**, which it had held since the early thirteenth-century election of Theobald (Thibaut), count of Champagne, as king of Navarre. Later Navarre passed first to the Fébus clan of Foix, and then early in the sixteenth century to the French house of Albret, which soon embraced Protestantism. All of Navarra was conquered by Fernando of Aragón in 1512, though the region of Basse-Navarre north of the watershed was returned to the French Henri II d'Albret in 1530, who ruled – as did his descendants – from Pau.

The Wars of Religion

His daughter, the militantly Calvinist **Jeanne d'Albret**, created an important secondary theatre in the **Wars of Religion** racking France at this time, defeating the Catholic troops of Charles IX at nearby Navarrenx. Like the Cathars before them, the Protestants were especially strong in the south of France, but also claimed a considerable number of adherents in the west. Jeanne's more easy-going son, Henri III of Béarn and Navarre, put himself in line for the French Crown by marrying Marguerite of Valois in 1572. Accordingly when he acceded to the throne of France in 1589 as **Henri IV**, his inheritance of Foix-Béarn and Basse-Navarre was incorporated into France, and the Pyrenean boundary of southwestern France was thus finalized. But as a Protestant, Henri was unacceptable in the Catholic north, and it was only after four years of fighting against the ultra-Catholic league led by the Guise family, and his own eventual conversion to Catholicism ("Paris is worth a Mass", he reputedly said) that he efffectively became king of all France.

Henri set about reconstructing the country and attempting to accommodate the religious factions that had been at war since 1562. The 1598 **Edict of Nantes** accorded the Huguenots – as the Protestants were also called – freedom of worship in specified places, the right to education and public office on par with Catholics, their own courts and the retention of certain fortresses as a guarantee against renewed attack. But Henri's assassination in 1610 ended royal protection for the growing numbers of Protestants in the French Pyrenees. The new King Louis XIII's agent **Cardinal Richelieu**, having crushed the Protestant strongholds of La Rochelle and Montpellier, then set about razing their various Pyrenean fortresses.

Franco-Spanish war and the Treaty of the Pyrenees

In 1635 an ascendant France and a weakened Spain were again at war, and by 1640 the Catalans had taken advantage of this to declare themselves an **independent republic**, under the presumed protection of Louis XIII. Their marching song, "Els Segadors" (The Reapers), was later to become the Catalan national anthem. Louis annexed Roussillon from the Spanish Crown and came personally to supervise the siege of Perpignan, which fell on September 9, 1642. The inhabitants were grateful, and looked forward to an independent Catalonia, but this was never to be: Barcelona fell to Spanish forces in 1652 and Catalonia was effectively split in two. In July 1654 the French besieged Villefranche-de-Conflent, which capitulated after eight days, and in October the key Cerdanyan town of Puigcerdà also fell to France. The French razed the walls of Villefranche in 1656, fearing that the Spanish might retake the city, which was somewhat rash, since the town soon became theirs by the **Treaty of the Pyrenees**. This, negotiated by the respective foreign ministers of France and Spain on a neutral island in the River Bidasoa near Bayonne in 1659, provided for permanent French control of Roussillon and part of the Cerdagne. The Spanish paid a heavy price when the details were thrashed out the following year at Llívia, ancient capital of the Cerdanya/Cerdagne. They ceded Perpignan – then one of the most important towns in Europe – and the fortified port of Collioure. Puigcerdà and Llívia remained Spanish, but the surrounding territory became French, leaving Llívia as an enclave. The Catalans had forever lost the prospect of a united, independent country.

With **Louis XIV,** the Roi Soleil or "Sun King", reigning alone after the death of Cardinal Mazarin in 1661, **Sébastien le Prestre de Vauban** began fortifying dozens of towns for the king along the north slopes of the Pyrenees, his most famous work being **Mont-Louis** in the Cerdagne. Even Vauban, however, fell out of favour for his criticism of Louis' war-mongering and wealth-amassing, financed by taxation from which aristocrats and clergy were exempt.

Although the **boundary** envisioned by the treaty was not formally delineated until the mid-nineteenth century, it proved one of the most stable and peaceful in Europe. For the Pyrenean population, especially in the upland of Cerdanya/Cerdagne, the treaty's terms conferred dubious benefits: age-old local customs were superseded by centralizing states; the power of the Church – whose dioceses frequently overlapped the new boundaries – was severely challenged; and smuggling was an inevitable consequence of zealous customs services. For the first time many Pyreneans, especially on the French side, became liable to conscription and thus saw parts of the wider world, often settling far away in the lowlands – the beginning of the massive mountain depopulation that continues to this day. Not only the Catalans but the Basques at the opposite end of the range suffered progressive erosion of the *fors/fueros*, ancient charters which had guaranteed some degree of home rule.

War of the Spanish Succession

With the death of the Habsburg King Carlos II of Spain in 1700, the throne was offered to the grandson of Louis XIV, Philippe d'Anjou, provided he renounce his rights to the throne of France. Louis XIV's acceptance of the deal, which put a Bourbon on the throne of Spain and gave him indirect control there, guaranteed war with Habsburg Austria, whose Archduke Charles had already been named as successor. England too was drawn into the conflict, fearing a combined French-Spanish power. The **War of the Spanish Succession** lasted thirteen years from 1701, with Holland, Portugal, Denmark, Austria and England arrayed against France, Spain and Bavaria. Peace was eventually achieved by the treaties of **Utrecht** (1713) and **Rastatt** (1714), with Philippe remaining as **King Felipe V** of Spain, but his realm was divested of all territory in Belgium, Luxembourg, Italy and Sardinia, with Gibraltar and Menorca being ceded to England. In revenge for its support of the Austrian claimant, Felipe V suppressed what little remained of Catalunya's autonomy. The war effort had effectively bankrupted the French, and Louis XIV, his sun well and truly set, died in 1715.

The French Revolution and the Peninsular War

On the evening of July 28, 1789, a group of strangers arrived in the Roussillonais town of Prades, sounded the alarm bell and forced open the salt store, instrument of the hated *gabelle* (salt tax). The **French Revolution** had reached the eastern

Pyrenees, and within days all Crown agents and tax-gatherers had been beaten up and ejected from Roussillon. But the euphoria was short-lived. After the solidarity of the anti-tax riots, the Revolution degenerated into a settling of old personal scores, of village against village; peasants went armed just to tend their vines. People soon realized that they had swapped a despised but distant monarchy for a system of government that would far more effectively pervade every aspect of their lives, not least in the suppression of the traditional regions such as Bigorre and Béarn and their replacement with new, gerrymandered *départements* designed to sever old loyalties. **Land reform**, with its abolition of feudal dues and tithes, was popular on the plains but less significant in the mountains where there was already a complex system of communal grazing rights. There was no support for the war with royalist Prussia and Austria who were determined to crush the Revolution, and men became fugitives rather than be conscripted, turning instead to smuggling. The **Terror** of 1792–95 claimed few Pyrenean lives, but when it did peasants suffered disproportionately.

The Peninsular War

Soon after becoming emperor of France in 1804, **Napoleon** sensed an opportunity to take over Spain. The Spanish fleet was defeated at the Battle of Trafalgar in 1805, precipitating the abdication of Carlos IV. In April 1808 Napoleon summoned the disgraced Spanish royal family to Bayonne, deported Carlos IV and his wife to Italy and imprisoned their sons Fernando and Carlos in France. Napoleon then installed his own brother, Joseph Bonaparte, as king of Spain. Among Spanish intellectuals, opposition was initially muted by the hope that French rule would prove a liberalizing force, but optimism quickly evaporated, and Britain and Portugal joined Spain against France in the **Peninsular War** (1808–14). Napoleon organized hospitals for his troops at Bagnères-de-Bigorre, Cauterets, Barèges and Capvern, revitalizating these spa towns. The emperor also planned various civil engineering projects in the Pyrenees to support his troops in Spain, including roads across passes above Marcadau and Gavarnie, but his army was forced back before anything came of them. His men retreated along the famous pilgrim route via Roncesvalles and were pursued eastwards along the foothills by the **Duke of Wellington**. Wellington's armies were rapturously received by a people sick of Napoleonic bellicosity – scoring extra points by paying for supplies rather than just requisitioning them – and many of his officers returned after the war to settle at Pau.

Seeds of the Spanish Civil War

Between 1810 and 1813 a *Cortes* or Spanish parliament attempted to found a liberal regime in the framework of a constitutional monarchy. But Fernando VII, upon being restored to the throne in 1814, immediately abolished this embryonic parliament and remained an implacable opponent of any liberalization, presiding at the same time over the loss of most of Spain's colonies in South America. Upon his death in 1833 the crown was claimed both by his daughter Isabella II (a child under the regency of her mother), and by his brother Carlos, backed by the Church, the conservatives and the Basques. The **First Carlist War** (1833–39) ended with victory for the (relatively speaking) liberals supporting Isabella, who came of age in 1843. Her reign was a long record of scandal, political crisis and constitutional compromise, until army generals forced Isabella to abdicate in 1868.

The experimental **First Republic** (1873–75) failed, and following the **Second Carlist War** the throne went to Isabella's son Alfonso XII.

Thereafter, attempts to balance monarchism with parliamentary government were only partly successful. Working-class **political movements** such as the Socialist Workers' Party were developing rapidly: the socialist trade union, the UGT, formed in 1888, took hold in the industrialized Basque country, while the anarchists' rival union, the CNT, was especially well represented in Catalunya. The loss of Cuba, Puerto Rico and the Philippines to the US in 1898, and the "Tragic Week" of rioting in Barcelona in 1909 – following a call-up of army reserves to fight in Morocco – represented significant blows to national morale.

During World War I Spain was neutral, but internal turbulence continued, and in 1923 **General Miguel Primo de Rivera** established a dictatorship. After his death in 1930, the success of antimonarchist parties in the municipal elections of 1931 led to the abdication of the king and the foundation of the **Second Republic**.

Catalunya declared itself an independent republic two days after the municipal elections on April 14, 1931, but had to settle for a statute of limited autonomy granted by Madrid the following year. A relatively dynamic region, it had long felt itself exploited by the rest of Spain. Meanwhile the Madrid government was too paralysed by the expectations of left-wingers and the potential for right-wing reaction to accomplish any substantive agrarian or tax reform. Additionally, the various brews of extreme political ideology that had been fermenting in Spain since the previous century were ready to explode. Anarchism, communism and socialism all derived some impetus from the Russian Revolution, while at the other end of the spectrum was the **Falange** – a black-shirted quasi-fascist youth group founded in 1923 by José Antonio Primo de Rivera, son of the dictator.

The **army** was divided between anti-monarchists, monarchists who supported the Bourbon dynasty and monarchists who supported the Carlist line – whose power base was conservative Navarra. But they were united in their opposition to left-wing government, and though General José Sanjurjo's 1934 coup attempt failed, it spawned the infamous **Spanish Military Union**, whose members included General Manuel Goded and **General Francisco Franco**, openly warning of another rebellion should the Catholic right fail to win the coming election. When the left-wing Frente Popular (Popular Front) won the election of February 1936 by a tiny majority, the stage was set.

Events in France 1810–1938

Following the end of Napoleonic rule, France endured over half a century of turbulence despite nominal restoration of the monarchy in 1815. There were reversals of revolutionary tenets under a series of reactionary kings or self-styled emperors, alternating with growing popular discontent and periods of liberal retrenchment, all taking place against a backdrop of growth in industrial and economic power.

The trauma of defeat in the 1870 Franco-Prussian War resulted in the definitive **declaration of a republic**, and indirectly in the growing influence of the political Left; the Spanish UGT had a near-exact counterpart in the French CGT, which eschewed political organization in favour of "direct action". As in Spain, socialist and communist parties found it difficult to co-operate, even given the opportunity presented by the aftermath of World War I, in which the 25 percent casualty rate among the French ranks had dealt the old social order a fatal blow. The scale of demographic decimation can be gauged by the memorial cenotaphs in every

French Pyrenean village, with their long lists of the dead – often far more numerous than the current local population.

The Catholic right, whose **Action Française** shock troops dated from the early 1900s, mirrored analogous groupings in Spain. Faced by the growing threat of both Nazism across the Rhine and homegrown fascism, the French Left papered over its internal differences and – in the same year as the Spanish Popular Front victory – won a more convincing mandate in the Parisian Chamber of Deputies. Encouraged by a wave of spontaneous sit-ins and wildcat strikes celebrating the poll triumph, the first **Front Populaire** government of 1936–37, headed by **Léon Blum**, nearly succeeded in ratifying the sorts of reforms – nationalization of key industries, forty-hour week, collective bargaining – which Spain could only contemplate. But within a year these measures had been stymied by a corollary proposal on currency exchange control. Similarly blunted by "reasons of state" (ie fear of the English and the Germans) were Blum's ineffectual attempts, despite his evident personal sympathy with the Spanish Frente Popular, to intervene openly in the Civil War – or even just supply armaments to the Republicans – until the fall of his second government in 1938.

The Spanish Civil War

On July 17, 1936, the military garrison in Morocco rebelled under the leadership of Franco, the agreed signal for revolt throughout Spain. Sanjurjo, by now in exile in Portugal, was the Military Union's choice for provisional head of state but was killed when his plane crashed between Portugal and Burgos. Another Franco rival, Goded, was captured by Republican loyalists in Barcelona and shot, allowing Franco to be proclaimed commander of the rebels – and "Head of State" – in October 1936.

The **Nationalists**, as the rebels styled themselves, had expected a short campaign, but the **Spanish Civil War** (1936–39) turned out to be long and bloody. In the Pyrenees, only Navarra immediately joined the Nationalists, who had convinced the heirs of the Carlists to join Franco's Falange. Gipuzkoa and Bizkaia, which had recently benefited from a home-rule statute similar to Catalunya's, remained devoutly Republican as did Catalunya and Aragón, whose mountain villages were particularly attracted by anarchism, an ideology that shared their traditional values of equality and personal liberty. Whatever their precise stripe, Republicans were overwhelmingly secular and virulently anticlerical, and the beginning of the conflict saw numerous churches or monasteries sacked, with priests and nuns murdered or raped.

Although the Nationalists initially had little popular support, they gradually swept the country by a mixture of audacity and deliberate terror, backed by a flood of arms and men from Nazi Germany and Italy. The Republicans were far less effectively supplied by Russia, Mexico and very sporadically by France, and reinforced by the socialist International Brigade. An international arms embargo and declaration of nonintervention was universally and selectively winked at by interested parties. Nominally a civil war, the Spanish conflict was really the opening act of World War II, and the first "modern" conflict: Italian and German airmen demonstrated the efficacy of terror bombing of civilian targets, and radio was first used as a propaganda weapon.

In the north, their foothold in Navarra allowed the Nationalists to attack both east and west. The Basque country was overwhelmed by the end of 1937, followed by a major Nationalist offensive into Aragón during March 1938. As the

△ Spanish Republican refugees, 1938

Nationalists advanced eastwards, **Republican** soldiers, marooned in the valleys of Alto Aragón and Catalunya, fled north across the high passes into France, joined or preceded by their families and other civilians fearful of a Falangist victory. Many Republicans believed – or perhaps deluded themselves – that theirs was a tactical withdrawal, hoping to be saved by a pan-European war in the wake of Hitler's provocations in Czechoslovakia. But by early 1939 it was all over, with refugees arriving at ordinary frontier crossings like Le Perthus, sometimes in columns of thousands, which totalled well over half a million by war's end. The French gave them an at best grudging welcome, interning the refugees in squalid concentration camps, for example at Argelès-Plage, where Republican poet Antonio Machado died of pneumonia in February 1939, a month before the Nationalists captured Madrid.

World War II

When **World War II** began in autumn 1939, the desperation of camp life, civic and monetary incentives from the French government and a further opportunity to combat fascism impelled nearly ten thousand Spanish refugees to volunteer to serve in the French army. But the capitulation of France in spring 1940 ironically led to a growing refugee movement back into Spain. Small numbers began making their way over the Pyrenees, intent on reaching England via neutral Spain or Portugal, to join the Free French forces. There was also regular transport from France into Spain of Swiss gold ingots as payment for humanitarian food aid to occupied Europe from the US.

The Germans were initially content to leave the south of France, including the Pyrenees up to the Arnegi-Valcarlos border crossing, under the control of the collaborationist **Vichy** government, but the Allied landings in North Africa of November 1942, only briefly opposed by Vichy troops in Morocco and Algeria, left the area vulnerable to attack from across the Mediterranean. Hitler immediately ordered the formal occupation of the south, prompting a new wave of escapes over Pyrenean passes.

Escapees and escape routes

These later refugees fell into four categories: **Allied forces**, mainly airmen who had been shot down; **évadé(e)s**, who had escaped prison or internment in France (though the word *évadé(e)s* could be applied to all escapees); **réfractaires**, French people who were in trouble with the Vichy or German authorities for falling foul of Occupation rules; and **Jews**.

Their guides were known as **passeurs** in French, **pasadores** in Castilian. Some knew the old contraband trails from lengthy experience, but the majority were ordinary working people who smuggled occasionally for a little extra money. Another contingent was made up of Spanish Republicans who, having fled from the frying pan into the fire, lived in hiding along the border, especially around the Cerdanya/Cerdagne. Some clergy were involved, as well as a few shepherds, a handful of mountain guides and even a scattering of mayors and customs officers. Altogether, about three thousand French (including two hundred women) were active in the Pyrenean escape routes, and five hundred Spaniards.

Until the **German occupation** of the French Pyrenees on November 11, 1942, it was left to the French themselves to patrol the frontier, a task entrusted to no more than eight hundred customs officers, policemen and support staff, and these were easily circumvented by well-established methods. Fugitives and their guides, for example, could take the Sunday afternoon train to Latour-de-Carol, stroll up to the frontier to mingle with the local Spanish and French who by custom gathered there to chat, and then just drift away onto the Spanish side. In Vichy Marseille, the American and Mexican consulates simply provided escapees with exit visas and put them on the train to Spain via Cerbère and Portbou.

However, from late 1942 the frontier was patrolled by over a thousand German military police, backed by as-numerous mobile units. In addition, there were about a hundred undercover Nazi agents in the region, assisted by French volunteer forces and informers motivated by money, anti-Semitism or both. Though the Germans were mostly older men considered unsuitable for the rigours of combat, these frontier guards were nevertheless formidable – tough Bavarian or Austrian mountaineers, well trained and well equipped, using reconnaissance aircraft to track their quarry. The Spanish had about eight hundred border guards and police on their side, and additionally 30,000 troops were also stationed not more than 30km south of the frontier.

The **escape organization** that developed to counter this intensified border security was run like a business, and an occasionally ruthless one. Known by the codename **MAURICE**, it had a substantial annual budget for transport, false documents, food, the hiring of guides and other expenses. Much of the money was raised by loans from sympathizers, for whom coded messages were broadcast on the BBC to acknowledge the receipt of funds and confirm later repayment. The cost of each crossing depended on the negotiating skill of the organizer and the difficulties of the route involved: if transport had to be arranged to the start of a crossing, the cost burgeoned as fuel was scarce. As particularly "hot" items, Jews had to pay – or be paid for – at many times the normal going rate to be guided out of the country. Those who demurred, and attempted to flee via the normal daily rail link between Oloron and Canfranc, were liable to be returned by the Spanish authorities or sent to an internment camp.

Early in the war the **consequences** of arrest on the French side were not too harsh: imprisonment, a fine or perhaps "volunteering" for the Vichy Foreign Legion. Later, the penalties became more severe: about a thousand escapees died in concentration camps in France or elsewhere, as did 150 of the five hundred *passeurs* who were caught. Crossing the border did not always mean safety; Spain might have been neutral but it was a pro-fascist country, and no official could be trusted. Anyone captured on the Spanish side would be sent to one of the local **internment camps**, where conditions were so bad as sometimes to be fatal – and approximately one in seven escapees ended up interned. Despite these hazards, about 35,000 civilians succeeded in escaping into Spain, including approximately 5000 Jews, 2000 Belgians, 500 Dutch, 800 Poles and around 1000 members of the Resistance, moreover, some 700 highly trained British, American and Canadian airmen were spirited across the border and returned to combat.

Spain: abortive invasion

Although the Spanish Civil War had left more than half a million dead, destroyed a quarter of a million houses and sent a third of a million Spaniards into exile in France and Latin America, Franco was in no mood for reconciliation. He set up **tribunals** which sentenced thousands of Republicans to death and interned nearly two million others in concentration camps until "order" had been restored. The Falange was the only permitted political organization, and censorship was rigidly enforced.

As World War II ground towards its conclusion, exiled **Spanish Republicans** distinguished themselves fighting for the Allies, especially among the ranks of the French Resistance, with many units active in the French Pyrenees from 1942 onward. Implacable foes of Franco and fascists in general, the Basques even formed their own Gernika Batallion, which in April 1945 was instrumental in crushing a large German force in southwest France, still being supplied by Spain.

Some months before this, about 15,000 Spanish Republicans, understandably concluding that total Allied victory would encompass the overthrow of Franco's pro-Nazi regime, had attempted to occupy the Spanish Pyrenean valleys as a prelude to uprisings across Spain. With minimal, half-hearted support from the French Resistance and the British SOE, they invaded on **October 19, 1944** along the entire length of the Pyrenees, principally in the Val d'Aran, but also at Luzaïde, Urdizeto, Benasque and the valleys of Roncal and Pineta. Although they arrived fully supplied to avoid relying on locals and thus provoking reprisals against them, the Republican guerrillas in any case found many villages already forcibly depopulated, and the wells poisoned. After some initial success in Aran, "**Reconquista de España**" (as the operation, partial subject of the 2006 film *Pan's Labyrinth*, was called) failed to take Vielha or seal off the Bonaigua pass and the half-built tunnel, and was forced to withdrew after a week. Subsequently, Franco's regime strongly reinforced its border defences against repeat incursions, and vicious reprisals (especially in Aran) were exacted anyway.

Surviving Spanish Resistance members resident in France, for the most part ardent communists, were for many years shabbily treated by the French government in respect of (belated) decorations and pensions, and still tend to segregate themselves from locally born fighters at comemorative ceremonies. On the Spanish side, only in spring 2001 were official references to the combatants of 1944 – and a few guerrilla cells who battled on in Spain until the early 1960s – as "bandits" and "brigands" struck from the official record, though the survivors failed to gain the right to military pensions.

The Pyrenees after the wars

By the end of World War II, during which Spain was neutral if actively pro-Nazi, Franco ranked as the last remaining fascist head of state in Europe, and had sanctioned more judicial deaths than any other ruler in Spanish history. Spain remained politically and economically isolated into the early 1950s, home to thousands of Nazi war criminals beyond the reach of extradition, despite diplomatic recognition of Franco's regime by much of Europe. With the economy at a standstill, Pyrenean villagers moved down to the towns in a usually fruitless search for work, accelerating the **depopulation** of the mountains. Mismanagement of the economy was so blatant that by 1953 the country was exporting less than it had twenty years earlier. The traditional livelihood of **smuggling** across the Pyrenees mushroomed into a major enterprise, but even this was dwarfed by the corruption of army officers and customs officials who imported luxury goods on false documents, an illicit trade equal to half the official imports.

Franco's otherwise probable overthrow was only averted in 1953 by the hotting up of the Cold War and his acceptance of token **American aid**, on condition that he provide space for four American air bases and a naval base; Spain's pariah status definitively ended the same year in a concordat with the Vatican, establishing Catholicism as the state religion, and subsequently in 1955 with its belated admission to the UN. The economy was revitalized far more by remittances from tourism and Spaniards working in northern Europe than by US loans, resulting in exponential economic growth through the 1960s. This merely accelerated the death of traditional Pyrenean agriculture, as **mechanized farming** on the plains progressively marginalized mountain life. A Spain of increasing urbanization and lowland agriculture required massive amounts of water and power, supplied by a plethora of dams in Catalunya and Aragón; their flooding of Pyrenean pastoral valleys, combined with punitive neglect on Madrid's part in failing to provide the most basic services to the overwhelmingly pro-Republican mountaineers, finished off any hope of subsistence in much of the Pyrenees.

Charles de Gaulle had emerged **in France** as the undisputed leader of the Free French government-in-exile, leaving the Allies little choice but to co-operate with him. After the liberation, an uneasy coalition of Right and Left – the Conseil National de la Résistance – gave rise to a provisional government for the demoralized and bankrupt nation. By 1947, thanks to the Cold War and the Marshall Plan, the Left – as well as (temporarily) de Gaulle – had been excluded from what became the Fourth Republic, though not before a new constitution had been agreed upon, providing for women's suffrage, the nationalization of key industries, trade union rights and the rudiments of a welfare state.

In the French Pyrenees themselves, hundreds of communities had been burnt by the Germans in reprisal for supporting the Resistance. Thousands of villagers who had been driven out decided to remain in the valley towns after the war, and even today many villages are still abandoned entirely or in part – though this changed somewhat after 1968 (see below).

If thoroughgoing political reform had been deferred, France during the 1950s transformed itself from a primarily agricultural country into a modern industrial giant, its growth rate often rivalling that of West Germany, with whom it established in 1957 the European Coal and Steel Community, predecessor to the Common Market/EC/EU. Although the country became a member of NATO, France's military resources soon became embroiled in the **Algerian colonial rebellion**, which following on the 1954 catastrophic defeat in Indochina became an eight-year experience nearly as traumatic as the German occupation. By 1958 hard-line rightists among the army and the so-called **pieds noirs** – a million civilian settlers in Algeria virulently opposed to its possible independence – threatened to take on both loyal army units and the native rebels. De Gaulle returned from political limbo, dissolving the Fourth Republic and demanding extraordinary powers to sort out Algeria. For his pains, as president of the Fifth Republic, de Gaulle provoked an even graver military revolt in 1961, with the **OAS** – a rogue faction intent on preventing any settlement – mounting several attempts on his life. But Algerian independence was finally granted in 1962, prompting a flood of refugees – mostly Jews, *pieds noirs* and *harkis* (Arabs who had fought for the central government) – into France. The *pieds noirs* in particular, many of them settling in southern France, would later support a resurgence in assorted racist and fascist activities, including the Front National.

Cracks in the old facade

De Gaulle's style in diplomacy was idiosyncratic, to put it mildly; by the mid-Sixties he had ruffled numerous feathers by blocking British entry to the Common Market, rebuking American policy in Vietnam, calling for a "free Québec", partly withdrawing from NATO and refusing to sign any nuclear test-ban treaties. Even at home he was increasingly unpopular, not just among the rightist fringe; a young challenger on the Left, **François Mitterrand**, nearly upset him in the 1965 presidential elections.

Yet despite these rumblings of discontent, the events of **May 1968** took everyone by surprise. What started as a provincial student protest against the paternalistic education system quickly escalated into broad-spectrum agitation by both blue-collar and white-collar workers as well as academics, culminating in a protracted general strike. *Autogestion* – workers' self-management – was the dominant slogan, but beyond specific demands for reform, there was general sentiment that all French institutions were too hierarchical and elitist. De Gaulle dropped out of sight for two weeks, consulting with army commanders, his private plane at the ready should he have to flee the country; upon his return, he dissolved parliament and, to quell the "revolution", demanded a fresh electoral mandate from the frightened silent majority – who complied.

Although the protesters could point to few specific gains except in education, the events of 1968 changed French society in subtler ways over the next two decades; there was a perceptible lessening in formality and authoritarianism, and various alternative movements (like the Green Party) can trace their start to the "days of May". Numerous self-employed professionals who felt themselves thwarted by the return to "normality" in the towns **fled south**, as had generations of dissidents before them, to the shelter of the Cévennes and the Pyrenees, forming the advance guard of the **nouveaux ruraux** (new rurals) who would slowly repopulate the abandoned villages and eventually set up tourism-related enterprises.

Spain's increasing prosperity as the 1960s became the 1970s merely underlined the intellectual and financial bankruptcy of Franco's regime, and its inability to cope with popular demands. The need for contemporary education and skills plus a creeping invasion of outside culture made the anachronism of the ruling ideology starkly clear. Franco's only reaction was to step up the pace of show trials and executions of his opponents, mirroring the repression of the early 1940s. Basque nationalists, whose 1973 assassination of Admiral Carrero Blanco effectively destroyed Franco's last hope of a like-minded successor, were singled out for particularly harsh treatment. When Franco finally died in November 1975, few expected much of his second-choice heir as head of state, the Bourbon prince **Juan Carlos**, cynically nicknamed *El Breve* (The Brief) for the anticipated duration of his reign.

Much to his credit, over the next seven years the new Spanish king oversaw a cautious, gradual but steady progress towards "democracy without adjectives", the demand of street activists in the late 1970s. The first **free elections of 1977** returned a coalition government, with the extreme Left and Right marginalized. Recognizing that his own future depended on the continuation of democracy, Juan Carlos declined to support the **attempted coup** of February 1981 by disaffected elements of the Guardia Civil and the army; its collapse, and attendant further discrediting of those nostalgic for the old order, set the stage for the landmark elections of October 1982.

Meanwhile, **in France**, the 1970s had been dominated by the two presidential terms of centre-rightist **Valéry Giscard d'Estaing**, who defeated Mitterrand in 1974 and 1978. Despite a series of scandals and the defection of Giscard's prime minister **Jacques Chirac** to form his own party, the Left were incapable of presenting a united front for the 1978 polls in particular. Few would have predicted the decisive result of the French elections of May 1981.

The first post-war Socialist governments

In May 1981 Parisians gathered spontaneously at the place de Bastille to celebrate the victory of Mitterrand's Socialists, the first left-of-centre triumph in France since the 1930s. Just over a year later, Felipe González's PSOE – the Spanish Socialists – also came to power with massive support, an even more dramatic reversal considering the nearness of the Falangist past. Despite enjoying substantial goodwill at the outset, both movements eventually foundered on domestic and international realities, amidst unprincipled betrayals of campaign promises and party manifestos. As a result, the French Socialists lost power between 1986 and 1989, between 1993 and 1996 and after 2002, while their Spanish counterparts only just squeaked back into office in 1993 before being eased out in 1997, not to return until 2004.

The presence of four Communist ministers in the first post-1981 French cabinet reflected inital commitment to an aggressively leftist agenda; by 1984, in the face of capital flight and bureaucratic foot-dragging, Mitterrand was compelled to appoint a centrist cabinet under Prime Minister **Laurent Fabius**, but 1986 saw the return of the Right under **Jacques Chirac**'s Gaullists. This uneasy arrangement under a sitting Socialist president – because parliamentary and presidential elections were then out of sync in France – was referred to as **cohabitation**. Chirac's monetarist fumblings and flirtations with **Jean-Marie Le Pen**'s overtly racist Front National resulted in a centre-left parliamentary coalition returning by a bare margin in 1989, under Social-Democrat prime minister **Michel Rocard**. Though some of Chirac's privatization programmes were stalled, the unpopularity of Rocard's own austerity measures resulted in **Édith Cresson** replacing him in 1991. Her abrasiveness and numerous gaffes prompted her sacking in 1992 in favour of **Pierre Bérégovoy**, a confidant of Mitterrand's. All these comings and goings virtually guaranteed a landslide coalition victory of the RPR and the UDF, the two conservative parties, in 1993; two months later, Bérégovoy – accused of accepting a private loan from a dubious character – shot himself, leaving no explanatory note.

This thumbnail summary of French politics to the early 1990s merely hints at the malaise which gripped the French scene. Scandal had been a near-constant feature of public life since 1981; equally disappointing was the Socialists' failure to change traditional militarism, all-pervasive secrecy and environmental-unfriendliness in one of the most centralized states in the world. In the Pyrenees especially, despite lip service to ecological considerations, mega-projects such as the Somport tunnel were only slowed or modified rather than halted.

Spain by contrast enjoyed a certain stability throughout the 1980s; the PSOE was convincingly re-elected in 1986, and only began to falter visibly in 1989 as recession hit. Yet there was a similar pattern of compromise on core issues, which often made the PSOE government indistinguishable from de jure conservative governments elsewhere in Europe. **Felipe González** had entered office in 1982 partly on an anti-NATO platform, but campaigned for continued membership in the 1986 referendum on the issue, which went narrowly in favour. Control of inflation, as stipulated by the EC, had a higher priority than employment, and loss-making state-owned industries were drastically overhauled, and many privatized. **Labour measures** such as cuts in unemployment benefits, a pay freeze for civil servants and a differential minimum-wage law for under-25s resulted in general strikes co-ordinated by the PSOE's own trade union, the powerful UGT (resurrected after 1975).

By the early 1990s it became obvious that prolonged time in office had made the PSOE not just corrupt but complacent, with only the lack of compelling alternatives and enduring suspicion of the Right maintaining the status quo. The PSOE barely survived a strong 1993 challenge by the centre-right Partido Popular (PP) under its uncharismatic chief **José María Aznar**, and continued to govern only with support from the Catalan nationalist party, lacking an outright majority. As in France, spectacular scandals regularly erupted, eroding the PSOE's position still further. Most damaging of these was the discovery of **GAL** (Grupo Antiterrorista de Liberación), an ostensibly rogue anti-terrorist unit which had been kidnapping and/or assassinating suspected ETA members and fellow-travellers throughout the 1980s. The press and an independent judiciary – both interfered with repeatedly by the government – exposed a clear chain of command extending up to the highest echelons of the PSOE.

France: the Right in power – and out again

Prime Minister **Edouard Balladur**'s centre-right government was beleagured early in 1994 by riotous objections from youth, Air France workers, farmers and fishermen to various monetarist measures, causing Balladur to back down and lose the respect of his natural constituency. Political violence in the south of France and corruption scandals continued unabated, adding – along with stubbornly high unemployment – to the support for fringe parties on the Left and Right.

Meanwhile **Mitterrand**, terminally ill with prostate cancer, clung to office until mid-1995, despite revelations about his war record as an official in the Vichy regime before he belatedly joined the Resistance. Yet when he **died** in January 1996, after fourteen years as president, he was mourned as a man of culture and vision, a tenacious political operator and a committed European.

The **May 1995 presidential elections** saw Socialist Lionel Jospin pitted against four rightist contenders; in the run-off, **Jacques Chirac** narrowly edged him out. One of Chirac's first decisions was the **abolition of conscription**, in favour of professional armed forces. The decree – not actually implemented until 2001 – provoked impassioned dismay from left-wing parties, for whom conscription represented social levelling and the revolutionary spirit expressed in the national anthem: "*Aux Armes, Citoyens …*". Another Chirac move was to delay signing the Nuclear Non-Proliferation Treaty until France had carried out a final series of **nuclear tests** in the South Pacific. These caused almost universal condemnation, boycotts and attacks on French embassy buildings, but most French opinion shrugged this off, while their navy captured Greenpeace's *Rainbow Warrior II*, almost ten years to the day after French secret service agents had bombed and sunk the first *Rainbow Warrior* in Auckland harbour.

Chirac's new prime minister was technocrat **Alain Juppé**, who had to balance election pledges of job creation and maintenance of social benefits against tax cuts, a continued strong franc and a reduced budget deficit. This soon all came unstuck when Chirac announced that fiscal rectitude would take precedence over social comfort, and Juppé proposed changes in social security and "downsizing" of the rail network. The response was an all-but-general **strike** in November and December, when five million public-sector workers took to the streets with considerable support from becalmed private-sector commuters. Amazingly, Juppé survived by abandoning some proposals and postponing others. A new tax to pay off the social security deficit was imposed, though cuts in the health service proceeded; the economically depressed Pyrenean regions, always net beneficiaries of every sort of public welfare programme from crêches to SNCF buses, were starkly affected by every policy wobble.

The UDF-RPR coalition stumbled through 1996, fulfilling predictions by Mitterrand and Giscard d'Estaing that Chirac's opportunism and impetuousness would quickly make his government a laughing stock. Although Chirac and Juppé enjoyed a huge parliamentary majority, valid until spring 1998, hanging on to the bitter end was not for Chirac. Incredibly, he called **snap elections** for late May 1997, perhaps hoping for a smaller but less fractious majority – and an end to future potential cohabitation by making the start of the next parliamentary and presidential terms coincide in 2002.

In the event Chirac totally misjudged the public mood and the Socialists' ability to attract potential coalition partners, while his ploy to strengthen the presidency backfired spectacularly. **Jospin** and his allies, the Communists, the Greens and the anti-Maastricht Citizens' Movement, swept back to power; 38 Communists, seven Greens and more than a hundred women took seats. The cohabitation Chirac had gone to such lengths to avoid had come to pass a year earlier than it otherwise would have.

Spain: Aznar's two terms

Despite the ongoing woes of the PSOE, the Spanish **elections of March 1996** yielded yet another **hung parliament**, though this time Aznar's PP had a plurality of fifteen seats over the PSOE. Denied the "absolute majority" he thought was his throughout the campaign, Aznar had to assemble a **coalition** with the Catalan, Basque and Canary Island nationalist parties (whom he had denounced as "greedy parasites") to get a parliamentary majority. In return for their support, these regional parties – including those in the Pyrenees – expected disproportionate benefits to their regions.

González, for his part, failed to draw the proper conclusion from the result: "A couple more weeks of campaigning and we would have won" was his off-the-cuff reaction, dismissing the idea of retirement. The close finish initially denied the PSOE the urgently needed self-reflection that a crushing defeat and a quick change of leadership would have provided. But early in 1998, **González** finally **resigned** the leadership of the party he had dominated for 23 years.

Aznar failed to win an outright majority in 1996 for two significant reasons. At the last moment, memories of the long, repressive Franco era unnerved many voters wary of losing hard-won decentralization and the PSOE-established social benefits system – a vital lifeline in many poorer regions, including the Pyrenees. The electoral weight of Andalucía, González's power-base, fulfilled its traditional role of offsetting the conservative North by supplying many of the discredited PSOE's surviving MPs.

During his first term as prime minister, Aznar gradually moved his party towards the "reforming centre", sidelining PP hardliners in hopes of gaining the electorate's confidence and a working majority not dependent on regional nationalists. Economically, the PP continued as the PSOE had begun: withdrawing subsidies from ailing industries such as shipbuilding, accelerating privatization of former state-owned industries, reducing corporate taxes and "liberalizing" labour laws.

The PSOE replaced González with former transport minister **José Borrell**, not his preferred choice of successor. González hovered constantly in the background, making it impossible for Borrell to stamp his own mark on the party. By 1999 Borrell had succumbed to scandal, replaced by the party hierarchy's – and González's – original nominee, **Joaquín Almunia**. With a general election now looming and the PSOE still trailing in the polls, Almunia fashioned an electoral pact with the ex-Communist Izquierda Unida (United Left), hoping that their combined votes would overturn a likely Aznar victory. But the **March 2000 election** was a stunning **triumph for Aznar** and the PP, who took 183 of the 350 parliamentary seats; for the first time since the death of Franco the Right were in power with a clear majority.

The electorate had been unconvinced by the "shotgun marriage" between the PSOE and the IU (bitter enemies since the Civil War), which smacked more of an opportunistic patchwork than a government-in-waiting, as well as by warnings during the campaign that, once in power with an overall majority, the PP's social-democratic mask would come off and wholesale dismantling of the social welfare systems would ensue. Moreover, large numbers of voters seemed unwilling to risk the indisputable economic gains of Aznar's tenure – unemployment below twenty percent for the first time since 1988 – while many of the Left's traditional supporters didn't bother to vote. Almunia promptly **resigned** from leadership of the PSOE, which retained just 125 seats. Party delegates spurned the old guard by electing as replacement a young (born 1961) unknown, **José Luís Rodríguez Zapatero**, a member of the moderate-socialist "Nueva Vía" (New Way) faction with in PSOE.

In 2001 the always-enigmatic Aznar announced that he would not lead the PP after the next general election, and by late 2003 had anointed as his successor the deputy prime minister **Mariano Rajoy**. Why Aznar, styled *el pequeño bigotudo* ("the little guy with the moustache") by self and others, chose to resign (he was only 52 when Rajoy's appointment was rubber-stamped by the PP ruling council) remains a mystery; presumably Aznar's ambitions were of a grander order – perhaps a Europe-wide, NATO or UN post as a reward for being at the forefront of Donald Rumsfeld's "New Europe". As likely, he chose to exit before all the gloss had rubbed off the PP's accomplishments: unemployment remained the highest in the EU, the **economy** overall was slowing, while labour law and social-security benefit "reforms" prompted an acrimonious general strike in June 2002. After years in opposition spent rooting out sleaze in the PSOE government, the PP was now also vulnerable to charges of cronyism and **corruption**.

But worse was to come on November 19, 2002, when the single-hulled oil-tanker **Prestige** broke up off Galicia, releasing almost 100,000 tonnes of crude oil over the next six months. Lack of preparedness and the studied indifference of various PP officials (including the head of the Galician *autonomía* and Madrid's minister of the environment) were ameliorated only by shoreline clean-up by thousands of volunteers and soldiers; though the EU quickly banned single-hulled vessels, the damage from the worst-ever local environmental disaster was protracted, with invisible carcinogenic pollutants contaminating the Galician fisheries for years and slicks reaching the Canaries and Ireland. Normally placid, pro-PP Galicia bridled at the perceived incompetence of the government; when Aznar proposed visiting the stricken area in December, he was advised to stay away for his own safety.

Aznar procured another hostage to fortune with his enthusiastic support for the inexorable American and British **march to war** over the winter of 2002–03, despite the opposition of ninety percent of Spaniards to the Iraq adventure. Madrid's relations with the Basque country remained tense, as did those with Catalunya following the December 2003 formation of a left-wing, pro-separatist regional government. Yet all indicators pointed to a third PP victory in the parliamentary **elections** set for **March 14, 2004**.

France: the second cohabitation

Jospin's victory inevitably raised unrealistic expectations of how much a left-of-centre government could accomplish, given limitations set by Brussels and economic globalization. But to its credit, the new government quickly adopted a consensual strategy, with decisions reached through debate and sounding out public opinion, in contrast to Juppé's top-down style. Thus it was able to propose a huge **increase in taxation** for social programmes, borne equally by corporations and individuals, without seriously denting its popularity.

Jospin's **poll ratings** remained high through 1999, despite increased friction with Chirac, dissension in the Left coalition itself and some predictable back-pedalling on campaign stances. Despite his execrating the practice on the hustings, Jospin soon surpassed all previous French prime minsters in **privatizations** of major state enterprises, selling off over $20 billion worth; unlike in other countries, though, small shareholders were made to benefit. In the **March 1999 Euro-elections**, the Greens overtook the Communists as France's second party of the "Left"; accordingly, at the Greens' September party conference there were murmurings that they should press Jospin for more action on such issues as the future of nuclear power, a 35-hour work-week, GM foods and regional languages, or consider leaving the government (where Green **Dominique Voynet** was minister of environment). By year's end universal health cover including the unemployed had been introduced, as well as a Pacte Civile de Solidarité (giving cohabiting couples, including gays, almost the same rights as married couples), and equal representation for women on all parties' candidacy lists in national and regional elections, as well as in municipal contests in towns of more than three thousand inhabitants. The long-promised **35-hour working week**, designed to reduce unemployment, was finally implemented in February 2000, initially pleasing nobody. Public unions threatened to strike, freelancers demanded the right to work as much as they liked, and owners warned that it would make French industry uncompetitive.

Despite Jospin's government having pulled France out of a long recession, and despite the 35-hour week proving far more popular with time, its **re-election** in 2002 was by no means certain. However, the UDF and RPR were still beset by sleaze, and French patience with the arrogance and corruption of the traditional elite had worn thin to the point of transparency. Future cohabitations, at least, seemed far less likely: as per a September 2000 referendum, France's presidential term, formerly seven years, would be brought into step with the five-year parliamentary term as from the 2002 elections.

Even by French standards, the year 2001 was rich in **high-profile scandals**, some posthumously besmirching Mitterrand's legacy. Former foreign minister and Mitterrand crony Roland Dumas was imprisoned for embezzling funds from state-owned Elf Aquitaine; Chirac narrowly escaped impeachment for involvement in criminal corruption in the matter of non-official perks for himself and family while mayor of Paris from 1977 to 1995; and Mitterrand's son Jean-Christophe was convicted for illegal arms trafficking to Angola. France's highest court ruled that Chirac would enjoy immunity from prosecution only as long as he stayed in office.

The "earthquake"

Against a backdrop of ongoing sleaze and voter apathy, the **presidential elections of spring 2002** promised at first to be a yawn. Once again Jospin was squaring off against Chirac and Le Pen – as well as thirteen other splinter-party candidates. At the outset, Jospin seemed to stand a good chance; he'd performed well on the economy, remained personally scandal-free and had been further boosted by the election of gay Socialist Bertrand Delanoë as mayor of Paris in March 2001, the first time any Left party controlled the capital since the Commune of 1871. However, Jospin's authority had been dented by his energetic sponsorship of an autonomy statute for Corsica, only to have it declared unconstitutional in January 2002. Moreover, Jospin had never overcome his charisma deficit, being described by one journalist as akin to that of a retired Swedish professor of religious studies. The glad-handing, high-living Chirac, despite his scandal-splattered history and poor achievement record, had by contrast lost little of his ability to charm.

The shock-horror announcement on the eve of April 21 and the first round of the presidential poll was that, at 16 percent, Jospin had been eliminated by none other than Le Pen at 16.9 percent; Chirac had a plurality of 19.9 percent. This result, characterized in the press as an "**earthquake**", sent ripples across the country and abroad as it emerged that nearly thirty percent of voters had abstained, while others had voted for fringe candidates in protest against the mainstream parties. The leftist tally had been dissipated amongst several hopefuls (even Trotskyite Arlette Laguiller polled 5.7 percent), thus dooming Jospin's bid. Jospin (temporarily) resigned from the Socialist Party, handed over the leadership to François Hollande and lapsed into a nine-month public silence: a sad end to a fundamentally decent and (by French standards) honest politician.

This result acted as a wake-up call for those who had abstained or voted frivolously in the first round, as nearly a million took to the Parisian streets on May 1 to protest the ascendancy of Le Pen – who'd run a shrewd campaign, playing on voter alienation and fear of crime, while downplaying his core racist message. The Socialists and Communists were reduced to endorsing Chirac to keep Le Pen out, and Chirac duly romped home with 82 percent of the vote in the May 5 second round.

With the **parliamentary elections** set for June 9–16, Chirac's supporters cobbled together an umbrella group of right-wing parties, the Union for a Presidential Majority, to scotch any chance of another cohabitation. The Socialists, severely shaken by Jospin's defeat, failed to put up a real fight, and the Right took 369 of 577 seats in the National Assembly; the Greens, with just three seats, nearly disappeared from the electoral map, while the Communists fared scarcely better.

Chirac named little-known **Jean-Pierre Raffarin** as prime minister, and (surprisingly for the centralizing Right) promulgated a bill devolving considerable power to the regional assemblies, ending the absolute domination of Paris for the first time since 1789. He also survived an assassination attempt by a rifle-toting neo-Nazi, widely diagnosed as an indirect consequence of the loony right being denied any parliamentary representation despite polling its typical thirteen percent of the vote nationwide. New interior minister **Nicolas Sarkozy** presided over a well-publicized, controversial drive against vice, and earmarked extra funds for policing as part of a general anti-crime drive. In November 2002 the UPM was renamed the Union pour un Mouvement Populaire, incorporating Démocratie Libérale as well as the RPR and UDF.

Spain: the Zapatero era

During morning rush hour on March 11, 2004, three days before **parliamentary elections**, ten terrorist **bombs** planted on four crowded Madrid commuter trains killed nearly two hundred and injured almost 1,500. Aznar and his ministers crassly tried to reap electoral benefit from the tragedy by pinning the blame, from the first hours of the aftermath, on ETA, the PP's favourite bugbear, despite ETA's immediate denial of responsibility. Over the next three days, however, police investigations indicated – despite the government's best efforts to hide the fact – that a local, Moroccan "franchise" of al-Qaeda, not the Basques, was responsible. In their fury at being manipulated and lied to by the Aznar government, and at being put in harm's way by its eager support of the Iraq war, the Spanish electorate turned out in force, both at street demos and at the polling booths, and handed the **PSOE a plurality** of nearly 43 percent of the vote and 164 seats; the PP plunged to just under 38 percent and 148 seats. No other single party won more than ten seats, but among these minor victors were the Catalan Republican Left with eight seats – one of the separatist entities on whom the PSOE, though declining to form a coalition, would have to rely on for support as a minority government. Prime Minister-elect Zapatero immediately announced the **withdrawal** of the 1,300 Spanish troops serving in **Iraq** by June 30, 2004; some observers noted, with alarm, that it was the first European election in decades to be swung, albeit indirectly, by terrorist action. On April 3, police cornered four more terrorists in a Madrid suburban apartment, presumed members of the "**Moroccan Islamic Combatant Group**" and key actors in the March 11 atrocity, who proceeded to blow themselves (and a policeman) up.

Since then, Zapatero's record has been competent if unspectacular as his government grapples with Spain's ongoing economic and constitutional problems. The **economy** – dominated by tourism, an overheated construction industry and consumer spending – is superficially buoyant, even as multinational companies quit Spain for the lower-wage environments of the newer central European EU members. Even the mainstay of tourism is threatened by lower-cost destinations

Catalan and Basque nationalism

Although the **Basque and Catalan separatist movements** both aim for the preservation of a distinctive language and culture as much as political autonomy, they also differ markedly. The long-standing Catalan complaint is of a relatively successful region milked by the rest of Spain, while Basque concerns centre on non-Basque-speaking immigrant labour and exploitation by a non-Basque elite. Among the Basque provinces, urbanized Bizkaia and Gipuzkoa are Basque-nationalist, but more rural Navarra and Araba are conservative and Spanish-loyalist, while French Basques view themselves as separate from both their Spanish counterparts and the rest of France.

Relations between Madrid and the Spanish Basque regions, never smooth, deteriorated considerably after Franco's Civil War victory, when the 1936 statute of autonomy granted by the Republicans to Gipuzkoa and Bizkaia was rescinded, the Basque language banned in public and "politically unreliable" teachers dismissed. The local Catholic Church's opposition to atheistic socialism had made it pro-Nationalist during the war, but from the 1950s, it encouraged part-time Basque schools or *ikastolak*, which had enrolled 33,000 pupils by 1975.

A poll just before Franco died highlighted the relative strengths of the two principal minority Pyrenean languages: 90 percent of Catalan housewives understood Catalan, 77 percent spoke it, 62 percent read it and 38 percent wrote it; for the Basque country the figures were 50 percent, 46 percent, 25 percent and 11 percent respectively. By 1996 a survey of Catalans showed that 95 percent understood, 80 percent spoke, 84 percent read and 53 percent wrote their language – a testimony to almost-universal schooling in Catalan since the 1980s. However, Barcelona is increasingly a Castilian-speaking island in Catalunya owing to large immigrant communities from Latin America augmenting existing Andalucian internal migrants, such that Catalan linguistic dominance is again a countryside phenomenon.

The failure of the 1895-founded **Basque National Party** (PNV) to gain lasting political autonomy for Gipuzkoa and Bizkaia, followed by Francoist repression, led to the emergence during the early 1950s of ETA (see box on pp.518–519 for full coverage), rarely exceeding a thousand full-time activists, whose violent actions triggered widespread reprisals, including mass arrests, torture and show trials. Meanwhile, there was little violence in Catalunya itself and no counterpart there to ETA: a 1963 petition against language restrictions, or a pointed rendition of the traditional anthem "Els Segadors" in Franco's presence, typified the Catalan approach.

The first post-Franco elections of 1977 gave **Pacte Democratico per Catalunya** – an alliance of Catalan regionalist parties – ten seats in the Madrid parliament; among the Basques, the PNV won eight seats and left-wing nationalist party **Euskadi Eskerra** won one. The PNV and Euskadi Eskerra theoretically advocated independence via constitutional means – in contrast to **Herri Batasuna** (HB), linked Sein Finn-style to ETA. During the 1980s HB typically won about ten percent representation in the Basque regional parliament, but deputies always refused to take their seats, leaving the PNV in complete control.

Although Catalunya's twentieth-century experience mirrored that of the Basque country – a Republican-era autonomy statute, followed by severe cultural repression after 1939 – relations with Madrid are somewhat more cordial. Catalunya is effectively run day-to-day by its **Generalitat** (regional government), which controls education, health, social security, tourism, commerce, agriculture and cultural matters, while collecting and disbursing about half of local taxation. Centre-right regional parliaments prevailed from 1978 until late 2003, viewed as better advocates of Catalan business interests, and – by participating in the 1993–2000 coalition governments – better able to extract concessions from Madrid. In 2002 Catalan supremo Artur Mas called for renegotiation of the 1978 autonomy charters, sparking a predictably gruff reaction from the obsessively centralizing PP regime. In December 2003 local Socialist leader Pasqual Maragall, now president of the Generalitat, formed a coalition with the pro-independence Republican Left Party and a Green–Communist alliance, excluding Jordi Pujol's long-ruling centre-right Convergence and Union party.

For many Basques, the denial of de jure independence still grates, though alone thus far among Spain's *autonomías*, the Basque provinces collect and disburse all of their own tax revenues. During 2003–04 Basque premier Juan José Ibarretxe tabled nebulous **proposals** for a “free association” of Araba, Gipuzkoa and Bizkaia with Spain: essentially a state within a state, with representation in the European Union, to be ratified by referendum in the Basque country. In early 2005 his regional parliament approved a more specific blueprint for a “**Basque free state**” with its own courts, passports and international diplomatic representation. Prime Minister Zapatero dimissed the proposals as unconstitutional and the plan was rejected by the Madrid Cortes, but Ibarretxe and Co. threatened to put the plan to a regional referendum.

Urban-proletariat-based ETA never flourished in the overwhelmingly rural **French Basque regions**. Grievances there focus on a perceived Parisian policy of relegating the Pays Basque to “Third World” status, promoting tourist-related industries at the expense of others. Teachers in the Basque-language primary schools around Bayonne were finally recognized as state employees in November 1989, and, since signing the European Charter on Regional and Minority Languages in May 1999, Paris must acknowledge the existence of **regional languages** such as Euskera (and Catalan, Gascon or Occitan), allowing them to be read, spoken, taught and broadcast. But by a 1999 French Supreme Court decision, the government is not obliged to accord them official status – ie no title deeds, weddings or trial transcripts in minority languages. The chances of a separate Pays-Basque *département*, governed from Bayonne, being hived off from Pyrénées-Atlantiques any time soon seem fairly remote, though such a proposal now figures in public debate, to the dismay of pundits who balefully predict the balkanization of France.

Early in 2004 the Catalan and Basque sagas began to overlap again. **Josep Lluis Carod-Rovira**, head of the Republican Left party and prime minister of the Generalitat, was obliged to resign when it emerged that he'd secretly met top ETA members in Perpignan, after which ETA declared Catalunya off-limits for terrorist activity. The PP attempted to capitalize on this “coincidence”, but their demonization strategy backfired, with Carod-Rovira's party increasing its Cortes presence in the March 2004 polls. In September 2004, taking their cue from the Basque assembly, the Catalan parliament voted overwhelmingly to become a “nation” – exact definition pending, aside from even more local fiscal control – and forwarded the proposal to Madrid, where following modifications it passed the Cortes, with Zapatero's blessing, in late March 2006. In June that year, a new, stronger autonomy charter for Catalunya was approved by a 74-percent ‘yes’ referendum vote, despite opposition from the PP – who foretold the accelerated break-up of Spain – and from separatist hardliners who thought the new deal didn't go far enough. It now seems clear that whatever increased autonomy the Catalans secure in future, the Basques will settle for nothing less – and vice versa.

△ Nationalist rally for regionalist Basque schools, Bayonne 1979

like Tunisia, Croatia and Bulgaria. Red tape hampering business start-ups, a clunky educational system and nonexistent government support for innovation seem intractable structural problems.

Zapatero has been confronted by the same **nationalist demands** from the autonomous regions as his predecessor, Aznar. It is a given that any concessions the Basques receive in terms of greater control over their own affairs, the equally fractious Catalans will immediately demand the same – and vice versa. Following the late 2005 resolution by the Catalan parliament (see p.547) for even greater autonomy, two high-ranking generals – José Mena Aguado and Alfonos Pardo de Santayana – were sacked and reprimanded respectively for warning that the present constitution permitted the armed forces to intervene in guaranteeing the unity of Spain, and toasting the army in that capacity – reawakening fears across the political spectrum that the strait-jacket centralization of the Franco era was returning. It's impossible to predict where this ongoing tug-of-war will end in one of the most decentralized European states, given that Spain's 1978 Constitution recognizes the right of the "regions and nationalities" to autonomy but also declares "the indissoluble unity of the Spanish nation".

France on the streets – again

Early 2003 saw France, and its articulate, telegenic foreign minister **Dominique de Villepin**, lead "Old Europe's" fight against the US and UK's slide towards war in Iraq. Chirac threatened to use France's Security Council veto if the US tabled a resolution with an ultimatum leading to war, but Bush's "coalition of the willing" simply bypassed the UN; Franco-American relations briefly plummeted to their nadir whilst jingos in the States renamed frites "freedom fries".

During the remainder of 2003, however, Raffarin's government ran into a domestic ditch. Large-scale unemployment held steady at ten percent, while pension reforms (including a proposal for retirement at 70) were vigorously resisted by successive waves of **strikes** and protest **marches** – and discussions to curtail the vaunted health service hadn't even been opened.

The government relented temporarily, while still insisting that reform was essential. Ambitious new finance minister **Nicolas Sarkozy** proposed privatizations and public-sector parsimony: the healthcare budget would shrink, but so would defence spending, in tandem with consumer-focused tax breaks. But March 2004 **regional elections** saw the Left **storm back** to take control of over three-quarters of the local assemblies. Worse was to follow: in a May 2005 referendum, 55 percent of French voters **rejected** the proposed new **EU constitution** which all major political parties had urged them to ratify. Opponents – principally far Left, far Right, Greens – saw it as wedding France to an "Anglo-Saxon", neoliberal Europe; many were voting against globalization or paternalism as much as against the constitution itself.

In the wake of this stark rebuff, Chirac sacked Raffarin as prime minister and replaced him with Dominique de Villepin; Nicolas Sarkozy – now leader of Chirac's UMP party – became interior minister. Both men were jockeying for position as Chirac's successor, now that former favourite Alain Juppé had been convicted on corruption charges while running Paris's city hall and barred from public office for ten years pending appeal. But by late 2006 both Sarkozy and de Villepin would in turn have their reputations seriously undermined.

Nicolas Sarkozy's test came with the **civil unrest** that swept urban France in November 2005, triggered by the accidental electrocution of two teenagers fleeing police on October 27 in a run-down Paris "suburb" consisting of neglected, deprived housing estates. Within a week, rioting had spread to other Parisian banlieues and many regional cities, as disaffected youths torched first cars or buses, then schools and police and power stations. "Sarko" (the interior minister's nick-name), had stirred up matters in October by calling estate-dwellers *racaille* (rabble), and in June by suggesting that crime-ridden neighbourhoods be hosed out with Karcher power-cleaners. After three weeks, the final tally was 9000 vehicles and property worth €200 million up in smoke, and nearly 3000 people arrested.

The **causes** of the unrest were hotly debated. Some tried to blame Muslim radicals, given that the worst-affected areas were home almost exclusively to North or West Africans, but a complete breakdown in relations between the police and youths, institutionalized racism and local unemployment approaching fifty percent were the true factors. As some rioters themselves said between bouts of vandalism and arson, "We hate France and France hates us… One way or another we're heading for prison. It might as well be for actually doing something."

Dominique de Villepin emerged from the riots in better shape than his putative rival, but the issue of **youth employment** soon strained his credibility as well. Attempting to tackle France's stagnant growth and stubborn budget deficit with labour-market "flexibility", he launched new legislation giving small companies the right to dismiss without cause employees on the job for under two years. Such measures are common elsewhere, but from the historical perspective of hard-won labour rights, this seemed an attack on the cherished **French exception** whereby the state protects workers' rights, the national agricultural and industrial base, and French culture generally, eschewing neoliberal or "Anglo-Saxon" capitalism. In November 2005 a million workers marched against the new labour law, with three-quarters of the population sympathizing.

In 2006, the measure was to be extended to cover the *contrat première embauche* (**CPE**), or first employment contract, to encourage firms to hire under-26s without risk of being saddled with them forever. Students and the young, however, saw it differently: why should they be denied rights their elders took for granted? In March students in Paris **occupied the Sorbonne**, in conscious imitation of May 1968. Once again, they were brutally driven out by riot police. And just as in 1968, people protested across France in their millions – only this time in the hope not that France would radically change, but that everything would remain the same. A contemporary survey concluded that the most desired job among young people in France, as with their elders, was civil-servant-for-life. On April 10 Dominique de Villepin withdrew the law.

Following the CPE debacle, Nicolas Sarkozy looked again more like **Chirac's probable successor**, notwithstanding the intense personal animosity between them. De Villepin's fortunes declined following allegations he had instructed judges to investigate Sarkozy's alleged role in the **Clearstream scandal**, in which French officials took bribes in a 1991 deal to sell frigates to Taiwan. Sarkozy vigorously and successfully defended himself, suggesting there was a plot to discredit him.

A new potential winner emerged for the Socialists in late 2006: **Ségolène Royal**. After a strong start occupying centrist ground previously rare in French politics – promoting an anti-elitist agenda while talking tough on family values plus law and order – her campaign stalled in the final run-up to the first-round vote of 22 April 2007, where Royal finished five percentage points behind Sarkozy, whilst dark horse centrist **François Bayrou** polled a respectable third. The second round on May 6, with (like the first) an impressive 85 percent voter turnout, saw "Sarko" square off against "Ségo", the first female candidate ever to make it this far, with Sarkozy prevailing by 53 percent to 47 percent. Sarkozy, a deeply polarizing figure proposing to undertake the economic reforms France urgently needs, seems poised to lead his UMP party to a plurality if not a majority in the June 2007 parliamentary elections versus the Socialists and Bayrou's new Parti Democratique.

General trends

Besides social exclusion and contending economic blueprints, salient contemporary issues in **France** are the interrelated ones of **racism** (surveys consistently show the country as one of the most unabashedly bigoted in Europe), relations with the **Muslim and African world**, remorse (or lack thereof) for the fate of its **Jews** during World War II and **immigration**, resulting in a community of five million Muslims, largest in Europe. While some far-rightists consider Jews, particularly North African ones, no better than Muslims, in 1997 French Catholic bishops formally apologized for the Church's complicity in the 1942 rounding-up of local Jews. The main exploiter of these anxieties has historically been Jean-Marie Le Pen's quasi-fascist **Front National**, which – though deprived of its parliamentary seats through creative gerrymandering – still gets between seven and fourteen percent nationwide (and even more in recent presidential polls).

More mainstream politicians have jumped on the **nativist bandwagon** at critical times. Charles Pasqua, Balladur's interior minister, restricted granting of residence permits or citizenship to immigrants or their descendants and introduced random street ID checks. Under Juppé, police evicted hundreds of unsuccessful Malian asylum-seekers from the Paris church where they had sought refuge; in a countervailing gesture which temporarily reduced tensions, Jospin's government amnestied them, as well as thousands of other illegals who had been working in France for years. But in December 2003 Raffarin's government set expulsion targets for illegal immigrants – beginning with some radical imams – and enacted a controversial (though popular) bill banning "ostensibly religious" garb, notably Islamic headscarves, from schools and hospitals.

Since the November 2005 disturbances there have been renewed moves to deport illegal immigrants and even legal residents in trouble with the law. But in the through-the-looking-glass world of contemporary French politics, a few Arabs and black Africans mended fences with Le Pen and/or indulged in anti-Semitic rants, to the extent of mooting a vote for Le Pen in the 2007 presidential poll to eliminate Sarkozy – who is one-quarter Jewish – in the first round. The celebratory scenes following France's 1998 World Cup victory, when blacks, whites and *beurs* (French-born of North African descent) embraced in the streets two days before Bastille Day, while Chirac hailed the "tricolour and multicolour" triumph, seem in light of subsequent events to belong to a distant age in a different country.

Spain, though now a major European (and international) player, still lacks sustained, incremental investment in its human resources. For example, conscription was phased out by 2002, leaving a professional army – and a 125,000-man staff shortfall for numerous social projects which used to rely on conscientious-objector volunteers, in the absence of funds for salaried positions. Local **unemployment** is still stubbornly high, though Catalunya, especially Girona province, is noticeably better off.

Many of the young people you'll see in seasonal jobs at Catalan Pyrenean resorts are migrants from remote provinces (or distant countries ranging from Latin America to Bulgaria), working on short-term internships or otherwise without employment security. The latter are part of the 3.7 million **immigrants** (8.7 percent of the population) resident in Spain, including nearly a million Muslim (North) Africans. In contrast with France, successive amnesties have legalized most of them, keeping social security coffers brimming, reversing population decline, and reining in incipient Christian–Muslim tension.

Nearly seven decades after the putative **end of the Civil War**, a generation with no memory of Franco has begun to question the return-to-democracy's "don't ask, don't tell, don't blame" coping strategy – which contributed substantially to the vacuousness and amorality of public life. Every few months yet another mass grave is uncovered, usually of civilians shot by Nationalists during the opening months of the war, as witnesses who always literally knew where the bodies were buried finally speak out, and volunteer diggers are recruited. Accompanying this has been an avalanche of published and recorded memoirs by veterans of the conflict, and the formation of "historical memory" groups across the country, as the main post-Franco taboo is definitively breached.

The 1978 Spanish constitution concedes significant **devolution of powers** to the seventeen autonomous regions, or *autonomías*, of Spain. Each has its own president, parliament and civil service – an expensive duplication of functions, with enhanced risk of vote-buying and corruption. Variable **statutes of autonomy** apply to Catalunya, Aragón, Navarra and Gipuzkoa, which include the entire Spanish Pyrenees. However, Madrid still reserves too many powers for the system to embody true federalism. Especially in Aragón, political authority theoretically exists for local initiatives, but funds have often proved insufficient.

While Spain is no longer so starry-eyed about **the EU**, a vast majority of Spaniards still backs European integration, reflected in Spain's referendum ratifying the EU Constitution early in 2005, the first member state to do so – even if France and Holland's rejection made this approval academic. Although Spain – until now the largest recipient of EU aid – will lose seven billion euros in annual funding following the EU's 2004–07 enlargements, most citizens remember the 120 billion euros accrued to the country since 1986 through EU "convergence" grants for infrastructure improvement, as well as subsidies under the Common Agricultural Policy.

Mountain agriculture at least has long since ceased to be viable on either slope of the Pyrenees as ancient terraces crumble back into wilderness; any repopulation is due to the *nouveaux ruraux/neo-rurales* in search of alternative lifestyles, and to people renovating second homes. France offers a range of subsidies for permanent mountain-dwellers, but **full-time Pyrenean residence** remains a precarious undertaking. Solar panels, Internet-capable telephony and mobile phones do mean that self-employment and residence are now feasible in previously abandoned, non-viable spots, which conventional state utilities have historically refused to supply.

The **single European market** has had considerable impact on foothill/coastal towns like Perpignan, Girona, Jaca and Bayonne, which funnel much of the freight and transit personnel moving north and south. The effect of EU money is highly visible in the Pyrenees, where it funds civil-engineering projects otherwise beyond the means of local government. Many of these risk transforming the mountains into a cluster of tame theme parks linked by motorways, where genuine indigenous culture and wildlife have been destroyed. That said, commercial exploitation is still far below the level prevailing in the Alps, even as the Pyrenees have "arrived" as a popular overseas tourist destination since the mid-1990s.

Wildlife

There is ample wildlife in the Pyrenees, despite the effects of hunting and environmental damage (see "The Environment", p.559). The range is especially rewarding for bird-spotters, with a variety of resident indigenous species, and enormous numbers of migrating birds to be seen at critical passes in autumn. The round-up below picks out the major animal species that you might encounter (as well as the disappearing species that you probably won't), and details some of the more interesting Pyrenean flora. However, this is only a general guide to occurrence and habitat. For something more specific, see the list of recommended wildlife titles on p.570.

Birds

The **lammergeier** or bearded vulture (*gypaète barbu* in French; *quebrantahuesos* in Castilian) was long persecuted by herdsmen fearing for their livestock, but lately has made a significant recovery. It is easily identified by the pinkish-gold breast of the adult, a long wedge-shaped tail, narrow wings and enormous size – weight up to 6kg, wingspan approaching 3m. Lammergeiers can most reliably be seen at Gavarnie, in the Aspe/Ossau region, in the Valle de Ordesa and in their principal strongholds of the Echo, Ansó and Roncal valleys northwest of Jaca.

The lammergeier's diet consists mainly of bone marrow, which it exposes by dropping bones onto a rocky surface from a height of 30–50m (hence the Castilian name, meaning "breaks-bones"). To locate its meal, the solitary lammergeier often works in conjunction with a flock of **griffon vultures**, which are similar in size, but lack the wedge-shaped tail, and have a distinctive white head and neck, as well as black wingtips. Only when the griffons (see p.474 for more about them) have finished stripping the carcass does the lammergeier move in. Flocks of griffon vultures patrol much of the Pyrenees, especially in the Basque country and the Aspe/Ossau valleys.

Occasionally, the rare **black vulture** is seen in the Western Pyrenees, particularly in the Valle de Echo or over the Iparla ridge, either with griffons or on its own. This bird can be distinguished from the griffon by its longer and more rounded tail, its much darker plumage and a black area around the eye.

Unlike the above species, the **Egyptian vulture** (*percnoptère* in French; *acantilados alimoche* in Castilian) is found in the Pyrenees only during the breeding season, when it can be seen in the Aspe, Ossau and Soule valleys or around the Ordesa region. The smallest of the vultures – with a wingspan of about 150cm – the Egyptian has white plumage and black wingtips. Nicknamed Marie-Blanque or La Dame Blanche in the French valleys, its arrival in the April skies announces the start of spring.

The **golden eagle** (*aigle royal* in French; *aguila real* in Castilian) is glimpsed everywhere in the high mountains, each breeding pair having a territory of between 90 and 130 square kilometres. You can identify juveniles by the white patches on the wing underside, but for adult birds over five years old, identification is easiest by size (around 80cm from beak to tail, with a wingspan of 3m) and the open V-shape of its upturned wings as it soars. Whereas the golden eagle and the scarcer **Bonelli's eagle** – dark on top, paler underneath, with a dark, striped tail – are seen all year round, the **booted eagle** and the **short-toed eagle** appear only during the summer breeding season. The booted is the smallest European eagle, with a wingspan of up to 120cm. It has a long, narrow tail and is either pale with an almost white front and white-flecked head, or uniformly mahogany-coloured with slender white stripes along the front of the wings. The short-toed eagle is often almost pure white with darker banding all round the wings, and a disproportionately large head. A unique characteristic is its habit of hovering motionless over its intended prey, commonly snakes, with its legs dangling freely.

The acrobatic kites are perhaps the most entertaining birds to watch, their permanent population supplemented by autumn migrators. The **red kite** (*milan royal* in French; *milano* in Castilian) has a deeply forked tail, and continuously twists in the air as it manoeuvres over carrion. The **black kite** (*milan noir* in French; *milano negro* in Castilian) is darker than the red kite, its tail shorter and straighter-edged, and its wingspan smaller at 115cm. It is most often seen circling over municipal rubbish dumps, unconcerned by the comings and goings of the trucks.

Since it is seldom seen in flight, except when flushed out of hiding, the **ptarmigan** (*lagopède alpin* in French; *perdiz blanca* in Castilian) is difficult to spot. It's found in pairs around the central Pyrenees during summer, and in winter in flocks, when the birds are almost totally snow-camouflage white, except for a black tail and red "eyebrows".

Several smaller but distinctive high-altitude birds are the playful, acrobatic **alpine chough**, a slim crow with a curved yellow beak, sometimes seen with its red-beaked cousin, the **common chough**; the **snow finch**, like a large sparrow, but noticeably black and white in flight; and the **wall-creeper**, red, grey and black, with a thin curved beak and usually found on or near cliffs. Lower down, the **white-backed woodpecker** has its only western European home among the broad-leaved trees of the Pyrenees, while the much larger but elusive, red-crested **black woodpecker** prefers pine woodland.

△ Griffon vulture feeding, Spanish Pyrenees

Mammals

The most agile and conspicuous wild mammal of the high mountains is the **isard** or **Pyrenean chamois** (*rebeco* or *camuza* in Castilian; *sarrio* in Aragonese), a member of the antelope family closely related to the larger Alpine chamois. Living among the peaks in summer and descending in the winter, they are numerous in the Parc National des Pyrénées and the contiguous Parque Nacional de Ordesa y Monte Perdido. Those around Port d'Espagne, near Cauterets, as well as in Ordesa are uncharacteristically tame because of their contact with tourists. Gavarnie, the Sierra del Cadí, Canigou and Aigüestortes are other good places to see them. A few individuals manage to survive at high altitudes during the snowy months, so brace yourself for the surprise of isards darting across ski runs, or the path of your lift.

The **mouflon** (*muflón* in Castilian), which resembles a large, sturdy sheep with curling black horns, is a recently reintroduced species. Bones found near Perpignan show that they inhabited the region thousands of years ago, but Corsica, Sardinia and Cyprus were this sheep's only modern natural strongholds. Mouflon now thrive in the Carlit Massif and on Pic Pibeste near Lourdes, with its congenial, Mediterranean microclimate.

The dark-bristled **wild boar** (*sanglier* in French; *jabalí* in Castilian) is nocturnal, and nomadic during hunting season, covering up to 40km between dusk and dawn. You may see it at its mud-wallow, to which the beast returns regularly, but are more likely to notice signs of its presence than the animal itself. Large areas of disturbed woodland earth are indicative that a wild boar has been rooting around with its tusks, foraging for beechnuts and acorns. Boar are much disliked locally, owing to their habit of damaging fields; they have become a prolific pest since the 1990s owing to mild winters and overzealous reintroduction programmes by hunting clubs.

Red deer and the much smaller, slim-horned **roe deer** live in the central Pyrenees, both favouring calcareous zones where open pasture meets forest and the necessary combination of food and cover is provided. Dawn and dusk are the best times to view deer, when feeding activity is most intense; they are elusive animals, though, and local advice will usually be needed to find them. On the Spanish side, however, hunting reserves set aside for them have proven too small for exploding populations; hungry animals have wandered out of the limited areas, resulting in numerous traffic accidents and demands from hunters to be allowed to cull the surplus.

The **marmot** (*marmotte* in French; *marmota* in Castilian) is effectively the mascot of the range; they were long extinct locally and had to be reintroduced, but now they have multiplied to the point of becoming pests. See the box on p.8 for the full story on the creature.

The Pyrenean **wildcat** (*chat sauvage* in French; *gato montés* in Castilian) is genetically much the same as that found in other parts of Europe; it looks like a domestic tabby, only much larger, with a distinctively thick tail and squat head. Pyrenean wildcats prefer south-facing forests well below alpine habitats, where their preferred prey of fieldmice and voles is abundant; they dislike snow, and descend as necessary in winter. Wildcats are protected on both sides of the Pyrenees, and are actually increasing in numbers and expanding their range, but are shy and seldom seen.

Wildcats shouldn't be confused with the **genet**, which inhabits lower altitudes up to about 1000m. Neither a feline nor a member of the weasel family, these curious creatures have a cat-like head, a leopard-spotted body and an outsize ringed tail. They're an introduced species, having been brought as pets from North Africa by the Moors – and subsequently escaping into the wild. Opportunist carnivores, they will eat anything from frogs to rabbits.

Stoats are another small, sinuous carnivore, of the weasel family, which prey on small rodents and rabbits. In their reddish-brown summer fur with a black-tipped tail they are fairly conspicuous, but in winter they become white to camouflage themselves in the snow, at which time they are called **ermines** (same in French; *armiños* in Castilian). A larger relative is the **pine marten** (*martre* in French; *marta garduña* in Castilian), which remains a warm brown colour all year round, and is found up to the tree line in the Pyrenees in coniferous and mixed woodland. The **red squirrel** (*ardilla roja* in Castilian; *écureuil rouge* in French) favours much the same habitat and – not subject to competition from greys as in Britain – remains relatively abundant, though prone to the disturbing habit of dashing across the road – and under one's car wheels. **Rabbits** and **hares** are both present; among these, the snowy hare (*lièvre variable* in French) changes like the ermine from tawny to white in winter, and thrives at high elevations where its splayed paws, covered with coarse fur, enable it to sprint across snow. **Bats** also frequent the Pyrenees up to 2000m altitude, the most striking of several species being *Pleocotus auritus* with its outsized ears.

Extinct and endangered species

The Pyrenean **ibex** (*bouquetin* in French; *cabra montés* in Castilian, *bucardo* in Aragonese), a stocky species of wild goat, is effectively extinct. Until 1999 the slopes of the Valle de Ordesa supported the range's single herd, but conservation-programme blunders, a harsh winter or two, inbreeding and bad luck doomed it; the last individual died in January 2000, struck by a falling tree. However, cells from the fresh corpse were quickly rescued, and cloning of new specimens is planned, with the less hardy Gredo ibex serving as surrogate mothers. Some five thousand of the latter survive, though they're a distinct subspecies of those formerly native in the Pyrenees. Hunting was the principal cause of the Pyrenean ibex's demise, their distinctive ribbed horns a much-esteemed trophy during the nineteenth century.

The small, unaggressive Pyrenean subspecies of **brown bear** (*ours* in French; *oso pardo* in Spanish) is also extinct as a native population. For a complete discussion of bear vicissitudes (and the controversy they've provoked), see the box on p.386.

The only other large local carnivore is the rare **lynx** (same in French; *pardelo* in Castilian), which has long been persecuted. Out of a total French/Spanish population of some six hundred, just a few dozen remain in the western French Pyrenees, but these are vulnerable to loss of habitat through deforestation. Wildcats (see opposite) are sometimes mistaken for them.

Few have heard of the **desman** (same in French; *almizclera* or *desmán* in Castilian), yet this trunk-nosed, aquatic, mole-like mammal is one of the great curiosities of the Pyrenees, with its only living relatives in southern Russia. All attempts to study the creature have failed, since in captivity specimens die almost immediately, and it is extremely scarce in the wild. Needing undisturbed and unpolluted streams to survive, the desman has been sighted in the Baronnies, in the Aspe and the streams of the Eastern Pyrenees, which are amongst the cleanest in the range; the parks and reserves south of the watershed are promising too, especially Aigüestortes, the headwaters of the Ara and Roncal's Parque Natural Pirenaico. Not exceeding 25cm in length (including the tail), it dives for small crustaceans, insects and other invertebrates, consuming daily up to two-thirds its body weight in food.

Another, slightly less endangered aquatic mammal is the **otter** (*loutre* in French; *nutria* in Castilian). It nests among the roots of riverside trees, but is a famously strong swimmer, capable of up to six minutes of submersion; preferred otter prey are amphibians and the rare native **trout** now restricted to the headwaters of the Río Ara on the Spanish side. A successful protection regimen at the Parc Natural dels Aiguamolls de l'Empordà has resulted in the release and tagging of adolescent individuals across the range, but progress in restocking areas depopulated of otters several decades ago is threatened by various dams proposed for Aragón (see box on p.405).

The turkey-like **capercaillie** (*grand tétras* in French; *urogallo* in Castilian) survives in small numbers in the Pyrenees, protected – not entirely effectively – in the national parks and in Andorra. Although evolved to survive in extreme winter conditions and on a near-starvation diet, it cannot tolerate human interference, and a conservation campaign – made feasible by the long lifespan (average. 15 years) of the surviving adults – has been launched on the Spanish side. Despite its size the capercaillie is a very elusive bird, but you might see one breaking noisily from cover, or witness the late-winter mating display of the cock, when it throws back its green-ringed neck, dances and sings. The hen is duller, mostly brown flecked with white, and with smaller bright red "eyebrows" than the male.

Amphibians, reptiles and butterflies

The slow-moving **fire salamander** (*salamandre jaune et noire* in French; *salamandra común* in Spanish) is like a soft-skinned lizard, with brilliant yellow-and-black markings that warn potential predators of its toxic skin secretions. They are primarily nocturnal, and usually only seen by day in damp weather on paths and roads. The smaller, camouflaged Pyrenean **brook salamander** (*tritón pirenaico* in Castilian) is endemic to the mountains between 1500m and 2200m, and found in cold lakes and streams; oddly, they fall into a stupor when the water temperature exceeds 15°C, at which time they're easy prey for the local trout. Salamanders are only aquatic during the four warmest months of the year, hibernating on land otherwise. The most spectacular local **frog**, known as the *ranita de San Antón* in Castilian, has almost harlequin-pattern markings in red, green and black.

A true reptile, the **Iberian rock lizard** can be found, unlike most of its sun-loving relatives, at surprisingly high altitudes in the Pyrenees. Several **snakes** occur in the area, none of them poisonous except the **asp viper**. Like most snakes, this species, with a dark wavy or zigzag pattern along the spine, only bites if under threat of attack and needs merely to be left alone. The only snake capable of enduring really low temperatures, it may even interrupt its November-to-February hibernation to take advantage of a sunny winter day.

Numerous **butterflies** (French *papillon*; Castilian *mariposa*) dwell in the Pyrenees, even to quite high altitudes, with July and August being the best months; the Val d'Aran is one of the prime locales for them. Apollo butterflies are white, with distinctive red or yellow eyespots on the wings, whereas the humbler clouded apollo could be mistaken for a small cabbage white. The endemic Gavarnie blue is a rather disappointing shade of grey, but the slightly more widespread Alcon and Eros blues can equal the colour of the gentians it feeds among. Ringlets are a group of medium-sized brown butterflies, with wings marked by black eyespots. They are difficult to distinguish, even for experts, but two species and seven subspecies are endemic to the Pyrenees.

Flora and fungi

Pyrenean high-altitude flora resembles that of the Alps in many ways, but with the warmer average temperatures, the tree line of the Pyrenees can be much higher in a few favoured positions, reaching 2600m on southern slopes of the Néouvielle Massif, or 2100m in the Marcadau valley. The highest-altitude **trees** are Pyrenean mountain pines (either *Pinus uncinata* or *Pinus mugo*, and hybrids), with distinctive hooked tips to the cone-scales – hence the French name of *pin crochet*. Black pines (*Pinus nigra*, ssp. *salzmanii*) are the next most tolerant of alpine conditions, occurring up to about 2100m; lower down, in roughly descending order of occurrence, Scots pine, beech, silver fir, birch and poplar form dense forests, with some of the finest being in the Ordesa National Park. Lower still (below about 1000m) grow maple, hornbeam, sweet chestnut and various deciduous oaks. To the east, near the Mediterranean coast, appear groves of umbrella-shaped stone pine, whose edible seeds are gathered as pine nuts (*pignon* in French; *piñon* in Spanish).

Because of the rainfall disparity between some of the dry Spanish slopes and the much wetter French slopes, especially in the east, the vegetation in one country is often very different from that at a similar altitude on the opposite side of the border. The underlying igneous and metamorphic rocks are hard and slow-weathering, but often overlaid with more plant-friendly limestone. The range's altitude has made the mountains an effective barrier, preventing the spread of many lower-altitude Spanish species northwards into France, and vice versa. June and July are the best months for finding the medium- and high-altitude wildflowers in bloom, but a few species begin as early as May, while others carry on into August, with a few exceptional autumn flowers.

More than 3300 species of **plants** are recorded for the Pyrenees, about 180 of them endemic (found growing wild nowhere else). Two unspectacular and very similar species of **Pyrenean yam**, with tiny green flowers, a swollen starchy root and tropical relatives, are ancient relicts of a warmer climate. Both are confined to the Pyrenees, with the rarer one living only in the Noguera Ribagorçana gorge. **Xatardia** is a stocky, green-flowered, celery-like plant restricted to a few high screes in the east of the range. A much more attractive relict from the Tertiary period is the **ramonda**, named after Ramond de Carbonnières, the doyen of Pyrenean exploration during the late eighteenth century. Although not rare, it is restricted to limestone slopes in northeastern Spain and the Pyrenees. Resembling its distant relative the African violet, it has fleshy wrinkled leaves and, in summer, small purple flowers with a central yellow cone of stamens.

Other endemics are more flamboyant. The long-leaved **butterwort**, clinging spectacularly to the cliffs at Gavarnie, has "flypaper" leaves that trap and digest insects. The large purple **storksbill** sports almost garish flowers, while the ashy and western **cranesbills** have more subtle shades of soft pink on their trumpet-shaped flowers. More delicate still are the little **horned pansies**, with fragrant violet blooms. The rare **silvery vetch** has spikes of pea flowers that are white with thread-like violet veining. The Pyrenean and Aragonese **columbines** have long-spurred flowers of a wonderful blue, while their relative, the Pyrenean **adonis**, or pheasant's eye, produces huge golden bowl-shaped flowers over feathery foliage in early summer. The higher areas of the Pyrenees are home to tussocky **fescue** grasses (*genus Festuca*), many species of which are endemic to these mountains. South-facing slopes in Alto Aragón turn yellow with **broom** during early summer.

Several **primroses** in subtle shades of lilac to red can be found in rocky or marshy places, but their smaller and more delicate relatives the **rock jasmines** are mostly restricted to high-altitude cliffs and screes; *Androsace ciliata* and *A. cylindrica* are two of the rarest, confined to the central areas around Gavarnie and Monte Perdido.

The **Pyrenean snowbell** has deeply fringed violet flowers and favours damp, shady conditions in the west of the range.

Growing mostly above the tree line, though sometimes in shady woodland, are many species of **saxifrage**, five of them endemic to the Pyrenees. Their flowers are usually small, numerous and starry, coloured white or pinkish in loose sprays. The endemic **water saxifrage** grows in mountain bogs and along streams up to about 2500m, its white flowers appearing in midsummer; the cliff-dwelling **Pyrenean saxifrage** has a large rosette of lime-encrusted leaves, which eventually produces a tall red-stemmed spike of flowers before dying. The **paniculate** (or livelong) **saxifrage** is similar to the Pyrenean but has a smaller, more ragged rosette, with yellow and white flowers only at the top. The most spectacular of this group, the **purple saxifrage**, has large, stemless flowers over carpets of tiny leaves, and grows on the highest peaks.

Succulent **stonecrops** (*Sedum* spp.), with yellow, white or pink flowers, and frequently red leaves, grow in dry, open places, often with little soil. The equally fleshy, but neatly rosetted, **houseleeks** produce occasional spikes of reddish flowers, and are capable of surviving at altitudes of nearly 3000m. A smaller, pale pink-flowered species of houseleek is endemic to the Sierra del Cadí.

Globularias are dwarf shrubs, with spherical tufted heads of blue or purple flowers and a long flowering period from May to August. There are numerous types of **daisy**, some with large flowers, like the endemic purple **Pyrenean aster**, and the even larger **shasta daisy** – the latter now widely cultivated as a garden plant. The huge **cardoon knapweed** brandishes spectacular purple thistle heads, up to 7cm across, in late-summer meadows; parts of this plant, a close relative of the artichoke, are edible and sometimes appear stewed in restaurants.

Members of the heather family cover large areas, and add colour to the slopes all through the summer. **Bilberries** (April–July), **bearberries** (June–Sept) and **cowberries** all have greenish-white or pinkish, often bell-shaped flowers, followed by edible berries. The prostrate, mat-forming **creeping azalea** (May–July) produces tiny pink flowers, but its bigger cousin the **wild rhododendron** (May–Aug) or alpenrose has clusters of conspicuous red flowers. Various species of **heather** itself provide colour from May to October.

The higher alpine meadows are home to some gorgeous members of the lily family, such as the chocolate or deep purple bells of the **Pyrenean fritillary**; the large white trumpets of **Saint Bruno's lily**; the yellow **Turk's-cap lily**, which prefers cliffs or rockpiles; the **dogstooth violet**, which takes its name from the pointed white oval bulb, not the magenta blossom; and *Brimeura*, a small amethyst **hyacinth**. Belonging to the same family, but crocus-like in shades of pink and white, are *Bulbocodium*, *Colchicum* and pink-purple *Merendera*, most of these autumn-blooming. The **true crocuses** bloom either in early summer amongst receding snow-patches, or in autumn as the season cools. During spring, half a dozen small members of the **daffodil family** appear, usually in damp meadows and often in great quantity; the rush-leaved narcissus, rock narcissus and lesser wild daffodil are among the more common. **Buttercups** are also well represented, for example the glacier crowfoot (*Ranunculus glacialis*), conspicuous as shiny white or pink flowers on high-altitude glacial moraines or screes, to 3000m and beyond. They are followed, in summer, by the deep, purplish-blue, so-called "English" **iris** (*Iris latifolia, ex-xiphioides*), which despite its name is more or less confined in the wild to the Pyrenees, forming spectacular, early-summer clusters on treeless slopes at 1600–2000m elevation. This species is the parent of many cultivated forms in northern Europe, and shouldn't be confused with the more widespread, lower-altitude Spanish iris (*Iris xiphium*).

Thirteen types of **gentian** are recorded for the Pyrenees, at elevations over 1500m, but they can be tricky to identify. Most species are small and delicate, with starry or trumpet-shaped flowers of a piercing blue that can mirror the sky or mountain tarns, but the more robust yellow gentians can attain a metre in height. The most common are the large, deep-blue trumpet gentians, *Gentiana acaulis* (*ex-kochiana*) and closely related species. Another legendary alpine dweller which may grow with them is the **edelweiss**, though the fuzzy whitish flowers can be disappointing up close and lack the gentian's charisma.

Numerous blue **bellflowers** occur, including a number of endemics. The taller ones grow in open or woodland areas, but the real gems nestle in crevices of the limestone, or run delicate stems through the debris of scree slopes. With them, but in contrasting shades of purplish-red through to pale pink, are **wild carnations** and **pinks** (*Dianthus* spp.), which often have powerful fragrances according to the kind of soil or rock rooted in; the fringed pink, thriving up to 2000m, is one of the most attractive.

A number of alpine or central European **orchids** grow in woodland and meadows on the French side, while lower areas on the Spanish side and at the hotter eastern and western ends of the range, are home to more Mediterranean species. *Epipactis parviflora* and *Dactylorhiza caramulensis* are two specialities of the area, but the endangered **lady's slipper** still survives in a few places in the east.

During late summer and autumn local people harvest the abundant **wild fungi**. Robust ceps, crinkly yellow chanterelles and saffron milk-caps are favourites, but most in demand are the brown honeycombed morels of springtime, scarce but almost worth their weight in gold when gathered and dried. You will see favourite picking grounds jealously signposted against nonresidents on the Spanish side (*Cota de Setas – Prohibido Coger Hongos sín Autorización*/Mushroom Reserve – Forbidden to Pick Fungi without a Permit).

The environment

Permanent human populations may be lower in most of the Pyrenees than they were during the nineteenth century, but the landscape is nonetheless threatened, and since the early 1980s French and Spanish conservationists have focused considerable attention on the region. Concerns are numerous: the potential extinction of endangered species, massacres of migrating birds, the health of forests and the obstruction of waterways and inundation of valleys by hydroelectric and water-transfer schemes. Environmental protests get some hearing these days, and occasionally succeed in stopping or at least modifying destructive projects. However, there are still formidable obstacles to be overcome, not least the mind-set of governmental officials in Spain, from regional levels all the way to the top.

The biggest contemporary threat to the Pyrenean environment is the uncontrolled building of second homes – usually apartment blocks – something apparently unstoppable in light of the money being made by developers, investors and town or village councils. The Spanish government is beginning to combat planning corruption, but Pyrenean towns and villages, especially on the southern slopes, have been and continue to be transformed by usually unoccupied buildings. A major economic consequence is the savaging of local short-term tourism facilities, with modest hotels pushed to the wall and reduced takings for bars and restaurants – those saddled with a huge mortgage for a second home are unlikely to eat out too often.

Natural reserves

Among the qualifications for national park status, as defined by the International Union for the Conservation of Nature and Natural Resources (IUCN), are that there should be no hunting and no exploitation other than that consistent with the "natural" way of life of mountain people, such as grazing or wild-food gathering. So far there are just three full-fledged **national parks in the Pyrenees**, and only two of those – the Parc National des Pyrénées in France and the adjoining Parque Nacional de Ordesa y Monte Perdido in Spain – actually meet the IUCN criteria. The Parc Nacional d'Aigüestortes i Sant Maurici in Catalunya is not officially recognized by the IUCN because of its numerous hydroelectric installations, a source of constant friction with conservationists.

Other areas of the Pyrenees are administered under less stringent conservation schemes. In Spain there are the *parques naturales* of Cadí-Moixeró, Alt Pirineu, Maladeta-Posets, the Sierra y Cañones de Guara, the Garrotxa, Larra-Belagoa and Los Valles (de Ansó y Hecho). France has various *réserves naturelles*, including that of Néouvielle – but these do not entirely protect wildlife from hunting.

Hunting

Hunting in the Pyrenees is **controlled** in a number of ways besides the outright ban in national parks. Various private reserves limit hunter numbers by charging high fees; permits are issued by auction or the drawing of lots; certain animals are designated as protected species; the hunting calendar is restricted; and voluntary management plans have been implemented by (French more than Spanish) hunting associations.

In some instances these restraints have been effective. There are around 15,000 **isards** on the French side of the range and probably a similar number on the Spanish, a reasonably healthy situation that leads hunters to insist that further kill limits are unnecessary. Herds have territories of just a few square kilometres, so those within the protected areas are fairly safe; the animals at risk – solitary old males, youngsters rejected by their mothers and mature males driven off by rivals – are those that stray outside the protected reserves.

Even if an animal is classified as a protected species, it isn't necessarily safe. Tragically the last native female Pyrenean brown bear was killed in the Vallée d'Aspe by a wild boar-hunter during the winter of 2005. Pigeon-hunters often illegally kill other species, such as vultures and kestrels, in the barrages of shot aimed at the dwindling flocks of pigeons. Two recent avian bright spots are the total ban on hunting at certain critical passes used by migratory birds, and a steady increase in lammergeier populations in the Western Pyrenees, thanks to EU-funded conservation projects and growing awareness amongst country people that these raptors feed only on already-dead livestock.

Ski and golf development

Given the inconsistent snow record of the Pyrenees, **downhill ski development** has lagged far behind that of the Alps, especially on the Spanish side of the range. A 1999 EU report advised, in light of **global warming**, that no new developments should plan to have a base point of under 2000m elevation; a more recent, late-2003 study by the UN Environment Programme warned that any resort worldwide (except for Scandanavia) with a base station of under 1500m would be non-viable by 2030, and predicted the demise of many Alpine (let alone Pyrenean) resorts by that date. At present, most Pyrenean ski centre base-stations lie at 1600–1850m, and many French stations have a *top* lift point of under 2000m. On the Spanish side, the 1990s saw Llessui and La Tuca close down through combinations of financial mismanagement and unco-operative climate, while Panticosa and Cerler narrowly escaped **closure** through massive investment in snow canons and new lifts. However, all the snow canons in the world will not make a difference if average winter temperatures remain too high. While many French Pyrenean centres have got away with lower siting owing to severe Atlantic weather, a half-dozen minor resorts – including Hautacam, Mijanès-Donezan and Guzet-Neige – now spend much of each winter inoperative, and are clearly on the way out, joining Goulier-Neige which shut permanently in 1999. In France, most ski stations are publicly owned and run at a loss, kept going as the major local employer and spur to the mountain economy. Despite the worsening climatic situation, more downhill ski resorts are planned – with similar justification – on the Spanish side, as young people in the high mountain valleys cannot live on the proceeds of a three-month summer season.

Expanding the network of **cross-country** ski destinations has not yet proven sufficiently attractive to planners or investors. Though a lower-profit game, it's also lower-risk and lower-impact – if warm, dry winters force them to fold, there's no hardware left littering the slopes and no scarred mountainsides where pistes used to be.

Existing downhill stations frantic over recent poor winters are, in accordance with the above-cited reports, looking to the **highest slopes** of the range to alleviate their problems – one rejected **expansion** plan at Candanchú hoped to blast away part of the Pico d'Aspe to lengthen its ski runs. There is now an accepted correlation between the clearance of forests for the construction of pistes and resorts and a higher incidence of **avalanches**, with devastating effects on settlements downhill.

Worse, other resorts propose to drain natural lakes to feed new **snow canons**. Ski centres in Spanish Catalunya are almost totally dependent on these monsters, which in the nine resorts concerned use up enough electricity over a season to power a town of 15,000 people – and render the industry grossly unprofitable given the huge consumption bills and per-canon set-up cost of €10,000. Environmental campaigners Ecologistas en Acción highlight a vicious circle: lack of snow increases canon use, which boosts CO_2 emissions, increases average winter temperatures and further reduces snow; they suggest a "green" energy source for the snow canons as a way out.

An as-yet unapproved French scheme – to link the domain of La Mongie with that of Saint-Lary-Soulan – demands exemption from the ban on development in the Parc National des Pyrénées and the Réserve Naturelle de Néouvielle. On the Spanish side, Formigal and Astún will be united into one "macro"-station via the Valle de Izas, notwithstanding opposition from Ecologistas en Acción and the region's failed bids to host the 1998 and 2010 **Winter Olympics**. Further east, Cerler is set to grow by fifty percent, up to the boundaries of the Parque Natural Posets-Maladeta; Baqueira-Beret wishes to expand into the Val d'Arreu, a move vigorously opposed by the group Ipcena, which notes that the EU must approve this since the particular valley has been included in the "Nature Net" of high-value sites. In Andorra, the Pal-Alins joint station and the Grau Roig domain have both grown since 2005, despite the objections of two local conservationist groups.

Although climate change makes further investment in downhill ski infrastructure extremely risky, and local surveys show that the number of skiers will not grow significantly, funds continue to pour in. The main potential beneficiaries are developers who have constructed thousands of apartments around Jaca since the 1980s; the cheapest interest rates ever in Spain mean a continued orgy of building despite the uncertainties of climate and Olympic-hosting. In fact, proposals for new ski centres are a means, not an end, for speculators wishing to justify yet more of the **urbanizaciones** (chalet complexes) that blight nearly every alpine village on the Spanish side not falling within the protection zone of a national park; the Cerdanya and the Val d'Aran in particular have been almost completely disfigured. Once the blocks are up and sold, developers couldn't care less whether the adjacent ski resort remains viable. **Golf courses** are the latest pretext for more *urbanizaciones* at lower altitudes; there are six new golf courses in the Alto Aragón area alone – each with a thousand-plus apartments built alongside. Such projects have obvious repercussions in terms of visual disturbance, sewage pollution and increased traffic.

Forest fires

Forest fires have so far had less impact in the Pyrenees than in drier parts of Spain and France, but throughout the range fires have been breaking out progressively earlier in the year – yet another symptom of global warming. Many are deliberately set by shepherds attempting to clear fresh grazing land, or are the result of burning field-stubble in early spring, with flames escaping into adjacent woodland (and doing nothing, incidentally, for ambient air quality). In the Albères, on the Mediterranean side of the range, there has been talk of planting more cork oak, a species highly resistant to fire. Improved husbandry of vineyards and olive groves through the clearance of undergrowth and the construction of firebreaks has given some protection to vegetation in the vulnerable Alt Empordà region, behind Catalunya's Mediterranean coast, but the nearby Cap de Creus promontory in Catalunya seems to burn with depressing regularity every few years.

Hydroelectric power – and new dams

Although **hydroelectric power** is in principle more acceptable than fossil-fuelled or nuclear alternatives, and can be almost benign environmentally, neither Spain nor France has devoted much effort to make it so in the Pyrenees. Valleys have been scoured and flooded in an entirely unaesthetic way, with almost no money spent on landscaping or tidying up. Tunnel-sized feed pipes have been routed through once-wooded areas, and substations send out their rhythmic roar day and night even in the remotest locations. High-tension pylons are strung across otherwise empty sky, while leftover construction and maintenance materials, including rusty, aerial cable cars, deface the most unexpected places. In 1999 it was officially agreed by assorted power companies and Alto Aragón municipalities that €200,000 was to be budgeted for hauling away the rubbish from a dozen badly affected lakes near the frontier; to date nothing has been done. Virtually no major river is untouched, and multilingual warning notices advise you to keep away from the banks downstream from dams in case the power company instigates sudden changes in water level.

The pace of hydroelectric development on the French side, which hit its stride between the world wars, has now slowed down considerably as France enjoys a kilowatt surplus. Indeed, a proposed 400,000-volt high-tension "superhighway" **exporting power** through the Couserans to Graus in Aragón, distinctly unpopular during the planning stages on both sides of the frontier, appears to have died a quiet death.

The Spaniards were latecomers to the hydro-game: while the very first dams appeared in the hills of Catalunya early in the 1900s, most Spanish projects were commissioned after World War II, and proposals for **new dams** are still on the drawing boards for depopulated Alto Aragón and Navarra – with the bulk of accumulated water to be sent, in all cases, down to farms and towns in the flatlands, or even as far away as the giant plantations and golf courses of southern Spain, by means of giant **trasvases**, or pipelines. Under Franco, dams served a dual purpose: as prestige projects proving that the country was "developing", and as a convenient way to clear the hills of potentially independent-minded folk. While paying token homage to rural dwellers as the repositories of original folkloric values, authoritarian regimes have always distrusted them as unlikely to fit in well with their social-engineering schemes. In democratic Spain there has been a subtle shift: many projects approved under Franco remain valid, and Pyrenean dwellers are expected to sacrifice their homes and livelihoods for the benefit of the millions in the thirsty cities and fields of Valencia, Almería and Murcía in the south. But they are not going quietly – those affected are considerably more sophisticated than the villagers terrorized into leaving Jánovas in 1960 (see box on p.405). Encouraged by the success of anti-dam movements in India and Turkey, locals have mounted vigorous, if not always successful **campaigns against hydro-projects** in Spain.

The future of dams on the Noguera Pallaresa near Rialp, the Río Ésera at Santaliestra and the Río Gállego at Biscarrués (see p.437) remains uncertain, and the €20-billion National Water Plan (NWP), designed in the late 1990s to ostensibly alleviate the natural imbalance in water resources between northern and southern Spain but effectively to benefit the then-ruling PP's major sponsors in the agricultural and construction sectors – has largely been shelved by the current PSOE government.

The NWP's biggest component in the Pyrenees was the enlargement of the **Yesa reservoir**, originally built in 1960; it caused the abandonment of three villages with 1500 people and inundated 2500 hectares of arable land – with token or no compensation. The PSOE government has so far kept its 2004 campaign promise that the new Yesa dam will be "only" 25m higher than the existing one, and a planned *trasvase* to the Mediterranean coast has been cancelled. But even this scaled-down enlargement will destroy rich farmland and the economy of two villages, while inundating a number of Roman and early Christian monuments in the Canal de Berdún (including part of the original Camino de Santiago). The extra water will go to irrigate rice-fields in a semi-desert near Bardenas, and address an alleged shortfall of drinking water for Zaragoza. Opponents of enlargement charge that Zaragoza loses nearly half its mains water to leaks at present, doesn't bill for roughly the same fraction and hasn't adequately explored the option of obtaining potable water from the Ebro, its own river. Moreover, the Bardenas irrigation zone is apparently not authorized to expand more than eight percent anyway, and its current water-delivery systems are obsolete and inefficient.

The **Itoiz dam**, a 135-metre-high structure on the Río Irati downstream from Auritze and Aribe, has had an even stormier history. The project was first conceived during the early 1970s to irrigate farms on the plains near Pamplona. When plans were revived in 1985 locals mobilized in opposition, citing the inundation of three villages and the ecological value of the Itoiz valley with its two nature reserves. By 1992 the Navarran government had dismissed these arguments and began to build. Environmental activists went to the Spanish supreme court – and won. The judges ruled that nature reserves could not be flooded, and ordered a reduction in dam height from 135m to 25m – which would completely undermine the project's economic viability. The Navarran parliament responded in 1995 by dissolving the nature reserves and ordering that construction resume. Faced with the limits of the local justice system, a direct-action group called **Solidarios con Itoiz** (ScI) then formed. With members of the press invited to watch, in 1996 eight members of ScI overpowered a security guard at the dam site and severed critical cables with power-grinders, delaying further construction for a year. For their pains, the eco-saboteurs got arrested and were given a thorough beating by the Guardia Civil, plus a draconian five-year sentence at their subsequent trial. Free on bail, they conducted a tour of Europe during 1999 to publicize their cause, beginning with a press conference at the European Parliament and culminating in various attention-getting stunts – before disappearing. Though the "ScI 8" are now officially "wanted", the authorities have made no particular effort to haul them in, to avoid further embarrassment. In early 2000 the last Spanish legal obstacle to the high dam was overcome, and the dam is nearing completion.

Marc Dubin, updates by Richard Cash

Books

The following books will greatly enrich a visit to the Pyrenees. Not all are concerned exclusively with the range, but certain titles dealing with all of France or Spain have been included because they contain much that is relevant to the mountains and their cultures. In-print books, whose publishers tend to change frequently, can be found on any book-retailing website such as Ⓦwww.amazon.com/.co.uk; most out-of-print books are easily and affordably available on such used-book sites as Ⓦwww.abe.co.uk/com, Ⓦwww.biblio.com or Ⓦwww.bookfinder.com, or at a library. Books marked with the symbol are especially recommended.

Travel and memoirs

Rosemary Bailey *Life in a Postcard: Escape to the French Pyrenees.* In which the author buys a minor Romanesque monastery on the outskirts of Mosset (see p.103) and proceeds to restore – and then live in – it. Part cautionary tale, part chronicle of expat/Parisian/local-born interactions; more engaging than typical "new life in the sun" British TV programmes. In her more recent *The Man Who Married a Mountain*, Bailey sets off in search of the grand nineteenth-century eccentric and mountaineer Henry Russell, visiting all the venues of his colourful life.

Hilaire Belloc *The Pyrenees.* Originally written in 1909, this is inevitably dated but still fascinating to dip into on a wealth of topics (eg why the Somport and Portalet passes have always been militarily strategic). His tips on Pyrenean high-altitude navigation remain valid, Spanish *botas* (goat-hairy insides and all) are extolled, and even back then maps on the Spanish side lagged behind their French counterparts. Easily findable on the recommended websites; later editions (1916, 1923) are far cheaper.

Simon Calder and Mick Webb *Backpacks' Boots and Baguettes: Walking in the Pyrenees*. Humorous to the point of flippancy, but there's as much hitching as walking here, and Calder in particular revels in his own nerdy persona, especially in a wimpy, whimpering account of the Chemin de Mâture (see p.397).

Norbert Casteret *The Descent of Pierre Saint-Martin* (o/p) chronicles the exploration of what was then the world's deepest-known cave system. Other translated titles by Casteret, the greatest Pyrenean speleologist, include *Ten Years Under the Earth* (o/p), *My Caves* (o/p), *Cave Men New and Old* (o/p) and *The Darkness Under the Earth* (o/p).

Eleanor Elsner *Romance of the Basque Country and the Pyrenees* (o/p). Published in 1927, but still a treasure for its old photographs and anecdotes.

Nina Epton *The Valley of Pyrene* (o/p). Record of a tour through the Ariège in the 1950s; encounters with luminaries – including Dalí – enhance the account.

Robin Fedden *The Enchanted Mountains: A Quest in the Pyrenees*. Short, elegiac account of several 1950s summers spent mountaineering on the Spanish side between Espot and Benasque, with wonderful period detail.

Nancy Louise Frey *Pilgrim Stories: On and Off the Road to Santiago, Journeys Along an Ancient Way in Modern Spain*. Not a guidebook per se, but an analysis by a trained anthropologist of the variety and motivations of modern pilgrims on the *Camino/Chemin*, and most intriguingly what happens to them when they return home.

Norman Lewis *Voices of the Old Sea*. Set between 1948 and 1950, this blend of novel and social record movingly charts the lives of two remote Costa Brava villages and the breakdown of the old ways upon the arrival of tourism.

Edwin Mullins *The Pilgrimage to Santiago*. While just a brief section of the medieval route from Paris to Santiago de Compostela includes the Pyrenees, this provides a good overview of the Santiago legend and the pilgrimage it sparked. Mullins, an amiable if sedentary cicerone, who never walks when he can ride a vintage car or a spirited horse, points out churches along the way, giving incisive accounts of their social and architectural background.

Henry Myhill *The Spanish Pyrenees* (o/p). The Spanish side as it was in the early 1960s; excellent for its historical speculation and human anecdotes, less commendable for an obvious pro-Francoist bias.

Matthew Parris *A Castle in Spain* Parris and his sister acquire a ruined sixteenth-century mansion in the Catalan Pyrenees, and restore it, via assorted misadventures, as the "castle" of the title.

John Sturrock *The French Pyrenees* (o/p). Another detailed historical travelogue, though the author rarely gets out of his car. Sturrock starts at the west coast and works east, stopping abruptly at the border, with the exception of a detour to Roncesvalles.

History, society and politics

Raymond Carr *Modern Spain, 1875–1980* and *The Spanish Tragedy: The Civil War in Perspective*. Two of the best concise narratives on the modern era, by the acknowledged top non-Spanish historian of the country.

Alfred Cobban *A History of Modern France* (3 vols: 1715–99, 1799–1871 & 1871–1962). Complete and very readable account of the main political, economic and social strands in French history from Louis XIV's death to the middle of the de Gaulle era.

Roger Collins *Early Medieval Spain, 400–1000*. As it says on the tin: a broad overview of this period from a distinguished historian.

Daniele Conversi *The Basques, the Catalans and Spain: Alternative Routes to Nationalist Mobilisation*. Scholarly exploration of the differing evolutions of Basque and Catalan nationalism.

Natalie Zemon Davis *The Return of Martin Guerre*. A man presents himself as a woman's long-lost husband, and persuades many doubters, despite his extremely tenuous resemblance to the missing spouse. A titillating hoax which actually occurred in the Pyrenean foothill village of Artigat during the sixteenth century, which inspired a movie and a musical.

J.H. Elliot *Imperial Spain 1469–1716*. Best introduction to the centuries immediately after unification – academically respected and a gripping tale.

Jonathan Fenby *France on the Brink*. Slightly alarmist diagnosis of France's woes (as of 2003), putting the blame squarely on its complacent, greedy ruling class.

Christopher Hibbert *The French Revolution*. Good, concise popular history of the period and salient events, in particular the descent into mob violence.

John Hooper *The New Spaniards*. A 1994 update of a perceptive 1986 portrait of post-Franco Spain and the new generation by the *Guardian*'s long-time Madrid correspondent. Though the revision in turn is due for rewriting, still the best one-volume introduction to contemporary Spain.

Mark Kurlansky *The Basque History of the World*. Eminently readable, unconventional chronicle of this mysterious people, from prehistory to the ETA era. Black-and-white illustrations, maps and even recipes illuminate Basque contributions to European cuisine, economic growth, Catholicism, banking and international relations (hence the title).

Peter Sahlins *Boundaries: The Making of France and Spain in the Pyrenees*. Using the partition of the Cerdanya/Cerdagne as a model, this explores the process of instilling French and Spanish national identities in a formerly unified area of the Catalan Pyrenees; academic and groaning with charts and tables, but has its readable moments.

Giles Tremlett *Ghosts of Spain: Travels Through A Country's Hidden Past*. The "ghosts" in question are those of the 160,000 civilian victims of political assassination and revenge killing during the Civil War, which in a consensus of amnesia were until the millennium largely unacknowledged. The first three chapters of this 2006 work by the *Guardian's* Spain correspondent – exploring Spain's coming to terms with this denial – are the best, followed by more pedestrian analyses of conventional topics like regionalism, tourism, corruption and flamenco.

Alexander Werth *France 1940–1955* (o/p). Excellent, engaged portrayal of the most taboo period in French history: the Occupation, followed by the early Cold War and colonial-struggle years in which the same political tensions and heart-searchings were at work; that said, written with perhaps too little hindsight, in 1956.

The Cathars

In its anti-centralist, anticlerical essentials, the Cathar heresy still fascinates both French and foreign readers, with the French audience served by two Toulouse-based publishers – Éditions Privat and Éditions Loubatières – specializing in works about the sect. The following are the best titles available in English.

Emmanuel Le Roy Ladurie *Montaillou: Cathars and Catholics in a French Village, 1294–1324*. Life in a recidivist Cathar village in the Pays de Sault, as recorded by the Inquisition early in the fourteenth century, and stored away until the 1970s in the Vatican archives. Hard going in places but a fascinating insight into medieval life, from the pastoral cycle to superstitions to sex scandals.

Zoé Oldenbourg *Massacre at Montségur*. English translation of a standard (1961) history of the Cathar crusades. Vivid and partisan (ie extremely sympathetic to the Cathars), stressing the connection between the suppression of the heresy and that of Languedoc separatism. Good appendices give some insight into Cathar beliefs – and the Church's horror of them.

Stephen O'Shea *The Perfect Heresy: The Life and Death of the Cathars*. A superbly written, succinct overview of the sect, its antecedents and the crusade against them, explaining the heresy in the social context of its time (and in ours, mentioning some of the weirder after-lives and commercial exploitations of the doctrine). End notes, elaborating on the main text, encompass echoes of Catharism amongst everybody from The Singing Nun to modern rappers.

Jonathan Sumption *The Albigensian Crusade*. Lively, somewhat revisionist account in which the Cathars are made out to be nearly as contemptible as their adversaries, who are given more depth than usual. Good on the cultural clash between the dour Normans, who largely staffed and directed the campaign, and the anarchistic Languedocians – as well as the extensive Aragonese involvement in the wars.

René Weis *The Yellow Cross: The Story of the Last Cathars, 1290–1329*. Weis picks up where Le Roy Ladurie leaves off, exploiting primary archival sources to forensically re-create events and fully rounded characters of the final resurgence of Catharism on both sides of the range; includes useful sketch maps and photos of the locales as they are now.

The Spanish Civil War

Gerald Brenan *The Spanish Labyrinth: An Account of the Social and Political Background of the Spanish Civil War*. As the subtitle says: not a straight history of the war, but one of the best non-academic studies on Spanish rural society of the time.

Ronald Fraser *Blood of Spain: The Experience of Civil War*. This quasi-oral history of 1936–39 gives a voice to the people who fought in and lived through the war on both sides.

George Orwell *Homage to Catalonia*. Journalist Orwell cut his teeth on this – if not his most celebrated book, certainly his best reportage. A forthright account of battles on the Aragón front, followed by Orwell's injury and disillusionment with the factional fighting among the Republican forces.

Paul Preston *Franco*. Penetrating, monumental biography of Franco and his regime, demonstrating how he won the Civil War, how he held power so long and what his ultimate significance was. Preston's more recent *Concise History of the Spanish Civil War* is a compelling introduction to the subject, more digestible than Hugh Thomas' tome.

Hugh Thomas *The Spanish Civil War*. Massive, exhaustive political study of the period, still the best single telling of the convoluted story.

World War II: French occupation and resistance

Marc Bloch *Strange Defeat: A Statement of Evidence Written in 1940*. Moving personal study of the reasons for France's defeat and subsequent caving-in to Nazism. Found among the papers of this Sorbonne historian and Resistance member after his death at the hands of the Gestapo in 1942.

Emilienne Eychenne *Les Pyrénées de la Liberté, 1939–1945* (Éditions Empire, France). History of World War II escapes over the Pyrenees into Spain, by a historian who has made this her special subject.

H.R. Kedward *In Search of the Maquis: Rural Resistance in South France 1942–44*. Slightly dry, but full of fascinating detail about the brave and often mortal struggle of the countless ordinary people in the region who fought to drive the Germans from their country.

Ian Ousby *Occupation: The Ordeal of France 1940–1944*. Revisionist 1997 account which shows how relatively late resistance was and how widespread collaboration – and why. Good mix of salient events and how it felt to live through these times.

Paul Webster *Pétain's Crime: The Full Story of French Collaboration in the Holocaust*. The fascinating, alarming story of the Vichy regime's eager collaboration with the deportations of Jews and the bravery of those, especially the Communist-dominated resistance in occupied France, who attempted to prevent it.

Art and architecture

Xavier Barral I Altet *The Romanesque: Towns, Cathedrals and Monasteries*. Concise, without stinting on illustrations, and highly readable but authoritative introduction to the genre; especially good on townscapes and castles, and ample emphasis on Pyrenean monuments.

Michael Jacobs *The Road to Santiago de Compostela*. A good architectural guide to the Spanish section of the pilgrimage route, but only about one-fourth of the book's coverage falls within this Rough Guide.

Bertrand Lorquin *Aristide Maillol*. Short and surprisingly reticent monograph on the sculptor by the curator of the Paris Maillol museum – and son of Maillol's last model, Dina Vierny.

Meyer Schapiro *Romanesque Art: Selected Papers* (1977 or 1993 edition). An excellent illustrated survey of Romanesque art and architecture in Spain and southern France, including its Visigothic and Mozarabic predecessors and the social function of portal sculpture in particular, though most examples fall outside the Pyrenees.

Ann Sieveking *The Cave Artists* (o/p). Comprehensive introduction to late-Paleolithic cave-painting, with explanations of the theories on meaning and layout; two chapters devoted to the Pyrenees.

Rolf Toman ed. *Romanesque: Architecture, Sculpture, Painting*. Huge, sumptuously illustrated volume of essays on every aspect of the style across Europe; only two chapters specifically devoted to France and Spain, but most of the major Pyrenean monuments are discussed, and placed cogently in their historical, religious and social context.

Sarah Whitfield *Fauvism*. Although its reproductions can't do justice to the vibrant colours of Matisse and the artists in his circle, this serves well as an introduction to this artistic movement.

The Pyrenees in literature

Victor Català (pseudonym of Caterina Albert i Paradis) *Solitude*. 1905 tale of sex, death and greed in and around a Pyrenean *ermita* that's considered the most important pre-Civil War Catalan novel.

Javier Cercas *Soldiers of Salamis*. Worldwide bestseller set in and around Girona and filmed (with considerable licence) in 2003, this novelized quest by Cercas' journalist alter ego for the truth behind a historical incident at the end of the Civil War – a Republican soldier inexplicably spares an escaped, top-ranking Falangist prisoner, poet and ideologue Rafael Sánchez Mazas – proves a humane and often funny sleuthing into mythopoeia, memory, artistic agitation, loyalty and the ubiquity of the war's consequences in Spanish life three generations later.

Julio Llamazares *The Yellow Rain*. Ainelle is an actual Spanish Pyrenean village between Biescas and Fiscal; this novella chronicles its post-Civil-War abandonment through the interior monologue of the last fictional inhabitant, waiting for death. By turns terse and overwrought, starkly graphic and magical-realist, it suffers somewhat in translation from the oft-reprinted Castilian original.

Pierre Loti *Ramuntcho* (in French). Cloyingly tragic romance, a sort of early, high-class Mills & Boon-type affair, set in the French Basque country.

The Song of Roland (translated by Glyn Burgess). Written around the end of the eleventh century, this mini-saga conjures up the whole legend of Roland and the famous ambush near Roncesvalles in the Basque Pyrenees.

Walking, climbing and rafting guides

The Confraternity of Saint James publishes numerous small A5 guides, usually the best and most current available, for each section of the route. *The Camino Francés*, despite the name, covers the stretch from Saint-Jean to Pamplona; *Arles to Puenta la Reina* goes via Jaca. Both have good route and facilities details, but no maps. Order them direct from ⓦwww.csj.org.uk.

GR11, Senderos de Gran Recorrido/Senda Pirenaica (PRAMES, Spain). In Castilian. Comes in three packagings: the complete range, covered in a two-ring binder – you extract sections and carry them about in the case provided; paperbound in three separate volumes – *Andorra/Catalunya, Aragón, Navarra/Gipuzkoa*; or as one volume, with 47 route maps at 1:40,000. Invaluable, and updated regularly (current pages available for the binder edition), though as ever for things Spanish some of the timings are way out.

Les Guides Rando (Rando Éditions, France). Compact, definitive, region-by-region guides for the French side, designed to be used in conjunction with the same company's 1:50,000 *cartes des randonnées*.

Ton Joosten *Pyrenean Haute Route* Now that Georges Véron's classic volume has well and truly vanished, the only guide to the trail in English, with decent maps and altitude plots. Be aware, though, that the route chosen is idiosyncratically personal and often doesn't correspond to the classic itinerary.

Paul Lucia *Through the Spanish Pyrenees, GR11: A Long-Distance Footpath*. Now in its third edition, with somewhat brisk time-courses, altitude profiles and lists of available facilities, but poor maps and coverage of variants.

Kev Reynolds *Walks and Climbs in the Pyrenees*. Soon due in a fifth edition, this is the standard English-language guide for trekkers and scramblers by the foreigner who knows these mountains best, covering the most spectacular parts of the range. Reynolds' *Classic Walks in the Pyrenees* (o/p) is a bit more clearly presented for route-planning, if rather purple in the prose; his 2004-issued *The Pyrenees*, bulky and expensively produced, serves the same purpose, though it falls somewhere between the chairs of coffee-table book and trail guide.

Patrick Santal *White Water Pyrenees*. All you possibly need to know about every worthwhile (and a few not so worthwhile – they tell you) rafting and kayaking river in the range, in this English translation of a French guide. Meticulous ratings, diagrams, instructions and outfitter contacts (as of 2000) in what's clearly a labour of love.

Douglas Streatfeild-James & others *Trekking in the Pyrenees*. The best and always the most current English-language west-to-east guide to the GR10 and its variants, also including choice bits of the Camino de Santiago and most of the GR11. Easy-to-use sketch maps, and plenty of practical details for villages you're likely to overnight in, but some time-courses are unrealistically fast.

Derek Walker *Rock Climbs in the Pyrenees*. The first English guide for climbers; serious stuff, including Pic du Midi d'Ossau and the palisades of the Valle de Ordesa.

Wildlife field guides

In case of difficulty ordering the following through the usual web sources, you may need to use a specialist mail-order dealer. A good UK one is Summerfield Books (ⓣ017683/41577, ⓦwww.summerfieldbooks.com), which stocks not only new botanical titles, but also rare or out-of-print natural history books on all topics.

The system of Linnaean classification is in a state of flux concerning small flora, where entire families have been suppressed in recent decades, and various species have been renamed or even assigned to a different genus. So while you may find photos of the live specimens in front of you, don't always expect to have a currently correct identification.

Marjorie Blamey and Christopher Grey-Wilson (o/p) *The Alpine Flowers of Britain and Europe*. Comprehensive field guide, with coloured drawings, but relatively rare and dated (1979).

John A. Burton, William Oliver and Guy Troughton *Field Guide to the Mammals of Britain and Europe*. A bargain: well illustrated and thorough, covering over 160 species.

John A. Burton, Nicholas Arnold and Denys W. Ovenden *Field Guide to the Reptiles and Amphibians of Britain and Europe*. For all those alpine newts, lizards and frogs.

Lance Chilton *Plant List for the Pyrenees*. Slim but dense A5 pamphlet updated in 2005, cataloguing every tree and plant known to occur in the range, whether as a native or introduced species. Order direct from ⓦwww.marengowalks.com.

Jacquie Crozier and James McCallum *A Birdwatching Guide to the Pyrenees* (o/p). Illustrated and mapped guidelet, detailing eighteen regions in Spain, France and Andorra; includes practical directions and checklist.

Pierre Delforge *Orchids of Britain and Europe*. The best, most up-to-date (if slightly pricey) guide, though beware of small inaccuracies in the translation from the French.

Hermann Heinzel, Richard Fitter and John Parslow *Birds of Britain and Europe with North Africa and the Middle East*. One of the best general guides to the subject, though maps could be better.

Lionel Higgins and Norman Riley *Field Guide to the Butterflies of Britain and Europe* (o/p). Not specific to the Pyrenees, but an excellent start.

Oleg Polunin and B. E. Smythies *Flowers of South-West Europe* (o/p). Covers all of Spain, Portugal and southwest France, including the Pyrenees; taxonomy is vintage 1988 despite relatively recent (1997) printing, but still unsurpassed for its introductions, plates, line drawings and keys.

A.W. Taylor *Wild Flowers of the Pyrenees* (o/p). Slender volume that's the only guide specifically dedicated to the range. Easy to use, but somewhat elderly (1971), not comprehensive and extremely rare (ie expensive).

Language

Language

Language

One of the features of the Pyrenees is its numerous regional languages – linguists recognize Catalan, Aranés, Aragonese, Occitan, Gascon and Euskera. There will be little opportunity to learn any of these on a short visit, though a smattering of French and Castilian Spanish should serve you adequately for most purposes.

French

French (français) is far from an easy language, despite the vocabulary it shares with English, but the bare essentials are not difficult to master, and they make all the difference. Even just saying "Bonjour Monsieur/Madame" when you enter a shop will usually get you a smile and helpful service. People working in tourist offices, hotels and so forth almost always speak better English than you do French, and so tend to reply in it when you're struggling to stammer out something in French – be grateful, not insulted.

Differentiating words is the initial problem in understanding spoken French, as it's hard to get people to slow down – if all else fails, get them to write what they've said, as you're bound to recognize more words that way. Even outside the Basque, Occitan/Gascon and Catalan areas, there are districts where the language of daily life is a strong dialect of French. Don't be dismayed – though you'll probably never understand an overheard conversation, any attempt to make yourself understood in school-book French should meet with a sympathetic response and a fairly comprehensible reply.

French learning materials

Rough Guide French Phrasebook. A mini-dictionary-style phrasebook with both English–French and French–English sections, along with cultural tips for tricky situations, and a comprehensive menu reader.

Streetwise French Dictionary/Thesaurus: The User-friendly Guide to French Slang and Idioms by Ian Pickup, R. J. Hares and Luc Nisset-Raidon. The most compact and – obviously critical for something like this – current of the various purported slang guides.

Dictionary of Modern Colloquial French by René James Herail and Edwin A. Lovatt. An alternative, if bulkier, French–English dictionary of street-level vernacular.

Collins Gem French Dictionary This is the compact (approx 3 x 4 inches) version of the best single-volume French-English/English-French desktop dictionary; be sure to get the most current edition.

Breakthrough French vol. 1 (with CD) & vol. 2 (with 3 cassettes), Euro Edition by Stephanie Rybak. Excellent two-phase teach-yourself course, purchasable together or separately.

A Vous La France, by Brian Page (2 cassettes sold separately). Excellent beginner's course for adults. The intermediate continuation is **France Extra**, by Alan Moys (o/p); **France Parler** (o/p) is the advanced volume, hardest to find. BBC Publications issued all of these.

A brief guide to speaking French

Pronunciation

One easy rule to remember is that **consonants** at the ends of words are usually silent. *Pas plus tard* (not later) is thus pronounced "pa-plu-tarr". But when the following word begins with a vowel, you elide the two: *pas après* (not after) becomes "pazapray".

Vowels are the hardest sounds to get right. Approximately:

a	as in t**a**r
e	as in g**e**t
é	between g**e**t and g**a**te
è	between g**e**t and g**u**t
eu	like the **u** in h**u**rt
i	as in mach**i**ne
o	as in h**o**t
ô, au	as in **o**ver
ou	as in f**oo**d
u	as in a pursed-lip version of **u**se

More awkward are the **combinations** in/im, en/em, an/am, on/om, un/um at the ends of words, or followed by consonants other than n or m. Again, roughly:

in/im	like the **an** in **an**xious
an/am, en/em	like the **don** in **Don**caster when said with a nasal accent
on/om	like the **don** in **Don**caster said by someone with a heavy cold
un/um	like the **u** in **u**nderstand

Consonants are much as in English, except that: ch is always "sh", ç is "s", c is "s" before i or e only, but always hard at the end of a word, h is silent, th is the same as t, ll is like the y in yes, x is variably silent or similar to English x, w is "v" and r is growled (or rolled).

Gender

French nouns, along with their pronouns and articles, are divided into masculine and feminine. Thus the endings of adjectives change to agree with the gender of the nouns they qualify. If you know some grammar, you will know what to do. If not, stick to the masculine form, which is the simplest – it's what we have done in the glossary, except for adjectives of nationality which have the feminine final 'e' or 'ne' in brackets.

Basics

today	aujourd'hui	**man**	un homme
yesterday	hier	**woman**	une femme
tomorrow	demain	**here**	ici
in the morning	le matin	**there**	là
in the afternoon	l'après-midi	**this one**	ceci
in the evening	le soir	**that one**	celà
now	maintenant	**open**	ouvert
later	plus tard	**closed**	fermé
at one o'clock	à une heure	**big**	grand
at three o'clock	à trois heures	**small**	petit
at ten-thirty	à dix heures et demie	**more**	plus
at midday	à midi	**less**	moins

a little	un peu	**bad**	mauvais
a lot	beaucoup	**hot**	chaud
cheap	bon marché	**cold**	froid
expensive	cher	**with**	avec
good	bon	**without**	sans

Question Words

where?	où?	**how many/how much?**	combien?
how?	comment?	**at what time?**	à quelle heure?
when?	quand?	**what is.../which is...?**	quel est...?
why?	pourquoi?		

Talking to People

When addressing people, plain *bonjour* by itself is not enough; you should always use *Monsieur* for a man, *Madame* for a woman, *Mademoiselle* for a younger woman or a girl. This isn't as formal as it seems, and it has its uses when you've forgotten someone's name or want to attract someone's attention.

Excuse me	Pardon	**I'll be right with you**	J'arrive
Do you speak English?	Parlez-vous anglais?	**Please speak slower**	S'il vous plaît, parlez moins vite
How do you say it in French?	Comment ça se dit en français?	**OK/agreed**	d'accord
What's your name?	Comment vous appelez-vous?	**please**	s'il vous plaît
My name is...	Je m'appelle...	**thank you**	merci
I'm	Je suis	**hello**	bonjour
...English	...anglais[e]	**goodbye**	au revoir
...Irish	...irlandais[e]	**good morning/ afternoon**	bonjour
...Scottish	...écossais[e]	**good evening**	bonsoir
...Welsh	...gallois[e]	**good night**	bonne nuit
...American	...américain[e]	**How are you?**	Comment allez-vous?/ Ça va?
...Australian	...australien[ne]	**Fine, thanks**	Très bien, merci
...Canadian	...canadien[ne]	**I don't know**	Je ne sais pas
...New Zealander	...néo-zélandais[e]	**Let's go**	Allons-y
yes	oui	**See you tomorrow**	À demain
no	non	**See you soon**	À bientôt
I understand	Je comprends	**Leave me alone**	Fichez-moi la paix! (aggressive)
I don't understand	Je ne comprends pas	**Please help me**	Aidez-moi, s'il vous plaît
(I'm) sorry	(Je suis) désolé[e]		
Sorry	Pardon/Je m'excuse		

Getting around

bus (long-haul)	autobus, bus, car	**train/taxi/ferry**	train/taxi/ferry
bus (shuttle)	navette	**boat**	bâteau
bus station	gare (routière)	**plane**	avion
bus stop	arrêt, halte routière	**railway station**	gare (SNCF)
car	voiture	**platform**	quai

What time does it leave?	À quelle heure part-il?
What time does it arrive?	À quelle heure arrive-t-il?
a ticket to...	un billet pour...
single ticket	aller simple
return ticket	aller retour
Validate/Cancel your ticket	Compostez votre billet
valid for...	valable pour...
ticket office	vente de billets
How many kilometres?	Combien de kilomètres?
How many hours?	Combien d'heures?
hitchhiking	autostop
on foot	à pied
Where are you going?	Où allez-vouz?
I'm going to...	Je vais à...
I want to get off at...	Je voudrais descendre à...
the road to...	la route pour...
the path to...	le sentier pour...
Beware! Field set with animal traps	Attention! Piégé
near	près/pas loin
far	loin
left	à gauche
right	à droite
straight on	tout droit
on the other side of	à l'autre côté de
on the corner of	à l'angle de
next to	à côté de
behind	derrière
in front of	devant
before	avant
after	après
under	sous
to cross	traverser
bridge	pont
old town	vieille ville

Cars

to park the car	garer la voiture
car park	un parking
no parking	défense de stationer/ stationnement interdit
service station	garage
petrol station	poste d'essence
fuel	essence
(to) fill it up	faire le plein
petrol can	bidon
inflate the tyres	gonfler les pneus
oil	huile
The battery is dead	La batterie est morte
spark plugs	bougies
to break down	tomber en panne
traffic lights	feux
insurance	assurance

Accommodation

a room for one/two people	une chambre pour une/deux personnes
a double bed	un lit double
a room with a shower/toilet	une chambre avec douche/WC
A room with a (full) bath	une chambre avec salle de bain
for one/two/three nights	pour une/deux/trois nuits
Can I see it?	Puis-je la voir?
a room on the courtyard	une chambre sur la cour
a room over the street	une chambre sur la rue
first floor	premier étage
second floor	deuxième étage
with a view	avec vue
key	clef
to iron	repasser
do laundry	faire la lessive
sheets	draps
blankets	couvertures
quiet	calme
noisy	bruyant
hot water	eau chaude
cold water	eau froide
Is breakfast included?	Est-ce que le petit déjeuner est compris?

I would like breakfast	Je voudrais prendre le petit déjeuner	**campsite**	un camping/terrain de camping/air de camping
I don't want breakfast	Je ne veux pas le petit déjeuner	**tent**	une tente
Can we camp here?	Est-ce q'on peut camper ici?	**tent space**	un emplacement
		youth hostel	auberge de jeunesse

Numbers

1	un/une	**22**	vingt-deux
2	deux	**30**	trente
3	trois	**40**	quarante
4	quatre	**50**	cinquante
5	cinq	**60**	soixante
6	six	**70**	soixante-dix
7	sept	**75**	soixante-quinze
8	huit	**80**	quatre-vingts
9	neuf	**90**	quatre-vingt-dix
10	dix	**95**	quatre-vingt-quinze
11	onze	**100**	cent
12	douze	**101**	cent-et-un
13	treize	**200**	deux cent
14	quatorze	**300**	trois cent
15	quinze	**500**	cinq cent
16	seize	**1000**	mille
17	dix-sept	**2000**	deux mille
18	dix-huit	**5000**	cinq mille
19	dix-neuf	**first**	première
20	vingt	**second**	deuxième
21	vingt-et un	**third**	troisième

Days and dates

January	janvier	**Sunday**	dimanche
February	février	**Monday**	lundi
March	mars	**Tuesday**	mardi
April	avril	**Wednesday**	mercredi
May	mai	**Thursday**	jeudi
June	juin	**Friday**	vendredi
July	juillet	**Saturday**	samedi
August	août	**August 1**	le premier août
September	septembre	**March 2**	le deux mars
October	octobre	**July 14**	le quatorze juillet
November	novembre	**November 23**	le vingt-trois novembre
December	décembre	**2008**	deux mille huit

French menu reader

Basic terms

pain	bread	**bouteille**	bottle
beurre	butter	**verre**	glass
lait	milk	**fourchette**	fork
huile	oil	**couteau**	knife
poivre	pepper	**cuillère**	spoon
sel	salt	**table**	table
sucre	sugar	**l'addition**	the bill
vinaigre	vinegar		

Typical snacks

un sandwich/une baguette au — a sandwich with...
- **jambon** — ham
- **fromage** — cheese
- **saucisson** — salami
- **à l'ail** — garlic
- **poivre** — pepper
- **pâté (de campagne)** — with pâté (country-style)

croque-monsieur — grilled cheese and ham sandwich

croque-madame — grilled cheese and bacon, sausage, chicken or an egg

oeufs — eggs
- **au plat** — fried
- **à la coque** — boiled
- **durs** — hard-boiled
- **brouillés** — scrambled

omelette... — omelette...
- **nature** — plain
- **aux fines herbes** — with herbs
- **au fromage** — with cheese

salade de... — salad of...
- **tomates** — tomatoes
- **betteraves** — beets
- **carottes rapées** — grated carrots
- **coeurs de palmiers** — hearts of palm
- **concombres** — cucumber
- **fonds d'artichauts** — artichoke hearts

crêpe... — thin pancake...
- **au sucre** — with sugar
- **au citron** — with lemon
- **au miel** — with honey
- **à la confiture** — with jam
- **à la crème de marrons** — with chestnut purée

Some food terms

cuit	cooked	**fumé**	smoked
cru	raw, uncooked	**pané**	breaded
emballé	wrapped	**salé**	salted/spicy
à emporter	to take away	**sucré**	sweetened

Soups (soupes)

bisque	shellfish soup	**pistou**	parmesan, basil and garlic paste, sometimes added to soup
bouillabaisse	fish soup	**potage**	thick soup, usually vegetable
bouillon	broth or stock		
bourride	thick fish soup		
consommé	clear soup		

rouille red pepper, garlic and saffron mayonnaise served with fish soup

velouté thick soup, usually fish or poultry

Starters (hors d'oeuvres)

assiette anglaise/ assiette de charcuterie plate of cold meats

salad composée mixed salad, with cold meat and vegetables

crudités raw vegetables with dressings

hors d'oeuvres variés combination of the previous two plus smoked or marinated fish

Fish (poisson), seafood (fruits de mer) and shellfish (crustacés or coquillages)

anchois anchovies

anguilles eels

baudroie monkfish, anglerfish

brème bream

cabillaud cod, unsalted

cal(a)mar squid

carrelet plaice

claire type of oyster

colin hake

congre conger eel

coques cockles

coquilles Saint-Jacques scallops

crabe crab

crevettes grises shrimps

crevettes roses prawns

dorade, daurade sea bream

ecrevisse freshwater crayfish

éperlan smelt or whitebait

escargots snails

espadon swordfish

favou(ille) tiny crab

flétan halibut

gambas king prawns

grenouilles (cuisses de) frogs (legs)

homard lobster

huîtres oysters

langouste spiny lobster

langoustines saltwater crayfish

limande lemon sole

lotte de mer monkfish

loup de mer sea bass (Mediterranean)

louvine similar to sea bass

maquereau mackerel

merlan whiting

morue salt cod

moules (marinière) mussels (with shallots in white wine sauce)

palourdes clams

poulpe octopus

praires small clams

raie skate

rouget red mullet

sandre zander (pike-like fish)

saumon salmon

Saint-Pierre John Dory

sardines sardines

sole sole

thon tuna

truite trout

truitelle baby trout

turbot turbot

violet, figue de mer sea-squirt

Terms (fish)

aïoli garlic mayonnaise

anchoïoade anchovy paste or sauce

béarnaise sauce made with egg yolks, white wine, shallots and vinegar

colbert	fried in egg and breadcrumbs
darne	fillet or steak
la douzaine	a dozen (ie oysters)
frit	fried
friture	assorted deep-fried small fish
fumé	smoked
fumet	fish stock
gigot de mer	large fish baked whole
grillé	grilled
hollandaise	butter and vinegar sauce
à la meunière	in butter, lemon and parsley sauce
mousse(line)	mousse
raito	red wine, olive, caper, garlic and shallot sauce

Meat (viande), game (gibier) and poultry (volaille)

agneau	lamb
andouille, andouillette	tripe sausage
bavette d'échalote	cheap steak fried with shallots
boeuf	beef
biche	doe venison
bifteck	steak
boudin blanc	white-meat sausage
boudin noir	black pudding
caille	quail
canard	duck
caneton	duckling
cervelle	brains
chateaubriand	porterhouse steak
cheval	horse meat
chevreau	kid goat
contrefilet	sirloin roast
coquelet	cockerel
couer	heart (esp. of duck)
dinde, dindon, dindonneau	turkey of different ages and genders
entrecôte	ribsteak
faux filet	sirloin steak
foie	liver
foie gras	fattened liver of duck or goose
fraises de veau	veal testicles
fricadelles	meatballs
gigot d'agneau	leg of lamb
langue	tongue
lapin, lapereau	rabbit, young rabbit
lard, lardons	bacon, diced bacon
lièvre	hare
marcassin	young wild boar
merguez	spicy North African sausage
mouton	mutton
oie	goose
palombe	wild dove
porc, pieds de porc	pork, pig's trotters
poulet	chicken
poulette	young chicken
poussin	baby chicken
ris	sweetbreads
rognons	kidneys
rognons blancs	testicles
sanglier	wild boar
toro	bull meat
travers de porc	spare ribs
tripes	tripe
truie	sow
veau	veal
venaison	venison

Dishes and terms (meat and poultry)

aile	wing
blanc	breast or white meat
blanquette, daube estouffade, navarin, ragoût	regional types of stews
à la broche	spit-roasted
brochette	kebab
canard à l'orange	roast duck with an orange-and-wine sauce
carré	best end of neck, chop or cutlet

cassoulet	casserole of beans, carrots and meat, usually sausage
choucroute	pickled cabbage with peppercorns, sausages, bacon and salami
civet	game stew
confit	meat preserve, often served baked or roasted
coq au vin	chicken cooked until it falls off the bone with wine, onions and mushrooms
côte	chop, cutlet or rib
cou	neck
croustillant	in a pastry crust
en croûte	in pastry
cuisse	thigh-and-leg portion
epaule	shoulder
farci	stuffed
au feu de bois	cooked over wood fire
au four	baked
galantine	cold dish of meat in aspic
garni	garnished (with vegetables)
gésier	gizzard
gigot de...	leg of any meat
graisse	fat
grillade	mixed grill
grillé	grilled
hâchis	chopped meat or hamburger
jambonneau	joint, shank
jarret	knuckle
magret de canard	cured duck breast slices
marmite	casserole
médaillon	round piece
mi-cuit	blanched
mijoté	stewed
museau	muzzle
os	bone
pavé	thick slice
persillade	cooked in parsley and oil
poêlé	pan-fried
rillade	coarse pork-and-goose paté
rôti	roast
sauté	lightly cooked in butter
steak au poivre (vert/rouge)	steak in a peppercorn sauce (green/red)
steak tartare	raw chopped beef usually accompanied by a raw egg yolk
terrine	solid loaf of finely puréed substance (duck liver, raspberry, etc)
tête de veau	calf's head in jelly
tournedos	thick slices of fillet

Terms for steaks

bleu	almost raw
saignant	rare
à point	medium rare
bien cuit	well done
très bien cuit	very well cooked

Garnishes and sauces

beurre blanc	sauce of white wine and shallots, with butter
bordelaise	in a red wine, shallots and bone marrow sauce
à la boulangère	baked with potatoes and onions
à la bourgeoise	with carrots, onions, celery, bacon and braised lettuce
chasseur	white wine, mushrooms and shallots
diable	strong mustard seasoning

forestière	with bacon and mushroom
fricassée	rich, creamy sauce
mornay	cheese sauce
pays d'auge	cream and cider
à la périgordine	in a truffle and foie gras sauce
piquante	gherkins or capers, vinegar and shallots
provençale	tomatoes, garlic, olive oil and herbs

Vegetables (légumes)

artichaut	artichoke
asperges	asparagus
avocat	avocado
betterave	beetroot
carotte	carrot
céleri	celery
champignons	mushrooms; types include: **de bois, cèpes, chanterelles, girolles, grisets, mousserons, pleurotes**
chicorée frisée	curly chicory
chou (rouge)	(red) cabbage
choufleur	cauliflower
citrouille	pumpkin
cogollos	lettuce hearts
concombre	cucumber
cornichon	gherkin
cresson	watercress
échalotes	shallots
endive	chicory
épinards	spinach
fenouil	fennel
fèves	broad beans
flageolet	white beans
haricots verts, rouges, blancs, beurres	beans (string/French, kidney, white, butter)
laitue	lettuce
lentilles	lentils
maïs	corn
navet	turnip
oignon	onion
oseille	sorrel
panais	parsnip
petits pois	peas
pignons	pine nuts
pissenlits	dandelion leaves
poireau	leek
pois chiche	chickpeas
poivron (vert, rouge)	sweet pepper (green, red)
pommes (de terre)	potatoes
primeurs	spring greens
radis	radishes
riz	rice
salade verte	green salad
sarrasin/sarrazin	buckwheat
seigle	rye
tomates	tomatoes
truffes	truffles

Herbs (herbes) and spices (épices)

ail	garlic
anis	aniseed
basilic	basil
cannelle	cinnamon
ciboulettes	chives
estragon	tarragon
genièvre	juniper (berry)
gingembre	ginger
girofle	clove
laurier	bay leaf
marjolaine	marjoram
menthe	mint
moutarde	mustard
persil	parsley
piment	pimento
pistou	ground basil, olive oil and garlic
raifort	horseradish
romarin	rosemary
safran	saffron
serpolet	wild thyme

Some vegetable dishes and terms

allumettes	very thin-sliced chips
biologique	organic
farci	stuffed
gratin dauphinois	potatoes baked in cream and garlic
gratiné	browned with cheese or butter
jardinière	with mixed diced vegetables
à la parisienne	sautéed in butter with white wine sauce, and shallots
parmentier	with potatoes
pommes château fondantes	quartered potatoes sautéed in butter
pommes lyonnaise	fried onions and potatoes
râpée	grated or shredded
ratatouille	mixture of aubergine, courgette, tomatos, and garlic
rémoulade	mustard mayonnaise and herb dressing
salade niçoise	salad of tomatoes, radishes, cucumber, hard-boiled eggs, anchovies, onion, artichokes, green peppers, beans, basil and garlic
sauté	lightly fried in butter
à la vapeur	steamed

Fruits (fruits) and nuts (noix)

abricot	apricot
amandes	almonds
ananas	pineapple
banane	banana
brugnon, nectarine	nectarine
cacahouètes	peanuts
cassis	blackcurrants
cérises	cherries
citron	lemon
citron vert	lime
coing	quince
dattes	dates
figues	figs
fraises	strawberries
fraises de bois	wild strawberries
framboises	raspberries
grenade	pomegranate
groseilles	redcurrants or gooseberries
marrons	chestnuts
melon	melon
mirabelles	small yellow plums
myrtilles	blueberries
noisette	hazelnut
noix	nuts
orange	orange
pamplemousse	grapefruit
pastèque	watermelon
pêche (blanche)	(white) peach
pistache	pistachio
poire	pear
pomme	apple
prune	plum
pruneau	prune
raisins	grapes
rhubarbe	rhubarb

Terms

beignet	fritter
compôte de...	stewed...
coulis	sauce of puréed fruit
flambé	set aflame in alcohol
frappé	iced

Desserts (desserts or entremets) and pastries (pâtisserie)

barquette	small boat-shaped flan
bavarois	the mould for a mousse or custard
bombe	an ice-cream dessert made in a round or conical mould
brioche	sweet, eggy breakfast roll
charlotte	custard and fruit in almond fingers
clafoutis	fruit tart, usually with berries
coupe	a serving of ice cream
crème caramel	caramelized pudding
crème Chantilly	vanilla-flavoured and sweetened whipped cream
crème fraîche	sour cream
crème pâtissière	thick pastry-filling made with eggs
crêpes suzettes	thin pancakes with orange juice and liqueur
fromage blanc	cream cheese, more like strained yoghurt
gateaux	fruit pies, usually apple, peach or pear
gaufre	waffle
gênoise	rich sponge cake
glace	ice cream
îles flottantes/oeufs à la neige	soft meringues floating on custard
lait caillé	cream-based dessert, like Italian panna cotta
macaron	macaroon
madeleine	small, scalloped-edge sponge cake
palmiers	caramelized puff pastries
parfait	frozen mousse, sometimes ice cream
petits fours	bite-sized cakes or pastries
poires belle hélène	pears and ice cream in chocolate sauce
sablé	shortbread biscuit
savarin	a filled, ring-shaped cake
tarte tatin	upside-down apple tart
tartelette	small tart
truffes	truffles (the chocolate or liqueur-filled variety)
tiramisu	mascarpone cheese, chocolate and cream
yaourt, yogourt	yoghurt

Cheese (fromage)

There are dozens of distinct Pyrenean cheeses, most of them named after their place of origin; *chèvre* is goat's cheese, *brebis* is ewe's cheese. *Le plateau de fromages* is the cheeseboard, and bread, but not butter, is served with it. Some useful phrases: *une petite tranche de celui-ci* (a small piece of this one); *puis-je le gouter?* (may I taste it?)

Regional dishes

Catalonia

bouillinade	fish stew flavoured with dry Banyuls wine
perdreau à la Català	partridge cooked with bitter oranges
cargolade	small grilled snails
bolet	wood mushroom, often fried in olive oil, to accompany game dishes
louillade	stew of mixed vegetables and **charcuterie**, popular winter dish in the Cerdagne
bunyetes	custard doughnuts
rosquillas	almond cake

Béarn

tourin	Onion, garlic and tomato soup
cousinette	Mixed soup that often includes beet, sorrel or chicory
garbure	A very thick soup using carrots, turnips, cabbage, parsley, and beans in poultry, lamb or pork stock
poule au pot	Boiled chicken with vegetables
tourtière	Puff pastry flavoured with rum or plums soaked in Armagnac

Pays Basque

axoa	veal-based dish, typical of Ezpeleta
bar	sea bass
gasna, (ardi) gazna	type of hard sheep's cheese, often served with Itsasu cherry jam
pipérade	omelette with peppers and tomatoes, served as a main dish but often just the vegetables served as an accompaniment
ttoro	fish stew
chipirons, txiporons	small squid, either casseroled or stuffed and baked
piballes	baby eels
tripotcha	veal tripe cooked with spices
loukinkas	small garlic sausages
jambon de Bayonne	ham from Bayonne, eaten cold and thinly sliced
gâteau Basque	almond-custardy pie in a crumb crust, occasionally topped with cherry conserve
touron	marzipan garnished with pistachio nuts
macarons	macaroons, especially from Saint-Jean-de-Luz
mamia	Same as **cuajada** (see Spanish Sweets, p.593)
marmite	grilled cod in a spicy mussel-and-scallop sauce

Castilian Spanish

Although Spain, like France, has its regional dialects and six recognized written languages, **Castilian** Spanish (**castellano**) – the language of the central *meseta* – is understood over most of the peninsula. Once you get into it, Castilian is – as John Hooper memorably put it – the easiest language to speak badly, and you'll be helped everywhere by people keen to understand even the most faltering attempt. English is spoken, but only in the main tourist areas to any extent, and wherever you are you'll get a far better reception if you at least try communicating with Spaniards in their own tongue. Being understood, of course, is only half the problem – grasping the reply, often rattled out at a furious pace, may prove more difficult.

The following pages contain lists of useful words and phrases that will enable you generally to get what you want. Anyone travelling for some length of time, however, should invest in a decent dictionary or phrasebook. A cursory glance at a Spanish **dictionary** might bewilder – until 1994 CH, LL and Ñ were separate letters, and in older dictionaries will still be found after C, L and N respectively.

Euskera and Catalan

After French and Castilian, the two most prevalent languages in the Pyrenees are Euskera and Catalan. There are almost no written records of **Euskera**, the Basque tongue, before the Middle Ages, even though it had been spoken for over a thousand years by then. Current scholarship asserts that Euskera was the indigenous, non-Indo-European language spoken on the Iberian peninsula before the Roman occupation; alternative theories linking it to Caucasian languages like Georgian are in eclipse. There are currently about half a million Euskera-speakers in Spain and France, at the western end of the Pyrenees.

Gascon, the native tongue of Béarn and several valleys all the way to Bayonne, is the westernmost variant of Occitan, and continued in official use until the eve of the Revolution. Long of merely folkloric value, it's making a modest comeback in the media (Ràdio Pais, 89.8 FM) and in a chain of optional primary schools, *les Calandretas*.

Catalan, a Romance language evolved from medieval Provençal, survived centralizing campaigns either favouring Castilian or actively suppressing *Català* (as it calls itself), from the fifteenth to the twentieth century. Although the teaching, printing and broadcasting of Catalan was prohibited under Franco, it is again a flourishing language, spoken by between three and four million people around the eastern part of the range. Currently all signposting in Catalunya (as well as rural restaurant menus) is solely in Catalan, the official language.

To the outsider, **written** Catalan is a far easier language to comprehend than Euskera – with a knowledge of both high-school Castilian and French you can get the gist of most tourist pamphlets or trekking booklets in *Català*. **Spoken** ***Català***, with its harsh sound and strong dialects, is much harder to follow. The **sounds of letters** in Catalan are often completely different from those of Castilian; the most important points of divergence are summarized below, enabling you to at least pronounce place names recognizably. Though Catalans in particular are delighted if you make some attempt to use their language, all Basques and Catalans understand and speak Castilian or French as the case may be, if sometimes grudgingly. Thus the basic French and Spanish vocabularies given in this section should be sufficient to make yourself understood as you travel through either end of the Pyrenees.

Castilian and Catalan learning materials

Rough Guide Spanish Phrasebook Mini-dictionary-style phrasebook, with Castilian–English and English–Castilian sections, cultural tips and menu readers.

Get By in Spanish. One of BBC-Active's excellent book-plus-cassette crash courses which gets you to survival-level Spanish within a couple of weeks; revised in 2007.

Breakthrough Spanish vol. 1 & 2, Euro Edition by Sandra Truscott. The best teach-yourself course, regularly revised, which aims to give you reasonable fluency in three months; purchasable stand-alone or with 3+4 cassettes.

Collins Gem Spanish Dictionary. This is the compact (approx 3 x 4 inches) version of the best single-volume Spanish–English/English–Spanish desktop dictionary; be sure to get the most current edition.

Teach Yourself Catalan by Anna Poch and Alan Yates. A not very ambitious primer, presented in English; available with or without companion CD.

Catalan: A Comprehensive Grammar by Max Wheeler, Alan Yates and Nicolau Dols. Exactly as it says; some coverage of dialects as well, though not Pyrenean ones.

Parla Català (Pia, Spain). The only available English–Catalan phrasebook.

Routledge Catalan Dictionary Big and thorough, but hardly portable and not error-free.

However, **local terms** can be useful for interpreting maps and signs in the Basque and Catalan regions (as well as inFrench valleys where there are strong dialects), so a comprehensive "Mountain Terminology" section appears on p.596. When travelling with internationally published maps, be aware that these usually lag well behind nationalistically motivated **name-changing campaigns** in every region of the Pyrenees. Often the local-vernacular name is proudly displayed on an official highways-division sign, but equally often Castilian or French signs have been suitably "edited" with spray paint.

Catalan pronunciation

ig/tg sound like "tch" in scratch; thus *Contraig* is pronounced "contraytch", *Mitg* sounds like "meetch"

ç is like S; *plaça* is pronounced "plassa"

c followed by E or I is a soft S-sound, not a TH as in Castilian

g followed by E or I is like the "zh" in Zhivago; otherwise hard

j is soft as in French, unlike the Castilian *jota*

ll strong L, except when medial: thus "*Ripoll*" sounds like "ripole", "*llac*" like "lak", but "*Mulleres*" sounds like "muyeres"

l.l pronounced as two separate "l"s

l-l pronounced as two separate "l"s

ny replaces the Castilian Ñ

t can sound like D, as in the words *viatge* (pronounced "veeadzheh") or *dotze* (pronounced "dodzeh"). Almost silent when final: thus "Pont de Suert" sounds like "Pon de Swear"

ui is same as U – the I is silent; thus *maduixa* sounds like "madusha", *puig* like "pootch"

x is like CH when initial, SH when medial, but as in English for certain loan-words like *excursionista*

y in the final syllable is all but silent: thus "*Morunys*" sounds like "morunsh", "*Montgrony*" like "montgron"

A brief guide to speaking Castilian Spanish

Pronunciation

The rules of **pronunciation** are pretty straightforward and, once you get to know them, strictly observed. Unless there's an accent, words ending in d, l, r and z are **stressed** on the last syllable, all others on the second to last. All **vowels** are pure and short; combinations of letters have predictable, regular results.

a as in f**a**ther

e as in g**e**t

i as in pol**i**ce

o as in r**o**le

u as in r**u**le

c is a theta (lisped) before E and I, hard otherwise: *cerca* is pronounced "thairka"

g varies similarly: a guttural "H" sound (like the *ch* in loch) before E or I, a hard G elsewhere – *gigante* becomes "higante"

h always silent

j the same sound as a guttural G: *jamón* is pronounced "hamon"

ll sounds like an English Y: *tortilla* is pronounced "torteeya"

n is as in English unless it has a tilde (accent) over it (**Ñ**), when it becomes NY: *mañana* sounds like "manyana"

qu is pronounced like an English K
r is rolled, **RR** doubly so
v sounds like B, *vino* becoming "beano"
x has an S sound before consonants, normal X before vowels. More common in Basque, Gallego or Catalan words, where it's "sh" or "zh"
z is the same as a soft C, so *cerveza* becomes "thervaytha". Catalan does not lisp c or z before i or e

Gender

Spanish **nouns**, along with their pronouns and articles, are divided into masculine and feminine. Thus the endings of adjectives (and pronouns) generally change to agree with the gender of the nouns they qualify. If you know some grammar, you will know what to do. If not, stick to the masculine form, which is the simplest – it's what we have done in the glossary.

Basics

yes	sí	**with**	con
no	no	**without**	sin
OK	vale	**good**	buen(o)
please	por favor	**bad**	mal(o)
thank you	gracias	**big**	gran(de)
here	aquí	**small**	pequeño
there	allí	**more**	más
this	este	**less**	menos
that	eso	**a lot**	mucho
now	ahora	**a little bit**	un poco
later	más tarde	**today**	hoy
open	abierto	**tomorrow**	mañana
closed	cerrado	**yesterday**	ayer

Talking to people

hello	hola	**What's your name?**	¿Cómo se llama usted?
goodbye	adiós	**I'm...**	Soy...
good morning	buenos días	**...English**	...inglés(a)
good afternoon/ evening	buenas tardes	**...Scottish**	...escosés(a)
		...Irish	...irlandés(a)
good night	buenas noches	**...American**	...estadunidense
see you later	hasta luego	**...Canadian**	...canadiense
sorry	lo siento/disculpeme	**I want...**	Quiero...
excuse me	con permiso/perdón	**I'd like...**	Querría...
How are you?	¿Cómo está (usted)?	**Do you know... ?**	¿Sabe... ?
You're welcome	De nada no hay de qué	**I don't know**	No sé
I (don't) understand	(No) entiendo	**There is (is there)?**	(¿)Hay (?)
Do you speak English?	¿Habla (usted) inglés?	**Give me...**	Deme...
		(one like that)	(un tal)
I don't speak Spanish	No hablo castellano	**How much?**	¿Cuánto?
		Do you have... ?	¿Tiene... ?
My name is...	Me llamo...	**... the time**	la hora

What is there to eat?	¿Qué hay para comer?
What's that?	¿Qué es eso?
What's this called in Spanish?	¿Cómo se llama este en español?
When?	¿Cuando?
Where?	¿Donde?

Getting about

How do I get to... ?	¿Cómo se va a... ?
left, right, straight	izquierda, derecha, erecho
old inter-village track	camino
trail	sendero, senda
forest road	pista forestal
bus	autobús
train	tren
shuttle bus	naveta
Where is... ?	¿Dónde esta... ?
... the bus station	la estación de autobuses
... the train station	la estación de ferrocarriles
... the post office	el correo (la oficina de correos)
... the toilet	los aseos/servicios
Where does the bus to... leave from?	¿De dónde sale el autobús para... ?
Is this the train for Jaca?	¿Es este el tren para Jaca?
I'd like a (single/return) ticket to...	Querría un billete (sencillo/de ida y vuelta) para...
What time does it leave (arrive at...)?	¿A qué hora sale (llega en...)?

Accommodation

Do you have... ?	¿Tiene... ?
... a room	una habitación
... with two beds/double bed	con dos camas/cama matrimonial
It's for one person (two people)	Es para una persona (dos personas)
... for one night (one week)	... para una noche (una semana)
It's fine, how much do you charge?	Está bien, ¿cuanto cobra?
It's too expensive	Es demasiado (caro)
Don't you have anything cheaper?	¿No tiene algo más barato?
Can one... ?	¿Se puede... ?
camp (near) here?	acampar aquí (cerca)?
Is there a hostel/refuge/hostal nearby?	¿Hay un albergue/refugio/hostal aquí cerca?

Numbers

1	un/uno/una
2	dos
3	tres
4	cuatro
5	cinco
6	seis
7	siete
8	ocho
9	nueve
10	diez
11	once
12	doce
13	trece
14	catorce
15	quince
16	diez y seis *or* dieciséis
17	diez y siete *or* diecisiete
18	diez y ocho *or* dieciocho
19	diez y nueve *or* diecinueve
20	veinte
21	veintiuno
30	treinta
40	cuarenta
50	cincuenta

60	sesenta	**500**	quinient(os)/(as)
70	setenta	**700**	setecient(os)/(as)
80	ochenta	**1000**	mil
90	noventa	**2000**	dos mil
100	cien(to)	**first**	primer(o)/(a)
101	ciento uno	**second**	segund(o)/(a)
200	doscient(os)/(as)	**third**	tercer(o)/(a)

Days and dates

January	enero	**November**	noviembre
February	febrero	**December**	diciembre
March	marzo	**Monday**	lunes
April	abril	**Tuesday**	martes
May	mayo	**Wednesday**	miércoles
June	junio	**Thursday**	jueves
July	julio	**Friday**	viernes
August	agosto	**Saturday**	sábado
September	se(p)tiembre	**Sunday**	domingo
October	octubre	**2008**	dos mil ocho

Spanish menu reader

Basics

pan	bread	**miel**	honey
mantequilla	butter	**botella**	bottle
huevos	eggs	**vaso**	glass
ajo	garlic	**tenedor**	fork
aceite	oil	**cuchillo**	knife
pimienta	pepper (black)	**cuchara**	spoon
sal	salt	**mesa**	table
azúcar	sugar	**desayuno**	breakfast
vinagre	vinegar	**la cuenta**	the bill

Typical Spanish snacks

The most usual **fillings for bocadillos** are *lomo* (pork loin), *tortilla* and *calamares* (all possibly served hot), *jamón* (*york* or, much better, *serrano*), *chorizo*, *salchichón* (or regional sausages like the small, spicy Catalan *botifarras*), *queso* (cheese) and *atún* (tuna, probably canned).

Standard tapas and raciones

aceitunas	olives	**callos**	tripe
albondigas	meatballs	**caracoles**	snails
arroz a la cubana	rice topped with fried egg and red sauce	**carne en salsa**	meat in red sauce
		champiñones	mushrooms
boquerones	anchovies (marinated)	**chorizo**	spicy sausage
calamares	squid	**empanadilla**	fish/meat turnover

ensaladilla	Russian salad	**patatas alli olli**	potatoes in mayonnaise-garlic sauce
escalibada	aubergine and pepper salad	**patatas bravas**	spicy potatoes
gambas	shrimps	**patatas riojanas**	potato stew with flecks of vegetable and *chorizo*
habas	beans	**pimientos**	peppers
habas con jamón	beans with ham	**pintxo moruno**	kebab
hígado	liver	**pulpo**	octopus
huevo cocido	hard-boiled egg	**riñones al Jerez**	kidneys in sherry
jamón serrano	top-grade cured ham	**salchichon**	salami
jamón york	low-grade pressed ham	**tortilla española**	potato omelette
longaniza	spicy sausage	**tortilla francesa**	plain omelette
morcilla	blood pudding		
navajas	razor clams		

Soups (sopas)

sopa de mariscos	seafood soup	**gazpacho**	cold tomato and cucumber soup with garlic and other spices
caldo de gallina	chicken soup	**sopa de cocido**	meat broth/soup
sopa de pescado	fish soup	**sopa de pasta (fideos)**	noodle soup
caldo verde/gallego	thick cabbage-based broth		
caldillo	clear fish soup		

Seafood (mariscos)

almejas	clams	**vieiras**	scallops
berberechos	cockles	**arroz con mariscos**	rice topped with assorted seafood
calamares	squid	**arroz a la banda**	like paella but without chicken
centolla	spider-crab	**chipirones en su tinta**	squid in ink
cigalas	king prawns	**merluza/calamares a la romana**	hake/squid (or almost anything else) fried in batter
conchas finas	large scallops	**paella**	classic Valencian dish with saffron rice, peas, chicken, seafood
gambas	shrimps	**zarzuela de mariscos**	seafood casserole
langosta	lobster		
langostinos	crayfish		
mejillones	mussels		
nécora	sea-crab		
ostras	oysters		
percebes	goose-barnacles		
pulpo	octopus		
sepia	cuttlefish		

Fish (pescados)

anchoas	anchovies (fresh)	**bonito**	mature tuna
anguila	eel	**callos de bacalao**	filleted rings from choice cod-jaw meat
angulas	elvers (baby eel)	**cazón**	shark
atún	tuna	**jurelas**	similar to anchovies
bacalao	cod (often salted)		

lenguado	sole
lubina	sea bass
merluza	hake
mero	perch
pez espada	swordfish
rape, sapito	monkfish
raya	ray, skate
rodaballo	turbot
salmonete	red mullet
sardinas	sardines
trucha	trout

Meat (carne) and poultry (aves)

butifarra	bratwurst
callos	tripe
carne de buey	beef, ox
cerdo	pork
chuletas	chops
ciervo	venison
cochinillo	suckling pig
codorniz	quail
conejo	rabbit
cordero	lamb
criadillas	testicles
escalope *or* **milanesa**	breaded schnitzel
fabada asturiana	hotpot with butter beans, black pudding, etc
habas con jamón	ham and beans
hígado	liver
jabalí	wild boar
lengua	tongue
lomo	loin (of pork)
manitas de cerdo	pig's knuckles
pato	duck
pavo	turkey
perdiz	partridge
pintada	guinea fowl
pollo	chicken
rebeco	chamois
riñones	kidneys
solomillo	pork flank steak
ternera	veal

Vegetables (verduras o legumes)

ac(i)elga	chard
alcachofas	artichokes
alubias	beans
arroz	rice
berenjena	aubergine
boletus	ceps
calabacín	courgette/zucchini
cardo, cardón	cardoon thistle stems
cebollas	onions
champiñones, setas	mushrooms
cogollos	lettuce hearts
coliflor	cauliflower
endivia	endive
espinacas	spinach
garbanzos	chickpeas
grelos	turnips
guisantes	peas
habas	broad beans
judías blancas	haricot beans
judías verdes, rojas, negras	green, red, black beans
lechuga	lettuce
lentejas	lentils
patatas (fritas)	potatoes (fried)
pepino	cucumber
pimientos	peppers
pimientos de padrón	medium-hot small green peppers
puerros	leeks
repollo	cabbage
tomate	tomatoes
trigueros	green asparagus
zanahorias	carrots
ajo blanco	purée of garlic, bread crumbs, almonds, oil
ensalada (mixta/verde)	(mixed/green) salad
menestra/panacha de verduras	vegetable medley
pimientos rellenos	stuffed peppers
pisto manchego	ratatouille
verduras con patatas	boiled potatoes with greens

Fruits (frutas)

albaricoques	apricots	melocotónes	peaches
arándanos	blueberries	melón	melon
chirimoyas	custard apples	naranjas	oranges
cerezas	cherries	pavías	nectarines
ciruelas	plums, prunes	peras	pears
datiles	dates	piña	pineapple
frambuesas	raspberries	plátanos	bananas
fresas	strawberries	sandía	watermelon
higos	figs	toronja/pomelo	grapefruit
limón	lemons	uvas	grapes
manzanas	apples		

Sweets (postres)

arroz con leche	rice pudding	membrillo	quince paste
cuajada	sheep-milk-based dessert, like Italian panna cotta, served with honey	nata	whipped cream
flan (de huevo)	crème caramel (egg-based)	natillas	custard
helados	ice cream	pasta/tarta de queso	cheesecake
macedonia	fresh fruit salad	requesón	whipped or beaten sweet-whey dessert, served with honey
melocotón en almíbar	peaches in syrup	yogur	yoghurt

Cheese

Cheeses (*quesos*; *formatges* in Catalan) are on the whole local, though you'll get the hard, slightly salty, sheep-based *queso manchego* everywhere. The best Pyrenean variety is *roncalés*, a sheep-milk product from the Valle de Roncal.

Some common terms

al ajillo	in garlic	cazuela, cocido	stew
al punto	medium rare	chilindrón	tomato, olive-oil and pepper sauce served on poultry and meat
asado	roast	en salsa	in (usually tomato) sauce
a la Navarra	stuffed with ham	frito	fried
a la parilla/plancha	grilled	guisado	casserole
a la romana/rebozado	fried in egg batter	hojaldre	in puff pastry
al horno	baked	jarrete	joint (of meat)
ali olli	with garlic mayonnaise	muy hecho	well done
¡Bon Profit! (Catalan)/¡Buen provecho! or ¡Aproveche! (Castilian)	bon appétit!	rehogado	baked
		salteado	stir-fried

Regional food

Catalunya: recipes and dishes

amanida (catalana)	salad (with salami)	**faves estofades**	pork and broad beans
arròs negre	rice cooked in squid ink	**fideuà**	paella made with noodles, not rice
bacallá	salt cod, served *a l'all* (with garlic) or *a l'all cremat* (creamed garlic)	**galtes de porc**	roast pig cheek
cabrit	goat, kid	**mongets (amb ventresca)**	white beans (with pancetta)
calçots	grilled baby spring onions (Jan–March)	**pa amb tomaquet**	tomato-ed and garlic-ed bread, usually a late breakfast, though available all day
carn d'olla	thick meat soup	**peus de porc**	pigs' feet
escalivada	baked or fried mixture of aubergines, tomatoes and peppers, often on toast	**rap**	monkfish
escudella	thick soup based on ham or veal stock	**samfaina**	ratatouille
espinacs a la catalana	spinach, pine nuts and raisins	**suquet de peix**	fish soup
esqueixada	salt-cod and tomato salad	**trinxat**	Cerdanyan hot-pot made from bacon, winter cabbage and potatoes or turnips
faves a la catalana	Catalan version of *fabada asturiana*	**xireta**	haggis, usually with rice and lamb bits

Catalunya: desserts

crema catalana	scorched-top custard	**menjar blanc**	almond pastry
flan	flan as elsewhere, but often flavoured	**pijama**	medley of various *flans* and *gelats*
gelat	ice cream	**trufes**	truffles (frozen)
mel i mató, recuit	same as Castilian *requesón*		

Catalunya: meat, game, poultry

ànec	duck	**llebre**	hare
botifarra	bratwurst-like sausage	**pernil**	ham
cansalada	bacon	**pollastre**	chicken
carn	meat	**senglar**	boar
conill	rabbit	**vedella**	veal
guatlles	quails	**xai**	lamb

Catlunya: seafood

anxoves	anchovies	**sèpia**	cuttlefish
llobarro	sea bass	**truita**	trout, or omelette
musclos	mussels	**xipirons**	baby squid

Catalunya: fruits & vegetables

albergínia	aubergine	**maduixas**	strawberries
cigrons	garbanzos	**pebrots**	peppers
codony	quince	**pèsols**	peas
llentics	lentils	**suc**	fruit juice

Catalunya: cooking terms

a la brasa grilled
barrejat mixed, assortment
civet any game stew
confit tender roast poultry thigh-leg, usually *de ànec*
esmorzar de forquilla savoury breakfast of meats, cheese, wine
farcit stuffed
graellada barbecued
pastís tureen, pâté
pastisso cake, tart

Aragón

boliches bean and sausage hot-pot
chireta haggis made with rice and blood pudding
guiso bony pork stewed in a sweet sauce
migas fry-up of breadcrumbs, bacon and spices
magras wind-dried raw ham, served thinly sliced
menestra de Tudela vegetable stew, using artichokes, beans, asparagus and anything else in season
salmorej egg concoction like a potato and rice omelette, eaten with lots of garlic or an unusual poached-egg stew
sopa de cana Christmas mix of milk, bread, cinnamon and turkey fat
ternasco lamb back, stewed or baked (quality varies); also in Catalunya
guirlache almond-and-toffee dessert

Basque Country

alubias de Tolosa reddish-black beans stewed with cabbage, *guindilla* peppers and blood sausage: the national dish of Gipuzkoa
ajoarriero salted cod, served with potatoes, red peppers, tomatoes and garlic
angulas baby eels (now rare), sautéed with garlic and hot peppers
calderete potato stew with sausage
gulas fake *angulas*, made from compressed Pacific pollack
Idiazábal a smoked cheese, identifiable by its yellow rind
marmitako fish, potato, pepper and tomato stew
merluza a la vasca hake in sauce
pimientos de piquillo red, sweet-hot peppers stuffed with cod
pochas greenish-white autumn beans
salmí pigeon prepared in wine and herbs

ttoro	mixed fish stew
txangurro	spider crab
txipirones en su tinto	tiny squid cooked in their own ink
txistorra	a spicy sausage

Mountain terminology

Eastern and Central Pyrenees

Agua/aigue/aygue	Water
Aigüeta	Small stream
Artigue/artiga	Pasture, meadow
Bal/ball/bat/batch/ val/vall	Valley
Barrage/presa	Dam
Borde/borda	Isolated cottage
Boum	Deep lake
Brèche	Gap in a ridge-line
Caillaouas	Rocky
Camí	Inter-village drovers' track
Campana	Pointed rock
Can, cal	Isolated lowland farmhouse
Cap	Highest point on a ridge; also means coastal cape, or the rear/back side of something
Cirque/circ/cirro	Alpine amphitheatre
Clot	Depression or narrow valley
Col/coll/collado/ coret/cuello	Pass or saddle
Corral	Enclosure for animals
Cortal	Shepherd's hut
Coma/Coume	Bare incline between trees
Desfiladero/ garganta/ congost(o)/foz	Gorge
Embalse	Reservoir
Eras/Eres	Grain barns, usually by a threshing cirque
Escalette/escaleta	Natural rock steps
Estanyet/estanyol	Small lake, pond
Estibe/estive	High pasture
Étang/estany/llac	Lake
Faja/faxa/feixa	Natural terrace in limestone
Farge/fragua	Forge
Font/fount/fuente	Source of a river
Gave	River (Béarn)
Gorg	Tarn
Grange/granja/ grangera	Barn
Grau	Pass
Hont/hount	Source of a river
Hourquette/forqueta/ horcado	Steep pass
Ibón/laquette	Tarn, small lake
Lis/lit	Avalanche couloir
Mas/masia	Farmstead (Catalunya/ Roussillon)
Né/ner/nère	Black
Neste	River (Bigorre)
Noguera	River (Catalunya)
Obaga/ubago/umbria	North-facing slope
Oule/oulette	Small "bowl" in terrain
Pántano/Pantà	Reservoir
Passerelle/passarella	Suspension bridge, catwalk
Peña/Peyre	Prominent rock outcrop
Port/porteille/puerto	Pass (implies long use as a trade or pilgrimage route)
Prat/prado/pradère	Meadow
Pic/puig/pique	Peak
Pujol/puy/puyo/pouey	High point
Raillère/ralhère	Avalanche gallery
Ribera/ribèra	Riverbank or river valley
Río/riu	River

Salhèt	Riverbank
Salto/sault	Waterfall, cascade
Seilh	Glacier
Serre/serra	Serrated, tooth-like ridge
Soula/solana/soulane	South-facing slope
Soum/turon/turoun	Rounded summit
Tartera/tartère	Scree slope
Tozal/tuc/tuca	Peak
Veinat	District, neighbourhood

Basque Pyrenees

Aran	Valley
Ardi	Sheep
Arri	Stone
Artz	Bear
Artzain	Shepherd
Beltz	Black
Bide	Route
Celhay/selhai	Plateau
Chara	Wood
Chipi/tchipi/txipi	Small
Churi/chouri/txuri	White
Çuby/(t)zubi	Bridge
Erreka	River
Etche/etxe	House
Etchola/etxda	Hut
Gain/gagna	Summit
Gorri	Red
Goyen/gora	High
Handi	Big
Harri	Stone
Hegi	Hill
Ibar	Valley
Ichouri/itxurri	Slope
Ithourri	River source
Kayolar/cayolar	Pastoral hut
Larra/larria	Moor, pasture
Lepo	Pass
Orri/orry	Pastoral hut
Mendi	Mountain
Oyhan	Forest
Portilloua	Pass
Tiki/ttipi	Small
Ur	Water

Glossary

ABBATIALE (French) Abbey church.

ABONO (Castilian) (Multi-)day ski-lift pass.

APLEC (Catalan) A pilgrimage to a rural shrine.

APSE Semicircular or polygonal terminations at the east end of a church.

AYUNTAMIENTO In Spain, the town hall; **AJUNTAMENT** in Catalan.

BAROQUE Late-Renaissance period of art and architecture, distinguished by extreme ornateness.

BARRIO (Castilian) Suburb or quarter.

BASTIDE Grid-plan fortified town established in southern France during the thirteenth century.

CAMINO DE SANTIAGO/CHEMIN DE SAINT-JACQUES The medieval pilgrims' route to the shrine of St James at Santiago de Compostela in northwest Spain; two main branches, plus many minor ones, cross the Pyrenees.

CARRER (Catalan) Street.

CATALONIA The geographical and cultural homeland of the Catalan people, disregarding the frontier established between France and Spain in 1659.

CATALUNYA The autonomous region of Spain comprising the provinces of (from northwest to southeast) Lleida, Girona, Barcelona and Tarragona.

CATHARISM Heretical religion of the twelfth to fourteenth centuries, with strongholds in the Ariège, Aude and Pays de Sault.

CESTA PUNTA The most spectacular, high-speed version of *pelota/pelote*, played by teams of two; sometimes called **JAÏ ALAÏ**, after the three-sided court it's played on.

CLAVIJAS Fixed peg-and-chain for hauling yourself up rock faces.

CLOCHER-MUR Triangular bell wall, either freestanding or at one end of the church, topped with decorative detail and often attributed to the Knights Templars.

CLOISTER Colonnaded walled courtyard, usually Romanesque and square, adjoining a monastic church on its south side.

COLEGIATA (Castilian) Large parish church, not quite ranking with a cathedral.

COMARCA/COMARQUE (Castilian/Catalan) Equivalent to an English county.

COMEDOR Formal dining room of a hotel, or at the rear of a *bar/restaurante*.

COMMUNE Smallest administrative division of the French Pyrenees.

CORREOS/CORREUS (Castilian/Catalan) Post office.

DÉPARTEMENT One of the French administrative provinces created after the Revolution, replacing traditional feudal duchies.

DOLMEN Neolithic stone monument, consisting of two or more upright slabs and a capping stone, thought to be either tombs or – from their frequent position on ridgelines – shepherds' shelters.

ERMITA/ERMITAGE (Spain/France). A wayside chapel, usually (but not always) out in the country.

FORFAIT/FORFET (French/Catalan) Daily or multi-day ski-lift pass.

FRESCO Wall painting, made more durable by being applied to wet plaster.

FRONTÓN Outdoor playing court for *pelota/pelote*, found in most Basque villages.

GENERALITAT The governing authority of Spanish Catalunya.

GOTHIC Architectural style prevalent from the twelfth until the sixteenth century, distinguished by pointed arches and rib-vaulting.

HALLE(S) In France, a covered produce market.

HOSPICE/HOSPITAL/HÔPITAU Medieval travellers' hostel built by religious or chivalric orders, often at the foot of strategic passes.

HÔTEL DE VILLE The town hall of a larger town in France.

ISARD (French/Catalan) Pyrenean chamois or izard, ubiquitous at higher elevations; called *rebeco* in Castilian, *sarrio* in Aragonese.

KALEA (Euskera) Street.

MAIRIE Municipal office of a French village.

MAJESTAT Carved medieval wooden image of a fully dressed, crucified Christ, formerly common in Catalunya; most examples were destroyed during the church-sackings of 1936.

MAS, MASIA A Catalan farmstead, usually isolated; precedes the proper name of the farm, which may be a family surname or some nearby natural feature.

MENJADOR Catalan for *comedor*.

MIRADOR A viewing point or platform intended for trekkers or motorists in the mountains.

MODERNISME/MODERNISTA (noun/adjective) Catalan version of Art Nouveau, prevalent between 1890 and 1925, relying heavily on stylized or grotesque curved forms from the natural world.

MOZARABIC Pertaining to the religion, art/architecture or culture of Mozarabs, medieval Spanish Christians living under Muslim rule.

MUDÉJAR Pertaining to the religion, art/architecture or culture of medieval Spanish Muslims living under Christian rule.

NAVE Main body of a church.

PASADOR/PASSEUR (Castilian/French) Person who during World War II guided refugees and Allied servicemen over the Pyrenees from occupied France into neutral Spain.

PELOTA/PELOTE (Castilian/French) A court ball-game originating in the Basque country, and played in several versions.

PETANCA/PÉTANQUE (Catalan/French). A game, similar to English bowls, where two teams of one to three persons each compete to pitch heavy balls as close as possible to a *cochonnet* or wooden marker jack 6–10m distant. From the Provençal *pied tanqués* or "feet together", after the small circle within which bowlers must stand as they pitch.

PLAÇA Catalan spelling of plaza.

(LA) POSTE (French) The post office.

RAMBLA Elongated rectangular promenade in a Catalan town, usually tree-shaded, pedestrianized and equipped with café tables.

RETABLE/RETABLO (French/Castilian). Intricately carved altarpiece.

ROMANESQUE Unadorned architectural style prevalent from the ninth to the thirteenth centuries, characterized by rounded arches and naively sculpted portals and column-capitals.

ROMERÍA (Spanish) Religious procession to a rural shrine, often with a venerated image.

SALLE CAPITULAIRE (French) Chapter house off a Romanesque cloister, often with fine rib-vaulting.

SANTUARI(O) (Catalan/Castilian) Remote religious shrine, larger and more exalted than an *ermita* – may have permanent staff.

TEMPLE Protestant church in France.

TRANSEPT Transverse arms of a church, perpendicular to the nave.

TRINQUET Smaller indoor/enclosed version of a *frontón.*

TYMPANUM Vertical, half-circular space above a Romanesque church portal, often decorated with a relief of Christ in Majesty.

URBANIZACIÓ(N) (Catalan/Castilian) Can mean any new apartment development, but in this guide refers to ski-chalet complexes surrounding Spanish Pyrenean villages.

VARIANT(E) An alternate routeing of the long-distance trails GR10, GR11 and HRP.

Acronyms

ARP *Alto Ruta Pirenaico* (Castilian); see **HRP**.

CAF *Club Alpin Français*, the French Alpine Club, administering many staffed refuges.

CEC *Centre Excursionista de Catalunya*, rival to the FEEC (see below).

CIMES *Centre d'Information Montagne et Sentiers*; administers some refuges in the Ariège.

EDF *Électricité de France*; power corporation responsible for all dams and dynamos in the Pyrenees.

ENHER Spanish power company active across the Pyrenees.

FAM *Federación Aragonesa de Montañismo*; Aragonese alpine club and refuge-managers.

FECSA Catalan power company restricted to the Catalan Pyrenees.

FEEC *Federació de Entitats Excursionistes de Catalunya*; important alpine club and refuge operator in Catalunya.

FNM *Federación Navarra de Montaña.*

GR *Gran recorrido* (Castilian), *gran recorregut* (Catalan), *grande randonnée* (French); long-distance trekking route for which you need overnighting/mountaineering gear.

HRP *Haute Randonnée Pyrénéenne*; strenuous, longitudinal traverse of the range, sticking close to the watershed.

ICONA *Instituto Nacional Para la Conservación de la Naturaleza*; Spanish administrative body responsible for certain picnic grounds, unattended campsites and unstaffed shelters.

PNP *Parc National des Pyrénées*; administers most mountain refuges within its area.

PR *Pequeño recorrido* (Castilian), *petit recorregut* (Catalan) *petite randonnée* (French), resort-based walking itinerary which takes a day or less, without special experience or equipment

RENFE *Red Nacional de Ferrocarriles*; the Spanish state rail corporation.

SNCF *Société Nationale des Chemins de Fer*; the French state rail corporation.

Travel store

Kenya
Marrakesh **D**
Morocco
South Africa, Lesotho & Swaziland
Syria
Tanzania
Tunisia
West Africa
Zanzibar

Travel Specials
First-Time Africa
First-Time Around the World
First-Time Asia
First-Time Europe
First-Time Latin America
Travel Health
Travel Online
Travel Survival
Walks in London & SE England
Women Travel
World Party

Maps
Algarve
Amsterdam
Andalucia & Costa del Sol
Argentina
Athens
Australia
Barcelona
Berlin
Boston & Cambridge
Brittany
Brussels
California
Chicago
Chile
Corsica
Costa Rica & Panama
Crete
Croatia
Cuba
Cyprus
Czech Republic
Dominican Republic
Dubai & UAE
Dublin
Egypt
Florence & Siena
Florida
France
Frankfurt
Germany
Greece
Guatemala & Belize
Iceland
India
Ireland
Italy
Kenya & Northern Tanzania
Lisbon
London
Los Angeles
Madrid
Malaysia
Mallorca
Marrakesh
Mexico
Miami & Key West
Morocco
New England
New York City
New Zealand
Northern Spain
Paris
Peru
Portugal
Prague
Pyrenees & Andorra
Rome
San Francisco
Sicily
South Africa
South India
Spain & Portugal
Sri Lanka
Tenerife
Thailand
Toronto
Trinidad & Tobago
Tunisia
Turkey
Tuscany
Venice
Vietnam, Laos & Cambodia
Washington DC
Yucatán Peninsula

Dictionary Phrasebooks
Croatian
Czech
Dutch
Egyptian Arabic
French
German
Greek
Hindi & Urdu
Italian
Japanese
Latin American Spanish
Mandarin Chinese
Mexican Spanish
Polish
Portuguese
Russian
Spanish
Swahili
Thai
Turkish
Vietnamese

Computers
Blogging
eBay
iPhone
iPods, iTunes & music online
The Internet
Macs & OS X
MySpace
PCs and Windows
PlayStation Portable
Website Directory

Film & TV
American Independent Film
British Cult Comedy
Chick Flicks
Comedy Movies
Cult Movies
Film
Film Musicals
Film Noir
Gangster Movies
Horror Movies
Kids' Movies
Sci-Fi Movies
Westerns

Lifestyle
Babies
Ethical Living
Pregnancy & Birth
Running

Music Guides
The Beatles
Blues
Bob Dylan
Book of Playlists
Classical Music
Elvis
Frank Sinatra
Heavy Metal
Hip-Hop
Jazz
Led Zeppelin
Opera
Pink Floyd
Punk
Reggae
Rock
The Rolling Stones
Soul and R&B
Velvet Underground
World Music (2 vols)

Popular Culture
Books for Teenagers
Children's Books, 5-11
Conspiracy Theories
Crime Fiction
Cult Fiction
The Da Vinci Code
His Dark Materials
Lord of the Rings
Shakespeare
Superheroes
The Templars
Unexplained Phenomena

Science
The Brain
Climate Change
The Earth
Genes & Cloning
The Universe
Weather

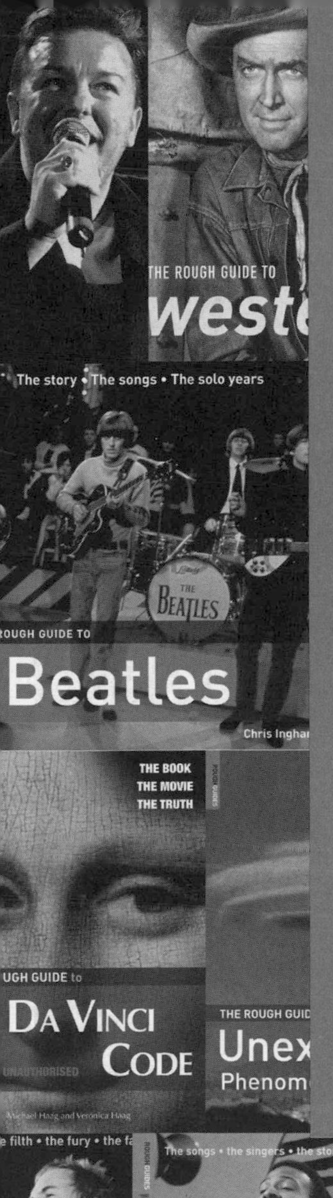
THE ROUGH GUIDE TO
The story • The songs • The solo years
Beatles
Chris Inghar
THE BOOK
THE MOVIE
THE TRUTH
Da Vinci
Code
UNAUTHORISED
Michael Haag and Veronica Haag
THE ROUGH GUID
Unex
Phenom

the filth • the fury • the fa
ROUGH GUIDES
The songs • the singers • the stories • the soul
H GUIDE to
unk
THE ROUGH GUIDE to
Soul and R&B

ROUGH GUIDES
THE ROUGH GUIDE to
The Rolling Stones
Sean Egan
THE ROUG
Blo

Spanish
Pyrenees
walking, trekking,
skiing & snowshoeing
holidays & short breaks
guided & independent
www.altoaragon.co.uk
altoaragon@arrakis.es
Alto Aragón

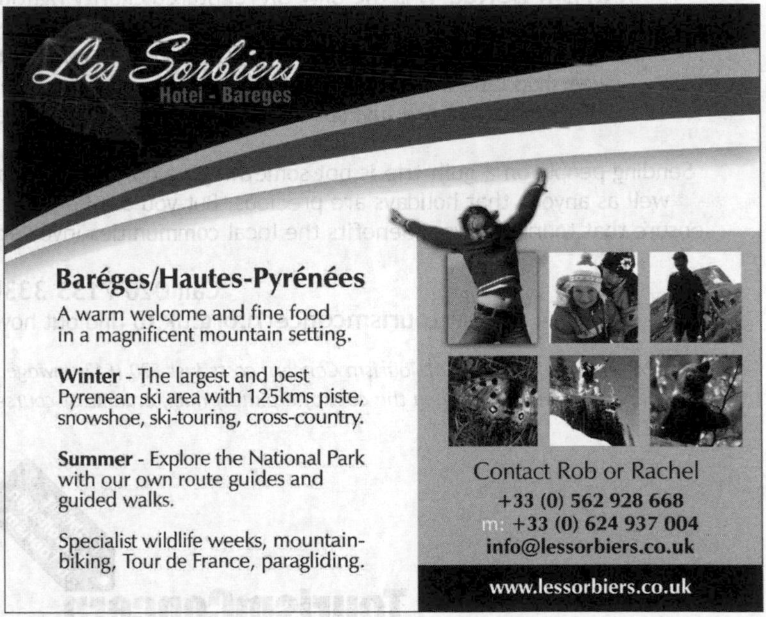

NOTES

NOTES

NOTES

NOTES

NOTES

Small print and

Index

A Rough Guide to Rough Guides

Published in 1982, the first Rough Guide – to Greece – was a student scheme that became a publishing phenomenon. Mark Ellingham, a recent graduate in English from Bristol University, had been travelling in Greece the previous summer and couldn't find the right guidebook. With a small group of friends he wrote his own guide, combining a highly contemporary, journalistic style with a thoroughly practical approach to travellers' needs.

The immediate success of the book spawned a series that rapidly covered dozens of destinations. And, in addition to impecunious backpackers, Rough Guides soon acquired a much broader and older readership that relished the guides' wit and inquisitiveness as much as their enthusiastic, critical approach and value-for-money ethos.

These days, Rough Guides include recommendations from shoestring to luxury and cover more than 200 destinations around the globe, including almost every country in the Americas and Europe, more than half of Africa and most of Asia and Australasia. Our ever-growing team of authors and photographers is spread all over the world, particularly in Europe, the USA and Australia.

In the early 1990s, Rough Guides branched out of travel, with the publication of Rough Guides to World Music, Classical Music and the Internet. All three have become benchmark titles in their fields, spearheading the publication of a wide range of books under the Rough Guide name.

Including the travel series, Rough Guides now number more than 350 titles, covering: phrasebooks, waterproof maps, music guides from Opera to Heavy Metal, reference works as diverse as Conspiracy Theories and Shakespeare, and popular culture books from iPods to Poker. Rough Guides also produce a series of more than 120 World Music CDs in partnership with World Music Network.

Visit www.roughguides.com to see our latest publications.

Rough Guide travel images are available for commercial licensing at www.roughguidespictures.com

Rough Guide credits

Text editor: Sarah Eno
Layout: Link Hall
Cartography: Karobi Gogoi
Picture editor: Jj Luck
Production: Aimee Hampson
Proofreader: Jennifer Speake
Cover design: Chloë Roberts
Photographer: Marc Dubin

Editorial: **London** Kate Berens, Claire Saunders, Ruth Blackmore, Polly Thomas, Richard Lim, Alison Murchie, Karoline Densley, Andy Turner, Keith Drew, Edward Aves, Nikki Birrell, Alice Park, Sarah Eno, Lucy White, Ruth Tidball, Jo Kirby, James Smart, Natasha Foges, Joe Staines, Duncan Clark, Peter Buckley, Matthew Milton, Tracy Hopkins; **New York** Andrew Rosenberg, Steven Horak, AnneLise Sorensen, Amy Hegarty, April Isaacs, Sean Mahoney, Ella Steim, Anna Owens, Joseph Petta
Design & Pictures: **London** Scott Stickland, Dan May, Diana Jarvis, Mark Thomas, Jj Luck, Chloë Roberts, Nicole Newman, Sarah Cummings; **Delhi** Umesh Aggarwal, Ajay Verma, Jessica Subramanian, Ankur Guha, Pradeep Thapliyal, Sachin Tanwar, Anita Singh, Madhavi Singh
Production: Katherine Owers, Aimee Hampson
Cartography: **London** Maxine Repath, Ed Wright, Katie Lloyd-Jones; **Delhi** Jai Prakash Mishra, Rajesh Chhibber, Ashutosh Bharti, Rajesh Mishra, Animesh Pathak, Jasbir Sandhu, Karobi Gogoi, Amod Singh, Alakananda Bhattacharya, Athokpam Jotinkumar
Online: **New York** Jennifer Gold, Kristin Mingrone, Cree Lawson; **Delhi** Manik Chauhan, Narender Kumar, Rakesh Kumar, Amit Kumar, Amit Verma, Rahul Kumar, Ganesh Sharma, Debojit Borah
Marketing & Publicity: **London** Niki Hanmer, Louise Maher, Jess Carter, Anna Paynton, Nikki Causer; **New York** Geoff Colquitt, Megan Kennedy, Katy Ball; **Delhi** Reem Khokhar
Editorial coordinator: Emma Traynor
Manager India: Punita Singh
Series editor: Mark Ellingham
Reference director: Andrew Lockett
Publishing coordinator: Helen Phillips
Editorial team assistant: Roísín Cameron
Publishing director: Martin Dunford

SMALL PRINT

Publishing information

This sixth edition published August 2007 by
Rough Guides Ltd,
80 Strand, London WC2R 0RL
345 Hudson St, 4th Floor,
New York, NY 10014, USA
14 Local Shopping Centre, Panchsheel Park,
New Delhi 110017, India
Distributed by the Penguin Group
Penguin Books Ltd,
80 Strand, London WC2R 0RL
Penguin Group (USA)
375 Hudson Street, NY 10014, USA
Penguin Group (Australia)
250 Camberwell Road, Camberwell,
Victoria 3124, Australia
Penguin Books Canada Ltd,
10 Alcorn Avenue, Toronto, Ontario,
Canada M4V 1E4
Penguin Group (NZ)
67 Apollo Drive, Mairangi Bay, Auckland 1310,
New Zealand

Cover concept by Peter Dyer.
Typeset in Bembo and Helvetica to an original design by Henry Iles.
Printed and bound in Singapore by SNP Security Printing Pte Ltd

632pp includes index
A catalogue record for this book is available from the British Library
ISBN: 9781843537663

3 5 7 9 8 6 4

Help us update

We've gone to a lot of effort to ensure that the sixth edition of **The Rough Guide to the Pyrenees** is accurate and up to date. However, things change – places get "discovered", opening hours are notoriously fickle, restaurants and rooms raise prices or lower standards. If you feel we've got it wrong or left something out, we'd like to know, and if you can remember the address, the price, the time, the phone number, so much the better.

We'll credit all contributions, and send a copy of the next edition (or any other Rough Guide if you prefer) for the best letters. Everyone who writes to us and isn't already a subscriber will receive a copy of our full-colour thrice-yearly newsletter. Please mark letters: "**Rough Guide Pyrenees Update**" and send to: Rough Guides, 80 Strand, London WC2R 0RL, or Rough Guides, 4th Floor, 345 Hudson St, New York, NY 10014. Or send an email to **mail@roughguides.com**

Have your questions answered and tell others about your trip at **www.roughguides.atinfopop.com**

Acknowledgements

Marc would like to thank Jordi of Fonda Biayna in Bellver de Cerdanya, the management of Pensió Santa Maria in Taüll, Niki Forsyth and Richard Cash in the Valle d'Echo, Richard and Sandra Loder in Santa Engràcia, David and Consell Bardaji in Taüll, Rob and Rachel Williamson in Barèges, Jonathan and Myriam Peat in Castillon-en-Couserans, and Luk and Micheline Peters at Thuès-entre-Valls for their hospitality and assistance; Peter Derbyshire in Luz-St-Sauveur for the usual inside tips; Carol Coulter at Skycars for travel facilities; the Zedón for coming along on both trips; and Sarah Eno for lightning-quick and largely painless editing.

Readers' letters

Thanks to all those readers of the fifth edition who took the trouble to write in with their amendments and additions.

Photo credits

All photography © Rough Guides except the following:

SMALL PRINT

Cover

Front image: Parque Nacional © 4cornersimages
Back image: View of San Sebastián from Mount Igueldo © Getty

Introduction

p.8 Marmot sitting upright on hind legs © Malcolm Park/Alamy

Things not to miss

06 Cremallera de Nuria train © Art Directors/Trip/Jean-Dominique Dallet
15 Cirque de Gavarnie © Ian Cumming/Getty Images
16 Canyoning in the Pyrenees abseiling through a waterfall © Picture Contact/Alamy
19 Ride up the mountain or col aubisque pyrenees in the Tour de France 2005 © Rupert Rivett/Alamy
20 Men's Pyramid dance, July Festival, Taüll © Marc Dubin
21 Gliding over Pyrenees, Puigcerda, Spain © Chris Bradley/Axiom
22 Kayaking on the le Saison, Pyrenees, France © Gareth McCormack/Alamy
26 The Cave of Niaux © Charles Jean Marc/Corbis Sygma

Pyrenean food and drink colour section

Eating tapas at a bar in the old part of town, San Sebastian, Spain © Alex Segre/Alamy
1996, Biarritz, France – Two garlic plants and a string of red chili peppers hang from a blue wall © Owen Franken/Corbis

Black and whites

p.82 The Cathar Chateau De Peyrepertuse © SAS/Alamy
p.182 Seu d'Urgell Kathedrale Kreuzgang © Bildarchiv Monheim GmbH/Alamy
p.208 Group of young skiers and snowboarders taking a ski lift, Soldeu ski resort, Andorra © The Photolibrary Wales/Alamy
p.276 Estany de Sant Maurici with reflection of Els Encantats, Aigüestortes National park Pyrenees Catalonia Spain © A.P./Alamy
p.328 Walker in the Pyrenees © Lyndsey Maiden/Alamy
p.534 13 Apr 1938, Luchon, France: Seeking Peace refugees in flight from Spain across the Pyrenees © Bettmann/Corbis
p.547 October 1979, Bayonne, France – Children demonstrate to show their support of regionalist Basque schools © Jacques Pavlovsky/Sygma/Corbis
p.553 Griffon Vulture at a feeding site in the Spanish Pyrenees © Philip Mugridge/Alamy

Index

Map entries are in colour

A

B

C

D

E

INDEX

F

G

INDEX

Q

R

INDEX

T

Map symbols

maps are listed in the full index using coloured text

	International boundary		Church (regional maps)
	Chapter division boundary		Abbey
	Motorway		Mountain refuge
	Road		Lighthouse
	Dirt road		Point of interest
	Steps		Bus stop
	Tunnel		Airport
	Footpath	P	Parking
	Railway	*i*	Tourist office
	Cable car and stations		Post office
	Wall		Downhill skiing area
	Mountain peak		Cross-country skiing area
	Mountain pass		Campsite
	Gorge/cliff face		Traffic barrier
	Cave		Building
	Waterfall		Church
	Hot spring, spa		Park
	Ruins		Forest
	Historic bridge		Beach
	Museum		Cemetery
	Castle